site, www.damron.com, we extensively list hotlines, social or support groups as well as services like the state tourism board or the personal guide with a limo.

Accommodations Most accommodations (especially B&Bs) require advance reservations. It's a good idea to request a brochure ahead of time, and to be clear about deposit and cancellation policies when making reservations.

Bars & Nightclubs Many codes apply only a few nights a week, especially when we've noted "theme nights." You should call the bar to verify what is scheduled for which nights. Bars coded **BW** (beer/wine) might not serve both.

Restaurants All restaurants listed are gay-friendly; those with mostly gay/lesbian clientele are coded **MW**.

Cafes are casual hangouts serving coffee and pastries, but not full menus.

Entertainment & Recreation Something touristy, maybe a little kitschy, unusual, or commonly overlooked, that even your friends who've lived there all their lives won't mind doing with you.

Publications If you want to know what's new, get one when you get to town. They're usually free and distributed in many of the locations we list. Your best bet, however, is to go right to the local LGBT or alternative bookstore to get the latest issue and/or lowdown.

Gyms are workout facilities, not bathhouses. They're mostly straight, unless coded **MW** or **MO**.

Men's Clubs include sex clubs, bathhouses, playspaces, and sex-oriented groups.

Men's Services are mostly telephone-dating services.

Cruisy Areas In many cities, you're more likely to meet vice cops than partners at public grounds. Try the local bar or bathhouse instead if you're bent on picking up. To avoid entrapment, read the notice about "Cruisy Areas," page 4.

Unconfirmed means we've called, several times, but no one answered. The phone still works but everything else may be different. Definitely call first.

Events Calendar Lists those "can't-miss" events for the upcoming year – from circuit parties to bear jamborees to street fairs and festivals.

Tour Operators A brief description of what kinds of tours the tour operator offers.

As Damron has done since 1964, we reward the best letters (those packed with new info of openings and closings we haven't already found) with a ***FREE COPY*** of next year's edition.

Table of Contents

United States of America

Table of Contents

Who We Are

In 1964, a businessman published a book of all the gay bars he knew from his constant travels across the United States. This book could fit comfortably in the palm of your hand. Despite its small size, it was an impressive accomplishment. Each one of the listings he had visited himself. Every last copy of that book he sold himself. The name of this pioneering businessman—Bob Damron.

Forty years later, his little book, the Damron Men's Travel Guide (originally Bob Damron's Address Book), is still a bestseller. And it has remained the model for the countless gay travel guides to follow in its wake. Today, Damron's ever-expanding list of titles includes: the Damron Women's Traveller for lesbians; the Damron City Guide, a full-color map guide; and Damron Accommodations, with thousands of expanded B&B listings and color photos.

How We Maintain the Accuracy of Our Listings

Our editors contact every single listing in our database annually, usually by phone, fax, or email. They also receive updated information directly from business owners and you, our readers. If you send in new, verifiably correct information, Damron will send you a free copy of the next edition as our way of saying a very sincere "thank you" for your help.

PLEASE READ THIS NOTICE ABOUT "CRUISY AREAS"

Certain locations are categorized as "Cruisy Areas." These areas include but are not limited to parks, rest stops, and beaches. Information regarding these areas is furnished to Damron by various sources and, due to time and other constraints, Damron is unable to investigate these areas. Areas marked as "AYOR" (At Your Own Risk) may involve risk and the reader should proceed with caution. However, the absence of an AYOR rating does not guarantee the safety or security of any area. Therefore, Damron makes no warranty or representation as to the safety, security, or status of those areas marked as cruisy areas. Damron urges readers to avoid sexual activity within Cruisy Areas.

BEWARE — MOST POLICE DEPARTMENTS IN THE USA HAVE COPIES OF THE MEN'S TRAVEL GUIDE.

the Damron Men's Travel Guide

Publisher	**Damron Company**
President & Editor-in-Chief	**Gina M. Gatta**
Managing Editor	**Erika O'Connor**
Roving Editor	**Ian Philips**
Editorial Assistants	**Maggie Dolan** **Allison Lui**
Director of Art & Advertising	**Kathleen Pratt**
Cover Photo	**Mary Burroughs**
Cover Design	**Rick Avila**

Board of Directors

Gina M. Gatta, Edward Gatta, Jr., Louise Mock

In Memory of Bob Damron and Dan Delbex

How to Contact Us

Mail: PO Box 422458, San Francisco, CA 94142-2458
Web: www.damron.com
Phone: 415/255-0404 & 800/462-6654
[9am-5pm (PST) Mon-Fri]
Fax: 415/703-9049

instinct
AMERICA'S #1
GAY MEN'S MAGAZINE
www.instinctmagazine.com

BEST
PLACES TO WORK
2009 for GLBT Equality
100% CORPORATE EQUALITY INDEX
www.gayparislasvegas.com
800-630-7933
Everything's Sexier in Paris LAS VEGAS
Must be 21 or older to gamble. Know When To Stop Before You Start.®
Gambling Problem? Call 1-800-522-4700.
© 2009, Harrah's License Company, LLC. All rights reserved. P9-072

Chat with me on
gay.com
Member Name: ThomTheLair

NASTY PIG
265A WEST 19TH STREET, NYC • WWW.NASTYPIG.COM

N2N
SHOP N2NBodywear.com
Grown in
Los Angeles

MENU
FUNC.
SET
ME & MICHAEL AT THE BRIDGE

CASTRO
GODARD'S
"TWOORTHREETHINGS
I KNOW ABOUT HER"
MENU
FUNC.
SET
THE HOOD

MENU
FUNC.
SET
SF PRIDE BABY!

TAG
Approved® 2010
TAG Approved®
Accommodations Program
Before checking in, check out our expanding gay-friendly world.
1,500 LGBT-welcoming hotels worldwide meeting six gay-friendly qualifications and ready to serve the LGBT community whenever you travel for pleasure, business or for meetings and events.
www.tagapproved.com

sfpride.org
40th ANNUAL SAN FRANCISCO
PRIDE
Celebration & Parade
JUNE 26-27 2010
PHOTO FIDEL LIRIO
ad space generously donated by
DAMRON

USA

ALABAMA

Statewide

PUBLICATIONS

► **Ambush Mag 504/522-8049** *LGBT newspaper for the Gulf South (TX through FL)*

Southern Voice 404/876-1819 *weekly LGBT newspaper for AL, FL (panhandle), GA, LA, MS, TN w/ resource listings*

Anniston

CRUISY AREAS

Cheaha Park [AYOR] Cheaha Scenic Dr *early evenings, head toward the walking trail (beware of cops!)*

Auburn

ACCOMMODATIONS

Black Bear Camp Men's Retreat [MO,R,SW,N,NS,WI,WC,GO] 10565 US Hwy 280 W, Waverly **334/887-5152** *hot tub, kitchen*

CRUISY AREAS

Rest Area [AYOR] Hwy 280 (30 miles E of Alexander City & 5 miles W of Auburn) *evenings*

Birmingham

ACCOMMODATIONS

The Tutwiler Hotel [GF,WI,WC] 2021 Park Pl N (at 21st St N) **205/322-2100** *also restaurant & lounge*

BARS

C&G's Place/ Our Place [M,NH,V,GO] 2115 7th Ave S (at 22nd St) **205/276-3823** *4pm-midnight, till 2am Fri-Sat*

The Garage Cafe [GF,F,E] 2304 10th Terrace S (at 23rd St S) **205/322-3220** *11am-close, from 3pm Sun-Mon, great sandwiches, live music*

The Phoenix [MW,NH,K,DS] 5120 5th Ave S **205/595-5120** *[CW] dancing & lessons Wed, [L] party monthly, [F] Sun*

Steel Urban Lounge [GF,D,F] 2300 1st Ave N **205/324-0666** *opens 4pm, clsd Sun-Mon*

Wine Loft [GF] 2200 1st Ave N **205/323-8228** *wine bar, light food served*

NIGHTCLUBS

Al's Lakeview Yacht Club [MW,D,DS,18+] 2627 7th Ave S **205/322-1682** *24hrs*

Pulse [MW,D,DS,18+] 2824 5th Ave S (at 29th St) *6pm-close*

The Quest Club [M,D,DS,PC,WC,$] 416 24th St S (at 5th Ave S) **205/251-4313** *24hrs, [19+] Wed-Sun, patio*

Steel Urban Lounge [GF,D] 2300 1st Ave N (at 23rd St) **205/324-0666** *4pm-2am, clsd Sun, upscale lounge*

CAFES

Chez Lulu [E] 1909 Cahaba Rd **205/870-7011** *lunch & dinner Tue-Sun, Sun brunch, clsd Mon, plenty veggie, also bakery*

Java and Jams [E,F,WI] 321 N 20th St **205/321-5282** *open 7am, from 8am Sat, live music wknds*

Safari Cup [F] 300 Richard Arrington Jr Blvd **205/326-0019** *6am-6pm, full menu, plenty veggie*

RESTAURANTS

Bottega Cafe & Restaurant [WC] 2240 Highland Ave S (btwn 22nd & 23rd) **205/939-1000** *5:30pm-10pm, clsd Sun, full bar*

Highlands Bar & Grill [WC] 2011 11th Ave S (at 20th St) **205/939-1400** *5:30pm-10pm, clsd Sun-Mon*

John's [WC] 112 21st St N (btwn 1st & 2nd Ave N) **205/322-6014** *lunch weekdays & dinner Mon-Sat, clsd Sun, full bar*

Rojo 2921 Highland Ave S **205/328-4733** *11am-10pm, clsd Mon, wknd brunch, Latin & American cuisine*

Silvertron Cafe 3813 Clairmont Ave S (at 39th St S) **205/591-3707** *7am-10pm, 11am-9pm Sun, also full bar, more gay Mon*

Taj India 2226 Highland Ave S **205/939-3805** *lunch & dinner, Indian, plenty veggie*

Entertainment & Recreation

Terrific New Theatre 2821 2nd Ave S (in Dr Pepper Design Complex) **205/328-0868**

Men's Services

Erotica

Alabama Adult Books 801 3rd Ave N (at 8th) **205/322-7323** *24hrs, super-arcade*

Birmingham Adult Books [★] 7610 1st Ave N (at 76th St) **205/836-1580** *24hrs, booths*

The Downtown Bookstore 2731 Rev Abraham Woods Blvd (at 28th St) **205/328-5525** *arcade, booths*

Pleasure Books 7606 1st Ave N (at 76th St) **205/836-7379** *arcade, booths*

Cruisy Areas

Cahaba River Rd Park [AYOR] at Jefferson/ Shelby county line (on Hwy 280 E, exit before Cahaba River bridge & turn left) *follow trail; noon & late afternoon popular*

Cullman

Cruisy Areas

Heritage Park [AYOR] Cherokee Ave *hospital side of park*

Daphne

Cruisy Areas

Spanish Fort Overlook [AYOR] scenic overlook, off Hwy 98 (from I-10, exit at Daphne/ Spanish Fort at Hwy 98) *great view of Mobile Bay (beware of cops!)*

Decatur

Restaurants

The Waffle House 710 6th Ave NE (btwn Layfayette & Walnut) **256/355-2871** *24hrs, popular after-hours*

Dothan

Nightclubs

Club Imagination [MW,D,TG,K,DS,18+,PC] 4129 Ross Clark Circle NW (off Hwy 431 N) **334/792-6555** *6pm-4am, clsd Sun-Tue*

Eufaula

Cruisy Areas

Rest Area [AYOR] southbound on Hwy 431 (S of town) *busier evenings*

Fairhope

Cruisy Areas

Wilson Park [AYOR] downtown (next to post office) *late nights, street cruising w/ cars circling park*

Foley

Nightclubs

Club Evolution [MW,D,DS] 8380 Hwy 59 **251/943-5557** *9pm-close, from 6pm Fri-Sat, clsd Tue*

Geneva

Accommodations

Spring Creek Campground & Resort [M,BYOB,SW,N,WI,GO] 163 Campground Rd (at Hwy 52 & Country Rd 4) **334/684-3891** *cabins, tent & RV sites, some theme wknds w/ DJ*

Gulf Shores

Cruisy Areas

Bon Secour Wildlife Refuge [AYOR] on Hwy 180, mile marker 12 (turn left on Mobile St Dr & take to beach) *walk right 1 mile, nude beach & dunes past beach homes*

Huntsville

Bars

Club Ozz [MW,NH,D,E,DS,WC] 1204 Posey (at Larkin) **256/534-5970** *6pm-2am, [D,DS] Th-Sun*

Partners [MW,D,F,E,K,WC,GO] 627 Meridan St (at Pratt Ave) **256/539-0975** *5pm-2am, from 6pm wknds*

Cruisy Areas

Monte Sano Scenic Overlook [AYOR] Governors Dr (on left before Monte Sano Blvd)

Jacksonville

Cruisy Areas

Germania Springs Park [AYOR] off N Hwy 21 (Pelham Rd) (past JSU campus) *afternoons (beware cops!)*

Mobile

see also Pensacola, Florida

Info Lines & Services

Pink Triangle AA Group 2201 Government St (at Cornerstone MCC) **251/479-9994 (AA#), 251/476-4621 (church)** *7pm Tue, Th & Sat*

Accommodations

Berney/ Fly B&B [GF,21+,SW,NS,WI,WC] 1118 Government St **251/405-0949** *Victorian B&B, full brkfst, close to gay bars*

Bars

Bacchus [MW,NH] 54 S Conception St **251/445-4099** *8pm-close Wed-Sat*

Gabriel's Downtown [MW,K,V,PC] 55 S Joachim St (off Government) **251/432-4900** *7pm-close, patio*

Midtown Pub [MW,NH,K] 153 S Florida St (at Emogene) **251/450-1555**

Nightclubs

B-Bob's Downtown [M,D,B,DS,P,WC] 213 Conti St (at Joachim) **251/433-2262** *6pm-close, from 7pm Sat, 2-level multi-venue club, home den of Gulf Coast Bears, also gift shop*

Vision's Twist [MW,D,E,K,WI,WC] 266 Dauphin St (at Jackson) **251/431-9002** *4pm-close Tue-Sun*

Men's Services

Montgomery

Accommodations

The Lattice Inn [GS,SW,WI,WC,GO] 1414 S Hull St (at Clanton) **334/262-3388**

Rocky Mount B&B [GF,NS] 2364 Rocky Mount Rd, Prattville **334/285-0490, 800/646-3831** *Victorian house on 50 acres, full brkfst*

Nightclubs

Club 322 [MW,D,DS] 322 N Lawrence St **334/263-4322** *5pm-close, from 9pm Fri-Sat, clsd Mon-Tue*

Men's Services

Cruisy Areas

Woodmere Park [AYOR] Woodmere Blvd (at Eastern)

Steele

Accommodations

Bluff Creek Falls [M,SW,PC,WI,GO] 1125 Loop Rd **256/538-0678, 205/515-7882** *secluded campground w/ waterfalls, bluffs, 50 minutes from Birmingham*

Sylacauga

Cruisy Areas

Noble Park [AYOR] N Broadway Ave *after dark, park near pavilions*

Tuscaloosa

Men's Services

▶ **Megaphone 205/535-3200** *Meet and Chat Live with HOT local men. FREE to listen & respond to ads. Video and text chat at GayMates.com. Use FREE code 4889.*

Cruisy Areas

Bowers Park [AYOR] from McFarland Blvd turn E onto 37th St, then turn N onto Bowers Park Dr

Jack Warner Pkwy Parks [AYOR] along Black Warrior River *formerly River Rd Parks, check out 4th park near boat ramp*

ALASKA

Statewide

Entertainment & Recreation

▶ **Out in Alaska** PO Box 82096, Fairbanks 99708 **877/374-9958** *adventure travel throughout Alaska for LGBT travelers*

Anchorage

Info Lines & Services

AA Gay/ Lesbian 336 E 5th Ave (at Community Center) **907/344-2474** *6pm 1st Mon*

Gay/ Lesbian Helpline **907/258-4777, 888/901-9876** *6pm-11pm*

Identity, Inc 336 E 5th Ave **907/929-4528** *community center, newsletter*

Accommodations

A Wildflower Inn B&B [GS,NS,WI,GO] 1239 I St (at 13th) **907/274-1239, 877/693-1239** *convenient, downtown location, close to hiking trails & scenic vistas, fun hosts*

Alaska Bear Company B&B [GS,NS,GO] 535 E 6th Ave (btwn Eagle & Fairbanks) **907/277-2327**

Alaska Heavenly Lodge [GF,NS] 34950 Blakely Rd (at Mile 49 Sterling Hwy), Cooper Landing **907/595-2012, 866/595-2012** *hot tub, cedar sauna*

Alaska's North Country Castle B&B [GF,NS] 14600 Joanne Ct **907/345-7296** *private decks, ocean & mtn views, full brkfst*

Anchorage Jewel Lake B&B [GS,NS,GO] 8125 Jewel Lake Rd **907/245-7321, 877/245-7321** *full brkfst, kids ok*

City Garden B&B [GS,NS,WI,GO] 1352 W 10th Ave (at N St) **907/276-8686** *beautiful views of Mt McKinley, 10-minute walk to downtown area*

Copper Whale Inn [GS,WI,NS,WC,GO] 440 L St **907/258-7999, 866/258-7999** *downtown*

Earth B&B & Tours [GF,NS,WI] 1001 W 12th Ave **907/279-9907** *close to downtown*

Gallery B&B [GS,WC,GO] 1229 G St (at 12th) **907/274-2567** *lesbian-owned*

Inlet Tower Hotel & Suites [GS,WI,WC] 1200 L St (at 12th) **907/276-0110, 800/544-0786** *also bar & restaurant*

Bars

Kodiak Bar [MW,F] 225 E 5th Ave (btwn Cordova & Barrow) **907/258-5233** *3pm-2:30am, till 5am Fri-Sat*

Mad Myrna's [MW,NH,D,F,K,DS] 530 E 5th Ave (at Fairbanks) **907/276-9762** *3pm-2:30am, till 3am Fri-Sat*

Raven [MW,NH,WC] 708 E 4th Ave **907/276-9672** *1pm-2:30am, till 3am wknds*

Restaurants

China Lights 12110 Business Blvd, Eagle River **907/694-8080** *11:30am-10pm, till 10:30pm wknds*

Garcia's 11901 Business Blvd #104 (next to Safeway), Eagle River **907/694-8600** *11am-10:30pm, from noon wknds, till midnight Fri-Sat, Mexican*

Simon & Seafort's 420 L St (btwn 4th & 5th) **907/274-3502** *lunch weekdays, dinner nightly, seafood & prime rib, full bar*

Entertainment & Recreation

Out North 3800 DeBarr Rd **907/279-3800, 907/279-8099** *community-based & visiting-artist exhibits, screenings & performances*

Bookstores

Title Wave Books 1360 W Northern Lights Blvd **907/278-9283** *9am-9pm, till 10pm Fri-Sat, 11am-7pm Sun, LGBT section; also at 415 W 5th Ave, 907/258-9283*

Publications

Anchorage Press 907/561-7737 *alternative paper*

Erotica

Le Shop 305 W Dimond Blvd (at C St) **907/522-1987** *8am-1:30am*

Fairbanks

Accommodations

All Seasons B&B Inn [GF,NS,WI,WC] 763 7th Ave (at Barnette St) **907/451-6649, 888/451-6649** *elegant, downtown, AAA 3 stars, full brkfst*

Billie's Backpackers Hostel [GF,F] 2895 Mack Rd **907/479-2034**

Cafes

Hot Licks Ice Cream 3453 College Rd **907/479-7813** *seasonal*

Erotica

Fantasyland Video 1765 Richardson Hwy **907/488-0879** *24hrs, arcade*

Haines

Accommodations

The Guardhouse Boarding House [MW,NS,GO] 15 Seward Dr **907/766-2566, 866/290-7445** *in former jail of Fort William H. Seward, great views of Lynn Canal, bald eagle-watching opportunities, lesbian-owned*

Homer

Accommodations

Island Watch Vacation Rental [GF,NS,WI,WC] 4241 Claudia St (at W Hill Rd) **907/235-2265, 888/649-2176** *also cabin, kitchen*

Sadie Cove Wilderness Lodge [GF,NS] Kachemak Bay State Park **907/235-2350, 888/283-7234** *tree planted for every guest to offset carbon emissions, built from hand-milled driftwood, uses nonpolluting alternative energy, 3 full meals a day*

Cafes

Spit Sister Cafe [GS,WI] Homer Spit Rd (at Harbor View Boardwalk #5) **907/235-4921 (summer), 907/299-6868/ 6767 (winter)** *5am-5pm, coffee, pastries, salads & more*

Entertainment & Recreation

Alaska Fantastic Fishing Charters 800/478-7777 *deluxe cabin cruiser for big-game fishing (halibut)*

Juneau

Accommodations

Alaska Suites Juneau [GF,NS] 2141-2145 Crowhill Rd, Douglas **907/789-3772** *1-bdrm condos, water-view balconies*

Pearson's Pond Luxury Suites & Adventure Spa [GF,NS,WI] 4541 Sawa Circle **907/789-3772, 888/658-6328** *B&B resort & spa*

The Silverbow [GF,NS,WI] 120 Second St **907/586-4146, 800/586-4146**

Restaurants

Hangar on the Wharf 2 Marine Way Ste 106 **907/586-5018** *lunch & dinner, full bar, great fish & chips*

Cruisy Areas

Cope Park [AYOR] *mornings & afternoons (summers)*

Ketchikan

Accommodations

Anchor Inn by the Sea [GF,NS] 4672 S Tongass Hwy **907/247-7117, 800/928-3308**

Entertainment & Recreation

Southeast Sea Kayak [GF] 1621 Tongass Ave, Ste 101B **907/225-1258, 800/287-1607**

McCarthy

Accommodations

Ma Johnson's Hotel [GF,NS] **907/554-4402** *inside America's largest nat'l park, Wrangell St Elias*

Palmer

Accommodations

Alaska Garden Gate B&B [GS,NS,WI,GO] 950 S Trunk Rd **907/746-2333** *full brkfst, hot tub, lesbian-owned*

Seward

Entertainment & Recreation

Puffin Fishing Charters [GS] PO Box 606, 99664 **907/278-3346, 800/978-3346** *day fishing trips*

Sitka

Cafes

Backdoor Cafe 104 Barracks (behind Old Harbor Books on Lincoln St, no street sign) **907/747-8856** *6:30am-5pm, till 2pm Sat, clsd Sun*

Entertainment & Recreation

Esther G Sea Taxi 215 Shotgun Alley **907/738-6481** *marine wildlife tours*

ARIZONA

Apache Junction

EROTICA

The Sunvalley Resort [MW,SW,AYOR] 10145 E Apache Tr (exit Crismon Rd off I-60 E, 30 minutes from Phoenix) **480/380-9843** *24hrs, sauna*

Bisbee

ACCOMMODATIONS

Casa de San Pedro B&B [GF,SW,NS,WI,WC,GO] 8933 S Yell Ln (at Hwy 92 & Palominas Rd), Hereford **520/366-1300, 888/257-2050** *full brkfst*

Copper Queen Hotel [GF,SW,NS,WC] 11 Howell Ave **520/432-2216** *restored historic landmark, restaurant*

David's Oasis Camping Resort [MW,21+,SW,WI,GO] 5311 W Double Adobe Rd, McNeal **520/979-6650** *bar & internet cafe*

Doublejack Guesthouse [M,NS,WI] 1-B Temby Ave (at Opera Dr) **520/559-6708**

Eldorado Suites [GF,NS] 55 OK St **520/432-6679** *on National Historic Register, territorial architecture, 1- & 2-bdrm suites, kitchens*

Sleepy Dog Guest House [GF,NS] 212A Opera Dr **520/432-3057, 520/234-8166 (cell)** *reclaimed miner's cabin, very quiet, kitchen, patio, great views, very dog-friendly, lots of stairs*

BARS

Copper Rainbow Bistro [MW,BW,PC,WC] 5311 W Double Adobe Rd, McNeal **520/979-6650** *5pm-10pm Fri-Sat, 2pm-7pm Sun*

St Elmo's [GF,E] 36 Brewery Gulch Ave **520/432-5578** *10am-2am, live bands Fri-Sat*

Bullhead City

includes Laughlin, Nevada

BARS

The Lariat Saloon [MW,NH,MR,WC] 1161 Hancock Rd (at 95) **928/704-1969** *10am-2am, patio*

CRUISY AREAS

Adult Theater Hwy 95 (S of town) *bookstores w/ arcade & theater*

Karen's Adult Bookstore Hwy 95 (near Mohave Jct, S of town)

Flagstaff

ACCOMMODATIONS

Arizona Sled Dog Inn [GS,NS,WI,GO] 10155 Mountainaire Rd **928/525-6212, 800/754-0664** *beautiful B&B in Coconino Nat'l Forest, near historic Flagstaff, huskies on premises, cedar sauna, hot tub, full brkfst*

The Historic Hotel Monte Vista [GF,NS] 100 N San Francisco St (at Aspen) **928/779-6971, 800/545-3068** *historic 1927 lodging, full bar*

Inn at 410 [GF,WI,WC] 410 N Leroux St **928/774-0088, 800/774-2008** *1894 estate, full brkfst*

Motel in the Pines [GF,WC] 80 W Pinewood Rd I-17 N, exit #322 (exit 322), Munds Park **928/286-9699, 800/574-5080** *20 miles from Flagstaff*

Starlight Pines B&B [GS,NS,WI,GO] 3380 E Lockett Rd (at Fanning) **928/527-1912, 800/752-1912** *full brkfst*

BARS

Charly's Pub & Grill [GF,F,E,WC] 23 N Leroux (at Aspen, at Weatherford Hotel) **928/779-1919** *8am-2am*

Monte Vista Lounge [GF,D,E,K] 100 N San Francisco St (at Hotel Monte Vista) **928/774-2403** *noon-2am, from 11am Fri-Sun*

CAFES

Macy's European Coffee House [F] 14 S Beaver St **928/774-2243** *6am-10pm, vegetarian/ vegan*

Restaurants

Cafe Olé [BW,WC] 119 S San Francisco (at Butler) **928/774-8272** *lunch & dinner, clsd Sun, Mexican*

Granny's Closet 218 S Milton Rd **928/774-8331** *lunch & dinner, also sports bar*

Pasto [BW,WC] 19 E Aspen (at San Francisco) **928/779-1937** *5pm-9pm, clsd Mon, Italian*

Retail Shops

Crystal Magic 1 N San Francisco St **928/779-2528** *books, gifts & more*

Erotica

Image 620 E Rte 66, Ste 100 **928/226-8335** *videos & adult gifts*

Cruisy Areas

Rest Area [AYOR] off I-40 (17 miles W of Flagstaff)

Thorpe Park [AYOR]

Golden Valley

Erotica

Pleasure Palace Adult Bookstore 3583 US Hwy 68 #7 **928/565-5600**

Jerome

Accommodations

The Cottage Inn Jerome [GS,GO] **928/634-0701, 928/649-6759** *full brkfst*

Mile High Grill & Inn [GF,GO] 309 Main St **928/634-5094** *cool hotel, also daily restaurant (brkfst to burgers)*

Restaurants

Red Rooster Cafe 363 S Main St **928/634-7087** *11am-3pm, till 4pm wknds*

Kingman

Accommodations

Kings Inn Best Western [GF,F,SW,WC] 2930 E Andy Devine **928/753-6101, 800/750-6101**

Lake Havasu City

Info Lines & Services

Lake Havasu City AA 877/652-9005

Accommodations

Nautical Inn [GF,SW] 1000 McCulloch Blvd **928/855-2141, 800/892-2141**

Lake Powell

Accommodations

Dreamkatchers of Lake Powell B&B [GS,GO] **435/675-5828**

Mesa

Entertainment & Recreation

Broadway Palm Dinner Theatre 5247 E Brown Rd **480/325-6700** *a variety of musicals*

Erotica

Castle Megastore 8315 E Main St **480/986-6114** *24hrs*

Cruisy Areas

Granite Reef Recreation Area [AYOR] Power Rd (at Salt River) *go past mile marker 22 to dirt lot on left, follow trail on E side of dirt lot*

Phoenix

see also Scottsdale & Tempe

Info Lines & Services

1N10 602/475-7456 *7pm Th, youth age 14-22 only, HIV peer education, call for location*

Phoenix Lambda Center 2622 N 16th St (at Virginia Ave) **602/635-2090** *space for many 12-step programs*

Accommodations

► **Arizona Royal Villa Complex** [MO,SW,N,NS,WI,GO] 4312 N 12th St **602/266-6883, 888/266-6884** *hot tub*

► **Arizona Sunburst Inn** [MO,R,SW,N,NS,WI,GO] 6245 N 12th Pl (at Rose Ln) **602/274-1474, 800/974-1474** *hot tub*

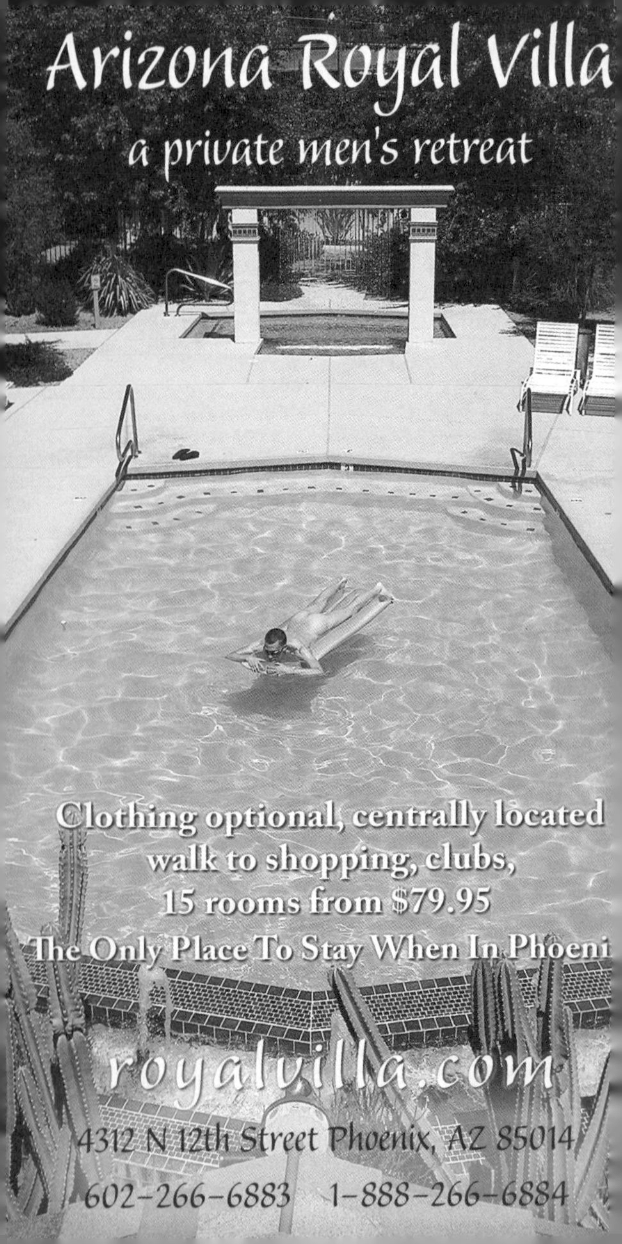
Arizona Royal Villa
a private men's retreat
Clothing optional, centrally located
walk to shopping, clubs,
15 rooms from $79.95
The Only Place To Stay When In Phoeni
royalvilla.com
4312 N 12th Street Phoenix, AZ 85014
602-266-6883 1-888-266-6884

Cantera Fountains [GF,SW,NS,WI,GO] 2228 E Campbell Ave **480/266-9008, 602/445-6274** *condo, fully equipped kitchen, hot tub*

Claremont House B&B [MW,SW,N,NS,WC,GO] 502 W Claremont Ave (btwn Maryland & Bethany Home, enter 7th Ave) **602/249-2974** *full brkfst, hot tub*

Clarendon Hotel & Suites [GS,SW,WI,WC,GO] 401 W Clarendon Ave (at 3rd Ave) **602/252-7363** *modern boutique hotel in midtown*

Hotel San Carlos [GF,F,SW,WI] 202 N Central Ave **602/253-4121, 866/253-4121** *boutique hotel, rooftop pool, restaurant*

Maricopa Manor B&B Inn [GS,SW,WI,WC,GO] 15 W Pasadena Ave **602/274-6302, 800/292-6403** *hot tub*

Rainbow Casita [M,N,NS,WI,GO] 2707 N 20th Ave (at Thomas Rd) **602/628-5781, 623/695-8588**

ZenYard [GS,SW,NS,WI,GO] 830 E Maryland Ave **602/680-7631, 866/594-0242** *private suites w/ kitchens, eco-friendly living, saltwater pool, koi pond, herbal gardens, full brkfst*

Bars

Amsterdam [MW,F,E,K] 718 N Central Ave (btwn Roosevelt & Fillmore) **602/258-6122** *4pm-2am, till 4am wknds, also Club Miami [D]*

Apollo's [M,NH,K,S,WI] 5749 N 7th St (S of Bethany Home) **602/277-9373** *8am-2am, till 2am wknds, diverse crowd, patio*

Bar 1 [M,NH,WI] 3702 N 16th St **602/266-9001** *4pm-2am*

The Bunkhouse Saloon [M,NH,K] 4428 N 7th Ave (at Indian School) **602/200-9154** *8am-2am, from 10am Sun, patio*

Cash Inn Country [W,D,CW,K,WC] 2140 E McDowell Rd (at 22nd St) **602/244-9943** *2pm-close, from noon wknds*

Charlie's [M,D,CW,WC] 727 W Camelback Rd (at 7th Ave) **602/265-0224** *2pm-2am, noon-4am Fri-Sat*

Cherry Bar [M,NH,B,F,K,GO] 1028 E Indian School Rd (at N 10th Pl) **602/277-7729**

Cheuvront Wine Bar [GS] 1326 N Central Ave **602/307-0022** *11am-10pm, till midnight Fri-Sat, 4pm-9pm Sun*

Cruisin' 7th [M,DS,K,TG,WC] 3702 N 7th St (near Indian School) **602/212-9888** *6am-2am, from 10am Sun, hustlers*

Dick's Cabaret [M,D,S] 3432 E Illini (off University, behind Radisson Hotel) **602/274-3425** *7pm-2am, till 3am Fri-Sat, "all male nude review," no alcohol*

The Door [M,NH] 1126 N Scottsdale Rd, Tempe **480/967-3667** *4pm-2am, from 2pm wknds, theme nights*

Homme [MW,NH,D,K] 138 W Camelback Rd (btwn 3rd & Central Aves) **602/234-3023** *4pm-2am, from 6pm Fri-Sat*

Ice Pics [MW,V] 3108 E McDowell Rd (at 32nd St) **602/267-8707** *4pm-2am,*

Incognito Lounge [MW,D,S,MR,WC] 2424 E Thomas Rd (at 24th St) **602/955-9805** *3pm-1am, till 3am Fri-Sat, clsd Mon-Wed*

Kobalt [MW,E] 3110 N Central Ave **602/264-5307** *noon-2am*

Oz [MW,NH] 1804 W Bethany Home Rd (at 19th) **602/242-5114** *noon-2am*

Plazma [MW,NH,E,V] 1560 E Osborn Rd (at N 16th St) **602/266-0477** *4pm-2am, till 1am Sun*

Pumphouse II [M,NH,K,S,V] 4132 E McDowell Rd (at 41st St) **602/275-3509** *noon-2am*

Retro Bar [M,D,NH,K] 3114 E Cactus Rd **602/493-0355** *2pm-2am*

The Rock/ La Roca [MW,NH,D,K] 4129 N 7th Ave (at Indian School) **602/248-8559** *noon-2am*

Roscoe's on 7th [MW,F] 4531 N 7th St (at Minnezona) **602/285-0833** *11am-1am, sports bar*

Taylor's Tavern [MW,NH] 15615 N Cave Creek Rd (btwn Greenway Pkwy & Greenway Rd) **602/867-2463** *3pm-1am, till 2am Fri-Sat*

Velocity [M,D,K] 2303 E Indian School Rd **602/956-2885** *noon-close*

Wild Card [MW,NH,D,K,DS,V] 801 N Arizona Ave, Chandler **480/857-3088** *2pm-2am*

Nightclubs

Club Dwntwn [M,D] 702 N Central Ave *Latin night Fri*

Karamba [★M,D,MR-L,WC] 1724 E McDowell (at 16th St) **602/254-0231** *4pm-close, clsd Mon-Wed, Latin wknds*

Cafes

Copper Star Coffee [WI] 4220 N 7th Ave (at Indian School) **602/266-2136** *6am-close, coffee in a converted gas station*

Restaurants

Alexi's [WC] 3550 N Central (in Valley Bank Bldg at Osborn) **602/279-0982** *lunch Mon-Fri, dinner nightly, clsd Sun, int'l, full bar, patio*

Barrio Cafe [E,GO] 2814 N 16th St **602/636-0240** *lunch Tue-Fri, dinner Tue-Sun, Sun brunch, clsd Mon, Mexican, live music*

Coronado Cafe 2201 N 7th St **602/258-5149** *lunch Mon-Sat, dinner Tue-Sat, clsd Sun*

Durant's 2611 N Central Ave **602/264-5967** *lunch Mon-Fri, dinner nightly, American*

Fez 3815 N Central Ave (S of Clarendon) **602/287-8700** *11am-midnight, sleek Mediterranean, full bar*

Green 2240 N Scottsdale Rd #8, Tempe **480/941-9003** *11am-9pm, clsd Sun, new American vegetarian/ vegan*

Harley's Bistro [MW] 4221 N 7th Ave (N of Indian School) **602/234-0333** *lunch Sun-Fri, dinner nightly, clsd Mon, Italian*

Los Dos Molinos 8646 S Central Ave **602/243-9113** *lunch & dinner, clsd Sun-Mon, homecooking*

MacAlpines's Soda Fountain 2303 N 7th St **602/262-5545** *11am-7pm, great milkshakes*

Mi Patio 3347 N 7th Ave **602/277-4831** *10am-10pm, 11am-9pm Sun, Mexican*

My Florist Cafe [P] 534 W McDowell Rd **602/254-0333** *7am-midnight, salads & sandwiches, full bar*

Persian Garden Cafe 1335 W Thomas Rd (at N 15th Ave) **602/263-1915** *lunch & dinner, clsd Sun-Mon*

Portland's 105 W Portland St (at Central Ave) **602/795-7480** *lunch Tue-Fri, dinner Mon-Sat, clsd Sun, also wine bar*

Rose & Crown 628 E Adams St **602/256-0223** *11am-2am, British pub*

Ticoz 5114 N 7th St (N of Camelback) **602/200-0160** *11am-11pm, till midnight Fri-Sat, Latin cuisine, full bar*

Vincent's on Camelback [WC] 3930 E Camelback Rd (at 40th St) **602/224-0225** *lunch Mon-Fri, dinner Mon-Sat, clsd Sun, Southwestern, some veggie*

Wild Thaiger 2631 N Central Ave (S of Thomas Rd) **602/241-8995** *lunch & dinner, Thai*

Z Pizza 53 W Thomas Rd **602/234-3289** *11am-9pm, till 9:30pm Fri-Sat, healthy pizza*

Entertainment & Recreation

Nearly Naked Theatre 100 E McDowell Rd (in the Little Theatre at Phoenix Theatre) **602/254-2151 (tickets), 602/274-2432 (office)** *for mature audiences*

Phoenix Metropolitan Men's Chorus PO Box 16462 85011 **602/717-4264** *gay choral group*

Soul Invictus 1022 NW Grand Ave (near W Van Buren St) *queer-friendly art gallery & cabaret*

The
HOTTEST
24 hour place in Phoenix to meet
BEARS & LEATHERMEN
Big, Butch & Friendly...
CHUTE
Always Play Responsibly!
PRIVATE MEN'S HEALTH CLUB
1440 E. Indian School Road
Phoenix, AZ 85014
602-234-1654
ATM Available
Credit Cards Accepted
WWW.CHUTEAZ.COM

Stray Cat Theatre 132 E 6th St, Tempe **480/820-8022** *provocative, off-the-beaten-path productions*

Retail Shops

Exposed Studio & Gallery [WC,GO] 4225 N 7th Ave (btwn N Indian School & Glenrosa) **602/248-8030** *11am-5pm, till 4pm Sat, clsd Sun, "new & established artists of all mediums"*

Movies on Central [WC] 4700 N Central #121 (at Highland) **602/274-0994** *noon-10pm, till 11pm Fri-Sat, LGBT video rentals & sales*

▶ **Off Chute Too** 4115 N 7th Ave (at Indian School Rd) **602/274-1429** *10am-8pm, till 10pm Fri-Sat, till 6pm Sun, LGBT gift shop in Melrose District*

Root Seller Gallery 4015 N 16th St #H (at Indian School) **602/265-7668** *10am-7pm, 11am-5pm Sun, LGBT books & gifts*

Unique on Central [WC] 4700 N Central Ave #205 (at Highland) **602/279-9691, 800/269-4840 (mail order)** *9am-9pm, noon-8pm Sun, cards & gifts*

Publications

Echo Magazine 602/266-0550, 888/324-6624 *bi-weekly LGBT news-magazine*

Ion Arizona Magazine 602/308-4662 x4 *entertainment guide*

'N Touch Magazine 602/308-4662 x5 *LGBT newsmagazine*

Gyms & Health Clubs

Alternatives Health & Wellness Center [GF,MR,TG,GO] 4314 N 7th Ave (at Indian School Rd) **602/266-0801** *11am-9pm, emphasizes spirituality*

Men's Clubs

▶ **Chute** [MO,B,L,V,18+] 1440 E Indian School Rd **602/234-1654** *24hrs, private rooms, gym, steam room*

Flex Complex [SW,PC] 1517 S Black Canyon Hwy (btwn 19th Ave & I-17) **602/271-9011** *24hrs*

Men's Services

▶ **Megaphone 602/993-4567** *Meet and Chat Live with HOT local men. FREE to listen & respond to ads. Video and text chat at GayMates.com. Use FREE code 4889.*

Erotica

Adult Shoppe 111 S 24th St (at Jefferson) **602/306-1130** *24hrs; also 5021 W Indian School Rd (at 51st Ave), 623/245-3008 & 2345 W Holly St, 602/253-7126*

Castle Megastore 300 E Camelback (at Central) **602/266-3348** *24hrs; also 5501 E Washington, 602/231-9837; 8802 N Black Canyon Fwy, 602/995-1641; 8315 E Apache Tr, 480/986-6114*

Fascinations 10242 N 19th Ave #1-7 **602/943-5859**

International Bookstore 3640 E Thomas Rd (at 36th St) **602/955-2000**

Pleasure World/ Bookcellar [V] 4029 E Washington (at 40th St) **602/275-0015** *also 1838 NW Grand Ave, 602/252-6446 & 6327 N 59th Ave, 623/939-3411*

Tuff Stuff 1716 E McDowell Rd (at 17th St) **602/254-9651, 877/875-4167** *10am-6pm, till 5pm Sat, clsd Sun-Mon, leather shop*

Cruisy Areas

Dreamy Draw Park [AYOR] Squaw Peak Pkwy (Hwy 51) (off Northern) *go E along the driveway to the back—popular w/ 9-5ers; be alert—major crackdown on cruising in Phoenix!*

Papago Park [AYOR] Galvin Pkwy (btwn McDowell Rd & Van Buren St) *be alert—major crackdown on cruising in Phoenix!*

Washington Park [AYOR] 21st Ave (N of Bethany Home) *nights; be alert—major crackdown on cruising in Phoenix!*

Prescott

Info Lines & Services

Prescott Pride Center [WC] 111 Josephine St **928/445-8800** *1pm-3pm Tue, 3pm-5pm Th, 2pm-6pm Sat, call for calendar of events*

Accommodations

Briar Wreath Inn B&B [GF,NS,WI] 232 S Arizona Ave (at Gurley) **928/778-6048, 928/215-0499 (cell)** *full brkfst, hot tub*

Cruisy Areas

Heritage Park [AYOR] Willow Creek Rd (3 miles S of Hwy 89)

Scottsdale

Accommodations

Inn at Eagle Mountain [GF,SW,NS] 9800 N Summer Hill Blvd, Fountain Hills **480/816-3000, 800/992-8083** *on 18-hole golf course*

Mondrian Hotel [GF,SW,NS] 7353 E Indian School Rd **480/308-1100, 888/697-1791** *hip boutique hotel, hot tub, gym, restaurant & bar*

Scottsdale Thunderbird Suites [GF,SW,NS,WI,WC] 7515 E Butherus Dr (at Scottsdale Rd) **480/951-4000, 800/951-1288** *full brkfst, gym, hot tub, full bar*

Bars

BS West [MW,D,K,V,WC] 7125 E 5th Ave (in pedestrian mall) **480/945-9028** *2pm-2am*

Nightclubs

Forbidden [M,D] 6820 E 5th Ave (at Indian Scool Rd) **480/994-5176** *clsd Sun-Wed*

Restaurants

AZ-88 7553 E Scottsdale Mall **480/994-5576** *11:30am-1am (food till 12:30am), from 5pm wknds, upscale, bar popular w/ gay men Fri-Sat evenings*

Malee's 7131 E Main **480/947-6042** *lunch & dinner, dinner only Sun, Thai, full bar*

Erotica

Zorba's Adult Book Shop 2924 N Scottsdale Rd (N of Thomas) **480/941-9891** *24hrs, video rentals & arcade*

Sedona

Accommodations

A-Lodge at Sedona—A Luxury B&B Inn [GS,SW,NS,WI] 125 Kallof Pl **928/204-1942, 800/619-4467** *Mission-style B&B inn w/ Red Rock views*

Apple Orchard Inn [GF,SW,NS,WC] 656 Jordan Rd **928/282-5328, 800/663-6968** *full brkfst*

Double H B&B [M,GO] 1475 S Hogan Ln (btwn 89-A & Zalesky), Cottonwood **928/649-0691, 928/451-0484** *secluded Santa Fe-style home w/ panoramic mtn vistas*

Iris Garden Inn [GS,NS,WI,WC] 390 Jordan Rd **928/282-2552, 800/321-8988** *motel, jacuzzi*

Sedona Rouge Hotel & Spa [GF,SW,NS,WI,WC] 2250 W Hwy 89-A **928/203-4111, 866/312-4111** *chic hotel, restaurant & bar*

Southwest Inn at Sedona [GF,SW,NS,WI] 3250 W Hwy 89-A **928/282-3344, 800/483-7422** *spa, workout room*

Restaurants

Judi's 40 Soldiers Pass Rd **928/282-4449** *lunch & dinner, clsd Sun, full bar*

Piñon Bistro [WC,GO] 1075 Hwy 260 (Rte 89-A), Cottonwood **928/649-0234** *dinner Th-Sun only, lesbian-owned*

Retail Shops

Sedona Green Gallery & Gifts 273 N Hwy 89A #P (btwn Jordan & Mesquite) **928/282-2335** *10-15% discount to self-identifying gay & lesbian customers*

Cruisy Areas

Beaverhead Flat Rd Scenic Viewpoint [AYOR] Beaverhead Flat Rd (1 1/2 miles off Hwy 179) *look for scenic overlook sign & follow gravel to parking lot*

Tempe

Restaurants

Restaurant Mexico 423 S Mill Ave **480/967-3280** *11am-9pm, till 10pm Fri-Sat, clsd Sun*

Bookstores

Changing Hands 6428 S McClintock Dr **480/730-0205** *new & used, LGBT section*

Erotica

Modern World 1812 E Apache (at McClintock Dr) **480/967-9052** *24hrs*

Tucson

Info Lines & Services

AA Gay/ Lesbian 3269 N Mountain Ave (at MCC) **520/624-4183** *8pm Th*

Wingspan, Southern Arizona's LGBT Community Center 425 E 7th **520/624-1779, 520/624-0348 (crisis#)** *11am-9pm, till 7pm Fri, 10am-4:30pm wknds, resources, youth support, library, film festival & more*

Accommodations

Adobe Desert Vacation Rentals [GS,NS,WI] **520/578-3998**

Adobe Rose Inn B&B [GF,SW,NS,WI] 940 N Olsen Ave (at E 2nd) **520/318-4644, 800/328-4122** *full brkfst, hot tub*

Armory Park Guesthouse [GF,GO] 219 S 5th Ave **520/206-9252** *renovated 1896 residence (owner's) w/ 2 detached guest units*

Catalina Park Inn [GS,NS,GO] 309 E 1st St **520/792-4541, 800/792-4885** *stately 1927 residence, full brkfst, near University of Arizona*

Desert Trails B&B [GF,SW,NS] 12851 E Speedway Blvd **520/885-7295, 877/758-3284** *adobe hacienda on 3 acres bordering Saguaro Nat'l Park, also guesthouse*

The Herbert House [GF,NS,WI,GO] 231 S Herbert Ave **520/882-4537** *rental home in historic district, full kitchen, covered porch, patio*

Hotel Congress [GS,F,WI] 311 E Congress St **520/622-8848, 800/722-8848** *landmark hotel, also Cup Cafe & full bar & club*

La Casita Del Sol [NS,WI,GO] 407 N Meyer Ave (btwn Church Ave & Franklin Ave) **520/623-8882** *1880s adobe guesthouse*

Natural B&B & Retreat [GS,NS,WI,GO] **520/881-4582, 888/295-8500** *nonallergenic, full brkfst, massage available*

Randolph Park Hotel & Suites [GF,SW,WC] 102 N Alvernon Wy **520/795-0330, 800/227-6086** *full brkfst, jacuzzi*

Royal Elizabeth B&B Inn [GS,SW,NS,WI,GO] 204 S Scott Ave (at Broadway) **520/670-9022, 877/670-9022** *historic 1878 downtown mansion, full brkfst, hot tub*

Bars

Ain't Nobody's Bizness [W,D,WC] 2900 E Broadway #118 (at Tucson) **520/318-4838** *3pm-2am, till 10pm Mon-Tue, [M] Sat for Latin Night*

Congress Tap Room [GF,NH,D,A,E] 311 E Congress (at Hotel Congress) **520/622-8848** *11am-2am, dance club from 9pm, theme nights*

Coyote Moon Pub [MW,D,CW,F,K] 915 W Prince Rd **520/293-7339** *3pm-1am, 11am-2am wknds, Buzztime trivia*

IBT's (It's About Time) [MW,D,S,WC] 616 N 4th Ave (at University) **520/882-3053** *noon-2am*

Venture-N [M,L] 1239 N 6th Ave (at Stone) **520/882-8224** *9am-2am, patio*

Woody's [M,V,WC] 3710 N Oracle (at Prince) **520/292-6702** *noon-2am, from 10am wknds*

The Yard Dog Saloon [GS,TG,WI,WC] 2449 N Stone (N of Grant) **520/624-3858** *noon-2am*

Cafes

The Cottage Bakery Cafe 800 N Kolb **520/722-1129** *7am-6pm, 8am-3pm Sun, clsd Mon*

Revolutionary Grounds [F,WI] 606 N 4th Ave (at E 5th St) **520/620-1770** *7am-7pm, till 11pm Fri-Sat, noon-7pm Sun, also leftist bookstore*

Restaurants

Blue Willow 2616 N Campbell (at Grant) **520/327-7577** *7am-9pm, from 8am wknds, brkfst served all day*

Cafe Poca Cosa 110 E Pennington St **520/622-6400** *11am-9pm, till 10pm Fri-Sat, clsd Sun-Mon, Mexican-influenced bistro, patio*

Colors Food & Spirits [MW,E] 5305 E Speedway **520/323-1840** *4pm-10pm, till midnight Fri, 10am-10pm Sun*

The Grill on Congress 100 E Congress (at Scott) **520/623-7621** *24hrs, full bar*

Bookstores

Antigone Books [WC] 411 N 4th Ave (at 7th St) **520/792-3715** *10am-7pm, till 9pm Fri-Sat, noon-5pm Sun, LGBT*

Publications

Ion Arizona Magazine **602/308-4662** *entertainment guide*

'N Touch Magazine *LGBT newsmagazine*

The Observer **520/622-7176**

Men's Services

Erotica

The Bookstore Southwest 5754 E Speedway Blvd **520/790-1550**

Caesar's Adult Shop 2540 N Oracle Rd (btwn Glen & Grant) **520/622-9479**

Continental Adult Shop 2655 N Campbell (at Grant) **520/327-8402** *24hrs, private rooms, arcade*

Hydra 145 E Congress (at 6th) **520/791-3711** *vinyl, leather, toys, shoes*

Cruisy Areas

Tanque Verde Falls/ Reddington Pass *upper Tanque Verde Falls, clothing-optional, gay area is beyond straight area*

White Mountains

Accommodations

Arizona High Country Campground [MW,WI,GO] 5064 Sawmill Rd (1 mile off Hwy 260), Clay Springs **928/739-4383** *10 campsites & RV hookups, near recreation areas, lesbian-owned*

Yuma

Bars

The Closet Lounge [MW,E,DS] 3780 S 4th Ave **928/726-6077** *10am-2am*

Erotica

Triple X Adult Super Store 3125 S Ave 3-E (32nd) **928/344-1799**

ARKANSAS

Statewide

Publications

Metro Star 918/835-7887 *monthly LGBT news publication serving AR, KS, MO & OK*

Batesville

Cruisy Areas

Riverside Park [AYOR]

Crossett

Cafes

Crosses Grocery & Cafe [★] 4223 Hwy 16 (E of Elkins, outside Fayetteville) **479/643-3307** *6am-9pm*

Eureka Springs

Accommodations

11 Singleton House B&B [GS,NS] 11 Singleton **800/833-3394** *1890s Victorian, full brkfst, jacuzzi, award-winning garden*

1905 Basin Park Hotel [GS,SW,WI,WC] 12 Spring St **479/253-7837, 877/643-4972** *1905 historic hotel*

Autumn Moon Cottage [GS,NS,GO] on Lake Lucerne **479/253-6813, 800/835-5184** *2-story cottage near historic downtown, jacuzzi, lesbian-owned*

A Byrds Eye View [GS,NS,WI,GO] 36 N Main (at Douglas) **479/253-0200, 888/210-8401** *in heart of downtown, porch*

Candlestick Cottage Inn [GF,NS,WI,GO] 6 Douglas St (at N Main) **479/253-6813, 800/835-5184** *romantic setting, full brkfst, lesbian-owned*

Cliff Cottage Inn & Eureka Springs Cottages [GS,NS,WI] in historic downtown **479/253-7409, 800/799-7409** *B&B & cottages in heart of downtown, full gourmet brkfst in B&B, hot tub*

Gardener's Cottage [GS,NS] in historic district **479/253-9111, 800/833-3394** *cottage for 2, jacuzzi*

Heart of the Hills Inn [GS,NS,GO] 5 Summit (on Historic Loop) **479/253-7468, 800/253-7468** *historic inn near downtown, full brkfst*

Home Suite Home [GF,NS,WI,GO] **888/933-4050** *suites or whole cottage, jacuzzi*

Lookout Lodge [GF,NS] 3098 E Van Buren **479/253-9335, 877/253-9335** *boutique hotel, private entrances, pets very welcome*

Mount Victoria [GF] 28 Fairmount St **479/253-7979, 888/408-7979** *elegant suites, garden, full brkfst*

Out on Main [GS,NS,WI,GO] 269 N Main St (at Magnetic Rd) **479/253-8449** *3-room cottage, full kitchen*

Palace Hotel & Bath House [GF,NS,WI] 135 Spring St **479/253-7474** *historic bathhouse open to all*

Pond Mountain Lodge & Resort [GS,SW,NS,WC,GO] **479/253-5877, 800/583-8043** *mtntop inn on 150 acres*

Red Bud Manor Inn [GF,WI,WO] 7 Kingshighway **479/253-9649, 866/253-9649**

Roadrunner Inn [GF,R,NS,WI] 3034 Mundell Rd **479/253-8166, 888/253-8166** *guestrooms & log cabins, lake views*

Silver Ridge Resort [GF] 132 Silver Ridge Rd **479/253-8719, 800/410-4641** *private cabins surrounded by 1,000 acres of mtn woodlands, jacuzzis*

Texaco Bungalow [GS,GO] 77 Mountain St **888/253-9093**

TradeWinds [GS,SW,WI,GO] 141 W Van Buren (at 23 N) **479/253-9774, 800/242-1615** *motel reminiscent of the motor inns of the '40s & '50s, jacuzzis*

Wildflower Cottages [GS,NS] 22 Hale **479/253-9173, 866/847-9776** *private cottages, hot tub*

▶ **The Woods Resort** [MW,NS,GO] 50 Wall St (off Hwy 62) **479/253-8281** *cottages, jacuzzis, kitchens, treehouse hot tub*

Bars

Chelsea's Corner Cafe [GF,D,WI] 10 Mountain St (at Center St) **479/253-6723** *11am-2am, till 10pm Sun, patio*

Eureka Live [GS,D,F] 35 N Main **479/253-7020** *4pm-1:30am, clsd Sun-Mon, more gay Wed*

Henri's [GS,NH,F] 19 Spring St **479/253-5795** *noon-2am, clsd Tue, gay night Wed*

The Lumberyard Bar & Grill [GS,F,E,K,GO] 105 E Van Buren **479/253-0400** *3pm-2am, from noon wknds*

Pied Piper Pub & Inn [GF,F,V] 82 Armstrong (at Main St) **479/363-9976, 866/363-9976** *noon-midnight, full bar*

Tiki Torch Club [GS,F,E,K,V] 75 S Main St **479/253-2305**

Restaurants

Autumn Breeze [NS] Hwy 23 S (1/2 mile off Hwy 62) **479/253-7734** *5pm-9pm, clsd Sun, cont'l, check site for winter schedule*

Cottage Inn 450 Hwy 62 W **479/253-5282** *5pm-9pm, clsd Mon-Wed, Mediterranean, full bar*

Ermilio's 26 White St **479/253-8806** *5pm-9pm, Italian, full bar*

Gaskins Cabin Steak House [GS,BW,R] 2883 Hwy 23 N (Hwy 187) **479/253-5466** *5pm-9pm, till 8pm Sun, clsd Mon-Tue, steak, seafood, full bar*

Marquee's 309 W Van Buren **479/253-8102** *4pm-9pm, clsd Tue, from noon wknds, also bar*

Entertainment & Recreation

Diversity Pride Events **479/253-2555** *produces events during Valentine's & Spring, Summer, Fall Diversity Wknds & more, for LGBTs & PFLAGs of all ages to enjoy together*

Bookstores

Gazebo Books 86 Spring St **479/253-9556**

Publications

Metro Star **918/835-7887** *monthly LGBT news publication serving AR, KS, MO & OK*

Fayetteville

Info Lines & Services

AA Gay/ Lesbian 568 W Sycamore **479/443-6366 (AA#)** *7pm Tue, 10am Sat*

PRIDE Arkansas Union A659 (University of Arkansas) *official LGBT student association, call for office hours*

Accommodations

Hilton Garden Inn Bentonville [GF,SW,WI,WC] 2204 SE Walton Blvd (Exit 85, off I-540), Bentonville **479/464-7300, 877/782-9444**

Nightclubs

Tangerine [MW,D,K,DS,18+] 21 N Block Ave **479/443-4600** *9pm-2am, clsd Sun-Tue*

Cafes

The Common Grounds 412 W Dickson (at West) **479/442-3515** *9am-close, full bar, also restaurant*

Bookstores

Hastings Bookstore 2999 N College Ave (Fiesta Square Shopping Center) **479/521-0244** *9am-11pm, till midnight Fri-Sat, 11am-11pm Sun*

Passages 930 N College Ave (at North St) **479/442-5845** *New Age bookstore*

Cruisy Areas

Flat Rock Beach [AYOR] 10 miles W of town *nude beach*

Helena

Accommodations

The Edwardian Inn [GF,NS] 317 Biscoe **870/338-9155, 800/598-4749** *60 miles from Memphis, classic Revival mansion, full brkfst*

Foxglove B&B [GF,NS] 229 Beech **870/338-9391, 800/863-1926** *107-year-old mansion, full brkfst*

Hot Springs

Accommodations

Park Hotel of Hot Springs [GS,WI] 211 Fountain St (at Central Ave) **501/624-5323, 800/895-7275**

The Rose Cottage [GF] 218 Court St (at Exchange St) **501/623-6449** *kids/ pets ok, jacuzzi*

Nightclubs

Jesters [MW,D,K,DS,V] 1010 E Grand Ave **501/624-5455** *8pm-4am, till 8pm Sun*

Cruisy Areas

Degray Lake [AYOR] lakeside area *afternoon in the woods*

Rest Area [AYOR] off Hwy 70 (btwn Hot Springs & I-30)

Jonesboro

Cruisy Areas

Craighead Forest Park [AYOR] *seasonal (beware of cops!)*

Little Rock

Accommodations

Legacy Hotel & Suites [★GF,WI,WC] 625 W Capitol Ave (at Gaines) **501/374-0100, 888/456-3669** *nat'l historic property in downtown area*

Bars

Backstreet [MW,D,K,DS,S,V,PC,WC] 1021 Jessie Rd #Q (btwn Cantrell & Riverfront) **501/664-2744** *9pm-5am, clsd Mon-Th, [18+] Fri & Sun, also Discovery Sat*

Sidetracks [M,NH,CW,B,L,OC,WI,WC] 415 Main St, North Little Rock **501/244-0444** *5pm-2am, also restaurant*

Nightclubs

UBU [MW,D,MR,TG,E,K,DS,PC,WC,GO] 824 W Capitol (at Izard) **501/375-8580** *8pm-2am Fri, from 9pm Sat, clsd Sun-Th*

Restaurants

Juanita's [E,R] 1300 S Main **501/372-1228** *11am-close, clsd Sun, live music*

Lilly's Dim Sum, Then Some [GO] 11121 N Rodney Parham Rd **501/716-2700** *11am-9pm, till 10pm Fri-Sat, noon-9pm Sun, contemporary Asian, plenty veggie, lesbian-owned*

Vino's Pizza [BW] 923 W 7th St (at Chester) **501/375-8466** *11am-close, from 11:30am Sat, from noon Sun*

Entertainment & Recreation

The Arts Scene 201 Maple St (at Broadway), N Little Rock **501/372-2130, 501/697-0196** *10am-6pm Sat-Sun, gallery & art market; also Friday Night Art Party, 8pm-1am 2nd Fri, live music, performance & films*

The Weekend Theater [GO] 1001 W 7th St (at Chester) **501/374-3761** *plays & musicals on wknds*

Bookstores

Wordsworth Books & Co 5920 R St **501/663-9198** *9am-7pm, till 6pm Fri-Sat, noon-5pm Sun, independent*

Retail Shops

A Twisted Gift Shop 1007 W 7th St (at Chester) **501/376-7723** *noon-midnight, gift shop*

Wild Card 400 N Bowman (at Maralynn) **501/223-9071** *10am-6pm, clsd Sun, novelties & gifts*

Erotica

Adult Video 2923 W 65th St (off I-30 W) **501/562-9628** *24hrs, arcade*

Cupids 3920 W 65th St (off I-30, exit 135) **501/565-2020** *24hrs, arcade*

Cruisy Areas

Reservoir Park [AYOR] Cantrell Rd (2 miles E of I-430, exit 9)

Mountain Home

Accommodations

Black Oak Resort [GS,SW,NS] PO Box 100, Oakland 72661 **870/431-8363** *quiet mtn resort*

CALIFORNIA

Statewide

PUBLICATIONS

▶ **Outword Magazine** **916/329-9280** *statewide LGBT newspaper w/ N & S CA editions*

Amador City

ACCOMMODATIONS

Imperial Hotel [GF,NS] 14202 Hwy 49 (at Water St) **209/267-9172** *B&B, brick Victorian hotel, full brkfst, restaurant & bar (Wed-Sun)*

Anaheim

see Orange County

Angeles Nat'l Forest

CRUISY AREAS

Beach in the Upper Big Tujunga Canyon (UBTC) [AYOR] Hwy 2, exit Angeles Crest Hwy, head N, turn left to UBTC Rd, turn right (btwn marker 4.5 & 4.8) *little nude beach along creek*

Antelope Valley

see Lancaster

Arcata

see also Eureka

INFO LINES & SERVICES

Queer Humboldt PO Box 45, 95518-0045 **707/834-4839** *"Humboldt County's online resource for the LGBT community," includes links & events calendar, check out www.queerhumboldt.org*

BARS

The Alibi [MW,NH,F,E,YC] 744 9th St **707/822-3731** *cocktail lounge w/ live music, also restaurant (8am-midnight)*

CAFES

Cafe Mokka [E] 5th & J **707/822-2228** *from noon, coffee & soups (bread bowls), live music, also Finnish sauna & hot tubs*

North Coast Co-op 811 I St **707/822-5947** *6am-10pm, co-op store w/ bakery, deli & espresso cafe*

RESTAURANTS

Wildflower Bakery & Cafe [★BW] 1604 G St **707/822-0360** *8am-8pm, till 9pm Th-Sat, vegetarian, organic beer & wine*

BOOKSTORES

Northtown Books 957 H St **707/822-2834** *10am-7pm, till 9pm Fri-Sat, noon-5pm Sun, LGBT section*

EROTICA

Pleasure Center 1731 G St #D **707/826-1708**

CRUISY AREAS

Aldergrove Marsh [AYOR] Alder Grove Rd (off West End Rd) *parking lot on left after Ericson Way*

Azalea State Reserve [AYOR] along Mad River (on N Bank Rd) *6 miles N of Arcata*

Arnold

ACCOMMODATIONS

Dorrington Inn at Big Trees [GS,GO] 3450 Hwy 4 (at Boards Crossing), Dorrington **209/795-2164, 888/874-2164** *cottages & suites, 3 hours from San Francisco, 18 miles from Bear Valley*

Atascadero

EROTICA

Diamond Adult World 7253 El Camino Real **805/462-0404** *8am-midnight*

CRUISY AREAS

Atascadero Lake Park & Zoo [AYOR] off Rte 41 *parking lot*

Bakersfield

Info Lines & Services

Gay AA 1001 34th St **661/322-4025 (AA#), 661/324-0371 (Alano Club #)** *7:30pm Mon & Th*

Bars

The Mint [GS,A,E] 1207 19th St (at M) **661/325-4048** *6am-2am, live music*

Nightclubs

The Casablanca Club [GS,NH,D,E,C,DS,V,WC] 1825 N St (at 19th St) **661/324-0661** *8pm-2am, clsd Mon*

Bookstores

Russo's Books 9000 Ming Ave #1-4 **661/665-4686** *9am-9pm, till 10pm Fri-Sat, 10am-8pm Sun, 2 other locations, independent*

Men's Services

Erotica

Deja Vu 1524 Golden State Hwy (at Chester Ave) **661/322-7300** *noon-2am, arcade*

Cruisy Areas

Gordon's Ferry [AYOR] Round Mountain Rd (at China Grade Loop), Oildale

Yokuts Park [AYOR] W of Hwy 99 (at Beach Park) *take W Truxtun Ave to Empire Dr entrance*

Barstow

Accommodations

Best Western Desert Villa Inn [GF,SW,WC] 1984 E Main St **760/256-1781** *hotel in Mojave Desert w/ fitness center, full restaurant & lounge*

Benicia

see Vallejo

Berkeley

see East Bay

Big Bear Lake

Accommodations

Alpine Retreats [GS,NS,GO] 433 Edgemoor (at Big Bear Blvd) **909/725-4192, 909/878-4155 (reservations)** *3 cottages, indoor spas, fireplaces, private entrances*

Eagles' Nest B&B [GF] 41675 Big Bear Blvd **909/866-6465, 888/866-6465** *guest lodge & 5 cottages, full brkfst*

Grey Squirrel Resort [GS,SW,WI,GO] 39372 Big Bear Blvd **909/866-4335, 800/381-5569** *20 cabins & 30 private rental homes, lesbian-owned*

Hillcrest Lodge [GS,WC] 40241 Big Bear Blvd **909/866-7330, 800/843-4449** *motel, nonsmoking rooms available, cabins, jacuzzi suites*

Knickerbocker Mansion Country Inn [GS,NS,WI,WC,GO] 869 Knickerbocker Rd **909/878-9190, 877/423-1180** *log mansion on lake, full brkfst*

Rainbow View Lodge [GS,NS] 2726 View Dr (at Hilltop), Running Springs **909/867-1810, 888/868-1810** *cottages w/ themed decor*

Shore Acres Lodge [GF,SW,WC] 41693 Big Bear Blvd **877/754-2327** *cabins, also rental homes, hot tub*

Switzerland Haus [GF,NS] 41829 Switzerland Dr **909/866-3729, 800/335-3729** *B&B-inn*

Big Sur

Accommodations

Eagle's Nest [GF,WI,GO] Pfeiffer Ridge #10 **831/667-2587, 888/742-9321** *guesthouse on private road, wraparound deck w/ views of Pfeiffer Ridge & Pacific Ocean, full kitchen*

Lucia Lodge [GF,NS] 62400 Hwy 1 **831/667-2391, 866/424-4787** *oceanview cabins (newly remodeled), restaurant, Rock Slide Lounge, store*

Cruisy Areas

Julia Pfiefer Burns State Park [AYOR] 20 miles S of Big Sur *sunrise to sunset*

Bishop

Cruisy Areas

Keough Hot Springs [AYOR] Hwy 395 (6 miles S of Bishop) *take Keough Hot Springs Rd exit, go W a half mile, turn right & continue 50 yds*

Bradley

Accommodations

Sapaque Valley Ranch [GS,NS,GO] 48491 Sapaque Valley Rd (btwn Byron/ Hesperia & Interlake Rd) **805/472-2750** *cottage & hacienda on private woodland*

Burlingame

see also San Francisco

Accommodations

Embassy Suites San Francisco Airport on the Bay [GF,SW,WI,WC] 150 Anza Blvd **650/342-4600, 800/362-2779** *full-service all-suite hotel, on San Francisco Bay, 2 miles from SFO, pets ok, fitness center*

Burney

Accommodations

Burney Mountain Guest Ranch [GF,SW,NS,WC,GO] 22800 Hat Creek, Powerhouse #2 (at Hwy 299), Cassel **530/335-4087** *cabins, close to some of best fly-fishing in state*

Cambria

Accommodations

Blue Dolphin Inn [GF,WI,WC] 6470 Moonstone Beach Dr **805/927-3300, 800/222-9157** *inn on Cambria's Moonstone Beach*

The J Patrick House B&B [★GF,NS] 2990 Burton Dr (1/2 mile off Hwy 1) **805/927-3812, 800/341-5258** *authentic log cabin, fireplaces*

Leopold Cove [GF,NS,GO] 2183 Sherwood Dr **805/927-5396, 800/240-2277** *vacation home overlooking the Pacific Ocean*

Pelican Cove Inn [GF,SW,NS,WC] 6316 Moonstone Beach Dr **805/927-1500, 800/222-9160** *B&B-inn, full brkfst*

Sea Otter Inn [GF,SW,NS,WI,WC] 6656 Moonstone Beach Dr **805/927-5888, 800/966-6490**

Cruisy Areas

Fiscalini Ranch Preserve both sides of Hwy 1 (S of Cambria Dr)

Capistrano Beach

Accommodations

Capistrano Seaside Inn [GF,WC] 34862 Pacific Coast Hwy **949/496-1399, 800/252-3224 (reservations only)** *outdoor jacuzzi, ocean views, across from beach*

Carmel

see also Monterey

Accommodations

Best Western Carmel Mission Inn [GF,SW] 3665 Rio Rd **831/624-1841, 800/348-9090** *near Monterey Bay, pets ok, also restaurant & lounge*

Carmel Resort Inn [GF,NS,WI] Carpenter Ave (btwn 1st & 2nd Ave) **831/624-3113, 800/454-3700**

Carmel River Inn [GF,SW,NS] Hwy 1 at Carmel River Bridge **831/624-1575, 800/966-6490**

Cypress Inn [GF] Lincoln & 7th **831/624-3871, 800/443-7443** *pets very welcome, owned by Doris Day*

Restaurants

Rio Grill 101 Crossroads Blvd **831/625-5436** *lunch & dinner daily, Sun brunch, "Creative American," full bar*

Cruisy Areas

Garland Ranch Regional Park [AYOR] Rte G16 (9 miles E of Carmel), Carmel Valley

Garrapata State Beach [AYOR] 10 miles S of crossroads (on right side of Hwy 1) *nude sunbathing*

Chico

Info Lines & Services

Stonewall Alliance Center 2889 Cohasset Rd #5 (at Cameo Dr) **530/893-3336** *HIV testing & counseling, recorded info, meetings*

Men's Services

▶ **Megaphone 888/634-2628** *Meet and Chat Live with HOT local men. Call for your local number or visit us online at GayMates.com. Use FREE code 4889.*

Cruisy Areas

Deer Pens [AYOR] 8th & Forest Sts

Chino

Restaurants

Riverside Grill 5258 Riverside Dr (at Central) **909/627-4144** *8am-9pm, till 3pm Sun-Tue, comfort food*

Chula Vista

see also San Diego

Men's Services

▶ **Megaphone 619/734-1110** *Meet and Chat Live with HOT local men. FREE to listen & respond to ads. Video and text chat at GayMates.com. Use FREE code 4889.*

Erotica

F St Bookstore [WC] 1141 3rd Ave (btwn Naples & Oxford) **619/585-3314**

Clearlake

includes major towns of Lake County

Accommodations

Blue Fish Cove Resort [GF,SW] 10573 E Hwy 20, Clearlake Oaks **707/998-1769** *lakeside resort cottages, boat facilities & rentals*

Edgewater Resort [SW,NS,GO] 6420 Soda Bay Rd (at Hohape Rd), Kelseyville **707/279-0208, 800/396-6224** *"gay-owned, straight-friendly," also camping, theme wknds, lesbian-owned*

Gingerbread Cottages B&B [GS,SW,NS,WI] 4057 E Hwy 20, Nice **707/274-0200, 888/880-5253** *lake-front w/ private beach, fireplaces, antiques & art, hot tub*

Sea Breeze Resort [GS,SW,NS,WC,GO] 9595 Harbor Dr, Glenhaven **707/998-3327** *lakefront cottages, full kitchens*

Bookstores

Wild About Books 14290 Olympic Dr, Ste A (at Lakeshore Dr) **707/994-9453** *10am-6pm, clsd Sun, independent*

Cloverdale

see also Healdsburg

Accommodations

Vintage Towers B&B [GF,NS,WI] 302 N Main St (at 3rd) **707/894-4535, 888/886-9377** *Queen Anne mansion, full brkfst*

Restaurants

Thai Time Asian Bistro [GO] 116 E 1st St **707/894-9820** *lunch & dinner*

Concord

see East Bay

Men's Services

▶ **Megaphone 925/695-1100** *Meet and Chat Live with HOT local men. FREE to listen & respond to ads. Video and text chat at GayMates.com. Use FREE code 4889.*

Corning

Cruisy Areas

Woodson Bridge State Recreational Area [AYOR] 5 miles E of Corning (on Sacramento River)

Costa Mesa

see Orange County

Cupertino

Accommodations

Cypress Hotel [GF,SW,WI] 10050 S De Anza Blvd **408/253-8900, 800/499-1408** *luxury hotel*

Cruisy Areas

Stevens Creek Canyon Park [AYOR] Foothill Blvd *at first road, turn left below the dam, go down, then go up to the top parking area on the right*

Dana Point

see Orange County

Danville

see East Bay

Davis

see also Sacramento

Info Lines & Services

LGBT Resource Center [WI,WC] University House Annex **530/752-2452** *10am-5pm, clsd wknds, info, referrals, meetings, library*

Cafes

Mishka's Cafe [★] 514B 2nd St **530/759-0811** *7:30am-11pm*

Bookstores

The Avid Reader 617 2nd St **530/758-4040** *10am-10pm, general independent, readings*

Men's Services

Desert Hot Springs

see also Palm Springs & Joshua Tree Nat'l Park

Accommodations

El Morocco Inn & Spa [GF,SW,WI] 66810 4th St (at Mesquite) **760/288-2527, 888/288-2523**

Two Bunch Palms Resort & Spa [GF,SW,NS,WI] 67425 Two Bunch Palms Trail (at Palm Canyon Dr) **760/329-8791, 800/472-4334** *also restaurant & full bar*

East Bay

includes major cities of Alameda and Contra Costa Counties: Alameda, Antioch, Berkeley, Concord, Danville, Fremont, Hayward, Lafayette, Newark, Oakland, Pleasant Hill, Richmond, San Leandro, Walnut Creek

Info Lines & Services

East Bay AA 510/839-8900 (AA#) *variety of LGBT-friendly mtgs*

La Peña [MR,NS,WC] 3105 Shattuck Ave, Berkeley **510/849-2568** *multicultural center & cafe, hosts meetings, dances, performance art, events*

Lighthouse Community Center 1217 A St (near 2nd St), Hayward **510/881-8167** *LGBT support groups & social events*

Pacific Center for Human Growth [WC] 2712 Telegraph Ave (at Derby), Berkeley **510/548-8283** *4pm-10pm Mon-Fri*

Rainbow Community Center of Contra Costa County 3024 Willow Pass Rd #200 (btwn Parkside & Esperanza), Concord **925/692-0090** *10am-5pm Mon-Fri*

Accommodations

Doubletree Hotel Berkeley Marina [GF,SW,WI,WC] 200 Marina Blvd, Berkeley **510/548-7920, 800/222-8733** *views of Golden Gate Bridge & San Francisco skyline*

Hotel Durant [GS,F,NS,WI] 2600 Durant Ave, Berkeley **510/845-8981**

Sheraton Pleasanton [GF,SW,WC] 5990 Stoneridge Mall Rd, Pleasanton **925/463-3330**

W Silicon Valley [GF,SW] 8200 Gateway Blvd, Newark **510/494-8800** *hot tub, pets ok, also restaurant & lounge*

Washington Inn [GF,NS,WC] 495 10th St (at Broadway), Oakland **510/452-1776** *historic boutique hotel, also restaurant*

Waterfront Hotel [GF,SW,NS,WC] 10 Washington St, Oakland **510/836-3800, 888/842-5333**

Woodfin Suite Hotel [GF,SW,NS,WC] 5800 Shellmound St (at Shellmound Wy), Emeryville **510/601-5880, 888/433-9042** *1- & 2-bdrm suites, full brkfst, hot tub*

Bars

The Alley [GS,P] 3325 Grand Ave (btwn Lake Park & Elwood Aves), Oakland **510/444-8505** *4pm-2am, camptastic sing-along piano bar from 9pm, more gay Th, also restaurant*

Bench & Bar [★M,D,MR-L,K,DS,P,S,YC,WC] 510 17th St, Oakland **510/444-2266** *4pm-2am, Latin Fri, Latin gay cowboy night Sat*

Cafe Van Kleef [GF,E,$] 1621 Telegraph Ave (at Broadway), Oakland **510/763-7711** *4pm-2am, clsd Sun, eclectic crowd & live-music scene—from cabaret to blue grass to jazz*

Easy Lounge [GF,NH,D,V] 3255 Lakeshore Ave, Oakland **510/338-4911** *4:30pm-2am, from 2pm Sat-Sun, cool lounge w/ theme nights*

Rainbow Room [MW,NH,D,E,WC] 21859 Mission Blvd (at Sunset), Hayward **510/582-8078** *2pm-2am, from 11am wknds*

Velvet [W,NH] 3411 Macarthur Blvd (at 35th), Oakland **510/531-3321** *6pm-close*

The Vibe Lounge [MW,D,MR-AF,K,V,DS] 2272 Telegraph Ave (at W Grand), Oakland **510/451-3777** *4pm-2am*

White Horse [MW,D,K,WC] 6551 Telegraph Ave (at 66th), Oakland **510/652-3820** *1pm-2am, from 3pm Mon-Tue, popular wknds (also Sun beer bust), [K] Tue*

World Famous Turf Club [MW,D,K,DS,WC] 22519 Main St (at A St), Hayward **510/881-9877** *1pm-2am, from noon Sat-Sun, huge patio*

Nightclubs

Club 1220 [MW,D,CW,K,WC] 1220 Pine St (at Civic Dr), Walnut Creek **925/938-4550** *4pm-2am, theme nights*

Cafes

Au Coquelet Cafe [F,BW] 2000 University Ave, Berkeley **510/845-0433** *6am-1:30am*

Bittersweet 5427 College Ave (in Rockridge District), Oakland **510/654-7159** *9am-7pm, till 9pm Fri-Sat*

Caffe Strada [★WC] 2300 College Ave (at Bancroft), Berkeley **510/843-5282** *6:30am-midnight, students, great patio*

Cole Coffee 6255 College Ave (btwn 62nd & 63rd Sts), Oakland **510/653-5458** *7am-7pm, hip hide-away in lovely Rockridge*

Raw Energy [GO] 2050 Addison St (btwn Shattuck & Milvia), Berkeley **510/665-9464** *7:30am-7:30pm, 11am-4pm Sat, clsd Sun, organic juice cafe*

Restaurants

Arizmendi Bakery & Pizzeria 3265 Lakeshore Ave, Oakland **510/268-8849** *7am-7pm, till 3pm Mon, clsd Sun, excellent pastries, breads & pizzas*

Bette's Oceanview Diner 1807 4th St (at Hearst), Berkeley **510/548-9494** *6:30am-2:30pm, till 4pm wknds, sandwiches & pizza*

Cactus Taqueria 5642 College Ave (at Shafter, in Rockridge), Oakland **510/658-6180** *11am-10pm, till 9pm, Mexican*

César [★] 1515 Shattuck Ave (in "Gourmet Ghetto," next door to Chez Panisse), Berkeley **510/883-0222** *noon-11pm, Spanish tapas, full bar till midnight; also 4039 Piedmont Ave, Oakland*

Cheeseboard Collective 1504 Shattuck Ave, Berkeley **510/549-3183** *10am-6pm, till 5pm Sat, clsd Sun*

Connie's Cantina [★] 3340 Grand Ave (btwn Lake Park Ave & Mandana Blvd), Oakland **510/839-4986** *10:30am-9pm, clsd Sun, delicious homemade Mexican food, plenty veggie, patio*

Dopo [★] 4293 Piedmont Ave **510/652-3676** *lunch & dinner, clsd Sun, Italian, wine list, worth the wait*

La Mediterranée [BW] 2936 College Ave (at Ashby), Berkeley **510/540-7773** *10am-10pm*

Le Cheval [★BW,WC] 1007 Clay St, Oakland **510/763-8495** *11am-9:30pm, from 5pm Sun, Vietnamese,*

Lois the Pie Queen [★] 851 60th St (off Martin Luther King Jr Hwy), Oakland **510/658-5616** *8am-2pm, Southern homecooking & killer desserts*

Mama's Royal Cafe [★BW,WC] 4012 Broadway (at 40th), Oakland **510/547-7600** *7am-2:30pm, from 8am wknds, come early for excellent wknd brunch*

Rockridge Cafe [★] 5492 College Ave (at Forest), Oakland **510/653-1567** *7:30am-3pm, great brkfsts, plenty veggie*

Zachary's Chicago Pizza [★BW] 5801 College Ave, Oakland **510/655-6385** *11am-10pm, till 10:30pm Fri-Sat, pizza that is worth the crowds & the long wait!*

Entertainment & Recreation

Oakland East Bay Gay Men's Chorus 800/706-2389

Bookstores

Black Oak Books 1491 Shattuck Ave, Berkeley **510/486-0698** *11am-9pm, independent, new & used, some LGBT titles, readings*

Diesel, A Bookstore 5433 College Avenue, Oakland **510/653-9965** *10am-9pm, till 10pm Fri-Sat, till 6pm Sun, independent*

Laurel Book Store [WC,GO] 4100 MacArthur Blvd (2 blks from High St), Oakland **510/531-2073** *10am-7pm, till 6pm Sat, clsd Sun, general, LGBT section, readings, lesbian-owned*

Pendragon Books 5560 College Ave (at Oceanview), Oakland **510/652-6259** *9am-10pm, from 10am Sun, used books, great to browse while waiting for a table in Rockridge; also 2 Berkeley locations*

Retail Shops

Ancient Ways [★] 4075 Telegraph Ave (at 41st), Oakland **510/653-3244** *11am-7pm, extensive occult supplies, classes, readings*

Collectors Realm 3 2566 Telegraph Ave (btwn Parker & Dwight), Berkeley **510/540-1182** *noon-8pm, gay vintage porn*

Paws & Claws [GO] 2023 MacArthur Blvd (at Fruitvale), Oakland **510/336-0105** *"a natural pet food store & bathhouse"*

Publications

San Francisco Bay Times 415/626-0260 *bi-weekly, good Bay Area resource listings*

Men's Clubs

Steamworks [★PC] 2107 4th St (at Addison), Berkeley **510/845-8992** *24hrs, call for recorded info*

Erotica

Golden Gate Books/ El Cerrito Secrets 10601 San Pablo Ave (at Moeser Ln), El Cerrito **510/528-1569** *8am-1am, arcade*

Good Vibrations [★WC] 2504 San Pablo (at Dwight Wy), Berkeley **510/841-8987** *noon-7pm, till 9pm Fri-Sat, clean, well-lighted sex toy store, also mail order, workshops & events*

Lingerie Etc 2298 Monument Blvd (at Buskirk), Pleasant Hill **925/676-2962**

Not Too Naughty 15670 E 14th St, San Leandro **510/278-4944** *arcade*

Cruisy Areas

Aquatic Park [AYOR] Bolivar Dr (off I-80, at Ashby Ave exit), Berkeley

Bushrod Park [AYOR] Shattuck Ave (btwn 59th & 60th Sts), Oakland *near tennis courts*

Central Park (aka Lake Elizabeth) [AYOR] Paseo Padre Ave & Stevenson Blvd, Fremont *trails right of lake & parking lot*

Gateway Exit [AYOR] Hwy 24, first exit after Caldecott Tunnel (if coming from Oakland), Orinda *stay right, parking lot & woods ahead*

Heather Farm Park [AYOR] Ygnacio Valley Rd, Walnut Creek *take Ygnacio Valley Rd for 2 miles E of Hwy 680, turn right into park on San Carlos Rd*

Hillcrest Park [AYOR] off Larkspur Dr, Antioch *take Hillcrest exit off Hwy 4, take left off Hillcrest Rd onto Larkspur Rd, park is on right after 6 blocks*

Keller Beach [AYOR] Miller-Knox Regional Park, Richmond *take Garrard Blvd exit of Hwy 580 after tunnel on Dornan Dr*

Lake Temescal Park [AYOR] Broadway Ave (at State Hwy 13), Oakland *afternoons*

Oyster Bay Park [AYOR] btwn San Leandro Marina & Oakland Airport (along the bay), San Leandro *take Doolittle to Williams, go W toward bay & make right when Williams ends*

El Cajon

Men's Services

▶ **Megaphone 619/387-0383** *Meet and Chat Live with HOT local men. FREE to listen & respond to ads. Video and text chat at GayMates.com. Use FREE code 4889.*

Elk

Restaurants

Queenie's Roadhouse Cafe [GO] 6061 S Hwy 1 **707/877-3285** *8am-3pm, clsd Tue-Wed, fabulous all-day brkfsts*

Elk Grove

Cruisy Areas

Elk Grove Park [AYOR] *take Hwy 99 to Elk Grove Blvd exit, head E & turn right at East Stockton, rear entrance to park is on left*

Encinitas

Accommodations

Ocean Inn [GF,WC] 1444 N Hwy 101, Leucadia **760/436-1988, 800/546-1598** *mission decor*

Escondido

Men's Services

▶ **Megaphone 760/708-0800** *Meet and Chat Live with HOT local men. FREE to listen & respond to ads. Video and text chat at GayMates.com. Use FREE code 4889.*

Erotica

F St Bookstore [WC] 237 E Grand Ave (at Broadway) **760/480-6031** *9am-2am*

Romantix Adult Superstore [WC] 2322 S Escondido Blvd **760/745-6697** *9am-2am*

Eureka

see also Arcata

Accommodations

Abigail's Elegant Victorian Mansion [GF,NS] 1406 C St **707/444-3144** *1878 nat'l historic landmark, sauna*

Carter House Victorians [GF,NS,WC] 301 L St **707/444-8062, 800/404-1390** *enclave of 4 unique inns, full brkfst, restaurant, wine shop*

Trinidad Bay B&B [GF,NS,WI,GO] 560 Edwards St (at Trinity), Trinidad **707/677-0840** *full brkfst*

Trinidad Escape [MW,WI] **707/677-3457**

Bars

Lost Coast Brewery [GF,F,BW,WI,WC] 617 4th St (btwn G & H Sts) **707/445-4480** *11am-1am, kitchen open till midnight*

The Shanty [GS,NH,GO] 213 3rd St (at C St) **707/444-2053** *noon-2am*

Cafes

North Coast Co-op 25 4th St (at B St) **707/443-6027** *6am-9pm, co-op store w/ bakery, deli & espresso cafe*

Ramone's Cafe & Bakery 209 E St (Old Town) **707/445-2923** *7am-6pm*

Restaurants

Chalet House of Omelettes 1935 5th St (at U St) **707/442-0333** *6am-3pm, brkfst & lunch*

Folie Deuce [BW,R,WC] 1551 G St, Arcata **707/822-1042** *dinner Tue-Sat, clsd Sun-Mon, bistro*

Hurricane Kate's 511 2nd St (Old Town) **707/444-1405** *lunch & dinner, clsd Sun-Mon, Caribbean/ Southeast Asian fusion, some veggie, wine*

Bookstores

Booklegger [WC] 402 2nd St (at E St) **707/445-1344** *10am-5:30pm, 11am-4pm Sun, mostly used, LGBT section*

Erotica

Good Relations [WC] 223 2nd St **707/441-9570, 877/506-8364** *queer-owned/ run*

Cruisy Areas

Hilfiker Reserve [AYOR] off Hilfiker Ln *last parking lot & wood trails*

Fairfield

see Vacaville

Ferndale

Accommodations

The Gingerbread Mansion Inn [★GF,NS,WI] 400 Berding St **707/786-4000, 800/952-4136** *grand Victorian lady, full brkfst*

Fontana

Erotica

Romantix Adult Superstore 14589 Valley Blvd (at Cherry) **909/350-4717** *24hrs*

Fort Bragg

see also Mendocino

Accommodations

Aslan Beach House [GF,NS] 24600 N Hwy 1 **707/964-1952** *beach house, hot tub, partial ocean view*

The Cleone Gardens Inn [GF,NS] 24600 N Hwy 1 **707/964-2788, 800/400-2189 (N CA only)** *country garden retreat on 2.5 acres, cottages, hot tub*

The Weller House Inn [GF,NS,WI] 524 Stewart St (at Pine) **707/964-4415, 877/893-5537** *1886 Victorian, full brkfst*

Restaurants

Cowlick's 250B N Main St **707/962-9271** *delicious homemade ice cream, including mushroom ice cream (in-season)—it's actually quite good!*

Purple Rose 24300 N Hwy 1 **707/964-6507** *5pm-9pm, clsd Mon-Tue, Mexican*

Entertainment & Recreation

Skunk Train California Western foot of Laurel St **707/964-6371, 866/457-5865**

Bookstores

Windsong Books & Records 324 N Main (at Redwood Ave) **707/964-2050** *10am-5:30pm, till 4pm Sun, mostly used*

Fountain Valley

see Orange County

Fremont

see East Bay

Men's Services

▶ **Megaphone 510/401-0101** *Meet and Chat Live with HOT local men. FREE to listen & respond to ads. Video and text chat at GayMates.com. Use FREE code 4889.*

Fresno

Info Lines & Services

Community Link 559/266-5465 *LGBT support, including LGBT youth group, also publishes Newslink*

Fresno AA 559/221-6907 *call or check website (www.fresnoaa.org) for meetings*

Accommodations

The San Joaquin Hotel [GF,SW,WI,WC] 1309 W Shaw Ave (at Fruit) **559/225-1309, 800/775-1309**

Bars

The Den [M,NH,CW,B,L,MR,V,OC] 4538 E Belmont Ave (at Maple) **559/255-3213** *5pm-2am, patio, popular beer busts & other events, "Fresno's Bear & Leather Bar"*

Red Lantern [M,NH,CW,MR-L,WI,WC] 4618 E Belmont Ave (at Maple) **559/251-5898** *2pm-2am, Latin night Sat very popular, patio*

Nightclubs

Express [★M,D,DS,V,GO,$] 708 N Blackstone (btwn Olive & Belmont, on Bremer) **559/445-0878** *9pm-2am, clsd Mon-Tue, theme nights, Latin night Th [DS], 3 themed rooms & 4 bars Fri-Sat, patio*

Restaurants

Cafe Rousseau 568 E Olive Ave (in Tower District) **559/445-1536** *lunch Tue-Fri, dinner from 5:30pm, clsd Sun-Mon, cont'l, also wine bar*

Irene's Cafe [BW] 747 E Olive Ave (in Tower District) **559/237-9919** *8am-9pm, some veggie, popular hamburgers*

Sequoia Brewing Company [E] 777 E Olive (in Tower District) **559/264-5521** *11am-10pm, till midnight Fri-Sat, till 9pm Sun, microbrewery with restaurant, live music*

Veni Vidi Vici [E,R] 1116 N Fulton (S of Olive Ave, in Tower District) **559/266-5510** *California fine dining, nightclub later*

Men's Services

Erotica

G-Spot [★GO] 1141 N Van Ness Ave (at Olive Ave) **559/264-6900** *10am-10pm, till midnight Fri-Sat*

Suzie's Adult Superstores 1267 N Blackstone **559/497-9613** *24hrs*

Wildcat Book Store 1535 Fresno St (at G St) **559/237-4525** *video arcade*

Cruisy Areas

LA-SF Time Out [AYOR] US 99 (at Kingsburg, S of Fresno) *go to cheap motel next to rest area; rest stop activity discouraged*

Garden Grove

see Orange County

Men's Services

Gaviota

Cruisy Areas

Vista Point [AYOR] Hwy 101 S (1/2 S of Gaviota Beach) *parking lot & nearby woods*

Grass Valley

see Nevada City

Gualala

Accommodations

Breakers Inn [GS] 39300 S Hwy 1 **707/884-3200, 800/273-2537** *oceanfront*

North Coast Country Inn [GF,NS] 34591 S Hwy 1 **707/884-4537, 800/959-4537** *hot tub*

Restaurants

Redwood Grill [BW,WC,GO] 35517 S Hwy 1 (at Ocean View Dr) **707/884-1639** *lunch & dinner, brkfst wknds, clsd Mon, patio, lesbian-owned*

Bookstores

The Four-Eyed Frog 39138 Ocean Dr (in Cypress Village) **707/884-1333**

Half Moon Bay

Accommodations

Mill Rose Inn [GF,NS,WI] 615 Mill St **650/726-8750, 800/900-7673** *classic European elegance by the sea, full brkfst, hot tub*

Restaurants

Moss Beach Distillery [★WC] 140 Beach Wy (at Ocean) **650/728-5595** *lunch & dinner, Sun brunch, steak & seafood, patio, even own ghost*

Pasta Moon [★WC] 315 Main St (at Mill) **650/726-5125** *lunch & dinner, Italian, full bar*

Hayward

see East Bay

Men's Services

Healdsburg

see Russian River & Sonoma County

Hemet

Cruisy Areas

Gibbel Park [AYOR] 2500 W Florida Ave (at Kirby, enter here) *very discreet*

Hermosa Beach

Accommodations

Quality Inn & Suites [GF,WI,WC] 901 Aviation Blvd **310/374-2666, 800/553-1145**

Erotica

Tender Box 809 Pacific Coast Hwy (at 7th) **310/318-2882**

Huntington Beach

see Orange County

Men's Services

Idyllwild

Accommodations

Alderwood Cabins [GF,NS] 25690 Alderwood St **951/659-3571** *1920s cabins on 2 wooded acres*

The Cedar Street Inn & Spa [GF] 25870 Cedar St **951/659-4789, 877/659-4789** *inn & cabins, on-site massage & spa services*

Quiet Creek Inn & Vacation Rentals [GF,NS,WI,GO] 26345 Delano Dr (at Toll Gate Rd) **951/659-6110, 800/450-6110** *vacation rentals*

The Rainbow Inn [GS,NS,WI,GO] 54420 S Circle Dr **951/659-0111** *full brkfst, patio, also conference center*

Strawberry Creek Inn B&B [GF,NS,WC,GO] 26370 Hwy 243 (at S Cir Dr) **951/659-3202, 800/262-8969** *relaxing getaway w/ sundeck, garden & hammocks*

Restaurants

Cafe Aroma [E] 54750 North Circle **951/659-5212** *7am-9pm, till 10pm Fri-Sat, great ambience & food, live music most nights*

Imperial Beach

Erotica

Romantix Adult Superstore 1177 Palm Ave (at Florida) **619/575-5081** *24hrs*

Irvine

see Orange County

Joshua Tree Nat'l Park

includes Twentynine Palms

Accommodations

The Desert Lily [GF] PO Box 139, 92252-0800 **760/366-4676, 877/887-7370** *artist-owned adobe-style B&B on 5 acres, also self-catering cabins, seasonal (clsd July-Aug)*

Desert Wonderland [GS,GO] **805/452-4898** *in high desert near Joshua Tree Nat'l Park*

Joshua Desert Retreats [GS,NS,SW,GO] Witt Rd (at Amboy Hwy), Twentynine Palms **310/558-5544** *10 vacation homes, weekly & monthly*

Joshua Tree Highlands Houses [GS,NS,WI,WC,GO] **760/366-3636** *private modern desert vacation rentals, fully equipped, each home on 5 acres, near Joshua Tree Nat'l Park*

Moon Way Lodge [GS,WI,NS,GO] **760/835-9369**

Sacred Sands [GS,NS,GO] HC1 Box 1071 A, 63155 Quail Springs Rd (at Desert Shadows), Joshua Tree **760/424-6407** *guest retreat in Joshua Tree Nat'l Park, private outdoor living, spa*

Spin & Margie's Desert Hideaway [GF] 64491 29 Palms Hwy **760/366-9124** *hacienda-style B&B, suites w/ private patios, cool trading post on-site*

Starland Retreat [M,N,18+] Yucca Valley **760/364-2069**

Restaurants

The Crossroads Cafe & Tavern 61715 29 Palms Hwy **760/366-5414** *7am-8pm, till 9pm Fri-Sat, clsd Wed*

Julian

Accommodations

The Artists' Loft [GF] Strawberry Hill **760/765-0765** *B&B & cabins in mtns E of San Diego*

Kernville

Accommodations

River View Lodge [GS,NS,GO] 2 Sirretta St **760/376-6019** *resort on Kern River, jacuzzi*

Klamath

Accommodations

Rhodes' End B&B [GF,NS] 115 Trobitz Rd **707/482-1654** *full brkfst, hot tub*

Laguna Beach

see Orange County

Men's Services

Lake Tahoe

see also Lake Tahoe, Nevada

Accommodations

Alpine Inn & Spa [GS,SW] 920 Stateline Ave (Lake Ave/ Hwy 50), South Lake Tahoe **530/544-3340, 800/826-8885** *motel just steps from casino*

Black Bear Inn [GS,NS,WI,GO] **530/544-4451, 877/232-7466** *full brkfst, hot tub, fireplaces*

The Cedar House Sport Hotel [GF,WI] 10918 Brockway Rd, Truckee **530/582-5655, 866/582-5655**

Sierra Views Vacation Home Cabin [GS,SW,NS] **530/582-8703** *3-bdrm cabin on pine-treed lot, dog-friendly*

Spruce Grove Cabins [GF,NS] 3599-3605 Spruce Ave, South Lake Tahoe **530/544-0549, 800/777-0914**

Tahoe Moon Properties [GF,SW,NS] **530/581-2771, 866/581-2771**

Tahoe Valley Lodge [GF,SW,NS,WI] 2241 Lake Tahoe Blvd (at Tahoe Keys Blvd), South Lake Tahoe **530/541-0353, 800/669-7544** *motel*

Restaurants

Driftwood Cafe [WC] 4119 Laurel Ave (at Poplar) **530/544-6545** *7am-3pm, homecooking*

Passaretti's [BW] 1181 Emerald Bay Rd/ Hwy 50, South Lake Tahoe **530/541-3433** *11am-9pm, Italian*

Cruisy Areas

El Dorado Beach [AYOR] btwn Rufus Allen Blvd & Lakeview, South Lake Tahoe

Private Beach [AYOR] off Pine St (near Park), South Lake Tahoe *private beach behind resorts*

Lancaster

includes Palmdale

Lathrop

Cruisy Areas

Mossdale Landing County Park [AYOR] Manthey Rd *parking lot & nearby woods*

Livermore

see East Bay

Lodi

Erotica

Intimates Adult Superstore [AYOR] 203 N Houston Ln **209/369-6191** *also arcade*

Long Beach

Info Lines & Services

AA Gay/ Lesbian 2017 E 4th St (at Cherry, at Gay & Lesbian Center) **562/434-4455** *7pm Mon [MW] & 7pm Fri [M]*

The Gay & Lesbian Center of Greater Long Beach 2017 E 4th St (at Cherry) **562/434-4455** *9am-9pm, by appt Sat, Gay & Bisexual Men's Rap Th, also newsletter*

Accommodations

Beachrunners' Inn [GS,NS] 231 Kennebec Ave (at Junipero & Broadway) **562/856-0202, 866/221-0001** *B&B, near beach, hot tub*

The Coast Long Beach Hotel [GF,SW,WI] 700 Queensway Dr **562/435-7676, 800/716-6199** *full brkfst, gym*

Hotel Maya [GS] 700 Queensway Dr **562/435-7676**

Queen Mary [GF,NS,WC] 1126 Queens Hwy **562/435-3511** *historic ocean liner*

Turret House B&B [GS,GO] 556 Chestnut Ave (at Sixth St) **562/624-1991, 888/488-7738** *restored Victorian, hot tub*

The Varden Hotel [GS,WI,NS,WC] 335 Pacific Ave (at 3rd St) **562/432-8950, 877/382-7336**

Bars

The Brit [M,NH,WC] 1744 E Broadway (at Cherry) **562/432-9742** *10am-2am, patio*

The Broadway [MW,NH,K,WC] 1100 E Broadway (at Cerritos) **562/432-3646** *10am-2am, [K] Fri-Sat*

CasaVino [GF,F] 51 S Pine Ave (at Ocean Blvd) **562/216-1590** *5pm-close, clsd Mon, some LGBT events, also art gallery*

Club Broadway [W,NH,V,WC] 3348 E Broadway (at Redondo) **562/438-7700** *11am-2am*

The Crest [M,L] 5935 Cherry Ave (at South) **562/423-6650** *2pm-2am*

The Falcon [M,NH,WC] 1435 E Broadway (at Falcon) **562/432-4146** *7am-2am*

Flux [MW,NH,WI] 17817 Lakewood Blvd (at Artesia), Bellflower **562/633-6394** *noon-2am, patio, theme nights*

Liquid Lounge [MW,NH,F,E,K] 3522 E Anaheim St **562/494-7564** *11am-1am, till 2am Fri-Sat, [K] Fri-Sat, patio*

Mineshaft [★M,B] 1720 E Broadway (btwn Gaviota & Hermosa) **562/436-2433** *10am-2am*

Paradise Piano Bar & Restaurant [MW,NH,F,E,P] 1800 E Broadway Blvd (at Hermosa) **562/590-8773** *3pm-1am, from 10am Sat-Sun*

Pistons [M,B,L] 2020 E Artesia (at Cherry) **562/422-1928** *6pm-2am, till 3am Fri-Sat, from 3pm Sun, till midnight Mon, patio, Leather Night Fri*

Que Será [GS,D,A,E] 1923 E 7th St (at Cherry) **562/599-6170** *9pm-2am Tue, from 5pm Wed-Sat, from 3pm Sun, clsd Mon, theme nights, [$] after 9pm*

Silver Fox [M,K,V,WC] 411 Redondo (at 4th) **562/439-6343** *4pm-2am, from noon wknds, popular happy hour, [K] Wed & Sun*

Sweetwater Saloon [M,NH,WC] 1201 E Broadway (at Orange) **562/432-7044** *6am-2am, popular days, cruisy*

Nightclubs

Boy's Room [M,D,E,S,WC] 3428 E Pacific Coast Hwy (at Redondo, at the Executive Suite) **562/597-3884** *9pm-2am Fri only*

Club Asia [M,D,MR-A] 740 E Broadway **562/436-7900** *9pm-2am 2nd Sat*

Club Ripples [★M,D,MR,F,E,K,DS,S,V,YC] 5101 E Ocean (at Granada) **562/433-0357** *noon-2am, patio, theme nights, T-dance Sun, Bear Bar every 2nd Sat, Arriba Arriba every 3rd Sat*

Executive Suite [★MW,D,E,WC] 3428 E Pacific Coast Hwy (at Redondo) **562/597-3884, 310/547-4730** *8pm-close Th-Sat*

Cafes

Coffee Haven [M] 1708 E Broadway (at Gaviota) **562/437-3785** *7am-midnight, from 7:30am Sun*

Hot Java [WI] 2101 E Broadway Ave **562/433-0688** *6am-11pm, till midnight Fri-Sat, also soups, sandwiches, salads*

The Library [WI] 3418 E Broadway **562/433-2393** *6am-midnight, till 1am Fri-Sat, from 7am wknds*

Restaurants

Hamburger Mary's [MW,D] 740 E Broadway (at Alamitos) **562/436-7900** *11am-2am, full bar w/ theme nights*

The House of Madame JoJo [★MW,BW,WC] 2941 E Broadway (btwn Temple & Redondo) **562/439-3672** *5:30pm-close, clsd Mon, cont'l*

Omelette Inn 108 W 3rd St (at Pine) **562/437-5625** *7am-2:30pm*

Original Park Pantry [WC] 2104 E Broadway (at Junipero) **562/434-0451** *6am-10pm, till 11pm Fri-Sat, int'l*

Bookstores

Open 2226 E 4th St (btwn Cherry & Junipero, in heart of Retro Row) **562/499-6736** *11am-7pm, till 8pm Sat, till 6pm Sun, clsd Mon, general; also films, art & events*

Retail Shops

Hot Stuff [GO] 2121 E Broadway (at Junipero) **562/433-0692** *11am-7pm, 10am-6pm Sat, noon-5pm Sun, cards, gifts & adult novelties, serving community since 1980*

Men's Clubs

1350 Club [18+] 510 W Anaheim St (at Neptune), Wilmington **310/830-4784** *24hrs*

Men's Services

▶ **Megaphone 562/485-4008** *Meet and Chat Live with HOT local men. FREE to listen & respond to ads. Video and text chat at GayMates.com. Use FREE code 4889.*

Erotica

The Crypt on Broadway 1712 E Broadway (btwn Cherry & Falcon) **562/983-6560** *10am-midnight, leather, toys*

The RubberTree 5018 E 2nd St (at Granada) **562/434-0027** *gifts for lovers, women-owned*

Cruisy Areas

Please Note: All cruisy areas for Long Beach have been removed by request of various LGBT community organizations.

Los Angeles

Los Angeles is divided into 8 geographical areas:
LA–Overview
LA–West Hollywood
LA–Hollywood
LA–West LA & Santa Monica
LA–Silverlake
LA–Midtown
LA–Valley
LA–East LA & South Central

LA—Overview

Info Lines & Services

Alcoholics Anonymous 323/936-4343 & 735-2089 (en español), 800/923-8722 *call or check web (www.lacoaa.org) for meetings*

Crystal Meth Anonymous 213/488-4455 *call or check website (www.crystalmeth.org) for meetings in LA County*

LA Gay & Lesbian Center 1625 N Schrader Blvd (McDonald/Wright Building) **323/993-7400** *9am-9pm, till 1pm Sat, clsd Sun, wide variety of services*

LA Gay & Lesbian Center's Village at Ed Gould Plaza 1125 N McCadden Pl (at Santa Monica) **323/860-7302** *6pm-10pm, 9am-5pm Sat, clsd Sun, cybercenter, cafe, theaters, library, classes, call for events & hours*

Los Angeles Convention & Visitors Bureau 800/228-2452, 213/624-7300 *visit at seemyLA.com*

Nightclubs

Rohan Bisset Presents [M,D] **323/378-6441** *after-hours dance parties*

Entertainment & Recreation

The Celebration Theatre 7051 Santa Monica Blvd (at La Brea) **323/957-1884** *LGBT theater, call for more info*

The Ellen DeGeneres Show *you know you want to dance w/ Ellen! check out ellen.warnerbros.com for tickets*

The Gay Mafia Comedy Company [MW,GO] **323/634-2820** *improv/ sketch comedy*

Gay Men's Chorus 323/467-9741, 800/MEN-SING

The Getty Center 1200 Getty Center Dr, Brentwood **310/440-7300** *10am-6pm, till 9pm Fri-Sat, clsd Mon, LA's shining city on a hill & world-class museum; of course, it's still in LA so you'll need to make reservations for parking (!)*

Griffith Observatory enter on N Vermont St (in Griffith Park) **213/473-0800** *noon-10pm, from 10am wknds, clsd Mon*

Highways 1651 18th St (at the 18th Street Arts Center), Santa Monica **310/315-1459 (reservation line)** *"full-service performance center"*

IMRU Gay Radio KPFK LA 90.7 FM *7pm Mon*

Moonlight Rollerway Gay Skate [MW] 5110 San Fernando Rd (N of W Colorado St, near LA Zoo), Glendale **818/241-3630** *8pm Wed only*

Outfest 213/480-7088 *LGBT media arts foundation that sponsors the annual LGBT film festival each July (see listing & ad in Film Festival Calendar)*

Purple Circuit Hotline 818/953-5072 *LGBT theater listings*

Publications

Adelante Magazine 323/256-6639 *bilingual LGBT magazine*

► **Frontiers Newsmagazine** 323/930-3220 *huge LGBT news-magazine w/ listings for everything*

Frontiers Yellow Pages 323/930-3220 *annual survival guide to LGBT Southern CA & Bay Area*

► **Gloss Magazine** 510/451-2090 *CA arts/ entertainment magazine, bi-weekly*

Gorgeous Magazine 323/436-7546 *bi-monthly*

IN Los Angeles 323/848-2200 *gay news & entertainment magazine for LA*

► **Odyssey Magazine** 323/874-8788 *dish on LA's club scene*

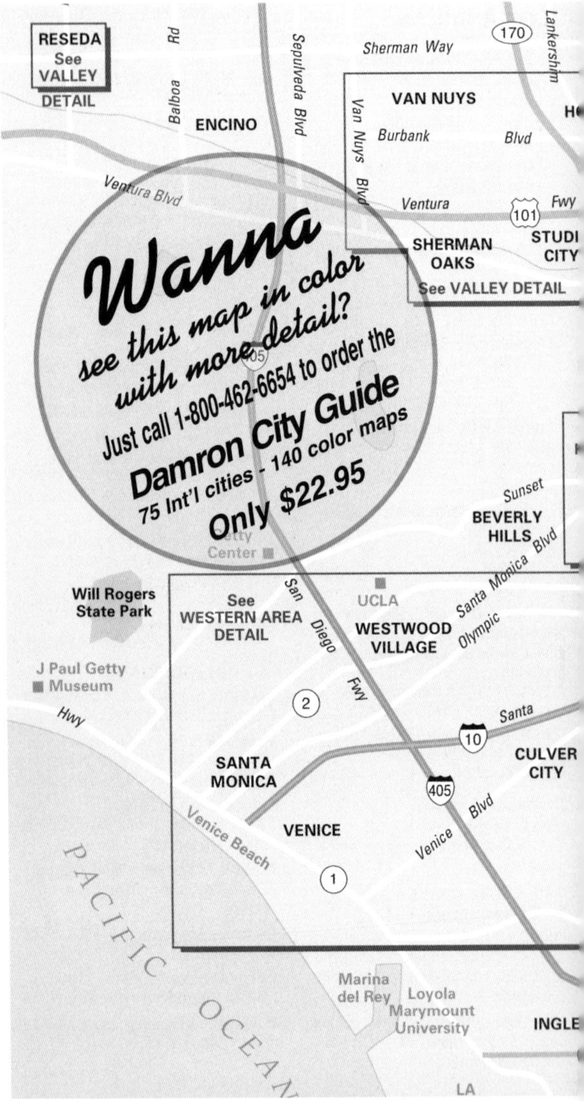
RESEDA
See
VALLEY
DETAIL
Balboa Rd
Sepulveda Blvd
Sherman Way
170
Lankershim
VAN NUYS
Van Nuys Blvd
Burbank Blvd
ENCINO
Ventura Blvd
Ventura Fwy
101
SHERMAN
OAKS
STUDI
CITY
See VALLEY DETAIL
Wanna
see this map in color
with more detail?
Just call 1-800-462-6654 to order the
Damron City Guide
75 Int'l cities - 140 color maps
Only $22.95
Sunset
BEVERLY
HILLS
Santa Monica Blvd
Getty
Center
Will Rogers
State Park
See
WESTERN AREA
DETAIL
San Diego Fwy
UCLA
WESTWOOD
VILLAGE
Olympic
J Paul Getty
Museum
Hwy
2
Santa
10
CULVER
CITY
SANTA
MONICA
405
Venice Blvd
Venice Beach
VENICE
1
PACIFIC
OCEAN
Marina
del Rey
Loyola
Marymount
University
INGLE
LA

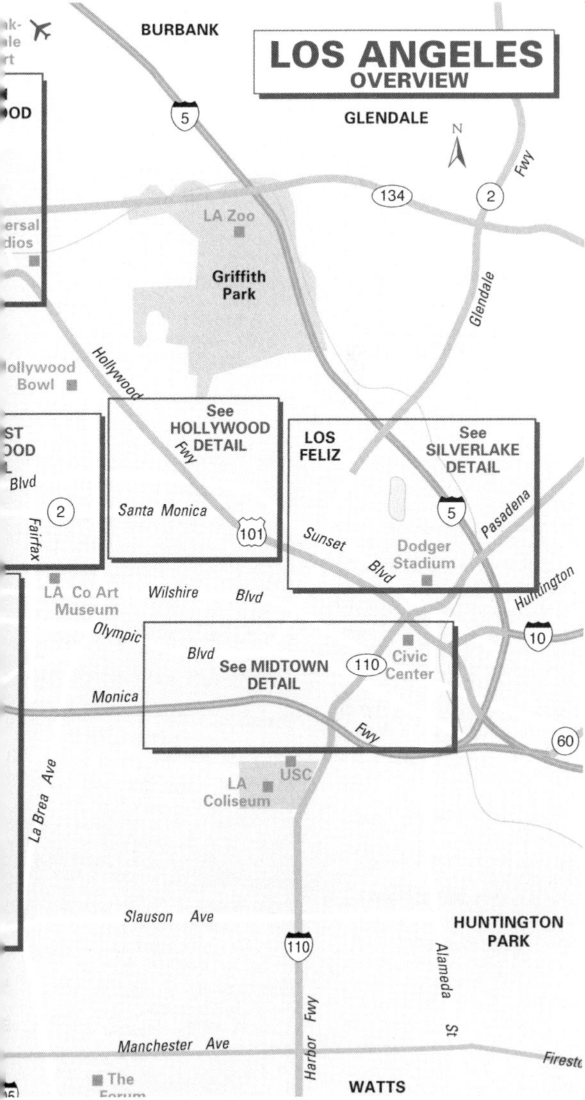
LOS ANGELES
OVERVIEW
BURBANK
GLENDALE
N
5
134
2
Fwy
LA Zoo
Griffith
Park
Glendale
ersal
dios
ollywood
Bowl
Hollywood
Fwy
See
HOLLYWOOD
DETAIL
LOS
FELIZ
See
SILVERLAKE
DETAIL
ST
OOD
Blvd
2
Fairfax
Santa Monica
101
Sunset
Blvd
Dodger
Stadium
Pasadena
Huntington
LA Co Art
Museum
Wilshire
Blvd
Olympic
Blvd
See MIDTOWN
DETAIL
110
Civic
Center
10
Monica
Fwy
60
USC
LA
Coliseum
La Brea
Ave
Slauson
Ave
110
HUNTINGTON
PARK
Alameda
St
Manchester
Ave
Harbor
Fwy
Firest
The
Forum
WATTS

Cruisy Areas

Beach in the Upper Big Tujunga Canyon (UBTC) [AYOR] Hwy 2, exit Angeles Crest Hwy, head N, turn left to UBTC Rd, turn right (btwn marker 4.5 & 4.8), Angeles Nat'l Forest *little nude beach along creek*

The Usual Suspects: Griffith Park, Elysian Park, Echo Park, Santa Fe Dam Regional Park, Whitsett Park [AYOR] *don't bother: LAPD & the rangers are waiting for you*

LA—West Hollywood

Info Lines & Services

West Hollywood Convention & Visitors Bureau 800/368-6020, 310/289-2525

Accommodations

Chamberlain [★GS,SW,WC] 1000 Westmount Dr (near Holloway) **310/657-7400, 800/201-9652** *boutique hotel, rooftop pool, restaurant & lounge*

The Elan Hotel Los Angeles [GS,NS,WI,WC,GO] 8435 Beverly Blvd (at Croft) **323/658-6663, 888/611-0398** *hip & trendy, fitness room*

The Grafton on Sunset [GS,SW,WC] 8462 W Sunset Blvd (at La Cienega) **323/654-4600, 800/821-3660** *sundeck, panoramic views, located in heart of Sunset Strip*

The Grove Guesthouse [MW,SW,WI,GO] **323/876-7778, 888/524-7683** *1-bdrm villa, hot tub*

Holloway Motel [GS,NS] 8465 Santa Monica Blvd (at La Cienega) **323/654-2454, 888/654-6400** *centrally located*

Hotel Le Petit [GF,SW,WC] 8822 Cynthia St (at Larrabee) **310/854-1114, 800/835-7997** *all-suite hotel, hot tub*

Hyatt West Hollywood [GS,SW,NS,WI,WC] 8401 Sunset Blvd (at Kings Rd) **323/656-1234, 800/233-1234** *on the Sunset Strip, rooftop pool*

Le Parc Suite Hotel [★GF,F,SW,WC] 733 N West Knoll Dr (at Melrose) **310/855-8888, 800/578-4837** *deluxe-class all-suite hotel, tennis courts, also restaurant*

The London West Hollywood [GF,SW,WI] 1020 N San Vicente Blvd **866/282-4560** *luxury hotel including dining in Gordon Ramsay's restaurant*

Mondrian [GF] 8440 Sunset Blvd **323/650-8999, 800/697-1791** *home of trendy Skybar & Asia de Cuba restaurant*

Ramada Plaza Hotel—West Hollywood [GF,F,SW,WC] 8585 Santa Monica Blvd (at La Cienega) **310/652-6400, 800/845-8585** *art deco, poolside WiFi, 15% off w/ mention of Damron*

San Vicente Inn-Resort [M,SW,N,GO] 845 N San Vicente Blvd (at Santa Monica) **310/854-6915, 800/577-6915** *hot tub, steam room, cruisy*

Sunset Marquis Hotel & Villas [GS,SW,WI,WC] 1200 Alta Loma Rd (1/2 block S of Sunset Blvd) **310/657-1333, 800/858-9758** *full brkfst, sauna, hot tub*

Bars

Club Nur [★MW,D] 8811 Santa Monica Blvd (at Eleven Restaurant) **323/855-0800** *Th only, Middle Eastern night*

Comedy Store [GF] 8433 Sunset Blvd (at La Cienega) **323/650-6268** *8pm-2am, legendary stand-up club*

East/ West Lounge [★GS] 8851 Santa Monica Blvd (at San Vicente) **310/360-6186, 877/395-6864** *4:30pm-2am, clsd Mon, très hip lounge that blends the best of both East & West Coasts, [K] Tue*

Fubar [★M,D,K,S] 7994 Santa Monica Blvd (at Crescent Hts) **323/654-0396** *4pm-2am, theme nights, [K] Tue, [D,$] Fri-Sun, go-go boys Sat*

Gold Coast [★M,NH,WC] 8228 Santa Monica Blvd (at La Jolla) **323/656-4879** *11am-2am, from 10am wknds*

Here Lounge [MW,P] 696 N Robertson Blvd (at Santa Monica) **310/360-8455** *4pm-2am, swanky & stylish, DJ nightly, [W] Th-Fri, also juice bar*

Improvisation [GF,F] 8162 Melrose Ave (at Crescent Heights) **323/651-2583** *stand-up comedy, also restaurant*

Micky's [★M,D,F,V,YC,GO] 8857 Santa Monica Blvd (at San Vicente) **310/657-1176** *noon-2am, after-hours wknds, patio*

Mother Lode [★M,NH,K,WC] 8944 Santa Monica Blvd (at Robertson) **310/659-9700** *3pm-2am, beer bust Sun*

The Normandie Room [GS,NH,WC] 8737 Santa Monica Blvd (at Hancock) **310/659-6204** *5pm-2am, "No homophobes, no heterophobes, no assholes," great cosmopolitans*

Numbers [★M,NH,F,WC,GO] 8745 Santa Monica Blvd (at Hancock, 2nd flr) **310/652-7700** *5pm-2am, restaurant/bar, upscale cont'l menu*

Smack [M] 8279 Santa Monica Blvd (at Sweetzer, at O-Bar) **323/822-3300 (O-Bar#), 323/654-0650** *9pm Th only, "world's fastest open bar": serves as many free cocktails in 5 minutes as possible at 9:15pm, 11:15pm & 12:15pm*

Trunks [M,NH,V,YC] 8809 Santa Monica Blvd (at Larrabee) **310/652-1015** *1pm-2am*

Viper Room [GF,D,E,$] 8852 Sunset Blvd (btwn San Vicente & Larrabee) **310/358-1881, 310/358-1881 (ticketing)** *doors open btwn 7pm-8pm nightly, live bands*

Nightclubs

Area [GF,D] 643 N La Cienega Blvd **310/652-2012** *10pm-2am Th-Sat, more gay last Sun for Sundays*

Cherry Pop [M,D] 661 N Robertson Blvd (at Santa Monica, at Ultra Suede) *9pm Sat only*

Eleven Restaurant & Nightclub 8811 Santa Monica Blvd (at Larrabee St) **310/885-0800** *lunch & dinner, more gay for the bar atmosphere till 2am*

The Factory [★M,D,V,$] 652 N La Peer Dr (at Santa Monica) **310/659-4551** *9pm-2am Fri-Sat, theme nights*

La Plaza [M,D,MR-L,DS,$] 739 N La Brea Ave (at Melrose) **323/939-0703** *9pm-2am, from 8pm Fri-Sat, clsd Tue, shows nightly at 10:15pm & midnight*

Rage [★M,D,F,DS,V,18+,YC,WC] 8911 Santa Monica Blvd (at San Vicente) **310/652-7055** *noon-2am*

The Ruby [GF,D,A,18+,$] 7070 Hollywood Blvd (at Sycamore) **323/467-7070** *10pm-3am, patio, theme nights: including '70s & '80s night, hip-hop, goth, electronica, house*

Rusty's [★MW,D,F] 7213 Sunset Blvd (btwn Poinsettia & Formosa, at Falcon restaurant & bar) **323/850-5350 (Falcon #)** *Tue only*

Ultra Suede [GS,D,A,E] 661 N Robertson Blvd (at Santa Monica) **310/659-4551** *10pm-2am Wed-Sat, theme nights, [W] for Girlbar Fri*

Cafes

Cafe Marco [WI] 1051 N Havenhurst Dr **323/650-7742** *6:30am-10pm, coffeehouse*

Champagne French Bakery & Cafe [F] 8917-9 Santa Monica Blvd **310/657-4051** *6:30am-9pm, till 11pm Fri-Sat, coffees & pastries as well as brkfst, lunch & dinner, some outdoor seating*

Mäni's Bakery [F,WC] 519 S Fairfax Ave (at Maryland Dr) **323/938-8800** *7:30am-10pm, till 11pm Sat*

Urth Caffe [F] 8565 Melrose Ave (btwn Robertson & La Cienega) **310/659-0628** *6:30am-11:30pm, organic coffees, teas & treats, plenty veggie & vegan, patio*

Who's On Third Cafe 8369 W 3rd St (at Orlando) **323/651-2928** *8am-5pm*

Restaurants

The Abbey [★MW,WC] 692 N Robertson Blvd (at Santa Monica) **310/289-8410** *8am-2am, full bar, patio*

AOC 8022 W Third St (at Crescent Heights Blvd) **323/653-6359** *dinner nightly, wine bar, eclectic, upscale*

Bossa Nova [BW,WC] 685 N Robertson Blvd (at Santa Monica) **310/657-5070** *11am-midnight, Brazilian, patio*

Cafe La Boheme [WC] 8400 Santa Monica Blvd (btwn Benecia Ave & Fox Hills Dr) **323/848-2360** *5pm-10pm Fri-Sat, till 11pm Sun-Th, eclectic Californian, full bar, patio*

Canter's Deli [WC] 419 N Fairfax (btwn Melrose & Beverly) **323/651-2030** *24hrs, hip after-hours, Jewish/ American, full bar*

Eat-Well [★] 8252 Santa Monica Blvd (at La Jolla) **323/656-1383** *7am-9:30pm, 8am-3pm wknds, comfort food diner*

Falcon [GS] 7213 Sunset Blvd (btwn Poinsettia & Formosa) **323/850-5350** *dinner, California/ cont'l fusion, hosts Rusty's [MW] Tue*

Fiesta Cantina [★M] 8851 Santa Monica Blvd (at San Vicente) **310/652-8865** *4pm-2am, from noon Fri-Sun, Mexican, sidewalk patio & rooftop bar*

Fogo de Chao 133 N La Cienega Blvd, Beverly Hills **310/289-7755** *lunch Mon-Fri, dinner nightly, Brazilian churrascaria*

Hamburger Mary's Bar & Grill [MW,TG,E,K,DS,S,V,GO] 8288 Santa Monica Blvd **323/654-3800** *11am-midnight, till 1am Fri-Sat, from 10am wknds (Sun brunch), full bar, theme nights*

Hedley's 640 N Robertson Blvd **310/659-2009** *lunch & dinner, also wknd brunch, clsd Sun night & Mon*

Il Piccolino Trattoria [WC] 350 N Robertson Blvd (btwn Melrose & Beverly) **310/659-2220** *lunch & dinner, clsd Sun, patio*

Joey's Cafe 8301 Santa Monica Blvd **323/822-0671** *8am-10pm, a little bit coffeehouse, a little bit diner, popular at lunch*

Kokomo Cafe [WC] 7385 Beverly Blvd (between La Brea Ave & Fairfax Ave) **323/933-0773** *diner*

Koo Koo Roo [BW,WC] 8520 Santa Monica Blvd (at La Cienega Blvd) **310/657-3300** *11am-11pm, till 10pm Sun, lots of healthy chicken dishes*

Louise's Trattoria [BW] 7505 Melrose Ave (at Gardner) **323/651-3880** *11am-10pm Italian, great foccacia bread, patio*

Lucques [WC] 8474 Melrose Ave (at La Cienega) **323/655-6277** *lunch Tue-Sat, dinner nightly, French, full bar, patio*

Marix Tex Mex [MW,WC] 1108 N Flores (btwn La Cienega & Fairfax) **323/656-8800** *11:30am-11pm, from 11am wknds, great margaritas, patio*

Mark's Restaurant [★] 861 N La Cienega Blvd (at Santa Monica) **310/652-5252** *7pm-10pm, Sun brunch from 11am, full bar*

Nyala 1076 S Fairfax (at Whitworth Dr) **323/936-5918** *many Ethiopian, Nigerian & other African restaurants to choose from on this block; Damron recommends Nyala, 1076 S Fairfax Ave, 323/936-5918*

O-Bar [GS] 8279 Santa Monica Blvd (at Sweetzer) **323/822-3300** *6pm-2am, full bar, hosts Smack Th [M] for "boys who like boys who like blazers"*

Real Food Daily [★BW,WC] 414 N La Cienega (btwn Beverly & Melrose) **310/289-9910** *11:30am-10pm, till 11pm Fri-Sat, Sun brunch 10am-3pm, organic vegan, patio*

Sante Libre 345 N La Brea (btwn Melrose & Beverly) **323/857-0412** *9am-10pm, pastas, salads & wraps*

Tango Grill [MW,BW,WC] 8807 Santa Monica Blvd (at San Vicente) **310/659-3663** *11:30am-11:30pm, Argentinian*

Tart 115 S Fairfax Ave **323/556-2608, 800/334-1658** *7am-midnight, Southern*

Taste 8454 Melrose Ave (at La Cienega) **323/852-6888** *lunch & dinner, wknd brunch, upscale eclectic, full bar*

Bookstores

Book Soup 8818 W Sunset Blvd (at Larrabee) **310/659-3110, 800/764-2665** *9am-10pm, till 7pm Sun, LGBT section*

Your leading resource for everything gay in Southern California!
FRONTIERS
INLA
News
Entertainment
Nightlife
WET ONES
323.930.3220 frontierspublishing.com
Use MyGayGo Mobile Media App wherever you travel in the U.S. and find the gay friendliest businesses in any area.
mygaygo.com

Retail Shops

665 Leather 8722 Santa Monica Blvd (at Huntley Dr) **310/854-7276** *noon-8pm, till 10pm Fri-Sat, custom leather & neoprene, also accessories & toys*

Dogspunk/ West Hollywood Tattoo [GO] 8206 Santa Monica Blvd (2nd flr, above 20/20 Video) **213/422-4801** *tattoo studio featuring Dave Davenport (aka "Dogspunk"), named best gay tattoo artist by Frontiers magazine*

Dorothy's Surrender 7985 Santa Monica Blvd #111 (at Laurel, in French Market) **323/650-4111** *10am-11pm, gifts, magazines*

Flight 001 8235 W 3rd St (at S Harper Ave) **323/966-0001, 877/354-4481** *11am-6pm, cool travel gear*

Gyms & Health Clubs

The Easton Gym [GF] 8053 Beverly Blvd (at Crescent Hts) **323/651-3636**

The Fitness Factory [★] 650 N La Peer Dr (at Santa Monica) **310/358-1838** *6am-9pm, till 8pm Fri, 7am-5pm Sat, 8am-1pm Sun*

Men's Clubs

Melrose Spa [★18+,PC] 7269 Melrose Ave (at Poinsettia) **323/937-2122** *24hrs*

Slammer [18+,PC] 3688 Beverly Blvd (2 blocks E of Vermont) **213/388-8040** *8pm-4am, from 2pm wknds*

Men's Services

► **Megaphone 323/648-3999** *Meet and Chat Live with HOT local men. FREE to listen & respond to ads. Video and text chat at GayMates.com. Use FREE code 4889.*

Erotica

Chi Chi LaRue's 8932 Santa Monica Blvd (at San Vicente) **800/997-9072** *10am-midnight, till 2am Th-Sun*

Circus of Books 8230 Santa Monica Blvd (at La Jolla) **323/656-6533** *6am-2am*

The New Unicorn Bookstore 8940 Santa Monica Blvd (at Robertson Blvd) **310/652-6253**

Pleasure Chest 7733 Santa Monica Blvd (at Genesee), N Hollywood **323/650-1022** *10am-midnight, till 1am Th-Sat*

LA—Hollywood

Accommodations

► **Coral Sands Hotel** [M,SW] 1730 N Western Ave (at Hollywood Blvd) **323/467-5141, 800/367-7263 (CA) & 800/421-3650 (US)** *hot tub, sauna, weights, cruisy for party & play crowd*

Holiday Inn Hollywood [GF,F,SW,WI,WC] 2005 N Highland (at Franklin) **323/876-8600, 866/696-3157** *exercise room, jacuzzi*

Hollywood Hotel - The Hotel of Hollywood [GF,SW,NS,WI,WC] 1160 N Vermont Ave (at Santa Monica) **323/315-1800, 800/800-9733**

Hollywood Metropolitan Hotel [GF,NS,WC] 5825 Sunset Blvd (btwn Bronson & Van Ness) **323/962-5800, 800/962-5800** *also restaurant*

Bars

Boardner's [GS,D,F,K] 1652 N Cherokee Ave **323/462-9621** *4pm-2am, "a Hollywood legend & best-kept secret since 1942"*

Faultline [★M,B,L,V,WC] 4216 Melrose Ave (at Vermont) **323/660-0889** *5pm-2am, from 2pm wknds, clsd Mon-Tue, patio*

Spotlight [M,NH,WC] 1601 N Cahuenga (at Hollywood) **323/467-2425** *6am-2am*

The Stone Bar [M,NH] 5221 Hollywood Blvd (at N Kingsley Dr) **323/466-6061**

Nightclubs

Arena/ Circus Disco [★M,D,MR-L,S,V] 6655 Santa Monica Blvd (at Seward, Circus behind Arena) **323/462-1291** *9pm-2am Tue-Wed & Fri-Sat, theme nights*

Avalon [GS,D,$] 1735 Vine St **323/462-8900** *one of LA's best dance music clubs, call for events*

Cinespace [GS,F,E,R] 6356 Hollywood Blvd (2nd flr) **323/817-3456** *6pm-2am Th-Sat only, theme nights, "Dinner & a Movie" 8pm Sat*

coral sands

CS
CS

MOTEL

1730 N Western Ave.
Hollywood, CA 90027

INFO: (323) 467-5141
FAX: (323) 467-4683
www.coralsands-la.com

For Reservation Only:

(800) 367-7263 California

(800) 421-3650 U.S. Continental

A legend in the gay community

Miss Kitty's [GS,D,A,E,C,S,$] 6510 Santa Monica Blvd (at Wilcox, at Dragonfly) *monthly, fetish/ goth/ rock 'n' roll dance club, w/ electro cabaret*

Tempo [M,D,MR-L,E,S] 5520 Santa Monica Blvd (at Western) **323/466-1094** *9pm-2am, 7pm-3am Th-Sat, from 2pm Sun, live bands Sat, beer bust Sun*

TigerHeat [GS,D,TG,E,DS,V,18+,$] 1735 Vine St (N of Hollywood Blvd, at Avalon nightclub) **323/462-1291** *9:30pm-3am Th only*

Restaurants

Hollywood Canteen 1006 N Seward St (at Santa Monica) **323/465-0961** *5pm-11pm, till 2am Th, 6pm-2am Fri-Sat, clsd Sun, classic*

La Poubelle [WC] 5907 Franklin Ave (at Bronson) **323/465-0807** *5:30pm-midnight, French/ Italian, full bar*

Lucy's Cafe El Adobe 5536 Melrose Ave (near Gower St) **323/462-9421** *11:30am-11pm, clsd Sun, Mexican, patio*

Musso & Frank Grill 6667 Hollywood Blvd (near Las Palmas) **323/467-5123** *11am-11pm, clsd Sun-Mon, the grand-dame diner/ steak house of Hollywood: great pancakes, potpies & martinis!*

Off Vine [BW] 6263 Leland Wy (at Vine) **323/962-1900** *lunch & dinner, wknd brunch*

Prado [WC] 244 N Larchmont Blvd (at Beverly) **323/467-3871** *lunch & dinner, dinner only Sun, Caribbean*

Quality [WC] 8030 W 3rd St (at Laurel) **323/658-5959** *8am-3:30pm, home-style brkfst*

Roscoe's House of Chicken & Waffles 1514 N Gower (at Sunset) **323/466-7453** *8:30am-midnight, till 4am Fri Sat*

Sushi Hiroba 776 N Vine St **323/962-7237** *lunch Mon-Fri, dinner nightly*

Bookstores

Skylight Books [★] 1818 N Vermont Ave (at Melbourne Ave) **323/660-1175** *10am-10pm, way cool independent in Los Feliz, great fiction & alt-lit sections*

Retail Shops

Mr S Leather & Fetters USA Los Angeles 4232 Melrose Ave (at New Hampshire) **323/663-7765, 800/746-7677 (orders)** *2pm-10pm, till 8pm Sun, clsd Mon-Tue, erotic goods, custom leather & latex*

Panpipes Magickal Marketplace 1641 N Cahuenga Blvd **323/462-7078** *noon-7pm, till 9pm Wed & Sat, clsd Mon, "nation's oldest occult store" w/ custom spells & classes*

Y-Que Trading Post 1770 N Vermont Ave **323/664-0021** *noon-8pm, kitsch boutique that's home to the "Free Wynona" & "Free Martha" T-shirts*

Gyms & Health Clubs

Gold's Gym [GF] 1016 N Cole Ave (near Santa Monica & Vine) **323/462-7012** *5am-midnight, 7am-9pm Sat-Sun*

Men's Clubs

Flex [SW] 4424 Melrose Ave (btwn Normandie & Vermont) **323/663-7786** *24hrs, patio, steam*

▶ **Hollywood Spa** [★PC] 1650 N Ivar (near Hollywood & Vine) **323/463-5169, 800/772-2582** *24hrs*

Jack [PC] 1037 N Sycamore Ave (at Santa Monica) **323/472-6495** *8pm-dawn, from 2pm Sun*

Men's Services

Masseur For Men [MO] **323/369-2601** *full-body massage for men*

Erotica

X Spot 6775 Santa Monica Blvd (at Highland) **323/463-0295** *24hrs*

LA—West LA & Santa Monica

Accommodations

Casa Malibu [GF,F] 22752 Pacific Coast Hwy, Malibu **310/456-2219**

The Georgian Hotel [GF,F,WI,WC] 1415 Ocean Ave (btwn Santa Monica & Broadway), Santa Monica **310/395-9945, 800/538-8147**

HOLLYWOOD
The Sexiest Spot in Hollywood!
World Famous
The HOLLYWOOD Spa
YOUR ULTIMATE PLAYGROUND™
Always Open
toll free 800spaclub
hollywoodspa.com

Hotel Angeleno [GS,SW,NS,WI] 170 N Church Ln (at Hwy 405) **310/476-6411, 866/264-3536** *boutique hotel w/ landmark circular shape, gym*

Hotel Palomar [GS,SW,WC] 10740 Wilshire Blvd (at Selby Ave) **310/475-8711, 800/475-8711**

The Inn at Venice Beach [GF,WI,WC] 327 Washington Blvd (at Via Dolce), Marina Del Rey **310/821-2557, 800/828-0688** *European-style inn*

The Linnington [MW,GO] **310/422-8825** *B&B, jacuzzi, lesbian-owned*

W Los Angeles [GF,F,SW] 930 Hilgard Ave (at Le Conte) **310/208-8765, 800/421-2317** *suites, gym, day spa*

Bars

The Dolphin [MW,NH,K,WC] 1995 Artesia Blvd (at Green Ln), Redondo Beach **310/318-3339** *7pm-2am, patio, [D] Tue & Fri-Sat, [K] Sun,Tue & Th*

Roosterfish [★M,NH] 1302 Abbot Kinney Blvd (at Cadiz), Venice **310/392-2123** *11am-2am, patio*

Nightclubs

Bubble Lounge [MW,D] 2537 Lincoln Blvd (N of Washington, at the Garter), Venice *10pm Wed only, slick lounge*

Club Papi Los Angeles [M,D,MR-L] 652 N La Peer Dr (at the Factory, at Santa Monica Blvd) **323/692-9573** *9pm-4am, monthly party, call for dates*

Cafes

The Novel Cafe 212 Pier Ave, Santa Monica **310/396-8566** *7am-1am, from 8am Sat, 8am-midnight Sun, coffeehouse that doubles as used bookstore*

Restaurants

12 Washington 12 Washington Blvd (at Pacific), Venice **310/822-5566** *5pm-10pm, till 11pm Fri-Sun, cont'l*

Axe 1009 Abbot Kinney, Venice **310/664-9787** *lunch & dinner, clsd Mon, healthy, plenty veggie*

Baja Cantina 311 Washington Blvd (at Sanborn), Venice **310/821-2252** *10:30am-1am, also brunch wknds, full bar*

Border Grill [★] 1445 4th St (at Broadway), Santa Monica **310/451-1655** *lunch & dinner from famous "Two Hot Tamales" chefs*

Cantalini's Salerno Beach Restaurant [★E,BW] 193 Culver Blvd (at Vista del Mar), Playa del Rey **310/821-0018** *lunch Mon-Fri, dinner nightly, Italian, homemade pastas, live music Sun nights*

Cora's Coffee Shop 1802 Ocean Ave (N of Pico Blvd), Santa Monica **310/451-9562** *6:30am-3pm, from 7am wknds, clsd Mon, organic*

Drago [WC] 2628 Wilshire Blvd (btwn 26th & Princeton), Santa Monica **310/828-1585** *lunch Mon-Sat, dinner nightly, Sicilian Italian*

Gjelina [BW] 1429 Abbot Kinney Blvd, Venice **310/450-1429** *pizzas & small plates*

Golden Bull [GS] 170 W Channel Rd (at Pacific Coast Hwy), Santa Monica **310/230-0402** *4:30pm-10pm, till 11pm wknds, Sun brunch, American, full bar*

Hamburger Habit [★] 11223 National Blvd (at Sepulveda) **310/478-5000** *10am-11pm, till midnight Fri-Sat*

Joe's 1023 Abbot Kinney Blvd, Venice **310/399-5811** *lunch Tue-Fri, dinner nightly, wknd brunch, clsd Mon, French/Californian*

Real Food Daily [BW,WC] 514 Santa Monica Blvd (btwn 5th & 6th), Santa Monica **310/451-7544** *11:30am-10pm, organic vegan*

Wokcano 1413 5th St, Santa Monica **310/458-3080** *11am-12:30am, till 1:30am Fri-Sat, sushi bar & Chinese cafe*

Bookstores

Diesel, A Bookstore 3890 Cross Creek Rd, Malibu **310/456-9961** *10am-7pm, till 9pm Fri-Sat, till 6pm Sun, independent*

Retail Shops

David Aden Gallery 361 Vernon #8 (at 4th Ave), Venice Beach **310/396-2949** *9am-5pm or by appt, large collection of male fine-art photography*

odyssey
odysseymagazine.net
photo by Justin Monroe
MARYTV.NET
It's hollywood babes...

Men's Clubs

Roman Holiday 12814 Venice Blvd (at Beethoven) **310/391-0200** *24hrs*

Men's Services

► **Megaphone 310/883-2299** *Meet and Chat Live with HOT local men. FREE to listen & respond to ads. Video and text chat at GayMates.com. Use FREE code 4889.*

Erotica

Pleasure Island 18426 Hawthorne Blvd (btwn Artesia & 190th), Torrance **310/793-9477** *11am-midnight, till 2am Fri-Sat*

LA—Silverlake

Accommodations

Sanborn GuestHouse [GS,NS,WI,GO] 1005 1/2 Sanborn Ave (near Sunset) **323/666-3947** *private unit w/ kitchen*

Silver Lake Gardens [M,WI,GO] 966 Manzanita St (at Delmar) **323/664-4987**

Bars

AKBar [★GS,NH,D,WC] 4356 W Sunset Blvd (at Fountain) **323/665-6810** *7pm-2am, hip Silverlake hangout*

Bigfoot Lodge [GS,D,K] 3172 Los Feliz Blvd **323/662-9227** *5pm-2am, "LA's only log cabin lounge"*

Cha Cha Lounge [GF,NH,GO] 2375 Glendale Blvd (at Silverlake) **323/660-7595** *5pm-2am, hipster lounge*

Eagle LA [★M,L,WC] 4219 Santa Monica Blvd (at Hoover) **323/669-9472** *4pm-2am, from 2pm wknds, uniform bar*

Good Luck Bar [GF] 1514 Hillhurst Ave (nr Hollywood Blvd) **323/666-3524** *7pm-2am, from 8pm wknds, stylish dive bar*

Little Joy [GS,NH,MR-L] 1477 W Sunset Blvd (at Portia) **213/250-3417** *6pm-2am, from 1pm wknds*

MJ's [★M,NH,D,B,L,WC] 2810 Hyperion Ave (at Rowena) **323/660-1503** *4pm-2am, from 2pm Fri-Sun, theme nights*

The Other Side [M,NH,E,P,OC] 2538 Hyperion Ave (at Griffith Park) **323/661-0618** *noon-2am*

Silverlake Lounge 2906 Sunset Blvd (at Silver Lake Blvd) **323/663-9636** *3pm-2am, rock 'n' roll club [GS,E] w/ live bands till Fri-Sun when more gay [M,MR-L,DS]*

Nightclubs

Dada Dance Haus [MW,D] 3211 Beverly Blvd (at Dillon St, at Medusa Lounge) *Wed only, electro & neo-disco*

Dragstrip 66 [★GS,D,A,DS,$] 1154 Glendale Blvd (btwn W Sunset & Park Ave, at the Echoplex) **323/969-2596** *9pm-2am , quarterly event, trashy pansexual rock 'n' roll club*

The Echo [GS,D,E] 1822 W Sunset Blvd (at Glendale Blvd) **213/413-8200**

Le Barcito [M,MR-L,DS] 3909 Sunset Blvd (at Hyperion) **323/644-3515** *6pm-2am, from 5pm Sun*

Cafes

The Coffee Table 2930 Rowena Ave **323/644-8111** *7am-11pm, patio, fab mosaic magic*

Restaurants

Casita Del Campo [★] 1920 Hyperion Ave **323/662-4255** *11am-midnight, till 2am Fri-Sat, Mexican, patio*

Cha Cha Cha [MW,WC] 656 N Virgil Ave (at Melrose) **323/664-7723** *lunch & dinner, Caribbean, plenty veggie*

El Conquistador [BW] 3701 W Sunset Blvd (at Lucille) **323/666-5136** *lunch Tue-Sun, dinner nightly, Mexican, patio*

The Flying Leap Cafe 2538 Hyperion Ave (below The Other Side bar) **323/661-0618** *dinner Tue-Sun, Sun brunch, cont'l, full bar, also Mary's Metro Station*

The Good Microbrew & Grill 3725 Sunset Blvd (at Lucille) **323/660-3645** *11am-10pm, till 11pm Fri, 9am-10pm wknds, plenty veggie*

Home 1760 Hillhurst Ave, Los Feliz **323/669-0211** *9am-10pm, patio*

The Kitchen [GO] 4348 Fountain Ave (at Sunset Blvd) **323/664-3663** *5pm-1am, from 11am Sat, till 10pm Sun, cozy diner*

Michelangelo Pizzeria Ristorante 2742 Rowena **323/660-4843** *lunch & dinner*

Square One Dining 4854 Fountain Ave (at Vermont Ave) **323/661-1109** *8am-3pm, great brkfst*

Bookstores

Serifos 3814 W Sunset Blvd **323/660-7467** *independent*

Retail Shops

Rough Trade Gear 3915 Sunset Blvd **323/660-7956** *noon-10pm, 10am-midnight Fri-Sat, till 8pm Sun*

Syren 2809 1/2 W Sunset Blvd **213/289-0334** *noon-10pm, clsd Mon, leather & latex*

Gyms & Health Clubs

Body Builders [GF] 2516 Hyperion Ave (at Tracy) **323/668-0802**

Erotica

Circus of Books 4001 Sunset Blvd (at Sanborn) **323/666-1304** *6am-2am*

Romantix Adult Superstore 3147 N San Fernando Rd **323/258-2867** *24hrs*

LA—Midtown

Bars

Cafe Club Fais Do-Do [GF,F,E] 5257 W Adams Blvd (btwn Fairfax & La Brea) **323/954-8080** *8pm-2am, live music, also Cajun restaurant*

Nightclubs

Coco Bongo [MW,D,MR-L,DS,S,18+] 3311 S Main St **213/748-2682** *9pm-2am, clsd Mon-Tue*

Jewel's Catch One Disco [GS,D,A,MR-AF,K,WC] 4067 W Pico Blvd (2 blocks E of Crenshaw) **323/734-8849 (hotline), 323/737-1159** *call for hours, clsd Wed-Th, theme nights*

Shits & Giggles [MW,D] 740 S Broadway (btwn 7th & 8th Sts, enter rear) *10pm-2am Fri only*

Restaurants

Cassell's 3266 W 6th St (at Vermont) **213/387-5502** *10:30am-4pm, clsd Sun, great burgers*

Ciudad [E,WC] 445 S Figueroa St (at 5th St) **213/486-5171** *lunch & dinner & late night cocktails*

Opus 3760 Wilshire Blvd (at S Western) **213/738-1600** *lunch & dinner, upscale contemporary, full bar*

Men's Clubs

Bears & Bellies [SW] 615 S Kohler (at Midtown Spa) **213/680-1838** *1st Wed of the month*

Klyt [MR-L] 132 E 4th St **213/972-9145** *24hrs, steam room & dry sauna*

Midtowne Spa—Los Angeles [SW] 615 S Kohler (at Central) **213/680-1838** *24hrs*

LA—Valley

includes San Fernando & San Gabriel Valleys

Bars

The Bullet [M,L,WC] 10522 Burbank Blvd (at Cahuenga), North Hollywood **818/762-8890** *noon-2am, patio*

Clear [GS,D] 11916 Ventura Blvd (btwn Laurel Canyon & Colfax), Studio City **818/980-4811** *8pm-2am, clsd Mon, hip cocktail lounge, patio*

Cobra [★M,D,CW,MR-L,WC] 10937 Burbank Blvd (1 block E of Vineland), North Hollywood **818/760-9798** *4pm-9pm, till 2am Wed-Sun, CW dance lessons Sun*

Silver Rail [MW,NH] 11518 Burbank Blvd (btwn Colfax & Lankershim) **818/980-8310** *4pm-2am, from noon wknds*

Nightclubs

C Frenz [★MW,NH,D,MR,K,C,S,WC,GO] 7026 Reseda Blvd (at Sherman Way), Reseda **818/996-2976** *3pm-2am, till 3am Sat, patio, theme nights: [S] Tue, [K] Th, Azucar Fri (Latin & hip-hop), beer bust Sun*

Oil Can Harry's [M,D,CW,S] 11502 Ventura Blvd (at Tujunga & Colfax), Studio City **818/760-9749** *7:30pm-2am, from 9pm Fri, from 8pm Sat, clsd Sun-Mon & Wed, dance lessons Tue & Th, classic disco Sat*

Cafes

Aroma 4360 Tujunga Ave, Studio City **818/508-0677** *6am-11pm, from 7am Sun, coffeehouse w/ small bookstore*

Restaurants

Du-Par's 12036 Ventura Blvd (at Laurel Canyon), Studio City **818/766-4437** *24hrs, plush diner schmoozing; also 75 W Thousand Oaks Blvd, Thousand Oaks*

Gourmet 88 230 N San Fernando Blvd, Burbank **818/848-8688** *11:30am-10pm, till 11pm Fri-Sat, Mandarin*

Retail Shops

Perfect Beat 12434 Oxnard St, N Hollywood **310/273-3337** *10am-6pm Mon-Fri, club music*

Gyms & Health Clubs

Gold's Gym 6233 N Laurel Canyon Blvd (at Oxnard), North Hollywood **818/506-4600**

Men's Clubs

► **The North Hollywood Spa** [M] 5636 Vineland (at Burbank) **818/760-6969, 800/772-2582** *24hrs, no membership required*

Men's Services

► **Megaphone 818/996-7000** *Meet and Chat Live with HOT local men. FREE to listen & respond to ads. Video and text chat at GayMates.com. Use FREE code 4889.*

Erotica

Eros Station 15164 Oxnard St, Van Nuys **818/994-6100** *10am-1am, videos & toys, also playspace w/ female "fantasy guides"*

Romantix Adult Superstore 21625 Sherman Wy (at Nelson), Canoga Park **818/992-9801**

Cruisy Areas

Chatsworth Park South [AYOR] 22360 Devonshire St, Chatsworth *parking lot & nearby woods*

LA—East LA & South Central

Bars

Annex [M,NH,MR-AF,K,WC] 835 S La Brea (at Arbor Vitae), Inglewood **310/671-7323** *6pm-2am, from 2pm Fri, [K] Mon & Sat-Sun*

Chico Bar [★M,D,MR-L,S] 2915 W Beverly Blvd (at Garfield), Montebello **323/721-3403** *9pm-2am, theme nights*

Erotica

Joe's Adult Books 4535 W Century Blvd, Inglewood **310/419-9064** *arcade*

Manhattan Beach

see also LA—West LA & Santa Monica

Accommodations

Sea View Inn at the Beach [GF,SW,WI] 3400 Highland Ave **310/545-1504** *nonsmoking rooms available, courtyard*

Restaurants

The Local Yolk [WI,WC] 3414 Highland Ave (at Rosecranz) **310/546-4407** *6:30am-2:30pm*

Marin County

includes Corte Madera, Mill Valley, San Anselmo, San Rafael, Sausalito, Tiburon

Info Lines & Services

AA Gay/ Lesbian 415/499-0400 *check website (www.aasf.org) for meeting times*

Spectrum Center for LGBT Concerns [WC] 1000 Sir Francis Drake Blvd #10, San Anselmo **415/457-1115** *drop-in hours: noon-5pm Mon, Tue & Th, 2pm-6pm Wed*

Accommodations

Acqua Hotel [GF,NS,WI,WC] 555 Redwood Hwy, Mill Valley **415/380-0400, 888/662-9555** *boutique hotel*

Casa Madrona Hotel & Spa [GF] 801 Bridgeway, Sausalito **415/332-0502, 800/288-0502** *overlooks SF skyline*

The Lodge at Tiburon [GF,SW,NS,WI] 1651 Tiburon Blvd, Tiburon **415/435-3133, 866/823-4669** *on 3 acres of landscaped gardens, also restaurant & bar*

Lunar Marine Boat & Breakfast [NS,WI,GO] **415/482-8027**

Marin Suites Hotel [GF,SW] 45 Tamal Vista Blvd (at Lucky Dr), Corte Madera **415/924-3608, 800/362-3372** *all-suite hotel w/ full kitchens*

Panama Hotel Restaurant & Inn [GF,F,NS,WI,WC] 4 Bayview St, San Rafael **415/457-3993, 800/899-3993** *cottages, some shared baths, also restaurant*

Waters Edge Hotel [GS,NS,WI,WC] 25 Main St, Tiburon **415/789-5999, 877/789-5999**

Restaurants

Guaymas 5 Main St (at ferry dock), Tiburon **415/435-6300** *gourmet Mexican, great views of the Bay*

Entertainment & Recreation

Black Sand Beach heading to San Francisco: take last exit before Golden Gate Bridge, go right on Outlook Rd, look for dirt parking lot, Golden Gate Nat'l Rec Area *popular nude beach, look for trail*

Bookstores

Book Passage [★] 51 Tamal Vista Blvd, Corte Madera **415/927-0960, 800/999-7909** *9am-9pm, beloved independent that draws the biggest names to read*

The Depot Bookshop & Cafe 87 Throckmorton, Mill Valley **415/383-2665** *7am-7pm, independent, also cafe w/ patio*

Retail Shops

Cowgirl Creamery 80 4th St (at Tomales Bay Foods), Pt Reyes Station **415/663-9335** *10am-6pm Wed-Sun, handmade cheeses, picnic lunches to go*

Mendocino

see also Fort Bragg

Accommodations

Agate Cove Inn [GF,NS] 11201 N Lansing **707/937-0551, 800/527-3111** *full brkfst, fireplaces*

The Alegria Quartet & Oceanfront Inn Cottages [GF,NS,WI] 44781 & 44800 Main St **707/937-5150, 800/780-7905** *in the village, ocean views*

Blair House & Cottage [GF,NS] 45110 Little Lake St (at Ford St) **707/937-1800, 800/699-9269** *in former "home" of Jessica Fletcher of Murder, She Wrote*

Brewery Gulch Inn [GS,NS,WI] 9401 N Hwy 1 **707/937-4752, 800/578-4454** *oceanview B&B made of eco-salvaged redwood, full gourmet brkfst, jacuzzi*

Dennen's Victorian Farmhouse [GF,NS] 7001 N Hwy 1 (at Hwy 128) **707/937-0697, 800/264-4723** *full brkfst*

Glendeven Inn [GF,NS,WI] 8205 N Hwy 1 (1.7 miles S of Mendocino), Little River **707/937-0083, 800/822-4536** *full brkfst, farmhouse on the coast*

Hill House Inn [GS] 10701 Palette Dr **707/937-0554, 800/422-0554** *also restaurant*

The Inn at Schoolhouse Creek [GS,NS,WI,WC] 7051 N Hwy 1, Little River **707/937-5525, 800/731-5525** *B&B w/ cottages & suites, full brkfst, hot tub, fireplaces*

John Dougherty House [GF,NS,GO] 571 Ukiah St (at Kasten St) **707/937-5266, 800/486-2104**

Little River Inn Resort & Spa [GF,NS,WI] 7901 Hwy 1, Little River **707/937-5942, 888/466-5683** *resort w/ spectacular ocean views*

MacCallum House Inn [GS,NS,WC] 45020 Albion St (at Lansing) **707/937-0289, 800/609-0492** *also restaurant & Grey Whale bar & cafe*

Mendocino Coastal Reservations [GF] **800/262-7801, 707/937-5033**

Mendocino Hotel & Garden Suites [GF,NS] 45080 Main St **707/937-0511, 800/548-0513** *garden cottages*

Orr Hot Springs [GF,R,SW,N] 13201 Orr Springs Rd, Ukiah **707/462-6277** *mineral hot springs, hostel-style cabins, private cottages & campsites, clothing-optional, guests must bring all own food*

Packard House [NS,WI,GO] 45170 Little Lake St (at Kasten St) **707/937-2677, 888/453-2677** *full brkfst*

Sea Gull Inn [GF,NS,WI,WC] 44960 Albion St **707/937-5204, 888/937-5204**

Stanford Inn by the Sea & Spa [GF,SW,NS,WI,WC] Coast Hwy 1 & Comptche-Ukiah Rd **707/937-5615, 800/331-8884** *full brkfst, fireplaces*

Stevenswood Resort & Indigo Eco Spa [GS,WI,WC,GO] 8211 N Hwy 1 **707/937-2810, 800/421-2810** *resort w/ forest spas & hot tubs*

Restaurants

Cafe Beaujolais [R,WC] 961 Ukiah St **707/937-5614** *lunch & dinner*

Bookstores

Gallery Bookshop Main & Kasten St S **707/937-2665** *9:30am-6pm, independent*

Menlo Park

see Palo Alto

Mill Valley

see Marin County

Modesto

see also Stockton

Accommodations

Rodeway Inn [GF,SW,WI] 936 McHenry Ave (at Roseburg Ave) **209/523-7701**

Bars

Brave Bull [MW,D,MR-L,E,K,S] 701 S 9th **209/529-6712** *7pm-2am, clsd Mon, [K] Wed, Latin Night Th [DS,S]*

Tiki Lounge [★MW,NH,MR,TG] 932 McHenry Ave (at Roseburg Ave) **209/577-9969** *2pm-2am*

Cafes

Cafe Genowa 3025 McHenry Ave (at Rumble) **209/571-3337** *8am-5pm*

Deva Cafe [F] 1202 J St **209/572-3382** *7am-3pm, 8am-noon Sun, patio*

Restaurants

Minnie's Restaurant 107McHenry Ave **209/524-4621** *lunch Tue-Fri, dinner Tue-Sun, clsd Mon, full bar*

Retail Shops

Mystical Body 121 Mchenry Ave **209/527-1163** *noon-8pm, clsd Sun-Mon, body piercing*

Erotica

L'Amour Shoppe 1507-B 9th St **209/521-7987**

Liberty Adult Book Store 1030 Kansas Ave **209/524-7603**

Suzie's Adult Superstores 115 McHenry Ave (at Needham) **209/529-5546** *8am-midnight, bookstore w/ arcade*

Cruisy Areas

McHenry Ave Recreation Area [AYOR] River Rd (N of Modesto) *go N on McHenry to River Rd & turn left*

Tuolumne River Regional Park [AYOR] S Santa Cruz Ave *parking lot & nearby woods*

Monterey

Accommodations

Asilomar Conference Grounds [GF,SW,WI] 800 Asilomar Blvd, Pacific Grove **831/372-8016, 888/733-9005** *Arts & Crafts-style buildings designed by Julia Morgan in pine & cypress forest*

Gosby House Inn [GF,NS,WC] 643 Lighthouse Ave (at 18th), Pacific Grove **831/375-1287, 800/527-8828** *B&B, full brkfst*

Monterey Fireside Lodge [GF,WI] 1131 10th St **831/373-4172, 800/722-2624** *hot tub, fireplaces, nonsmoking rooms available*

The Monterey Hotel [GF] 406 Alvarado St **831/375-3184, 800/966-6490** *turn-of-the-century boutique hotel*

Nightclubs

Franco's Club [MW,D,MR-L] 10639 Merritt, Castroville **831/633-2090, 831/758-9266** *10pm-2am Sat only*

Restaurants

Old Fisherman's Grotto 39 Fisherman's Wharf #1 **831/375-4604** *11am-9pm*

Tarpy's Roadhouse 2999 Hwy 68 (at Canyon Dr) **831/647-1444** *lunch & dinner, Sun brunch, patios & gardens, full bar*

Entertainment & Recreation

Ag Venture Tours [GF] PO Box 2634, 93942 **831/761-8463**

Monterey Bay Aquarium 886 Cannery Row **831/648-4800** *come for the otters, stay for the day*

Morro Bay

see San Luis Obispo

Mountain View

Nightclubs

King of Clubs Nightclub [MW,NH,D,MR,TG,K] 893 Leong Dr (at Moffett Blvd) **650/968-6366** *7pm-2am, from 8:30pm Tue, theme nights*

Men's Services

Myers Flat

Accommodations

Giant Redwoods RV & Camp [GF] **707/943-3198** *campsites, RV, located off the Avenue of the Giants on the Eel River*

Napa Valley

Accommodations

Beazley House B&B Inn [GF,NS,WI,WC] 1910 First St, Napa **707/257-1649, 800/559-1649** *historic inn, full brkfst, pet-friendly*

Brannan Cottage Inn [GF,NS,WI] 109 Wapoo Ave, Calistoga **707/942-4200** *B&B in Victorian cottage, full brkfst*

The Chablis Inn [GF,SW,NS,WC] 3360 Solano Ave (Redwood Rd at Hwy 29), Napa **707/257-1944, 800/443-3490** *motel, hot tub, kids/ pets ok*

The Chanric Inn [GS,SW,NS,WI,GO] 1805 Foothill Blvd, Calistoga **707/942-4535, 877/281-3671** *full brkfst*

Chateau de Vie [GS,SW,WI,GO] 3250 Hwy 128, Calistoga **707/942-6446, 877/558-2513** *chateau w/ gardens, full brkfst, hot tub*

Embassy Suites Hotel [GF,SW,WI,WC] 1075 California Blvd, Napa **707/253-9540**

Garnett Creek Inn [GF,NS] 1139 Lincoln Ave, Calistoga **707/942-9797** *on historic main street*

The Ink House B&B [GF,NS] 1575 St Helena Hwy, St Helena **707/963-3890** *Italianate Victorian, full brkfst*

The Inn on First [GS,GO] 1938 1st St, Napa **707/253-1331, 866/253-1331**

La Belle Epoque B&B Inn [GF,NS,WI] 1386 Calistoga Ave, Napa **707/257-2161, 800/238-8070** *in historic Old Town, full brkfst*

Meadowlark Country House [GS,SW,N,NS,GO] 601 Petrified Forest Rd, Calistoga **707/942-5651, 800/942-5651** *B&B, full brkfst, hot tub, clothing-optional mineral pool, sauna & hot tub*

The Mount View Hotel & Spa [GF,SW,WI] 1457 Lincoln Ave, Calistoga **707/942-6877, 800/816-6877** *hotel & cottages, full-service day spa, also restaurant & bar/ cafe*

Napa River Inn [GF,WI] 500 Main St (at 5th), Napa **707/251-8500, 877/251-8500** *luxury boutique hotel w/ spa, located in historic Napa Mill*

Stone Oaks Vineyard B&B [GS,SW,NS,WI] Silverado Trail, Napa **707/226-7439** *jacuzzi*

Yountville Inn [GF,SW,NS] 6462 Washington St, Yountville **707/944-5600** *alongside Hopper Creek, spa, private patios*

Restaurants

Brannan's [GO] 1374 Lincoln Ave (at Washington), Calistoga **707/942-2233** *lunch & dinner, brunch wknds, new American/ Wine Country cuisine, full bar, live jazz wknds*

Flat Iron Grill [GO] 1440 Lincoln Ave (at Washington), Calistoga **707/942-1220** *dinner, New York neighborhood-style restaurant, traditional American classics*

Redd [R] 6480 Washington St, Yountville **707/944-2222** *lunch Mon-Sat, dinner nightly, Sun brunch, American*

Tra Vigne 1050 Charter Oak Ave (Hwy 29), St Helena **707/963-4444** *11:30am-10pm, Italian, also wine bar, reservations recommended*

Entertainment & Recreation

Harbin Hot Springs [★GF] 18424 Harbin Springs Rd, Middletown **707/987-2477, 800/622-2477 (CA only)** *nonprofit retreat & workshop center, massage available, some sundecks clothing-optional*

Lavender Hill Spa [GF] 1015 Foothill Blvd (at Lincoln Ave), Calistoga **707/942-4495, 800/528-4772** *9am-9pm*

Bookstores

Copperfield's Books 1330 Lincoln Ave, Calistoga **707/942-1616** *10am-8pm, till 9pm Fri-Sat, till 6pm Sun*

Men's Services

► **Megaphone 707/266-2021** *Meet and Chat Live with HOT local men. FREE to listen & respond to ads. Video and text chat at GayMates.com. Use FREE code 4889.*

Cruisy Areas

Red Rock Beach [AYOR] Stinson Beach *nude beach 1 mile S of Stinson Beach, off Hwy 1*

Vista Point [AYOR] Rte 12/121 bridge over Napa River, Napa *parking lot & nearby woods N of bridge on E side*

Nevada City

Accommodations

The Flume's End [GS] 317 S Pine St **530/265-9665** *creekside Victorian, full brkfst*

Cafes

Java John's 306 Broad St **530/265-3653** *6:30am-5pm*

Restaurants

Friar Tucks [★WC] 111 N Pine St (at Commercial) **530/265-9093** *dinner from 5pm, American/ fondue, full bar*

Cruisy Areas

Hoyt's Crossing [AYOR] Hwy 49 *take to Hoyt Trail & follow till crosses Yuba River, near upstream end of Miner's Tunnel, nude sunbathing*

Newport Beach

see Orange County

Oakland

see East Bay

Oceanside

Men's Services

► **Megaphone 760/405-4005** *Meet and Chat Live with HOT local men. FREE to listen & respond to ads. Video and text chat at GayMates.com. Use FREE code 4889.*

Orange County

includes Anaheim, Costa Mesa, Garden Grove, Huntington Beach, Irvine, Laguna Beach, Newport Beach, Santa Ana

Info Lines & Services

AA Gay/ Lesbian Laguna Beach **714/556-4555 (AA#)** *call or visit www.oc-aa.org for meeting times*

The Center Orange County 1605 N Spurgeon St, Santa Ana **714/953-5428** *9am-5pm Mon-Fri or by appt or event*

Accommodations

Best Western Laguna Brisas Spa Hotel [GS,SW,NS,WI,WC] 1600 S Coast Hwy (at Bluebird), Laguna Beach **949/497-7272, 888/296-6834** *resort hotel, in-room whirlpool spas*

Best Western Raffles Inn & Suites [GF,SW,WI] 2040 S Harbor Blvd, Anaheim **714/750-6100, 800/654-0196** *in walking distance of Disneyland*

By The Sea Inn [GF,SW,WC] 475 N Coast Hwy, Laguna Beach **949/497-6645, 800/297-0007** *hot tub, easy beach access*

Casa Laguna Inn & Spa [GF,SW,WI,NS,GO] 2510 S Coast Hwy, Laguna Beach **949/494-2996, 800/233-0449** *inn & cottages overlooking the Pacific*

Embassy Suites Anaheim North [GF,SW,WI,WC] 3100 E Frontera, Anaheim **714/632-1221** *minutes from Disneyland*

Fairfield Inn Placentia [GF,SW,WI,WC] 710 W Kimberly Ave, Placentia **714/996-4410, 800/233-6583**

Holiday Inn Costa Inn [GF,SW,WI,WC] 3131 S Bristol St (at Baker St), Costa Mesa **714/913-9055, 800/362-1655**

Holiday Inn Express Newport Beach [GF,SW,WI] 2300 West Coast Hwy, Newport Beach **949/722-2999, 800/633-3199**

Holiday Inn Laguna Beach [GF,F,SW,WI,WC] 696 S Coast Hwy, Laguna Beach **949/494-1001, 888/465-4329**

Holiday Inn & Suites Anaheim [GF,SW,WC] 1240 S Walnut, Anaheim **714/535-0300, 800/824-5459** *walk to Disneyland, also restaurant*

Laguna Cliffs Marriott Resort & Spa [GF,SW,WC] 25135 Park Lantern, Dana Point **949/661-5000, 800/533-9748**

Laguna Magical Cottages [GS] 217 & 223 Nyes Pl, Laguna Beach **949/494-4554** *2 rental cottages on Laguna Beach*

Marriott Ontario Airport [GF,SW,WI] 2200 E Holt Blvd, Ontario **909/975-5000, 800/284-8811** *fitness center w/ tennis*

St Regis Monarch Beach [GF,SW,NS,WI,WC] One Monarch Beach Resort, Dana Point **949/234-3200**

Surf & Sand Resort [GF,F,SW] 555 S Coast Hwy, Laguna Beach **949/497-4477, 888/869-7569**

Bars

Club Bounce [MW,D,E,K] 1460 S Coast Hwy, Laguna Beach **949/494-0056** *2pm-2am, [K] Mon-Tue, upstairs dance bar Fri-Sat*

Frat House [★MW,D,MR,DS,S,YC,WC] 8112 Garden Grove Blvd (at Beach Blvd), Garden Grove **714/373-3728** *3pm-2am, [D] Wed-Sun, [DS,S] Th-Sun*

Metro Q Bar & Grill [MW,F] 19092 Beach Blvd (at Garfield), Huntington Beach **714/968-6677** *11:30-close*

Tin Lizzie Saloon [M,NH,WC] 752 St Clair (at Bristol), Costa Mesa **714/966-2029** *11:30am-2am*

Nightclubs

Bravo [GS,D,A,MR-L,F,DS,S] 1490 S Anaheim Blvd, Anaheim **714/533-2291** *theme nights, Latin music Wed & Fri-Sat, more gay Th & Sat night, goth & electronica Th & Sun*

Club Lucky Sundays [★M,D,E,S,18+,$] 14988 Sand Canyon Ave (at Tia Juana's), Irvine **949/551-2998** *9pm-2am Sun only, go-go boys*

El Calor [GF,D,MR-L,DS] 2916 W Lincoln Ave (at E Beach Blvd), Anaheim **714/527-8873** *8pm-2am, Latin music, also restaurant*

Lions Den [MW,D,K,DS,YC] 719 W 19th St (at Pomona), Costa Mesa **949/645-3830** *9pm-2am, clsd Mon-Tue, theme nights, [K] Wed, only gay Fri for Fiesta Latina [MW,MR-L,DS]*

Cafes

Avanti Cafe [F,BW] 259 E 17th St (at Westminster), Costa Mesa **949/548-2224** *11am-10pm, till 8pm Sun, brkfst, lunch & dinner, veggie & vegan, "hella fierce rockin' world food"*

The Koffee Klatch [WI] 1440 S Coast Hwy (btwn Mountain & Pacific Coast Hwy), Laguna Beach **949/376-6867** *7am-11pm, till midnight Fri-Sat*

Zinc Cafe [F,BW,WC] 350 Ocean Ave (at Broadway), Laguna Beach **949/494-6302** *7am-9pm, till 3pm Mon-Tue, patio, full cafe menu, also market*

RESTAURANTS

Cafe Zoolu [BW,WC] 860 Glenneyre, Laguna Beach **949/494-6825** *5pm-10pm, clsd Mon, Californian, some veggie*

The Cottage 308 N Coast Hwy (at Aster), Laguna Beach **949/494-3023** *brkfst, lunch & dinner, homestyle cooking, some veggie*

Dizz's As Is 2794 S Coast Hwy, Laguna Beach **949/494-5250** *open 5pm, seating at 6pm, clsd Mon, int'l, full bar, patio*

Madison Square & Garden Cafe 320 N Coast Hwy, Laguna Beach **949/494-0137** *8am-3pm, clsd Tue, dog-friendly*

Sorrento Grille 370 Glenneyre St, Laguna Beach **949/494-8686** *dinner only, upscale American bistro & martini bar*

Sundried Tomato Cafe [GO] 361 Forest Ave #103, Laguna Beach **949/494-3312** *lunch & dinner, full bar*

ENTERTAINMENT & RECREATION

Men Alive 866/636-2548 *gay men's chorus of Orange County*

West St Beach Laguna Beach

PUBLICATIONS

Orange County/ Long Beach Blade 949/494-4898

EROTICA

A-Z Bookstore 8192 Garden Grove Blvd (at Beach), Garden Grove **714/534-9349**

Garden of Eden 12061 Garden Grove Blvd, Garden Grove **714/534-9805** *24hrs*

Pink Kitty [GO] 17955 Sky Park Cir Ste A, Irvine **949/660-4990** *10am-6pm*

MEN'S SERVICES

▶ **Megaphone 714/905-0050** *Meet and Chat Live with HOT local men. FREE to listen & respond to ads. Video and text chat at GayMates.com. Use FREE code 4889.*

CRUISY AREAS

Calafia State Beach [AYOR] to the left, off the fwy (from Hwy 5 S), San Clemente

Eisenhower Park [AYOR] Orange

Fairview Park [AYOR] Costa Mesa

Fullerton Dam [AYOR] on Harbor Blvd, Fullerton *park*

Heisler Park [AYOR] N side of park, Laguna Beach *also take path to the ocean, then climb over the rocks to the right; beware cops (!)*

Santiago Park [AYOR] off I-5 (at Main St), Santa Ana *parking lot & nearby woods, early evenings*

William Mason Regional Park [AYOR] Culver St & University Ave, Irvine

Oroville

CAFES

Mug Shots [GF,WI,GO] 2040 Montgomery St **530/538-8342** *6am-7pm, 7am-4:30pm wknds*

Oxnard

MEN'S SERVICES

▶ **Megaphone 805/200-0299** *Meet and Chat Live with HOT local men. FREE to listen & respond to ads. Video and text chat at GayMates.com. Use FREE code 4889.*

CRUISY AREAS

Oxnard Shores Beach [AYOR] 5th St (past Harbor Blvd) *head to sand dunes*

Pacifica

CRUISY AREAS

Grey Whale Cove Beach [AYOR] Hwy 1 *3 miles S of Pacifica on Devil's Slide, large parking lot on left, nude beach*

San Pedro Mountain Park [AYOR] Linda Mar & Odstaad Dr

Palm Springs

Info Lines & Services

AA Gay/ Lesbian 760/324-4880 (AA#) *call for meeting schedule*

Desert Pride Center 611 S Palm Canyon #201 (at The Sun Center) **760/327-2313** *10am-9pm, till 2pm Fri-Sat, clsd Sun, programs & services, 12-step meetings*

Accommodations

The 550 [★M,B,V,SW,N,GO] 550 Warm Sands Dr (at Ramon) **760/323-7505, 800/798-8781** *hot tub, kitchens*

► **All Worlds Resort** [★M,SW,N,WI,GO] 526 Warm Sands Dr (at Ramon) **760/542-9577, 800/798-8781** *4 pools & 4 spas & large steam room*

Another World [M,SW,N,WI,GO] 526 Warm Sands **760/323-7505, 800/798-8781** *luxury clothing-optional resort*

Bacchanal Resort [★M,SW,N,NS,WI,GO] 589 S Grenfall Rd (at Parocela) **760/323-0760, 800/806-9059** *full brkfst, kitchens, 9-man hot tub*

BauHouse in the Desert [GS,SW,NS,WC] 2470 S Yosemite Dr (at Camino Real & Hwy 111) **760/320-6800** *rental home, jacuzzi*

Caliente Tropics Resort [GS,F,SW,NS,WC,GO] 411 E Palm Canyon Dr **760/327-1391, 888/277-0999** *pet-friendly motor hotel, jacuzzi*

Calla Lily Inn [GF,SW,NS,WI] 350 S Belardo Rd (at Baristo) **760/323-3654, 888/888-5787** *"a tranquil oasis"*

► **Camp Palm Springs** [★M,SW,N,WI,GO] 1466 N Palm Canyon Dr (at Monte Vista) **760/322-2267, 800/793-0063 or 747-7969 (CA only)** *kitchens, sauna*

Canyon Club Hotel [M,SW,N,WI,GO] 960 N Palm Canyon Dr (btwn Tachevah & El Alameda) **760/778-8042, 877/258-2887** *clothing-optional, kitchens, hot tub & patios*

▶ **Casa Ocotillo** [★M,SW,NS,V,N,WI,GO] 240 E Ocotillo Ave **760/327-6110, 800/996-4108** *intimate & elegant resort-style accommodations in a 1934 Mexican hacienda—"the ultimate get-away for the discriminating traveler"*

▶ **CCBC Resort Hotel** [★M,SW,N,WC,GO] 68-369 Sunair Rd (btwn Melrose & Palo Verde), Cathedral City **760/324-1350, 800/472-0836** *JocKuzzi Spa, steam room, saltwater pool, waterfall & cave, jail & dungeon*

Century Palm Springs [★M,SW,N,WI] 598 Grenfall Rd (btwn Ramon & Sunny Dunes) **760/323-9966, 800/475-5188** *'50s guesthouse w/ sleek retro style*

Chaps Inn [M,SW,WI,WC,GO] 312 E Camino Monte Vista **760/327-8222, 800/445-8916 (also TTY)** *catering to leather & bears mostly, hot tub*

Chestnutz [M,SW,N,NS,WI,GO] 641 San Lorenzo Rd (at Random) **760/325-5269, 800/621-6973** *full brkfst, hot tub, gym*

Desert Eclipse Resort [M,SW,N,WI,WC,GO] 537 Grenfall Rd (at Ramon) **760/325-0655, 800/798-0655** *studios, hot tub*

▶ **Desert Paradise Resort Hotel** [★M,SW,N,NS,WI,GO] 615 Warm Sands Dr (at Parocela) **760/320-5650, 800/342-7635** *jacuzzi, firepit, outdoor shower, clothing-optional throughout*

Desert Star Bungalows [GF,SW,NS,WI] 1611 Calle Palo Fierro **760/778-1047, 800/399-1006** *boutique hotel made up of bungalows w/ fully equipped kitchen*

The East Canyon Hotel & Spa [★M,SW,NS,WI,GO] 288 E Camino Monte Vista **760/320-1928, 877/324-6835** *boutique hotel, day spa, winner of Out & About's 5 Palm Award*

PALM SPRINGS' FINEST PLACE TO STAY
Casa Ocotillo
CUSTOM DESIGNED BATHS
2-MAN SHOWERS
ALL KING BEDS
GATED OFF-STREET PARKING
HEATED POOL & HOT TUB
PETS
The Ultimate Getaway for the Discriminating Traveler
800-996-4108 ■ 760-327-6110
WWW.CASAOCOTILLO.COM

WORLD'S FOREMOST GAY & LESBIAN HOTELS™
MEMBER
the hacienda
at warm sands
www.thehacienda.com
800.359.2007
Palm Springs

▼4 POOLS
▼2 JACUZZIS
▼STEAM ROOM
▼OUTDOOR FIREPLACE
▼FULLY EQUIPPED GYM
▼OUTDOOR COOLING MIST
▼CLOTHING ALWAYS OPTIONAL
No shirt, No shoes GOOD service
NO PANTS! Even BETTER service.
BROCHURES & RESERVATIONS:
800 962-0186
www.innexile.com
760 327-6413
545 WARM SANDS DR.
PALM SPRINGS, CA 92264
INN
Exile
A MAN'S RESORT

La Dolce Vita
Resort & Spa
20 Rooms & Suites
2 Heated Pools, 2 Hot tubs
Steam Room, Gym, AVEDA
Free Wi-Fi, Amazing Views
Massages
Facials
Body Scrubs
Body Wraps
Full service Waxing
1491 S. Via Soledad, Palm Springs, CA
760.325.2686 LaDolceVitaResort.com 877.644.4111

El Mirasol Villas [M,SW,N,NS,WI,GO] 525 Warm Sands Dr (at Ramon) **760/327-5913, 800/327-2985** *newly renovated bungalows in a garden setting, steam room & jacuzzi*

► **The Hacienda at Warm Sands** [★M,V,SW,N,NS,WI,WC,GO] 586 Warm Sands Dr (at Parocela) **760/327-8111, 800/359-2007** *2 pools & hot tub*

Helios Resort [★M,SW,N,NS,WI,WC,GO] 280 East Mel Ave **760/323-2868, 877/435-4677** *resort, hot tub, tropical gardens, mtn views, "come & stay in the playground of the porn stars"*

The Horizon Hotel [GF,SW,WI] 1050 E Palm Canyon Dr **760/323-1858, 800/377-7855** *jacuzzi*

Hotel Zoso [GF,SW,WI] 150 S Indian Canyon Dr **760/325-9676** *4-acre resort, restaurant & bar, spa*

Hyatt Regency Suites Palm Springs [GF,SW,WI] 285 N Palm Canyon Dr **760/322-9000, 800/554-9288** *also restaurant & bar*

► **Inn Exile** [★M,F,SW,N,WI,GO] 545 Warm Sands Dr (at Ramon) **760/327-6413, 800/962-0186** *resort, hot tub, gym, steam, also Skivvies Cafe, 6pm-10pm, pizzas & snacks*

► **INNdulge Palm Springs** [★M,SW,N,NS,WI,GO] 601 Grenfall Rd (at Parocela) **760/327-1408, 800/833-5675** *hot tub, Out & About-rated 5 Palms*

La Casa Contenta [GS,SW,NS,WC] **760/322-2500, 800/777-4606** *prestigious 5-bdrm estate property w/ lush gardens, lots of privacy*

► **La Dolce Vita Resort** [M,SW,N,NS,WI,WC,GO] 1491 S Via Soledad (at Sonora & S Palm Canyon) **760/325-2686, 877/644-4111** *full brkfst, jacuzzi, Out & About-rated 4 Palms*

Mojave [GF,SW,NS,WC] 73721 Shadow Mountain Dr, Palm Desert **760/346-6121, 866/846-8358** *boutique hotel, hot tub, spa services*

Mountain View Villa [GS,SW,NS] on Farrell Dr **305/294-1525** *vacation rental at Mesquite Country Club*

Rendezvous [GF,SW,WI] 1420 N Indian Canyon Dr **760/320-1178** *'50s chic*

Ruby Montana's Coral Sands Inn [GS,SW,WI,WC,GO] 210 W Stevens Rd (at N Palm Canyon) **760/325-4900, 866/820-8302** *resort, kitschy 1950s chic*

Santiago Resort [M,SW,N,NS,WI,GO] 650 San Lorenzo Rd (at Mesquite) **760/322-1300, 800/710-7729** *clothing-optional, hot tub, sauna & shower garden, brkfst & lunch included*

Sun & Fun Vacation Rentals [GS,SW,NS,GO] **760/322-7961, 877/322-7961** *rental houses & condos*

► **Terrazzo Resort** [M,SW,NS,WI,WC,GO] 1600 E Palm Canyon Dr (btwn Calle Marcus & Sunrise) **760/778-5883, 866/837-7996** *resort, full brkfst*

The Three Thirty Three B&B [GS,NS,GO] 333 E Ramon Rd **760/320-7744 (9am-8pm PST)** *intimate 3-bdrm B&B, hot tub [N], bear-friendly*

Tortuga del Sol [M,SW,N,NS,WI,GO] 715 San Lorenzo **760/416-3111, 888/541-3777** *resort, jacuzzi*

► **Triangle Inn Palm Springs** [★M,SW,N,GO] 555 San Lorenzo Rd (at Random Rd) **760/322-7993, 800/732-7555** *hot tub, 2 sundecks*

Villa Mykonos [MW,SW,WI] 67-590 Jones Rd (at Cree), Cathedral City **800/471-4753** *timeshare condos & rental units*

Villa Royale [★GF,SW] 1620 Indian Trail **760/327-2314, 800/245-2314** *jacuzzi, also Europa Restaurant*

► **Warm Sands Villas** [★M,SW,N,NS,WI,GO] 555 Warm Sands Dr (at Ramon) **760/323-3005, 800/357-5695** *hot tub*

Bars

Alternate Route [MW,D,K,WC] 120 S Palm Canyon Dr **760/883-5900** *3pm-2am, from noon Sun*

Azul [MW,NH,V] 369 N Palm Canyon Dr **760/325-5533** *11am-2am, from 10am Sun, also restaurant*

The Barracks [M,L] 67-625 E Palm Canyon (at Canyon Plaza), Cathedral City **760/321-9688** *2pm-2am, cruisy, also LeatherSmiths leather store*

Club Whatever [MW,NH,K] 36-737 Cathedral Canyon Dr (at Commercial), Cathedral City **760/321-0031** *2pm-2am, patio, wknds [C,DS]*

Georgie's Alibi [M,NH,F,V] 369 N Palm Canyon Dr **760/325-5533** *11am-2am, from 10am Sun*

Hunter's Video Bar [★M,D,V] 302 E Arenas Rd (at Calle Encilia) **760/323-0700** *10am-2am, go-go boys Fri*

Score [M,NH,V] 301 E Arenas Rd **760/327-3299** *6am-2am*

SpurLine [M,NH,K,V] 200 S Indian Canyon Dr (at Arenas) **760/778-4326** *noon-2am, lounge, [K] Th, beer bust Sun*

Streetbar [★M,NH,E,K,WC] 224 E Arenas Rd (at Indian) **760/320-1266** *10am-2am, patio*

Studio One Eleven [M,D,K] 67-555 E Palm Canyon Dr (at E Eagle Canyon Way), Cathedral City **760/324-5717** *4pm-midnight, till 2am wknds*

Tool Shed [M,NH,L] 600 E Sunny Dunes Rd (at Palm Canyon) **760/320-3299** *7am-2am*

Toucan's Tiki Lounge [MW,D,E,DS,S] 2100 N Palm Canyon Dr (at Via Escuela) **760/416-7584** *noon-2am, [E] Mon, [DS] Wed & Sun, go-go dancers wknds*

Nightclubs

Confession [MW,D,S,V,$] 611 S Palm Canyon Dr (in the Sun Center) **760/416-0950** *noon-close, till 2am Fri, till 4am Sat*

Cafes

Palm Springs Koffi [★WI,GO] 515 N Palm Canyon Dr (at Alejo) **760/416-2244** *5:30am-8pm*

Restaurants

Amici 71380 Hwy 111, Rancho Mirage **760/341-0738** *lunch & dinner, Sun brunch, Italian, patio, also full bar*

Bangkok Five 70-026 Hwy 111, Rancho Mirage **760/770-9508** *dinner nightly, Thai*

Billy Reed's [WC] 1800 N Palm Canyon Dr (at Vista Chino) **760/325-1946** *7am-9pm, till 10pm Fri-Sat*

Blame It on Midnight [M,E,GO] 777 E Tahquitz Canyon Wy, Stes 101-109 (at the Courtyard) **760/323-1200** *5pm-10pm, till 11pm Fri-Sat, live music Th-Sun, also full bar, patio*

Blue Coyote Grill 445 N Palm Canyon Dr **760/327-1196** *11am-10pm, till 11pm Fri-Sat, Southwestern*

Bongo Johnny's 214 E Arenas Rd **760/866-1905** *8am-10pm, till 11pm Fri-Sat, burgers & sandwiches*

Boscoso 707 N Palm Canyon Dr (at Merito, in Uptown) **760/325-4002** *from 5pm, Northern Italian, also lounge*

The Chop House [R] 262 S Palm Canyon Dr **760/320-4500** *from 5pm, steak*

Copley's 621 N Palm Canyon Dr (btwn E Tamarisk Rd & E Granvia Valmonte) **760/327-9555** *6pm-10pm, Sun brunch, "creative contemporary American cuisine," full bar*

Davey's Hideaway [P] 292 E Palm Canyon Dr **760/320-4480** *from 5pm, steak, seafood & pasta, patio, full bar*

Dink's Restaurant & Ultra Lounge 2080 Palm Canyon Dr **760/327-7676** *lunch & dinner, swank lounge*

El Gallito [BW] 68820 Grove St (at Palm Canyon), Cathedral City **760/328-7794** *10am-9pm, home-made Mexican*

Hamburger Mary's 415 N Palm Canyon Dr **760/778-6279** *11am-close, full bar*

Las Casuelas 368 N Palm Canyon Dr (btwn Amado & Alejo) **760/325-3213** *11am-10pm, Mexican*

Look 139 E Andreas Rd **760/778-3520** *11am-10pm, patio bar till 2am*

Warm Sands Villas
PALM SPRINGS • SINCE 1933
DESERT HOSPITALITY AT ITS BEST
28 UNIQUE GUESTROOMS
HEATED POOL/SPA & OUTDOOR MISTING SYSTEM
CONTINENTAL BREAKFAST & EVENING SOCIAL HOUR
WIRELESS INTERNET ACCESS
CLOTHING OPTIONAL
WEEKLY AND MIDWEEK DISCOUNTS
WARMSANDSVILLAS.COM
1 800 357 5695

Lotza Mozza 119 S Indian Canyon **760/325-5571** *10am-9pm, till 10pm Fri-Sat, pizza & pasta*

Matchbox 155 S Palm Canyon Dr (in Mercado Plaza, 2nd level) **760/778-6000** *4pm-11pm, till 1am Fri-Sat pizza*

Ming's Chinese Cuisine 35300 Date Palm Dr, Cathedral City **760/770-3663** *11:30am-9pm, clsd Sun*

Pomme Frite 256 S Palm Canyon Dr **760/778-3727** *dinner nightly, lunch wknds, clsd Tue, Belgian beer & French food*

Red Tomato & House of Lamb [BW,WC] 68-784 E Palm Canyon (btwn Date Palm & Cathedral Canyon), Cathedral City **760/328-7518** *4pm-10pm, Italian*

Rick's Restaurant 1973 N Palm Canyon Dr **760/416-0090** *6am-3pm, Cuban/American*

Rock Garden Cafe 777 S Palm Canyon Dr **760/327-8840** *7am-10pm, Greek, patio*

Shame on the Moon [R,WC] 69-950 Frank Sinatra Dr (at Hwy 111), Rancho Mirage **760/324-5515** *5pm-10:30pm, cont'l, full bar, patio*

Sherman's Deli & Bakery 401 E Tahquitz Canyon Wy **760/325-1199** *7am-9pm, till 2pm Th, kosher-style deli*

Spencer's Restaurant [R] 701 W Baristo Rd **760/327-3446** *9am-2:30pm & 5pm-10pm, Sun brunch, upscale contemporary*

Tootie's Texas Barbeque 68-703 Perez Rd, Cathedral City **760/202-6963** *11am-8pm, clsd Sun, the name says it all*

Towne Center Cafe 44491 Town Center Wy, Palm Desert **760/346-2131** *Greek diner*

Wang's in the Desert 424 S Indian Canyon Dr **760/325-9264** *from 5:30pm, Chinese*

Zin American Bistro 198 S Palm Canyon (at Arenas) **760/322-6300** *lunch Th-Mon, dinner nightly*

Entertainment & Recreation

CopyKatz Celebrity Review 49500 Seminole Dr (at I-10, at Morongo Casino), Cabazon **760/770-6611, 800/252-4499** *celebrity impersonators*

The Living Desert Zoo & Gardens [$] 47-900 Portola Ave, Palm Desert **760/346-5694** *9am-5pm (8am-1pm June-Aug), zoo & endangered species conservation center*

Palm Springs Caballeros PO Box 8057, 92263-8057 **760/322-3112** *gay men's chorus*

Ruddy's 1930s General Store Museum 221 S Palm Canyon Dr **760/327-2156** *10am-4pm Th-Sun, clsd summers, "the most you can spend is 95¢"*

Bookstores

Q Trading Company 606 E Sunny Dunes Rd (at Indian Canyon) **760/416-7150, 800/756-2290** *10am-6pm, LGBT, also cards, gifts, videos*

Retail Shops

Bear Wear Etc 319 E Arenas Rd **760/323-8940** *10am-6pm, till 10pm Th-Sat, noon-5pm Sun, men's clothing, leatherwear & resortwear*

The Drag Bag 650 E Sunny Dunes #3 **760/322-9500** *noon-5pm, clsd Sun-Mon, everything a drag queen needs*

GayMartUSA 305 E Arenas Rd (at Indian Canyon) **760/416-6436** *10am-midnight*

Mischief 210 E Arenas Rd (at Indian Canyon) **760/322-8555**

Tuff Stuff 407 Industrial Pl (Palm Canyon & Sunny Dunes) **760/864-8539** *10am-6pm, clsd Sun-Mon*

Publications

The Bottom Line 760/323-0552 *the desert's LGBT bar guide & classifieds*

Desert Daily Guide 760/320-3237 *LGBT weekly*

▶ **Odyssey Magazine 323/874-8788** *dish on L.A. & Palm Springs' club scene*

Gyms & Health Clubs

Basic Gym 1584 S Palm Canyon Dr (at E Olancha) **760/320-1009** *7am-8pm, 8am-6pm Sat, 11am-3pm Sun*

Gold's Gym [GF] 4070 Airport Center Dr (at Ramon) **760/322-4653**

▶ **World Gym Palm Springs** [M,WC,GO] 1751 N Sunrise Way (at Vista Chino) **760/327-7100** *5am-10pm, from 6am wknds, day passes available, steam & sauna, club-quality sound system*

Men's Services

▶ **Megaphone 760/406-8222** *Meet and Chat Live with HOT local men. FREE to listen & respond to ads. Video and text chat at GayMates.com. Use FREE code 4889.*

Erotica

Gear Leather & Fetish 650 E Sunny Dunes #1 (at S Calle Palo Fierro) **760/322-3363** *noon-7pm, till midnight Fri-Sat, leather, fetish & piercing*

Hidden Joy Book Shop 68-424 Commercial (at Cathedral Canyon), Cathedral City **760/328-1694** *24 hrs, arcade*

Perez Images 68-366 Perez Rd, Cathedral City **760/321-1033** *24hrs*

Cruisy Areas

Cahuilla Hills Park [AYOR] Palm Desert

Palmdale

see Lancaster

Palo Alto

Accommodations

Creekside Inn [GS,SW,NS,WI,WC] 3400 El Camino Real (at Page Mill Rd) **650/493-2411, 800/492-7335** *restaurant & lounge*

Hotel Avante [GS,SW,NS] 860 El Camino Real, Mountain View **650/940-1000, 800/538-1600** *jacuzzi, in heart of Silicon Valley*

Restaurants

Junnoon [R] 150 University Ave **650/329-9644** *lunch Mon-Fri, dinner nightly, Indian*

Bookstores

Books Inc 855 El Camino Real **650/321-0600** *9:30am-9pm, 10am-8pm Sat, 11am-6pm Sun, general, LGBT section*

Men's Services

▶ **Megaphone 650/223-0505** *Meet and Chat Live with HOT local men. FREE to listen & respond to ads. Video and text chat at GayMates.com. Use FREE code 4889.*

Pasadena

Bars

The 35er [GS,NH,F] 12 E Colorado Blvd (Old Town) **626 /356-9315** *3pm-1am, from 1pm wknds, more gay on Tue*

Boulevard/ Club S Karaoke [M,NH,K,P] 3199 E Foothill Blvd (at Sierra Madre Villa) **626/356-9304** *6pm-2am, from 3pm Fri-Sun*

Restaurants

Chandra [WC] 400 S Arroyo Pkwy **626/577-6599** *11am-10:30pm, Thai, full bar*

Twin Palms [NS] 101 W Green St (at De Lacey Ave) **626/577-2567** *lunch & dinner, huge menu, great patio, full bar*

Men's Services

▶ **Megaphone 626/720-2999** *Meet and Chat Live with HOT local men. FREE to listen & respond to ads. Video and text chat at GayMates.com. Use FREE code 4889.*

Erotica

Romantix Adult Superstore 45 E Colorado Blvd (at Raymond) **626/683-9468**

Paso Robles

Accommodations

Asuncion Ridge Vineyards & Inn [GF,GO] 11010 Fuentes Rd (at El Monte) **805/461-0675**

Entertainment & Recreation

Cinema e Vino Paradiso [GO] **323/422-0987** *wine tasting, dinner & classic films under the stars at selected CA wineries*

Wine Attic 1305 13th St Alley (at downtown Paso Robles) **805/227-4107** *open daily, e-wine show w/ wines, beers, & sake; also private wine country tours*

Pescadero

Accommodations

Costanoa [GS] 2001 Rossi Rd (at Hwy 1) **650/879-1100, 877/262-7848** *coastal lodge & camp w/ tent bungalows & cabins, also general store & restaurant, 1 hour S of San Francisco*

Petaluma

Restaurants

Bricks [★] 16 Kentucky St (in Lanmart Bldg) **707/766-8162** *dinner from 5pm, handmade pizzas, paninis*

Bookstores

Copperfield's Books 140 Kentucky St (btwn Western & Washington, downtown) **707/762-0563** *10am-9pm, till 6pm Sun, new & used books, also great little cafe*

Cruisy Areas

Lucchesi Park [AYOR]

Placerville

Accommodations

Albert Shafsky House B&B [GF,NS,WI,GO] 2942 Coloma St (at Spring St/ Hwy 49) **530/642-2776** *full brkfst, lesbian-owned*

Rancho Cicada Retreat [M,SW,N,GO] PO Box 225, Plymouth 95669 **209/245-4841, 877/553-9481** *riverside retreat, campsites, tents & cabins*

Retail Shops

Tony Matthews 447 Main St (at Bedford) **530/626-9161**

Cruisy Areas

Lumsden Park [AYOR] Wiltse Rd *parking lots & woods*

Pleasant Hill

see East Bay

Point Reyes

Cruisy Areas

Hagmire Pond [AYOR] Hwy 1 (at milepost 20.53) *nude sunbathing & woods; walk right across meadow & look for pond on the right, walk up hill to right of pond*

Pomona

Bars

Alibi East [M,D] 225 S San Antonio Ave (at 2nd) **909/623-9422** *10am-2am, till 4am Fri-Sat, also Back Alley Bar [M], from 9pm Fri-Sat*

The Hookup [MW,F,K,V,WC,GO] 1047 E 2nd St (at Pico) **909/620-2844** *noon-2am, beer bust Sun*

Nightclubs

The Brick Nightclub [MW,D,F] 340 S Thomas St **909/629-6333** *9pm-4am, from 3pm Sun, clsd Mon-Tue*

Erotica

Mustang Books & Videos 961 N Central (at Foothill Blvd), Upland **909/981-0227** *24hrs, arcade*

Redding

Bars

Top Shelf [MW,NH,D,K,WC,GO] 2151 Market St (at Gold St, off Pine St) **530/247-1691** *6pm-2am*

Erotica

Secrets Adult Superstore 2131 Hilltop Dr **530/223-2675**

Cruisy Areas

Clear Creek Rd [AYOR] 13 miles W of Hwy 273 (4 miles W of old 99) *nude beach, summers*

Redlands

Cruisy Areas

Ford Park [AYOR] Ford St (at Parkford Dr) *take I-10 E & exit at Ford St, turn right & first street you come to (Prospect) turn right again; park begins where street stops; take sidewalk adjacent to tennis court that goes up hill*

Sylvan Park [AYOR] 601 N University St (exit 10 E at University St) *make left when going under bridge; weekdays only*

Redondo Beach

see also Los Angeles—West LA & Santa Monica

Accommodations

Best Western Sunrise Hotel [GF,SW,WI] 400 N Harbor Dr **310/376-0746, 800/334-7384** *hot tub, kids ok*

Palos Verdes Inn [GF,F,SW,WI,WC] 1700 S Pacific Coast Hwy **310/316-4211, 800/421-9241** *jacuzzi*

Riverside

see also San Bernardino

Nightclubs

El Destino Cabaret & Bistro [M,D,MR] 83085 Indio Blvd, Indio **760/775-0686** *9pm-2am Wed-Sun*

Menagerie [MW,D,K,DS,WC] 3581 University Ave (at Orange) **951/788-8000** *4pm-2am*

VIP Nightclub & Restaurant [MW,D,F,K,DS,18+] 3673 Merrill Ave (at Magnolia) **951/784-2370** *3pm-2am*

Men's Services

Erotica

Romantix Adult Superstore 3945 Market St (at 9th) **951/788-5194** *24hrs*

Cruisy Areas

Fairmount Park [AYOR] off Rte 60 (at Market St exit)

Riverton

Cruisy Areas

Bull Creek Rd [AYOR] off Hwy 50 *trail along river*

Russian River

includes Cazadero, Forestville, Guerneville & Monte Rio

see also Sonoma County

Info Lines & Services

AA Meetings in Sonoma County **707/544-1300 (AA#), 800/224-1300** *call for meeting times*

Russian River Chamber of Commerce & Visitors Center 16209 First St (on the plaza), Guerneville **707/869-9000, 877/644-9001** *10am-6pm, also 24hr recorded tourist info*

▶ **Sonoma County Tourism Bureau** **800/576-6662**

Accommodations

5 Seasons Resort & Spa [GS,SW,NS,WI,WC] 14880 River Rd, Guerneville **707/869-8139** *cottages, hot tub, full-service spa*

Applewood Inn [GF,F,SW,NS,WI,WC,GO] 13555 Hwy 116 (at Mays Canyon), Guerneville **707/869-9093, 800/555-8509** *full brkfst*

boon hotel & spa [GS,SW,NS,GO] 14711 Armstrong Woods Rd, Guerneville **707/869-2721, 877/668-8545**

Dawn Ranch Lodge [GF,F,SW,NS,WI,WC,GO] 16467 River Rd (at Brookside Ln), Guerneville **707/869-0656, 800/734-3371** *51 cottages & cabins, also restaurant & full bar*

Duncans Cottage [MW,WI,GO] 6056 Ross Branch Rd (Ross Station), Sebastopol **707/696-1578**

Eagle's Peak [M,GO] 11644 Our Peak Rd (at McPeak Rd), Forestville **707/480-3328, 877/891-6466** *vacation house w/ deck & spa on 26 acres*

Far Reaches [GF,GO] Highland Terrace (at Huckleberry St), Monte Rio **415/864-4554** *cottage, large deck*

Fern Grove Cottages [GF,SW,NS,WI] 16650 River Rd, Guerneville **707/869-8105** *restored 1920s cottages, kids/ pets ok*

Grandma's House [MW,WC,GO] 20280 River Blvd, Monte Rio **707/865-1865, 800/433-6673** *rental home on river, private beach, lesbian-owned*

HearthSide Cabin [GS,WI,GO] 2320 Cazadero Hwy, Cazadero **415/255-1099** *2-bdrm cabin (sleeps 6), hot tub*

Highland Dell Resort [GF,WI] 21050 River Blvd (at Bohemian Hwy), Monte Rio **707/865-2300** *riverside hotel w/ full bar & restaurant*

▶ **Highlands Resort** [MW,SW,N] 14000 Woodland Dr, Guerneville **707/869-0333** *country retreat on 4 wooded acres, hot tub*

Huckleberry Springs Country Inn & Spa [GS,V,SW,NS] 8105 Old Beedle, Monte Rio **707/865-2683, 800/822-2683** *private cottages, spa, massage therapy, no smoking anywhere on property*

Inn at Occidental [GF,NS,WC] 3657 Church St, Occidental **707/874-1047, 800/522-6324** *luxury Sonoma Wine Country inn, full brkfst*

Las Nubes [GF,GO] 20635 Monte Rio Ave (at Bohemian Ave), Monte Rio **707/869-9030, 800/997-3312** *tree-house-like atmosphere w/ total privacy*

New Dynamic Inn [GF,NS,WI,WC] 14030 Mill St (at Main St), Guerneville **707/869-5082**

Pacha Mama Home [MW,NS,WI,GO] **415/608-5174** *2-bdrm home on wooded hillside, hot tub, wood stove, dog-friendly, near river, lesbian-owned*

Rio Villa Beach Resort [GF,NS,WI,GO] 20292 Hwy 116 (at Bohemian Hwy), Monte Rio **707/865-1143, 877/746-8455** *cabins on the river*

River Gem Resort [GS,NS] 20284 Hwy 116 (at F St), Monte Rio **707/865-1467, 800/865-1467** *historic riverfront cottages*

Russian River Getaways [MW,SW,NS,WI,GO] 14070 Mill St (at 4th St), Guerneville **707/869-4560, 800/433-6673** *vacation rental service*

HIGHLANDS RESORT

GUERNEVILLE
RUSSIAN RIVER

CABINS, ROOMS & CAMPING
FIREPLACES
~
POOL & HOT TUB: NUDE SUNBATHING!
~
QUIET & RELAXING
EASY WALK TO TOWN
~
14000 WOODLAND DRIVE ~ P O BOX 346
GUERNEVILLE, CALIFORNIA 95446
707.869.0333
WWW.HIGHLANDSRESORT.COM

Just add men.
{ The Woods has everything else. }
Clothing Optional Pool
Individual Cottages
& Cabins
The Woods
RESORT AT THE RUSSIAN RIVER
877 887 9218 www.rrwoods.com

▶ **Russian River Resort/ Triple R Resort** [★MW,E,P,V,SW,N,WC,GO] 16390 4th St (at Mill), Guerneville **707/869-0691, 800/417-3767** *hot tub, bar, restaurant*

Village Inn & Restaurant [GS,NS,WC,WI,GO] 20822 River Blvd, Monte Rio **707/865-2304, 800/303-2303** *historic inn w/ restaurant & full bar*

West Sonoma Inn & Spa [GS,SW,NS,WI,WC] 14100 Brookside Ln (at Main St), Guerneville **707/869-2470, 800/551-1881** *6-acre resort a short walk from Johnson's Beach, spa, some jacuzzis*

Westside Lodge [GF,NS,WI,GO] 12320 Westside Rd, Forestville **800/433-6673** *2-flr 1936 cabin-style home (sleeps 8)*

▶ **The Woods Resort** [M,SW,N,NS,WC,GO] 16484 4th St (at Mill St), Guerneville **707/869-0600, 877/887-9218** *cottages, guest cabins & suites, [WI] in lobby*

Bars

Club Yamagata [M,NH,D,F,E,S,WI,WC] 16225 Main St (at Armstrong Woods Rd), Guerneville **707/869-9875** *4pm-2am, from 2pm Fri-Sat*

Mc T's Bullpen [GS,NH,WI,WC] 16246 1st St (at Church), Guerneville **707/869-3377** *10am-2am, sports bar, patio*

The Pink Elephant [GF,NH] 9895 Main St, Monte Rio **707/865-0500** *10am-2am*

Rainbow Cattle Co [★GS,NH] 16220 Main St (at Armstrong Woods Rd), Guerneville **707/869-0206** *6am-2am, DJ Bruce Sat*

Nightclubs

RiverSpace [GS,D] 16135 Main St, Guerneville *open for special events & holiday wknds, check local listings*

Cafes

Coffee Bazaar [★WI] 14045 Armstrong Woods Rd (at River Rd), Guerneville **707/869-9706** *6am-8pm, soups, salads & sandwiches*

Coffee Catz [E,WI,WC] 6761 Sebastopol Ave (at Hwy 116), Sebastopol **707/829-6600** *7am-6pm, till 8pm Th, till 10pm Wed & Fri-Sat*

Front Street Coffee [WI] 6544 Front St (Hwy 116), Forestville **707/887-9647** *6am-2pm, 7am-1pm Sat, clsd Sun*

Roasters Espresso Bar [E,WI] 6656 Front St (Hwy 116), Forestville **707/887-1632** *6am-6pm, from 7am Sat-Sun*

Roasters Espresso Bar [E,WI] 992 Gravenstein Hwy S (Hwy 116), Sebastopol **707/829-3882** *6am-6pm, from 7am Sat-Sun, organic coffee*

Restaurants

Aioli [BW] 6536 Front St, Forestville **707/887-2476** *8am-5pm, from 10am Sat, clsd Sun-Mon, gourmet deli, outdoor seating*

Chef Patrick [BW,WC] 16236 Main St (at Hwy 116), Guerneville **707/869-9161** *lunch & dinner, clsd Wed*

Boon Eat + Drink [BW] 16248 Main St (at Hwy 116), Guerneville **707/869-0780** *lunch & dinner, clsd Tue-Wed, American*

Cape Fear Cafe 25191 Main St, Duncans Mills **707/865-9246** *9am-2:30pm & 5pm-9pm*

Farmhouse Inn Restaurant [BW] 7871 River Rd, Forestville **707/887-3300, 800/464-6642** *dinner, clsd Tue-Wed*

Garden Grill 17132 Hwy 116, Guerneville **707/869-3922** *7:30am-8pm, clsd Tue-Wed, great burgers & sandwiches, some veggie, patio*

Main Street Station [C,BW] 16280 Main St (at Church St), Guerneville **707/869-0501** *11am-7pm, Italian restaurant & pizzeria, cabaret dinner shows nightly*

Mosaic [TG,WC] 6675 Front St (Hwy 116), Forestville **707/887-7503** *lunch, dinner, Sun brunch, also wine lounge*

River Inn Grill [★WC] 16141 Main St, Guerneville **707/869-0481** *8am-8pm, till 2pm Sun-Mon, local favorite*

Seahorse [MW,WC] 16390 4th St (at Triple R Resort), Guerneville **707/869-0691**

Tahoe Chinese Restaurant 6492 Mirabel Rd, Forestville **707/887-9772** *lunch & dinner Mon-Fri, dinner only Sat, clsd Sun, some veggie*

Underwood Bar & Bistro 9113 Graton Rd, Graton **707/823-7023** *lunch & dinner, clsd Sun*

Willow Wood Market Cafe [★] 9020 Graton Rd, Graton **707/823-0233** *8am-9pm, from 9am Sat*

Entertainment & Recreation

The Nude Beach [AYOR] on Russian River at Wohler Bridge, Guerneville

Pegasus Theater [WC] 20347 Hwy 116 (at Bohemian Hwy), Monte Rio **707/522-9043** *classic to contemporary plays*

Retail Shops

Bruce's Barber Shop 16190 Main St #C (in the Russian River Realty Bldg), Guerneville *11am-5:30pm, Tue till 5pm, Fri till 6pm, 9am-2pm Sat, clsd Sun-Mon*

Guerneville 5 &10 [GO] 16252 Main St, Guerneville **707/869-3404** *10am-6pm, old-fashioned five & dime*

Nexus 16218 Main St **707/869-3374** *home decor*

Sonoma Nesting Company [GO] 16151 Main St, Guerneville **707/869-3434** *antiques and home decorating*

Touch of Greene [GO] 16377 B Main St, Guerneville **707/869-3180** *11am-5pm, clsd Mon-Tue, bath & body shop, massage, lesbian-owned*

Up the River 16212 Main St (at Armstrong Woods Rd), Guerneville **707/869-3167** *cards, gifts, T-shirts & more*

Vine Life 16359 Main St (at Mill St), Guerneville **707/869-1234** *11am-5pm, wine, cards & gifts*

Cruisy Areas

Steelhead Beach Regional Park [AYOR] 9000 River Rd, Forestville *beach & woods*

Sacramento

Info Lines & Services

Gay AA 916/454-1100 *call or visit www.aasacramento.org for times*

Lambda Community Center 1927 L St **916/442-0185** *noon-6pm Mon-Fri, youth groups, discussion groups, referrals*

Accommodations

Citizen Hotel [GF,NS,WC] 926 J Street **916/447-2700**

Governors Inn [GF,SW,NS,WI] 210 Richards Blvd (at I-5) **916/448-7224, 800/999-6689** *internet, hot tub, exercise room*

Inn & Spa at Parkside [GS,WI,GO,WC] 2116 6th St (at U St) **916/658-1818, 800/995-7275** *B&B inn, full brkfst, jacuzzi, also full-service spa*

Verona Village River Resort [GS] 6985 Garden Hwy, Nicolaus **530/656-1321** *RV space, restaurant, full bar, store, marina*

Bars

The Bolt [M,NH,B,L] 2560 Boxwood St (at El Camino) **916/649-8420** *5pm-2am, from 2pm wknds, patio, volleyball in summer*

The Depot [★M,NH,TG,E,S,V,WC] 2001 K St **916/441-6823** *4pm-2am, till 4am Fri-Sat, from 2pm wknds*

L Wine Lounge [GF,F] 1801 L St (at 19th St) **916/443-6970** *upscale wine lounge, also restaurant*

The Mercantile Saloon [★M,NH,WC] 1928 L St (at 20th St) **916/447-0792** *10am-2am*

Nightclubs

Badlands [M,D,S,V] 2003 K St **916/448-8790** *4pm-2am, from 2pm wknds, patio & balcony*

Club 21 [W,D,MR,V,GO,WC,$] 1119 21st St (btwn K & L Sts) **916/443-1537** *5pm-2am, clsd Mon, more gay for Club Bojangles men's night Wed & Sun [18+]*

Club Bojangles [M,D,MR,V,18+,WC,$] 1119 21st St (btwn K & L Sts, at Club 21) **916/443-1537** *9pm-2am Wed & Sun only*

Club Papi Sacramento [M,D,MR-L] 2000 K St (at Faces) **415/675-9763** *monthly party from 9pm-3am, call for dates*

Faces [★MW,D,TG,K,S,V,WC,$] 2000 K St (at 20th St) **916/448-7798** *4pm-2am, 3 bars w/ various theme nights featuring Latin, CW & HiNRG dance music, patio*

Head Hunters Video Lounge & Grill [MW,E,F] 1930 K St (at 20th St) **916/492-2922** *dinner Tue-Sun, Sun brunch, bar open till 2am*

Silk Bar & Cafe [GF,D,$] 1011 Del Paso Blvd (at Globe) **916/922-9994** *11am-2am, cafe [F] by day, hip-hop/dance music by night*

Cafes

Butch N Nellies Coffee Co. [WI] 1827 I St **916/443-6133** *7am-7pm, from 8am Sun*

N Street Cafe [WI] 2022 N Street **916/491-4008** *6:30am-6pm, 8am-3pm Sat-Sun*

Restaurants

Chops 1117 11th St (at L St, across from State Capitol Building) **916/447-8900** *lunch Mon-Fri, dinner nightly, steak & seafood, full bar*

Dragonfly Restaurant 1809 Capitol Ave **916/498-9200** *11am-9pm, till 11pm Th-Sat, Asian-inspired tapas, also sushi, outdoor seating, full bar*

Hamburger Patty's [K] 1630 J St (at 17th) **916/441-4340** *11am-10pm, full bar*

Hot Rod's Burgers 2007 K St **916/443-7637** *11am-2am, till 3am Fri-Sat*

Ink Eats & Drinks 2730 N St (at 28th) **916/456-2800** *lunch, dinner, late-night brkfst (till 1am, till 4am Th-Sat), wknd brunch, full bar, DJ wknds*

Jack's Urban Eats 1230 20th St (at Capitol Ave) **916/444-0307** *11am-8pm, till 9pm Wed-Sat; also 2535 Fair Oaks Blvd, 916/481-5225*

Paesanos 1806 Capitol Ave (at 18th) **916/447-8646** *11:30am-9:30pm, from noon wknds, Italian, funky artwork, patio, full bar; also 8519 Bond Rd, 916/690-8646*

Paesanos Pronto [WC] 1501 16th St **916/444-5850** *from 11am, Italian paninis & salads*

Rick's Dessert Diner 2322 K St (btwn 23rd & 24th) **916/444-0969** *10am-midnight, till 1am wknds, from noon Sun*

Sofia Restaurant 815 11th St (at H St) **916/441-0030** *lunch & dinner Mon-Fri, dinner only Sat, clsd Sun, Italian, patio, full bar*

Thai Palace 3262 J St (33rd St) **916/447-5353** *lunch & dinner*

Zócalo 1801 Capitol Ave (at 18th St) **916/441-0303** *11am-10pm, Mexican, full bar*

Entertainment & Recreation

Lambda Players 1018 R St **916/444-8229** *LGBT theater company*

Lavender Library, Archives & Cultural Exchange of Sacramento 1414 21st St **916/492-0558** *4:30pm-8pm Th-Fri, noon-6pm wknds, clsd Mon-Wed*

Publications

▶ **Gloss Magazine 510/451-2090** *CA arts/ entertainment magazine, bi-weekly*

MGW (Mom Guess What) 916/441-6397

▶ **Outword Magazine 916/329-9280** *statewide LGBT newspaper w/ N & S CA editions*

Men's Clubs

Folsom Park Sauna [MO,$] 9261 Folsom Blvd #401 **916/363-1247** *10am-10pm, bathhouse*

The Power Inn Men's Club 4931 Jackson St (at Madison) **916/879-4611** *noon-1am, hot tub*

Men's Services

▶ **Megaphone 916/340-1414** *Meet and Chat Live with HOT local men. FREE to listen & respond to ads. Video and text chat at GayMates.com. Use FREE code 4889.*

Erotica

G Spot [★GO] 2009 K St (at 20th) **916/441-3200**

Goldie's I 201 N 12th St (at North B St) **916/447-5860** *24hrs; also Goldies II, 2138 Del Paso Blvd, 916/922-0103*

Kiss-N-Tell 4201 Sunrise Blvd (at Fair Oaks) **916/966-5477** *clean, well-lighted erotica store; also 2401 Arden Wy, 916/920-5477*

L'Amour Shoppe 2531 Broadway (at 26th) **916/736-3467** *9am-1am*

Suzie's Adult Superstores 5138 Auburn Blvd **916/332-1051** *24hrs; also 4177 Florin Rd, 916/429-8480, 24hrs*

Cruisy Areas

American River Access [AYOR] off La Rivera Dr, near Howe Ave & Watt Ave

Beach & levee on American River [AYOR] at end of N 10th St, off Richards Blvd

San Bernardino

see also Riverside

Info Lines & Services

AA Gay/ Lesbian 909/825-4700 *call or visit www.inlandempireaa.org for times*

Nightclubs

The Lark [MW,D,CW,E,K,WC,GO] 917 Inland Center Dr **909/884-8770** *3pm-2am, from 6pm Mon, beer bust Sun, huge patio*

Men's Clubs

Total Body Therapy Spa 808 N Arrowhead Ave (enter on 8th St) **909/888-7242** *24hrs*

Men's Services

Erotica

Bearfacts Book Store 1434 E Baseline **909/885-9176** *24hrs, arcade*

Le Sex Shoppe 304 W Highland Ave **909/881-3583** *24hrs, arcade*

Cruisy Areas

Cajon Pass [AYOR] Cajon Pass (off Rte 138, W of I-15, in San Bernardino Nat'l Forest), Cajon Junction *parking lot & nearby woods*

San Clemente

see Orange County

San Diego

Info Lines & Services

AA Gay/ Lesbian 1730 Monroe Ave (at The Live & Let Live Alano Club) **619/298-8008** *10:30am-10pm, from 8:30am wknds, see www.lllac.org for meetings*

San Diego LGBT Community Center 3909 Centre St (at University) **619/692-2077** *9am-10pm, till 7pm Sat, clsd Sun*

Accommodations

Balboa Park Inn [GF,NS] 3402 Park Blvd (at Upas) **619/298-0823, 800/938-8181** *theme rooms*

Beach Area B&B/ Elsbree House [GF,NS] 5054 Narragansett Ave (at Sunset Cliffs Blvd) **619/226-4133, 800/607-4133** *B&B & 3-bdrm condo near beach*

Best Western Blue Sea Lodge [GF,SW,WC] 707 Pacific Beach Dr **858/488-4700, 800/258-3732** *beachfront hotel, hot tub*

The Bristol Hotel [GS,WI,WC] 1055 First St **619/232-6141, 800/662-4477** *restaurant & bar, great collection of pop art*

Carole's B&B Inn [GF,SW,WI,NS] 3227 Grim Ave **619/280-5258, 800/975-5521** *comfy early California bungalow, full brfkst*

Casa Granada [GS,NS,WI,GO] 1720 Granada Ave (at Dante St) **619/501-5911, 866/524-2312** *near beach*

Crown City Inn [GF,SW,WI,WC] 520 Orange Ave, Coronado Island **619/435-3116, 800/422-1173** *near beach, also restaurant*

Front Street [MW,GO] 2068 Front St (at Hawthorn) **619/507-9201**

Gaslamp Vacations [GS,SW,WI,NS] 1446 Front St (at Beech St) **619/446-6329, 888/470-6111** *30 vacation rental properties*

Handlery Hotel & Resort [GF,SW,NS,WI,WC] 950 Hotel Circle N **619/298-0511, 800/676-6567** *in Mission Valley, minutes from Hillcrest*

Hillcrest House B&B [GS.WI] 3845 Front St (at University) **619/990-2441**

► **Hillcrest Inn Hotel** [MW,WI,WC] 3754 5th Ave (btwn Robinson & Pennsylvania) **619/293-7078, 800/258-2280**

Hilton Garden Inn Carlsbad Beach [GF,SW,NS,WI,WC] 6450 Carlsbad Blvd (at Palomar Airport Rd), Carlsbad **760/476-0800, 877/782-0801**

Holiday Inn Express Old Town [GF,SW,NS,WI,WC] 3900 Old Town Ave **619/299-7400**

Keating House [GF,NS,WI,GO] 2331 2nd Ave (at Juniper) **619/239-8585, 800/995-8644** *Victorian B&B, full brkfst*

Kings Inn Hotel [GS,SW,WI,WC] 1333 Hotel Circle S (Backman St) **619/297-2231, 800/785-4647**

Mike's Place [M,WI,GO] 1252 Lincoln Ave (at Washington St) **619/992-7466** *private guest cottage*

Park Manor Suites [GF,WI] 525 Spruce St (btwn 5th & 6th) **619/291-0999, 800/874-2649** *1926 hotel, bar [P] & 2 restaurants, popular Fri happy hour*

Sunburst Court Inn [GS,NS,WI,GO] 4086 Alabama St (at Polk) **619/294-9665, 866/217-5490** *all-suite inn*

W San Diego [GF,SW,NS,WI,WC] 421 W B St **619/398-3100, 877/WHOTELS (reservations only)** *rooftop bar, also restaurant*

Bars

Airport Lounge [GF,D,F,YC] 2400 India St (in Little Italy) **619/685-3881** *8pm-2am Th-Sat, futuristic airplane-themed restaurant to match the planes booming by overhead*

Bourbon Street [★M,E,V] 4612 Park Blvd (at Adams) **619/291-4043** *4pm-2am, front bar [E] & lounge [DJ], patio, [K] Tue, go-go boys Sat*

The Brass Rail [MW,D,WC] 3796 5th Ave (at Robinson) **619/298-2233** *7pm-2am, from 2pm Fri-Sun, clsd Tue, theme nights, Latin night Sat*

The Caliph [M,E,K,P,OC,WC] 3100 5th Ave (at Redwood) **619/298-9495** *11am-2am, piano bar*

Cheers [M,NH] 1839 Adams Ave (at Park) **619/298-3269** *11am-2am, patio*

The Flame [★MW,D] 3780 Park Blvd (at University) **619/295-4163** *patio*

Flicks [★M,K,V,YC] 1017 University Ave (at 10th Ave) **619/297-2056** *2pm-2am, wet underwear contest Sat*

The Hole [M,NH,L] 2820 Lytton St (at Rosecrans) **619/226-9019** *4pm-close, from noon wknds, tropical patio*

Kickers [★MW,D,CW,WC] 308 University Ave (at 3rd Ave) **619/491-0400** *Th & Sat only, also dance lessons*

The Loft [M,NH,WC] 3610 5th Ave (at Brookes) **619/296-6407** *11am-2am*

No 1 Fifth Ave (no sign) [M,NH,V] 3845 5th Ave (at University) **619/299-1911** *noon-2am, patio*

Pecs [M,NH,B,L,WC] 2046 University Ave (at Alabama) **619/296-0889** *noon-2am, from 10am Sun, patio, cruisy*

Redwing Bar & Grill [M,NH] 4012 30th St (at Lincoln, North Park) **619/281-8700** *11am-2am, patio*

San Diego Eagle [M,NH,L,WC] 3040 North Park Wy (at 30th) **619/295-8072** *4pm-2am, from 2pm Fri-Sun*

SRO Lounge [M,NH,OC] 1807 5th Ave (btwn Elm & Fir) **619/232-1886** *10am-2am, cocktail lounge, Ladies Night Out 1st & 3rd Sat [W,TG]*

Nightclubs

► **Bacchus House** [★M,D,MR,TG,E,DS,S,V,YC,WC,GO] 3054 University Ave (at 30th St) **619/299-2032** *4pm-2am, clsd Mon, theme nights*

Numbers [★MW,D,S,V,WC] 3811 Park Blvd (at University) **619/294-7583** *G Spot [W] Fri, Recharge [M] Sat, patio*

Rich's [★M,D,V,S,YC] 1051 University Ave (at Vermont) **619/295-2195** *open Wed-Sun, theme nights, L.L. Bear [B,L] 3rd Sat*

Universal [GS,D] 1202 University (at Vermont) **619/692-1900** *also lounge & restaurant*

Cafes

Babycakes [BW] 3766 5th Ave (at Robinson) **619/296-4173** *9am-11pm, patio*

The Big Kitchen [WC] 3003 Grape St (at 30th) **619/234-5789** *8am-2pm*

Claire de Lune 2906 University Ave **619/688-9845** *5am-midnight, till 1am Fri-Sat*

Cream Coffee Bar [WI] 4496 Park Blvd (University Heights) **619/260-1917** *7am-11pm*

Espresso Roma UCSD Price Center #76 (at Voight), La Jolla **858/450-2141** *7am-10pm*

Extraordinary Desserts 2929 5th Ave **619/294-2132** *also store in Little Italy: 1430 Union, 619/249-7001, the name says it all*

Gelato Vero Caffee [WI] 3753 India St **619/295-9269** *7am-midnight, great desserts (yes, the gelato is truly delicious) as well as coffee*

Twiggs [E] 4590 Park Blvd (at Madison Ave, University Heights) **619/296-0616** *7am-11pm, live music*

Urban Grind [★GO] 3797 Park Blvd (at University) **619/294-2920** *7am-11pm*

Restaurants

Adams Avenue Grill [BW,WC,GO] 2201 Adams Ave (at Mississippi) **619/298-8440** *brkfst, lunch & dinner, bistro*

Apertivo 3926 30th St **619/297-7799** *dinner Tue-Sun, clsd Mon, Italian tapas & wine bar*

Aqua Blu [WC] 734 5th Ave (near G St) **619/544-6456** *lunch & dinner, "fusion seafood," upscale*

Arrivederci 3845 4th Ave **619/299-6282** *lunch & dinner*

Bai Yook Thai 1260 University Ave **619/296-2700** *lunch & dinner, dinner only Sun*

Baja Betty's [★MW,WC] 1421 University Ave (at Normal St) **619/269-8510** *11am-midnight, till 1am Fri-Sat, Mexican, also tequila bar, patio*

Brian's American Eatery [BW] 1451 Washington St **619/296-8268** *6:30am-10pm, 24hrs Fri-Sat*

Cafe Eleven [WC,GO] 1440 University Ave (at Normal) **619/260-8023** *11am-close, Sun brunch from 10am, country French, patio*

California Cuisine [WC] 1027 University Ave (at 10th Ave) **619/543-0790** *5pm-10pm, some veggie, also bar*

Celadon 3671 5th Ave (btwn Brookes & Penn) **619/297-8424** *lunch & dinner, upscale Thai*

City Deli 535 University Ave (at 6th Ave) **619/295-2747** *7am-midnight, till 2am wknds, NY deli, full bar*

Cody's La Jolla [E,R] 8030 Girard Ave (at Coast Blvd S), La Jolla **858/459-0040** *brkfst & lunch daily, dinner Th-Sun*

The Cottage 7702 Fay (at Klein), La Jolla **858/454-8409** *7:30am-3pm, dinner June-Sept*

CrazeeBurger [BW] 4201 30th St (at Howard) **619/282-6044** *11am-9pm, till 11pm Fri-Sat*

Crest Cafe [WC] 425 Robinson (btwn 4th & 5th) **619/295-2510** *7am-midnight*

Dish 1220 University Ave (at Universal Lounge) **619/296-3474** *from 5pm Th-Sat, from 9am Sun, upscale*

Gulf Coast Grill 4130 Park Blvd **619/295-2244** *lunch & dinner, also Sun brunch, New Orleans-inspired menu*

Hash House A Go Go 3628 5th Ave **619/298-4646** *brkfst, lunch & dinner, clsd Mon, great brkfst*

Hawthorn's 2895 University Ave **619/544-0940, 619/295-1688** *dinner nightly, Sun brunch, clsd Mon, seasonal food & wine, American, also popular lounge*

Hawthorn's 2895 University Ave **619/295-1688** *dinner Tue-Sun, Sun brunch, clsd Mon, upscale, also lounge*

Hula's Bar & Grill 142 University Ave **619/501-2506** *11am-1am, from 8am wknds*

Inn at the Park [★M] 525 Spruce St (btwn 5th & 6th, at Park Manor Suites) **619/296-0057** *dinner nightly, also bar [P]*

Jimmy Carter's Mexican Cafe 3172 5th Ave (at Spruce) **866/920-9163** *7am-9pm*

Kemo Sabe [R] 3958 5th Ave **619/220-6802** *5:30pm-close, int'l*

Kous Kous 3940 4th Ave, Ste 110 (beneath Martinis on Fourth) **619/295-5560** *5pm-11pm, Moroccan*

Lips [DS] 3036 El Cajon Blvd **619/295-7900** *5pm-close, Sun gospel brunch, clsd Mon, "the ultimate in drag dining," Bitchy Bingo Wed, celeb impersonation Th, DJ wknds*

Magnolias [E] 342 Euclid Ave, Ste 403 **619/262-6005** *Southern, live jazz*

Martinis Above Fourth [MW,C,P,GO] 3940 4th Ave, Ste 200 (btwn Washington & University) **619/400-4500** *5pm-11pm, 4pm-midnight Fri-Sat, clsd Sun-Mon*

The Mission 3795 Mission Blvd (at San Jose), Mission Beach **858/488-9060** *7am-3pm*

Modus Supper Club [WC] 2202 4th Ave (at Ivy) **619/236-8516** *5pm-2am, clsd Mon, patio*

Ono Sushi 1236 University Ave **619/298-0616** *lunch wknds, dinner nightly*

The Prado 1549 El Prado (in Balboa Park) **619/557-9441** *lunch & dinner, Latin/ Italian fusion*

Roberto's 3202 Mission Blvd **858/488-1610** *the best rolled tacos & guacamole, multiple locations*

Rudford's [★] 2900 El Cajon Blvd (at Kansas St) **619/282-8423** *24hrs, homestyle cooking*

Saigon on Fifth 3900 5th Ave, Ste 120 **619/220-8828** *11am-midnight, Vietnamese*

South Park Bar & Grill [E] 1946 Fern St (at Grape St) **619/696-0096** *5pm-9pm, till midnight Wed-Sat, bar till 2am*

Taste of Szechuan 670 University Ave **619/298-1668** *11:30am-11pm*

Terra 3900 block of Vermont St (at 10th Ave) **619/293-7088** *lunch & dinner, clsd for dinner*

Urban Mo's [★MW,D,E,WC] 308 University Ave (at 3rd) **619/491-0400** *9am-2am, 10am-midnight Sun, 3 full bars (Club Mo's), patio*

Veg N Out 3442 30th St (North Park) **619/546-8411** *11am-9pm, from noon Sun, veggie burgers, dogs, sandwiches & more*

Waffle Spot 1333 Hotel Circle S (at King's Inn) **619/297-2231** *7am-2pm*

Entertainment & Recreation

Diversionary Theatre 4545 Park Blvd #101 (at Madison) **619/220-0097 (box office #), 619/220-6830** *LGBT theater*

Torrey Pines Beach State Park ("Blacks Beach") *popular nude beach*

Bookstores

Groundwork Books Collective [WC] UCSD Student Center 0323 (at Gilman Dr), La Jolla **858/452-9625** *10am-4pm Mon-Th only, alternative, LGBT section*

VULCAN
STEAM AND SAUNA
steam room
sauna
whirlpool
patio sundeck
private rooms
community rooms
bunkroom
lockers
4 tv lounges
open 24 hours
619.238.1980
805 W. Cedar St.
San Diego, CA 92101
downtown
across from the trolley

Obelisk the Bookstore [★WC] 1029 University Ave (at 10th) **619/297-4171** *10am-10pm, LGBT*

Traveler's Depot 1655 Garnet Ave (in Pacific Beach) **858/483-1421** *10am-7pm, noon-5pm*

Retail Shops

Auntie Helen's [WC] 4028 30th St (at Lincoln) **619/584-8438** *10am-4:30pm, clsd Sun-Mon, thrift shop benefits PWAs*

Babette Schwartz [GO] 421 University Ave (at 5th Ave) **619/220-7048** *11am-9pm, till 5pm Sun, campy novelties & gifts*

Flesh Skin Grafix 1155 Palm Ave, Imperial Beach **619/424-8983** *tattoos & piercing*

Mankind 3425 5th Ave (at Upas St) **617/497-1970** *11am-10pm, noon-6pm Sun*

Publications

The Bottomline 3314 4th Ave **619/291-6690** *bi-weekly, news, entertainment & listings, covers San Diego & Palm Springs*

► **Gay/ Lesbian Times** 1730 Monroe Ave, Ste A **619/299-6397, 800/438-8786** *LGBT newsmagazine*

San Diego PIX 1010 University Ave **877/727-5446**

Gyms & Health Clubs

Frog's Athletic Club 901 Hotel Circle S (at Washington), Mission Valley **619/291-3500**

PowerHouse Gym 734 University Ave #D (at 7th Ave) **619/296-7878** *5am-11pm, 8am-8pm wknds*

Urbanbody Gym 3148 University Ave (at Iowa St, North Park) **619/795-9712**

Men's Clubs

► **Club San Diego** [★PC] 3955 4th Ave (btwn Washington & University) **619/295-0850** *24hrs*

► **Vulcan Steam & Sauna** [★PC] 805 W Cedar St (at Pacific Hwy) **619/238-1980** *24hrs*

Men's Services

► **Megaphone 619/308-0800** *Meet and Chat Live with HOT local men. FREE to listen & respond to ads. Video and text chat at GayMates.com. Use FREE code 4889.*

Erotica

Adult Emporium [GO] 3576 Main St (at 32nd St) **619/239-1878** *24hrs*

Barnett Ave Adult Superstore 3610 Barnett Ave (near intersection of Barnett & Jessop Ln) **619/224-0187** *24hrs*

The Crypt 3847 Park Blvd (at University) **619/692-9499**

Gemini Adult Books [WC] 5265 University Ave (at 52nd) **619/287-1402**

Pleasures & Treasures [GO] 2228 University Ave **619/822-4280** *clsd Tue*

Romantix Adult Superstore 1407 University Ave (at Richmond) **619/299-7186** *also Hillcrest location*

Cruisy Areas

Please Note: All cruisy areas for San Diego have been removed because the SDPD aggressively polices these areas.

San Francisco

San Francisco is divided into 7 geographical areas:

SF–Overview
SF–Castro & Noe Valley
SF–South of Market
SF–Polk Street Area
SF–Downtown & North Beach
SF–Mission District
SF–Haight, Fillmore, Hayes Valley

SF—Overview

Info Lines & Services

AA Gay/ Lesbian 1821 Sacramento St **415/674-1821** *check www.aasf.org for meeting times*

The Center for Sex & Culture 2215-R Market St, PMB 455, 94114 **415/255-1155** *very queer-friendly classes, events, readings & more*

Crystal Meth Anonymous 415/835-4747

GLBT Hotline of San Francisco 415/355-0999 *5pm-9pm Mon-Fri, peer-counseling, info*

LYRIC (Lavender Youth Recreation/ Information Center) 127 Collingwood (btwn 18th & 19th) **415/703-6150, 800/969-6884 (nationwide) & 246-7743 (CA only)** *Talkline 6:30pm-9:30pm Mon-Sat, peer-run support line for LGBT youth under 24, at 415/863-3636 (in SF) or 800/246-7743 (in CA) or 800/969-6884 (nationwide)*

Magnet [★] 4122 18th St **415/581-1600** *center for total gay men's health (mind & body) in heart of the Castro*

► **San Francisco Convention & Visitors Bureau 415/391-2000, 800/637-5196 (reservations line)** *see ad in front color section*

The San Francisco LGBT Community Center 1800 Market St (at Octavia) **415/865-5555** *noon-10pm, from 9am Sat, clsd Sun, cafe, classes & more*

Nightclubs

► **GusPresents.com** *The host with the most—Gus is always throwing one hell of a party for the boys!*

Restaurants

Beach Chalet Brewery & Restaurant [E] 1000 Great Hwy (at Fulton St) **415/386-8439**

Entertainment & Recreation

Betty's List 415/503-1375 *LGBT directory & community calendar at www.bettyslist.com*

Black Sand Beach first exit past Golden Gate Bridge (Alexander) (go left under fwy, right on Outlook Rd, look for dirt parking lot), Golden Gate Nat'l Rec Area *popular nude beach, look for trail*

Castro Theatre 429 Castro (at Market) **415/621-6120** *art house cinema, many LGBT & cult classics, live organ evenings*

Cruisin' the Castro Tours tour meets at the rainbow flag at Harvey Milk Plaza (corner of Castro & Market) **415/255-1821** *"The 'original' historical walking tour of the Castro, the world's largest gay mecca. Fun & easy!"*

Femina Potens 2199 Market St (at Sanchez) **415/864-1558** *nonprofit art gallery & performance space promoting women & transfolk in the arts*

Frameline 415/703-8650 *LGBT media arts foundation that sponsors annual SF Int'l LGBT Film Festival in June*

The Intersection for the Arts [GF] 446 Valencia St (btwn 15th & 16th Sts) **415/626-2787, 415/626-3311 (box office)** *San Francisco's oldest alternative arts space (since 1965!) w/ plays, art exhibitions, live jazz, literary series, performance art & much more*

Local Tastes of the City Tours [GO] **415/665-0480, 888/358-8687** *explore the history & culture of local neighborhoods, including Chinatown & North Beach/ Little Italy, as "we eat our way through San Francisco"*

The Marsh 1062 Valencia (at 22nd St) **415/826-5750 (event info) & 641-0235 (office), 800/838-3006 (box office)** *queer-positive theater*

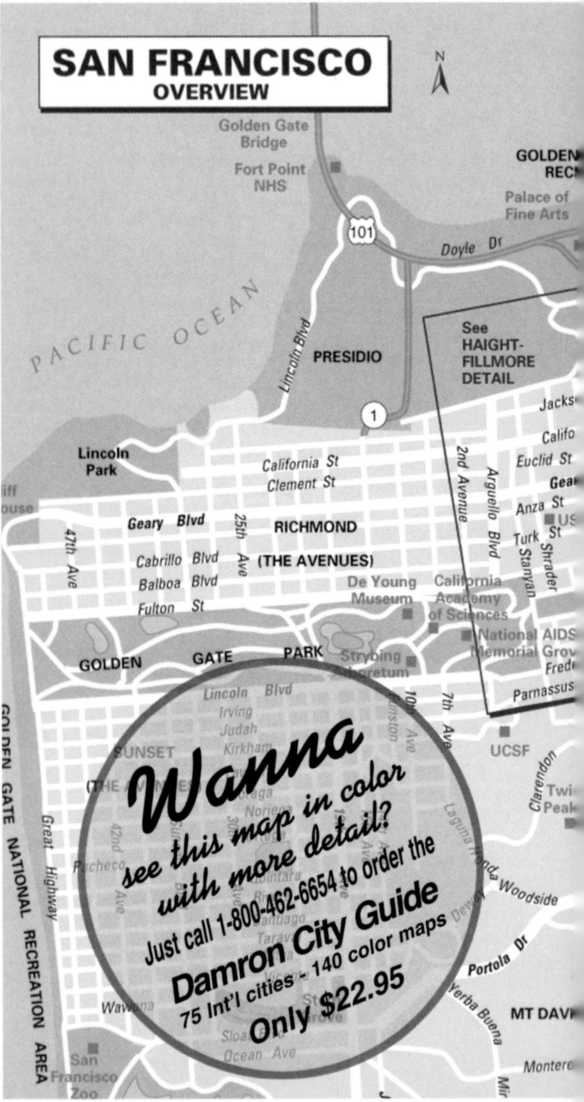
SAN FRANCISCO
OVERVIEW
N
Golden Gate Bridge
Fort Point NHS
101
PACIFIC OCEAN
Doyle Dr
Palace of Fine Arts
Lincoln Blvd
PRESIDIO
See HAIGHT-FILLMORE DETAIL
1
Lincoln Park
California St
Clement St
Geary Blvd
25th Ave
47th Ave
RICHMOND
(THE AVENUES)
Cabrillo Blvd
Balboa Blvd
Fulton St
2nd Avenue
Arguello Blvd
Euclid St
Anza St
Turk St
Stanyan
Shrader
De Young Museum
California Academy of Sciences
National AIDS
GOLDEN GATE PARK
Parnassus
UCSF
Lincoln Blvd
Irving
Judah
Kirkham
SUNSET
Great Highway
GOLDEN GATE NATIONAL RECREATION AREA
Woodside
Portola Dr
Yerba Buena
San Francisco Zoo
Ocean Ave
Wanna
see this map in color
with more detail?
Just call 1-800-462-6654 to order the
Damron City Guide
75 Int'l cities - 140 color maps
Only $22.95

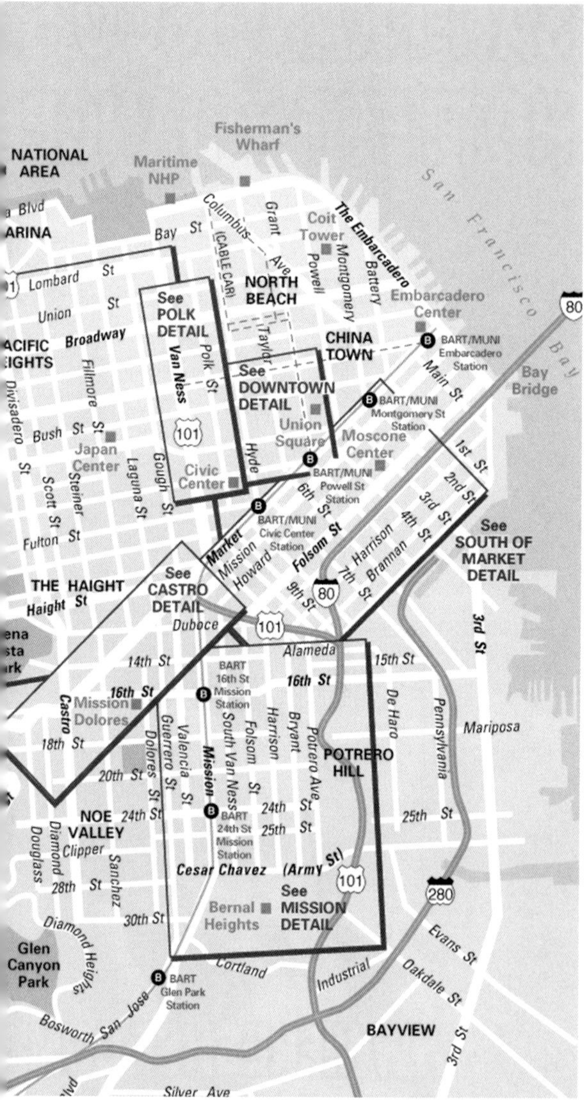
Fisherman's Wharf
NATIONAL AREA
Maritime NHP
San Francisco Bay
Columbus
Grant
Coit Tower
The Embarcadero
Bay St
(CABLE CAR)
Ave
Powell
Montgomery
Battery
ARINA
Lombard St
Union St
NORTH BEACH
Embarcadero Center
80
See POLK DETAIL
ACIFIC IGHTS
Broadway
Van Ness
Polk St
Taylor
CHINA TOWN
BART/MUNI Embarcadero Station
Bay Bridge
Main St
See DOWNTOWN DETAIL
Divisadero St
Fillmore
Bush St
Japan Center
101
Union Square
BART/MUNI Montgomery St Station
Moscone Center
Scott St
Steiner
Laguna St
Gough St
Hyde
Civic Center
BART/MUNI Powell St Station
1st St
2nd St
3rd St
6th St
Fulton St
BART/MUNI Civic Center Station
Market
Mission
Howard
Folsom St
Harrison
Brannan
4th St
7th St
See SOUTH OF MARKET DETAIL
THE HAIGHT
Haight St
See CASTRO DETAIL
9th St
80
Duboce
101
3rd St
Alameda
15th St
14th St
BART 16th St Mission Station
16th St
16th St
Castro
Mission Dolores
De Haro
Pennsylvania
Mariposa
18th St
Guerrero St
Valencia St
Dolores St
South Van Ness
Folsom St
Harrison
Bryant
Potrero Ave
POTRERO HILL
20th St
Mission
NOE VALLEY
24th St
BART 24th St Mission Station
24th St
25th St
25th St
Douglass
Diamond
Clipper
Sanchez
28th St
Cesar Chavez (Army St)
101
See MISSION DETAIL
Bernal Heights
280
30th St
Diamond Heights
Evans St
Glen Canyon Park
BART Glen Park Station
Cortland
Industrial
Oakdale St
Bosworth
San Jose
BAYVIEW
3rd St
Silver Ave

SAN FRANCISCO'S
HOTTEST T-DANCE
RubySkye
POUR HOMME
FRESH
POUR HOMME
RubySkye
WWW.FRESHSF.COM

GUS PRESENTS
BOY BAR
FULL FRONTAL FRIDAYS
IN THE CASTRO!
CHEAP DRINKS!
RED HOT GO-GO BROS!
SICK MUSIC by MATT!
2369 market @ castro
pm-2am
GUSPRESENTS.COM
MYSPACE.COM/BOY_BAR
Now Showing On
NAKED SWORD
NAKEDSWORD.COM
Blue Angel

▶ **National AIDS Memorial Grove** [WC] Golden Gate Park (on corner of Middle Drive East & Bowling Green Dr) **415/765-0497, 888/294-7683** *guided tours available 9am-noon every 3rd Sat*

The New Conservatory Theatre Center 25 Van Ness Ave, Lower Lobby (at Market) **415/861-8972** *LGBT theater in historic Masonic Bldg*

San Francisco Pride 1800 Market St, PMB #Q31 94102 **415/864-3733**

Steve Silver's Beach Blanket Babylon [★] 678 Beach Blanket Babylon Ave (formerly Green St) (btwn Powell & Columbus, in Club Fugazi) **415/421-4222** *the USA's longest running musical revue & wigs that must be seen to be believed; also restaurant & full bar*

Theatre Rhinoceros 2926 16th St (at S Van Ness) **415/861-5079 (box office), 415/552-4100** *LGBT theater*

Victorian Home Walks [GO] **415/252-9485** *custom-tailored walking tours w/ San Francisco resident*

Yerba Buena Center for the Arts [GF] 701 Mission St (at 3rd St) **415/978-2787 (box office), 415/978-2700 (administrative)** *annual season includes wide variety of contemporary dance, theater & music, also film theater & gallery*

Publications

BAR (Bay Area Reporter) **415/861-5019** *the weekly LGBT newspaper*

Bay Times **415/626-0260** *bi-weekly, good Bay Area resource listings*

▶ **Gloss Magazine** **510/451-2090** *CA arts/ entertainment magazine, bi-weekly*

Men's Clubs

SF Jacks **415/267-6999** *2nd & 4th Mon, doors open 7:30pm-8:30pm only, mandatory clothes check, call hotline for location*

Steamworks [★PC] 2107 4th St (at Addison), Berkeley **510/845-8992** *24hrs, live DJ Fri-Sat*

Men's Services

▶ **Megaphone** **415/430-1199** *Meet and Chat Live with HOT local men. FREE to listen & respond to ads. Video and text chat at GayMates.com. Use FREE code 4889.*

SF—Castro & Noe Valley

Accommodations

24 Henry & Village House [M,NS,WI,GO] 24 Henry St & 4080 18th St (btwn Sanchez & Noe) **415/864-5686, 800/900-5686** *B&B, some shared baths, 1-bdrm apt also available*

Albion House Inn [GF,NS] 135 Gough St (at Fell) **415/621-0896, 800/400-8295** *European full brkfst*

Andrew Whelan House [GS,NS,WI,GO] 300 Castro St (at 16th St) **415/621-7736** *Victorian home & garden, shared baths*

Beck's Motor Lodge [GF,WC] 2222 Market St (at Sanchez) **415/621-8212, 800/955-2325** *in the heart of the Castro (ie, cruisy)*

▶ **Belvedere House** [★MW,NS,WI,GO] 598 Belvedere St (at 17th St) **415/731-6654, 877/226-3273** *wall-to-wall books, art & style*

Casa Buena Vista [GF,NS,WI] Corona Heights (near Market & Castro) **916/974-7409, 916/813-3119 (cell)** *rental apts*

Casa Francisquita [GS] 4336 20th St (at Castro St) **415/431-9907** *apt rental in the gay district*

Casa Luna SF [MW,NS,GO] 4060 17th St (at Castro) **415/738-8121 x9, 888/992-8833** *apt*

Castillo Inn [WI] 48 Henry St **415/864-5111, 800/865-5112**

Castro Suites [GS,NS,WI,GO] 927 14th St (at Noe) **415/437-1783** *furnished apts, kitchen*

Edwardian San Francisco [GF,NS] 1668 Market St (btwn Franklin & Gough) **415/864-1271, 888/864-8070** *some shared baths, hot tub, jacuzzi*

Inn on Castro [MW,NS,WI,GO] 321 Castro St (btwn 16th & 17th) **415/861-0321** *full brkfst*

Le Grenier [MW] 347 Noe St (at 16th St) **415/864-4748** *2-rm suite (sleeps up to 3)*

Noe's Nest B&B [GF,NS] 1257 Guerrero St (btwn 24th & 25th Sts) **415/821-0751** *kitchens, fireplace*

Olive's Gate Guesthouse [GS,NS,WI,GO] 3796 23rd St (at Church) **415/821-6039** *studio apt in Noe Valley, lesbian-owned*

▶ **The Parker Guest House** [★M,NS,WI,GO] 520 Church St (at 17th) **415/621-3222, 888/520-7275** *guesthouse complex w/ gardens, steam spa*

Terrace Place [M,WI,GO] **415/241-0425** *guest suite*

Tom's Place [M,L,WI,GO] 4510 18th St (at Douglass) **415/861-0516** *slinged play area*

Travelodge Central [GF] 1707 Market St (at Valencia) **415/621-6775, 800/578-7878 (reservations)** *nonsmoking rooms available, close to LGBT center*

▶ **The Willows Inn** [MW,NS,WI,GO] 710 14th St (at Church) **415/431-4770, 800/431-0277** *"amenities, comfort, great location"*

BARS

440 Castro [★M,NH,B,L] 440 Castro St **415/621-8732** *noon-2am, very cruisy*

Amber [GS] 718 14th St (at Market) **415/626-7827** *6pm-2am, from 7pm wknds, smoking bar*

The Bar on Church [M,NH,D] 198 Church St (at Market) *5pm-2am, from 3pm wknds*

Blackbird [GS,GO] 2124 Market St **415/503-0630** *6am-2am*

Boy Bar [M,D] 2369 Market St (at Castro, at the Cafe) *Fri only*

The Cafe [MW,D,YC] 2369 Market St (at Castro) **415/861-3846** *4pm-2am, from 3pm Sat, from 2pm Sun, deck overlooking Castro & Market*

Cafe du Nord [GF,A,F,E] 2170 Market St (at Sanchez) **415/861-5016** *live music, theme nights*

CAV Wine Bar & Kitchen [GS] 1666 Market St (at Gough) **415/437-1770** *5:30pm-11pm, till midnight Fri-Sat, clsd Sun, also restaurant*

The Edge [M,NH,L] 4149 18th St **415/863-4027** *noon-2am, classic cruise bar*

Harvey's [★MW,NH,E,DS,WC] 500 Castro St **415/431-4278** *11am-11pm, 9am-2am wknds, also restaurant*

Last Call Bar [M,NH] 3988 18th St **415/861-1310** *noon-2am*

The Lookout [M,F] 3600 16th St (at Market) **415/431-0306** *11am-2am*

Martuni's [GS,NH,P] 4 Valencia St (at Market) **415/241-0205** *4pm-2am, lounge, great martinis*

▶ **Midnight Sun** [★M,V] 4067 18th St (at Castro) **415/861-4186** *2pm-2am, from 1pm Sat-Sun*

The Mint [MW,K] 1942 Market St (at Buchanan) **415/626-4726** *noon-2am, popular karaoke bar nights, also sushi restaurant*

The Mix [M,NH] 4086 18th St **415/431-8616** *3pm-2am, from 8am wknds, heated patio*

Moby Dick [M,NH,V] 4049 18th St (at Hartford) *2pm-2am, from noon wknds*

Pan Dulce [MW,D,MR-L] 2369 Market St (at the Cafe) **415/861-3846** *9pm-2am Th only, "The Castro's Biggest Latino Party!"*

Pilsner Inn [★M,NH,YC] 225 Church St (at Market) **415/621-7058** *10am-2am, great patio*

Q Bar [★M,NH,D,WC] 456 Castro St **415/864-2877** *4pm-2am, from 2pm wknds, sidewalk patio*

SF Badlands [★M,NH,D,V,WC] 4121 18th St (at Castro) **415/626-9320** *2pm-2am, Sun beer bust*

Trigger [M,D] 2344 Market St (at Castro) **415/551-2582** *4pm-2am*

Twin Peaks Tavern [M,OC] 401 Castro St (at Market & 17th) **415/864-9470** *noon-2am, from 8am Th-Sun*

Nightclubs

Tingel Tangel Club [MW,D,TG] *monthly cabaret happening, check tingeltangel-club.com for details*

Cafes

Cafe Flore [★MW,WI] 2298 Market St (at Noe) **415/621-8579** *7am-2am, full bar, great patio to see & be seen, come early for a seat*

Caffe Trieste [★E] 1667 Market St (at Gough) **415/551-1000** *6:30am-10pm, till 11pm Fri-Sat, great coffee, live music*

Duboce Park Cafe [F] 2 Sanchez St (at Duboce) **415/621-1108** *7am-8pm, outdoor seating*

Jumpin' Java [WI] 139 Noe St (at 14th St) **415/431-5282** *6:30am-7:30pm, 7am-8pm wknds, popular w/ boys who like to cruise & cybercruise at the same time*

Lovejoy's Tea Room [★] 1351 Church St (at Clipper) **415/648-5895** *11am-6pm, clsd Mon-Tue, for a tea party fit for a queen*

Orbit Room Cafe 1900 Market St (at Laguna) **415/252-9525** *2pm-2am, till midnight Sun, also bar*

Samovar Tea Lounge 498 Sanchez St (at 18th St) **415/626-4700** *10am-10pm*

Starbucks [B] 4094 18th St (at Castro) **415/626-6263** *always a bear jamboree*

Sweet Inspiration [F] 2239 Market St **415/621-8664** *8am-11pm, 8am-12:30am Fri-Sat, fabulous desserts*

Restaurants

2223 Market [WC] 2223 Market St **415/431-0692** *dinner, Sun brunch, full bar*

Anchor Oyster Bar [MW,BW] 579 Castro St (at 19th) **415/431-3990** *11:30am-10pm, from 4pm Sun*

Bagdad Cafe [MW] 2295 Market St **415/621-4434** *open till midnight, 24hrs Th-Sat, American*

Blue [★BW] 2337 Market St (btwn Castro & Noe) **415/863-2583** *11:30am-11pm, wknd brunch from 10:30am, homecooking served w/ style*

Catch [E] 2362 Market St **415/431-5000** *lunch and dinner [R], wknd brunch, seafood*

Chloe's [★] 1399 Church St (at 26th St) **415/648-4116** *8am-4pm, come early for wknd brunch*

Chow [★] 215 Church St (at Market) **415/552-2469** *8am-11pm, till midnight wknds, patio*

Cove Cafe [MW,WC] 434 Castro St **415/626-0462** *8am-9pm, till 10pm Fri-Sat*

Eric's Chinese Restaurant [★] 1500 Church St (at 27th St) **415/282-0919** *11am-9pm*

Firewood Cafe 4248 18th St (at Diamond St) **415/252-0999** *11am-11pm, rotisserie chicken, pastas, oven-fired pizzas, salads*

Home [★] 2100 Market St (at Church) **415/503-0333** *11am-midnight, wknd brunch 10am-2pm, American*

It's Tops 1801 Market St (at Octavia) **415/431-6395** *8am-3pm & 8pm-3am (Wed-Sat), vintage diner*

La Mediterranée [BW] 288 Noe (at Market) **415/431-7210** *11am-10pm, till 11pm Sat-Sun*

Lime [★] 2247 Market St **415/621-5256** *5pm-midnight, wknd brunch, fusion small plates, full bar*

Nirvana Restaurant & Bar [MW] 544 Castro St (btwn 18th & 19th) **415/861-2226** *Southeast Asian, patio*

Orphan Andy's [GO] 3991 17th St **415/864-9795** *24hrs, diner*

Poesia Osteria Italiana 4072 18th St (at Collingwood) **415/252-9325** *dinner nighly, great food & full bar*

The Sausage Factory [MW,BW] 517 Castro St **415/626-1250** *11:30am-midnight, pizza & pasta*

Sparky's 242 Church St (at Market) **415/626-8666** *24hrs, diner, popular after-hours*

Squat & Gobble 3600 16th St **415/552-2125** *8am-10pm, popular wknds for brkfst, outdoor seating*

Sumi [MW] 4243 18th St (at Diamond) **415/626-7864** *5:30pm-10pm, cont'l/ Japanese*

Thailand Restaurant 438-A Castro St **415/863-6868** *11am-10pm, plenty veggie*

Triple Crown [GO] 1772 Market St (near Gough) **415/863-3516** *dinner nightly, Sun brunch, DJs by night*

Zuni Cafe [★] 1658 Market St (at Franklin) **415/552-2522** *lunch & dinner, clsd Mon, upscale cont'l/ Mediterranean, full bar*

Entertainment & Recreation

Castro Country Club [MW] 4058 18th St (at Hartford) **415/552-6102** *11am-11pm, till 1am Fri-Sat, open holidays, alcohol- & drug-free space*

Heart of the Castro Wedding Chapel 4052 18th St (at Hartford) **415/626-7743**

Pink Triangle Park near Market & Castro *"in remembrance of LGBT victims of the Nazi regime"*

Bookstores

A Different Light 489 Castro St **415/431-0891** *10am-10pm, till 11pm Fri-Sat, LGBT, readings, cruisy late nights & wknds*

Aardvark Books 227 Church St **415/552-6733** *10:30am-10:30pm, mostly used, good LGBT section*

Books, Inc [WC] 2275 Market St **415/864-6777** *9:30am-11pm, till 10pm Sun, LGBT section, readings*

Get Lost [★] 1825 Market St (at Guerrero) **415/437-0529** *10am-7pm, till 6pm Sat, 11am-5pm Sun, stylish travel book store, LGBT section*

Retail Shops

Best in Show 545 Castro St (btwn 18th & 19th) **415/864-7387** *11am-8pm, 11am-7pm Sat, 11am-6pm Sun*

Cold Steel America 2377 Market St (at 17th St, 2nd flr) **415/621-7233** *noon-8pm, piercing & tattoo studio; also 1783 Haight St, 415/933-7233*

De La Sole Footwear 4126 18th St **415/255-3140** *11am-7pm, till 8pm Sat*

Kenneth Wingard 2319 Market St (btwn Castro & Noe) **415/431-6900**

Rolo 2351 Market St **415/431-4545** *11am-8pm, till 7pm Sun, designer labels*

Under One Roof [WC] 549 Castro **415/503-2300, 800/525-2125** *10am-8pm, 11am-7pm Sun, 100% donated to AIDS relief*

Gyms & Health Clubs

Gold's Gym Castro [MW] 2301 Market St **415/626-4488** *day passes available*

The Gym SF [MO,GO] 2275 Market St **415/863-4700** *day passes available*

▶ **Sun Days Tanning Center** 3985 17th St (at Market & Castro Sts) **415/626-8222** *8am-10pm, 10am-6pm Sun*

Men's Clubs

▶ **Eros** [PC] 2051 Market St (btwn Church & Dolores) **415/864-3767** *open 2pm Sat-Sun, 4pm weekdays, safer-sex club, theme nights, massage available, day passes*

Erotica

Auto-Erotica 4077-A 18th St, 2nd flr **415/861-5787** *"purveyor of vintage porn & fine dildos"*

Castro Gulch 2353 Market St (at Castro) **415/934-8524** *10am-midnight, till 2am Fri-Sat, toys, videos, DVDs, men's sexy clothing, fetish items*

Chaps 4057 18th St (btwn Castro & Hartford) **415/863-1699** *10am-11pm, till midnight Fri-Sat*

Rock Hard 518 Castro St (at 18th St) **415/437-2430** *9:30am-11pm, till midnight Fri-Sat, toys, DVDs, lube, leather, cockrings & more*

Cruisy Areas

Collingwood Park [AYOR] (btwn 18th & 19th Sts) *Castro merry-go-round, after bars close*

SF—South of Market

Accommodations

Americania Hotel [GF,SW,NS,WC] 121 7th St (at Mission) **415/626-0200**

Holiday Inn Civic Center [GF,SW,WI,WC] 50 8th St **415/626-6103, 800/972-3124**

Hotel Vitale [GF,NS,WI,WC] 8 Mission St **415/278-3700, 888/890-8688** *4-star, full-service waterfront luxury hotel, rooftop spa, restaurant & bar*

Hotel Whitcomb [GF,WI,WC] 1231 Market St (btwn 8th & 9th) **415/626-8000, 800/227-4747** *landmark hotel on Pride route, also restaurant & Starbucks on-site*

The Mosser Hotel [GS,NS] 54 4th St (btwn Market & Mission) **415/986-4400, 800/227-3804** *1913 landmark, also restaurant & full bar*

National Hotel [GF] 1139 Market St **415/864-9343** *hostel*

► **Renoir Hotel** [GS,NS,WC] 45 McAllister (at Market St) **415/626-5200, 800/576-3388** *boutique-style*

Vagabond Inn San Francisco [GS,WI,WC] 385 9th St (at Harrison) **415/431-5131, 800/522-1555** *motel, close to SOMA bars*

W San Francisco [GF,SW,WI,WC] 181 Third St **415/777-5300, 877/WHOTELS (reservations only)** *also XYZ restaurant & bar*

The Westin San Francisco Market Street [GF,NS] 50 3rd St **415/974-6400, 888/627-8561** *sauna*

Bars

Chaps II [★M,L] 1225 Folsom St (at 8th) **415/255-2427** *7pm-2am, from 3pm Fri-Sun*

Dada SF Studio [GS,GO] 86 2nd St (btwn Market & Mission) **415/357-1367** *4pm-midnight, till 2am Th-Sat, from 8pm Sat, clsd Sun, art gallery*

The Eagle Tavern [★M,L,E] 398 12th St (at Harrison) **415/626-0880** *noon-2am, great beer bust Sun, patio*

Hole in the Wall Saloon [★M,NH,L] 1369 Folsom (btwn 9th & 10th) **415/431-4695** *noon-2am, "a nasty little biker bar"*

Lone Star Saloon [★M,B,L] 1354 Harrison St (btwn 9th & 10th) **415/863-9999** *noon-2am, from 9am wknds, patio, bear bar, beer bust wknds*

Powerhouse [M,NH,L] 1347 Folsom St (at Dore Alley) **415/552-8689** *4pm-2am, theme nights, popular wknds w/ DJ, patio, cruisy*

Nightclubs

Asia SF [★GS,D,MR-A,S,$] 201 9th St (at Howard) **415/255-2742** *10pm-close Wed-Sat, theme nights, go-go boys, also Cal-Asian restaurant w/ en-drag dinner service*

Bootie [★GF,D,A,E,$] 375 11th St (at Harrison, at DNA Lounge) **415/626-1409 (DNA info line)** *9pm-close 2nd & 4th Sat, mashups, bootlegs, bastard pop*

Club Dragon [★M,D,MR-A,S,$] 1151 Folsom St (at Eight) **415/431-1151** *9pm-3am Fri, go-go boys*

The Crib SF [MW,D,V,18+,$] 715 Harrison St (at 3rd) *9:30pm-2am Th only, "all-video pop club"*

Eight [★GS,D,$] 1151 Folsom St (btwn 7th & 8th St) **415/431-1151** *9pm-3am, clsd Mon-Wed, theme nights, smoking patio*

Endup [GS,D,MR] 401 6th St (at Harrison) **415/646-0999 (info line), 415/357-0827** *theme nights, popular Sun mornings*

► **GusPresents.com** *The host with the most–Gus is always throwing one hell of a party for the boys!*

The Stud [★MW,D,YC] 399 9th St (at Harrison) **415/863-6623** *5pm-2am, theme nights, outrageous Trannyshack Tue, Hot Mess Sat*

Trannyshack [★M,D,TG,E,GO] **415/863-6623** *occasional events, check trannyshack.com for info*

Cafes

Brain Wash [★E,BW] 1122 Folsom St (at 7th St) **415/861-3663, 415/431-9274** *7am-11pm, 8am-10pm Sun, laundromat & cafe*

Restaurants

Ame [R] 689 Mission St (at 3rd St, in St Regis Hotel) **415/284-4040** *lunch & dinner, full bar*

Ananda Fuara 1298 Market St (at 9th) **415/621-1994** *8am-8pm, till 3pm Wed, clsd Sun, vegetarian*

Bacar Restaurant & Wine Salon [★E,R,WC] 448 Brannan St (btwn 3rd & 4th) **415/904-4100** *dinner nightly, Sun brunch*

Butter 354 11th St (btwn Folsom & Harrison) **415/863-5964** *6pm-2am, clsd Mon, "white trash bistro," full bar, theme nights*

Don Ramon's Mexican Restaurant 225 11th St (btwn Howard & Folsom) **415/864-2700** *lunch Tue-Fri, dinner nightly, clsd Mon, some veggie, full bar*

Fringale [WC] 570 4th St (btwn Bryant & Brannan) **415/543-0573** *lunch Tue-Fri & dinner nightly, French bistro*

Levende Lounge [E] 1710 Mission St (at Duboce) **415/864-5585** *dinner Wed-Sat, Boogie Brunch Sun, clsd Mon, full bar, live DJs nightly*

Orson [GO] 508 4th St *5pm-11pm, clsd Sun*

Rocco's Cafe [★] 1131 Folsom St (at 7th) **415/554-0522** *brkfst & lunch daily, dinner Wed-Sat only*

The Slanted Door [★R] 1 Ferry Building #3 **415/861-8032** *lunch & dinner, Vietnamese, full bar*

Supperclub [E] 657 Harrison St (btwn 2nd & 3rd) **415/348-0900** *6:30pm-close, live performance art & acrobatics, also full bar & nightclub*

Tu Lan 8 6th St (at Market) **415/626-0927** *lunch & dinner, clsd Sun, Vietnamese, dicey neighborhood but delicious (& cheap) food*

Woodward's Garden [WC] 1700 Mission St (at Duboce) **415/621-7122** *dinner from 6pm, clsd Sun-Mon*

Yank Sing [★] 101 Spear St (One Rincon Center, at Mission) **415/957-9300** *11am-3pm Mon-Fri, 10am-4pm wknds, dim-sum heaven!*

Entertainment & Recreation

111 Minna Gallery [GS,D,E] 111 Minna St (at 2nd St) **415/974-1719** *[D] Wed for Qool, call for events*

Retail Shops

A Taste of Leather 1285 Folsom (btwn 9th & 10th) **415/252-9166** *noon-8pm, till 9pm Fri-Sat, till 6pm Sun*

Dandelion [GO] 55 Potrero Ave (at Alameda St) **415/436-9500, 888/548-1968** *10am-7pm, till 6pm Fri-Sat, noon-5pm Sun*

Mr S Leather & Fetters USA San Francisco 385 8th St (at Harrison) **415/863-7764, 800/746-7677 (orders)** *11am-7pm, erotic goods, custom leather & latex*

Stompers 323 10th St (at Folsom) **415/255-6422, 888/BOOTMAN** *11am-6pm, noon-4pm Sun, clsd Mon, boots, cigars & gloves*

Stormy Leather 1158 Howard St (btwn 7th & 8th) **415/626-1672, 800/486-9650** *noon-7pm, leather, latex, toys & magazines*

Gyms & Health Clubs

Gold's Gym San Francisco [★] 1001 Brannan St (at 9th) **415/552-4653** *day passes available*

Men's Clubs

▶ **Blow Buddies** [★MO,L,V,PC,GO] 933 Harrison (btwn 5th & 6th) **415/777-4323** *open late Wed-Sun, clsd Mon-Tue*

Mack Folsom Prison [MO,L,PC] 1285 Folsom (at 9th) **415/252-1221** *6pm-6am, 24hrs wknds, fetish parties*

Erotica

City Entertainment 960 Folsom St (btwn 5th & 6th) **415/543-2124** *10am-2am, 24hrs wknds, the best in adult entertainment*

Folsom Gulch 947 Folsom (btwn 5th & 6th) **415/495-6402** *10am-2am, 24hrs Fri-Sat, hot arcade action, serving the gay community for over 25 years!*

Secrets 1036 Market St (at 7th) **415/863-7115** *lots of arcade action*

Cruisy Areas

Folsom St [AYOR] btwn 5th & 6th *late*

SF—Polk Street Area

Accommodations

Broadway Manor Inn [GF,WI,WC] 2201 Van Ness Ave (at Broadway) **415/776-7900, 800/727-6239** *motel close to Fisherman's Wharf*

Cathedral Hill Hotel [GF,SW] 1101 Van Ness Ave **415/776-8200, 800/622-0855** *also restaurant & lounge*

The Monarch Hotel [GF] 1015 Geary St (at Polk) **415/673-5232, 800/777-3210** *Edwardian boutique-style hotel*

Nob Hill Motor Inn [GF,NS,WI,WC] 1630 Pacific Ave (at Van Ness Ave) **415/775-8160, 800/343-6900** *hotel*

The Phoenix Hotel [★GF,SW,WI] 601 Eddy St (at Larkin) **415/776-1380, 800/248-9466** *1950s-style motor lodge, fave of celebrity rockers, also Bambuddha lounge & restaurant*

San Francisco City Center Hostel [GF,NS,WI] 685 Ellis St (at Larkin) **415/474-5721, 888/464-4872** *hostel, shared & private rooms available, free brkfst, kids ok*

Bars

The Cinch [M,NH,WI,WC] 1723 Polk St (at Clay) **415/776-4162** *6am-2am, patio, lots of pool tables & no attitude, [D] Th-Sat, [DS] Fri*

Deco Lounge [M,NH,DS,P] 510 Larkin (at Turk) **415/346-2025** *10am-2am, theme nights*

Edinburgh Castle [GF,NH,E] 950 Geary St (at Polk) **415/885-4074** *5pm-2am, Scottish pub w/ single malts & authentic fish & chips*

Gangway [M,NH] 841 Larkin St (btwn Geary & O'Farrell) **415/776-6828** *8am-2am*

Kimo's [M,NH,GO] 1351 Polk St (at Pine) **415/885-4535** *8am-2am, live bands upstairs*

Lush Lounge [★GS,NH,WC] 1092 Post (at Polk) **415/771-2022** *4pm-2am*

Nightclubs

Bearracuda [M,D,B] 510 Larkin (at Deco Lounge) **415/346-2025** *10pm-3am 1st & 3rd Sat*

Cockblock [MW,D] 155 Fell St (at Rickshaw Shop) *10pm-2am 2nd Sat*

Divas [M,NH,D,TG,DS] 1081 Post St (at Larkin) **415/474-3482** *6am-2am, TS/TVs & their admirers*

HOM T-Dance [M,D] 124 Ellis St (at Infusion Lounge) *1st Sun only*

Wunderland [M,D] 181 Eddy St (at Taylor) *10pm-4am Sat*

Cafes

La Boulange de Polk 2310 Polk St (at Green St) **415/345-1107** *7am-6:30pm, till 6pm Sun, clsd Mon, French bakery & cafe, outdoor seating, Parisian down to the attitude*

Quetzal Internet Cafe [★E,V,BW,WI] 1234 Polk St (at Sutter) **415/673-4181, 888/673-4181** *6:30am-10pm, roasts own coffee*

Restaurants

Antica Trattoria 2400 Polk St (at Union) **415/928-5797** *dinner, clsd Mon, Italian, wine served*

Grubstake II [MW,BW] 1525 Pine St (at Polk) **415/673-8268** *5pm-4am, from 10am wknds, diner*

Rex Cafe 2323 Polk St **415/441-2244, 415/441-9244** *from 5pm, dinner, also brunch 10am-3pm Sat-Sun*

Street 2141 Polk St (btwn Broadway & Vallejo) **415/775-1055** *dinner, clsd Mon, incredible hamburgers*

Bookstores

Books Inc Opera Plaza [★] 601 Van Ness Ave (at Turk) **415/776-1111** *8:30am-9:30pm, general, LGBT section, readings*

Erotica

Frenchy's 1020 Geary St (at Polk) **415/776-5940** *24hrs*

Good Vibrations [★W] 1620 Polk St (btwn Sacramento & Clay) **415/345-0400**

The Polk Gulch 1038 Polk St (at Post) **415/775-9076** *hot arcade action till midnight*

Cruisy Areas

Polk St [AYOR] btwn Geary & California Sts *hustlers*

SF—Downtown & North Beach

Accommodations

Adante Hotel [GS,NS,WC] 610 Geary St (at Jones) **415/673-9221, 888/423-0083** *in Union Square/ Theater District, kids ok*

Andrews Hotel [GF,NS,WI] 624 Post St (at Taylor) **415/563-6877, 800/926-3739** *Victorian hotel, also Italian restaurant*

Argonaut Hotel [GF,NS,WC] 495 Jefferson St (at Hyde) **415/563-0800, 866/415-0704** *boutique hotel in Fisherman's Wharf*

Dakota Hotel/ Hostel [GF,WI] 606 Post St (at Taylor) **415/931-7475** *near Union Square*

Executive Hotel Vintage Court [GF,NS,WI,WC] 650 Bush St (at Powell) **415/392-4666, 888/388-3932** *also world-famous 5-star Masa's restaurant, French*

Galleria Park Hotel [GS,WI,WC] 191 Sutter St (at Kearny) **415/781-3060, 800/792-9639** *boutique hotel*

Grand Hyatt San Francisco [GF,WI] 345 Stockton St (at Sutter) **415/398-1234, 800/233-1234** *restaurant & lounge, gym*

Halcyon Hotel [GF,NS,WI] 649 Jones St (at Post) **415/929-8033, 800/627-2396**

Handlery Union Square Hotel [GF,SW,WI,WC] 351 Geary St **415/781-7800, 800/995-4874** *steps from Union Square*

Harbor Court Hotel [GF,SW,WI,WC] 165 Steuart St (btwn Howard & Mission) **415/882-1300, 866/792-6283** *in the heart of the Financial District, gym*

Hotel Abri [GF,WI] 127 Ellis St (at Powell) **415/392-8800, 866/778-6169** *boutique hotel*

Hotel Adagio [GF,WC] 550 Geary St **415/775-5000, 800/228-8830**

Hotel Bijou [GS,NS,WI,WC] 111 Mason St (at Eddy) **415/771-1200, 800/771-1022**

The Hotel California [GF,NS] 580 Geary St (at Jones) **415/441-2700, 800/227-4223** *also popular Millennium gourmet vegetarian restaurant & bar*

Hotel Carlton [GF] 1075 Sutter (at Larkin) **415/673-0242, 800/922-7586** *also Saha restaurant, Arabic-fusion*

Hotel Diva [GF,NS,WI] 440 Geary (at Mason) **415/885-0200, 800/553-1900** *hip hotel, gym*

Hotel Drisco [GF,NS] 2901 Pacific Ave **415/346-2880, 800/634-7277**

Hotel Fusion [GS,NS,WI,WC] 140 Ellis St (at Powell St) **415/568-2525, 866/753-4244**

Hotel Griffon [GS,WI,WC] 155 Steuart St (at Mission) **415/495-2100, 800/321-2201** *also restaurant, bistro/cont'l*

Hotel Mark Twain [GF,WI,WC] 345 Taylor St (at Ellis) **415/673-2332, 877/854-4106** *also Fish & Farm restaurant*

Hotel Metropolis [GF,WI,NS] 25 Mason St **800/553-1900** *near Union Square shopping*

Hotel Monaco [GF] 501 Geary St (at Taylor) **415/292-0100, 866/622-5284** *pets ok, also Grand Cafe restaurant, French*

Hotel Nikko San Francisco [GF,SW,NS,WC] 222 Mason St **415/394-1111, 866/645-5673** *health club & spa, also ANZU restaurant*

Hotel Palomar [GS,WI] 12 4th St (at Market) **415/348-1111, 866/373-4941** *boutique hotel*

The Hotel Rex [GF,WC] 562 Sutter St (at Powell) **415/433-4434, 800/433-4434** *full bar*

Hotel Triton [GF,WI,WC] 342 Grant Ave (at Bush) **415/394-0500, 800/433-6611** *designer theme rooms*

Hotel Union Square [GF,WI] 114 Powell St **800/553-1900** *1930s art deco lobby, original art by Gladys Perint Palmer in rms*

Hyatt Regency San Francisco [GF,NS,WI] 5 Embarcadero Center (at California) **415/788-1234, 800/233-1234** *luxury waterfront hotel*

The Inn at Union Square [GF,NS,WI] 440 Post St **415/397-3510, 800/288-4346** *steps from Union Square*

JW Marriott Hotel San Francisco [GF,NS,WI,WC] 500 Post St (at Mason) **415/771-8600, 800/605-6568**

Kensington Park Hotel [GF,NS,WI] 450 Post St **800/553-1900** *on Union Square, also Farallon Restaurant*

King George Hotel [GS,F,WI,WC] 334 Mason St (at Geary) **415/781-5050, 800/288-6005** *also The Windsor Tearoom*

Larkspur Hotel [GF,WI,NS] 524 Sutter St (at Powell) **415/421-2865, 800/919-9779** *B&B-inn on Union Square, afternoon tea, wine hour*

Luz Hotel [GS] 725 Geary Blvd (at Leavenworth) **415/928-1917** *clothing-optional jacuzzi*

The Maxwell/ Frank Hotel [GS,WC] 386 Geary St (at Mason) **415/986-2000, 800/553-1900** *1908 art deco masterpiece, full brkfst*

Nob Hill Hotel [GS,NS,WC] 835 Hyde St (btwn Bush & Sutter) **415/885-2987, 877/662-4455** *European-style hotel, jacuzzi*

Petite Auberge [GF,NS] 863 Bush St (at Taylor) **415/928-6000, 800/365-3004**

Prescott Hotel [GF,NS,WI] 545 Post St (btwn Taylor & Mason) **415/563-0303, 866/271-3632** *small luxury hotel*

Radisson Hotel Fisherman's Wharf [GF,SW,WI,WC] 250 Beach St **415/392-6700, 800/333-3333**

San Francisco Downtown Hostel [GS,WI,WC] 312 Mason St (at O'Farrell) **415/788-5604, 800/909-4776** *hostel, shared baths, open kitchen*

Serrano Hotel [GF,WI,WC] 405 Taylor St (at O'Farrell) **415/885-2500, 866/289-6561** *in heart of Theater District*

Sir Francis Drake Hotel [GF,WI] 450 Powell St (at Sutter) **415/392-7755, 800/795-7129** *1928 landmark, also restaurant & Starlight Room*

The Stratford Hotel [GS,WI,WC] 242 Powell St (at Geary) **415/397-7080, 877/922-5928** *near Union Square*

The Touchstone Hotel [GF,WC] 480 Geary St (btwn Mason & Taylor) **415/771-1600, 800/620-5889** *in Theater District, full brkfst*

Tuscan Inn [GF,WC] 425 N Point St (at Mason) **415/561-1100, 888/648-4626**

Union Square Plaza Hotel [GF] 432 Geary St **415/776-7585, 800/841-3135** *1 block from Union Square*

Vertigo Hotel [GS,NS,WI,WC] 940 Sutter St (at Leavenworth) **415/885-6800, 800/808-9675** *boutique hotel*

Villa Florence Hotel [GF,WI] 225 Powell St (at Geary) **415/397-7700, 866/823-4669** *Union Square boutique hotel, also Kuleto's restaurant, Italian*

Bars

Aunt Charlie's Lounge [M,NH,DS] 133 Turk St (at Taylor) **415/441-2922** *10am-midnight, till 2am Fri- Sat*

Bourbon & Branch [GS,R] 501 Jones St (at O'Farrell) *in Prohibition-era speakeasy, drinks are worth the price*

Nightclubs

▶ **Fresh @ Ruby Skye** [★M,D,$] 420 Mason (at Geary) **415/693-0777** *monthly Sun T-dance, check local listings for dates*

Cafes

Caffe Trieste [★] 601 Vallejo St **415/392-6739** *get a taste of the real North Beach (past & present)*

Restaurants

Ar Roi 643 Post St (at Jones) **415/771-5146** *lunch Mon-Sat, dinner nightly, Thai*

The Buena Vista 2765 Hyde St (at Beach) **415/474-5044** *9am-2am, from 8am wknds, the restaurant that introduced Irish coffee to America*

Cafe Claude [E,BW] 7 Claude Ln (near Bush & Kearny) **415/392-3515** *11:30am-10:30pm, from 5:30pm Sun, live music Th-Sat, as close to Paris as you can get in SF*

Canteen 817 Sutter St **415/928-8870** *great brkfst*

Le Colonial 20 Cosmo Pl (btwn Taylor & Jones) **415/931-3600** *dinner only, Vietnamese, full bar*

Dottie's True Blue Cafe [GO] 522 Jones St (at Geary) **415/885-2767** *7:30am-3pm, clsd Tue, great brkfst*

Golden Era [★] 572 O'Farrell St **415/673-3136** *11am-9pm, clsd Tue, vegetarian/ vegan*

Mario's Bohemian Cigar Store Cafe [BW,WI] 566 Columbus Ave (at Union) **415/362-0536** *10am-close, great foccacia sandwiches*

Millennium 580 Geary St (at Jones) **415/345-3900** *dinner only, Euro-Mediterranean, upscale vegetarian*

Entertainment & Recreation

Razz Room [★GS,C,WC] 222 Mason (at Nikko Hotel) **415/394-1189** *cabaret w/ world-class performers*

Sunday's A Drag@The Starlight Room [MW,E,$] 450 Mason St (at Powell) **415/395-8595** *Sun brunch, noon & 2:30pm drag shows*

Bookstores

Book Passage 1 Ferry Bldg #42 **415/835-1020** *10am-8pm, from 8am Sat, 10am-7pm Sun-Mon, independent*

City Lights Bookstore 261 Columbus Ave (at Pacific) **415/362-8193** *10am-midnight, historic beatnik bookstore, many progressive titles, LGBT section, whole floor dedicated to poetry*

Erotica

Nob Hill Adult Theater [MO,$] 729 Bush St (at Powell) **415/781-9468 (info line)** *9am-2:30am, male dancers, over 25 shows daily*

SF—Mission District

includes Bernal Heights

Accommodations

Bernal Heights Duplex, Carriage House [GS,NS,WI] 3 Porter St (at Crescent) **415/601-6460** *1-bdrm & studio apt vacation rentals*

Elements [★GS,F,WI] 2516 Mission St (at 21st St) **415/647-4100, 866/327-8407** *hostel w/ private or shared rooms*

The Inn San Francisco [GF,NS,WI] 943 S Van Ness Ave (btwn 20th & 21st) **415/641-0188, 800/359-0913** *Victorian mansion, hot tub*

Bars

Argus Lounge [GS,NH] 3187 Mission St, Bernal Heights (at Valencia) **415/824-1447** *4pm-2am*

El Rio [★GS,NH,MR,E] 3158 Mission St (at Cesar Chavez) **415/282-3325** *5pm-close Mon-Th, from 3pm wknds, patio*

Esta Noche [M,D,MR-L,TG,S] 3079 16th St (at Mission) **415/861-5757** *1pm-2am, salsa & disco in a classic Tijuana dive*

Lexington Club [★W,NH,GO] 3464 19th St (btwn Mission & Valencia) **415/863-2052** *5pm-2am, from 3pm Fri-Sun*

Lone Palm [GS] 3394 22nd St (at Guerrero) **415/648-0109** *4pm-2am, a bar for grown ups (we know you're out there)*

Nihon [GS,D,F] 1779 Folsom St (at 14th St) **415/552-4400** *6pm-close, clsd Sun, whiskey lounge, also Japanese restaurant*

Phone Booth [MW,NH] 1398 S Van Ness Ave (at 25th) **415/648-4683** *noon-2am, from 1pm wknds*

Pop's Bar [GS,NH,WC] 2800 24th St (btwn York & Bryant) **415/401-7677** *4pm-2am, photobooth*

Stray Bar [GS,NH,GO] 309 Cortland Ave, Bernal Heights (at Bocana) **415/821-9263** *4pm-2am, from 2pm wknds*

Truck Bar [MW,NH,F,GO] 1900 Folsom St (at 15th) **415/252-0306** *11pm-2am, from 4pm Sat, from 2pm Sun*

Wild Side West [GS,WC] 424 Cortland, Bernal Heights (at Wool) **415/647-3099** *1pm-2am, patio, magic garden*

Zeitgeist [★GS,F] 199 Valencia St (at Duboce) **415/255-7505** *9am-2am, divey biker bar & beer garden*

Nightclubs

Club Papi SF [M,D,MR-L] 550 Barneveld (at space550, 2 blocks off Bayview) **415/675-9763** *monthly party from 10pm-4am, call for dates*

Heavy Rotation [MW,D] 3158 Mission St (at El Rio) **415/282-3325** *10pm 2nd Fri, queer dance party, all sizes welcome!*

Mighty [GF,D] 119 Utah St (at 15th St) **415/762-0151 (info line), 415/626-7001 (office)**

Sundance Saloon [★M,D,CW,GO,$] 550 Barneveld Ave (at space550, 2 blocks off Bayshore Blvd at Industrial) **415/820-1403** *5pm-10:30pm Sun (lessons at 5:30pm) & 6:30pm-10:30pm Th (lessons at 7pm)*

Cafes

Dolores Park Cafe [★F,E] 501 Dolores St (at 18th St) **415/621-2936** *7am-8pm, outdoor seating overlooking Dolores Park, live music Fri*

Farleys [E] 1315 18th St (at Texas St, Potrero Hill) **415/648-1545** *6:30am-10pm, from 7:30am Sat & 8am Sun*

The Revolution Cafe [E] 3248 22nd St (btwn Mission & Bartlett) **415/642-0474** *9am-1am*

Tartine Bakery [★] 600 Guerrero St (at 18th St) **415/487-2600** *8am-7pm, from 9am Sun, French bakery w/ a line out the door*

Restaurants

Aslam's Rasoi 1037 Valencia St (at 21st) **415/695-0599** *5pm-11pm, Indian & Pakistani*

Boogaloos [★] 3296 22nd St (at Valencia) **415/824-4088** *8am-3pm, worth the wait*

Charanga [★BW,WC] 2351 Mission St (at 20th St) **415/282-1813** *5:30pm-close, clsd Sun-Mon, Cuban-Caribbean tapas*

Circolo 500 Florida St (at Mariposa) **415/553-8560** *5pm-close, clsd Mon, Latin-Asian fusion, full bar*

Delfina [★R] 3621 18th St (at Dolores) **415/552-4055** *5:30pm-10pm, excellent Tuscan cuisine, full bar, patio (summers)*

El Farolito [★] 2779 Mission St (at 24th) **415/824-7877** *10am-3am, delicious, cheap burritos & more*

Mabel's Just For You [★MW] 722 22nd St (at 3rd St) **415/647-3033** *7:30am-3pm, Southern brkfst*

Maverick 3316 17th St (btwn Mission & Valencia) **415/863-3061** *dinner nightly, also wknd brunch, upscale American, great wine selection*

Medjool [★WC] 2522 Mission St (at 21st St) **415/550-9055** *5pm-10pm, till 11pm Fri-Sat, clsd Sun, tapas, also cafe, lounge & rooftop bar*

Moki's Sushi & Pacific Grill 615 Cortland Ave (at Moultine) **415/970-9336** *dinner nightly*

Pauline's Pizza Pie [★MW,BW] 260 Valencia St (btwn 14th & Duboce) **415/552-2050** *5pm-10pm, clsd Sun-Mon, gourmet pizza*

Picaro [BW,WC] 3120 16th St (at Valencia) **415/431-4089** *5pm-10pm, from 9:30am wknds, Spanish tapas bar*

Pork Store Cafe [★BW] 3122 16th St (at Valencia) **415/626-5523** *8am-4pm daily & 7pm-3am Fri-Sat, American/diner food, great breakfasts; also 1451 Haight St, 415/864-6981*

Range [★] 842 Valencia St (btwn 19th & 20th Sts) **415/282-8283** *dinner nightly, California contemporary, full bar*

Slow Club [WC] 2501 Mariposa (at Hampshire) **415/241-9390** *lunch Mon-Fri, dinner Mon-Sat, wknd brunch, full bar*

Entertainment & Recreation

Metronome Ballroom [GS,$] 1830 17th St (at De Haro) **415/252-9000** *dance lessons, salsa to swing, dance parties wknds, call for events*

Bookstores

Dog Eared Books 900 Valencia St (at 20th) **415/282-1901** *10am-10pm, till 8pm Sun, new & used, good LGBT section*

Modern Times Bookstore [WC] 888 Valencia St **415/282-9246** *10am-9pm, 11am-6pm Sun, progressive, LGBT section, readings*

Retail Shops

Black & Blue Tattoo [★W] 381 Guerrero (at 16th St) **415/626-0770**

Body Manipulations 3234 16th St (btwn Guerrero & Dolores) **415/621-0408** *noon-7pm, from 2pm Mon-Th, piercing (walk-in basis), jewelry*

Erotica

Good Vibrations [★W,WC] 603 Valencia St (at 17th St) **415/522-5460, 800/289-8423** *11am-7pm, till 8pm Th, till 9pm Fri-Sat, clean, well-lighted sex toy store, also mail order*

Mission St News 2086 Mission St (at 17th) **415/626-0309** *24hrs*

SF—Haight, Fillmore, Hayes Valley

Accommodations

555 Haight Guesthouse [GS,NS] 555 Haight St **415/551-2555, 800/785-5504** *hostel*

The Chateau Tivoli [GF,NS,WI] 1057 Steiner St (at Golden Gate) **415/776-5462, 800/228-1647** *historic SF B&B*

Edward II Inn & Suites [GF,WI] 3155 Scott St **415/922-3000, 800/473-2846** *European-style B&B w/ own pub & gym*

Francisco Bay Inn [GF,NS,WI] 1501 Lombard St (at Franklin) **415/474-3030, 800/410-7007** *motel, free parking*

Hayes Valley Inn [GS,NS,WI] 417 Gough St (at Hayes) **415/431-9131, 800/930-7999** *European-style pension, shared baths*

Heritage Marina Hotel [GF,SW] 2550 Van Ness Ave **415/776-7500, 866/714-6835** *vintage '50s hotel in the Marina District*

Hotel Del Sol [★GS,NS,SW,WI,WC] 3100 Webster St (at Greenwich) **415/921-5520, 877/433-5765**

Hotel Kabuki [GF,WC] 1625 Post St (at Laguna) **415/922-3200, 800/333-3333** *in Japantown*

Hotel Majestic [GF,NS,WI,WC] 1500 Sutter St (at Gough) **415/441-1100, 800/869-8966** *one of SF's earliest grand hotels, also restaurant, full bar*

Hotel Tomo [GF,NS,WI] 1800 Sutter St (at Buchanan) **415/921-4000, 888/822-8666** *in Japantown, restaurant & bar*

Inn 1890 [GS,NS,GO] 1890 Page St (near Stanyan) **415/386-0486, 888/INN-1890** *Victorian near Golden Gate Park*

Inn at the Opera [GF,NS,WC] 333 Fulton St (at Franklin) **415/863-8400, 800/325-2708**

Jackson Court [GF,NS,WI] 2198 Jackson St (at Buchanan) **415/929-7670**

The Laurel Inn [GF,NS] 444 Presidio Ave **415/567-8467, 800/552-8735**

Metro Hotel [GF,F,WI] 319 Divisadero St (at Haight) **415/861-5364** *European-style pension*

Queen Anne Hotel [★GF,NS,WI,GO] 1590 Sutter St (at Octavia) **415/441-2828, 800/227-3970** *1890 landmark*

San Francisco Fisherman's Wharf Hostel [GS,F,WI,NS,WC] Fort Mason, Bldg 240 (at Franklin) **415/771-7277, 800/909-4776** *hostel, shared baths*

Shannon-Kavanaugh Guest House [GF,NS,GO] 722 Steiner St (at Hayes) **415/563-2727** *1-bdrm garden apt in house on SF's famous "Postcard Row"*

Stanyan Park Hotel [GF,NS,WC] 750 Stanyan St (at Waller) **415/751-1000** *historic Victorian*

Bars

Jade Bar [GF] 650 Gough St (at McAllister) **415/869-1900** *5pm-2am, from 8pm Sun, upscale cocktails & Asian-inspired "nibbles"*

Marlena's [M,NH,DS,P,WC] 488 Hayes St (at Octavia) **415/864-6672** *noon-2am, [DS] Sat, Cheers for drag queens (a friendly oasis in hip & het Hayes Valley)*

Rickshaw Stop [★GF,F,E] 155 Fell St (btwn Van Ness & Franklin) **415/861-2011** *Wed-Sat only, hipster bar, nightclub (live bands) & restaurant*

Traxx [M,NH] 1437 Haight St (at Masonic) **415/864-4213** *noon-2am*

Nightclubs

The Underground [GS,D,A] 424 Haight St (at Webster) **415/864-7386** *5:30pm-2am, clsd Mon, theme nights, call for events, more gay Sat*

Cafes

Blue Bottle Coffee Company [★] 315 Linden St (at Gough St) **415/252-7535** *7am-5pm, from 8am wknds, organic coffee & treats from kiosk in front of artists' workshop—wonderful hidden treat*

Restaurants

Absinthe Brasserie & Bar 398 Hayes St (at Gough) **415/551-1590** *lunch & dinner, bar till 2am Fri-Sat, clsd Mon*

Burma Superstar [★] 309 Clement St **415/387-2147** *lunch & dinner, Burmese food that will rock your world*

Cheese Steak Shop 1716 Divisadero St (btwn Bush & Sutter) **415/346-3712** *9am-10pm, from 11am Sun, from 10am Mon, best cheese steak outside Philly, also veggie versions*

Citizen Cake [★] 399 Grove St (at Gough) **415/861-2228** *8am-10pm Tue-Fri, from 10am Sat, 10am-5pm Sun, clsd Mon*

Eliza's [★] 2877 California (at Broderick) **415/621-4819** *lunch Mon-Wed, dinner nightly, excellent Chinese food & stylish decor*

Ella's 500 Presidio Ave (at California) **415/441-5669** *brkfst & lunch Mon-Fri, dinner Wed-Sun, popular wknd brunch*

Garibaldi's [WC,GO] 347 Presidio Ave (at Sacramento) **415/563-8841** *open for lunch weekdays & dinner nightly, Mediterranean, full bar*

Greens [★] Fort Mason, Bldg A (near Van Ness & Bay) **415/771-6222** *lunch Tue-Sat, dinner Mon-Sat, Sun brunch, gourmet vegetarian, spectacular view of the Golden Gate Bridge*

Little Star Pizza [★BW] 846 Divisadero St (btwn Fulton & McAllister Sts) **415/441-1118** *5pm-10pm, till 11pm Fri-Sat, clsd Mon, Chicago-style deep dish pizza*

Memphis Minnie's BBQ [★] 576 Haight St **415/864-7675** *11am-10pm,till 9pm Sun, clsd Mon*

Nopa 560 Divisadero St (at Hayes) **415/864-8643** *dinner 6pm-1am, bar from 5pm, urban rustic*

Park Chow [★] 1238 9th Ave (btwn Irving & Lincoln) **415/665-9912** *11am-10pm, brunch from 10am wknds, eclectic & affordable*

Patxi's Chicago Pizza 511 Hayes St (at Octavia St) **415/558-9991** *11am-10pm, clsd Mon, Chicago-style deep dish pizza, also thin crust*

Pluto's Fresh Food for a Hungry Universe 627 Irving St (btwn 7th & 8th Aves) **415/753-8867** *11am-10pm, design your own sandwiches*

Suppenküche [BW,GO] 601 Hayes (at Laguna) **415/252-9289** *dinner, Sun brunch, German cuisine served at communal tables*

Thep-Phanom [★BW] 400 Waller St (at Fillmore) **415/431-2526** *5:30pm-10:30pm, excellent Thai food, worth the wait!*

Vivande Porta Via 2125 Fillmore St **415/436-4430** *lunch & dinner, also mail order*

Bookstores

Bibliohead Bookstore 334 Gough St (at Hayes) **415/621-6772** *eclectic used books, queer section*

The Booksmith 1644 Haight St **415/863-8688, 800/493-7323 (in US)** *cool independent, big-name author readings*

Retail Shops

Flight 001 525 Hayes St (btwn Octavia & Laguna) **415/487-1001, 877/354-4481** *11am-7pm, till 6pm Sun, way cool travel gear*

Timbuk 2 Store 506 Hayes St **415/252-9860**

Gyms & Health Clubs

Kabuki Springs & Spa 1750 Geary Blvd (at Fillmore) **415/922-6000** *10am-9:45pm, traditional Japanese bath w/ extensive menu of spa sevices*

Cruisy Areas

Buena Vista Park [AYOR] Haight St (btwn Baker & Central) *evenings in northern & highest part*

Land's End [AYOR] NW tip of SF *inquire locally*

San Jose

includes Campbell & Los Gatos; see also Cupertino, Santa Clara & Sunnyvale

Info Lines & Services

AA Gay/ Lesbian 274 E Hamilton Ave, Ste D, Campbell **408/374-8511** *24hr helpline, check www.aasanjose.org for meeting schedule*

Billy DeFrank Lesbian/ Gay Community Center [WC] 938 The Alameda **408/293-2429, 408/293-3040** *10am-9pm, till 2pm Sat, clsd Sun-Mon*

Accommodations

Hotel De Anza [GF,F,WC,NS] 233 W Santa Clara St **408/286-1000, 800/843-3700** *art deco gem*

Hotel Montgomery [GF] 211 S 1st St **408/282-8800, 866/823-0530** *recently added to Nat'l Register of Historic Places, also restaurant*

Moorpark Hotel [GF,SW,WC] 4241 Moorpark Ave **408/864-0300, 877/740-6622** *also bar & restaurant*

Bars

Hunters [MW,NH,D,MR,TG,K,V,WC] 349 S 1st St (at San Salvadore) **408/947-1975** *4pm-2am*

Mac's Club [M,NH] 39 Post St (btwn 1st & Market) **408/288-8221** *noon-2am, patio*

Renegades [M,NH,B,L] 501 W Taylor St (at Coleman Ave) **408/275-9902** *noon-2am, patio*

Nightclubs

Splash [M,D,K,DS,V,GO,$] 65 Post St (at 1st) **408/993-0861** *9pm-2am Th-Sat, theme nights*

Restaurants

Eulipia Restaurant & Bar 374 S 1st St (at San Carlos) **408/280-6161** *dinner only, clsd Mon*

Pasta Pomodoro 1205 The Alameda (at Race) **408/292-9929** *Italian*

Vin Santo 1346 Lincoln Ave **408/920-2508** *lunch Wed-Fri, dinner nightly, clsd Mon, Northern Italian, wine bar*

Entertainment & Recreation

Tech Museum of Innovation 201 S Market St (at Park Ave) **408/294-8324** *10am-5pm, IMAX Dome Theater, a must-see for digital junkies*

Retail Shops

Scott's Super Video 840 Willow St #700 (at Bird) **408/298-7013** *large gay/ lesbian video selection*

Publications

ON Newsmagazine 1346 The Alameda 7-106 **408/947-7374** *LGBT newspaper*

Men's Clubs

▶ **Watergarden** [★WI,18+,PC] 1010 The Alameda **408/275-1215** *24hrs, great outdoor patio & jacuzzi, Latino Th*

Men's Services

▶ **Megaphone 408/514-1111** *Meet and Chat Live with HOT local men. FREE to listen & respond to ads. Video and text chat at GayMates.com. Use FREE code 4889.*

Erotica

Leather Masters 969 Park Ave (at Race St) **408/293-7660** *noon-8pm, clsd Sun-Mon, fetish clothes, toys, etc*

Party Time 1456 W San Carlos St **408/998-0925** *arcade*

Pleasures from the Heart 1565 Winchester Blvd, Campbell **408/871-1826** *11am-10pm, intimate apparel, toys & gifts, women-owned*

San Luis Obispo

Info Lines & Services

Wayne McCaughan Community Pride Center 11573 Los Osos Valley Rd, Ste B (at Madonna Rd) **805/541-4252** *9am-6pm, clsd wknds*

Accommodations

The Madonna Inn [GF] 100 Madonna Rd **805/543-3000, 800/543-9666** *one-of-a-kind theme rooms (our fave is the Caveman Room)*

The Palomar Inn [GS,WI] 1601 Shell Beach Rd, Shell Beach **805/773-4204, 888/384-4004** *motel*

EMBRACE
YOUR
DESIRE
California's #1
Resort-Like Baths
Go To
TheWatergarden.com
• Photo Gallery
• Discount Offers
• Poolside Temperature
• Membership & Current Photo I.D. Required
• One-Time Membership Available
• Must Be 18 Years Or Older
Photo: Ovideo Sainz
THE
WATERGARDEN
GAY AND BISEXUAL
MEN'S CLUB & BATHS
1010 THE ALAMEDA
SAN JOSE, CALIFORNIA
(408) 275-1215
WWW.THEWATERGARDEN.COM
OPEN 24 HOURS/7 DAYS A WEEK

Sycamore Mineral Springs Resort [GF] 1215 Avila Beach Dr **805/595-7302, 800/234-5831** *hot mineral spring spa, integrative retreat center, also restaurant*

▶ **Temptation Ranch at Hidden Springs** [★M,SW,N,NS,WI,GO] **888/213-7733** *cabins & house & bunkhouse on private lake, hot tub, gym*

Cafes

Linnaea's Cafe [E] 1110 Garden St (near Marsh) **805/541-5888** *6:30am-11pm*

Outspoken, A Beverage Bistro [GO] 1422 Monterey (at California) **805/545-7664** *6:30am-5:30pm, 8am-2pm Sat, clsd Sun, cafe & juice bar*

West End Espresso & Tea [GO] 670 Higuera St #A (at Nipomo) **805/543-4902, 805/544-3581** *6am-7pm, till 9:30pm Th, till 8pm Fri-Sat, outdoor seating*

Restaurants

Big Sky Cafe 1121 Broad St (btwn Higuera & Marsh Sts) **805/545-5401** *7am-10pm, 8am-9pm Sun-Th*

Novo 726 Higuera St **805/543-3986** *lunch & dinner*

Bookstores

Coalesce Bookstore 845 Main St, Morro Bay **805/772-2880** *10am-5:30pm, 11am-4pm Sun, general, LGBT section*

Volumes of Pleasure [WC,GO] 1016 Los Osos Valley Rd, Los Osos **805/528-5565** *10am-6pm, noon-5pm Sun, general, LGBT section*

Publications

GALA News & Reviews **805/541-4252** *news & events for Central California coast*

San Rafael

see Marin County

San Ramon

see East Bay

Santa Ana

see Orange County

Santa Barbara

see also Ventura

Info Lines & Services

Pacific Pride Foundation 126 E Haley St #A-11 **805/963-3636** *9am-5pm Mon-Fri, social/ educational & support services*

Accommodations

Inn of the Spanish Garden [GF,SW,NS,WC] 915 Garden St (at Carrillo) **805/564-4700, 866/564-4700** *luxury hotel*

Old Yacht Club Inn [GF,NS,WI] 431 Corona Del Mar Dr **805/962-1277, 800/676-1676** *only B&B on beach*

The Orchid Inn at Santa Barbara [GS,NS,WI,WC,GO] 420 W Montecito St **805/965-2333, 877/722-3657** *1900s Victorian*

White Jasmine Inn [GS,NS] 1327 Bath St (at Sola) **805/966-0589** *4 different homes w/ 4 different personalities, full brkfst, fireplaces*

Nightclubs

Flavor [★MW,D] 15 W Ortega St (at Wildcat Lounge) **805/962-7970** *9pm-2am Sun only*

Cafes

Our Daily Bread 831 Santa Barbara St **805/966-3894** *6:30am-5:30pm, 7am-4pm Sat, clsd Sun, bakery/ cafe*

Reds Cafe [E,WI] 211 Helena Ave **805/966-5906** *11am-10pm, later wknds, clsd Mon*

Restaurants

Joe's Cafe 536 State St **805/966-4638** *look for the neon sign*

The Natural Cafe 508 State St **805/962-9494** *11am-9pm*

Opal Restaurant & Bar 1325 State St **805/966-9676** *lunch (Mon-Sat) & dinner nightly, full bar*

Sojourner Cafe [BW,WC] 134 E Canon Perdido (at Santa Barbara) **805/965-7922** *11am-11pm*

Entertainment & Recreation

Santa Barbara Mission 2201 Laguna St **805/682-4713** *the "queen of the missions"; take a self-guided tour btwn 9am-5pm daily & find out why*

Bookstores

Chaucer's Books [★] 3321 State St (at Las Positas Rd, Loreto Plaza) **805/682-6787** *9am-9pm, till 6pm Sun*

Erotica

For Adults Only 223 Anacapa **805/963-9922** *24hrs*

The Riviera Adult Superstore 4135 State St (at Hwy 154 intersection) **805/967-8282** *10am-midnight, pride items, community resources*

Santa Clara

Accommodations

Biltmore Hotel & Suites [GF,SW,NS,WI] 2151 Laurelwood Rd (at Montague Expwy) **408/988-8411, 800/255-9925**

Nightclubs

A Tinker's Damn (TD's) [M,D] 46 N Saratoga Ave (at Stevens Creek) **408/243-4595** *3pm-2am, from 1pm wknds*

Erotica

Hot Stuff 56 Saratoga Ave **408/241-9971** *arcade*

L'Amour Shoppe 2329 El Camino Real **408/296-7076** *24hrs, arcade*

Santa Cruz

Info Lines & Services

AA Gay/ Lesbian 5732 Soquel Dr, Soquel **831/475-5782 (AA#)** *call or visit www.aasantacruz.org for meetings*

The Diversity Center [WI] 1117 Soquel Ave **831/425-5422** *open daily, call for events*

Accommodations

Pleasure Point Inn [GF,NS,WI] 2-3655 E Cliff Dr **831/475-4657** *overlooks Monterey Bay*

Nightclubs

Blue Lagoon [GS,D,A,TG,V,WC] 923 Pacific Ave **831/423-7117** *3:30pm-2am, theme nights, live bands some nights*

Restaurants

Betty Burgers 505 Seabright Ave (at Murray) **831/423-8190** *11am-10pm, retro burger joint, outdoor seating, some veggie*

Cafe Limelight [TG,WC,GO] 1016 Cedar St (at Locust St) **831/425-7873** *lunch & dinner, clsd Mon, European*

Cilantros Mexican Restaurant 1934 Main St (in Town Center strip mall), Watsonville **831/761-2161** *lunch & dinner*

Crêpe Place [WC] 1134 Soquel Ave (at Seabright, across from Rio Theater) **831/429-6994** *11am-midnight, from 9am Sat-Sun, full bar, garden patio*

Saturn Cafe [GO] 145 Laurel St (at Pacific) **831/429-8505** *10am-3am, vegetarian diner*

Silver Spur 2650 Soquel Dr **831/475-2725** *6am-3pm, clsd Sun*

Bookstores

Bookshop Santa Cruz [WC] 1520 Pacific Ave **831/423-0900** *9am-10pm*

Gyms & Health Clubs

Kiva Retreat House Spa 702 Water St (at Ocean) **831/429-1142** *noon-11pm, till midnight Fri-Sat, women only 9am-1:30pm Sun*

Men's Services

▶ **Megaphone 831/515-1020** *Meet and Chat Live with HOT local men. FREE to listen & respond to ads. Video and text chat at GayMates.com. Use FREE code 4889.*

Erotica

Frenchy's Cruzin Books & Video 3960 Portola Dr (at 41st Ave) **831/475-9221** *arcade, adult novelties, lingerie, & DVDs*

Cruisy Areas

Laguna Creek Beach [AYOR] 7 miles N of town

Santa Rosa

see also Sonoma County

Info Lines & Services

AA Meetings in Sonoma County 707/544-1300 (AA#), 800/224-1300 *call or visit www.sonomacountyaa.org for meeting times*

Nightclubs

The Vine [GF,D,F] 528 7th St **707/393-7104** *4:30pm-2am Wed-Sat, theme nights*

Cafes

A' Roma Roasters [MW,E,WC,GO] 95 5th St (Railroad Square) **707/576-7765** *6am-close, from 7am Sat-Sun*

Restaurants

Syrah 205 5th St (at Davis) **707/568-4002** *lunch Tue-Sat & dinner nightly, creative California/ French*

Bookstores

Sawyer's News 733 4th St (btwn D & E Sts) **707/542-1311** *7am-7pm*

Men's Services

▶ **Megaphone 707/583-1112** *Meet and Chat Live with HOT local men. FREE to listen & respond to ads. Video and text chat at GayMates.com. Use FREE code 4889.*

Erotica

Santa Rosa Adult Books 3301 Santa Rosa Ave (at Todd) **707/542-8248**

Sausalito

see Marin County

Sebastopol

see Russian River & Sonoma County

Sequoia Nat'l Park

Accommodations

Wuksachi Lodge [GF] **559/253-2199, 866/807-3598** *mtn views, near hiking & skiing, [WI] in common areas, also restaurant & lounge*

Sonoma County

see also Petaluma, Russian River & Sonoma County

Info Lines & Services

AA Meetings in Sonoma County 707/544-1300 (AA#), 800/224-1300 *call or check www.sonomacountyaa.org for meeting times*

► **Sonoma County Tourism Bureau 707/522-5800, 800/576-6662** *see ad on p. 97*

Accommodations

A Wine Country Teahouse [MW,GO] 9556 Frederica Ave, Kenwood **707/833-6998** *B&B in authentic Japanese teahouse*

Beltane Ranch [GF] 11775 Sonoma Hwy (Hwy 12), Glen Ellen **707/996-6501** *1892 New Orleans-style ranch house*

Best Western Dry Creek Inn [GS,SW] 198 Dry Creek Rd, Healdsburg **707/433-0300, 800/222-5784**

Camellia Inn [GF,SW,NS] 211 North St, Healdsburg **707/433-8182, 800/727-8182** *Italianate Victorian, full brkfst*

The Gaige House [GF,SW,WI] 13540 Arnold Dr, Glen Ellen **707/935-0237, 800/935-0237** *in the Wine Country*

Glenelly Inn & Cottages [GF,NS,WI] 5131 Warm Springs Rd, Glen Ellen **707/996-6720** *B&B, full brkfst*

Grape Leaf Inn [GF,WI] 539 Johnson St, Healdsburg **707/433-8140, 866/433-8140** *Queen Anne Victorian, full brkfst*

Hyatt Vineyard Creek Hotel [GF,SW,WI,WC] 170 Railroad St (at Third St), Santa Rosa **707/284-1234** *resort, seafood restaurant*

Madrona Manor [GF,F,SW,NS,WC] **707/433-4231, 800/258-4003** *elegant Victorian country inn, full brkfst, also restaurant*

Magliulo's Rose Garden Inn [GF,WC] 681 Broadway (at Andrieux), Sonoma **707/996-1031** *one of Wine Country's most romantic Victorian B&Bs*

Midnight Sun Inn [GF,NS] 428 Haydon St (at University), Healdsburg **707/433-1718** *full brkfst, jacuzzi*

Thistle Dew Inn [GF,NS,WI,GS] 171 W Spain St (at First St W), Sonoma **707/938-2909, 800/382-7895** *located in Wine Country, whirlpool baths & fireplaces, free use of bikes*

Trojan Horse Inn [GF,NS] 19455 Sonoma Hwy (btwn W Spain & W Napa), Sonoma **707/996-2430, 800/899-1925** *romantic 100-year-old inn, full brkfst*

Vine Hill Inn B&B [GF,SW,NS] 3949 Vine Hill Rd, Sebastopol **707/823-8832** *B&B in restored 1897 farmhouse*

Bars

Black Cat Bar & Cafe [W,NH,D,F,E,GO] 10056 Main St, Penngrove **707/793-9480**

Cafes

Coffee Catz [E,WI] 6761 Sebastopol Ave #300 (in Gravenstein Station), Sebastopol **707/829-6600** *6:30am-6pm, till 10pm Wed (open mic), till 10pm Fri & Sat (live bands) garden*

Screamin' Mimi's 6902 Sebastopol Ave (intersection of Hwy 12 & 116), Sebastopol **707/823-5902** *espresso drinks & homemade ice cream*

Restaurants

Estate 400 W Spain St, Sonoma **707/933-3663** *lunch & dinner, Sun brunch, clsd Mon, Italian*

Mom's Apple Pie 4550 Gravenstein Hwy N, Sebastopol **707/823-8330** *pie worth stopping for on your way to & from Russian River!*

Singletree Inn [GO] 165 Healdsburg Ave, Healdsburg **707/433-8263** *7am-2:30pm, till 3pm wknds, good brkfsts, famous BBQ sandwiches, some veggie, local wines, outdoor seating*

Slice of Life 6970 McKinley St, Sebastopol **707/829-6627** *11am-9pm, from 9am Sat-Sun, clsd Mon, vegan & vegetarian*

Entertainment & Recreation

River's Edge Kayak & Canoe Company [GO] **707/433-7247** *river excursions*

Erotica

The Sensuality Shoppe 2371-A Gravenstein Hwy S, Sebastopol **707/829-3999** *11am-6pm, toys, books, videos, woman-owned/ run*

Springville

Accommodations

Great Energy [MW,SW,NS] PO Box 473, 93265 **559/539-2382** *retreat in foothills of Sierra Nevada mtns*

Stockton

see also Modesto

Nightclubs

Paradise Club [MW,D,E,V,YC] 10100 N Lower Sacramento Rd (near Grider) **209/477-4724** *6pm-2am, from 3pm Sun*

Erotica

Jaybird Books 332 N California (at Miner) **209/941-8607**

Suzie's Adult Superstores 3126 E Hammer Ln **209/952-6900** *24hrs, arcade*

Cruisy Areas

Oak Park [AYOR] Alpine Ave

Sunnyvale

see also San Jose

Accommodations

Wild Palms Hotel [GF,SW,WC] 910 E Fremont Ave (at Wolfe Ave) **408/738-0500, 800/538-1600** *hot tub*

Men's Services

▶ **Megaphone 408/331-7400** *Meet and Chat Live with HOT local men. FREE to listen & respond to ads. Video and text chat at GayMates.com. Use FREE code 4889.*

Sutter Creek

Accommodations

The Foxes Inn of Sutter Creek [GF,NS,WI,GO] 77 Main St (at Keys St) **209/267-5882, 800/987-3344** *full brkfst*

The Sea Ranch

Accommodations

Getaway [GF,SW,NS,GO] 38249 Green Vale Close **707/785-3823** *2-bdrm rental home, deck w/ hot tub, ocean views, lesbian-owned*

Tiburon

see Marin County

Twentynine Palms

see Joshua Tree Nat'l Park

Ukiah

Bars

Perkins St Lounge [GF,D] 228 E Perkins St **707/462-0327** *3pm-2am*

Upland

Nightclubs

Oasis [M,D,DS,WC] 1386 E Foothill Blvd #H (at Grove) **909/920-9590** *6pm-2am Wed-Sat, from 8pm Sun, drag Th & Sun [18+]*

Erotica

Mustang Books 961 N Central (at Foothill) **909/981-0227** *24hrs, arcade [AYOR]*

Sensations Love Boutique 1656 W Foothill Blvd (at Mountain) **909/985-1654**

The Toy Box 1999 W Arrow Rte (at Central) **909/920-1135** *24hrs*

Vacaville

Info Lines & Services

Solano Pride Center 1125 Missouri St #203-D, Fairfield **707/427-2356** *call for meeting times*

Erotica

Secrets Adult Super Store 564 Parker Rd (at Union Ave), Fairfield **707/437-9297** *arcade*

Cruisy Areas

Lee Bell Park [AYOR] Travis Blvd (at Union Ave), Fairfield

Vallejo

includes Benicia

Bars

Town House Cocktail Lounge [GF,NH,GO] 401-A Georgia St (at Marin) **707/553-9109** *1pm-2am, from 10am Sat-Sun*

Bookstores

Bookshop Benicia [WC] 856 Southampton Rd, Benicia **707/747-5155** *10am-8pm, till 6pm wknds*

Van Nuys

Men's Services

▶ **Megaphone 818/465-0500** *Meet and Chat Live with HOT local men. FREE to listen & respond to ads. Video and text chat at GayMates.com. Use FREE code 4889.*

Erotica

Diamond Adult World 6406 Van Nuys Blvd (at Victory) **818/997-3665** *24hrs*

Ventura

see also Santa Barbara

Info Lines & Services

AA Gay/ Lesbian 805/389-1444 (AA#), 800/990-7750 *call or visit www.aaventuracounty.org for meetings*

Ventura County Rainbow Alliance 4567 Telephone Rd, Ste 100 **805/339-6340** *9am-8pm, LGBT center*

Bars

Paddy McDermott's [MW,D,E,K] 2 W Main St (at Ventura) **805/652-1071** *2pm-2am, beer busts*

Erotica

Three Star Books 359 E Main St **805/653-9068** *24hrs*

Cruisy Areas

Surfers Point [AYOR] N of the Ventura Pier (btwn fairgrounds & Ocean) *go N along beach to Hobo's Jungle*

Victorville

Bars

Ricky's [MW,D] 13728 Hesperia Rd #12 **760/951-5400** *6pm-2am, clsd Mon*

Westside 15 [MW,NH] 16868 Stoddard Wells Rd (off I-15) **760/243-9600** *5pm-2am, from 4pm Sat, from 3pm Sun, ladies night Th*

Erotica

Oasis Adult Dept Store 14949 Palmdale Rd **760/241-0788** *arcade*

Cruisy Areas

Deep Creek Hot Springs [AYOR] Apple Valley *from I-15, take Bear Valley Cutoff & turn right onto Central Rd; go left onto Ocotillo Rd for 2 miles & turn right onto Bowen Ranch Rd (unmarked dirt road)*

Grady Trammel Park [AYOR] 3/4 mile N of West Side 15 bar (on Stoddard Wells Rd) *watch out for rangers (!)*

Walnut Creek

see East Bay

Men's Services

▶ **Megaphone 925/300-9999** *Meet and Chat Live with HOT local men. FREE to listen & respond to ads. Video and text chat at GayMates.com. Use FREE code 4889.*

Whittier

Info Lines & Services

Together in Pride AA 11931 Washington Blvd (at Good Samaritan MCC) **562/696-6213 (church #)** *call for meeting times*

Erotica

Romantix Adult Superstore 10614 Whittier Blvd **562/695-6301** *24hrs*

Willits

Accommodations

Black Hawk Weyr [MW,NS,WC,GO] **415/225-2624** *vacation cabin on forested mountainside, sleeps 5, lesbian-owned*

Restaurants

Purple Thistle 50 S Main St **707/459-4750** *lunch Tue-Fri, dinner nightly, clsd Sun-Mon*

Bookstores

Leaves of Grass 15 S Main St **707/459-3744** *10am-6pm, noon-5pm Sun*

Yosemite Nat'l Park

Accommodations

The Ahwahnee Hotel [GF,F,SW] Yosemite Valley Floor **559/252-4848, 866/875-8456 (reservations)** *incredibly dramatic & expensive grand fortress*

Highland House B&B [GF] 3125 Wild Dove Ln (at Jerseydale Rd), Mariposa **209/966-3737**

The Homestead [GF,NS] 41110 Rd 600, Ahwahnee **559/683-0495, 800/483-0495** *cottages & 2-bdrm house*

June Lake Villager [GF] 2640 Hwy 158 (2.5 miles W of Hwy 395), June Lake **760/648-7712, 800/655-6545** *cottages, cabins & suites 20 minutes from Yosemite*

Narrow Gauge Inn [GF,SW,NS] 48571 Hwy 41, Fish Camp **559/683-7720, 888/644-9050** *mtnside country inn, 4 miles from Yosemite, hot tub*

Queen's Inn by the River [GS,NS,WI,WC,GO] 41139 Hwy 41, Oakhurst **559/683-4354** *garden w/ river view, lesbian-owned*

Tenaya Lodge at Yosemite [GF,SW] 1122 Hwy 41, Fish Camp **559/683-6555, 888/514-2167** *resort w/ spa services, forest & mtn views, pets ok*

Yosemite Big Creek Inn B&B [GS,NS,WI] 1221 Hwy 41, Fish Camp **559/641-2828** *B&B, full brkfst, hot tub*

The Yosemite Bug Rustic Mountain Resort [GF,F,SW,NS,WI,WC] 6979 Hwy 140, Midpines **209/966-6666, 866/826-7108** *hostel w/ dorms, cabins, private rooms & tents*

Yosemite View Lodge [GF,SW,WC] 11136 Hwy 140, El Portal **209/379-2681, 888/742-4371** *3 pools, 2 restaurants & lounge*

Yosemite's Apple Blossom Inn B&B [GF,NS,WC] **559/642-2001, 888/687-4281** *20 minutes from S entrance to Yosemite, hot tub*

Cruisy Areas

Rest Stop [AYOR] at turn to Glacier Point on road to valley

Colorado

Statewide

Publications

Colorado Pride Guide **303/377-1826** *LGBT business & travel directory, visit www.GayColorado.com for free copy*

▶ **Out Front Colorado** **303/778-7900** *statewide LGBT newspaper*

Aspen

Accommodations

Aspen Mountain Lodge [GF,SW,NS] 311 W Main St **970/925-7650, 800/362-7736** *full brkfst, hot tub*

Hotel Aspen [GF,SW,NS,WI] 110 W Main St **970/925-3441, 800/527-7369** *hot tub, après-ski wine & cheese*

Hotel Lenado [GF] 200 S Aspen St **970/925-6246, 800/321-3457** *full brkfst, hot tub, bar*

St Moritz Lodge [GF,SW,NS,GO] 334 W Hyman Ave **970/925-3220, 800/817-2069** *also condos & hostel, hot tub*

Restaurants

Jimmy's 205 S Mill St (at Hopkins) **970/925-6020** *5:30pm-11pm, also bar*

Syzygy [E,WC] 520 E Hyman, 2nd flr **970/925-3700** *seasonal, 6pm-10:30pm, bar till 2am*

Bookstores

Explore Booksellers & Bistro [F,WI,WC] 221 E Main (at Aspen) **970/925-5336, 800/562-7323** *10am-10pm, also gourmet vegetarian restaurant*

Beaver Creek

Accommodations

Beaver Creek Lodge [GF,SW,NS,WI,WC] 26 Avondale Ln (at Village Rd) **970/845-9800, 800/583-9615** *also restaurant, mtn chic, steam room, workout room*

Boulder

Info Lines & Services

Boulder Pride 2132 14th St (at Pine) **303/499-5777** *LGBT resource center*

Accommodations

The Briar Rose B&B [GF,NS,WI] 2151 Arapahoe Ave (at 22nd St) **303/442-3007, 888/786-8440** *full organic brkfst*

Zelda's B&B [MW,WI,GO] 4256 Redwood Ct (at 30th St) **303/859-0844**

Cafes

Walnut Cafe [★WC] 3073 Walnut (at 30th) **303/447-2315** *7am-3pm, patio*

Bookstores

Left Hand Books 1200 Pearl St #10 (E of Broadway) **303/443-8252** *10am-9pm, noon-6pm Sun*

Retail Shops

Enchanted Ink [GO] 1200 Pearl St #35 (at Broadway) **303/440-6611** *tattoos, piercing, henna, RN-owned*

Men's Services

Cruisy Areas

Dream Canyon [SW,N] Lost Angel Rd (off Sugarloaf Mtn Rd) *inquire locally for detailed directions*

Breckenridge

Accommodations

The Bunkhouse Lodge [MO,N,GO] 13203 Hwy 9 **970/453-6475** *full brkfst, hot tub, also Bunkhouse Bar [CW,BYOB]*

Valdoro Mountain Lodge [GS,SW,NS,WI,WC] 500 Village Rd **970/453-4880, 800/436-6780** *condos w/ access to pool, massage facilities & outdoor hot tub*

Colorado Springs

(includes Manitou Springs)

Info Lines & Services

Pikes Peak Gay/ Lesbian Community Center 719/471-4429 *2pm-6pm, call for events*

Accommodations

Authentic B&B Inns of the Pikes Peak Region 888/892-2237, 719/660-7084

Blue Skies Inn B&B [GS,NS,WI] 402 Manitou Ave (at Mayfair), Manitou Springs **719/685-3899, 800/398-7949** *Gothic Revival, full brkfst*

Old Town Guesthouse [GF,NS,WI,WC] 115 S 26th St **719/632-9194, 888/375-4210** *full brkfst, hot tub*

Pikes Peak Paradise [GF,NS,WI,GO] Woodland Park **719/687-6656, 800/728-8282** *full brkfst, hot tub, mansion w/ view of Pikes Peak, surrounded by national forest*

Quality Inn & Suites–Garden of the Gods [GF,SW,WI,WC] 555 W Garden of the Gods **719/593-9119, 800/828-4347**

Two Sisters Inn–A B&B [★GF,NS] 10 Otoe Pl, Manitou Springs **719/685-9684, 800/274-7466**

Bars

Bijou Bar & Grill [MW,D,F,K,NS] 2510 E Bijou **719/473-5718** *3pm-2am, till midnight Sun & Tue, clsd Mon, patio*

Club Q [★M,NH,D,F,E,K,S,18+,WC,GO] 3430 N Academy Blvd (at N Carefree) **719/570-1429** *6pm-2am, till 4am Sat, clsd Mon*

DJ's Bar & Grill [MW,NH,D,TG,F,K,DS,S,WC] 1110 E Filmore St (at Nevada) **719/473-2425** *11am-2am*

Underground [M,NH,D,F,GO] 110 N Nevada Ave (at Kiowa St) **719/578-7771** *4pm-2am, goth night Sun*

Nightclubs

Club Hush [MW,D,DS] 3738 Astrozon Blvd (at S Academy Blvd) **719/393-7400** *6pm-2am Wed-Sun*

Cafes

Spice of Life an Ingredients Emporium 727 Manitou Ave, Manitou Springs **719/685-5284**

Restaurants

Dale Street Cafe Bistro 115 E Dale (at Nevada) **719/578-9898** *lunch & dinner, brunch wknds*

Entertainment & Recreation

Out Loud 719/471-0468 *men's chorus*

Men's Clubs

Buddies [MO,MR,V,18+,N,PC,GO] 3430 B N Academy Blvd (N Carefree) **719/591-7660** *3pm-4am, clsd Mon, beer bust Sun, video booths, darkrooms*

Men's Services

Erotica

First Amendment Adult Bookstore 220 E Fillmore (at Nevada) **719/630-7676**

Romantix Adult Superstore 1613 Lashelle Wy (off B St) **719/538-9675**

XXX-Treme Mature Fantasy Store 620 Peterson Rd (Platte -Hwy 24) **719/638-0200**

Cruisy Areas

Palmer Park [AYOR] *many undercover cops*

Denver

Info Lines & Services

Gay/ Lesbian AA 303/322-4440

The GLBT Center of Colorado (The Center) [WC] 1050 Broadway **303/733-7743** *10am-6pm Mon-Fri, extensive resources & support groups*

Sketchin'-OUT (Crystal Meth Anonymous) [WC] 1050 Broadway (at The Center) **303/733-7743** *7pm Fri; also Ray of Light (Narcotics Anonymous) 7pm Wed*

Accommodations

The Brown Palace [GF,WI] 321 17th St **303/297-3111, 800/321-2599** *stained glass canopy, sun in every room*

Capitol Hill Mansion B&B [GF,NS,WI] 1207 Pennsylvania (at 12th) **303/839-5221, 800/839-9329** *full brkfst, hot tub*

Castle Marne [GF,WI] 1572 Race St **303/331-0621, 800/926-2763** *1889 mansion on Nat'l Register of Historic Places, some jacuzzis*

The Curtis [GF,SW,WI] 1405 Curtis St **303/571-0300, 800/525-6651** *hip hotel, hot tub*

OUT FRONT
Colorado
Colorado's leading GLBT
publication – Since 1976
www.OutFrontColorado.com
303.778.7900

Elyria's Western Guest House [M,NS,GO] 1655 E 47th Ave (near I-70 & Brighton, check in here) **303/291-0915** *historic neighborhood*

The Gregory Inn, LoDo [GF,NS] 2500 Arapahoe St (at 25th St) **303/295-6570, 800/925-6570** *full brkfst, jacuzzis*

Hotel Monaco [GF,NS,WI] 1717 Champa St (at 17th) **303/296-1717, 800/990-1303** *gym, spa, also Italian restaurant*

Hotel Teatro [GF] 1100 14th St **303/228-1100, 888/727-1200** *luxury boutique hotel, 2 restaurants*

The Oxford Hotel [GF,F,WI] 1600 17th St **303/628-5400, 800/228-5838** *health club & spa, also restaurant & art deco lounge*

Radisson Hotel Denver Stapleton Plaza [GF,SW,WI,WC] 3333 Quebec St (at 35th) **303/321-3500, 800/333-3333** *gym, restaurant*

Ramada Inn Denver Downtown [GS,SW,WI,WC] 1150 E Colfax Ave (at Downing) **303/831-7700, 800/272-6232** *hotel in the heart of Capitol Hill, hot tub, full brkfst*

Residence Inn Denver City Center [GF,NS] 1725 Champa St **303/296-3444, 800/331-3131** *all-suite hotel, 8th-flr patio w/ hot tub*

Bars

The Atrium Bar & Grill [GS,D,S] 554 S Broadway **303/744-1923** *7am-2am, dancing/DJ Fri-Sat*

Barker Lounge [M,NH] 255 S Broadway (at Byers) **303/778-0545** *noon-2am, also large patio with bar, dogs welcome*

Bender's Tavern [GF,F,E,K] 314 E 13th Ave (at Grant) **303/861-7070** *noon-2am, live bands, [K] Tue & Th*

BJ's Carousel [★MW,NH,TG,F,K,DS,S,WC,GO] 1380 S Broadway (at Arkansas) **303/777-9880** *4pm-2am, from 10am Sat-Mon, male strippers Tue, [K] Wed, [C,DS] Fri-Sat, also restaurant, dinner Wed-Sun*

Boyztown [M,NH,S,WI] 117 Broadway (btwn 1st & 2nd Aves) **303/722-7373, 303/777-9378** *3pm-2am, from noon Fri-Sun, male dancers Tue-Sun*

Broadways [M,NH,WI] 1027 Broadway (at 11th Ave) **303/623-0700** *2pm-2am, from noon Sat-Sun, cool mix of folk, [K] Th*

Charlie's [★M,D,CW,WC] 900 E Colfax Ave (at Emerson) **303/839-8890** *11am-2am, 2 clubs, also restaurant*

The Compound [★M,NH,D,A] 145 Broadway (at 2nd Ave) **303/722-7977** *7am-2am, [D] Fri-Sat*

Da Hook Up [MW,D,E] 5190 Brighton Blvd (at Safari Club) **303/295-2819**

Dazzle [GF,F,E] 930 Lincoln St (btwn 9th & 10th Aves) **303/839-5100** *from 4pm Sun-Th, from 11am Fri, also Sun brunch (9:30am-1pm), jazz club & restaurant*

Denver Detour [★W,NH,E,WC] 5110 W Colfax Ave (at Sheridan) **303/861-1497** *11am-2am, lunch & dinner daily, [K] 2nd & 4th Fri*

Denver Eagle [M,NH,B,L,WC,GO] 1475 36th St (at Blake) **303/291-0250** *levi/leather/cruise bar*

The Denver Wrangler [M,B,WC] 1700 Logan Ave (at 17th Ave) **303/837-1075** *11am-2am, levi/bear bar, popular Sun beer bust*

El Chapultepec [★GF,F,E,$] 1962 Market St (at 20th) **303/295-9126** *9am-2am, live jazz & blues, 1-drink minimum per set*

El Potrero [GS,MR-L,E,F] 320 S Birch St (at Leetsdale Dr), Glendale *Mexican restaurant early, Latino gay bar late (Wed, Sat-Sun)*

Her Bar [W,D,E,K] 629 E Colfax Ave **303/832-2687** *Boyz night Wed*

JR's Bar [★M,NH,K,DS,V,GO] 777 E 17th Ave (at Clarkson) **303/831-0459** *3pm-2am*

Lannie's Clocktower Cabaret [GF,F,E,C] 16th St Mall at Arapahoe (in historic D&F Tower) **303/293-0075** *upscale cabaret w/ variety of acts weekly including drag (Tue) & burlesque (Th)*

Mo's of Denver [MW,V,WC] 1037 Broadway **720/235-8593** *3pm-2am*

Mozart Lounge [MW,E] 1417 Krameria (btwn 14th & Colfax) **303/388-0701** *piano bar*

R&R Denver [MW,NH] 4958 E Colfax Ave (at Elm) **303/320-9337** *3pm-2am, from 1pm Fri, from 11am wknds*

Rock Bar [GS] 3015 E Colfax **303/322-4444** *dive bar, theme nights*

tHERe Coffee Bar & Lounge [W,E,TG,WI,GO] 1526 E Colfax (btwn Humboldt & Franklin) **303/830-8437** *10am-midnight, till 1am Sat, till 10pm Sun-Tue, also cafe*

Nightclubs

La Rumba [GF,D,E,$] 99 W 9th Ave (at Broadway) **303/572-8006** *salsa dancing & lessons Th & Sat, more gay Fri for Lipgloss (Brit-pop & indie music)*

Pure Nightlife [M,D] 2549 Welton St **303/570-1390** *gay Sat only*

Tracks [GS,D,MR] 3500 Walnut St (at 35th) **303/863-7326** *9pm-2am, clsd Sun-Wed, 2 rooms, theme nights*

Cafes

Bump & Grind Cafe 439 E 17th Ave (at Pennsylvania) **303/861-4841** *brkfst & lunch 7am-3:30pm, popular Petticoat Bruncheon w/ drag servers 10am-2pm wknds, clsd Mon-Tue*

City, O City 206 E 13th Ave (at Sherman) **303/832-7313** *7am-2am, from 8am wknds, vegetarian/ vegan, also bar*

Common Grounds [WI] 3484 W 32nd Ave (Howell) **303/458-5248** *also 1601 17th St, 303/296-9248 [WI]*

Java Creek [WI,WC] 287 Columbine St (at 3rd Ave) **303/377-8902** *7am-6pm, 8:30am-3pm Sun, patio*

The Market at Larimer Square [F] 1445 Larimer Sq **303/534-5140** *6am-11pm, till midnight Fri-Sat, till 10pm Sun*

Paris on the Platte [F,WI] 1553 Platte St (at 15th) **303/455-2451** *7am-1am, till 3am Fri-Sat, from 8am wknds, soups, salads, sandwiches, popular after-hours*

Wired Coffee & Art [WI] 19 E Bayaud **303/733-3977** *8:30am-5:30pm, clsd Mon*

Restaurants

Alto [E,WC] 1320 15th St (at Larimer, LoDo) **303/893-2586** *dinner Tue-Fri, contemporary northern Italian*

Annie's Cafe [★] 4012 E 8th Ave **303/355-8197** *7am-10pm, from 8am Sat, diner*

The Avenue Grill 630 E 17th Ave (at Washington) **303/861-2820** *11:30am-11pm, till midnight Fri-Sat, 5pm-10pm Sun*

Benny's Restaurante y Tequila Bar [NS] 301 E 7th Ave (at Grant St) **303/894-0788** *lunch & dinner, patio*

Devil's Food 1020 S Gaylord St (at E Tennessee) **303/733-7448** *6am-4pm, 7am-3pm wknds, desserts & brkfst*

Dixon's Downtown Grill [WC] 1610 16th St (at Wazee) **303/573-6100** *7am-close, from 8am wknds, American*

Duo 2413 W 32nd Ave (at Zuni) **303/477-4141** *dinner nightly, wknd brunch, hip, organic, creative American, full bar*

The Earl of Sandwich [GO] 1431 Ogden St (btwn 14th Ave & Ogden Theatre) **303/832-7411** *10am-4pm, clsd Sun, sandwiches & salads*

Fruition 1313 E 6th Ave **303/831-1962** *5pm-10pm, till 8pm Sun, contemporary French, seasonal menu*

Hamburger Mary's Bar & Grille [★GS,D,K] 700 E 17th Ave (at Washington St, across from JR's bar) **303/832-1333** *11am-2am, from 10am Sun, also Club M*

Il Vicino 550 Broadway **303/861-0801** *11am-10pm, till 11pm Fri-Sat, pizza*

Joseph's Southern Food, Carry Out & Drive In [GO] 2868 Fairfax St (at 29th) **303/333-5332** *11am-8pm Tue-Sat, traditional Southern, also bakery, ice cream parlor, candy*

Las Margaritas Uptown [★GO] 1035 E 17th Ave (at Downing) **303/830-2199** *11am-1am, Mexican, also bar*

Le Central [BW] 112 E 8th Ave (at Lincoln St) **303/863-8094** *lunch & dinner, brunch Sat-Sun, "affordable French"*

Pete's Kitchen [★] 1962 E Colfax Ave **303/321-3139** *24hrs, diner, popular after bars close*

Racine's 650 Sherman St (at 6th Ave) **303/595-0418** *brkfst, lunch, dinner, late night & Sun brunch, full bar*

Steuben's 523 E 17th Ave **303/830-1001** *11am-11pm, till midnight Fri, 10am-midnight Sat, till 11pm Sun, American comfort food served up hip, patio, full bar*

Sunny Gardens 6460 E Yale Avenue **303/691-8830** *Chinese, plenty veggie/vegan*

Thai Pot Cafe 1550 S Colorado Blvd (at E Florida) **303/639-6200** *Thai*

Tom's Home Cookin' [GO] 800 E 26th Ave (Clarkson St) **303/388-8035** *11am-3pm, clsd Sat-Sun, Southern comfort food*

Vesta Dipping Grill 1822 Blake St (near 18th St) **303/296-1970** *5pm-10pm Sun-Th, till 11pm Fri-Sat, upscale*

WaterCourse Foods 837 E 17th Ave (at Clarkston) **303/832-7313** *7am-9pm, till 10pm Fri-Sat, vegetarian/ vegan*

Wazee Supper Club 1600 15th St (at Wazee) **303/623-9518** *11am-2am, noon-midnight Sun, classic comfort food, full bar*

Zaidy's Deli 121 Adams (at First) **303/333-5336** *6:30am-5pm, till 8pm Th-Sat, 7:30am-5pm Sun; also 15th at Lawrence, 303/893-3600*

Entertainment & Recreation

Colorado OUT Spoken PBS KBDI, channel 12 **303/861-0829** *10pm Sun, LGBT news & entertainment TV program*

Denver Gay Men's Chorus **303/832-3462**

Mercury Cafe [F,E,NS] 2199 California St **303/294-9281** *5:30pm-close, swing, tango, salsa dancing, live shows, also restaurant, dinner only Tue-Sun, wknd brunch*

Pride Radio **303/631-2957** *gossip & music*

Rocky Mountain Rainbeaus **303/863-7739** *all-inclusive, all-levels, high-energy square dance club*

Bookstores

Tattered Cover Book Store [WC] 2526 Colfax Ave (at Elizabeth) **303/322-7727, 800/833-9327** *7am-9pm, from 9am Sat, 10am-6pm Sun, local independent, coffee shop; also 1628 16th St, 303/ 436-1070*

Retail Shops

Arco Iris Design 82 S Broadway (Bayau Ave) **303/765-5116** *pride jewelry & design*

Bound By Design 1332 E Colfax (at Humboldt) **303/830-7272, 303/832-TAT2** *piercing & tattoos*

Heaven Sent Me [WC] 116 S Broadway (btwn Alameda & Virginia) **303/733-9000** *11am-7pm, pride items, clothing, gifts*

Hysteria [GF] 114 S Broadway (at Bayaud Ave) **303/733-3373** *11am-7pm, from noon Sat, till 5pm Sun, clsd Tue, feminist/ queer-friendly sex-toy shop*

Needz [GO] 135 Broadway (at 1st Ave) **303/722-0969** *10am-10pm, noon-6pm Sun, cards, gifts, sexy menswear & toys for adults*

Rockmount Ranch Wear 1626 Wazee St **303/629-7777, 800/775-2566** *7am-5pm, 11am-4pm wknds, makers of the shirts worn in Brokeback Mountain*

Publications

Gayzette 720/435-8914 *LGBT monthly publication*

▶ **Out Front Colorado 303/778-7900** *statewide bi-weekly LGBT newspaper, since 1976*

PINK Magazine 303/316-4688, 877/769-7465 *LGBT business directory & lifestyle magazine*

Men's Clubs

CCC (Community Country Club) [V,PC] 2151 Lawrence St (at 21st) **303/297-2601**

Denver Swim Club [★MO,V,YC,SW,PC] 6923 E Colfax Ave (at Olive) **303/322-4023**

Midtowne Spa—Denver [PC] 2935 Zuni St (at 29th) **303/458-8902** *24hrs, sundeck, whirlpool, private rooms, basement play area*

Men's Services

▶ **Megaphone 303/433-6789** *Meet and Chat Live with HOT local men. FREE to listen & respond to ads. Video and text chat at GayMates.com. Use FREE code 4889.*

Erotica

Circus Cinema 5580 N Federal Blvd **303/455-3144** *24hrs*

Crypt Adult Entertainment 139 Broadway (btwn 1st & 2nd) **303/778-6584** *10am-2am, till 4am Fri-Sat, all-male theaters & arcades*

The Crypt on Broadway 8 Broadway (at Ellsworth) **303/733-3112** *11am-11pm, till 8pm Sun, leather, clubwear & more*

Dove Theater 3480 W Colfax **303/893-0037** *8:30am-12:30am, 24hrs wknds*

Pleasure Entertainment Center 127 S Broadway (at Bayaud) **303/722-5852** *open 23hrs; also 3250 W Alameda, 303/934-2373 & 3490 W Colfax, 303/825-6505*

Romantix Adult Superstore 633 E Colfax Ave (at Washington) **303/831-8319** *24hrs*

Cruisy Areas

Cheesman Park [AYOR] near Pavilion *beware of undercover cops!*

Durango

Accommodations

Leland House B&B [★GF,NS,WC] 721 E 2nd Ave **970/385-1920, 800/664-1920** *rooms & suites, full brkfst*

Mesa Verde Far View Lodge [GF,NS,WI] 1 Navajo Hill, Mesa Verde National Park **602/331-5210, 800/449-2288** *inside nat'l park at 8250' elevation, views of 4 states*

Rochester Hotel [★GF,NS,WC] 726 E 2nd Ave **970/385-1920, 800/664-1920** *Western-style house, full brkfst*

Englewood

Bookstores

Isis Books & Gifts [WC] 2775 S Broadway (at Yale) **303/761-8627, 800/808-0867 (orders)** *10am-7pm, till 6pm Fri-Sat, noon-5pm Sun, New Age, metaphysical, wellness center*

Estes Park

Accommodations

Mountain Sage Inn [GF,NS] 553 W Elkhorn Ave **970/586-2833, 800/552-2833**

Stanley Hotel [GF] 333 Wonderview Ave **800/976-1377, 970/586-3371** *1909 lodge near Rocky Mtn Nat'l Park, the inspiration for Stephen King's The Shining*

Fort Collins

Info Lines & Services

The Lambda Community Center 212 South Mason St **970/221-3247** *10am-3pm Mon-Fri, or by appt*

Accommodations

Archer's Poudre River Resort [GF,GO] 33021 Poudre Canyon Hwy, Bellvue **970/881-2139, 888/822-0588**

Bars

Choice City Shots [MW,NH,D,K,S,WC,GO] 124 LaPorte Ave (at College) **970/221-4333** *6:30pm-midnight, till 1:30am Fri-Sat*

Grand Junction

Restaurants

Leon's Taqueria 505 30th Rd **970/242-1388** *11am-9pm*

Erotica

24 Road Video Exchange 639 24 Rd (at Mesa Mall) **970/243-4112** *10am-midnight, till 10pm Sun*

Cruisy Areas

Hawthorne Park [AYOR]

Walker Wildlife Area [AYOR] Hwy 6/50 W, past Mesa Mall (near the CO River) *in the woods*

Hotchkiss

Accommodations

Leroux Creek Inn & Vineyards 12388 3100 Rd **970/872-4746**

Restaurants

North Fork Valley Restaurant & Thirsty Parrot Pub [E] 140 W Bridge St **970/872-4215** *11am-8pm, American/ Mexican*

Lakewood

see also Denver

Erotica

Romantix Adult Superstore 1569 N Wadsworth Blvd (at Colfax) **303/232-2332** *8am-2am, till midnight Sun*

Leadville

Accommodations

The Ice Palace Inn B&B [GF,NS,GO] 813 Spruce St **719/846-8272, 800/754-2840** *historic Victorian, mtn views, fireplaces, hot tub*

New Raymer

Accommodations

Colorado Cattle Company & Guest Ranch [GF,SW,NS] 70008 WCR 132 **970/437-5345** *guests participate in cattle work & horseback riding in this Wild West adventure*

Pine

Accommodations

Platte River Cabins [GF,GO] 16525 Pine Valley Rd **303/838-9195** *riverfront vacation cabins, private fishing*

Pueblo

Bars

Pirate's Cove [MW,NH,WC] 105 Central Plaza (off 1st & Union) **719/543-2683** *4pm-2am, 2pm-midnight Sun, clsd Mon*

Cruisy Areas

City Park Pueblo Blvd & Thatcher *N side near gazebo*

San Acacio

Accommodations

Luna Creative Retreats [GF,TG,GO] 401 Directa **719/206-0622** *artists retreat*

Stratton

Accommodations

Claremont Inn [GS,GO] 800 Claremont Dr (off exit 419, I-70) **888/291-8910** *B&B-inn 2 hours from Denver, full brkfst, commitment ceremonies*

Vail

Accommodations

Antlers at Vail [GF,SW] 680 W Lionshead Pl **970/476-2471, 800/843-8245** *apts, kitchens, hot tub*

Restaurants

Larkspur Restaurant & Market [WC] 458 Vail Valley Dr (in the Golden Peak Lodge) **970/479-8050** *lunch & dinner, seasonal hours, fine dining, also bar, patio, ski-in/ out*

Sweet Basil [WC] 193 E Gore Creek Dr **970/476-0125** *lunch & dinner, bar*

Winter Park

Accommodations

Bear Paw Inn [GF,NS] 871 Bear Paw Dr **970/887-1351** *massive log lodge on top of mtn w/ spectacular views of Rocky Mtn Nat'l Park, jacuzzi*

CONNECTICUT

Statewide

PUBLICATIONS

▶ **Metroline 860/231-8334** *regional newspaper & entertainment guide, covers CT, RI & MA*

Bethel

CAFES

Molten Java [E,GO] 102 Greenwood Ave **203/739-0313** *6am-10pm, till 11pm Fri-Sat, 8am-8pm Sun*

RESTAURANTS

Bethel Pizza House 206 Greenwood Ave **203/748-1427** *11am-11pm, till midnight Fri-Sat*

Bridgeport

RESTAURANTS

Bloodroot Restaurant 85 Ferris St (at Harbor Ave) **203/576-9168** *lunch Tue & Th-Sat, dinner Tue-Sat, brunch only Sun, clsd Mon, vegetarian*

BOOKSTORES

Bloodroot [WC] 85 Ferris St (at Harbor Ave) **203/576-9168** *clsd Mon, call for hours, also vegetarian restaurant*

MEN'S SERVICES

EROTICA

Boston Book & Video 2053 Boston Ave **203/335-9705**

Romantix Adult Superstore 410 North Ave **203/332-7129**

Bristol

EROTICA

Amazing Superstore 167 Farmington Ave **860/582-9000**

CRUISY AREAS

Rockwell Park [AYOR] Rte 72

Danbury

ACCOMMODATIONS

Maron Hotel & Suites [GF,WC] 42 Lake Ave Extension (off I-84) **203/791-2200, 866/811-2582** *kids/ pets ok*

BARS

Triangles Cafe [★MW,D,K,S,GO] 66 Sugar Hollow Rd, Rte 7 **203/798-6996** *5pm-1am, till 2am Fri-Sat, patio*

RESTAURANTS

Goulash Place [BW] 42 Highland Ave **203/744-1971** *lunch & dinner, clsd Mon, Hungarian*

Sesame Seed 68 W Wooster St **203/743-9850** *lunch & dinner, clsd Sun, Mediterranean/ Italian, funky decor, plenty veggie*

Thang Long [BYOB] 56 Padanaram Rd (near North Street Shopping Center) **203/743-6049** *lunch & dinner, Vietnamese*

East Haven

EROTICA

Romantix Adult Superstore 815-817 Foxon Rd **203/468-8597** *24hrs*

Enfield

EROTICA

Bookends 44 Enfield St/ Rte 5 **860/745-3988**

Groton

ACCOMMODATIONS

Flagship Inn & Suites [GF,WI,WC] 470 Gold Star Hwy (Rte 184, off I-95) **860/445-7458, 888/800-0770** *gym passes, in-room movies*

Hartford

ACCOMMODATIONS

Butternut Farm [GS,NS] 1654 Main St, Glastonbury **860/633-7197** *full brkfst*

The Mansion Inn [GF] 139 Hartford Rd (at Main St), Manchester **860/646-0453** *B&B, full brkfst, in-room fireplaces*

Bars

Chez Est [★MW,D,F,K,DS] 458 Wethersfield Ave (at Main St) **860/525-3243** *3pm-1am, till 2am Fri-Sat*

The Polo Club [MW,D,E,K,DS,S] 678 Maple Ave (btwn Preston & Mapleton) **860/278-3333** *8pm-1am, till 2am Fri-Sat, clsd Mon-Tue*

Nightclubs

Hartford Polo Club [MW,D,DS,18+] 678 Maple Ave **860/278-3333** *9pm Th-Sat*

The Kitty Kat Party [W,D] 960 Main St (at Room 960) **860/593-3093**

Cafes

Tisane Tea & Coffee Bar [F,E,WI] 537 Farmington Ave (at Kenyon) **860/523-5417** *7am-1am, 8am-1:30am wknds, also bar, men's night Tue*

Restaurants

Arugula [R,WC] 953 Farmington Ave, West Hartford **860/561-4888** *lunch & dinner, dinner only Mon, clsd Sun, Mediterranean*

Peppercorns Grill 357 Main St **860/547-1714** *lunch Mon-Fri, dinner nightly, clsd Sun, Northern Italian*

Pond House Cafe [BYOB,WC] 155 Asylum Ave **860/231-8823** *lunch & dinner Tue-Sat, Sun brunch, patio*

Trumbull Kitchen 150 Trumbull St (at Pearl St) **860/493-7417** *lunch Mon-Fri, dinner nightly, global cuisine/ tapas*

Entertainment & Recreation

Real Art Ways [WI] 56 Arbor St **860/232-1006** *contemporary art, cinema, performance, also lounge*

Retail Shops

▶ **MetroStore** 493 Farmington Ave (at Sisson Ave) **860/231-8845** *8:30am-8pm, till 5:30pm Tue, Wed & Sat, clsd Sun, magazines, travel guides, leather, DVD rentals & more*

Publications

▶ **Metroline 860/233-8334** *regional newspaper & entertainment guide, covers CT, RI & MA*

Men's Services

▶ **Megaphone 860/242-3600** *Meet and Chat Live with HOT local men. FREE to listen & respond to ads. Video and text chat at GayMates.com. Use FREE code 4889.*

Erotica

Aircraft Book & News 349 Main St (at Pratt), East Hartford **860/569-2324** *adult videos & DVDs, toys*

Amazing Express 1870 Berlin Tpke/ Rte 15, Wethersfield **860/257-8663**

Erotic Zone [AYOR] 35 W Service Rd (at Hwy 91 N) **860/549-1896** *hustlers*

Very Intimate Pleasures 100 Brainard Rd (exit 27, off I-91) **860/246-1875**

Cruisy Areas

Bushnell Park [AYOR] S of Asylum Ave (downtown exit off I-84)

Kent

Accommodations

Inn at Kent Falls [GS,SW,NS,WI,WC,GO] 107 Kent Cornwall Rd **860/927-3197** *B&B in Colonial on 2.5 acres*

Manchester

Info Lines & Services

True Colors 945 Main St Ste 211 **860/649-7386, 888/565-5551** *support & mentoring for LGBT youth*

Meriden

Cruisy Areas

Hubbard Park [AYOR]

Middletown

Entertainment & Recreation

Wednesday Night Supper Club [M,B,F] 825 Saybrook Rd (at Tommy's Restaurant) **860/346-8686** *6:30pm-close Wed only*

Milford

Erotica

Romantix Adult Superstore 120 Boston Post Rd **203/877-3492**

Mystic

Accommodations

House of 1833 B&B Resort [GF,SW,NS,GO] 72 N Stonington Rd **860/536-6325, 800/367-1833** *Greek Revival mansion, full brkfst*

The Mare's Inn B&B [GF,NS,WC,GO] 333 Colonel Ledyard Hwy, Ledyard **860/572-7556** *great birding, near casinos, full brkfst, lesbian-owned*

Mermaid Inn of Mystic [MW,WI,GO] 2 Broadway **860/536-6223, 877/692-2632** *B&B w/ village location & river views, full brkfst, lesbian-owned*

The Old Mystic Inn [GF,NS,WI,GO] 52 Main St (at Rte 27), Old Mystic **860/572-9422** *full brkfst*

New Britain

Cruisy Areas

Martha Hart Park [AYOR] off Corbin Ave

New Haven

Info Lines & Services

New Haven Gay/ Lesbian Community Center 14 Gilbert St **203/387-2252**

Accommodations

Omni New Haven Hotel at Yale [GF,WI,WC] 155 Temple St (at Chapel) **203/772-6664, 800/843-6664**

Bars

168 York St Cafe [MW,F,GO] 168 York St **203/789-1915** *3pm-1am, till 2am Fri-Sat, also restaurant, dinner Mon-Sat, Sun brunch, patio*

The Bar [GS,D,F,WC] 254 Crown St **203/495-8924** *4pm-1am, more gay Tue*

Center Street Lounge [GF,D,GO] 1 Center St (at Orange) **203/777-7264**

Partners [MW,NH,D,L,K] 365 Crown St (at Park St) **203/776-1014** *5pm-1am, till 2am Fri-Sat, [L] 1st & 3rd Sat*

Nightclubs

Center Street Lounge [MW,D,GO] 29 Center St (at Orange) **203/231-1491** *8pm-close Th-Sat*

Gotham Citi Cafe [GS,D,18+,WC] 130 Crown St (at Church) **203/498-2484** *9pm-4am clsd Sun-Wed, more gay Sat*

Cafes

Atticus Cafe 1082 Chapel St **203/776-4040** *7am-9pm, also bookstore*

Restaurants

Beach Head Cafe [E] 3 Cosey Beach Ave, East Haven **203/469-5450** *4pm-close, from 1pm Sun, seafood, Italian, patio*

Claire's Corner Copia [WC] 1000 Chapel St (at College St) **203/562-3888** *8am-9pm, till 10pm Fri-Sat, vegetarian*

Soul de Cuba 238 Crown St **203/498-2822** *lunch & dinner, clsd Mon, Cuban, full bar*

Erotica

Fairmont Theatre 33 Main St Annex **203/467-3832**

Very Intimate Pleasures 170 Boston Post Rd, Orange **203/799-7040**

Cruisy Areas

East Rock State Park [AYOR] lower parking lot *days*

New London

Bars

Frank's Place [M,D,E,WC] 9 Tilley St (at Bank), New London **860/442-2782** *4pm-1am, till 2am Fri-Sun, patio*

O'Neill's Brass Rail [M,WI] 52 Bank St **860/443-6203** *11am-1am, till 2am Fri-Sat*

Erotica

Amazing 591 Rte 12 #8, Groton **860/448-0787**

Norfolk

Accommodations

Manor House B&B [GF,NS] 69 Maple Ave **860/542-5690, 866/542-5690** *1898 Victorian Tudor estate, full brkfst, fireplaces, whirlpool*

North Stonington Village

Accommodations

Antiques & Accommodations [GF,NS,WI] **800/554-7829** *B&B*

Norwalk

Info Lines & Services

Triangle Community Center 16 River St (Mechanic St entrance) **203/853-0600** *call for info*

Cruisy Areas

Merritt Pkwy Park & Ride [AYOR] Rte 15, exit 38 (Rte 123, New Canaan Ave) *main lot, turn right*

Old Saybrook

Accommodations

The Copper Beech Inn [GF,NS] 46 Main St, Ivoryton **860/767-0330, 888/809-2056** *full brkfst, also upscale French restaurants*

Ridgefield

Restaurants

Caputo's East Ridge Cafe 5 Grove St **203/894-1940** *11:30am-10pm, also mellow, upscale bar*

Cruisy Areas

Riverside on Rte 7 [AYOR] opposite Ridgefield Motor Inn

Stamford

Cruisy Areas

Cove Island Park [AYOR] intersection of Cove Rd & Weed Ave

Waterbury

Bars

Fletchers Cafe [M,D,K,S,GO] 34 Brook St **203/596-7944** *8pm-1am, till 2am Fri-Sat*

Nightclubs

Twisted Wednesdays [M,D,MR] 52 E Main St (at Kriola) **203/597-7313**

Erotica

Video Books of Waterbury 90 S Main St **203/573-1066**

Cruisy Areas

Lakewood Park/ Twin Lakes Annex [AYOR] Farmwood Rd *days*

Westport

Bars

Cedar Brook Cafe [MW,D,K,S,WC] 919 Post Rd E **203/221-7429** *8pm-1am, till 2am Fri-Sat, 6pm-11pm Sun, clsd Tue*

Entertainment & Recreation

Sherwood Island State Park Beach left to gay area

West Redding

Restaurants

The Station House [BW,WI] 3 Side Cut Rd **203/938-8933** *6:30am-2:30pm, from 8am wknds, great cheddar corn pancakes*

Willimantic

Erotica

Dan's Adult World 1110 Main St **860/456-3780**

DELAWARE

New Castle

EROTICA

Bob's Discount Books 174 S DuPont Hwy (near 13/40 split) **302/328-4812** *clsd Sun, arcade*

Rehoboth Beach

INFO LINES & SERVICES

Camp Rehoboth Community Center 37 Baltimore Ave **302/227-5620** *9am-5:30pm Mon-Fri, 10am-4pm wknds, community center, HIV testing & counseling, also magazine*

Gay & Lesbian AA 302/856-6452 (Southern Delaware Intergroup #)

Narcotics Anonymous 37 Baltimore Ave (at Camp Rehoboth center) **302/227-5620** *5:30pm Sun*

ACCOMMODATIONS

An Inn by the Bay [GS,NS,GO] 205 Savannah Rd, Lewes **302/644-8878, 866/833-2565** *hot tub*

At Melissa's B&B [GS,NS] 36 Delaware Ave (btwn 1st & 2nd) **302/227-7504, 800/396-8090**

Bellmoor Inn [GF,SW,WI] 6 Christian St **302/227-5800, 800/425-2355** *upscale inn & spa*

Breakers Hotel & Suites [GF,WC] 105 Second St **302/227-6688, 800/441-8009** *hotel adjacent to Lake Gerar*

Cabana Gardens B&B [GS,SW,NS,GO] 20 Lake Ave (at 3rd St) **302/227-5429** *ocean views, rooftop deck*

Canalside Inn [GS,SW,NS,WI,WC,GO] Canal at 6th **302/226-2006, 866/412-2625** *inn w/in walking distance of beach*

Delaware Inn B&B [GF,SW,GO] 55 Delaware Ave **302/227-6031, 800/246-5244** *near beach*

The Homestead at Rehoboth B&B [GF,SW,NS,WI,WC,GO] 35060 Warrington Rd **302/226-7625** *small dogs ok, lesbian-owned*

Lazy L at Willow Creek [GS,SW,WI,GO] 16061 Willow Creek Rd (at Hwy 1), Lewes **302/644-7220** *full brkfst, hot tub, very pet-friendly, lesbian-owned*

The Lighthouse Inn B&B [GS,NS,WI,GO] 20 Delaware Ave **302/226-0407**

Pine-n-Brine 101 [GF,NS,WC,GO] 29 Maryland Ave, #101 **410/757-6951** *2-bdrm condo*

The Ram's Head [MO,SW,N,GO] 35006 Warrington Rd **302/226-9171** *hot tub & sauna, gym*

Rehoboth Guest House [MW,NS,WI,GO] 40 Maryland Ave (btwn 1st & 2nd Sts) **302/227-4117, 800/564-0493** *Victorian beach house*

The Royal Rose Inn [GS,GO] 41 Baltimore Ave **302/226-2535** *sundeck*

Sea Witch Manor Inn & Spa [GS,NS,WC,GO] 71 Lake Ave (at Rehoboth Ave) **302/226-9482, 866/732-9482** *Hollywood-themed, full brkfst, hot tub*

▶ **Silver Lake Guest House** [MW,NS,WI,GO] 20388 Silver Lake Dr **302/226-2115, 800/842-2115** *near Poodle Beach*

Summer Place Hotel [GS] 30 Olive Ave (at 1st) **302/226-0766, 800/815-3925** *also apts, near beach*

BARS

The Blue Moon [★MW,E,DS] 35 Baltimore Ave (btwn 1st & 2nd) **302/227-6515** *6pm-2am, clsd Jan, also restaurant, dinner, Sun brunch, plenty veggie*

Dogfish Head Brewings & Eats [GF,F,E] 320 Rehoboth Ave **302/226-2739** *micro-brewery, wood-grilled food*

Double L Bar [M,L,B] 622 Rehoboth Ave **302/227-0818** *3pm-2am, patio*

Finbar [GF,F,E] 316-318 Rehoboth Ave **302/227-1873** *from 3pm, from noon Sat-Sun, traditional pub, popular happy hour, also restaurant*

Frogg Pond [GF,NH,F,E,K] 3 S 1st St (near Rehoboth Ave) **302/227-2234** *11am-1am, from 10am Sun, popular happy hour, popular w/ women in summer, women's T-dance Sun*

Rigby's Bar & Grill [GS,F] 404 Rehoboth Ave (at State St) **302/227-6080** *3pm-1am, from 10am Sun*

Nightclubs

Sky Bar [★MW,D,WC] 234 Rehoboth Ave (at Cloud 9) **302/226-1999** *nightly, men's dance 10pm Fri-Sat, Ladies Tea 5pm Fri-Sat, [K] Mon & Th*

Cafes

The Coffee Mill [WI,GO] 127B Rehoboth Mews **302/227-7530, 888/227-7530** *7:30am-11pm, till 5pm (off-season), lesbian-owned*

Lori's Cafe [GO] 39 Baltimore Ave (at 1st) **302/226-3066** *seasonal, call for hours, courtyard*

Restaurants

Abstractions Sushi Bar & Restaurant 203 Rehoboth Ave **302/226-0877** *5pm daily (March-Jan)*

Aqua Grill [E,P] 57 Baltimore Ave **302/226-9001** *seasonal, deck, full bar*

Back Porch Cafe [WC] 59 Rehoboth Ave **302/227-3674** *lunch & dinner, Sun brunch, seasonal*

Blue Plate Diner 329 Savannah Rd, Lewes **302/644-8400** *Fri-Mon (seasonal)*

Buttery 102 2nd St, Lewes **302/645-7755** *lunch, dinner, Sun brunch, fine dining in elegant Victorian, reservations suggested*

Cafe Sole 44 Baltimore Ave **302/227-7107** *lunch daily, dinner Wed-Sun, casual, patio, also full bar*

Celsius [WC] 50-C Wilmington Ave **302/227-5767** *dinner (clsd Th), Sun brunch, French-Mediterranean*

Cloud 9 [★D,WC] 234 Rehoboth Ave (at 2nd) **302/226-1999** *4pm-2am, Sun brunch from 11am, fusion bistro, also Sky Bar nightly, men's dance 10pm Fri-Sat*

The Cultured Pearl 301 Rehoboth Ave (2nd flr) **302/227-8493** *dinner, lunch Th-Mon (clsd Mon-Wed off-season), pan-Asian, cocktail lounge*

Dish 26 Baltimore Ave **302/226-2112** *dinner Th-Sun, "a retro dining gallery," also Lava Lounge*

Dos Locos [★] 208 Rehoboth Ave (across from Fire Company) **302/227-3353** *11:30am-10pm, till 11pm Fri-Sat, Mexican*

Eden [★WC] 23 Baltimore Ave **302/227-3330** *dinner Wed-Sat, seasonal, "bold" American, wine list & martini bar*

Espuma 28 Wilmington Ave **302/227-4199** *6pm-10pm, clsd Mon, modern Mediterranean, full bar from 5pm*

Fins 243 Rehoboth Ave **302/226-3467** *4:30pm-9pm, till 10pm Fri-Sat, fish house & raw bar*

Go Fish! 24 Rehoboth Ave **302/226-1044** *11:30am-9:30pm (in-season), seafood & authentic British fish & chips*

Hobo's Deli 56 Baltimore Ave **302/226-2226** *from 11am (in-season)*

Iguana Grill 52 Baltimore Ave **302/227-0948** *lunch & dinner (summers), Southwestern, full bar, patio*

Jerry's Seafood 108 2nd St, Lewes **302/645-6611** *lunch & dinner daily, "home of the crab bomb"*

Just in Thyme 31 Robinson St **302/227-3100** *seafood & steak by candlelight, also Sun brunch, local favorite*

La La Land 22 Wilmington Ave **302/227-3887** *6pm-1am (seasonal), seafood, full bar, patio*

Mariachi [NS,WC] 14 Wilmington Ave **302/227-0115** *11am-10pm, till 11pm Fri-Sat, Mexican-Latin American, 2 bars*

Planet X Cafe 35 Wilmington Ave **302/226-1928** *seasonal, lunch, dinner, Sun brunch, some veggie*

Purple Parrot Grill [K,DS,WC] 134 Rehoboth Ave **302/226-1139** *lunch & dinner daily, brunch Sun, karaoke & drag shows wknds*

Retro Cafe & Grille 10 Wilmington Ave (on the beach block, 1/2 block from boardwalk) **302/227-9752** *8am-3pm, open daily during season, wknds only off season*

Seaside Thai 19 Rehoboth Ave **302/227-9525** *1 block from beach*

Tijuana Taxi [WC] 33401 Tenley Ct **302/644-8294** *lunch & dinner, full bar*

Venus on the Halfshell [★] 136 Dagsworthy St, Dewey Beach **302/227-9292** *seasonal, waterside Asian-inspired restaurant w/ fun Morocco-Meets-the-Far-East setting*

Entertainment & Recreation

Cape Henlopen State Park Beach 42 Cape Henlopen Dr, Lewes **302/645-8983** *8am-sunset*

Poodle Beach S of boardwalk at Queen St *popular gay beach*

Bookstores

Lambda Rising [WC] 39 Baltimore Ave (btwn 1st & 2nd) **302/227-6969** *noon-8pm, till 10pm Fri-Sat, 10am-midnight summers, LGBT*

Retail Shops

Leather Central 4284A Hwy 1 (on the service road) **302/227-0700** *10am-6pm, till 5pm Sun, clsd Tue-Wed, leather uniforms, toys, accessories*

The Pelican Loft Home & Garden Gift Shop [GO] 49 Baltimore Ave **302/226-5080** *lesbian-owned*

Publications

Letters from Camp Rehoboth **302/227-5620** *newsmagazine w/ events & entertainment listings*

Gyms & Health Clubs

Body Shop 401 N Boardwalk (at Virginia) **302/226-0920** *8am-7pm, till 6pm Sun, on the beach, $12 day pass*

The Firm Fitness Center 6 Camelot Shopping Center/ Rte 1 **302/227-8363** *$10 day pass*

Gold's Gym 3712 Hwy 1, #11 **302/226-4653** *6am-10pm, 7am-8pm Sat, 8am-5pm Sun*

Midway Fitness Midway Shopping Center #28B (on Rte 1, NW of John J Williams Hwy) **302/645-0407** *$12 day pass, racquetball*

Men's Services

▶ **Megaphone 888/634-2628** *Meet and Chat Live with HOT local men. Call for your local number or visit us online at GayMates.com. Use FREE code 4889.*

Wilmington

Nightclubs

Baxter's [MW,D,K] 2006 Pennsylvania Ave **302/654-9858** *4pm-2am, from 5pm Sat, from 6pm Sun, lounge, also restaurant*

Crimson Moon [M,D,DS,V] 1909 W 6th St (at Union) **302/654-9099**

Restaurants

Eclipse 1020 Union St **302/658-1588** *lunch Mon-Fri, dinner nightly, upscale*

The Green Room 11th & Market St (at Hotel Dupont) **302/594-3154** *brkfst, lunch & dinner, Sun brunch, full bar*

Mrs Robino's [WC] 520 N Union (at Pennsylvania) **302/652-9223** *11am-9pm, till 10pm Fri, 3pm-10pm Sat, noon-9pm Sun, family-style Italian, bar*

Men's Services

▶ **Megaphone 302/397-0111** *Meet and Chat Live with HOT local men. FREE to listen & respond to ads. Video and text chat at GayMates.com. Use FREE code 4889.*

District of Columbia

Washington

Info Lines & Services

▶ **Kasper's Livery Service** [GO] 4301 Massachusetts Ave NW #1006 **202/554-2471, 800/455-2471** *limousine service serving DC, MD & VA*

Triangle Club 2030 P St NW (at 21st St NW) **202/659-8641** *various 12-Step groups, call for times*

Accommodations

Artist Inn Residence B&B [GS,NS,WI,GO] 1824 R St NW **202/667-6707** *B&B & private art gallery*

Beacon Hotel & Corporate Quarters [GF] 1615 Rhode Island Ave NW (at 17th) **202/296-2100**

► **The Bed & Breakfast at the William Lewis House** [★M,GO] 1309 R St NW (at 13th) **202/462-7574, 800/465-7574** *turn-of-the-century, hot tub, full brkfst wknds*

Bloomingdale Inn [GF] 2417 1st St NW (at Bryant) **202/319-0801** *Victorian town house*

The Carlyle Suites Hotel [GS,F,WI,WC] 1731 New Hampshire Ave NW (btwn R & S Sts) **202/234-3200, 800/964-5377** *art deco, also bar, popular gay Sun brunch*

Chez Aimee [GF,NS,WI] **202/669-7708, 202/669-7708 (cell)** *flat in 1910-era rowhouse in Adams Morgan district*

Comfort Inn Downtown DC–Convention Center [GS,WI,WC] 1201 13th St NW **202/682-5300, 877/424-6423** *near Dupont Circle, internet access*

DC GuestHouse [GS,WI,GO] 1337 10th St NW **202/332-2502** *full brkfst*

The District Hotel [GS,WI] 1440 Rhode Island Ave NW (btwn 14th & 15th) **202/232-7800, 800/350-5759** *conveniently located in Dupont/ Logan Circle Historic District*

Doubletree Hotel–Washington [GF,WI] 1515 Rhode Island Ave NW **202/232-7000** *boutique hotel*

Dupont at The Circle [GS,NS,WI] 1604 19th St NW (at Q St) **202/332-5251** *Victorian at Dupont Circle*

The Embassy Inn [GF,WI] 1627 16th St NW **202/234-7800, 800/423-9111** *small hotel w/ B&B atmosphere*

Embassy Suites Alexandria [GS,SW] 1900 Diagonal Rd, Alexandria, VA **703/684-5900, 800/362-2779** *full brkfst*

Embassy Suites Hotel at the Chevy Chase Pavilion [GF,SW,WC] 4300 Military Rd NW **202/362-9300, 800/362-2779**

Embassy Suites Tysons Corner [GF,SW,WC] 8517 Leesburg Pike, Vienna, VA **703/883-0707, 800/362-2779** *full brkfst*

Embassy Suites Washington, DC [GF,SW,WI] 1250 22nd St NW **202/857-3388, 800/362-2779** *full brkfst*

Hotel Helix [GF,WC,WI] 1430 Rhode Island Ave NW **202/462-9001, 800/706-1202** *full-service boutique hotel, also Helix Lounge*

Hotel Madera [GF,WI,WC] 1310 New Hampshire Ave NW (at N) **202/296-7600, 800/430-1202** *boutique hotel, Firefly bistro adjacent*

Hotel Monaco Washington DC [GF,WC,WI] 700 F St NW (at 7th) **202/628-7177, 800/649-1202** *boutique hotel*

Hotel Palomar [GF,F,SW,WC] 2121 P St NW (at 21st St) **202/448-1800, 800/546-7866** *in Dupont Circle*

Hotel Rouge [GF,WI,WC] 1315 16th St NW (at Rhode Island) **202/232-8000, 800/368-5689** *ultra-hip, high-tech luxury hotel, also restaurant & bar*

Kalorama Guest House at Kalorama Park [GS,NS,WI] 1854 Mintwood Pl NW (at Columbia Rd) **202/667-6369** *Victorian town house*

Kalorama Guest House at Woodley Park [GS,NS,WI] 2700 Cathedral Ave NW (off Connecticut Ave) **202/328-0860, 800/974-9101**

Morrison-Clark Historic Inn & Restaurant [GF,WI] 1015 L St NW (at Massachusetts Ave NW) **202/898-1200, 800/322-7898** *hotel in 2 Victorian town houses w/ very popular restaurant*

Otis Place B&B [GS,WI,GO] 1003 Otis Place NW (at 10th St) **202/483-0241, 877/893-3233** *1910 Victorian town house*

The River Inn [GF,WI,WC] 924 25th St NW (at K St) **202/337-7600, 888/874-0100** *also Dish + Drinks restaurant*

Savoy Suites Hotel [GF,WI,WC] 2505 Wisconsin Ave NW (at Calvert, in Georgetown) **202/337-9700, 800/944-5377** *also Italian restaurant*

Swann House Historic B&B [GS,SW,WI] 1808 New Hampshire Ave NW (at Swann St) **202/265-4414** *Victorian mansion in Dupont Circle, swimming, roof deck*

Topaz Hotel [GF,WI,WC] 1733 N St NW **202/393-3000, 800/424-2950** *boutique hotel, also restaurant & bar*

Toutorsky Mansion [GF,WI,GO] 1720 16th St NW (at Riggs) **202/302-1472**

Washington Plaza [GF,SW] 10 Thomas Cir NW (at 14th & Massachusetts) **202/842-1300, 800/424-1140** *full-service hotel, also restaurant*

Bars

1409 Playbill Cafe [MW,F] 1409 14th St NW **202/265-3055** *4pm-1am, till 3am Fri-Sat, also theater*

Back Door Pub [M,D,MR-AF,F,S,WC] 1104 8th St SE, 2nd flr (at L St) **202/546-5979** *5pm-2am, till 3am Fri-Sat*

DC Eagle [★M,L,WC] 639 New York Ave NW (btwn 6th & 7th) **202/347-6025** *4pm-2am, 2pm-3am Fri-Sat*

DIK Bar/ Windows [M,D,K,OC] 1637 17th St NW (near 16th St NW, upstairs) **202/328-0100, 202/234-5747** *4pm-2am*

EFN Lounge/ Motley Bar [MW,NH,D] 1318 9th St NW (at O St) **202/341-8281** *5pm-2am, till 3am Fri-Sat, theme nights*

The Fireplace [M,NH,MR,V,WC] 2161 P St NW (at 22nd St) **202/293-1293** *1pm-2am, till 3am Fri-Sat*

Green Lantern [M,NH,B,K,V] 1335 Green Court NW (in alley L St, btwn 13th & 14th) **202/347-4533** *4pm-2am, till 3am wknds*

Halo [MW,NH] 1435 'P' St NW **202/797-9730** *5pm-close*

JR's [★M,NH,F,V,YC] 1519 17th St NW (at Church) **202/328-0090** *2pm-2am, till 3am Fri, 1pm-3am Sat, 1pm-2am Sun, cruisy, hot cocktail hour*

Larry's Lounge [MW,NH,F,WC,GO] 1840 18th St NW (at T St) **202/483-1483** *4pm-1am, till 2am Fri-Sat, also Malaysian restaurant*

Mr Henry's Capitol Hill [★GF,MR,E,NS] 601 Pennsylvania Ave SE (at 6th St) **202/546-8412** *11:30am-11:30pm, live jazz Fri, also restaurant*

Nellie's Sports Bar [M,NH] 900 U St NW (at 9th) **202/332-6355** *5pm-midnight, till 2am wknds, gay sports bar*

Omega [★M,MR,K,DS,S,V] 2122 P St NW (enter rear) **202/223-4917** *4pm-2am, from 8pm Sat, from 7pm Sun*

Remington's [★M,D,CW,K,DS,V] 639 Pennsylvania Ave SE (btwn 6th & 7th) **202/543-3113** *4pm-2am, till 3am Fri-Sat, 6pm-2am Sun, 2 flrs, T-dance Sun*

Nightclubs

Apex [MW,D,K,V,YC,WC,$] 1415 22nd St NW (btwn O & P Sts) **202/296-0505** *9pm-3am Th, till 4am Fri-Sat, clsd Sun-Wed*

Bachelors Mill [★M,D,MR-AF,S,WC] 1104 8th St SE (downstairs at Back Door Pub) **202/546-5979** *5pm-2am, till 3am wknds, 2 flrs*

Calor [M,D] **888/269-3349** *occasional parties, call for date & location*

Chief Ike's Mambo Room [GF,D,E,WC] 1725 Columbia Rd NW (btwn 17th & 18th) **202/332-2211** *4pm-2am, till 3am Fri, 6pm-3am Sat, clsd Sun, live music Wed-Th, also restaurant, American*

Club Fuego [MW,D,MR-L] 1818 New York Ave (at Bladensburg Rd NE) *10:30pm-3am Fri only, salsa, merengue, Latin pop*

Cobalt/ 30 Degrees Lounge [M,D,E,DS] 1639 R St NW (at 17th) **202/232-4416** *5pm-2am, till 3am Fri-Sat*

Delta Elite [MW,D,MR-AF] 3734 10th St NE (at Perry St NE, in Brookland) **202/529-0626** *ladies night Fri, men's night Sat*

Fab Lounge [MW,D,MR] 2022 Florida Ave NW (at Connecticut) **202/797-1122** *5pm-close*

Taint [MW,D,E] 1940 9th St NW (at U St NW, at DC9) *monthly electro-rock indie dance party, queer performance & video*

Town Danceboutique [M,D,DS,18+] 2009 8th St NW (at U St NW) **202/234-8696** *9pm-4am Fri-Sat, 18+ Fri*

Ziegfield's/ Secrets [M,D,DS,S] 1824 Half St SW **202/863-0670** *9pm-close Wed-Sun, [DS] downstairs, strippers upstairs*

Cafes

Cosi [★WI] 1647 20th St NW **202/332-6364** *7am-11pm, till midnight Fri-Sat, 8am-10pm Sun, full bar from 4pm, make your own s'mores*

Jolt 'n' Bolt [★] 1918 18th St NW (at Florida) **202/232-0077** *7am-11pm, till 8:30pm wknds, patio*

Soho Tea & Coffee [F,WI,WC] 2150 P St NW (at 22nd St) **202/463-7646** *open 7:30am till late, patio*

Restaurants

18th & U Duplex Diner [GS] 2004 18th St NW (at Ave U) **202/265-7828** *6pm-close, American comfort food, full bar*

2 Amys Pizza 3715 Macomb St NW **202/885-5700** *lunch & dinner Tue-Sun, dinner only Mon*

Acadiana [R] 901 New York Ave NW **202/408-8848** *lunch Mon-Fri, dinner nightly, brunch Sun, Cajun, great bourbon selection*

Annie's Paramount Steak House [★] 1609 17th St NW (at Corcoran) **202/232-0395** *10am-11:30pm, till 1am Th & Sun, 24hrs Fri-Sat, full bar*

Armand's Chicago Pizza 4231 Wisconsin Ave NW (at Veazey) **202/363-5500** *11am-10pm, till 11pm Fri-Sat, noon-10pm Sun, full bar; also Capitol Hill location: 226 Massachusetts Ave NE, 202/547-6600*

Asylum 2471 18th St NW **202/319-9353** *5pm-2am, till 3am Fri, from 11am wknds, plenty veggie, also bar*

Banana Cafe & Piano Bar [E,P,GO] 500 8th St SE (at E St) **202/543-5906** *11am-10:30pm, till 11pm Fri-Sat, till 10pm Sun, Puerto Rican/ Cuban, some veggie, famous margaritas*

Beacon Bar & Grill [★] 1615 Rhode Island Ave NW (at 17th, at Beacon Hotel) **202/872-1126** *brkfst, lunch & dinner, popular Sun brunch, patio*

Busboys & Poets [E,WI] 2021 14th St NW (at V St) **202/387-7638** *8am-midnight, till 2am Fri-Sat, 10am-midnight Sun, also bookstore, live jazz & poetry*

Cafe Japoné [★MR-A,K] 2032 P St NW (at 21st) **202/223-1573** *6pm-1:30am, till 2:30am Fri-Sat, Japanese, full bar, live jazz*

Cafe Luna [★MW] 1633 P St NW (at 17th) **202/387-4005** *10am-11pm, till midnight wknds*

Chartwell Grill [WC] 1914 Connecticut Ave (in The Churchill Hotel) **202/797-2000** *6:30am-10:30pm, also lounge till 12:30am, till 11pm Sun, cont'l*

Dupont Italian Kitchen & Bar 1637 17th St NW (at R St) **202/328-3222, 202/328-0100** *11:30am-11pm, bar 4pm-2am*

Floriana's [GO] 1602 17th St NW (at Q St NW) **202/667-5937** *dinner nightly, Italian, full bar, patio*

Food For Thought [NS] 1811 14th St NW (at the Black Cat) **202/667-4490** *8pm-1am, 7pm-2am Fri-Sat, mostly vegan/ veggie, indie/ punk music shows, readings*

Guapo's [WC] 4515 Wisconsin Ave NW (at Albemarle) **202/686-3588** *lunch & dinner, Mexican, full bar*

The Islander [E,K] 1201 U St NW (at 12th) **202/234-4955** *lunch & dinner, Caribbean, full bar*

Jack's 1527 17th St NW **202/332-6767** *lunch Tue-Sun, dinner nightly, wknd brunch, also bar*

Jaleo [E,WC] 480 7th St NW (at E St) **202/628-7949** *lunch & dinner, tapas, full bar, Sevillanas dancers Wed*

La Frontera Cantina 1633 17th St NW (btwn R & Q Sts) **202/232-0437** *11am-11pm, till 1am Fri-Sat, Tex-Mex*

Lauriol Plaza 1835 18th St NW (at S St) **202/387-0035** *11:30am-11pm, till midnight Fri-Sat, Latin American*

Logan Tavern [GO] 1423 P St NW **202/332-3710** *lunch & dinner, wknd brunch, American comfort food, also neighborhood bar [GF]*

Occidental Grill 1475 Pennsylvania Ave NW (btwn 14th & 15th) **202/783-1475** *lunch Mon-Sat, dinner nightly, clsd Sun, upscale, political player hangout*

Perry's 1811 Columbia Rd NW (at 18th) **202/234-6218** *5:30pm-11:30pm, popular drag Sun brunch, contemporary American & sushi, full bar*

Rasika 633 D St NW **202/637-1222** *lunch Mon-Fri, dinner Mon-Sat, clsd Sun, Indian*

Rice 1608 14th St NW (at 'Q') **202/234-2400** *Thai*

Rocklands 2418 Wisconsin Ave NW (at Calvert) **202/333-2558** *11am-10pm, till 9pm Sun, BBQ & take-out*

Sala Thai 2016 P St NW (at 21st) **202/872-1144** *lunch & dinner*

Skewers [★E] 1633 P St NW (at 17th) **202/387-7400** *11am-11pm, noon-midnight wknds, Middle Eastern, belly dancing Sat, full bar*

Soul Vegetarian 2606 Georgia Ave NW **202/328-7685** *11am-9pm, till 3pm Sun (brunch), all-vegan menu*

Stars Bistro 2120 P St NW **202/464-6464** *lunch & dinner, brunch wknds, singing servers*

Thai Tanic 1326 14th St NW (at Rhode Island Ave) **202/588-1795** *Thai, plenty veggie*

Trio 1537 17th St NW (at Q St NW) **202/232-6305** *8am-midnight, American, full bar, sidewalk cafe*

Twist Dupont [GS,WC] 1731 New Hampshire (at 18th & R Sts, in the Carlyle Suites) **202/518-5011** *lunch & dinner, also art deco bar, internet access*

Entertainment & Recreation

Anecdotal History Tours [GF] **301/294-9514** *guided tours*

Bike & Roll [GF] 1100 Pennsylvania Ave NW (off 12th St) **202/842-2453**

Gay Men's Chorus of Washington 202/293-1548

Hillwood Museum & Gardens [R] 4155 Linnean Ave NW (at Tilden St NW) **202/686-5807, 877/445-5966** *10am-5pm Tue-Sat, Fabergé, porcelain, furniture & more*

Lesbian & Gay Chorus of Washington, DC 202/546-1549

Phillips Collection 1600 21st St NW (at Q St) **202/387-2151** *clsd Mon, America's first museum of modern art, near Dupont Circle*

Bookstores

ADC Map & Travel Center 1636 I St NW (at 17th St) **202/628-2608, 800/544-2659** *9am-6:30pm, till 5:30pm Fri, 11am-5pm Sat, clsd Sun, extensive maps & travel guides*

G Books [GO] 1520 U St NW, BSMT (btwn 15th St & U St) **202/986-9697** *4pm-10pm, from 11pm Fri-Sat, new & used LGBT books, magazines, pride items, etc*

Kramerbooks & Afterwords Cafe & Grill [E,F,WC] 1517 Connecticut Ave NW (at Q St) **202/387-1400** *7:30am-1am, 24hrs wknds, also cafe & bar*

Lambda Rising [WC] 1625 Connecticut Ave NW (btwn Q & R Sts) **202/462-6969** *10am-10pm, till midnight Fri-Sat, LGBT*

Retail Shops

Leather Rack 1723 Connecticut Ave NW (btwn R & S Sts) **202/797-7401**

Pleasure Place [WC] 1063 Wisconsin Ave NW, Georgetown (btwn M & K Sts) **202/333-8570** *10am-10pm, till midnight Wed-Sat, noon-7pm Sun, erotica, clubwear, leather, adult toys, DVDs, clothing & more; also at* 1710 Connecticut Ave NW (btwn Florida Ave & R St) **202/483-3297**

Pulp 1803 14th St NW **202/462-7857** *11am-7pm, till 5pm Sun, cards, gifts, music*

Universal Gear 1529 14th St NW **202/319-0136** *11am-10pm, till midnight Fri-Sat, casual, club, athletic & designer clothing*

Publications

Metro Weekly 202/638-6830 *lesbian/ gay newsmagazine, extensive club listings*

Washington Blade 202/797-7000 *huge LGBT newspaper w/ extensive resource listings*

Gyms & Health Clubs

Results—The Gym [GF] 1612 U St NW (at 17th St) **202/234-5678** *also cafe*

Washington Sports Club 1835 Connecticut Ave NW (at Columbia & Florida) **202/332-0100**

Men's Clubs

Crew Club 1321 14th St NW (at Rhode Island) **202/319-1333** *24hrs*

Men's Services

► **Megaphone 202/822-1666** *Meet and Chat Live with HOT local men. FREE to listen & respond to ads. Video and text chat at GayMates.com. Use FREE code 4889.*

Erotica

Pleasure Place [WC] 1063 Wisconsin Ave NW, Georgetown (btwn M & K Sts) **800/386-2386** *10am-10pm, till midnight Wed-Sat, noon-7pm Sun, erotica, clubwear, leather, adult toys, DVDs, clothing & more*

Pleasure Place 1710 Connecticut Ave NW (btwn Florida Ave & R St) **202/483-3297** *10am-10pm, till midnight Wed-Sat, noon-7pm Sun, erotica, clubwear, leather, adult toys, DVDs, clothing & more*

Cruisy Areas

Rock Creek Park [AYOR] Beach Dr N, above 16th St

FLORIDA

Statewide

Publications

► **Ambush Mag 504/522-8049** *LGBT newspaper for the Gulf South (TX through FL)*

HOTSPOTS! Magazine 954/928-1862 *"South Florida's largest gay publication"*

Southern Voice 404/876-1819 *weekly LGBT newspaper for AL, FL (panhandle), GA, LA, MS, TN w/ resource listings*

Amelia Island

Accommodations

Ash Street Inn [GS,SW,NS,WI,WC] 102 S 7th St (at Ash St) **904/277-6660, 800/277-6660** *B&B, full brkfst, jacuzzi*

Florida House Inn [GF,NS,WI] 20 S 3rd St **904/261-3300, 800/258-3301** *B&B in Florida's oldest surviving hotel, restaurant & bar/ grille [E]*

The Hoyt House [GF,SW,NS,WI,WC] 804 Atlantic Ave **904/277-4300, 800/432-2085** *1905 Queen Anne mansion, full brkfst, hot tub*

Restaurants

Beech Street Grill [E] 801 Beech St (at 8th St), Fernandina Beach **904/277-3662** *6pm-9pm*

Brett's Waterway Cafe 1 Front St **904/261-2660** *lunch & dinner, seafood*

Cruisy Areas

Burney Park [AYOR] off A1A

Apalachicola

Accommodations

Coombs House Inn [GF,NS,WI,WC] 80 6th St **850/653-9199, 888/244-8320** *Victorian B&B, full brkfst*

Auburndale

Bars

Twisters [M,NH,BW,GO] 404 Eaker St (at Hwy 92) **863/965-9018** *noon-2am, till midnight Sun*

Nightclubs

Boots [MW,NH,D,K,WC] 340 Havendale Blvd **863/268-8294** *2pm-2am, clsd Sun*

Boca Raton

Bars

Joe & Craig's Place [MW,NH,GO] 1929 N Federal Hwy (US 1) **561/347-8044, 866/311-2638** *6pm-midnight, till 2am Fri-Sat*

Restaurants

Kyojin 21073 Powerline Rd **561/218-1708** *lunch & dinner, Japanese buffet*

Sapa 499 S Federal Hwy **561/353-4600** *lunch Mon-Fri, dinner nightly, sushi & Thai, full bar*

Bonifay

Cruisy Areas

Wayside Park Hwy 79 *parking lot & woods 6 miles N of Bonifay at Holmes Creek bridge*

Boynton Beach

see West Palm Beach

Bradenton

see also Sarasota

Accommodations

Summer House [GF,SW,NS] 111 & 113 36th St, Holmes Beach **941/778-2333, 800/431-0278** *cottage-style inn*

Men's Services

Erotica

C&J [AYOR] 4949 14th St W **941/755-9076**

XTC Supercenter 1008 Cortez Rd W **941/708-6969**

Cruisy Areas

ManGroves [AYOR] Manatee Ave (off Palma Sola Bay) *on right, after crossing the first bridge, toward Anna Maria Island (beware cops!)*

Cape Canaveral

Restaurants

Izzy's Bistro [BW] 6615 N Atlantic Ave **321/783-4548** *4pm-10pm, clsd Sun, seafood & steak*

Erotica

Fairvilla Megastore 500 Thurm Blvd **321/799-9961** *9am-2am, from 10am Sun, clean, well-lighted adult store w/ emphasis on couples: "store for lovers"*

Cape Coral

see Fort Myers

Chipley

Cruisy Areas

Blue Lake Park [AYOR] Hwy 77 (S of I-10)

Clearwater

see also Dunedin, New Port Richey, Port Richey & St Petersburg

Accommodations

Holiday Inn Select [GF,SW,WI,WC] 3535 Ulmerton Rd **727/577-9100, 888/465-4329** *close to airport & beach*

Bars

Pro Shop Pub [★M,NH,B,GO] 840 Cleveland St (at Prospect) **727/447-4259** *1pm-2am*

Retail Shops

Skinz 2027 Gulf to Bay Blvd (aka State Rd 60, at Hercules Rd) **727/441-8789** *10am-6pm, men's & women's swimwear, gymwear & clubwear, also online store*

Men's Services

▶ **Megaphone 727/230-0030** *Meet and Chat Live with HOT local men. FREE to listen & respond to ads. Video and text chat at GayMates.com. Use FREE code 4889.*

Erotica

Dundee Erotica 12880 US 19 N **727/524-3604** *24hrs*

Cocoa

Erotica

Showboat Adult World [AYOR] 1800 W King St (on Rte 520) **321/633-5588** *9am-2am*

Cocoa Beach

Accommodations

Beach Place Guesthouses [GF,NS,WI,GO] 1445 S Atlantic Ave **321/783-4045**

Restaurants

Lobster Shanty [WC] 2200 S Orlando Ave **321/783-1350** *11:30am-9pm, till 10pm Fri-Sat, full bar*

Mango Tree [WC] 118 N Atlantic Ave **321/799-0513** *6pm-10pm, clsd Mon, fine dining, single malt Scotch bar*

Crestview

Cruisy Areas

Shoal River Park [AYOR] Hwy 85 (2 miles S of Crestview)

Daytona Beach

Accommodations

Acapulco Hotel & Resort [GF,F,SW,WC] 2505 S Atlantic Blvd (at Int'l Speedway Blvd) **386/761-2210** *jacuzzi*

The August Seven Inn [GF,NS,WI,GO] 1209 S Peninsula Dr (at Silver Beach) **386/248-8420, 877/797-3836** *historic Victorian 1 block from ocean, full brkfst*

Mayan Inn [GF,SW,WC] 103 S Ocean Ave **386/252-2378, 800/448-2286** *ocean views, lounge*

The Villa B&B [GF,SW,N,NS,WI,GO] 801 N Peninsula Dr **386/248-2020, 888/248-7060** *historic Spanish mansion, spa*

Bars

Streamline Lounge [GF,D,E] 140 S Atlantic Ave (at Streamline Hotel) **386/258-6937** *11am-3am, penthouse lounge*

Cafes

Java Joint & Eatery 2201 N A1A, Flagler Beach **386/439-1013** *7am-4pm*

Restaurants

Anna's Trattoria [BW] 304 Seabreeze Blvd **386/239-9624** *5pm-10pm, clsd Sun-Mon, Italian*

Barnacles Restaurant & Lounge 869 S Atlantic Ave, Ormond Beach **386/673-1070** *4pm-10pm*

The Clubhouse 600 Wilder Blvd (at Daytona Beach Golf & Country Club) **386/257-0727** *6am-7:30pm, American*

Frappes North [E,WC] 123 W Granada St (at S Yonge St), Ormond Beach **386/615-4888** *lunch Tue-Fri, dinner nightly, clsd Mon, "organically groovy" American, patio, full bar*

Sapporo 501 Seabreeze Ave **386/257-4477** *lunch Mon-Fri, dinner nightly, Japanese steak house & sushi bar, full bar*

Publications

Watermark 407/481-2243 (Orlando office) *bi-weekly LGBT newspaper for Central FL*

Men's Services

▶ **Megaphone 888/634-2628** *Meet and Chat Live with HOT local men. Call for your local number or visit us online at GayMates.com. Use FREE code 4889.*

Erotica

The Banned Bookstore 701 N Ridgewood Ave **386/248-0072** *9am-1am, noon-midnight Sun*

X-Mart Boutique 2591 W International Speedway Blvd **386/252-8707** *24hrs*

Cruisy Areas

Boylston Beach Ramp & Seawall [AYOR] off A1A (across from Bel-Aire Plaza & also S on 1400 block) *around bandshell*

De Land

Cruisy Areas

Rest Stop [AYOR] I-4 (10 miles E toward Daytona Beach)

Delray Beach

Accommodations

Crane's BeachHouse [GF,NS,SW] 82 Gleason St (at Atlantic Ave) **561/278-1700, 866/372-7263** *hotel*

Bookstores

Shining Through 426 E Atlantic Ave **561/276-8559** *metaphysical/ New Age, some LGBT titles, also incense, candles, crystals & gifts*

Dunedin

see also St Petersburg

Cruisy Areas

Honeymoon Island State Recreation Area [AYOR] end of Causeway Blvd *nude sunbathing & beach*

Edgewater

Cruisy Areas

Menard-May Park [AYOR] S Riverside Dr (at E Ocean Ave)

Floral City

Accommodations

Our Country Home [MW,NS,WC,GO] 12495 S Istachatta Rd (off CR 48) **813/388-3313** *private home on 5 acres near bike trails & canoeing, pets ok*

Florida City

Accommodations

Ramada Inn [GF,WC] 124 E Palm Dr (at US 1) **305/247-8833, 800/272-6232** *located at the start of the FL Tpke, the gateway to the FL Keys*

Fort Lauderdale

Info Lines & Services

Gay/ Lesbian Community Center of South Florida [WC] 1717 N Andrews Ave (btwn Sunrise & Oakland) **954/463-9005** *10am-10pm, noon-5pm wknds, outreach*

▶ **Greater Fort Lauderdale Convention & Visitors Bureau** 100 E Broward Blvd, Ste 200 **800/227-8669 (code 187), 954/765-4466** *call for free Rainbow Vacation Planner*

Lambda South Inc [WC] 1231-A E Las Olas Blvd (alley access only) **954/761-9072** *meeting space for LGBT in recovery*

Accommodations

▶ **Alcazar Resort** [MO,SW,N,NS,WI,GO] 555 N Birch Rd (at Terramar) **954/567-2525, 888/830-9931** *at the beach*

Aragon Inn [M,WI,GO] 2520 NE 6th Ave (at NE 26th St), Wilton Manors **954/566-2900, 888/642-9466**

Bamboo Resort [MO,SW,N,NS,WI,GO] 2733 Middle River Dr (near 26th St NE) **954/565-7775, 800/479-1767**

▶ **The Blue Dolphin** [MO,V,SW,WI,WC,GO] 725 N Birch Rd (at Vistamar) **954/565-8437, 800/893-2583** *rooms & apts, near beach*

Bungalow Six Resort [M,SW,GO] 2726 NE 6th Ln (at 27th St), Wilton Manors **954/561-5454, 877/210-6317**

▶ **The Cabanas** [★M,SW,NS,WI,GO] 2209 NE 26th St **954/564-7764, 866/564-7764** *riverfront, kayaks available, clothing-optional jacuzzi, spa*

▶ **Cheston House** [MO,SW,N,NS,WI,GO] 520 N Birch Rd (at Viramar) **954/566-7950, 866/566-7950** *on beach*

▶ **Coconut Cove Guesthouse** [MO,SW,NS,WI,GO] 3012 Granada St (at Birch St & A1A) **954/523-3226, 888/414-3226** *courtyard gardens*

greater FORT LAUDERDALE
Fabulous scenery.
Fabulous scene.
Greater Fort Lauderdale is as warm and inviting as the sand between your toes. Come play on miles of Blue Wave beaches and yacht-lined waterways, and enjoy this destination's new restaurant scene, arts and entertainment, and vibrant gay community. Request your free Rainbow Vacation Calendar now at sunny.org/glbt or call 800-22-SUNNY.
greater FORT LAUDERDALE
sunny.org/glbt

Coconut Cove
GUESTHOUSE
Ft. Lauderdale Beach
STOP BY FOR A TOUR
A Clothing Optional Resort For Gay Men . . .
YOUR HOST DAVID
CHECK OUT OUR VIDEO AT GAYFLL.COM
Unlike any other gay resort in Fort Lauderdale.
Come experience the difference
954.523.3226 or 888.414.3226
CoconutCoveGuesthouse.com
3012 Granada Street, Fort Lauderdale Beach, FL
THE CLOSEST GAY GUESTHOUSE TO THE BEACH

Retro
SCHUBERT
Resort
"An unprecedented level of service and attention to detail... on one acre of lush tropical paradise!
SCHUBERT
RESORT
LOWER YOUR SPENDING...
WITHOUT LOWERING
YOUR STANDARDS
Stay 2 Nights In One Of Our King Suites, Receive a 3rd Night FREE!*
oversized suites · minutes to wilton drive
forever clothing optional · pet friendly
WWW.SCHUBERTRESORT.COM
954.763.7434 · 866.763.7435
855 N.E. 20TH AVE., FT LAUDERDALE, FL 33304
* April 15th to December 15th - Holidays & Black-Out Dates Excluded

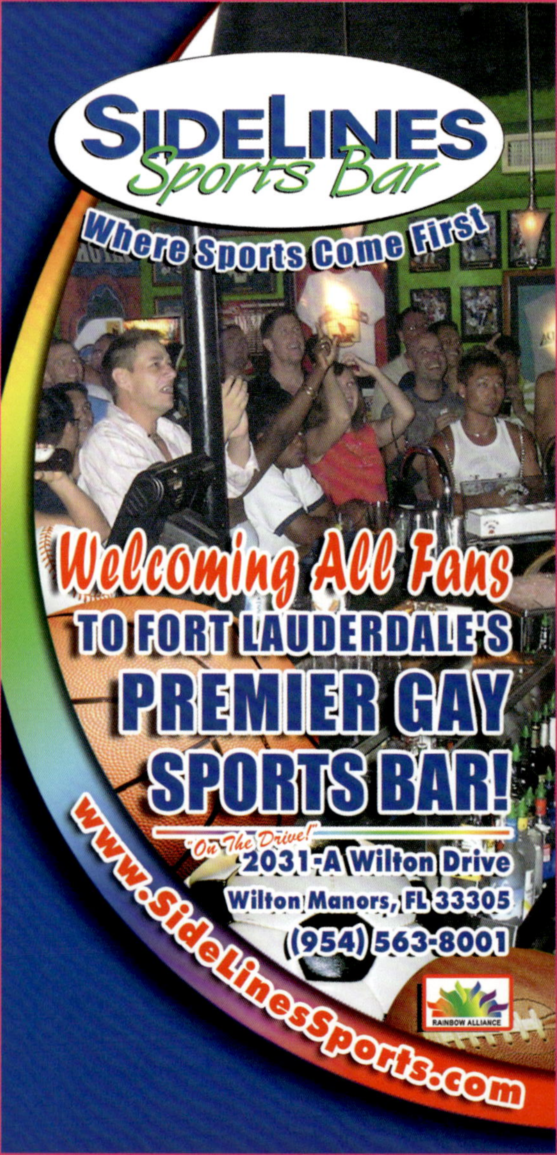
SIDELINES
Sports Bar
Where Sports Come First
Welcoming All Fans
TO FORT LAUDERDALE'S
PREMIER GAY
SPORTS BAR!
"On The Drive!"
2031-A Wilton Drive
Wilton Manors, FL 33305
(954) 563-8001
RAINBOW ALLIANCE
www.SideLinesSports.com

ALCAZAR
RESORT
FORT LAUDERDALE BEACH
954.567.2525 | 888.830.9931
WWW.ALCAZARRESORT.COM

A PREMIER FT. LAUDERDALE MEN'S RESORT
THE BLUE DOLPHIN
Guest Rooms, Efficiencies & 1 Bedroom Apartments
Just a short walk to Fort Lauderdale's Gay Beach
BlueDolphinHotel.com
A complimentary Continental breakfast is included. All our rooms have private bathrooms, Cable TV, AC, Phone, Refrigerator and Coffee making service for those late risers! Onsite laundry facilities, BBQ amenities and free parking available.
725 N. Birch Road · Ft. Lauderdale, FL 33304
(954) 565-8437 800-893-BLUE(2583)

WILTON MANORS ONLY GAY MEN'S RESORT & SPA
The Cabanas
GUESTHOUSE & SPA
YOU TRAVEL . . . WE HOST
CLOSEST TO NIGHTLIFE
CLOTHING OPTIONAL
FULL SERVICE SPA
STEAM ROOM
KAYAKS
THECABANASGUESTHOUSE.COM
954.564.7764 · 866.564.7764
2209 N.E. 26TH STREET, FT. LAUDERDALE, FL 33305 USA

Cheston House
REDISCOVER YOUR PLAYFUL SIDE
RELAX • UNWIND • PLAY
520 N. Birch Road, Fort Lauderdale, FL 33304
www.ChestonHouse.com
954.566.7950 · 866.566.7950

Giant Hot Tub · Internet Access · Continental Breakfast
Clothing-Optional
Coral Reef
GUEST HOUSE
CoralReefGuesthouse.com
888.365.6948 or 954.568.0292
2609 NE 13 Court, Ft. Lauderdale, FL

Elysium Resort
FORT LAUDERDALE
Paradise Awaits ...
552 N. Birch Road • Fort Lauderdale, FL
800.533.4744 • 954.564.9601
www.ElysiumResort.net

THE GRAND
RESORT AND SPA
FORT LAUDERDALE BEACH'S LARGEST MEN'S RESORT
Voted A Top 10 Gay Spa in the Country
954.630.3000 • 800.818.1211
539 N. BIRCH ROAD • FORT LAUDERDALE
WWW.GRANDRESORT.NET

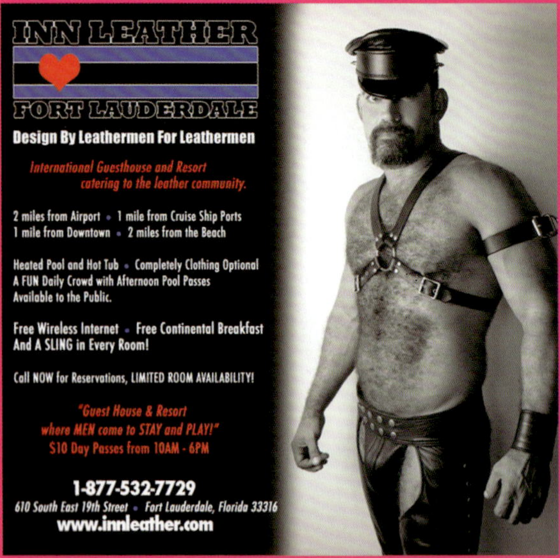
INN LEATHER
FORT LAUDERDALE
Design By Leathermen For Leathermen
International Guesthouse and Resort catering to the leather community.
2 miles from Airport • 1 mile from Cruise Ship Ports
1 mile from Downtown • 2 miles from the Beach
Heated Pool and Hot Tub • Completely Clothing Optional
A FUN Daily Crowd with Afternoon Pool Passes Available to the Public.
Free Wireless Internet • Free Continental Breakfast
And A SLING in Every Room!
Call NOW for Reservations, LIMITED ROOM AVAILABILITY!
"Guest House & Resort where MEN come to STAY and PLAY!"
$10 Day Passes from 10AM - 6PM
1-877-532-7729
610 South East 19th Street • Fort Lauderdale, Florida 33316
www.innleather.com

Exquisite accommodations, unparalleled amenities, impeccable service. Without a doubt the finest gay guesthouse in the world.
PINEAPPLE POINT
GUESTHOUSE & RESORT
got pineapple?
OUT&ABOUT
White Gloves Award
IGLTA
Read Our Reviews On
TripAdvisor.com & PinkChoice.com
315 NE 16th Terrace, Fort Lauderdale, FL
PINEAPPLEPOINT.COM 954.527.0094 · 888.844.7295

WINDAMAR
BEACH RESORT
OWNED AND OPERATED BY TOWNHOUSE OF NYC
THERE IS NO BETTER PLACE TO RELAX AND HAVE FUN
THE FRIENDLIEST IN FORT LAUDERDALE
One block to the ocean,
Continental breakfast, Weekend BBQ,
Heated pool, Jacuzzi, Wi-fi
543 Breakers Ave. Fort Lauderdale, Florida 33304
954 561 0039 WWW.WINDAMAR.COM

▶ **Coral Reef Guesthouse** [MO,SW,N,WI,WC,GO] 2609 NE 13th Ct (off Sunrise Blvd) **954/568-0292, 888/365-6948** *12-man jacuzzi, very secluded*

The Deauville Hostel & Crewhouse [GF,SW,WI] 2916 N Ocean Blvd (Oakland Park Blvd & A1A) **954/568-5000** *budget accommodations for backpackers, tourists, students in the heart of Fort Lauderdale Beach*

The Dunes Guest House [MO,SW,NS,WI,GO] 2835 Terramar St (at Orton) **954/568-6161, 800/425-8105**

Ed Lugo Resort [GF,SW,WI,GO] 2404 NE 8th Ave (Wilton Manors) **954/275-8299**

▶ **Elysium Resort** [MO,SW,NS,WI,GO] 552 N Birch Rd (at Terramar) **954/564-9601, 800/533-4744** *sundeck, near beach*

Embassy Suites Hotel [GF,SW,WI,WC] 1100 SE 17th St **954/527-2700, 800/362-2779** *full brkfst, hot tub*

The Flamingo—Inn Amongst the Flowers [MO,SW,NS,WI,GO] 2727 Terramar St (near Birch) **954/561-4658, 800/283-4786** *luxury hotel*

▶ **The Grand Resort & Spa** [MO,SW,N,NS,WI,WC,GO] 539 N Birch Rd (at Windamar) **954/630-3000, 800/818-1211** *sundeck, spa, gym, clothing-optional courtyard*

▶ **Inn Leather Guesthouse** [★MO,L,SW,N,WI,GO] 610 SE 19th St (at SW 1st Ave) **954/467-1444, 877/532-7729** *sling in each room, dungeon, hot tub*

Liberty Apartment & Garden Suites [MW,SW,WI,WC,GO] 1501 SW 2nd Ave (at Sheridan), Dania Beach **954/927-0090, 877/927-0090** *furnished apts, weekly rates*

▶ **Manhattan Tower** [GF,SW] 701 Bayshore Dr, **954/224-7301** *apt hotel, full kitchens*

Manor Inn [MO,SW,N,NS,WI,GO] 2408 NE 6th Ave (at NE 24th St), Wilton Manors **954/566-8223, 866/682-7456** *B&B, hot tub*

Mary's Resort [M,SW,NS,WI,GO] 1115 Tequesta St (at 11th Ave) **954/523-3500, 866/805-6570**

The New Zealand House B&B [M,SW,N,WI,WC,GO] 908 NE 15th Ave (at Sunrise) **954/523-7829, 888/234-5494** *Key West-style guest-house*

► **Orton Terrace** [MO,SW,N,WI,GO] 606 Orton Ave (at Terramar) **954/566-5068, 800/323-1142** *1- & 2-bdrm apts*

Palm Plaza Resort [★MO,L,SW,N,WI,WC,GO] 2801 Riomar St (at Birch) **954/260-6568** *tropical garden, near beach*

► **Pineapple Point Guest House** [MO,SW,N,NS,WI,WC,GO] 315 NE 16th Terr (at NE 3rd Ct) **954/527-0094, 888/844-7295** *luxury guesthouse, gym*

The Royal Palms Resort [M,SW,NS,WI,GO] 2901 Terramar St (at Birch) **954/564-6444, 800/237-7256**

► **The Schubert Resort** [MO,SW,NS,WI,WC,GO] 855 NE 20th Ave **954/763-7434, 866/763-7435** *full-service resort*

Sea Grape House Inn [M,SW,N,NS,WI,GO] 1109 NE 16th Pl (at Dixie Hwy) **954/525-6586, 800/377-8802** *2 clothing-optional pools, 7-man spa*

► **Villa Venice Resort** [MO,SW,NS,WI,WC,GO] 2900 Terramar St (at Orton) **954/564-7855, 877/284-5522** *2 blocks to beach*

W Hotel Fort Lauderdale [GF] 401 N Fort Lauderdale Beach Blvd **954/414-8200**

Windamar Beach Club [MW] 533 Orton Ave **954/563-7062**

► **Windamar Beach Resort** [M,SW,N,WI,GO] 543 Breakers Ave (near Bayshore) **954/561-0039, 866/554-6816** *steps from the gay beach, clothing-optional throughout*

► **The Worthington Guest House** [MO,SW,NS,GO] 543 N Birch Rd (at Terramar) **954/563-6819, 800/445-7036** *resort, clothing-optional hot tub*

Bars

Bill's [M,NH,CW,K,WC] 2209 Wilton Dr (off NE 23rd St) **954/567-5978** *2pm-2am, till 3am Fri-Sat, from noon Sat-Sun*

Boardwalk [★M,NH,S,18+] 1721 N Andrews Ave **954/463-6969** *3pm-2am, till 3am Fri-Sat, strippers from 5pm*

Corner Pub [GS,NH,GO] 1915 N Andrews **954/564-7335** *11am-2am, till 3am Fri-Sat, from 9am Sun*

Cubby Hole [M,NH,B,L,F,WC] 823 N Federal Hwy (at 8th St) **954/728-9001** *11am-2am, till 3am Fri-Sat, internet access*

The Depot [M,NH,K] 1243 NE 11th Ave **954/524-3990** *noon-2am, till 3am Fri-Sat*

Exit 66 [GS,D] 219 S Ft Lauderdale Beach Blvd **954/357-9981** *home of Crobar & Alegria events*

Georgie's Alibi [★MW,F,V,NS,WC] 2266 Wilton Dr (at NE 4th Ave) **954/565-2526** *11am-2am, till 3am Fri-Sat, sports bar*

Jackhammer in Exile [★M,D,B,L,WC] 2232 Wilton Dr (at Boom in Wilton Manors) *Sun only T-dance*

Johnny's/ 11 Nightclub [M,NH,F,S,WC] 1116 W Broward Blvd (at 11th Ave) **954/522-5931** *2pm-2am, till 3am Fri-Sat, from noon Sun, male dancers nightly*

Matty's on the Drive [M,NH,WC] 2426 Wilton Dr, Wilton Manors **954/564-1799** *11am-2am, till 3am Fri-Sat*

Mona's [M,NH,K] 502 E Sunrise Blvd (at 6th Ave) **954/489-1129** *noon-2am, till 3am wknds*

Monkey Business [M,NH,C,DS] 2740 N Andrews Ave **954/565-3550** *9am-2am, till 3am wknds*

Naked Grape [GF] 2039 Wilton Dr (at NE 20th St), Wilton Manors **954/563-5631** *2pm-midnight, till 1am Fri-Sat, clsd Sun-Mon, wine bar*

PJ's Corner Pocket [M,NH,K,S] 1208 NE 4th Ave **954/533-0257** *noon-2am, clsd Mon*

Ramrod [★M,B,L] 1508 NE 4th Ave (at 16th St) **954/763-8219** *3pm-2am, till 3am wknds, cruisy, patio, also LeatherWerks leather store*

Scandals [M,D,CW,B,E,K,OC,WC] 3073 NE 6th Ave, Wilton Manors **954/567-2432** *noon-2am, patio*

▶ **Sidelines Sports Bar** [MW] 2031 Wilton Dr, Wilton Manors **954/563-8001** *2pm-2am, from noon wknds*

Smarty Pants [★M,NH,E,K,DS,WC] 3038 N Federal Hwy (at Oakland Park Blvd) **954/561-1724** *9am-2am, till 3am Sat, noon-2am Sun*

The Stable Bar [M,NH] 205 E Oakland Park Blvd (at Andrews) **954/565-4506** *2pm-2am, noon-3am Fri-Sat*

Nightclubs

Boom [★M,D,E,K,DS,V,GO] 2232 Wilton Dr, Wilton Manors **954/630-3556** *4pm-2am, 2pm-3am wknds, T-dance Sun*

Dudes Bar [MO,E,P,S,V] 3270 NE 33rd St **954/568-7777** *4pm-2am, till 3am Fri-Sat, live music 6pm, male dancers nightly*

Karnival Beach Club [MW,D,NH,V] 900 E Sunrise Ln **954/588-3363** *noon-2am, till 3am Sat*

Living Room [M,D] 300 SW 1st Ave (at Brickell) **888/992-7555** *gay Fri only*

Purgatory [GS,D,V] 1000 W State Rd 84 **954/357-4700** *call for events*

The Sea Monster [MW,D,TG,WC,GO] 2 S New River Dr W (under the Andrews Drawbridge, across from Las Olas shopping center) **954/474-0183** *9pm-3am, 4pm-2am Sun, clsd Mon-Th, Latin night Fri*

Torpedo [M,D,S] 2829 W Broward Blvd (at 28th Ave) **954/587-2500** *10pm-4am nightly*

Voodoo Lounge [M,D,DS] 111 SW 2nd Ave (at Moffat St) **954/522-0733** *gay Sun only for afternoon Babylon T-dance & drag show*

Cafes

Cafe Emunah [F] 3558 N Ocean Blvd **954/561-6411** *11am-10pm, till 4pm Fri, sunset-1am Sat, kosher, kabbalistic cafe & teabar*

Ciao Cafe [F,E,BW,WC,GO] 411 S Fort Lauderdale Beach Blvd (at Las Olas Blvd) **954/463-4054** *8am-11pm, "Fort Lauderdale's only gay cafe on the beach"*

Fantasia's of Boston 1826 E Sunrise Blvd (next to Gateway Theater) **954/522-4886** *noon-9:30pm*

Island City Bistro [WI] 2037 Wilton Dr, Wilton Manors **954/563-2266** *5pm-10pm, from 11am wknds, clsd Mon*

Java Boys [★WI] 2230 Wilton Dr, Wilton Manors **954/564-8828** *8am-midnight, coffee, tea & desserts*

Jimmies Chocolates & Cafe 148 N Federal Hwy, Dania Beach **954/921-0688** *bistro w/ fresh fare & wine*

The Storks [WC] 2505 NE 15th Ave (at NE 26th St, Wilton Manors) **954/567-3220** *6:30am-midnight, from 7am wknds, patio; also at 1109 E Las Olas Blvd, 954/522-4670*

Restaurants

Canyon 1818 E Sunrise Blvd **954/765-1950** *dinner, Southwestern, full bar*

Christine's 2671 E Oakland Park Blvd **954/566-1919** *lunch & dinner, clsd Sun-Mon, live jazz nightly*

Dogma Grill 900 S Federal Hwy **954/525-1319** *11am-8pm, gourmet hot dog grill, plenty veggie*

The Floridian 1410 E Las Olas Blvd **954/463-4041** *24hr diner*

The Four Rivers [D] 1201 N Federal Hwy #3-A **954/616-1152** *Thai lounge, full bar*

Galanga 2389 Wilton Dr, Wilton Manors **954/202-0000** *dinner nightly, lunch weekdays, Thai, also sushi*

Grandma's French Cafe 3354 N Ocean Blvd (N of Oakland Park Blvd) **954/564-3671** *noon-10pm, dinner only Mon, also ice cream parlor*

Hi-Life Cafe [R] 3000 N Federal Hwy (at Oakland Park Blvd, in the Plaza 3000) **954/563-1395** *dinner, clsd Mon, bistro*

Himmarshee Grille 210 SW 2nd St **954/524-1818** *lunch & dinner, creative & upscale*

Humpy's 2244 Wilton Dr, Wilton Manors **954/566-2722, 877/448-6797** *11am-10pm, till 2am Th-Sat, pizza & panini*

Kitchenetta 2850 N Federal Hwy **954/567-3333** *dinner nightly, clsd Mon*

Kyojin 3485 N Federal Hwy **954/568-2208** *lunch & dinner, Japanese buffet*

LaBamba 4245 N Federal Hwy **954/568-5662** *more gay Tue night*

Lester's Diner [★] 250 State Rd 84 **954/525-5641** *24hrs, more gay late nights*

Lips [DS] 1421 E Oakland Park Blvd (at Dixie Hwy) **954/567-0987** *6pm-close, from noon Sun, clsd Mon, "the ultimate in drag dining"*

Maracas Mexican Gar & Grill 3001 N Federal Hwy **954/537-2002** *more gay Mon*

Peter Pan Diner 1216 E Oakland Park Blvd **954/565-7177** *24hrs*

Rosie's Bar & Grill [★] 2449 Wilton Dr, Wilton Manors **954/563-0123** *11am-11pm, till 1am Fri-Sat, full bar*

Sebastian's Restaurant [GF,BW,WC,GO] 17 S Fort Lauderdale Beach Blvd #228 (at Beach Place) **945/530-7433** *on the beach, 2nd floor*

Simply Delish Cafe [R] 2287 Wilton Dr, Wilton Manors **954/565-8646** *8am-2pm, clsd Mon*

Sublime 1431 N Federal Hwy **954/539-9000** *5:30pm-10pm, clsd Mon, vegan/ vegetarian*

Tasty Thai 2254 Wilton Dr, Wilton Manors **954/396-3177** *lunch & dinner*

Tequila Sunrise Mexican Cafe 4711 N Dixie Hwy **954/938-4473** *11:30am-10pm, till 11pm Th-Sat, 1pm-10pm Sun, monster margaritas*

Tropics Cabaret & Restaurant [MW,P,WC] 2000 Wilton Dr (at 20th) **954/537-6000** *lunch & dinner, Sun brunch, also piano bar, till 3am Sat*

Victoria Park Diner 1730 E Sunrise Blvd **954/759-0022** *6:30am-10pm*

The Wine Cellar [GO] 199 E Oakland Park Blvd **954/565-9021** *dinner, clsd Mon, Eastern European*

Entertainment & Recreation

Gay Tea Cruise [M,D,F,DS] **888/211-3266** *1st Sun*

Gold Coast Roller Rink [MW,TG] 2604 S Federal Hwy **954/547-3419** *8pm-2am Tue, gay skate*

Laffing Matterz [GF,WC] 219 S Andrews Ave (NW corner at Las Olas) **954/763-5236** *7:15pm Wed-Fri, 6:45pm Sat, 4:30pm Sun, unique dinner-theater*

South Florida Lambda Chorale 6278 N Federal Hwy #611 **866/937-4644** *LGBT choir*

Bookstores

Pride Factory 850 NE 13th St **954/463-6600** *10am-11pm, 11am-9pm Sun, books, clothing, gifts*

Retail Shops

Audace 813 E Las Olas Blvd (at 8th St) **954/522-7503, 888/522-7502** *10am-10pm, till midnight Fri-Sat, men's underwear & sportswear*

Bottoms & Tops [GO] 2258 Wilton Dr (in Shoppes of Wilton Manors), Wilton Manors **954/561-6670** *designer men's apparel*

GayMartUSA 2240 Wilton Dr (at NE 6th Ave) **954/630-0360** *10am-midnight, clothes & gifts*

LeatherWerks [L,18+,GO] 501 NE 13th St (at NE 4th Ave) **954/761-1236** *11am-8pm, noon-6pm Sun, leatherwear & gear, adult toys; also inside the Ramrod (8pm-close)*

Out of the Closet 2097 Wilton Dr, Wilton Manors **954/358-5580** *10am-7pm, till 6pm Sun, very cruisy*

To The Moon [GO] 2205 Wilton Dr (at 6th Ave), Wilton Manors **954/564-2987** *11am-12am, pride gifts, cards, & candy candy candy!*

Publications

The 411 Magazine 954/568-1880 *weekly entertainment guide*

The Rimmer 954/240-8954 *monthly "fun & sleaze magazine" for gay men*

South Florida Blade 954/568-1880

Gyms & Health Clubs

Island City Health & Fitness 2270 Wilton Dr, Wilton Manors **954/318-3900** *5am-11pm, 8am-8pm wknds, also variety of classes*

Men's Clubs

Club Fort Lauderdale [★SW,18+,PC] 110 NW 5th Ave (at Broward) **954/525-3344** *24hrs, multilevel sundeck, outdoor whirlpool, steam cavern, sauna*

Clubhouse II [V,PC] 2650 E Oakland Park Blvd **954/566-6750** *24hrs, gym, [L] Tue*

Slammer [MO,BYOB,PC] 321 W Sunrise Blvd **954/524-2625** *8pm-close*

Men's Services

► **Megaphone 954/761-7070** *Meet and Chat Live with HOT local men. FREE to listen & respond to ads. Video and text chat at GayMates.com. Use FREE code 4889.*

Erotica

Fetish Factory 855 E Oakland Park Blvd **954/563-5777** *11am-9pm, noon-6pm Sun, fetishwear, toys, books, magazine, videos*

Hustler Hollywood 1500 Sunrise Blvd (at NE 15th Ave) **954/828-9769**

Rock Hard 2301 Wilton Dr, Wilton Manors **954/318-7625**

Tropixxx Video 1514 NE 4th Ave (at 16th St), Wilton Manors **888/464-5988**

Cruisy Areas

Beach at Sebastian St [AYOR]

Fort Lauderdale Beach [★AYOR] opposite 18th St NE (btwn Oakland Park & Sunrise Blvds) *dune area cruisy all night & gay beach during the day*

Pompano Beach [AYOR] 16th St & A1A (N of Atlantic)

Fort Myers

Info Lines & Services

Gay AA Lambda Drummers [WC] 3049 McGregor Blvd (at St John the Apostle MCC) **239/275-5111 (AA#)** *8pm Tue & Sat in social hall*

Accommodations

The Hibiscus House B&B [GF,NS,WI,WC] 2135 McGregor Blvd **239/332-2651**

Holiday Inn Gulfside [GF,SW,WC] 6890 Estero Blvd (at Bonita Beach Rd), Fort Myers Beach **239/463-5711, 888/465-4329** *beachfront, kids ok*

Lighthouse Resort Inn & Suites [★GF,SW,NS,WI,WC] 1051 5th St, Fort Myers Beach **239/463-9392, 800/778-7748** *resort across the street from Fort Myers Beach*

Bars

The Office Pub [M,NH,B] 3704 Cleveland Ave (at Grove) **239/936-3212** *noon-2am, theme nights*

Tubby's [M,K,S,GO] 4350 Fowler St (off Colonial Blvd) **239/274-5001** *2pm-2am*

Nightclubs

The Bottom Line (TBL) [MW,D,K,DS,V,WC] 3090 Evans Ave (at Hanson) **239/337-7292, 800/839-6823** *2pm-2am*

Restaurants

McGregor Food & Spirits Company [GO] 15675 McGregor Blvd, Ste 24 **239/437-3499** *11:30am-2am, from 5pm Sun, pub fare, some outdoor dining, also full bar*

Oasis [BW,WC] 2260 Martin Luther King Blvd (at Hendry St) **239/334-1566** *7am-3pm, 8am-2pm wknds*

Men's Services

► **Megaphone 239/337-3100** *Meet and Chat Live with HOT local men. FREE to listen & respond to ads. Video and text chat at GayMates.com. Use FREE code 4889.*

Cruisy Areas

Bowditch Point Recreational Park [AYOR] 50 Estero Blvd (at end of street), Fort Myers Beach

Bunche Beach [AYOR] John Morris Pkwy *S end of beach*

Horton Park [AYOR] Everest Pkwy (go E on Del Prado to end), Cape Coral *open sunrise to sunset*

Jaycee's Park [AYOR] at the end of Beach Blvd, Cape Coral *also "Treeline Road," just past rest area at same exit off I-75 for the park*

Fort Pierce

Erotica

► **The Lion's Den Adult Superstore** 7100 Okeechobee Rd (exit 129, off I-95) **318/633-9994** *24hrs*

Fort Walton Beach

see Pensacola

Gainesville

Info Lines & Services

Free to Be AA 1624 NW 5th Ave (United Church of Gainesville) **352/372-8091 (AA#)** *7:30pm Sun, LGBT AA group*

Pride Community Center 3131 NW 13th St **352/377-8915** *3pm-7pm, noon-4pm Sat, clsd Sun, also switchboard*

Bars

Spikes [MW,NH,WC] 4130 NW 6th St **352/376-3772** *5pm-2am, till 11pm Sun*

The University Club [★MW,D,K,DS,S,YC,WC] 18 E University Ave (enter rear) **352/378-6814** *5pm-2am, from 9pm Sat, till 11pm Sun, patio*

Restaurants

Book Lovers Cafe 505 NW 13th St (at 5th Ave, in Books Inc) **352/384-0090** *10am-9pm, vegetarian cafe & used bookstore*

Entertainment & Recreation

Ponte Vedra LGBT Beach *Go N from Gainesville on Waldo Rd to N 301, then E on I-10. I-10 becomes 95. Go S on 95, then take a left. Go E onto Butler Blvd, which ends at A1A. Turn right onto A1A & then drive 5 to 7 minutes looking for Guana Boat Landing parking lot on the right. Park in a parking lot or get ticketed.*

Bookstores

Goerings Book Store 1717 NW 1st Ave **352/377-3703** *10am-9:30pm, till 5pm Sun, independent, LGBT section*

Wild Iris Books [TG,E,WC] 802 W University Ave (at 8th St) **352/375-7477** *11am-8pm, clsd Sun-Mon, feminist/ LGBT*

Cruisy Areas

Bolen's Bluff Dock [AYOR] US 441 S (past Praynes Prairie, on the right) *days*

High Springs

Accommodations

Grady House [GF,NS] 420 NW 1st Ave **386/454-2206** *B&B in historic 1917 Craftsman home, full brkfst*

Holiday

Bars

Frank & Tony's Pub [MW,NH,B,K,S,BW,GO] 2419 Grand Blvd (near Sunray Blvd) **727/942-9734** *3pm-2am, patio*

Hollywood

see also Miami

Bars

Trixie's Show Bar [M,NH,TG,DS] 600 S Dixie Hwy (S of Hollywood Blvd) **954/923-9322** *5pm-2am*

Restaurants

Sushi Blues Cafe [E] 2009 Harrison St **954/929-9560** *lunch Mon-Fri, dinner nightly, sushi, steaks & sandwiches, live blues 9:30pm Fri-Sat, also full bar*

Men's Services

Erotica

Adult Books & Videos [AYOR] 4205 N State Rd 7 (US 441) (at Stirling)

Hollywood Spice 600 N State Rd 7 (btwn Hollywood Blvd & Johnson St) **954/983-4687** *arcade*

Pleasure Emporium 1321 S 30th Ave **954/927-8181**

Sensations Video 106 S State Rd 7 **954/894-7701**

Cruisy Areas

Holland Park [AYOR] Johnson St (at Intracoastal)

Inverness

Accommodations

Camp David [MO,SW,N] 2000 S Bishop's Point Rd **352/344-3445** *camping/ RV retreat, membership req'd*

Islamorada

Accommodations

Casa Morada [GF,SW] 136 Madeira Rd **305/664-0044, 888/881-3030** *luxury all-suite hotel w/ private island*

Lookout Lodge Resort [GF,NS,WI] 87770 Overseas Hwy, mile marker 88 (at Plantation Blvd) **305/852-9915, 800/870-1772** *waterfront resort*

Jacksonville

Info Lines & Services

Free to Be LGBT AA 1562 LaSalle St **904/399-8535 (AA#)** *6:30pm Mon*

Accommodations

Comfort Inn Oceanfront [GF,F,SW] 1515 N 1st St, Jacksonville Beach **904/241-2311, 800/654-8776** *oceanfront, w/ restaurant & gym*

The French Bull Beach House [MO,WI,GO] 130 10th Ave N (at 3rd St), Jacksonville Beach

Hilton Garden Inn Jacksonville JTB/ Deerwood Park [GF,SW,WI,WC] 9745 Gate Pkwy (at Southside Blvd) **904/997-6600, 877/782-9444** *jacuzzi, 15 minutes to beach*

Spring Hill Suites Jacksonville [GF,SW,NS] 4385 Southside Blvd (at J Turner Butler Blvd) **904/997-6650, 888/287-9400** *studio suites, jacuzzi*

Bars

616 [MW,NH,B,K] 616 Park St (at I-95) **904/358-6969** *4pm-2am, patio*

AJ's Bar & Grill [W,D,F,E,WC] 10244 Atlantic Blvd (in Regency Walk Shopping Center) **904/805-9060** *4pm-2am, men very welcome, live music*

Bo's Coral Reef [MW,NH,D,F,DS] 201 5th Ave N (at 2nd St), Jacksonville Beach **904/246-9874** *2pm-2am*

Boot Rack Saloon [M,CW,BW,WC] 4751 Lenox Ave (at Cassat Ave) **904/384-7090** *3pm-2am, cruise bar, patio, also toy store*

InCahoots [M,D,A,MR,E,K,DS,V,WC] 711 Edison Ave (btwn Riverside & Park) **904/353-6316** *8pm-2am, from 4pm Sun, clsd Mon-Tue, 3 bars*

The Metro [★MW,D,DS,P,S,V,18+,WC] 2929 Plum St **904/388-8719** *4pm-2am, till 4am Fri-Sat, 6 bars, male strippers, Latino night Tue, also The Loft [NS]*

The Norm [W,D,E,WC] 2952 Roosevelt Blvd (at College) **904/384-9929** *4pm-close, everyone welcome*

Park Place Lounge [MW,NH,D,WC] 931 King St (at Post) **904/389-6616** *noon-2am*

Nightclubs

The Pearl [GS,D] 1101 Main St (E 1st St) **904/791-4499** *theme nights*

Restaurants

Al's Pizza 1620 Margaret St, Ste 201 **904/388-8384** *11am-10pm, till 11pm Fri-Sat, noon-9pm Sun, in Riverside/ Little 5 Points area*

Biscotti's [★] 3556 Saint Johns Ave (Talbot Ave) **904/387-2060** *10:30am-10pm, till midnight Fri, 8am-midnight Sat, 8am-9pm Sun, killer desserts, also cafe*

Bistro Aix 1440 San Marco Blvd **904/398-1949** *11am-10pm, till 11pm Fri, 5pm-11pm Sat, 5pm-9pm Sun, French bistro*

Derby House 1068 Park St **904/356-0227** *7am-2pm, till 9pm Fri-Sat, very popular wknds for brkfst*

European Street Cafe [★BW,WC,GO] 2753 Park St (at King) **904/384-9999** *10am-10pm, deli, patio*

The Grape Wine Bar & Bistro 10281 Midtown Pkwy #119 (at St Johns Town Center) **904/642-7111** *restaurant, wine bar, also retail shop*

Mossfire Grill 1537 Margaret St **904/355-4434** *lunch & dinner, Southwestern, full bar*

Bookstores

Borders 8801 Southside Blvd, Ste 10 **904/519-6500** *9am-11pm, till 9pm Sun, LGBT section*

Retail Shops

Metro Gift Shop 2929 Plum St (inside The Metro) **904/388-8719** *2am-2pm leatherwear, gifts & club supplies*

Rainbows & Stars 1046 Park St (in historic 5 Points) **904/356-7702** *clsd Mon-Tue, 10am-7pm Wed-Fri, noon-7pm Sat, noon-5pm Sun, pride giftstore*

Men's Clubs

Club Jacksonville [★SW,PC] 1939 Hendricks Ave **904/398-7451** *24hrs*

Men's Services

▶ **Megaphone 904/721-9999** *Meet and Chat Live with HOT local men. FREE to listen & respond to ads. Video and text chat at GayMates.com. Use FREE code 4889.*

Erotica

Insurrection 5110 University Blvd W (btwn Phillips Hwy & I-95) **904/730-0754**

Cruisy Areas

Willow Branch Park [AYOR] Park St (btwn Willow Branch Ave & Cherry St) *take Roosevelt Blvd to McDuff Ave & head toward river*

Key Biscayne

Cruisy Areas

Bear Cut Park [AYOR] in Crandon Beach Park *head W on beach; beware cops (even undercover)!*

Key Largo

Erotica

Adult Video Outlet 102700 Overseas Hwy **305/453-1320** *9am-2am*

Key West

Info Lines & Services

Gay/Lesbian Community Center 513 Truman Ave **305/292-3223** *many meetings & groups, call for info*

Keep It Simple (Gay/ Lesbian AA) 305/296-8654 (AA #) *8pm*

▶ **Key West Business Guild 305/294-4603, 800/535-7797** *see ad in front color section*

Accommodations

Alexander Palms Court [GF,SW,WC,GO] 715 South St (at Vernon) **305/296-6413, 800/858-1943**

Alexander's Guest House [MW,SW,N,WI,WC,GO] 1118 Fleming St (at Frances) **305/294-9919, 800/654-9919** *sundecks, whirlpool, private patios*

Ambrosia House Tropical Lodging [GF,SW,WI,WC] 615 & 618-622 Fleming St (at Simonton) **305/296-9838** *sea captain's house, lagoon pool; also Ambrosia Two*

Andrews Inn [GF,SW,NS,WI] Zero Whalton Ln (at Duval) **305/294-7730, 888/263-7393** *steps from Duval St, tropical courtyard*

The Artist House [GS,NS] 534 Eaton St (at Duval) **305/296-3977, 800/582-7882** *full brkfst (seasonal), jacuzzi, garden*

www.islandhousekeywest.com
1 800-890-6284
305-294-6284
IHKeyWest@aol.com
IsLAnd HouSe
"The best gay men's resort in the world..."
BOYZ Magazine

Avalon B&B [GF,SW,WI] 1317 Duval St (at United) **305/294-8233, 800/848-1317** *restored Victorian, near beach*

Beach Bungalow & Beach Guest Suite [GS,NS,WI] **305/293-9611, 800/407-8417** *vacation rental, 3-day-minimum stay*

Big Ruby's Guesthouse [M,SW,N,WI,NS,WC,GO] 409 Appelrouth Ln (at Duval & Whitehead) **305/296-2323, 800/477-7829** *full brkfst, evening wine, hot tub*

Blue Parrot Inn [GF,SW,N,WC,GO] 916 Elizabeth St (at Olivia) **305/296-0033, 800/231-2473** *historic Bahamian home, sundeck, 2 cats on premises*

Casa de Luces [GF,NS,WI,WC] 422 Amelia St (at Whitehead) **305/294-5269, 800/833-0372** *early 1900s Conch house & condos, jacuzzi*

▶ **Coral Tree Inn/ Oasis/ Coconut Grove Guest House** [★MO,SW,N,NS,WI,WC,GO] 817 & 822 & 823 Fleming St (at Margaret) **305/296-2131, 800/362-7477** *3 historic homes w/ roof decks w/ 50-mile vistas of the Gulf of Mexico, 3 hot tubs, gym*

Cuban Club Suites [GF] 1102-1108 Duval St (at Virginia) **305/294-5269, 800/833-0372** *award-winning historic hotel*

Curry House [GS,SW,NS,WI] 806 Fleming St (at William) **305/294-6777, 800/633-7439** *full brkfst, patio*

Cypress House & Guest Studios [GF,SW,NS,WI,WC] 601 Caroline (at Simonton) **305/294-6969, 800/525-2488** *1888 Grand Conch mansion, sundeck*

Duval House [GF,SW,NS] 815 Duval St (at Petronia) **305/292-9491, 800/223-8825** *Victorians w/ gardens, sundeck*

Duval Quarters [GF,NS] 415 Julia St **305/292-4040, 305/393-4828** *private garden*

Equator Guest House [MO,SW,N,NS,WI,WC,GO] 818 Fleming St (at William) **305/294-7775, 800/278-4552**

The Grand Guest House [MW,WI,NS,GO] 1116 Grinnell St **305/294-0590, 888/947-2630** *in converted rooming house built in 1880s for cigar workers*

Heartbreak Hotel [MW,GO] 716 Duval St (near Petronia) **305/296-5558** *kitchens*

Heron House [GF,SW,NS,WI,WC] 512 Simonton St (at Fleming) **305/294-9227, 800/294-9227** *evening wine*

Heron House Court [GF,SW,NS,WC] 412 Frances St (at Eaton) **800/932-9119** *luxury guesthouse, hot tub*

▶ **Island House** [MO,F,SW,N,NS,WI,GO] 1129 Fleming St (at White) **305/294-6284, 800/890-6284** *some shared baths, hot tub, sauna, steam, gym, very cruisy*

Key West Harbor Inn B&B [GS,SW,NS,WI] 219 Elizabeth St (at Greene) **305/296-2978, 800/608-6569** *hot tub*

Knowles House B&B [GS,SW,N,NS,GO] 1004 Eaton St (at Grinnell) **305/296-8132, 800/352-4414** *restored 1880s Conch house*

La Te Da [★MW,S,21+,SW,WI,WC,GO] 1125 Duval St (at Catherine) **305/296-6706, 877/528-3320** *full brkfst, tropical setting, also restaurant & 3 bars*

Marquesa Hotel [★GF,SW,NS,WI,WC] 600 Fleming St (at Simonton) **305/292-1919, 800/869-4631** *also Cafe Marquesa 6pm-10:30pm, full bar*

Marrero's Guest Mansion [GF,SW,NS,WI] 410 Fleming St (btwn Duval & Whitehead) **305/294-6977, 800/459-6212** *1890 mansion, wknd sunset cocktails*

The Mermaid & the Alligator—A Key West B&B [GS,SW,NS,WI,GO] 729 Truman Ave (at Windsor Ln) **305/294-1894, 800/773-1894** *full brkfst*

Nassau House [GF,SW,NS,WI,WC] 1016 Fleming St (at Grinnell) **305/296-8513, 800/296-8513** *sundeck, hot tub*

The New Orleans House Guesthouse [M,SW,GO] 724 Duval St, upstairs (at Angela) **305/293-9800, 888/293-9893**

Old Town Manor [GF,NS,WI] 511 Eaton St (at Duval) **305/292-2170, 800/294-2170**

Pier House Resort & Caribbean Spa [GF,SW,NS,WI,WC] 1 Duval St (at Front) **305/296-4600, 800/723-2791** *private beach, hot tub, restaurants, bars, spa*

Pilot House Guest House [GS,SW,N,NS,WI,WC] 414 Simonton St (at Eaton) **305/293-6600, 800/648-3780** *Victorian mansion, hot tub*

Seascape Tropical Inn [GF,SW,NS] 420 Olivia St (at Duval) **305/296-7776, 800/765-6438** *also cottages, hot tub, sundeck*

Sheraton Suites Key West [GF,SW,NS,WI,WC] 2001 S Roosevelt Blvd **305/292-9800, 800/452-3224** *also restaurant*

Simonton Court Historic Inn & Cottages [GF,SW,NS,WI] 320 Simonton St (at Caroline) **305/294-6386, 800/944-2687** *built in 1880s*

Travelers Palm [GF,SW] 915 Center St **305/294-9560, 800/294-9560** *in Old Town Key West, shared jacuzzi*

Tropical Inn [GF,SW,WI] 812 Duval St (at Petronia) **305/294-9977, 888/611-6510** *hot tub, sundeck*

Bars

The 801 Bourbon Bar [★MW,NH,D,C,DS,P,S] 801 Duval St (at Petronia) **305/296-1992** *10am-4am, from noon Sun, also Saloon One [M,L]*

Bobby's Monkey Bar [M,NH,E,K,WC] 900 Simonton St (at Olivia) **305/294-2655** *noon-4am*

Bourbon Street Pub [★M,S,V,SW,WC] 724 Duval St (at Angela) **305/296-1992** *11am-4am, from noon Sun, popular daytime bar, start your "Duval Crawl" here*

Hog's Breath Saloon [GF,F,E] 400 Front St **305/296-4222**

Kwest Men [★M,S] 705 Duval St **305/292-8500** *3pm-4am, strippers*

La Te Da [★MW,C,P,WC,GO] 1125 Duval St (at Catherine) **305/296-6706** *3 bars & restaurant*

Virgilio's [GS,D,F,E] 524 Duval St (at Fleming in La Trattoria) **305/296-8118** *7pm-4am, martini bar, garden*

Nightclubs

Aqua [★MW,D,E,K,DS,V] 711 Duval St **305/294-0555** *3pm-2am, till 4am Th-Sat, also Wet Bar, from 9pm Fri-Sat, garden w/ waterfall*

Bottle Cap Lounge [GS,D,E] 1128 Simonton St. **305/296-2807** *noon-4am*

Cafes

Croissants de France [BW] 816 Duval St **305/294-2624** *7:30am-6pm, restaurant open till 3pm, French pastries, patio*

Restaurants

Antonia's [★] 615 Duval St (at Southard) **305/294-6565** *6pm-11pm, Italian, full bar*

Bo's Fish Wagon [★] 801 Caroline (at Williams) **305/294-9272** *lunch, dinner, "seafood & eat it"*

Cafe Sole 1029 Southard St (at Frances) **305/294-0230** *dinner nightly, Sun brunch, romantic, candlelit backyard*

Camille's 1202 Simonton (at Catherine) **305/296-4811** *brkfst, lunch & dinner, bistro, hearty brkfst*

Half Shell Raw Bar 231 Margaret St **305/294-7496** *11am-10pm, waterfront, full bar*

Hurricane Hole 5130 Overseas Hwy **305/294-8025, 305/294-0200** *11:30am-10pm, Sun brunch, dockside bar*

Kelly's Caribbean Bar Grill & Brewery 301 Whitehead St (at Caroline) **305/293-8484** *lunch & dinner, owned by actress Kelly McGillis*

La Trattoria Venezia 524 Duval St (at Fleming) **305/296-1075** *5:30pm-10:30pm, Italian, full bar*

Lobos Mixed Grill [BW] 5 Key Lime Sq (south of Southard St) **305/296-5303** *11am-6pm*

Louie's Backyard [★] 700 Waddell Ave (at Vernon) **305/294-1061** *11:30am-1am, fine dining, deck*

Mangia Mangia [BW] 900 Southard St (at Margaret St) **305/294-2469** *dinner only, fresh pasta, patio*

Mangoes [WC] 700 Duval St (at Angela) **305/292-4606** *lunch & dinner, bar till 1am, "Floribbean" cuisine, full bar*

New York Pizza Cafe 1075 Duval St (Duval Square) **305/292-1991** *11am-10pm*

Pisces 1007 Simonton St (at Truman) **305/294-7100** *6pm-11pm, French seafood, full bar*

Restaurant at La Te Da [★P] 1125 Duval St (at La Te Da accommodations) **305/296-6706, 877/528-3320** *brkfst, lunch & dinner, fusion*

Rooftop Cafe 308 Front St (at Fitzpatrick) **305/294-2042** *brkfst, lunch & dinner, best Key Lime pie, full bar*

Salsa Loca 618 Duval St (in Cowboy Bills) **305/292-1865** *clsd Mon, tasty, inexpensive Mexican*

Seven Fish [★] 632 Olivia St (at Elizabeth) **305/296-2777** *6pm-10pm, clsd Tue*

Square One [WC] 1075 Duval St (at Truman) **305/296-4300** *6pm-10pm, American, full bar*

Upper Crust 611 Duval St **305/293-8890** *noon-11pm, excellent pizza*

Entertainment & Recreation

BluQ Sailing [M,GO] 201 William St (at Caroline) **305/923-7245** *all-gay sails, meals included*

Fort Zachary Taylor Beach *more gay to the right*

Gay & Lesbian Trolley Tour **305/294-4603** *10:50am Sat, check out all of the gay hotspots & historical points, look for rainbow-decorated trolley*

Islescapes Gourmet Dinner Cruises Schooner Wharf (at Pier 1) **305/923-3319** *romantic setting w/ gorgeous sunsets*

The Key West Butterfly & Nature Conservatory [GO] 1316 Duval Street **305/296-2988, 800/839-4647**

Moped Hospital 601 Truman **866/296-1625** *forget the car—mopeds are a must for touring the island*

SkinnyDipperCruises.com Garrison Bight Marina (Palm Ave) **305/240-0517** *clothing-optional chartered cruises*

Bookstores

Key West Island Books 513 Fleming St (at Duval) **305/294-2904** *10am-9pm, new & used rare books, LGBT section*

Retail Shops

Fast Buck Freddie's [WC] 500 Duval St (at Fleming) **305/294-2007** *10am-6pm, till 8pm Th-Fri, till 10pm Sat, from 11am Sun, clothing, gifts*

Fausto's Food Palace 522 Fleming St (at Duval) **305/296-5663** *8am-8pm, till 7pm Sun, cruisy grocery store*

Frank's In Touch 706-A Duval St (at Angela) **305/294-1995** *9am-9pm, gay gifts*

Gyms & Health Clubs

Body Zone South 2740 N Roosevelt Blvd **305/292-2930**

Men's Services

▶ **Megaphone 305/390-0390** *Meet and Chat Live with HOT local men. FREE to listen & respond to ads. Video and text chat at GayMates.com. Use FREE code 4889.*

Erotica

Fairvilla Megastore 520 Front St **305/292-0448** *9am-midnight, clean, well-lighted adult store w/ emphasis on couples: "store for lovers"*

Leather Master 418 Appelrouth Ln (btwn Duval & Whitehead) **305/292-5051** *11am-10pm, noon-8pm Sun, custom leather, toys & more*

Truman Adult Books & Video 922 Truman Ave **305/295-0120** *10am-2am, 24hr wknds, arcade*

Cruisy Areas

Higgs Beach [AYOR] on White St

Little Hamaca Park [AYOR] on Government Rd *from downtown, go E on Flagler Rd, turn right on Government & follow past airport to park at end of road*

Lake Worth

see also West Palm Beach

Info Lines & Services

Compass LGBT Community Center [WC] 201 N Dixie Hwy **561/533-9699** *10am-9pm, till 5pm Fri, 4pm-8pm Sat, clsd Sun*

Bars

The Bar [MW,NH,D,K] 2211 N Dixie Hwy **561/370-3954** *2pm-2am, noon-midnight Sun*

The Mad Hatter Bar & Grill [M,NH,K,V,OC,GO] 1532 N Dixie Hwy (16th Ave) **561/547-8860** *1pm-2am, 1pm-midnight Sun*

Nightclubs

Mojito [GS,D] 129 N Federal Hwy (btwn 1st & 2nd) **561/582-3232** *check listings for gay theme nights*

Cafes

Mother Earth Coffee [E,GO] 410 Second Ave N **877/262-2384** *8am-10pm, till midnight Fri-Sat, fair trade, organic beans*

Restaurants

The Cottage 522 Lucerne Ave **561/586-0080** *dinner only, also bar*

Lakeland

see also Tampa

Accommodations

Sunset Motel [GF,SW,WC,GO] 2301 New Tampa Hwy **863/683-6464** *motels, apts & private home on 3 acres*

Swan Park Inn B&B [GS,SW,N,NS,WC,GO] 118 E Park St **863/248-2235, 888/211-1671** *remodeled 1915 Four Square*

Bars

Pulse [M,D,TG,DS,S,WC] 1030 E Main St **863/683-6021** *4pm-2am, till midnight Sun, [DS] Th, [DS,S] Fri-Sat*

Men's Services

▶ **Megaphone 863/248-0100** *Meet and Chat Live with HOT local men. FREE to listen & respond to ads. Video and text chat at GayMates.com. Use FREE code 4889.*

Cruisy Areas

Lake Morton [AYOR] *beware cops (including undercover)!*

Largo

Erotica

Buddies of Largo 13801 66th St **727/539-7979**

Candlelight Adult Theatre 11455 66th St **727/544-9500**

Madeira Beach

see St Petersburg

Madison

Accommodations

The Mystic Lake Manor [MO,R,SW,N,WI,WC,GO] **850/973-8435** *full brkfst, hot tub*

Marathon

Accommodations

Tropical Cottages [GF,V,NS,GO] 243 61st St Gulf **305/743-6048** *motor-court-style resort, near water sports, pets ok*

Entertainment & Recreation

Bahia Honda State Park & Beach 12 miles S of Marathon

Melbourne

Accommodations

Beach Bungalow [GF,NS] 312 Wavecrest Ave, Indialantic by the Sea **321/984-1330, 321/594-4194** *beachfront town homes*

Crane Creek Inn B&B [GS,SW,NS,WI] 907 E Melbourne Ave **321/768-6416** *full brkfst, hot tub, on the waterfront*

Bars

Cold Keg [★MW,D,C,DS,18+,WC] 4060 W New Haven Ave (1/2 mile E of I-95) **321/724-1510** *2pm-2am, amateur strip contest Th*

Erotica

Hot Flixx 3369 Sarno Rd (Bldg A) **321/752-8805**

Miami

Miami is divided into 3 geographical areas:
Miami–Overview
Miami–Greater Miami
Miami–Miami Beach/ South Beach

Miami—Overview

Info Lines & Services

Switchboard of Miami 305/358-4357 (helpline #), 305/358-1640 (office #) *24hrs, gay-friendly info & referrals for Dade County*

Entertainment & Recreation

Sailboat Charters of Miami [MW] 3400 Pan American Dr (at S Bayshore Dr) **305/772-4221** *private sailing charters aboard all-teakwood 46-foot clipper to Bahamas & the Keys*

Miami—Greater Miami

Accommodations

Miami River Inn [GF,SW,WI,WC] 118 SW S River Dr **305/325-0045, 800/468-3589** *B&B located in Miami's Little Havana district, jacuzzi*

Bars

Rocks on the Mile [MW,D,F,K] 94-96 Miracle Mile, Coral Gables **305/444-7933** *5pm-2am, clsd Sun*

The Shack Bar [GS,NH,E,P,R] 709 NE 79th St (at Magnum Lounge) **305/757-3368** *6pm-midnight, till 3am wknds, clsd Mon, patio*

Nightclubs

Azucar [MW,D,MR-L,DS] 2301 SW 32nd Ave (at Coral Wy) **305/441-6974** *10:30pm-5am Th-Sat, 8pm-3am Sun, clsd Mon-Wed*

Club Boi [M,D,MR-AF] 726 NW 79th St (1 block W of I-95) **305/836-8995** *11pm-close Tue & Fri-Sat*

Discotekka [M,D,18+] 950 NE 2nd Ave (at Metropolis Nightclub) **305/371-3773** *after hours Wed-Sun*

Kaffe Krystal [GF,D] 10855 SW 72nd St **305/274-1112** *clsd Mon-Tue, theme nights*

Sandal Club [★MO,D,MR-L,DS,S,GO] 1060 NE 79th St (1/2 mile E of Biscayne Blvd) **305/758-3556, 786/597-4927** *10pm-5am, nude dancers*

Vlada Lounge [M,D,DS] 3215 NE 2nd Ave (at NE 32nd St) **305/381-5015**

Cafes

Gourmet Station 7601 Biscayne Blvd (at NE 71st St) **305/762-7229** *8am-9pm, till 8pm Fri, 11am-4pm Sat, clsd Sun*

Restaurants

Jimmy's East Side Diner [GF] 7201 Biscayne Blvd **305/754-3692** *7am-4pm*

The Magnum Lounge & Restaurant [GS,NH,E,P,R] 709 NE 79th St **305/757-3368** *6pm-midnight, bar open 5pm-2am, till 3am wknds, clsd Mon, cont'l*

Ortanique on the Mile [★] 278 Miracle Mile (at Salzedo), Coral Gables **305/446-7710** *Caribbean, full bar*

Royal Bavarian Schnitzel Haus 1085 NE 79th St **305/754-8002** *5pm-11pm, till midnight Fri-Sat*

Bookstores

Lambda Passages Bookstore 7545 Biscayne Blvd (at 76th) **305/754-6900** *11am-9pm, noon-6pm Sun, LGBT/ feminist*

Men's Clubs

Club Aqua Miami [MO,SW,PC] 2991 Coral Wy **305/448-2214** *24hrs*

Erotica

Cloverleaf Book & Video 14907 NW 7th Ave **305/681-2001** *24hrs*

Happy Books 9514 S Dixie Hwy (at 95th) **305/670-9203** *24hrs*

J&R Book & Video 7455 Bird Rd (at Palmetto/826) **305/262-6570** *24hrs*

Miami Playground 2657 NW 36th St **305/638-4957** *24hrs*

Cruisy Areas

Matheson Hammock Beach [AYOR] on Old Cutler Rd (S of Kendall Dr) *also Indian Hammocks Park on 117 Ave in Kendall, btwn 107th & 117th Aves & Sunset & Kendall Drs*

Miami—Miami Beach/ South Beach

Accommodations

Aqua Hotel & Lounge [GS,WI] 1530 Collins Ave **305/538-4361** *boutique hotel, jacuzzi*

Beachcomber Hotel [GF,NS,WI] 1340 Collins Ave (at 13th St) **305/531-3755, 888/305-4683** *intimate art deco hotel*

The Blue Moon Hotel [GF,SW] 944 Collins Ave **305/673-2262, 800/553-7739** *Mediterranean-style hotel, also bar*

Bresaro Suites at the Mantell [GS,SW,GO] 255 W 24th St **305/772-5665** *in 1942 art deco bldg, kitchens, no more than 2 people per suite*

The Cardozo Hotel [GF,F,WI,WC] 1300 Ocean Dr **305/535-6500, 800/782-6500** *Gloria Estefan's plush hotel*

The Century [GF,F,NS,WI,WC] 140 Ocean Dr **305/674-8855, 888/982-3688** *restored art deco, Joia restaurant, celebrity hangout*

Chesterfield Hotel, Suites & Day Spa [GS] 855 Collins Ave **305/531-5831, 877/762-3477** *super stylish hotel*

Circa 39 Hotel [GF,SW,NS,WI,WC] 3900 Collins Ave (at 39th St) **305/538-4900, 877/824-7223** *art deco hotel, also evening lounge*

The Colony Hotel [GF,F,WI,WC] 736 Ocean Dr (at 7th St) **305/673-0088** *stylish art deco*

Crescent Suites [GF,NS] 1420 Ocean Dr, Miami Beach **305/531-5197, 800/880-9041** *art deco boutique all-suite property in heart of South Beach*

Delano Hotel [GF,F,SW,WC] 1685 Collins Ave **305/672-2000, 800/697-1791** *hip hotel, great bar scene (see & be seen)*

The European Guesthouse [MW,WI,GO] 721 Michigan Ave (btwn 7th & 8th) **305/673-6665** *B&B, full brkfst, hot tub*

Florida Hotel Network [★] **800/293-2419** *reservations & rentals*

Fontainebleau [GF,F,SW,WC] 4441 Collins Ave **305/538-2000, 800/548-8886** *includes Tresor & Sorrento resorts, billion-dollar renovation in 2008*

The Hotel [GF,F,SW,NS,WI,WC] 801 Collins Ave **305/531-2222, 877/843-4683** *interior design by Todd Oldham, also Wish restaurant & Spire bar*

Hotel Astor [★GF,F,WI,WC] 956 Washington Ave (at 10th St) **305/531-8081, 800/270-4981**

Hotel Impala [GS,F,NS,WI,WC] 1228 Collins Ave **305/673-2021, 800/646-7252** *luxury boutique hotel near beach*

Hotel Nash [GF,F,SW,NS,WC] 1120 Collins Ave **305/674-7800, 800/403-6274** *sleek & modern new boutique hotel, also restaurant & spa, near gay beach*

Hotel Ocean [★GS,F,WI,WC] 1230-38 Ocean Dr **305/672-2579, 800/783-1725** *great location, jacuzzi*

Hotel Shelley [GS,WI] 844 Collins Ave **305/531-3341** *1930s art deco hotel*

The Indian Creek Hotel [GF,F,SW,WI,WC] 2727 Indian Creek Dr **305/531-2727, 800/491-2772** *oasis of serenity w/ art deco flair*

Island House Miami Beach [GS,N,NS,GO] 82nd St **305/864-2422, 800/382-2422** *patio, jacuzzi*

Island House South Beach [MO,GO] 1428 Collins Ave **305/864-2422, 800/382-2422** *SoBe's largest men's guesthouse, full brkfst*

The Kent [GS,F,WI,WC] 1131 Collins Ave (at 11th St) **305/604-5068, 866/826-5368** *on the beach, garden*

The Loft Hotel [GS,WI] 952 Collins Ave **305/534-2244** *affordable boutique hotel*

Miami Habitat [GS,NS] **305/673-3958, 800/385-4644** *furnished apts & hotel rooms*

The Nassau Suite Hotel [GS,NS] 1414 Collins Ave **305/532-0043, 866/859-4177** *renovated art deco, near beach*

The National Hotel [GS,F,SW,WI,WC] 1677 Collins Ave **305/532-2311, 800/327-8370** *on beach*

The New Casablanca on the Ocean [GS,SW] 6345 Collins Ave (at 63rd St) **305/868-0010, 800/813-6676** *studios & town houses*

Ocean Surf Hotel [GF,WC] 7436 Ocean Terrace (near 75th St & Collins Ave) **305/866-1648, 800/555-0411** *restored art deco in quiet North Beach*

The Park Central [GF,F,SW,WI] 640 Ocean Dr **305/538-1611** *ocean views*

The Pelican [★GS,F,WI,WC] 826 Ocean Dr (btwn 8th & 9th Sts) **305/673-3373, 800/773-5422** *designer theme rooms*

The Raleigh, Miami Beach [GF,SW,WI,WC] 1775 Collins Ave (at Ocean Front) **305/534-6300, 800/848-1775**

The Savoy Hotel [GS,SW,NS,WI,WC] 425 Ocean Dr (at 5th St) **305/532-0200, 800/237-2869** *art-deco-meets-eclectic-boutique hotel*

The Shelborne Beach Resort [GS,F,SW,WI,WC] 1801 Collins Ave (at 18th) **305/531-1271, 800/327-8757** *full brkfst, tropical gardens*

South Seas [GF,F,SW,WI] 1751 Collins Ave **305/538-1411, 800/345-2678** *clean & basic, beach access*

The Tides [GS,F,SW,WI] 1220 Ocean Dr **305/604-5070, 800/439-4095** *private beach area*

The Tropics Hotel & Hostel [GS,SW] 1550 Collins Ave (btwn 15th & 16th Sts) **305/531-0361** *near beach & attractions*

Villa Paradiso Guesthouse [GF] 1415 Collins Ave **305/532-0616** *studios*

The Wave Hotel [GF] 350 Ocean Dr **305/673-0401, 800/501-0401** *tropical style*

The Winterhaven [GS,WI,WC] 1400 Ocean Dr **305/531-5571, 800/553-7739** *ocean views*

BARS

Boy Bar [M,NH] 1220 Normandy (at Rue Notre Dame) **305/864-2697** *4pm-5am, cruisy, backroom*

Buck15 Lounge [GS] 707 Lincoln Ln **305/538-3815** *10pm-5am, clsd Mon, gallery lounge, more gay Th*

Creme Lounge [MW,NH,D] 725 Lincoln Ln (upstairs from Score) **305/535-1163** *open Tue & Th-Sat, theme nights*

Palace Bar & Grill [MW,F,DS,GO] 1200 Ocean Dr (at 12th St) **305/531-7234** *noon-midnight, later Th-Sat*

NIGHTCLUBS

Click [M,D] 247 23rd St (at Aerobar) *10pm Sun only*

Halo [MW] 1625 Michigan Ave **305/534-8181** *3pm-3am, from noon Sun, lounge w/ DJ wknds*

Score [★MW,D,K,DS,V] 727 Lincoln Rd (at Meridian) **305/535-1111** *4 bars, lounge opens 3pm, dance club 10pm-5am Tue & Th-Sat*

Twist [★M,D,K,DS,S,V,WC] 1057 Washington Ave (at 11th) **305/538-9478** *1pm-5am, cruisy*

CAFES

News Cafe [★] 800 Ocean Dr (at 8th St) **305/538-6397** *24hrs, healthy sandwiches, also bookstore & bar*

RESTAURANTS

11th Street Diner 1065 Washington (at 11th) **305/534-6373** *24hrs, full bar*

A Fish Called Avalon [R,WC] 700 Ocean Dr (at Avalon Hotel) **305/532-1727** *6pm-11pm, full bar, seafood*

Balans 1022 Lincoln Rd (btwn Michigan & Lennox) **305/534-9191** *8am-midnight, till 1am Fri-Sat, int'l*

Big Pink 157 Collins (at 2nd St) **305/532-4700** *8am-midnight, open late wknds, "real food for real people"*

David's Cafe II 1654 Meridian Ave **305/672-8707** *24hrs, Cuban*

El Rancho Grande 1626 Pennsylvania Ave (S of Lincoln) **305/673-0480** *11:30am-11pm, Mexican*

The Front Porch 1418 Ocean Dr (at Penguin Hotel) **305/531-8300** *lunch & dinner, healthy homecooking, full bar*

Gem [R] 671 Washington Ave (btwn 6th & 7th), Miami Beach **305/674-0977** *brunch show Sun 11am-4pm*

Joe's Stone Crab 11 Washington Ave (near South Point Dr) **305/673-0365** *lunch & dinner, dinner only Sun-Mon, seasonal*

Larios on the Beach 820 Ocean Dr (at 8th) **305/532-9577** *11:30am-midnight, Cuban*

Nemo 100 Collins Ave (at 1st St) **305/532-4550** *chic decor, Pacific Rim & South American cuisine*

Nexxt Cafe [★] 700 Lincoln Rd (at Euclid Ave) **305/532-6643** *11:30am-11pm, till midnight Fri-Sat*

Prime 112 112 Ocean Dr **305/532-8112** *lunch Mon-Fri, dinner nightly, steak house*

Ruby J's Restaurant & Bar [GF,NH,TG,E,K,DS,WC] 239 Sunny Isles Blvd (at 163rd St & Collins Ave), Sunny Isles Beach **305/945-2040** *6pm-close, clsd Sun-Mon, Madame's cabaret Sat nights*

Spiga 1228 Collins Ave (at 12th St) **305/534-0079** *homemade pastas*

Sushi Rock Cafe [★] 1351 Collins Ave (at 14th) **305/532-2133** *noon-midnight, 2pm-1am wknds, full bar*

Tiramesu 721 Lincoln Rd **305/532-4538** *lunch & dinner, Italian*

Yuca 501 Lincoln Rd (at Drexel Ave) **305/532-9822** *noon-11:30pm, New Cuban cuisine*

Entertainment & Recreation

Beach Scooter Rentals 1341 Washington Ave **305/538-7878**

Fritz's Skate & Bike 730 Lincoln Rd (at Euclid & Meridian) **305/532-1954, 877/699-5252** *rentals, in pedestrian mall*

The Gay Beach 12th St & Ocean *where the boys are*

Lincoln Rd Lincoln Rd (btwn Bay Rd & Collins Aves) *pedestrian mall that embodies the rebirth of South Beach—fabulous restaurants, stores, galleries, museums, theaters, people at every step*

World Erotic Art Museum 1205 Washington Ave (at 12th St), Miami Beach **305/532-9336, 866/969-9326**

Bookstores

The 9th Chakra 530 Lincoln Rd (btwn Drexel & Pennsylvania) **305/538-0671, 866/538-0671** *New Age books, supplies, gifts*

Books & Books Inc 927 Lincoln Rd **305/532-3222** *10am-11pm, till midnight Fri-Sat, independent, LGBT section*

Gyms & Health Clubs

Crunch [★] 1676 Alton Rd (btwn 16th & 17th) **305/531-4743**

David Barton Gym [GF] 2323 Collins Ave **305/534-1660**

Men's Services

Men's Clubs

Flex *www.flexbaths.com, opening soon*

Erotica

Pleasure Emporium 1019 5th St **305/673-3311** *24hrs*

Pleasure Place 425 Washington Ave (S of 5th), Miami Beach **305/604-8771, 800/386-2386** *erotica, clubwear, leather, adult toys, DVDs, clothing & more*

Sensations Video 1317 Washington Ave **305/534-2330** *24hrs*

X Spot 19800 S Dixie Hwy **305/255-2190** *24hrs*

Cruisy Areas

Haulover Beach Park [AYOR] North Miami Beach *popular nude beach, N of station #27; beware of cops (even undercover)!*

Mt Dora

Accommodations

Adora Inn [GS,NS,WI,GO] **352/735-3110** *full brkfst*

Naples

see also Fort Myers

Info Lines & Services

Lesbian/ Gay AA 2651 Davis Blvd (at New Attitudes Club) **239/262-6535 (AA#)** *8pm Th*

Bars

Bambusa Bar & Grill [GF,NH,F,V,GO] 600 Goodlette Rd N (at 5th Ave N) **239/649-5657** *4pm-midnight, [K] Sat, also restaurant*

Snappers Nightclub [MW,NH,D,TG,E,K,DS,WC] 2634 Tamiami Trail E (at Bay Shore Dr) **239/775-4114** *3pm-2am*

Cafes

Sunburst Cafe [WC] 2340 Pine Ridge Rd (at Airport Pulling Rd) **239/263-3123** *7am-3pm*

Restaurants

Caffe dell'Amore [BW,WC] 1400 Gulf Shore Blvd N (at Banyan Blvd) **239/261-1389** *open Oct-May only; dinner, Italian*

Patric's [GS,E] 13040 Livingson Rd **239/248-0120** *11am-9:30pm, cont'l, jazz piano*

Narnaja

Erotica

Dixie Adult Super Store 27338 S Dixie Hwy **305/247-5127**

New Smyrna Beach

Accommodations

Night Swan B&B [GF,NS,WI,WC] 512 S Riverside Dr **386/423-4940, 800/465-4261** *B&B on Intracoastal Waterway, full brkfst*

Ocala

Bars

Copa/ Tropix [M,D,DS,F] 2330 S Pine Ave **352/351-5721** *2pm-2am*

Bookstores

Barnes & Noble 4414 SW College Rd **352/237-1581** *9am-10pm, till 11pm Fri-Sat, LGBT section*

Orlando

Info Lines & Services

Gay, Lesbian & Bisexual Community Center of Central Florida 946 N Mills Ave **407/228-8272** *noon-9pm, till 5pm Fri-Sat, clsd Sun, full-service community center, helpline, extensive referrals*

Accommodations

Advantage Vacation Homes [GF,SW,NS] 7799 Styles Blvd (off Hwy 192), Kissimmee **407/396-2262, 800/527-2262** *large selection of pool homes & condominiums near Walt Disney World*

Clarion Hotel Universal [GF,SW,WI,WC] 7299 Universal Blvd **407/351-5009, 800/445-7299** *near Universal Studios, 2 jacuzzis, sundeck*

33 YEARS!
THE NEW
Parliament House
RESORT
www.parliamenthouse.com
VOTED
ORLANDO'S
BEST GAY CLUB!
World's Most Famous
ALL GAY Resort
& Entertainment complex...
130 Rooms - Pool - Dance Club - Western Bar
Piano Bar - Café - Video Bar - Pool Bar - The Footlight Theater
Spacious Courtyard - Beach - On Beautiful Rock Lake
410 N. Orange Blossom Trail - Orlando FL
(407) 425-7571 - Fax (407) 425-5881

EO Inn & Urban Spa [GS,F,NS,WI] 227 N Eola Dr (at Robinson) **407/481-8485, 888/481-8488** *boutique hotel, rooftop terrace, hot tub, cafe on-site*

Grand Bohemian Hotel Orlando [GF,SW,NS,WC] 325 S Orange Ave **407/313-9000, 866/663-0024** *luxury hotel in downtown Orlando*

Holiday Villas [GF,SW,NS,WI] 2941 Lucayan Harbour Cir, Kissimmee **407/397-0700, 800/344-3959** *luxury villas just 4 miles from Walt Disney World, hot tub*

Mid-Century Modern Rental Home [GF,SW,NS] **407/758-1190** *restored 1950s rental home, near Disney*

The Orlando-Mulford Retreat [GS,GO] 2830 Muford Ave (at East End Ave), Winter Park **407/898-4299**

► **Parliament House Resort** [★MW,D,MR,F,S,YC,SW,WC,GO] 410 N Orange Blossom Tr **407/425-7571** *also 6 bars (open at 8pm)*

The Perri House Inn [GF,SW] 10417 Vista Oaks Ct, Lake Buena Vista **407/876-4830, 800/780-4830** *quiet oasis 3 miles from Disney*

Ramada Plaza Gateway [GF,F,WC] 7470 Hwy 192 W, Kissimmee **407/396-4400, 800/327-9170** *1 mile from Walt Disney World*

► **Rick's B&B** [M,N,SW,WI,GO] PO Box 22318, 32830 **407/396-7751, 407/414-7751 (cell)** *full brkfst, patio, near Walt Disney World*

Sheraton Studio City [GF,SW,WI,WC] 5905 International Dr **407/351-2100, 800/327-1366** *world-class amenities combined w/ elegance & sophisticated excitement of 1940s & 1950s Hollywood, also bar & restaurant*

South Beach Orlando Luxury Suites [GS,SW,WC] 4786 W Irlo Memorial Hwy, Kissimmee **407/997-2700**

The Veranda B&B [GF,SW,NS,WC] 115 N Summerlin Ave **407/849-0321, 800/420-6822** *hot tub*

Westgate Palace Resort [GF,SW,NS,WI,WC] 6145 Carrier Dr **407/996-6000, 877/996-6151** *hotel, all 2-bdrm suites, kitchens*

The Winter Park Sweet Lodge [GS,GO] 271 S Orlando Ave (at Fairbanks Ave), Winter Park **407/644-6099** *motel*

Bars

Bar Codes [M,NH] 4453 Edgewater Dr **407/412-6917** *4pm-2am, patio*

Copper Rocket [GF,BW,WC] 106 Lake Ave (at 17-92), Maitland **407/645-0069** *11:30am-2am, from 4pm wknds, till midnight Sun, also restaurant*

Hank's [M,NH,BW,WC] 5026 Edgewater Dr **407/291-2399** *noon-2am, patio*

The New Phoenix [MW,NH,D,E,K,DS] 7124 Aloma Ave (at Forsythe), Winter Park **407/678-9070** *6pm-2am, from 4pm Th-Sat*

Paradise [M,NH,CW,L,K,WI] 1300 N Mills Ave (btwn Virginia & Colonial) **407/898-0090** *4pm-2am, from noon wknds, theme nights*

The Peacock Room [GF,NH,E] 1321 N Mills Ave (at Montana) **407/228-0048** *4:30pm-2am, from 8pm wknds, trendy lounge, art shows*

Savoy [M,S] 1913 N Orange Ave **407/898-6766** *5pm-2am, male dancers nightly, buffet Fri*

Western Bar [M,CW,L,F,P,S] 410 N Orange Blossom Tr (at Parliament House) **407/425-7571** *6pm-2am, from noon wknds, also restaurant*

Wylde's [MW,NH] 3530 S Orange Ave **407/852-0612** *5pm-2am, underwear Tue*

Nightclubs

► **Parliament House Resort** [★MW,D,MR,F,S,V,18+,SW,WC,GO] 410 N Orange Blossom Tr **407/425-7571** *10:30am-3am, 6 bars*

Pulse Orlando [M,D,K,S,18+] 1912 S Orange Ave **407/649-3888** *9pm-2am, clsd Sun & Mon, theme nights*

Revolution [GS,D,MR,DS,S,V,18+,WC] 375 S Bumby Ave **407/228-9900** *4pm-close, theme nights, go-go dancers, patio, more gay Sat*

Cafes

White Wolf Cafe & Antique Shop [E,BW,WC] 1829 N Orange Ave (at Princeton) **407/895-9911** *11am-10pm, till 9pm Mon, till 11pm Fri-Sat, clsd Sun*

Restaurants

The Beacon 100 S Eola Dr **407/841-5444** *dinner, Sun brunch, also bar*

Blue Bistro & Grill 815 N Mills Ave **407/898-5660** *lunch & dinner, dinner only Sat, clsd Sun, upscale American*

Brian's 1409 N Orange Ave (at Virginia) **407/896-9912** *6am-4pm, popular Sun*

Dexter's Thornton Park [E] 808 E Washington St **407/648-2777** *lunch & dinner, brunch Sat-Sun, American, also wine bar; also Winter Park location, 407/629-1150*

Funky Monkey Wine Company 912 N Mills Ave (at E Marks St) **407/427-1447** *lunch & dinner*

Hamburger Mary's Orlando [E,K,V,WC,GO] 110 W Church St (at Garland) **321/319-0600** *11am-11pm, till midnight Th-Sat, full bar*

Hue 629 E Central Blvd (at N Summerlin Ave) **407/849-1800** *lunch & dinner, wknd brunch, new American, full bar*

Pom Pom's 67 N Bumby Ave **407/894-0865** *11am-close, from noon wknds, tea & sandwiches*

The Rainbow Cafe [MW] at Parliament House **407/425-7571** *7am-11pm, till 3am Fri-Sun*

Stonewall Bistro [WC.GO] 741 W Church St **407/373-0888** *11am-midnight, till 10pm Sun*

Entertainment & Recreation

The Enzian Theater [BW] 1300 S Orlando Ave (at Magnolia), Maitland **407/629-1088** *art house cinema & cafe*

Gay Orlando Talk WPRK 91.5 FM **407/896-8431** *noon Fri, LGBT radio*

Indian River Cruises [R,GO] Cocoa Beach **321/223-6825**

Universal Studios Florida 1000 Universal Studios Plz **407/363-8000, 877/801-9720**

Walt Disney World Resort **407/939-6244** *don't even pretend you came to Orlando for any other reason*

Bookstores

Mojo 930 N Mills Ave (at E Marks St) **407/896-0204** *1pm-8pm, 3pm-6pm Sun, LGBT bookstore*

Urban Think Bookstore 625 E Central Blvd **407/650-8004** *11am-9pm, till 6pm Sun-Mon, LGBT section, also bar*

Retail Shops

The Back Room [GO] 5026 Edgewater Dr (outside Hanks Bar) **407/298-2802** *7pm-midnight, till 1:30am Fri-Sat, DVDs, cards, erotica, sex toys, lube, video head cleaner*

Harmony Designs [WC,GO] 496 N Orange Blossom Tr **407/481-9850** *3:30pm-10pm, pride store*

Knowledge For Spiritual Living [GF] 729 Thornton Ave (at SR 50 & 17-92) **407/463-2248**

Urban Body 12 N Summerlin Ave (btwn Central & Washington) **407/481-7979** *11am-8pm, clsd Mon, noon-6pm Sun, men's clothing*

Publications

The 411 Magazine 954/568-1880 *weekly entertainment guide*

Orlando Gay Yellow Pages 101 Wymore Rd #228, Altamonte Springs 32174 **407/788-2008, 877/428-6334**

Watermark 407/481-2243 *bi-weekly LGBT newspaper for Central FL*

What's Happening Magazine **407/690-0809**

Men's Clubs

Club Orlando [SW,PC] 450 E Compton St **407/425-5005** *24hrs*

Men's Services

▶ **Megaphone 407/657-4500** *Meet and Chat Live with HOT local men. FREE to listen & respond to ads. Video and text chat at GayMates.com. Use FREE code 4889.*

Erotica

Fairvilla Megastore 1740 N Orange Blossom Tr **407/425-6005** *9am-2am, from 10am Sun, clean, well-lighted adult store w/ emphasis on couples: "store for lovers"*

Midnight News at Parliament House **407/425-7571**

Video Express 2 496 N Orange Blossom Trail **407/839-8835** *11am-midnight, till 1am Fri-Sat*

Cruisy Areas

Mead Botanical Gardens [AYOR] Denning Rd & Garden St, Winter Park *take I-4 to Fairbanks exit & go E to Denning Rd, turn right & go 1 mile, on left*

Split Oak Park [AYOR] Narcoossee Rd *Take Narcoossee Rd, 5 miles S of 417, to Clapp Sims Duda Rd & turn left. Go for 1.5 miles to park. If you go past Boggy Creek Rd (7-11), you passed the turnoff by 1/2 mile.*

Turkey Lake Rest Area [AYOR] *take FL Turnpike N from I-4 to milepost 263 btwn exits 259 & 265*

Palm Beach

Restaurants

Ta-boo [WC] 221 Worth Ave **561/835-3500** *11:30am-10pm, till midnight Fri-Sat, cont'l*

Erotica

Adult Video Warehouse 501 Northlake Blvd, North Palm Beach **561/863-9997**

Panama City

Accommodations

Beach Vacation Rentals [GF,SW,NS] **770/569-9215** *pet-friendly condos*

Casa de Playa [MW,SW,NS,GO] 20304 Front Beach Rd, Panama City Beach **850/236-8436** *guesthouse, steps from Gulf of Mexico, jacuzzi, patios*

Wisteria Inn [GS,SW,NS] 20404 Front Beach Rd, Panama City Beach **850/234-0557** *tropical inn, hot tub*

Bars

La Royale Lounge & Liquor Store [MW,NH,WC] 100 Harrison (at Beach Dr) **850/763-1755** *3pm-3am, till 4am Fri-Sat, from 7pm Sun, courtyard*

Splash Bar [M,NH,S,V,18+,YC,WC,GO] 6520 Thomas Dr, Panama City Beach **850/236-3450** *6pm-2am, till 4am Th-Sat, male dancers Th-Sat, also pride shop*

Nightclubs

Fiesta Room [MW,D,DS,WC] 110 Harrison Ave (at Beach Dr) **850/763-1755** *3pm-3am*

Cruisy Areas

Tyndall Bridge [AYOR] on Tyndall Pkwy (toward Air Force base) *parking lot*

Panama City Beach

Erotica

Condom Knowledge 7510-A Thomas Dr **850/230-3961** *9am-11pm; also 13208 Front Beach Rd*

Pensacola

Info Lines & Services

Rainbow Group AA Gay/ Lesbian 461 Massachusetts (at W St) **850/433-4191 (AA#)** *7pm Fri*

Accommodations

The Compound Campground [M,SW,N,WI,PC,GO] 7962 Hickory Hammock Rd (at Ward Basin Rd), Milton **850/983-8017** *21+, hot tub, shower/ bath facilities, tent & RV camping, day passes, safe & friendly atmosphere*

Gulf-Front Villa [GF,SW,NS,WI,WC] Fort Morgan Rd, Gulf Shores, AL **865/522-8547** *private condo, panoramic views, on golf course on the Gulf of Mexico*

Bars

Round-Up [★M,NH,B,L,WC] 560 E Heinberg **850/433-8482** *2pm-3am, patio, very bear- & leather/ levi-friendly*

Nightclubs

Emerald City [★MW,D,DS,S,18+,WC] 406 E Wright St (at Alcaniz) **850/433-9491** *3pm-3am (happy hour bar), dance club from 9pm, clsd Tue, patio*

Cafes

End of the Line Cafe [★E] 610 E Wright St **850/429-0336** *10am-10pm, 11am-5pm Sun, clsd Mon, vegetarian, events*

Cruisy Areas

The Bluffs [AYOR] Scenic Dr *beware of cops!*

Pompano Beach

Restaurants

J Marks Restaurant [E,GO] 1490 23th St (at Copans Rd) **954/782-7000** *11am-10pm, till 11pm Fri-Sat, full bar*

Port Charlotte

Nightclubs

Charlotte's Web [GS,D,E] 1193 Enterprise Dr **941/627-4777** *7pm-2am, till midnight Sun*

Cruisy Areas

Kiwanis Park [AYOR] Donora St (at Helena Ave)

Ollie's Pond Park [AYOR] Gobron Ave *take Collingswood to Wintergarden, turn E, go to Gobron & turn right, park at end*

Port Richey

see also St Petersburg

Bars

Waterside Landing [MW,D,K,S,WC] 7737 Grand Blvd (2 blocks off US 19) **727/841-7900** *4pm-2am, from 6pm Sun*

Erotica

Pure Pleasure 12419 US Hwy 19 (N of SR 52) **727/697-3699** *24hrs*

Port St Lucie

Nightclubs

Rebar [MW,NH,D,V,WC,GO] 8283 S Federal Hwy (at Fiesta Square) **772/340-7777** *4pm-2am, till midnight Sun, video bar*

Sarasota

Info Lines & Services

Gay AA 7225 N Lockwood Ridge Rd (in Pierce Hall, Church of the Trinity MCC) **941/355-0847 (church #)** *7pm Sun & 7pm Th*

Accommodations

The Cypress [GF,NS,WI] 621 Gulfstream Ave S **941/955-4683** *B&B inn overlooking Sarasota Bay, full brkfst*

Siesta Holidays [GF,SW,NS,WI] 1011 Crescent St, Siesta Key **941/312-9882, 800/720-6885** *2 locations, near Crescent Beach*

Bars

ID Martini Lounge [MW,NH] 1732 N Honore **941/592-2936** *4pm-2am, clsd Mon*

Witness Cafe [MW,NH,D,F,K,GO] 5100 Tamiami Tr (at Mecca Dr) **941/351-4949** *2pm-2am, also restaurant*

Restaurants

Caragiulos 69 S Palm Ave **941/951-0866** *lunch Mon-Fri, dinner nightly, Italian-American*

Publications

Watermark 813/966-7295 (Tampa office) *bi-weekly LGBT newspaper for Central FL*

Men's Services

▶ **Megaphone 941/870-0800** *Meet and Chat Live with HOT local men. FREE to listen & respond to ads. Video and text chat at GayMates.com. Use FREE code 4889.*

Erotica

Tamiami Books 7338 S Tamiami Tr **941/923-7626**

Cruisy Areas

Gravel Pit Lake [AYOR] Honore Ave (N of 17th St) *road has no sign, turn right after passing power lines*

Satellite Beach

Erotica

Space Age Books & Temptations 63 Ocean Blvd **321/773-7660**

South Beach

see Miami Beach/ South Beach

St Augustine

see also Jacksonville

Accommodations

Alexander Homestead [GF,NS,WI] 14 Sevilla St **904/826-4147, 888/292-4147** *Victorian inn, full brkfst*

Casa Monica [GF,SW,NS,WC] 95 Cordova St **904/827-1888, 800/648-1888** *historic 1888 hotel*

Channel Marker 71 Barrier Island Inn & Restaurant [GF,SW,NS] 7601 A1A S (10 miles S of St Augustine) **904/461-4288, 866/461-4288** *on Intracoastal Water Way*

The Dolphin [MW,NS,GO] **617/216-8960** *1930s beach cottage 100 yds from ocean, large deck, lesbian-owned*

The Inn at Camachee Harbor [GF,WI] 201 Yacht Club Dr (at May St) **904/825-0003, 800/688-5379**

Ocean Blue II [GF,WC] 2701 Anahma Dr (at Vilano Rd) **904/819-5555, 866/877-9297**

Our House B&B [GS,WI,GO] 7 Cincinnati Ave **904/824-9204** *B&B in Victorian home in antiques district, full brkfst*

Saragossa Inn B&B [GS,NS] 34 Saragossa St (at Sevilla) **904/808-7384, 877/808-7384** *full brkfst*

Restaurants

Collage [★R] 60 Hypolita St **904/829-0055** *lunch Tue-Fri, dinner nightly, "artful global dining"*

Cruisy Areas

Riverdale Park [AYOR] CR 305 *take Hwy 207 to CR 305, follow through Racey Point & then Riverdale, days*

Vilano Beach Walkway [AYOR] *go N on A1A 2 miles, 2nd crosswalk over A1A, beachside*

St Petersburg

see also Tampa

Accommodations

Bay Palm Resort [GF,SW,NS,WI,GO] 4237 Gulf Blvd, St Petersburg Beach **727/360-7642** *mention Damron guide for 10% discount (restrictions apply)*

Berwin Oak Guesthouse [MO,NS,GO] 5103 28th Ave S (at 51st St S), Gulfport **727/321-4272, 727/543-6953 (cell)** *comprised of 3 apts, courtyard w/ bar, deck & hot tub*

Changing Tides Cottages [MW,NS,WI] 225 Boca Ciega Dr, Madeira Beach **727/397-7706**

Dicken's House B&B [GS,WI,GO] 335 8th Ave NE **727/822-8622, 800/381-2022** *near museums, full brkfst*

GayStPete House [M,SW,NS,WI,WC,GO] 4505 5th Ave N (at 45th) **727/365-0544** *clothing-optional pool & hot tub, close to bars, beaches & downtown*

Inn at the Bay B&B [GF,NS,WI,WC] 126 4th Ave NE (at 1st St) **727/822-1700, 888/873-2122** *full brkfst, jacuzzis*

Mansion House [GF,SW,NS,WI] 105 Fifth Ave NE **727/821-9391, 800/274-7520** *historic B&B inn, full brkfst*

Sea Oats by the Gulf [GF,WC] 12625 Sunshine Ln, Treasure Island **727/367-7568, 866/715-9595** *directly on the Gulf of Mexico*

SunCoast Gay Suites 350 16th Ave NE (at Locust) **727/806-8006**

Villa Da Costa [GS,GO] 7555 46th Ave N **727/546-1477**

Bars

B&G Bar [MW,NH,K,18+] 10387 Gandy Blvd **727/242-7287** *2pm-2am*

Christopher Street Bar [M,D,DS,S,WI] 13344 66th St N (at Ulmerton Rd), Largo **727/538-0660, 727/520-4111 (info line)** *2pm-2am*

Club Nautico [MW,D,DS,K] 4900 66th St N **727/546-7274** *2pm-2am, theme nights*

Detour [M,NH,D,K,WI,WC] 2612 Central Ave (at 26th) **727/327-8204** *2pm-2am, patio*

Haymarket Pub [M,NH,WC] 8308 4th St N (at 83rd) **727/577-9621** *5pm-2am, upscale*

Lucky Star Lounge [GS] 2760 Central Ave (28th St) **727/327-7359** *2pm-2am*

Oar House [MW,NH,F,K] 4807 22nd Ave S **727/327-1691** *9am-2am, from 1pm Sun*

Bars

Partners Sports Cafe [MW,NH,F,E,DS] 2924 5th Ave N (nr 34th St S) **727/321-0088** *11am-2pm*

Pepperz [★MW,D,K,WC] 4918 Gulfport Blvd S (at 49th), Gulfport **727/322-9702** *2pm-2am*

Sporters Bar [M,NH,B,CW,L,WC,GO] 187 Dr Martin Luther King St N **727/821-1986** *2pm-2am*

Nightclubs

Georgie's Alibi [MW,NH,D,F,DS,S,V,WC,GO] 3100 3rd Ave N (at 31st St N) **727/321-2112** *11am-2am, patio*

Restaurants

Central Avenue Oyster Bar 249 Central Ave **727/897-9728** *11am-10pm, clsd Sun, upscale*

Louis Pappas Market Cafe 1530 4th St N **727/822-0900** *11am-9pm, till 7pm Sun, Greek*

Sea Porch Cafe 3400 Gulf Blvd (at Don Cesar Beach Resort) **727/360-1884** *open daily for breakfast, lunch & dinner*

Skyway Jack's 2795 34th St S **727/867-1907** *5am-3pm, Southern cooking (diner-style)*

Retail Shops

The MC Film Festival 1901 N 15th St (at 8th Ave) **813/247-6233** *LGBT pride gift store*

Publications

Watermark 813/655-9890 (Tampa office), 877/926-8118 *bi-weekly LGBT newspaper for Central FL*

Men's Clubs

Club F2F 3150 46th Ave N (at US19) **727/471-0720** *call for hours*

Men's Services

▶ **Megaphone 727/490-0800** *Meet and Chat Live with HOT local men. FREE to listen & respond to ads. Video and text chat at GayMates.com. Use FREE code 4889.*

Erotica

XTC Adult Supercenter 4800 34th St S **727/865-6977** *arcade*

Cruisy Areas

Fort DeSoto Park [AYOR] Pinellas Bayway S *days, beautiful beach, after leave North Beach parking lot & cross rainbow bridge*

Mirror Lake Park [AYOR] Mirror Lake Dr (near 3rd Ave N) *evenings, along beach past mangrove*

North Shore Park [AYOR]

Tallahassee

Info Lines & Services

The Family Tree 310 Blount St #205 **850/222-8555** *LGBT community center, call for hours*

Accommodations

Hampton Inn Quincy [GF,SW,WI,WC] 165 Spooner Rd (Pat Thomas Pkwy), Quincy **850/627-7555**

Men's Services

▶ **Megaphone 850/385-9900** *Meet and Chat Live with HOT local men. FREE to listen & respond to ads. Video and text chat at GayMates.com. Use FREE code 4889.*

Erotica

Rick's Toy Box 618 W Tennessee St **850/577-9000**

X-Mart Adult Supercenter [AYOR] 5021 W Tennessee (US 90) (Capital Circle W) **850/575-2169** *24hrs, arcade*

Tampa

see also St Petersburg

Accommodations

Bonita Casitas [GS,WI] 1813 E 5th Ave **813/334-1857**

Don Vicente de Ybor Inn [GS] 1915 Republica de Cuba **813/241-4545, 866/206-4545** *historic boutique hotel*

Gram's Place Hostel [GS,P,BYOB,N,NS] 3109 N Ola Ave **813/221-0596** *hot tub*

Sawmill Camping Resort [★MW,D,E,K,SW,N,GO] 21710 US Hwy 98, Dade City **352/583-0664** *RV hookups, cabins, tent spots*

Bars

2606 [★M,L,S,WC,GO] 2606 N Armenia Ave (at St Conrad) **813/875-6993** *2pm-3am, strippers wknds, also leather shop from 9pm*

Baxter's [M,NH,K,S,WC] 1519 S Dale Mabry (at W Neptune) **813/258-8830** *noon-3am*

Chelsea Lounge [M,NH,K] 1502 N Florida **813/228-0139** *3pm-3am*

City Side [MW,NH,K] 3703 Henderson Blvd (at Dale Mabry) **813/350-0600** *11am-3am, patio*

Keith's Bar [M,NH,S,GO] 14905 N Nebraska (at Bearss) **813/971-3576** *1pm-3am, strippers Fri*

Lounge 714/ The Forge [M,D] 1327 E 7th Ave (at 14th St), Ybor City **813/247-2711** *4pm-close, from 1pm Sun, patio*

Midtown Tavern [M,NH,GO] 9002 N Florida Ave (at Busch) **813/915-0819** *3pm-3am*

Spurs [MW,D,CW,V,WC] 1701 E 8th Ave (at 17th St) **813/247-7877** *8pm-1am Fri-Sat, 3pm-8pm Sun, clsd Mon-Th*

Streetcar Charlie's [MW,F] 1811 N 15th St (at 8th Ave) *theme nights*

Nightclubs

G Bar [★MW,D,DS,V,18+] 1401 E 7th Ave **813/247-1016** *4pm-3am, clsd Sun-Mon, theme nights*

Metro Tampa [M,D] 2606 N Armenia Ave (at Cypress) **813/876-4650** *3pm-3am, from 1pm Sun*

Steam Fridays [M,D,18+] 1507 E 7th Ave (at the Honeypot) *10pm Fri only, 3 flrs*

Valentines Nightclub [M,D,K,DS,S] 7522 N Armenia Ave (btwn Sligh & Waters) **813/936-1999** *3pm-3am*

W T-Dance [M,D] 1801 E 7th Ave (at 18th)

Ybor City Social Club/ Eagle Club [M,D,B,L] 1909 N 15th St (btwn 8th & 9th), Ybor City *2pm-3am*

Cafes

Sacred Grounds Coffeehouse [MW,E] 4819 E Busch Blvd **813/983-0837** *7pm-close, from noon Mon, open mic Mon*

Restaurants

Columbia 2117 E 7th Ave **813/248-4961** *11am-close, from noon Sun, Cuban & Spanish, historical restaurant*

Crabby Bill's 401 Gulf Blvd, Indian Rocks Beach **727/595-4825** *inexpensive seafood joint*

Ho Ho Chinese [WC] 2502 W Columbus Dr **813/254-9557** *11am-10pm, dinner only wknds, full bar*

Publications

Watermark 813/655-9890 *bi-weekly LGBT newspaper for Central FL*

Men's Clubs

Club Tampa [★PC] 215 N 11th St **813/223-5181** *24hrs*

Rainbow Cabaret [AYOR,WI] 4421 N Hubert Ave (behind Playhouse Theatre) **813/877-7585** *24hrs, sauna, jacuzzi*

Ybor Resort & Spa [MO,WI,PC] 1512 E 8th Ave **813/242-0900**

Men's Services

Erotica

Buddies Video 4322 W Crest Ave (at Hillsborough) **813/876-8083** *24hrs*

Playhouse Theatre 4421 N Hubert Ave (at Alva) **813/873-9235** *24hrs*

Tres Equis 6220 Adamo Dr (behind Goldrush topless bar) **813/740-8664** *24hrs*

XTC Adult Supercenter 330 E Fowler Ave **813/930-0069** *24hrs*

Xtreme Adult Books & Video 1212 E Fowler Ave **813/558-0112** *24hrs*

Cruisy Areas

Al Lopez Park [AYOR] N Himes Ave (1 blk S of Hillsborough), West Tampa *take I-275 N toward Ocala, take Hillsborough exit, then go W on Hillsborough Ave for 2 1/2 miles, turn left on Himes Ave*

Picnic Island [AYOR] Picnic Island Blvd (across from the military base, on E side) *gay beach at end of park, past the last parking lot & beyond the mangroves*

Titusville

Cruisy Areas

Playalinda Beach [AYOR] Rte 407 E

Venice

Cruisy Areas

Casperson Beach [AYOR] *at S end of Harbor Dr, beware cops (!), heavy police presence*

Venus

Accommodations

Camp Mars [M,SW,N,GO] 326 Goff Rd **863/699-6277** *campground w/ cabins, tents, RV hookups, 2 hours from Fort Lauderdale & Miami*

West Palm Beach

Accommodations

Grandview Gardens B&B [GF,SW,NS,WI,WC,GO] 1608 Lake Ave (at Palm) **561/833-9023** *1925 Spanish-Mediterranean home*

Hibiscus House B&B [GS,SW,NS,WI,GO] 501 30th St **561/863-5633, 800/203-4927** *full brkfst, pet-friendly*

Scandia Lodge [GS,SW,NS,GO] 625 S Federal Hwy (at 6th Ave), Lake Worth **561/586-3155** *10 minutes to West Palm Beach*

Bars

Fort Dix [★M,NH,WC] 6205 Georgia Ave (at Colonial) **561/533-5355** *noon-3am, till 4am Fri-Sat, patio, DJ wknds*

HG Rooster's [★M,NH,F,K,S,WC] 823 Belvedere Rd (btwn Parker & Lake) **561/832-9119** *3pm-3am, till 4am Fri-Sat*

Nightclubs

Dolche [MW,D,DS] 3097 Forest Hill Blvd **561/574-5700** *theme nights*

The Lounge [GS,D] 517 Clematis St *theme nights*

Monarchy [GS,D] 221 Clematis St

Respectable Street [GF,D,A,E,18+] 518 Clematis St **561/832-9999** *9pm-3am, till 4am Fri-Sat, clsd Sun-Tue, retro & new wave nights*

Restaurants

Rhythm Cafe [BW] 3800-A S Dixie Hwy **561/833-3406** *6pm-10pm, clsd Sun-Mon*

Thai Bay 1900 Okeechobee Blvd (in Palm Beach Market Pl) **561/640-0131** *lunch weekdays & dinner nightly*

Entertainment & Recreation

MacArthur Beach Singer Island, N Palm Beach

Bookstores

Changing Times Bookstore 911 Village Blvd #806 (at Palm Beach Lakes) **561/640-0496** *10am-7pm, till 5pm Sat, noon-5pm Sun, LGBT section*

Retail Shops

Eurotique 3111 45th St #16 (at Village Blvd) **561/684-2302, 800/486-9650** *11am-7pm, noon-6pm Sat, clsd Sun, PVC, leather, books, videos*

Studio 205 & Java Juice Bar 600 Lake Ave (at L St), Lake Worth **561/533-5272** *10am-6pm, till 5pm Sun, gay pride items, books & home accessories*

Men's Services

▶ **Megaphone 561/909-1100** *Meet and Chat Live with HOT local men. FREE to listen & respond to ads. Video and text chat at GayMates.com. Use FREE code 4889.*

Erotica

Redlight Adult Video Outlet 3900 W Industrial Wy **561/844-9779** *booths*

Cruisy Areas

Bert Winters Park [AYOR] Ellison Wilson Rd, Juno Beach

Jupiter Beach [AYOR] Jupiter *going S on A1A, it's the 3rd catwalk past Jupiter Key on the left*

Wilton Manors

see Fort Lauderdale

Winter Haven

Accommodations

Ranch House Inn & Suites [GF,SW,WI,WC] 1911 Cypress Gardens Blvd **863/324-5994, 800/366-5996** *motel, restaurant*

Bars

Old Man Frank's [GF,NH,F,WC] 1005 S Lake Howard Dr (at Central) **863/294-9179** *11am-2am, from noon-midnight Sun, on the lake, smoking allowed*

Georgia

Statewide

Publications

Southern Voice 404/876-1819 *weekly LGBT newspaper for AL, FL (panhandle), GA, LA, MS, TN w/ resource listings*

Athens

Accommodations

Ashford Manor B&B [GF,SW,NS,WI,GO] 5 Harden Hill Rd (at Main St), Watkinsville **706/769-2633** *refrigerators, some private porches*

Bars

The Globe [GF,F] 199 N Lumpkin (at Clayton) **706/353-4721** *11am-2am, till midnight Sun, 40 single-malt scotches*

Nightclubs

Forty Watt Club [GF,E,WC] 285 W Washington St (at Pulaski) **706/549-7871** *call for hours, live music venue*

Cafes

Espresso Royale Cafe [WC] 297 E Broad St (at Jackson) **706/613-7449** *7am-midnight Mon-Fri, from 8am wknds, best coffee in Athens*

Restaurants

The Bluebird 493 E Clayton (N Thomas St) **706/549-3663** *8am-3pm, popular brunch wknds, all veggie*

The Grit [WC] 199 Prince Ave **706/543-6592** *11am-10pm Mon-Fri, dinner 5pm-10pm, great wknd brunch 10am-3pm*

Cruisy Areas

Ben Burton Park [AYOR] Mitchell Bridge Rd (just before Oconee River Bridge)

Kangaroo Truck Stop [AYOR] Hwy 29 N

Atlanta

Info Lines & Services

Galano Club 585 Dutch Valley Rd (at Monroe) **404/881-9188** *meetings throughout the day, LGBT recovery club*

Accommodations

The Gaslight Inn [GS,NS,WI,GO] 1001 St Charles Ave NE **404/875-1001** *1913 craftsman-style B&B*

The Georgian Terrace Hotel [GF,SW,WI,WC] 659 Peachtree St **404/897-1991, 800/555-8000** *hosted Gone with the Wind world-premier reception in 1939, kids ok*

Glenn Hotel [GS] 110 Marietta St NW **404/521-2250, 866/404-5366** *boutique hotel, also restaurant & rooftop lounge*

Hill Street Resort B&B [GS,SW,WI,GO] 729 Hill St SE **404/627-4281** *full brkfst, hot tub*

Holiday Inn Atlanta South [GS,SW,WI,WC] 6288 Old Dixie Hwy (at Tara Blvd), Jonesboro **770/968-4300, 800/972-2404**

Hotel Indigo [WI] 683 Peachtree St NE **404/874-9200** *cozy, stylish no-frills hotel, workout room, also restaurant*

In the Woods Campground & Resort [M,N,GO] 142 Casey Ct (at Hwy 327 & Hwy 51), Canon **706/246-9512** *campground w/ 36+ campsites & 20+ RV hookups*

Microtel Inn & Suites [GF,WI,WC] 1840 Corporate Blvd **404/325-4446**

Midtown Guest House [GS,SW,NS,WI,GO] 770 Penn Ave **404/931-8791** *in the heart of midtown*

Sheraton Atlanta Hotel [GF,F,SW,WC] 165 Courtland St (at International Blvd) **404/659-6500, 800/325-3535** *3 restaurants, full bar, gym*

Stonehurst Place Bed & Breakfast [GS,NS,WI,GO] 923 Piedmont Ave NE **404/881-0722, 877/285-2246**

W Atlanta [GF,SW,NS,WI,WC] 111 Perimeter Center W **770/396-6800, 877/WHOTELS (reservations only)** *also restaurant*

Bars

3-Legged Cowboy [★M,D,CW,E,WC] 931 Monroe Dr #B (at Midtown Promenade) **404/876-0001** *6pm-2am, clsd Sun-Mon*

Amsterdam [★M,D,F,V] 502 Amsterdam Ave NE **404/892-2227** *11:30am-close, video & sports bar*

Atlanta Eagle [★M,D,B,L,GO] 306 Ponce de Leon Ave NE (at Argonne) **404/873-2453** *3pm-3am, clsd Sun, also leather store*

BJ Roosters [M,NH,K,DS,GO] 2345 Cheshire Bridge Rd (at La Vista) **404/634-5895** *2:30pm-3am*

Blake's on the Park [★MW,NH,F,P,S,V] 227 10th St (at Piedmont) **404/892-5786** *11am-3am, till midnight Sun*

Bulldogs [★M,NH,D,L,MR-AF,V] 893 Peachtree St NE (btwn 7th & 8th) **404/872-3025** *2pm-4am Sun-Fri, till 3am Sat, cruise bar*

Burkhart's Pub [MW,NH,F,K,S,WC] 1492-F Piedmont Ave (at Monroe, in Ansley Square) **404/872-4403** *4pm-2:30am, from 2pm wknds, till midnight Sun, patio*

Eastside Lounge [GS,D,MR] 485-A Flat Shoals Ave **404/521-9666** *9pm-2:30am, from 8pm Fri-Sat, clsd Sun*

Eddie's Attic [GS,E] 515-B N McDonough St (at Trinity Place), Decatur **404/377-4976** *4:30pm-12:30am Mon-Th, till 2am Fri & Sat, open 1 hr before showtime Sun, live music, comedy, also restaurant, rooftop deck*

Felix's on the Square [M,F] 1510-G Piedmont Ave NE (Ansley Square) **404/249-7899** *2pm-3am, from 1pm Sat, 1pm-midnight Sun*

Friends on Ponce [MW,NH,V] 736 Ponce de Leon NE (at Ponce de Leon Pl) **404/817-3820** *2pm-3am, from noon Sat, till midnight Sun, rooftop patio*

Halo Lounge [GS,F] 817 W Peachtree (6th St, btwn W Peachtree & Peachtree) **404/962-7333** *4pm-3am, from 6pm Sat, clsd Sun*

Le Buzz [MW,NH,D,F,K,DS,S,WC] 585 Franklin Rd A-10 (at S Marietta Pkwy, in Longhorn Plaza), Marietta **770/424-1337** *7pm-3am, clsd Sun, DJ Fri, patio*

Mary's [MW,NH,D,K,V] 1287B Glenwood Ave (at Flat Shoals) **404/624-4411** *5pm-3am, clsd Sun, friendly cocktail bar*

Mixx [M,NH,D] 1492-B Piedmont Ave (at Monroe, in Ansley Square) **404/228-4372** *4pm-1am, till 3am Fri-Sat, clsd Mon*

Model T [M,NH,F,K,DS,OC,WC] 699 Ponce de Leon NE #11 (at Barnett) **404/872-2209** *noon-3am, till midnight Sun, cruisy, [DS] Fri-Sat*

New Order Lounge [M,NH,E,OC,WC] 1544 Piedmont Ave NE (at Monroe, in Ansley Mall) **404/874-8247** *2pm-2am Mon-Th, till 3am Fri-Sat, till midnight Sun*

Opus I [M,NH,WC] 1086 Alco St NE (at Cheshire Bridge) **404/634-6478** *11am-3am, from 9am Sat, 12:30pm-midnight Sun*

The Stage Door [MW,K,DS,GO] 4431 Hugh Howell Rd, Tucker **770/414-9292** *5pm-4am, 3pm-3am Sat-Sun*

Swinging Richard's [M,S,$] 1400 Northside Dr NW (btwn I-75 & Northside Dr) **404/352-0532** *6:30pm-close, clsd Sun-Mon, gay strip club, nude dancers*

Tripps [M,NH,F] 1931 Piedmont Circle (at Cheshire Bridge) **404/724-0067** *11am-3am, 12:30pm-midnight Sun*

Woofs on Piedmont [★M,NH,F,GO] 2425 Piedmont (at Lindbergh) **404/869-9422** *11:30am-2am, 12:30pm-midnight Sun, sports bar*

NIGHTCLUBS

Bazzaar [GS,D,MR,F] 654 Peachtree St (at Ponce de Leon) **404/885-7505** *6pm-3am, lounge w/ food served*

Black Ice Lounge [M,D,MR-AF] 138 Edgewood **404/423-7871** *open Th-Sun, theme nights*

Body Shop [M,D] 2675 Johnson Rd **404/636-1233** *after hours club: open 2am Sat & major holidays only*

Chaparral [M,D,MR-L] 2715 Buford Hwy **404/634-3737** *10pm-4am, more gay Fri & Sun*

Club 708 [M,D,E,MR-AF] 708 Spring St **404/874-8125** *10pm-6am, clsd Mon-Tue, go-go dancers*

Grown & Sexy Sundays [M,D,MR-AF] 495 Peachtree St (at Django's) **404/246-9000** *7pm-midnight Sun only*

The Heretic [★M,D,L,F,S,WC] 2069 Cheshire Bridge Rd (at Piedmont) **404/325-3061** *9am-3am, clsd Sun, 3 bars, patio, call for theme nights, also Heretic Leathers toy shop*

Magnum Saturdays [M,MR-AF] 708 Spring St NW **404/246-9000**

Masquerade [GF,D,F,E,18+,$] 695 North Ave NE **404/577-8178, 404/577-2002** *hours vary*

Paris Decatur [W,D] 308H Ponce De Leon Pl, Decatur **404/687-1965**

Phase One [GS,D,MR-AF,S] 4933 Memorial Dr, Decatur **404/296-4895** *hrs vary, call for theme nights*

Sunday Night Live [M,D,MR-AF,DS,18+] 4001 Presidential Pkwy (at Club Europe) **780/991-6929** *8pm Sun only*

Sutra Lounge [GF,D] 1136 Crescent Ave (at 13th) **404/607-1160** *hrs vary Mon, Th-Sat*

Traxx [M,D,MR-AF,E] 1287 Columbia Dr, Decatur **866/602-5553** *Sat only*

Who's Who? [MW,D,MR-AF] 79 Poplar St (at The Mark Ultralounge) **678/904-0050** *10pm-3am Wed only*

Wild Mustang/ Jungle [★MW,D,DS,$] 2115 Faulkner Rd NE (off Cheshire Bridge Rd NE) **404/844-8800** *9pm-close, clsd Wed & Sun, also 11pm Mon for Stars of the Century [DS]*

CAFES

Apache Cafe [MR,F,E] 64 3rd St NW **404/876-5436** *food served, poetry readings, events, gallery*

Australian Bakery Cafe 48 S Park Square, Marietta **678/797-6222** *7am-5:30pm, 8am-4pm wknds; also 463 Flat Shoals Rd, 404/ 653-0100*

Caribou Coffee 1551 Piedmont Ave NE (at Monroe) **404/733-5539** *6am-10pm, till 11pm Fri-Sat, 7am-9pm Sun, locations throughout the city*

Intermezzo [WI] 1845 Peachtree Rd NE **404/355-0411** *10:30am-3am, classy, full bar, great desserts, [WI] till 7pm*

Urban Grounds 38 N Avondale Rd, Avondale Estates **404/499-2136** *6:30am-9pm, till 10pm Fri, 7:30am-10pm Sat, 8am-4pm Sun*

Restaurants

Agnes & Muriel's [★BW] 3133 Piedmont Rd **404/814-9103** *lunch & dinner, wknd brunch, clsd Mon, patio*

Apres Diem 931 Monroe Dr #C-103 **404/872-3333** *11:30am-midnight, till 2am Fri-Sat, from 11am wknds, brunch Sat-Sun, French bistro, live jazz Wed, full bar*

Bacchanalia/ Star Provisions/ Quinones 1198 Howell Mill Rd NW **404/365-0410** *lunch Wed-Sat & dinner Mon-Sat, upscale*

Beleza 905 Juniper St (at 8th) **678/904-4582** *5:30pm-1am, till 2am wknds, clsd Sun-Mon, Brazilian, also cocktails*

The Colonnade 1879 Cheshire Bridge Rd NE **404/874-5642** *lunch Wed-Sun, dinner nightly, traditional Southern*

Cowtippers [TG,WC] 1600 Piedmont Ave NE (at Monroe) **404/874-3751** *11:30am-11pm, till midnight Fri-Sat, steak house*

Ecco [R] 40 7th St **404/347-9555** *5:30pm-10pm, till 11pm Fri-Sat, till 10pm Sun, Italian*

Einstein's [★WC] 1077 Juniper (at 12th) **404/876-7925** *11am-11pm, till midnight Fri-Sat, from 10am Sun, wknd brunch, full bar, patio*

The Flying Biscuit Cafe [★BW,WC] 1655 McLendon Ave (at Clifton) **404/687-8888** *7am-10pm, till 10:30pm Fri-Sat, healthy brkfst all day; multiple locations*

Gilbert's Cafe 219 10th St **404/872-8012** *lunch & dinner, food till 2am, bar till 3am, till midnight Sun*

Joe's On Juniper 1049 Juniper St **404/875-6634** *11am-2am, till midnight Sun, American*

The Lobby at Twelve [R] 361 17th St **404/961-7370** *brkfst, lunch & dinner, upscale American*

Majestic Diner [★AYOR] 1031 Ponce de Leon (at Highland) **404/875-0276** *24hrs, diner right from the '50s, cantankerous waitresses included*

Murphy's [★WC] 997 Virginia Ave NE (at N Highland Ave) **404/872-0904** *11am-10pm, till midnight Fri, from 8am wknds*

Nickiemoto's 990 Piedmont Ave NE **404/253-2010** *lunch & dinner, pan-Asian/ sushi, Drag-a-Magki drag show Mon*

No Más! Cantina [GO] 180 Walker St **404/574-5678** *lunch & dinner daily, wknd brunch, Mexican, also huge furniture & gift store*

R Thomas Deluxe Grill [BW,WC] 1812 Peachtree Rd NE (btwn 26th & 27th) **404/872-2942** *24hrs, healthy Californian/ juice bar, popular late night*

Repast [R] 620 N Glen Iris Dr **404/870-8707** *5:30pm-10pm, till 10:30pm Fri-Sat, clsd Sun, upscale American*

Ria's Bluebird Cafe [★BW,TG,WC] 421 Memorial Dr **404/521-3737** *8am-3pm, gourmet brunch in quaint old diner in Grant Park*

Roxx Tavern & Diner 1824 Cheshire Brg Rd NE (at Manchester) **404/892-4541** *lunch & dinner, Sun brunch, patio*

Slice [WI,GO] 259 Peters St **404/588-1820** *11am-midnight, till 3am Fri, noon-3am Sat, noon-midnight Sun, pizza & martinis, second location 85 Poplar St (404/917-1820)*

Swan Coach House 3130 Slaton Dr NW **404/261-0636** *11am-2:30pm, clsd Sun, also gift shop & art gallery*

Sweet Devil Moon [D,E] 980 Piedmont Ave **404/347-3600** *4pm-midnight, from 3pm Fri-Sun, Boys Night Out Wed, Peruvian tapas*

Table 1280 1280 Peachtree St NE (at Woodruff Arts Center) **404/897-1280** *11am-8pm Tue-Sat, till 6pm Sun, Sun brunch, clsd Mon, also lounge, upscale American & tapas*

TWO urban licks [E,R] 820 Ralph McGill Blvd **404/522-4622** *dinner nightly, great grill, full bar, live blues*

Veni Vidi Vici [WI] 41 14th St **404/875-8424** *lunch Mon-Fri, dinner nightly, upscale Italian*

Wasabi 180 Walker St **404/574-5680** *lunch Th-Fri, dinner nightly, clsd Sun, sushi*

Watershed 406 W Ponce de Leon Ave, Decatur **404/378-4900** *11am-10pm, Sun brunch, wine bar, also gift shop, owned by Emily Saliers of the Indigo Girls*

Entertainment & Recreation

AIDS Memorial Quilt/ NAMES Project 637 Hoke NW **404/688-5500** *visit The Quilt at the foundation offices*

Ansley Park Playhouse 1545 Peachtree St **404/875-1193** *some LGBT-themed productions*

Atlanta Gay Men's Chorus 1379 Tullie Rd, Ste 200, 30329-2308 **404/320-1030**

Krause Gallery 291 Peters St SW **404/522-6205** *1pm-5:30pm, noon-6pm Th-Sat, clsd Sun, contemporary art & photography*

Lambda Radio Report WRFG 89.3 FM **404/523-8989** *6pm Tue, LGBT radio program*

Little 5 Points, Moreland & Euclid Ave S of Ponce de Leon Ave *hip & funky area w/ too many restaurants & shops to list*

Martin Luther King, Jr Center for Non-Violent Social Change 449 Auburn Ave NE **404/526-8900** *includes King's birth home, the church where he preached in the '60s & his gravesite*

Piedmont Park [AYOR] NE of Piedmont at 10th *hilltop sunbathing*

Wertz Contemporary 264 Peters St **404/420-4342** *art drawn from Africa & the African Diaspora*

Bookstores

Brushstrokes/ Capulets [GO] 1510-J Piedmont Ave NE (near Monroe) **404/876-6567** *10am-10pm, till 11pm Fri-Sat, LGBT variety store*

Oakwells 403 W Ponce de Leon Ave, Decatur **404/373-5190** *6am-7pm, LGBT section*

▶ **Outwrite Bookstore & Coffeehouse** [★F,WC] 991 Piedmont Ave (at 10th) **404/607-0082** *10am-11pm, LGBT, music, videos, gifts, cafe*

Retail Shops

Atlanta Leather Company 2111 Faulkner Rd NE (at Chesire Bridge Rd) **404/320-8989** *11am-8pm, noon-6pm Sun, leather, fetish*

▶ **The Boy Next Door** 1447 Piedmont Ave NE (btwn 14th & Monroe) **404/873-2664** *10am-8pm, noon-6pm Sun, clothing*

The Junkman's Daughter 464 Moreland Ave (at Euclid) **404/577-3188** *11am-7pm, till 8pm Fri, till 9pm Sat, from noon Sun, hip stuff*

Piercing Experience 1654 McLendon Ave NE (at Clifton) **404/378-9100, 800/646-0393** *noon-8pm, till 9pm Fri-Sat, till 6pm Sun*

Publications

David Atlanta 404/876-1819 *gay entertainment magazine w/ extensive nightlife calendar, maps & directory*

Southern Voice 404/876-1819 *weekly LGBT newspaper for AL, FL (panhandle), GA, LA, MS, TN w/ resource listings*

Gyms & Health Clubs

The Blue Med Spa 190 10th St **404/815-8880** *10am-7pm, from 1pm Sun*

The Fitness Factory [★GF] 749 Moreland Ave SE **404/627-3977** *full gym*

Men's Clubs

Club Eros Atlanta [MO,PC] 2219 Faulkner Rd **404/287-4482** *8pm-6am, clsd Mon-Tue, "social club exists to support homosexual males who share the ideals of the swingers lifestyle & the right of private assembly," check web (www.cluberosatlanta.com) for details*

The Den [MO,MR-AF,PC] 334 N Clarendon Ave, Ste D, Scottsdale **404/292-7746**

Flex [SW,WI] 76 4th St NW (at Spring St) **404/815-0456** *24hrs*

Men's Services

▶ **Megaphone 404/244-7000** *Meet and Chat Live with HOT local men. FREE to listen & respond to ads. Video and text chat at GayMates.com. Use FREE code 4889.*

Erotica

Inserection 1739 Cheshire Bridge Rd **404/262-9113**

Inserection 505 Peachtree St NE **404/888-0878** *call for other locations*

Lollipop Adult Treats 3165 Roswell Rd (at Peachtree St) **404/816-8299** *24hrs*

The Poster Hut, Inc 2175 Cheshire Bridge Rd (at Piedmont Rd) **404/633-7491**

Southern Nights Videos 2205 Cheshire Br Rd (at Woodland Ave NE) **404/728-0701** *24hrs*

Starship 2275 Cheshire Bridge Rd **404/320-9101, 800/215-1053** *24hrs, many locations in Atlanta*

Cruisy Areas

Piedmont Park [AYOR] 10th St (at Monroe)

Augusta

see also Aiken, South Carolina

Accommodations

► **Parliament Resort** [MO,L,V,18+,BYOB,SW,N,WI,PC,GO] 1250 Gordon Hwy **706/722-1155** *24hrs, motel complex w/ hot tub, pride shop, cafe, video lounge, maze, novice dungeon*

Nightclubs

Club Argos [NH,D,TG,K,DS,V,GO] 1923 Walton Way (at Heckle) **706/481-8829** *7pm-3am, clsd Sun, 2 stories*

Big Canoe

Accommodations

Shooting Star Falls [GF,GO] 6243 Windflower Dr **404/358-7432** *rental cabin in mtns, 2 fireplaces, hot tub*

Blue Ridge

Accommodations

Black Bear Cabin Rentals [GF,NS] 1901 Appalachian Hwy **706/632-4794, 888/902-2246** *67 cabins in the Blue Ridge Mtns*

Carrollton

Cruisy Areas

Lake Carroll Park [AYOR]

Cartersville

Erotica

► **The Lion's Den Adult Superstore** 33 Kent Dr (exit 296, off I-75) **770/607-5113** *24hrs*

Columbus

Erotica

Foxes Cinema 3009 Victory Dr **706/689-2211**

MACA Bookstore 3016 Victory Dr **706/689-2212** *9am-11:30pm, booths*

Cruisy Areas

Cooper Creek Park [AYOR] 4816 Milgen Rd

Flat Rock Park [AYOR] 6250 Warm Springs Road

Dahlonega

Accommodations

Mountain Laurel Creek [GS,NS,GO] 202 Talmer Grizzle Rd (at Hwy 19 & McDonald Rd) **706/867-8134** *B&B, full brkfst, jacuzzi, garden, creek*

Restaurants

Smith House 84 S Chestatee St **706/867-7000, 800/852-9577** *lunch & dinner, clsd Mon, family-style Southern*

Dalton

Restaurants

Dalton Depot 110 Depot St **706/226-3150** *11am-9pm, till 10pm Th-Sat, from 11:30am Sun*

Decatur

see Atlanta

Dewy Rose

Accommodations

The River's Edge [M,F,E,SW,N,NS,WC] 2311 Pulliam Mill Rd **706/213-8081** *cabins, camping, RV*

Lake Lanier

Entertainment & Recreation

Gay Cove btwn Athens Park Rd & Frank Boyd Rd (Channel Marker 21) *a rainbow rendezvous for the pleasure-boating crowd—look for the rainbow flag*

Macon

Nightclubs

Club Synergy [★MW,D,K,S,WC] 425 Cherry St (at MLK, Jr Blvd) **478/755-9383** *9pm-close, clsd Sun-Tue, 4 bars*

Cruisy Areas

Central City Park [AYOR] Walnut St (at 7th)

Rest Area [AYOR] I-475 bypass (off I-75, after Mercer University Dr)

Marietta

see Atlanta

Rabun Gap

Accommodations

The York House [GF,NS,WC] 416 York House Rd **706/746-2068, 800/231-9675** *1896 historic country inn, located btwn Clayton & Dillard, full brkfst*

Savannah

Info Lines & Services

First City Network 307 E Harris St **912/236-2489** *info & events line, social group, newsletter*

Accommodations

912 Barnard Victorian B&B [MW,NS,GO] 912 Barnard St **912/234-9121** *fireplaces, period furnishings, garden*

The Azalea Inn [GF,SW,NS] 217 E Huntingdon St (at Abercorn St) **912/236-2707, 800/582-3823** *19th-c Italianate, vintage gardens, full Southern brkfst*

Catherine Ward House Inn [GS,WI] 118 E Waldburg St (at Abercorn) **912/234-8564, 800/327-4270** *Victorian Italianate B&B, full brkfst*

Kehoe House [GF,WI] 123 Habersham St **912/232-1020, 800/820-1020** *period antiques & modern conveniences, full brkfst*

Mansion on Forsyth Park [GF,NS,WI,WC] 700 Drayton St **912/238-5158, 888/711-5114** *restored Victorian mansion in historic district*

My Beach House Rentals on Tybee [MW,WI] 1204 2nd Ave, Tybee Island **912/484-8397** *oceanfront condos & vintage beach condos*

Park Avenue Manor [GF,NS] 107-109 W Park Ave **912/233-0352** *1889 Victorian B&B, full brkfst*

Statesboro Inn [GF,WI] 106 S Main, Statesboro **912/489-8628, 800/846-9466** *on Nat'l Register of Historic Places, full brkfst*

Thunderbird Inn [GF,NS,WI,GO] 611 W Oglethorpe Ave (at MLK Blvd) **912/232-2661, 866/324-2661**

Tybee Beach Condo [NS,WC,GO] 1217 Bay St Unit 105B (at Hwy 80 E), Tybee Island **404/320-3280, 404/933-5347** *20 minutes to Savannah*

Tybee Vacation Rentals [GF,SW,NS,WI] 1207 Hwy 80 E (at McKenzie), Tybee Island **912/786-5853, 866/359-0297** *rental homes, cottages & condos, some gay-owned*

Under the Rainbow Inn [GS,NS,GO] 104-106 West 38th St **912/790-1005**

Bars

Blaine's Backdoor Bar & Meat Rack Deli [M,NH,B,L,F,WC,GO] 13 E Perry St (enter rear) **912/233-6765** *2pm-3am, clsd Sun*

Chuck's Bar [GS,NH,YC] 305 W River St **912/232-1005** *8pm-3am, from 7pm Th-Sat, clsd Sun*

Venus Di Milo [MW] 38 MLK Jr Blvd **912/447-0901** *5pm-3am, clsd Sun*

Nightclubs

Club One [MW,D,F,C,DS,S,V] 1 Jefferson St (at Bay) **912/232-0200** *5pm-3am, till 2am Sun, "home of the Lady Chablis"*

Restaurants

Churchill's Pub 13 W Bay St **912/232-8501** *5pm-10pm, till 11pm Fri-Sat, from noon Sat*

Clary's Cafe 404 Abercorn (at Jones) **912/233-0402** *7am-4pm, 8am-5pm Sat, 8am-4pm Sun, country cookin'; also 4330 Habersham St, 912/351-0302, open till 9pm*

The Distillery [WC] 416 W Liberty St **912/236-1772**

Fannie's on the Beach 1613 Strand Ave (at Silver Ave), Tybee Island **912/786-6109** *noon-11pm, till 2am wknds*

Firefly Cafe [WC] 321 Habersham St **912/234-1971**

Wright Square Cafe [GO] 21 E York St **912/238-1150** *7:30am-5pm, from 9am Sat, clsd Sun, large chocolate selection, patio*

Entertainment & Recreation

Savannah Walks, Inc [GF] **888/728-9255** *walking tours of downtown Savannah*

Men's Services

▶ **Megaphone 912/344-9494** *Meet and Chat Live with HOT local men. FREE to listen & respond to ads. Video and text chat at GayMates.com. Use FREE code 4889.*

Erotica

Home Run Video & News [GO] 4 E Liberty St (at Bull St) **912/236-5192** *large LGBT section*

Sea Island

Restaurants

The Georgian Room [R] 100 Cloister Dr (in The Cloister) **912/634-4353, 800/732-4752 x 4347** *6pm-10pm, clsd Sun-Mon, upscale American, coat & tie required*

Unadilla

Accommodations

Lumberjack's Camping Resort [M,SW,GO] 50 Hwy 230 (at Hwy 41) **478/783-2267, 877/888-1688** *200 campsites & 85 RV hookups, on 150 acres, jacuzzi, also restaurant*

Erotica

▶ **Lion's Den** 790 Pine St (Exit 121, off I-75) **478/627-2782** *24hrs*

▶ **The Lion's Den Adult Superstore** 790 Pine St (exit 121 off I-75) **478/627-2782**

Valdosta

Cruisy Areas

Langdale Park [AYOR] N Valdosta Rd *days*

Washington

Accommodations

Holly Court Inn [GF,WI] 301 S Alexander Ave (at Water St) **706/678-3982, 866/465-5928** *historic home 1 hour from Augusta & Athens, full brkfst*

HAWAII

Please note that cities are grouped by islands:
Hawaii (Big Island)
Kauai
Maui
Molokai
Oahu (includes Honolulu)

Statewide

Accommodations

Pacific Ocean Holidays Oahu **808/545-5252, 800/735-6600** *"Hawaii vacations for gay men & women"*

Entertainment & Recreation

Hawaii Scuba Divers 866/926-3483 *"gay-friendly scuba diving lessons & tours in the state of Hawaii"*

HAWAII (BIG ISLAND)

Info Lines & Services

▶ **Leis of Hawaii 888/534-7644** *personalized Hawaiian greeting service, complete w/ fresh flower leis*

Men's Services

▶ **Megaphone 808/930-3300** *Meet and Chat Live with HOT local men. FREE to listen & respond to ads. Video and text chat at GayMates.com. Use FREE code 4889.*

Captain Cook

Accommodations

Affordable Hawaii at Pomaika'i (Lucky) Farm B&B [GS,NS] 83-5465 Mamalahoa Hwy **808/328-2112, 800/325-6427** *working, century-old Kona farm, full brkfst*

Aloha Guest House [GS,N,NS,WI,WC,GO] 84-4780 Mamalahoa Hwy **808/328-8955, 800/897-3188** *full brkfst, hot tub, ocean views*

Areca Palms Estate B&B [GF,NS] **808/323-2276, 800/545-4390** *full brkfst, jacuzzi*

Diver Dan's B&B Hawaii [M,GO] PO Box 842, 96726 **808/328-9546** *view of Kona coastline, diving & snorkeling*

Hale Lana at Kealakekua Bay [GF,NS,WI,GO] 82-6277 Kahauloa St (at Kahauloa Rd) **808/328-7338** *luxurious pole house rental near snorkeling at Kealakekua Bay, hot tub*

Horizon Guest House [GS,SW,NS,WC,GO] **808/328-2540, 888/328-8301** *full brkfst*

Ka'awa Loa Plantation [GS,NS,WI,WC,GO] PO Box 1280, Kealakekua 96750 **808/323-2686** *plantation-style B&B on 5-acre start-up coffee farm & orchard near Kealakekua Bay, hot tub*

Kealakekua Bay B&B [GS,NS] **808/328-8150, 800/328-8150** *villa & 2-bdrm guesthouse*

Rainbow Plantation B&B [GF,NS] **808/323-2393, 800/494-2829** *on coffee & macadamia plantation, kayak rentals*

Hilo

Info Lines & Services

Aloha Coast Realty, LLC [GO] 330 Kamehameha Ave (at Mamo) **808/934-7600, 808/987-9243 (cell)** *Big Island real estate agents*

Accommodations

Mele Kohola [GF,NS,WI] 15-991 Paradise Dr (Paradise Ala Kai) **808/965-0400** *vacation rental*

Oceanfront B&B [GF,WC] 1923 Kalanianaole St (3 miles from intersection of Hwys 11 & 19) **808/934-9004, 800/363-9524** *2 units w/ ocean views*

Cafes

Kope-Kope [WI] 1261 Kilauea Ave #220 (in Hilo Shopping Center) **808/933-1221** *6:30am-9pm, from 7:30am wknds, till 3pm Sun, espresso bar*

Restaurants

Cafe Pesto 308 Kamehameha Ave **808/969-6640** *pizzas, salads, pastas*

The Planet Cafe [E,BYOB,WO] 187 Kilauea Ave (at Ponahawii) **808/640-1777** *7am-8pm, 9am-3pm Sat-Sun*

Entertainment & Recreation

Richardson Beach at end of Kalanianaole Ave (Keaukaha)

Bookstores

Borders 301 Maka'ala St (at Kanoelehua Hwy) **808/933-1410** *LGBT section*

Retail Shops

Pride Project [GO] 223-B Kilauea Ave (at Ponahawaii) **808/935-5566** *LGBT community center & thrift store*

Cruisy Areas

Reeds "Gay" Bay Tearooms [AYOR] Banyan Dr *1st beach S of the hotels*

Honaunau-Kona

Accommodations

Dragonfly Ranch Healing Arts Center [GS,NS,WI] 1 1/2 miles down City of Refuge Rd **808/328-2159** *near ancient sanctuary w/ friendly dolphins*

Kailua-Kona

Accommodations

1st Class B&B Kona Hawaii [GF,NS,WI] 77-6504 Kilohana St **808/329-8778, 888/769-1110** *full brkfst, ocean views*

KonaLani Coffee Plantation Inn [MW,NS,WI,GO] 76-5917H Mamalahoa Hwy **808/324-0793** *B&B inn, full brkfst*

Puako B&B [GS,SW,NS,GO] 25 Puako Beach Dr **808/882-1331, 800/910-1331** *on Kohala coast, 30 minutes N of Kona Int'l, "the most Hawaiian B&B on the island of Hawaii"*

Royal Kona Resort [GF,F,E,SW,WC] 75-5852 Ali'i Dr **808/329-3111, 800/222-5642** *overlooking Kailua Bay, private beach*

BARS

Mask-querade Bar & Grill [★MW,NH,D,B,E,K] 75-5660 Kopiko St (at Cathedral Plaza) **808/329-8558** *10am-2am, only gay & lesbian bar on the island*

RESTAURANTS

Huggo's [E,K] 75-5828 Kahakai Rd (on Kailua Bay) **808/329-1493** *11:30am-2:30pm, dinner 5pm-10pm, bar open later, waterfront dining, seafood & steak, also bar, patio*

GYMS & HEALTH CLUBS

Hawaii Healing Ohana Spa [GO] 75-5799 Ali'i Dr A3 (Ali'i Sunset Plaza) **808/331-1050**

CRUISY AREAS

67 Beach Old Puako Rd *take Rte 19 N to Puako Beach Rd, take 1st right onto Old Puako Rd, look for telephone pole #67*

Honokohau Beach [AYOR] 5 miles S of airport, Kailua-Kona *far N end of beach*

Kahaluu Beach Park [AYOR]

Kamuela

ACCOMMODATIONS

Waimea Views Guest House [GS,WI,WO] 65-1546 Kawaihae Rd (at Paki Pl) **808/885-8559** *on the slopes of Mauna Kea*

Kehena

ACCOMMODATIONS

Kehena Beach Guesthouse [GS,GO] 12-7114 Waioleka St, Puna Beach Palisades **808/965-8625**

Ninole

ACCOMMODATIONS

Pu'u Puanani Vacation Estate [GS,NS,GO] **808/963-6789** *2 units in 1 guesthouse on 11 acres, hot tub, ocean views*

Pahala

ACCOMMODATIONS

Hale O Luna [GS,NS,WI,GO] 963181 Pikake St (at Hwy 11) **808/640-1113** *grand restored plantation home*

Pahoa

ACCOMMODATIONS

Absolute Paradise B&B [M,SW,N,NS,WI,GO] **808/965-1828, 888/285-1540** *B&B, outdoor hot tub, some shared baths*

Coconut Cottage B&B [GS,GO] 13-1139 Leilani Ave (at Oneloa St) **808/965-0973, 866/204-7444**

Hale Hulili [GS,NS,WI,GO] 14-3551 Kahoolawe Circle (at Flower Rd) **323/864-9226, 800/662-4464** *Hawaiian-style rental home in the rain-forest*

Hale 'Ohai [GS,NS,GO] **415/255-2497 (CA #)** *unique modern rental home amid giant monkeypod ('ohai) trees; 15-minute walk to clothing-optional beach*

Isle of You—Hawaii Farm & Retreat [M,NS,GO] **808/965-1639** *cabin & yurts on naturist farm retreat*

Kalani Oceanside Retreat [GS,F,SW,N,NS,WI,WC,GO] **808/965-7828, 800/800-6886** *coastal wellness retreat & spa, hot tub*

Pamalu—Hawaiian Country House [GS,SW,NS,WI,GO] **808/965-0830** *country retreat on 5 secluded acres*

Paradise Cliffs B&B [MW,NS,WI,GO] **808/965-8640** *B&B, ocean views, lesbian-owned*

Scott St Properties [NS,WI,GO] 12-86 Anuenue Wawae, Kaimu **800/484-6394x8466** *cozy treehouse*

Entertainment & Recreation

Kehena Beach off Hwy 137 (trailhead at 19-mile marker phone booth) *lava rock trail to clothing-optional black-sand beach*

Rainbow Adventures [GO] **808/965-9011** *custom-made remote land & sea excursions*

Cruisy Areas

Steam Vents [AYOR] 3 miles S of Pahoa on Keaau-Pahoa Rd *early evenings*

Volcano Village

Accommodations

The Chalet Kilauea Collection [GF,NS] 998 Wright Rd **808/967-7786, 800/937-7786** *full brkfst, hot tub*

Hale Ohia Cottages [GS,NS,WI,GO] **808/967-7986, 800/455-3803** *hot tub*

Volcano Artist Cottage [GF,WI] 19-3834 Old Volcano Rd (at Wright Rd) **808/985-8979**

Kauai

Info Lines & Services

▶ **Leis of Hawaii 888/534-7644** *personalized Hawaiian greeting service, complete w/ fresh flower leis*

Men's Services

▶ **Megaphone 808/240-3300** *Meet and Chat Live with HOT local men. FREE to listen & respond to ads. Video and text chat at GayMates.com. Use FREE code 4889.*

Anahola

Accommodations

Aliomanu Palms—A Beachfront Vacation Rental [GS] 4880 Aliomanu Rd (at Kuhio Hwy) **831/438-2800** *vacation rental, located on the beach*

Mahina Kai Ocean Villa [★GS,SW,N,NS,GO] 4933 Aliomanu Rd **808/822-9451, 800/337-1134** *B&B villa, hot tub, near gay beach*

Hanalei

Nightclubs

Tahiti Nui [GF,D,F,E,K,WC] 5-5134 Kuhio Hwy (near Hanalei Center) **808/826-6277** *11am-2am, also restaurant*

Kalaheo

Accommodations

Kalanikai B&B [M,SW,NS,WI,GO] 2777 Wawae Dr **808/332-5149, 888/552-2777** *hot tubs, on sunny S shore*

Kapaa

Accommodations

17 Palms Kauai [GS,NS,WI,WC,GO] **808/822-5659, 888/725-6799** *2 secluded cottages 200 steps from beach*

Anuenue Plantation B&B [M,NS,WI,GO] **808/823-8335, 888/371-7716** *plantation house w/ mtn views, full brkfst*

Fern Grotto Inn [GS,WI,NS] 4561 Kuamoo Rd (at Kuhio Hwy), Kapaa **808/821-9836**

Mohala Ke Ola B&B Retreat [GF,SW,NS,WI,GO] 5663 Ohelo Rd (at Kuamoo Rd/ Hwy 580) **808/823-6398, 888/465-2824** *jacuzzi, lomilomi massage*

Restaurants

Eggbert's [★] 4-484 Kuhio Hwy (in Coconut Plantation Marketplace) **808/822-4422** *7am-2am, also Hula Girl Grill for dinner*

Mema 4-369 Kuhio Hwy (in shopping center) **808/823-0899** *lunch Mon-Fri, dinner nightly, Thai & Chinese*

Cruisy Areas

Cocunut Marketplace 484 Kuhio Hwy (NW corner)

Donkey Beach [AYOR] off Hwy 56, N of Kapaa (btwn 11 & 12-mile markers) *walk along cane field, down through ironwood trees & then to the right on the dirt road to the beach*

Kilauea

Accommodations

Kauai Vacation Hideaway [MW,NS,WC] North Shore **808/828-0228, 888/858-6562** *over-looks Pacific, private path to secluded beach, jacuzzi, 4-day minimum*

Cruisy Areas

Secret Beach [AYOR] *inquire locally*

Lihue

Accommodations

Hilton Kauai Beach Resort [GF,SW] 4331 Kauai Beach Dr **808/245-1955, 888/805-3843** *jacuzzi, also restau-rant/ bar*

Entertainment & Recreation

Lydgate State Park Beach off Hwy 56 btwn Lihue & Kapaa (S of Wailua River) *gay beach btwn the condos & the golf course*

Bookstores

Borders Bookstore & Cafe 4303 Nawiliwili Rd (in Kukui Grove Center) **808/246-0862** *9am-10pm, till 11pm Fri-Sat, 8am-8pm Sun, large LGBT section*

Poipu Beach

Accommodations

The Makahuena [GS,SW] 1661 Pe'e Rd **808/742-2482, 800/367-5004**

Poipu Plantation B&B Inn & Vacation Rental Suites [GS,NS,WI,GO] 1792 Pe'e Rd **808/742-6757, 800/634-0263** *rooms & cottages, hot tub*

Princeville

Accommodations

Kauai Oceanfront Condo [GS,SW,NS] 5300 Ka Haku Rd **610/793-7539**

Puunene

Restaurants

Roy's Poipu Bar & Grill 2360 Kiahuna Plantation Dr **808/742-5000** *5:30pm-9:30pm, Hawaiian fusion*

Wailua

Restaurants

Caffe Coco [E,BYOB] 4-369 Kuhio Hwy **808/822-7990** *lunch Tue-Fri, dinner nightly, clsd Mon*

Waimea

Accommodations

▶ **Aston Waimea Plantation Cottages** [GF,SW] **808/338-1625, 800/992-4632** *seaside cottages from restored plantation homes*

MAUI

Info Lines & Services

Both Sides Now *LGBT community resources & events*

▶ **Leis of Hawaii 888/534-7644** *personalized Hawaiian greeting service, complete w/ fresh flower leis*

Men's Services

▶ **Megaphone 808/270-3300** *Meet and Chat Live with HOT local men. FREE to listen & respond to ads. Video and text chat at GayMates.com. Use FREE code 4889.*

Haiku

Accommodations

Hale Malie Maui [GF,NS,WI,WC,GO] 65 N Holokai Rd **808/573-6848, 888/203-2113** *condo, ocean views, lush tropical gardens, near windsurfing & big wave surfing*

Huelo Point Flower Farm [GF,SW,WI] **808/572-1850** *vacation rentals, oceanfront estate*

Hana

Accommodations

The Guest Houses at Malanai [GF,NS,GO] Hana Hwy **808/248-8818**

Hale Ohia [GS] 49625 Hana Hwy (at mile marker 27) **808/248-7045** *rental home, hot tub*

Hana Accommodations [GS,GO] **808/248-7868, 800/228-4262** *studios & tropical cottages, hot tub*

Na Pualani 'Ohana [GS,GO] **808/248-8935** *studios & suites*

Huelo

Accommodations

Cliff's Edge [GF,WI] **808/572-4530, 866/262-6284** *rental properties*

Kaanapali

Accommodations

The Royal Lahaina Resort [GF,F, SW,WC] 2780 Kekaa Dr **808/661-3611, 800/222-5642** *full-service resort*

Kihei

Info Lines & Services

AA Gay/ Lesbian 131 S Kihei Rd (at Bridge Center) **808/244-9673** *6pm Fri*

AA Gay/ Lesbian Kalama Park South Pavilion **808/244-9673** *7:30am Sun*

Accommodations

Andrea's Maui Condos [GS,SW,NS,WC,GO] **800/289-1522** *1- & 2-bdrm beachfront condos, lesbian-owned*

► **Anfora's Dreams** [GS,SW,GO] **323/467-2991, 800/788-5046** *rental condo near ocean, hot tub*

Best Western Maui Oceanfront Inn [GS] 2980 S Kihei Rd **808/879-7744, 800/263-3387** *hotel*

Eva Villa [GF,WI,WC] 815 Kumulani Dr **808/874-6407, 800/884-1845** *near Wailea beaches*

Koa Lagoon [GF,SW,WC] 800 S Kihei Rd **808/879-3002, 800/367-8030** *oceanfront suites*

Maui Studio [GS,SW,NS,GO] 1993 S Kihei Rd #401 **808/357-0802** *inexpensive rentals*

▶ **Maui Sunseeker Resort** [MW,NS,WI,GO] 551 S Kihei Rd (at Wailana Place) **808/879-1261, 800/532-6284** *beachfront island hideaway*

Two Mermaids on Maui B&B [GS,SW,NS,GO] 2840 Umalu Pl **808/874-8687, 800/598-9550** *jacuzzi, near beach*

Nightclubs

Oceans Bar & Grill [GF,D,K] 1819 S Kihei Rd (in Kukui Mall) **808/891-2414** *10pm-2am*

Cafes

Cafe at La Plage 2395 S Kihei Rd (at Kam Beach I) **808/875-7668** *7am-5pm, till 3pm Sun*

Restaurants

Jawz Tacos 1279 S Kihei Rd **808/874-8226** *11am-9pm, fresh fish tacos*

Stella Blues [E,WC] 1279 S Kihei Rd (in Azeka II Shopping Center) **808/874-3779** *7:30am-11pm*

Erotica

The Love Shack 1913 S Kihei Rd **808/875-0303** *men's intimate apparel, DVDs*

Cruisy Areas

Kalama Park [AYOR]

Kula

Accommodations

The Upcountry B&B [GF] 4925 Lower Kula Rd (at Copp St) **808/878-8083** *jacuzzi, pets ok*

Lahaina

Accommodations

▶ **Aston Maui Kaanapali Villas** [GF,F,SW,WC] 45 Kai Ala Dr **808/667-7791, 866/774-2924** *private condos on the beach*

Restaurants

Betty's Beach Cafe 505 Front St **808/662-0300** *8am-9pm, full bar*

Lahaina Coolers 180 Dickenson St **808/661-7082** *8am-1am, int'l, patio*

Retail Shops

Skin Deep Tattoo 626 Front St (across from the Banyan Tree) **808/661-8531** *10am-10pm, till 8pm Sun, tattooing, adult toys, T-shirts*

Cruisy Areas

Front St [AYOR] along Beach Walk

Makawao

Accommodations

Hale Ho'okipa Inn B&B [GF,NS,WI,WC] 32 Pakani Pl **808/572-6698, 877/572-6698** *gracious old Hawaiian plantation home; also Kipa Cottage, 1-bdrm + loft*

Restaurants

Casanova Restaurant & Deli [D,E] 1188 Makawao Ave **808/572-0220** *lunch & dinner, Italian, full bar till 2am, live music Wed-Sat*

Makena

Entertainment & Recreation

Little Beach at Makena [MW] *Pilani Hwy S to Wailea, right at Wailea Ike Dr, left on Wailea Alanui Dr to public beach, then take trail up hill at right end of beach*

Wailuku

Accommodations

Maalaea Kai Condo [GF] 70 Hauoli St (Maalaea Village), Wailuku **562/301-3820**

Molokai

Kaunakakai

Restaurants

Kanemitsu Bakery & Coffee Shop 79 Ala Malama St **808/553-5855** *5:30am-6:30pm, clsd Tue, great sweet bread*

Oahu

Publications

Odyssey Magazine Hawaii **808/955-5959** *everything you need to know about gay Hawaii*

Aiea

Erotica

Video Warehouse 98-019 Kamehameha Hwy (at Hekaha St) **808/487-1750** *24hrs, booths*

Honolulu

Info Lines & Services

The Center *LGBT community website, alohapridecenter.org*

Gay/ Lesbian AA 277 Ohua (at Waikiki Health Center, ground flr) **808/946-1438 (Oahu Central Office #)**

▶ **Leis of Hawaii 888/534-7644** *personalized Hawaiian greeting service, complete w/ fresh flower leis*

Accommodations

Aqua Coconut Plaza [GF,SW,WC] 450 Lewers St (at Ala Wai, Waikiki) **808/923-8828** *boutique hotel near the Kuhio (gay) District*

Aqua Palms & Spa [GF,SW,NS,WC] 1850 Ala Moana Blvd (at Kalia & Ena) **808/947-7256, 866/406-2782** *boutique hotel w/ retro-Hawaiian style, full spa*

▶ **Aston Waikiki Circle Hotel** [GF,NS] 2464 Kalakaua Ave (at Uluniu St, Waikiki) **808/923-1571, 877/997-6667** *overlooking Waikiki Beach*

▶ **Aston Waikiki Joy Hotel** [★GF,F,K,SW,NS,WC] 320 Lewers St (at Kalakaua Ave, Waikiki) **808/923-2300, 866/774-2924** *boutique hotel*

at the "Home of World Famous Hula's"
Stay & Play
Waikiki Grand Hotel
Book Online NOW!*
waikikigrand.com dhbhotel.com
*TWO FREE MAI TAIs @Hula's per Stay!
HULA'S
2007
BEST
BARS
HONOLULU
BAR & LEI STAND
WAIKIKI
BEACH BAR AND DISCO
GO TO: HULAS.COM
Catamaran
Smoke Lounge
FREE W I F I
Pool Table
Dancing
DJs Nightly
GoGo Boyz
Food Specials
(Fri - Mon
5pm - 9pm)
FREE Online
iMacs

Suite Paradise
Beautiful Newly Renovated Suites
Steps from Queens Surf beach, Hula's and Gym
Waikiki's Only Gay Place to Stay
For Reservation Call Toll-free:
1-877-902-2121
(808) 926-5555
www.cabana-waikiki.com
THE CABANA WAIKIKI

▶ **The Cabana at Waikiki** [★M,GO] 2551 Cartwright Rd (off Kapahulu Ave) **808/926-5555, 877/902-2121** *1-bdrm suites w/ kitchens & lanais, 8-man spa, 1 block to gay Queen's Surf beach & 1/2 block to Hula's*

Hotel Renew [GF,WI] 129 Paoakalani Ave (Waikiki Beach) **808/687-7700**

Waikiki GLBT Vacation Rentals [GF,SW,NS,WC] **808/922-1659** *ask for Walt Flood*

Waikiki Grand Hotel [M,NS] 134 Kapahulu Ave **808/923-1814, 888/336-4368** *rentals above Hula's Bar, close to gay beach*

Bars

Angles [MW,NH,D,S,V] 2256 Kuhio Ave, 2nd flr (at Seaside, Waikiki) **808/926-9766, 808/923-1130 (infoline)** *10am-2am, DJ Wed-Sun, male dancers Th & Sun, catamaran cruise 1pm Sun*

Chiko's Tavern [GS,F,K] 930 McCully St **808/949-5440** *4pm-2am*

In Between [M,NH,K] 2155 Lau'ula St (off Lewers, across from Planet Hollywood, Waikiki) **808/926-7060** *4pm-2am*

Tapa's Restaurant & Lanai Bar [GS,E,F,GO] 407 Seaside, 2nd flr (at Kuhio Ave) **808/921-2288** *9am-2am, lanai bar, also restaurant for dinner & Sun brunch*

Nightclubs

Bar 7 [GS,D,MR-A,S,YC] 1349 Kapiolani Blvd (below China House restaurant, at Piikoi) **808/955-2640** *9pm-4am, [DS] Sat*

Fusion Waikiki [★M,D,TG,K,DS,S,V] 2260 Kuhio Ave, 2nd flr (at Seaside) **808/924-2422** *10pm-4am, from 8pm Fri-Sat, [K] Mon-Tue, [DS,S] Fri-Sat*

▶ **Hula's Bar & Lei Stand** [★M,D,TG,F,S,V,YC,WI] 134 Kapahulu Ave (2nd flr of Waikiki Grand Hotel) **808/923-0669** *10am-2am, near gay beach, go-go boys Th & Sun, weekly catamaran cruise*

Cafes

Cafe Hula Girl [WI,GO] 1888 Kalakaua Ave, C106 (in Waikiki Landmark Building) **808/979-2299** *8am-10pm, internet cafe, patio*

Mocha Java Cafe 1200 Ala Moana Blvd (in Ward Center) **808/591-9023** *8am-9pm, till 6pm Sun, outdoor seating*

Restaurants

Arancino Trattoria 2155 Kalakaua Ave (in Waikiki Beach Marriott) **808/922-4405**

Cafe Che Pasta [MW,D,E] 1001 Bishop St, Ste 108 (enter off Alakea St) **808/524-0004** *lunch & dinner Mon-Fri, clsd Sun, full bar*

Cafe Sistina [WC] 1314 S King St **808/596-0061** *lunch Mon-Fri, dinner nightly, northern Italian, full bar, live music wknds*

Cha Cha Cha 342 Seaside Ave **808/923-7797**

Cheeseburger in Paradise 2500 Kalakaua Blvd **808/923-3731** *7am-11pm, full bar*

Crouching Lion Inn Bar & Grill [MR,E,K,GO] 51-666 Kamehameha Hwy, Kaaawa **808/237-8981** *11am-9pm, full bar*

Eggs 'n' Things 1911-B Kalakaua Ave **808/949-0820** *6am-2pm, 5pm-10pm*

Hula Grill 2335 Kalakaua Ave (in Outrigger Hotel) **808/923-4852**

Indigo [E] 1121 Nu'uanu Ave **808/521-2900** *lunch Tue-Fri, dinner Tue-Sat, Eurasian*

Keo's in Waikiki [★R] 2028 Kuhio Ave **808/951-9355** *7am-11am & 4pm-10pm*

La Cucaracha 2446 Koa Ave **808/924-3366** *noon-11pm, Mexican, full bar*

Lulu's 2586 Kalakaua Ave **808/926-5222** *7am-4am, full bar*

Rock Island Cafe 131 Kaiulani Ave (off Kalakaua, in King's Village Waikiki) **808/923-8033** *old-fashioned soda fountain*

Sergios 449 Kapahulu Ave (nr the Zoo) **808/737-4461**

Singha Thai [E] 1910 Ala Moana Blvd **808/941-2898, 800/482-8424** *4pm-10pm*

Tikis 2570 Kalakaua Ave (in ResortQuest Hotel) **808/923-8454**

Entertainment & Recreation

Dolphin Quest 5000 Kahala Ave (at Kahala Hotel & Resort) **808/739-8918, 800/248-3316**

Honolulu Gay/ Lesbian Cultural Foundation 1877 Kalakaua Ave **808/381-1952** *last wknd of May Honolulu Rainbow Film Festival*

LikeHike 808/455-8193 *gay hiking tours every other Sun*

Queen's Surf Beach Kapiolani Park (off Kalakaua) *popular gay beach at far end of Kuhio Beach*

Rainbow Sailing Charters [MW,GO] **808/347-0235** *day & overnight sailing adventures, whale-watching, snorkeling, sunset cocktail cruises & commitment ceremonies, lesbian-owned*

Retail Shops

Bethel Street Gallery [GO] 1140 Bethel St (at Pauahi St) **808/524-3552** *11am-5pm, till 4pm Sat, clsd Sun-Mon, contemporary art by Hawaiian artists*

Douglas Simonson—Artists Studio 808/737-6275 *call for app't & location*

Eighty Percent Straight 134 Kapahulu Ave, Ste B (in Waikiki Grand Hotel) **808/923-9996** *10am-11pm, till midnight Fri-Sat, noon-11pm Sun, LGBT clothing, books, videos, cards, toys*

Over Easy Down Under 2301 Kuhio Ave, Ste 220 (Level 2, Waikiki Town Center) **808/926-4994** *10am-10pm, clsd Sun, men's swimwear & activewear*

Publications

Expression 808/393-7994 *monthly glossy LGBT magazine*

Odyssey Magazine Hawaii 808/955-5959 *everything you need to know about gay Hawaii*

Men's Clubs

Max's Gym [★V,18+,PC] 438 Hobron Ln, 4th flr (at Ala Moana Blvd, in Eaton Square) **808/951-8232** *24hrs, also Cafe Max*

Men's Services

▶ **Megaphone 808/599-6999** *Meet and Chat Live with HOT local men. FREE to listen & respond to ads. Video and text chat at GayMates.com. Use FREE code 4889.*

Erotica

Backseat Betty's 1687 Kapiolani Blvd **808/946-7301** *10am-2am*

Velvet Video 2155 Lau'ula St, 2nd flr (above In Between, Waikiki) **808/924-0868** *24hrs, booths, toys*

Waikiki Adult Video Entertainment 2270 Kuhio St (at Seaside Ave) **808/924-9283**

Cruisy Areas

Ala Moana Beach Park [AYOR] *near Waikiki Yacht Club*

Alan Davis Beach Rte 27 *turn past Sandy Beach but before Makapuu Point Lighthouse*

Diamond Head Rd [AYOR] *on trails across the street from the lighthouse*

Kailua

Accommodations

Haku's Hale [M,SW,WC,GO] **808/261-5834, 808/271-3368** *beautiful cottage attached to 1960s Hawaiian estate, 20 minutes from Waikiki*

Wahiawa

Erotica

Divine Pleasures 55 S Kamehameha Hwy (at Olive St), Wahiawa **808/621-8090** *24hrs, hustlers*

Windward Coast

Accommodations

Ali'i Bluffs Windward B&B [GS,SW,NS,GO] 46-251 Ikiiki St, Kane'ohe **808/235-1124, 800/235-1151**

Idaho

Statewide

Publications

Diversity Newsmagazine **208/286-6519** *statewide LGBT newspaper, monthly*

Boise

Info Lines & Services

The Community Center 305 E 37th St **208/336-3870** *volunteer staff*

Accommodations

Bed & Buns [MO,N,NS,WI,GO] **208/866-2759, 208/362-1802** *B&B, hot tub*

Courtyard by Marriott [GF,NS] 222 S Broadway Ave **208/331-2700, 800/321-2211**

Bars

The Lucky Dog [M,NH,B,L] 2223 W Fairview Ave (at 23rd) **208/333-0074** *2pm-2am, from noon wknds, patio, lounge*

Neurolux [GF,D,E] 111 N 11th St (at W Idaho) **208/343-0886** *noon-2am, live music*

Nightclubs

The Balcony Club [★MW,D,WC,GO] 150 N 8th St #226 (at Idaho) **208/336-1313** *4pm-2am, theme nights*

Emerald City Club [MW,D,TG,DS,WI,WC] 415 S 9th St (at Borah) **208/342-5446** *10am-2am*

Cafes

Big City Coffee 5517 W State St **208/853-9161** *6am-6pm, till 4pm Sun*

Flying M Coffeehouse [WI] 500 W Idaho (at 5th St) **208/345-4320** *6:30am-11pm, till 6pm Sun*

Lucy's Coffee & Espresso [WI] 1079 Broadway Ave **208/344-5907** *6am-10pm, 7am-8pm Sun, organic, fair trade coffee, gourmet pastries*

Tully's 794 Broad St **208/343-2953** *7am-9pm, till 11pm Fri-Sat, 9am-8pm Sun*

Restaurants

Lucky 13 Pizza 3662 S Eckert Rd **208/344-6967** *11am-10pm*

Entertainment & Recreation

The Flicks [F,E,BW,WC] 646 Fulton St **208/342-4222** *opens 4pm, from noon Fri-Sun, 4 movie theaters, patio*

Retail Shops

The Record Exchange 1101 W Idaho St (at 11th) **208/344-5383** *7am-10pm, from 9am wknds, till 7pm Sun, gifts, cards, music, also cafe*

Men's Services

Erotica

The O!Zone 1615 Broadway Ave **208/395-1977, 888/326-3713**

Pleasure Boutique 5022 Fairview (at Orchard) **208/433-1161** *toys, videos*

Cruisy Areas

Ann Morrison Park [AYOR] near baseball fields

Coeur d'Alene

see also Spokane, Washington

Accommodations

The Clark House on Hayden Lake [★GF,NS,WI,GO] 5250 E Hayden Lake Rd, Hayden Lake **208/772-3470, 800/765-4593** *mansion on 12-acre estate, full brkfst, hot tub*

Bars

Mik-N-Mac's [GS,NH,D,K,S] 406 N 4th (at Wallace) **208/667-4858** *4pm-2am, till 1am Mon*

Idaho Falls

Cruisy Areas

Freeman Park [AYOR] Science Center Dr (N of town)

Lava Hot Springs

see also Pocatello

Accommodations

Lava Hot Springs Inn [GF,SW,NS,WI] **208/776-5830, 800/527-5830** *full brkfst*

Bookstores

Aura Soma Lava 196 E Main St **208/776-5800, 800/757-1233** *7am-8pm, metaphysical & LGBT books*

Moscow

Bookstores

Bookpeople 521 S Main (btwn 5th & 6th) **208/882-7957** *9am-8pm*

Nampa

Cafes

Flying M Coffeegarage 1314 2nd St S **208/467-5533**

Pocatello

Nightclubs

Charleys [MW,D,E,WC] 331 E Center **208/232-9606** *5pm-2am, from 7pm Sun*

Cafes

Main St Coffee & News 234 N Main (btwn Lander & Clark) **208/234-9834** *6:30am-4pm, from 8am Sat, from 9am Sun*

Erotica

Main Street Video 657 N Main **208/235-9457**

Pegasus Book Store 246 W Center **208/232-6493**

The Silver Fox 143 S 2nd St (at Center) **208/234-2477**

Cruisy Areas

Ross Park [AYOR] *upper level*

Powell

Cruisy Areas

Jerry Johnson Hot Springs [AYOR] US 12 *days*

Twin Falls

Cafes

Caffe Mocha [F,WC] 591 Addison Ave W (at 8th St) **208/736-2003** *6am-6pm*

Restaurants

Pizza Planet 720 Main St (at 8th St), Buhl **208/543-8560** *11am-8pm, also video/ DVD store*

Cruisy Areas

City Park [AYOR] Shoshone & 4th Ave E

Rock Creek Park [AYOR] W on Hwy 30 *days*

Illinois

Publications

Out & About Illinois 11227 W Glen Ave, Peoria **309/693-3725**

Alsip

see also Chicago

Erotica

Slightly Sinful 12300 S Cicero (at 123rd) **708/388-6902**

Alton

see also St Louis, Missouri

Nightclubs

Bubby & Sissy's [MW,D,K,DS,WC] 602 Belle St (at 6th) **618/465-4773** *3pm-2am, till 3am Fri-Sat, clsd Mon, [DS] Fri-Sat*

Cruisy Areas

Rock Springs Park [AYOR] College Ave (at Rock Springs Dr)

Arlington Heights

see Chicago

Atkinson

Erotica

► **The Lion's Den Adult Superstore** 313 S State St (Exit 27, off I-80) **309/936-7066** *24hrs*

Aurora

see also Chicago

Erotica

Denmark Book Store 1300 US Hwy 30 (2 miles S of Rte 34) **630/898-9838** *24hrs*

Belleville

see St Louis, Missouri

Bloomington

Info Lines & Services

Connections Community Center [WI] 313 N Main St (at Monroe St) **309/827-2437, 866/694-5297** *call for hours & meeting times, LGBT library, HIV testing*

Bars

Bistro [MW,D,WI,WC] 316 N Main St (at Jefferson) **309/829-2278** *8pm-1am, from 4:30pm Fri, till 2am Fri-Sat*

The Shark [MW,NH] 3 Finance Dr **309/662-0717** *5pm-close*

Cafes

Coffee Hound [WI] 407 N Main St **309/827-7575** *6:30am-6pm, 8am-5pm Sun*

Kelly's Bakery & Cafe 113 N Center St **309/820-1200** *7am-6pm, till 2pm Sat, clsd Sun*

Blue Island

see also Chicago

Nightclubs

Club Krave [MW,NH,TG,K,C,DS,S,WC] 13126 S Western (at Grove) **708/597-8379** *8pm-2am, till 3am Fri-Sat, clsd Sun-Mon*

Bradley

Restaurants

La Villetta 801 W Broadway St **815/939-4960** *11am-9pm, till 8pm Sun, Italian*

Buckley

Erotica

▶ **The Lion's Den Adult Superstore** 362-E 800 North Rd (exit 272, off I-57) **217/394-2601** *24hrs*

Calumet City

see also Chicago & Hammond, Indiana

Cruisy Areas

Clayhole Woods, Shabonna Woods & Sandridge Forest Preserves [AYOR]

Carbondale

Info Lines & Services

AA Lesbian/ Gay 618/549-4633

Accommodations

The New Ranch [MO,SW,N,NS,GO] **618/833-7926** *wooded creekside campsite*

Nightclubs

Club Traz [GF,NH,D,E,S,V,GO] 213 E Main St **618/549-4270** *9pm-2am, clsd Mon-Tue & Th*

Flirt [MW,D,DS] 1215 E Walnut (at Sky Bar) *monthly party, check myspace.com/melissathebartender for dates*

Cruisy Areas

Crab Orchard Lake [AYOR] Cambria Neck Ln *exit off Rte 13 onto Cambria Rd, drive 1 mile N, on right side of Cambria Rd is side road called Cambria Neck Ln, turn right onto it*

Centreville

see also St Louis, Missouri

Nightclubs

Boxers 'n' Briefs [M,D,F,S,18+,WC,$] 55 Four Corners Ln (next to PT's Show Club) **618/332-6141** *7pm-4am, till 6am Fri-Sat, till 3am Sun, clsd Mon, nude dancers*

Champaign/ Urbana

Accommodations

Sylvia's Irish Inn [GF,NS,WI] 312 W Green St, Urbana **217/384-4800**

Bars

Mike 'N Molly's [GF,E] 105 N Market St, Champaign **217/355-1236** *4pm-2am, live music, beer garden*

Nightclubs

Chester Street [MW,D,DS,WC,GO] 63 Chester St (at Water St), Champaign **217/356-5607** *5pm-2am*

Cafes

Aroma Cafe [E] 118 N Neil St, Champaign **217/356-3200** *7am-10pm, from 8am wknds, live music Th*

Cafe Kopi [F,NS,WI] 109 N Walnut, Champaign **217/359-4266** *7am-midnight, full bar*

Espresso Royale 602 E Daniel (at 6th St), Champaign **217/328-1112** *7am-midnight*

Pekara Bakery & Bistro 116 N Neil St, Champaign **217/359-4500** *7am-9pm, from 8am Sun*

Restaurants

Boltini Lounge 211 N Neil, Champaign **217/378-8001** *4pm-2am, till 11pm Sun, also full bar, upscale*

The Courier Cafe 111 N Race St, Urbana **217/328-1811** *7am-11pm*

Dos Reales 1407 N Prospect Ave, Champaign **217/351-6879** *11am-10pm, Mexican*

Farren's Pub & Eatery 308 N Randolph St, Champaign **217/359-6977** *11am-9pm, till 10pm Fri, noon-10pm Sat, clsd Sun, American, full bar*

Fiesta Cafe [GO] 216 S 1st St (at White, near U of IL campus), Champaign **217/352-5902** *11am-11pm, bar till 1am, Mexican*

The Great Impasta 156C Lincoln Sq, Urbana **217/359-7377** *11am-9pm, till 10pm Fri, 5pm-10pm Sat, clsd Sun*

Radio Maria 119 N Walnut St, Champaign **217/398-7729** *lunch Tue-Fri, dinner Tue-Sat, brunch Sun, clsd Mon, eclectic Mexican cuisine, also tapas bar till 2am*

Silvercreek 402 N Race St, Urbana **217/328-3402** *lunch & dinner Mon-Sat, brunch Sun*

Retail Shops

Dandelion 9 Taylor St, Champaign **217/355-9333** *11am-6pm, noon-5pm Fri, vintage & used clothing*

Gyms & Health Clubs

Refinery [GF] 2302 W John St, Champaign **217/355-4444** *24hrs*

Erotica

Fantasy's 3604 N Cunningham (Cunningham exit off I-74 E), Urbana **217/328-1199** *24hrs, video booths*

Holiday Video/I-Block Arcade 213 S Neil St (btwn White & Clark), Champaign **217/351-8897** *video booths, basement theater*

Illini Video Arcade 33 E Springfield Ave (S Neil exit, off I-74), Champaign **217/359-8529** *24hrs*

Urbana News 602 Cunningham (next to Five Points Tavern), Urbana **217/384-0188** *24hrs*

Cruisy Areas

Crystal Lake Park [AYOR] at Park & University Sts, Urbana

Chicago

Chicago is divided into 5 geographical areas:
Chicago—Overview
Chicago—North Side
Chicago—Boystown/ Lakeview
Chicago—Near North
Chicago—South Side

Chicago—Overview

includes some listings for Greater Chicagoland; please check individual cities like Oak Park as well

Info Lines & Services

AA/ Newtown Alano Club [WC] 909 W Belmont Ave, 2nd flr (btwn Clark & Sheffield) **773/529-0321** *5pm-11pm, from 8:30am wknds*

The Center on Halsted 3656 N Halsted St (at Waveland) **773/472-6469, 773/472-1277 (TTY)** *8am-10pm, LGBT center, organic grocery store, cafe, theater, gym, technology center*

Center on Halsted Info Line 773/929-4357, 773/871-2273 (LGBT violence hotline) *8am-10pm, live counselors w/ info on wide variety of LGBT issues*

OPALGA (Oak Park Area Lesbian & Gay Association) Center 947 Garfield St, Oak Park **708/848-0273, 708/386-3463 (youth programs)** *9am-noon & 1pm-2pm Mon-Tue & Th-Fri, group also hosts variety of social & educational events*

Entertainment & Recreation

About Face Theatre 773/784-8565 *roving LGBT theater company w/ popular Youth Theatre as well*

Bailiwick Arts Center 1229 W Belmont Ave **773/883-1090 (box office #)** *many LGBT-themed productions, popular Pride Series*

Cafe Pride 716 W Addison St (at Broadway, at Lake View Presbyterian) **773/281-2655 (church #)** *coffeehouse for LGBT youth (17-24) only, 8pm-midnight Fri*

Chicago Neighborhood Tours [GF] 77 E Randolph St (at Chicago Cultural Center) **312/742-1190** *the best way to make the Windy City your kind of town*

GayCo 3656 N Halsted (at the Center) **312/458-9400, 773/478-6376** *sketch-comedy revues based on LGBT themes*

The Hancock Observatory 875 N Michigan Ave (in John Hancock Center) **312/751-3681, 888/875-8439** *9am-11pm, renovated 94th-flr observatory w/ outside Skywalk*

Heartland Cafe 7000 N Glenwood Ave (in Rogers Park) **773/465-8005** *cafe w/ full bar, theater, lots of live music*

Leather Archives & Museum 6418 N Greenview Ave **773/761-9200** *noon-8pm Th-Fri, till 5pm Sat-Sun, membership required (purchase at door)*

The Neo-Futurarium 5153 N Ashland Ave **773/275-5255** *alternative theater group*

Second City [GF,E] 1616 N Wells St (at North) **312/337-3992, 877/778-4707** *legendary comedy club, call for reservations*

Willis/ Sears Tower Skydeck 233 S Wacker Dr (enter at Jackson Blvd) **312/875-9696** *see the city from the 99th & 103rd floors of North America's tallest building*

Windy City Performing Arts 3023 N Clark St #329 **773/404-9242** *includes Windy City Gay Chorus, Aria: Windy City Women's Ensemble & Unison: Windy City Lesbian & Gay Singers*

Publications

The Alternative Phone Book 619 W Stratford Pl **773/472-6319** *directory of local businesses*

boi magazine 773/975-0264 *slick glossy w/ bar listings, articles, photos & circuit dish*

Chicago Free Press 773/868-0005 *LGBT newspaper*

Gay Chicago 773/327-7271 *weekly, extensive resource listings*

Identity 773/871-7610 *monthly news & features for LGBTs of color*

Nightspots 773/871-7610 *weekly LGBT nightlife magazine*

PINK Magazine 773/769-6328, 877/769-7465 *LGBT business directory & lifestyle magazine*

Windy City Times 773/871-7610 *weekly LGBT newspaper & calendar guide*

Men's Clubs

Windy City Bondage Club 312/409-7613 (hotline #) *members-only club for bondage & BDSM w/ play parties; guests welcome*

Men's Services

Cruisy Areas

Humboldt Park [AYOR] North Ave & Sacramento *near pavilion & bushes*

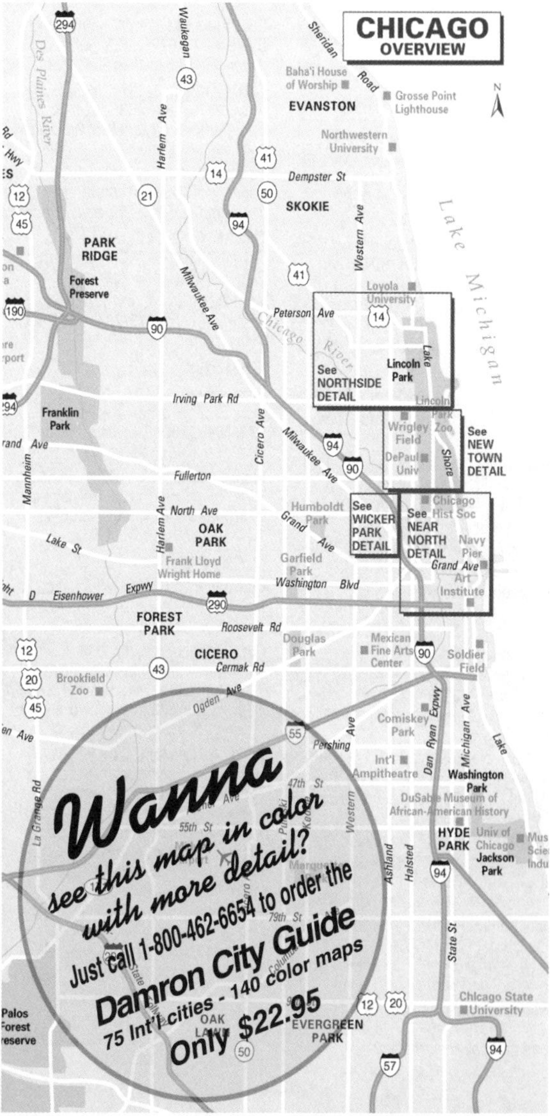
CHICAGO
OVERVIEW
Sheridan Road
Baha'i House of Worship
Grosse Point Lighthouse
EVANSTON
Northwestern University
Waukegan
Des Plaines River
Harlem Ave
Dempster St
SKOKIE
Western Ave
Lake Michigan
PARK RIDGE
Forest Preserve
Milwaukee Ave
Loyola University
Peterson Ave
Chicago River
See NORTHSIDE DETAIL
Lincoln Park
Lake Shore
Franklin Park
Irving Park Rd
Cicero Ave
Lincoln Park Zoo
Wrigley Field
DePaul Univ
See NEW TOWN DETAIL
Mannheim
Fullerton
North Ave
Humboldt Park
See WICKER PARK DETAIL
Chicago Hist Soc
See NEAR NORTH DETAIL
Navy Pier
Grand Ave
OAK PARK
Lake St
Frank Lloyd Wright Home
Garfield Park
Washington Blvd
Art Institute
Eisenhower Expwy
FOREST PARK
Roosevelt Rd
Douglas Park
Mexican Fine Arts Center
Soldier Field
CICERO
Cermak Rd
Brookfield Zoo
Ogden Ave
Dan Ryan Expwy
Comiskey Park
Pershing
Michigan Ave
Int'l Ampitheatre
Washington Park
47th St
DuSable Museum of African-American History
La Grange Rd
55th St
HYDE PARK
Univ of Chicago
Jackson Park
Ashland
Halsted
79th St
State St
Palos Forest Preserve
OAK LAWN
EVERGREEN PARK
Chicago State University
Wanna see this map in color with more detail?
Just call 1-800-462-6654 to order the
Damron City Guide
75 Int'l cities - 140 color maps
Only $22.95

Marquette Park [AYOR] 7100 S Kedzie Avenue (at 71st Street W) *use S entrance*

Chicago—North Side

Accommodations

The Ardmore House [M,WI,GO] 1248 W Ardmore Ave (at Magnolia) **773/728-5414** *Victorian B&B, full brkfst wknds, hot tub*

Ashland Arms [M,WI,GO] 6408 N Clark St (at Devon) **312/498-9979**

House 5863 [GS,NS,WI,GO] 5863 N Glenwood (at Admore) **773/944-5555** *contemporary B&B near historic Andersonville neighborhood*

Bars

The Anvil [M,NH,V] 1137 W Granville (E of Broadway) **773/973-0006** *9am-2am*

Big Chicks [MW,NH,D,F,V,WI,WC] 5024 N Sheridan (btwn Foster & Argyle) **773/728-5511** *4pm-2am, from 3pm wknds, patio, Sun BBQ*

Cattle Call [MW,D,CW,DS] 1547 W Bryn Mawr *4pm-2am*

Chicago Eagle [MW,L,WC] 5015 N Clark St (at Argyle) **773/728-0050** *8pm-4am, till 5am Sat, dress code Tue & Fri-Sat*

Crew [MW,F,V] 4804 N Broadway St (at Lawrence) **773/784-2739** *11:30am-midnight, 11am-2am Fri-Sun sports bar & grill, patio*

El Gato Negro [GS,D,MR-L,TG,E] 1461 W Irving Park (btwn Clark & Ashland) **773/472-9353** *noon-2am, till 3am Sat, live shows Sun*

Green Mill [★GS,E] 4802 N Broadway St (at Lawrence) **773/878-5552** *noon-4am, till 5am Sat, noted jazz venue, hosts the Uptown Poetry Slam*

Jackhammer [★M,NH,D,L,S,V] 6406 N Clark St (at Devon) **773/743-5772** *4pm-4am, till 5am Fri-Sat, from 2pm wknds, 3 bars patio*

Marty's [GF,F] 1511 W Balmoral Ave (at Clark) **773/561-6425** *5pm-2am, upscale wine & martini bar*

Scot's [M,NH] 1829 W Montrose (at Damen) **773/528-3253** *3pm-2am, 11am-3am Sat, till 2am Sun*

Sofo [M,NH,V] 4923 N Clark St (at Argyle) **773/784-7636** *5pm-2am, 3pm-3am Sat, till 2am Sun, video bar, backyard beer garden*

T's [GS,NH,F,WC] 5025 N Clark St (at Winnemac) **773/784-6000** *5pm-2am, 11am-3am, till 2am Sun, also restaurant*

Touché [★M,L] 6412 N Clark St (at Devon) **773/465-7400** *5pm-4am, 3pm-5am Sat, noon-4am Sun*

Wild Pug [M,D,WC] 4810 N Broadway St (at Lawrence) **773/784-4811** *4pm-2am*

Nightclubs

Atmosphere [MW,D,C,S,GO] 5355 N Clark St (at W Balmoral Ave) **773/784-1100** *6pm-2am, till 3am Sat, 3pm-2am Sun, clsd Mon, [S] Th-Sat*

Planet Claire [GS,D,V] 4000 N Sheridan Rd (at Irving Park, at the Holiday Club) **773/348-9600 (Holiday Club #)** *10pm-2am Fri only, New Wave*

Cafes

Charmer's Cafe [MW,WI,WC] 1500 W Jarvis (at Greenview) **773/743-2233** *6am-10pm, from 7am wknds*

Coffee Chicago [F,WI] 5256 N Broadway St (btwn Berwyn & Foster) **773/784-1305** *7am-9pm, till 9:30pm Fri, from 8am Sat, till 9pm Sun, also sandwiches, soups, smoothies, ice cream*

KOPI: A Traveler's Cafe [E] 5317 N Clark St (at Summerdale) **773/989-5674** *8am-11pm, till midnight Fri-Sat, from 9am Sat, from 10am Sun, coffee & tea, soup, sandwiches, & pastries; also boutique & gallery w/ travel books & art from around the world*

Metropolis Coffee [★WI] 1039 W Granville Ave (at Kenmore) **773/764-0400** *6:30am-8pm, from 7am Sat, from 7:30am Sun*

Restaurants

Andie's [WC] 5253 N Clark (btwn Berwyn & Farragut) **773/784-8616** *10:30am-midnight, till 10:30pm Sun, eastern Mediterranean, plenty veggie, full bar*

Deluxe Diner/ Maria's 6349 N Clark St (at Devon) **773/743-8244 (Deluxe #), 773/743-9900 (Maria's #)** *24hr diner & pizza/ Italian restaurant till 11pm*

Fireside 5739 N Ravenswood (at Rosehill) **773/561-7433, 877/878-7433** *11am-4am, till 5am Sat, 10am-4am Sun, Cajun & pizza, patio, full bar*

Hamburger Mary's [MW,E,K,DS] 5400 N Clark St (at Balmoral) **773/784-6969** *opens 11am, from 10am Sun, also full bar*

Pauline's 1754 W Balmoral (at Ravenswood) **773/561-8573** *7am-3pm, hearty brkfsts, home of 5-egg omelette*

Reza's Restaurant [WC] 5255 N Clark (btwn Berwyn & Farragut) **773/561-1898** *lunch, dinner & wknd brunch, Mediterranean/ Persian, plenty veggie, full bar*

Svea Restaurant [WC] 5236 N Clark (btwn Berwyn & Farragut) **773/275-7738** *7am-2:30pm, till 3:30pm wknds, Swedish/ American comfort food*

Tedino's [★WC] 5335 N Sheridan (at Broadway) **773/275-8100** *11am-11pm, till midnight wknds, pizza, full bar*

Thai Pastry & Restaurant 4925 N Broadway St, Unit E (at Argyle) **773/784-5399** *11am-10pm, till 11pm Fri-Sat*

Tweet [WI] 5020 N Sheridan Rd (at Argyle) **773/728-5576** *9am-3pm, clsd Tue, brkfst & brunch, cash only*

Unique So Chique Tea & Chocolate Room [GO] 4600 N Magnolia, Ste C (entrance on Wilson, next to Starbucks) **773/561-0324** *noon-6pm, from 10am Sat, clsd Mon, also boutique*

Entertainment & Recreation

Hollywood Beach [★] at Hollywood & Sheridan Sts *"the" gay beach*

Retail Shops

Enjoy, An Urban General Store 4727 N Lincoln Ave (Lincoln Square) **773/334-8626** *from 11am, from 10am Sat-Sun, cards & gifts, pride items*

Gaymart 3457 N Halsted St (at Cornelius) **773/929-4272** *11am-7pm, noon-8pm Fri, till 6pm Sun, lots of kitsch & pride items*

Mephisto Leathers North America [MW,GO] 6410 N Clark St (at Devon, btwn Jackhammer & Touché) **773/508-0900, 800/910-0666** *noon-midnight, till 4am Th, till 5am Fri, till 6am Sat, 4pm-midight Sun-Mon*

Specialty Video Films [GO] 5307 N Clark St (at Berwin Ave) **773/878-3434** *10am-11pm, till midnight Fri-Sat, foreign, cult, art house, LGBT & erotic videos*

Gyms & Health Clubs

Cheetah Gym 5248 N Clark St (at Foster) **773/728-7777**

Sir Spa [GS,GO] 5151 N Clark St **773/217-7000**

Men's Clubs

Man's Country [PC,S] 5015 N Clark St (at Argyle) **773/878-2069** *24hrs, nude strippers Fri-Sat*

Erotica

Admiral Theater 3940 W Lawrence Ave (at Pulaski) **773/478-8111**

Banana Video 4923 N Clark (at Argyle, 2nd flr) **773/561-8322** *4pm-6am, arcade*

Cruisy Areas

Hollywood Beach [AYOR] along lake (at 5700 N)

Lincoln Park [AYOR] E of Lake Shore Dr (btwn Foster & Montrose)

Chicago—Boystown/ Lakeview

Accommodations

Best Western Hawthorne Terrace [GF,WI,WC] 3434 N Broadway St (at Hawthorne Pl) **773/244-3434, 866/378-9790** *in heart of Chicago's gay community, gym*

City Suites Hotel [GF,WI] 933 W Belmont Ave (btwn Clark & Sheffield) **773/404-3400, 800/248-9108** *European style*

Inn at Lincoln Park [GS,WI,GO] 601 W Diversey Pkwy (at N Clark St) **773/348-2810, 866/774-7275** *vintage Victorian inn in Lincoln Park*

Majestic Hotel [GF,NS,WI] 528 W Brompton Ave (at Addison) **773/404-3499, 800/727-5108** *romantic 19th-c atmosphere*

Roscoe Rooms [M,NS,GO] 1951 W Cornelia (at Damen) **773/281-4546, 773/392-4546** *2 rms in Queen Cottage in heart of Roscoe Village*

▶ **Villa Toscana B&B** [MW,NS,WI,GO] 3447 N Halsted St (at Cornelia) **773/404-2643, 800/404-2643** *1890s coach house*

The Willows [GS,WI] 555 W Surf St (at Broadway) **773/528-8400, 800/787-3108** *19th-c French flair*

Bars

3160 [MW,NH,E,WC] 3160 N Clark St (at Belmont) **773/327-5969** *3pm-2am, till 3am Sat*

Beat Kitchen [GF,F,E] 2100 W Belmont (btwn Hoyne & Damen) **773/281-4444** *4pm-2am, from 11:30am Fri-Sun, till 3am Sat, live bands, also grill*

Blues [★GF,E] 2519 N Halsted St (at Wrightwood) **773/528-1012, 773/549-9436** *8pm-2am, till 3am Sat, classic Chicago blues spot*

Bobby Love's [MW,NH,K,WC] 3729 N Halsted St (at Waveland) **773/525-1200** *3pm-2am, from noon wknds, till 3am Sat*

Buck's Saloon [M,NH] 3439 N Halsted St (btwn Cornelia & Newport) **773/525-1125** *noon-2am, till 3am Sat, 11am-2am Sun, beer garden on the street*

Cell Block [M,D,B,L,WC] 3702 N Halsted St (at Waveland) **773/665-8064** *4pm-2am, from 2pm wknds, also Holding Cell from 10pm Fri-Sat w/ strict leather/ latex/ uniform code*

Charlie's Chicago [M,D,CW,K] 3726 N Broadway St (btwn Waveland & Grace) **773/871-8887** *3pm-4am, till 5am Sat, club music after 1am*

The Closet [★MW,NH,V] 3325 N Broadway St (at Buckingham) **773/477-8533** *5pm-4am, noon-5am Sat, till 4am Sun, video bar*

Cocktail [MW,NH,D,S,V,WC] 3359 N Halsted St (at Roscoe) **773/477-1420** *4pm-2am, from 2pm wknds, till 3am Sat, go-go dancers Tue & Th*

Little Jim's [★M,NH] 3501 N Halsted St (at Cornelia) **773/871-6116** *noon-4am, till 5am Sat*

The Lucky Horseshoe Lounge [M,NH,S] 3169 N Halsted St (at Briar) **773/404-3169** *3pm-2am, 2pm-3am Sat, till 2am Sun, dancers nightly*

Manhandler Saloon [★M,NH,V] 1948 N Halsted St (at Armitage) **773/871-3339** *noon-4am, till 5am Sat, patio*

Minibar [MW,NS] 3341 N Halsted St (at Roscoe) **773/871-6227** *5pm-2am, from 11am wknds, small lounge, specialty martinis*

The North End [M,NH,WC] 3733 N Halsted St (at Grace) **773/477-7999** *2pm-2am, from 11am wknds, sports bar*

Roscoe's [★MW,NH,D,F,S,V] 3354-56 N Halsted St (at W Roscoe) **773/281-3355** *3pm-2am, 1pm-3am Sat, till 2am Sun, 6 bars, patio cafe in summer*

Sidetrack [★MW,NH,V,WC] 3349 N Halsted St (at Roscoe) **773/477-9189** *3pm-2am, from 1pm wknds, upscale video bar*

Stardust Thursdays [W,D,F] 954 W Belmont (at Berlin) **312/523-9467**

Winebar [MW,F] 3341 N Halsted St (at Roscoe) **773/871-6227** *dinner 5pm-11pm, bar till 3am*

NIGHTCLUBS

Berlin [★MW,D,TG,S,V,WC] 954 W Belmont (at Sheffield) **773/348-4975** *5pm-4am, from 8pm Sun-Mon*

Boom Boom Room [★GS,D] 2200 N Ashland (at Green Dolphin Street bar) **773/395-0066, 312/649-0101 (promoter's #)** *11pm-4am Mon only*

Circuit [M,D,MR,S] 3641 N Halsted St (at Addison) **773/325-2233** *9pm-4am, till 5am Sat, clsd Tue-Wed, theme nights, Latin nights Th & Sun (T-dance)*

Hydrate [★GS,D,E,DS,S] 3458 N Halsted St (at Cornelia) **773/975-9244** *8pm-4am, till 5am Sat, opens earlier in summer, [DS] Wed, [S] Th*

Planet Earth [GS,D] 2350 N Clark St (at Fullerton Pkwy, at Neo nightclub) **773/528-2622** *10pm-4am Th, New Wave*

Smart Bar [★GF,D,A,E] 3730 N Clark St (downstairs at the Metro) **773/549-0203** *10pm-4am, till 5am Sat, clsd Mon-Tue, theme nights*

Spin [MW,D,DS,S,V,YC] 800 W Belmont (enter on Halsted) **773/327-7711** *4pm-2am, from 2pm wknds, 3 bars*

CAFES

Caribou Coffee [WI] 3300 N Broadway St (at Aldine) **773/477-3695** *from 5:30am, from 6:30am Sat, from 7am Sun*

The Coffee & Tea Exchange 3311 N Broadway St (at Roscoe) **773/528-2241** *8am-8pm, till 7pm Fri, 9am-7pm Sat, 10am-6pm Sun, fair-trade coffee & tea*

Starbucks [WI] 3358 N Broadway St (at Roscoe) **773/528-0343** *5:30am-9pm*

RESTAURANTS

44th Ward Dinner Party 3542 N Halsted St **312/857-2911** *5:30pm-midnight, till 2am wknds, grilled cheese sandwiches*

Angelina Ristorante [WC] 3561 N Broadway St (at Addison) **773/935-5933** *5:30pm-11pm, Sun brunch, Italian, full bar*

Ann Sather's [★] 909 W Belmont Ave (at Sheffield) **773/348-2378** *7am-3pm, till 4pm Sat-Sun, Swedish diner & Boystown fixture*

Arco de Cuchilleros [MW] 3445 N Halsted St (btwn Newport & Cornelia) **773/296-6046** *5pm-11pm, till midnight Fri-Sat, 4pm-10pm Sun, clsd Mon, tapas, full bar, patio*

Cesar's 2924 N Broadway (at Oakdale) **773/296-9097** *"home of the killer margaritas"*

Chicago Diner [BW] 3411 N Halsted St (at Roscoe) **773/935-6696** *11am-10pm, from 10am wknds, till 11pm Fri-Sat, hip & vegan*

Cornelia's [E,WC] 750 W Cornelia Ave (at Halsted) **773/248-8333** *dinner only, upscale Italian, full bar, live music nightly*

Firefly 3335 N Halsted St (at Roscoe) **773/525-2505** *5pm-1:30am, till midnight Sun, clsd Tue, romantic French bistro*

Home Bistro [★BYOB] 3404 N Halsted St (at Roscoe, btwn Addison & Belmont) **773/661-0299** *dinner only, clsd Mon-Tue*

Horizon Cafe 3805 N Broadway St (corner w/ Halsted & Grace) **773/883-1565** *7am-9pm, till 10pm Fri-Sat, diner, brkfst anytime*

Joy's Noodles & Rice 3257 N Broadway St (at Melrose) **773/327-8330** *11am-10pm, till 11pm Fri-Sat, plenty veggie, patio*

Kit Kat Lounge & Supper Club [C,DS,GO] 3700 N Halsted St (at W Waveland Ave) **773/525-1111** *5:30pm-1am, brunch Sun (seasonal), clsd Mon, great martini menu*

Kitsch'n On Roscoe 2005 W Roscoe (at Damen) **773/248-7372** *9am-9pm, till 3pm Mon, brunch wknds, comfort food for hipsters, full bar*

RAM
BOOKSTORE
CHICAGO'S
BIGGEST
AND BEST
BACKROOM!
3511 N Halsted
525-9528

Las Mananitas [★GS] 3523 N Halsted St (at Cornelia) **773/528-2109** *11am-11pm, till midnight Fri-Sat, Mexican, full bar, strong margaritas*

Mon Ami Gabi 2300 N Lincoln Park W (at Belden) **773/348-8886** *dinner only, French bistro*

Nancy's Pizza 2930 N Broadway (at Oakdale) **773/883-1977** *deep-dish pizza*

Nookie's Tree [★] 3334 N Halsted St (at Roscoe) **773/248-9888** *7am-midnight, 24hrs wknds*

Panino's Pizzeria [WC] 3702 N Broadway (at Waveland) **773/472-6200** *11:30am-11pm, from noon Sat, till 10pm Sun, Italian, full bar*

Pick Me Up Cafe & All Nite Express Lounge 3408 N Clark St (at Roscoe) **773/248-6613** *11am-3am, 24hrs Fri-Sat, brkfst all day*

The Raw Bar & Grill [E,WC] 3720 N Clark St (at Waveland) **773/348-7291, 773/348-7961** *11am-2am, till 3am Sat, seafood*

Yoshi's Cafe [★] 3257 N Halsted St (at Melrose) **773/248-6160** *dinner Tue-Sun, also Sun brunch, Asian-inspired French*

Bookstores

Unabridged Books [★] 3251 N Broadway St (at Aldine) **773/883-9119** *10am-9pm, till 7pm wknds, LGBT section*

Retail Shops

Bears Like Us 3732 N Broadway St (at Waveland) **773/857-7393** *noon-8pm, till midnight Fri-Sat, bearwear & more for the "Bear Lifestyle"*

Specialty Video Films [GO] 3221 N Broadway St (at Belmont) **773/248-3434** *10am-11pm, foreign, cult, art house, LGBT & erotic videos*

Uncle Fun 1338 W Belmont (at Racine) **773/477-8223** *heaven for kitsch lovers*

Universal Gear 3153 N Broadway St (at Belmont) **773/296-1090** *10am-9pm, till 10pm Fri-Sat, 11am-8pm Sun, casual, club, athletic & designer clothing*

Men's Clubs

Steamworks Men's Gym/ Sauna [★PC] 3246 N Halsted St (N of Belmont) **773/929-6080** *24hrs*

Erotica

Adult Fantasy 2928 N Broadway St (at Oakdale) **773/525-9705** *24hrs*

Batteries Not Included 3420 N Halsted St (at Newport) **773/935-9900** *11am-midnight, till 1am Fri, 10am-2am Sat; also 1439 N Milwaukee Ave, 773/489-2200*

▶ **Cupid's Leather Sport** 3505 N Halsted St (at Cornelia) **773/868-0914** *11am-midnight*

Cupid's Treasures 3519 N Halsted St (at Cornelia) **773/348-3884** *11am-midnight*

The Pleasure Chest 3436 N Lincoln Ave (btwn Roscoe & Addison) **773/525-7152** *10am-10pm, till midnight Fri-Sat*

▶ **The Ram Bookstore** 3511 N Halsted St (at Cornelia) **773/525-9528** *24hrs*

Cruisy Areas

Belmont Rocks [AYOR] S of Belmont (at the lake)

Chicago—Near North

Accommodations

Allegro Chicago [GF,F,E,WI,WC] 171 W Randolph St (at LaSalle) **312/236-0123, 866/672-6143** *Kimpton hotel, upscale lounge & restaurant*

Comfort Inn & Suites Downtown [GF,WI] 15 E Ohio St (at State St) **312/894-0900, 888/775-9223** *boutique hotel, art deco decor, gym*

Dana Hotel & Spa [GF,F,NS,WC] 660 N State St (at Erie) **312/202-6000, 888/301-7946**

Flemish House of Chicago [GS,NS,WI,GO] 68 E Cedar St (btwn Rush & Lake Shore Dr) **312/664-9981** *B&B, studios & apts in greystone row house*

Gold Coast Guest House B&B [GF,NS,WI] 113 W Elm St (btwn Clark & LaSalle) **312/337-0361** *long-term rates available*

The Hotel Burnham [GF,WI] One W Washington St (at State) **312/782-1111, 877/294-9712** *Chicago landmark*

Hotel Cass—Holiday Inn Express [GF,F,WI] 640 N Wabash Ave (btwn Ontario & Erie) **312/787-4030, 800/799-4030**

Hotel Indigo Chicago [GF,WI,WC] 1244 N Dearborn Pkwy (btwn Goethe & Division) **312/787-4980, 800/972-2494** *designer hotel, gym, restaurant & lounge*

Hotel Monaco [GF,WI] 225 N Wabash (at S Water & Wacker Pl) **312/960-8500, 800/397-7661** *4-star luxury hotel, gym, also restaurant*

Hyatt Regency Chicago [GF,WI] 151 E Wacker Dr (at Michigan Ave) **312/565-1234, 800/233-1234** *fitness center, restaurant, cafe & bar*

Millennium Hotels & Resorts [GF,F,WC] 163 E Walton Pl (Michigan Ave) **312/751-8100, 800/621-8140** *gym, restaurant & martini bar*

Old Town Chicago Guest House [GS,NS,WI] 1442 N North Park Ave (at Wells) **312/440-9268** *whole house or rent by room*

Palmer House Hilton [GF,SW] 17 E Monroe St (at State St) **312/726-7500** *fitness center, shopping arcade*

Parkview Hotel Chicago [GF,WC] 1816 N Clark St (at Lincoln) **312/664-3040, 800/329-7466 (reservations)**

W Chicago—City Center [GF,NS,WI,WC] 172 W Adams St (at LaSalle) **312/332-1200, 877/WHOTELS (reservations only)** *in the Loop, also restaurant & bar*

W Chicago—Lakeshore [GF,SW,NS,WI,WC] 644 N Lake Shore Dr (at Ontario) **312/943-9200, 877/WHOTELS (reservations only)** *overlooking Lake Michigan, also restaurant & bar*

Bars

Club Foot [GF,NH,D,A] 1824 W Augusta Blvd (in Wicker Park) **773/489-0379** *8pm-2am, till 3am Sat, kitschy*

Davenport's [GS,C,P] 1383 N Milwaukee (in Wicker Park) **773/278-1830** *7pm-midnight, till 2am Fri-Sat, till 11pm Sun, clsd Tue*

Second Story Bar [M,NH] 157 E Ohio St (at Michigan Ave) **312/923-9536** *noon-2am, till 3am Sat*

Nightclubs

Baton Show Lounge [MW,DS,WC] 436 N Clark St (btwn Illinois & Hubbard) **312/644-5269** *showtimes at 8:30pm, 10:30pm, 12:30am, clsd Mon-Tue, reservations advised, since 1969!*

Chances Dances [MW,D] 2011 W North Ave (at Damen & Milwaukee, at Subterranean) *9pm 3rd Mon only*

Crobar [★GF,D] 1543 N Kingsbury (at Sheffield) **312/266-1900** *10pm-4am, clsd Mon-Th, occasional gay nights Sun*

The Rails [★M,D,MR-AF,MR-L,S,$] 1675 N Elston Ave (at North Ave, at Prop House in Wicker Park) **773/486-2086 (Prop House #)** *11pm-4am Fri only*

Sound Bar/ Y Bar [GS,D] 226 W Ontario (btwn Franklin & Wells) **312/787-4480** *10pm-4am Fri, till 5am Sat, clsd Sun-Th*

Underground Wonder Bar [GF,E,MR,P] 10 E Walton St (at State St) **312/266-7761**

Cafes

Earwax Cafe & Film 1561 N Milwaukee Ave (in Wicker Park) **773/772-4019** *9am-10pm, food served (burgers, burritos, salads & vegan soups & stews), also film section w/ 1,000 DVDs*

Restaurants

Blackbird 619 W Randolph St (at Des Plaines) **312/715-0708** *lunch Mon-Fri, dinner nightly, clsd Sun*

Fireplace Inn 1448 N Wells St (at North Ave) **312/664-5264** *4:30pm-1am, 11:30am-1am Fri-Sat, BBQ, patio, full bar*

Hot Chocolate [WC] 1747 N Damen Ave (in Wicker Park) **773/489-1747** *lunch, dinner & dessert, wknd brunch, clsd Mon*

Ina's 1235 W Randolph St (at Racine) **312/226-8227** *brkfst, lunch & dinner, full bar, free parking*

Japonais 600 W Chicago Ave (at Larrabee) **312/822-9600** *lunch Mon-Fri, dinner nightly, upscale Japanese, lounge*

Kiki's Bistro 900 N Franklin St (at Locust) **312/335-5454** *lunch Mon-Fri, dinner nightly, clsd Sun, French, full bar*

Lou Mitchell's 565 W Jackson St (at Jefferson) **312/939-3111** *great brkfst*

Manny's 1141 S Jefferson St (at Roosevelt) **312/939-2855** *5am-8pm, clsd Sun, killer corned beef*

Moonshine 1824 N Division St (at Honore, in Wicker Park) **773/862-8686** *lunch & dinner, American, also bar*

Nacional 27 325 W Huron (at N Orleans) **312/664-2727** *5:30pm-9:30pm, till 11pm Fri-Sat, clsd Sun, Nuevo Latino, live music Tue & Th, salsa dancing 11pm-2am Fri-Sat*

Park Grill 11 N Michigan Ave (in Millennium Park) **312/521-7275** *11am-10pm, classic American, seasonal outdoor dining*

Parthenon Restaurant 314 S Halsted St (near W Jackson) **312/726-2407** *11am-midnight, full bar, Greek, "best gyros in Chicago"*

Shaw's Crab House [WC] 21 E Hubbard St (at State St) **312/527-2722** *lunch & dinner, full bar*

Topolobampo/ Frontera Grill 445 N Clark St (btwn Illinois & Hubbard) **312/661-1434** *lunch & dinner, Sat brunch (Frontera only), clsd Sun, Mexican*

Vermilion [★WC] 10 W Hubbard St (at State) **312/527-4060** *lunch Mon-Fri, dinner nightly, Latin-Indian fusion, full bar, patio, upscale*

Bookstores

After-Words New & Used Books 23 E Illinois (at State) **312/464-1110** *10:30am-10pm, till 11pm Fri-Sat, noon-7pm Sun, internet access*

Quimby's Bookstore [★WC] 1854 W North Ave (at Wolcott, in Wicker Park) **773/342-0910** *noon-10pm, from 11am Sat, noon-6pm Sun, alternative literature & comics*

Retail Shops

Flight 001 1133 N State St (at Division) **312/944-1001, 877/354-4481** *11am-7pm, till 6pm Sun, way cool travel gear*

Gyms & Health Clubs

Cheetah Gym 1934 W North Ave (at Damen, in Wicker Park) **773/394-5900**

Erotica

Bijou Theatre 1349 N Wells St (at North Ave) **312/943-5397** *24hrs*

Erotic Warehouse [WC] 1246 W Randolph (at Elizabeth) **312/226-5222** *24hrs*

Frenchy's 872 N State St (at E Chestnut) **312/337-9190** *24hrs*

Hubbard Books 109 W Hubbard (at Clark) **312/828-0953** *24hrs*

Wells Books 178 N Wells (at Lake) **312/263-9266** *7am-10pm, 9am-9pm Sun*

Chicago—South Side

Bars

Club Escape [MW,D,DS,MR-AF,F] 1530 E 75th St (at Stoney Island) **773/667-6454** *4pm-2am, till 3am Sat*

Inn Exile [M,D,V,WI,WC] 5758 W 65th St (at Menard, near Midway Airport; 1 mile W of Midway hotel center at 65th & Cicero) **773/582-3510** *8pm-2am, till 3am Sat*

Jeffery Pub [★MW,D,MR-AF,DS,WC] 7041 S Jeffery (at 71st) **773/363-8555** *5pm-4am, from 1pm Fri, noon-5am Sat, noon-4am Sun, clsd Mon*

Nightclubs

Escapades [M,D,V] 6301 S Harlem (at 63rd) **773/229-0886** *9pm-5am*

Bookstores

57th St Books 1301 E 57th St, Hyde Park (at Kimbark St) **773/684-1300** *10am-9pm, till 8pm Sat-Sun, LGBT section, readings*

Barbara's Bookstore [★WC] 1218 S Halsted St (at W Roosevelt) **312/413-2665** *9am-10pm, from 10am wknds, till 8pm Sun, women's/ LGBT section; also at Macy's, 111 N State St, 312/781-3033; also 1100 Lake St, Oak Park, 708/848-9140*

De Kalb

Nightclubs

Otto's [GF,E] 118 E Lincoln Hwy **815/758-2715** *live music venue*

Erotica

Paperback Grotto 157 E Lincoln Hwy (at 2nd) **815/758-8061**

Decatur

Bars

The Flashback Lounge [MW,NH,D,K] 2239 E Wood St (at 22nd) **217/422-3530** *9am-2am*

Restaurants

Robbies 122 Merchant St **217/423-0448** *11am-9pm, till 2pm Sat, clsd Sun, American, full bar*

Erotica

Romantix Adult Superstore 2015 N 22nd St **217/362-0105** *24hrs, booths*

Cruisy Areas

Fairview Park [AYOR] in the back

Du Quoin

Accommodations

The Pit [MW,18+,SW,N,GO] 7403 Persimmon Rd **618/542-9470** *primitive camping*

Elgin

see Chicago

Elk Grove Village

see also Chicago

Nightclubs

Hunter's Night Club [★M,D,TG,E,K,S,V,WC,GO] 1932 E Higgins (at Busse) **847/439-8840** *4pm-2am, till 4am Th-Sat, patio*

Cruisy Areas

Busse Woods Forest Preserve [AYOR] off Hwy 72 (Higgins Rd) (W of Arlington Heights Rd)

Elkhart

Cafes

Bluestem Bake Shop 107 Governor Oglesby St **217/947-2222** *9am-4pm, clsd Mon, soup, sandwiches & baked goods*

Evanston

see Chicago

Forest Park

see also Chicago

Nightclubs

Hideaway [M,D,K,DS,V] 7301 W Roosevelt Rd (at Marengo) **708/771-4459** *3pm-2am, till 3am Fri-Sat, male dancers*

Galesburg

Accommodations

The Fahnestock House [GS,NS,GO] 591 N Prairie St (at Losey) **309/344-0270** *full brkfst, Queen Anne Victorian, clsd Nov-Jan*

Men's Clubs

▶ **Hole in the Wall** [MO,B,L,MR,F,V,18+,N,PC,WC,GO] 1438 Knox Hwy 9 (off I-74 at Exit 51) **309/289-2375** *10am-11pm, 24hrs Th-Sun, clsd Mon-Tue, steam room*

Erotica

Romantix Adult Superstore 595 N Henderson St (at Losey) **309/342-7019**

Granite City

see St Louis, Missouri

Hoffman Estates

Cruisy Areas

Beverly Lake Forest Preserve [AYOR] Rte 72 (btwn 25 & 59)

Ina

Cruisy Areas

Rend Lake [AYOR] off I-57 (S of Mt Vernon, N of Carbondale) *near boat ramp, beware of cops*

Iuka

Accommodations

Priapus Pines [MO,21+,SW,N,PC,GO] **618/822-2559** *clothing-optional campground on 60 acres, RV hookups*

Joliet

Info Lines & Services

Community Alliance & Action Network 68 N Chicago St **815/726-7906** *10:30am-1:30pm & 7pm-9pm Mon, Wed & Fri (or by appointment), LGBT community center*

Nightclubs

Maneuvers & Co [MW,D,TG,DS] 118 E Jefferson (at Chicago) **815/727-7069** *8pm-2am, till 3am Fri-Sat, patio, frequent events*

Cruisy Areas

Hammill Woods [AYOR] Rte 59 (2 miles N of Hwy 52) *beware of cops*

Kankakee

Cruisy Areas

Kankakee River State Park [AYOR] Rte 102 *across from main entrance, Dan Uze Area*

LaGrange

Cruisy Areas

Possum Hollow Woods [AYOR] 31st St (W of LaGrange Rd)

Leroy

Cruisy Areas

Moraine View State Park [AYOR] *around Dawson Lake & Timber Point*

Long Grove

Retail Shops

The Long Grove Popcorn Shoppe [GO] 318 Old McHenry Rd **847/821-9101** *10am-5pm, try the "Pride Pop," also gourmet coffee & doggie treats*

Marion

Erotica

▶ **The Lion's Den Adult Superstore** 1642 Rte 148 (exit 45, off I-57) **618/995-1586** *24hrs*

Monticello

Restaurants

The Brown Bag 212 W Washington St **217/762-9221** *9am-7pm, till 8pm Tue & Fri, till 4pm Sat, clsd Sun*

Morris

Erotica

Forty-Seven Video 50 Gore Rd (N of exit 112, off I-80) **815/942-8309** *24hrs*

HOLE IN THE WALL
CENTRAL ILLINOIS' FIRST AND FINEST
PRIVATE MEN'S CLUB
holeinthewallmensclub.org
LOCATED JUST NORTH OF EXIT 51, OFF I-74 3 MILES EAST OF GALESBURG (35 MINUTES WEST OF PEORIA)
COLD BEER HOT PIZZA and HOTTER MEN!
CALL FOR RATES, HOURS & DIRECTIONS
309-289-2375
WE KNOW WHAT YOU WANT, AND WE'VE GOT IT!
COME EARLY - STAY LATE
OPEN 24 HRS FRI THRU SUN
PRIVATE ROOMS (WITH FULL USE OF OUR EXTENSIVE LIBRARY OF DVD & VIDEOS OR BRING YOUR OWN),
LOCKERS,
2 RELAXATION AREAS,
INDOOR & OUTDOOR - GANG SHOWERS,
LARGE STEAM ROOM,
EXERCISE EQUIPMENT
INFRARED DRY HEAT SAUNAS,
GROUP HOT TUB, PRIVATE OUTDOOR SMOKING AREA,
CLOTHING OPTIONAL SUNBATHING,
HOT SNACKS AND COLD DRINKS AVAILABLE

Normal

Cafes

Coffeehouse & Deli 114 E Beaufort **309/452-6774** *7am-10pm, vegetarian/ vegan*

Restaurants

Micheleo's Pizza 116 E North St **309/454-4444** *11am-close*

North Riverside

Bars

Rumors [M,NH,F,S,V,GO] 2433 Desplaines Ave **708/443-1227** *3pm-3am, from noon wknds*

O'Fallon

Restaurants

Paulo's at the Mansion [WC,GO] 1680 Mansion Wy (at Lakepointe Center Dr) **618/624-0629** *4pm-10pm Tue-Sat, steakhouse*

Oak Park

see also Berwyn & Chicago

Info Lines & Services

OPALGA (Oak Park Area Lesbian & Gay Association) Center 947 Garfield St **708/848-0273, 708/386-3463 (youth programs)** *9am-noon & 1pm-2pm Mon-Tue & Th-Fri, group also hosts variety of social & educational events*

Bars

Velvet Rope [MW,E,F] 728 W Lake St **708/358-8840** *4pm-1am, till 2am wknds*

Oakwood

Erotica

Oasis Books & Video 502 N Oakwood **217/354-4820** *24hrs, arcade*

Ottawa

Erotica

Brown Bag Video 3042 N Rte 71 (at I-80, exit 93) **815/434-0820** *24hrs*

Cruisy Areas

Matthiessen State Park [AYOR] 1 mile E of I-39 (at Exit 54) *river area*

Peoria

Accommodations

Hotel Pere Marquette [GF] 501 Main St **309/637-6500, 800/447-1676** *buffet brkfst*

Bars

Apostrophe [GS,WI] 5901 N Prospect Rd (Junction City Shopping Ctr) **309/691-2111** *11am-1am, clsd Mon, pizza & wings*

Buddies On Adams [MW,NH,K,WI] 807 SW Adams St (at Oak St) **308/282-2125** *6pm-1am, till 4am Fri-Sat, clsd Mon*

Sparky's Ringside Bar & Grille [GS,NH,K] 1914 N Wisconsin Ave **309/682-0826** *10am-1am, sports bar*

Nightclubs

Diesel [MW,D,DS] 629 Main St

Cafes

One World [NS,WI] 1245 W Main St **309/672-1522** *7am-11pm, from 8am Sun*

Restaurants

Two 25 225 NE Adams St (at Mark Twain Hotel) **309/282-7777** *lunch Mon-Fri, dinner nightly, clsd Sun*

Erotica

Brown Bag Video 801 SW Adams (at Oak) **309/676-3003**

The Green Door 2610 W Farmington Rd (near Sterling Ave) **309/674-4337**

Swingers World 335 SW Adams (at Harrison) **309/676-9275** *24hrs*

Prospect Heights

see Chicago

Quincy

Nightclubs

Irene's Cabaret [★MW,D,B,L,MR,TG,F,E,K,DS,WC,GO] 124 N 5th St (at Washington Park, enter rear) **217/222-6292** *9pm-2:30am, from 7pm Fri-Sat, till 3:30am Sat, from 3pm Sun*

Erotica

Chelsea Entertainment 5000 Gardner Expwy (2 miles S of Quincy) **217/224-7000**

Cruisy Areas

Parker Heights Park [AYOR] *parking lot by archery range*

Rock Island

see also Davenport, Iowa

Bars

Augie's [MW,NH,TG,K,WC] 313 20th St (at 3rd) **309/788-7389** *3pm-3am, from noon wknds*

Erotica

Centennial Video Center 309 20th St **309/794-1682** *arcade, booths*

TR Video 8210 42nd St W **309/787-1852** *24hrs*

Rockford

Nightclubs

The Office Niteclub [★MW,D,E,DS,S,V] 513 E State St (btwn 2nd & 3rd) **815/965-0344** *5pm-2am, noon-midnight Sun*

Restaurants

Lucerne's Fondue & Spirits [WC] 845 N Church St (at Whitman) **815/968-2665** *5pm-11pm, clsd Mon (also Sun summers)*

Maria's 828 Cunningham St (at Corbin) **815/968-6781** *4:30pm-9pm, clsd Sun-Mon*

Schiller Park

Cruisy Areas

Schiller Woods [AYOR] Irving Park Rd (btwn N Cumberland Ave & River Rd)

Springfield

Info Lines & Services

The Phoenix Center 109 E Lawrence Ave **217/528-5253** *8:30am-4:30pm, clsd wknds, Phoenix Cafe group from 6pm Tue & Fri*

Accommodations

The Henry Mischler House [GF,NS] 802 E Edwards St (btwn 8th & 9th Sts) **217/525-2660, 800/525-2660** *full brkfst*

The State House, a Clarion Collection Hotel [GF,WC] 101 E Adams (at First St) **217/528-5100** *hotel, full brkfst*

Bars

Scandals [M,D,DS] 2901 Chatham Rd **217/546-6009** *11am-1am*

The Station House [MW,NH,D,WC] 304-306 E Washington (btwn 3rd & 4th Sts) **217/525-0438** *2pm-1am, till 3am Th-Sat, from noon wknds*

Restaurants

Caitie Girls 400 E Jefferson (in St Nicholas Hotel) **217/528-1294** *lunch Tue-Fri, dinner nightly, Sun brunch, clsd Mon*

Lil' Jimmy's Diner [GO] 1629 1/2 Peoria Rd (at North Grand Ave) **217/753-1055** *6am-2pm, till 8pm Fri*

Retail Shops

New Age Tattoos & Body Piercings 2915 S MacArthur Blvd **217/546-5006** *11am-8pm, till 6pm Sun*

Men's Services

Cruisy Areas

Douglas Park [AYOR] MacArthur & Mason

Riverside Park [AYOR] Peoria Rd N, past river

Utica

Accommodations

Landers House [GF,WI] 115 E Church St **815/667-5170** *full brkfst*

The Willows Hotel [GF,WI,WC] 325 Clark St **815/667-3400** *full brkfst*

Washington Park

see St Louis, Missouri

Waukegan

see also Chicago

Cruisy Areas

Green Belt Forest Preserve Hwy 120 E, right on Green Bay Rd

Wood River

see also Alton

Indiana

Anderson

Erotica

After Dark 2012 Mounds Rd **765/649-7597** *10am-11pm, till midnight Fri-Sat, noon-10pm Sun, adult novelties, lingerie, videos, magazines*

Bloomington

Bars

Uncle Elizabeth's [MW,NH] 1614 W 3rd St **812/331-0060** *4pm-3am, 5pm-midnight Sun, dance floor, drag shows, patio*

Cafes

Soma Coffee House [WI] 322 E Kirkwood Ave (below Laughing Planet) **812/331-2770** *7am-11pm, from 8am Sun*

Restaurants

Laughing Planet Cafe 322 E Kirkwood Ave (enter on Grant) **812/323-2233** *11am-9pm, outdoor seating*

Village Deli [MW] 409 E Kirkwood **812/336-2303** *7am-8pm, 8am-8pm wknds*

Entertainment & Recreation

BloomingOut WFHB 91.3 & 98.1 & 100.7 & 106.3FM **812/325-7870 & 323-1200** *6pm Th, "your midwest queer connection"*

Retail Shops

Athena Gallery [WC] 116 N Walnut **812/339-0734** *10:30am-7pm, till 8:30pm Fri, noon-5pm Sun, clothing, drums, incense, gifts, etc*

Erotica

College Ave Bookstore 1013 N College Ave (at 14th) **812/332-5160** *24hrs*

Cruisy Areas

Cascades Park [AYOR] *beware of cops late evenings!*

Columbus

Cruisy Areas

Nobblitt Park [AYOR] 17th St (1 1/2 blocks W of Washington) *walk to train bridge*

Crothersville

Erotica

▶ **The Lion's Den Adult Superstore** 11769 E State Rte 250 (exit 41, off I-65) **812/524-2429** *24hrs*

Elkhart

see also South Bend

Bars

The Club [MW,K] 23861 Hwy 33 E **574/875-9999** *5pm-3am Th-Sat only*

Evansville

Nightclubs

Someplace Else [MW,D,K,DS] 930 Main St (at Sycamore) **812/424-3202** *4pm-3am, 4pm-midnight Sun*

Erotica

Bookmart of Evansville 519 N Main (by Lucky Lady) **812/423-2011** *24hrs*

Exotica 4605 Washington Ave **812/401-7399**

Fulton Ave Bookmart 201 S Fulton Ave (at 2nd) **812/421-0222**

Cruisy Areas

Mesker Park [AYOR] *police patrols are heavy*

Fort Wayne

Info Lines & Services

Gay/ Lesbian AA 501 W Berry St (at Plymouth church) *6:30pm Tue, 1pm Sun*

Up the Stairs Community Center 514 E Washington Blvd **260/422-2450** *7pm-10pm, till midnight Fri-Sat, youth group, library, space for various groups including lesbian/ gay helpline, also newspaper*

Accommodations

Worthington Mansion B&B [NS,WI,GO] 805 W Wayne St (at Van Buren) **260/424-6564, 866/404-6564** *full brkfst*

Nightclubs

After Dark [M,D,K,DS,S,WC,GO] 1601 S Harrison St (at Grand St) **260/456-6235** *noon-3am, 6pm-1am Sun, strippers*

Babylon [MW,D] 112 Masterson St **260/456-7005** *6pm-3am, also Lion's Den & Gallery bars*

Cafes

Firefly [E,WI] 3523 N Anthony Blvd **260/373-0505** *6:30am-8pm, from 8am wknds*

Retail Shops

Boudoir Noir 512 W Superior St **260/420-0557** *10am-midnight, noon-8pm Sun, gifts, toys, leather*

Publications

Reality 260/409-2920 *LGBT publication*

Cruisy Areas

Swinney Park [AYOR] *be alert—major crackdown on cruising in Fort Wayne*

Gary

see also Chicago, Illinois

Erotica

Romantix Adult Superstore 8801 Melton Rd/ US 20 (at Ripley Rd) **219/938-2194** *24hrs*

Trucker's World [AYOR] 25th Ave & Burr St (off I-80/ 94)

Goshen

see also South Bend

Cafes

The Electric Brew [E] 136 S Main St **574/533-5990** *6:30am-10pm, till 11pm Fri-Sat, clsd Sun, "Goshen's original coffeehouse"*

Hammond

Accommodations

Sibley Court Yard Inn [MO,NS,PC,GO] 629 Sibley St (at Calumet Ave) **219/933-9604** *gay men's guesthouse w/ bathhouse facilities: steam room, sauna, hot tub, private courtyard*

Bars

Dick's R U Crazee [M,NH] 1221 E 150th St **219/852-0222** *7pm-3am, till midnight Sun*

Hebron

Erotica

► **The Lion's Den Adult Superstore** 18010 Colorado St (exit 240, off I-65) **219/696-1276** *24hrs*

Indiana Dunes

Accommodations

The Gray Goose Inn B&B [GS,WI] 350 Indian Boundary Rd (at I-95), Chesterton **219/926-5781, 800/521-5127** *full brkfst*

Indianapolis

Info Lines & Services

AA Gay/ Lesbian 317/632-7864, 317/631-5099 (en español) *various LGBT meeting, check web (www.indyaa.org) for meeting times & locations*

Accommodations

Adam's Mark Hotel [GF,SW] 2544 Executive Dr (off Airport Expy) **317/248-2481, 800/444-2326** *seasonal pool, [WI] in lobby, restaurant & lounge*

The Kendall Inn [GF,NS,WC] 5830 N Post Rd **317/638-6000** *luxury inn in historic Fort Harrison in NE Indianapolis*

Kurt's B&B Inn [MO,SW,N,GO] **317/291-5728** *8 miles from downtown bars & 3 miles from Indy 500*

Sycamore Knoll B&B [GS,NS,WI,GO] 10777 Riverwood Ave, Noblesville **317/776-0570** *1886 estate near the White River, full brkfst, lesbian-owned*

Yellow Rose Inn [GS,NS] 1441 N Delaware St **317/636-7673** *Victorian B&B, rooftop hot tub*

Bars

501 Eagle [★M,D,B,L] 501 N College (at Michigan St) **317/632-2100** *5:30pm-3am, from 7:30pm Sat, 4pm-12:30am Sun*

Cosmos [M,NH,F,E,K,WI,GO] 243 N State Ave (at Washington) **317/634-9999** *5pm-close, "pianoke" singalongs*

Downtown Olly's [M,NH,V,WC] 822 N Illinois St (at St Clair) **317/636-5597** *7am-3am Mon-Th, 24hrs Fri-Sat, till 12:30am Sun, sports & video bar, brkfst, lunch, dinner*

The Metro Restaurant & Nightclub [★MW,F,K,P,WC] 707 Massachusetts Ave (at College) **317/639-6022** *3pm-3am, 11am-12:30am Sun, patio, also restaurant, giftshop*

Noah Grant's Grill House & Raw Bar [GF,NH,F,E] 65 S 1st St (at W Oak St), Zionsville **317/732-2233** *clsd Sun-Mon, wine bar & bistro, full restaurant serving lunch & dinner, Sun brunch, patio*

Varsity Lounge [M,NH,F,K] 1517 N Pennsylvania St (S of 16th) **317/635-9998** *10am-3am, till midnight Sun*

Zonie's Closet [GS,K,DS] 1446 E Washington (at Arsenal) **317/266-0535** *8am-3am, noon-midnight Sun, [DS] Fri-Sat*

Nightclubs

Greg's [★M,D,CW,V,WC] 231 E 16th St (at Alabama) **317/638-8138** *4pm-3am, 4pm-midnight Sun, DJ Th-Sat, patio*

Talbott Street [★GS,D,DS,GO] 2145 N Talbott St (at 22nd St) **317/931-1343** *9pm-3am, till 1am Sun, clsd Mon-Wed, theme nights*

The Ten [★MW,D,DS,S,WC] 1218 N Pennsylvania St (at 12th, enter rear) **317/638-5802** *6pm-3am, till 1am Wed, till midnight Sun, clsd Mon-Tue*

The Unicorn Club [★M,D,S,PC] 122 W 13th St (at Illinois) **317/262-9195** *8pm-3am, till 12:30am Sun, male strippers nightly*

Cafes

Ah Barista Cafe [F,WI] 201 S Capitol Ave (btwn Maryland & South Sts) **317/638-2233** *7am-3pm Mon-Fri, brkfst & lunch menu*

Bjava 5510 Lafayette Rd **317/280-1236** *6am-5pm, 7am-3pm Sat, clsd Sun*

Cornerstone Coffeehouse [F,WI] 651 E 54th St (at N College Ave, Broad Ripple) **317/726-1360** *6am-10pm, 7am-10pm Sat, 7am-9pm Sun*

Henry's on E Street [★F,WI,GO] 627 N East St (next door to Out Word Bound Books) **317/951-0335** *7am-7pm, till 11pm Fri, 9am-3pm Sat-Sun, winter/summer hours vary*

Hubbard & Cravens 4930 N Pennsylvania St (in Broad Ripple) **317/251-5161** *6am-7pm, 7am-3pm Sun*

Monon Coffee Company 920 E Westfield Blvd (at Guilford) **317/255-0510** *6:30am-8pm, till 10pm Fri, from 7am Sat, 8am-8pm Sun*

Restaurants

14 West 14 W Maryland St **317/636-1414** *lunch & dinner, seafood & steaks, patio*

Adobo Grill 110 E Washington **317/822-9990** *lunch Fri-Sun, dinner nightly, Mexican, full bar, also Fiesta Fridays [D] w/ salsa dancing*

Aesop's Tables [BW,WC] 600 N Massachusetts Ave (at East) **317/631-0055** *lunch & dinner, clsd Sun, authentic Mediterranean*

Agio [NS] 635 Massachusetts Ave (at East) **317/488-0359** *lunch Mon-Fri, dinner nightly, cont'l*

Creation Cafe 337 W 11th St (in Buggs' Temple) **317/955-2389** *7am-9pm, till 10pm wknds, outdoor seating*

English Ivy's 944 S Alabama (at 10th) **317/822-5070** *lunch & dinner, till 3am Mon-Sat, 11am-midnight Sun, eclectic, also full bar*

Hoaglin To Go 448 Massachusetts Ave **317/423-0300** *8am-2:30pm, market till 6pm*

India Garden 830 Broad Ripple Ave (btwn Carrollton & Guilford) **317/253-6060** *lunch & dinner, Indian; also 207 N Delaware St, 317/634-6060, lunch & dinner*

Mama Carolla's [★WC] 1031 E 54th St (at Winthrop) **317/259-9412** *5pm-9:30pm, till 10pm Sun-Mon, traditional Italian*

Mikado [★WC] 148 S Illinois St (at Georgia) **317/972-4180** *11:30am-10:30pm, till 11:30pm Sat, till 10pm Sun, Japanese, enjoy the saketini*

Naked Tchopstix [★BW] 6253 N College Ave (in Broad Ripple) **317/252-5555** *lunch & dinner 7 days, Korean, Japanese, Chinese cuisine, also sushi bar*

Oakley's Bistro [★] 1464 W 86th St (at Ditch Rd) **317/824-1231** *lunch & dinner, clsd Sun-Mon, gourmet cont'l, reservations suggested*

Pancho's Taqueria [★] 7023 Michigan Rd (at Westlane) **317/202-9015** *11am-9pm 7 days, authentic Mexican*

Red Eye Cafe [WI] 250 S Meridian St (N of Union Station) **317/972-1500** *24hrs, diner, beer*

Sawasdee 1222 W 86th St (at Ditch Rd) **317/844-9451** *lunch Mon-Sat, dinner nightly, Thai, some veggie*

Scholars Inn 725 Massachusetts Ave **317/536-0707** *dinner nightly, Sun brunch, also swank lounge*

Shanghai Lil 8505 Keystone Crossing (across from Keystone Mall) **317/205-9335** *lunch & dinner 7 days, upscale Chinese & Japanese, full bar*

Three Sisters Cafe 6360 Guilford Ave (at 64th) **317/257-5556** *8am-9pm, till 3pm Sun, plenty veggie & vegan, popular Sun brunch*

Usual Suspects 6319 Guilford Ave (at Broad Ripple) **317/251-3138** *5pm-10pm, till 11pm Fri-Sat, till 9pm Sun, clsd Mon, eclectic, full bar, patio*

Yats [★WC] 659 Massachusetts Ave (at Walnut) **317/686-6380** *11am-9pm, till 10pm Fri-Sat, till 7pm Sun, Cajun; also 5463 N College Ave, 317/253-8817 & 8352 E 96th St, 317/585-1792*

Entertainment & Recreation

Indianapolis Men's Chorus PO Box 2919 46206-2919 **317/931-9464** *various concerts throughout season*

Theatre on the Square 627 Massachusetts Ave (at East) **317/685-8687**

Bookstores

Big Hat Books 6510 Cornell Ave **317/202-0203** *10am-6pm, noon-5pm Sun, general independent*

Bookmamas 9 S Johnson Ave (at E Washington St, in Irvington) **317/375-3715** *open Wed-Sat, call for hours, used bookstore*

Out Word Bound [★GO] 625 N East St (at Massachusetts Ave) **317/951-9100** *from 11am daily, LGBT, special events*

Retail Shops

All My Relations 1008 Main (at 10th) **317/227-3925** *noon-6pm, till 7pm Wed-Th, 10am-6pm Sat, New Age/metaphysical store, also classes*

Discount News Company 130 N Delaware St (btwn Market & Ohio) **317/632-9331** *clsd Sun, old-fashioned newsstand, some gay titles*

For the Love of Dogs 5537 E Washington **317/375-8592** *dog bakery*

The Magic Candle 204 S Audubon Rd (S of Washington) **317/357-8801** *10am-7pm, 1pm-5pm Sun, pagan supplies, books, gifts, also classes*

Metamorphosis [18+] 828 Broad Ripple Ave (at Carrollton) **317/466-1666** *1pm-9pm, till 5pm Sun, tattoo & piercing parlor*

Metropolis 707 Massachusetts Ave (upstairs at The Metro) **317/639-1029** *4pm-2am, 1pm-12:30am Sun, also restaurant & nightclub*

Publications

Nuvo 317/254-2400 *Indy's alternative weekly*

The Word 317/725-8840 *LGBT newspaper*

Men's Clubs

▶ **Club Indianapolis** [18+,SW,PC] 620 N Capitol Ave (at North & Walnut) **317/635-5796** *24hrs, steam, sauna, gym, outdoor patio*

The Works [L,V,PC,GO] 4120 N Keystone Ave (at 38th) **317/547-9210** *24hrs*

Men's Services

▶ **Megaphone 317/322-9000** *Meet and Chat Live with HOT local men. FREE to listen & respond to ads. Video and text chat at GayMates.com. Use FREE code 4889.*

Erotica

Annex Bookstore 6767 E 38th St (at Massachusetts) **317/549-3522** *arcade, 10am-midnight Mon-Sat*

Fat Dicks Video 822 N Illinois St (behind Downtown Olly's) *noon-7pm, videos & magazines*

Southern Nights Videos 3760 Commercial Dr (at 38th St) **317/329-5505** *10am-midnight, clsd Sun, videos, DVDs, toys, etc*

Cruisy Areas

Damron does not list here as there are 9 cops to every 1 cruiser [AYOR]

Kokomo

Cruisy Areas

Highland Park [AYOR] near "Old Ben"

La Porte

Restaurants

Holy Macaroni Cafe & PizzAria [MR,NS,WC,GO] 4318 W US Hwy 20 (E of I-94 & Hwy 20/35 interchange) **219/872-3046** *11am-9pm, till 10pm Fri-Sat, clsd Sun-Mon*

Lafayette

Info Lines & Services

Pride Lafayette, Inc 658 Main St, Ste 218 **765/423-7579** *community center 6pm-8pm Tue, Th & Fri, support/ social activities*

Nightclubs

Zoolegers [MW,D] 644 Main St (at Columbia) **765/742-6321** *8pm-3am, clsd Sun*

Erotica

Fantasy East 2315 Concord Rd (at Teal) **765/474-2417** *open daily, books & videos*

Lake Station

Nightclubs

Encompass Nightclub & Lounge [★MW,D,F,E,C,DS,P,S,V,WC] 2415 Rush St (at I-80/94 & Ripley St) **219/962-4640** *8pm-3am, 7pm-1am Sun*

Logansport

Cruisy Areas

Spencer Park [AYOR] near tennis courts & trails along Eel River

Lowell

Accommodations

Inn Town B&B [GF,NS,WI] 1651 E Commercial Ave (Rte 2 or 181st) (at Burr St) **219/696-3338** *full brkfst*

Madison

Cruisy Areas

Clifty St Park [AYOR] btwn poplar & oak groves

Vaughn Dr [AYOR] along river

Marion

Erotica

Pleasures 1311 Johnson St **765/662-3688** *10am-11pm, till midnight Fri-Sat, noon-10pm Sun, adult novelties, lingerie, videos, magazines*

Michigan City

Accommodations

Duneland Beach Inn & Restaurant [GF] 3311 Pottawattamie Trail (at Duneland Beach Dr) **219/874-7729, 800/423-7729** *B&B/ restaurant/ bar, 1 block away from Lake Michigan, private beach, 60 miles from Chicago*

Tryon Farm Guest House [GF,NS] 1400 Tryon Rd (at Hwy 212) **219/879-3618** *full brkfst, hot tub*

Mishawaka

see also South Bend

Accommodations

The Beiger Mansion [GF,SW,NS,WI,GO] 317 Lincolnway E **574/255-6300, 800/437-0131** *B&B in 4-level neo-classical limestone mansion*

Entertainment & Recreation

GLBT Resource Center of Michiana [GO] **574/254-1411** *temporarily without a location, call for updates*

Morgantown

Accommodations

Camp Buckwood [MO,SW,GO] 8670 Spearsville Rd **812/597-2450** *lodge w/ tents & RV sites*

Muncie

Cafes

The MT Cup 1606 W University Ave (at N Dill St) **765/287-1995** *7:30am-3am, till midnight Sun-Tue, sandwiches & baked goods*

Cruisy Areas

McCulloch Park [AYOR] on Broadway (past the Muncie Mall)

New Albany

see Louisville, KY

Noblesville

see Indianapolis

Richmond

Erotica

Exotic Fantasies 12 S 11th St **765/935-5827** *9am-midnight, till 1am Th-Sat, noon 10pm Sun, toys, DVDs, arcade*

South Bend

Accommodations

Council Oak Inn [MO,N,NS,GO] near airport **574/273-6416, 574/315-7098** *B&B in private home, full brkfst, private decks*

Innisfree B&B [GF,NS] 702 W Colfax **574/283-0740** *1892 Queen Anne minutes from Notre Dame, full brkfst*

Bars

Bryan's Piano Bar [GF,F,E] 2410 Mishawaka Ave **574/251-0542** *3pm-close*

Jeannie's Tavern [GF,TG,GO] 621 S Bendix (at Ford St) **574/288-2962** *11am-2am*

Vickies Inc [GS,NH,TG,F,GO] 112 W Monroe (at S Michigan Ave) **574/232-4090** *2pm-midnight Mon-Sat, open some Sundays, football party every Sat in season*

Nightclubs

Starzbar [★M,D,S,WC] 1505 S Kendall St (at Indiana) **574/288-7827** *9pm-3am, from 8pm Fri-Sat, clsd Sun*

Truman's Nightclub & Lounge/ Little T's [★MW,D,F,K,DS] 100 N Center St, Mishawaka **574/259-2282, 574/259-7507** *8pm-3am, from 10pm Fri-Sat, Little T's sports bar [K] open 8pm-2am Fri-Sat, till 12:30am Sun, also gift shop*

Cafes

Lula's Cafe [E] 1637 Edison Rd **574/273-6216** *7:30am-11:30pm, from 9am Sat, from 10am Sun*

Erotica

Pleasureland Museum 114 W Mishawaka Ave (at Main) **574/259-6776** *10am-10pm, clsd Sun*

Romantix Adult Superstore 2715 S Main St (at Ewing) **574/291-1899** *9:30am-3am, clsd Sun*

Cruisy Areas

Rum Village Park [AYOR] W Ewing Ave

Terre Haute

Nightclubs

ZimMarss Nightclub & Restaurant [MW,D,TG,F,DS,S] 1500 Locust St (at 15th St) **812/232-3026** *5pm-3am, 7pm-12:30am Sun, clsd Mon, also restaurant*

Cruisy Areas

Deming Park [AYOR]

Fairbanks Park [AYOR] S 1st Ave

Valparaiso

Accommodations

Inn at Aberdeen [GF,NS,WI,WC] 3158 S State Rd 2 **219/465-3753, 866/761-3753** *1880s Queen Anne, full brkfst*

Vincennes

Cruisy Areas

George Rodgers Clark Memorial Park [AYOR]

Zionsville

see Indianapolis

Iowa

Statewide

Publications

Accessline 319/232-6805 *LGBT newspaper*

Lavender Magazine 612/436-4660, 877/515-9969 *LGBT newsmagazine for IA, MN, ND, SD, WI*

Ames

Restaurants

Lucullan's Italian Grill 400 Main St (at Burnett) **515/232-8484** *dinner Tue-Sun, Italian, full bar*

Erotica

Romantix Adult Superstore 117 Kellogg (at Lincoln Wy) **515/232-7717** *24hrs*

Boone

Cruisy Areas

Roadside Park [AYOR] 1 mile W on US-30

Burlington

Accommodations

Arrowhead Motel, Inc [GF,WI,WC,GO] 2520 Mt Pleasant St **319/752-6353**

Restaurants

Steve's Place [WC] 852 Washington (at Central Ave) **319/754-5868** *10am-2am, noon-6pm Sun, also bar*

Erotica

Risque IV 421 Dry Creek Ave, West Burlington **319/753-5455**

Cruisy Areas

Hunt Woods [AYOR] 1 mile S of town *days*

Cedar Falls

see Waterloo

Cedar Rapids

Info Lines & Services

Gay/ Lesbian Resource Center 6300 Rockwell Dr NE **319/366-2055** *support groups, referrals*

Nightclubs

Club Basix [MW,D,L,TG,DS,GO] 3916 1st Ave NE (btwn 39th & 40th) **319/363-3194** *5pm-2am, from noon wknds*

Restaurants

Hamburger Mary's [MW,DS,E] 222 Glenbrook Dr SE **319/378-4627** *11am-2am, also full bar*

The Happy Chef 1906 Blairs Ferry Rd NE **319/395-7793** *24hrs, all-American, salad bar*

Entertainment & Recreation

CSPS Arts Center 1103 3rd St SE **319/364-1580** *many LGBT events*

Erotica

Adult Shop 630 66th Ave SW (at 6th St) **319/362-4939** *24hrs*

Adult Shop North 5539 Crane Ln NE **319/294-5360**

Clinton

Erotica

ABC Books 135 5th Ave S **563/242-7687**

Council Bluffs

see also Omaha, Nebraska

Accommodations

Historic Wickham B&B [GS,WI,GO] 616 S 7th Street **712/328-1872**

Erotica

Romantix Adult Superstore 3216 1st Ave (at Broadway) **712/328-2673** *24hrs*

Romantix Adult Superstore 50662 189th St **712/366-1764** *24hrs*

Davenport

see also Rock Island, Illinois

Accommodations

Traveler Motel [GS] 433 14th St (near I-74 & US 61), Bettendorf **563/355-0285** *XXX motel*

Bars

Mary's on 2nd [MW,NH,D,E,V,WC] 832 W 2nd St **563/884-8014** *4pm-2am, patio*

Nan's Piano Bar [GF,E] 421 W River Dr (at the Freight House) **563/323-5081** *4:30pm-midnight, till 2am wknds, clsd Mon*

Nightclubs

Club Fusion [MW,D,DS,S,GO] 813 W 2nd St (at Warren) **563/326-3452** *4pm-2am, patio, deck*

Connections [MW,D,DS,K] 822 W 2nd St **563/322-1121** *4pm-2am*

Erotica

TR Video 3727 Hickory Grove Rd (at Fairmont & Hickory Grove) **563/386-7914**

Venus News 902 W 3rd St **563/322-7576**

Cruisy Areas

Credit Island Park [AYOR] W River Dr (W end) *daytime*

Davenport Levee [AYOR] under the Centennial Bridge *dusk*

Le Clair Park [AYOR] on riverfront from Main to Ripley *late*

Des Moines

Accommodations

The Cottage B&B [GF] 1094 28th St (at Cottage Grove) **515/277-7559**

Hotel Fort Des Moines [GF,SW,NS,WI,WC] 1000 Walnut St (at 10th St) **515/243-1161, 800/532-1466**

Ramada Inn Clive [GF,SW,WI,WC,GO] 1600 NW 114th St (at University Ave), Clive **515/226-1600, 866/981-6100**

The Renaissance Savery Hotel [GF,F,SW,WC] 401 Locust St (at 4th) **515/244-2151, 800/798-2151** *luxury hotel & spa*

Bars

The Blazing Saddle [★M,D,L,DS,S,WC] 416 E 5th St (btwn Grand & Locust) **515/246-1299** *2pm-2am, from noon wknds*

Buddies Corral [GF,K] 418 E 5th St (btwn Grand & Locust) **515/244-7140** *noon-2am*

Rio Video/ Patio Bar [M,NH,S,V] 1500 SE 1st **515/288-0382** *3pm-2am*

Nightclubs

The Garden [MW,D,K,S,V,YC,WC] 112 SE 4th St **515/243-3965** *4pm-2am, clsd Mon-Tue, patio*

Cafes

Baby Boomer's [F,GO] 313 E Locust (at E 4th St) **515/244-9107** *6am-2pm, 7am-noon Sat, clsd Sun-Mon, great brkfst*

Drake Diner [F,WC] 1111 25th St (btwn University & Cottage Grove) **515/277-1111** *7am-10pm, till 11pm Fri-Sat, award-winning chili, patio, full bar*

Java Joe's [E,WI] 214 4th St (at Court Ave) **515/288-5282** *7am-11pm, till 12:30am Fri-Sat, from 9am Sun*

Ritual Cafe [E] 1301 E Locust St **515/288-4872** *7am-7pm, till 11pm Fri-Sat, 9am-3pm Sun*

Zanzibar's Coffee Adventure 2723 Ingersoll (at 28th St) **515/244-7694** *6:30am-9pm, till 11pm Fri-Sat, 8am-6pm Sun*

Restaurants

Cafe di Scala [E,WC] 644 18th St (at Woodland) **515/244-1353** *dinner Th-Sat only*

Chicago Dog & Deli 523 Euclid (at 6th) **515/243-3085** *8am-5pm, till 3pm Sat, clsd Sun*

Paradise Pizza 2025 Grand, West Des Moines **515/222-9959** *11am-9pm, till 10pm Fri-Sat, clsd Mon*

Entertainment & Recreation

First Friday Breakfast Club, Inc [MO,R] 1501 Woodland (at 15th) **515/288-2500, 515/284-0880** *7am-8:15am 1st Fri, gay & bisexual men, cont'l brkfst, guest speakers, call to reserve*

Bookstores

Borders 4100 University #115 (at 42nd, Water Tower mall), West Des Moines **515/223-1620** *9am-10pm, till 11pm Fri-Sat, 11am-8pm Sun, LGBT section, also cafe*

Retail Shops

Liberty Gifts 333 E Grand Ave, Ste 105 (entrance on E 4th St) **515/508-0825** *11am-6pm, till 7pm Fri-Sat, noon-5pm Sun, clsd Mon, pride store*

Men's Services

▶ **Megaphone 515/267-0900** *Meet and Chat Live with HOT local men. FREE to listen & respond to ads. Video and text chat at GayMates.com. Use FREE code 4889.*

Erotica

Gallery Book Store 1000 Cherry (at 10th) **515/244-2916** *24hrs*

Minx Love Boutique 1510 NE Broadway **515/266-2744** *also Minx Show Palace*

Romantix Adult Superstore 1401 E Army Post Rd (at SE 14th St) **515/256-1102** *24hrs*

Romantix Adult Superstore 2020 E Euclid (at Delaware) **515/266-7992** *24hrs*

Cruisy Areas

West River Dr [AYOR] N of downtown, by the river (off 2nd Ave N)

Dubuque

Cafes

Cafe Manna Java [GO] 269 Main St (at 4th St) **563/588-3105** *7am-9pm*

Erotica

Adult Warehouse 975 Jackson St **563/588-9184**

Cruisy Areas

Julien Dubuque Monument Park [AYOR]

Fort Dodge

Erotica

Romantix Adult Superstore 15 N 5th St (on the square) **515/955-9756**

Iowa City

Info Lines & Services

AA Gay/ Lesbian 500 N Clinton (at church) **319/338-9111 (AA#)** *5pm Sun & Wed*

Bars

Deadwood [★GF,NH] 6 S Dubuque St **319/351-9417** *10am-2am, from noon Sun, mostly straight, college crowd*

Studio 13 [MW,D,DS,S,19+,GO] 13 S Linn St (in the alley btwn Linn & Dubuque Sts) **319/338-7145** *7pm-2am, clsd Mon-Tue*

Restaurants

The Mill [E] 120 E Burlington St **319/351-9529** *lunch & dinner, wknd brunch, live music*

Bookstores

Prairie Lights Bookstore [WC] 15 S Dubuque St (at Washington) **319/337-2681** *9am-10pm, till 6pm wknds, also cafe*

Retail Shops

New Pioneer Co-op & Bakehouse [GF] 22 S Van Buren **319/338-9441** *7am-10pm, health food store & deli; also Coralville location at 1101 2nd St, 319/358-5514*

Publications

Outlook Magazine PO Box 1733, 52244

Erotica

Romantix Adult Superstore 315 Kirkwood Ave (at Gilbert) **319/351-9444** *24hrs*

Marshalltown

Erotica

Adult Odyssey 907 Iowa Ave E **641/752-6550** *videos, toys, leather*

Newton

Accommodations

La Corsette Maison Inn [GF,NS] 629 1st Ave E **641/792-6833** *upscale B&B w/ 4-star restaurant*

Erotica

▶ **The Lion's Den Adult Superstore** 7717 Hwy F 48 West (Exit 159, off I-80) **641/792-9301** *24hrs*

Ottumwa

Erotica

Cinema X 317 E Main St (downtown exit, off Rte 34) **641/683-1481** *clsd Mon*

Cruisy Areas

Greater Ottumwa Park [AYOR]

Sioux City

Nightclubs

Jones Street Station [GS,D,MR,TG,K,DS,V,WC,GO] 412 Jones St (at 5th St) **712/258-6338** *7pm-2am, clsd Sun-Mon*

Erotica

Romantix Adult Superstore 511 Pearl St **712/277-8566** *24hrs*

Waterloo

Accommodations

Stella's Guesthouse [MW,NS,GO] 324 Summit Ave (at Chicago) **319/232-2122** *B&B in 107-year-old home, full brkfst, hot tub, shared baths*

Bars

Monica's [GF,NH,E,K,WC,GO] 324 E 4th St (at Mulberry) **319/233-1319** *4pm-12pm, till 2am Fri-Sat, clsd Mon*

Nightclubs

Kings & Queens Knight Club [GF,D,TG,DS,V,YC,WC] 304 W 4th St (at Jefferson) **319/232-3001** *6pm-2am Wed-Sat*

Erotica

Adult Cinema 16 315 E 4th St (at Mulberry) **319/234-7459**

Romantix Adult Superstore 1507 La Porte Rd (at Lock) **319/234-9340** *24hrs*

KANSAS

Statewide

Publications

The Liberty Press 316/652-7737 *Kansas statewide LGBT newspaper*

Abilene

Erotica

▶ **The Lion's Den Adult Superstore** 2349 Fair Rd (exit 272 off I-70) **785/263-9898**

Great Bend

Cruisy Areas

Fort Zarah Rest Area [AYOR] on Santa Fe Trail (on Hwy 56) *2 miles E of Great Bend*

Hutchinson

Cruisy Areas

Carey Park [AYOR] Main St (at the very S end)

Junction City

Nightclubs

Xcalibur Club [GS,D,E,DS,18+,GO] 384 Grant Ave **785/762-2050** *6pm-2am, clsd Mon-Tue, [B] 4th wknd*

Erotica

After Dark Video 785/762-4747 *24hrs, cruisy*

Kansas City

see also **Kansas City, Missouri**

Entertainment & Recreation

2nd Friday Art Walk downtown **913/371-0024** *5pm-8pm 1st Fri, art galleries & food*

Men's Services

▶ **Megaphone 913/904-9974** *Meet and Chat Live with HOT local men. FREE to listen & respond to ads. Video and text chat at GayMates.com. Use FREE code 4889.*

Cruisy Areas

Pierson Park [AYOR] Wyandotte County (off Nieman Rd) *Mon-Fri*

Lawrence

Nightclubs

Granada [GS,D,E,WC] 1020 Massachusetts (at 11th) **785/842-1390** *hours vary, clsd Sun, live bands*

Jazzhaus [GF,E] 926-1/2 Massachusetts St **785/749-3320, 785/749-1387** *8pm-2am, clsd Sun*

Wilde's Chateau [GS,D] 2412 Iowa St **785/856-1514** *9pm-2am Wed-Sat*

Cafes

Henry's 11 E 8th St (btwn Massachusetts St & New Hampshire St) **785/331-3511** *8am-2am, also full bar upstairs*

Java Break [GO] 17 E 7th St (at New Hampshire) **785/749-5282** *24hrs, sandwiches, desserts*

Restaurants

Teller's Restaurant & Bar [WC] 746 Massachusetts St (at 8th) **785/843-4111** *11:30am-10pm, till 11pm Fri-Sat, 9am-10pm Sun, Italian*

Bookstores

The Dusty Bookshelf [GO] 708 Massachusetts St **785/749-4643** *10am-8pm, till 10pm Fri-Sat, noon-6pm Sun, LGBT section*

Cruisy Areas

Memorial Drive [AYOR] E of Jayhawk Blvd

Riverfront Park [AYOR] Hwy 24/40 (at N 2nd St)

Liberal

Bookstores

Second Street Bookstore 11 W 2nd St **620/624-8105** *10am-7:30pm, from noon Sun, gay magazine section*

Manhattan

Bookstores

The Dusty Bookshelf [E,GO] 700 N Manhattan **785/539-2839** *10am-8pm, till 6pm Sat, noon-5pm Sun*

Cruisy Areas

Tuttle Creek Park [AYOR]

Olathe

Cruisy Areas

Cedar Lake [AYOR] on Lone Elm Rd

Overland Park

Accommodations

Holtze Executive Village [GF,SW,NS,WI,WC] 11400 College Blvd **913/344-8100, 888/446-5893** *suites in authentic Colorado-style lodge*

Bars

The Fox [M,NH,TG,V] 7520 Shawnee Mission Pkwy (at Metcalf) **913/384-0369** *1pm-2am, from 6pm Fri-Mon*

Salina

Cruisy Areas

Thomas Park [AYOR] 1/2 mile S of I-70 (at 9th St exit)

Topeka

Info Lines & Services

AA Gay/ Lesbian 4425 SW 19th (at MCC) **785/215-7436** *8pm Fri*

Bars

The Tool Shed Tap [M,NH,D,CW,B,L,GO] 921 S Kansas Ave (near 10th St) **785/234-0482** *3pm-2am*

Bookstores

Barnes & Noble 6130 SW 17th St #101 **785/273-9600** *9am-11pm, LGBT section*

Erotica

Sinsations 4720 SW Topeka Blvd (S from I-470) **785/862-5002** *video arcade*

Cruisy Areas

Gage Park [AYOR] *beware of cops!*

Shunga Park [AYOR] 29th St & Fairlawn Rd

Wichita

Info Lines & Services

One Day at a Time Gay AA 156 S Kansas Ave (at MCC, enter on English) **316/522-7411, 316/522-2321** *8pm Mon, Wed & Th*

Accommodations

Hawthorn Suites [GF,WC] 2405 N Ridge Rd **316/729-5700** *brkfst buffet*

Bars

J's Lounge [MW,E,K,C,WC] 513 E Central (at Emporia) **316/262-1363** *4pm-2am, cabaret, patio, "an upscale dive"*

The Other Side [MW,NH] 1315 E Central **316/262-7825** *4pm-2am*

Side Street [M,D,CW,L,WC] 1106 S Pattie (near Lincoln & Hydraulic) **316/267-0324** *2pm-2am, patio*

The Store [W,NH] 3210 E Osie (btw Harry & Hillside) **316/683-9781** *2pm-2am, men welcome*

Nightclubs

Fantasy Complex [MW,D,CW,DS,S,18+,WC] 3201 S Hillside (at 31st) **316/682-5494** *8pm-2am Th-Sun, also South Forty Fri-Sat [CW]*

Cafes

Riverside Perk 1144 Bitting Ave (at 11th) **316/264-6464** *7am-10pm, till midnight Fri-Sat, from 10am Sun, internet access; also Lava Lounge juice bar next door*

The Vagabond [WI] 614 W Douglas Ave **316/303-1110** *7am-2am, also art gallery & bar, theme nights*

Restaurants

Moe's Sub Shop 2815 S Hydraulic (at Wassall) **316/524-5511** *11am-8pm, clsd Sun*

Old Mill Tasty Shop 604 E Douglas (at St Francis) **316/264-6500** *11am-3pm, from 8am Sat, clsd Sun, old-fashioned soda fountain, lunch menu*

River City Brewing Company 150 N Mosley St **316/263-2739** *11am-10pm, till 11pm wknds, American, also live music*

Riverside Cafe 739 W 13th (at Bitting) **316/262-6703** *6am-8pm, till 2pm Sun*

Uptown Bistro 301 N Mead (at 2nd) **316/262-3232** *lunch & dinner daily, noon-8pm Sun*

Entertainment & Recreation

Cabaret Oldtown Theatre 412 1/2 E Douglas (at Topeka) **316/265-4400** *edgy, kitschy productions*

Mosley Street Melodrama [F,$] 234 N Mosley St (btwn 1st & 2nd St) **316/263-0222** *melodrama, homestyle buffet & full bar!*

Wichita Arts 334 N Mead **316/462-2787** *promotes visual & performing arts; ArtScene publication has extensive cultural calendar*

Retail Shops

Holier Than Thou Body Piercing 1115 E Douglas Ave (at Washington) **316/266-4100** *noon-8pm, clsd Sun-Mon*

Publications

The Liberty Press 316/652-7737 *statewide LGBT newspaper*

Men's Services

Erotica

Circle Cinema/ Video 2570 S Seneca St (at Crawford St) **316/264-2245** *24hrs*

Fetish Lingerie 2150 S Broadway (btwn E Clark & E Kinkaid Sts) **316/264-7800** *leather, toys, clubwear, all sizes available*

Las Vegas Adult Video 8323 W Kellogg **316/722-7808** *24hrs*

Priscilla's 6143 W Kellogg (at Dugan) **316/942-1244**

Xcitement Video 1306 E Harry (at Pattie) **316/269-9036** *24hrs*

Cruisy Areas

Chisholm Trail Park [AYOR] Oliver & 29th St *days*

Kentucky

Ashland

Cruisy Areas

Central Park [AYOR] *beware of cops on bikes!*

Campbellsville

Cruisy Areas

Green River Dam [AYOR] Hwy 55 (below dam)

Covington

see also Cincinnati, Ohio

Accommodations

Amos Shinkle Townhouse B&B [GF,GO] 215 Garrard St (at 3rd St) **859/431-2118, 800/972-7012** *in Covington's Riverside Historic District, hot tub*

Bars

Bar Monet [MW,D,F,K,S] 837 Willard St **859/491-2403** *4pm-1am*

Rosie's Tavern [GS,NH,GO] 643 Bakewell St (at 7th St) **859/291-9707** *3pm-2:30am*

Yadda Club [MW,NH,MR,F,E,K,WC] 404 Pike St (at Main St) **859/491-5600** *8pm-2:30am Wed-Sat, patio*

Cruisy Areas

Devou Park [AYOR] Covington exit, off Rte 75

Harned

Accommodations

Kentucky Holler House [GS,NS] **270/547-4507** *rental cabin on 31 acres*

Jamestown

Cruisy Areas

Kendall Recreation Area [AYOR] below Wolf Creek Dam (10 miles S on Hwy 127) *also pull-off areas & overlook above dam*

Lexington

Info Lines & Services

Gay/ Lesbian AA 472 Rose St (at St Augustine's Chapel) **859/225-1212 (AA#)** *8pm Mon & Wed, also 7:30pm Fri at 205 E Short St*

GLSO Pride Center of the Bluegrass 389 Waller Ave #100 **859/253-3233** *10am-3pm Mon-Fri*

Accommodations

The Bear & Boar B&B Resort [MO,SW,GO] Wood Creek Lake, London **606/862-6557** *also camping, theme parties*

Bars

The Bar Complex [★MW,D,DS,S,WC] 224 E Main St (at Esplanade) **859/255-1551** *4pm-2am, till 11:30pm Mon-Wed*

Crossings [M,NH,L,S,WC] 117 N Limestone St **859/233-7266** *4pm-2am, clsd Sun*

Mia's [MW,NH,F] 127 N Limestone **859/455-9903** *4pm-2:30am, from 11am wknds for brunch*

Nightclubs

The Dame [GF,D] 367 E Main St *more gay Fri for 80s night*

Niche [M,DS] 1203 Versailles Rd **859/389-9713**

Restaurants

Alfalfa Restaurant [E] 141 E Main St **859/253-0014** *lunch & dinner, brunch wknds, healthy multi-ethnic, folk music wknds*

Natasha's Bistro & Bar [E] 112 Esplanade (at Main St) **859/259-2754, 888/901-8412 (shop #)** *lunch & dinner, clsd Sun, eclectic dining, plenty veggie, also live theater & music*

Bookstores

Joseph-Beth [WC] 161 Lexington Green Circle **859/273-2911, 800/248-6849** *9am-10pm, till 11pm Fri-Sat, 11am-9pm Sun, also cafe*

Sqecial Media 371 S Limestone St **859/255-4316** *10am-8pm, noon-6pm Sun, also pride items*

Publications

GLSO (Gay/ Lesbian) News **859/253-3233** *local news & calendar*

Erotica

Book Novelty 940 Winchester Rd **859/252-2093**

Romantix Adult Superstore 933 Winchester Rd **859/252-0357** *24hrs*

Cruisy Areas

Jacobson Park [AYOR] Richmond Rd (3 miles W of Lexington) *take 3 rights inside park to sunbathing area*

Woodland Park [AYOR] E High St

Louisville

Info Lines & Services

Gay AA 1432 Highland Ave (at MCC) **502/587-6225** *4:30pm & 6pm Sun, 7:30pm Tue, 6:30pm Wed, 7pm Fri*

Accommodations

21c Museum Hotel [GF] 700 W Main **502/217-6300, 877/217-6400** *boutique hotel w/ museum*

The Brown Hotel [GF] 335 W Broadway (at 4th) **502/583-1234, 888/888-5252**

Columbine B&B [GF,NS,WI,GO] 1707 S 3rd St (near Lee St) **502/635-5000, 800/635-5010** *1896 Greek Revivial mansion, full brkfst*

Galt House Hotel & Suites [GF] 140 N 4th St (at W Main) **502/589-5200, 800/843-4258** *waterfront hotel*

Holiday Inn Southwest [GF,F,SW,WC] 4110 Dixie Hwy (at I-264) **502/448-2020**

Hyatt Regency Louisville [GF,SW,WI,WC] 320 W Jefferson St (at 3rd) **502/581-1234** *tennis*

Inn at the Park [GF,NS] 1332 S 4th St (at Park Ave) **502/638-0045** *restored mansion, full brkfst*

Bars

Magnolia Bar [GF,NH,YC] 1398 S 2nd St (at Magnolia) **502/637-9052** *4pm-4am*

Teddy Bears Bar & Grill [M,NH,WC] 1148 Garvin Pl (at St Catherine) **502/589-2619** *11am-4am, from 1pm Sun*

Tink's Pub [MW,NH,K,DS] 2235 S Preston St **502/634-8180** *4pm-close, from 2pm Sun*

Tryangles [M,K,S,WC] 209 S Preston St (at Market) **502/583-6395** *4pm-4am, from 1pm Sun*

Woody's Tavern [M] 208 E Burnett Ave **502/635-9221** *4pm-4am*

Nightclubs

Boots [★M,L] 120 S Floyd St (in Connections Complex) **502/585-5752** *9pm-2am, till 4am Fri-Sat, dress code, fireplace, patio*

The Connection Complex [★MW,D,C,P,V,WC] 120 S Floyd St (at Market) **502/585-5752** *7pm-4am, till 2am Mon-Tue, 5 bars*

Fuzion [M,D,DS] 1335 Story Ave **502/588-8861** *5pm-close, clsd Mon*

Starbase Q [M,D,K,V] 921 W Main St (at 9th St) *industrial video bar*

Restaurants

El Mundo [★] 2345 Frankfort Ave **502/899-9930** *11:30am-10pm, full bar till 2am Th-Sat, clsd Sun-Mon, Mexican*

Lynn's Paradise Cafe [★MW,WI,GO] 984 Barret Ave (at Baxter) **502/583-3447** *7am-10pm, from 8am wknds, also bar*

Mayan Cafe 813 E Market St **502/566-0651** *lunch Mon-Fri, dinner nightly, clsd Sun, Mayan/ Mexican*

Porcini 2370 Frankfort Ave **502/894-8686** *dinner nightly, clsd Sun, Italian*

Proof on Main 702 W Main St (at 7th) **502/217-6360** *brkfst & lunch Mon-Fri, dinner nightly, upscale, American w/ Tuscan influence*

Ramsi's Cafe on the World 1293 Bardstown Rd **502/451-0700** *11am-1am, till 2am Fri-Sat, Sun brunch, eclectic menu*

Rudyard Kipling [E] 422 W Oak St **502/636-1311** *6:30pm-close Fri-Sat, full bar, occasionally open for plays & special events*

Third Avenue Cafe 1164 S 3rd St (at W Oak) **502/585-2233** *11am-9pm, till 10pm Fri-Sat, clsd Sun, vegan/ vegetarian, patio*

Vietnam Kitchen 5339 Mitscher Ave **502/363-5154** *Vietnamese, plenty veggie*

Windy City Pizza [GO] 2622 S 4th St **502/636-3708** *clsd Sun-Mon*

Zen Garden 2240 Frankfort Ave **502/895-9114** *lunch & dinner, clsd Sun, Asian, vegetarian*

Entertainment & Recreation

Pandora Productions PO Box 4185 40204 *LGBT-themed productions*

Voices of Kentuckiana 502/583-1013 *LGBT chorus*

Bookstores

Borders 3024 Bardstown Rd (in Gardiner Lane Shopping Center) **502/456-6660, 800/844-7323** *9am-9pm, 10am-6pm Sun; also 4600 Shelbyville Rd, Shelbyville Plaza, 502/893-0133*

Carmichael's 1295 Bardstown Rd (at Longest Ave) **502/456-6950** *8am-10pm, till 11pm Fri-Sat, from 10am Sun, large LGBT section*

Publications

The Letter *LGBT newspaper*

Men's Services

► **Megaphone 502/561-6666** *Meet and Chat Live with HOT local men. FREE to listen & respond to ads. Video and text chat at GayMates.com. Use FREE code 4889.*

Erotica

Arcade Adult Bookstore 2822 7th St (at Arcade) **502/637-8388**

Blue Movies 140 W Jefferson St (at 2nd) **502/585-4627** *24hrs*

Louisville Manor 4600 Dixie Hwy **502/449-1443** *24hrs*

Metro Station 4948 Poplar Level Rd **502/968-2353**

Showboat Adult Bookstore 3524 S 7th St (at Berry Blvd) **502/361-0007** *hustlers*

Theatair X 4505 Hwy 31 (1/2 mile N of I-65), Clarksville, IN **812/282-6976** *24hrs*

Madisonville

Cruisy Areas

Grapevine Lake [AYOR]

Madisonville City Park [AYOR] Park Ave (off Pennyrile Pkwy) *go W thru 3 traffic lights, go left & drive 1 mile*

Midway

Cafes

Quirk Cafe & Coffee [WI,GO] 131 E Main St (inside Le Marché boutique mall) **859/846-4688** *10am-4pm, till 9pm Fri-Sat*

Morehead

Cruisy Areas

Cave Run State Park [AYOR]

Daniel Boone Campground [AYOR]

Newport

see also Cincinnati, Ohio

Bars

The Crazy Fox Saloon [GS,NH] 901 Washington Ave (at 9th) **859/261-2143** *3pm-2:30am*

Cruisy Areas

James Taylor Park [AYOR] on Newport Levee

Owensboro

Bars

Equals Bar [MW,D,E,K] 1006 E 4th St (at Hathaway) **270/313-0820** *4:30-2am*

Paducah

Erotica

Romantix Adult Superstore 243 Brown (at Irvin Cobb Dr) **270/442-5584**

Radcliff

Restaurants

Gyros Express 661 Knox Blvd **270/351-2009** *11am-9pm, till 5pm Sun, Greek*

Somerset

Cruisy Areas

Alpine Rest Area [AYOR] S Hwy 27 Daniel Boone Nat'l Forest

Upton

Erotica

► **The Lion's Den Adult Superstore** 2833 Weldon Loop (exit 76 off I-65) **270/369-8171**

Whitesburg

Cruisy Areas

Carr Creek Dam [AYOR] Hazard

Louisiana

Statewide

Publications

▶ **Ambush Mag 504/522-8049** *oldest LGBT newspaper for the Gulf South (Texas through Florida)*

Southern Voice 404/876-1819 *weekly LGBT newspaper for AL, FL (panhandle), GA, LA, MS, TN w/ resource listings*

Alexandria

Nightclubs

Unique Bar & Lounge [★MW,D,TG,K,DS,S,WC] 3217 Industrial St **318/448-0555** *9pm-3am, clsd Sun-Tue*

Erotica

Alexandria Adult Emporium 3117 Masonic Dr (across from Bringhurst Park) **318/561-0306** *arcade*

Capri Video #3 1820 N MacArthur Dr (off Hwy 1) **318/767-1669** *arcade*

Cruisy Areas

Bringhurst Park [AYOR] 3016 Masonic Dr

Baton Rouge

Info Lines & Services

Freedom of Choice/ Gay AA 7747 Tom Dr (at MCC) **225/388-0069 (AA#)** *8pm Th & 8pm Sat*

Bars

George's Place [★MW,NH,K,S,V,WC] 860 St Louis **225/387-9798** *3pm-2am, from 5pm Sat, clsd Sun, [S] Fri*

Hound Dog [MW,NH,WC] 668 Main St (at 7th) **225/344-0807** *2pm-2am, from 4pm Mon-Tue, clsd Sun*

Nightclubs

Splash [★MW,D,DS,18+,WC] 2183 Highland Rd **225/242-9491** *9pm-2am, clsd Sun-Tue*

Restaurants

Drusilla Seafood 3482 Drusilla Ln (at Jefferson Hwy) **225/923-0896** *11am-10pm, till 9pm wknds*

Ralph & Kacoo's 6110 Bluebonnet Blvd (off I-10 & Perkins) **225/766-2113** *11am-9:30pm, till 10:30pm Fri-Sat, Cajun, full bar*

Publications

▶ **Ambush Mag 504/522-8049** *LGBT newspaper for the Gulf South (TX through FL)*

Men's Services

▶ **Megaphone 888/634-2628** *Meet and Chat Live with HOT local men. Call for your local number or visit us online at GayMates.com. Use FREE code 4889.*

Erotica

Grand Cinema Station 10732 Florida Blvd **225/272-2010**

Cruisy Areas

Capitol Lakes Park [AYOR] New Orleans *also adjacent area*

Manchac Park [AYOR] Hwy 73 (N of Bayou Manchac)

Breaux Bridge

Accommodations

Maison des Amis [GF] 111 Washington St (at Bridge St) **337/507-3399**

Egan

Erotica

▶ **The Lion's Den Adult Superstore** 191 Bocage Rd (exit 72 off I-10) **337/783-5000** *24hrs*

Gretna

see New Orleans

Harvey

see New Orleans

Houma

Erotica

Conxxxion 239 N Hollywood Rd **985/868-8100**

Lafayette

Info Lines & Services

AA Gay/ Lesbian 115 Leonie St **337/991-0830 (AA#)** *call for times & locations*

Bars

Back Side [MW,NH,GO] 209 Jefferson St (at Sound Factory) **337/269-0430** *4pm-2am, noon-midnight Sun*

Sadies Niteclub [GS,D,NH,18+] 425 Jefferson **337/267-7404** *4pm-2am, 8pm-midnight Sun*

Nightclubs

Seven [MW] 533 Jefferson St **337/264-8000** *7pm-2am Wed-Sat*

Sound Factory [M,D,K,DS,YC,GO] 209 Jefferson St (at Cypress) **337/269-6011** *9pm-2am, till midnight Sun*

Cruisy Areas

Acadiana Park, Beaver Park & Moore Park [AYOR]

Lake Charles

Accommodations

Aunt Ruby's B&B [GS] 504 Pujo St (at Hodges) **337/430-0603** *full brkfst*

Nightclubs

Crystal's [MW,D,CW,F,DS,WC,GO] 112 W Broad St **337/433-5457** *9pm-2am, till 4am Fri*

Restaurants

Pujo St Cafe [GO] 901 Ryan St (at Pujo) **337/439-2054** *11am-9pm, till 10pm Fri-Sat, clsd Sun, full bar*

Cruisy Areas

Pindarosa Park [AYOR] Sampson St, Westlake

Prien Lake Park & Tuten Park [AYOR]

Metairie

see New Orleans

Monroe

Bars

The Corner Bar [MW,NH,MR,E,K,DS,18+,GO] 512 N 3rd St (at Pine) **318/329-0046** *8pm-2am, 3pm-midnight Sun, clsd Mon & Wed, seasonal hrs*

Cruisy Areas

Forsythe Park [AYOR] Forsythe Ave (at Riverside Dr)

Natchitoches

Accommodations

Chez des Amis B&B [GS,NS,WI,GO] 910 Washington St (btwn Texas & Pavie) **318/352-2647** *full brkfst*

New Iberia

Erotica

Leisure Time Entertainment 7600 Hwy 90 W **337/364-1883** *24hrs, arcade*

New Orleans

Info Lines & Services

AA Lambda Center 638 Papworth Ave #101, Metairie **504/838-3399 (general AA office #)** *daily meetings, call for schedule*

Lesbian/ Gay Community Center of New Orleans [WC] 2114 Decatur St (btwn Elysian Fields & Frenchmen) **504/945-1103** *2pm-8pm, noon-6pm Fri-Sat, clsd Sun, call first*

Accommodations

1896 O'Malley House B&B [GS,NS,WI,GO] 120 S Pierce St (at Canal St) **504/488-5896, 866/226-1896**

5 Continents B&B [GS,WI,GO] 1731 Esplanade Ave (at Claiborne) **504/324-8594, 800/997-4652** *full brkfst*

Aaron Ingram Haus [GS,WI,GO] 1012 Elysian Fields Ave (btwn N Rampart & St Claude) **504/949-3110** *guesthouse, apts, courtyard*

American Creole House [GS,WI] 1124 St Charles Ave (at Caliope) **504/522-7777, 800/999-7891**

Andrew Jackson Hotel [GF,WI] 919 Royal St (btwn St Philip & Dumaine) **504/561-5881, 800/654-0224** *historic inn*

Antebellum Guest House [GS,N,NS,WI,GO] 1333 Esplanade Ave (at Maris St) **504/943-1900** *B&B in historic 1830s Grand Greek Revival near French Quarter, antique interiors, full brkfst, clothing-optional hot tub & private courtyard*

Ashton's B&B [GF,NS,WI] 2023 Esplanade Ave (at Galvez) **504/942-7048, 800/725-4131**

B&W Courtyards B&B [GF,NS,WI,GO] 2425 Chartres St (btwn Mandeville & Spain) **504/945-9418, 800/585-5731** *three 19th-c bldgs connected by courtyards, hot tub*

Biscuit Palace Guest House [GF,WI,WC] 730 Dumaine (btwn Royal & Bourbon) **504/525-9949** *1820s Creole mansion in the French Quarter*

Block-Keller House [GS,NS,GO] 3620 Canal St (at Telemachus) **504/483-3033, 877/588-3033**

Bon Maison Guest House [GS,NS,GO] 835 Bourbon St (btwn Lafitte's & Bourbon Pub) **504/561-8498**

Bourbon Orleans Hotel [★GF,F,SW] 717 Orleans (at Bourbon St) **504/523-2222**

▶ **Bourgoyne Guest House** [★MW] 839 Bourbon St (at Dumaine St) **504/524-3621, 504/525-3983** *1830s Creole mansion furnished w/ antiques, courtyard*

The Burgundy B&B [GS,NS,WI,GO] 2513 Burgundy St (at St Roch) **504/942-1463, 800/970-2153** *1890s "double shotgun" in Faubourg Marigny, close to French Quarter, hot tub [N]*

Chez Palmiers B&B [GS,SW,NS,WI,GO] 1744 N Rampart St **877/233-9449**

The Cornstalk Hotel [GF,WI] 915 Royal St **504/523-1515, 800/759-6112**

Creole Inn [GS,NS,WI,GO] 2471 Dauphine St (at Spain) **504/948-3230** *B&B in private home*

Crescent City Guest House [GS,N,NS,WI,GO] 612 Marigny St (at Chartres) **504/944-8722, 877/281-2680** *near French Quarter, hot tub*

The Degas House [GF,WI] 2306 Esplanade Ave (at Tonti St) **504/821-5009, 800/755-6730** *full brkfst*

Elysian Guest House [MW,NS,WI,GO] 1008 Elysian Fields Ave (at Rampart St) **504/324-4311** *hot tub*

Empress Hotel [GF] 1317 Ursulines Ave (btwn Treme & Marais) **504/529-4100, 888/524-9200** *small Euro-style hotel*

The Frenchmen Hotel [★GS,SW,NS,WI,WC] 417 Frenchmen St (where Esplanade, Decatur & Frenchmen intersect) **504/948-2166, 800/831-1781**

The Green House Inn [MW,SW,NS,WI,GO] 1212 Magazine St (at Erato) **504/525-1333, 800/966-1303** *gym, hot tub*

Historic Rentals [GS,WI,GO] **800/537-5408** *1- & 2-bdrm apts in French Quarter*

Hotel Maison de Ville [GF,SW,WI] 727 Rue Toulouse (btwn Bourbon & Royal Sts) **504/561-5858, 800/634-1600**

Hotel Monteleone [GF] 214 Royal St **504/523-3341, 800/535-9595**

Inn The Quarter Reservation Service [GF,NS] **888/523-5235**

Kerlerec House [GS,NS,WI,GO] 928 Kerlerec St (at Dauphine St) **504/944-8544** *1 block from the French Quarter, gardens*

La Dauphine, Residence des Artistes [GS,NS,WI,GO] 2316 Dauphine St (btwn Elysian Fields & Marigny) **504/948-2217** *B&B, no unregistered overnight guests*

La Maison Marigny B&B on Bourbon [GS,NS,WI,GO] 1421 Bourbon St (at Esplanade) **504/948-3638, 800/570-2014** *on the quiet end of Bourbon St*

► **Lamothe House Hotel** [★GS,SW,NS,WI,GO] 621 Esplanade Ave (btwn Royal & Chartres) **504/947-1161, 800/367-5858**

Le Papillon Guesthouse [GS,NS,GO] 2011 N Rampart St (at Touro St) **504/948-4993, 504/884-4008 (cell)**

Lions Inn [GS,SW,N,NS,WI,GO] 2517 Chartres St (btwn Spain & Franklin) **504/945-2339, 800/485-6846** *1850s home, hot tub, patio*

Maison Dupuy Hotel [GF,SW] 1001 Toulouse St **504/586-8000, 800/535-9177**

Mentone B&B [GF,NS,WI] 1437 Pauger St (at Kerlerec) **504/943-3019** *suite in Victorian home in Faubourg Marigny district*

New Orleans Guest House [GS,NS,WI,GO] 1118 Ursulines Ave (at N Rampart) **504/566-1177, 800/562-1177** *1848 Creole cottage, courtyard*

The Olivier House [★GF,SW,WI,WC] 828 Toulouse **504/525-8456, 866/525-9748**

Pierre Coulon Guest House [GS,NS,GO] **504/943-6692, 866/328-1497** *quiet apt*

Royal Barracks Guest House [GF,NS,WI] 717 Barracks St (at Bourbon) **504/529-7269, 888/255-7269**

Royal Street Courtyard [GS,WI,GO] 2438 Royal St (at Spain) **504/943-6818, 888/846-4004** *historic 1850s guesthouse, hot tub*

St Charles Guest House [GF,SW,NS,WI] 1748 Prytania St (at Felicity) **504/523-6556**

Ursuline Guest House [★GS,NS,WI,WC,GO] 708 Ursuline Ave (btwn Royal & Bourbon) **504/525-8509, 800/654-2351** *hot tub*

W New Orleans–French Quarter [GF,SW,WI,WC] 316 Chartres St **504/581-1200, 877/WHOTELS (reservations only)** *also Bacco restaurant*

Bars

700 Club [MW,V] 700 Burgundy **504/561–1095** *noon- 5am, til midnight Sun*

All Ways Lounge [M,NH,D,CW,E,WI] 2240 St Claude Ave (at Marigny) **504/947–0505** *11am-2am, dance lessons 8pm Wed, also The Barn theater space*

Big Daddy's [MW,NH,WC] 2513 Royal St (at Franklin) **504/948–6288** *24hrs, occasional shows*

Bourbon Pub & Parade [★MW,D,DS,S,V,18+,YC,WI] 801 Bourbon St (at St Ann) **504/529–2107** *24hrs, theme nights, Sun T-dance*

Cafe Lafitte in Exile/ The Balcony Bar [★M,D,S,V] 901 Bourbon St (at Dumaine) **504/522–8397** *24hrs, Balcony Bar upstairs w/ cyberbar*

The Corner Pocket [★M,NH,DS,S] 940 St Louis (at Burgundy) **504/568–9829** *noon-2am, 24hrs Fri-Sat, male dancers nightly, New Meat Amateur Dance Contest Fri, hustlers*

Country Club [★GS,F,C,S,SW,N] 634 Louisa St (at Royal) **504/945–0742** *11am-1am, not your father's country club!*

Cutter's [MW,NH,WC] 706 Franklin Ave (at Royal) **504/948–4200** *3pm-3am*

The Double Play [M,NH,TG] 439 Dauphine (at St Louis) **504/523–4517** *24hrs*

The Four Seasons [★M,NH,E,K,DS,GO] 3229 N Causeway Blvd (at 18th), Metairie **504/832–0659** *3pm-close, also the Out Back Bar summers, patio*

The Friendly Bar [★M,NH,WC] 2301 Chartres St (at Marigny) **504/943–8929** *11am-close*

Good Friends Bar [★M,NH,K,P,WC] 740 Dauphine (at St Ann) **504/566–7191** *also Queens Head Pub upstairs Sun only, popular piano sing-along 4pm-8pm*

JohnPaul [M,D,E,DS] 940 Elysian Fields Ave (at N Rampart) **504/948–1888** *noon-close, 120" big screen for sporting events*

Le Roundup [M,NH,TG] 819 St Louis St (at Dauphine) **504/561-8340** *24hrs, very MTF-friendly crowd*

Masquerades Lounge [MW,NH,F,K] 3505 Division St, Metairie **504/888-4101** *noon-2am, till 3am Fri-Sat, from 5pm Sun; also Two Jokers Grill, 504/454-5101, 11am-8pm, till midnight Fri-Sat*

Napoleon's Itch [★M,E,NS] 734 Bourbon (at St Ann, in Bourbon Orleans Hotel) *noon-2am, till 4am Fri-Sat, wine & martini bar*

Ninth Circle [M,NH,TG] 700 N Rampart (at St Peter) **504/524-7654** *noon-3am, 24hrs wknds*

Orlando's Society Page Lounge [M,NH,TG] 542 N Rampart (at Toulouse) **504/299-0156** *6pm-2am, from 3pm wknds*

Phoenix [★M,NH,B,L,F,GO] 941 Elysian Fields Ave (at N Rampart) **504/945-9264** *24hrs, cruise room, beer busts, also The Eagle [D] 9pm-5am*

Rawhide 2010 [★M,NH,D,A,B,L,V] 740 Burgundy St (at St Ann) **504/525-8106** *1pm-5am, underground sound*

The Sanctuary [MW,NH,E,K,WC] 2301 N Causeway Blvd (at 34th), Metairie **504/834-7979** *5pm-close, live shows Sat, monthly drag shows*

Spotted Cat [GF,E] 623 Frenchmen St **504/943-3887** *2pm-3am, excellent live jazz in the Faubourg Marigny*

Tubby's Golden Lantern [M,NH,DS,S] 1239 Royal St (at Barracks) **504/529-2860** *noon-4am, [DS] Fri-Sun*

NIGHTCLUBS

Oz [★M,D,E,DS,S,V,YC,WC] 800 Bourbon St (at St Ann) **504/593-9491** *24hrs*

Starlight by the Park [MW,NH,DS,WC] 834 N Rampart (at Dumaine) **504/561-8939** *noon-2am, 24hrs Fri-Sun, also courtyard bar*

CAFES

Cafe Rose Nicaud [WI] 632 Frenchmen St (btwn Royal & Chartres) **504/949-3300** *7am-7pm*

CC's Coffee House [WI] 941 Royal St **504/581-6996** *7am-7pm*

Croissants d'Or 617 Ursulines St **504/524-4663** *7am-2pm, clsd Tue, delicious pastries*

Marigny Perks [MW,F] 2401 Burgundy **504/948-7401**

Royal Blend Coffee & Tea House 621 Royal St **504/523-2716** *8am-5:30pm, on a quiet, hidden courtyard, also salads & sandwiches*

Z'otz [E] 8210 Oak St **504/861-2224** *7am-2am, coffee shop & art space*

RESTAURANTS

13 Monaghan's [WC] 517 Frenchmen St **504/942-1345** *11am-4am, brkfst, lunch & dinner all the time, some veggie, full bar*

Angeli on Decatur [WI] 1141 Decatur St (at Gov Nicholls) **504/566-0077** *11am-2am, till 4am Fri-Sat, pizza*

Bluebird Cafe [★] 3625 Prytania St (btwn Foucher & Antonine) **504/895-7166** *7am-2pm, from 8am wknds, clsd Mon-Tue, great brkfsts, cash only*

Bywater Bar-B-Que [GO] 3162 Dauphine St (at Louisa) **504/944-4445, 504/947-0000** *11am-9pm, clsd Wed; also Lorenzo's Pizzeria*

Cafe Amelie 912 Royal St (in Princess of Monaco Courtyard) **504/412-8965** *lunch & dinner, Sun brunch, clsd Mon-Tue, Creole*

Cafe Negril [E] 606 Frenchman St (at Chartres St) **504/944-4744** *dinner, clsd Sun-Mon, Caribbean*

Casamento's 4330 Magazine St (at Napoleon Ave) **504/895-9761** *lunch, dinner Th-Sat, clsd Sun-Mon (also clsd June-Aug), best oyster loaf in city*

Clover Grill [★] 900 Bourbon St (at Dumaine) **504/598-1010** *24hrs, diner fare*

Commander's Palace [★R] 1403 Washington Ave (at Coliseum St, in Garden District) **504/899-8221** *lunch Mon-Fri, dinner nightly, jazz brunch wknds, upscale Creole, dress code*

EAT New Orleans 900 Dumaine St (at Dauphine) **504/522-7222** *lunch & dinner, wknd brunch, clsd Mon, Cajun/ Creole, some veggie, cute waiters*

Feelings Cafe [P] 2600 Chartres St (at Franklin Ave) **504/945-2222** *dinner Th-Sun, also Sun brunch, Creole, also piano bar*

Fiorella's Cafe 45 French Market Pl (at Gov Nicholls & Ursulines) **504/553-2155** *noon-midnight, till 2am Fri, 11:30am-2am Sat, 11:30am-midnight Sun, homecooking*

La Peniche 1940 Dauphine St (at Touro St) **504/943-1460** *8am-9pm, clsd Tue-Wed, Southern comfort foods, popular for brkfst*

Lafitte's Restaurant 2031 St Charles Ave (in Pontchartrain Hotel) **504/524-0581, 800/777-6193** *brkfst, lunch & dinner, Creole, the setting for part of Anne Rice's The Witching Hour*

Marigny Brasserie 640 Frenchmen St **504/945-4472** *lunch Mon-Fri, dinner nightly, wknd brunch, French*

Meauxbar Bistro 942 N Rampart St **504/569-9979** *6pm-10pm, clsd Sun-Mon*

Mona Lisa [BW,GO] 1212 Royal St (at Barracks) **504/522-6746** *11am-10pm, from 5pm Tue-Wed, Italian*

Mona's 504 Frenchmen St **504/949-4115** *11am-10pm, till 11pm Fri-Sat, noon-9pm Sun, cheap Middle Eastern eats, some veggie*

Moon Wok 800 Dauphine St **504/523-6910** *11am-9pm, till 10pm Fri-Sat, Chinese*

Nola [WC] 534 St Louis St (btwn Chartres & Decatur) **504/522-6652** *lunch wknds, dinner nightly, fusion Creole from Emeril Lagasse*

Olivier's [WC] 204 Decatur St **504/525-7734** *5pm-10pm, Creole*

Orleans Grapevine 718-720 Orleans Ave **504/523-1930** *4pm-10:30pm, till 11:30pm Fri-Sat, wine bar & bistro*

Petunia's 817 St Louis (at Bourbon) **504/522-6440** *8am-3pm, till 10pm Th-Sun, Cajun/ Creole, full bar*

Praline Connection [E] 542 Frenchmen St (at Chartres) **504/943-3934** *11am-10pm, soul food*

Quartermaster 1100 Bourbon St **504/529-1416** *24hrs, "The Nellie Deli," sandwiches & more*

Sammy's Seafood 627 Bourbon St (across from Pat O' Brien's) **504/525-8442** *11am-11pm, Cajun/ Creole*

The Upperline Restaurant 1413 Upperline **504/891-9822** *dinner Wed-Sun, Creole, fine dining, full bar*

ENTERTAINMENT & RECREATION

Cafe du Monde 800 Decatur St (at St Ann, corner of Jackson Square) **504/525-4544, 800/772-2927** *till you've had a beignet—fried dough, powdered w/ sugar, that melts in your mouth—you haven't been to New Orleans & this is "the" place to have them 24hrs a day*

Gay Heritage Tour 909 Bourbon St **504/945-6789** *call for details, departs from Alternatives giftshop*

Haunted History Tour **504/861-2727, 888/644-6787** *guided 2-1/2-hour tours of New Orleans' most famous haunts, including Anne Rice's former home*

Mardi Gras World 1380 Port of New Orleans Pl **504/362-8211, 800/362-8213** *tour this year-round Mardi Gras float workshop*

Pat O'Brien's [GF,F] 718 St Peter St (btwn Bourbon & Royal) **504/525-4823, 800/597-4823** *more than just a bar—come for the Hurricane, stay for the kitsch*

Preservation Hall [NS,$] 726 St Peter St **504/522-2841, 888/946-5299** *8pm-midnight, set begins at 8:30pm, come & hear the music that started jazz: New Orleans-style jazz!*

St Charles Streetcar St Charles St (at Canal St) **504/248-3900 (RTA Rideline #)** *it's not named Desire, but you should still ride it, Blanche, if you want to see the Garden District*

Bookstores

Barnes & Noble [WC] 1601 Westbank Expwy, Harvey **504/263-1146** *9am-10pm, till 11pm Fri-Sat, 10am-9pm Sun*

FAB (Faubourg Marigny Art & Books) 600 Frenchmen St (at Chartres) **504/947-3700** *noon-10pm, LGBT*

Garden District Book Shop 2727 Prytania St (at Washington) **504/895-2266** *10am-6pm, till 4pm Sun, independent*

Kitchen Witch Cook Books [GF] 631 Toulouse St (at Royal St) **504/528-8382** *10am-7pm, clsd Tue, cook books from rare to campy*

Retail Shops

Alternatives 909 Bourbon St (at Dumaine) **504/524-5222** *11am-6pm, LGBT cards, gifts*

Angela King Gallery 241 Royal St **504/524-8211, 504/566 -1944**

Dress to Kill 227 Dauphine **504/587-7012** *10am-10pm, till 11pm Wed-Sat, sexy footwear (up to size 14)*

Hit Parade [★] 741 Bourbon St **504/524-7700** *3pm-11pm, 11am-2am Fri-Sat, 11am-midnight Sun, LGBT books, designer circuit clothing & more*

NOLA Tattoo 1820 Hampson St (Uptown, at Riverbend) **504/524-6147** *tattoos & piercing*

Rab-Dab 918 Royal St **504/525-6662** *noon-6pm, men's clothing/ clubwear & gifts*

Second Skin Leather 521 St Philip St (btwn Decatur & Chartres) **504/561-8167** *noon-8pm, till 10pm Fri-Sat*

Wicked Orleans 1201 Decatur St (at Gov Nicholls) **504/529-4384, 866/297-9207 (outside LA)** *11am-6pm, leather & goth clothes*

Publications

▶ **Ambush Mag 504/522-8049** *LGBT newspaper for the Gulf South (TX through FL)*

Southern Voice 404/876-1819 *weekly LGBT newspaper for AL, FL (panhandle), GA, LA, MS, TN w/ resource listings*

Men's Clubs

The Club New Orleans [★18+,PC] 515 Toulouse St (at Decatur) **504/581-2402** *24hrs, 5 levels, gym, sauna & steam room, rooftop sundeck*

Flex—New Orleans [V] 700 Baronne St **504/598-3539** *24hrs, 5 flrs, gym, sauna & steam room*

Men's Services

▶ **Megaphone 504/733-3939** *Meet and Chat Live with HOT local men. FREE to listen & respond to ads. Video and text chat at GayMates.com. Use FREE code 4889.*

Erotica

Airline Adult Books 1404 26th St (off Bainbridge), Kenner **504/468-2931** *24hrs, super-arcade w/ 30 rooms*

Bourbon-Strip Tease 205 Bourbon St **504/581-6633** *10am-1am, erotic lingerie, dancewear, adult novelties*

Chartres St Conxxxion 107 Chartres St (off Canal St) **504/586-8006** *24hrs*

Panda Bear [WC] 415 Bourbon St (at St Louis) **504/529-8064** *leather & toys*

Paradise Adult Video [WC] 41 W 24th St (at Crestview), Kenner **504/461-0000** *arcade*

Shreveport

Accommodations

Twenty-Four Thirty-Nine Fairfield [GF] 2439 Fairfield Ave **318/424-2424, 877/251-2439** *1905 Victorian*

Bars

Korner Lounge II [M,NH] 800 Louisiana (near Cotton) **318/222-9796** *3pm-2am*

Nightclubs

Central Station [★MW,D,CW,DS,TG,WC] 1025 Marshall (btwn Fairfield & Creswell) **318/222-2216** *5pm-close, till 4am Fri-Sat*

Erotica

Capri Video 2010 Nelson St **318/221-5427** *10am-midnight, includes 2 theaters*

Fun Shop Too 9434 Mansfield Rd **318/688-2482** *clsd Sun, adult, novelty & gag gifts & toys*

Slidell

see also New Orleans

Bars

Billy's [MW,NH] 2600 Hwy 190 W **985/847-1921** *5pm-2am*

Tallulah

Erotica

▶ **The Lion's Den Adult Superstore** 238 Hwy 193 (exit 186 off I-20) **318/633-9994** *24hrs*

Maine

Albion

Accommodations

Twin Ponds Lodge [MO,SW,N,WI] 96 York Town Rd (at Libby Hill Rd) **207/437-2200**

Aroostook County

Accommodations

Magic Pond Wildlife Sanctuary & Guest House [W,NS,GO] Blaine **207/429-8787, 207/947-2240** *artist-owned cottage*

Augusta

includes Hallowell

Accommodations

The Benjamin Wales House B&B [GS,GO] 49 Middle St (at Chestnut St), Hallowell **207/512-2461, 877/323-4712**

Maple Hill Farm B&B Inn [GS,NS,WI,WC,GO] Hallowell **207/622-2708, 800/622-2708** *historic Victorian farmhouse, full brkfst, swimming pond [N]*

Nightclubs

PJ's (aka Papa Joe's) [★MW,D,F,P] 80 Water St (btwn Laurel & Bridge) **207/623-4041** *4pm-1am Wed-Sat*

Restaurants

Slate's [E] 167 Water St (Franklin), Hallowell **207/622-9575** *lunch & dinner, brunch only Sun*

Bangor

Accommodations

Maine Wilderness Lake Island [MW] 26 5th St **207/990-5839** *seasonal rental cabins*

Bars

Fuzion [GS,NH,D,K,DS] 123 Franklin St **207/942-3112** *9pm-2am*

Bookstores

Pro Libris Bookshop 10 3rd St (at Union) **207/942-3019** *10am-6pm, clsd Sun-Mon, new & used*

Cruisy Areas

Valley Avenue Park [AYOR] along river bank

Bar Harbor

Accommodations

Aysgarth Station [GF,NS,WI] 20 Roberts Ave **207/288-9655** *10-minute drive from Acadia, cats on premises*

Central House Inn [GS,NS,GO] 51 Clark Point Rd (at Rte 102), Southwest Harbor **207/244-0100, 877/205-0289** *weekly vacation rental, 4-bdrm house, also cottage, kitchen, kids ok*

The Colonial Inn [GF,SW] 321 High St (at US1), Ellsworth **207/667-5548, 888/667-5548**

Manor House Inn [GF,NS,WI] 106 West St (near Bridge St) **207/288-3759, 800/437-0088** *open April-Oct, 1887 Victorian mansion, full brkfst, some rooms w/ whirlpools*

Restaurants

Mama DiMatteo's [GO] 34 Kennebec Pl (at Rodick St) **207/288-3666** *4:30pm-10pm, full bar*

Entertainment & Recreation

ImprovAcadia 15 Cottage St (2nd flr) **207/288-2503** *live improvised theater*

Cruisy Areas

Lake Wood [AYOR] off Crooked Rd (1 mile from Hulls Cove) *follow trail to the "Ledges"*

Thompson Island [AYOR] Mt Desert Island *beware of cops!*

Bath

Accommodations

The Galen C Moses House [GS,NS,WI,GO] 1009 Washington St **207/442-8771, 888/442-8771** *full brkfst*

The Inn at Bath [GS,NS,WC] 969 Washington St **207/443-4294, 800/423-0964** *1810 Greek Revival B&B, full brkfst*

Bingham

Erotica

Bingham Village Video 10 Murray St (at Rte 201) **207/672-4900**

Boothbay Harbor

Accommodations

Sur La Mer Inn [GF,NS,GO] 18 Eames Rd, PO Box 663, 04538 **207/633-7400, 800/791-2026** *luxury oceanfront B&B*

Brunswick

Bookstores

Gulf of Maine Books 134 Maine St (at Pleasant) **207/729-5083** *9:30am-5:30pm, clsd Sun*

Camden

Accommodations

Norumbega Inn [GF,NS,GO] 63 High St **207/236-4646** *inn, circa 1886*

Corea

Accommodations

The Black Duck Inn on Corea Harbor [GS,NS,WI,GO] **207/963-2689** *full brkfst, restored farmhouse on harbor, also cottages*

Deer Isle

Restaurants

Fisherman's Friend School St, Stonington **207/367-2442** *open April-Dec, 11am-9pm, till 10pm Fri-Sat*

Dexter

Accommodations

Brewster Inn [GF,NS,WI,WC] 37 Zions Hill **207/924-3130** *historic mansion, full brkfst*

Farmington

Bookstores

Devany, Doak & Garrett Booksellers 193 Broadway **207/778-3454** *10am-5pm, till 5:30pm Th, till 6:30pm Fri, 9am-5pm Sat, noon-3pm Sun, LGBT section*

Freeport

Accommodations

The Royalsborough Inn [GF,NS,WI] 1290 Royalsborough Rd, Durham **207/865-6566, 800/765-1772** *full brfkst, spa services, massage, also alpaca farm*

Restaurants

Harraseeket Lunch & Lobster Co 162 Main St **207/865-9377, 800/342-6423** *open May-Oct*

Hancock

Restaurants

Le Domaine Restaurant & Inn 207/422-3395, 800/554-8498 *open June-Oct, 6pm-9pm, Sun brunch, clsd Mon*

Kennebunkport

Accommodations

The Colony Hotel [GF,F,SW,NS,WI] 140 Ocean Ave (at Kings Hwy) **207/967-3331, 800/552-2363** *May-Oct, oceanfront property w/ private beach, also rental cottages*

White Barn Inn [GF,SW,F,NS,WI] 37 Beach St **207/967-2321** *also restaurant*

Restaurants

Bartley's Dockside by the bridge **207/967-5050** *lunch & dinner, full bar*

Kittery

see also Portsmouth, New Hampshire

Erotica

Amazing 92 Rte 236 N (1 mile from traffic circle), Eliot **207/439-6285**

Lewiston

Accommodations

Ware Street Inn B&B [GF,NS,WI] 52 Ware St (at College St) **207/783-8171, 877/783-8171**

Bars

The Sportsman's Club [★MW,NH,D,E,K,DS] 2 Bates St (at Main) **207/784-2251** *7pm-1am, clsd Mon-Tue, "oldest gay bah in Maine"*

Erotica

Paris Book Store 297 Lisbon St (at Chestnut) **207/783-6677**

Naples

Accommodations

Lambs Mill Inn [GS,NS,WI,GO] **207/693-6253** *1890s farmhouse on 20 acres, full brkfst, hot tub, lesbian-owned*

Restaurants

Sydney's Rte 302 **207/693-3333** *dinner April-Nov only, full bar*

Newcastle

Accommodations

The Tipsy Butler B&B [GF,NS,WI] 11 High St **207/563-3394** *on the Damariscotta River*

Ogunquit

Accommodations

Beauport Inn & Suites on Clay Hill [GS,SW,NS,WC] 339 Agamenticus/ Clay Hill Rd **207/361-2400, 800/646-8681** *English country manor on 11 acres, full brkfst*

Beaver Dam Campground [GF,SW] 551 School St, Rte 9, Berwick **207/698-2267** *campground on beautiful 20-acre spring-fed pond*

Belm House Vacation Units [MW,WI,GO] **207/641-2637** *rental units w/ kitchens*

Black Boar Inn [MW,NS,GO] 277 Main St **207/646-2112** *B&B built in 1674, full gourmet brkfst, tea, also weekly cottages*

Distant Sands B&B [GS,NS,GO] **207/646-8686** *18th-c farmhouse, full brkfst, overlooks Ogunquit River & ocean, also cottage*

The HideAway 65 Main St **207/646-3787** *guesthouse*

Leisure Inn [GF,NS,WI] 73 School St **207/646-2737** *seasonal*

MainEscape Rental House [MW,GO] 66 Cottage St (at Shore Rd) **954/816-5286** *located in village center, weekly rentals June-Aug*

Meadowmere Resort [GF,SW,NS,WI,WC] 74 S Main St (at Rte 1) **207/646-9661, 800/633-8718** *health club & spa*

Moon Over Maine B&B [MW,NS,WI,GO] Berwick Rd **207/646-6666, 800/851-6837** *hot tub*

Morning Dove [MW,NS,WI,GO] 13 Bourne Ln **207/646-3891**

Ogunquit Beach Inn [M,WI,GO] 67 School St **207/646-1112, 888/976-2463** *5 minutes to beach*

The Ogunquit Inn [MW,NS,WI,GO] 17 Glen Ave **207/646-3633, 866/999-3633** *clsd Nov-April, Victorian B&B*

Ogunquit-by-the-Sea Lodging [M,NS,WI,GO] 44 School St (at Main St) **207/646-4132** *charming 1- & 2-bdrm self-catering vacation units rented weekly in Ogunquit Village Center; rooms by the night; near beach & nightlife*

OgunquitCottages.com [MW,NS,GO] 25 Mill St, N Reading, MA 01864 **207/646-3840, 978/664-5813** *weekly rentals, seasonal (June-Sept), near bars & beach*

Rockmere Lodge B&B [GS,NS,GO] 150 Stearns Rd **207/646-2985** *Maine shingle cottage, near beach*

Two Village Square [★M,SW,NS,WI,GO] 14 Village Square Ln **207/646-5779, 412/683-0218 (winter #)** *open May-Oct, Victorian w/ ocean views, hot tub*

Yellow Monkey Guest Houses/ Hotel [GS,WC,GO] 280 Main St **207/646-9056** *seasonal, jacuzzi, ocean view, gym*

Bars

Front Porch Cafe [GS,F,P] 9 Shore Rd (at Beach St) **207/646-3976, 207/646-4005** *seasonal, 4pm-1am, from 11:30am wknds*

Vine Cafe [F] 478 Main St **207/646-0288, 877/646-0288** *seasonal, 4pm-close, also restaurant, good wine selection*

Nightclubs

Maine Street [★MW,D,F,K,C,GO] 195 Main St/ US Rte 1 **207/646-5101** *5pm-1am, T-dance from 3pm wknds, seasonal*

Cafes

Bread & Roses 246 Main St **207/646-4227** *7am-11pm, seasonal*

Fancy That Cafe Main St (near the Square) **207/646-4118** *April-Oct, 6:30am-11pm*

Restaurants

Amore Breakfast 309 Shore Rd **207/646-6661** *brkfst only, seasonal*

Angelina's Ristorante 655 Main St **207/646-0445** *dinner, Italian*

Arrows [★R] Berwick Rd (2 miles W of Rte 1) **207/361-1100** *open April-Dec, 6pm-9pm, clsd Mon, eclectic*

Clay Hill Farm [P] 220 Clay Hill Rd, Cape Neddick (York) **207/361-2272** *dinner, seafood, also piano bar*

Five-O [★] 50 Shore Rd **207/646-5001** *5pm-midnight, martini bar & restaurant, full bar*

Jonathan's [E,WC] 92 Bourne Ln **207/646-4777** *dinner nightly, steak/ seafood, full bar*

La Pizzeria [BW,GO] 25 Main St (Rte 1) **207/646-1143** *open April-Dec, lunch & dinner*

Wild Blueberry Cafe [E] 82 Shore Rd **207/646-0990** *brkfst, lunch & dinner, jazz brunch 10am-1pm Sun*

Entertainment & Recreation

Ogunquit Playhouse US Route 1 **207/646-5511 (box office), 207/646-2402** *summer theater, some LGBT-themed productions*

Cruisy Areas

Ogunquit Beach [AYOR] off Rte 1 *200 yds N of beach entrance*

Portland

Accommodations

Auberge by the Sea B&B [GF,NS,WI] 103 East Grand Ave, Old Orchard Beach **207/934-2355** *private beach path*

The Inn at St John [GS,NS,WI,GO] 939 Congress St **207/773-6481, 800/636-9127** *unique historic inn*

The Inn by the Sea [GF,SW,NS,WC] 40 Bowery Beach Rd, Cape Elizabeth **207/799-3134, 800/888-4287** *condo-style suites*

The Percy Inn [GF,NS] 15 Pine St (at Longfellow Square) **207/871-7638, 888/417-3729** *B&B at Longfellow Square*

The Pomegranate Inn [GF,NS,WI] 49 Neal St **207/772-1006, 800/356-0408** *upscale B&B, full brkfst*

Sea View Motel [GS,SW,NS,WI,WC] 65 W Grand Ave (at Atlantic Ave), Old Orchard Beach **207/934-4180, 800/541-8439** *year-round oceanfront motel*

West End Inn [GF,NS,WI] 146 Pine St **207/772-1377, 800/338-1377** *1870 town house*

Wild Iris Inn [GF,NS] 273 State St **207/775-0224, 800/600-1557** *in downtown Portland*

Bars

Blackstones [M,NH,WC] 6 Pine St (off Longfellow Square) **207/775-2885** *4pm-1am, from 1pm wknds, [L] 3rd Sat, theme nights*

Una [GS,F] 505 Fore St (at Cotton St) **207/828-0300** *4:30pm-1am, tapas, wine bar, lounge*

The Wine Bar [GS,F] 38 Wharf St **207/772-6976** *5pm-close*

Nightclubs

Styxx [★MW,D,E,DS,GO] 3 Spring St **207/828-0822** *7pm-1am, clsd Tue-Wed*

Cafes

Coffee by Design 43 Washington Ave **207/879-2233**

North Star Music Café [W] 225 Congress St (at Washington Ave) **207/699-2994**

Restaurants

Becky's 390 Commercial St **207/773-7070** *4am-10pm, great brkfst & chowdah*

Katahdin 106 High St (at Spring) **207/774-1740** *5pm-9pm, till 10pm Fri-Sat, clsd Sun-Mon, American menu, bar*

Siam Restaurant [BW,WC,GO] 339 Fore St (at Pearl) **207/773-8389** *lunch Tue-Fri, dinner nightly, clsd Mon, Thai*

Street & Co [★BW,WC] 33 Wharf St (btwn Dana & Union) **207/775-0887** *5:30pm-9:30pm, till 10pm Fri-Sat, seafood*

Walter's Cafe 15 Exchange St **207/871-9258** *lunch Mon-Sat, dinner nightly, seafood/ pasta*

Entertainment & Recreation

Maine Gay Men's Chorus PO Box 10391, 04104-0391 **207/772-1384**

Bookstores

Longfellow Books 1 Monument Way **207/772-4045** *9am-7pm, till 6pm Sat, 9:30am-5pm Sun, LGBT section*

Retail Shops

Communiques 3 Moulton St (at Commercial) **207/773-5181** *8:30am-6pm, till 7pm Th-Sat, cards, gifts, clothing*

The Corner General Store 154 Middle St **207/253-5280** *8am-1am, great wine selection*

Men's Services

Erotica

Condom Sense 424 Fore St (at Union) **207/871-0356** *10am-8pm, till 9pm Th, till 10pm Fri-Sat, till 6pm Sun*

Video Expo 666 Congress St (at State) **207/774-1377**

Cruisy Areas

Cutter Street [AYOR] *at the foot of the street on the Eastern Promenade*

Rockland

Accommodations

Captain Lindsey House Inn [GF,NS,WC] 5 Lindsey St **207/596-7950, 800/523-2145**

The Old Granite Inn [GF,NS,WI,WC] 546 Main St **207/594-9036, 800/386-9036** *1880s stone guesthouse, full brkfst, harbor views*

Rockport

Restaurants

Chez Michel Rte 1, Lincolnville Beach **207/789-5600** *dinner, Sun brunch, clsd Mon, full bar, some veggie*

Lobster Pound Rte 1, Lincolnville Beach **207/789-5550** *11:30am-8pm May-Oct, full bar, patio*

Searsport

Accommodations

Wildflower Inn B&B [GS,NS,WI,GO] 2 Black Rd S/ US Rte 1 **207/548-2112, 888/546-2112** *close to hiking, kayaking, biking & antiquing, lesbian-owned*

Tenants Harbor

ACCOMMODATIONS

Eastwind Inn [GF,F] **207/372-6366, 800/241-8439** *clsd Dec-April, full brkfst, rooms & apts, at water's edge, also restaurant*

Waterville

EROTICA

Treasure Chest [★GO] 5 Sanger Ave (at Main) **207/873-7411**

Video 54 [★GO] 18 Water St (at Sherwin St) **207/873-4201**

White Mtns

ACCOMMODATIONS

Mountain Village Inn [GF,NS,WI] 164 Main St, Kingfield 04947 **207/265-2030, 866/577-0741** *rural & sophisticated B&B, full brkfst*

York Harbor

RESTAURANTS

York Harbor Inn Rte 1A **207/363-5119, 800/343-3869** *lunch Mon-Sat, dinner nightly, Sun brunch, also the Cellar Pub, also lodging*

MARYLAND

Annapolis

INFO LINES & SERVICES

AA Gay/ Lesbian 199 Duke of Gloucester St (at St Anne's Parish) **410/268-5441** *8pm Tue*

ACCOMMODATIONS

Two-O-One B&B [GS,NS,WI,GO] 201 Prince George St (at Maryland Ave) **410/268-8053** *full brkfst*

William Page Inn B&B [GS,NS,WI,GO] 8 Martin St **410/626-1506, 800/364-4160** *renovated 1908 home, full brkfst, jacuzzi*

RESTAURANTS

Cafe Sado 205 Tackle Cir (at Castle Marina Rd), Chester **410/604-1688** *lunch & dinner, sushi/ Asian fusion*

Baltimore

INFO LINES & SERVICES

AA Gay/ Lesbian 410/663-1922 *6:30pm Sat, call for other mtg times*

Gay, Lesbian, Bisexual & Transgender Community Center of Baltimore 241 W Chase St (at Read) **410/837-5445** *call for hours*

ACCOMMODATIONS

Abacrombie Fine Food & Accommodations [GS,NS] 58 W Biddle St (at Cathedral) **410/244-7227, 888/922-3437** *also restaurant*

Biltmore Suites [GF] 205 W Madison St (at Park) **410/728-6550, 800/868-5064** *Victorian hotel*

Embassy Suites Hotel Baltimore at BWI [GF,SW,WI,WC] 1300 Concourse Dr, Linthicum **410/850-0747, 800/362-2779** *full brkfst*

Harbor Inn Pier 5 [GS,F,WI,WC] 711 Eastern Ave (at President) **410/539-2000, 866/583-4162** *on waterfront, full brkfst, restaurant, cigar bar*

Tremont Park Hotel [GS,WC] 8 E Pleasant St **410/576-1200, 800/873-6668**

BARS

Baltimore Eagle [★M,L,WC] 2022 N Charles St (enter on 21st) **443/524-3333** *3pm-2am, leather store, video store, cruise bar, patio*

Blue Parrot [MW,NH,F,K,DS] 5860 Belair Rd **410/254-3785** *11am-2am, patio*

Club Bunns [MW,D,MR-AF,S] 608 W Lexington St (at Greene St) **410/234-2866** *3pm-2am, till midnight Mon-Tue, male strippers Wed*

Club Gypsies [MW,NH] 4020 E Lombard **410/522-1602** *6pm-2am*

Club Phoenix [MW,D,MR,F,K,DS,V] 1 W Biddle St **410/837-3906** *4pm-2am, from noon-midnight Sun*

The Drinkery [M,NH,K] 205 W Read St (at Park) **410/225-3100** *11am-2am*

The Gallery Bar & Studio Restaurant [MW,WC] 1735 Maryland Ave (at Lafayette) **410/539-6965** *2pm-1:30am, dinner Mon-Sat*

Grand Central [★MW,D,F,K,DS,V,18+] 1001 N Charles St (at Eager) **410/752-7133** *4pm-close, 3 bars*

Hippo [★MW,D,TG,E,K,DS,P,V,WC] 1 W Eager St (at Charles) **410/547-0069, 410/576-0018** *4pm-2am, 3 bars*

Jay's on Read [M,P] 225 W Read St **410/225-0188** *4pm-1am, clsd Sun*

Leon's [MW,NH,F,WC] 870 Park Ave (at Chase) **410/539-4993, 410/539-4850** *11am-2am, also Tyson's Place restaurant, Sun brunch*

The Quest [M,NH] 3607 Fleet St (at Conkling) **410/563-2617** *4pm-2am*

The Rowan Tree [GS,K] 1633 S Charles St **410/468-0550** *noon-2am, "where diversity is our name"*

Ziascoz [GS,NH,K,MR-AF] 1313 E Pratt St **410/276-5790** *5pm-2am*

Nightclubs

Club 1722 [GS,D,MR,18+,BYOB,PC] 1722 N Charles St (at Lafayette) **410/547-8423** *afterhours club, Fri & Sat only, 2am-close*

The Paradox [★GS,D,MR,F,E,V,WC] 1310 Russell St (at 13th) **410/837-9110** *11pm-5am, midnight-6am Sat, more gay Sat*

Cafes

Donna's Coffee Bar [BW] 800 N Charles St **410/385-0180** *7:30am-9pm, from 9am Sat-Sun, till 10pm Fri-Sat*

Restaurants

Alonso's [NS,WC] 415 W Cold Spring Ln (at Keswick Rd) **410/235-3433** *4pm-10:30pm, from 11:30am Fri-Sat, pizza & burgers, full bar*

Cafe Hon [WC] 1002 W 36th St (at Roland) **410/243-1230** *7am-9pm, 9am-close wknds*

Golden West Cafe 1105 W 36th St **410/889-8891** *brkfst, lunch & dinner, New Mexican*

Loco Hombre 413 W Cold Spring Ln (at Roland) **410/889-2233** *4pm-10pm, till 11pm Fri-Sat, from 11:30am Fri-Sun, wknd brunch*

Mount Vernon Stable & Saloon 909 N Charles St (btwn Eager & Read) **410/685-7427** *11am-midnight, from 10am wknds, some veggie, Sun brunch, also bar*

Neo Viccino 1317 N Charles St **410/347-0349** *11am-11pm, till 9pm Sun, New American, full bar*

Night of the Cookers 885 N Howard St **410/383-2093** *5pm-close, clsd Mon, Sun brunch, Southern cooking, full bar, live jazz*

XS Baltimore 1307 N Charles St **410/468-0002** *7am-midnight, till 2am Fri-Sat, sushi restaurant, cafe & lounge*

Publications

Baltimore OUTloud 410/244-6780

Gay Life 410/837-7748 *LGBT newspaper*

Men's Services

Erotica

Big Top Books 429 E Baltimore **410/547-2495** *8am-11:30pm, 24hr Th-Sat*

Chained Desires 136 W Read St **410/528-8441, 888/886-8442** *11am-8pm, till 9pm Fri-Sat, clsd Mon, custom leather crafts & apparel, adult toys*

Greenmount Books 3222 Greenmount Ave (at 33rd St) **410/467-0403** *10am-midnight, from noon Sun*

Sugar [GO] 927 W 36th St (at Roland) **410/467-2632**

Cruisy Areas

Druid Hill Park [MR-AF,YC,AYOR] W side of town (near Park Cir)

Lake Montebello Park [AYOR] Lake Montebello Terr (at Harford Rd) *in the woods*

Wyman Dell Park [AYOR] Charles St (btwn 29th & 33rd) *hustlers on the sidewalk, cruising on the Wyman Park Dr side*

Beltsville

see Washington, District of Columbia

Boonsboro

Nightclubs

Deer Park Lodge [M,D,DS,GO] 21614 National Pike **301/797-7672** *7pm-2am, till midnight Sun, clsd Mon-Wed*

College Park

see Washington, District of Columbia

Cumberland

Accommodations

Rocky Gap Lodge & Golf Resort [GF,SW] 16701 Lakeview Rd NE, Flintstone **301/784-8400, 800/724-0828** *expansive property w/ forests, lake & elegantly rustic lodge*

Restaurants

Acropolis 47 E Main St, Frostburg **301/689-8277** *4pm-10pm, clsd Sun-Mon, full bar*

Au Petit Paris [R,WC] 86 E Main St, Frostburg **301/689-8946** *6pm-9:30pm, clsd Sun-Mon, also lounge*

Edgewood

Erotica

Bush River Books & Video 3909 Pulaski Hwy (Rte 40), Abingdon **410/676-9051** *24hrs*

Frederick

Cruisy Areas

Gambrill State Park [AYOR] W of Frederick (off I-70) *go to the summit, turn left*

Greenbelt

see also Washington, District of Columbia

Cruisy Areas

Greenbelt Park [AYOR]

Hagerstown

Retail Shops

Rainbow Connection LLC [GO] 14 1/2 E Washington St (at Potomac St) **301/739-6629** *10am-7pm, till 6pm Sat, clsd Sun; pride gifts & more*

Havre de Grace

Accommodations

La Clé D'Or [GS,GO] 226 N Union Ave (at Chesapeake Bay) **410/939-6562, 888/484-4837** *1868 home of the Johns Hopkins family, full brkfst*

Hyattsville

see Washington, District of Columbia

Laurel

see also Washington, District of Columbia

Bars

PW's Sports Bar & Grill [MW,NH,F,K,WI,GO] 9855 N Washington Blvd (at Whiskey Bottom Rd) **301/498-4840** *5am-2am, sports bar*

Erotica

Route 1 News Agency 106 Washington Blvd (at Main) **410/880-4253**

Potomac

see Washington, District of Columbia

Princess Anne

Accommodations

The Alexander House Booklovers B&B [GF,NS] 30535 Linden Ave (at corner of Beckford) **410/651-5195** *literary-themed B&B, full brkfst*

Rock Hall

Accommodations

Tallulah's on Main [GS,NS,WC,GO] 5750 Main St (at Sharp St) **410/639-2596** *small suite hotel*

Rockville

see also Washington, District of Columbia

Restaurants

The Vegetable Garden 11618 Rockville Pk **301/468-9301** *lunch Mon-Fri, dinner nightly, vegetarian/ vegan*

Cruisy Areas

Lake Needwood [AYOR] N of Rte 28 (off Avery Rd)

Salisbury

Erotica

Salisbury News Agency 616 S Salisbury Blvd (near Vine) **410/543-4469**

Silver Spring

see Washington, District of Columbia

Massachusetts

Acton

Restaurants

Acton Jazz Cafe [E,NS,$] 452 Great Rd/ Rte 2-A **978/263-6161** *6pm-midnight, jazz jam 4pm Sun, full bar*

Amherst

see also Northampton

Bookstores

Amherst Books 8 Main St **413/256-1547, 800/503-5865** *6:30am-9pm, till 5pm Sun, independent, LGBT section*

Food For Thought [★WC] 106 N Pleasant St (at Main) **413/253-5432** *9:30am-6pm, till 7pm Wed-Th, 10am-6pm Sat, noon-5pm Sun, progressive bookstore*

Attleboro

Erotica

State Line Video 1124 Washington St (off I-95, Broadway exit), South Attleboro **508/761-4900** *arcade*

Barre

Accommodations

Jenkins Inn & Restaurant [GF,F,NS,WI,GO] **978/355-6444, 800/378-7373** *also restaurant & full bar*

Winterwood [GF,NS] 19 N Main St, Petersham **978/724-8885** *Greek Revival mansion, fireplaces, full brkfst*

Restaurants

Barre Mill 90 Main St, South Barre **978/355-2987, 978/355-6417** *4:30pm-9pm Wed-Sat, noon-8pm Sun, clsd Mon-Tue, Italian*

Berkshires

Accommodations

The B&B at Howden Farm [GS,NS,GO] 303 Rannapo Rd, Sheffield **413/229-8481** *on 250-acre working farm, full brkfst*

Broken Hill Manor [GF,NS,WI,GO] 771 West Rd (at Rte 23), Sheffield **413/528-6159, 877/535-6159** *B&B, full brkfst*

Cornell Inn [GF,NS,WI,WC] 203 Main St, Lenox **413/637-0562, 800/637-0562** *same-sex wedding ceremonies happily facilitated, full brkfst*

Gateways Inn [GF,NS] 51 Walker St (at Church St), Lenox **413/637-2532, 888/492-9466** *neoclassical inn, also bar & restaurant*

Guest House at Field Farm [GF,TG,NS,WI] 554 Sloan Rd, Williamstown **413/458-3135**

Hallig Hilltop House [GF,SW,NS,GO] 68 West St, Mt Washington **413/644-0076** *turn-of-the-century Dutch Colonial, surrounded by state park, near hiking & skiing*

Harrison House [GF,GO] Lenox **413/637-1746** *"eclectic upscale B&B," fireplaces*

Mount Greylock Inn [GS,GO] 6 East St, Adams **413/743-2665** *some views of Mt Greylock, cat on premises*

River Bend Farm B&B [GF,NS] 643 Simonds Rd, Williamstown **413/458-3121** *historic home, seasonal*

The Rookwood Inn [GS,NS,WI] 11 Old Stockbridge Rd (at Walker St/ Rte 183), Lenox **413/637-9750, 800/223-9750** *Victorian inn near Tanglewood & skiing*

Topia Inn [GS,NS,WI,WC,GO] 10 Pleasant St (at Rte 8), Adams **413/743-9605, 888/868-6742** *eco-friendly B&B, organic gourmet brkfst, lesbian-owned*

The Village Inn [GF,NS] 16 Church St, Lenox **413/637-0020, 800/253-0917** *antique-furnished 1771 New England inn, also restaurant*

Walker House [GS,NS,WI] 64 Walker St, Lenox **413/637-1271, 800/235-3098** *1804 guesthouse*

Windflower Inn [GF,SW,NS,WI] 684 S Egremont Rd, Great Barrington **413/528-2720, 800/992-1993** *country inn in the Berkshires, full brkfst*

Cafes

Cafe Topia [E,BW,WI,WC,GO] 27 Park St (at Rte 8), Adams **413/743-9600** *6pm-11pm Fri-Sat only, Mediterranean food*

Restaurants

Cafe Latino 1111 Mass MoCa Wy, North Adams **413/662-2004** *lunch & dinner, Sun brunch, seaonal hours, contemporary Latin American*

Cafe Lucia 80 Church St, Lenox **413/637-2640** *dinner only, clsd Mon, seasonal*

Church Street Cafe 65 Church St, Lenox **413/637-2745** *lunch & dinner, seasonal, American bistro*

Gateways [WC] 51 Walker St, Lenox **413/637-2532** *5pm-9pm, clsd Sun-Mon*

Mezze Bistro & Bar 16 Water St, Williamstown **413/458-0123** *5pm-9pm Sun-Mon, till 10pm Fri-Sat, seasonal hours*

Entertainment & Recreation

Tanglewood [E] 197 Rte 183, Lenox **888/266-1200** *summer home of the Boston Symphony/ Pops*

Williamstown Theatre Festival just E of Rte 2 & Rte 7 junction, Williamstown **413/597-3400, 413/458-3200** *call for season calendar*

Erotica

Amazing 1021 South St/ Rte 20, Pittsfield **413/496-8055**

Cruisy Areas

Onota Lake [AYOR] parking lot near woods, Pittsfield

Boston

Info Lines & Services

Fenway Community Health Center 1340 Boylston St **617/267-0900, 888/242-0900** *HIV services, LGBT recovery groups*

Gay AA 12 Channel St #604 **617/426-9444 (AA#)**

GLBT Helpline 617/267-9001, 888/340-4528 *6pm-11pm*

Accommodations

463 Beacon St Guest House [GS,NS,WI,GO] 463 Beacon St **617/536-1302** *residential area, minutes from Boston's heart*

Appleton Studio [GF,NS,WI,GO] 30 Appleton St (at Berkely) **617/720-0522, 800/347-5088** *spacious studio apt, also weekly/ monthly rentals*

Beacon Hill Hotel & Bistro 25 Charles St (Chestnut St) **617/723-7575**

Carolyn's B&B [GF,NS] 102 Holworthy St (at Huron Ave), Cambridge **617/864-7042** *near Harvard Square*

▶ **Chandler Inn** [GF,NS,WI] 26 Chandler St **617/482-3450, 800/842-3450** *European-style hotel*

The Charles Street Inn [GS,NS,WC,GO] 94 Charles St (at Mount Vernon, Beacon Hill) **617/314-8900, 877/772-8900** *B&B, jacuzzi, lesbian-owned*

BOSTON
On the edge of historic Back Bay and the wonderfully eclectic South End, Boston's most exciting small hotel offers visitors a myriad of fringe benefits.
All rooms newly renovated
BOSTONS BEST VALUE.
Complimentary continental breakfast served daily in Fritz, one of Boston's most frequented gay bars.
1-800-842-3450
www.chandlerinn-fritz.com
CHANDLER INN
HOTEL
26 Chandler at Berkeley, Boston, MA 02116 (617) 482-3450

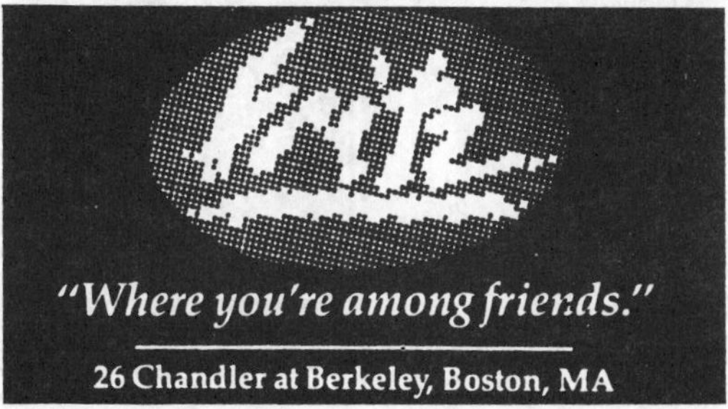
fritz
"Where you're among friends."
26 Chandler at Berkeley, Boston, MA

Clarendon Square Inn [GS,NS,WI,GO] 198 W Brookline St (btwn Tremont & Columbus) **617/536-2229** *restored Victorian town house, hot tub*

Encore B&B [GF,NS,GO] 116 W Newton St (at Tremont) **617/247-3425** *19th-c town house in Boston's South End*

Holiday Inn Express & Suites Boston Downtown [GF,WI,NS,WC] 280 Friend St (at Causeway) **617/720-5544** *modern decor*

Holiday Inn Select Boston Government Center [GF,SW,WI,WC] 5 Blossom St (Cambridge St) **617/742-7630** *close to shops, restaurants & entertainment, full brkfst*

Hotel 140 [GS,NS,WC] 140 Clarendon St (at Stuart St) **617/585-5600** *gym, close to South End*

The Liberty Hotel [GF,NS,WI,WC] 215 Charles St (at Cambridge St) **617/224-4000, 866/507-5245** *in the former Charles St Jail*

Nine Zero Hotel [GF] 90 Tremont St (at Bosworth) **617/772-5800, 866/646-3937** *luxury hotel, full brkfst, jacuzzi*

▶ **Oasis Guest House** [★GS,NS,WC,GO] 22 Edgerly Rd **617/267-2262, 800/230-0105** *in Back Bay*

Papa-Nona's [GS,WI] **781/289-0851** *1-bdrm apt*

Rutland Square House B&B [GS,NS,GO] 56 Rutland Square **617/247-0018** *Victorian town house*

Taylor House B&B [GS,NS,WI,GO] 50 Burroughs St, Jamaica Plain **617/983-9334, 888/228-2956** *Italianate Victorian*

Whitman House Inn [NS,WI,GO] 17 Worcester St (at Norfolk St), Cambridge **617/913-6189**

BARS

The Alley [★M,NH,D,B,L,WC,GO] 14 Pi Alley (at 275 Washington St) **617/263-1449** *2pm-2am, from noon wknds, cruisy*

Boston Eagle [M,NH] 520 Tremont St (near Berkeley) **617/542-4494** *3pm-2am, from noon Sun*

Boston Ramrod [★M,D,B,L,WC] 1254 Boylston St (at Ipswich, 1 block from Fenway Park) **617/266-2986** *noon-2am*

► **Club Cafe Lounge & Video Bar** [★MW,D,F,E,K,P,V,WC] 209 Columbus (at Berkeley) **617/536-0966** *11:30am-2am, Sun brunch from 10:30am, [D] 6pm-close Sun, also restaurant*

Encore [GS,E] 275 Tremont St (at Stuart St, in hotel) **617/728-2162** *lounge & cabaret*

► **Fritz** [★M,NH] 26 Chandler St (in the Chandler Inn) **617/482-4428** *noon-2am, brunch Sat-Sun, sports bar*

Jacque's [★M,TG,C,DS,$] 79 Broadway (at Stuart) **617/426-8902** *11am-midnight, from noon Sun*

Johnny D's Restaurant & Music Club [D,E] 17 Holland St (in Davis Square), Somerville **617/776-2004** *12:30pm-1am, from 9am wknds, live music nightly*

Milky Way Lounge & Lanes [GS,F,E,K] 284 Amory St, Jamaica Plain **617/524-3740** *6pm-1am, live music, poetry, bowling, also restaurant*

Paradise [M,D,S,V] 180 Massachusetts Ave, Cambridge **617/868-3000** *7pm-1am, till 2am Th-Sat*

Ryles [GS,F,E] 212 Hampshire St (at Cambridge St, in Inman Square), Cambridge **617/876-9330** *great wknd jazz brunch*

Sister Sorel [MW,NH] 647 Tremont **617/266-4600** *also restaurant, dinner only, wknd brunch*

Nightclubs

dbar [GS] 1236 Dorchester Ave, Dorchester **617/265-4490** *5pm-2am, from 11:30am Sun, also restaurant, dinner nightly*

Epic Saturday [M,D] 279 Tremont St (at Stuart, at the Roxy) **617/338-7699** *10:30pm Sat only*

The Estate [MW,D,19+,$] 1 Boylston Pl **617/536-2100** *gay Th only*

The Glam Life [MW,D,19+,$] 1 Boylston Pl (at Estate) **617/536-2100** *Th only, hip-hop*

HBF Entertainment [MW,MR] **617/792-3823** *Boston's LGBT hip hop events*

Hot Mess Sundays [M,D] 275 Tremont St (at Stuart St, at Underbar) **617/292-0080** *Sun only*

Machine [★M,D,V,S,YC,WC] 1256 Boylston St (below Boston Ramrod) **617/536-1950** *10pm-2am, theme nights*

The Middle East [GF,A,F,E,YC,$] 472 Massachusetts Ave (in Central Square), Cambridge **617/497-0576** *11am-1am, till 2am wknds, live music*

Night Gallery Video Bar [GS,V] 835 Beacon St (btwn Arundel & Miner, at An Tua Nua) *Th-Sat only*

Rise [GS,D,PC] 306 Stuart St (btwn Berkeley & Arlington) **617/423-7473** *1:30am-6:30am Fri-Sat & holiday Sun only*

Cafes

1369 Cafe 757 Massachusetts Ave (in Central Square), Cambridge **617/576-4600** *7am-11pm, from 8am wknds, till 10pm Sun, coffee & baked goods; also 1369 Cambridge St (Inman Square), 617/576-1369*

Berkeley Perk [F,GO] 69 Berkeley St (at Chandler) **617/426-7375** *6am-5pm, 7:30am-4pm Sat, 8am-noon Sun (clsd Sun summers)*

Diesel Cafe [GO] 257 Elm St (in Davis Square), Somerville **617/629-8717** *7am-midnight, from 8am wknds*

Fiore's Bakery [GO] 55 South St, Jamaica Plain **617/524-9200** *7am-7pm, 8am-6pm wknds, bakery & organic coffees*

Francesca's [★MW,WC] 564 Tremont St (at Clarendon) **617/482-9026** *8am-11pm, pastries*

JP Licks [★] 352 Newbury St **617/236-1666** *"homemade ice cream cafe"—& yes, they serve coffee too*

June Bug Cafe [WI,GO] 403A Centre St, Jamaica Plain **617/522-2393** *8am-11pm, from 9am Sat-Sun, also sandwiches*

South End Buttery 314 Shawmut Ave (at Union Park St) **617/482-1015** *cupcakes! also brkfst, lunch & dinner*

True Grounds [E] 717 Broadway, Somerville **617/591-9559** *7am-9pm, from 8am wknds, brkfst, lunch*

Restaurants

28 Degrees 1 Appleton St (at Tremont St) **617/728-0728** *upscale restaurant & lounge*

33 Restaurant & Lounge 33 Stanhope St **617/572-3311** *dinner nightly, Sun brunch, French/ Italian, patio*

BarLola [E] 160 Commonwealth Ave (at Dartmouth) **617/266-1122** *4pm-2am, from noon wknds, Spanish tapas lounge*

Boston Pita Pit [WC,GO] 479 Harvard St (at Commonwealth), Brookline **617/738-7482** *10:30am-midnight, till 2:30am wknds, plenty veggie*

Casa Romero 30 Gloucester St **617/536-4341** *dinner, Mexican, also bar*

Charlie's Sandwich Shoppe 429 Columbus Ave (at Pembroke St) **617/536-7669** *great brkfst, clsd Sun*

City Girl Cafe [BW,GO] 204 Hampshire St (at Prospect), Cambridge **617/864-2809** *11am-9pm, from 10am Sat, till 3pm Sun, clsd Mon, Italian, great sandwiches*

▶ **Club Cafe** [★E,P,V,WC] 209 Columbus (adjacent to Club Cafe) **617/536-0966** *lunch, dinner & Sun brunch, also 3 bars*

Geoffrey's Cafe 4257 Washington St, Roslindale **617/325-1000** *4pm-1am, from 10am wknds, popular Disco brunch*

Icarus [E] 3 Appleton St (off Tremont) **617/426-1790** *dinner only, jazz Fri*

Laurel 142 Berkeley St (at Columbus) **617/424-6711** *lunch weekdays & dinner nightly, Sun brunch*

My Thai Cafe 3 Beach St, 2nd flr **617/451-2395** *11am-10pm, till 11pm Fri-Sat, Asian, vegetarian/ vegan*

Om 92 Winthrop, Cambridge **617/576-2800** *noon-3pm & 5pm-1am Mon-Fri, 5pm-2am only Th-Sat, American*

Pho Republique 1415 Washington St (at Union Park St) **617/262-0005** *5:30pm-1am, French-Vietnamese, plenty veggie*

Rabia's [WC] 73 Salem St (at Cross St) **617/227-6637** *11am-10:30pm, fine Italian*

Ristorante Lucia 415 Hanover St **617/367-2353** *great North End pasta*

Sage 1395 Washington St (at Union Park St) **617/248-8814** *Italian fine dining nightly, also Sun brunch, bar till 1am*

Sorellina [R] 1 Huntington Ave **617/412-4600** *5:30pm-10:30pm, till 11pm Fri-Sat, till 10pm Sun, Italian*

Stix 35 Stanhope St **617/236-6363** *dinner nightly, lounge , clsd Sun-Mon*

Trattoria Pulcinella 147 Huron Ave (at Concord), Cambridge **617/491-6336** *5pm-10pm, fine Italian*

Veggie Planet 47 Palmer St (at Club Passim), Cambridge **617/661-1513** *11:30am-10:30pm, vegetarian, also live music venue*

Entertainment & Recreation

Boston Gay Men's Chorus **617/542-7464** *diverse array of classical & pop, concerts usually held in Dec, March & June*

Club Passim 47 Palmer St, Cambridge **617/492-5300** *folk music & cultural center*

Freedom Trail **617/357-8300** *start at the Visitor Information Center in Boston Common (at Tremont & West Sts), the most famous cow pasture & oldest public park in the US, then follow the red line to some of Boston's most famous sites*

Isabella Stewart Gardner Museum 280 The Fenway **617/566-1401** *Venetian palazzo filled w/ Old Masters to Impressionists, gorgeous courtyard, clsd Mon*

The Mapparium 200 Massachusetts Ave (in Mary Baker Eddy Library) **617/450-7000** *10am-4pm, clsd Mon, the map's out of date, but where else can you walk through a 30-ft stained-glass globe?*

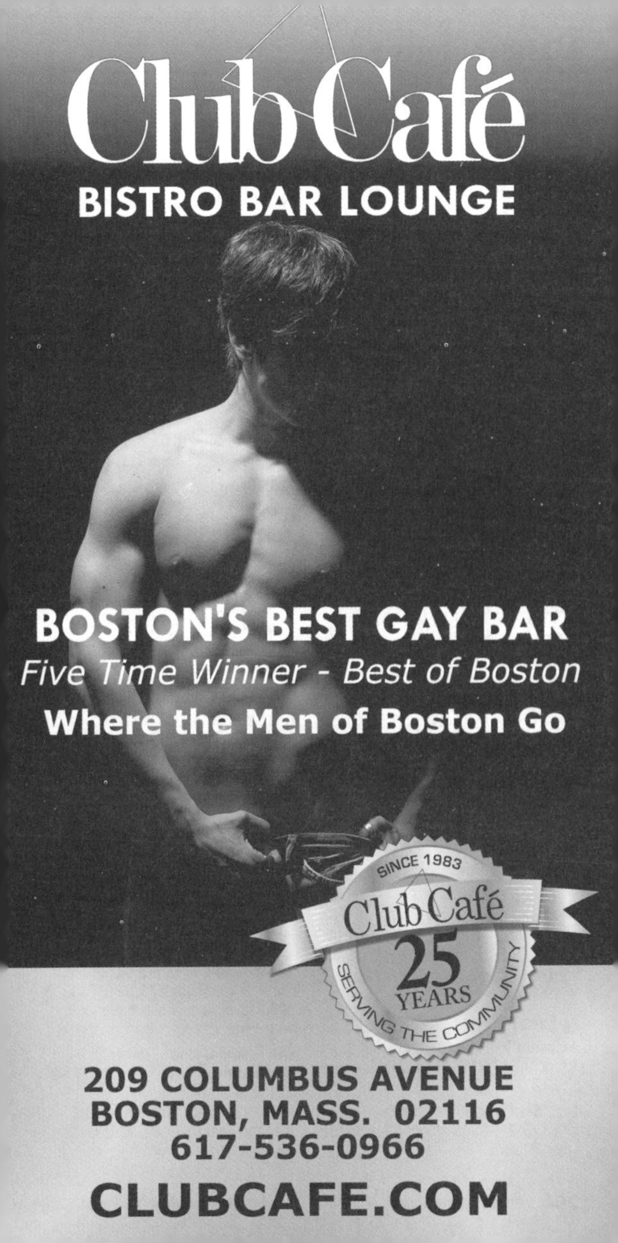
Club Café
BISTRO BAR LOUNGE
BOSTON'S BEST GAY BAR
Five Time Winner - Best of Boston
Where the Men of Boston Go
SINCE 1983
Club Café
25
YEARS
SERVING THE COMMUNITY
209 COLUMBUS AVENUE
BOSTON, MASS. 02116
617-536-0966
CLUBCAFE.COM

Museum of African American History/ Black Heritage Trail 46 Joy St (at Smith Ct, on Beacon Hill) **617/725-0022** *10am-4pm, clsd Sun, exhibits in the Abiel Smith School, the nation's first public school for black childen*

New Repertory Theatre 321 Arsenal St, Watertown **617/923-8487 (box office), 617/923-7060**

The Theater Offensive **617/661-1600** *"New England's premier presenter of LGBT theater," also Out on the Edge festival in Oct*

Urban Adventours 890 Commonwealth Ave (at St Paul) **617/233-7595, 800/979-3370** *guided bike tours & bike rentals*

Bookstores

Calamus Bookstore [★] 92-B South St **617/338-1931, 888/800-7300** *9am-7pm, noon-6pm, LGBT, also cards, music, jewelry, videos, magazines*

The Globe Corner Bookstore 90 Mt Auburn (Harvard Square), Cambridge **617/497-6277, 800/358-6013** *travel books & maps*

Trident Booksellers & Cafe [F,BW,WI,WC] 338 Newbury St (off Mass Ave) **617/267-8688** *8am-midnight, good magazine browsing*

Publications

Bay Windows **617/266-6670** *LGBT newspaper*

Gyms & Health Clubs

Revolution Fitness [GF] 209 Columbus **617/536-3006**

Men's Services

▶ **Megaphone** **617/423-6666** *Meet and Chat Live with HOT local men. FREE to listen & respond to ads. Video and text chat at GayMates.com. Use FREE code 4889.*

Erotica

Amazing Express 1258 Boylston St (at Ipswich) **617/859-8911** *also 57 Stuart St, 617/ 338-1252*

Eros Boutique 581-A Tremont St, 2nd flr **617/425-0345** *10am-10pm, fetish-wear & toys*

Good Vibrations [★WC] 308 Harvard St, Brookline **617/264-4400** *noon-7pm, till 8pm Th-Sat, clean, well-lighted sex toy store, also mail order, workshops & events*

Hubba Hubba 534 Massachusetts Ave (at Brookline, in Central Square), Cambridge **617/492-9082** *fetish & drag gear*

Marquis de Sade 92 South St **617/426-2120** *10am-11pm*

Cruisy Areas

Carson Beach [AYOR] William J Day Blvd

Charles River Esplanade [AYOR] across foot bridge at end of Dartmouth St, near lagoon *go to the right*

The Fens (FenwayVictory Gardens) [AYOR] near the Ramrod bar

Brookline

see Boston

Cambridge

see Boston

Cape Ann

Retail Shops

Bearskin Neck Leathers 7 Bearskin Neck **978/546-2258**

Cape Cod

see also Provincetown listings

Info Lines & Services

Gay/ Lesbian AA 460 W Main St (at Cape Cod Human Services Bldg), Hyannis **508/775-7060** *6pm Sun*

Accommodations

Cape Cod Guest House [MW,NS,GO] 77 Lake Shore Dr (Rte 28 & Sandwich Rd), East Falmouth **774/521-6333** *clothing-optional hot tub overlooks water, canoes available, pet-friendly*

The Colonial House Inn & Restaurant [GF,SW,NS,WI,GO] 277 Main St, Rte 6A, Yarmouthport **508/362-4348, 800/999-3416** *dinner & light brkfst included, jacuzzi, also restaurant & lounge*

The Crow's Nest of West Dennis [GS,NS,WI,GO] 230 Main St (at Station Ave), West Dennis **508/760-3335, 877/240-2769** *B&B, dogs ok*

Josiah Sampson House [GF,NS,WI,GO] 40 Old Kings Rd, Cotuit **508/428-8383** *1793 Federal-style house on National Register of Historic Places, some fireplaces*

Lamb & Lion Inn [GF,NS,SW] 2504 Main St (Rte 6A), Barnstable **508/362-6823, 800/909-6923** *1740s inn w/ additions, courtyard*

Night Heron Cottage B&B [GF,NS,WI,GO] 35 Lucinda Ct, Eastham **508/255-7063, 845/797-1737** *near birding, beaches, kayaking & canoeing, lesbian-owned*

White Swan B&B [GF,NS,WI] 146 Manomet Point Rd **508/224-3759, 888/988-7666** *in 200-year-old farmhouse, open year-round, at mouth of Cape Cod*

Woods Hole Passage [GF,WI] 186 Woods Hole Rd, Falmouth **508/548-9575, 800/790-8976** *full brkfst, near beaches*

Nightclubs

Club 477/ Mallory Dock [MW,D,WC] 477 Yarmouth Rd, Hyannis **508/771-7511, 800/393-6161** *6pm-1am, T-dance from 3pm (summer), Cape Cod's largest gay complex, patio*

Cruisy Areas

Boardwalk [AYOR] Jarvis St (off 6-A, exit 1), Sandwich *nights*

Crow's Pasture [AYOR] N on 6-A to South St, past cemetery, Dennis *in dunes*

Kalmus Park Beach [AYOR] end of Ocean St, Hyannis *behind parking lot*

Ryder Woods Conservation Area [AYOR] Rte 130 to Cotuit Rd (toward Mashpee for 3.5 miles), Sandwich *trails along the lake*

Skaket Beach [AYOR] Dennis *off to the right*

Chelsea

see Boston

Dedham

Erotica

Amazing Express 530 Providence Hwy/ Rte 1 **781/320-9377**

Greenfield

Accommodations

Brandt House [GF,NS,WI] 29 Highland Ave **413/774-3329, 800/235-3329** *16-rm estate on hill, full brkfst, formal garden*

The Charlemont Inn [GF,E,NS,GO] Rte 2, Mohawk Trail, Charlemont **413/339-5796** *restaurant, full bar*

Restaurants

Hope & Olive 44 Hope St **413/774-3150** *lunch & dinner, clsd Mon*

Bookstores

World Eye Bookshop 156 Main St **413/772-2186** *9:30am-6:30pm, 9am-5pm Sat, noon-5pm Sun, LGBT section*

Haverhill

Cafes

Wicked Big Cafe [WI,WC,GO] 19 Essex St (at Wingate) **978/556-5656** *7am-5pm, 8am-2pm Sat, clsd Sun*

Ipswich

Cruisy Areas

Crane's Beach [AYOR] 1/2 mile to the right

Lenox

see Berkshires

Lowell

Erotica

Tower News 101 Gorham St **978/452-8693**

Lynn

Bars

Fran's Place [MW,D,K,S,WC] 776 Washington (at Sagamore) **781/598-5618** *3pm-1am, also sports bar*

The Pub at 47 Central [M,NH,D,L,K,DS,V,GO] 47 Central Ave **781/586-0551** *2pm-1am, DJ wknds*

Martha's Vineyard

Accommodations

Arbor Inn [GF,NS] 222 Upper Main St, Edgartown **508/627-8137, 888/748-4383** *B&B, some shared baths*

The Inn at Babson Court [GF,NS,GO] 55 Western Ave, Gloucester **978/281-4469** *overlooks Gloucester Harbor, brkfst kitchens, cloistered garden & fountain*

Martha's Vineyard Surfside [GF,WC] 7 Oak Bluffs Ave, Oak Bluffs **508/693-2500, 800/537-3007**

The Shiverick Inn [GS,NS,WI,GO] 5 Pease's Pt Wy, Edgartown (at Pent Ln) **508/627-3797, 800/723-4292** *restored 1840 mansion, full brkfst*

Restaurants

The Black Dog Tavern [WC] Beach St Extension #21 **508/693-9223** *brkfst, lunch & dinner, seasonal*

Le Grenier 96 Main St, Vineyard Haven **508/693-4906** *dinner, French*

Louis' Cafe [GO] 350 State Rd, Vineyard Haven **508/693-3255** *Italian, plenty veggie*

Bookstores

Bunch of Grapes 44 Main St, Vineyard Haven **508/693-2291, 800/693-0221** *9am-6pm, till 9:30pm Fri & summers, some LGBT titles*

Medford

Erotica

Amazing Express 423 Mystic Ave/ Rte 38 **781/391-7438**

Nantucket

Accommodations

The Chestnut House [GF,WI,NS] 3 Chestnut St **508/228-0049** *also cottage*

New Bedford

Bars

Le Place [★MW,D,K] 20 Kenyon St **508/990-1248** *2pm-2am*

The Rainbow's End [MW,D,F,K,S,WC] 426 N Front St (at Philips Ave) **508/997-0466** *5pm-2am, DJ Fri-Sat, [S] Fri*

Erotica

Amazing Express 10 Sconticut Square/ Rte 6, Fairhaven **508/991-8191**

Newburyport

Restaurants

Glenn's Restaurant & Cool Bar [E,WC] 44 Merrimac St **978/465-3811** *5:30pm-9pm, till 10pm Fri-Sat, clsd Mon, bar open till midnight, from 4pm wknds*

Newton

see Boston

North Adams

see Berkshires

Northampton

see also Amherst

Accommodations

Clarion Hotel & Conference Center [GF,SW,NS,WI,WC] 1 Atwood Dr **413/586-1211, 800/582-2929** *also restaurants & bar*

Corner Porches [GS,NS] 82 Baptist Corner Rd, Ashfield **413/628-4592** *full brkfst, shared bath, pets on premises, 30 minutes from Northampton*

The Hotel Northampton [GF,NS,WI,WC] 36 King St **413/584-3100, 800/547-3529** *in the heart of downtown, also Gothic Gardens bldg & 4-rm cottage*

Bars

The Iron Horse [GF,F,E,NS] 20 Center St **413/584-0610** *7pm-close, live music, all ages*

Nightclubs

Diva's [★MW,D,E,K,DS,S,YC] 492 Pleasant St (at Conz St) **413/586-8161** *9pm-2am, clsd Sun-Mon, theme nights, [18+] Sun-Fri*

Pearl Street [GS,D,E,YC] 10 Pearl St **413/584-7771** *7pm-1am, live music*

Cafes

Haymarket Cafe [★F] 185 Main St **413/586-9969** *7am-10pm, till 11:30pm Fri-Sat, also restaurant*

Restaurants

Bela [WC,GO] 68 Masonic St **413/586-8011** *noon-8:45pm, clsd Sun-Mon, vegetarian*

Bueno Y Sano 134 Main St **413/586-7311** *11am-10pm, till 9pm Sun, Mexican*

Paul & Elizabeth's [BW,WC] 150 Main St (in Thorne's Marketplace) **413/584-4832** *lunch & dinner, Sun brunch, seafood*

Union Station 125A Pleasant St **413/586-5366** *dinner, clsd Mon, steak & seafood*

Retail Shops

Oh My A Sensuality Shop 2-C Conz St (in Maplewood Shops) **413/584-9669** *11am-6pm, till 8pm Fri-Sat, noon-5pm Sun, informative, helpful & intimate sex toy store*

Pride & Joy [WC,GO] 20 Crafts Ave **413/585-0683** *open 7 days, LGBT books & gifts*

Publications

▶ **Metroline 860/233-8334** *covers CT, RI & MA*

The Rainbow Times 413/204-8959, 866/310-8512 *bi-weekly LGBT news magazine for western MA, Capital District of NY, northern CT & southern VT*

Cruisy Areas

Northampton Meadows [AYOR] next to the Connecticut River (dirt roads) *not far from I-91 rest areas*

Pulaski Park [AYOR] Main St *summer nights*

Northborough

Erotica

Amazing Superstore 15 Belmont St/ Rte 9 **508/366-3807**

Plymouth

Accommodations

Symphony Hollow B&B at the Round House [GS,GO] 82 Mayflower Rd, Plympton **781/640-6936**

Provincetown

see also Cape Cod listings

Info Lines & Services

▶ **Provincetown Business Guild 508/487-2313, 800/637-8696**

Accommodations

1807 House [MW,NS,WI,GO] 54 Commercial St (btwn W Vine & Point St) **508/487-2173, 888/522-1807** *50 ft from beach*

Admiral's Landing Guest House [M,NS,WI,GO] 158 Bradford St (btwn Conwell & Pearl) **508/487-9665, 800/934-0925** *1840s Greek Revival home & studio efficiencies*

Aerie House & Beach Club [MW,WI,GO] 184 Bradford St (at Miller Hill) **508/487-1197, 800/487-1197** *bay views, hot tub, sundeck*

Ampersand Guesthouse [M,NS,WI,GO] 6 Cottage St **508/487-0959, 800/574-9645** *1880s Greek Revival, sundeck*

Anchor Inn Beach House [★GS,NS,WC] 175 Commercial St **508/487-0432, 800/858-2657** *private beach*

Bayberry Accommodations [MW,NS,WI,GO] 16 Winthrop St **508/487-4605, 800/422-4605** *newly renovated, award-winning home*

Beachfront Realty 139 Commercial St **508/487-1397** *vacation rentals*

Beaconlight Guest House [★M,NS,WI,GO] 12 Winthrop St **508/487-9603, 800/696-9603** *hot tub, sundecks, parking, award-winning*

Benchmark Inn & Central [MW,SW,NS,WI,WC,GO] 6-8 Dyer St **508/487-7440, 888/487-7440** *hot tub, sauna, harbor views*

The Black Pearl Inn [MW,GO] 11 & 18 Pearl St **508/487-0302, 800/761-1016** *renovated 19th-c sea captain's home, hot tub, "friends of Bill welcome"*

▶ **Boatslip Resort** [★M,SW,GO] 161 Commercial St **508/487-1669, 877/786-9662** *seasonal, also several bars & popular T-dance*

The Bradford Carver House [MW,NS,GO] 70 Bradford St **508/487-0728, 800/826-9083** *restored mid-19th-c home, centrally located*

▶ **Brass Key Guesthouse** [★M,SW,NS,WI,WC,GO] 67 Bradford St (at Carver) **508/487-9005, 800/842-9858** *luxury inn w/ hot tub*

Burch House [GS,WI] 116 Bradford St **508/487-9170** *seasonal, studios w/ kitchenettes, some shared baths*

Cape Inn [GS,SW,NS,WC] **508/487-1711, 800/422-4224** *also restaurant & bar*

Captain's House B&B [M,B,NS,GO] 350-A Commercial St (at Center) **508/487-9353, 800/457-8885** *hot tub, patio*

Carl's Guest House [MO,N,NS,GO] 68 Bradford St (at Court St) **508/487-1650, 800/348-2275** *sundeck*

Carpe Diem Guesthouse & Spa [MW,NS,WI,GO] 12 Johnson St **508/487-4242, 800/487-0132** *full German brkfst, hot tub*

The Carriage House Guesthouse [GS,GO] 7 Central St **508/487-8855, 800/309-0248** *1700s guesthouse, hot tub*

Chicago House [MW,NS,WI,GO] 6 Winslow St (at Bradford) **508/487-0537, 800/733-7869** *rooms & apts*

► **Christopher's by the Bay** [MW,NS,WI,GO] 8 Johnson St (at Bradford) **508/487-9263, 877/487-9263** *full brkfst, some shared baths, patio*

The Clarendon House [GS,NS] 118 Bradford St (btwn Ryder & Alden) **508/487-1645, 800/669-8229** *also pet-friendly cottage, hot tub, roof deck, full brkfst*

The Commons Guest House & Bistro [GS,GO] 386 Commercial St (at Pearl) **508/487-7800, 800/487-0784** *deck w/ full bar, also restaurant*

Crown & Anchor [MW,SW,NS,WI,GO] 247 Commercial St **508/487-1430** *also cabaret & poolside bars*

Crowne Pointe Historic Inn & Shui Spa [MW,SW,NS,WI,WC,GO] 82 Bradford St **508/487-6767, 877/276-9631** *luxurious inn, full brkfst, 2 large jacuzzis, spa, restaurant*

Designer's Dock [GS,WI,GO] 349 Commercial St **508/776-5746, 800/724-9888** *weekly condos in town & on beach, seasonal*

Dexter's Inn [MW,NS,GO] 6 Conwell St (at Railroad) **508/487-1911, 888/521-1999** *sundeck*

Dyer's Antique Barn Guest Suites [MW,SW] 9 Winthrop St (at Commercial) **508/487-2061** *seasonal self-catering units*

Enzo [GS] 186 Commercial St **508/487-7555, 888/873-5001** *Italian restaurant & piano bar on premises*

Fairbanks Inn [★MW,NS,WI,GO] 90 Bradford St **508/487-0386, 800/324-7265**

Four Gables [GS,GO] 15 Race Rd **866/487-2427**

Gabriel's at The Ashbrooke Inn [★MW,NS,WI,GO] 102 Bradford St **508/487-3232, 800/969-2643** *full brkfst, hot tub*

The Gallery Inn [M] 3 Johnson St **508/487-3010, 800/676-3010** *seasonal*

Gifford House Inn [MW,WI,GO] 9 Carver St **508/487-0688, 800/434-0130** *seasonal, also several bars & 11 Carver restaurant (dinner only, seafood)*

Gracie House [MW,NS,GO] 152 Bradford St (at Conwell) **508/487-4808** *historic, restored Queen Anne, lesbian-owned*

Grand View Inn [MW,NS,GO] 4 Conant St **508/487-9193, 888/268-9169** *decks*

Harbor Hill at Provincetown [GF,GO] 4 Harbor Hill Rd **508/487-0541** *condo resort in West End, 500 yds from Nat'l Seashore*

Heritage House [MW,GO] 7 Center St **508/487-3692** *shared baths, lesbian-owned*

The Inn at Cook Street [GF,NS,GO] 7 Cook St **508/487-3894, 888/266-5655** *intimate & quiet*

Inn at the Moors [GF,SW,NS,WI,GO] 59 Provincelands Rd **508/487-1342, 800/842-6379** *motel, across from Nat'l Seashore Province Lands, seasonal*

John Randall House [MW,NS,WI,GO] 140 Bradford St (at Standish) **508/487-3533, 800/573-6700** *open year-round*

Labrador Landing [MW,GO] 47 Commercial St **917/597-1500** *luxury cottages on West End*

▶ **Land's End Inn** [GS,NS,GO] 22 Commercial St **508/487-0706, 800/276-7088** *seasonal*

Lotus Guest House [MW,WI,GO] 296 Commercial St (at Standish) **508/487-4644, 888/508-4644** *seasonal, decks, garden*

Moffett House [MW,GO] 296-A Commercial St **508/487-6615, 800/990-8865** *levi/ leather-friendly*

The Oxford [MW,NS,WI,GO] 8 Cottage St **508/487-9103, 888/456-9103** *newly renovated Revival, parking*

Prince Albert Guest House [M,NS,GO] 164-166 Commercial St **508/487-1850**

Provincetown Inn [GS,SW,WC] 1 Commercial St (at Rotary) **508/487-9500, 800/942-5388** *waterfront, private beach, poolside bar & grill, theater*

The Ranch Guestlodge [MO,B,L,N,NS,WI,GO] 198 Commercial St **508/487-1542, 800/942-1542** *shared baths, sundeck [N], also bar for guests*

Ravenwood Guest House [MW,NS,WC,GO] 462 Commercial St (at Cook) **508/487-3203** *1830 Greek Revival, also apts & cottage, private beach, lesbian-owned*

The Red Inn [GF,NS,WC,GO] 15 Commercial St (at Point) **508/487-7334, 866/473-3466**

Revere Guesthouse [MW,NS,GO] 14 Court St (btwn Commercial & Bradford) **508/487-2292, 800/487-2292** *restored 1820s captain's home, also apt*

Romeo's Holiday [MW,N,WI,GO] 97 Bradford St (btwn Gosnold & Masonic) **508/487-6636, 877/697-6636** *hot tub*

Rose & Crown Guest House [GS,GO] 158 Commercial St **508/487-3332** *also cottage*

Sandbars [GS] 570 Shore Rd, Beach Pt, North Truro **800/223-0088 x160** *seasonal, oceanfront rooms, private beach*

Seasons, An Inn for All [MW,NS,WI,GO] 160 Bradford St (at Pearl) **508/487-2283, 800/563-0113** *Victorian B&B, full brkfst*

The Secret Garden Inn [MW,NS] 300-A Commercial St **508/487-9027, 866/786-9646**

Shiremax Inn [MW,GO] 5 Tremont St (btwn Franklin & School) **508/487-1233, 888/744-7362** *seasonal, also apt*

Snug Cottage [GS,NS,WI,GO] 178 Bradford St **508/487-1616, 800/432-2334** *boutique B&B*

Somerset House [MW,NS,WI,GO] 378 Commercial St (at Pearl) **508/487-0383, 800/575-1850**

The Stone Lion Inn [GF,NS,WI] 130 Commercial St, Wellfleet **508/349-9565** *full brkfst, 17 miles from P-Town*

Sunny West End Guest Apartment [MW,NS,GO] **508/487-9055** *sunny rental apt*

Sunset Inn [MW,N,NS,GO] 142 Bradford St (at Center) **508/487-9810, 800/965-1801** *seasonal, some shared baths*

Surfside Hotel & Suites [GS,SW,NS,WI] 543 Commercial (at Kendall Ln) **508/487-1726, 800/421-1726** *seasonal, waterfront hotel w/ lots of amenities, private beach*

The Tucker Inn [MW,NS,WI,GO] 12 Center St **508/487-0381, 800/477-1867** *1870s house & 1 cottage (weekly rental), full brkfst*

Victoria House [MW,GO] 5 Standish St **508/487-4455, 877/867-8696**

Watership Inn [M,WI,GO] 7 Winthrop St **508/487-0094, 800/330-9413** *sundeck*

West End Inn [GF,GO] 44 Commercial St **508/487-9555, 800/559-1220** *seasonal*

Westville Cottage [GS,NS,WI,GO] Pleasant St (at Kings Wy) **203/710-5733** *private condo for 2*

White Porch Inn [M,WI] 7 Johnson St **508/364-2549, 866/922-0333**

White Wind Inn [MW,GO] 174 Commercial St (at Winthrop) **508/487-1526, 888/449-9463** *well-appointed*

BARS

► **The Boatslip Resort** [★MW,D,F,YC] 161 Commercial St **508/487-1669, 877/786-9662** *seasonal, popular T-dance 4pm daily, special events, outdoor/ waterfront grill*

Governor Bradford [GF,F,E,K,DS] 312 Commercial St (at Standish) **508/487-2781** *11am-1am, from noon Sun, "drag karaoke" Sat (nightly in season), also restaurant in summer*

PiedBar [★MW,D,F,E,P,S,WC] 193-A Commercial St (at Court St) **508/487-1527** *seasonal May-Oct, noon-1am, mostly men 6:30pm-9:30pm at After Tea T-Dance*

Porchside Lounge [M,NH,P] 11 Carver St (in the Gifford House) **508/487-0688** *5pm-1am, Lobby Bar from 10pm, also restaurant*

Vault [MO,B,L] 247 Commercial St (downstairs in the Crown & Anchor) **508/487-1430** *9pm-1am Th-Sun only*

Wave Video Bar [MW,NH,K] 247 Commercial St (in the Crown & Anchor) **508/487-1430** *6pm-1am, from noon in season, T-dance Sun from 6pm*

Nightclubs

Atlantic House (The "A-House") [★M,D] 6 Masonic Pl **508/487-3169** *10pm-1am, 3 bars, weekly theme parties, also The Little Bar [M,NH] & the Macho Bar [M,L]*

Club Purgatory [MW,D,L] 9-11 Carver St (at Bradford St, in the Gifford House) **508/487-8442** *5pm-1am, theme nights*

Paramount [★MW,D,E,C,DS,$] in the Crown & Anchor **508/487-1430** *10pm-1am wknds, seasonal*

Cafes

Joe's 148-A Commercial St (btwn Atlantic & Conant) **508/487-6656** *7:30am-close, great coffee w/ a view*

Post Office Cafe Cabaret [MW,E] 303 Commercial St (upstairs) **508/487-3892** *8am-11pm, seasonal hours*

Restaurants

Bayside Betsy's [WC] 177 Commercial St **508/487-6566** *lunch & dinner, bar till 10pm, on waterfront*

Big Daddy's Burritos 205 Commercial St **508/487-4432** *11am-10pm (May-Oct), Tex-Mex, burritos, veggie wraps, salads & nachos*

Bubala's by the Bay [★] 183-185 Commercial **508/487-0773** *brunch & dinner, bar till 1am, patio*

Ciro & Sal's [R] 4 Kiley Ct (btwn Bangs St & Lovett's Ct) **508/487-6444** *dinner from 5:30pm, bar from 5pm, Northern Italian*

Fanizzi's [★WC] 539 Commercial St (at Kendall Lane) **508/487-1964** *open daily year round, full bar*

Front Street Restaurant [BW] 230 Commercial St **508/487-9715** *seasonal, bistro 6pm-10:30pm, bar till 1am*

Lobster Pot [WC] harborside (at 321 Commercial St) **508/487-0842** *11:30am-10pm (April-Nov), seafood, some veggie*

Lorraine's [★MW,BW,GO] 133 Commercial St **508/487-6074** *dinner, clsd Th-Sun off-season, Mexican*

The Mews Restaurant & Cafe [★E,WC] 429 Commercial St (btwn Lovett's & Kiley) **508/487-1500** *dinner, Sun brunch, also Cafe Mews upstairs, waterfront dining*

Napi's Restaurant [WC] 7 Freeman St **508/487-1145, 800/571-6274** *dinner (lunch Oct-April), int'l/ seafood, plenty veggie*

The Red Inn [★GF,NS,WC,GO] 15 Commercial St (at Point) **508/487-7334, 866/473-3466** *dinner from 5:30pm, brunch Th-Sun, clsd Jan-April, reservations a must, full bar*

Sal's Place [★] 99 Commercial St **508/487-1279** *seasonal, seafood/ Italian, deck, on the water*

Spiritus Pizza [★] 190 Commercial St **508/487-2808** *noon-2am, great espresso shakes & late-night hangout for a slice*

Entertainment & Recreation

Art's Dune Tours [GO] 4 Standish St **508/487-1950, 800/894-1951** *day trips, sunset tours & charters through historic sand dunes & Nat'l Seashore Park*

Dolphin Fleet Whale Watch [GF,WC] 70 Shank Painter Rd (at MacMillan Wharf) **800/442-3188** *3-hr day & evening cruises*

Herring Cove Beach [AYOR]

Ptown Bikes [GO] 42 Bradford **508/487-8735** *9am-6pm, rentals*

Spaghetti Strip *nude beach, 1.5 miles S of Race Point Beach*

Theatre Go Round 508/487-0931 *many LGBT-themed plays*

Bookstores

Now, Voyager Bookstore & Gallery 357 Commercial St **508/487-0848** *10am-10pm (summers), LGBT & general books, cards*

Provincetown Bookshop 246 Commercial St **508/487-0964** *hours vary*

Retail Shops

Piercings by the Bearded Lady [GO] 336 Commercial St #4 **508/487-7979** *noon-8pm, seasonal*

Recovering Hearts [WC] 2-4 Standish St **508/487-4875** *10am-11pm (in summer), call for off-season hours, recovery, LGBT & New Age titles*

Publications

Provincetown Banner 167 Commercial St **508/487-7400** *newspaper*

Provincetown Magazine 508/487-1000 *seasonal, Provincetown's oldest weekly magazine*

Gyms & Health Clubs

Mussel Beach Health Club [MW] 35 Bradford St (btwn Montello & Conant) **508/487-0001** *6am-9pm, till 8pm in winter*

Provincetown Gym [MW] 82 Shank Painter Rd (at Winthrop) **508/487-2776**

Erotica

MG Leather Inc [GO] 338 Commercial St (at Standish St) **508/487-4036** *leather, fetish*

Cruisy Areas

Dick Dock [AYOR] behind Boatslip Beach Club *late*

Herring Cove Beach [AYOR]

Quincy

see also Boston

Nightclubs

My House Sundays [MW,D,DS] 609 Washington St *from 3pm Sun, drag shows at 11pm*

Randolph

Bars

Randolph Country Club [★MW,D,F,K,C,S,V,SW,WC] 44 Mazzeo Dr **781/961-2414** *2pm-2am, from 10am summer, 2 dance clubs, cabaret, poolside grill, volleyball*

Raynham

Erotica

Video Xtra 1832 Rte 44 **508/821-7800**

Rockport

Accommodations

Seven South Street Inn [GF,SW,NS,WI] 7 South St **888/284-2730, 978/546-6708** *4-course gourmet brkfst*

Salisbury

Bars

Hobo's Cafe & Lounge [MW,NH,K,GO] 5 Broadway **978/465-4626**

Saugus

Nightclubs

Tabú [GF,D,K] 168 Broadway (Rte 1 N, Godfried's Plaza) **781/231-5111** *from 10pm*

Shelburne Falls

Restaurants

Cafe Martin [WC,GO] 24 Bridge St (at Water St) **413/625-2795** *11am-9pm, clsd Mon, brunch Sun, full bar*

Somerville

see Boston

Springfield

Bars

Pure [M,NH,F,WC] 234 Chestnut St (E of Main) **413/205-1483** *1am-2am from noon Sun*

Nightclubs

Oz Nightclub [M,NH,D,K] 397 Dwight St (at Taylor) *7pm-2am*

Xstatic [M,D,S] 240 Chestnut St **413/736-2618, 800/710-2618** *7pm-2am, nude dancers*

Men's Services

▶ **Megaphone 413/271-3700** *Meet and Chat Live with HOT local men. FREE to listen & respond to ads. Video and text chat at GayMates.com. Use FREE code 4889.*

Erotica

Amazing 486-B Bridge St **413/747-9812**

Stoneham

Cruisy Areas

Sheep's Fold Conservation Area [AYOR] Rte I-93 exit 33 (off Rte 28) *top of the hills*

Taunton

Bars

Bobby's Place [MW,D,K] 62 Weir St (at Route 44, 138 & 140, at Taunton Green) **508/824-9997** *5pm-1am, till 2am Fri-Sat, from 2pm Sun*

Waltham

Bookstores

Synchronicity Transgender Bookstore 13 Felton St (at Moody) **781/899-2212** *over 100 TG titles*

Watertown

see Boston

Weymouth

Erotica

Amazing Express 138 Bridge St, North Weymouth **781/335-0446**

Williamstown

see Berkshires

Worcester

Info Lines & Services

AA Gay/ Lesbian [NS] 1 Freeland St **508/752-9000** *7pm Sat*

Bars

MB Lounge [MW,NH,P,WI,WC] 40 Grafton St (at Franklin) **508/799-4521** *5pm-close, from 3pm Fri-Sun*

Nightclubs

Blu Ultralounge & Nightclub [M,D] 105 Water St **508/756-2227** *7:30pm-2am, from 9pm Sat, clsd Sun-Mon*

Restaurants

86 Winter Street [★GO] 65 Water St **508/459-5400** *lunch Wed-Fri, dinner Wed-Sun, clsd Mon-Tue, live jazz Sun*

Retail Shops

Glamour Boutique 850 Southbridge St, Auburn **508/721-7800** *noon-8pm, 3pm-6pm Sun, large-size dresses, wigs, etc*

MICHIGAN

Ann Arbor

Info Lines & Services

Lesbian/ Gay AA 734/482-5700

Bars

\'aut\ Bar [★MW,NH,F,WC] 315 Braun Ct (at Catherine) **734/994-3677** *4pm-2am, from noon Sun, patio, also restaurant (lunch, dinner & Sun brunch), American/ Mexican*

Nightclubs

The Necto [GS,D,V,18+,YC] 516 E Liberty **734/994-5436** *9pm-2am, theme nights, gay night Fri*

Cafes

Cafe Verde [★F] 214 N Fourth Ave **734/994-9174** *7am-9:30pm, 9am-8pm Sun, fair trade & organic coffee & tea*

Restaurants

Dominick's [WC] 812 Monroe St (at Tappan Ave) **734/662-5414** *10am-10pm, clsd Sun, Italian, full bar*

The Earle [BW,WC] 121 W Washington (at Ashley) **734/994-0211** *5:30pm-10pm, till 11:30pm Fri-Sat, 5pm-9pm Sun, cont'l*

Seva 314 E Liberty **734/662-1111** *11am-9pm, from 10am wknds, vegetarian, also cafe & wine bar*

Zingerman's Delicatessen [GO] 422 Detroit St (at Kingsley) **734/663-3354** *7am-10pm, also ship food worldwide*

Entertainment & Recreation

The Ark [GF,E] 316 S Main St (btwn William & Liberty) **734/761-1451** *concert house*

Bookstores

Common Language [WC] 317 Braun Ct **734/663-0036** *11am-10pm, till midnight Fri-Sat, till 7pm Sun, LGBT*

Crazy Wisdom Books 114 S Main (btwn Huron & Washington) **734/665-2757** *10am-10pm, till 11pm Wed-Sat, 11am-6pm Sun, holistic & metaphysical*

Nicola's Books 2513 Jackson Ave (at Maple, in Westgate) **734/662-0600** *9am-9pm, till 6pm Sun*

Battle Creek

Nightclubs

Partners [MW,D,K,S,V,WC] 910 North Ave (at Morgan) **269/964-7276** *7pm-2am, clsd Mon*

Erotica

Romantix Adult Superstore 686 W Michigan (at Grand) **269/964-3070**

Bellaire

Accommodations

Applesauce Inn B&B [GF] 7296 S M-88 **231/533-6448, 888/533-6448** *B&B in 100-year-old farmhouse*

Bellaire B&B [GS,WI,GO] 212 Park St (at Antrim) **231/533-6077, 800/545-0780** *stately 1879 home, full brkfst, jacuzzi*

Big Bay

Accommodations

Big Bay Depot Motel [GF,WI,GO] **906/345-9350**

Big Rapids

Erotica

Fantasies Unlimited 13480 Northland Dr **231/796-8052**

Cheboygan

Erotica

Fantasies Unlimited 1116 E State St **231/627-4665**

Coldwater

Erotica

▶ **The Lion's Den Adult Superstore** 570 Jonesville Rd (exit 16, off I-69) **517/278-9577** *24hrs*

Copemish

Accommodations

Jeralan's Farm B&B [GF,NS] 18361 Viaduct Rd **231/378-2926, 866/250-8444** *B&B in 1872 farmhouse on 120 acres of woods & ponds*

Detroit

Info Lines & Services

Affirmations Lesbian/ Gay Community Center 290 W 9 Mile Rd (enter on Troy), Ferndale **248/398-7105, 800/398-4297** *11am-close, 10am-10pm, clsd Sun, also cafe*

Helpline 800/398-4297 *4pm-9pm Tue-Sat, support & resources line*

Together We Can (Gay/ Lesbian AA) **313/831-5550, 313/831-2555**

Accommodations

The Atheneum Suite Hotel [GF,WC] 1000 Brush St (at Lafayette) **313/962-2323, 800/772-2323** *luxury all-suite hotel, restaurant & lounge, gym*

Milner Hotel [GF] 1538 Centre St **313/963-3950, 877/645-6377** *downtown*

Shorecrest Motor Inn [GF,WC] 1316 E Jefferson Ave **313/568-3000, 800/992-9616** *downtown, also restaurant*

Bars

Adam's Apple [M,NH,K] 18931 W Warren (at Artesian) **313/240-8482** *3pm-2am, from noon wknds*

Club Gold Coast [★M,D,DS,S,WC,WI] 2971 E 7 Mile Rd (at Conant) **313/366-6135** *4pm-2am, from 7pm wknds, till 5am Fri-Sat, male dancers nightly*

Detroit Eagle [★M,D,L,WC] 1501 Holden (at Trumbull) **313/873-6969** *8pm-2am, from 9pm Sat-Sun, clsd Mon-Tue, patio*

Diamond Jim's Saloon [M,NH,D,CW,B,L,MR,F,K,GO] 19650 Warren (1 block E of Evergreen) **313/336-8680** *noon-2am, dance lessons, also Round Up Grill*

Gigi's [M,D,TG,K,DS,S,GO] 16920 W Warren (at Clayburn, enter rear) **313/584-6525** *noon-2am, from 2pm wknds, dancers*

Hayloft Saloon [M,NH,B,L,OC,WC] 8070 Greenfield Rd (S of Joy Rd) **313/581-8913** *3pm-2am, cruise bar for leathermen, bears, daddies, mature men*

Male Box Bar [M,NH,D,K,DS,18+,GO] 3537 E 7 Mile Rd **313/893-7696** *2pm-2am*

Menjo's [★M,D,V,YC] 928 W McNichols Rd (at Hamilton) **313/863-3934** *1pm-2am, popular happy hour*

Pronto [★MW,F,V] 608 S Washington (at 6th St), Royal Oak **248/544-7900** *11am-2am Wed-Sat, patio, also restaurant*

R&R Saloon [M,NH,D,L,F] 7330 Michigan Ave (at Central) **313/849-2751** *2pm-2am, till 4am Wed & wknds*

Soho [MW,K] 205 W 9 Mile (at Woodward), Ferndale **248/542-7646** *4pm-close, from 6pm wknds*

Stingers Lounge [MW,NH,F,DS,GO] 19404 Sherwood (at 7 Mile) **313/892-1765** *6pm-5am, from 8pm wknds*

Wednesday at Via Nove [MW,F] 344 W 9 Mile Rd, Ferndale **248/336-9936** *gay Wed only, till 2am, Italian restaurant w/ full bar*

The Woodward Bar & Grill [★M,D,MR,F,K,V] 6426 Woodward Ave (at Milwaukee, rear entrance) **313/872-0166** *2pm-2am, lounge, DJ Th-Sun*

The Works Detroit [GS,D,V] 1846 Michigan Ave (at Rosa Parks) **313/961-1742** *10pm-3am Th, till 5am Fri, till 6am Sat, mostly gay men Sat*

Nightclubs

Backstreet [★M,D,18+,WC,$] 15606 Joy Rd (at Greenfield) **313/838-6699** *9pm-2am Wed & Sat, 5 levels*

Inuendo [MW,MR,D,K,DS] 744 E Savannah (at 6 1/2 Mile & I-75), Highland Park **313/891-5798** *10pm-5am, till 2am Sun-Wed, clsd Mon & Tue*

Leland City Club [GF,D,A,18+] 400 Bagley St (at Leland Hotel) *10pm-4:30am Fri-Sat, goth/ alternative crowd*

Luna [GF,D,A] 1815 N Main St (at 12 Mile), Royal Oak **248/589-3344** *from 9pm, clsd Sun-Tue, goth/alternative crowd, theme nights*

Nine [MW,D,K] 141 W 9 Mile (at Woodward), Ferndale **248/582-7227** *more men Fri*

Off Broadway East [MR-AF,D,MR,YC] 12215 Harper Ave (at Dickerson) **313/526-8401** *9pm-2am, Wed & Sat popular*

Pandora's Box [★W,D,MR-AF,K,DS,S,WC] 6221 E Davison (at Mound) **313/892-8120** *9pm-2am Th-Sat, more women Sat*

Posh [GS,D,$] 22061 Woodward Ave, Ferndale **248/541-POSH** *10pm-close Th-Sat*

The Rainbow Room [MW,D,K,DS,18+] 6640 E 8 Mile Rd (btwn Mound Rd & Van Dyke Ave) **313/891-1020** *7pm-2am Wed-Sun*

Temple [GS,D,MR-AF,TG,WC] 2906 Cass Ave (btwn Charlotte & Temple) **313/832-2822** *11am-2am, popular wknds*

CAFES

Avalon International Breads [GO] 422 W Willis (at Cass) **313/832-0008** *6am-6pm, clsd Sun-Mon*

Coffee Beanery Cafe [WI] 28557 S Woodward Ave (S of 12 Mile), Berkley **248/336-9930** *7am-11pm*

Trixie's Cafe [E] 25925 Gratiot Ave, Roseville **586/776-9002** *2pm-1am, from 6pm Sun, hosts open mics*

RESTAURANTS

Amici's Living Room 3249 12 Mile Rd, Berkley **248/544-4100** *gourmet pizza & martinis*

Atlas Global Bistro 3111 Woodward Ave **313/831-2241** *lunch & dinner, Sun brunch, American/int'l, upscale*

Cass Cafe [WI] 4620 Cass Ave (at Forest) **313/831-1400** *11am-2am, 5pm-1am Sun, full bar*

Como's [WC] 22812 Woodward (at 9 Mile), Ferndale **248/548-5005** *11am-2am, till 3:30am Th-Sat, Italian, Sun brunch, full bar, patio*

Elwood Bar & Grill 300 Adams (at Brush, by Comerica Park) **313/962-2337** *11am-8pm, till 2pm Mon, clsd Sun (unless there's a Tiger's game); Art Deco diner*

Inn Season 500 E 4th St, Royal Oak **248/547-7916** *lunch & dinner, Sun brunch, clsd Mon, organic vegetarian*

La Dolce Vita [MW,WC] 17546 Woodward Ave (at McNichols) **313/865-0331** *lunch & dinner, Sun brunch, clsd Mon, Italian, patio*

Pete's Place Broadway Cafe [BYOB] 1225 Woodward Hts (at Hilton Rd), Ferndale **248/544-4215** *10am-10pm, till midnight Fri-Sat*

Pronto [★MW] 608 S Washington (at 6th St), Royal Oak **248/544-7900** *11am-10pm, patio, also video bar*

Starving Artist [GO] 212 W 9 Mile (1/2 block W of Woodward), Ferndale **248/545-5650** *lunch & dinner, clsd Sun-Mon, full bar*

Sweet Lorraine's Cafe & Bar [★WC] 29101 Greenfield Rd (at 12 Mile), Southfield **248/559-5985** *11am-10pm, till 11pm Fri-Sat, till 9:30pm Sun, modern American, some veggie*

Traffic Jam & Snug 511 W Canfield St (at SE corner of 2nd Ave) **313/831-9470** *11am-10:30pm, till midnight Fri-Sat, from noon Sat, till 8pm Sun, eclectic, plenty veggie, also full bar, bakery, dairy & brewery*

Via Nove 344 W 9 Mile Rd, Ferndale **248/336-9936** *Italian, also bar*

Vivio's 2460 Market St (btwn Gratiot & Russell) **313/393-1711** *lunch & dinner, clsd Sun, Italian, full bar*

ENTERTAINMENT & RECREATION

Charles H Wright Museum of African American History 315 E Warren Ave (at Brush) **313/494-5800**

Detroit Together Men's Chorus 2441 Pinecrest, Ferndale **248/544-3872**

Motown Historical Museum 2648 W Grand Blvd **313/875-2264**

BOOKSTORES

Chosen Books [WC] 120 W 4th St, Royal Oak **248/543-5758** *noon-10pm, LGBT*

Just 4 Us [GO] 211 W 9 Mile Rd (at Woodward), Ferndale **248/547-5878** *noon-8pm, till 10pm Th-Fri, 10am-8pm Sat, 11am-5pm Sun, also cafe*

RETAIL SHOPS

Royal Oak Tattoo 820 S Washington Ave (at Lincoln), Royal Oak **248/398-0052** *noon-8pm, till 9pm Fri-Sat, clsd Sun, tattoo & piercing studio*

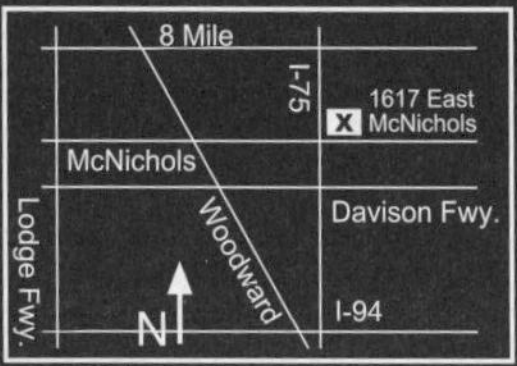

8 Mile
I-75
1617 East McNichols
McNichols
Davison Fwy.
Lodge Fwy.
Woodward
N
I-94

Publications

Between the Lines 734/293-7200 *statewide LGBT weekly*

Metra Magazine PO Box 71844, Madison Heights 48071 **248/543-3500** *covers IN, IL, MI, OH, PA, WI & Ontario, Canada*

Men's Clubs

▶ **Body Zone Health Club** [★MO,V,18+,PC,GO] 1617 E McNichols (at I-75) **313/366-9663** *24hrs, gym & steam, sauna & tanning, day passes, "Detroit's busiest gay health club"*

TNT Health Club [★MO,V,18+,PC,GO,$] 13333 W 8 Mile Rd (at Schaefer, enter rear) **313/341-7250** *24hrs*

Men's Services

▶ **Megaphone 313/962-5000** *Meet and Chat Live with HOT local men. FREE to listen & respond to ads. Video and text chat at GayMates.com. Use FREE code 4889.*

Erotica

24hr Video 17438 Woodward Ave (N of McNichols Rd) **313/869-2955** *11am-4am*

Blue Moon Video 7041 W 8 Mile Rd (2 blocks W of Livernois) **313/340-1730** *11am-1am, till 10pm Sun*

Escape Adult Bookstore 18728 W Warren Ave (8 blocks W of Southfield) **313/336-6558** *10am-10pm, noon-8pm Sun*

Fifth Wheel Adult Books 9320 Michigan Ave (at Wyoming) **313/846-8613**

Noir Leather [WC] 124 W 4th St (at S Center St), Royal Oak **248/541-3979** *11am-9pm, till 10pm Fri-Sat, noon-7pm Sun, leather, S&M gear, toys, fetishwear*

Uptown Book Store 16541 Woodward Ave (at 6 Mile Rd), Highland Park **313/869-9477**

Douglas

see Saugatuck

Escanaba

Erotica

Sensual Arts Adult Bookstore [GO] 615 N Lincoln Rd **906/786-9020**

Flint

Bars

MI [★MW,D,MR] 2406 N Franklin St (at Davison) **810/234-9481** *3pm-2am*

Pachyderm Pub [MW,NH,D,MR,TG,K,F,P,GO] G-1408 E Hemphill Rd (btwn I-475 & Saginaw St), Burton **810/744-4960** *3pm-2am, from 5pm wknds, video bar & restaurant, patio*

State Bar [★MW,D,WC] 2510 S Dort Hwy **810/767-7050** *2pm-2am*

The Zoo [MW,D,F,GO] 4511 S Saginaw St (at Bristol Rd) **810/249-0267** *2pm-close Tue-Sun, theme nights*

Nightclubs

Club Triangle [★MW,D,S,18+] 2101 S Dort (at Lippincott) **810/767-7550** *9pm-close Wed-Sun*

Purple Moon [MW,D] 2525 S Dort Hwy **810/424-9579** *9pm-2am*

Cafes

The Good Beans Cafe [E,WC,GO] 328 N Grand Traverse (at 1st Ave) **810/237-4663** *7:30am-4pm, till 9pm Th-Fri, open some wknds*

Men's Services

▶ **Megaphone 810/597-0597** *Meet and Chat Live with HOT local men. FREE to listen & respond to ads. Video and text chat at GayMates.com. Use FREE code 4889.*

Erotica

Fantasies Unlimited G3030 Pierson Rd **810/789-6608**

Frankfort

Accommodations

Wayfarer Lodgings [GF,NS,WI] 1912 S Scenic Hwy (M-22) **231/352-9264, 800/735-8564**

Grand Rapids

Accommodations

Radisson Riverfront Hotel [GF,WC,WI] 270 Ann St NW (at Turner Ave) **616/363-9001, 1-800/333-3333**

Bars

The Apartment [M,NH,WC] 33 Sheldon NE (at Library) **616/451-0815** *noon-2am, from 2pm Sun*

Diversions [★MW,D,K,V,18+,WC] 10 Fountain St NW (at Division) **616/451-3800** *8pm-2am, also cafe*

Pub 43 [MW,NH,F] 43 S Division St **616/458-2205** *3pm-2:30am*

Nightclubs

Rumors Nightclub [MW,D,DS,S,V,WC,GO] 69 S Division Ave (at Oakes St) **616/454-8720** *4pm-2am*

Throwback's [M,D,F,K,S,18+,WC,GO] 245 N Division (at Lyon) **616/451-2337** *3pm-2am, from noon Sun*

Cafes

Discussions [GO,WC] 6 Jefferson SE (at Fulton) **616/301-3553** *10am-1:30am, till 3am Fri-Sat, 1pm-1am Sun*

Restaurants

Brandywine 1345 Lake Dr SE (in East Town) **616/774-8641** *7am-9pm, 7:30am-9pm Sat, 8am-4pm Sun, 7am-8pm Mon*

Cherie Inn [WC] 969 Cherry St (at Lake Dr) **616/458-0588** *7am-2pm, till 3pm wknds, clsd Mon*

Gaia Cafe 209 Diamond Ave SE (at Cherry St) **616/454-6233** *8am-8pm, till 3pm wknds, clsd Mon, vegetarian*

Men's Clubs

Diplomat Health Club [PC] 2324 S Division Ave (at Whithey) **616/452-3754** *24hrs*

Men's Services

Erotica

Cina-Mini I 1358 Plainfield NE (at Spencer) **616/454-2444** *also at 415 Bridge St NW, 616/ 454-7531*

Grayling

Erotica

Fantasies Unlimited 6131 M-72 West **989/348-4665**

Houghton

Erotica

Backroom Multi Entertainment [GO] 109 Sheldon Ave (at Bridge) **906/482-0637**

Ionia

Men's Clubs

Ionia Eagle 3935 W Bluewater Hwy (at Johnson Rd) **616/293-3755** *camping, cruising & accommodations owned by gay truckers*

Kalamazoo

Info Lines & Services

Kalamazoo Gay/ Lesbian Resource Center 629 Pioneer St **269/349-4234** *educational/ support groups, youth group, hotline*

Bars

Partners Kalamazoo [MW,NH,D] 562 Portage St (at Walnut) **269/383-1814** *4pm-2am, theme nights*

Lansing

Bars

Esquire [MW,NH] 1250 Turner (at Clinton) **517/487-5338** *3pm-2am, from noon Wed*

Nightclubs

Spiral [M,D,V,18+] 1247 Center St (at Clinton) **517/371-3221** *8pm-2am, clsd Mon-Tue, theme nights*

X-cel [★GS,D,S,YC,$] 224 S Washington Square (at Washtenaw St) **517/484-2399** *9pm-2am, clsd Mon, gay Tue*

Bookstores

Everybody Reads 2019 E Michigan Ave **517/346-9900** *11am-7pm, 10am-4pm Sun, cool general bookstore, also coffeehouse*

Retail Shops

Splash of Color 515 E Grand River Ave, Ste F, East Lansing **517/333-0990** *open daily, tattoo & piercing studio*

Men's Services

► **Megaphone 517/318-0333** *Meet and Chat Live with HOT local men. FREE to listen & respond to ads. Video and text chat at GayMates.com. Use FREE code 4889.*

Erotica

Fantasies Unlimited 3208 S MLK Blvd **517/393-1159**

Marquette

Accommodations

The Landmark Inn [GF,WI] 230 N Front St **906/228-2580, 888/752-6362** *historic boutique hotel overlooking Lake Superior, 3 restaurants*

Erotica

Backroom Obsessions [GO] 215 S Front St (at Main) **906/228-2210**

Cruisy Areas

Presque Isle Point [AYOR]

Mount Pleasant

Cruisy Areas

Mission Creek Park [AYOR] Harris St *summers*

Muskegon

Nightclubs

Club Mo'z [M,D,MR,18+,YC,WC,GO] 80 E Seaway Dr (entrance on Norton Ave), Muskegon Heights **231/830-0190** *3pm-2am*

Parma

Erotica

► **Lion's Den** 2101 N Concord Rd (Exit 127, off I-94), Albion **517/531-5051** *24hrs*

► **The Lion's Den Adult Superstore** 2101 N Concord Rd (exit 127, off I-94) **517/531-5051** *24hrs*

Perry

Erotica

► **The Lion's Den Adult Superstore** 2890 Lansing Rd (exit 105, off I-69) **517/625-1019** *24hrs*

Petoskey

Accommodations

Coach House Inn [GO] 1011 N US 31 (at Mitchell) **231/347-8281, 877/347-8088** *basic amenities*

Pontiac

Erotica

Fantasies Unlimited 974 Joslyn Ave **248/338-2442**

Cruisy Areas

Hawthorne Park [AYOR] N Telegraph Rd (at Dixie Hwy)

Port Huron

Nightclubs

Gruv [MW,D] 402 Quay St **810/984-2131** *10pm-2am Wed, Fri-Sat*

Seekers [MW,D,S] 3301 24th St (btwn Oak & Little) **810/985-9349** *7pm-2am, from 4pm Fri-Sat, from 2pm Sun*

Cruisy Areas

Pine Grove Park [AYOR]

Saginaw

Nightclubs

The Mixx Nightclub [MW,D,F,K,V,18+,WC] 115 N Hamilton **989/498-4022** *5pm-close Wed-Sun*

Saugatuck

Accommodations

Beechwood Manor Inn & Cottage [GS,NS,WI,GO] 736 Pleasant St **269/857-1587, 877/857-1587** *upscale inn, full brkfst*

The Belvedere Inn & Restaurant [GF,NS,GO] 3656 63rd St **269/857-5777** *boutique inn in 1913 mansion, full gourmet brkfrst*

Bentley Waterfront Suites [GF,NS,GO] 326 Water St **269/857-5416** *down-town & on the water*

Bird Center Resort [GF,WI] 584-586 Lake St **269/857-3900, 269/857-1750** *3 cottages across from Sautatuck Harbor, 2 w/ hot tubs*

The Bunkhouse B&B at Campit [MW,SW,NS,WI,GO] **269/543-4335, 877/226-7481**

Campit Outdoor Resort [MW,SW,WI,GO] 6635 118th Ave, Fennville **269/543-4335, 877/226-7481** *seasonal, campsites & RV hookups, also B&B, membership required*

Douglas House B&B [GS,NS,GO] 41 Spring St, Douglas **269/857-1119, 248/478-9392 (winter)** *near gay beach*

The Dunes Resort [MW,D,TG,F,E,DS,SW,WC,GO] 333 Blue Star Hwy, Douglas **269/857-1401** *motel & cottages, open year-round*

Hidden Garden Cottages & Suites [GF,NS,WI] 247 Butler St **269/857-8109, 888/857-8109** *cottages & suites for 2*

Hillby Thatch Cottages [GS,NS] 1438-1440 71st St, Glenn **847/864-3553**

Hooten Inn [GS] 6541 Blue Star Hwy (at Washinton) **269/857-1039** *boutique motel*

The Hunter's Lodge [GS,NS] 2790 Blue Star Hwy (at US 31), Douglas **269/857-5402** *motel in rustic lodge*

J Paules Fenn Inn [GF,NS] 2254 S 58th St, Fennville **269/561-2836, 877/561-2836** *full brkfst*

The Kingsley House B&B [GF,NS,WI,GO] 626 West Main St, Fennville **269/561-6425, 866/561-6425** *B&B in Victorian Queen Anne mansion, full brkfst*

Kirby House [GS,SW,NS,WI,GO] 294 W Center (at Blue Star Hwy) **269/857-2904, 800/521-6473** *full brkfst, Queen Anne manor*

Lake Street Commons [GF,NS,WI,GO] 790 Lake St **269/857-1680** *suites w/ kitchen & private decks, jacuzzi*

Maple Ridge Cottages [GS,NS,GO] 713-719 Maple **269/857-5211 (Pines #)** *quaint 2-brdm & 1-bath cottages w/ private hot tubs*

Moore's Creek Inn [GF,NS] 820 Holland St (at Lucy) **269/857-5241** *full brkfst, old-fashioned farmhouse*

The Newnham SunCatcher Inn [GF,SW,NS,GO] 131 Griffith (at Mason) **269/857-4249** *full brkfst, hot tub, lesbian-owned*

The Park House Inn B&B [GF,NS,WI] 888 Holland St **269/857-4535, 866/321-4535** *B&B in one of Saugatuck's oldest residences, full brkfst, also cottages*

The Pines Motor Lodge [GS,NS,GO] 56 Blue Star Hwy (at Center St), Douglas **269/857-5211** *boutique retro motel, also retro gift gallery*

The Spruce Cutter's Cottage [GS,GO] 6670 126th Ave (at Blue Star Hwy & M-89), Fennville **269/543-4285, 800/493-5888**

Timber Bluff [NS] 2731 Lakeshore Dr, Fennville **269/857-2586** *cottages on Lake Michigan*

The Timberline Motel [GF,SW] 3353 Blue Star Hwy **269/857-2147, 800/257-2147** *open year-round, jacuzzi*

Bars

Dunes Disco [MW,D,TG,E,C,DS,GO] 333 Blue Star Hwy (at the Dunes Resort) **269/857-1401** *9am-2am*

Cafes

Uncommon Grounds 127 Hoffman (at Water) **269/857-3333** *6:30am-10pm, coffee & juice bar*

The Yum Yum Gourmet Cafe & Gelateria [GS,GO] 98 Center St, lower level (at Union St), Douglas **269/857-4567**

Restaurants

Back Alley Pizza Joint 22 Main St, Douglas **269/857-7277** *11am-9pm, till 11pm Fri-Sat,*

Chequers 220 Culver St **269/857-1868** *11:30am-9pm, English pub, great fish & chips*

Everyday People Cafe [E] 11 Center St, Douglas **269/857-4240** *clsd Wed off season*

Kalico Kitchen 312 Ferry St, Douglas **269/857-2678** *7am-9pm winter, till 10pm summer*

Marro's Italian 147 Water St **269/857-4248** *dinner only, clsd Mon, nightclub till 2am Fri-Sat*

Monroe's Cafe-Grille 302 Culver St **269/857-1242** *8am-9pm, clsd Nov-March*

Phil's Bar & Grille 215 Butler St **269/857-1555** *11:30am-10pm, till 11pm Fri-Sat, noon-10pm Sun, patio*

Pumpernickel's 202 Butler St (at Mason) **269/857-1196** *8am-4pm*

Restaurant Toulouse [R,WC] 248 Culver St (at Griffith) **269/857-1561** *dinner nightly, lunch wknds (dinner only, clsd Mon-Wed winters), full bar*

The White House Bistro [E] corner of Mason & Griffith **269/857-3240** *4pm-10pm, 9am-midnight Sat, 9am-9pm Sun, live music*

The Wicks Park [E,WC] 449 Water St **269/857-2888** *dinner nightly, live music wknds*

Entertainment & Recreation

Earl's Farm Market [GO] 1630 Blue Star Hwy, Fennville **269/227-2074** *8am-9pm May-Oct only, pick your own berries!*

Oval Beach consult local map for driving directions, Douglas *popular beach on Lake Michigan*

Red Barn Play House Blue Star Hwy at 63rd St (E of exit 41 off US31/I-196) *regional community arts center, plays & events*

Bookstores

Open Door Music & Books 403 Water St **269/857-4565, 888/613-8570**

Singapore Bank Bookstore 317 Butler St (upstairs) **269/857-3785**

Retail Shops

Amaru Leather 322 Griffith St **269/857-3745** *"original & custom creations in leather by two resident designers"*

Circa Antiques, Arts & Accessories [GO] 12 Center St (at Union St), Douglas **269/857-7676** *10am-5pm, antiques, art & furnishings*

Groovy! Groovy! Retro Gift Gallery [GO] 56 Blue Star Hwy (at Center St), Douglas **269/857-2171** *seasonal hours, antiques, funky gifts & goods*

Hoopdee Scootee 133 Mason (at Butler) **269/857-4141** *seasonal, clothing, gifts*

Saugatuck Drug Store 201 Butler St **269/857-2300** *seasonal, old-fashioned corner drug store, including actual soda fountain!*

Gyms & Health Clubs

Pump House Gym 6492 Blue Star Hwy **269/857-7867** *day passes*

Cruisy Areas

Oval Beach [AYOR] *walk north*

Sawyer

Erotica

► **The Lion's Den Adult Superstore 269/426-6099**

South Haven

Accommodations

Yelton Manor B&B [GS,NS,WC] 140 North Shore Dr (at Dyckman) **269/637-5220** *full brkfst, jacuzzi*

Traverse City

Accommodations

Neahtawanta Inn [GF,SW,NS,WI,WC] 1308 Neahtawanta Rd **231/223-7315, 800/220-1415** *sauna*

Nightclubs

Side Traxx Nite Club [MW,D,V,GO] 520 Franklin **231/935-1666** *5pm-2am, cruise bar*

Bookstores

The Bookie Joint 124 S Union St (btwn State & Front) **231/946-8862** *10am-6pm, till 5pm Sat, 1pm-4pm Sun, pride gifts, used books*

Cruisy Areas

Westend Beach Hwy 31 (N of Munson Hospital)

Union Pier

Accommodations

Blue Fish Guest House & Cottage [GS,NS,GO] 10234 Community Hall Rd **269/469-0468 x112** *cottages & guesthouses*

Fire Fly Resort [GS,NS,GO] 15657 Lakeshore Rd **269/469-0245** *1- & 2-bdrm units*

Ypsilanti

see also Ann Arbor

Nightclubs

Club Divine [GS,D] 23 N Washington **734/485-4444** *more gay Sun, theme nights*

Minnesota

Statewide

Publications

Lavender Magazine 612/436-4660, 877/515-9969 *LGBT newsmagazine for IA, MN, ND, SD, WI*

Bemidji

Cruisy Areas

Diamond Point Park [AYOR] *summers*

The Indian Trail [AYOR] below Lake Blvd (btwn 10th & 12th St)

Duluth

see also Superior, Wisconsin

Accommodations

The Olcott House B&B Inn [GF,NS,WI,GO] 2316 E 1st St (at 23rd Ave) **218/728-1339, 800/715-1339** *Georgian colonial near Lake Superior, full brkfst*

Cafes

Jitters 102 W Superior St **218/720-6015** *7am-7pm, clsd Sun*

Bookstores

At Sara's Table Chester Creek Cafe [WI,WC] 1902 E 8th (at 19th) **218/724-6811, 218/724-6811** *7am-9pm, till 4pm Sun*

Men's Clubs

Duluth Family Sauna 18 N 1st Ave E **218/726-1388** *noon-10pm*

Erotica

Wabasha Books 114 E 1st St **218/723-1980**

Ely

Accommodations

Log Cabin Hideaways [GF,NS] 1321 N Hwy 21 **218/365-6045** *remote wilderness cabins, wood-fired sauna & hot tub, no running water/ electricity*

Hastings

Accommodations

Classic Rosewood [GF,NS] 620 Ramsey St **651/437-3297, 888/846-7966** *full brkfst*

Hinckley

Accommodations

Dakota Lodge B&B [GS,NS,WI,WC] **320/384-6052, 866/268-9266** *full brkfst, hot tub, fireplaces*

Kenyon

Accommodations

Dancing Winds Farmstay Retreat [GS,NS,GO] 6863 County 12 Blvd **507/789-6606** *farmstay on 20-acre working farm, pond, no pets*

Mankato

Cafes

The Coffee Hag [E,WC] 329 N Riverfront Dr **507/387-5533** *7am-10pm, till 11pm Fri-Sat*

Erotica

Pure Pleasure 2102 N Riverfront Dr **507/388-6871** *24hrs*

Minneapolis/ St Paul

Info Lines & Services

AA Intergroup 952/922-0880

OutFront Minnesota 310 38th St E #204, Minneapolis **612/822-0127, 800/800-0350** *info line w/ 24hr pre-recorded visitor info*

Quatrefoil Library 1619 Dayton Ave #105, St Paul **651/641-0969** *7pm-9pm, 10am-5pm Sat, 1pm-5pm Sun, LGBT library & resource center*

Accommodations

The Chambers [GF,WI,WC] 901 Hennepin Ave, Minneapolis **612/767-6900** *chic, art-filled hotel; also restaurant*

Cover Park Manor [GF,NS] 15330 58th St N (at Peller), Stillwater **651/430-9292, 877/430-9292** *full brkfst, in-room jacuzzi & fireplace*

Millennium Hotel Minneapolis [GF,F,SW,WI,WC] 1313 Nicollet Mall (btwn W Grant & 13th St), Minneapolis **612/332-6000, 866/866-8086** *also restaurant & bar*

The Saloon Hotel [M,WI,GO] 828 Hennepin Ave (btwn 8th & 9th), Minneapolis **612/288-0459** *shared baths*

Bars

19 Bar [M,NH,WC] 19 W 15th St (at La Salle), Minneapolis **612/871-5553** *3pm-2am, from 1pm wknds*

Bev's Wine Bar [GF] 250 3rd Ave N (at Washington Ave), Minneapolis **612/337-0102** *4:30pm-1am, from 6:30pm Sat, clsd Sun, patio*

Brass Rail [★M,E,K,DS,P,S,V,WC] 422 Hennepin Ave (at 4th), Minneapolis **612/333-3016** *noon-2am, dancers Th-Sat*

Bryant Lake Bowl [GF,A,F,E,WC] 810 W Lake St (near Bryant), Minneapolis **612/825-3737** *8am-2am, bar, theater & bowling alley*

Camp Bar [★M,D,F,K,S,V,WC] 490 N Robert St (at 9th St), St Paul **651/292-1844** *4pm-2am, bear party 4th Fri, also restaurant*

The Independent [GS,F] 3001 Hennepin Ave (in Calhoun Square, upstairs), Minneapolis **612/378-1905** *noon-2am, Sun brunch, great martini selection*

Jetset [MW,NS] 115 N First St (at 1st Ave N), Minneapolis **612/339-3933** *5pm-close, from 6pm Sat, clsd Sun-Mon, cool space*

Minneapolis Eagle [M,B,L,F] 515 Washington Ave S (btwn Portland & 5th Ave), Minneapolis **612/338-4214** *4pm-2am, from 10am Fri-Sat, dress code Fri-Sat, beer bust Sun, [B] 2nd Th*

Tickles [MW,E,F] 1032 3rd Ave NE **612/354-3846** *live entertainment/ piano Fri-Sun, also restaurant, dinner & wknd brunch*

The Town House [★MW,D,E,K,C,DS,P] 1415 University Ave W (at Elbert), St Paul **651/646-7087** *3pm-2am, from noon wknds, theme nights*

Nightclubs

The Bolt [M,D,MR,F,V,WC,GO] 513 Washington Ave S (at Portland), Minneapolis **612/338-0896** *4pm-2:30am, from 10:30am wknds, also Bolt Underground at 501 Washington*

Gay 90s [★MW,D,MR,F,E,K,DS,18+,WC] 408 Hennepin Ave (at 4th), Minneapolis **612/333-7755** *8am-2am (dinner nightly), 9-bar complex, also Men's Room [MO,L]*

Ground Zero/ The Front [★GS,D,A,S,WC] 15 NE 4th St (at Hennepin), Minneapolis **612/378-5115** *10pm-2am Fri-Sat only, more gay Sat for Bondage-A-Go-Go, also The Front lounge from 9pm*

Krave [M,D] 315 1st Ave N (at 3rd St N, at Karma), Minneapolis **612/340-1100** *seasonal monthly party, call for info*

Rumours/ Innuendo [M,D,B,K,DS] 213 E 4th St, St Paul **651/225-4528** *4pm-3am, theme nights*

The Saloon [★M,D,F,S,YC,WC,GO] 830 Hennepin Ave (at 9th), Minneapolis **612/332-0835** *10pm-close, grill open from 5pm Mon-Sat, theme nights, [18+] Mon & Th*

Cafes

Anodyne at 43rd [F,E,WC] 4301 Nicollet Ave S (at 43rd), Minneapolis **612/824-4300** *7am-10pm, till 8pm Sat*

Black Dog Coffee & Wine Bar [F] 308 Prince St (at Broadway), St Paul **651/228-9274** *7am-10pm, till 11pm Fri-Sat, 8am-8pm Sun*

Blue Moon 3822 E Lake St, Minneapolis **612/721-9230** *7am-11pm, from 8am Sun*

Cahoots 1562 Selby Ave (at Snelling), St Paul **651/644-6778** *6:30am-10:30pm, from 7am wknds*

Moose & Sadie's 212 3rd Ave N (at 2nd St), Minneapolis **612/371-0464** *7am-8pm, 9am-2pm wknds*

Uncommon Grounds [GS] 2809 Hennepin Ave (at 28th Ave), Minneapolis **612/872-4811** *noon-midnight, till 1am Fri-Sat, patio*

The Urban Bean 3255 Bryant Ave S (at 33rd), Minneapolis **612/824-6611** *6:30am-11pm, from 7am Sun, patio*

Vera's Cafe [BW] 2901 Lyndale Ave S (at 29th St W), Minneapolis **612/822-3871** *7am-11pm, cozy coffeehouse w/ baked goods & light meals*

White Rock Cafe 769 Cleveland, St Paul **651/699-5448** *7am-9pm, till 6pm Sun*

Wilde Roast Cafe [BW,WC,GO] 518 Hennepin Ave E (at Central), Minneapolis **612/331-4544** *7am-10pm, till 11pm Fri-Sat*

Restaurants

Al's Breakfast [★] 413 14th Ave SE (at 4th), Minneapolis **612/331-9991** *6am-1pm, from 9am Sun, great hash*

Azia 2550 Nicollet Ave S, Minneapolis **612/813-1200** *11am-2am, from 3pm Sun, Asian fusion, full bar*

Birchwood Cafe 3311 E 25th St, Minneapolis **612/722-4474** *7am-9pm, from 8am Sat, 9am-2pm Sun, organic, plenty veggie*

Brasa Premium Rotisserie 600 E Hennepin, Minneapolis **612/379-3030**

Cafe Barbette [MW,BW] 1600 W Lake St (at Irving), Minneapolis **612/827-5710** *8am-1am, till 2am Fri-Sat, French/ American*

Cafe Brenda [NS] 300 1st Ave N (at 3rd), Minneapolis **612/342-9230** *lunch Mon-Fri, dinner Mon-Sat, clsd Sun, vegetarian & seafood*

Campiello 1320 W Lake St (at Hennepin), Minneapolis **612/825-2222** *dinner & Sun brunch, Italian*

D'Amico Cucina [E] 100 N 6th St (btwn 1st & 2nd Aves), Minneapolis **612/338-2401** *dinner nightly, clsd Sun, full bar, live music Fri-Sat*

Figlio 3001 Hennepin Ave S (in Calhoun Square Mall), Minneapolis **612/822-1688** *lunch & dinner, bar till 2am*

Hard Times Cafe 1821 Riverside Ave, Minneapolis **612/341-9261** *6am-4am, vegan/ vegetarian, punk rock ambiance*

Joe's Garage 1610 Harmon Pl, Minneapolis **612/904-1163** *lunch & dinner, full bar till 1am, rooftop seating*

Lucia's Restaurant & Wine Bar [GS] 1432 W 31st St, Minneapolis **612/825-1572** *lunch & dinner, clsd Mon, American bistro*

Monte Carlo 219 3rd Ave N, Minneapolis **612/333-5900** *lunch & dinner, bar till 1am*

Murray's 26 S 6th St (at Hennepin), Minneapolis **612/339-0909** *lunch Mon-Fri, dinner nightly, steak & seafood*

Nye's Polonaise [E,P] 112 E Hennepin Ave, Minneapolis **612/379-2021** *11am-2am, from 4pm Sun, prime rib, piano bar, live polka & bands, full bar*

Palomino Euro Bistro 825 Hennepin Ave (at 9th St), Minneapolis **612/339-3800** *lunch Mon-Sat, dinner nightly, Italian/ Mediterranean*

Psycho Suzi's 2519 Marshall St NE, Minneapolis **612/788-9069** *11am-2am, tiki lounge*

Punch Neapolitan Pizza 704 Cleveland Ave S, St Paul **651/696-1066** *11am-9:30pm, till 10pm Fri-Sat*

Red Stag Supperclub [E,WC] 509 1st Ave NE (at 5th St), Minneapolis **612/767-7766** *11am-2am, from 9am Sat-Sun*

Royal Orchid [TG] 2401 Fairview Ave N, St Paul **651/639-9999** *11am-9pm, from noon Sat, clsd Sun, Thai*

Rudolph's Bar-B-Que [WC] 1933 Lyndale (at Franklin), Minneapolis **612/871-8969** *11am-2am, till 1am Sun, full bar*

Seward Cafe 2129 E Franklin Ave, Minneapolis **612/332-1011** *7am-3pm, 8am-4pm wknds, vegetarian cafe*

Trattoria da Vinci 400 Sibley St, St Paul **651/222-4050** *11am-9pm, till 10pm Fri, 5pm-10pm Sat, clsd Sun, Italian*

Entertainment & Recreation

Calhoun 32nd Beach [GS] 3300 E Calhoun Pkwy (33rd & Calhoun Blvd), Minneapolis **612/230-6400**

Fresh Fruit KFAI 90.3 FM, Minneapolis **612/341-0980 (on-air studio), 612/341-3144 (office)** *7:30pm-8:30pm Th, gay radio program, more LGBT programs 9pm-11pm Sun*

Illusion Theater 528 Hennepin Ave (8th floor), Minneapolis **612/339-4944** *some LGBT-themed productions*

Minnesota Transgender Health Coalition [TG] **612/823-1152**

One Voice Mixed Chorus **651/298-1954** *LGBTA community chorus*

Outward Spiral Theater **612/703-1258** *"theater from a Queer point of view"*

Patrick's Cabaret [GS] 3010 Minnehaha Ave S, Minneapolis **612/724-6273, 612/721-3595** *informal performance space w/ bi-weekly shows*

Suburban World Theater [F] 3022 Hennepin Ave S **612/822-9000** *historic theater, cinema, concerts, live performances*

Twin Cities Gay Men's Chorus 528 Hennepin Avenue #307, Minneapolis **612/339-7664**

Twin Lake Beach [N] in Wirth Park (33rd & Calhoun Blvd), Minneapolis *aka Hidden Lake, hard to find, inquire locally*

Bookstores

Birchbark Books 2115 W 21st St, Minneapolis **612/374-4023** *8am-7pm, 10am-5pm wknds, specializes in Native American art & literature, owned by Louise Erdrich*

Magus Books, Ltd 1309 1/2 SE 4th St (at 13th/ 14th), Minneapolis **612/379-7669, 800/996-2387** *10am-9pm, till 6pm wknds, from noon Sun, spirituality, also mail order*

Retail Shops

The Rainbow Road [WC] 109 W Grant (at LaSalle), Minneapolis **612/872-8448** *10am-10pm, LGBT retail & video*

Publications

Lavender Magazine 612/436-4660, 877/515-9969 *LGBT newsmagazine for IA, MN, ND, SD, WI*

Men's Services

Erotica

Denmark Books 459 W 7th St, St Paul **651/222-2928** *10am-midnight*

Fantasy Gifts 1437 University Ave, St Paul **651/256-7484** *10am-10pm, noon-6pm Sun*

Lickety Split 251 3rd Ave S, Minneapolis **612/333-0599**

Midwest Triple X 207 Washington Ave N, Minneapolis **612/332-8725**

SexWorld 241 2nd Ave N (at Washington), Minneapolis **612/672-0556** *24hrs*

Cruisy Areas

"Bare Ass" Beach [AYOR] E bank of the Mississippi (btwn the Franklin Ave & I-94 bridges), Minneapolis *especially summer afternoons*

Loring Park [AYOR] 15th St (near 35 W & I-94 exchange), Minneapolis

Moorhead

see also Fargo, North Dakota

Info Lines & Services

Pride Collective & Community Center 116 12th St S (in Pepp Bldg at Main Ave) **218/287-8034** *3pm-5pm Sat, referrals, support/ social groups*

Nightclubs

The I-Beam [MW,D,DS] 1021 Center Ave **218/233-7700** *9pm-2am Fri-Sat only*

Cafes

Atomic Coffee [E,GO] 16 4th St S (at Main) **218/299-6161** *6:30am-10pm, from 7am wknds, also gallery*

Rochester

Info Lines & Services

Gay/ Lesbian Community Service 507/281-3265 *Wed at 7pm*

Cruisy Areas

Eastwood Park [AYOR] County Rd 14 N (off US 52)

Soldiers Field Park [AYOR]

Rushford

Accommodations

Windswept Inn [GF,GO] 207 N Mill St **507/864-2545**

Two Harbors

Accommodations

Grand Superior Lodge [GS,SW,F] 2826 Hwy 61 E (near Gooseberry Falls State Park) **218/834-3796, 800/627-9565** *log cabins on Lake Superior, hot tub*

Wolverton

Restaurants

District 31 Victoria's [BW,R] 100 First St **218/995-2000** *5:30pm-9:30pm, clsd Sun*

Mississippi

Statewide

Publications

► **Ambush Mag 504/522-8049** *LGBT newspaper for the Gulf South (TX through FL)*

Southern Voice 404/876-1819 *weekly LGBT newspaper for AL, FL (panhandle), GA, LA, MS, TN w/ resource listings*

Bay Saint Louis

Accommodations

Nella's RV Park [GS] 16145 Hwy 603 (near I-10), Kiln **228/586-0053** *kids/ pets ok, friendly & clean, close to New Orleans*

Biloxi

Accommodations

Lofty Oaks Inn [GF,SW] 17288 Hwy 67 **228/392-6722, 800/280-4361** *full brkfst, hot tub*

Bars

Just Us Lounge [MW,NH,D,E,K,DS,S] 906 Division St (at Caillavet) **228/374-1007** *24hrs*

Erotica

Adult Theatre 222 Iberville Dr (at Biloxi) **228/435-5625**

Cruisy Areas

Hiller Park [AYOR] off Pass Rd

Gulfport

Bars

Salty Dawg Saloon [GF,NH,D,K,GO] 1105 Broad Ave (at Railroad) **228/864-0463**

Jackson

Info Lines & Services

Gay/ Lesbian Community Info Line 601/371-3019, 601/346-4379 *24hrs, switchboard for many organizations, including youth group*

Lambda AA 4866 N State St (at Unitarian Church) **601/856-5337** *6:30pm Mon & Wed, 8pm Sat*

Bars

Jack's Construction Site (JC's) [MW,NH,BYOB] 425 N Mart Plaza **601/362-3108** *5pm-2am, clsd Mon*

Nightclubs

Dick & Jane's [MW,D,DS,18+,YC] 206 E Capitol St *9pm-close Th-Sun*

Cruisy Areas

Battlefield Park [AYOR] Terry Rd (at Hwy 80) *afternoons*

Natchez

Accommodations

The Antebellum Music Room B&B at the Stone House [GF,WI] 804 Washington St **601/445-7466** *antebellum Greek Revival on Nat'l Historic Register, full Southern brkfst*

Historic Oak Hill Inn B&B [NS,GO] 409 S Rankin St (at Orleans St) **601/446-2500, 601/446-8641** *antebellum mansion near the Mississippi*

Mark Twain Guesthouse [GF] 25 Silver St **601/446-8023** *above Under the Hill Saloon*

Bars

Under the Hill Saloon [GF,NH,E,WI] 25 Silver St **601/446-8023** *10am-close*

Ovett

Accommodations

Camp Sister Spirit [W,F,NS,GO] **601/344-1411** *120 acres of camping & RV sites, volunteer-run, men welcome except during women-only events, clean & sober space, lesbian-owned*

Oxford

Cruisy Areas

Pat Lamar Park [AYOR]

Tupelo

Cruisy Areas

Chickasaw Village & Old Town Site Scenic Overlooks [AYOR] Natchez Trace Pkwy *closes at sunset*

Confederate Grave Site [AYOR] Hwy 78-Natchez Trace Pkwy interchange (5 miles N)

Vicksburg

Cruisy Areas

Rest Stop I-20 E (2nd rest stop)

Missouri

Statewide

Publications

Metro Star 918/835-7887 *monthly LGBT news publication serving AR, KS, MO & OK*

Ava

Accommodations

Cactus Canyon Campground [MO,N,GO] 16 miles E of Ava on Hwy 14 (N 1 mile on County 223) **417/683-9199**

Boonville

Men's Clubs

Megaplex Health Club & Spa 11674 Old Hwy 40 **660/882-0008**

Erotica

Passions LLC 17701 Old Five Dr **660/882-9426** *24hrs*

Branson

see also Springfield & Eureka Springs, Arkansas

Accommodations

Branson Stagecoach RV Park [GF,SW,GO] 5751 State Hwy 165 **417/335-8185, 800/446-7110** *pull-thru & back-in RV sites, cabins*

Eden Roc Resort Motel [GF,SW] 2652 State Hwy 176 (at Mineral Ct), Rockaway Beach **417/561-4163** *all rooms have lake views*

Cruisy Areas
Table Rock Lake Dam [AYOR] Fish Hatchery area

Cape Girardeau

Accommodations
Rose Bed Inn [GS,F,NS,WI,WC,GO] 611 S Sprigg St **573/332-7673, 866/767-3233** *B&B, full brkfst, hot tub, gourmet dining by reservation*

Nightclubs
Independence Place [MW,D,TG,DS] 5 S Henderson St (at Independence, at Holiday Happenings) **573/334-2939** *8:30pm-1:30am Mon-Th, from 7pm Fri-Sat, clsd Sun*

Cruisy Areas
Capaha Park [AYOR]

Clinton

Cruisy Areas
Sparrowfoot Park [AYOR] 4 miles S off Hwy 13 Lithuania *swimming & boat launch area at Truman Lake*

Columbia

Bars
The Arch & Column Pub [M,NH,K,WC,GO] 1301 Business Loop 70 E (at College) **573/441-8088** *5pm-1:30am, clsd Sun*

SoCo Club [MW,D,F,K,DS,V,WC] 128 E Nifong Blvd #E (at Providence Rd) **573/499-9483** *8pm-1:30am, from 6:30pm Sat, clsd Sun-Mon, [K] Tue, patio*

Cafes
Ernie's Cafe 1005 E Walnut (at 10th) **573/874-7804** *6:30am-3pm*

RagTag Cinemacafe [F,BW] 10 Hitt St (Broadway) **573/443-4359, 573/441-8504** *5pm-close, from 4pm Sat, from 1:30pm Sun, independent & alternative cinema, also theater, music & dance*

Restaurants
Main Squeeze 28 S 9th St (at Cherry St) **573/817-5616** *7am-8pm, till 3pm Sun, local organic ingredients, vegetarian*

Bookstores
The Peace Nook [GF] 804 C East Broadway (btwn 8th & 9th) **573/875-0539** *10am-9pm, noon-6pm Sun, LGBT section, books, pride products*

Erotica
Bocomo Bay [★] 1122-A Wilkes Blvd **573/443-0873**

Olde Un Theatre/ Midwest Adult Book Store 101 E Walnut St (at 1st) **573/442-6622** *8am-3am, 24hrs Fri-Sat*

Venus [GO] 1010 Old Hwy 63 S **573/442-4319**

Cruisy Areas
Cosmopolitan Park [AYOR] W side of town (off Business Loop 70)

Hannibal

Accommodations
Garden House B&B [GF,WI,NS,GO] 301 N 5th St (at Bird) **573/221-7800, 866/423-7800**

Restaurants
LaBinnah Bistro [BYOB,GO] 207 N 5th St (at Center) **537/221-8207** *dinner only, in a Victorian home*

Hermann

Accommodations
Healing Stone Retreat & Spa [GF,NS] **573/486-5000** *full brkfst*

Jefferson City

Accommodations
Jefferson Inn B&B [GF] 801 W High St **573/635-7196, 800/530-5009** *full brkfst*

Joplin

Publications
Metro Star 918/835-7887 *monthly LGBT news publication serving AR, KS, MO & OK*

Bars
Pla Mor Lounge [MW,NH,D,K] 532 S Joplin Ave **417/624-2722** *5pm-1am, clsd Sun-Mon*

Kansas City

see also Kansas City & Overland Park, Kansas

Info Lines & Services

Lesbian & Gay Community Center of Greater Kansas City 207 Westport Rd, Stes 212-218 **816/931-4420** *6pm-9pm Mon, Tue, Th-Fri, call for events*

Live & Let Live AA 3535 Broadway, 4th flr (at Knickerbocker Pl) **816/531-9668** *noon daily, 6pm Tue-Fri, 7pm Sat*

Accommodations

The Concourse Park B&B [M,GO] 300 Benton Blvd (at Anderson) **816/231-1196**

Ken's Place [MW,SW,N,WI,GO] 18 W 38th St (at Baltimore) **816/753-0533** *some shared baths, near gay bars*

The Porch Swing Inn [GF,WI,GO] 702 East St, Parkville **816/587-6282, 866/587-6282** *B&B, full brkfst, lesbian-owned*

Q Hotel & Spa [GF,WI,WC] 560 Westport Rd (at Mill St) **816/931-0001, 800/942-4233** *in Westport district, whirlpool, dry spa*

Sleep Inn [GF,SW,WI,WC] 7611 NW 97th Terrace (at Tiffany Springs Rd) **816/891-0111** *hotel*

Su Casa B&B [GF,SW,NS,WI] 9004 E 92nd St **816/965-5647, 816/916-3444 (cell)** *Southwest-style home*

Bars

Balanca's [GS,D,MR,F,E] 1809 Grand Ave **816/474-6369** *6pm-3am, from 2pm Sat, clsd Sun-Mon, 2 flrs*

Buddies [M,NH] 3715 Main St (at 37th) **816/561-2600** *6am-3am, clsd Sun*

Daddy's Backdoor [M,B,L] 1610 Main St **816/283-3201** *6pm-close, from 4pm Sun*

Missie B's/ Bootleggers [MW,NH,D,L,TG,K,DS,S] 805 W 39th St (at SW Trafficway) **816/561-0625** *noon-3am, 2 floors*

Outa Bounds [M,NH,F] 3601 Broadway St **816/756-2577** *11am-1:30am, till midnight Sun, gay sports bar*

OutaBounds [M] 3611 Broadway **816/931-0501** *11am-1:30am, sports bar*

The Redhead Lounge [MW,D,K,F] 529 Walnut St **816/527-0999** *11am-3pm, clsd Mon, theme nights*

Sidekicks [MW,D,CW,DS,WC] 3707 Main St (at 37th) **816/931-1430** *2pm-3am, from 4pm Sun, clsd Mon*

Sidestreet Bar [M,NH,GO] 413 E 33rd St (at Gilliam) **816/531-1775** *10am-1:30am, clsd Sun*

The View on the Hill [M,NH,GO] 204 Orchard St, KS **913/281-0833** *4pm-2am, from noon Sun, clsd Mon*

Nightclubs

Bar Azul [M,D,DS,MR-L] 4960 State Ave *10pm-2am Sat only, Latino night*

Mint [GS,D] 334 E 31st St **816/561-2640** *more gay Th, swank dance club*

NV [GF,D,V,WC] 220 Admiral Blvd (at Grand Blvd) **816/421-6852** *9pm-3am Th-Sun only, rooftop deck*

Cafes

Broadway Cafe [F,NS] 4106 Broadway (at Westport) **816/531-2432** *7am-9pm; also 301 Westport Rd, 816/931-9955*

Cafe Trio [★E,GO] 3535 Broadway Blvd (at 35th) **816/756-3227** *5pm-11pm, clsd Sun, also Starlet Lounge, live jazz*

Restaurants

Bistro 303 303 Westport Rd **816/753-2303** *dinner nightly, lunch wknds, also martini bar*

Blue Bird Bistro 1700 Summit **816/221-7559** *7am-10pm, 10am-2pm Sun, oranic fare*

Cafe Trio/ Starlet Lounge [P,GO] 4558 Main St **816/756-3227** *11am-midnight, clsd Sun, New American*

Classic Cup Cafe [WC] 301 W 47th St (at Central) **816/753-1840** *brkfst, lunch, dinner, Sun brunch*

The Corner Restaurant [WC] 4059 Broadway (at Main) **816/931-6630** *7am-7pm, till 5pm Sun, lots of veggie*

Mama's Diner [TG] 3906 Waddell St **816/531-6422** *6:30am-10pm, till 3pm Sun-Tue*

One 80 **816/389-4180** *11am-3am, from 10am wknds, pizzas, pasta & more*

Sharp's 63rd St Grill [WC] 128 W 63rd St **816/333-4355** *7am-10pm, from 8am wknds, full bar*

YJ's Snack Bar 128 W 18th St **816/472-5533** *8am-10pm, 24hrs Th-Sat, eclectic menu, inexpensive*

Entertainment & Recreation

First Fridays Art Walk Crossroads District (Baltimore & 20th) **816/994-9325** *5pm-10pm 1st Fri, art gallery walk, also live music & vendors*

Heartland Men's Chorus **816/931-3338**

Unicorn Theatre 3828 Main St (at 39th St) **816/531-7529** *contemporary American theater*

Retail Shops

Out There 205 Westport Rd (btwn Main & Broadway) **816/753-4757** *10am-7pm, till 6:30pm Sat, noon-5pm Sun, LGBT*

Men's Services

▶ **Megaphone** **816/326-9926** *Meet and Chat Live with HOT local men. FREE to listen & respond to ads. Video and text chat at GayMates.com. Use FREE code 4889.*

Erotica

Erotic City 8401 E Truman Rd (at I-435) **816/252-3370**

Hollywood at Home 9063 Metcalf (at 91st), Overland Park, KS **913/649-9666** *10am-11pm*

Video Mania 208 Westport Rd **816/561-6397**

Moberly

Cruisy Areas

Rothwell Park [AYOR]

Nelson

Erotica

▶ **The Lion's Den Adult Superstore** RR1 Hwy J Box 163 (Exit 84, off I-70) **660/859-2741**

Osage Beach

Accommodations

Utopian Inn [MW,NS,GO] 1962 Alcorn Hollow Rd, Roach **573/347-3605**

Overland

Erotica

Patricia's 10210 Page Ave (E of Ashby) **314/423-8422**

Poplar Bluff

Nightclubs

Sammy's [MW,D,DS] 200 Bartlett St **573/727-9779** *7pm-1:30am, clsd Sun-Wed*

Springfield

Info Lines & Services

AA Gay/ Lesbian [NS] 518 E Commercial St **417/823-7125 (AA #)** *6pm Sat*

Gay & Lesbian Community Center of the Ozarks [WC] 518 E Commercial St **417/869-3978** *transgender support group 7pm Sun, youth group 4pm Tue, many other groups, newsletter*

■ BARS

The Club 821 [GS,NH,GO] 821 W College St (at Grant) **417/866-4821** *4pm-1:30am, clsd Sun*

The Edge [MW,D,K,DS,WC,GO] 424 N Boonville **417/831-4700** *4pm-1:30am, clsd Sun*

Martha's Vineyard [MW,NH,D,DS,18+,WC,$] 217-221 W Olive St **417/864-4572, 417/831-6144** *5pm-1:30am, clsd Sun-Mon, also martini lounge, patio*

■ EROTICA

Patricia's 1918 S Glenstone (at Sunshine) **417/881-8444**

■ CRUISY AREAS

Lake Springfield Park [AYOR] *NW side, north of power plant, days*

Phelps Grove Park [AYOR]

St Ann

■ EROTICA

Spanky's Video 3419 N Lindbergh Blvd (S of I-70), Bridgeton **314/344-0016** *24hrs*

St Joseph

■ NIGHTCLUBS

Shaft Nightclub [MW,D,TG,DS,V,WI,GO] 615 Felix (at 6th St) **816/364-2625** *8pm-1:30am, from 5pm Fri, clsd Sun-Mon*

■ CRUISY AREAS

Riverfront Park [AYOR] downtown

St Louis

■ ACCOMMODATIONS

► **A St Louis Guesthouse** [M,N,NS,WI,GO] 1032 Allen Ave (at Menard) **314/773-1016** *in historic Soulard district, hot tub*

Brewers House B&B [MW,NS,WI,GO] 1829 Lami St (at Lemp) **314/771-1542, 888/767-4665** *1860s home, jacuzzi*

Dwell 912 B&B [GF,NS,WI,GO] 912 Hickory St (at Choteau) **314/599-3100**

Napoleon's Retreat B&B [GS,NS,WI,GO] 1815 Lafayette Ave (at Mississippi) **314/772-6979, 800/700-9980** *restored 1880s town house, full brkfst*

Park Avenue Mansion—A B&B Guesthouse [GS,WI] 2007 Park Ave (at Mississippi) **314/588-9004, 866/588-9004** *B&B inn, full brkfst, jacuzzi*

■ BARS

Hummel's Pub [MW,NH,F,K,GO] 7101 S Broadway **314/353-5080** *11am-1am*

Premium Lounge [GS] 4199 Manchester **314/652-8585** *opens 4pm, clsd Sun*

Absolutli Goosed Martini Bar, Etc [MW,NH,GO] 3196 S Grand (4 blocks S of Tower Grove Park) **314/772-0400** *4pm-midnight, till 1am Fri, 5pm-1am Sat, clsd Mon, also desserts, appetizers, patio*

Bad Dog Bar [M,NH,B,L,GO] 3960 Chouteau **314/652-0011** *4pm-1:30am, from 1pm Sat, clsd Sun*

Cicero's [GS,E] 6691 Delmar, University City **314/862-0009** *11am-12:30am, till 11pm Sun, Italian restaurant, tavern, live music venue*

Clementine's [★M,NH,L,F,WC] 2001 Menard (at Allen) **314/664-7869** *10am-1:30am, 11am-midnight Sun*

Club Escapades [MW,D,K,S] 133 W Main St (at 2nd), Belleville, IL **618/222-9597** *6pm-2am*

Grey Fox Pub [MW,NH,TG,DS,S] 3503 S Spring (at Potomac) **314/772-2150** *2pm-1:30am, noon-midnight Sun, patio*

JJ's Clubhouse & Bar [M,NH,B,L,WC] 3858 Market St (at Vandeventer) **314/535-4100** *3pm-3am*

Just John [MW,NH,D,K,V] 4112 Manchester Ave **314/371-1333** *3pm-1:30am, noon-midnight Sun*

Korner's Bar [MW,D,DS] 7109 S Broadway (at Blow St) **314/352-3088** *4pm-1:30am, clsd Sun-Mon*

Loading Zone [★MW,V,WC,GO] 16 S Euclid (at Forest Park Pkwy) **314/361-4119** *2:30pm-1:30am, show tunes Tue*

Novak's Bar & Grill [W,D,F,E,K,S,WC] 4121 Manchester (at Sarah) **314/531-3699** *4pm-3am, patio*

Rehab Lounge [GS] 4052 Chouteau **314/652-3700**

Soulard Bastille [M,NH,F] 1027 Russell (at Menard) **314/664-4408** *11am-1:30am*

Nightclubs

Atomic Cowboy [GS,F,E,WI] 4140 Manchester **314/775-0775** *11am-3am, from 5pm Sat-Sun, clsd Mon, also Fresh-Mex Mayan grill*

Attitudes [MW,D,DS,K] 4100 Manchester **314/534-0044** *7pm-3am*

Bubby & Sissy's [MW,D,E,K,DS,V,WC] 602 Belle St (at 6th St), Alton, IL **618/465-4773** *3pm-2am, till 3am Fri-Sat*

The Complex Nightclub & Restaurant [★MW,D,F,DS,V,WC] 3515 Chouteau Ave (at Grand) **314/772-2645** *9pm-3am, 5 bars, patio*

Cafes

Coffee Cartel [★WI] 2 Maryland Plaza (at Euclid) **314/454-0000** *24hrs*

MoKaBe's [★E,WC] 3606 Arsenal (at S Grand) **314/865-2009** *8am-midnight, from 9am Sun*

Soulard Coffee Garden Cafe [F] 910 Geyer Ave **314/241-1464** *6:30am-4pm*

Restaurants

Billie's Diner 1802 S Broadway **314/621-0848** *5am-2:30pm, midnight-1:30pm wknds*

Chez Leon [GO] 4580 Laclede Ave (at Euclid) **314/361-1589** *5:30pm-10pm, till 11pm Fri-Sat, 5pm-9pm Sun, clsd Mon, French bistro, full bar*

City Diner 3139 S Grand **314/772-6100** *7am-11pm, 24hrs Fri-Sat, till 10pm Sun*

Dressel's [E] 419 N Euclid (at McPherson) **314/361-1060** *11:30am-1:30am, till midnight Sun, great Welsh pub food, full bar*

Duff's [WC] 392 N Euclid Ave (at McPherson) **314/361-0522** *lunch & dinner, brunch wknds, clsd Mon, fine dining, full bar*

Imperial Palace 2543 N Grand Blvd **314/531- 1951** *soul food*

Majestic Cafe 4900 Laclede (at Euclid) **314/361-2011** *6am-9:30pm, bar till 1:30am, Greek-American diner fare*

Meskerem 3210 S Grand Blvd **314/772-4442** *lunch & dinner, Ethiopian, plenty veggie*

Park West Grille [E] 2917 S Jefferson **314/773-7275** *11am-1:30am, live music*

Rue 13 [D,C] 1311 Washington **314/588-7070** *5pm-3am, from 7pm wknds, sushi, full bar*

Ted Drewes Frozen Custard [★WC] 6726 Chippewa (at Jameson) **314/481-2652, 314/481-2124** *11am-10pm, seasonal, a St Louis landmark; also 4224 S Grand Blvd, 314/352-7376*

Terrene 33 N Sarah **314/535-5100** *dinner nightly, also bar, patio dining in season*

Tony's [R] 410 Market St (at Broadway) **314/231-7007** *dinner only, clsd Sun, Italian fine dining*

Van Goghz [WI] 3200 Shenandoah **314/865-3345** *brkfst, lunch & dinner, also martini bar*

Vin de Set 2017 Chouteau **314/241-8989** *rooftop bar & bistro*

The Wild Flower Restaurant & Bar 4590 Laclede Ave (at Euclid) **314/367-9888** *lunch & dinner, bar till 1:30am, clsd Tue, Sun brunch*

Entertainment & Recreation

Anheuser-Busch Brewery Tours/ Grant's Farm S 12th & Lynch **314/577-2626, 314/843-1700 (Grant's Farm)** *all-American kitsch: see the Clydesdales in their air-conditioned stables, or visit the Busch family estate that was once the home of Ulysses S Grant, www.grantsfarm.com*

Int'l Bowling Museum & Hall of Fame 111 Stadium Plaza (across from Busch Stadium) **314/231-6340** *5,000 years of bowling history (!) & 4 free frames*

Opera Theatre of Saint Louis [WC] 210 Hazel Ave (at Edgar & Big Bend) **314/961-0644 (box office)** *intimate theater w/ operas sung in English*

Bookstores

Left Bank Books [★] 399 N Euclid Ave (at McPherson) **314/367-6731** *10am-10pm, 11am-6pm Sun, strong LGBT section*

Retail Shops

▶ **Boxers** 1305 Washington Ave **314/454-0209** *11am-6pm, clsd Sun, men's underwear*

CheapTRX 3211 S Grand Blvd **314/664-4011** *alternative shopping, body piercing, tattoos*

Publications

Vital Voice 314/289-9666 *bi-weekly news & features publication*

Men's Clubs

Club St Louis [PC,SW,18+] 2625 Samuel Shepard Dr (at Jefferson) **314/533-3666** *24hrs*

Men's Services

▶ **Megaphone 314/209-0300** *Meet and Chat Live with HOT local men. FREE to listen & respond to ads. Video and text chat at GayMates.com. Use FREE code 4889.*

Erotica

Barbdwyr 15 S Vandeventer Ave **314/531-4711** *leather*

Patricia's 3550 Gravois (at Grand) **314/771-9405** *10am-10pm, noon-7pm Sun, fetish clothes, toys, videos, dating service*

Cruisy Areas

Creve Coeur Park [AYOR] Dorset Rd W (off Hwy 2-70)

St Peters

Erotica

Patricia's 1034 Venture Dr **636/928-2144**

A Unique
Shopping Experience
FIFTY UNDERWEAR BRANDS
TO TOUCH & FEEL
C-IN2
2(x)ist
N2N
BODYWEAR
DIESEL
Visit us in Saint Louis, Missouri
BOXERS
1305 Washington Ave, St. Louis, MO • 314.454.0209
Visit us
Online:
MensUnderwearStore.com®
WE'RE MORE THAN JUST UNDERWEAR

Steele

Erotica

▶ **The Lion's Den Adult Superstore** 36 E Outer Rd (exit 8, off I-55) **573/695-7294** *24hrs*

Steelville

Accommodations

Country's Getaway [MO,SW,N] 119 Big Bend Ln (near Hwy 8) **573/775-5534** *campground (open May 15-Oct 31), 100 miles SW of St Louis*

Waynesville

Erotica

▶ **The Lion's Den Adult Superstore** 25965 Hwy 17 (Exit 153, off I-44) **573/774-9957** *24hrs*

Montana

Statewide

Publications

Out Words 127 N Higgins Ave #202, Missoula **406/543-2224** *Montana's LGBT publication*

Billings

Bars

The Loft [★MW,D,WC] 1123 1st Ave N (at 12th) **406/259-9074** *10am-2am*

Erotica

Big Sky Books 1203 1st Ave N (at 12th St) **406/259-0051**

The Victorian [P] 2019 Minnesota Ave (at 21st) **406/245-4293** *noon-midnight, clsd Sun-Mon, fireplace, also HIV testing Wed-Sat & monthly Hep B/C testing*

Boulder

Accommodations

Boulder Hot Springs Inn & Retreat [GF,F,SW,N,NS,WC] **406/225-4339** *massage, workshops*

Bozeman

Accommodations

Gallatin Gateway Inn [GF,F,SW,WC] 76405 Gallatin Rd/ Hwy 191 **406/763-4672, 800/676-3522**

Lehrkind Mansion B&B [GS,NS,WI,GO] 719 N Wallace Ave **406/585-6932, 800/992-6932** *Queen Anne Victorian, full brkfst, hot tub*

Cafes

The Leaf & Bean [E,WC] 35 W Main **406/587-1580** *6am-10pm, from 7am Sun, till 11pm Fri-Sat; also 1500 N 19th Ave, 406/587-2132*

The Nova Cafe 312 E Main St **406/587-3973** *7am-2pm*

Retail Shops

Jeannette Rankin Peace Center 519 S Higgins Ave **406/543-3955** *10am-6pm, fair trade gift store; also peace resource center, events*

Erotica

Erotique 12 N Willson (at Main) **406/586-7825**

Butte

Restaurants

Matt's Place 2339 Placer (btwn Montana & Rowe) **406/782-8049** *11:30am-7pm, clsd Sun-Mon, classic soda-fountain diner*

Pekin Noodle Parlor 117 S Main, 2nd flr **406/782-2217** *5pm-11pm, till midnight Fri-Sat, till 10:30pm Sun-Mon, clsd Tue*

Pork Chop John's 2400 Harrison Ave **406/782-1783** *10:30am-10:30pm, till 9:30pm Sun; also 8 W Mercury, 406/782-0812*

Uptown Cafe [WC] 47 E Broadway **406/723-4735** *lunch weekdays & dinner nightly, bistro, full bar*

Erotica

Rocky Adult Book Store 121 W Broadway (at Montana) **406/723-7218**

Great Falls

Accommodations

Triple Crown Motor Inn [GS,NS,WI] 621 Central Ave (at 7th St) **406/452-1470, 866/452-1470**

Restaurants

Black Diamond Bar & Supper Club 64 Castner, Belt **406/277-4118** *5pm-10pm, clsd Mon, steaks & seafood, 20 miles from Great Falls*

Kalispell

Info Lines & Services

Flathead Valley Alliance **406/758-6707** *LGBT referral service*

Livingston

Accommodations

Yellowstone River Inn Cabins [GS,NS] 4950 Hwy 89 S **406/222-2429, 888/669-6993** *cabins 40 ft from Yellowstone River, full brkfst*

Missoula

Info Lines & Services

KISMIS Gay/ Lesbian AA 538 University Ave (at The Ark) **406/543-0011** *7pm Mon*

Western Montana Gay/ Lesbian Community Center 127 N Higgins Ave #202 **406/543-2224** *LGBT resource center*

Accommodations

Brooks St Motor Inn [GF,WC] 3333 Brooks St (at MacDonald) **406/549-5115, 800/538-3260** *motel, hot tub*

Bars

The Oxford [★GF] 337 N Higgins (at Pine) **406/549-0117** *8am-2am, 24hr cafe & casino*

Nightclubs

Club Q [MW,D,DS,V] 112 N Pattee (at Front, at Elks Lodge) **406/728-6963** *9pm-2am Sat & special event Fridays*

Cafes

The Catalyst 111 N Higgins **406/542-1337** *7am-6pm*

Restaurants

Montana Club/ Red Baron Casino [WC] 2620 Brooks **406/543-3200** *6am-10pm, till 11pm Fri-Sat, casino open till 2am*

Bookstores

Fact & Fiction [WC] 220 N Higgins **406/721-2881** *9am-8pm, 10am-5pm Sat, noon-4pm Sun*

University Center Bookstore 5 Campus Dr (at U of MT) **406/243-1234, 888/333-1995** *8am-6pm, from 10am Sat, clsd Sun, gender studies section*

Publications

Out Words 127 N Higgins Ave #202 **406/543-2224** *Montana's LGBT publication*

Cruisy Areas

McCormick Park [AYOR] W side of Orange St Bridge

Ovando

Accommodations

Lake Upsata Guest Ranch [GF,F,NS] **406/793-5890, 800/594-7687** *seasonal, cabins, hot tub, outings, meals provided*

Swan Valley

Accommodations

Holland Lake Lodge [GF,WC,GO] 1947 Holland Lake Rd (at Hwy 83) **406/754-2282, 877/925-6343** *resort w/ lakefront cabins, restaurant & bar*

Whitefish

Accommodations

Sunset Ridge [GS,GO] 1991 Ridgecrest Dr **406/862-8263** *spacious rental home*

NEBRASKA

Columbus

CRUISY AREAS

Pawnee Park [AYOR]

Grand Island

EROTICA

K&L Market 2008 E Hwy 30 **308/382-0910**

CRUISY AREAS

Ashley Park [AYOR] Capital & St Paul Rd

Kearney

RETAIL SHOPS

Hastings Entertainment 9 W 39th St **308/234-1130** *10am-11pm, some LGBT books, also adult section*

CRUISY AREAS

Harmon Park [OC,AYOR] 29th St & 5th Ave *near rock garden & stage area*

Lincoln

INFO LINES & SERVICES

Rainbow Group Gay/ Lesbian AA 2325 S 24 St (at Sewell, at St Matthew's) **402/438-5214** *7:30pm Mon*

BARS

Panic [MW,E,WC,GO] 200 S 18th St (at N St) **402/435-8764** *4pm-1am, from 1pm wknds, patio, internet access*

NIGHTCLUBS

The Q [MW,D,E,DS,S] 226 S 9th St (btwn M & N Sts) **402/475-2269** *8pm-1am, clsd Mon, bingo Tue [19+], also lounge*

BOOKSTORES

A Novel Idea Bookstore 118 N 14th **402/475-8663** *10am-6pm, 1pm-5pm Sun, used, rare & out-of-print books*

EROTICA

Romantix Adult Superstore 921 O St **402/435-9323** *24hrs*

CRUISY AREAS

15th St [AYOR] from A St to State Capitol

Pioneers & Van Dorn Parks [AYOR]

McCook

CRUISY AREAS

Rest Area [AYOR] 2 miles E of McCook, on Hwy 6 & 34

Norfolk

CRUISY AREAS

Tahazooka Park [AYOR]

Omaha

INFO LINES & SERVICES

AA Gay/ Lesbian 851 N 74th (at Presbyterian Church) **402/556-1880** *8:15pm Fri*

Rainbow Outreach Center 1719 Leavenworth St **402/341-0330** *7:30pm-9pm Th, 6pm-11pm Fri, 3pm-6pm Sun*

ACCOMMODATIONS

Castle Unicorn [GS,NS,WI,GO] 57034 Deacon Rd (at Hwy 34 & I-29), Pacific Jct, IA **712/527-5930** *medieval-style B&B*

The Cornerstone Mansion Inn [GF,NS,WI] 140 N 39th St (at Dodge) **402/558-7600, 888/883-7745** *1894 historic mansion, commitment ceremonies*

BARS

Connections [MW,D,K,WC,GO] 1901 Leavenworth St (at 19th) **402/933-3033** *4pm-1am, from 6pm Tue-Wed, clsd Mon*

DC's Saloon [MW,D,CW,S,WC] 610 S 14th St (at Jackson) **402/344-3103** *2pm-1am*

Flixx [M,NH,V] 1019 S 10th St **402/408-1020** *5pm-1am*

The Omaha Mining Company [M,D,S,18+,WC] 1715 Leavenworth St (btwn 17th & 18th) **402/449-8703** *2pm-1am, till 4am Fri-Sat, very cruisy*

NIGHTCLUBS

The Max [★M,D,DS,S,V,WC,$] 1417 Jackson (at 15th St) **402/346-4110** *4pm-1am, 5 bars, DJ Wed-Sun, patio, [$] Fri-Sat*

RESTAURANTS

Dixie Quick's [R] 1915 Leavenworth St **402/346-3549** *dinner Wed-Fri, brunch Tue-Fri & Sun, Southern*

French Cafe 1017 Howard St **402/341-3547** *lunch Mon-Fri, dinner Mon-Sat, Sun brunch, full bar*

Entertainment & Recreation

River City Mixed Chorus **402/341-7464** *LGBT chorus*

Bookstores

New Realities [WC] 1026 Howard St (in the Old Market) **402/342-1863** *10am-10pm, 11am-6pm Sun, progressive*

Next Millennium [WC] 3141 N 93rd St **402/393-1121, 866/414-7473** *11am-8pm, till 5pm wknds, from noon Sun, metaphysical books & gifts*

Retail Shops

Blue Flamingo 1716 S 10 St (at Hickory) **402/964-2740** *thrift store*

Villain's 3629 Q St **402/731-0202** *noon-8pm, till 5pm Sun, tattooing, piercing*

Men's Services

► **Megaphone 402/341-4000** *Meet and Chat Live with HOT local men. FREE to listen & respond to ads. Video and text chat at GayMates.com. Use FREE code 4889.*

Cruisy Areas

Glen Cunningham Lake [AYOR] along W side

Scottsbluff

Cruisy Areas

Riverside Zoo Park [AYOR]

Nevada

Statewide

Publications

Nevada Pride Guide 702/882-3766 *LGBT business directory, visit www.gaynevada.com*

Baker

Accommodations

Silver Jack Inn [GF] 10 Main St **775/234-7323** *motel & restaurant*

Carson City

Accommodations

West Walker Motel [GF,WI] 106833 Hwy 395, Coleville, CA **530/495-2263** *in Toiyabe Nat'l Forest nr W Walker River*

Men's Services

► **Megaphone 775/888-9995** *Meet and Chat Live with HOT local men. FREE to listen & respond to ads. Video and text chat at GayMates.com. Use FREE code 4889.*

Elko

Cruisy Areas

Elko City Park [AYOR]

Lake Tahoe

see Lake Tahoe, California

Las Vegas

Info Lines & Services

Alcoholics Together 900 E Karen, 2nd flr #A-202 (at Sahara, in Commercial Center) **702/737-0035** *noon & 8pm daily, call for directions*

The Gay/ Lesbian Community Center of Southern Nevada 953 E Sahara Ave #B-31 **702/733-9800** *11am-7pm, 10am-3pm Sat, clsd Sun*

Accommodations

► **Blue Moon Resort** [MO,SW,N,WI,WC,GO] 2651 Westwood Dr **702/784-4500, 866/798-9194** *private resort, coffeehouse, sundeck, steam room & jacuzzi grotto*

Lucky You B&B [M,SW,N,GO] **702/384-1129** *hot tub, sauna, shared baths*

► **Paris, Las Vegas Resort & Casino** [GF] 3655 Las Vegas Blvd S **702/946-7000** *see ad in front color section*

Bars

8 1/2 Ultra Lounge/ Piranha [MW,NH,V,WC] 4633 Paradise Rd (at Naples) **702/791-0100**

Backdoor Lounge [MW,NH,D,MR-L,WC] 1415 E Charleston (near Maryland Pkwy) **702/385-2018** *24hrs, patio*

Badlands Saloon [M,NH,D,CW,WC,GO] 953 E Sahara #22 (in Commercial Center) **702/792-9262** *24hrs*

The Buffalo [★M,B,L,V,WC] 4640 Paradise Rd #11 (at Naples) **702/733-8355** *24hrs*

Charlie's Las Vegas [★M,D,CW,WC] 5012 S Arville St (at Tropicana) **702/876-1844** *24hrs, dance lessons 7pm-9pm Mon, Th-Sat*

Escape Lounge [M,NH] 4213 W Sahara Ave **702/364-1167** *24hrs*

Flex [MW,D,DS,S] 4347 W Charleston (at Arville) **702/385-3539** *24hrs*

Freezone [MW,NH,D,TG,F,K,DS,S,YC,GO] 610 E Naples **702/794-2300** *24hrs, also restaurant*

Goodtimes [M,NH,D,WC] 1775 E Tropicana Ave (at Spencer, in Liberace Plaza) **702/736-9494** *24hrs, DJ Mon, [K] Wed, after-hours Fri-Sat*

The Las Vegas Eagle [M,L] 3430 E Tropicana (at Pecos) **702/458-8662** *24hrs, DJ Wed, Fri-Sat*

Las Vegas Lounge [GF,NH,TG,DS,S] 900 E Karen Ave (at Maryland Pkwy) **702/737-9350** *24hrs*

Snick's Place [MO,NH] 1402 S 3rd St (at Imperial) **702/385-9298** *24hrs*

The Spotlight Lounge [★M,NH,D,E] 957 E Sahara (at Commercial Center's entrance) **702/696-0202** *24hrs, theme nights*

NIGHTCLUBS

Blush [GS] 3131 S Las Vegas Blvd (at Wynn) **702/770-3633** *9pm-3am, clsd Sun-Mon, ultralounge, [$] Wed & Fri-Sat*

Fun Hog Ranch [M,D,B,L] 495 E Twain **702/791-7001** *24hrs*

The Gipsy [★M,D,S,V,YC] 4605 S Paradise Rd (at Naples) **702/731-1919** *9pm-close, go-go boys*

House of Blues [GF,D,F,S,$] 3950 Las Vegas Blvd S (at Hacienda Ave, in Mandalay Bay) **702/632-7600**

Krave [M,D] 3663 S Las Vegas Blvd (at Harmon St, next to Planet Hollywood) **702/836-0830** *11pm-close, clsd Mon*

Mix [$] 3950 Las Vegas Blvd S (at Mandalay Bay) **702/632-9500**

Pure Nightclub [GF,D,$] 3570 S Las Vegas Blvd (at Caesar's Palace) **702/731-7873** *10pm-4am, clsd Mon & Wed-Th, upscale, top DJs*

Restaurants

Bootlegger Bistro 7700 S Las Vegas Blvd **702/736-4939** *24hrs, a Vegas classic, Italian, musical entertainment nightly*

Border Grill 3950 Las Vegas Blvd S (at the Mandalay Bay Resort & Casino) **702/632-7403** *11:30am-close, Mexican, full bar, patio*

Carluccio's Tivoli Gardens 1775 E Tropicana (next to Liberace Museum) **702/795-3236** *4:30pm-10pm, clsd Mon, Italian, formerly owned by Liberace; check out the mirrored, autographed grand piano!*

Chicago Joe's 820 S 4th St **702/382-5637** *11am-10pm, from 5pm Sat, clsd Sun-Mon, Italian, in downtown arts district*

The Egg & I [★] 4533 W Sahara Ave (near Arville) **702/364-9686** *6am-3pm, also murder mystery dinners*

Firefly 3900 Paradise Rd #A **702/369-3971** *11am-2am, till 3am wknds, tapas, also bar*

Go Raw 2381 Windmill Ln **702/450-9007** *9am-9pm, 11am-6pm Sun, organic vegan, also juice bar; also at 2910 Lake East Dr, 702/254-5382*

Guy Savoy [R] 3570 Las Vegas Blvd (at Caesar's Palace) **877/346-4642** *5pm-10:30pm, clsd Mon-Tue, French*

Joël Robuchon [R] 3799 Las Vegas Blvd S (at MGM Grand Hotel) **702/891-7925** *5:30pm-10pm, till 10:30pm Fri-Sat, French*

Lindo Michoacan [★] 2655 E Desert Inn Rd (near Eastern) **702/735-6828** *11am-11pm, till midnight wknds, Mexican*

Lotus of Siam [★] 953 E Sahara Ave #A-5 (in Commercial Center) **702/735-3033** *lunch & dinner, Thai*

Mon Ami Gabi 3655 Las Vegas Blvd S (at Paris Las Vegas) **702/944-4224** *outdoor seating*

Wichcraft at MGM Grand **702/891-1111** *10am-5pm, till 8pm Fri-Sat, creative sandwiches, eat-in or take-out*

Entertainment & Recreation

Cupid's Wedding Chapel [GS] 827 Las Vegas Blvd S (1 block N of Charleston) **702/598-4444, 800/543-2933** *commitment ceremonies*

Erotic Heritage Museum 3275 Industrial Rd **702/369-6442** *3pm-midnight, from noon wknds, clsd Mon-Tue*

The Forum Shops at Caesars 3570 Las Vegas Blvd S (in Caesars Palace) *you saw it in Showgirls & many other movies, now come shop for yourself*

Kà by Cirque du Soleil at MGM Grand **702/796-9999, 877/264-1844** *6:30pm & 9:30pm Tue-Sat*

Liberace Museum 1775 E Tropicana Ave (at Spencer Ave) **702/798-5595** *this is one queen's closet you have to look into—especially if you love your pianos, clothes & cars covered w/ diamonds*

Mystère by Cirque du Soleil at Treasure Island **702/796-9999, 800/963-9634** *7:30pm & 10:30pm Wed-Sat, 4:30pm & 7:30pm Sun*

O by Cirque du Soleil at the Bellagio **702/796-9999, 800/963-9634** *7:30pm & 10:30pm Wed-Sun, showstopper in a specially constructed aquatic theater*

Onyx Theater 953 E Sahara Ave, Bldg 16 **702/732-7225** *alternative films & performances*

Red Rock Lanes 11011 W Charleston Blvd **702/797-7777**

Thanks Babs, the Day Tripper [GO] **702/370-6961**

Viva Las Vegas Wedding Chapel [GO] 1205 Las Vegas Blvd **800/574-4450**

Zumanity [18+] at New York-New York Hotel & Casino **702/740-6815, 866/606-7111** *7:30pm & 10:30pm Wed-Sun, explores human sexuality in an intimate, cabaret-style setting*

Bookstores

Borders [WC] 2323 S Decatur (at Sahara) **702/258-0999** *9am-11pm, till 9pm Sun, LGBT section, cafe*

Get Booked 4640 S Paradise #15 (at Naples) **702/737-7780** *10am-midnight, till 2am Fri-Sat, LGBT*

Retail Shops

Aristo [GO] 3200 Las Vegas Blvd #2065 (2nd floor of the Fashion Show Mall) **702/360-2070**

Glamour Boutique II 714 E Sahara Ave #250 **702/697-1800, 866/692-1800** *clsd Sun, large-size dresses, wigs, etc*

The Rack 953 E Sahara Ave, Ste 101, Bldg 16 (in Commercial Center) **702/732-7225** *leather, fetish*

Publications

Las Vegas Night Beat 702/369-8441

QVegas 702/650-0636 *monthly LGBT news & entertainment magazine*

Gyms & Health Clubs

▶ **Hands On Therapeutic Massage** 8335 S Las Vegas Blvd (at Cancun Resort) **702/458-8777** *licensed massage therapists visit home or hotel room, "open to all men & women," mention ad for discount*

The Las Vegas Athletic Club [GF] 2655 S Maryland Pkwy **702/734-5822** *day passes*

Men's Clubs

Entourage Vegas [MO,SW] 953 E Sahara Ave #A19 (near Paradise & Maryland, at Commercial Center entrance) **702/650-9191** *24hrs*

Hawks Gym [MO,PC,AYOR,GO,$] 953 E Sahara (at SE corner of Commercial Center) **702/731-4295** *24hrs wknds*

Power Exchange [TG,18+,$] 3610 S Highland Dr **702/255-4739** *cover charge for men*

Men's Services

▶ **Megaphone 702/932-7373** *Meet and Chat Live with HOT local men. FREE to listen & respond to ads. Video and text chat at GayMates.com. Use FREE code 4889.*

Erotica

Adult World/ Mini Theaters [V] 3781 Meade Ave (at Valley View) **702/579-9735** *24hrs*

Bare Essentials Fantasy Fashions [GO] 4029 W Sahara Ave (near Valley View Blvd) **702/247-4711** *exotic/ intimate apparel, toys*

Desert Adult Books 4350 N Las Vegas Blvd (at Craig Rd) **702/643-7982** *24hrs*

Fantasy World Arcade/ Theaters 6760 Boulder Hwy (btwn Sunset & Russell) **702/433-6311** *24hrs*

Industrial Road Adult Books 3427 Industrial Rd (at Spring Mtn) **702/734-7667** *24hrs*

Price Video 700 E Naples Dr #102 (at Swenson) **702/734-1342** *10am-10pm*

Rancho Adult Entertainment Center 4820 N Rancho #D (at Lone Mtn) **702/645-6104** *24hrs*

Romantix Adult Superstore 2923 S Industrial Rd (behind Circus Circus) **702/892-0699** *24hrs*

Tropicana Book & Video/ Adult Super Store 3850 W Tropicana (at Valley View) **702/798-0144** *24hrs, cruisy theaters*

Cruisy Areas

Jaycee Park [AYOR] Eastern & St Louis (N of Sahara)

Sunset Park [AYOR]

Laughlin

see Bullhead City, Arizona

Reno

Accommodations

Holiday Inn & Diamonds Casino [GF,SW,WI,WC] 1000 E 6th St (at Wells Ave) **775/786-5151** *restaurant*

Sands Regency Casino Hotel Downtown Reno [GF,E] 345 N Arlington Ave **775/348-2200, 866/386-7829**

Bars

1099 Club [★MW,NH,S,V,WC] 1099 S Virginia St (at Vassar) **775/329-1099** *10am-2am, patio*

Cadillac Lounge [MW,NH] 1114 E 4th St **775/324-7827** *noon-2am*

Carl's Pub [M,NH,D,L] 3310 S Virginia St (at Moana) **775/829-8886** *2pm-2am, till midnight Sun, patio, theme nights*

Five Star Saloon [M,NH,D,WC] 132 West St (at 1st) **775/329-2878** *24hrs*

The Patio [MW,NH] 600 W 5th St (btwn Washington & Ralston) **775/323-6565** *11am-2am*

Reflections [MW,D,WI] 3001 W 4th St **775/322-3001** *noon-9pm, till 3am Fri-Sat, till 8pm Sun*

Nightclubs

Neutron [★GS,D,YC] 340 Kietzke Ln (btwn Glendale & Mill) **775/786-2121** *2pm-close*

Tronix [★MW,D,MR,TG,S,V,YC,WC,GO] 303 Kietzke Ln (at E 2nd St) **775/333-9696** *9am-3am, 24hrs wknds*

Restaurants

Pneumatic Diner 501 W 1st St (in Truckee River Apts, 2nd flr) **775/786-8888 x106** *10am-11pm, from 9am Sat, from 8am Sun, vegetarian*

Entertainment & Recreation

Brüka Theatre 99 N Virginia St **775/323-3221** *alternative theater & performance space*

La Bussola & Center Gallery [MR,TG,GO] 254 W 1st St **775/348-8858** *art boutique representing over 85 artists, including many local LGBT artists; lesbian-owned*

Bookstores

Borders 4995 S Virginia St (at Kietzke) **775/448-9999** *9am-10pm, till 11pm Fri-Sat, till 9pm Sun*

Sundance Books 1155 W 4th St #106 (at Keystone) **775/786-1188** *9am-9pm, 10am-6pm wknds, independent*

Retail Shops

The Hidden Woman [TG] 1507 S Wells Ave #100 (at E Pueblo St) **775/826-8832** *10am-6pm, 11am-5pm Sat, specializes in transgender/ MTF clothing & accessories, also men's lingerie & clubwear*

Publications

Sierra Voice 775/322-7866 *monthly, bar & resource listings, community events, arts & entertainment*

Men's Clubs

Steve's [PC] 1030 W 2nd St (at Keystone) **775/323-8770** *24hrs, spa*

Men's Services

▶ **Megaphone 775/334-6666** *Meet and Chat Live with HOT local men. FREE to listen & respond to ads. Video and text chat at GayMates.com. Use FREE code 4889.*

Erotica

The Chocolate Walrus 1278 S Virginia St **775/825-2267** *10am-9pm, noon-6pm Sun, naughty chocolate confections*

Suzie's 195 Kietzke Ln (at E 2nd St) **775/786-8557** *24hrs*

Cruisy Areas

Crissie Caughlin Park [AYOR] W end of the park *days*

Tonopah

Accommodations

Best Western Hi-Desert Inn [GF,SW] 320 N Main St (at Florence) **775/482-3511, 877/286-2208** *hot tub, spa*

Tonopah Station House Ramada [GF,F,NS,WC] 1137 S Main St **775/482-9777, 866/611-9777** *casino/ bar, pets ok, restaurant*

Winnemuca

Cruisy Areas

Button Point [AYOR] I-80, exit 187 (3 miles E of Winnemuca)

New Hampshire

Statewide

Info Lines & Services

Rainbow Resources of NH Inc 800/750-2524 *LGBT info for NH, VT, ME & MA*

Claremont

Accommodations

The Goddard Mansion B&B [GF,NS,WI,GO] 25 Hillstead Rd **603/543-0603, 800/736-0603** *mtn views, near skiing*

Concord

Cruisy Areas

Rollings Park [AYOR] S end of town

Dover

Cafes

Cafe on the Corner 478 Central Ave **603/749-4711** *7am-9pm*

Durham

Accommodations

Three Chimneys Inn [GF,NS,WI,WC] 17 Newmarket Rd (Rte 108, off Rte 4) **603/868-7800, 888/399-9777** *1649 house, near Portsmouth, full brkfst, jacuzzi*

Exeter

Accommodations

Inn by the Bandstand [GF] 6 Front St (at Water) **603/772-6352, 877/239-3837**

Keene

Accommodations

E F Lane Hotel [GS,F,NS,WC] 30 Main St **603/357-7070, 888/300-5056** *rooms & suites, internet access*

Littleton

Accommodations

▶ **Beal House** [GF,WI] 2 W Main St **603/444-2661** *French country brkfst*

Manchester

Bars

313 [★MW,D,F,E,K,DS,P,V,NS,WC] 93 S Maple St (at S Willow) **603/628-6813** *6pm-1am, from 7pm Sun, "three clubs in one"*

The Breezeway [MW,NH,D,C,DS,GO] 14 Pearl St **603/621-9111** *4pm-1am, from noon Sun, theme nights*

Element Lounge [MW,D,F,K,DS] 1055 Elm St **603/627-2922** *3pm-1am*

Tudor of Manchester [M,NH,D,F] 361 Pine St (at Hanover) **603/626-4900** *3pm-1:30am, from noon wknds*

Men's Services

► **Megaphone 888/634-2628** *Meet and Chat Live with HOT local men. Call for your local number or visit us online at GayMates.com. Use FREE code 4889.*

Nashua

Nightclubs

The Amber Room [GS] 53 High St **603/881-9060** *more gay Fri for Male Encounter*

Newfound Lake

Accommodations

The Inn on Newfound Lake [GS,SW,NS,WI,GO] 1030 Mayhew Tpke Rte 3-A, Bridgewater **603/744-9111, 800/745-7990** *private beach on cleanest lake in NH, also restaurant, full bar*

Plymouth

Accommodations

Federal House Inn Historic B&B [GS,NS,WI,GO] 27 Rte 25 (Rte 3 traffic circle) **603/536-4644, 866/536-4644** *full brkfst, hot tub*

Portsmouth

Cafes

Breaking New Grounds 14 Market Square **603/436-9555** *6:30am-10pm, coffee, tea, espresso shakes*

Restaurants

The Dunaway Restaurant at Strawberry Banke [WC] 66 Marcy St (at State St) **603/373-6112** *lunch & dinner, Sun brunch*

Erotica

Moonlight Reader 940 Rte 1 Bypass N **603/436-9622**

Spaulding Book & Video [GO] 80 Spaulding Tpke **603/430-9760**

Surry

Accommodations

The Surry House [GS,SW,NS,GO] 50 Village Rd (at Crain Rd) **603/352-2268** *B&B in private home, full brkfst, lesbian-owned*

White Mtns

Accommodations

Brookhill B&B [GS,NS,WI] Rte 16 (at Intervale Cross Rd), Intervale **603/356-3061, 888/356-3061** *1- or 2-bdrm suite, full brkfst*

Eagle Mountain House & Golf Club 179 Carter Notch Rd, Jackson **603/383-9111, 800/966-5779**

The Horse & Hound Inn [GF,F,NS,WI,GO] 205 Wells Rd, Franconia **603/823-5501, 800/450-5501** *clsd April & Nov, also restaurant*

The Inn at Bowman [GS,SW,NS,WC,GO] 1174 Rte 2 (Presidential Hwy), Randolph **603/466-5006** *B&B gracing the White Mtns, hot tub*

Inn at Crystal Lake [GS,NS,GO] 2356 Eaton Rd (at Rte 16), North Conway **603/447-2120, 800/343-7336**

Mulburn Inn at Bethlehem [GS,NS,WI] 2370 Main St/ Rte 302 (at Turner), Bethlehem **603/869-3389, 800/457-9440** *Victorian B&B, hot tub*

The Notchland Inn [GS,F,NS,GO] Rte 302, Hart's Location **603/374-6131, 800/866-6131** *1860s mansion on 100 acres, full brkfst, also cottages*

Riverbend Inn B&B [GS,NS,WI,GO] 273 Chocorua Mtn Hwy (at Rte 113), Chocorua **603/323-7440, 800/628-6944** *full brkfst, located on the Chocorua River*

Top Notch Vacations [GF,NS] Rte 302, Glen **603/383-4133, 800/383-4111** *condos, cottages & chalets, mtn views*

Wildcat Inn & Tavern [GF,E,NS] Rte 16A, Jackson Village **603/383-4245, 800/228-4245** *full brkfst, also tavern & dining room*

Will's Inn [GF,SW,NS] Rte 302, Glen **603/383-6757, 800/233-6780** *traditional New England motor inn; 2-bdrm cottages available; also rental house, sleeps up to 34, rent by floor or whole house; beach on Saco River*

Bars

The Up Country Restaurant & Tavern [D,E,K,V,WI] Rte 16, North Conway **603/356-3336** *11am-1am, from 1pm wknds*

Restaurants

Polly's Pancake Parlor Rte 117 (exit 38 off 93 N), Sugar Hill **603/823-5575** *7am-2pm, till 3pm wknds, clsd winters*

The Red Parka Steakhouse & Pub Rte 302, Glen **603/383-4344** *open from 3pm, also bar*

Cruisy Areas

Scenic Rest Area [AYOR] on left of Rte 16 N, Chocorua

New Jersey

Statewide

Publications

Out in Jersey 743 Hamilton Ave, Trenton 08629 **609/213-9310** *publication for all of New Jersey's LGBTI community*

PM Entertainment Magazine 516/845-0759 *events, listings, classifieds & more for Long Island, NJ & NYC*

Asbury Park

Accommodations

Empress Hotel [GF] 101 Asbury Ave **732/774-0100** *also Empress Lobby Lounge on wknds*

Sixth Avenue House [GS,GO] 305 Sixth Ave (at Berg St) **732/361-6609**

Bars

Georgie's [MW,NH,F,K,DS] 812 5th Ave (at Main) **732/988-1220** *2pm-2am*

Nightclubs

Paradise [MW,D,E,P,SW] 101 Asbury Ave (at Ocean Ave) **732/988-6663** *4pm-2am, from 2pm Sat, from noon Sun, 2 dance flrs, also piano bar & tiki/ pool bar in summer*

Restaurants

Bistro Olé [★GO] 230 Main St **732/897-0048** *dinner nightly from 5pm, Spanish-Portuguese*

The Harrison Restaurant [★] 716 Cookman Ave **732/774-2200** *4pm-close, Sun brunch, clsd Tue*

Moonstruck [E] 517 Lake Ave (at Grand) **732/988-0123** *dinner only, clsd Mon-Tue, also bar, live music wknds*

Restaurant Plan B 705 Cookman Ave **732/807-4710** *lunch Tue-Sat, dinner nightly, Sun brunch, food served till 3am Fri-Sat, full bar*

Atlantic City

Accommodations

The Carisbrooke Inn [GF,NS,WI] 105 S Little Rock Ave, Ventnor **609/822-6392** *on a beach block 1 mile from Atlantic City*

▶ **Ocean House** [MO,V,SW,N,GO] 127 S Ocean Ave **609/345-8203** *intimate atmosphere*

Tropicana Casino & Resort [GF,SW] Brighton & The Boardwalk **609/340-4000, 800/345-8767**

Bars

Westside Bar & Lounge [M,D,B,L,MR,TG,K,WC] 511 N Arkansas Ave (at Bacharach Blvd) **609/344-0883** *4pm-4am, from noon Sat-Sun*

Restaurants

Dock's Oyster House [WC] 2405 Atlantic Ave **609/345-0092** *5pm-10pm, till 11pm Fri-Sat*

White House Sub Shop 2301 Arctic Ave (at Mississippi) **609/345-1564** *10am-10pm, till 11pm Fri-Sat, from 11am Sun*

Men's Services

Erotica

Atlantic City News 101 S Martin Luther King Jr Blvd (at Pacific) **609/344-9444** *24hrs*

Belmar

Cruisy Areas

Belmar Beach [AYOR] *under fishing pier*

Boonton

Nightclubs

Switch [MW,D,CW,F,S,18+] 202 Myrtle Ave (off Washington) **973/263-4000** *6pm-2am, from 4pm Sun*

Camden

see also Philadelphia, Pennsylvania

Entertainment & Recreation

The Walt Whitman House 328 Mickle Blvd (btwn S 3rd & S 4th Sts) **856/964-5383** *the last home of America's great & controversial poet*

Cape May

Accommodations

Beauclaires B&B Inn [GS,NS] 23 Ocean St (at Columbia Ave) **609/898-1222** *1/2 block from ocean*

Cottage Beside the Point [NS,GO] **609/204-0549** *studio*

Highland House [GF,NS] 131 N Broadway (at York) **609/898-1198** *B&B, gazebo*

The Virginia Hotel [GF] 25 Jackson St (btwn Beach Dr & Carpenter's Ln) **609/884-5700, 800/732-4236** *also The Ebbitt Room restaurant*

Bars

The King Edward Room [M] 301 Howard St (at The Chalfonte Hotel) **609/884-8409** *5pm-1am summer only*

Cruisy Areas

Cape May Promenade [AYOR] Beach Ave (btwn Broadway & 2nd)

Higbee Beach [AYOR]

Cherry Hill

see also Philadelphia, Pennsylvania

Nightclubs

Taylor's [M,D] 2310 W Marlton Pike **856/486-1001** *gay Sun eve only*

Cruisy Areas

Cooper River Park [AYOR] Cuthbert Blvd S (off Rte 70)

Cliffwood

Cruisy Areas

Cliffwood Beach [AYOR]

Collingswood

see Philadelphia, Pennsylvania

Elizabeth

Nightclubs

Club Miami [MW,D,K] 605 Westfield Ave (at Elmora) **908/282-0404** *clsd Mon-Tue*

Gay Night 652 New Point Rd (at Mango's) **908/289-6767**

Highland Park

Info Lines & Services

Pride Center of New Jersey 321 Raritan Ave **732/846-2232** *info line & meeting space for various groups*

Hoboken

Bars

The Cage [MW,NH,D] 32 Newark St **201/216-1766** *5pm-2am, till 3am Fri-Sat, theme nights*

Nightclubs

Maxwell's [★GF,A,F] 1039 Washington St **201/653-1703** *live music venue*

Jamesburg

Restaurants

Fiddleheads [BYOB,GO] 27 E Railroad Ave **732/521-0878** *lunch & dinner, Sun brunch, clsd Mon-Tue, upscale bistro*

Jersey City

Info Lines & Services

Hudson Pride Connections 32 Jones St **201/963-4779** *"serving the LGBT communities & all people living w/ HIV, since 1993"*

Accommodations

Hyatt Regency Jersey City [GF,SW,NS,WC] 2 Exchange Pl (on the Hudson) **201/645-4712** *luxury waterfront hotel, short ride to NYC*

Bars

Lamp Post [GS,F] 382 2nd St **201/222-1331** *11:30am-2am, till 3am Fri-Sat, more gay Wed for Musko*

LITM [GS] 140 Newark Ave (at Grove) **201/536-5557** *5pm-1am, till 2am Fri-Sat, 4pm-midnight Sun, also restaurant & gallery*

Restaurants

Baja 117 Montgomery St **201/915-0062** *lunch & dinner, Mexican, DJ wknds*

Lambertville

see New Hope, Pennsylvania

Long Branch

see Asbury Park

Morristown

Info Lines & Services

GAAMC (Gay Activist Alliance in Morris County) 21 Normandy Hts Rd (at Unitarian Fellowship) **973/285-1595** *info line 7:30pm-9pm, also recorded info*

New Brunswick

Bars

The Den [★M,D,CW,MR,F,DS,V,WC] 700 Hamilton St (at Douglas), Somerset **732/545-7354** *8pm-2am, from 9pm Sat, clsd Mon, DJ Fri-Sat*

Restaurants

The Frog & the Peach [WC] 29 Dennis St (at Hiram Square) **732/846-3216** *lunch Mon-Fri, dinner nightly, full bar, upscale*

Stage Left [★MW,WC] 5 Livingston Ave (at George) **732/828-4444** *full bar, expensive*

Newark

Nightclubs

Rainbow Party [M,D,DS] 181 NJ Rail Road Ave (at Guitar Bar) **973/207-4261** *Tue only*

Men's Services

► **Megaphone 973/679-2020** *Meet and Chat Live with HOT local men. FREE to listen & respond to ads. Video and text chat at GayMates.com. Use FREE code 4889.*

Erotica

Cameo Twin Theatre 469 Broad St **973/621-7622**

Little Theatre 562 Broad St

Ocean City

Cruisy Areas

58th St Pavilion [AYOR] *late*

Ocean Grove

Accommodations

Ashley House [GF,NS,WI,GO] 14 Surf Ave **732/502-0081** *1875 Victorian, full brkfst, lesbian-owned*

Paterson

Restaurants

E&V Restaurant 320 Chamberlain Ave **973/942-8080** *lunch & dinner nightly, clsd Mon, Italian*

Plainfield

Accommodations

The Pillars of Plainfield B&B [GS,NS,WI] 922 Central Ave (at 9th St) **908/753-0922, 888/645-5277** *full brkfst, Georgian/ Victorian mansion*

Princeton

Accommodations

Residence Inn by Marriott [GF,SW,NS,WI,WC] 4225 US Hwy 1 (at Raymond Rd) **732/329-9600, 800/331-3131** *hot tub, full brkfst*

Cruisy Areas

Herrontown Woods Park [AYOR] off Snowden Ln, btwn mailbox 586 & 603 (no sign, entrance looks like private driveway) *beware of cops!*

Red Bank

Bookstores

Earth Spirit 25 Monmouth **732/842-3855** *10am-10pm, till 11pm Fri-Sat, noon-5pm Sun, New Age bookstore & center*

River Edge

Nightclubs

Feathers [★M,D,K,S,V,YC,WC] 77 Kinderkamack Rd (at Grand) **201/342-6410** *9pm-2am, till 3am Sat, from 7pm Sun, theme nights*

Cruisy Areas

Park & Ride [AYOR] off Rte 4 (across the street from Feathers nightclub)

Rosemont

Restaurants

The Cafe [BYOB] 88 Kingwood-Stockton Rd (intersection of CR 519 & 604) **609/397-4097** *lunch Tue-Fri, dinner Wed-Sun, wknd brunch, clsd Mon*

Sandy Hook

Entertainment & Recreation

Gunnison Nude Beach Beach G parking lot (near Gunnison Park, S end) *at the beach go right (all the way) to the gay section, cruisy area year-round*

Sayreville

Nightclubs

Cagney's [D,K,E] 3276 Washington Rd **732/525-5586** *7pm-2am, live music*

Deko Lounge [M,D] 1979 Hwy 35 South **732/727-4141, 732/727-6410** *9pm-2am, gay Fri only*

Seaside Park

Cruisy Areas

Franklin Ave & Boardwalk [AYOR] *summers only*

Sergeantsville

see New Hope, Pennsylvania

Stockton

Accommodations

Woolverton Inn [GF,NS,WI,WC] 6 Woolverton Rd **609/397-0802, 888/264-6648** *full brkfst, jacuzzi*

Toms River

Cruisy Areas

Winding River [AYOR] Rte 37 (near Garden State Pkwy)

Trenton

Bars

The Mill Hill Saloon [GF,F,E] 300 S Broad (at Market) **609/394-7222** *11:30am-2am, from 5pm Sat, clsd Sun, Brew Cellar from 10pm, live bands from jazz to blues to rock to folk*

Cafes

Cafe Ole [F,NS] 126 S Warren St **609/396-2233** *bistro, hosts Trenton Q-Nite, queer coffeehouse, 6:30pm-9:30pm Fri*

Union

Restaurants

Rio 22 2185 Rte 22 West **908/206-0060** 4pm-10pm, till 1pm Fri-Sat, noon-9pm Sun, upscale

Westville

see **Philadelphia, Pennsylvania**

New Mexico

Abiquiu

Accommodations

Casita de Chuparosa [GF,NS,WI] **505/685-0823** vacation rental in O'Keeffe country, huge views, 2 bdrms, fireplace, gourmet kitchen w/ full brkfst provisions, near hiking trails

Alamogordo

Accommodations

Best Western Desert Aire Motor Inn [GF,SW,WC] 1021 S White Sands Blvd **505/437-2110, 800/637-5956**

Cruisy Areas

Alameda Park [AYOR] off White Sands Blvd nights

Foothills Park [AYOR] 1st St E (past Scenic Dr) days

Albuquerque

includes Bernalillo, Corrales, Placitas & Rio Rancho

Info Lines & Services

AA Gay/ Lesbian [NS,WC] **505/266-1900 (AA#)**

Common Bond Info Line 505/891-3647 24hrs, covers LGBT community

▶ **Steve Benoit, Associate Broker with Coldwell Banker Legacy Realtors** 2501 Rio Grande Blvd NW #B **505/235-7218, 505/848-3148** New Mexico's community-respected realtor; associate broker: buyer's agent, listing specialist, relocation manager

Accommodations

8 Dwelling [GS,SW,NS,WI,GO] 6800 Vista Del Norte Unit 1928 (at Osuna) **800/941-6759** *3-bdrm condo, private balcony, lesbian-owned*

Adobe Nido [GF,NS,WI] 1124 Major Ave NW **505/344-1310, 866/435-6436** *B&B, also aviary*

Albuquerque Grand Hotel [GF,SW] 2910 Yale Blvd SE (at Gibson) **505/843-7000, 800/227-1117** *4-star hotel, also Rojo Grille restaurant*

Bottger Mansion of Old Town [GF,TG,WI] 110 San Felipe **505/243-3639, 800/758-3639** *B&B*

Brittania & W E Mauger Estate B&B [GF,NS,WI] 701 Roma Ave NW (at 7th) **505/242-8755, 800/719-9189** *intimate Queen Anne house, full brkfst*

Casa Manzano B&B [GS,GO] 103 Forest Rd 321 (at State Rte 55), Tajique **505/384-9767**

Casas de Suenos [GS] 310 Rio Grande SW **505/247-4560, 800/665-7002**

La Casita B&B [GF,NS,WI] 317 16th St NW **505/242-0173** *adobe guesthouse*

Casitas at Old Town [GS,NS,GO] 1604 Old Town Rd NW **505/843-7479** *classic adobe bldg, private patios*

Golden Guesthouses [MW,NS,GO] 2645 Decker NW **505/344-9205, 888/513-GOLD** *lesbian-owned*

Hacienda Antigua B&B [GS,SW,NS] 6708 Tierra Dr NW (close to corner of 2nd & Osuna) **505/345-5399, 800/201-2986** *full brkfst, hot tub*

Hacienda of Old Town B&B [NS] 115 Laguna **505/245-7838, 505/848-3148** *condo rental*

Bars

Albuquerque Social Club [★MW,D,PC] 4021 Central Ave NE (enter rear) **505/255-0887** *3pm-midnight, till 2am Fri-Sat, noon-midnight Sun*

Ralli's 4th Street Pub & Grill [GS,D,E] 109 4th St NW **505/243-1093**

Sidewinders Ranch [M,D,CW,B,L,K,WC] 8900 Central SE (at Wyoming) **505/275-1616** *noon-2am, till midnight Sun*

Cafes

Java Joe's 906 Park Ave SW **505/765-1514** *6:30am-3:30pm, coffee & pastries, monthly art shows*

Restaurants

Artichoke Cafe 424 Central Ave **505/243-0200** *lunch Mon-Fri, dinner nightly, bistro*

Cafe Cubano at Laru Ni Hati [GO] 3413 Central Ave NE **505/255-1575** *9am-9pm, 10am-5pm Sun, clsd Mon, cigars & cheap Cuban food, also unisex hair salon*

Chef du Jour [WC] 119 San Pasquale SW (at Central) **505/247-8998** *lunch Tue-Fri, dinner Th-Sat*

El Patio [★YC,BW] 142 Harvard St SE **505/268-4245** *11am-9pm, from noon Sun, plenty veggie*

Flying Star Cafe [WC] 3416 Central SE (2 blocks W of Carlisle) **505/255-6633** *6am-11pm, till midnight Fri-Sat*

Frontier 2400 Central SE (at Cornell) **505/266-0550** *5am-1am, good breakfast burritos*

Martini Grille 4200 Central Ave NE **505/255-4111** *4pm-2am, from 5pm Sat-Sun, swank*

Romano's Macaroni Grill 2100 Louisiana NE (at Winrock Mall) **505/881-3400** *11am-10pm, Italian*

Sadie's Cocinita [★] 6230 4th St NW (near Osuna) **505/345-5339** *11am-10pm, 10am-9pm Sun, New Mexican*

Zinc Wine Bar & Bistro [E,R] 3009 Central Ave NE **505/254-9462** *lunch & dinner, brunch Sun, also Blues Cellar till 1am Mon-Sat, live jazz Th & Sat-Sun*

Entertainment & Recreation

New Mexico Gay Men's Chorus **505/268-6995**

Rainbow Ryders, Inc [GF] 5601 Eagle Rock Ave NE **505/823-1111, 800/725-2477** *scenic balloon rides*

Bookstores

Bird Song 1708 Central SE **505/268-7204** *11am-7pm, clsd Mon, used, LGBT section*

Page One 11018 Montgomery NE **505/294-2026, 800/521-4122** *9am-9pm, till 7pm Sun, "New Mexico's largest independent bookstore"*

Retail Shops

Newsland 2112 Central Ave SE (at Yale) **505/242-0694** *8am-8pm, till 7pm Sun, some LGBT magazines*

Men's Services

▶ **Megaphone 505/268-1111** *Meet and Chat Live with HOT local men. FREE to listen & respond to ads. Video and text chat at GayMates.com. Use FREE code 4889.*

Erotica

Castle Superstore 5110 Central Ave SE (at San Mateo) **505/262-2266**

Self Serve [GO] 3904B Central Ave SE (at Morningside) **505/265-5815**

Video Maxxx 810 Comanche NE (at I-25) **505/341-4000** *leather, novelties, books, etc*

Viewpoint [★] 6406 Central Ave SE (at San Pedro) **505/268-6373** *24hrs*

Chimayo

Accommodations

Casa Escondida B&B [GF,NS,WI] **505/351-4805, 800/643-7201** *full brkfst, hot tub*

Cloudcroft

Accommodations

High Rolls Hideaway [GS,NS] **505/682-2955, 888/288-8065** *1-bdrm cottage*

Clovis

Cruisy Areas

Main St [AYOR] btwn 2nd & 7th

Farmington

Accommodations

Days Inn [GF,WI,WC] 1901 E Broadway **505/325-3700**

Hobbs

Erotica

Oasis Video & Bookstore Hwy 132 & Hwy 83 (10 miles N of town) **575/392-2310**

Stateline Video 6100 W Carlsbad Hwy 62 (across from airport) **575/393-3616**

Las Cruces

Retail Shops

Spirit Winds Gifts & Cafe [E] 2260 S Locust St **575/521-0222** *7am-7pm, 9am-6pm Sun, patio*

Cruisy Areas

Burn Lake [AYOR] btwn W Amador & Westgate

Madrid

Accommodations

Madrid Lodging [GF,NS,WI,WC] 14 Opera House Rd **505/471-3450** *suite, hot tub*

Bars

Mineshaft Tavern [GF,F,E] 2846 State Hwy 14 **505/473-0743** *11am-close, also restaurant*

Cafes

Java Junction 2855 State Hwy 14 **505/438-2772** *7:15am-5pm, till 6pm wknds, also B&B*

Ramah

Accommodations

El Morro RV Park, Cabins & Cafe [GS,NS,WI,GO] 4018 Hwy 53 **505/783-4612** *in Zuni Mtns, full brkfst, lesbian-owned*

Ruidoso

Restaurants

Mountain Annie's [E,NS,WC] 2710 Sudderth (at Mechem) **575/257-7982** *7pm-10pm Th-Sat, dinner theater, patio*

Cruisy Areas

Cedar Creek [AYOR] off Mechem Dr

Santa Fe

Info Lines & Services

AA Gay/ Lesbian 1915 Rosina St (at Friendship Club) **505/982-8932** *6pm Tue*

Accommodations

Alexander's Inn [GS,NS,WI] 529 E Palace Ave (at Delgado) **505/986-1431, 888/321-5123** *vacation rentals w/ kitchens, hot tub*

Bishop's Lodge Resort & Spa [GF,SW,NS,WC] 1297 Bishops Lodge Rd **505/983-6377, 800/419-0492** *on 450 acres, hot tub, spa has indoor & outdoor treatment rooms*

Casa Santa Fe [GF,NS,GO] 123 Candelario **505/995-8270, 505/995-8277** *3-bdrm casa sleeps up to 7, fully equipped kitchen, private yard, lesbian-owned*

El Farolito B&B [GS,NS,WI,GO] 514 Galisteo St (at Paseo de Peralta) **505/988-1631, 888/634-8782** *adobe compound w/ casitas*

Four Kachinas Inn [GS,NS,WI,WC,GO] 512 Webber St **505/982-2550, 800/397-2564** *courtyard, near the Plaza*

Hacienda Las Barrancas [GF,NS,WI] 27 Country Rd 84-D (at Hwy 502) **505/455-2197, 866/455-2197** *adobe hacienda located in scenic Pojoaque River Valley N of Santa Fe, full brkfst*

Hacienda Nicholas [GS,NS,WI,WC] 320 E Marcy St **505/992-8385, 888/284-3170** *full brkfst*

Inn of the Anasazi [GF,WI,WC] 113 Washington Ave **505/988-3030, 800/688-8100** *luxury hotel 1/2 block from historic Plaza, also restaurant*

▶ **Inn of the Turquoise Bear B&B** [MW,NS,WI,GO] 342 E Buena Vista St **505/983-0798, 800/396-4104** *Out & About Editors' Choice Award 1999-03 & Santa Fe Heritage Preservation Award 1999, New Mexico Preservation Award 2000*

Inn on the Alameda [GF,WI,WC] 303 E Alameda **505/984-2121, 888/984-2121** *afternoon wine reception, hot tubs*

Las Palomas [GF,NS,WI,WC] 460 W San Francisco St **505/982-5560, 877/982-5560** *luxury hotel 3 blocks from historic Plaza*

The Madeleine Inn [GS,NS,WI] 106 Faithway St **505/982-3465, 888/877-7622** *Queen Anne Victorian, full brkfst, hot tub, also Balinese-style spa*

Marriott Residence Inn [GF,SW,NS,WI,WC] 1698 Galisteo St (at St Michaels) **505/988-7300, 800/331-3131** *suites, hot tub*

Michael's Casa Quintana [GS,NS,WI] 114 Quintana St **505/438-0997, 888/443-2272** *2 separate adobe rental homes*

Tano Road Casita [GS,NS] 15 Tano Pt Ln **505/989-7802, 505/989-7803** *studio guesthouse in quiet, residential area*

The Triangle Inn—Santa Fe [MW,WI,WC,GO] 14 Arroyo Cuyamungue (12 miles N of Santa Fe) **505/455-3375, 877/733-7689** *7 adobe casitas, nonsmoking available, hot tub, lesbian-owned*

The Water Street Inn [GF,NS,WI,WC] 427 W Water St **505/984-1193, 800/646-6752** *historic adobe inn, jacuzzi*

Bars

Silver Starlight Lounge [MW] 500 Rodeo Rd (at RainbowVision) **505/428-7781**

Nightclubs

Fusion [GS,D,F,GO] 135 W Palace Ave, 3rd flr (at Grant) **505/955-0400** *dinner Tue-Sat, lounge from 9pm Tue & Fri-Sat, clsd Sun-Mon, tapas & sushi*

Restaurants

Anasazi Restaurant [WC] 113 Washington Ave (at The Inn of the Anasazi) **505/988-3236** *brkfst, lunch, dinner & Sun brunch*

Cafe Pasqual's [★BW] 121 Don Gaspar (at Water St) **505/983-9340, 800/722-7672** *brkfst, lunch, dinner & Sun brunch, Southwestern*

The Compound Restaurant [★GS,NS,R] 653 Canyon Rd **505/ 982-4353** *lunch Mon-Sat & dinner nightly, upscale, Southwestern, patio*

Cowgirl BBQ 319 S Guadalupe (btwn Aztec & Guadalupe) **505/982-2565** *11am-2am, great margaritas*

Geronimo's 724 Canyon Rd (at Camino del Monte Sol) **505/982-1500** *dinner nightly, eclectic gourmet, full bar from 11am-11pm*

Mauka [★] 544 Agua Fria **505/984-1969** *lunch Mon-Fri, dinner nightly, Japanese, patio*

Santacafe [WC] 231 Washington Ave **505/984-1788** *lunch & dinner, Southwestern/ Asian*

Tune Up Cafe [BW] 1115 Hickox St (at Cortez) **505/983-7060** *7am-10pm, from 8am wknds, New Mexican*

Vanessie of Santa Fe [★MW,P] 434 W San Francisco (at Guadalupe) **505/ 982-9966** *5:30pm-9pm (bar 4:30pm-midnight), steak house, piano bar*

Entertainment & Recreation

Ten Thousand Waves [N] 3451 Hyde Park Rd (4 miles out of town) **505/992-5025 (info), 505/982-9304 (reservations)** *Japanese health spa & lodging, sit under the stars & look out at the mtns, clothing-optional in all tubs*

Bookstores

Downtown Subscription 376 Garcia St (at Acequia Madre) **505/983-3085** *7am-6pm, newsstand & coffee shop*

Retail Shops

The Ark 133 Romero St (at Agua Fria) **505/988-3709** *9:30am-7pm, 10am-6pm Sat, 11am-5pm Sun, spiritual*

Men's Services

▶ **Megaphone 505/216-3000** *Meet and Chat Live with HOT local men. FREE to listen & respond to ads. Video and text chat at GayMates.com. Use FREE code 4889.*

Silver City

Accommodations

West Street Inn 505/534-2302

Cafes

Shevek & Mi [BW,GO] 602 N Bullard St (at 6th St) **505/534-9168** *wknd & holiday brunch, Mediterranean cuisine, espresso, "the best service in town"*

Restaurants

Diane's Restaurant & Bakery [BW] 510 N Bullard **575/538-8722**

Taos

Accommodations

Adobe & Stars B&B [GS,NS,WI,WC] 584 State Hwy 150 (at Valdez Rim Rd) **575/776-2776, 800/211-7076** *full brkfst, kiva fireplaces, patios*

Casa Benavides B&B [GF,NS,WI,WC] 137 Kit Carson Rd **575/758-1772, 800/552-1772** *fireplaces, hot tubs, extensive gardens, mtn views, full brkfst*

Casa Europa Inn & Gallery [GS,NS,WI] 840 Upper Ranchitos Rd (at Ranchitos Rd) **575/758-9798, 888/758-9798** *full brkfst*

Casa Gallina [GS,NS,WC,GO] **575/758-2306** *3 adobe casitas in pastoral setting*

Dobson House [GF,NS] 484 Tune Dr **575/776-5738** *luxury suites, N of Taos, full brkfst, solar-powered eco-resort*

Dreamcatcher B&B [GF,NS,WI,WC] 416 La Lomita Rd (at Valverde) **575/758-0613, 888/758-0613** *full brkfst, hot tub*

The Historic Taos Inn [GF] 125 Paseo del Pueblo Norte **575/758-2233, 888/518-8267** *several adobe houses date from the 1800s, pueblo-style fireplaces, also restaurant & bar*

Orinda B&B [GS,NS,WI] 461 Valverde St (on Valverde Park) **575/758-8581, 800/847-1837** *full brkfst*

San Geronimo Lodge [★GS,SW,NS,WI,WC] 1101 Witt Rd (off Kit Carson) **575/751-3776, 800/894-4119** *full brkfst, hot tub & massage available*

Taos Rainbow Villa [GS,NS,GO] **302/233-6897** *rental home, lesbian-owned*

Restaurants

Sabroso [★E] 470 State Hwy 150, Arroyo Seco **575/776-3333** *5pm-10pm, American & Mediterranean, also full bar, patio*

Entertainment & Recreation

Llama Trekking Adventures **800/758-5262** *day hikes & multiday llama treks in Sangre de Cristo Mtns & Rio Grande Gorge*

Truth or Consequences

Accommodations

The Belair Inn [GS,NS,WI,GO] 705 N Date St (at 7th St) **505/740-4100** *"retro 1950s motel w/ 21st-century amenities"*

New York

Adirondack Mtns

Accommodations

The Cornerstone Victorian [GF] 3921 Main St (Rte 9), Warrensburg **518/623-3308** *close to skiing, hiking, Saratoga & more, 5-course gourmet brkfst*

Country Road Lodge B&B [GF,NS,WI] 115 Hickory Hill Rd (at State Rte 418), Warrensburg **518/623-2207** *full brkfst, secluded retreat*

The Doctor's Inn [GF,NS] 304 Trudeau Rd, Saranac Lake **518/891-3464, 888/518-3464** *full brkfst, some shared baths*

Falls Brook Yurts in Adirondacks [GF] John Brannon Rd, Minerva **518/761-6187** *access to hiking, fishing & boating*

Hudson River Beach House [MW,NS] **518/361-2375** *2-bdrm cottage w/ private beach on Upper Hudson River*

Jake's Adirondack Place [GS,NS,WI,GO] **609/273-7169** *3-bdrm rental home, hot tub, lesbian-owned*

King Hendrick Motel [GF,SW,WC] 1602 State Rte 9, Lake George **518/792-0418, 866/521-6883** *cabins available*

The Merrill Magee House [GF,NS,WC] 3 Hudson St (off Rte 9/ Main St), Warrensburg **518/623-2449, 888/664-4661** *Victorian country inn, full brkfst*

Rainbow Woods Campgrounds [MO] 134 Rte 74 (at Rte 9), Schroon Lake **518/532-9728** *summer campground*

Saranac Club & Inn [GS,NS,WI] 371 Park Ave (at Old Military Rd), Saranac Lake **518/891-7212, 866/595-9800** *hot tub, full brkfst*

Tea Island Resort [GF] 3020 Lake Shore Dr, Lake George **518/668-2776**

Albany

see Capital District

Restaurants

Bob's Lunch & Dairy Bar 4139 Rte 22 (Junction Rtes 22 & 29), Salem **518/854-7505** *11am-9pm April-Oct, great soft serve*

Angelica

Accommodations

Jones Pond Campground [MO,SW,N,WI,GO] 9835 Old State Rd **585/567-8100** *May-Oct 15, theme wknds, campsites & RV, guesthouse & log cabins*

Binghamton

see also Scranton, Pennsylvania

Info Lines & Services

AA Gay/ Lesbian 607/722-5983

NEMA 607/656-4388 *leather/ levi social club, visitors welcome*

Accommodations

Serenity Farms [GS,SW,GO] 386 Pollard Rd, Greene **607/656-4659** *B&B, camping, on 100 acres*

Bars

Merlin's [MW,NH,D,E,K] 201 State St **607/722-1022** *8pm-close, till 3am Fri-Sat, [18+] Wed-Fri & Sun*

Squiggy's [MW,NH,D,K,DS] 34 Chenango St (at Court) **607/722-2299** *6pm-1am, till 3am Fri-Sat, from 8pm Sat, clsd Sun*

Cafes

Lost Dog Cafe [★E,BW,WC] 222 Water St (at Henry) **607/771-6063** *11:30am-10pm, till 11pm Fri-Sat, clsd Sun*

Restaurants

The Whole in the Wall 43 S Washington St **607/722-5138** *11:30am-9pm, clsd Sun-Mon*

Erotica

North Street Bookshop 17 Washington Ave (at North), Endicott **607/785-1588**

Buffalo

Info Lines & Services

Lesbian/ Gay AA 18 Trinity Pl (at Pride Ctr) **716/852-7743** *8pm Mon, Wed & Fri*

Pride Center of Western NY 206 S Elmwood Ave **716/852-7743** *1pm-9pm Mon-Fri & 5pm-8pm Tue*

Accommodations

Beau Fleuve B&B [GF] 242 Linwood Ave **716/882-6116, 800/278-0245**

The Mansion on Delaware [GF] 414 Delaware Ave **716/886-3300**

Bars

Adonia's [MW,D,K,V] 20 Allen St **716/332-1205** *3pm-2am, till 4am Fri-Sat, from noon Sun*

Cathode Ray [M,NH,V,WC] 26 Allen St (at N Pearl) **716/884-3615** *1pm-4am, from 7am Sun*

Fugazi [GS,V] 503 Franklin St (near Allen St) **716/881-3588** *5pm-2am, from 8pm wknds, cocktail lounge*

K Gallagher's [GF,NH,MR,F,WC] 73 Allen St **716/885-2244** *11:30am-4am (most nights)*

OHM [GS,D,B,DS] 948 Main St (at Allen) **716/332-0510**

Q [MW,NH] 44 Allen St **716/332-2223** *3pm-4am, from noon wknds*

The Underground [M,NH,D,K] 274 Delaware Ave (at Johnson) **716/853-0092** *noon-4am*

Nightclubs

Club Marcella [MW,D,DS,WC,18+] 622 Main St **716/847-6850** *9pm-4am, clsd Mon-Tue*

Cafes

Allen Street Hardware Cafe [E] 245 Allen St (at College) **716/882-8843** *5pm daily*

Cafe 59 [WI] 59 Allen St (at Franklin) **716/883-1880** *8am-6pm, 10am-5pm Sat, clsd Sun*

Restaurants

Anchor Bar 1047 Main St **716/884-5083** *11am-10pm, till midnight Fri-Sat, home of the original Buffalo Chicken Wing*

Mothers 33 Virginia Pl (at Virginia St) **716/882-2989** *5pm-3am, 2pm-midnight Sun*

Rue Franklin 341 Franklin St (at W Tupper) **716/852-4416** *5:30pm-10pm, clsd Sun-Mon, upscale, contemporary French*

Tempo 581 Delaware Ave (in Allentown) **716/885-1594** *upscale Italian/American*

Towne Restaurant 186 Allen St **716/884-5128** *7am-5:30am, clsd Sun, Greek*

Entertainment & Recreation

Babeville 341 Delaware Ave (at W Tupper) **716/852-3835**

Buffalo United Artists 672 Main St **716/886-9239** *theater company*

Bookstores

Talking Leaves 3158 Main St (btwn Winspear & Hertel Aves) **716/837-8554** *10am-6pm, till 8pm Wed-Th, clsd Sun; also 951 Elmwood Ave, 716/884-9524*

Publications

About Magazine PO Box 112, 14205 **646/233-2153** *"the queer voice of western New York & southern Ontario"*

Outcome Buffalo 506 Linwood Ave Ste 6 **716/883-2756** *monthly*

Men's Services

Erotica

Adult Mart 3102 Delaware Ave (at Sheridan), Kenmore **716/877-5027** *24hrs*

Video Liquidators 1770 Elmwood Ave **716/874-7223** *24hrs*

Cruisy Areas

South Park Lake [AYOR] 15 minutes from downtown *best btwn 5pm & midnight*

Capital District

includes Albany, Cohoes, Schenectady & Troy

Info Lines & Services

Capital District Lesbian/ Gay Community Center 332 Hudson Ave, Albany **518/462-6138** *social & human service programs*

Gay AA 332 Hudson Ave (at L/G Community Center), Albany **518/462-6138** *7:30pm Sun, men only 7:30pm Mon*

Accommodations

The Morgan State House [GF,NS] 393 State St, Albany **518/427-6063, 888/427-6063** *1800s town house*

Bars

Alibi's [GS,F,YC,GO] 1100 Madison Ave (at N Allen), Albany **518/489-0606** *5pm-1am, till 4am Fri-Sat, casual martini lounge, also Peking restaurant*

Clinton Street Pub [MW,NH,D,E,K] 159 Clinton St, Schenectady **518/377-8555** *11am-close*

George Bar [MW,K,WI,WC] 720 Central Ave, Albany **518/459-1596**

Oh Bar [MW,NH,MR,K,V,WC] 304 Lark St (at Madison), Albany **518/463-9004** *2pm-4am*

Rocks [MW,NH,K,GO] 77 Central Ave (at Elk), Albany **518/472-3588** *2pm-4am*

Waterworks Pub [M,NH,D,F,E,K,18+,WC] 76 Central Ave (btwn Lexington & Northern), Albany **518/465-9079** *1pm-4am, garden bar, DJ wknds*

Nightclubs

Fuze Box [GS,D,E,GO] 12 Central Ave, Albany **518/432-4472** *2pm-4am, from 8pm Th-Sat, swing dancing*

Cafes

Muddy Cup [WI,GO] 1038 Madison Ave, Albany **518/458-6120** *7am-midnight, 7am-2am wknds, events*

Restaurants

Bomber's Burrito Bar [GO] 258 Lark St, Albany **518/463-9636** *11am-1am, lots of veggie*

Le Canard Enchainé 25 Quackenbush Sq (btwn Clinton & Broadway), Albany **518/465-1111** *noon-10pm, till 11pm Fri-Sat, French, full bar*

Debbie's Kitchen 456 Madison Ave (btwn Lark St & Washington Park), Albany **518/463-3829** *10am-9pm, 11am-6pm Sat, clsd Sun*

El Loco Mexican Cafe 465 Madison Ave (btwn Lark & Willett), Albany **518/436-1855** *lunch Wed-Sat, dinner nightly, clsd Mon, full bar*

Magnolia's [E] 462 Madison Ave, Albany **518/449-2492** *5pm-9pm, till 10pm wknds, Sun brunch, clsd Mon*

Yono's [E,WC] 25 Chapel St (at Sheridan), Albany **518/436-7747** *5:30pm-10pm, clsd Sun-Mon*

Retail Shops

Romeo's Gifts 299 Lark St (at Madison), Albany **518/434-4014** *noon-9pm, till 5pm Sun*

Men's Clubs

River Street Club [MO,V,N,NS,PC,WC,GO] 540 River St (at corner of River & Hoosick St), Troy **518/272-0340** *noon-11pm, till 2am Fri-Sat*

Cruisy Areas

Empire State Plaza [AYOR] Albany

Catskill Mtns

Info Lines & Services

Sullivan County Visitors Association **800/882-2287** *LGBT info for the Catskills*

Accommodations

Beds on Clouds [GS] 5320 Main St/ Rte 23 (at CR21), Windham **518/734-4692**

Bradstan Country Hotel [GF,C,P] 1561 Rte 17-B, White Lake **845/583-4114** *also piano bar & cabaret from 9pm-1am Fri-Sat*

Country Suite [GF,NS,WC,GO] Rte 23, Windham **518/734-4079** *B&B, Victorian-style farmhouse, full brkfst, some shared baths, antique shop*

Cuomo's Cove [GF,NS] 33 Cumo's Cove Rd (at South St), Windham **518/734-5903, 800/734-5903**

ECCE B&B [GS,NS,WI,GO] 19 Silverfish Rd, Barryville **845/557-8562, 888/557-8562** *B&B 300 ft above Upper Delaware River, full brkfst*

Inn at Stone Ridge [GF,F] Rte 209, Stone Ridge **845/687-0736**

Kate's Lazy Meadow Motel [GF,NS,WI] 5191 Rte 28, Mt Tremper **845/688-7200** *way-cool love shack owned by Kate Pierson of the B-52s*

Magical Land of Oz B&B [GS,GO] 753 Shandelee Rd, Livingston Manor **845/439-3418** *rooms have Oz theme, shared baths, hot tub*

Point Lookout Mountain Inn [GF,NS,WC] The Mohican Trail, Rte 23, East Windham **518/734-3381**

The Roxbury, Contemporary Catskill Lodging [GS,NS,WI,WC,GO] 2258 County Hwy 41 (at Bridge St), Roxbury **607/326-7200** *hip country motel, kids ok*

Village Green [GO] 12 Tinker St, Woodstock **845/679-0313**

Bars

Public Lounge [GF,GO] 2318 City Hwy 41 (Bridge St), Roxbury **607/326-4026** *5pm-9pm, till midnight Fri-Sat, clsd Mon-Tue*

Restaurants

Catskill Rose 5355 Rte 212, Mt Tremper **845/688-7100** *5pm-close Th-Sun, full bar, patio*

Entertainment & Recreation

Frog Hollow Farm Old Post Rd, Esopus **845/384-6424** *riding school*

Bookstores

Golden Notebook [WC] 29 Tinker St, Woodstock **845/679-8000** *10:30am-7pm*

Erotica

Exotic Gifts & Videos Old Rte 52 (at Rte 52), Liberty **845/292-1140**

Cherry Creek

Accommodations

The Cherry Creek Inn [GF] 1022 West Rd (CR68) (at Center Rd) **716/296-5105** *B&B, full brkfst*

Cooperstown

see Sharon Springs

Corning

Accommodations

Black Sheep Inn [GS] 8329 Pleasant Valley Rd (Rte 54), Hammondsport **607/569-3767, 877/274-6286**

Hillcrest Manor B&B [GF,NS,WI,GO] 227 Cedar St (at Fourth St) **607/936-4548** *elegant 1890 mansion in quiet neighborhood*

Rufus Tanner House B&B [GS,NS,WI,WC] 60 Sagetown Rd, Pine City **607/732-0213, 800/360-9259** *full brkfst, hot tub*

Croton-on-Hudson

Accommodations

Alexander Hamilton House [GS,SW,NS,WI] 49 Van Wyck St **914/271-6737** *full brkfst, 1889 Victorian*

Elmira

Bars

Chill [MW,NH,D,F,K,DS,GO] 200 W 5th **607/732-1414** *6pm-1:30am, clsd Sun-Tue*

Erotica

Deluxe Books 123 Lake St **607/734-9656**

Findley Lake

Accommodations

Blue Heron Inn [GF,NS] 10412 Main St (at Shadyside Rd) **716/769-7852** *B&B, full brkfst*

Fire Island

see also Long Island

Info Lines & Services

AA 631/669-1124 *call for meeting times*

Accommodations

A Summer Place Realty [MW,GO] Bayview Walk (at Main Walk), Cherry Grove **631/597-6140** *rentals, private homes & apts, also sales*

► **Belvedere Guest House for Men** [MO,SW,WC,GO] **631/597-6448** *Venetian-style palace, hot tub, jacuzzi, gym*

Dune Point Guesthouse [GF,NS,WC] **631/597-6261, 631/560-2200 (cell)** *hot tub*

GroveHotel [M,SW,N,WC,GO] Dock Walk, Cherry Grove **631/597-6600** *nonsmoking room available, also 4 bars*

Hotel Ciel [M,F,SW,WC] The Pines **631/597-6500** *also restaurant*

The Madison Fire Island Pines [M,SW,NS,WI,GO] **631/597-6061** *new guesthouse w/ full amenities*

Pines Bluff Overlook [M] 362 Ocean Walk (at Crown) **631/597-3064**

Bars

Blue Whale [★MW,D,F,WC] Fire Island Blvd, The Pines **631/597-6500** *seasonal, popular Low Tea dance*

Cherry's On the Bay [★MW,D,F,E,DS,P] 158 Bayview Walk, Cherry Grove **631/597-7859** *seasonal, noon-4am, patio, also restaurant*

Pines Bistro & Martini Bar [M,D,E,P] 36 Fire Island Blvd, The Pines **631/597-6862** *seasonal, opens 6pm*

Sip n' Twirl [M,D,E,P] 36 Fire Island Blvd, The Pines **631/597-3599** *seasonal, noon-4am, also piano bar*

Nightclubs

Ice Palace [MW,D,DS,WC] Bayview Walk, Cherry Grove **631/597-6600** *hours vary*

The Pavilion [★MW,D,WC] Fire Island Blvd, The Pines **631/597-6500** *seasonal, noon-8am Fri-Sun only, popular High Tea dance*

Cafes

Bay Bar Cafe [★M,F,WC] Fire Island Blvd, The Pines **631/597-6500** *coffee, smoothies, cocktails and food*

Restaurants

Cherry Grove Pizza Dock Walk (under the GroveHotel), Cherry Grove **631/597-6766** *seasonal, 11am-10pm*

Jumpin' Jack's Seafood Shack Ocean Walk, Cherry Grove **631/597-4174** *seasonal, lunch & dinner, also piano bar*

Marina Meat Market Harbor Walk, The Pines **631/597-6588** *great sandwiches*

Pines Pizza 36 Fire Island Blvd, The Pines **631/597-3597** *seasonal, 11am-11pm*

Entertainment & Recreation

Invasion of the Pines The Pines dock (July 4th wknd) *come & enjoy the annual fun as boatloads of drag queens from Cherry Grove arrive to terrorize the posh Pines*

Retail Shops

Index Fire Island Blvd, The Pines *men's retail store*

Gyms & Health Clubs

Aqua Gym Fire Island Blvd, The Pines *7am-6pm, $25 day pass*

Cruisy Areas

Meat Rack [AYOR] trail btwn Cherry Grove & W end of Pines *where the boys of Fire Island really work out*

Fredonia

Cafes

Intermezzo Coffeehouse by Monika's Delites 12 Park Pl (on Barker Common) **716/672-6070** *7am-8pm, 8am-4pm Sat, clsd Sun, gourmet soups, salads, sandwiches & desserts*

Geneva

Accommodations

Belhurst [GF,F] 4069 Rte 14 S (near Snell Rd) **315/781-0201** *fireplaces, also restaurant*

Glens Falls

Accommodations

Glens Falls Inn [GF,WI] 25 Sherman Ave **646/824-8379** *Victorian B&B, full brkfst*

Hamptons

see Long Island—Suffolk/ Hamptons

Hudson Valley

Hudson Valley includes Catskill, High Falls, Highland, Hudson, Hyde Park, Kinderhook, Kingston, New Paltz, Poughkeepsie, Rhinebeck & Saugerties

ACCOMMODATIONS

Barclay Heights B&B [GF,NS] 158 Burt St (at Trinity Place), Saugerties **845/246-3788** *full brkfst*

The Country Squire B&B [GS,NS,WI,GO] 251 Allen St (at 3rd), Hudson **518/822-9229**

The Day House [GF,NS,GO] 260 Main St (at Greene St), Catskill **518/943-4751**

Hudson City B&B [GS,NS,GO] 326 Allen St (at Rte 9-G/ 3rd St), Hudson **518/822-8044** *18th-c Victorian, hot tub*

Lefèvre House B&B [GS,NS,WI,GO] 14 Southside Ave, New Paltz **845/255-4747** *full brkfst, hot tub, kids ok*

Van Schaack House [GF,NS,GO] 20 Broad St (at Albany Rd), Kinderhook **518/758-6118** *B&B, full brkfst*

BARS

Congress [MW,NH,WC] 411 Main St (off Academy), Poughkeepsie **845/486-9068** *3pm-4am, 7pm Sat-Sun*

CAFES

Mod Cafe [GO] 395 Main St, Catskill **518/943-0420** *8am-3pm, from 5pm Th, clsd Sat-Sun*

Muddy Cup [WI,GO] 129 Main St, Beacon **845/838-0138** *6am-10pm*

Muddy Cup [WI,GO] 742 Warren St, Hudson **518/828-2210** *7am-10pm, from 8am wknds, events*

RESTAURANTS

Armadillo Bar & Grill 97 Abeel St, Kingston **845/339-1550** *lunch wknds, dinner Tue-Sat, clsd Mon*

Barnbabys Rte 32 N Chestnut (at Academy), New Paltz **845/255-2433**

Locust Tree Restaurant 215 Hugenot St (behind conference center), New Paltz **845/255-7888** *5pm-close, Sun brunch 11am-3pm, clsd Mon-Tue*

Northern Spy Cafe [WC] Rte 213, High Falls **845/687-7298** *dinner only, clsd Sun-Mon*

Quinn's Restaurant 330 Main St, Beacon **845/831-8065** *5am-1:30pm, great bread*

Terrapin 6426 Montgomery St, Rhinebeck **845/876-3330**

The Would Restaurant [GO] 120 North Rd (off Rte 9 W), Highland **845/691-9883** *dinner nightly, full bar, patio*

ENTERTAINMENT & RECREATION

Dia:Beacon Riggio Galleries 3 Beekman St (at Rte 9D), Beacon **845/440-0100** *modern art museum*

PUBLICATIONS

InsideOUT PO Box 165, Athens 12105 **518/943-9200** *LGBT newsmagazine*

EROTICA

Hamilton Book & Video 216 N Hamilton St (at Parker), Poughkeepsie **845/473-1776**

Ulster Video & Gifts 584 Ulster Ave, Kingston **845/331-6023**

Ithaca

INFO LINES & SERVICES

AA Gay/ Lesbian 607/273-1541

ACCOMMODATIONS

Juniper Hill B&B [GF,NS,WI,GO] 16 Elm St (at Main St), Trumansburg **607/387-3044, 888/809-1367** *full brkfst*

Noble House Farm [GF,NS,WC,GO] 215 Connecticut Hill Rd, Newfield **607/277-4798** *near gorges & wine tours*

William Henry Miller Inn [GF,WI] 303 N Aurora St (at E Buffalo St) **607/256-4553, 877/256-4553**

BARS

Common Ground [★MW,D,MR,E,WC] 1230 Danby Rd/ Rte 96-B (at Comfort) **607/273-1505** *5pm-1am, clsd Mon, also restaurant*

Felicia's Atomic Lounge [GF,F,E,P,GO] 508 W State St (Meadow St) **607/273-2219** *4pm-1am, clsd Mon*

CAFES

Sarah's Patisserie [MR,TG,GO] 200 Pleasant Grove Rd (at Hanshaw Rd) **607/257-4257** *10am-6pm, clsd Mon-Tue, lesbian-owned*

Restaurants

ABC Cafe [BW] 308 Stewart Ave (at Buffalo) **607/277-4770** *8am-11pm, clsd Mon, vegetarian*

Entertainment & Recreation

Out Loud Chorus 607/280-0374

Bookstores

Colophon Books Inc [WC] 205 N Aurora St **607/277-5608** *11am-7pm, clsd Sun-Mon*

Cruisy Areas

Stewart Park [AYOR]

Jamestown

Accommodations

Fairmount Motel [GF,GO] 138 W Fairmount (Rte 394) **716/763-9550** *near Lake Chautauqua*

Bars

Sky Club [MW,D] 108 Fairmount Ave **716/661-3212** *4pm-2am*

Sneakers [MW,D,WC] 100 Harrison (at Institute) **716/484-8816** *2pm-2am, clsd Tue*

Entertainment & Recreation

The Lucy-Desi Museum 300 N Main St **716/484-0800, 877/582-9326** *for those who love Lucy*

Little Falls

Accommodations

Stone Mill of Little Falls [GS,WI,WC,GO] 410 S Ann St **315/823-0208**

Cafes

Piccolo Cafe 365 S Ann St **315/823-9856** *lunch Mon-Fri, dinner Wed-Sun*

Long Island

Long Island is divided into 2 geographical areas:
Long Island—Nassau
Long Island—Suffolk/ Hamptons
see also Fire Island

Long Island—Nassau

Info Lines & Services

Gay/ Lesbian Switchboard of Long Island (GLSB of LI) 631/665-3700 *7pm-10pm weekdays only*

Bars

Blanche [M,NH,K,E,S] 47-2 Boundary Ave, South Farmingdale **516/694-6906** *5pm-4am, from 3pm Sun*

Kelli's Bar & Grill [MW,NH,D,GO] 2955 Merrick Rd, Bellmore **516/765-3892** *4pm-4am, from 3pm wknds*

Zen Lounge [M,D,K,GO] 121 Woodfield Rd, West Hempstead **516/489-1976** *8pm-4am, from 5pm Sun, clsd Mon*

Nightclubs

Shy Lounge [MW,D] 2686 Hempstead Tpke, Levittown **516/520-1332** *10pm-4am Wed for Deluxe and Sat for Gation*

Restaurants

RS Jones 153 Merrick Ave (off Sunrise), Merrick **516/378-7177** *dinner, clsd Mon, Tex-Mex*

Entertainment & Recreation

Jones Beach Field #6

Pride for Youth Coffeehouse [MW] 2050 Bellmore Ave, Bellmore **516/679-9000** *7:30pm-11:30pm Fri, ages 13-20, live music*

Publications

PM Entertainment Magazine 516/845-0759 *covers Long Island, NJ & NYC*

Erotica

Sugar Bush 102 Marine St (off Rte 110), Farmingdale **631/753-3931**

Long Island—Suffolk/ Hamptons

Accommodations

Comfort Inn [GF,SW,WC] 2695 Rte 112 (exit 64 off LI Expwy), Medford **631/654-3000, 800/626-7779 (out-of-state reservations only)** *also Gateway Lounge [F]*

East Hampton Village B&B [GS,NS,WI] 172 Newtown Ln (at McGuirk St), East Hampton **631/324-1858** *lovely turn-of-the-century home*

EconoLodge—Bay Shore [GS] 501 E Main St (at Saxon Ave), Bay Shore **631/666-6000, 800/553-2666** *close to beaches & ferries to Fire Island*

Hampton Resorts & Hospitality [GF,SW,WC] 1655 Country Rd 39, Southampton **631/283-6100** *boutique hotels, jacuzzi*

Mill House Inn [GF,NS,WI,WC] 31 N Main St (at Newtown Lane), East Hampton **631/324-9766** *B&B, full brkfst, kids/ dogs ok*

Stirling House B&B [GF,NS,WI,GO] 104 Bay Ave, Greenport **631/477-0654, 800/551-0654** *full brkfst, jacuzzi*

Bars

The Long Island Eagle [M,NH,L] 94 N Clinton St (at Union Blvd), Bay Shore **631/968-2750** *9pm-4am, from 4pm Sun*

Nightclubs

620 Lounge [GS,D] 620 Waverly Ave, Patchouge **631/291-9737** *9pm-4am Tue & from 10pm Fri gay nights*

Restaurants

Babette's 66 Newtown Ln, East Hampton **631/329-5377** *seasonal, brkfst, lunch & dinner, healthy*

Men's Services

Erotica

Sugar Bush 290A Knickerbocker Ave (btwn Sunrise & Vets Hwy), Bohemia **631/567-9779**

Cruisy Areas

Fowler Beach [AYOR] Southampton *go right*

Smith Point Park [AYOR] Fire Island Nat'l Seashore (at end of William Floyd Pkwy), Shirley

Middletown

Accommodations

Best Western Inn at Hunt's Landing [GF,SW,WI] 120 Rtes 6 & 209, Matamoras, PA **570/491-2400, 800/528-1234** *restaurant & bar*

Montgomery

Accommodations

The Borland House B&B [GF,WI] 130 Clinton St **845/457-1513**

New York City

New York City is divided into 9 geographical areas:
NYC—Overview
NYC—Soho, Greenwich & Chelsea
NYC—Downtown
NYC—Midtown
NYC—Uptown
NYC—Brooklyn
NYC—Queens
NYC—Bronx
NYC—Staten Island

NYC—Overview

Info Lines & Services

AA Gay/ Lesbian Intergroup at Lesbian/ Gay Community Center **212/647-1680**

LGBT Community Center [★WC] 208 W 13th (at 7th Ave) **212/620-7310** *tons of groups & resources, museum*

LOOK WHAT'S NEW
at the
GLBT
17TH
Original
EXPO
MARCH 20-21, 2010
JACOB JAVITS CONVENTION CENTER, 38TH ST. AND 11TH AVE., NYC
THE LARGEST EVENT FOR
THE GAY COMMUNITY
FEATURING:
RainbowWedding Network
PASSPORT MAGAZINE
travelshow
Passport Travel
3rd Annual Video Lounge
Rhode Island International Film Festival
2 DAYS OF NIGHTLIFE -
The Best in Gay Entertainment
PLAN TO VISIT
NEW YORK TO ATTEND THIS
FAMOUS EVENT
For information on exhibiting and attending:
RDP Group - 800-243-9774
info@rdpgroup.com
www.originalglbtexpo.com

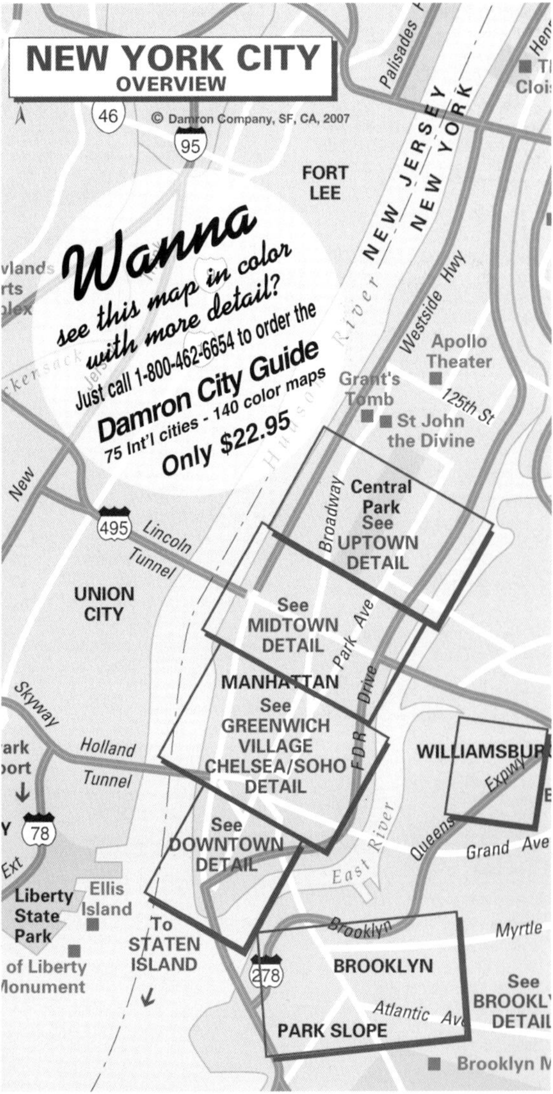
NEW YORK CITY
OVERVIEW
© Damron Company, SF, CA, 2007
46
95
FORT LEE
Palisades
NEW JERSEY
NEW YORK
Wanna
see this map in color
with more detail?
Just call 1-800-462-6654 to order the
Damron City Guide
75 Int'l cities - 140 color maps
Only $22.95
Hudson River
Westside Hwy
Apollo Theater
Grant's Tomb
125th St
St John the Divine
Central Park
See UPTOWN DETAIL
Broadway
New
495
Lincoln Tunnel
UNION CITY
See MIDTOWN DETAIL
Park Ave
MANHATTAN
See GREENWICH VILLAGE CHELSEA/SOHO DETAIL
FDR Drive
Skyway
Holland Tunnel
WILLIAMSBU
Expwy
78
Ext
See DOWNTOWN DETAIL
East River
Queens
Grand Ave
Liberty State Park
Ellis Island
of Liberty Monument
To STATEN ISLAND
Brooklyn
Myrtle
278
BROOKLYN
Atlantic Ave
PARK SLOPE
See BROOKL DETAIL
Brooklyn M

Accommodations

Manhattan Getaways [GS] **212/956-2010** *B&B rooms & private apts throughout Manhattan*

Nightclubs

Sholay Productions/ Desilicious [MW,D,MR] **212/713-5111** *monthly party, Bollywood, bhangra & house music, call for dates*

Entertainment & Recreation

Before Stonewall: A Lesbian & Gay History Tour meet: Washington Square Arch (at Big Onion Walking Tours) **212/439-1090**

Publications

Gay City News 646/452-4496 *LGBT newspaper, weekly*

HX Magazine 212/695-0270 *complete weekly guide to gay New York at night*

MetroSource 212/691-5127 *LGBT lifestyle magazine & resource directory*

New York Blade News 212/695-0270 *weekly LGBT newspaper*

Next 212/627-0165 *entertainment & nightlife paper*

PM Entertainment Magazine 516/845-0759 *events, listings, classifieds & more for Long Island, NJ & NYC*

Men's Services

NYC—Soho, Greenwich & Chelsea

Accommodations

Abingdon Guesthouse [GS,NS,WC] 21 8th Ave (at W 12th St) **212/243-5384** *quiet, mature clientele*

Chelsea 18th Street B&B [M,NS,WI,GO] **646/416-4176** *modern studio apts on 18th St in heart of gay Chelsea, kitchens*

Chelsea Inn [GS] 46 W 17th St (btwn 5th & 6th Aves) **212/645-8989, 800/640-6469** *European-style inn*

Chelsea Mews Guest House [MO,NS,GO] 344 W 15th St (btwn 8th & 9th Aves) **212/255-9174** *some shared baths*

▶ **Chelsea Pines Inn** [MW,WI,GO] 317 W 14th St (btwn 8th & 9th Aves) **212/929-1023, 888/546-2700** *some shared baths*

The Chelsea Savoy Hotel [GS,WI,WC] 204 W 23rd St (at 7th Ave) **212/929-9353, 866/929-9353**

Chelsea Star Hotel [GS,WI] 300 W 30th St (at 8th Ave) **212/ 244-7827, 877/ 827-6969**

▶ **Colonial House Inn** [MW,N,GO] 318 W 22nd St (btwn 8th & 9th Aves) **212/243-9669, 800/689-3779** *1850 brownstone in Chelsea, rooftop patio*

▶ **The GEM Hotel Chelsea** [GF,WI,WC] 300 W 22nd St (at 8th Ave) **212/675-1911**

▶ **The GEM Hotel-SoHo** [GF,WI,WC] 135 E Houston St (at Forsyth St) **212/358-8844**

Gershwin Hotel [GF,WI] 7 E 27th St (at 5th Ave) **212/545-8000** *artsy, seedy hotel w/ model's floor dorms & rooms*

Greenwich Village Home [MW,GO] **877/878-2263** *B&B in private town house, lesbian-owned*

Holiday Inn Downtown [GF,F,WI] 138 Lafayette St (btwn Canal & Howard, in Chinatown) **212/966-8898**

Hotel 17 [GF] 225 E 17th St **212/475-2845** *"East Village chic" budget hotel, shared baths*

▶ **Incentra Village House** [MW,NS,WI,GO] 32 8th Ave (at W 12th St) **212/206-0007** *in 2 red-brick buildings built in 1841*

The Jane [GS] 113 Jane St (at Hudson River Pk) **212/924-6700** *shared baths*

Lambda Mews Loft Soho [WC,GO] **212/213-8798**

Mercer Hotel [GF,F,NS,WI,WC] 147 Mercer St (at Prince St) **212/966-6060**

Your corner of the world

Soho Grand Hotel [GF,WI,WC] 310 W Broadway (at Canal St) **212/965-3000** *big, glossy, over-the-top hotel*

Tribeca Grand [GS,WI] 2 Ave of the Americas **212/519-6600**

W New York—Union Square [GS,WI,WC] 201 Park Ave S **212/253-9119, 877/WHOTELS (reservations only)** *also restaurant & bar*

Washington Square Hotel [GF,F,WI] 103 Waverly Pl (at MacDougal St) **212/777-9515, 800/222-0418** *renovated 100-year-old hotel, also North Square restaurant & lounge*

Bars

Ate Avenue [M,F] 169 8th Ave (at 19th St) **646/763-8355** *4pm-4am, from noon wknds*

Barracuda [★M,S] 275 W 22nd St (at 8th Ave) **212/645-8613** *4pm-4am, live DJs*

Beauty Bar [GS,D,E] 213 E 14th St (at 3rd Ave) **212/539-1389** *5pm-4am, from 7pm wknds, Drop Dead Gorgeous beauty pageant 1st Sun*

The Boiler Room [★M,NH] 86 E 4th St (at 2nd Ave) **212/254-7536** *4pm-4am*

Boots and Saddle [M,NH,B,L,MR,S,18+,YC] 76 Christopher St (at 7th Ave S) **212/929-9684** *noon-4am, go-go dancers*

Chi Chiz [M,NH,MR-AF,F,K,S] 135 Christopher St (at Hudson) **212/462-0027** *6pm-4am*

The Cock [M,K,S,$] 29 2nd Ave (1 blk above Houston) **212/473-9406** *11pm-4am, a "sleazy rock 'n' roll bar," live DJs*

Cubbyhole [MW,NH] 281 W 12th St (at 4th St) **212/243-9041**

DTOX [M,DS] 31 2nd Ave (at 2nd St) **212/777-0774** *6pm-4am*

Duplex [GF,C,P,$] 61 Christopher St (at 7th Ave) **212/255-5438** *4pm-4am, piano bar from 9pm*

Dusk [GS] 147 W 24th St (btwn 6th & 7th) **212/924-4490** *5:30pm-close, from 7:30pm Sat, clsd Sun*

The Eagle [★M,L] 554 W 28th St (btwn 10th & 11th) **646/473-1866** *10pm-4am*

Eastern Bloc [★MW,D,S,WC] 505 E 6th St (at Ave A) **212/777-2555** *7pm-4am, trendy lounge*

G Lounge [★M,GO] 225 W 19th St (at 7th Ave) **212/929-1085** *4pm-4am, lounge, live DJs*

Gym Sports Bar [M,NH] 167 8th Ave (btwn 18th & 19th) **212/337-2439** *4pm-close, from 1pm wknds, neighborhood sports bar*

The Hangar [M,DS,S] 115 Christopher St (at Bleecker) **212/627-2044** *3pm-4am*

▶ **The Monster** [★M,D,C,P,WC] 80 Grove St (at W 4th St, Sheridan Square) **212/924-3558** *4pm-4am, from 2pm wknds, piano bar, T-dance Sun*

Mr Black [★M,D] 35 E 21st (btwn B'way & Park Ave S) *10pm-4am Th-Sat*

Nowhere [MW,NH,TG] 322 E 14th St (btwn 1st & 2nd) **212/477-4744** *3pm-4am, [TG] Th*

Phoenix [MW,NH] 447 E 13th (at Ave A) **212/477-9979** *4pm-4am, patio*

Pieces [M,NH,D,K,C] 8 Christopher St (btwn 6th & 7th) **212/929-9291** *2pm-4am*

The Ramrod [M,NH,L,WC] 185 Christopher St (at Weehawken St) **212/242-9113** *noon-close*

Rawhide NYC [M,L,S] 212 8th Ave (at 21st) **212/242-9332** *10am-4am, from noon Sun, leather/ levi cruise bar, go-go men, beer blast wknds*

Secret Lounge [M] 525 W 29th St (at 10th Ave) **212/268-5580** *7pm-4am, clsd Sun-Wed, lounge*

Section 8 [MW,NH] 218 Ave A (btwn 13th & 14th) *4pm-close*

▶ **Splash** [★MO,D,S,V,YC] 50 W 17th St (at 6th Ave) **212/691-0073** *4pm-5am*

Stonewall Inn [M,NH,D,DS,B,E] 53 Christopher St (at 7th Ave) **212/488-2705** *1pm-4am,*

Ty's [M,NH,L,GO] 114 Christopher St (btwn Bleecker & Hudson) **212/741-9641** *3pm-4am*

Urge [M,NH,F,S] 33 2nd Ave (at 2nd St) **212/533-5757** *4pm-4am, cruisy lounge, go-go boys*

View Bar [★M,V] 232 8th Ave (at 22nd St) **212/929-2243** *4pm-4am, from 1pm wknds, theme nights*

NIGHTCLUBS

Alegria [★M,D] *8 parties a year, during holiday wknds & Black Party in March*

Basement [MW,D,E] 302 Broome St (at Forsyth, at Happy Endings) **212/334-9676** *11pm Th only*

Beige [GS] 40 E 4th St (at Bowery, at B-Bar) **212/475-2220** *11pm Tue only, swank lounge, garden*

Big Apple Ranch [MW,D,CW,BW,$] 39 W 19th St, 5th flr (btwn 5th & 6th, at Dance Manhattan) **212/358-5752** *8pm-1am Sat only, two-step lessons*

Happy Endings [GS,D,E] 302 Broome St (at Forsyth) **212/334-9676** *7pm-4am, clsd Sun-Mon, theme nights*

Hiro [GS,D] 371 W 16th (at 9th Ave, in the Maritime Hotel) **212/242-4300** *10pm-4am Th-Sun, more gay Asian Sun*

The Hose [GS] 225 Ave B, 2nd flr (btwn 13th & 14th Sts) **212/979-8506** *mostly gay Fri*

Mooseknuckle [M,B,L] 225 Ave B, 2nd flr (btwn 13th & 14th Sts, at The Hose) **212/979-8506** *10pm 1st Fri*

Pyramid [MW] 101 Ave A (at 7th St) **212/228-4888** *10pm-4am Fri for 1984 ('80s)*

Rush [M,D,S,18+] 579 6th Ave (off 16th St) **212/243-6100** *open Wed-Sat, young crowd, College Party Sat*

Saint-At-Large [★M,D] **212/674-8541** *producers of the Black Party in March*

Sea Tea [M,D,MR,F,P,S,GO,$] leaves from Pier 40 (at Christopher St) **212/675-2971** *6pm-10pm Sun (June-Oct)*

The Skinny [M,D] 215 W 28th St (at 7th) *10pm Th, dancing & debauchery*

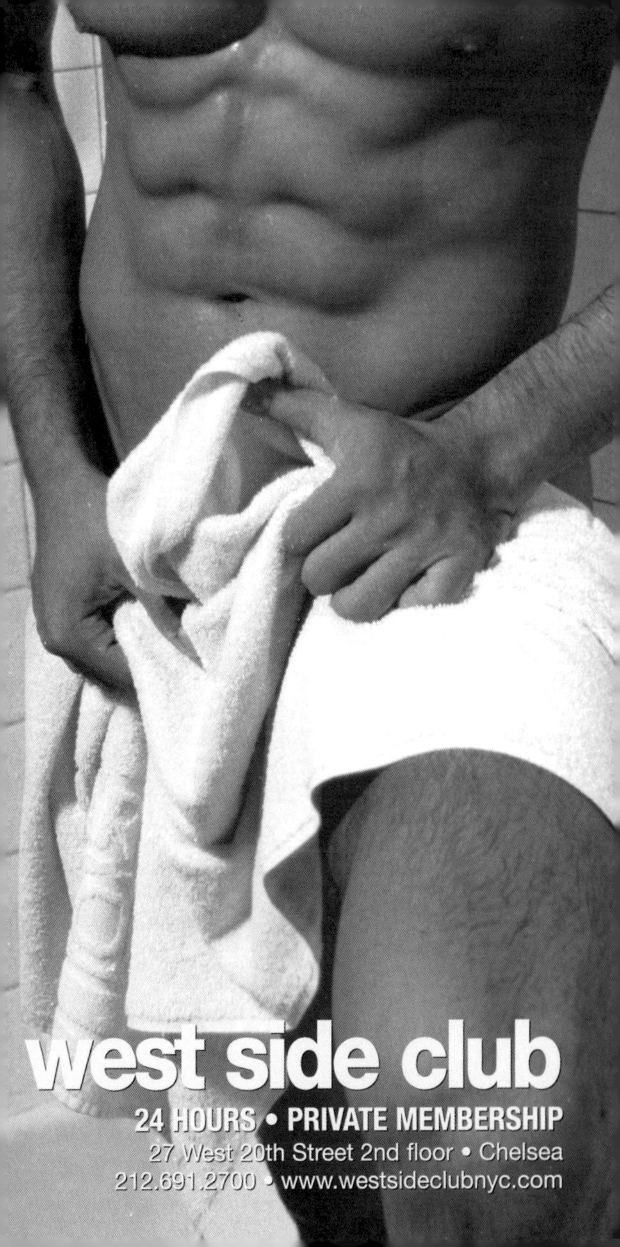
west side club
24 HOURS • PRIVATE MEMBERSHIP
27 West 20th Street 2nd floor • Chelsea
212.691.2700 • www.westsideclubnyc.com

Snapshot [MW,D,YC] 168 Delancey (at Clinton, at Delancey Lounge) **212/254-9920** *Tue only*

Snaxx [M,D] 360 W 23rd St (at 9th, in basement of Westside Tavern) **212/366-3738** *11pm-close Fri only*

XES Lounge [★M,D,K,C,V,GO] 157 W 24th St (at 7th Ave) **212/604-0212** *4pm-4am, smoking patio*

Cafes

Brown Cup Cafe 334 8th Ave (at 27th St) **212/675-7765** *7am-7pm, 8am-6pm Sat, clsd Sun*

Village Cafe [TG] 137 7th Ave (at W 10th St) **212/337-3133** *5:30pm-4am*

Restaurants

7A [★] 109 Ave A (at 7th St) **212/673-6583** *24hrs*

Agave 140 Seventh Ave (btwn 10th St & Charles) **212/989-2100** *noon-close, Southwestern, popular brunch*

Angelica Kitchen 300 E 12th St (at 1st Ave) **212/228-2909** *11:30am-10:30pm, vegetarian/ vegan*

Angon 320 E 6th (btwn 1st & 2nd Aves) **212/260-8229** *noon-11pm, Indian*

Antica Venezia 396 West St (at W 10th St) **212/229-0606** *dinner nightly, Italian*

ArtePasta 81 Greenwich Ave (at Bank St) **212/229-0234** *dinner nightly, Sun brunch, Italian*

Awash 338 E 6th (btwn 1st & 2nd Aves) **212/982-9589** *11am-11pm, Ethiopian*

Bayard's Ale House 533 Hudson (at Charles) **212/989-0313** *lunch & dinner, Cajun, full bar*

Benny's Burritos 93 Ave A (at 6th St) **212/254-2054** *11am-midnight, till 1am Fri-Sat, cheap & huge; also 113 Greenwich (at Jane), 212/727-0584*

Better Burger 178 Eighth Ave (at 19th St) **212/989-6688** *11am-midnight, burgers, hot dogs, salads & more, plenty veggie*

Blue Ribbon [WC] 97 Sullivan St (at Spring St) **212/274-0404** *4pm-4am, cont'l/ American, chef hangout*

Bone Lick Park [WC,GO] 75 Greenwich Ave (at 7th Ave) **212/647-9600** *BBQ, full bar*

Broadway East [WC] 171 E Broadway (btwn Rutgers & Jefferson), New York **212/228-3100** *mostly vegetarian, also wine bar & cafe*

Cola's [★] 148 8th Ave (at 17th St) **212/633-8020** *lunch & dinner, Italian*

Counter [BW,GO] 105 1st Ave (at 7th St) **212/982-5870** *4pm-midnight, 11am-1am wknds, vegan, '50s retro wine & martini bar*

Cowgirl Hall of Fame 519 Hudson St (at W 10th) **212/633-1133** *lunch, dinner, wknd brunch*

The Dish 201 8th Ave (btwn 20th & 21st) **212/352-9800, 212/352-3003** *brkfst, lunch & dinner, also bar*

East of Eighth 254 W 23rd St (at 8th) **212/352-0075** *lunch & dinner, bar open late*

Elmo 156 7th Ave (at 20th St) **212/337-8000** *lunch & dinner, also lounge*

Empire Diner 210 10th Ave (at 22nd St) **212/243-2736** *24hrs*

Les Enfants Terribles 37 Canal St (at Ludlow) **212/777-7518** *8am-4am, full bar & DJ, African/Moroccan, Brazilian, French*

Garage [E] 99 7th Ave S (at Grove St) **212/645-0600** *noon-3am, contemporary American, live jazz*

Gobo 401 Ave of the Americas (at W 8th) **212/255-3242** *11:30am-11pm, vegetarian/ vegan*

Gonzo [★] 140 W 13th St (btwn 6th & 7th Aves) **212/645-4606** *5pm-11pm, till midnight Fri-Sat, till 10:30pm Sun, great Tuscan menu, over 60 wines by the glass, full bar*

I Coppi 432 E 9th St (at 1st Ave) **212/254-2263** *5pm-11pm, 11am-3pm Sat-Sun*

Intermezzo 202 8th Ave (at 21st St) **212/929-3433** *noon-midnight, Italian, great wknd brunch*

Kate's Joint 58 Ave B (at 4th St) **212/777-7059** *10am-11pm, till 1am Fri-Sat, vegetarian*

LaVagna 545 E 5th St (btwn Aves A & B) **212/979-1005** *dinner only, affordable Italian*

Life Cafe 343 E 10th St (at Ave B) **212/477-8791** *10am-midnight, till 2am Fri-Sat, full bar, plenty veggie, artist hangout*

Lips [DS] 2 Bank St (at Greenwich) **212/675-7710** *6pm-midnight, till 1:30am Fri-Sat, gospel brunch Sun, full bar, "the ultimate in drag dining"*

Lucky Cheng's [★K,DS] 24 1st Ave (at 2nd St) **212/995-5500, 212/473-0516** *5:30pm-midnight, Asian/fusion, full bar, drag shows*

The Noho Star 330 Lafayette St (at Bleecker) **212/925-0070** *8am-midnight, from 10:30am wknds, eclectic European & Chinese*

Omai 158 9th Ave (at 19th St) **212/633-0550** *dinner nightly, Vietnamese*

Philip Marie 569 Hudson St (at 11th St) **212/242-6200** *noon-11pm*

The Pink Tea Cup 42 Grove St (btwn Bleecker & Bedford) **212/807-6755** *8am-midnight, till 1am Fri-Sat, Southern homestyle*

Sacred Chow [WC] 227 Sullivan St (at W 3rd St) **212/337-0863** *11am-10pm, till 11pm Fri-Sat, gourmet vegan*

Sigiri 91 1st Ave (btwn 5th & 6th Sts) **212/614-9333** *lunch & dinner, Sri Lankan*

Trattoria Pesce Pasta 262 Bleecker St (at 6th Ave) **212/645-2993** *noon-midnight*

Tribeca Grill [★R] 375 Greenwich St (btwn N Moore & Franklin) **212/941-3900** *lunch Sun-Fri, dinner nightly, chic neighborhood restaurant co-owned by Robert DeNiro, full bar, extensive wine list*

Veselka 144 2nd Ave (at 9th St) **212/228-9682** *24hrs, Ukrainian, great pierogi*

The Viceroy [★] 160 8th Ave (at 18th St) **212/633-8484** *11am-midnight, from 9am wknds, till 1am Sat, fusion, full bar*

Entertainment & Recreation

Leslie/ Lohman Gay Art Foundation & Gallery 26 Wooster St **212/431-2609** *noon-6pm, clsd Sun-Mon*

PS 122 150 1st Ave (at E 9th St) **212/477-5829** *it's rough, it's raw, it's real New York performance art*

Will Clark's Porno Bingo 8 Christopher St (at 6th Ave, at Pieces) *8pm Wed*

Retail Shops

DeMask 144 Orchard St **212/466-0814** *European fetish fashion*

Flight 001 96 Greenwich Ave (btwn Jane & 12th) **212/989-0001, 877/354-4481** *11am-8pm, noon-6pm Sun, way cool travel gear*

Nasty Pig 265 West 19th St (at 8th Ave) **212/691-6067** *noon-8pm, 1pm-6am Sun, rubber chaps, racing pants, rubber jocks, uniforms & harnesses*

Rainbows & Triangles 192 8th Ave (at 19th St) **212/627-2166** *11am-10pm, noon-9pm Sun, LGBT cards, books, gifts & more*

Universal Gear 140 8th Ave (btwn 16th & 17th) **212/206-9119** *casual, club, athletic & designer clothing*

Gyms & Health Clubs

19th St Gym [MW] 22 W 19th St (btwn 5th & 6th) **212/414-5800** *also day passes*

New York Sports Club [M] 128 8th Ave (btwn 16th & 17th) **212/627-0065** *day passes available*

Men's Clubs

▶ **West Side Club** [★M,PC] 27 W 20th St, 2nd flr (at 6th Ave) **212/691-2700** *24hrs*

Erotica

Blue Door Video 87 1st Ave (at 6th St) **212/995-2248** *gay movie theater*

Leather Man 111 Christopher St (at Bleecker) **212/243-5339**

Pleasure Chest 156 7th Ave S (at Charles) **212/242-2158**

Purple Passion [GO] 211 W 20th St (at 7th Ave) **212/807-0486** *fetishwear*

▶ **Unicorn** 277-C W 22nd St (at 8th Ave) **212/924-2921**

NYC—Downtown

Accommodations

Best Western Seaport Inn [GF,NS,WI,WC] 33 Peck Slip (near Front St) **212/766-6600, 800/468-3569**

Embassy Suites Hotel® New York City [WC] 102 North End Ave **212/945-0100, 877/692-4458** *upscale all-suite hotel located on water in downtown Manhattan*

Guild Hall Wall Street [GS,WC] 15 Gold St (at Platt) **212/232-7700, 212/232-7800 (reservations)** *high-tech boutique hotel, also restaurant & lounge*

Millenium Hilton [SW,WC] 55 Church St **212/693-2001, 877/692-4458** *hotel close to all lower Manhattan's finest*

Retail Shops

David Samuel Menkes Custom Leather 144 Fifth Ave #3 (at 19th St) **212/989-3706** *custom leather, fetish-wear*

NYC—Midtown

Accommodations

Bryant Park Hotel [GF,NS,WI,WC] 40 W 40th St (near Sixth Ave) **212/869-0100, 877/640-9300**

Buckingham Hotel [GF] 101 W 57th St (at 6th Ave) **212/246-1500, 888/511-1900** *studios & 1-bdrm suites, concierge, fitness center*

Courtyard by Marriott Times Square South [GF,NS,SW,WI,WC] 114 W 40th St (near Sixth Ave) **212/391-0088**

Doubletree Guest Suites® Times Square-New York City [NS,WI,WC] 1568 Broadway **212/719-1600, 877/692-4458** *all-suite hotel in heart of Times Square*

▶ **The GEM Hotel-Midtown West** [GF,WI,WC] 449 W 36th St (at 10th Ave) **212/967-7206**

Hampton Inn Times Square North [GF,WI,WC] 851 Eighth Ave (at 51st St) **212/581-4100, 212/974-7502**

Hilton New York [NS,WC] 1335 Ave of the Americas **212/586-7000, 877/692-4458** *also 2 restaurants*

Hilton Times Square [NS,WC] 234 W 42nd St (btwn 7th & 8th Aves) **212/840-8222, 877/692-4458** *hotel located on 42nd St near Times Square & Broadway*

Hotel 57 [GF,NS,WI,WC] 130 E 57th St (at Lexington) **212/753-8841, 800/497-6028** *upscale*

Hotel Grace [GF,SW,NS,WI,WC] 125 W 45th St (near Sixth Ave) **212/354-2323**

The Hotel Metro [GF,WI,WC] 45 W 35th St (at 5th Ave) **212/947-2500, 800/356-3870** *art deco hotel*

Hotel Roger Williams 131 Madison Ave (at 31st St) **212/448-7000, 888/448-7788** *cozy & sophisticated*

Hudson Hotel [GF,WI,WC] 356 W 58th St **512/554-6000, 800/697-1791** *magical hotel w/ trendy bars*

Park Central Hotel [GF,WC] 870 7th Ave (at 56th St) **212/247-8000, 800/346-1359** *also restaurant*

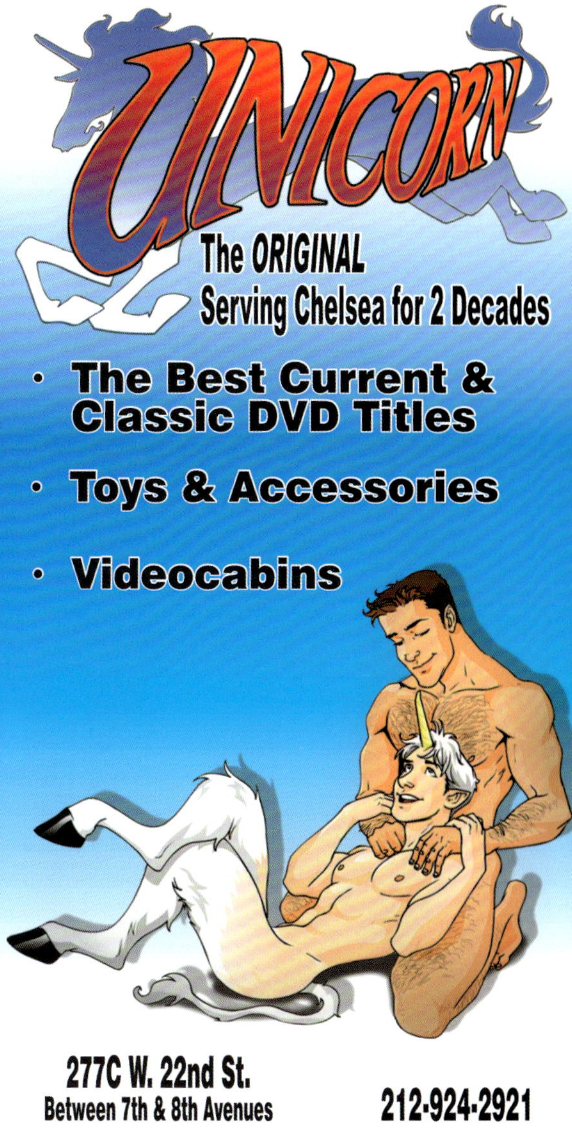
UNICORN
The ORIGINAL
Serving Chelsea for 2 Decades
• The Best Current & Classic DVD Titles
• Toys & Accessories
• Videocabins
277C W. 22nd St.
Between 7th & 8th Avenues
212-924-2921

The Pod Hotel [NS,WI,WC] 230 E 51st Street (near Second Ave) **212/355-0300, 800/742-5945**

Radisson Martinique [GS,WI] 49 W 32nd St (btwn Broadway & 5th) **212/736-3800** *also restaurant, cafe & cocktail lounge*

▶ **Travel Inn** [GF,SW,WC] 515 W 42nd St (at 10th Ave) **212/695-7171, 800/869-4630** *fitness center*

W New York—The Tuscany [GS,WI,WC] 120 E 39th St **212/686-1600, 877/WHOTELS (reservations only)** *also Parisian-style cafe-bar*

Bars

9th Avenue Saloon [M,NH] 656 9th Ave (at 46th St) **212/307-1503** *noon-4am*

Barrage [M] 401 W 47th St (at 9th Ave) **212/586-9390** *5pm-2am*

Don't Tell Mama [★GF,C,P,YC,$] 343 W 46th St (at 9th Ave) **212/757-0788** *4pm-4am, cover + 2 drink minimum for [C]*

Evolve [M,E,DS,S,V,GO] 221 E 58th St (at 2nd Ave) **212/355-3395** *4pm-4am, theme nights*

HK Hell's Kitchen [MW] 523 9th Ave (at 39th St) **212/913-9092** *swank lounge, theme nights, also restaurant*

Posh [M,NH] 405 W 51st St (at 9th Ave) **212/957-2222** *4pm-4am, popular happy hour, theme nights, DJ Fri-Sun*

The Ritz [M,D] 369 W 46th St (btwn 8th & 9th Aves) **212/333-2554** *great place for a drink pre- or post- theater*

Therapy [MW,F,E,C] 348 W 52nd St (at 9th) **212/397-1700** *5pm-4am*

Townhouse Bar [M,E,C,P] 236 E 58th St (btwn 2nd Ave & 3rd Ave) **212/754-4649** *4pm-3am, till 4am Fri-Sat, upscale, dress code*

Vlada [M] 331 W 51st St **212/974-8030** *4pm-3am, clsd Mon, slick gay lounge*

"Still one of the most reliable
GOOD TIME
places in the United States."
east side club
Temporary memberships available to out-of-town men with proper I.D.
227 East 56th Street • New York
212.PL3.2222 • www.eastsideclubnyc.com

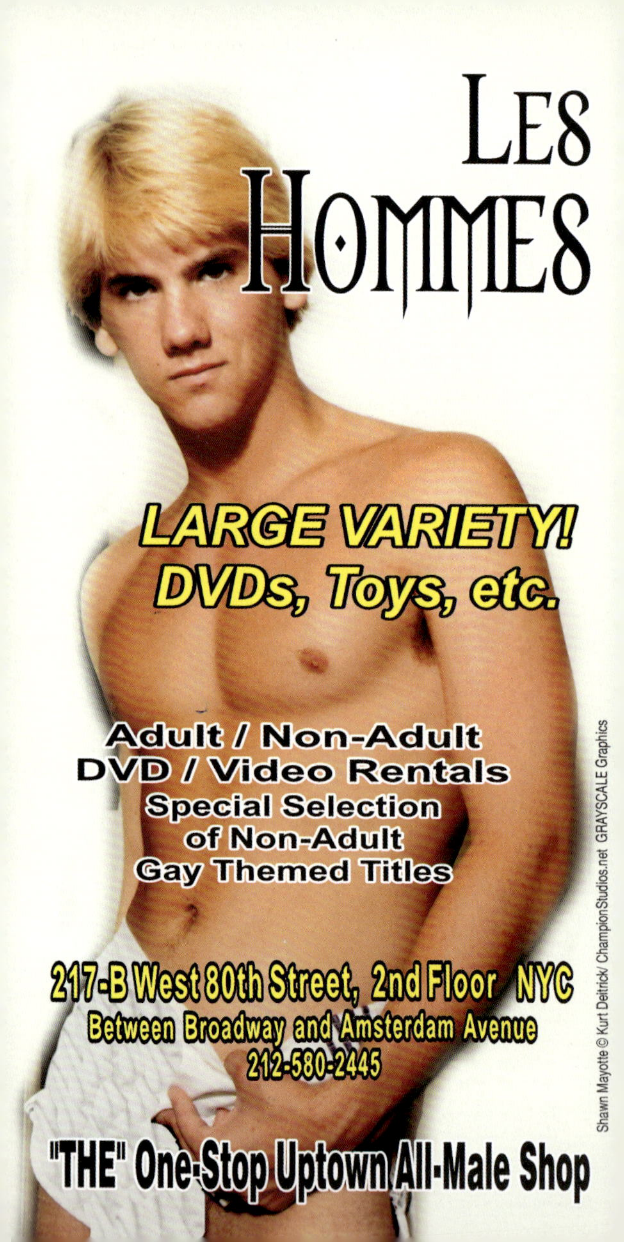
LES HOMMES
LARGE VARIETY!
DVDs, Toys, etc.
Adult / Non-Adult
DVD / Video Rentals
Special Selection
of Non-Adult
Gay Themed Titles
217-B West 80th Street, 2nd Floor NYC
Between Broadway and Amsterdam Avenue
212-580-2445
"THE" One-Stop Uptown All-Male Shop
Shawn Mayotte © Kurt Deitrick/ ChampionStudios.net GRAYSCALE Graphics

The Web [M,D,MR-A,S] 40 E 58th St (at Madison) **212/308-1546** *4pm-close, from 8pm wknds, theme nights, go-go boys*

Nightclubs

Asseteria [M,D,S] 135 W 41st St *11pm Sun only*

Escuelita [M,D,MR-L,TG,DS,S,18+,$] 301 W 39th St (at 8th Ave) **212/631-0588** *10pm-5am Th-Sun*

Jim Caruso's Cast Party [★GS,E,C] 315 W 44th St (btwn 8th & 9th Aves, at Birdland) **212/581-3080** *9:30pm-1am Mon only*

Night Life [M,D,MR-AF] **212/591-6852** *mostly African American, call for events*

Pacha [GS] 618 W 46th St **212/209-7500** *10pm-close Fri-Sat only*

Restaurants

44 1/2 [WC,GO] 626 10th Ave (at 44th St) **212/399-4450** *5:30pm-close, brunch wknds*

44 & X Hell's Kitchen [WC,GO] 622 10th Ave (at 44th St) **212/977-1170** *5:30pm-close, brunch wknds, American comfort food*

A Voce [R] 41 Madison Ave (at 26th) **212/545-8555** *lunch Mon-Sat, dinner nightly, Sun brunch, Italian*

Bamboo 52 344 W 52nd St (btwn 8th & 9th Aves) **212/315-2777** *noon-4am, from 4pm Sun, sushi, also sake bar, garden*

Bann 350 W 50th St (btwn 8th & 9th Aves) **212/582-4446** *lunch Mon-Fri, dinner nightly, Korean*

Beacon 25 W 56th St (btwn 5th & 6th) **212/332-0500** *lunch & dinner, wknd brunch, open-fire cooking, also bar*

Cafe Un Deux Trois [★] 123 W 44th St (at Broadway) **212/354-4148** *noon-midnight, brunch wknds, bistro*

Country [R] 90 Madison Ave (at 29th St) **212/889-7100** *brkfst, lunch & dinner, upscale American*

Mangia e Bevi 800 9th Ave (at W 53rd St) **212/956-3976** *noon-midnight, Italian*

Market Cafe [GO] 496 9th Ave (at 38th St) **212/967-3892**

Rice 'N' Beans [BW] 744 9th Ave (at 50th St) **212/265-4444** *11am-10pm, till 11pm Fri-Sat, Latin/ Brazilian, plenty veggie*

Vynl 754 9th Ave (at 51st St) **212/974-2003** *11am-11pm, also bar*

Entertainment & Recreation

Sex & the City Tour [R] 5th Ave, in front of the Pulitzer Fountain (at 58th St) **212/209-3370** *3 hours, reservations a must!*

Gyms & Health Clubs

Club H Fitness 423 W 55th St (at 9th Ave) **212/245-5802**

Men's Clubs

▶ **East Side Club** [★PC] 227 E 56th St, 6th flr (btwn 2nd & 3rd) **212/753-2222, 212/888-1884** *24hrs, day passes available*

NYC—Uptown

Accommodations

BB Lodges [GS,NS,WI,GO] 1598 Lexington Ave (btwn 101st & 102nd) **917/345-7914** *private rooms w/ private kitchens*

Country Inn the City [GF,NS] W 77th St (at Broadway) **212/580-4183** *studio apts in restored 1891 town house*

The Harlem Flophouse [NS,WI] **212/662-0678** *guesthouse, near Apollo Theatre*

Harlem Renaissance House [GS,NS,WI,GO] **212/226-1590** *in heart of Harlem's Striver Row District, fully restored Stanford White town house*

Hotel Newton [GS,NS,WC] 2528 Broadway **212/678-6500, 800/643-5553** *nearest hotel to Columbia University*

Bars

Brandy's Piano Bar [MW,P] 235 E 84th St (at 2nd Ave) **212/650-1944** *4pm-4am*

Suite [M,NH,K,DS] 992 Amsterdam (at 109th St) **212/222-4600** *5pm-4am*

Tool Box [M,NH,V] 1742 2nd Ave (at 91st St) **212/348-1288** *8pm-4am, cruisy*

Nightclubs

Code Red Thursday [MW,MR] 1 Bennett Ave (at Red Room Lounge) **718/200-9742** *7pm Th only*

Restaurants

Billie's Black [E,K,GO] 271 W 119th St (btwn St Nicholas Ave & Frederick Douglass Blvd) **212/280-2248** *noon-midnight, till 4am Fri-Sat, soul food, also full bar, live music Th-Fri*

Orbit East Harlem [E,K,R] 2257 1st Ave E (at E 116th St) **212/348-7818** *dinner nightly, Sun brunch, full bar, live jazz & blues*

Erotica

▶ **Les Hommes** 217-B W 80th St, 2nd flr (at Broadway) **212/580-2445**

Cruisy Areas

The Ramble [AYOR] in Central Park

NYC—Brooklyn

Info Lines & Services

Audre Lorde Project [TG] 85 S Oxford St **718/596-0342** *noon-6pm Mon & Fri, noon-9pm Tue-Th, 11:30pm-7pm Sat, clsd Sun, LGBT center for people of color*

Accommodations

The Loralei B&B [GS,NS,WI,GO] 667 Argyle Rd (at Foster Ave) **646/228-4656** *1904 Victorian*

Bars

The Abbey [GS,NH,D] 536 Driggs Ave (btwn N 7th & 8th), Williamsburg **718/599-4400** *3pm-4am*

Alligator Lounge [GS,F,K] 600 Metropolitan Ave (at Lorimer) **718/599-4440** *3pm-4am, free pizza from 6pm*

Bar 4 [GS,NH,E] 444 7th Ave (at 15th St, in Park Slope) **718/832-9800** *6pm-4am, DJ Fri-Sat*

Belleville Bistro & Lounge [MW,GO] 330 5th St (at 5th Ave) **718/832-9777** *theme nights, also restaurant*

Excelsior [MW] 390 5th Ave (btwn 6th & 7th) **718/832-1599** *6pm-4am, from 2pm wknds, patio*

Ginger's Bar [MW,NH,E] 363 5th Ave (btwn 5th & 6th Sts, in Park Slope) **718/788-0924** *5pm-4am, from 2pm wknds, patio*

Kili [★GS,NH,E] 81 Hoyt St (btwn State & Atlantic) **718/855-5574** *5pm-4am, funky local bar*

Metropolitan [MW,NH,D] 559 Lorimer St (at Metropolitan Ave), Williamsburg **718/599-4444** *3pm-4am, comfy bar w/ fireplaces*

R Bar [GF,NH] 451 Meeker Ave (Graham Ave) **646/523-1813** *5pm-close, more gay Tue*

Starlite Lounge [M,MR-AF] 1086 Bergen St (at Nostrand) **718/771-3340** *2pm-2am*

Sugarland [MW,D,E,K] 221 N 9th St (at Driggs Ave) **718/599-4044** *8pm-4am, from 4pm wknds*

Superfine [GS,E,GO] 126 Front St **718/243-9005** *11:30am-4am, clsd Mon, also restaurant, relaxed atmosphere, lesbian-owned*

Nightclubs

249 Bar & Lounge [MW,D] 249 4th Ave (btwn President & Carroll) **718/230-5740** *6pm-2am Th, till 4am Fri-Sat, from 4pm Sun*

Milk & Sugar [MW,D] 149 7th St (btwn 2nd & 3rd Aves, at Bell House) *11pm 2nd Sat*

Secret Faggot [MW,D,TG] 289 Kent St (at the Glasslands, Williamsburg) *10pm-4am Fri only, freaky queer dance party*

That's My Jam [MW,D] 262 Taaffe Pl (btwn Willoughby & Kalb, at Sputnik) **718/398-6666** *9pm 2nd Sat*

Tingel Tangel Club [MW,D,TG] 289 Kent St (at the Glasslands, Williamsburg) *monthly cabaret happening, check tingeltangelclub.com for details*

Cafes

Jacques Torres 66 Water St **718/875-9772** *9am-7pm, 10am-6pm Sun, chocolatier*

Outpost [MW,YC,BW,GO] 1014 Fulton St **718/636-1260** *8am-10:30pm, from 9am wknds, also lounge, art gallery*

Restaurants

Alma 187 Columbia St (at Degraw) **718/643-5400** *dinner nightly, wknd brunch, upscale Mexican, outdoor rooftop seating w/ view of Manhattan, also B61 Bar downstairs*

Aunt Suzie [E] 247 5th Ave (at Garfield Pl) **718/788-2868** *dinner only, Italian*

Beast 638 Bergen St (at Vanderbilt Ave) **718/399-6855** *dinner nightly, wknd brunch, also bar from 5pm*

Bogota Latin Bistro [E, GO] 141 5th Ave (at St John's Pl) **718/230-3805** *dinner nightly, wknd brunch, clsd Tue*

ChipShop/ The Curry Shop [★] 383 5th Ave (at 6th St) **718/244-7746** *noon-10pm, till 11pm Th-Sat, from 11am wknds, English/ Indian, home of the famous fried Twinkie!*

Faan 209 Smith St (at Baltic) **718/694-2277** *lunch & dinner, pan-Asian, also bar downstairs*

Johnny Mack's [E] 1114 8th Ave (btwn 11th & 12th) **718/832-7961** *4pm-11pm, till midnight Fri-Sat, Sun brunch*

Santa Fe Grill 62 7th Ave (at Lincoln) **718/636-0279** *5pm-close, from noon wknds, also bar*

Tini Wine Bar & Cafe 293 Van Brunt St (btwn Pioneer & King, at Home Made) **347/223-4135**

Entertainment & Recreation

Gloria Kennedy Gallery [GO] 111 Front St Gallery 222 (at Washington, in D.U.M.B.O.) **718/858-5254** *1pm-6pm Th-Fri, noon-5pm Sat, contemporary art gallery, lesbian-owned*

Erotica

Babeland 462 Bergen St (at 5th Ave) **718/638-3820**

Pink Pussy Cat Boutique 355 5th Ave **718/369-0088**

NYC—Queens

Bars

Albatross [GS,NH,GO] 36-19 24th Ave (at 37th), Astoria **718/204-9045** *6pm-4am, more gay wknds*

Bungalo [GS,F] 32-03 Broadway (at 32nd St) **718/204-7010** *5pm-4am, from 3pm wknds, gay night Wed, dress code*

Chueca [W,MR-L,GO] 69-04 Woodside Ave (at 69th St), Woodside **718/424-1171** *6pm-4am, clsd Mon-Tue, gay men welcome*

Friend's Tavern [M,NH,MR-L] 78-11 Roosevelt Ave, Jackson Hts **718/397-7256** *4pm-4am, DJ Wed-Sun*

Hell Gate Social [GS,D] 12-21 Astoria Blvd (at 14th St) **718/204-8313** *7pm-4am*

Nightclubs

Club Atlantis [MW,D,MR-L,DS] 76-19 Roosevelt Ave (at 77th St), Jackson Hts **718/457-3939** *4pm-4am*

Restaurants

Mezzo Mezzo 31-29 Ditmars Blvd **718/278-0444** *11am-1am, till 2am Th-Sun, Greek*

Mundo Cafe 31-18E Broadway (at 32nd St), Astoria **718/777-2829** *5pm-11:30pm, Mediterranean/ Turkish, plenty veggie*

Men's Clubs

Northern Men's Sauna [PC] 3365 Farrington St, Flushing **718/445-9775**

NYC—Bronx

Bars

Nina's Lounge [W,NH,D,GO] 3159 Bruckner Blvd (at Waterbury) **646/201-1983** *8pm-4am Fri-Sat*

No Parking [MW] 4168 Broadway (at 177th St) **212/923-8700** *6pm-3am, from 7pm Sat-Sun, swank lounge*

Nightclubs

Conceited Tuesdays [M,D,MR,18+] 1306 Union Port Rd (at Mi Gente Cafe) **718/822-9274** *9pm Tue only*

NYC—Staten Island

Nightclubs

Q s.i.n.y. [MW,D] 632 Midland Ave *also restaurant*

Nyack

Nightclubs

Barz [MW,D,A,K,S] 327 Rte 9 W **845/353-4444** *8pm-4am, from 3pm Sun, clsd Mon*

Olean

Bars

Mixers [MW,E,DS] 204 Coleman St **716/372-1004** *7pm-midnight, till 2am Fri-Sat, clsd Sun-Tue*

Orange County

Restaurants

Gigi's Folderol [P,WC] 795 Rte 284, Westtown **845/726-3822** *5pm-close, clsd Tue-Wed, [P] Fri-Sat*

Erotica

Exotic Gifts & Videos 658 Rte 211 E (exit 120, off Rte 17), Middletown **845/692-6664**

Ripley

Erotica

▶ **The Lion's Den Adult Superstore** 6306 Shortman Rd (Exit 61, off I-90, 1st exit in NY) **716/736-6400** *24hrs*

Rochester

Info Lines & Services

AA Gay/ Lesbian 17 Fitzhugh St (St Lukes & Simon Church) **585/232-6720 (AA#)** *8pm Sun*

Gay Alliance of the Genesee Valley (GAGV) 875 E Main St, 5th flr **585/244-8640**

Accommodations

Silver Waters Bed & Breakfast [GS,GO] 8420 Bay St (at Lummis), Sodus Point **315/483-8098**

Bars

Avenue Pub [★M,NH,D] 522 Monroe Ave (at Goodman) **585/244-4960** *4pm-2am, patio*

The Bachelor Forum [M,B,L] 670 University Ave (at Atlantic) **585/271-6930** *2pm-2am*

Muther's [★MW,D,DS,18+,GO] 40 S Union St (at Gardiner Park) **585/325-6216** *4pm-close, clsd Mon-Tue patio*

Nasty D's [MW,D,E,K,DS,V,GO] 140 Alexander St (at Broadway) **585/256-1000** *4pm-2am, from 2pm Sun, also restaurant*

Nightclubs

Tilt Nightclub [MW,D,DS] 444 Central Ave **585/232-8440** *open Th-Sat only*

Vertex [GS,D] 169 N Chestnut St **585/232-5498** *10pm-close Th-Sat, goth club*

Cafes

Little Theatre Cafe [★E,BW,WC] 240 East Ave **585/258-0412** *5pm-10pm, till 11pm Fri-Sat, till 8pm Sun*

Restaurants

The Grill at Union Hill Country Store 1891 Ridge Rd, Webster **585/265-4443** *6am-9pm, 7am-8pm Sun*

Triphammer Grill 60 Browns Race (btwn Platt & Commercial), High Falls **585/262-2700** *seasonal, lunch Mon-Fri, dinner Tue-Sat, clsd Sun, full bar, patio*

Retail Shops

Equal Grounds 750 South Ave (at Caroline) **585/242-7840** *7am-midnight, from 10am Sat-Sun, till 6pm Sun, clsd Mon, LGBT gifts & books, also coffeehouse*

Outlandish [GO] 274 N Goodman St (in the Village Gate) **585/760-8383** *11am-9pm, noon-5pm Sun*

Publications

Empty Closet 585/244-9030 *LGBT newspaper, resource listings*

Men's Clubs

Rochester Spa & Body Club [PC] 109 Liberty Pole Way **585/454-1074** *24hrs*

Men's Services

► **Megaphone 585/563-2820** *Meet and Chat Live with HOT local men. FREE to listen & respond to ads. Video and text chat at GayMates.com. Use FREE code 4889.*

Saratoga Springs

Accommodations

The Inn at Round Lake [GF,SW,NS,WI,GO] 14 Covel Ave (at Burlington), Round Lake **513/289-5018** *Victorian B&B in quaint village btwn Albany & Saratoga Springs*

The Mansion [GF,NS,WC,GO] 801 Rte 29, Rock City Falls **518/885-1607, 888/996-9977** *1860 Victorian mansion, full brkfst*

Saratoga B&B/ Saratoga Motel [GF,NS,GO] 434 Church St **518/584-0920** *1850 farmhouse, full brkfst*

Saratoga Rose Inn & Restaurant [GS,NS,GO] 4136 Rockwell St (at Rte 9N & Bay Rd), Hadley **518/696-2861, 800/942-5025** *full brkfst, hot tub*

Bars

Desperate Annie's [GF,NH] 12 Caroline St (off Broadway) **518/587-2455** *4pm-close*

Restaurants

Esperanto [★YC] 6 1/2 Caroline St (off Broadway) **518/587-4236** *11am-close, doughboys!*

Little India [BW] 60 Court St **518/583-4151** *lunch & dinner, clsd Mon*

Saratoga Rose Inn & Restaurant 4136 Rockwell St, Hadley **518/696-2861, 800/942-5025** *5pm-8:30pm*

Sharon Springs

Accommodations

American Hotel [GS,F,NS,WI,WC,GO] Main St/ Rte 10 **518/284-2105** *1847 Nat'l Register hotel, also restaurant & bar*

Cobblescote on the Lake [GF,WI, F,GO] 6515 State Hwy 80, Cooperstown **607/437-1146**

Edgefield [GS,NS,GO] 153 Washington St **518/284-3339** *well-appointed English Country house, near opera*

The TurnAround Spa Lodge [MW,F,NS,GO] 105 Washington St **518/284-9708, 212/628-9008** *small hotel & health spa, full brkfst, hot tub*

Retail Shops

The Finishing Touch 197 Main St (Rte 10) **518/284-2884** *call fro hours, gallery & gift shop*

Syracuse

Info Lines & Services

AA Gay/ Lesbian 315/463-5011 (AA#) *call for meeting schedule*

Accommodations

B&B Wellington [GF,NS] 707 Danforth St (at Carbon) **315/474-3641, 800/724-5006** *full brkfst wknds, kids ok*

Yellow Lantern Kampground [GF,SW] 1770 Rte 13 N, Cortland **607/756-2959** *205 campsites & RV hookups, short drive from Syracuse or Ithaca*

Bars

Rain Lounge [M,NH,MR,TG,E,K,GO] 218 N Franklin St (at Herald Pl) **315/474-3487** *4pm-2am*

Sugarpearl Espresso Bar & Lounge [GF,TG,F,E,GO] 600 Burnet Ave (at N Crouse) **315/422-7427** *7am-10pm*

X Bar [MW,NH,D,E] 205 N West St (at W Genessee) **315/471-9279** *3pm-2am, 5pm-1am Mon-Tue*

Nightclubs

The Mystic [MW,DS] 1203 Milton Ave **315/218-5897** *7pm-2am, clsd Mon-Tue*

Trexx [M,D,DS,S,V,18+WC] 319 N Clinton St (exit 18, off Rte 81) **315/474-6408** *8pm-2am, till 4am Fri-Sat, clsd Mon-Wed, go-go dancers, [DS] Sun, patio*

Bookstores

The Lavender Inkwell Bookshoppe 304 N McBride St **315/424-7191** *11am-6pm, 11am-3pm Sun, LGBT*

Men's Clubs

Clinton Street Spa [MO,18+,WI,PC,GO] 319-25 N Clinton St, 2nd flr (corner of Herald Pl) **315/466-5401**

Men's Services

Erotica

Boulevard Books 2576 Erie Blvd E (at Seeley) **315/446-1595** *24hrs*

Salt City Book & Video 2807 Brewerton Rd **315/454-0629** *24hrs*

Cruisy Areas

Thornden Park [AYOR] pink triangle rock

Utica

Nightclubs

That Place [M,D,YC,WC] 216 Bleecker St (at Genessee) *9pm-2am, clsd Sun-Tue*

Watertown

Bars

Clueless [M,NH,D,V,18+] 545 Arsenal St **315/782-9006** *8pm-2am, clsd Sun-Tue*

White Plains

Info Lines & Services

The LOFT 252 Bryant Ave **914/948-2932, 914/948-4922 (helpline)** *LGBT community center, call for hours, also newsletter*

North Carolina

Statewide

Publications

Night Out Carolinas 3044 Mt Vernon Dr, Gastonia **704/866-8956** *LGBT magazine for the Carolinas*

On Q Carolina Edition *LGBT publication*

Q Notes 704/531-9988 *bi-weekly LGBT newspaper for the Carolinas*

Asheville

includes Black Mountain

Info Lines & Services

Lambda AA Biltmore Village (at All Souls Episcopal Church) **828/254-8539 (AA#), 800/524-0465** *7pm Mon*

Accommodations

105 Main Street B&B [GF,NS,WI,GO] 105 N Main St, Mars Hill **828/680-9161** *1901 home in Appalachians, views of Blue Ridge Mtns*

1889 WhiteGate Inn & Cottage [★GS,NS,WI,GO] 173 E Chestnut St **828/253-2553, 800/485-3045** *full-service B&B, 3-course brkfst*

The 1900 Inn on Montford [★GF,NS,WI] 296 Montford Ave **828/254-9569, 800/254-9569** *English cottage, full brkfst, some jacuzzis*

A Bird's Nest Bed & Kitchen [MW,NS,WI,GO] 41 Oak Park Rd **828/713-0141, 800/770-9055** *lesbian-owned*

Abbington Green [GF,NS] 46 Cumberland Circle (at Cumberland Ave) **828/251-2454, 800/251-2454** *B&B in Montford historic district*

Another Point of View [GS,NS,GO] 99 Booter Rd, Fairview **828/628-0005** *apt on equestrian farm outside Asheville*

Asheville Cabins, Cottages & More [GS,NS,WI,GO] **828/255-0704, 828/231-2152** *3 private cabins, hot tubs, lesbian-owned*

Asheville's Downtown Loft [GS,NS,WI,GO] 55 1/2 Broadway St (at Walnut) **828/251-2002, 800/770-9055** *spacious loft in heart of downtown Asheville, lesbian-owned*

Biltmore Village Inn [GF,NS,WI,GO] 119 Dodge St (at Irwin) **828/274-8707, 866/274-8779** *luxury B&B near Biltmore Estate, mtn views*

Bittersweet Cottage [GS,NS,WI,GO] 458 Elk Mountain Scenic Hwy (at Beaverdam Rd) **828/712-2414** *"Arts & Crafts-style retreat" situated on Elk Mtn, 2 1-bdrm cottages*

The Hawk & Ivy B&B [GS,SW,NS,WI] 133 N Fork Rd, Barnardsville **828/626-3486, 888/395-7254** *holistic organic B&B, 1910 farmhouse, full brkfst*

Heron Cabin [GS,NS,GO] **828/683-5463, 828/216-4958** *19th-c log cabin, near hiking, kayaking & birding, also meditation hut*

Lofty Notions Campsite [MW,SW,GO] **828/287-0069** *campsite overlooking waterfall, lesbian-owned*

Lovers' Loop Retreat [GS,WC,GO] 1 mile from Blue Ridge Pkwy, I-40 & I-240 **828/296-0660**

Mountain Laurel B&B [MW,NS,WI,GO] 139 Lee Dotson Rd, Fairview **828/628-9903, 828/712-6289 (cell)** *25 miles from Asheville, full brkfst, lesbian-owned*

Richmond Hill Inn [GS,NS,WI] 87 Richmond Hill Dr **828/252-7313, 888/742-4536** *upscale resort, full brkfst, also restaurants*

Shoji Spa & Lodge [GS] 96 Avondale Heights Rd **828/299-0999**

Tanbark Ridge B&B [MO,NS,GO] **828/298-5879** *log home in secluded area*

The Tree House [W,TG,NS,GO] 190 Tessie Ln, Black Mountain **828/669-3889** *private, serene mtn guesthouse, near Asheville*

Bars

LaRue's Backdoor [MW,NH,DS,PC] 237 Haywood St **828/252-1014** *8pm-2am, clsd Sun-Tue*

O Henry's/ Straps [GS,NH] 237 Haywood St **828/254-1891** *2pm-2am; also Straps Fri-Sat [L]*

Smokey's After Dark [M,NH] 18 Broadway **828/253-2155** *4pm-2am*

Tressa's [GS,D,E] 28 Broadway **828/254-7072** *4pm-2:30am, from 6pm Sat, clsd Sun-Mon, jazz/ cigar bar*

Nightclubs

Closet at Nashwa [MW,D] 64 N Carter St *Wed only*

Club Hairspray [MW,NH,D,E,K,C,DS] 38 N French Broad Ave (at Patton Ave) **828/258-2027** *8pm-2am, clsd Sun, game room*

Fred's Speakeasy [GF,K,E] 122 College St **828/281-0920** *4:30pm-2am, till midnight Tue, clsd Sun-Mon, live music venue/ dive bar*

Scandals [MW,D,DS,V,18+,PC,WC] 11 Grove St (at Patton) **828/252-2838** *10pm-3am Th-Sun, 4 bars, 3 dance floors*

Cafes

Laurey's [★WC,GO] 67 Biltmore Ave **828/252-1500** *8am-6pm, till 4pm Sat, clsd Sun, "low-key" brkfst, delicious salads & cookies, dinners-to-go*

Restaurants

Barley's Taproom & Pizzeria [E] 42 Biltmore **828/255-0504** *11:30am-midnight, till 1am Fri-Sat, noon-11pm Sun, bar open later, live jazz, bluegrass & Americana*

Charlotte Street Grill & Pub [GO] 157 Charlotte St **828/253-5348, 828/252-2948** *lunch & dinner Mon-Sat, full bar noon-2am daily, some veggie, lesbian-owned*

Early Girl Eatery 8 Wall St **828/259-9292** *brkfst & lunch daily, dinner Tue-Sat, wknd brunch, Southern, local ingredients*

Firestorm Cafe & Books [WI] 48 Commerce St **828/255-8115** *10am-11pm, clsd Sun, vegetarian, also cafe & bookstore*

Laughing Seed Cafe [BW,WC] 40 Wall St (at Haywood) **828/252-3445** *11:30am-9pm, till 10pm Fri-Sat, Sun brunch from 10am, clsd Tue, vegetarian/ vegan, patio*

Nova 109 Broadway **828/505-2152** *lunch Mon-Fri, dinner nightly, clsd Sun, American*

Picnics Restaurant & Bake Shop [BW,WC,GO] 371 Merrimon Ave **828/258-2858** *11:30am-8pm, clsd Sun-Mon*

Table 48 College St **828/254-8980, 828/254-8983** *11am-2:30pm & 5:30pm-11pm, clsd Tue, moderately priced New American*

Tupelo Honey Cafe 12 College St **828/255-4404** *9am-3pm daily & 5:30pm-close Tue-Sun, "Southern home-cookin' w/ an uptown twist"*

Entertainment & Recreation

Fine Arts Theatre 36 Biltmore Ave **828/232-1536** *first-run art & independent films*

Bookstores

Downtown Books & News 67 N Lexington Ave (btwn Walnut & Hiawassee) **828/253-8654** *8am-6pm, till 8pm Fri-Sat, used books & new magazines, LGBT section*

Malaprop's Bookstore/ Cafe [E] 55 Haywood St (at Walnut) **828/254-6734, 800/441-9829** *8am-9pm, clsd Sun*

Montford's Books 31 Montford Ave **828/285-8805** *10am-7pm, till 8pm Fri-Sat, noon-5pm Sun, used books*

Publications

Stereotypd 828/505-2870 *LGBT newspaper for NC & SC*

Erotica

Bedtyme Stories 2334 Hendersonville Rd, Arden **828/684-8250, 770/844-1208**

Cruisy Areas

The Blue Ridge Parkway [AYOR] Sleepy Gap & Chestnut Cove overlooks (at mile marker 397 & 398)

Atlantic Beach

Accommodations

Palm Suites of Atlantic Beach [GF,SW,NS,WC] 602 W Ft Macon Rd **252/247-6400, 800/972-3297** *rental condos near beach*

Blowing Rock

Accommodations

Blowing Rock Victorian Inn [GF,NS,WI,GO] 242 Ransom St (at US 321) **828/295-0034** *B&B, full brkfst, jacuzzis*

Maple Lodge [GS,NS,GO] 152 Sunset Dr **828/295-3331, 866/795-3331** *English country house & 2-bdrm cottage, lesbian-owned*

Roaring River Chalets [GF,NS,WI,GO] 408 Roaring River Dr **828/295-0034** *chalet-style cabins on the headwaters of the New River; kitchenettes, living rooms*

Boone

Accommodations

Beech Mountaintop Villa [GF,SW,NS,WI] Beech Mtn Pkwy, Beech Mountain **865/522-8547** *condo, highest resort east of the Rockies, panoramic views*

Prospect Hill B&B Inn [GF,WI] 801 W Main St (Hwy 421 & 67), Mountain City, TN **423/727-0139, 800/339-5084**

Stonecliff/ Blue Ridge Mountain Cabin [GF,NS,GO] 182 Laurel Trail (btwn Fleetwood Trail & Railroad Grade Rd), Fleetwood **954/205-6594** *mtn cabin w/ stone fireplace near river & hiking, lesbian-owned*

Brevard

Accommodations

Ash Grove Resort Cabins & Camping [GS,NS,WI,GO] 749 E Fork Rd **828/885-7216** *camping & cabins on 14 wooded acres in Blue Ridge Mtns, hot tub*

Burnsville

Accommodations

Cabin Branch [GS,NS,GO] **828/628-0005**

Nu Wray Inn [GF,NS,GO] 102 Town Square **828/682-2329, 800/368-9729** *"heritage & hospitality since 1833," full brkfst*

Cary

Nightclubs

Icon Nightclub [MW,D,DS,K,MR-AF,18+,PC,WC] 300 E Durham Rd **252/266-6464**

Chapel Hill

see **Raleigh/Durham/Chapel Hill**

Charlotte

Info Lines & Services

Acceptance Group Gay/ Lesbian AA 1200 East Blvd (at church) **704/377-0244, 877/233-6853** *8pm Fri*

The Lesbian/ Gay Community Center 1401-B Central Ave (at Clement Ave) **704/333-0144** *5pm-8pm Tue-Th, 10am-1pm Fri-Sat, clsd Sun-Mon*

Accommodations

Doubletree Guest Suites Charlotte/ South Park [GF,SW] 6300 Morrison Blvd **704/364-2400, 800/222-8733** *all-suite hotel, fitness room*

Four Points by Sheraton [GS,SW,WI] 315 E Woodlawn Rd **704/522-0852** *close to Charlotte Eagle*

The Morehead Inn [GF,WI,WC] 1122 E Morehead St **704/376-3357, 888/667-3432** *antique-filled suites*

VanLandingham Estate [GF,NS,WI,GO] 2010 The Plaza **704/334-8909, 888/524-2020** *bungalow-style estate on Nat'l Historic Register*

Bars

Central Station [M,NH,DS,PC] 2131 Central Ave **704/313-4430** *5pm-2:30am*

Charlotte Eagle [★M,D,CW,B,L,V,GO] 4544-H South Blvd (at Woodlawn) **704/679-9901** *8pm-2am, from 3pm Sun, theme nights, also Jack Hammered Cafe [F], 5pm-10pm Mon-Fri*

Hartigan's Irish Pub [★GS,NH,D,CW,F,E,GO] 601 S Cedar St **704/347-1841**

Liaisons [★MW,NH,F,V,PC] 316 Rensselaer Ave (at South Blvd) **704/376-1617** *7pm-1am, till 2am Fri-Sat, restaurant Wed-Sun*

Morehead Street Tavern [GF,NH,D,F,E] 300 E Morehead St (btwn South Blvd & S Tryon) **704/334-2655** *11:30am-2am, from 5pm Sun, [18+] Sat*

Petra's Piano Bar [GS] 1917 Commonwealth Ave **704/332-6608** *5pm-2am, clsd Mon*

Sidelines Sports Bar & Billiards [GF,NH,F,V,PC,WC,GO] 4544-C South Blvd (at Woodlawn) **704/525-2608**

The Woodshed [M,NH,B,L,F,PC,WC] 4000 Queen City Dr (at Little Rock) **704/394-1712** *5pm-2am, from 3pm Sun, also patio bar*

Nightclubs

Chasers [M,D,S,V,PC,WC] 3217 The Plaza (at 36th) **704/339-0500** *5pm-2am*

Club Myxx [MW,D,MR-AF,S,PC] 3110 S Tryon St **704/525-5001** *10:30pm-close Sat only*

Dammit Janet [GS,D] 3746 N Davidson St *70s dance club, more gay Sun*

Fierce [M,D,DS] 10008 University City Blvd (at Buck Wild) *9pm-3am Th only*

Halo [GF,D] 820 Hamilton St **704/246-1752** *10pm-2am Fri-Sun only*

Scorpio's [MW,D,MR,DS,V,18+,PC,WC] 2301 Freedom Dr **704/373-9124** *9pm-3am Wed & Sun, also Diva's show bar*

Tremont Music Hall [GF,E] 400 W Tremont Ave **704/343-9494** *live music venue*

Velocity [★M,D,C,18+,PC,WC] 935 S Summit Ave (at Morehead St) **704/333-0060** *10pm-3:30am Fri, 9pm-2:30am Sat, clsd Sun-Th*

Cafes

Caribou Coffee [WI] 1531 East Blvd (near Scott) **704/334-3570** *6am-11pm, till midnight Fri-Sat, from 7am Sat-Sun, popular gay hangout Wed nights*

Smelly Cat Coffee [GF] 514 E 36th St **704/374-9656** *7am-8pm, till 10pm Th, till midnight Fri-Sat, 8am-5pm Sun*

Tic Toc Coffeeshop 512 N Tryon St (btwn 8th & 9th) **704/375-5750** *7am-3pm, clsd wknds*

Restaurants

300 East [WC] 300 East Blvd (at Cleveland) **704/332-6507** *11am-10pm, till 11pm Fri-Sat, Sun brunch, full bar*

Alexander Michael's [WC] 401 W 9th St (at Pine) **704/332-6789** *lunch & dinner, clsd Sun, pub fare, full bar*

City Hot Dogs [WC,GO] 1408 E Blvd #A-1 (at Scott Ave) **704/335-3700** *11am-8pm*

Cosmos Cafe 300 N College (at 6th) **704/372-3553** *11am-2am, from 5pm Sat, clsd Sun, some veggie, also martini lounge*

Lupie's Cafe [★] 2718 Monroe Rd (near 5th St) **704/374-1232** *11am-10pm, from noon Sat, clsd Sun, home-style cookin'*

The Pewter Rose Bistro [D,E] 1820 South Blvd (near East Blvd) **704/332-8149** *dinner nightly, lunch Mon-Fri, wknd brunch, outdoor dining, also nightclub*

Entertainment & Recreation

One Voice Chorus [GO] PO Box 9241 28299 **704/716-1129**

Bookstores

Paper Skyscraper [WC] 330 East Blvd (at Euclid Ave) **704/333-7130** *10am-7pm, till 6pm Sat, noon-5pm Sun, books & funky gifts*

White Rabbit Books & Things 920 Central Ave **704/377-4067** *10am-9pm, noon-6pm Sun, LGBT, gifts*

Publications

Q Notes 704/531-9988 *bi-weekly LGBT newspaper for the Carolinas*

Men's Services

▶ **Megaphone 704/556-0006** *Meet and Chat Live with HOT local men. FREE to listen & respond to ads. Video and text chat at GayMates.com. Use FREE code 4889.*

Erotica

Carolina Video Source 8829 E Harris Blvd (at Albemarle Rd) **704/566-9993**

Hwy 74 Video & News 3514 Barry Dr (at Wilkinson Blvd) **704/399-7907**

Independence News 3205 The Plaza (at 36th) **704/332-8430**

Cruisy Areas

Freedom Park [AYOR]

Duck

Accommodations

Advice 5¢, a B&B [GF,NS] 111 Scarborough Ln **252/255-1050, 800/238-4235** *seaside cottage on North Carolina's Outer Banks*

Durham

see Raleigh/Durham/Chapel Hill

Fayetteville

Nightclubs

Alias [MW,D,MR,TG,E,S,V,18+,PC,GO] 984 Old McPherson Church Rd (at Raeford Rd) **910/484-7994** *9pm-2:30am Th-Sat*

Club Emages [MW,D,MR,E,DS,S] 107 Swain St (at Bragg Blvd) **910/868-4279** *8pm-3am, clsd Mon-Tue, patio*

Erotica

Cupid's Boutique [GF] 137 N Reilly Rd (at Morganton) **910/860-7716**

Fort Video & News 4431 Bragg Blvd (near 401 overpass) **910/868-9905** *24hrs*

Priscilla's 3800 Sycamore Dairy Rd (at Bragg Blvd) **910/860-1776**

Franklin

Accommodations

Phoenix Nest [MW,NS,WC,GO] **850/421-1984** *seasonal mtn cabin, sleeps 4*

Gastonia

Bars

Night Owls [MW,D,C,DS] 420 W Main Ave **704/866-7333** *6pm-2:30am Th-Sun only*

Erotica

321 News & Video 1410 N Chester St **704/866-0075**

Cruisy Areas

W Main St [AYOR] from Chester St to Trenton St

Greensboro

Info Lines & Services

Live & Let Live AA 617 N Elm St (at Presbyterian Church) **336/854-4278 (AA#)** *8pm Tue; also Free Spirit, 8pm Sat, 2105 W Market St (at Episcopal Church)*

Accommodations

Biltmore Greensboro Hotel [GS,NS,WI,GO] 111 W Washington St (at Elm St) **336/272-3474, 800/332-0303** *fully restored historic hotel, gym*

O Henry Hotel [GF,SW,WC] 624 Green Valley Rd (at Benjamin Pkwy) **336/854-2000, 800/965-8259** *full brkfst, afternoon tea, bar/ restaurant popular w/ local gay community*

Bars

The Q [MW,NH,D,18+,WI] 708 W Market St **336/272-2587** *4pm-close, from 9pm Sat, from 7pm Sun, patio*

Nightclubs

Aldo's Underground [M,D,DS,MR-L] 2428 High Point Rd **336/340-5288** *10pm Fri only*

Artistika [MW,D,18+] 523 S Elm St **336/271-2686** *Tue only*

Tips [MW,D,MR-AF] 2519 High Point Rd **336/547-6286** *Th-Sun only*

Warehouse 29 [M,D,DS,S,V,18+,PC] 1011 Arnold St **336/333-9333** *9:30pm-2:30am Wed, Fri-Sun, T-dance Sun (summers), add'l summer hours, hosts Out at the Movies, also patio bar*

Restaurants

Much/ Level 2/ Heaven 113 Elm St **336/370-1311** *upscale restaurant & martini lounge, also nightclub*

Men's Services

▶ **Megaphone 336/617-2032** *Meet and Chat Live with HOT local men. FREE to listen & respond to ads. Video and text chat at GayMates.com. Use FREE code 4889.*

Erotica

New Vision Video & News 507 Mobile St (off Randleman Rd) **336/274-6443**

Xanadu 1205 E Bessemer **336/373-9849**

Greenville

Nightclubs

The Great American Mining Co of New Guinea, Inc [MW,D,K,DS,S,V,GO] 1008 B Dickinson Ave (at 10th St) **252/353-2623** *10pm-3am*

Erotica

Late Show Video [GO] 1101 Charles Blvd (at 10th St) **252/758-5883** *DVDs & toys*

Cruisy Areas

Green Springs Park [AYOR] 5th St (behind Pizza Hut)

Hickory

Nightclubs

Club Cabaret [MW,D,S,PC,WC] 101 N Center St (at 1st Ave) **828/322-8103** *9:30pm-close, clsd Mon-Wed*

Cafes

Taste Full Beans [GO] 29 2nd St NW **828/325-0108** *7am-5:30pm, till 3pm Sat, clsd Sun, art exhibits*

Hot Springs

Accommodations

The Duckett House Inn [GS,NS,WI,GO] **828/622-7621** *Victorian farmhouse, full brkfst, creek swimming, also a vegetarian restaurant*

Jacksonville

Cafes

Monster's Pizza & Corner Cafe 1108 Henderson Dr **910/347-6100** *6pm-midnight or later, internet access, full bar, patio*

Erotica

Priscilla's 113-A Western Blvd **910/355-0765**

Madison

Accommodations

Hunter House B&B [GS,SW,NS,WI,GO] 216 W Hunter St **336/445-4730** *patio, gardens, pets on premises*

Mooresville

Restaurants

Pomodoro's Italian American Cafe [BW,WC,GO] 350-J West Plaza Dr (at I-77) **704/663-6686** *11am-10pm, till 7pm Sun*

Mt Mitchell

Accommodations

Serendipity Cabin [GS,NS] 2160 S Toe River Rd, Burnsville **954/448-8371**

New Bern

Accommodations

Dockside Retreat [GF] 1507 Harbourside Dr **252/675-2049**

Harmony House Inn [GF,NS] 215 Pollock St **252/636-3810, 800/636-3113** *1850 Greek Revival, full brkfst*

Raleigh/Durham/Chapel Hill

Info Lines & Services

Common Solutions Gay/ Lesbian AA 505 Alexander Ave (at Episcopal Student Center), Durham **919/286-9499 (AA#)** *6:30pm Mon*

The Gay/ Lesbian Helpline **919/821-0055** *6:30pm-9:30pm Sun-Th*

Accommodations

Carol's Garden Inn [GF,NS,WI] 2412 S Alston Ave, Durham **919/740-1240, 877/922-6777** *on 3 acres, whirpools in 2 rms*

Fickle Creek Farm B&B [GS,NS,GO] **919/304-6287** *passive solar B&B on working farm, full brkfst, some shared baths*

Morehead Manor B&B [GS,NS,WI] 914 Vickers Ave (at Morehead), Durham **919/687-4366, 888/437-6333** *splendid colonial home, full brkfst*

The Oakwood Inn B&B [GF,NS,WI] 411 N Bloodworth St (at Oakwood), Raleigh **919/832-9712, 800/267-9712** *Victorian in the heart of Raleigh, full brkfst*

Bars

Blue Martini [GS,F,WI] 116 N West St, Raleigh **919/899-6464** *4pm-2am, tapas, martini bar*

Flex [★M,B,L,E,S,PC] 2 S West St (at Hillsborough), Raleigh **919/832-8855** *5pm-close, from 2pm Sun, [18+] Th*

Hibernian Restaurant & Pub [GF,F,E] 311 Glenwood Ave (at W Lane St), Raleigh **919/833-2258** *11am-2am daily*

Nightclubs

The Capital Corral (CC) [M,D,MR,P,18+,WI,PC,WC] 313 W Hargett St (at Harrington), Raleigh **919/755-9599** *8pm-close, from 6pm Sun, piano bar, more diverse Th*

Cat's Cradle [GF,A,E] 300 E Main St, Carrboro **919/967-9053** *live music venue*

Club Black Tie [GS,D,E,GO] 3201 New Bern Ave (at Milburnie), Raleigh **919/255-1314** *7pm-3am, from 8pm wknds, patio, [18+] Wed*

Legends/ View [MW,D,DS,S,YC,PC,WC] 330 W Hargett St, Raleigh **919/831-8888** *5pm-close, clsd Wed, theme nights, deck*

The Office [GF,D,YC,PC] 310 S West St, Raleigh **919/828-9994** *Fri-Sun only, preppy dance club, 3 rooms, martini lounge, [18+] Fri*

Stir [M,D] 201 E Franklin St, Chapel Hill **919/929-0024** *9pm Sun only*

Thrive [MW,D] 746 9th St (at Club 9) *11pm 4th Fri only*

Cafes

Bean Traders 105-249 W NC Hwy 54, Durham **919/484-2499** *6:30am-8pm, from 7:30am wknds*

Caribou Coffee 110 West Franklin St (at N Columbia St), Chapel Hill **919/933-5404** *7am-11pm, till midnight Fri-Sat, from 8am Sun*

Reverie: A Coffee Den [GO] 2522 Hillsborough St (at Pogue), Raleigh **919/839-2233**

Restaurants

The Borough [WI] 317 W Morgan St, Raleigh **919/832-8433** *4pm-2am, also bar*

Crooks Corner [WC] 610 Franklin St (at Merritt Mill Rd), Chapel Hill **919/929-7643** *dinner nightly, Sun brunch, clsd Mon, Southern cooking, full bar*

Elmo's Diner 776 9th St (in the Carr Mill Mall), Durham **919/416-3823** *6:30am-10pm, till 11pm Fri-Sat*

Irregardless Cafe [E] 901 W Morgan St (at Hillsborough), Raleigh **919/833-8898** *lunch Tue-Fri, dinner Tue-Sat, Sun brunch, clsd Mon*

Lantern 423 W Franklin St, Chapel Hill **919/969-8846** *Asian, also cocktail lounge*

Magnolia Grill [WC] 1002 9th St (at Knox), Durham **919/286-3609** *dinner, clsd Sun-Mon, upscale Southern, full bar*

Spotted Dog 111 E Main St, Carrboro **919/933-1117** *11:30am-midnight, clsd Mon, plenty veggie*

Sunrise Biscuit Kitchen 1305 E Franklin St, Chapel Hill **919/933-1324** *great brkfst, drive-thru only*

Weathervane Cafe [E,WC] 201 S Estes Dr (in the University Mall), Chapel Hill **919/929-9466** *7am-9pm, till 10pm Fri-Sat, 10:30am-6pm Sun, patio, full bar, great brunch*

Entertainment & Recreation

Bull City HQ 723 N Magnum St, Durham *performance & musical events, gallery*

Bookstores

Internationalist Books & Community Center 405 W Franklin St (at Kenan St), Chapel Hill **919/942-1740** *11am-8pm, noon-6pm Sun, progressive/ alternative, cooperatively run, nonprofit, literature readings & events*

Quail Ridge Books 3522 Wade Ave (at Ridgewood Center), Raleigh **919/828-1588, 800/672-6789** *9am-9pm, LGBT section*

Reader's Corner 3201 Hillsborough St (at Rosemary), Raleigh **919/828-7024** *10am-8pm, till 6pm Sat, noon-6pm Sun, used books*

The Regulator Bookshop 720 9th St (btwn Hillsborough & Perry), Durham **919/286-2700** *9am-9pm, 10am-6pm Sun*

White Rabbit Raleigh [WC] 309 W Martin St (btwn Dawson & Harrington), Raleigh **919/856-1429** *11am-9pm, noon-7pm Sun, LGBT, music, movies, cards & gifts*

Men's Services

Erotica

Capitol Blvd News 2236 Capitol Blvd, Raleigh **919/831-1400** *24hrs, DVDs & videos, arcade, toys*

Castle Video & News 1210 Capitol Blvd, Raleigh **919/836-9189** *24hrs*

Cherry Pie [18+] 1819 Fordham Blvd, Chapel Hill **919/928-0499** *drag bingo & other events*

Eagles/ Videos for the Mature 9016 Glenwood Ave, Raleigh **919/787-0016** *24hrs*

Frisky Business 1720 Hwy 70 E, Durham **919/957-4441** *adult toys, also classes*

Our Place 327 W Hargett (at Harrington), Raleigh **919/833-8968** *24hrs wknds*

Rocky Mount

Nightclubs

Liquid Nightclub [M,D,A,S,AYOR] 313 Falls Rd **252/266-6464** *8pm-close Wed, till 2am Fri, till 3am Sat only, seasonal*

Sanford

Erotica

Sanford Video & News 667 S Horner Blvd **919/774-9124**

Spruce Pine

Accommodations

The Lemon Tree Inn [GS,GO] 872 Greenwood Rd **828/765-6161**

Statesville

Accommodations

Madelyn's in the Grove [GS,NS,WI] 1836 W Memorial Hwy, Union Grove **704/539-4151** *B&B, full brkfst, "murder mystery" wknds*

Washington

Cafes

Back Water Jack's Tiki Bar [WC] 1052 E Main St (at Havens St) **252/975-1090** *lunch & dinner, also bar*

West Jefferson

Accommodations

Blue Ridge Hideaway [GF,NS,WI,GO] 115 Arbor Pl (at Skyline) **615/360-7099, 615/484-7171** *cozy log cabin, private river access, lesbian-owned*

Wilmington

Accommodations

Best Western Coastline Inn [GS,NS,WC,GO] 503 Nutt St **910/763-2800, 800/617-7732**

Blue Heaven B&B [GF,NS,WI] 517 Orange St **910/772-9929** *full brkfst*

Hidden Treasure Beach [GS,SW,WI,NS] 113 S 4th Ave (at K Ave), Kure Beach **910/458-3216** *4 private units w/ kitchens in long ranch house*

Rosehill Inn B&B [GF,NS,WI] 114 S 3rd St (at Dock St) **910/815-0250, 800/815-0250** *full brkfst, jacuzzi in 1 rm*

The Taylor House Inn [GS,NS] 14 N 7th St **910/763-7581, 800/382-9982** *romantic 1905 house, full brkfst*

Bars

Costello's [M,E,P,V,PC,WC,GO] 211 Princess St (btwn 2nd & 3rd) **910/470-9666** *7pm-2:30am*

Tool Box [M,NH,D,K,GO] 2325 Burnett Blvd **910/343-6988** *5pm-2am, from 3pm Sun*

Nightclubs

Ibiza [M,D,K,DS,S,YC,PC,WC,GO] 118 Market St (rear) **910/251-1301** *8pm-3am Th-Sun only*

Restaurants

Caffé Phoenix [GO] 9 S Front St **910/343-1395** *11:30am-10pm, Mediterranean food, some veggie*

Entertainment & Recreation

Cinematique 310 Chestnut St (at Thalian Hall) **910/343-3664, 910/343-1640** *classic, foreign & notable films*

Winston-Salem

Info Lines & Services

Alternative Resources of the Triad 111 W Washington St, Greensboro **336/324-6092** *7pm-10pm*

Accommodations

Henry F Shaffner House [GF,NS,WI] 150 S Marshall St (at High St) **336/777-0052, 800/952-2256** *Tudor-style Victorian B&B in downtown Winston-Salem*

Nightclubs

Club Odyssey [★MW,D,B,MR,TG,C,DS,18+,PC,WC,GO,$] 4019-A Country Club Rd (at Hedgecock Ave) **336/774-7071** *9pm-2:30am, till 3:30am Sat, clsd Mon*

Men's Services

▶ **Megaphone 336/201-5553** *Meet and Chat Live with HOT local men. FREE to listen & respond to ads. Video and text chat at GayMates.com. Use FREE code 4889.*

Erotica

New Vision Video & News 1045 N Cherry St (at N Huff) **336/725-8034** *also 3061 Kennersville Rd, 336/788-0020*

Parkview Video & News 3051 Waughtown St **336/788-9100**

North Dakota

Fargo

Info Lines & Services

Pride Collective & Community Center 116 12th St S (at Main Ave), Moorhead, MN **218/287-8034** *3pm-5pm Sat, referrals, support/social groups, check www.pridecollective.com for events*

Nightclubs

I-Beam [MW,D,DS] 1021 Center Ave (at 11th), Moorhead, MN **218/233-7700** *9pm-2am Fri-Sat only*

Cafes

Atomic Coffee [WI] 222 Broadway **701/478-6160** *7am-11pm, till 9pm Sun, clsd Mon-Tue*

Restaurants

Fargo's Fryn' Pan [★WC] 300 Main St (at 4th) **701/293-9952** *24hrs*

Retail Shops

One World Imports [GO] 614 Main Ave (at Broadway) **701/297-8882** *10am-7pm, till 6pm Fri-Sat, clsd Sun*

Zandbroz Variety 420 N Broadway **701/239-4729** *9am-8pm, noon-5pm Sun, books & gifts*

Men's Services

▶ **Megaphone 888/634-2628** *Meet and Chat Live with HOT local men. Call for your local number or visit us online at GayMates.com. Use FREE code 4889.*

Erotica

Romantix Adult Superstore 417 N Pacific Ave **701/235-2640** *24hrs*

Cruisy Areas

Island Park [AYOR] near pool

Grand Forks

Erotica

Romantix Adult Superstore 102 S 3rd St (at Kittson) **701/772-9021** *24hrs*

Mandan

Erotica

Risque's II 2113 Memorial Hwy **701/663-9013**

Minot

Erotica

Risque's 1514 S Broadway **701/838-2837**

Cruisy Areas

Rest Area [AYOR] Hwy 2 (10 miles E of town)

Ohio

Statewide

Publications

Gay People's Chronicle **216/631-8646** *Ohio's largest bi-weekly LGBT newspaper w/ extensive listings*

OUTlines Magazine 440/716-1495 *free bi-weekly club magazine covering Akron, Canton, Cleveland, Columbus, Dayton, Sandusky, Toledo & more*

Outlook Weekly 614/268-8525 *statewide LGBT newsweekly*

Akron

Info Lines & Services

AA Intergroup 330/253-8181 (AA#)

Akron Pride Center 1501 Aster Ave (at Firestone Blvd) **330/785-0088** *call for meeting schedule*

Bars

Adams Street Bar [★M,D,DS,P,S] 77 N Adams St **330/434-9794** *4:30pm-2:30am, from 9pm Sun, [P] Wed*

Club Amsterdam [MW,NH] 358 S Main St **330/376-9248** *3pm-2:30am, from 7pm Sun*

Cocktails [M,D,DS,V] 1009 S Main St **330/376-2625** *4pm-2:30am, clsd Sun, Daddy's [L] upstairs wknds*

Lydia's [MW,NH,E,K] 1400 S Arlington St (in Arlington Plaza) **330/773-3001** *6pm-2:30am, live blues*

The Office [GF,NH,MR,P,WI,WC] 778 N Main St (at Cuyahoga Falls Ave) **330/376-9550** *11am-2:30am , bistro & lounge, bi-sexual friendly*

Tear-Ez [MW,NH,DS,S,WC] 360 S Main (near Exchange St) **330/376-0011** *11am-2:30am, from noon Sun, male strippers Mon & Wed*

Nightclubs

Interbelt [MW,D,DS,S,V] 70 N Howard St (near Perkins & Main) **330/253-5700** *9pm-2:30am, from 10pm Th & Sun, clsd Tue, patio*

Square [M,D,E,WC,GO] 820 W Market St (btwn Portage Pass & Rhodes Ave) **330/374-9661** *5pm-2:30am, from 8pm Sat, from 7pm Sun*

Cafes

Angel Falls Coffee Company [WC,GO] 792 W Market St (btwn S Highland & Grand) **330/376-5282** *patio*

Restaurants

Aladdin's Eatery 782 W Market St **330/535-0110** *11am-10pm, Middle Eastern*

Bricco [GO] 1 W Exchange St (at S Main St) **330/475-1600** *11am-midnight, till 1am Fri-Sat, clsd Sun, Italian, also bar*

Bruegger's Bagels 1821 Merriman Rd **330/867-8394** *6am-4pm*

Men's Clubs

Akron Steam & Sauna [PC] 41 S Case (near River) **330/252-2791** *noon-midnight, till 6am Fri-Sat*

Men's Services

▶ **Megaphone 330/315-3000** *Meet and Chat Live with HOT local men. FREE to listen & respond to ads. Video and text chat at GayMates.com. Use FREE code 4889.*

Brunswick

see also Akron & Cleveland

Restaurants

Pizza Marcello 67-A Pearl Rd (near Boston Rd) **330/225-1211** *3pm-close, from noon wknds, Italian*

Canton

Nightclubs

Crew [MW,D,K,C] 304 Cherry Ave NE **330/452-2739** *6pm-2:30am, from 9pm Sat-Sun*

Chillicothe

Erotica

▶ **The Lion's Den Adult Superstore** 3216 S Bridge St (US 23 & Three Locks Rd) **740/663-5060** *24hrs*

Cincinnati

Info Lines & Services

AA Gay/ Lesbian 320 Resor Ave (in St John's Unitarian Church), Clifton **513/351-0422 (AA#)** *8pm Wed, call for locations of wknd meetings*

Gay/ Lesbian Community Center of Greater Cincinnati 4119 Hamilton Ave (near Blue Rock) **513/591-0200** *6pm-9pm, noon-4pm Sat, clsd Sun*

Accommodations

Cincinnatian Hotel [GF,WI,WC] 601 Vine St (at 6th St) **513/381-3000, 800/942-9000** *restaurant & lounge*

Crowne Plaza [GF,SW,WI,WC] 5901 Pfeiffer Rd (at I-71) **513/793-4500, 800/468-3597**

First Farm Inn [GF,NS,WC] 2510 Stevens Rd, Idlewild, KY **859/586-0199** *1800s farmhouse B&B, full brkfst, 20 minutes from Cincinnati*

Millennium Hotel Cincinnati [GF,SW,WI,WC] 150 W 5th St **513/352-2100, 800/876-2100** *centrally located hotel near gay bars & clubs & all of the city's major attractions, w/ city's only outdoor rooftop pool & sundeck, also 24hr business & fitness center*

The Vernon Manor Hotel [GF,WI,WC] 400 Oak St **513/281-3300, 800/543-3999** *restaurant, pub, gym*

Weller Haus B&B [GF,NS,WI] 319 Poplar St, Newport, KY **859/431-6829, 800/431-4287** *B&B in 2 side-by-side historic homes, 2 jacuzzis*

Bars

Below Zero Lounge [GS,F,E,K,V] 1122 Walnut St (at E Central Pkwy) **513/421-9376** *4pm-2:30am, 6pm-2:30am Sat-Sun, clsd Mon-Tue*

Golden Lion [M,NH,D,K] 340 Ludlow (at Telford), Clifton **513/281-4179** *11am-2:30am, from 1pm Sun, dive bar*

Junkers Tavern [GF,NH] 4158 Langland (at Pullan) **513/541-5470** *8:30am-1am*

Little Bit Bar [MW,NH,D,K,DS,V,WC] 2401 Vine St (at Hollister, Clifton Heights) **513/721-8484** *7pm-2:30am, clsd Mon*

Milton's [GF,NH] 301 Milton St (at Sycamore) **513/784-9938** *4pm-2:30am*

On Broadway [M,NH,CW,B,L,K,DS,V,GO] 817 Broadway **513/421-2555** *4pm-2:30am*

The Serpent [M,L] 4042 Hamilton Ave (at Blue Rock) **513/681-6969** *9pm-2:30am*

Shooters [M,D,CW,K,S] 927 Race St (at Court) **513/381-9900** *4pm-2:30am, [K] Wed*

Simon Says [★M,NH,P,WC] 428 Walnut St (at 5th) **513/381-7577** *11am-2:30am, from 1pm Sun*

The Subway [M,NH,D,F,S] 609 Walnut St (at 6th) **513/421-1294** *6am-2:30am, from 1pm Sun*

Nightclubs

Adonis [MW,D,TG,K,DS] 4601 Kellogg Ave **513/871-1542** *9pm-3am Fri-Sat only*

Bronz [MW,D,E,K,V,WC,GO] 4029 Hamilton Ave (at Blue Rock) **513/591-2100** *5pm-2:30am*

The Dock [★MW,D,DS,S,19+,WC] 603 W Pete Rose Wy (near Central) **513/241-5623** *10pm-3am, till 4am Fri-Sat, clsd Mon-Wed*

Cafes

College Hill Coffee Co [E,WI] 6128 Hamilton Ave **513/542-2739** *6:30am-6:30pm, till 10pm Fri, 8:30am-10pm Sat, 8:30am-4pm Sun, clsd Mon, live music Sat*

Zen & Now 4453 Bridgetown Rd **513/598-8999** *7am-10pm, till midnight Fri, 9am-midnight Sat, clsd Sun*

Restaurants

Boca [WC] 3200 Madison Rd, Oakley **513/542-2022** *dinner Tue-Sat, clsd Sun-Mon, nouvelle int'l, full bar*

Melt 4165 Hamilton Ave **513/681-6358** *11am-9pm, till 10pm Fri-Sat, eclectic, plenty veggie*

Myra's Dionysus 121 Calhoun St **513/961-1578** *11am-10pm, till 11pm Fri-Sat, from 5pm Sun, diverse menu, plenty veggie*

Entertainment & Recreation

Alternating Currents WAIF 88.3 FM **513/749-1444 (during show)** *3pm Sat, LGBT public affairs radio program*

Ensemble Theatre of Cincinnati 1127 Vine St **513/421-3555**

Know Theatre 1120 Jackson St (at Central Pkwy) **513/300-5669** *contemporary multicultural theater*

Retail Shops

Pink Pyramid 907 Race St (btwn 9th & Court) **513/621-7465** *noon-10pm, till 11pm Fri-Sat, 1pm-7pm Sun, pride items, also leather*

Publications

Gay People's Chronicle **216/631-8646** *Ohio's largest bi-weekly LGBT newspaper w/ extensive listings*

Greater Cincinnati GLBT News **513/241-7539** *see: www.greater-cincinnatiglbtnews.com*

Men's Services

► **Megaphone 513/821-4500** *Meet and Chat Live with HOT local men. FREE to listen & respond to ads. Video and text chat at GayMates.com. Use FREE code 4889.*

Cleveland

Info Lines & Services

AA Gay/ Lesbian 6600 Detroit Ave (at LGBT Center) **216/241-7387** *7pm Mon*

Cleveland Lesbian/ Gay Community Center [WC] 6600 Detroit Ave **216/651-5428, 888/429-8761** *noon-8pm Mon & Fri, till 10pm Tue-Th, clsd wknds*

Accommodations

Clifford House [GS,NS,GO] 1810 W 28th St (at Jay) **216/589-0121** *near downtown*

Flex Hotel/ Spa, LLC [M,SW,NS,WI,GO] 2600 Hamilton Ave (at 26th) **216/812-3304** *24hrs, in renovated art deco Greyhound bus station, steam room, sauna, gym & 20-man whirlpool*

Glendennis B&B [GS,WI] 2808 Bridge Ave (at 28th St) **216/589-0663** *3-rm suite, full brkfst*

J Palen House [GF,WI] 2708 Bridge Ave (at W 28th St) **216/664-0813** *restored Victorian, full brkfst*

Radisson Hotel Cleveland–Gateway [GF,WI,WC] 651 Huron Rd **216/377-9000, 888/201-1718** *also restaurant*

Stone Gables B&B [GS,WI,WC,GO] 3806 Franklin Blvd (at W 38th) **216/961-4654, 877/215-4326** *full brkfst, sauna*

Bars

A Man's World [M,D] 2909 Detroit Ave (at 29th St) **216/771-0369** *7am-2:30am, from noon Sun-Mon, DJ Sat, Sun eve [CW], patio*

Apex [★MW,NH,E,K] 11633 Lorain Ave (at W 117th St) **216/476-1970** *5pm-2:30am, from 7pm Sat, from 2pm Sun*

Club Argos [M,NH,D,B,MR,S,YC] 2032 W 25th St (at Lorain & 24th) **216/781-9191** *3pm-close, from noon wknds, alternative sports bar*

Cocktails Cleveland [★M,D,L,F,K,S,V] 9208 Detroit Ave (at W 93rd St) **216/961-3115** *4pm-2:30am, patio, "Cleveland's only Sun T-dance"*

The Hawk [MW,NH,WC] 11217 Detroit Ave (at 112th St) **216/521-5443** *noon-2:30am, from 1pm Sun*

Lady Z's [MW,NH,F,K,WI,WC] 4002 Jennings Rd **216/741-0100** *2pm-midnight, till 2:30am wknds, clsd Sun*

► **Leather Stallion Saloon** [★M,NH,B,L,F] 2205 St Clair Ave (near E 21st St) **216/589-8588** *3pm-2am, DJ Sun, patio*

Muggs [MW,NH,D,K] 3194 W 25th St (near Clark) **216/398-7012** *11am-2:30am, clsd Sun*

Twist [★MW,NH,D,P] 11633 Clifton (at 117th St) **216/221-2333** *11:30am-2:30am, from noon Sun*

Union Station Video Cafe [★MW,F,V,GO] 2814 Detroit Ave (at W 28th) **216/357-2997** *5pm-2:30am; also Bounce [D,DS] Fri-Sat*

View Ultra Lounge [GS,D,E] 618 Prospect Ave (at E 4th St) **216/664-1815** *theme nights*

Nightclubs

Bottoms Up [MW,D,F,K,DS] 1572 W 117th, Lakewood *11am-close, theme nights*

Cafes

Gypsy Beans & Baking Co [★WI] 6425 Detroit Ave (at W 65th St, next to Cleveland Public Theatre) **216/939-9009** *7am-9pm, till 11pm Fri-Sat, fresh-baked gourmet pastries, soups, sandwiches*

Lucky's Cafe 777 Starkweather Ave **216/622-7773** *7am-8pm, 8am-5pm wknds, popular wknd brunch (9am-2am), cafe & bakery, outdoor seating*

Phoenix Coffee [★WI] 2287 Lee Rd, Cleveland Heights **216/932-8227** *6am-10pm, till 11pm Fri, from 7am Sat, 7am-7pm Sun, cafe w/ specialty beverages, pastries, great sandwiches, outdoor seating*

Restaurants

Ali Baba [★BYOB] 12021 Lorain Ave (at W 120th St) **216/251-2040** *11:30am-10pm Th-Sat, the best Middle Eastern food you'll have outside the Middle East, plenty veggie*

Battiste & Dupree Cajun Grill & Bar 1992 Warrensville Ctr Rd **216/381-3341** *lunch & dinner, clsd Sun-Mon*

Cafe Tandoor 2096 S Taylor Rd (at Cedar), Cleveland Heights **216/371-8500, 216/371-8569** *lunch & dinner, 3pm-9pm Sun, Indian*

The Coffee Pot 12415 Madison Ave, Lakewood **216/226-6443** *6am-4pm, till 3pm Sat, till 2pm Sun, clsd Mon, diner*

Diner on Clifton [M] 11637 Clifton Blvd (at W 117th St) **216/521-5003** *7am-11pm*

Hecks [★WC] 2927 Bridge Ave (at W 30th) **216/861-5464, 800/677-8592** *lunch & dinner, gourmet burgers*

The Inn on Coventry [WC] 2785 Euclid Heights Blvd (at Coventry), Cleveland Heights **216/371-1811** *7am-8:30pm, from 8:30am Sat-Mon, till 3pm Sun-Mon, homestyle, popular Bloody Marys*

Jimmy O'Neill's Tavern 2195 Lee Rd, Cleveland Heights **216/321-1116** *5pm-midnight, till 11pm Sun, bar till 2:30am*

Johnny Mango World Cafe & Bar [NS,WC] 3120 Bridge Ave (btwn Fulton & W 32nd, in Ohio City) **216/575-1919** *11am-10pm, till 11pm Fri-Sat, healthy world food & juice bar, also full bar till 1am*

Latitude 41N [GO] 5712 Detroit Ave (at W 58th St, Detroit Shoreway) **216/961-0000** *8am-9pm, till 10pm Fri, till 3pm Sun, restaurant & cafe*

Lolita [★] 900 Literary Rd (at Professor Ave, in Tremont) **216/771-5652** *5pm-11pm, till 1am Fri-Sat, 4pm-9pm Sun, clsd Mon, upscale cont'l, full bar; also Lola's in Warehouse District downtown, both owned by Iron Chef Michael Symon*

Luchita's [★] 3456 W 117th St (at Governor) **216/252-1169** *lunch & dinner, clsd Mon, Mexican, full bar*

Luxe 6605 Detroit Ave (at W 65th St) **216/920-0600** *5pm-midnight, lounge till 2am, gourmet comfort food, also lounge, directly across from LGBT Center*

My Friend's Deli & Restaurant [WI,BW] 11616 Detroit Ave (at W 117th) **216/221-2575** *24hrs*

Pearl of the Orient 19300 Detroit Rd (in Beachcliff Market Sq), Rocky River **440/333-9902** *lunch & dinner, Chinese, some veggie, also restaurant on East Side*

Tommy's [WI] 1824 Coventry Rd, Cleveland Heights **216/321-7757** *9am-9pm, till 10pm Fri, 7:30am-10pm Sat, plenty veggie, great milkshakes*

Entertainment & Recreation

Rock & Roll Hall of Fame 1100 Rock & Roll Blvd (at E 9th & Lake Erie) **216/781-ROCK** *even if you don't like rock, stop by & check out IM Pei's architectural gift to Cleveland*

Bookstores

Borders Bookshop & Espresso Bar 2101 Richmond Rd (at Cedar, in LaPlace Mall), Beachwood **216/292-2660** *10am-10pm, till 9pm Sun*

Joseph-Beth Booksellers 24519 Cedar Rd (in Legacy Village shopping center), Lyndhurst **216/691-7000** *9am-9pm, till 11pm Fri-Sat, till 7pm Sun, LGBT section, active reading series, also bistro*

Loganberry Books 13015 Larchmere Blvd, Shaker Heights **216/795-9800** *10am-6pm, till 8pm Th, clsd Sun, used & rare books*

Mac's Backs 1820 Coventry Rd (next to Tommy's), Cleveland Heights **216/321-2665** *10am-9pm, till 10pm Fri-Sat, 11am-8pm Sun, great new & used, 3 floors, reading series, some LGBT titles*

Retail Shops

Big Fun 1814 Coventry Rd, Cleveland Heights **216/371-4386** *11am-8pm, till 10pm Fri-Sat, till 6pm Sun, kitschy variety store*

Dean Rufus House of Fun 1422 W 29th St (at Detroit) **216/348-1386** *1pm-midnight, till 2:30am Fri-Sat, clsd Mon, clothing, DVDs*

Goddess Blessed 15729 Madison Ave (at Hillard), Lakewood **216/221-8755** *11am-7pm, clsd Sun-Mon, goddess-focused & occult gifts & supplies, tarot readings, events & classes*

Kitsch City 6511 Detroit Ave **216/651-2489** *11am-7pm, noon-4pm Sun, clsd Mon, cards, gifts, T-shirts & more*

Publications

Erie Gay News 814/456-9833

Gay People's Chronicle 216/631-8646 *Ohio's largest bi-weekly LGBT newspaper w/ extensive listings*

OUTlines Magazine 440/716-1495 *free bi-weekly club magazine covering Akron, Canton, Cleveland, Columbus, Dayton, Sandusky, Toledo & more*

Men's Clubs

The Club Cleveland [★PC] 3219 Detroit Ave **216/961-2727** *24hrs*

Flex [★MR,SW,V,PC] 2600 Hamilton Ave **216/812-3304** *24hrs, in renovated art deco Greyhound bus station, steam room, sauna, gym & 20-man whirlpool*

Men's Services

► **Megaphone 216/912-6000** *Meet and Chat Live with HOT local men. FREE to listen & respond to ads. Video and text chat at GayMates.com. Use FREE code 4889.*

Erotica

Adult Mart [AYOR] 16700 Brookpark Rd (at W 150th) **216/267-9019**

Adult Mart 19121 Neff Rd **216/738-0133** *24hrs*

Bank News 4025 Clark Ave (at W 41st St) **216/281-8777** *general magazine store w/ section for adult videos, magazines, toys*

Body Language 11424 Lorain Ave (at W 115th St) **216/251-3330, 888/429-7733** *11am-11pm, till 6pm Sun, "one stop GLBT shop"*

Rocky's Entertainment & Emporium [AYOR] 13330 Brookpark Rd (at W 130th) **216/267-4659**

Columbus

Info Lines & Services

AA Gay/ Lesbian 614/253-8501, 800/870-3795 (in OH)

Stonewall Columbus Community Center/ Hotline [WC] 1160 N High St (at E 4th Ave) **614/299-7764** *9am-5pm, clsd wknds*

Accommodations

The Brewmaster's House [MO,NS,WI,GO] **614/449-8298** *full brkfst, historic house*

Columbus Gatehouse Inn [GF,SW,WI,WC] 2084 S Hamilton Rd (at Grove Rd) **614/864-8844**

Courtyard by Marriott [GF,SW,WI,WC] 35 W Spring St (at Front St) **614/228-3200, 800/321-2211**

Garden Manor Bed & Breakfast [GF,WI,GO] 108 N 20th St (at E Broad St) **614/832-4079, 866/925-4929**

Harrison House B&B [GF,NS,WI] 313 W 5th Ave (at Neil Ave) **614/421-2202, 800/827-4203**

Bars

AWOL [M,NH,K,WC] 49 Parsons Ave (at Oak) **614/621-8779** *2pm-2:30am*

Blazer's Pub [MW,NH,K] 1205 N High St (at 5th) **614/299-1800** *4pm-midnight, till 2am Th-Sat, clsd Sun*

Club 20 [M,NH,K] 20 E Duncan (at High) **614/261-9111** *noon-2:30am, from 1pm Sun, patio*

Club Diversity [MW,E,P] 863 S High St **614/224-4050** *4pm-midnight, noon-2:30am Sat, piano bar, [E] Fri-Sat*

Eagle Tavern [M,NH,F,K,S,18+] 1586 S High St (at Morrill) **614/444-6600** *11am-1am*

Exile [M,NH,L,S,WC] 893 N 4th St (at 2nd Ave) **614/299-0069** *9pm-2:30am*

Havana Video Lounge [★MW,NH,D,F,DS,S,V] 862 N High (at 1st Ave) **614/421-9697** *5pm-2:30am, martini lounge, male strippers Sun*

James' Club 88 [M,E] 55 W Long St **614/223-1213** *5pm-close, clsd Mon, live jazz & piano bar*

Liquid Lounge [W,D,F,K] 1100 N High St **614/298-3000** *4pm-2:30am, clsd Sun-Mon, men's night 10pm Th*

The Pyramid II [M,NH,DS,S] 211 N 6th St **614/228-6151** *4pm-2:30am, from 1pm wknds*

Q [M,D,TG,K,S,V,GO] 205 N 5th St (at Spring) **614/222-2401** *4pm-2am, from 1pm wknds, patio*

Score [MW,K] 145 N 5th St **614/849-0099** *4pm-2:30am, gay sports bar, drag bingo*

Slammers [W,D,F,E,WC] 202 E Long St (at N 5th St) **614/221-8880** *11am-12:30am, till 2:30am Fri-Sat, from 6pm wknds, open mic Tue, patio*

Somewhere Else [MW,F,E,K,DS,S] 1312 S High St (at Moler) **614/443-4300** *5pm-2:30am, from 7pm Sun-Mon, clsd Mon winters*

The South Bend Tavern [MW,NH,DS,WC] 126 E Moler St (at 4th St) **614/444-3386** *noon-2:30am*

Tremont [M,NH,OC] 708 S High St (at Frankfort) **614/445-9365** *1pm-2:30am*

Union Cafe [★MW,F,V,WI,WC] 782 N High St (at Hubbard) **614/421-2233** *11am-11pm, video bar, full menu*

Nightclubs

Axis [★M,D,C,DS,S,18+,WC,GO] 775 N High St (at Hubbard) **614/291-4008** *10pm-2:30am Fri-Sat only, also Pump lounge*

Tradewinds II [M,D,B,L,V,WC] 117 E Chestnut (at 3rd St) **614/461-4110** *4pm-2:30am, clsd Mon-Tue, 3 bars & restaurant*

Wall Street [★MW,D,CW,DS,P,YC,WC] 144 N Wall St (at Spring St) **614/464-2800** *9pm-2:30am, from 10pm Wed, 8pm-midnight Th, clsd Mon-Tue*

Cafes

Cup-O-Joe Cafe [F] 627 3rd St (at Sycamore) **614/221-1563** *6am-10:30pm, till 11pm Fri-Sat, from 7am wknds, till 10pm Sun*

Restaurants

Banana Leaf 816 Bethel Rd **614/459-4101** *11:30am-9:30pm, vegetarian Indian*

Betty's [E] 680 N High St **614/228-6191** *11am-2am, plenty veggie, also bar*

Blue Nile 2361 N High St (at W Patterson) **614/421-2323** *lunch & dinner, clsd Mon, Ethopian*

Cap City Diner 1299 Olentangy River Rd **614/291-3663** *11am-10pm, till 11pm Fri-Sat, till 9pm Sun*

Dragonfly 247 King Ave **614/298-9986** *5pm-10pm Tue-Sat, Sat brunch, clsd Sun-Mon, upscale vegetarian, patio*

L'Antibes [WC,GO] 772 N High St #106 (at Warren) **614/291-1666** *dinner from 5pm, clsd Sun-Mon, French*

Lemongrass [★R] 641 N High (at Russell) **614/224-1414** *lunch weekdays & dinner nightly, Asian cuisine*

Northstar Cafe [★] 951 N High St (at W 2nd Ave) **614/298-9999** *9am-10pm, plenty veggie*

Surly Girl Saloon [E] 1126 N High St **614/294-4900** *11am-2am, plenty veggie, also bar*

Tip Top Kitchen [E] 73 E Gay St (at N 3rd) **614/221-8300** *11am-2am, plenty veggie, also bar*

Whole World Bakery & Restaurant 3269 N High St **614/268-5751** *11am-8pm, Sun brunch, clsd Mon, vegetarian & vegan*

Bookstores

The Book Loft of German Village 631 S 3rd St (at Sycamore) **614/464-1774** *10am-11pm, till midnight Fri-Sat, LGBT section*

Retail Shops

Hausfrau Haven 769 S 3rd St (at Columbus) **614/443-3680** *10am-7pm, noon-5pm Sun, cards, wine & gifts*

Piercology [GO] 190 W 2nd Ave **614/297-4743** *noon-8pm, 1pm-7pm Sun, body-piercing studio*

Schmidt's Fudge Haus 220 E Kossuth St (in Historic German Village) **614/444-2222** *noon-close, old fashioned fudge & candy, gifts*

Torso 772 N High St (at Warren) **614/421-7663** *11am-10pm, till 5pm Sun-Mon, clothing*

Publications

Gay People's Chronicle **216/631-8646** *Ohio's largest bi-weekly LGBT newspaper w/ extensive listings*

OUTlines Magazine **440/716-1495** *free bi-weekly club magazine covering Akron, Canton, Cleveland, Columbus, Dayton, Sandusky, Toledo & more*

Outlook Weekly **614/268-8525** *statewide LGBT weekly*

Men's Clubs

▶ **The Club Columbus** [SW] 795 W 5th Ave (at Olentangy Rd) **614/291-0049** *gym, steam, sauna*

Flex Columbus [MO,V,PC] 1567 E Livingston Ave (at Geers Ave) **614/252-0730** *24hrs, lounge, steam room, glory room, dungeon, dry sauna, guest memberships*

Men's Services

▶ **Megaphone** **614/888-7777** *Meet and Chat Live with HOT local men. FREE to listen & respond to ads. Video and text chat at GayMates.com. Use FREE code 4889.*

Erotica

The Garden 1174 N High St (btwn 4th & 5th Ave) **614/294-2869** *11am-3am, noon-midnight Sun, adult toys*

▶ **The Lion's Den Adult Superstore** 3015 Morse Rd (at Westerville Rd) **614/475-1943** *24hrs*

▶ **The Lion's Den Adult Superstore** 4315 Kimberly Pkwy (off Hamilton Rd) **614/861-6770** *24hrs*

▶ **The Lion's Den Adult Superstore** 4375 Roberts Rd (Exit 10, off I-270) **614/529-8501** *24hrs*

North Campus Video 2465 N High St (at Hudson) **614/268-4021** *24hrs*

Danville

Accommodations

The White Oak Inn [GF,WI,NS,WC] 29683 Walhonding Rd **740/599-6107, 877/908-5923**

Dayton

Info Lines & Services

AA Gay/ Lesbian 20 W 1st St (off Main, at Christ Episcopal Church) **937/222-2211** *8pm Sat*

Dayton Lesbian/ Gay Center 937/274-1776

Bars

Argos Bar [MO,NH,L,GO] 301 Mabel Ave (near Linden & I-35) **937/252-2976** *6pm-2:30am*

MJ's Cafe [M,D,F,K] 119 E 3rd St **937/223-3259** *3pm-2:30am, deck*

Stage Door [M,L,WC] 44 N Jefferson (at 2nd) **937/223-7418** *noon-2:30am, from 2pm Wed & wknds*

Nightclubs

Aquarius [MW,D,DS,WC] 135 E 2nd **937/223-1723** *5pm-2:30am*

L Room [W,D] 42 N. Jefferson St **937/223-7418**

Masque [★M,D,DS,S,18+] 34 N Jefferson St (btwn 2nd & 3rd) **937/228-2582** *7pm-2:30am, till 5am wknds*

Cafes

Signatures Gourmet Coffee [GO] 313 W Main St (Third St), Fairborn **937/878-1000** *7am-9pm, 9am-2pm Sat, clsd Sun, live music Fri*

Restaurants

Cold Beer & Cheeseburgers [WC] 33 S Jefferson St (at 4th St) **937/222-2337** *11am-close, clsd Sun, grill, full bar*

The Spaghetti Warehouse 36 W 5th St (at Ludlow) **937/461-3913** *11am-10pm, till 11pm Fri, noon-11pm Sat, more gay Tue w/ Friends of the Italian Opera*

Bookstores

Books & Co 350 E Stroop Rd (at Farhills) **937/298-6540** *9am-11pm, till 8pm Sun*

Retail Shops

Q Gift Shop 1904 N Main St (at Ridge Ave) **937/274-4400** *noon-7pm, till 9pm Fri, LGBT gifts & movies*

Publications

Gay Dayton 937/623-1590 *monthly LGBT publication*

Men's Services

▶ **Megaphone 937/395-9001** *Meet and Chat Live with HOT local men. FREE to listen & respond to ads. Video and text chat at GayMates.com. Use FREE code 4889.*

Erotica

Adult Total X [V] 6388 N Dixie Dr (at Needmore Ave) **937/454-9999** *24hrs*

Deja Vu Love Boutique 1267 N Keowee St (off I-75) **937/222-1212** *10am-3am, 24hrs Th-Sat, novelties, toys, DVDs, arcade*

Findlay

Erotica

Findlay Adult Books & Video 623 Trenton Ave (at I-75, exit 159) **419/422-1301** *24hrs*

Heath

Erotica

▶ **The Lion's Den Adult Superstore** 6762 Hebron Rd/ SR 79 (exit 129b, off I-70) **740/928-4404** *24hrs*

Jeffersonville

Erotica

▶ **The Lion's Den Adult Superstore** 9021 W Lancaster Rd NW (exit 65, off I-71) **740/948-2446** *24hrs*

Kent

Bars

The Zephyr Pub [GF,E,WC] 106 W Main St **330/678-4848** *3pm-close*

Lima

Nightclubs

Somewhere in Time [MW,D,DS,S] 804 W North St **419/227-7288** *7pm-2:30am, from 8pm wknds*

Logan

Accommodations

Glenlaurel—A Scottish Country Inn & Cottages [GS,NS,WC,GO] 14940 Mt Olive Rd (off State Rte I-80), Rockbridge **740/385-4070, 800/809-7378** *full brkfst, hot tub*

Inn & Spa at Cedar Falls [GS,NS,WI] 21190 State Rte 374 **740/385-7489, 800/653-2557**

Lazy Lane Cabins [GF,NS] **740/385-3475, 877/225-6572** *secluded cabins sleep 2-8, hot tubs, fireplaces, satellite TV*

Lorain

Bars

Tim's Place [MW,NH,D,DS,WC] 2223 Broadway (btwn 22nd & 23rd) **440/246-9002** *8pm-2:30am, clsd Mon, patio*

Nightclubs

La Sala [GS,D,F,K,MR] 939 Broadway **440/242-2622** *8pm-2am, clsd Sun-Tue*

Mansfield

Bars

The Gee Spot Dance Club [GS,D] 470 Newman St **419/524-0007** *6pm-close, from 4pm Wed-Th*

Marengo

Erotica

▶ **The Lion's Den Adult Superstore** 511 State Rte 61 (exit 140, off I-71) **419/253-5200** *24hrs*

Marietta

Accommodations

Fourth St B&B [GS,NS,GO] **614/638-1187**

Monroe

Bars

Old Street Saloon [MW,NH,D,K,DS] 13 Old St **513/539-9183** *8pm-2am Th-Sat, till 1am Wed, clsd Sun-Tue*

Niles

Erotica

Niles Books 5970 Youngstown Warren Rd (off Rte 46) **330/544-3755**

Oberlin

Accommodations

Hallauer House B&B [GF,SW,WI] 14945 Hallauer Rd **440/774-3400, 877/774-3406** *eco-friendly historic inn 3 miles S of Oberlin*

Cafes

Java Zone 5 W College St #A **440/774-5282** *8am-9pm, till 10pm Sat-Sun, coffee, also sandwiches*

Restaurants

The Feve Bar & Grill [★NS] 30 S Main St **440/774-1978** *11am-midnight, popular wknd brunch (9:30am-2:30pm), plenty veggie, full bar (5pm-2am)*

Weia Teia [BW] 9 S Main St **440/774-8880** *lunch & dinner, Thai/Asian fusion, upscale, some veggie*

Bookstores

MindFair Books 13 W College St (shares storefront w/ Ben Franklin) **440/774-6463** *9am-6pm, till 8pm Fri, noon-5pm Sun*

Oxford

Cruisy Areas

Hueston Woods State Park [AYOR] *mornings & at dusk*

Perrysville

Accommodations

Circle JJ Ranch [M,21+] 1104 Amsterdam Rd SE, Scio **330/627-3101** *open April-Oct, special events, theme wknds*

Pickerington

Cafes

Planet Coffee & Tea Coffee Company 1252 Hill Rd N **614/861-2040** *6am-10pm, till 11pm Fri-Sat, wknd hours vary*

Quaker City

Erotica

▶ **The Lion's Den Adult Superstore** 65799 Batesville Rd (exit 193, off I-70) **740/758-5210** *24hrs*

Sandusky

Nightclubs

Crowbar [MW,NH,D,K,GO] 206 W Market St (at Jackson St) **419/624-0109** *4pm-2:30am*

Xcentricities [MW,D,DS,S] 306 W Water St (at Jackson St) **419/624-8118** *6pm-2:30am, from 2pm wknds, patio*

Restaurants

Mona Pizza Gourmet [MR,TG,GO] 135 Columbus Ave (at Market St) **419/626-8166** *11am-3am*

Cruisy Areas

Boeckling Boat Dock [AYOR]

Springfield

Nightclubs

Chances [GF,D,E,K] 1912-14 Edwards Ave (at N Belmont Ave) **937/324-0383** *8:30pm-2:30am, clsd Tue, patio*

Why Not III 5 N Murray **937/324-9758** *9:30pm-2:30am, till 1am Sun-Tue*

Why Not III 5 N Murray **937/324-9758** *9:30pm-2:30am, till 1am Sun-Tue*

Cruisy Areas

Clarence J Brown Reservoir Beach [AYOR]

Steubenville

Bars

PJ's [MW,D,F,GO] 169 N 4th St **740/283-2747** *11am-2:30am*

Toledo

Info Lines & Services

AA Gay/ Lesbian 2272 Collingwood Blvd (at St Mark's Episcopal Church) **419/380-9862** *8pm Wed*

Accommodations

Hotel Seagate [GF,SW,WC] 141 N Summit St (at Jefferson) **419/242-8885, 866/744-5711**

Mansion View Inn [GF,NS] 2035 Collingwood Blvd **419/244-5676** *1887 Victorian near downtown in Historic Old West End*

Bars

Outskirts [W,D,K] 1515 W Laskey Rd (btwn Jackman & Lewis) **419/476-1577** *3pm-2:30am, till 3:30am Fri-Sat, clsd Sun-Tue*

R House [M,D] 5534 Secor Rd (btwn Laskey & Alexis) **419/474-2929** *4pm-2:30am, patio*

Rip Cord [M,NH,K,S] 115 N Erie (btwn Jefferson & Monroe) **419/243-3412** *9am-2:30am, Sun brunch*

Nightclubs

Bretz [MW,D,K,DS,S,18+,WC] 2012 Adams St **419/243-1900** *6pm-2:30am, till 4:30am Fri-Sat, clsd Mon-Tue, patio*

Caesar's Show Bar [MW,D,F,DS,WC] 725 Jefferson **419/241-5140** *1pm-2:30am*

Men's Clubs

Diplomat Health Club [PC] 1313 N Summit (along Maumee River) **419/255-3700** *24hrs*

Men's Services

▶ **Megaphone 419/873-3000** *Meet and Chat Live with HOT local men. FREE to listen & respond to ads. Video and text chat at GayMates.com. Use FREE code 4889.*

Van Buren

Erotica

▶ **The Lion's Den Adult Superstore** 11681 State Rte 613 (Exit 164, off I-75) **419/299-8080** *24hrs*

Warren

Nightclubs

Club 441 [MW,D,S,WC] 441 E Market St (enter rear) **330/394-9483** *4pm-2:30am, from 2pm wknds*

The Funky Skunk [M,D,DS,K] 143 E Market St *9pm-close*

West Lafayette

Restaurants

Lava Rock Grill at Unusual Junction [WC,GO] 56310 US Hwy 36 **740/545-9772** *'50s-style diner in restored railroad station*

Yellow Springs

Restaurants

Winds Cafe & Bakery [WC] 215 Xenia Ave **937/767-1144** *lunch & dinner, Sun brunch, clsd Mon, full bar*

Bookstores

Epic Bookshop & Mermaid Cafe **937/767-7997** *9am-6pm, till 9pm Th-Sat, till 5pm Sun, spiritual, also cafe*

Youngstown

Info Lines & Services

The Mahoning Valley Pride Center 15223 Poland Ave

Bars

Our Bar [MW,NH,D] 2105 South Ave **330/743-0473** *4pm-2am, clsd Sun*

Nightclubs

Split Level [MW,D,DS,K] 169 S Four Mile Run Rd (at S Mahoning Ave) **330/318-9830**

Utopia Video Nightclub [MW,D,DS] 876 E Midlothian Blvd **330/781-9000** *5pm-close, clsd Mon*

Oklahoma

Statewide

Publications

Metro Star **918/835-7887** *monthly LGBT news publication serving AR, KS, MO & OK*

Bartlesville

Cruisy Areas

Johnstone Park [AYOR]

Enid

Erotica

Patricia's 4810-A W Garriott (at Garland) **580/233-5511** *toys & more*

Grand Lake

Accommodations

Southern Oaks Resort & Spa [GF,SW,NS,GO] 2 miles S of Hwy 28/ 82 Junction, Langley **918/782-9346** *19 cabins on 30 acres, basketball court, sand volleyball, hiking trails*

Restaurants

The Artichoke Restaurant & Bar 35896 S Hwy 82, Langley **918/782-9855, 866/682-9855** *5pm-10pm, clsd Sun-Mon*

Frosty's & Edna's Cafe Highway 28, Langley **918/782-9123** *6am-10pm*

Lighthouse Supper Club Highway 85 & Main, Ketchum **918/782-3316** *from 5pm, clsd Sun-Tue*

Lawton

Bookstores

Ingrid's Books 1124 NW Cache Rd **580/353-1488** *10am-10pm, clsd Sun, also adult novelties, magazines*

Cruisy Areas

The Strip [AYOR] Fort Sill Blvd, near Cache Rd *by car*

Norman

see also Oklahoma City

Info Lines & Services

GLBTF at University of Oklahoma **405/325-4452**

Restaurants

La Luna Mexican Cafe 529 Buchanan Ave (on historic Campus Corner) **405/329-9596** *11am-9pm, 11am-9:30pm Fri-Sat, clsd Sun, full cantina & bar*

Bookstores

Borders Books 300 Norman Center Ct **405/573-4907** *9am-11pm, 10am-10pm Sun, LGBT section*

Oklahoma City

see also Edmond & Norman

Info Lines & Services

AA Live & Let Live 3405 N Villa **405/947-3834**

YGLA (Young Gay/ Lesbian Alliance) 2242 NW 39th (at Red Rock North) **405/ 525-5165 , 405/524-6500** *drop-in testing 9am-5pm Mon-Th, till 4pm Fri, support group & more for LGBT youth (ages 13-20) 6pm-10pm Th*

Accommodations

Days Inn Oklahoma City Northwest [GF,SW,WI] 2801 NW 39th St (at I-44 & May Ave, Exit 124) **405/946-0741**

▶ **Habana Inn** [★MW,SW,NS,WC] 2200 NW 39th St (at Youngs) **405/528-2221, 800/988-2221 (reservations only)** *gay resort, also 3 bars, restaurant, gift shop*

Hawthorn Suites [GF,SW] 1600 NW Expy (Richmond Square) **405/840-1440, 800/527-1133 (reservations)** *all suites, full brkfst*

Waterford Marriott [GF,SW,NS,WI] 6300 Waterford Blvd **405/848-4782, 800/228-9290** *boutique hotel, also restaurant & bar*

Bars

Alibi's [GS,NH,TG,K,GO] 1200 N Pennsylvania (at NW 11th) **405/605-3795** *3pm-2am, from noon wknds*

Bearz 3020 [GS,NH,K] 3020 N Pennsylvania (at NW 29th St) **405/524-9306** *2pm-2am, [K] Th & Sun*

The Boom [MW,NH,K,DS,S,WI,WC] 2218 NW 39th St (at Penn) **405/601-7200** *11am-2am, clsd Mon*

▶ **The Finishline** [MW,NH,D,CW,WC] at Habana Inn **405/525-2900** *noon-2am, poolside bar*

Hi-Lo Club [MW,NH,D,E,DS] 1221 NW 50th St (btwn Western & Classen) **405/843-1722** *noon-2am, live bands weekly*

▶ **The Ledo** [MW,F,K,NS,WC] at Habana Inn **405/525-0730** *4pm-10:30pm, till 2am Fri-Sat, martini lounge*

Phoenix Rising [M,NH,D,CW,B,L,GO] 2120 NW 39th St (at Pennsylvania Ave) **405/601-3711** *4pm-2am, from 2pm Sun, patio*

Tramps [★M,D,S,WC] 2201 NW 39th St (at Barnes) **405/521-9888** *noon-2am, from 10am wknds*

Nightclubs

Angles [MW,D] 2117 NW 39th St **405/524-3431** *Fri-Sat only*

▶ **The Copa** [★MW,D,E,DS,K,S,WC] at Habana Inn **405/525-0730** *9pm-2am, clsd Mon, theme nights, male dancers Fri-Sat*

The Park [M,D,S,V,WC] 2125 NW 39th St (at Barnes/ Pennsylvania) **405/528-4690** *5pm-2am, from 3pm Sun (free buffet), patio, cruisy*

Wreck Room [★MW,D,DS,S,YC] 2127 NW 39th St (at Pennsylvania) **405/525-7610** *10pm-close Fri-Sat only, [18+] after 1am*

Cafes

The Red Cup [F,E,NS,WI] 3122 N Classen Blvd (at NW 30th St) **405/525-3430** *7am-5pm, till 10pm Th-Fri, 9am-10pm Sat, till 5pm Sun, coffeehouse, also sandwiches*

Restaurants

Bricktown Brewery Restaurant 1 N Oklahoma Ave (at Sheridan) **405/232-2739** *11am-10pm, till midnight Sat, from noon Sun, full bar*

Cheever's Cafe [R] 2409 N Hudson Ave (at NW 23rd) **405/525-7007** *11am-9:30pm, 5pm-10:30pm Sat, brunch Sun*

Earl's Rib Palace 216 Johnny Bench Dr, Ste BBQ (in Bricktown) **405/272-9898** *11am-9pm, till 10pm Fri-Sat, noon-8pm Sun, several locations in OKC*

▶ **Gusher's** [WC] at Habana Inn **405/525-0730** *11am-10:30pm, from 9am wknds, till 3:30am Fri-Sat (after-hours brkfst)*

Iguana Bar & Grill 9 NW 9th St (at N Santa Fe Ave) **405/606-7172** *lunch & dinner, Mexican*

Ingrid's Kitchen 3701 N Youngs (btwn Penn & May, on NW 36th) **405/946-8444** *7am-8pm, till 6:30pm Mon 10am-2pm Sun, German/ American bakery & deli*

La Luna Mexican Cafe 409 W Reno Ave (at Walker) **405/235-9596** *full bar*

Rococo Restaurant & Fine Wine 2824 N Pennsylvania (at NW 27th St) **405/528-2824** *lunch Mon-Fri, dinner nightly, Sun jazz brunch, full bar*

Someplace Else Deli & Bakery [★] 2310 N Western Ave **405/524-0887** *7am-6:30pm, 9:30am-4pm Sat, clsd Sun*

Sushi Neko 4318 N Western (btwn 42nd & 43rd) **405/528-8862** *11am-11pm, clsd Sun*

Entertainment & Recreation

Carpenter Square Theater 400 W Sheridan (at Stage Center) **405/232-6500** *occasional gay-themed material*

First Friday Gallery Walk from 28th at N Walker to 30th at N Dewey **405/525-2688** *open tour of Paseo Arts District galleries, first Fri & Sat*

Bookstores

Full Circle Bookstore [F] 50 Penn Pl, 1900 NW Expwy (in NE corner of 1st level) **405/842-2900, 800/683-7323** *10am-9pm, noon-5pm Sun, also cafe & coffee bar*

Nature's Treasures 6223 SE 15th St (btwn Sooner & Air Depot Blvd), Midwest City **405/741-4322** *10am-7pm, from noon Sun, New Age books*

Retail Shops

23rd St Body Piercing 411 NW 23rd St (btwn Hudson & Walker) **405/524-6824** *noon-9pm, 1pm-6pm Sun*

▶ **Jungle Red** [WC] at Habana Inn **405/524-5733** *novelties, leather, gifts*

Publications

Oklahoma Gazette 405/528-6000 *"Metro OKC's independent weekly"*

Standout Magazine [GO] **405/473-7891**

Men's Services

▶ **Megaphone 405/524-3838** *Meet and Chat Live with HOT local men. FREE to listen & respond to ads. Video and text chat at GayMates.com. Use FREE code 4889.*

Erotica

Christie's Toy Box 2904 S Perdue **877/684-2226** *multiple locations in OKC*

Naughty & Nice 3121 SW 29th St (at I-44) **405/681-5044** *24hrs*

Priscilla's 615 E Memorial **405/755-8600**

Cruisy Areas

Trosper Park [AYOR] *beware cops (!)*

Tulsa

Info Lines & Services

Dennis R Neill Equality Center [WC] 621 E 4th St (at Kenosha) **918/743-4297** *3pm-9pm, clsd Sun, also Pride store*

Gay/ Lesbian AA 2545 S Yale Ave (at Community of Hope) **918/627-2224** *7pm Mon, Wed & Fri, 5:30pm Sat*

Openarms Youth Project 2015-B S Lakewood Ave **918/838-7104** *social events, support groups, HIV testing*

Youth Services Tulsa [WI] 311 S Madison **918/582-0061** *6pm-8pm Tue youth group meeting, activity center, coffeeshop, [GS] shows Sat*

Accommodations

Crowne Plaza [GF,F,SW,WI,WC] 100 E Second St (at 2nd St) **918/582-9000, 800/980-6429**

Holiday Inn Select [GF,SW,WC] 5000 East Skelly Dr (at I-44 & Yale Ave) **918/622-7000, 800/836-9635** *kids/ pets ok*

Bars

Bamboo Lounge [M,NH,D,K,S,WC] 7204 E Pine **918/836-8700** *noon-2am*

Club 209 [GS,NS] 209 N Boulder Ave (at Brady) **918/584-9944** *5pm-2am, till midnight Sun, clsd Mon-Wed*

End Up [M,S] 5336 E Admiral Pl **918/836-0915** *4pm-2am*

New Age Renegade [MW,NH,K,C,S] 1649 S Main St (at 17th) **918/585-3405** *4pm-2am, patio*

Steve's Hideaway Lounge [M,E] 11730 E 11th St (at I-44) **918/437-0449** *2pm-2am*

Tulsa Eagle [★M,NH,K,L,WI,WC] 1338 E 3rd (at Peoria) **918/592-1188** *2pm-2am*

The Yellow Brick Road [MW,NH,WC] 2630 E 15th (at Harvard) **918/293-0304** *1pm-2am*

Nightclubs

Club Majestic [MW,D,DS,TG,YC,WC,GO] 124 N Boston (at Brady) **918/584-9494** *9pm-2am Th-Sun, drag shows Th & Sun*

Club Maverick [MW,D,CW,K] 822 S Sheridan (at 9th) **918/835-3301** *4pm-2am*

Cafes

Gypsy's Coffee House 303 N Cincinnati Ave **918/295-2181** *11am-midnight, till 3am Fri-Sat, clsd Mon*

Restaurants

White Lion Pub 6927 S Canton Ave (off 71st) **918/491-6533** *4pm-10pm, clsd Sun-Mon, British-style pub*

Wild Fork [WC] 1820 Utica Square **918/742-0712** *7am-10pm, clsd Sun*

Entertainment & Recreation

Council Oak Men's Chorale **918/748-3888**

Gilcrease Museum 1400 N Gilcrease Museum Rd **918/596-2700, 888/655-2278** *one of the best collections of Native American & cowboy art in the US*

Nightingale Theater 1416 E 4th St (at Quincy) **918/633-8666** *savvy, unconventional productions by the Midwestern Theater Troupe*

Philbrook Museum of Art 2727 S Rockford Rd (1 block E of Peoria, at end of 27th St) **918/324-7941** *clsd Mon, Italian villa built in the '20s oil boom complete w/ kitschy lighted dance flr, the gardens are a must in spring & summer*

Retail Shops

Brookside Piercing & Tattoo 3314 S Peoria **918/712-1122** *noon-10pm, till midnight Fri-Sat*

Publications

Urban Tulsa Weekly **918/592-5550** *"Tulsa Metro's only independent newsweekly"*

Men's Services

▶ **Megaphone** **918/663-2700** *Meet and Chat Live with HOT local men. FREE to listen & respond to ads. Video and text chat at GayMates.com. Use FREE code 4889.*

Erotica

Midtown Superstore 319 E 3rd St (at Elgin) **918/584-3112** *24hrs*

Oregon

Statewide

Publications

Just Out **503/236-1252** *LGBT newspaper w/ resource directory*

Arch Cape

Accommodations

Inn at Arch Cape [GS,NS,WI] 79340 Hwy 101 **503/738-7373, 800/352-8034** *'30s-style retreat, kitchens in all rooms, near beach & arts community*

Ashland

Info Lines & Services

The Abdill-Ellis Lambda Community Center 208 Oak St, Ste 112 **541/488-6990** *3pm-6pm, clsd wknds, meetings, events, library*

Gay/ Lesbian AA 208 Oak St #112 (at Old Armory) **541/732-1850** *6:30pm Mon*

Accommodations

The Arden Forest Inn [GS,NS,SW,WI,WC,GO] 261 W Hersey St **541/488-1496, 800/460-3912** *full brkfst*

Ashland Creek Inn [GF,NS,GO] 70 Water St **541/482-3315** *secluded forest location minutes to downtown Ashland, kitchens in all suites, multi-course gourmet brkfst*

Blue Moon B&B [GF,NS,WI,GO] 312 Helman St (at Hersey) **541/482-9228, 800/460-5453** *full brkfst*

Country Willows Inn [GF,SW,NS,WI,WC] 1313 Clay St **541/488-1590, 800/945-5697** *full brkfst, jacuzzi*

Lithia Springs Inn [GS,NS,WI] 2165 W Jackson Rd **541/482-7128, 800/482-7128** *full brkfst, natural hot-springs-fed whirlpools*

Romeo Inn B&B [GF,SW,NS,WI] 295 Idaho St **541/488-0884, 800/915-8899** *full brkfst, jacuzzi*

Cafes

Ashland Bakery/ Cafe [WC] 38 E Main **541/482-2117** *8am-3pm, also dinner from 5pm Wed-Sun*

Restaurants

The Black Sheep [NS] 51 N Main St (on the Plaza) **541/482-6414** *11:30am-1am, eclectic pub fare*

Geppetto's [WC] 345 E Main **541/482-1138** *8am-midnight, Italian, full bar*

Greenleaf Restaurant [BW] 49 N Main St (on The Plaza) **541/482-2808** *8am-8pm, creekside dining*

Bookstores

Bloomsbury Books 290 E Main St (btwn 1st & 2nd) **541/488-0029** *8am-10pm, from 9am Sat, 10am-9pm Sun*

Retail Shops

Travel Essentials 252 E Main St **541/482-7383, 800/258-0758** *10am-5:30pm, 11am-4pm Sun, luggage, books, accessories*

Cruisy Areas

Keno Rock Quarry *take Dead Indian Memorial Rd past Howard Prairie Lake to mile marker 18, turn right at Keno Rd, when you see pile of gravel on your left, turn right into quarry*

Astoria

Accommodations

Rosebriar B&B [GF] 636 14th St **503/325-7427, 800/487-0224** *upscale classic inn in former convent, full brkfst*

Beaverton

Restaurants

Swagat Indian Cuisine [BW] 4325 SW 109th Ave **503/626-3000** *lunch & dinner*

Bend

Accommodations

Dawson House Lodge [GF,NS,WI,GO] 109455 Hwy 97 N, Chemult **541/365-2232, 888/281-8375** *rustic inn w/ modern amenities, near Crater Lake*

Restaurants

Blacksmith Restaurant 211 NW Greenwood Ave **541/318-0588** *5:30pm-close, new American, upscale*

Cruisy Areas

Drake Park [AYOR] Riverside Dr *clsd winter*

Sawyer Park [AYOR] *evenings*

Corvallis

Bookstores

Book Bin 215 SW 4th St **541/752-0040** *8am-9pm, till 10pm Fri-Sat, 9am-7pm Sun*

Grass Roots Bookstore [WC] 227 SW 2nd St (btwn Jefferson & Madison) **541/754-7668** *9:30am-6pm, till 9pm Fri, 10am-5:30pm Sat, noon-5pm Sun, music section, espresso bar*

Cruisy Areas

Willamette Park Beach [N,AYOR] N of Willamette Park

Depoe Bay

Accommodations

Harbor Lights [GF,NS,WI,WC] 235 SE Bayview Ave **541/765-2322, 800/228-0448** *right on marina, also restaurant & bar*

Eugene

Info Lines & Services

Gay/ Lesbian AA [GS] 1414 Kincaid (at Koinonia Center) **541/342-4113** *7pm Wed, 8pm Fri*

LGBTQ Alliance [WC] **541/346-3360** *9am-5pm, various drop-in groups*

Accommodations

C'est La Vie Inn [GF,NS,WI] 1960 Willamette St **541/302-3014, 866/302-3014** *full brkfst*

Bars

Sam's Place Tavern [GF,NH,D,F,K,GO] 825 Wilson St (at 11th St W) **541/484-4455** *11am-2:30am, from 9am wknds, till midnight Sun*

Nightclubs

Diablo's Downtown Lounge [GF,D,F] 959 Pearl St **541/343-2346** *[K] Sun, open mic Tue, theme nights*

Cafes

Eugene Coffee Company [GO] 1840 Chambers (at 18th) **541/344-0002** *7am-6pm*

Restaurants

Glenwood Restaurant 1340 Alder St (at 13th St) **541/687-0355** *7am-10pm*

Keystone Cafe 395 W 5th (at Lawrence) **541/342-2075** *7am-2pm, till 3pm Fri-Sat, popular brkfst*

Retail Shops

High Priestess Piercing 675 Lincoln St (at 7th St) **541/342-6585** *11am-8pm, 11am-9pm Fri-Sat, piercing studio*

Erotica

Exclusively Adult 1166 South A St (at 10th St), Springfield **541/726-6969** *24hrs*

Cruisy Areas

Skinner Butte Park [AYOR]

Willamette River Beach [AYOR] on the Coast Fork *take 30th Ave, exit E off I-5, turn left at stop sign, right at Texaco station & park past the recycling center, then follow paths to paved road to beach*

Grants Pass

Cafes

Sunshine Natural Foods Cafe 128 SW H St (btwn 5th & 6th Sts) **541/474-5044** *9am-6pm, 9:30am-5pm Sat, clsd Sun*

Jacksonville

Accommodations

The TouVelle House [GF,SW,NS,WI] 455 N Oregon St (at E St) **541/899-8938, 800/846-8422** *1916 Craftsman on 1 1/2 acres*

Joseph

Accommodations

The Bronze Antler B&B [GF,NS,WI] 309 S Main **541/432-0230, 866/520-9769** *in 1925 Craftsman bungalow, mtn views, cat on premises*

Klamath Falls

Accommodations

Crystal Wood Lodge [GO] 38625 Westside Road **541/381-2322, 866/381-2322**

Cruisy Areas

Haglestein Park [AYOR] Hwy 97 (about 10 miles N of town, past Klamath Lake)

Moore Park [AYOR] *summers*

Lincoln City

Accommodations

Ashley Inn [GF,SW WI] 3430 NE Hwy 101 **541/996-7500, 888/427-4539**

A Vista D' Mar [GS,NS] 1421 NW Harbor **541/994-6300, 866/776-8659** *kitchens, beach access*

Restaurants

Dory Cove Restaurant [BW] 2981 SW Hwy 101 **541/557-4000** *11:30am-9pm, steak & seafood*

Mist Restaurant 2945 NW Jetty Ave **541/994-3877** *7am-9pm*

Medford

Erotica

Castle Megastore 1113 Progress Dr (at Bittle) **541/608-9540**

Cruisy Areas

Jackson County Sports Park [AYOR]

Touvelle Park [AYOR] along Rogue River

Newport

Accommodations

Cliff House B&B [GF,NS,WI] **541/563-2506** *oceanfront, full brkfst, hot tub, great view*

Restaurants

Mo's Annex [E] 657 SW Bay Blvd **541/265-7512** *11am-9pm, great chowder, live music*

Cruisy Areas

Yaquina Bay State Park [AYOR] off Hwy 101 (at N end of Yaquina Bay Bridge)

North Bend

Erotica

The Back Door [GO] 1754 Union Ave, Ste C (btwn Connecticut St & Montana St) **541/756-6477** *upscale adult bookstore & billiard supplies, arcades*

Ontario

Bookstores

Proud Mary's [GO] 31 SW 3rd Ave **541/889-4711** *10am-6pm, clsd Sun-Mon, LGBT*

Cruisy Areas

Ontario State Park [AYOR] on the Snake River

Parkdale

Accommodations

Old Parkdale Inn [GF,NS,WI] 4932 Baseline Rd **541/352-5551, 877/687-4669**

Portland

see also Vancouver, Washington

Info Lines & Services

Live & Let Live Club 1210 SE 7th **503/238-6091** *12-step meetings*

Q Center 69 SE Taylor **503/234-7837** *4pm-8pm Mon-Wed, 1pm-5pm Sun, LGBTQ community center*

Sexual Minority Youth Resource Center (SMYRC) 2100 SE Belmont **503/872-9664** *4pm-9pm Wed, Fri-Sat, drop-in center for LGBTQ youth*

Accommodations

The Ace Hotel [GS,NS,WI,WC] 1022 SW Stark St (at 11th) **503/228-2277** *hip hotel for "cultural influencers & opinion leaders on a budget"*

Forest Springs B&B [GS,NS,GO] 3680 SW Towle Ave, Gresham **503/674-8992, 877/674-9282** *full brkfst*

Hotel Deluxe [GF] 729 SW 15th Ave **503/219-2094, 866/895-2094**

Hotel Monaco Portland [GF,WI] 506 SW Washington (at 5th Ave) **503/222-0001, 888/207-2201** *also restaurant, gym*

Hotel Vintage Plaza [★GF,WI,WC] 422 SW Broadway **503/228-1212, 800/263-2305** *upscale, also restaurant*

Jupiter Hotel [★GF,NS,WI,WC] 800 E Burnside **503/230-9200, 877/800-0004** *boutique, also restaurant & lounge (7am-4am daily)*

The Kinley Manor Coach House [GS,NS,WI,GO] 924 NE Schuyler **503/249-7270** *rental home, fully equipped kitchen, laundry facilities, no partiers*

The Lion & the Rose [GS,NS,WI,GO] 1810 NE 15th Ave **503/287-9245, 800/955-1647** *in 1906 Queen Anne mansion*

The Mark Spencer Hotel [GF,NS] 409 SW Eleventh Ave (near Stark) **503/224-3293, 800/548-3934**

Painted Lady Inn [GS,NS] 1744 NE Clackamas St (at 17th) **503/331-1104**

Portland's White House B&B [GS,NS,WI,GO] 1914 NE 22nd Ave **503/287-7131, 800/272-7131** *in 1911 Greek Revival mansion*

Sheraton Portland Airport Hotel [GF,SW,NS,WI,WC] 82335 NE Airport Wy (at 82nd Ave) **503/335-2857, 800/743-7286**

Bars

Boxxes [★M,D,K,V,WI,WC] 1035 SW Stark (at SW 11th Ave) **503/226-4171** *5pm-close, also Brig [MW,D], also Red Cap Garage*

Candlelight Cafe & Bar [GF,F,E] 2032 SW 5th (at Lincoln) **503/222-3378** *11am-2:30am, live blues*

CC Slaughter's [★M,D,CW,F,K,V,WI,WC] 219 NW Davis (at 3rd) **503/248-9135, 888/348-9135** *3pm-2am, [K] Tue, also martini lounge, Bear Night 4th Fri*

Chopsticks Express II [GS,F,K,YC,WC] 2651 E Burnside St (at SE 26th) **503/234-6171** *11am-2am, karaoke*

Crush [GS,F] 1400 SE Morrison (at SE 14th) **503/235-8150** *4:30pm-2am, from 6pm Sat, 9am-midnight Sun, clsd Mon, wine & martini bar*

Darcelle XV [GS,D,F,C,DS,S,WC] 208 NW 3rd Ave (at NW Davis St) **503/222-5338** *6pm-11pm, till 2am Fri-Sat, clsd Sun-Tue*

Dirty Duck Tavern [M,NH,B,L,OC,BW,WC] 439 NW 3rd (at Glisan) **503/224-8446** *3pm-1am, 2pm-2am Fri, 3pm-2am Sat, noon-1am Sun, "home of the bears," hanky night & leather social 1st & 3rd Fri*

Doug Fir [★GF,F,E] 830 E Burnside (at NE 9th) **503/231-9663** *7am-3am, hipster log cabin lounge, also restaurant, live music*

Eagle PDX [M,L,V,WC] 610 NW Couch (at 6th, downstairs at Casey's) **503/224-9062** *8pm-2am Wed-Sat*

Eagle Portland [M,B,L,N] 835 N Lombard (at Albina) **503/283-9734** *11am-2:30am*

Flirt [★M,D,MR-AF,V,WC] 1035 SW Stark (at SW 11th Ave, at Boxxes) **503/226-4171** *9pm Tue, hip-hop*

Fox & Hound [★M,WC] 217 NW 2nd Ave (btwn Everett & Davis) **503/243-5530** *11am-2am, also restaurant, brunch wknds*

JOQ's Tavern [M,NH,F,WC] 2512 NE Broadway (at NE 24th Ave) **503/287-4210** *11am-2am*

Moonstar [GS,D] 7410 NE Martin Luther King Jr Blvd (btwn NE Knott & NE Graham) **503/285-1230** *11am-1:30am*

Northbank [MW,D,DS,F,K,NS,WC] 106 W 6th St (at Main), Vancouver, WA **360/695-3862** *2pm-2am*

Rotture [GF,F,E] 315 SE 3rd Ave **503/234-5683** *8pm-2:30am, live music venue, also restaurant*

Scandals Tavern [M,NH,F,WC,GO] 1125 SW Stark St (at 12th) **503/227-5887** *noon-2am, friendly bar*

Silverado [★M,D,F,K,S,WC,GO] 318 SW 3rd Ave (at Stark St) **503/224-4493** *9am-2:30am, strippers*

Starky's [★MW,NH,F,WC] 2913 SE Stark St (at SE 29th Ave) **503/230-7980** *11am-2am, also restaurant, Sun brunch, patio*

Vault Martini Bar [GS,F] 226 NW 12th Ave **503/224-4909** *4pm-1am, till 2am Th-Sat, 1pm-10pm Sun, full menu*

Vino Vixens [GS,NS] 2929 SE Powell Blvd **503/231-8466** *"Portland's first rock 'n' roll wine shop," retail & lounge, clsd Sun-Mon*

Zaytoon [GS,F,GO] 2236 NE Alberta (at 23rd) **503/284-1168** *5pm-1am, till 2:30am Fri-Sat, lesbian-owned*

Nightclubs

Casey's [MW,D,S] 610 NW Couch (at 6th) **503/224-9062** *7am-2:30am*

Delicious [MW,D] 205 NW 4th Ave (at Davis, at Crown Room) **503/222-6655** *10m Th only*

Embers [★M,D,F,DS,WC] 110 NW Broadway (at NW Couch St) **503/222-3082** *9am-3am, also restaurant*

Escape [MW,D] 333 SW Park (btwn SW Oak & SW Stark) **503/227-0830** *10:30pm-close Fri-Sat only, Portland's only all-ages gay club*

Holocene [GS,D,E,DS] 1001 SE Morrison (at E 10th) **503/239-7639** *many gay theme nights*

Pop Tart [W,D,MR] 1001 SE Morrison (at SE 10th Ave, at Holocene) **503/239-7639** *7pm 2nd Sun*

Cafes

Black Sheep Bakery [GO] 833 SE Main St **503/235-1419, 877/238-3426** *8am-3pm, clsd Sat-Sun*

Blend [WI] 2327 E Burnside **503/234-8610** *7am-6pm, from 8am Sun*

Bread & Ink Cafe [★BW,WC] 3610 SE Hawthorne Blvd (at 36th) **503/239-4756** *brkfst, lunch & dinner, packed for brunch on Sun*

Cup & Saucer Cafe [★F,NS] 3566 SE Hawthorne Blvd (btwn 34th & 36th) **503/236-6001** *7am-9pm, full menu, some veggie*

Elephant's Delicatessan 115 NW 22nd Ave **503/299-6304** *7am-7:30pm, 9:30am-6:30pm Sun, deli, desserts, coffee*

Half & Half [GS] 923 SW Oak St **503/222-4495** *7:30am-7:30pm, from 8am Sat, 8am-6pm Sun*

Haven Coffee [W,E,WI,WC,GO] 3551 SE Division St **503/236-6890** *7:30am-6pm*

Marco's Cafe & Espresso Bar [F] 7910 SW 35th (at Multnomah Blvd), Multnomah **503/245-0199** *7am-9pm, from 8am Sat, 8am-2pm Sun*

Mountain Village Coffee & Tea House [E,BW,GO] 445 NE 70th Ave **503/262-7613** *7am-10pm, 8am-midnight wknds, outdoor garden, community resource room*

The Pied Cow [WC] 3244 SE Belmont (at 33rd Ave) **503/230-4866** *4pm-midnight, till 1am Fri, noon-1am Sat, till midnight Sun, funky Victorian, great desserts, patio*

Pix Pâtisserie 3402 SE Division St **503/232-4407** *10am-midnight, till 2am Fri-Sat, dessert*

Three Friends Coffeehouse [WI] 201 SE 12th Ave (at Ash) **503/236-6411** *7am-10pm, from 8am Sun*

Voodoo Doughnut 22 SW 3rd Ave **503/241-4704** *24hrs, clsd 2pm Sun-6am Mon*

Restaurants

The Adobe Rose [BW] 1634 SE Bybee Blvd (at Milwaukee) **503/235-9114** *lunch & dinner, clsd Sun-Mon, New Mexican cuisine*

Andina 1314 NW Glisan St **503/228-9535** *lunch, dinner & tapas, Peruvian, full bar*

Aura Restaurant & Lounge [D,WC] 1022 W Burnside St (btwn SW 10th & 11th) **503/597-2872** *4:30pm-midnight, till 2:30am Fri-Sat, clsd Sun-Mon, also bar*

Bastas Trattoria 410 NW 21st (at Flanders) **503/274-1572** *dinner nightly, northern Italian, full bar till late*

Berbati's Pan [E] 19 SW 2nd Ave (btwn Burnside & Ankeny) **503/226-2122** *11am-2am, from 5pm Sun-Mon, Greek, full bar, live music venue*

Besaw's 2301 NW Savier (at NW 23rd) **503/228-2619** *7am-10pm Tue-Fri, from 8am Sat, 8am-3pm Sun-Mon, American*

Bijou Cafe [★WC] 132 SW 3rd Ave (at Pine St) **503/222-3187** *7am-2pm, from 8am wknds*

Bluehour [WC] 250 NW 13th Ave (at NW Everett St) **503/226-3394** *lunch Sun-Fri, dinner nightly, Sun brunch, extensive wine list*

Chameleon [MW] 2000 NE 40th Ave **503/460-2682** *5:30pm-9:30pm, lounge open later Fri-Sat, clsd Sun-Mon, Asian fusion, patio*

Daily Cafe in the Pearl 902 NW 13th Ave (at Kearney St) **503/242-1916** *7am-5pm, till 9pm Wed-Fri, 9am-9pm Sat, 9am-2pm Sun, Northwest cuisine*

Delta [WC] 4607 SE Woodstock (at 46th) **503/771-3101** *5pm-midnight, bar till 1am Fri-Sat, Southern*

Dingo's Mexican Grill [★GO] 4612 SE Hawthorne Blvd (at SE 39th) **503/233-3996** *noon-10pm, till 11pm Th, till 9pm Sun*

Dot's Cafe [★WC] 2521 SE Clinton (at 26th) **503/235-0203** *noon-2am, full bar*

Equinox 830 N Shaver St **503/460-3333** *dinner, brunch wknds, clsd Mon, int'l, patio*

Esparza's Tex-Mex Cafe [★] 2725 SE Ankeny St (at 28th) **503/234-7909** *11:30am-10pm, clsd Sun, funky*

Farm Cafe 10 SE 7th Ave (at E Burnside St) **503/736-3276** *5pm-11pm, Northwest cuisine*

Fish Grotto [★E,P,WC] 1035 SW Stark (at SW 11th Ave, at Boxxes) **503/226-4171** *5pm-10pm, till 9pm Sun-Mon, full bar*

Genies Cafe 1101 SE Division St **503/445-9777** *8am-3pm, brunch, house-infused vodkas*

Gypsy Restaurant & Lounge [K,WC] 625 NW 21st (btwn Hoyt & Irving) **503/796-1859** *4pm-2:30am, full bar, inexpensive*

Hobo's [GS,P,WC] 120 NW 3rd Ave (btwn Davis & Couch) **503/224-3285** *4pm-2:30am, piano bar, also restaurant*

Le Happy 1011 NW 16th Ave **503/226-1258** *5pm-1am, till 2:30am Fri, 6pm-2:30am Sat, clsd Sun, crêpes*

Mama Mia Trattoria 439 W 2nd Ave **503/295-6464** *lunch & dinner*

Masu [WI] 406 SW 13th Ave **503/221-6278** *dinner only, sushi*

Mayas Taqueria 1000 SW Morrison **503/226-1946** *11am-10pm, till 8pm Sun*

Mint [GO] 816 N Russell St **503/284-5518** *4pm-10pm, till 11pm Fri-Sat, fusion food, also 820 Lounge*

Montage [★WC] 301 SE Morrison **503/234-1324** *lunch Tue-Fri, dinner till 2am, till 4am Fri-Sat, Louisiana-style cookin', full bar*

Mother's Bistro & Bar 212 SW Stark St (at 2nd Ave) **503/464-1122** *brkfst, lunch & dinner, clsd Mon, American*

Nicholas' 318 SE Grand **503/235-5123** *11am-9pm, from noon Sun, Middle Eastern*

Noble Rot [BW] 1111 E Burnside St **503/233-1999** *5pm-midnight, clsd Sun, small plates, also wine bar*

Nostrana 1401 SE Morrison **503/234-2427** *lunch Mon-Fri, dinner nightly; fresh, local, wood-fired Italian*

Old Town Pizza 226 NW Davis **503/222-9999** *11:30am-11pm, till midnight Fri-Sat, clsd Sun, above Shanghai Tunnels, supposedly home to 100-year-old ghost*

Old Wives Tales [★BW,WC] 1300 E Burnside St (at 13th) **503/238-0470** *8am-9pm, till 10pm Fri-Sat, multi-ethnic vegetarian*

The Original Pancake House [★] 8600 SW 24th Ave **503/246-9007** *7am-3pm, clsd Mon-Tue, crowded on wknds*

Paley's Place 1204 NW 21st Ave (at NW Northrup St) **503/243-2403** *dinner nightly, Northwest cuisine*

Papa Haydn [R] 701 NW 23rd Ave (at NW Irving) **503/228-7317** *11am-9:30pm, till midnight Fri-Sat, 10am-10pm Sun, bistro, full bar; also at 5839 SE Milwaukee, 503/232-9440*

Paradox Cafe [★] 3439 SE Belmont **503/232-7508** *brkfst, lunch & dinner, vegetarian diner, killer Reuben*

Pizzacato [★BW] 505 NW 23rd (at Glisan) **503/242-0023** *11:30am-9pm, till 10pm Fri-Sat, many locations*

Pour 2755 NE Broadway **503/288-7687** *4:30pm-11pm, till close Fri-Sat, clsd Sun, wine bar & bistro*

Roux 1700 N Killingsworth St **503/285-1200** *dinner nightly, Sun brunch, New Orleans-inspired cuisine*

The Roxy [★MW,WC] 1121 SW Stark St (btwn 11th & 12th) **503/223-9160** *24hrs, clsd Mon, retro American diner*

Santa Fe Taqueria [★] 831 NW 23rd (at Kearney) **503/220-0406** *11am-midnight*

Saucebox [MW,D,WC,GO] 214 SW Broadway (at SW Oak) **503/241-3393** *5pm-close, clsd Sun-Mon, pan-Asian, full bar*

Under Wonder Lounge [GS,TG,DS,NS,GO] 128 NE Russell **503/493-0371** *5pm-midnight, open show nights only, full bar*

Vino Paradiso Wine Bar & Bistro [NS,BW,GO] 417 NW 10th Ave (btwn NW Glisan & Flanders) **503/295-9536** *4pm-11pm, 3pm-9pm Sun, clsd Mon, owned by Timothy Nishimoto of Pink Martini*

Vista Spring Cafe [BW,WC] 2440 SW Vista (at Spring) **503/222-2811** *11am-9:30pm, from noon wknds, till 9pm Sun*

Vita Cafe 3024 NE Alberta St **503/335-8233** *brkfst, lunch & dinner, mostly vegetarian, some free-range meat*

West Cafe 1201 SW Jefferson St (12th Ave) **503/227-8189** *lunch Mon-Fri, dinner nightly, Sun brunch, "comfort food w/ a twist"*

Wildwood [★R] 1221 NW 21st Ave (at Overton) **503/248-9663** *lunch Mon-Fri, dinner nightly, full bar, upscale*

Yakuza Lounge 5411 NE 30th Ave (at Killingsworth) **503/450-0893** *5pm-close, clsd Mon-Tue, Japanese, full bar*

Entertainment & Recreation

Brian Marki Fine Art [GO] 2236 NE Broadway **503/249-5659** *gallery*

Froelick Gallery [GO] 714 NW Davis St **503/222-1142**

Onda Arte Latina [GO] 2215 NE Alberta St **503/493-1909** *Latin American arts & crafts gallery*

Out Dancing [MW] 975 SE Sandy Blvd (at SE Ankeny St & SE 9th Ave) **503/236-5129** *LGBT dance lessons*

Portland Gay Men's Chorus 812 SW Washington #1050 (at the Stevens Bldg) **503/226-2588**

Sauvie's Island Beach 25 miles NW (off US 30) *follow Reeder Rd to the Collins beach area, park at the farthest end of the road, then follow path to beach; also "Rooster Rock," 22 miles E on Columbia River*

Wonder Ballroom 128 NE Russell St **503/284-8686** *live music venue*

Bookstores

Countermedia 927 SW Oak (btwn 9th & 10th) **503/226-8141** *11am-7pm, noon-6pm Sun, alternative comics, vintage gay books/ periodicals/ erotica*

Laughing Horse Bookstore [WC] 3652 SE Division St (at 37th) **503/236-2893** *11am-7pm, clsd Sun, alternative/ progressive*

Looking Glass Bookstore 7983 SE 13th Ave (in Stellwood) **503/227-4760** *9am-6pm, 10am-5pm Sun, clsd Mon, general, some LGBT titles*

Powell's Books [★WC] 1005 W Burnside St (at 10th) **503/228-4651, 800/878-7323** *9am-11pm, huge new & used bookstore, cafe, readings*

Reading Frenzy [WC] 921 SW Oak St (at 9th) **503/274-1449** *noon-6pm, zines, comics, LGBT selection*

Retail Shops

Hip Chicks Do Wine 4510 SE 23rd Ave (SE Holgate & 26th) **503/234-3790** *11am-6pm*

The Jellybean [WC] 721 SW 10th Ave (at Morrison) **503/222-5888** *10am-6pm, noon-5pm Sun, cards, T-shirts & gifts*

Presents of Mind [WC] 3633 SE Hawthorne (at 37th Ave) **503/230-7740** *10am-7pm, jewelry, clothing, unique gifts*

Robot Piercing 128 NW 23rd Ave **503/224-9916**

Under U 4 Men 507 SW Broadway St (at Washington) **503/274-2555** *10am-6pm, till 7pm Sat, noon-5pm Sun, designer underwear & in-store underwear models*

Publications

Just Out 503/236-1252 *LGBT newspaper w/ resource directory*

Gyms & Health Clubs

Inner City Hot Tubs [GF,R] 2927 NE Everett St (btwn 29th & 30th) **503/238-1065** *10am-11pm, wellness center*

Men's Clubs

Steam Portland [MO,PC,GO] 2885 NE Sandy Blvd **503/736-9999** *24hrs*

Men's Services

▶ **Megaphone 503/299-9911** *Meet and Chat Live with HOT local men. FREE to listen & respond to ads. Video and text chat at GayMates.com. Use FREE code 4889.*

Erotica

Fantasy for Adults 1512 W Burnside (near NE 39th) **503/295-6969**

Fat Cobra Video 5940 N Interstate Ave **503/247-3425** *also 5501 NW St Helens Rd, 503/222-0180*

Spartacus Leathers 302 SW 12th Ave (at Burnside) **503/224-2604**

Taboo Video 237 SE MLK Blvd **503/239-1678** *24hrs*

Cruisy Areas

Kelly Point [AYOR] on Marine Dr *follow trail to left of parking lot*

Roseburg

Info Lines & Services

Gay/ Lesbian Switchboard 541/464-4126 *24hrs, support & referrals*

Cruisy Areas

Stewart Park [AYOR] river trails & under bridge

Salem

Accommodations

Eagle Crest B&B [GF,NS] 4401 Eagle Crest Rd NW **503/588-8315**

Nightclubs

Southside Speakeasy [GS,NH,D,F,K,DS,GO] 3529 Fairview Industrial Dr SE (at Madrona) **503/362-1139** *11am-2am, from 3:30pm wknds*

Restaurants

Off Center Cafe [★WC] 1741 Center St NE (at 17th) **503/363-9245** *brkfst & lunch Tue-Fri, brunch wknds, clsd Mon*

Entertainment & Recreation

Confluence 503/587-7464 *"The Willamette Valley Mixed GALA Chorus"*

Bookstores

Borders 2235 Lancaster Dr NE **503/375-9588** *9am-10pm, till 11pm Sat, 10am-7pm Sun, LGBT section*

Erotica

Bob's Adult Bookstore 3815 State St (at Lancaster) **503/363-3846**

Cruisy Areas

Bush Park [AYOR] 12th & State Sts *days only*

Silverton

Accommodations

The Oregon Garden Resort [GF,WI] 895 W Main St **800/966-6490** *boutique-style resort*

Sunriver

Accommodations

DiamondStone Guest Lodges [GF,NS,WI] **541/536-6263, 866/626-9887** *Western hotel-style B&B, full brkfst*

Yachats

Accommodations

Ocean Odyssey [GF,NS] **541/547-3637, 800/800-1915** *vacation rental homes in Yachats & Waldport, on the coast*

The Oregon House [GF,NS,WI,WC] 94288 Hwy 101 **541/547-3329** *ocean views*

See Vue Motel [GS,NS,WI,GO] 95590 Hwy 101 **541/547-3227, 866/547-3237** *ocean view*

Shamrock Lodgettes [GF,GO] 105 Hwy 101 S (at Yachats Ocean Rd) **541/547-3312, 800/845-5028** *5-acre resort, hot tub*

PENNSYLVANIA

Abington

BARS

Kitchen Bar [GF,D,F,E] 1482 Old York Rd **215/576-9766** *7am-2am*

RESTAURANTS

Vintage Bar & Restaurant 1116 Old York Rd **215/887-8500** *11am-2am*

Allentown

see also Bethlehem

BARS

Candida's [MW,NH,F] 247 N 12th St (at Chew) **610/434-3071** *4pm-2am Mon-Tue, from 2pm Fri-Sun*

Stonewall, Moose Lounge Bar & Grille [★M,D,F,E,K,DS,S,V] 28-30 N 10th St (at Hamilton) **610/432-0706** *7pm-2am, clsd Mon, [18+] Th*

MEN'S SERVICES

▶ **Megaphone 484/244-0144** *Meet and Chat Live with HOT local men. FREE to listen & respond to ads. Video and text chat at GayMates.com. Use FREE code 4889.*

EROTICA

Adult World 880 S West End Blvd/ Rte 309, Quakerstown **215/538-1522**

CRUISY AREAS

Union Terrace Park [AYOR] Union & St Elmo's Sts

Upper Macungie Park [AYOR] Rte 100 (1 mile N of the I-78 exit)

Altoona

ACCOMMODATIONS

Blue Knob Mountaintop Villas [GF,SW,WI] Overland Pass, Blue Knob **865/522-8547** *private condos, panoramic views, on a golf course at a ski resort*

NIGHTCLUBS

Rumors [MW,D,F,K,GO] 1413 11th Ave (enter rear) **814/941-0803** *9pm-2am, clsd Sun, patio*

RESTAURANTS

Michael's Cafe [GO] 1413 11th Ave **814/941-0803** *11am-9pm, till 2pm Mon, clsd Sun, upscale, full bar*

EROTICA

Adult World Old Rte 220 (Bellwood exit, off I-99) **814/742-7781**

Beaver Falls

EROTICA

Video Hobby Land 7211 Big Beaver Blvd (on Rte 18) **724/847-3777**

Berwick

CRUISY AREAS

Test Track Park [AYOR] S Eaton St (off Rte 11)

Bethlehem

NIGHTCLUBS

Diamonz [W,D,F,E,K,WC] 1913 W Broad St (at Pennsylvania Ave) **610/865-1028** *4pm-2am, from 6pm Sun, also restaurant*

EROTICA

Green Door Video 1162 Pembroke Rd **610/865-5855** *also Cupid's Treasures 861 Stefko Blvd, 610/868-6616*

Bristol

EROTICA

Bristol News World 576 Bristol Pike/ Rte 13 N **215/785-4770**

CRUISY AREAS

Silver Lake Park [AYOR]

Butler

NIGHTCLUBS

Vertigo 100 Pillow St (at W Cunningham) *parties weekly, check myspace.com/butlervertigo*

CRUISY AREAS

Moraine State Park [AYOR] Bear Run area (south shore)

Edinboro

Cruisy Areas

Lakeside Commons [AYOR] Rte 6 N (behind the mall overlooking the lake), Waterford *days*

Elizabeth

Erotica

51 Video & Books - Adult Mart 931 Hayden (Rte 51) **412/384-6383** *24hrs*

Erie

Accommodations

The Boothby Inn [GF] 311 W 6th St **814/456-1888, 866/266-8429** *full brkfst*

Nightclubs

Craze [GS,D,K] 1607 Raspberry St **814/456-3027** *9pm-2am, clsd Sun, patio, [18+] Mon, drag shows Fri*

The Zone [MW,D,F] 133 W 18th St (at Peach) **814/452-0125** *8pm-2am*

Restaurants

Pie in the Sky Cafe [BYOB,R,WC] 463 W 8th St (at Walnut) **814/459-8638** *7:30am-2pm, dinner from 5:30pm Fri-Sat, clsd Sun-Mon*

Radicchio Deli [GO] 16501 State St (at E 10th St) **814/454-3616** *8am-3pm, till 9pm Fri, 11am-9pm Sat*

Retail Shops

Ink Assassins Tattoos & Piercings 2601 Peach St **814/455-6752** *noon-10pm, till 6pm Sun*

Publications

Erie Gay News 814/456-9833 *covers news & events in the Erie, Cleveland, Pittsburgh, Buffalo & Chautauqua County (NY) region*

Gay People's Chronicle 216/631-8646 *Ohio's largest bi-weekly LGBT newspaper w/ extensive listings*

Erotica

Eastern Adult Books - Adult Mart 1313 State St (btwn 13th & 14th) **814/459-7014** *24hrs*

Modern News 1113 State St (at 12th) **814/453-6932**

Cruisy Areas

Glenwood Park [AYOR] park on the hill (overlooking the zoo)

Gettysburg

Accommodations

Battlefield B&B [GS,WI,GO] 2264 Emmitsburg Rd (at Ridge Rd) **717/334-8804, 888/766-3897** *full brkfst, Civil War home*

Sheppard Mansion B&B [GS,NS,WI] 117 Frederick St (at High St), Hanover **717/633-8075, 877/762-6746** *full-service inn, full brkfst , also restaurant & bar*

Gibson

Accommodations

Hillside Campgrounds [★MO,D,SW,N,WI,21+GO] Creek Rd, 3 miles off I-81, at exit 219 **570/756-2007** *seasonal, campground, cabins, disco Fri-Sat*

Glen Mills

Accommodations

Sweetwater Farm B&B [GF,SW,NS,WI,WC] 50 Sweetwater Rd **610/459-4711, 800/793-3892** *1734 home w/ 7 guest rooms & 7 cottages*

Greensburg

Accommodations

Mountain View Inn [GF,SW,WC] 121 Village Dr (at Rte 30) **724/834-5300, 800/537-8709** *full brkfst*

Nightclubs

Longbada Lounge [★MW,D,K,DS,WC] 108 W Pittsburgh St (at Pennsylvania Ave) **724/837-6614** *9pm-2am, clsd Sun-Mon, patio*

Cruisy Areas

Harrison Ave [AYOR] off Otterman St

Harrisburg

Info Lines & Services

Central PA LGBT Center Coalition 200 N 3rd St, 8th flr *www.centralpalgbtcenter.org*

Bars

704 Strawberry [★M,K,V,OC,WC] 704 N 3rd St **717/234-4228** *4pm-2am*

The Brownstone Lounge [MW,NH,F,K,WC] 412 Forster St (btwn 3rd & 6th) **717/234-7009** *11am-2am, from 5pm wknds*

The Liquid 891 [★MW,D,TG,F,E,DS,V] 891 Eisenhower Blvd (near exit 19) **717/939-3590** *7pm-2am, till midnight Th, clsd Sun-Wed*

Neptune's Lounge [★MW,NH,D,YC] 268 North St (at 3rd) **717/233-0581** *4pm-2am, from 2pm Sun*

Nightclubs

Stallions [★M,D,E,K,DS,S,V,WC] 706 N 3rd St (enter rear) **717/232-3060** *7pm-2am, 18+ night Sun*

Men's Services

Cruisy Areas

Riverfront Park [AYOR] Front & State Sts

Irwin

Nightclubs

The Link [MW,D,F,E,DS,S] 91 Wendel Rd, Herminie **724/446-7717** *6pm-2am*

Johnstown

Nightclubs

Lucille's [MW,D,K,DS,S] 520 Washington St (near Central Park) **814/539-4448** *6pm-2am, clsd Sun-Mon, strippers*

Cruisy Areas

Central Park [AYOR]

Kutztown

Accommodations

Grim's Manor B&B [MW,NS,GO] 10 Kern Rd **610/683-7089** *stone farmhouse on 5 acres, full brkfst*

Lancaster

Accommodations

Cameron Estate Inn [GS,F,NS,WC,GO] 1855 Mansion Ln (at Donegal Springs Rd), Mount Joy **717/492-0111, 888/422-6376**

Candlelight Inn B&B [GF] 2574 Lincoln Hwy E (at Rte 896/ Hartman Bridge Rd), Ronks **717/299-6005, 800/772-2635** *full brkfst, jacuzzi*

The Railroad House B&B, Restaurant & Tavern [GS,NS,WI,WC,GO] 280 W Front St (at S Perry St), Marietta **717/426-4141** *full brkfst, also Sun bar [MW]*

Bars

Dad's Pub [GS,NH,F,K] 168 S Main St, Manheim **717/665-1960** *3:30pm-2am, from 11am Fri, Dog House & Club 168 [D] 8pm Fri-Sat*

Tally Ho [★MW,D,K,DS,YC] 201 W Orange (at Water) **717/299-0661** *6pm-2am*

Restaurants

The Loft above Tally Ho bar **717/299-0661** *lunch & dinner, clsd Sun, contemporary American/ French*

Erotica

The Den 53 N Prince St **717/299-1779**

Cruisy Areas

Lancaster County Park [AYOR]

Long's Park [AYOR] Rte 30 at Harrisburg Pike

Lebanon

Erotica

Hobbeze Lebanon Adult Gifts 1604 E Cumberland St/ Rte 422 (at 15th Ave) **717/273-6398**

Cruisy Areas

Union Canal Tunnel Park [AYOR]

Liverpool

Erotica

Adult Depot [GO] 64 Old Trail Rd (near Rte 11 & 104 Jct) **717/444-3894** *10am-1am, all-male theater, booths, toys*

Meadville

Restaurants

Peppercorn & Vine [18+,GO] 994 Market St **814/337-0005** *steak & seafood, also lounge*

Erotica

Park Ave News 1206 Park Ave **814/724-4690** *large selection of LGBT & adult publications*

Milford

Accommodations

Hotel Fauchere [GF,NS,WI,WC] 401 Broad St (at Catharine St) **570/409-1212** *historic boutique hotel, Hudson River School paintings throughout, full brkfst, also restaurant & bar*

Mt Haven Country Resort [GF,SW,WI] RD 1 Log Tavern Rd **570/296-7262, 800/553-1530**

New Hope

see also Lambertville & Sergeantsville, New Jersey

Accommodations

Ash Mill Farm B&B [GF,NS,WI,GO] 5358 York Rd (at Rte 202), Holicong **215/794-5373**

Cordials B&B of New Hope [MW,NS,WI,WC,GO] 143 Old York Rd (at Sugan Rd) **215/862-3919, 877/219-1009** *hot tub*

Fox & Hound B&B [GF,NS,WI] 246 West Bridge St **215/862-5082** *1850s stone manor, full brkfst wknds*

The Lexington House [★GS,SW,NS,GO] 6171 Upper York Rd **215/794-0811** *1749 country home, full brkfst*

The Mansion Inn [MW,SW,NS,GO] 9 S Main (at Bridge St) **215/862-1231** *B&B inn, full brkfst, jacuzzi*

The Nevermore [GF,SW,WC] 6426 Lower York Rd/ Rte 202 **215/862-5221, 800/467-3202** *also restaurant & lounge*

Silver Maple Organic Farm & B&B [GS,SW,NS,WI,WC,GO] 483 Sergeantsville Rd (Rte 523), Sergeantsville, NJ **908/237-2192** *200-year-old farmhouse, full brkfst, hot tub*

The Wishing Well Guesthouse [GS,NS,GO] 144 Old York Rd **215/862-8819** *B&B in restored farmhouse*

York Street House B&B [GF,NS] 42 York St, Lambertville, NJ **609/397-3007, 888/398-3199** *1909 Manor house*

Bars

Harlans [GS,C,F] 6426 Lower York Rd (at the Nevermore Hotel) **215/862-5225** *cabaret, dinner served, also hotel*

Restaurants

Eagle Diner [WC] 6522 York Rd **215/862-5575** *24hrs*

Havana [E,K] 105 S Main St **215/862-9897** *noon-midnight, from 11am wknds, bar till 2am*

Karla's 5 W Mechanic St (at Main) **215/862-2612** *noon-11pm, till midnight Fri-Sat, from 10am Sun, New American, full bar*

Mother's 34 N Main St **215/862-5857** *11am-9pm, till 10pm Fri-Sat*

Wildflowers 8 W Mechanic St **215/862-2241** *seasonal, noon-9:30pm, full bar*

Erotica

Grownups [GO] 2 E Mechanic St (at Main) **215/862-9304**

Le Chateau Exotique 27 W Mechanic St **215/862-3810** *fetishwear*

New Milford

Accommodations

Oneida Camp & Lodge [M,SW,N,WI,GO] **570/465-7011** *seasonal*

Philadelphia

Info Lines & Services

Colours 112 N Broad St, 11th Floor **215/496-0330** *serving the LGBTQ community of color, special emphasis on health*

William Way LGBT Community Center 1315 Spruce St (at Juniper) **215/732-2220** *10am-9pm, from noon Sat, till 7pm Sun*

Accommodations

Alexander Inn [GS,NS,WI,GO] Spruce (at 12th St) **215/923-3535, 877/253-9466** *restored hotel, fitness center*

Antique Row B&B [GF] 341 S 12th St (at Pine) **215/592-7802** *1820s town house, full brkfst*

The Conwell Inn [GS,SW,NS,WI,WC] 1331 W Berks St (at Montgomery Ave) **215/235-6200, 888/379-9737** *B&B on Temple University campus*

Embassy Suites Center City [GF] 1776 Ben Franklin Pkwy (at 18th) **215/561-1776, 800/362-2779**

The Gables B&B [GS,NS,WI,GO] 4520 Chester Ave **215/662-1918** *Victorian, garden*

Hampton Inn Center City Philadelphia [GS,SW,WI,WC] 1301 Race St (13th St) **215/665-9100, 800/426-7866** *jacuzzi, brkfst included*

Holiday Inn Historic District [GF,SW,NS,WI,WC] 400 Arch St (at Market) **215/923-8660, 800/972-2796**

The Independent Hotel [GS,WI,WC] 1234 Locust St (at 13th) **215/772-1440**

The Inn at Chester Springs [GF,SW,WI] 815 N Pottstown Pike (Exit 312), Exton **610/363-1100, 888/253-6119**

Latham Hotel [GF,WI,WC] 135 S 17th St (at Walnut) **215/563-7474, 877/528-4261**

Morris House Hotel [GF,NS,WI] 225 S 8th St **215/922-2446**

Philadelphia Marriott [GF,SW,NS,WC] 1201 Market St (btwn 12th & 13th) **215/625-2900, 800/320-5744** *near the gay area in Philly*

Rittenhouse Hotel [GF,NS,WI] 210 W Rittenhouse Square (at 19th) **215/546-9000, 800/635-1042** *also restaurants & bar*

Rodeway Inn [GF,NS,WI] 1208 Walnut St (btwn 12th & 13th) **215/546-7000, 877/424-6423**

Uncles Upstairs Inn [M,NS,GO] 1220 Locust St (at 12th) **215/546-6660**

Bars

12th Air Command Headquarters for Men [M,D,A,F,E,K,S] 254 S 12th St (btwn Locust & Spruce) **215/545-8088** *4pm-2am, from 2pm Sun (summer), [17+] Sat*

Bump [MW,F,D] 1234 Locust St (at 13th) **215/732-1800** *5pm-2am, also restaurant, Sun brunch from 11am*

Camac [M,NH,F] 1305 Locust St (at S 13th) **215/545-1430**

L' Etage [GS,D,F,C] 624 S 6th St (at Bainbridge) **215/592-0656** *7:30pm-1am, till 2am Fri-Sat, clsd Mon, [C] 1st Th, also restaurant downstairs, noon-11pm, from 10am wknds, crêperie*

The Khyber [GF,E,WC] 56 S 2nd St (btwn Market & Chestnut) **215/238-5888** *noon-2am, from 4pm Sat, live bands*

North Third [GS,F] 801 N 3rd (at Brown) **215/413-3666** *5pm-midnight, till 2am wknds, wknd brunch, also restaurant*

Stir Lounge [MW,NH,D,V] 1705 Chancellor St (at Rittenhouse Sq btwn Walnut & Spruce) **215/732-2700** *4pm-2am*

Tavern on Camac [MW,D,C,P] 243 S Camac St (at Spruce) **215/545-0900** *4pm-2am, 11:30am-3:30pm Sun brunch, also restaurant*

Uncle's [M,NH] 1220 Locust St (at 12th) **215/546-6660** *11am-2am*

Venture Inn [MW,NH,F] 255 S Camac (at Spruce) **215/545-8731** *11am-2am, from noon Sat*

The Westbury [MW,NH,F,WC,GO] 261 S 13th (at Spruce) **215/546-5170** *11am-2am, dinner till 10pm (till 11pm wknds)*

Woody's [★M,D,CW,F,K,S,V,YC,WC] 202 S 13th St (at Walnut) **215/545-1893** *11am-2am, [18+] Wed, Latin Th*

Nightclubs

Bike Stop [★M,D,L,K] 204-206 S Quince St (btwn 11th & 12th, Walnut & Locust) **215/627-1662** *4pm-2am, from 2pm wknds, cruisy, 4 flrs, [K] 5pm Sun*

Bob & Barbara's Lounge [GS,E,DS] 1509 South St **215/545-4511** *3pm-2am, from 6pm Sun, [DS] Th, live jazz Fri-Sat*

Fluid [GF,D,E,S,$] 613 S 4th St (at Kater) **215/629-3686** *9pm-2am, more gay wknds, theme nights*

Lounge 125 [GS,D,F,S,PC] 125 S 2nd St (at Chestnut) **215/351-9026** *midnight-3:30am, from 11pm Wed-Sat*

Pure [M,D,K,C,P,PC] 1221 St James St (off 13th & Locust) **215/735-5772** *9pm-3:30am Wed-Sun, also Pink Lounge nightly*

The Scene [MW,D] 417 N Columbus Blvd *4th Sat only*

Shampoo [GS,D,A] 417 N 8th St (at Willow) **215/922-7500** *9pm-2am, clsd Mon-Tue & Th, more gay Fri*

Sisters [W,D,F,E,K,WC] 1320 Chancellor St (at Juniper) **215/735-0735** *5pm-2am, from noon Sun, from 8pm Mon, also restaurant [MW], dinner Wed-Sat, Sun brunch*

Cafes

10th Street Pour House [WC] 262 S 10th St (at Spruce) **215/922-5626** *7:30am-3pm, from 8:30am wknds, popular brunch wknds*

Brew HaHa! [WI] 212 S 12th St (btwn Locust & Walnut) **215/893-5680** *7am-9pm, also newsstand*

Capogiro 119 S 13th St (at Sansom) **215/351-0900** *7:30am-11:30pm, till 1am Fri-Sat, gelato*

Cosi 1128 Walnut St **215/413-1608** *6:30am-midnight, from 7am wknds*

Green Line Cafe [F,E] 4239 Baltimore Ave **215/222-3431** *7am-11pm, 8am-8pm Sun*

Joe Coffee Bar [WI] 1100 Walnut St (at 11th St) **215/592-7384** *6:30am-8pm, till 6:30pm Mon, from 8am Sat, clsd Sun*

Restaurants

13th Street Pizza 209 S 13th St (at Chancellor St) **215/546-4453** *11am-4am, popular late night*

The Adobe Cafe [E] 4550 Mitchell St (at Greenleaf), Roxborough **215/483-3947** *lunch Th-Sun & dinner nightly, plenty veggie*

Alfa 1709 Walnut St (at 17th) **215/751-0201** *4:30pm-2am, also Walnut Room lounge*

The Caboose Grille 2 W Broad St, Souderton **215/721-1001** *lunch & dinner Tue-Sat, brkfst wknds, clsd Mon*

The Continental 138 Market St (at 2nd) **215/923-6069** *lunch, dinner, wknd brunch, also bar until 2am, eclectic, some veggie*

Figs [BYOB,WC] 2501 Meredith St **215/978-8440** *lunch Tue-Fri, dinner nightly, wknd brunch, clsd Mon, eclectic Mediterranean*

A Full Plate Cafe [MR,TG,BYOB,GO] 1009 Bodine St (at George St) **215/627-4068** *11am-9pm, till 10pm Fri, 10am-10pm Sat, till 3pm Sun, patio, lesbian-owned*

The Happy Rooster [E,K] 118 S 16th St (at Sansom St) **215/963-9311** *11:30am-11pm, from 3pm Sat, cont'l, upscale, full bar till 1am*

Knock 226 S 12th St **215/925-1166** *lunch & dinner, Sun brunch, American, also bar*

L2 [E] 2201 South St (at 22nd) **215/732-7878** *dinner nightly, clsd Mon, Asian/ fusion, also bar*

Liberties 705 N 2nd St (at Fairmount) **215/238-0660** *lunch & dinner, full bar till 2am*

Little Pete's 219 S 17th St (at Locust) **215/545-5508** *24hrs, diner*

Lolita [BYOB] 106 S 13th St (at Sansom) **215/546-7100** *5pm-10pm, upscale Mexican*

Mercato [BYOB] 1216 Spruce St **215/985-2962** *dinner, Italian*

Midtown II [TG] 122 S 11th St **215/627-6452** *24 hrs, diner, popular late night*

Mixto 1141-43 Pine St **215/592-0363** *lunch & dinner, brkfst wknds, Latin American*

More Than Just Ice Cream 1119 Locust St (at 12th) **215/574-0586** *11am-11pm, American*

My Thai 2200 South St (at 22nd) **215/985-1878** *5pm-10pm, till 11pm Fri-Sat, full bar*

New Harmony 135 N 9th St (at Cherry) **215/627-4520** *11am-11pm, vegan*

The Plough & the Stars [E] 123 Chestnut St (at 2nd) **215/733-0300** *lunch & dinner, popular wknd brunch, Irish pub fare, full bar till 2am, live music Sun*

Valanni 1229 Spruce St **215/790-9494** *dinner nightly, Sun brunch, Mediterranean/ Latin, full bar*

White Dog Cafe [E] 3420 Sansom St (at Walnut) **215/386-9224** *lunch & dinner, brunch Sun, full bar, cool Mon reading & Sun film series*

Zócalo 3600 Lancaster Ave (at 36th) **215/895-0139** *lunch Mon-Fri, dinner nightly, Mexican/ New Southwestern*

Entertainment & Recreation

The Walt Whitman House 328 Mickle Blvd (btwn S 3rd & S 4th Sts), Camden, NJ **856/964-5383** *the last home of America's great & controversial poet, just across the Delaware River*

Bookstores

Giovanni's Room [★] 345 S 12th St (at Pine) **215/923-2960** *11:30am-7pm, from 1pm Sun, legendary LGBT bookstore*

Robin's Bookstore 108 S 13th St **215/735-9600** *11am-7pm, noon-5pm Sun, oldest independent bookstore in Philly*

Retail Shops

Infinite Body Piercing 626 S 4th St (at South) **215/923-7335** *noon-10pm, till 8pm Sun*

Jean-Jacques Gallery [GO] 7118 Germantown Ave (at Mt Pleasant) **215/242-5440**

PHAG/ Philadelphia Home Art Garden 1225 Walnut St **215/627-0461** *11am-8pm, noon-6pm Sun, boutique*

Sherman Mills Art Supply [GO] 3510 Scotts Ln (just off Ridge Ave) **215/844-5262, 888/692-7878** *art supplies & gifts*

TLA Video 1520 Locust St (btwn 15th & 16th) **215/735-7887** *10am-midnight, extensive LGBT titles*

TLA Video 517 S 4th St (btwn 4th & Lombard) **215/735-7887** *11am-midnight, from 10am Fri-Sun, extensive LGBT titles*

TLA Video 7630 Germantown Ave **215/248-4448** *10am-11pm, extensive LGBT titles*

Publications

PGN (Philadelphia Gay News) **215/625-8501** *LGBT newspaper w/ extensive listings*

Gyms & Health Clubs

12th St Gym [SW] 204 S 12th St (btwn Locust & Walnut) **215/985-4092** *day passes*

Men's Clubs

Club Body Center [NS,WI,PC] 1220 Chancellor St (at 12th & Walnut) **215/735-7671** *24hrs, 5 flrs*

Philly Jacks [MO,18+,PC] **215/618-1519** *4 sex parties per month, call for location*

▶ **Sansom Street Gym** [★MO,V,PC] 2020 Sansom St **267/330-0151** *24hrs*

CLEANEST CLUB AROUND!
Philly's BEST!
OPEN 24HRS!
In & Out Privileges!
New Facility
with Sling Room!
WHERE MEN
MEET MEN
GYM & BATHS Where Men meet Men
Sansom Street GYM®
2020 Sansom Street, Philly PA
(267) 330-0151
WWW.SANSOMSTREETGYM.COM

Men's Services

▶ **Megaphone 215/877-3337** *Meet and Chat Live with HOT local men. FREE to listen & respond to ads. Video and text chat at GayMates.com. Use FREE code 4889.*

Erotica

▶ **Adonis Cinema Complex** 2026 Sansom St (at 20th) **215/557-9319** *24hrs*

Condom Kingdom 437 South St (at 5th) **215/829-1668** *safer sex materials & toys*

Danny's [★] 133 S 13th St (at Walnut) **215/925-5041** *24hrs*

Fantasy Island Adult Books 7363 State Rd **215/332-5454**

Passional Boutique 704 S 5th St (at Bainbridge) **215/829-4986, 877/826-7738** *noon-10pm*

Scorpio Adult Boutique & Video 205 S Juniper St (btwn Walnut & Locust) **215/545-2181**

Pittsburgh

Info Lines & Services

AA Gay/ Lesbian 412/471-7472 *call for times & location*

Gay/ Lesbian Community Center 5808 Forward Ave (at Murray, 2nd flr) **412/422-0114** *6pm-9pm Tue, Wed & Th, noon-9pm Sat, noon-6pm Sun, clsd Mon*

Accommodations

Arbors B&B [MO,NS,WI,GO] 745 Maginn St **412/231-4643** *in restored farmhouse, hot tub*

Camp Davis [MW,D,SW] 311 Red Brush Rd, Boyers **724/637-2402** *1 hour from Pittsburgh, cabins & campsites, variety of events*

The Inn on Negley [GF,NS,WI,WC] 703 S Negley Ave (at Elmer St) **412/661-0631**

The Inn on the Mexican War Streets [MW,F,NS,WI,GO] 604 W North Ave **412/231-6544**

Morning Glory Inn B&B [GF,WI] 2119 Sarah St **412/431-1707** *in 1862 Italianate-style Victorian townhouse*

The Parador Inn [GF,WI,GO] 939 Western Ave **412/231-4800, 888/540-1443** *Caribbean-style B&B, fireplaces, gardens*

The Priory [GF,NS,WI,WC] 614 Pressley St (near Cedar Ave) **412/231-3338, 866/377-4679** *Victorian, renovated 1888 monastery, fitness center*

Bars

5801 [★MW,F,V,WC] 5801 Ellsworth Ave (at Maryland) **412/661-5600** *4pm-2am, also restaurant Th-Sun, deck*

Blue Moon Bar & Lounge [M,NH,TG,S] 5115 Butler St **412/781-1119** *4pm-close, till 2am Wed-Sat*

Brewery Tavern [GF] 3315 Liberty Ave (at Herron Ave) **412/681-7991** *10am-2am, from 11am Sun*

Cattivo [MW,D,F] 146 44th St **412/687-2157** *4pm-2am Wed-Sun, clsd Mon-Tue*

Images [M,K,S,V] 965 Liberty Ave (at 10th St) **412/391-9990** *2pm-2am, go-go boys*

Leather Central [★M,D,L,F,V] 1226 Herron Ave (at Liberty, in Donny's basement) **412/682-9869** *9pm-2am Fri-Sat, 6pm-11pm Sun*

Pittsburgh Eagle [★M,D,L,WC] 1740 Eckert St (near Beaver) **412/766-7222** *9pm-2am Fri-Sat only*

PTown [MW,D] 4740 Baum Blvd **412/621-0111** *5pm-2am*

Real Luck Cafe [MW,NH,F,S,WC] 1519 Penn Ave (at 16th) **412/566-8988** *4pm-2am*

Remedy [GS,NH,MR] 5121 Butler St, Lawrenceville **412/781-6771** *3pm-2am, from 5pm Sun, also restaurant on upper level*

Spin [GS,E,WC] 5744 Ellsworth Ave, Shadyside **412/362-7746** *4pm-2am, bartini lounge*

There Video Lounge [MW,WC] 931 Liberty Ave (at Smithfield) **412/642-4435** *5:30pm-2am, from 8pm Sat-Sun*

Nightclubs

941 Saloon [★MW,D,K] 941 Liberty Ave (at Smithfield St, 2nd flr) **412/281-5222** *2pm-2am*

Pegasus [★MW,D,18+,YC] 818 Liberty Ave (at 9th) **412/281-2131** *10pm-2am, clsd Mon-Tue*

Privilege Ultra Lounge [MW,D,E] 1650 Smallman St (at 16th St) **412/253-7330** *10pm-2am, burlesque Fri, Blowpop Sat*

Cafes

Square Cafe [E,GO] 1137 S Braddock Ave **412/244-8002** *7am-3pm, from 8am Sun, live shows monthly, lesbian-owned*

Restaurants

Harris Grill 5747 Ellsworth Ave **412/362-5273** *11am-2am, from 10 Sun, full bar*

Quiet Storm 5430 Penn Ave (at Graham St) *8am-7pm, till 10pm Fri-Sat, till 4pm Sun, vegetarian/ vegan*

Zenith 86 S 26th St **412/481-4833** *11am-9pm, Sun brunch, clsd Mon-Wed, vegetarian/ vegan, also antiques store*

Entertainment & Recreation

Andy Warhol Museum 117 Sandusky St (at General Robinson) **412/237-8300** *10am-5pm, till 10pm Fri, clsd Mon, is it soup or is it art?—see for yourself*

Retail Shops

Slacker [WC] 1321 E Carson St (btwn 13th & 14th) **412/381-3911** *11am-9pm, till 11pm Fri-Sat, 11am-6pm Sun, magazines, clothing, leather, piercing*

Publications

Erie Gay News 814/456-9833 *covers news & events in the Erie, Cleveland, Pittsburgh, Buffalo & Chautauqua County, NY region*

▶ **Out 412/381-3350** *LGBT newspaper*

Men's Clubs

▶ **Club Pittsburgh** [★PC] 1139 Penn Ave (enter side) **412/471-6790** *24hrs, 3 flrs, gym, rooftop tanning deck*

Men's Services

▶ **Megaphone 412/937-9999** *Meet and Chat Live with HOT local men. FREE to listen & respond to ads. Video and text chat at GayMates.com. Use FREE code 4889.*

Erotica

Adult Mart 346 Blvd of the Allies **412/261-9119**

Cruisy Areas

Schenley Park [AYOR]

Poconos

Accommodations

The Arrowheart Inn [GS,NS,WI,GO] 3021 Valley View Dr (at Fox Gap Rd), Bangor **610/588-0241**

Frog Hollow [MW,GO] **570/595-2814** *secluded 1920s cottage*

Pocmont Resort & Conference Center [GF,SW,NS,WI,WC] Bushkill Falls Rd, Bushkill **570/588-6671, 800/762-6668**

Rainbow Mountain Resort [MW,D,TG,E,K,SW,WI,GO] **570/223-8484** *atop Pocono mtn on 26 acres, hot tub, also restaurant & bar, DJ Fri-Sat*

Stoney Ridge [MW,GO] **570/629-5036** *secluded log home*

The Woods Campground [MW,SW,18+] 845 Vaughn Acres Ln, Lehighton **610/377-9577**

Reading

Bars

The Peanut Bar & Restaurant [GF] 332 Penn St **610/376-8500, 800/515-8500** *11am-11pm, till midnight Fri-Sat, clsd Sun, a Reading landmark!*

The Red Star [★M,NH,D,L,MR,TG,DS,OC,GO] 11 S 10th St (at Penn St) **610/375-4116** *9pm-2am, clsd Sun-Tue*

Restaurants

Judy's On Cherry 332 Cherry St **610/374-8511** *lunch Tue-Fri, dinner Tue-Sat, clsd Sun-Mon, Mediterranean*

The Ugly Oyster 21 S 5th St (at Cherry) **610/373-6791** *11:30am-10pm, from noon Sat, clsd Sun, traditional Irish pub (bar open till 2am)*

Gyms & Health Clubs

Gold's Gym [GF] 1119 Bern Rd, Wyomissing **610/372-9131**

Men's Services

▶ **Megaphone 888/634-2628** *Meet and Chat Live with HOT local men. Call for your local number or visit us online at GayMates.com. Use FREE code 4889.*

Cruisy Areas

Mt Penn [AYOR] *btwn pagoda & fire tower & surrounding woodlands*

Scranton

Bars

Twelve Penny Saloon [MW,NH,TG,F,K,DS,WC,GO] 3501 Birney Ave, Moosic **570/941-0444** *6pm-2am, Fri-Sat [D]*

Gyms & Health Clubs

FitnessQUEST [GO] 6270 Rte 502 (at Rte 435), Moscow **570/842-2000**

Cruisy Areas

Court House Square [AYOR]

Shippensburg

Erotica

► **The Lion's Den Adult Superstore** 8071 Olde Scotland Rd (Penn exit 24, off I-81) **717/530-8032** *24hrs*

State College

Bars

Chumley's [★M,NH,WC] 108 W College **814/238-4446** *5pm-2am, from 6pm Sun*

Nightclubs

Indigo [GS,D,V,YC] 112 W College Ave **814/234-1031** *9pm-2am, clsd Mon-Wed, "Alternative" night Sun*

Cruisy Areas

The Wall [AYOR] 100 blk of College Ave

Sunbury

Bars

CC's [MW,D,K,DS] 555 Klinger Rd **570/286-6022** *7pm-2am Th-Sat, from 3pm Sun*

Cruisy Areas

Market St & Park [AYOR] downtown

Uniontown

Bars

Eddie's Tavern [GF,F,K] 200 Francis St **724/438-9563** *11am-midnight, try the wings*

Nightclubs

Club 231 [M,NH,D,TG,F,K,DS,GO] 231 Pittsburgh St/ Rte 51 (at Fulton) **724/430-1477** *8pm-close*

Cruisy Areas

Dunlap Creek Park [AYOR] off Rocky Point Rd

West Chester

Cruisy Areas

Court House Wall [AYOR] *late nights*

Wilkes-Barre

Info Lines & Services

NEPA Rainbow Alliance Resource Center 512 Northampton St #218, Kingston **570/606-4410**

Nightclubs

Twist [★M,D,F,WC] 1170 Hwy 315 (in Fox Ridge Plaza) **570/825-7300** *8pm-2am, from 6pm Sun, patio, also restaurant*

Erotica

Cinema 309 [AYOR] Rte 309 (Blackman St exit, off I-81) *behind Kmart, unconfirmed*

Cruisy Areas

Nesbitt Park [AYOR] Susquehanna River (N of Pierce St bridge), Kingston

Williamsport

Nightclubs

Club Z [MW,D,K,GO] 321 Pine St **570/322-6900** *5pm-2am, clsd Sun-Mon*

Erotica

Adult Playtime Boutique Rte 15, Montgomery **570/547-2663**

Cruisy Areas

Scenic Overlook [AYOR] 3 miles S, on Rte 15 N

York

Accommodations

Stone Crest York B&B & Retreats [GF,WI,GO] 321 Imperial Dr (at PA 182) **717/741-2105**

Nightclubs

Altland's Ranch [MW,CW,D,K] 8505 Orchard Rd, Spring Grove **717/225-4479** *8pm-2am Fri-Sat only*

Club XS [MW,D] 36 W 11th **717/846-6969** *4pm-2am*

Erotica

Cupid's Connection Adult Boutique 244 N George St (at North) **717/846-5029**

Rhode Island

Narragansett

Accommodations

Blueberry Cove Inn [GS,NS,WI] 75 Kingstown Rd **401/792-9865, 800/478-1426** *3 blks from beach*

Restaurants

Crazy Burger 144 Boon St **401/783-1818** *8am-9pm, great breakfast*

Newport

Info Lines & Services

Sobriety First [GF] 135 Pelham St (at Channing Memorial Church) **401/438-8860** *8pm Fri*

Accommodations

Architect's Inn [GF,NS,WI,GO] 2 Sunnyside Pl **401/847-7081, 877/466-2547** *1873 Victorian, fireplaces, near beach, shops & restaurants*

Brinley Victorian Inn [GS,NS,WI] 23 Brinley St **401/849-7645, 800/999-8523**

Francis Malbone House Inn [GF,NS,WC] 392 Thames St (at Memorial Blvd) **401/846-0392, 800/846-0392**

Hilltop Inn [GF,NS,WI,GO] 2 Kay St **800/846-2536**

Hydrangea House Inn [★GS,NS,GO] 16 Bellevue Ave **401/846-4435, 800/945-4667** *full brkfst, near beach*

Inn Bliss B&B [GS,NS,WI,GO] 10 Bliss Rd (at Broadway) **401/845-2547, 877/466-2547** *Victorian B&B, walk to beaches, mansions & downtown area, hot tub*

The Melville House Inn [★GF,NS,WI] 39 Clarke St **401/847-0640, 800/711-7184** *full brkfst*

The Spring Seasons Inn [GF,NS] 86 Spring St (btwn Mary St & Touro) **401/849-0004, 877/294-0004** *full brkfst*

Restaurants

Restaurant Bouchard 505 Thames St **401/846-0123** *dinner, clsd Tue*

Whitehorse Tavern [NS] 26 Marlborough (at Farewell) **401/849-3600** *lunch & dinner, Sun brunch, upscale dining, patio*

Erotica

Newport Video 228 JT Connell Hwy **401/847-4480** *arcade*

North Kingstown

Erotica

Amazing.net Video Store 6774 Post Rd/ Rte 1 **401/885-0209**

Pawtucket

Info Lines & Services

Gay & Lesbian AA 71 Park Place (at Park Place Congregational Church) **401/438-8860**

Providence

Info Lines & Services

Brothers in Sobriety 372 Wayland Ave (at Community Church) **401/438-8860** *7:30pm Sat*

GLBT Helpline of Rhode Island **401/751-3322**

Accommodations

Courtyard by Marriott [GF,NS] 32 Exchange Terr (at Memorial Blvd) **401/272-1191, 888/887-7955**

Edgewood Manor [GF,NS,WI] 232 Norwood Ave **401/781-0099, 800/882-3285** *1905 Greek Revival mansion, some fireplaces & whirlpools*

Hotel Dolce Villa [GS,NS] 63 DePasquale Square **401/383-7031** *boutique hotel, jacuzzis, kitchens*

The Hotel Providence [GS,WI,NS] 311 Westminister St **401/861-8000, 800/861-8990**

Renaissance Providence Hotel [GS,F,NS,WI,WC] 5 Avenue of the Arts **401/919-5000, 800/468-3571**

Bars

Alleycat [MW,NH,V,GO] 17 Snow St (at Washington) **401/272-6369** *3pm-1am, till 2am Fri-Sat*

Club Energy [MW,D] 69 Union St **401/331-2291** *noon-1am, till 2am wknds, theme nights*

Club Gallery [★MW,NH,D,WC] 150 Point St **401/751-7166** *noon-1am, till 2am Fri-Sat, from 4pm Sun, patio, fetish night Fri, mostly women Sat*

The Providence Eagle [M,B,L,WC] 198 Union St (at Weybosset) **401/421-1447** *3pm-1am, till 2am Fri, from noon wknds*

Sunset Bar & Grille [MW,D,F,E,K] 888 Charles St **401/726-8889** *6pm-1am Fri-Sat*

Union [M,B,L,K,P] 200 Union St (next to the Providence Eagle) **401/831-5366** *3pm-1am, till 2am Fri-Sat*

Wheels [MW,NH,V,WC] 125 Washington (at Mathewson) **401/272-6950** *noon-1am, till 2am Fri-Sat*

Nightclubs

Dark Lady [M,D,K,DS,V] 124 Snow St (at Weybosset) **401/831-4297** *9pm-1am, till 2am Fri-Sat*

Mirabar [M,D,S,WC] 35 Richmond St (at Weybosset) **401/331-6761** *3pm-1am, till 2am Fri-Sat, male dancers*

Therapy [GF,D,YC,WC] 7 Dike St (at Troy) **401/490-7202** *9pm-2am, till 4am Fri-Sat, clsd Sun-Mon, also gallery & cafe from 10am*

Trixx@XL [MO,S,18+] 257 Allens Ave (beside The Gay Mega-Plex) **401/461-9522** *9pm-1am, till 2am Fri-Sat, 6pm-1am Sun, clsd Mon, nude male dancers*

Cafes

Coffee Exchange 207 Wickenden St **401/273-1198** *6:30am-11pm, deck*

Nicks on Broadway 500 Broadway **401/421-0286** *lunch & dinner Wed-Sat, Sun brunch, clsd Mon-Tue*

Pastiche Fine Desserts 92 Spruce St **401/861-5190** *8:30am-11pm, 10am-10pm Sun*

Reflections Cafe [F] 8 Governor St (at Wickenden) **401/273-7278** *7am-10pm*

White Electric Coffee 711 Westminster **401/453-3007** *7am-6:30pm*

Restaurants

Al Forno [★] 577 S Main St **401/273-9760** *dinner only, clsd Sun-Mon*

Bravo Brasserie 123 Empire St **401/490-5112** *lunch Tue-Sat, dinner nightly, Sun brunch*

Camille's 71 Bradford St (at Atwell's Ave) **401/751-4812** *lunch & dinner, clsd Sun, full bar*

Downcity [WC] 151 Weybosset St **401/331-9217** *lunch weekdays, dinner nightly, wknd brunch, full bar*

Fellini Pizzeria [GO] 166 Wickenden St **401/751-6737**

Gay Latin Night [MW,D,MR-L] 44 Hospital St **401/490-3980** *9pm Sun only*

Haven Brothers Diner 72 Spruce St (in a truck outside City Hall) **401/861-7777** *5pm-3am, since the 1930s*

Julian's 318 Broadway (at Vinton) **401/861-1770** *9am-11pm, gourmet*

Local 121 121 Washington St **401/274-2121** *lunch Mon-Sat, dinner nightly*

Lot 401 44 Hospital St **401/490-3980** *dinner, clsd Sun-Mon, also club*

Taqueria Pacifica 103 Empire St **401/621-8785** *Mexican, plenty veggie*

Entertainment & Recreation

Cable Car Cinema 204 S Main St **401/272-3970** *art-house flicks & free popcorn refills*

Perishable Theatre 95 Empire St **401/331-2695** *plays, also late-night comedy*

Providence Gay Men's Chorus **401/455-4698**

WaterFire Waterplace Park **401/272-3111** *May-Oct only, bonfire installations along the Providence River at sunset, check local listings for dates*

Bookstores

Books on the Square 471 Angell St (at Wayland) **401/331-9097, 888/669-9660** *9am-9pm, 10am-6pm Sun, some LGBT*

Publications

▶ **Metroline 860/231-8845, 800/233-8334** *covers CT, RI & MA*

Options 401/724-5428 *LGBT community magazine*

Men's Clubs

Club Body Center [NS,WI,PC] 257 Weybosset St, 2nd flr (at Richmond) **401/274-0298** *24hrs*

The Gay Mega-Plex [PC,WC,GO] 257 Allens Ave **401/780-8769** *24hrs*

Men's Services

▶ **Megaphone 401/738-7788** *Meet and Chat Live with HOT local men. FREE to listen & respond to ads. Video and text chat at GayMates.com. Use FREE code 4889.*

Erotica

Adult Video News 255 Allens Ave (at Point) **401/785-1324** *9am-4am, 9am-midnight Sun, arcade*

Amazing 75 Empire St (at Weybosset) **401/274-4477**

Amazing.net Video Store 155 Newport Ave/ Rte 1A (Taylor St), E Providence **401/438-3070**

Amazing Super Store 15 Thurbers Ave (at Rte 1A) **401/467-7631**

Millenium Video 345 Charles St **401/277-9595**

Mister Sister 268 Wickenden St **401/421-6969** *fetishwear, sex toys, classes*

Cruisy Areas

State House Circle Road [AYOR] *nights*

Warwick

Erotica

Amazing 2318 Post Rd/ Rte 1 **401/739-3080**

Cruisy Areas

Salter Grove Park [AYOR] Narragansett Pkwy (off Post Rd)

Westerly

Cruisy Areas

Misquamicut State Beach [AYOR] go left before the bridge (at Fenway Beach)

SOUTH CAROLINA

Statewide

Publications

Q Notes 704/531-9988 *bi-weekly LGBT newspaper for the Carolinas*

Stereotypd 828/505-2870 *LGBT newspaper for NC & SC*

Aiken

see also Augusta, Georgia

Nightclubs

Marlboro Station [MW,D,S] 141 Marlboro St **803/644-6485** *10pm-close Fri-Sun*

Beaufort

Restaurants

Old House Restaurant [BYOB,WC,GO] Hwy 462 (at Hwy 336), Ridgeland **843/258-4444** *5pm-9pm, till 10pm Fri-Sat, clsd Sun*

Blacksburg

Erotica

Bedtyme Stories 145 Simper Rd (I-85, exit 100) **864/839-0007, 770/844-1208**

Bowman

Erotica

▶ **The Lion's Den Adult Superstore** 2269 Homestead Rd (exit 159 off I-26) **803/829-1781** *24hrs*

Charleston

Info Lines & Services

Acceptance Group (Gay AA) 67 Anson St (btwn Society & George, at St Stephen's Episcopal) **843/723-9633 (AA#)** *8pm Tue, 6:30pm Sat-Sun*

Accommodations

A B&B @ 4 Unity Alley [GS,NS] 4 Unity Alley **843/577-6660** *18th-c warehouse, full brkfst, parking inside*

Alice's Carriage House B&B [GF,SW,NS,WI] 22 New St (at Tradd St) **843/973-3458** *hot tub, courtyard*

Folly Flamingo [NS,GF] 116 E Ashley Ave (at Center St), Folly Beach **843/588-3351** *beach access*

Height of Folly [MO,N,WI,GO] 1309 E Ashley Ave, Folly Beach **843/588-6200** *beachfront apts, hot tub*

Phoebe Pember House [GF] 26 Society St (at East Bay) **843/722-4186** *also yoga classes*

Wentworth Mansion [GF,NS,WI] 149 Wentworth St **843/853-1886, 888/466-1886**

Bars

Dudley's on Ann [M,NH,K,18+,GO] 42 Ann St (at King St) **843/577-6779** *4pm-2am*

Patrick's Pub [MW,NH,TG,E,K,S,WC] 1377 Ashley River Rd/ Hwy 61 **843/571-3435** *6pm-2am, patio bar*

Nightclubs

Club Pantheon [M,D,MR,E,C,DS,GO] 28 Ann St (at King) **843/577-2582** *10pm-2am Fri-Sun only*

Deja Vu II [W,D,F,E,DS,S,PC,WC,GO] 4628 Spruill Ave **843/554-5959** *5pm-close Th, from 10pm Fri-Sat*

Cafes

Bear E Patch [WC] 1980A Ashley River Rd **843/766-6490** *7am-9pm, 8am-8pm Sat, clsd Sun*

Restaurants

82 Queen 82 Queen St **843/723-7591, 800/849-0082** *lunch & dinner daily, brunch Sun, Lowcountry cuisine*

Blossom Cafe [WC] 171 E Bay St **843/722-9200** *11:30am-10pm, till 11pm wknds, Sun brunch, seafood, courtyard*

Fat Hen [★E,BW] 3140 Maybank Hwy, St Johns Island **843/559-9090** *5:30pm-11pm, clsd Mon, French bistro, seafood*

Fig [WC] 232 Meeting St (near Hasell) **843/805-5900** *5:30pm-10:30pm, till 11pm Fri-Sat*

High Cotton 199 E Bay St **843/724-3815** *lunch Sat, brunch Sun, dinner nightly, Southern cuisine, full bar*

Hominy Grill 207 Rutledge Ave (at Cannon) **843/937-0930** *great brkfst*

Jim 'N Nick's Bar-B-Q 288 King St **843/577-0406** *10:30am-9pm, till 10pm Fri-Sat*

Joe Pasta 428 King St (at John) **843/965-5252** *11:30am-11pm, till midnight Fri-Sat, also full bar*

Magnolias 185 E Bay St #200 **843/577-7771** *lunch & dinner, brunch Sun, Southern*

Melvin's Legendary Bar-B-Que 538 Folly Rd **843/762-0511** *10:45am-9:30pm, clsd Sun*

Tropical Taxi 177 Meeting St (near Hasell) **843/723-1111** *7am-9pm, till 5pm Tue & Th, soups, sandwiches & desserts*

Vickery's of Beaufain Street [★] 15 Beaufain St (at St Philip) **843/577-5300** *11:30am-1am, from 11am Sun, Cuban influence, full bar*

Entertainment & Recreation

Historic Charleston Foundation 40 E Bay St **843/723-1623** *call for info on city walking tours (March-April only)*

Spoleto Festival USA 843/722-2764 *2-week avant-garde performing art festival in late May-early June*

Publications

Q Notes 704/531-9988 *bi-weekly LGBT newspaper for the Carolinas*

Cruisy Areas

Folly Beach [AYOR] western tip of island (make a right at the island's only traffic light & drive all the way to county park)

West Ashley Park [AYOR]

Columbia

Info Lines & Services

The Harriet Hancock Center for Gay & Lesbian SC 1108 Woodrow St **803/771-7713** *5:30pm-9pm, 1pm-3pm wknds, clsd Mon & Fri*

Primary Purpose Gay/ Lesbian AA 5220 Clemson (in the house behind St Martin's Church) **803/254-5301(AA#)** *7pm Sun*

Bars

The Alternative Watering Hole H20 [M,NH,DS,B,TG,K,PC,WC,GO] 220 State St (across the Gervais Bridge), W Columbia **803/794-8443** *6pm-2am*

Art Bar [GS,D,K] 1211 Park St **803/929-0198** *8pm-close*

Capital Club [M,NH,P,PC,WC] 1002 Gervais St **803/256-6464** *5pm-2am*

Nightclubs

Club Ice [GS,D,18+,PC] 920 Lady St (at Park) **803/765-1574** *10pm-close Th-Sat only*

PTS 1109 [MW,D,MR,TG,S,PC,GO] 1109 Assembly St (at Gervais St) **803/253-8900** *5pm-2am, till 6am Fri, till 3am Sat-Sun*

Entertainment & Recreation

Rainbow Radio 803/771-7713 *10am Sun, weekly LGBT radio program*

Retail Shops

Papa Jazz Record Shoppe 2014 Greene St **803/256-0095** *10am-7pm, 1pm-6pm Sun*

Men's Services

▶ **Megaphone 803/939-0666** *Meet and Chat Live with HOT local men. FREE to listen & respond to ads. Video and text chat at GayMates.com. Use FREE code 4889.*

Erotica

Video Magic 5445 Two Notch Rd **803/786-8125**

Cruisy Areas

Senate Street [AYOR] near the university

Florence

Cruisy Areas

Timrod Park [AYOR]

Greenville

Accommodations

Walnut Lane Inn [GF,WI,GO] 110 Ridge Rd (at Groce Rd), Lyman **864/949-7230, 800/949-4686** *full brkfst*

Bars

Sugar Shack [MW,D,E,DS,PC] 424 Laurens Rd **864/242-0294** *7pm-close Th-Sun*

Nightclubs

The Castle [★MW,D,DS,S,V,YC,PC] 8-B Legrande Blvd **864/235-9949** *9:30pm-3am Fri-Sun*

Bookstores

Out of Bounds 21 S Pleasantburg Dr **864/239-0106** *2pm- 8pm, till 6pm Sun, from 11am Fri-Sat*

Men's Services

▶ **Megaphone 864/421-0400** *Meet and Chat Live with HOT local men. FREE to listen & respond to ads. Video and text chat at GayMates.com. Use FREE code 4889.*

Hilton Head

Bars

Twist/ Two Dollar Bill's [MW,NH,TG,F] 32 Palmetto Bay Rd #D-2 (at Sea Pines Cir) **843/341-6933** *11am-2am, till midnight Sun*

Cruisy Areas

Coligny Circle Beach [AYOR] S of the Holiday Inn (at the end of Pope Ave)

Pinckney State Park [AYOR] Hwy 278 *days*

Mountain Rest

Accommodations

Crystal Lake Cottage [GS,NS,GO] **828/622-3336** *quiet 1-bdrm cottage on private lake in mtns of SC, near Highlands, NC*

Myrtle Beach

Info Lines & Services

The Center Project 307 Hwy 15 (at 3rd Ave S) **843/626-4953** *2pm-9pm, till 6pm Sat-Mon, LGBT community center*

Accommodations

Lillypad Studios [MO] 407 12th Ave S (at Ocean Blvd) **843/450-4225**

Bars

Time Out [★M,NH,D,K,DS,S,PC,WC] 520 8th Ave N (at Oak) **843/448-1180** *5pm-close, till 2am Sat, patio bar*

Nightclubs

Rainbow House [MW,D,DS,WC] 815 N Kings Hwy **843/626-7298** *3pm-5am, till 2am wknds, patio*

Restaurants

Cedar Hill Landing Seafood & Oyster Roast [E,WC] 5225 Hwy 17 (Business), Murrells Inlet **843/651-8706** *10am-10pm, full bar*

Erotica

X-citement Video 3106 Hwy 17 S **843/272-0744** *24hrs*

Cruisy Areas

Huntington Beach State Park [AYOR] Hwy 17 S *Mon-Fri*

Hurl Rock Park [AYOR] at 21st Ave S (south end)

Rock Hill

Info Lines & Services

Catawba Care Coalition 1151 Camden Ave **803/909-6363** *HIV/AIDS support & services, free testing, free condoms*

Bars

Hideaway [MW,NH,K,DS,PC] 405 Baskins Rd **803/328-6630** *8pm-close Th-Sat*

Spartanburg

Men's Services

South Dakota

Statewide

Publications

Lavender Magazine 612/436-4660, 877/515-9969 *LGBT newsmagazine for IA, MN, ND, SD, WI*

Batesland

Accommodations

Wakpamni B&B [GF,NS,WI] (on the Pine Ridge Indian Reservation) **605/288-1800** *rooms & tipis, full brkfst, dinner available*

Hot Springs

Entertainment & Recreation

Springs Bath House [GF] 146 N Garden St (at University, near River St) **605/745-4424, 888/817-1972** *10am-9pm (seasonal), 1880s bathhouse w/ hot mineral-water soaking pools (indoor & outdoor), massage center, day-spa services*

Murdo

Accommodations

Iversen Inn [GF,WI,GO] 108 E 5th St (btwn I-90 & Hwy 83) **605/669-2452** *refrigerators & microwaves*

Pierre

Cruisy Areas

LaFramboise Island [AYOR] off the causeway

Rapid City

Info Lines & Services

The Black Hills Center For Equality 1102 West Rapid St **605/348-3244** *11am-5pm, till 6pm Sat, clsd Sun, LGBT resource center*

Unified Live & Let Live AA 522 7th St #218 **605/209-9225** *8pm Fri*

Accommodations

Camp Michael B&B [M,NS,GO] 1103 12th St **605/342-5590**

Salem

Accommodations

Camp America [GF,SW,NS,GO] 25495 US 81 **605/425-9085** *35 miles W of Sioux Falls, camping, RV hookups, lesbian-owned*

Sioux Falls

Info Lines & Services

The Center 3600 S Minnesota Ave #5 **605/331-1153** *support groups, counseling, library & more*

Bars

Toppers [MW,K] 1213 N Cliff Ave **605/339-7686** *3pm-close, till 2am Fri-Sat, clsd Sun*

Nightclubs

Club David [MW,D,K,DS] 214 W 10th St (btwn Main & Dakota) **605/274-0700** *4:30pm-2am, also restaurant*

Erotica

Romantix Adult Superstore 311 N Dakota Ave (btwn 6th & 7th) **605/332-9316** *24hrs*

Cruisy Areas

Sherman Park [AYOR] Kiwanis (btwn 12th & 26th Sts)

Spearfish

Cafes

The Bay Leaf Cafe 126 W Hudson St **605/642-5462** *lunch & dinner, plenty veggie, espresso bar*

TENNESSEE

Statewide

Publications

Southern Voice 404/876-1819 *weekly LGBT newspaper for AL, FL (panhandle), GA, LA, MS, TN w/ resource listings*

Bristol

Accommodations

An Appalachian Mountain Vacation [GF,NS,WI,WC] 138 Moreland Dr, Butler **423/768-2446, 888/781-2399**

Chattanooga

Bars

Chuck's II [MW,NH,D,K,OC] 27-1/2 W Main (at Market) **423/265-5405** *6pm-1am, till 3am Fri-Sat, patio*

Nightclubs

Alan Gold's [★MW,D,F,DS,S,YC,WC] 1100 McCallie Ave (at Central) **423/629-8080** *4:30pm-3am*

Images [MW,D,F,DS,WC] 6005 Lee Hwy **423/855-8210** *5pm-3am, also restaurant*

Men's Services

▶ **Megaphone 423/535-9900** *Meet and Chat Live with HOT local men. FREE to listen & respond to ads. Video and text chat at GayMates.com. Use FREE code 4889.*

Clarksville

Cruisy Areas

Fairground Park [AYOR]

Gatlinburg

Accommodations

Big Creek Stables & Big Creek Outpost [GS,WC] 5019 Rag Mtn Rd, Hartford **423/487-5742, 423/487-3490** *cabins, camping, horseback riding*

Christopher Place, An Intimate Resort [GS,SW,NS,WC] 1500 Pinnacles Wy, Newport **423/623-6555, 800/595-9441** *full brkfst*

English Mountaintop Villa [GF,SW,NS,WI,WC] Cove Rd, Sevierville **865/522-8547** *private condo in Great Smoky Mtns National Park, panoramic views*

Four Seasons View [MW,NS,GO] 3588 Four Seasons Ln (at Little Cove Rd), Sevierville **386/837-1458** *private home in Wears Valley, sleeps 5, near Smoky Mtns, great views, hot tub*

Mountain Vista Cabins [MW,NS] 1805 Shady Grove Rd (at Old Birds Creek Rd), Sevierville **865/712-9897** *hot tub*

Stonecreek Cabins [MW,NS,GO] **865/429-0400** *23-acre paradise*

Greeneville

Accommodations

Timberfell Lodge [MO,F,SW,N,NS,GO] 2240 Van Hill Rd (exit 36, off I-81) **423/234-0833, 800/437-0118** *also camping & RV hookups, full brkfst, hot tub*

Jackson

Erotica

I-40 Bookstore [18+] 186 Providence Rd, Denmark **731/424-7226**

Cruisy Areas

Muse Park [AYOR]

Johnson City

Accommodations

Cabin on Twin Pine Lane [GF,NS] 142 Twin Pine Ln (at Airport Rd), Elizabethton **423/542-8962** *cabin in forest w/ views of mountains & waterfall, sleeps 5*

Safehaven Farm [GF,NS] 336 Stanley Hollow Rd, Roan Mountain **423/725-4262** *cabins, creekside privacy, fireplace, wraparound porch*

Nightclubs

New Beginnings [★M,D,F,DS,WC] 2910 N Bristol Hwy **423/282-4446** *9pm-3am, from 8pm Fri-Sat, clsd Mon*

Retail Shops

My Secret Closet 2910 N Bristol Hwy (inside New Beginnings) **423/282-4446** *10pm-3am Fri-Sat only, pride gifts*

Kingsport

Cruisy Areas

Sullivan St [AYOR] near library

Knoxville

Info Lines & Services

AA Gay/ Lesbian 2931 Kingston Pike (at Unitarian Church) **865/522-9667 (AA#)** *8pm Fri*

Bars

Kurt's Bar [M,NH,D,F,E,K,WC,GO] 4928 Homberg Dr (at Kingston Pike) **865/558-5720** *4pm-3am, from 9pm Mon-Tue, restaurant, patio*

Nightclubs

Club XYZ [MW,D,DS] 1215 N Central **865/637-4999** *5:30pm-3am, from 9pm Sat, from 7pm Sun*

The New Rainbow Club West [MW,D,F,K,DS,WC] 7211 Kingston Pike **865/588-8030** *5pm-3am*

Men's Services

Erotica

Town & Country News 6927 Clinton Hwy **865/947-9153**

West Knoxville News 5011 Kingston Pike **865/588-1972** *24hrs*

Cruisy Areas

The Block [AYOR] 100 Northview Dr (in Bearden area W of UT) *10pm-5am every night, hottest Fri-Sat after bars close*

Downtown [AYOR] btwn post office & library

IC King Park [AYOR] off Alcoa Hwy

Sharps Ridge [AYOR] off N Broadway

The Square [AYOR] intersection of Church, Market, Walnut & Union Sts

Memphis

Info Lines & Services

AA Intergroup 1835 Union Ave #302 **901/726-6750**

Memphis Gay/ Lesbian Community Center 892 S Cooper **901/278-6422, 901/278-4297 (hotline)** *24-hr recorded info, groups*

Accommodations

French Quarter Suites [GF] 2144 Madison **901/728-4000, 800/843-0353** *also Bourbon St Cafe*

Madison Hotel [GF,SW,NS] 79 Madison Ave **901/333-1200**

Shellcrest Guesthouse [GS,NS,WI,GO] 671 Jefferson Ave (at N Orleans St) **901/277-0223** *suites in Victorian*

Talbot Heirs Guesthouse [GF,NS] 99 S 2nd St (btwn Union & Peabody Pl) **901/527-9772, 800/955-3956** *suites w/ kitchens, funky decor*

Bars

Dru's Place [W,NH,D,BYOB] 1474 Madison (at McNeil) **901/275-8082** *11am-midnight, till 3am Fri-Sat, from noon Sun, beer & set-ups only*

Lorenz/Aftershock [MW,NH,D,DS,MR] 1528 Madison Ave (at Avalon) **901/274-8272** *11am-3am, patio*

The Metro [MW,D,F,K,WC] 1349 Autumn St (at Cleveland) **901/274-8010** *6pm-3am, from 4pm Sun*

Mollie Fontaine Lounge [GS,F] 679 Adams Ave **901/524-1886** *5pm-2am, clsd Sun-Tue*

Pumping Station [M,D,WC] 1382 Poplar (at Cleveland) **901/272-7600** *4pm-3am, from 3pm wknds, courtyard*

The Vault [GS,D,E,K] 529 S Highland St **901/452-6583** *5pm-3am, live jazz Wed*

Nightclubs

Backstreet [MW,D,K,C,18+,WC] 2018 Court Ave (at Morrison) **901/276-5522** *8pm-6am Wed-Sun only, beer & set-ups only*

Crossroads [MW,NH,K,DS] 1278 Jefferson (at Claybrook) **901/272-8801** *4pm-midnight, 3pm-3am Fri-Sun*

Cafes

Java Cabana [E] 2170 Young Ave (at Cooper) **901/272-7210** *6:30am-10pm, 9am-midnight Fri-Sat, noon-10pm Sun, clsd Mon, also art gallery*

Otherlands Coffee Bar [★F,E,WI] 641 S Cooper (at Central) **901/278-4994** *7am-8pm, live music till 11pm Fri-Sat, also gift shop*

P&H Cafe [F,E,BW,WC] 1532 Madison (at Adeline) **901/726-0906** *3pm-3am, from 5pm Sat, clsd Sun*

Restaurants

Automatic Slim's Tonga Club [WC] 83 S 2nd St (at Union) **901/525-7948** *lunch & dinner, Sun brunch, Caribbean & Southwestern, full bar*

Cafe Eclectic 603 N McLean Blvd (at Faxon Ave) **901/725-1718** *6am-10pm, 9am-3pm Sun*

Cafe Society [WC] 212 N Evergreen Ave (btwn McLean & Belvedere) **901/722-2177** *lunch Mon-Fri, dinner nightly, full bar*

Dish 948 S Cooper (at Young) **901/276-0002** *dinner till 10pm, bar till 3am Wed-Sun, Mediterranean tapas*

India Palace 1720 Poplar Ave **901/278-1199**

Leonard's Pit Barbecue 5465 Fox Plaza Dr **901/360-1963** *11am-9pm, Elvis ordered the pork sandwich at the original Leonard's (now closed), but the food is just as good here!*

Molly's La Casita 2006 Madison Ave (at N Morrison St) **901/726-1873** *Mexican*

Pie in the Sky 2149 Young Ave (at S Cooper) **901/276-7437** *pizza*

Quetzal 668 Union Ave **901/521-8388** *cafe & restaurant, gay events during the evening*

Saigon Le 51 N Cleveland **901/276-5326** *11am-9pm, clsd Sun, pan-Asian*

Sweet Bistro 938 S Cooper **901/726-4300** *11am-midnight Fri-Sat, Sun brunch, 5pm-10pm Wed-Th, clsd Mon-Tue, amazing desserts*

Tsunami 928 S Cooper **901/274-2556** *lunch & dinner, Pacific rim cuisine*

Entertainment & Recreation

Center for Southern Folklore [F] 119 S Main St (at Peabody Pl) **901/525-3655** *11am-6pm, clsd Sun, open later for shows, live music, gallery, also cybercafe*

Graceland 3734 Elvis Presley Blvd **901/332-3322, 800/238-2000** *no visit to Memphis would be complete w/out a trip to see The King*

Memphis Rock 'N Roll Tours **901/359-3102** *historical tour of Memphis music scene*

Bookstores

Davis-Kidd Booksellers 387 Perkins Rd Ext (at Poplar & Walnut Grove) **901/683-9801** *9am-9pm, till 8pm Sun, some LGBT titles, also cafe*

Retail Shops

Inz & Outz [WC] 553 S Cooper **901/728-6535** *10am-7pm, till 8pm Fri-Sat, noon-5pm Sun, pride items, books*

Publications

Triangle Journal News **901/857-8523** *LGBT newspaper*

Men's Services

Erotica

Airport Book Mart 2214 Brooks Rd E (at Airways) **901/345-0657**

Cherokee Books 2947 Lamar **901/744-7494**

Getwell Books 1275 Getwell (at Park) **901/454-7765**

Paris Theater 2432 Summer Ave (at Hollywood) **901/323-2665**

Romantix Adult Superstore 1617 Getwell Rd **901/744-4513**

Romantix Adult Superstore 2220 E Brooks Rd **901/396-9050**

Romantix Adult Superstore 5939 Summer Ave **901/373-5760**

Nashville

Info Lines & Services

AA Gay/ Lesbian 615/831-1050 *call for info*

Accommodations

The Big Bungalow B&B [GF,E,NS] 618 Fatherland St **615/256-8375** *full brkfst, live music, massage available*

Doubletree Nashville [GF,WI] 315 4th Ave N **615/244-8200** *also restaurant & lounge, fitness center*

Top O' Woodland Historic B&B Inn [GF] 1603 Woodland St (at 16th) **615/228-3868, 888/228-3868** *full brkfst*

Bars

Blue Gene's [M,B,K,WI] 1715 Church St **615/329-3508** *4pm-3am, from 3pm wknds, clsd Mon*

Purple Heys [MW,NH,F,WC] 1401 4th Ave S (btwn Lafayette & Chestnut) **615/244-4433** *11am-3am*

Stirrup Nashville [M,NH,MR,F,WC] 1529 4th Ave S (at Mallory Ave) **615/782-0043** *noon-3am, patio*

Trax [M,NH,K,WI] 1501 2nd Ave S (at Carney) **615/742-8856** *noon-3am*

Tribe/ Red [MW,F,E,V,WC,GO] 1517 Church St (at 15th Ave S) **615/329-2912** *4pm-midnight, till 2am wknds, upscale, full restaurant*

Vibe [MW,D,DS] 1715 Church St (at 17th & 18th) **615/329-3838** *9pm Sat only, patio*

Nightclubs

Play Dance Bar [M,D,MR,TG,E,DS,18+,WC] 1519 Church St **615/322-9627** *9pm-3am Wed-Sun*

Cafes

Bongo Java [E] 2007 Belmont Blvd **615/385-5282** *7am-11pm, from 8am wknds, coffeehouse, deck, also serves brkfst, lunch & dinner*

Fido [F] 1812 21st Ave S **615/777-3436** *7am-11pm, till midnight Fri-Sat, from 8am wknds, also full menu*

Restaurants

Battered & Fried 1008 Woodland St **615/226-9283** *lunch & dinner, seafood, full bar, also Wave sushi bar*

Beyond the Edge 112 S 11th St **615/226-3343** *11am-2am, pizza & sandwiches, full bar*

Cafe Coco [E,BW] 210 Louise Ave **615/321-2626** *24hrs, patio*

Calypso Cafe 2424 Elliston Pl **615/321-3878** *11am-9pm, 11:30am-8:30pm wknds, Caribbean*

International Market 2010 Belmont Blvd (at International) **615/297-4453** *10:30am-9pm, Thai/ Chinese, plenty veggie*

Mad Donna's 1313 Woodland St (at 14th) **615/226-1617** *11am-10pm, till 11pm Sat, clsd Mon, also lounge, drag bingo Tue*

The Mad Platter [R,WC] 1239 6th Ave N (at Monroe) **615/242-2563** *lunch Mon-Fri, dinner Wed-Sun*

Rumba 3009 W End Ave **615/321-1350** *4pm-close, from 5pm Sun, Latin/ Asian*

Rumours Wine & Art Bar 2304 12th Ave S **615/292-9400** *5pm-midnight, clsd Sun*

Sky Blue Coffeehouse & Bistro 700 Fatherland St (at S 7th St) **615/770-7097** *brkfst & lunch*

Sole Mio 311 3rd Ave S **615/256-4013** *11am-10pm, till midnight Fri-Sat, clsd Mon, Italian*

The Standard at the Smith House 167 8th Ave N (btwn Church & Commerce) **615/254-1277** *dinner Tue-Sat, clsd Sun-Mon*

Entertainment & Recreation

NashTrash Tours [R] tours leave from the Farmers Market (900 8th Ave N) **615/226-7300, 800/342-2132** *campy tours of Nashville w/ the Jugg Sisters*

Tennessee Repertory Theater 505 Deaderick St (at the Tennessee Performing Arts Center) **615/244-4878**

Bookstores

Davis-Kidd Booksellers 2121 Green Hills Village Dr **615/385-2645** *9am-9pm, till 10pm Fri-Sat, 10am-7pm Sun, LGBT section*

Outloud Books & Gifts [GO] 1703 Church St (btwn 17th & 18th Ave) **615/340-0034** *10am-10pm, till 11pm Fri-Sat, LGBT, also cafe*

Publications

Inside Out Nashville 615/831-1806 *LGBT newspaper & bar guide*

Out & About Newspaper 617 Hart Ln (at Ben Allen Rd) **615/596-6210** *LGBT newspaper for Nashville, Knoxville, Chattanooga & Atlanta area, monthly*

Men's Services

Erotica

▸ **Lion's Den** 2807 Nolensville Pike **615/254-8891** *24hrs*

The Metro News [WI] 822 5th Ave S **615/256-1310** *24hrs*

Cruisy Areas

J Percy Priest Dam [AYOR]

Pigeon Forge

Entertainment & Recreation

Dollywood 1020 Dollywood Ln **800/365-5996** *Dolly Parton's "wholesome Smoky Mtn theme park," 35 miles SE of Knoxville*

Sewanee

Accommodations

Boxwood Cottage B&B [MO,NS,GO] 293 Anderson Cemetery Rd **931/598-5012** *mtn-top log cabin near state park, full brkfst*

Waverly

Restaurants

Pizza Villa [GO] 241 E Commerce St (at Cooley) **931/296-4411**

Texas

Statewide

Publications

▶ **Ambush Mag 504/522-8049** *LGBT newspaper for the Gulf South (TX through FL)*

Abilene

Cruisy Areas

Kirby Park [AYOR]

Amarillo

Info Lines & Services

OUTstanding Amarillo 616 S Harrison (at 7th) **806/337-1688** *7pm-10pm Fri, LGBT community center*

Bars

212 Club [MW,NH,D,DS,WC] 212 W 6th St (at Harrison) **806/372-7997** *2pm-2am*

Kick Back [MW,NH,K,GO] 521 E 10th St (at Lincoln) **806/371-3535** *3pm-2am, clsd Sun*

R&R [GF,NH,GO] 701 S Georgia **806/342-9000** *4pm-2am*

Sassy's [MW,D,K,DS] 309 W 6th St **806/374-3029** *3pm-2am Th, 6pm-3am Fri-Sat*

Restaurants

Furrbie's [GO] 210 W 6th Ave **806/220-0841** *clsd Mon, 11am-4pm, 11am-7:30pm Sat, 11:30am-3pm Sun*

Erotica

Fantasy Gifts & Video 440 N Lakeside **806/372-6500**

Studio One 9000 Triangle Dr **806/376-5379** *24hrs*

Arlington

see also Dallas & Fort Worth

Info Lines & Services

Tarrant County Lesbian/ Gay Alliance 817/877-5544 *info line, meetings*

Accommodations

A&A's Executive Inn & Suites [GF,SW,WI] **817/652-3100**

Nightclubs

The 1851 Club [MW,D,K,DS,V,WC] 1851 W Division (at Fielder) **817/801-9303** *3pm-2am*

Austin

Info Lines & Services

Lambda AA (Live & Let Live) [NS,WC] 7801 N Lamar Blvd (at W Anderson Ln) **512/444-0071, 512/832-6767 (en español)** *8pm daily, also 6:30pm Mon-Tue & Th-Fri, 10am Sat, 11am Sun*

Q 3408 West Ave (2 blks W of Guadalupe & 34th) **512/420-8557** *2pm-10pm Tue-Sat, support & information for GBTQI men 18-29*

Accommodations

Austin Folk House [GS,NS,WC] 506 W 22nd St (at Nueces) **512/472-6700, 866/472-6700** *B&B in restored 1880 house*

Brava House [GF,NS,WI] 1108 Blanco St (at W 11th) **512/478-5034, 866/892-5726** *1880s Victorian close to downtown & 6th Street*

Days Inn North [GF,SW,WC] 820 E Anderson Ln/ Hwy 183 (at I-35) **512/835-4311, 866/835-4311** *200-car (free) parking lot, good for truckers & tour buses*

Driskill Hotel [GF,F,WC] 604 Brazos St (at 6th) **512/474-5911, 800/252-9367** *even if you don't stay in this landmark hotel, be sure to check out the lobby*

Hotel San Jose [★GS,SW,NS,WC,GO] 1316 S Congress Ave **512/444-7322, 800/574-8897** *small boutique hotel*

Kimber Modern [GS,WI,WO] 110 The Circle **512/912-1046**

Mi Yard B&B [GF,NS,WI] 2307 Riverside Farms Rd (of I-35) **512/789-3486** *minutes from downtown Austin, hot tub*

Mt Gainor Inn B&B [GS,NS,WI] 2390 Prochnow Rd (at Mt Gainor Rd), Dripping Springs **512/858-0982, 888/644-0982**

Omni Austin Hotel Downtown [GF,F,SW,WI,WC] 700 San Jacinto (at 8th) **512/476-3700, 800/843-6664** *rooftop pool, also health club*

Park Lane Guest House [GS,SW,WC,GO] 221 Park Ln (at Drake) **512/447-7460, 800/492-8827** *full brkfst, also cottage*

Robin's Nest [GF] 1007 Stewart Cove **512/266-3413** *B&B in 3 homes on Lake Travis*

Star of Texas Inn [GF,NS] 611 W 22nd St (at Rio Grande) **512/472-6700, 866/472-6700** *neo-classical Victorian, full brkfst*

Bars

'Bout Time [★MW,NH,TG,K,DS,WI,WC] 9601 N Ih 35 (at Rundberg) **512/832-5339** *2pm-2am, volleyball court*

Casino El Camino [GF,NH,F,WI,WC] 517 E 6th St (at Red River) **512/469-9330** *4pm-2am, psychedelic punk jazz lounge, great burgers*

Chain Drive [M,D,L,WC] 504 Willow St (at Red River) **512/480-9017** *4pm-2am, clsd Tue, live music Wed, Bear Bust 2nd Sun, cruisy*

Charlie's Austin [★M,D,DS,S,18+,YC,NS,WC] 1301 Lavaca (at 13th) **512/474-6481** *11:30am-2am, from 2pm wknds, smoking patio*

The Peacock [GF] 515 Pedernales St (1.25 miles E of I-35) (E Sixth St) **512/276-8979** *8pm-2am Sat-Tue, 5pm-2am Wed-Fri, retro-cool cocktail lounge that mixes vintage cocktails*

Rainbow Cattle Company [MW,D,K,CW,WI] 305 W 5th St (btwn Guadalupe & Lavaca) **512/472-5288** *3pm-2am, from 8pm wknds, clsd Mon, CW dance classes Tue, Latino night Sun*

Rusty Spurs [MW,D,CW] 405 E 7th Street (E of Trinity) **512/482-9002** *4pm-2am, till midnight Sun, clsd Mon*

Nightclubs

Cock Pit [M,D,S] 113 San Jacinto Blvd (btwn 1st & 2nd) **512/457-8010** *2pm-2am, theme nights, patio*

Kiss & Fly [M,D] 404 Colorado **512/476-7799** *9pm-close Wed-Sat, from 5pm Sun*

Oil Can Harry's [★M,D,K,S,DS,YC,WI,WC] 211 W 4th St (btwn Lavaca & Colorado) **512/320-8823** *2pm-close, patio, [18+] after 10pm Mon-Fri*

Rain [M,D,K] 217-B W 4th St (at Colorado St) **512/494-1150** *4pm-close, from 3pm Fri-Sun, upscale gay lounge*

Cafes

Austin Java Cafe & Coffeehouse [F] 1608 Barton Springs Rd (at Kinney Ave) **512/482-9450** *7am-11pm, till midnight Fri, from 8am Sat, till 11pm Sun; also 1206 Parkway (at 12th & Lamar), 512/476-1829 & 300 W 2nd St, Ste 100, 512/481-9400*

Bouldin Creek Coffeehouse [F] 1501 S 1st St (at Elizabeth) **512/416-1601** *7am-midnight, from 9am wknds, vegetarian; occasional live music*

Joe's Bakery & Coffee Shop 2305 E 7th St (at Morelos & Northwestern) **512/472-0017** *7am-3pm, clsd Mon, Tex-Mex*

Little City Espresso Bar & Cafe [F,BW,WI,WC] 916 Congress Ave (at E 11th St) **512/476-2489** *popular gay hangout*

Spider House Patio Bar & Cafe [F,BW,E] 2908 Fruth St (at West Dr) **512/480-9562** *7am-2am, plenty veggie, patio*

Restaurants

The Belmont 305 W 6th St **512/457-0300** *11:30am-2am, from 5pm wknds, swank midcentury modern eatery & lounge*

Castle Hill Cafe [WC] 1101 W 5th St (at Baylor) **512/476-0728** *lunch weekdays & dinner nightly, clsd Sun, romantic*

Chuy's 1728 Barton Springs Rd **512/474-4452** *11am-10pm, till 11pm Fri-Sat, Tex-Mex, full bar*

Eastside Cafe [BW,WC] 2113 Manor Rd (at Coleto, by bright yellow gas station) **512/476-5858** *11:30am-9:30pm, 10am-10pm wknds*

El Sol y La Luna [★E,WC,GO] 600 E 6th St (at Red River) **512/444-7770** *7am-11pm, till 2pm Fri-Sat, 9am-4pm Sun, great brkfst, Latin American*

Fonda San Miguel 2330 W North Loop (at Hancock Rd) **512/459-4121** *dinner only Mon-Sat, popular Sun brunch, Mexican, full bar*

Galaxy 1000 W Lynn **512/478-3434** *7am-10pm, quick, stylish & tasty*

Imperia 310 Colorado St **512/472-6770** *dinner only, upscale Asian, full bar*

Jo's Hot Coffee & Good Food [WC,GO] 1300 S Congress Ave (at James) **512/444-3800** *7am-9pm, till 10pm Sat; also 242 W 2nd St, 512/469-9003*

Katz's [WC] 618 W 6th St (at Rio Grande) **512/472-2037** *24hrs, NY-style deli, full bar*

The Kitchen Door [GO] 3742 Far West Blvd (at Hart Ln) **512/794-1100** *7am-7pm, clsd Sun; also at 221 W 6th St, 512/476-1000*

Mother's Cafe & Garden [★] 4215 Duval St (at 43rd) **512/451-3994** *11:15am-10pm, from 10am wknds, vegetarian*

Nueva Onda [GO] 2218 College Ave (off S Congress & Oltorf) **512/447-5063** *7:30am-3pm, from 8am Sun, Mexican, some veggie, patio*

Pangaea [GF] 409 Colorado St **512/472-8882** *9pm-2am Th-Sat, safari-themed ultra lounge*

Romeo's [E,WC] 1500 Barton Springs Rd (near Lamar) **512/476-1090** *11am-10pm, till 11pm Fri-Sat, Italian, some veggie, full bar, live music nightly*

Threadgill's [E] 6416 N Lamar (at Koenig) **512/451-5440** *10am-10pm, till 9pm Sun, great chicken-fried steak, live music Wed; also 301 W Riverside Dr, 512/472-9304, beer garden, live music*

Entertainment & Recreation

Austin Cabaret Theatre 701 W Riverside Drive (at the Long Center) **512/453-2287**

Barton Springs [N] Barton Springs Rd (in Zilker Park) *natural swimming hole*

Bat Colony Congress Ave Bridge (at Barton Springs Dr) *everything's bigger in Texas—including the colony of bats that flies out from under this bridge every evening March-Oct*

Capital City Men's Chorus **512/477-7464** *call for events*

Historic Austin Tours 209 E 6th St (in the Visitor Information Center, open 9am-5pm, till 6pm Sat-Sun) **512/478-0098, 866/468-8784** *free guided & self-guided tours of the Capitol, Congress Ave & 6th St, Texas State Cemetery, Hyde Park*

Queer Radio on KOOP 91.7 FM **512/472-1369** *"Outcast" 6pm-6:30pm Sun, queer culture*

Zachary Scott Theatre Center 1510 Toomey Rd (off S Lamar Blvd) **512/476-0541** *diverse theater*

Bookstores

Bookpeople 603 N Lamar Blvd (at 6th) **512/472-5050, 800/853-9757** *9am-11pm, clsd Thanksgiving Day, independent, readings*

Resistencia Bookstore 1801-A S 1st St (at W Annie) **512/416-8885** *emphasis on Chicana/o, Latina/o & Native American titles, also some LGBT of color titles, readings*

Retail Shops

Tapelenders [GO] 1114 W 5th St (at Baylor) **512/472-0844** *10am-10pm, till midnight Fri-Sat, noon-10pm Sun, LGBT videos, novelties*

Publications

▶ **Ambush Mag 504/522-8049** *LGBT newspaper for the Gulf South (TX through FL)*

Austin Chronicle 512/454-5766 *Austin's alternative weekly paper, has extensive online gay guide as well as events calendar (check out www.austinchronicle.com)*

L Style G Style 512/443-6677 *glossy mag*

Gyms & Health Clubs

Hyde Park Gym [GF] 4125 Guadalupe (at 42nd St) **512/459-9174** *5am-10pm, 7am-7pm Sat, 8am-7pm Sun, day passes*

Men's Clubs

Midtowne Spa—Austin [PC] 5815 Airport Blvd (at Koenig) **512/302-9696** *24hrs, outdoor hot tub, sundeck*

Men's Services

▶ **Megaphone 512/480-8400** *Meet and Chat Live with HOT local men. FREE to listen & respond to ads. Video and text chat at GayMates.com. Use FREE code 4889.*

Erotica

Adult Video Megaplexxx 7111 S Ih 35 **512/442-5430** *24hrs, arcade*

Forbidden Fruit 512 Neches (btwn 5th & 6th) **512/478-8358** *woman-owned & operated*

New Video 7901 S Ih 35 **512/280-1142** *24hrs, arcade*

Cruisy Areas

Hippie Hollow-Lake Travis [AYOR]

Beaumont

Info Lines & Services

Lambda AA 1385 Calder Ave **409/832-1107** *8pm Wed & Sat*

Bars

Orleans Street Pub & Patio [MW,NH,D,K,DS] 650 Orleans St **409/835-4243** *7pm-2am, clsd Sun*

Nightclubs

Copa [★MW,D,E,DS,WC] 304 Orleans St (at Liberty) **409/832-4206** *9pm-2am Wed-Sun*

Men's Services

▶ **Megaphone 409/812-0333** *Meet and Chat Live with HOT local men. FREE to listen & respond to ads. Video and text chat at GayMates.com. Use FREE code 4889.*

Brownsville

Nightclubs

Valentinos Night Club [MW,D,E] 765 Central Blvd **956/504-6874** *10pm-3am*

Brownwood

Restaurants

Uncle Roy's Catfish & Seafood Grill 705 Melwood Ave **325/641-1838** *11am-8pm, till 10pm Fri-Sat, bar till midnight nightly*

Bryan

Bars

Revolution Cafe & Bar [GF,NH,TG,F,E,WI] 211 B S Main St (btwn 26th & 28th) **979/823-4044** *3pm-2am, clsd Mon, live jazz/ funk/ reggae nightly*

Nightclubs

Halo Bar [MW,D,DS,V,18+,WC] 121 N Main St (at William J Bryan Pkwy) **979/823-6174** *9:30pm-2am Th-Sat, 2 levels*

Corpus Christi

Info Lines & Services

Clean & Serene AA 1315 Craig (at church) **361/992-8911, 866/672-7029** *8pm Fri*

Accommodations

Anthony's By The Sea [GS,SW,WI,WC,GO] 732 S Pearl St, Rockport **361/729-6100, 800/460-2557** *4 blocks from water, full brkfst, lesbian-owned*

The Belles by the Sea [GS,SW,NS] **361/749-6138** *Euro-style inn on dunes of Mustang Island & Port Aransas, hot tub*

Christy Estates Suites [GF,SW,WC] 3942 Holly Rd (at Weber) **361/854-1091, 800/678-4836** *hot tubs & spas, nonsmoking rooms available*

Port Aransas Inn [GS,SW,WI,WC] 1500 11th St (at Ave G), Port Aransas **361/749-5937, 800/241-8871** *standard rms, apts & 3-bdrm condo; near beach & restaurants*

Bars

Get Happy [MW,NH,D,F,K,GO] 526 S Staples (at Park St) **361/881-8910** *noon-2am*

The Hidden Door [M,NH,D,WC] 802 S Staples St (at Coleman) **361/882-5002** *noon-2am, patio*

The Rose [W,NH] 213 S Staples **361/881-8181** *6pm-2am, from 3pm Sun, clsd Mon*

Nightclubs

Sixx [M,E,DS,S,18+] 1212 Leopard St **361/888-7499** *9pm-2am Wed & Sun, till 4am Fri-Sat*

Entertainment & Recreation

Robert James Provisioners [GF,MR,TG,GO] 837 Redmond **361/937-4880** *8am-10pm, sailboat charters*

Men's Services

Crockett

Accommodations

Warfield House B&B [GS,SW,GO] 712 Houston Ave (in Town Square) **936/544-4037** *turn-of-the-century B&B, pool, hot tub*

Dallas

see also Arlington, Fort Worth

Info Lines & Services

Gay/ Lesbian Switchboard **214/528-0022** *9am-9pm, 10am-5pm Sat, noon-5pm Sun*

John Thomas Gay/ Lesbian Community Center [WC] 2701 Reagan St (at Brown) **214/528-0144, 214/528-0022** *9am-9pm, 10am-6pm Sat, noon-5pm Sun*

Lambda AA 2438 Butler #106 **214/267-0222, 214/887-6699 (Central Office #)** *call for meeting details*

Accommodations

Amelia's Place [GF,WI] 5425 Gaston Ave #112 **214/827-3779** *downtown apt, full brkfst*

Bailey's Uptown Inn [GF,NS,WI] 2505 Worthington St (at Hibernia) **214/720-2258**

Daisy Polk Inn [GF,NS,WI] 2917 Reagan St (at Dickason Ave) **214/522-4692** *B&B in 1909 Arts & Crafts home*

Holiday Inn Select Dallas Central [GS,SW,WI,WC] 10650 N Central Expwy (at Meadow) **214/373-6000, 888/477-STAY**

Hotel Zaza [GF,SW] 2332 Leonard St **214/468-8399, 800/597-8399**

Melrose Hotel [GF,P,SW,WC] 3015 Oak Lawn Ave (at Cedar Springs) **214/521-5151, 800/635-7673** *full brkfst, nonsmoking rooms available, also piano bar & lounge*

Quality Inn Market Center [GF,SW,WI,WC] 1955 Market Center Blvd (at Turtle Creek Blvd) **214/747-9551**

The Stoneleigh Hotel [GF,WI,WC] 2927 Maple Ave (at Randall St) **214/871-7111** *landmark hotel, gym, also restaurant*

Bars

Barbara's Pavillion [M,NH,WC] 325 Centre St (1blk W of Zang) **214/941-2145** *4pm-2am, from 6pm Sat, patio*

Cross Bar [M,NH,K] 5334 Lemmon Ave (at Hudnall) **214/443-8336** *noon-2am*

Dallas Eagle [M,B,L] 2515 Inwood Rd #107 (at Maple, enter rear) **214/357-4375** *4pm-2am, till 4am Fri-Sat*

Grapevine [GS] 3902 Maple Ave (at Shelby) **214/522-8466** *3pm-2am, classic dive bar*

The Hidden Door [M,NH,L,WC] 5025 Bowser Ave (at Mahanna) **214/526-0620** *7am-2am, from noon Sun, patio*

Illusions [MW,NH,K,DS] 4100 Maple Ave (at Throckmorton) **214/252-0552** *4pm-2am, from noon wknds, potlucks Sun*

Jack's Backyard [GS,F] 2303 Pittman St (at W Commerce St) **214/741-3131** *11am-2am, also bar*

JR's Bar & Grill [★MW,F,E,V,YC,WI,WC] 3923 Cedar Springs Rd (at Throckmorton) **214/528-1004** *11am-2am, from noon Sun, upscale*

Mickey's [M,E,V] 3851 Cedar Springs Rd **214/219-6425** *3pm-2am*

The Mining Co [★M,D,L] 3903 Cedar Springs Rd (at Reagan) **214/521-4204** *5pm-4am, clsd Mon-Wed*

Pekers [MW,NH,E,K,C,WC] 2615 Oak Lawn Ave, Ste 101 (btwn Fairmount & Brown) **214/528-3333** *10am-2am*

Pub Pegasus [M,NH,WC] 3326 N Fitzhugh (at Travis) **214/559-4663** *noon-2am, patio*

Rush [M,NH,D,DS] 3903 Lemmon Ave (at Reagan) **214/780-0955** *4pm-2am, from 2pm Sat, from noon Sun*

Sue Ellen's [★W,D,E,WC] 3014 Throckmorton (at Cedar Springs) **214/559-0707** *5pm-2am, 2pm-close wknds, patio*

Tin Room [M,NH] 2514 Hudnall St (at Maple Ave) **214/526-6365** *10am-2am, from noon Sun*

Woody's [MW,K,V,WC] 4011 Cedar Springs Rd (btwn Douglas & Throckmorton) **214/520-6629** *2pm-2am, sports bar, patio*

Zippers [M,NH,S] 3333 N Fitzhugh (at Travis) **214/526-9519** *noon-2am*

Nightclubs

Alexandre's [GS,E] 4026 Cedar Springs Rd (at Knight St) **214/559-0720** *9am-2pm, from 2pm Sun-Mon, live music*

Club Cherries [M,S] 2506 Knight (at Maple) **214/520-8251** *noon-2am*

Havana Bar & Grill [GS,D,MR-L,DS] 4006 Cedar Springs Rd (at Throckmorton) **214/526-9494** *grill 5pm-10pm Wed-Sun, lounge from 10pm*

Joe's Dallas [MW,NH,D,F,K,E,WC,$] 4125 Maple Ave (at Throckmorton) **214/521-2024** *noon-2am, patio*

Kaliente [M,D,MR-L,K,DS] 4350 Maple Ave (at Hondo) **214/520-6676** *9pm-2am, clsd Tue, salsa & Tejano*

Round-Up Saloon [★M,D,CW,K,WC] 3912 Cedar Springs Rd (at Throckmorton) **214/522-9611** *3pm-2am, from noon wknds, 6 bars, patio*

Station 4 [★MW,D,C,DS,S,V,18+] 3911 Cedar Springs Rd (at Throckmorton) **214/526-7171** *9pm-4am Wed-Sun, also Rose Room cabaret, patio*

Cafes

Buli [WI] 3908 Cedar Springs Rd **214/528-5410** *7am-midnight*

Opening Bell Coffee [E,BW] 1409 S Lamar St, Ste 012 **214/565-0383** *7am-10pm, till midnight wknds, clsd Sun*

Restaurants

Ali Baba Cafe 1901 Abrams Rd (near La Vista Dr) **214/823-8235** *lunch and dinner, clsd Sun, Middle Eastern*

Bangkok Orchid [GO,BYOB,WC] 331 W Airport Fwy (N Beltline), Irving **972/252-7770** *lunch & dinner, clsd Mon, ask for Danny*

Black-Eyed Pea [WC] 3857 Cedar Springs Rd (at Reagan) **214/521-4580** *11am-10pm, Southern homecookin'*

Blue Mesa Grill 5100 Beltline Rd (at Tollway), Addison **972/934-0165** *11am-10pm, till 10:30pm Fri-Sat, 10am-9pm Sun, great fajitas, full bar*

Bread Winners [GS,WC] 3301 McKinney Ave **214/754-4940** *brkfst & lunch daily, dinner Tue-Sun, Sun brunch, int'l, full bar*

The Bronx Restaurant & Bar [WC,GO] 3835 Cedar Springs Rd (at Oak Lawn) **214/521-5821** *lunch & dinner, Sun brunch, clsd Mon*

Cafe Brazil 3847 Cedar Springs Rd **214/461-8762** *open 24 hrs*

Cosmic Cafe [F,E] 2912 Oak Lawn Ave **214/521-6157** *11am-10:30pm, till 11pm Fri-Sat, noon-10pm Sun, veggie, also yoga & meditation*

Cremona Bistro & Cafe 2704 Worthington St (at Howell) **214/871-1115** *lunch weekdays & dinner nightly, Italian, full bar, patio, live music Fri-Sat*

Dream Cafe [BW,WI,WC] 2800 Routh St (in the Quadrangle) **214/954-0486** *7am-9pm, till 8pm Fri-Sat, brkfst served till 5pm*

Fitness Essentials [WC,GO] 3878 Oak Lawn, Ste 100E (near Avondale) **214/528-5535** *9am-7pm, till 6pm Sat, clsd Sun, organic, plenty veggie*

Hung Dinger [DS,C,TG] 4000-E Cedar Springs Rd (at Throckmorton) **214/522-4864** *11am-midnight, clsd Mon-Tue, wknd brunch; kitschy Italian supperclub*

Hunky's [★BW,WC,GO] 4000 Cedar Springs Rd (at Throckmorton) **214/522-1212** *11am-10pm, till 11pm Fri-Sat, from noon Sun, burgers & salads, patio*

Lucky's Cafe 3531 Oak Lawn **214/522-3500** *7am-10pm, classic comfort food, great brkfst*

McCormick & Schmick's Seafood Restaurant 307 NorthPark Center (at W Northwest Hwy) **214/891-0100, 888/226-6212** *11am-10pm, till 9pm Sun, fresh seafood, full bar*

Monica Aca y Alla [★TG,E,WC] 2914 Main St (at Malcolm X) **214/748-7140** *lunch Mon-Fri, dinner Tue-Sun, brunch wknds, trendy, contemporary Mexican, full bar, live music wknds, Latin jazz/ salsa*

Rocco's [WI] 2916 McKinney Ave **214/871-9207, 214/871-9208** *lunch & dinner, pizza & pasta*

Stephan Pyles 1807 Ross Ave, Ste 200 **214/580-7000** *lunch Mon-Fri, dinner Mon-Sat, clsd Sun, Southwestern cuisine*

Thai Soon 101 S Coit, Ste 401 (at Beltline) **972/234-6111** *lunch & dinner*

Vitto [BW,WC,GO] 316 W 7th St (at Bishop) **214/946-1212** *lunch Mon-Sat, dinner nightly, Italian*

Ziziki's [WC] 4514 Travis St, #122 (in Travis Walk) **214/521-2233** *11am-10pm, Sun brunch, Greek, full bar*

Entertainment & Recreation

Lambda Weekly KNON 89.3 FM **972/263-5305** *noon Sun, LGBT radio show for northern TX*

Turtle Creek Chorale (TCC) 3630 Harry Hines Blvd (at Sammons Center for the Arts) **214/526-3214, 800/746-4412** *world-famous male choir w/ several subscription concerts yearly & many CDs*

Retail Shops

Obscurities 4000-B Cedar Springs **214/559-3706** *11am-9pm, 2pm-8pm Sun, clsd Mon, tattoo & piercing*

Tapelenders [GO] 3926 Cedar Springs Rd (at Throckmorton) **214/528-6344** *9am-midnight, LGBT T-shirts, books, video rentals*

Union Jack 3920 Cedar Springs Rd **214/528-9600** *men's clothing & underwear*

Publications

Dallas Voice 214/754-8710 *LGBT newspaper w/ extensive resource listings*

Men's Clubs

Club Dallas [★SW,PC] 2616 Swiss Ave (at Good Latimer) **214/821-1990** *24hrs, full gym, steam room, sauna, sundeck*

Midtowne Spa—Dallas [★PC] 2509 Pacific (at Hawkins) **214/821-8989** *24hrs, 3 flrs, rooftop sundeck & hot tub, weekend cookouts*

Men's Services

► **Megaphone 214/615-0100** *Meet and Chat Live with HOT local men. FREE to listen & respond to ads. Video and text chat at GayMates.com. Use FREE code 4889.*

Erotica

Alternatives 1720 W Mockingbird Ln (at Hawes) **214/630-7071** *24hrs*

Amazing Superstore 11327 Reeder Rd (at Royal/ I-35) **972/241-3944** *24hrs, bookstore w/ arcade*

Leather Masters, Dallas 3000 Main St **214/528-3865** *noon-10pm, clsd Sun-Mon, custom leather & more*

Lido Theatre 7035 John Carpenter Fwy (at Mockinbird Ln) **214/630-7127**

Mockingbird Video 708 W Mockingbird Ln (at I-35 & Halifax) **214/631-3003** *24hrs, bookstore w/ arcade*

Odyssey Video 11505 Anaheim Dr (at Forest Ln) **972/484-4999** *24hrs*

Paris Adult Book & Video Store 11118 Harry Hines Blvd **972/263-0774** *24hrs, bookstore w/ arcade*

Cruisy Areas

Reverchon Park [AYOR] 3505 Maple Ave (at Turtle Creek Blvd)

Tom Braniff Park [AYOR] off SH 114 (at Tom Braniff exit) *beware cops (!)*

Denison

Bars

Good Time Lounge [MW,K,DS] 2520 Hwy 91 N **903/463-6086** *7pm-2am Wed-Sun*

Denton

Cafes

Cupboard Natural Foods 200 W Congress St (at Elm) **940/387-5386** *8am-9pm, 10am-8pm Sun, health food store & cafe*

El Paso

see also Ciudad Juárez, Mexico

Info Lines & Services

El Paso GLBT Community Center [F] 216 S Ochoa **206/600-4297** *24-hr hotline, events, pride store, De Ambiente Cafe*

Lambda Line 206/350-4283

Bars

Briar Patch [MW,NH,K] 508 N Stanton (at Missouri) **915/577-9555** *noon-2am, patio*

Chiquita's Bar [MW,NH,MR-L,WC] 310 E Missouri (at Stanton) **915/351-0095** *2pm-2am*

The Whatever Lounge [MW,D,MR-L,K,WC] 701 E Paisano St (at Ochoa) **915/533-0215** *2pm-2am*

Nightclubs

The New Old Plantation [★MW,D,DS,V,WC] 301 S Ochoa St (at Paisano) **915/533-6055** *9pm-2am, till 4am Fri-Sat, [DS] Sun, also Generation Q II pride store upstairs*

San Antonio Mining Co [★MW,D,DS,V,WC] 800 E San Antonio Ave (at Ochoa) **915/533-9516** *3pm-2am*

Restaurants

The Little Diner 7209 7th St, Canutillo **915/877-2176** *11am-8pm, clsd Wed, true Texas fare*

Men's Services

► **Megaphone 915/541-8888** *Meet and Chat Live with HOT local men. FREE to listen & respond to ads. Video and text chat at GayMates.com. Use FREE code 4889.*

Erotica

Tres Equis 2230 Texas Ave (at Palm) **915/532-6171**

Venus Adult Theatre & Books 4812 Montana (near Reynolds) **915/566-8061**

Fort Worth

see also Arlington & Dallas

Info Lines & Services

Tarrant County Lesbian/ Gay Alliance 817/877-5544 *info line & newsletter*

Accommodations

Crossroads Campground [MO,SW] 1409 CR 495 (at Hwy 16), Desdemona **254/758-2788**

Hotel Trinity InnSuites Hotel [GF,NS,WC] 2000 Beach St **817/534-4801, 800/989-3556**

Bars

Best Friends Club [MW,NH,D] 2620 E Lancaster Ave **817/534-2280** *3pm-2am, [K] Wed along w/ CW dance lessons, [D] wknds*

Crossroads [M,NH] 515 S Jennings Ave (at Pennsylvania) **817/332-0071** *11am-2am, from noon Sun*

Stampede [MW,NH,CW] 621 Hemphill St **817/335-0196** *11am-2am, noon-midnight Sun*

Nightclubs

Copa Cabana [M,D,DS,MR-L] 1002 S Main St **817/882-9504**

Rainbow Lounge [M,D,DS,WC] 651 S Jennings Ave (at Pennsylvania) **817/819-5277** *1pm-2:30am, theme nights*

Entertainment & Recreation

Fort Worth Men's Chorus 817/731-7878

Men's Services

Erotica

The Bright Lights 12313 I-30 W (at Linkcrest) **817/244-3220** *24hrs*

Cruisy Areas

Benbrook Dam [AYOR] *parking lot & woods*

Trinity Park [AYOR] *parking lot & woods*

Fredericksburg

Accommodations

Town Creek B&B [GS] 304 N Edison (at W Travis) **830/997-6848, 877/777-6848** *full brkfst*

Galveston

Accommodations

Cottage by the Gulf [GF,WC,GO] 810 Ave L (at Seawall & 8th) **409/770-9332** *6 private rental homes, patio*

Galveston House I & II [GF,NS,GO] 2415 51st St (at Stewart St) **409/750-1966** *vacation homes near beach*

Lost Bayou Guesthouse B&B [GS,NS,WI,GO] 1607 Ave L (at 16th) **409/770-0688** *1890 Victorian home survived hurricane of 1900*

Oasis Beach Cottage [GF,NS,GO] **713/256-3000** *on the Gulf of Mexico*

Bars

3rd Coast Beach Bar [M,DS,S] 3102 Seawall (at 31st) **409/765-6911** *noon-2am*

Pink Dolphin [M,DS,K] 904 Avenue M (at 9th & Seawall) **409/621-1808** *10am-2am*

Robert's Lafitte [M,DS,WC] 2501 Q Ave (at 25th St) **409/765-9092** *7am-2am, from 10am Sun, [DS] wknds*

Nightclubs

Groove [MW,D,S,K] 2409 Market **409/789-9134** *6pm-2am, clsd Mon*

Cafes

Mod Coffee & Tea House [F] 2126 Post Office St (at 22nd) **409/765-5659** *7am-10pm*

Restaurants

Eat Cetera 408 25th St **409/762-0803** *11am-7pm, clsd Sun, sandwiches*

Luigi's 2328 The Strand (at Tremont) **409/763-6500** *lunch & dinner, clsd Sun, Italian*

Mosquito Cafe 628 14th St (at Winnie) **409/763-1010** *11am-9pm, 8am-9pm Sat, till 3pm Sun, clsd Mon*

The Spot 3204 Seawall Blvd (at 32nd St) **409/621-5237** *good burgers, great view, also Tiki Bar*

Star Drug Store 510 23rd St **409/766-7719** *9am-4pm, old-fashioned drug store & soda fountain*

Men's Services

▶ **Megaphone 888/634-2628** *Meet and Chat Live with HOT local men. Call for your local number or visit us online at GayMates.com. Use FREE code 4889.*

Cruisy Areas

The Dunes [AYOR] at East Beach off Hwy 87

Groesbeck

Accommodations

Rainbow Ranch Campground [MW,SW,NS,GO] 1662 LCR 800 **254/729-8484, 888/875-7596** *cabins, campsites & RV hookups, on Lake Limestone*

Gun Barrel City

Accommodations

Circle J Ranch & Cattle Co [M,18+,SW,N,PC,GO] **903/479-4189** *campground (cabins, tents, RVs) 1 hour from Dallas*

Bars

Friends [MW,NH,F,WC] 410 S Gun Barrel/ Hwy 198 **903/887-2061** *4pm-midnight, from 3pm wknds, till 1am Sat, patio*

Houston

Info Lines & Services

Gay & Lesbian Switchboard Houston 713/529-3211 *24hr crisis hotline*

Houston GLBT Community Center 3400 Montrose # 207 (at Hawthorne) **713/524-3818** *noon-9pm*

Lambda AA Center [WC] 1201 W Clay (btwn Montrose & Waugh) **713/521-1243**

Accommodations

The Lovett Inn [★GS,SW,NS,WI,GO] 501 Lovett Blvd, Montrose (at Whitney) **713/522-5224, 800/779-5224** *sundeck, hot tub*

Robin's Nest B&B Inn [GF,WI] 4104 Greeley St **713/528-5821, 800/622-8343** *Victorian & Craftsman in Montrose Museum District, lush gardens*

Sycamore Heights B&B [GF,NS,WI,GO] 245 W 18th St **713/861-4117** *circa 1905, garden*

Bars

The 611 Club [★M,NH] 611 Hyde Park (at Stanford) **713/526-7070** *7am-2am, from noon Sun*

Beer Island [GF,NH,GO] 2631 White Oak Dr (at Studewood) **713/862-4670** *3pm-2am, very dog-friendly*

Blur [MW,D] 710 Pacific St (at Crocker) **713/529-3447** *10pm-2am, clsd Mon-Tue*

Boom Boom Room [GF] 2518 Yale St **713/868-3740** *4pm-2am, from 10am wknds, clsd Mon, wine & panini bar*

Brazos River Bottom (BRB) [★M,D,CW] 2400 Brazos (btwn Hadley & McIlhenny) **713/528-9192** *noon-2am*

Chances [W,D,E,WC] 1100 Westheimer (at Waugh) **713/523-7217** *2pm-2am*

Club Adam/ Eden [MW,D,CW,18+] 522 W Nasa Pkwy, Webster **281/554-3336** *7pm-2am*

Cousins [MW,NH,DS] 817 Fairview (at Converse) **713/528-9204** *11am-2am, from noon Sun*

Crocker [MW,NH,WI] 2312 Crocker St **713/529-3355** *11am-2am, theme nights*

Dean's Credit Clothing [GF] 316 Main **713/227-3326** *vintage clothing store 10am-2am, cocktail lounge from 7pm, also live music*

Decades [MW,NH] 1205 Richmond (btwn Mandel & Montrose) **713/521-2224** *11am-2am, from noon Sun*

EJ's [M,D,E,S] 2517 Ralph (at Westheimer) **713/527-9071** *7am-2am, from 10am Sun, 4 bars, patio*

George [M,NH,CW,GO] 617 Fairview (at Stanford) **713/528-8102** *7am-2am, from noon Sun, sports bar, patio*

Guava Lamp [MW,K,V,WC] 570 Waugh **713/524-3359** *4pm-2am, from 2pm Sun, swanky lounge, [K] Wed & Sun*

In & Out [MW] 1537 N Shepherd **713/589-9780** *4pm-2am*

JR's [★M,K,DS,S,V,WC] 808 Pacific (at Grant) **713/521-2519** *noon-2am, patio*

Mary's [★MW,NH,L,S,WC] 1022 Westheimer (at Waugh) **713/527-9669** *7am-2am, from 10am Sun, also patio bar*

Meteor [M,V,GO] 2306 Genesee (at Fairview) **713/521-0123** *4pm-2am*

Michael's Outpost [M,NH,E,OC] 1419 Richmond (at Mandell) **713/520-8446** *3pm-2am, from noon wknds*

Montrose Mining Co [★M,CW,L] 808 Pacific (at Grant) **713/529-7488** *4pm-2am, till 3am Fri-Sat, patio*

Privé Lounge [GS] 910 Westheimer **713/522-2542** *5pm-2am, from noon Wed-Sat, from 2pm Sun, rooftop patio*

Rainbow Room [MW,D,E] 527 Barren Springs Dr (at Ella Blvd) **281/872-0215** *3pm-2am*

Ripcord [M,L,WC] 715 Fairview (at Crocker) **713/521-2792** *1pm-2am, till 4am Fri-Sat, popular after-hours*

Tony's Corner Pocket [MW,NH,K,S] 817 W Dallas (btwn Arthur & Crosby) **713/571-7870** *noon-2am, large 2-level deck*

Whispers [MW,D,K] 226 1st St E (off I-59), Humble **281/359-2900** *4pm-midnight, till 2am Th-Sat*

Nightclubs

Crystal [M,D,DS,MR-L] 6684 Southwest Fwy (at Colorado) **713/278-2582** *Latino club, theme nights*

Numbers [GF,D,E,V,YC] 300 Westheimer (at Taft) **713/526-6551** *also live music*

Ranch Hill Saloon [MW,NH,D,CW,K,WC,GO] 24704 I-45 N, Spring **281/298-9035** *1pm-2am*

South Beach Nightclub [★M,D,S] 810 Pacific **713/521-0107, 713/529-7623** *9pm-5am, clsd Mon-Tue*

True Colors [MW,D,MR-AF] 2727 Crossview **713/266-6505**

Viviana's Nite Club [M,D,MR-L] 4624 Dacoma St **713/681-4101** *5pm-2am, till 5am wknds*

Cafes

Dirk's Coffee 4005 Montrose (btwn Richmond & W Alabama) **713/526-1319** *6am-11pm, till midnight Fri-Sat, 7am-10pm Sun*

Empire Cafe 1732 Westheimer Rd **713/528-5282** *7:30am-10pm, till 11pm Fri-Sat*

The Path of Tea 2340 W Alabama St **713/252-4473** *10am-9pm, till 11pm Fri-Sat, 1pm-6pm Sun, tea house*

Restaurants

Aka 2390 W Alabama St **713/807-7895** *noon-11pm, sushi*

Baba Yega's [★WC] 2607 Grant (at Pacific) **713/522-0042** *11am-10pm, till 11pm Fri-Sat, from 10am Sun, full bar, patio*

Barnaby's Cafe [★BW,WC] 604 Fairview (btwn Stanford & Hopkins St) **713/522-0106** *11am-10pm, till 11pm Fri-Sat; also 1701 S Shepherd, 713/520-5131*

Beaver's 2310 Decatur (at Sawyer) **713/864-2328** *11am-10pm, till midnight Fri-Sat, clsd Mon, BBQ*

Black-Eyed Pea [★WC] 2675 Wilcrest **713/266-0928** *11am-10pm, Southern*

Brasil [BW] 2604 Dunlavy (at Westheimer) **713/528-1993** *7:30am-1am, bistro, plenty veggie*

Cafe Annie 1728 Post Oak Blvd (at San Felipe) **713/840-1111** *lunch Tue-Fri, dinner Mon-Sat, clsd Sun, fine dining*

Captain Benny's Half Shell [BW] 8506 S Main **713/666-5469** *11am-10pm*

Chapultepec [BW] 813 Richmond (btwn Montrose & Main) **713/522-2365** *24hrs, Mexican*

El Tiempo Cantina 1308 Montrose Blvd **713/807-8996** *11am-9pm, till 10pm Wed-Th, till 11pm Fri-Sat, Mexican seafood*

House of Pies [★] 3112 Kirby Dr (at Richmond/ Alabama) **713/528-3816** *24hrs*

Java Java Cafe [★] 911 W 11th (at Shepherd) **713/880-5282** *7:30am-3pm, from 8:30am wknds*

Julia's Bistro 3722 Main St (at W Alabama) **713/807-0090** *lunch Mon-Fri, dinner Mon-Sat, clsd Sun, Mexican*

Kelley's Country Cookin' 8015 Park Pl (at Gulf Fwy) **713/645-6428** *6am-10pm, till 11pm wknds, great brkfst*

La Strada [★E] 322 Westheimer Rd **713/523-1014** *lunch & dinner, Sun brunch, clsd Mon, Italian*

Magnolia Bar & Grill [WC] 6000 Richmond Ave (at Fountainview Dr) **713/781-6207** *11am-10pm, till 11pm Fri-Sat, from 10:30am Sun, Cajun, full bar*

Mo Mong 1201 Westheimer #B (at Montrose) **713/524-5664** *11am-10pm, clsd Sun, Vietnamese, full bar*

Ninfa's [★] 2704 Navigation Blvd **713/228-1175** *11am-11pm, Mexican, full bar*

Ninos 2817 W Dallas (btwn Montrose & Waugh Dr) **713/522-5120** *lunch Mon-Fri, dinner Mon-Sat, clsd Sun, Italian, full bar*

Spanish Flowers [BW] 4701 N Main (at Airline) **713/869-1706** *24hrs, till 10pm Tue, from 9am Wed, Mexican*

Tafia [GO] 3701 Travis St **713/524-6922** *dinner Tue-Sat, Mediterranean, also bar*

Entertainment & Recreation

After Hours KPFT 90.1 FM (also 89.5 Galveston) **713/526-4000, 713/526-5738 (request line)** *1am-4am Sat, LGBT radio*

Beer Can House 222 Malone St **713/926-6368** *noon-5pm Sat-Sun only; 50,000+ beer cans cover the building!*

DiverseWorks Art Space 1117 East Fwy (I-10 at N Main) **713/223-8346, 713/335-3443** *gallery noon-6pm Wed-Sat, call for events, some LGBT-themed art & performance*

Dominic Walsh Dance Theater 2311 Dunlavy St, Ste 210 **713/652-3938** *contemporary dance theater, annual Illumination Project benefits Baylor Int'l Pediatric AIDS Initiative, call for events*

Mukuru **713/623-6796 x226** *arts for AIDS, see www.mukuru.org for events*

Orange Show Center for Visionary Art 2401 Munger St **713/926-6368** *performance, music, public art; produces annual Art Car Parade*

Queer Voices **713/526-5738, 713/529-6929** *9pm Mon*

Unhinged Productions *LGBT theater company (see www.u-p.org for events)*

Retail Shops

Black Hawk Leather 711 Fairview **713/522-1414** *noon-8pm, 2pm-7pm Sun*

The Chocolate Bar 1835 W Alabama St **713/520-8599** *chocolate gifts & yummy desserts*

Hollywood Super Center 2409 Grant St (at Crocker St) **713/527-8510** *10am-2am, gifts, novelties*

Lucia's Garden 2216 Portsmouth (at Greenbriar) **713/523-6494** *clsd Sun, spiritual herb center*

Publications

abOUT Magazine 711 Hyde Park Blvd **713/492-0485**

OutSmart **713/520-7237** *free monthly LGBT newsmagazine*

Gyms & Health Clubs

Houston Gym [GF,GO] 1501 Durham Rd (at Washington & Eigel) **713/880-9191** *5am-10pm, 8am-8pm wknds*

YMCA Downtown [GF,SW] 1600 Louisiana St (btwn Pease & Bell) **713/659-5566** *5am-10pm*

Men's Clubs

The Club Houston [★SW,PC] 2200 Fannin St (at W Gray) **713/659-4998** *24hrs*

Midtowne Spa—Houston [★SW,PC] 3100 Fannin (at Elgin) **713/522-2379** *24hrs*

Men's Services

▶ **Megaphone 713/225-5500** *Meet and Chat Live with HOT local men. FREE to listen & respond to ads. Video and text chat at GayMates.com. Use FREE code 4889.*

Erotica

Eros 1207 [GO] 1207 Spencer Hwy (at Allen Genoa) **713/944-6010**

Leather Forever 604 Westheimer (at Stanford) **713/526-6940**

Loveworks 25170 I-45 N, Spring **281/292-0070**

Kilgore

Erotica

Texas Adult Video [GS,GO] 1907 Industrial Blvd **903/986-2090** *large selection of gay erotica*

Killeen

Nightclubs

The Beach [D,DS,S] 1607 E Veterans Memorial Blvd **254/519-2005** *9pm-close Th-Sat*

Longview

Bars

Decisions [MW,D,CW,K,DS,WC] 2103 E Marshall (2 blocks E of Eastman Rd) **903/757-4884** *5pm-2am, 2 bars, DJ Fri-Sun, [DS] Fri & Sun*

Cruisy Areas

Hinsley Park [AYOR]

Teague Park [AYOR]

Lubbock

Info Lines & Services

AA Lambda 4501 University Ave (at MCC) **806/792-5562** *8pm Fri*

Accommodations

LaQuinta Inns & Suites North [GF,NS,WI,WC,GO] 5006 Auburn St (at Winston) **806/749-1600**

Nightclubs

Club Luxor [GS,D,K,DS] 2211 4th St **806/744-3744** *9pm-2am Wed-Sun*

Heaven Nightclub [GF,D,MR,DS,18+,YC] 1928 Buddy Holly Ave (at I-27) **806/762-4466** *Th-Sun*

Cruisy Areas

McKenzie Park [AYOR]

McAllen

see Rio Grande Valley

Mission

Accommodations

Seldom Rest Ranch [GF,WC,GO] 3900 Bentsen Palm Dr (I-83) **956/585-1215** *outdoor hot tub, located 10 miles outside Mexico & 1 hour from beach*

Mt Vernon

Accommodations

The Veranda [GS,F,SW,NS,WI] 3264 County Rd SE 4115 **903/588-2402** *B&B on 68 private acres, lake, jacuzzi, gourmet restaurant Fri-Sat*

Odessa/ Midland

Erotica

B&L Adult Bookstore 5890 W University Blvd (at Mercury), W Odessa **432/381-6855**

County Line 6947 Commerce, Odessa **432/552-0055** *24hrs*

Plano

see also Dallas

Restaurants

Roy's Hawaiian Seafood [WC] 2840 Dallas Pkwy (btwn Park & Parker) **972/473-6263** *5:30pm-9pm, till 10pm Wed-Fri, till 11pm Sat, Hawaiian fusion*

Rio Grande Valley

includes McAllen

Bars

PBD's [M,D,DS,S,WC] 2908 N Ware Rd (at Daffodil), McAllen **956/682-8019** *8pm-2am, clsd Mon, [S] Fri-Sat*

Trade Bar [MW,D,S,18+,YC,GO] 2010 Nolana (at Bicentennial), McAllen **956/630-6304** *10pm-3am Tue & Th-Sat*

San Angelo

Cruisy Areas

Downtown River [AYOR]

San Antonio

Info Lines & Services

Lambda AA 319 Camden Rm #4 (Madison Square Presbyterian Church) **210/979-5939** *8:15pm daily*

Accommodations

1908 Ayres Inn [GS,NS,WI,WC,GO] 124 W Woodlawn Ave (at N Main) **210/736-4232** *Nat'l Historic Place in historic Monte Vista neighborhood, built by architect Atlee B. Ayres, eclectic mix of chic furnishings & luxurious surroundings*

Alamo Lodge [GF,SW,WC] 1126 E Elmira (at Wilmington) **210/222-9463, 210/222-9820**

Arbor House Suites B&B [GS,NS,WC,GO] 109 Arciniega (btwn S Alamo & S St Mary's) **210/472-2005, 888/272-6700** *hot tub*

Beauregard House B&B [GF,NS,WI] 215 Beauregard St **210/222-1198, 888/667-0555** *Victorian in historic district*

Beckman Inn [GF,NS] 222 E Guenther St **210/229-1449, 800/945-1449** *B&B in King William historic district*

Brackenridge House [GF,SW,WI] 230 Madison **210/271-3442, 800/221-1412** *B&B in historic King William district*

Das Liszt Ferienhaus [GF] 200 Loretta Pl **210/422-8810** *3-bdrm rental near River Walk*

Fiesta B&B [M,NS,WI,GO] 1823 Saunders Ave (at Trinity) **210/226-5548, 210/887-0074** *full brkfst*

The Painted Lady Inn on Broadway [MW,NS,WI,WC,GO] 620 Broadway (at 6th) **210/220-1092** *full brkfst, private art deco suites, rooftop deck & spa*

Bars

2015 Place [M,NH,K] 2015 San Pedro (at Woodlawn) **210/733-3365** *4pm-2am, patio, [K] Wed*

The Annex [M,NH,WC] 330 San Pedro Ave (at Euclid) **210/223-6957** *2pm-2am, cruise bar*

Club Unity [MW,NH] 1210 E Elmira **210/320-3787** *noon-2am*

Cobalt Club [MW,NH,WC] 2022 McCullough (at Ashby) **210/734-2244** *7am-2am, from 10:30am Sun*

Electric Company [MW,D,S,18+] 820 San Pedro Ave (at W Laurel) **210/212-6635** *9pm-3am Wed-Sun*

The Flying Saucer [GF] 11255 Huebner Rd #212 (at I-10) **210/647-7468** *11am-1am, till 2am Th-Sat, noon-midnight Sun, large beer selection*

Gotham [GS,NH,WC] 223 3rd St (at N Alamo) **210/527-1707** *1pm-2am*

Lava Lounge [GS,D,MR-L] 2702 N St Mary's St **210/320-1740**

One-Oh-Six Off Broadway [M,NH,F] 106 Pershing St (at Broadway) **210/820-0906** *noon-2am*

Pegasus [M,K,L,S] 1402 N Main Ave (btwn Laurel & Evergreen) **210/299-4222** *2pm-2am*

Silver Dollar Saloon [MW,D,CW,K,WC] *bar moving; check local listings for new location*

Sparks [M,E,S] 8011 Webbles **210/599-3225** *5pm-2am*

Nightclubs

The Bonham Exchange [★MW,D,V,18+,GO] 411 Bonham St (at 3rd/ Houston) **210/271-3811, 210/271-9219** *4pm-2am, 9pm-4am Fri-Sat, in 111-year-old mansion*

Club Venom [M,D,K,DS] 2407 N St Mary's St **210/738-8180**

Heat [M,D,S] 1500 N Main Ave (at Evergreen) **210/227-2600** *9pm-2am, clsd Mon*

The Industry [GS,D] 8021 Pinebrook Dr **210/584-0103**

The Saint [M,D,DS,S,18+] 1430 N Main (at Evergreen) **210/225-7330** *4pm-2am*

Cafes

Candlelight Coffeehouse & Wine Bar [WI] 3011 N St Mary's (at Rte 281) **210/738-0099** *4pm-midnight, Sun brunch 10am-2pm, clsd Mon*

Timo's Coffee House 2021 San Pedro **210/733-8049** *8am-8pm, 10am-4pm Sat, clsd Sun*

Restaurants

Chacho's [E,K] 7870 Callaghan Rd (at I-10) **210/366-2023** *24hrs, Mexican*

Giovanni's Pizza & Italian Restaurant 913 S Brazos (at Guadalupe) **210/212-6626** *11am-7pm*

Lulu's Bakery & Cafe [WC] 918 N Main (at W Elmira) **210/222-9422** *24hrs, Tex-Mex*

Luther's Cafe [GO] 1425 N Main Ave **210/223-7727** *11am-3am*

Madhatter's Tea [BYOB,WC] 320 Beauregard **210/212-4832** *9am-9pm, till 3pm Sun-Mon, patio*

El Mirador [BW,WC] 722 S St Mary's St (at Durango St) **210/225-9444** *6:30am-9pm, till 2pm Sun, Tex-Mex, plenty veggie, patio*

Taco Taco Cafe 145 E Hildebrand **210/822-9533** *7am-2pm*

WD Deli 3123 Broadway St **210/828-2322** *10:30am-5pm, till 4pm Sat, clsd Sun*

Retail Shops

On Main/ Off Main 120 W Mistletoe Ave **210/737-2323** *10am-6pm, till 5pm Sat, clsd Sun, gifts, cards & T-shirts*

ZEBRAZ.com 1608 N Main Ave (at E Park Ave) **210/472-2800, 800/788-4729** *9am-midnight, till 10pm Sun-Tue, LGBT dept store, also online version*

Publications

Ignite SA *LGBT publication for San Antonio*

Men's Clubs

Alternative Club Inc [SW,PC] 827 E Elmira St (at St Mary's) **210/223-2177** *noon-9am, 24hrs wknds*

Executive Health Club [PC] 402 Austin St **210/299-1400** *24hrs*

Men's Services

▶ **Megaphone 210/375-1155** *Meet and Chat Live with HOT local men. FREE to listen & respond to ads. Video and text chat at GayMates.com. Use FREE code 4889.*

Erotica

Broadway News 2202 Broadway (at Appler St) **210/223-2034**

Dreamers Apollo 2376 Austin Hwy (at Walzem) **210/653-3538** *24hrs*

Encore Video 1031 NE Loop 410 **210/821-5345**

Cruisy Areas

Please Note: All cruisy areas for San Antonio have been removed because the San Antonio Park Rangers aggressively police these areas.

South Padre Island

Accommodations

Upper Deck Hotel & Bar [M,SW,N,WI,WC,GO] 120 E Atol St (at Padre Blvd) **956/761-5953** *bar 2pm-close, from noon wknds*

Terrel

Erotica

Dreamers 6086 W Hwy 80 (Frontage Rd exit) **972/524-1449** *24hrs*

Tyler

Accommodations

Cross Timber Ranch B&B [GS,SW,NS,WI,GO] 6271 FM 858 (at Hwy 64), Ben Wheeler **903/833-9000, 877/833-9002** *full brkfst*

Cruisy Areas

Bergfeld Park [AYOR]

Waco

Info Lines & Services

Eddie & Velma Dwyer Community Center 507 Jefferson (at N 5th St) **254/757-1284** *gay & lesbian center*

Nightclubs

Club Trix [MW,D,V] 110 S 6th St **254/714-0767** *10pm-2am Wed-Th, 8pm-2am Fri-Sat*

Cruisy Areas

Midway Park [AYOR]

Wichita Falls

Bars

Odds [MW,D,K,DS,18+,BW] 1205 Lamar (at 12th) **940/322-2996** *4pm-2am, from 3pm Sun, [K] Th*

Cruisy Areas

Lucy Park [AYOR]

Wimberley

Accommodations

Bella Vista [GS,SW,NS,GO] 2121 Hilltop **512/847-6425**

Utah

Bryce Canyon

Accommodations

The Red Brick Inn of Panguitch B&B [GF] 161 N 100 West (at 200 North), Panguitch **435/676-2141, 866/733-2745** *full brkfst*

Holladay

Restaurants

Loco Lizard Cantina [TG,WC] 1612 Ute Blvd (in Kimball Jct Shopping Ctr) **435/645-7000** *11am-10pm, till 11pm Fri-Sat, brunch wknds, Mexican, full bar*

Logan

Cruisy Areas

Logan Canyon [AYOR] *Zanavoo loop*

Moab

Accommodations

Los Vados Canyon House [GS,SW,NS] **801/532-2651** *retreat house in a red rock canyon*

Mayor's House B&B [GF,SW,NS,GO] 505 Rose Tree Ln (at 400 E) **435/259-6015, 888/791-2345** *hot tub, full brkfst*

Mt Peale Resort Inn, Lodge & Cabins [GS,NS,GO] 1415 E Hwy 46 (at mile marker 14), Old La Sal **435/686-2284, 888/687-3253** *B&B & cabins, full brkfst, hot tub, lesbian-owned*

Red Cliffs Lodge [GF,SW,NS,WC] Hwy 128 (at mile marker 14) **435/259-2002, 866/812-2002** *resort, on Colorado River, hot tub*

Ogden

Accommodations

North Fork B&B [M,NS,GO] **801/540-5490** *in 4,000-sq-ft home, 1 hour from Salt Lake, jacuzzi, weight room*

Men's Services

Park City

Accommodations

Resort Quest Park City [GF] **800/243-2932** *vacation rentals*

Men's Services

Salt Lake City

Info Lines & Services

Utah Pride Center 361 N 300 W, 1st flr **801/539-8800, 888/874-2743** *info, resource center, meetings, coffee shop, programs, youth activity center & much more*

Accommodations

Anniversary Inn [GF] 460 S 1000 E **801/363-4900, 800/324-4152** *elaborate, kitschy theme rms*

Anton Boxrud B&B [GF,NS,WI] 57 S 600 E (at S Temple) **801/363-8035, 800/524-5511** *full brkfst, hot tub*

Hotel Monaco Salt Lake City [GF,WC,WI] 15 W 200 S **801/595-0000, 877/294-9710** *restaurant & bar, gym*

Parrish Place [GF,NS,WI] 720 E Ashton Ave **801/832-0970, 888/832-0869** *Victorian mansion, hot tub*

Peery Hotel [★GF,NS,WI,WC] 110 W 300 S **801/521-4300, 800/331-0073** *full brkfst, also 2 restaurants, full bar*

Under the Lindens [★M,NS,WI,GO] 128 S 1000 E (downtown) **801/355-9808** *studios, hot tub, commitment ceremonies, mention Damron for discount*

Bars

Club Edge [GS,D] 615 North 400 West **801/755-6389**

Club Try-Angles [M,NH,D,F,PC,GO] 251 W 900 S **801/364-3203** *2pm-2am*

Jam [MW,NH,D,K,BW] 751 North 300 West **801/891-1162** *5pm-2am, clsd Sun*

Radio City [M,WC] 147 S State St (btwn 1st & 2nd) **801/532-9327** *10am-2am, beer only*

Speakeasy [GF,E] 63 West 100 South **801/521-7000** *live jazz & blues, some gay theme nights*

The Tavernacle Social Club [GF,F,K,P,NS,PC] 201 E 300 South **801/519-8900** *5pm-close, from 8pm Sun-Mon, "Duelin' Pianos"*

The Trapp [MW,D,CW,PC,WC] 102 S 600 W **801/531-8727** *11am-2am, patio, food Sun*

W Lounge [GS,D,NS,PC] 358 SW Temple **801/359-0637** *8pm-2am*

Nightclubs

Area 51 [GS,D] 451 South 400 West **801/534-0819** *80s & goth theme nights Tue, Th & Sat*

Club Babylon [MW,D] 400 S West Temple (at Bliss Nightclub) **801/364-2547** *Sat only*

Club Manhattan [GF,D,E,WC] 5 E 400 S (at Main) **801/364-7651** *9pm-2am, more gay Sat for Latin salsa*

Gossip [★M,D] 579 W 200 S (at 600 W, at Club Sound) **801/328-0255** *gay 10pm-2am Fri only, live bands rest of the week*

Pachanga [M,D,MR-L] 1051 East 2100 South (at Karamba) **801/637-9197** *9pm Sun only, gay Latin night*

Cafes

Coffee Garden [WC] 878 E 900 S **801/355-3425** *6am-11pm, till midnight Fri-Sat, 7am-11pm Sun, light fare*

Restaurants

Bambara 202 S Main St **801/363-5454** *lunch Mon-Fri, brkfst & dinner daily, upscale American*

Blue Plate Diner 2041 S 2100 E **801/463-1151** *7am-9pm, till 10pm Fri-Sat*

Cafe Med 420 E 3300 South **801/493-0100** *lunch & dinner, Mediterranean*

Cafe Trio Downtown 680 S 900 E **801/533-8746** *11am-10pm, Italian*

Cedars of Lebanon [WI,E] 152 E 200 South **801/364-4096** *lunch & dinner, dinner only Sun, Lebanese, veggie/vegan-friendly*

Citris Grill 2991 E 3300 South **801/466-1202**

Lamb's Grill Cafe [E,WC] 169 S Main St **801/364-7166** *7am-9pm, from 8am Sat, clsd Sun, live jazz wknds*

Market St Grill [WC] 48 W Market St **801/322-4668** *brkfst & lunch Mon-Sat, dinner nightly, Sun brunch, seafood/steak, full bar*

The Metropolitan [R] 173 W Broadway **801/364-3472** *lunch Mon-Fri, dinner nightly, clsd Sun, upscale New American*

New Yorker [WC] 60 W Market St **801/363-0166** *lunch Mon-Fri, dinner nightly, clsd Sun, fine dining, steak*

Nick-N-Willy's Pizza 4536 S Highland Dr **801/273-8282** *11am-8pm, till 9pm wknds*

Red Iguana [★] 736 W North Temple **801/322-1489** *lunch & dinner, Mexican*

Rio Grande Cafe [★WC] 270 S Rio Grande **801/364-3302** *lunch Mon-Sat & dinner nightly, Mexican, full bar*

Sage's Cafe 473 E 300 S **801/322-3790** *lunch & dinner, brkfst wknds, clsd Mon-Tue, vegan/ vegetarian*

Stoneground 249 E 400 South **801/364-1368** *11am-11pm, 5pm-9pm Sun, pizza & more*

Vertical Diner 2280 S West Temple **801/484-8378** *10am-9pm, vegetarian diner*

Entertainment & Recreation

Lambda Hiking Club 801/583-7064 *hiking & other activities*

Plan B Theatre Company 138 West 300 South (at Rose Wagner Performing Arts Center, btwn W Temple & 200 West) **801/355-2787** *at least one LGBT-themed production each season*

Salt Lake Men's Choir 801/355-2787, 888/451-2787

Bookstores

Golden Braid Books 151 S 500 E **801/322-1162, 801/322-0404 (cafe)** *10am-9pm, till 6pm Sun, also Oasis Cafe, 8am-9pm, till 10pm wknds*

Sam Weller's 254 S Main St **801/328-2586** *10am-7pm Mon-Sat*

Retail Shops

Cahoots [WC,GO] 878 E 900 S (at 900 E) **801/538-0606** *10am-9pm, unique gift shop*

Gypsy Moon Emporium 1011 E 900 S **801/521-9100** *call for hours, Celtic & goddess-oriented gifts*

Publications

Q Salt Lake 801/649-6663, 800/806-7357 *bi-weekly LGBT newspaper*

Men's Services

▶ **Megaphone 801/595-0005** *Meet and Chat Live with HOT local men. FREE to listen & respond to ads. Video and text chat at GayMates.com. Use FREE code 4889.*

Erotica

All For Love [TG,WC] 3072 S Main St (at 33rd St S) **801/487-8358** *clsd Sun, lingerie & S/M boutique*

Blue Boutique Sugarhouse 1400 E 2100 South **801/485-2072** *also piercing*

Cahoots [WC,GO] 878 E 900 S (at 900 E) **801/538-0606** *9am-5pm, gift store that also carries gay adult magazines, cards, calendars & toys*

Mischievous 559 S 300 W (at 6th St S) **801/530-3100** *clsd Sun*

Cruisy Areas

Memory Grove [AYOR] Canyon Rd (below the Capitol, on the E side)

Sugarhouse Park [AYOR] 21st S *also btwn 13th & 17th E*

Torrey

Accommodations

Capitol Reef Inn & Cafe [GF] 360 W Main St **435/425-3271** *seasonal, hot tub, also restaurant [BW], plenty veggie*

SkyRidge Inn B&B [GF,NS,WI] **435/425-3222, 800/448-6990** *full brkfst, hot tubs, near Capitol Reef Nat'l Park*

Zion Nat'l Park

Accommodations

Canyon Vista B&B [GF,NS] 2175 Zion Park Blvd (at Hwy 9), Springdale **435/772-3801**

Red Rock Inn [GS,NS,WC,GO] 998 Zion Park Blvd, Springdale **435/772-3139** *cottages w/ canyon views, full brkfst, hot tub, lesbian-owned*

Restaurants

Cafe Soleil [GO] 205 Zion Park Blvd **435/772-0505** *coffee drinks, sandwiches, salads, wraps*

VERMONT

Statewide

INFO LINES & SERVICES

Vermont Gay Tourism Association *Vermont's official office to promote gay & lesbian travel throughout the state, see www.vermontgaytourism.com*

Arlington

ACCOMMODATIONS

Arlington Inn [GF,WI] Historic Rte 7-A **802/375-6532, 800/443-9442** *inn, also restaurant, dinner from 5:30pm, clsd Sun-Mon*

Barre

EROTICA

La Trend 129 Main St (upstairs from Planet Rock) **802/661-0073**

Bellow Falls

ACCOMMODATIONS

Private Suite at the Witch Mountain House [M,NS,GO] 6 Hapgood St **802/428-2018** *private guest suite in 1885 home*

Brattleboro

ACCOMMODATIONS

Frog Meadow Farm [M,NS,WI,GO] 34 Upper Spring Hill Rd, Newfane **802/365-7242, 877/365-7242**

RESTAURANTS

Peter Haven's [GO] 32 Elliott St (at Main) **802/257-3333** *6pm-10pm, clsd Sun-Mon, cont'l*

BOOKSTORES

Everyone's Books [WC] 23 Elliott St **802/254-8160** *9:30am-6pm, till 5:30pm Mon, till 8pm Fri, till 7pm Sat, 11am-5pm Sun*

Bridgewater Corners

RESTAURANTS

Blanche & Bill's Pancake House US Rte 4 **802/422-3816** *7am-2pm Th-Sun, great flapjacks & maple syrup*

Brookfield

RESTAURANTS

Ariel's Restaurant & Pond Village Pub Rte 65 (at Stone Rd) **802/276-3939** *dinner, clsd Sun-Tue, eclectic, overlooking Sunset Lake*

Burlington

INFO LINES & SERVICES

R.U.1.2? Community Center 34 Elmwood Ave (across from Burlington post office) **802/860-RU12 (7812)** *drop-in & cybercenter, support & advocacy, events*

ACCOMMODATIONS

The Black Bear Inn [GS,SW,NS,WI] 4010 Bolton Access Rd, Bolton Valley **802/434-2126, 800/395-6335** *mtn-top inn on 6,000 acres, full brkfst, hot tub*

The Inn at Essex [GF,SW,WI,WC] 70 Essex Way, Essex **802/878-1100, 800/727-4295**

One of a Kind B&B [NS,WI] 53 Lakeview Terrace **802/862-5576, 877/479-2736**

NIGHTCLUBS

Metronome/ Nectar's [GF,D,F,E] 182 Main St **802/865-4563, 802/658-4771** *clsd Mon-Tue*

CAFES

Muddy Waters [BW] 184 Main St **802/658-0466** *7:30am-11pm, till midnight Fri-Sat, till 10pm Sun, coffeehouse, try the white hot chocolate*

Radio Bean Coffeehouse [E] 8 N Winooski Ave (at Pearl) **802/660-9346** *8am-midnight, till 2am Th-Sat, 10am-11pm Sun, cool bohemian coffeehouse, live bands & open mic nights*

RESTAURANTS

Bluebird Tavern [BW,GO] 317 Riverside Ave **802/428-4696** *3pm-11pm, from 9am wknds for brunch*

Daily Planet 15 Center St (at College) **802/862-9647** *4pm-close, also bar till 2am*

Loretta's [GO] 44 Park St (near 5 Corners), Essex Junction **802/879-7777** *lunch weekdays, dinner nightly, clsd Sun-Mon, Italian*

Parima Thai 185 Pearl St **802/864-7917** *lunch & dinner, courtyard garden*

Shanty on the Shore 181 Battery St **802/864-0238** *11am-10pm, seafood, views of Lake Champlain*

Silver Palace 1216 Williston Rd **802/864-0125** *11:30am-9pm, till 10pm Fri-Sat, 3pm-9pm Sun, Chinese, full bar*

Retail Shops

Peace & Justice Store 21 Church St (at Pearl) **802/863-2345** *10am-6pm, till 8pm Fri-Sat, noon-6pm Sun, fair trade retail store*

Cruisy Areas

The Loop [AYOR] downtown Bank, College & St Pauls Sts

Chester

Accommodations

Chester House Inn [GS,NS,WI,WC,GO] 266 Main St **802/875-2205, 888/875-2205** *inn circa 1780, also restaurant [BW]*

Dorset

Cruisy Areas

Dorset Quarry [AYOR] on Rte 30 & Kelly Rd

Greensboro

Accommodations

Highland Lodge [GF,WC,NS,WI,WC] 1608 Craftsbury Rd **802/533-2647** *includes brkfst & dinner*

Jay Peak

Accommodations

Four Seasons Apartments [GS,NS] 10 Elm St (at Main St), North Troy **802/578-7103**

Grey Gables Mansion [GF,NS,WI] 122 River St, Richford **802/848-3625, 800/299-2117** *circa 1888 B&B inn, full brkfst*

Phineas Swann B&B [GS,NS,WI,GO] **802/326-4306** *restored Victorian on Trout River, full brkfst*

Killington

Accommodations

Salt Ash Inn [GF,F,SW,WI,WC] 4758 Rte 100A (at Rte 100), Plymouth **802/672-3748, 800/725-8274** *1830s country inn, full brkfst, hot tub, pub, near skiing*

Restaurants

Grist Mill Killington Rd (on Summit Pond) **802/422-3970** *lunch & dinner, New England fare*

Ludlow

Accommodations

Cavendish Inn [GF,F,NS,WI,WC] 1589 Main St (off Rte 131), Cavendish **802/226-7080, 877/282-7460**

Happy Trails Motel [GF,NS,WI] 321 Rte 103 S **802/228-8888, 800/228-9984** *seasonal hot tub, near skiing*

Restaurants

Cappuccino's Restaurant 41 Depot St **802/228-7566** *dinner, clsd Mon-Tue, meat, pasta & seafood*

Lyndonville

Restaurants

Miss Lyndonville Diner Rte 5 **802/626-9890** *6am-3pm, till 8pm Wed-Th & Sun, till 9pm Fri-Sat*

Manchester

Accommodations

Hill Farm Inn [GF,NS] 458 Hill Farm Rd (at Historic Rte 7-A), Arlington **802/375-2269, 800/882-2545** *full brkfst*

Cafes

Little Rooster Cafe Rte 7-A, Manchester Center **802/362-3496** *7am-2:30pm, clsd Wed (winters)*

Restaurants

Bistro Henry [R] 1942 Rte 11/ 30 (.5 mile E of Rte 7) **802/362-4982** *dinner only, clsd Mon, Mediterranean, also bar*

Chantecleer Rte 7-A N, Manchester Center **802/362-1616** *call for hours, seasonal*

Bookstores

Northshire Bookstore 4869 Main St, Manchester Center **802/362-2200, 800/437-3700** *10am-7pm, till 9pm Th-Sat*

Marshfield

Accommodations

Marshfield Inn & Motel [GF,WI,GO] 5630 US Rte 2 **802/426-3383**

Montgomery Center

Cafes

Trout River Traders [GF,F,WI,GO] 91 Main St (at Rte 242) **802/326-3058** *9am-5pm, tapas & dinner till 9pm Fri-Sat, Sun brunch, also gift shop*

Montpelier

Restaurants

Julio's 54 State **802/229-9348** *11:30am-11pm, till midnight Wed & Fri-Sat, Mexican*

Sarducci's [WC] 3 Main St **802/223-0229** *11:30am-9:30pm, from 4:30pm Sun, Italian, full bar*

Wayside Restaurant [WC] Rte 302 **802/223-6611** *6:30am-9:30pm*

Retail Shops

Phoenix Rising 34 State St **802/229-0522** *10am-5:30pm, till 6pm Fri, 11am-5pm Sat, noon-4pm Sun, metaphysical, jewelry, gifts, pride items, music*

Plainfield

Accommodations

Comstock House [GF,WI,GO] 1620 Middle Rd **802/272-2693** *1891 house on former dairy farm overlooking Winooski River Valley, full brkfst*

Richmond

Restaurants

The Kitchen Table Bistro 1840 Main St **802/434-8686** *5pm-9pm, seasonal menu, local food*

Rutland

Accommodations

The Inn of the Six Mountains [GF,SW,WC] 2617 Killington Rd, Killington **802/422-4302, 800/228-4676** *hotel, full brkfst, jacuzzi*

Lilac Inn [WC] 53 Park St, Brandon **802/247-5463, 800/221-0720** *full brkfst*

Maplewood Inn [GS,NS,WI] 1108 S Main St (Rte 22-A), Fair Haven **802/265-8039, 800/253-7729** *1843 Greek Revival B&B w/ beautiful antiques, full brkfst*

Cruisy Areas

Clarendon Gorge [AYOR] off Route 7 on Gorge Rd (S of Rutland) *nude sunbathing by Mill River*

Saxtons River

Accommodations

The Inn at Saxtons River [GF,NS,WI,GO] 27 Main St (at Academy Ave) **802/869-2110** *historic Victorian inn w/ charming pub & restaurant, located in quaint New England village*

Shelburne

Restaurants

Bistro Sauce Falls Rd (at Shelburne Shopping Park) **802/985-2830** *lunch & dinner, Sun brunch, local food*

St Albans

Restaurants

Jeff's Maine Seafood 65 N Main St **802/524-6135** *lunch daily, dinner Tue-Sat, clsd Sun*

St Johnsbury

Accommodations

Comfort Inn & Suites [GF,SW,WI,WC] 703 US Rte 5 S (at I-91) **802/748-1500, 800/424-6423** *hotel, hot tub*

Restaurants

Elements 98 Mill St **802/748-8400** *dinner, clsd Sun-Mon, local food*

Stowe

Accommodations

Arbor Inn [GS,SW,NS] 3214 Mountain Rd **802/253-4772, 800/543-1293** *full brkfst, hot tub*

Fitch Hill Inn [GS,WI] 258 Fitch Hill Rd, Hyde Park **802/888-3834, 800/639-2903** *full brkfst, hot tub*

The Green Mountain Inn [GF,F,SW,NS,WI,WC] 18 Main St **802/253-7301, 800/253-7302**

Northern Lights Lodge [GF,SW,WI,GO] 4441 Mountain Rd **802/253-8541, 800/448-4554** *full brkfst, hot tub, sauna*

The Old Stagecoach Inn [GF,NS,WI] 18 N Main St (at Stowe St), Waterbury **802/244-5056, 800/262-2206** *historic village inn, full brkfst, also full bar*

Timberholm Inn [GS,NS,WI] 452 Cottage Club Rd **802/253-7603, 800/753-7603** *full brkfst, hot tub*

Townshend

Accommodations

Townshend State Park [GF] 2755 State Forest Rd **802/365-7500, 888/409-7579** *open Memorial Day wknd to Labor Day wknd, campground, hiking*

Vergennes

Restaurants

Basin Harbor Club 4800 Basin Harbor Rd **802/475-2311, 800/622-4000** *brkfst & dinner, Sun jazz brunch (seasonal), eclectic New England fare, upscale*

Waterbury

Accommodations

The Belding House B&B [GS,NS,GO] 746 Rte 100 (at VT Rte 100B), Moretown **802/496-7420** *fireplaces, full brkfst*

Grünberg Haus B&B & Cabins [GS,NS,WI] 94 Pine St, Rte 100 S **802/244-7726, 800/800-7760** *full brkfst, also cabins May-Oct*

Moose Meadow Lodge [GS,NS,WI,GO] 607 Crossett Hill **802/244-5378**

Restaurants

Cider House BBQ & Pub [GO] 1675 US Rte 2 **802/244-8400** *lunch Th-Sat, dinner nightly, full bar, patio*

Wells River

Accommodations

The Gargoyle House [M,N,NS,WI,GO] 3351 Wallace Hill Rd (at US 302 & I-91) **802/429-2341**

West Dover

Accommodations

Deerhill Inn [GS,SW,NS,WI] 14 Valley View Rd **802/464-3100, 800/993-3379** *inn w/ restaurant*

Inn at Mount Snow [GF,NS,WI,GO] 401 Rte 101 **802/464-8388, 866/587-7669** *at foot of Mt Snow, near skiing*

The Inn at Sawmill farm [GS,NS,WC] 7 Crosstown Rd (at Rte 100) **802/464-8131, 800/493-1133**

Red Oak Inn [GF,SW,NS] 45 Rte 100 (at Rte 9) **802/464-8817** *also tavern*

Wilmington

Accommodations

Nordic Hills Lodge [GS,SW,NS,WI] 34 Look Rd (at Route 101) **802/464-5130, 800/326-5130** *fireplace, game room, exercise room, full restaurant & bar*

Windham

Accommodations

A Stone Wall Inn [GS,NS,GO] 578 Hitchcock Hill Rd **802/875-4238** *B&B inn, hot tub*

Woodstock

Accommodations

The Ardmore Inn [GF,NS,WI] 23 Pleasant St **802/457-3887, 800/497-9652** *1880s Greek Revival, full brkfst, jacuzzi*

Cabin in the Woods [GF,SW,NS] 1944 Chateauguay Rd, Bridgewater Corners **802/672-5141 (no calls after 9pm EST)** *secluded rustic cabin, hot tub, swimming hole, fireplace, seasonal May-Oct*

Deer Brook Inn [GF,NS,WI,GO] 535 Woodstock Rd **802/672-3713**

Village Inn of Woodstock [GF,NS,WI] 41 Pleasant St **802/457-1255, 800/722-4571** *full brkfst*

Virginia

Alexandria

see also Washington, District of Columbia

Accommodations

Hotel Monaco Alexandria [GF,F,WC] 480 King St **703/549-6080, 800/368-5047**

Arlington

see also Washington, District of Columbia

Info Lines & Services

Arlington Gay/ Lesbian Alliance *monthly meetings & outreach events (see: www.agla.org)*

Bars

Freddie's Beach Bar & Restaurant [MW,F,E,K,DS,WC] 555 S 23rd St **703/685-0555** *11am-2am, from 4pm Mon, wknd brunch, patio*

Cafes

Java Shack [MW] 2507 N Franklin Rd (at Wilson Blvd & N Barton) **703/527-9556** *7am-8pm, till 10pm Fri-Sat*

Cruisy Areas

Seabee Memorial [AYOR] Memorial Dr

Bowling Green

Accommodations

Column Wood B&B [GF,NS,WI,GO] 233 N Main St (at Broaddus Ave) **804/633-5606, 866/633-9314** *full brkfst*

Bristol

Erotica

Exotic Illusions Adult Video 2003 W State St (at 20th St) **276/466-6909** *24hrs*

Cape Charles

see also Norfolk & Virginia Beach

Accommodations

Cape Charles House B&B [GF,NS] 645 Tazewell Ave (at Fig) **757/331-4920** *1912 colonial revival home w/ antiques*

Sea Gate B&B [GF,WI,GO] 9 Tazewell Ave **757/331-2206** *full brkfst*

Restaurants

The Chesapeake Restaurant & Nightclub [E] 307 Mason Ave **757/331-3123** *lunch & dinner, clsd Mon-Tues*

Charlottesville

Accommodations

The Barboursville Inn [GS,GO] 12421 Albano Rd, Barboursville **540/832-0550**

The Inn at Court Square [GF,NS] 410 E Jefferson St **434/295-2800, 866/466-2877** *period antiques, jacuzzi*

The Summer Kitchen B&B [GS,NS,GO] 6482 Dick Woods Rd **540/456-7009** *full brkfst, hot tub, sauna, lesbian-owned*

Nightclubs

Club 216 [★MW,D,S,YC,PC,WC] 216 W Water St (enter on South St) **434/296-8783** *10pm-5am Fri-Sat, some Sun events*

Restaurants

Escafe [E,GO] in West End downtown mall (next to the Omni Hotel) **434/295-8668** *5:30pm-11pm, 4:30pm-9:30pm Sun, clsd Mon, Asian/ American fusion, full bar*

Erotica

Pamela's Secrets 3051 S Main St, Harrisonburg **540/432-6403**

Sneak Reviews Video 2244 Ivy Rd **434/979-4420**

Cruisy Areas

Chris Green Lake [AYOR] Rte 29 to Airport Rd

Chincoteague Island

Accommodations

1848 Island Manor House [GS,NS,WI,GO] 4160 Main St (at Smith St) **757/336-5436, 800/852-1505** *B&B, full brkfst*

Danville

Cruisy Areas

Ballou Park [AYOR]

Hampton

see also Newport News

Cafes

The Java Junction [F] 768 Settlers Landing Rd **757/722-6300** *7am-7pm, from 8am wknds, till 3pm Sun*

Cruisy Areas

Grandview Beach [AYOR] nude beach past rock mounds

Harrisonburg

Cafes

Artful Dodger Coffeehouse [D,E,WC] 47 W Court Square **540/432-1179** *8am-2am, noon-midnight Sun, also bar*

Luray

see Shenandoah Valley

Lynchburg

Cruisy Areas

Blackwater Creek area [AYOR]

Peaks View Park [AYOR]

Newport News

see also Norfolk & Virginia Beach

Bars

Corner Pocket [MW,NH,F,E,WC] 6157 Jefferson Ave (at Mercury) **757/825-0440** *5pm-2am, full menu till midnight*

Erotica

Video Store II 9903 W Jefferson **757/596-3454**

Norfolk

see also Virginia Beach

Info Lines & Services

Saturday Night Live Gay/ Lesbian AA 1301 Colley Ave (at First Lutheran Church) **757/625-1953 (church #)** *8pm Sat*

Accommodations

B&B @ Historic Page House Inn [GF,NS,WI] 323 Fairfax Ave **757/625-5033, 800/599-7659** *B&B in 1899 mansion*

Tazewell Hotel & Suites [GF,WI,WC] 245 Granby St (at Tazewell St) **757/623-6200**

Bars

The Garage [M,NH,F,K,WC] 731 Granby St (at Brambleton) **757/623-0303** *9am-2am, from 11am Sat, from noon Sun*

Hershee Bar [W,D,F,E,WC] 6117 Sewells Pt Rd (at Norview) **757/853-9842** *4pm-2am*

Nutty Buddy's [M,D,MR,F,DS,WC] 143 E Little Creek Rd **757/853-9842** *4pm-2am Wed-Sun, also restaurant*

Skip's [M,NH,F] 3822 Hampton Blvd **757/489-2345** *5pm-2am, from 10am Sat*

The Wave [M,D,F,S,WC] 4107 Colley Ave (at 41st St) **757/440-5911** *4pm-2am, from 5pm Sat, clsd Sun, also restaurant*

Cafes

Oasis Cafe [GO] 142 W York St #101A (in York Center bldg) **757/627-6161** *7:30am-4pm Mon-Fri*

Restaurants

Charlie's Cafe [BW] 1800 Granby St (at 18th) **757/625-0824** *7am-2pm*

Enrico's Ristorante [WC] 4012 Colley Ave **757/423-2700** *11am-10pm, till 11pm Fri, 5pm-11pm Sat, clsd Sun, Greek & Italian*

Tortilla West 508 Oropax St **757/440-3777** *Mexican, plenty veggie/ vegan*

Retail Shops

Kindred Spirit 7510-C Granby St (at Wards Corner) **757/480-0424** *10am-7pm, till 5pm Sat, from noon Sun, gifts, books, massage, readings & more*

Men's Services

▶ **Megaphone 757/498-3555** *Meet and Chat Live with HOT local men. FREE to listen & respond to ads. Video and text chat at GayMates.com. Use FREE code 4889.*

Erotica

Leather & Lace 149 E Little Creek Rd (at Granby) **757/583-4334**

Onley

Accommodations

Neptune Vacation Suites [GF,WI,GO] 21033 Front St (at Main St) **757/630-5193** *suites w/ retro '60s TV theme*

Petersburg

Accommodations

▶ **Centre Hill Inn** [GF,GO] 131 Franklin St **804/861-5822**

▶ **Walker House B&B** [GF,NS,WI,GO] 3280 S Crater Rd (at Wagner) **804/861-5822** *antebellum farmhouse*

Bookstores

Minerva Books [WC,GO] 233 Bartow Alley (at W Bank St) **804/732-2440** *11am-6pm clsd Sun-Mon*

Erotica

Thriller Books 1919 E Washington (on Rte 36) **804/733-0064**

Richmond

Info Lines & Services

AA Gay/ Lesbian 1205 W Franklin (at St James Episcopal Church) **804/355-1212**

Accommodations

Omni Richmond Hotel [GF,SW,WC] 100 S 12th St (at Cary St) **804/344-7000, 800/843-6664** *views of city & James River*

Bars

Babes of Carytown [W,D,CW,F,E,K,WC] 3166 W Cary St (at Auburn) **804/355-9330** *11am-2am, from noon Sat, 10am-8pm Sun*

Barcode [M,NH,K,V] 6 E Grace St (btwn 1st & Foushee Sts) **804/648-2040** *11am-2am, from 3pm wknds*

Godfrey's [MW,D,F,K,DS] 308 E Grace St (btwn 3rd & 4th) **804/648-3957** *lunch Tue-Fri, dinner Wed-Sun, clsd Mon, also restaurant*

Nightclubs

Club Colours [MW,D,MR-AF,F,S,WC] 536 N Harrison St (at Broad) **804/353-9776** *11:30pm-3am Wed & Sat*

Fieldens [★M,D,S,BYOB,PC] 2033 W Broad St **804/359-1963** *midnight-close Fri-Sat, 3 levels, not a sex club*

Restaurants

Galaxy Diner 3109 W Cary St **804/213-0510** *11am-midnight, till 2am wknds, some veggie, full bar*

The Village 1001 W Grace **804/353-8204** *8am-2am, bar till 2am, American*

Entertainment & Recreation

Richmond Triangle Players 2033 W Broad St (at Fieldens Cabaret Theater) **804/346-8113** *alternative theater group*

Venture Richmond 804/788-6466 *tour the James River, lots of shops, restaurants, etc*

Bookstores

Carytown Books [WC] 4021 MacArthur **804/261-7710** *10am-7pm, till 5pm Sun, LGBT section*

Phoenix Rising [WC] 19 N Belmont Ave **804/355-7939, 800/719-1690** *11am-7pm, clsd Tue, LGBT*

Men's Services

Erotica

Quality Books 8 S Crenshaw Ave **804/257-7146**

Cruisy Areas

Deep Run Park [AYOR] Ridgefield Pkwy (at Gaskins)

Forest Hill Park [AYOR] at 42nd St

Texas Beach/ North Bank Park [AYOR] N side of James River (at Texas Ave) *also Great Shiplock Park*

Roanoke

Bars

Backstreet Cafe [MW,NH,F] 356 Salem Ave (off Jefferson) **540/345-1542** *7pm-2am, till midnight Sun, clsd Mon*

Cuba Pete's [GF,NH,F,K,WC] 120 Church Ave SW (at First St SW, inside Macado's) **540/342-7231** *11am-2am, more gay wknds, also Macado's restaurant*

Nightclubs

The Park [★MW,D,DS,V,YC,WC] 615 Salem Ave **540/342-0946** *9pm-close Fri-Sun*

Publications

Blue Ridge Lambda Press **540/382-1103** *covers western VA*

Men's Services

▶ **Megaphone 888/634-2628** *Meet and Chat Live with HOT local men. Call for your local number or visit us online at GayMates.com. Use FREE code 4889.*

Shenandoah Valley

Info Lines & Services

SVGLA (Shenandoah Valley Gay/ Lesbian Assoc) 540/574-4636 *24-hr touchtone info & weekly meetings, also dances & potlucks*

Accommodations

Frog Hollow B&B [GS,GO] 492 Greenhouse Rd (at Rte 11), Lexington **540/463-5444** *full brkfst, hot tub*

Mayneview B&B [GF,NS] 439 Mechanic St, Luray **540/743-7921** *full brkfst, near Luray Caverns, wineries & hiking*

The Olde Staunton Inn [GS] 260 N Lewis St, Staunton **540/886-0193, 866/653-3786** *B&B, hot tub*

Piney Hill B&B [GS,NS,GO] 1048 Piney Hill Rd (at Mill Creek Crossroads), Luray **540/778-5261, 800/644-5261** *1750s farmhouse in Shenandoah Valley, hot tub*

Shenandoah Valley B&B [GF,NS] 402 E Beverley St (at Coalter), Staunton **540/885-1733, 866/466-1733** *full brkfst*

White Fence B&B [GF,NS] 275 Chapel Rd, Stanley **540/778-4680, 800/211-9885** *full brkfst, jacuzzi*

Urbanna

Accommodations

Inn at Urbanna Creek [GF,NS] **804/758-4661** *1870s home 2 hours from DC*

Virginia Beach

see also Norfolk

Accommodations

Capes Ocean Resort Hotel [GF,SW,NS,WI,WC] 2001 Atlantic Ave (at 20th St) **757/428-5421, 800/456-5421** *oceanfront rooms, private balconies, some jacuzzis*

Bars

In Between [MW,F,GO] 5266 Princess Anne Rd (btwn Witchduck & Newton Rds) **757/490-9498** *4pm-2am, from 5pm Sat, also restaurant, Sun brunch*

Klub Ambush [MW,NH,D,F,K,DS,GO] 475 S Lynnhaven Rd (at Lynnhaven Pkwy) **757/498-4301** *5pm-2am*

Rainbow Cactus [M,D,CW,F,DS,WC] 3472 Holland Rd (at Diana Lee) **757/368-0441** *7pm-2am, clsd Mon-Tue*

Restaurants

Alexander's on the Bay 4536 Oceanview Ave **757/464-4999** *dinner only, seafood, upscale, Chesapeake Bay views*

Publications

Lambda Directory 757/486-3546

Men's Services

▶ **Megaphone 757/821-7373** *Meet and Chat Live with HOT local men. FREE to listen & respond to ads. Video and text chat at GayMates.com. Use FREE code 4889.*

Erotica

Nancy's Nook 1301 Oceana Blvd **757/428-1498** *24hrs*

Washington

Accommodations

Gay Street Inn [GF,NS,WI,GO] 160 Gay St **540/675-3288** *restored 1860s farmhouse in historic Town of Washington*

Waverly

Erotica

Country Bookstore 111 S County Dr (Rte 460) (at Rte 40) **804/834-1122**

Windsor

Accommodations

Blackwater Campground [GF,SW] 7651 Whispering Pines Trail **757/357-7211** *RV hookups & primitive camping*

WASHINGTON

Auburn

CRUISY AREAS

Isaac Evans Park [AYOR] Green River Rd (off 104th Ave SE)

Bainbridge Island

BOOKSTORES

Eagle Harbor Book Co 157 Winslow Wy E **206/842-5332** *9am-7pm, till 9pm Th, till 6pm Sat, 10am-6pm Sun*

Bellevue

see Seattle

Bellingham

BARS

Rumors [MW,D,F,WC] 1119 Railroad Ave (at Chestnut) **360/671-1849** *4pm-2am*

CAFES

Tony's Cafe [WC] 1101 Harris Ave (at 11th), Fairhaven **360/738-4710** *7am-6pm*

RESTAURANTS

Bobbylees Pub & Eatery [GF,NH,D,GO,WC] 108 W Main St (Washington Ave), Everson **360/966-8838** *11am-2am*

Skylark's Hidden Cafe [E] 1308-B 11th St (at McKenzie) **360/715-3642** *7am-midnight, outdoor seating, full bar, live jazz wknds*

BOOKSTORES

Village Books 1200 11th St (at Harris) **360/671-2626** *9am-10pm, 11am-8pm Sun, new & used*

EROTICA

Great Northern Bookstore 1308 Railroad Ave (at Holly) **360/733-1650**

CRUISY AREAS

Teddy Bear Cove [AYOR]

Bender Creek

ACCOMMODATIONS

Triangle Recreation Camp [MW,PC] PO Box 1226, Granite Falls 98252 *members-only camping on 80-acre nature conservancy, (see www.camptrc.org)*

Bremerton

INFO LINES & SERVICES

AA Gay/ Lesbian 700 Callahan Dr (at St Paul's Episcopal) **360/475-0775** *7:30pm Tue*

BARS

Brewski's [GF,NH,F,WC] 2810 Kitsap Wy (enter off Wycuff St) **360/479-9100** *11am-2am, from 10am wknds*

Centralia

CRUISY AREAS

Fort Borst Park [AYOR] Harrison Ave

Coupeville

ACCOMMODATIONS

Morris Farmhouse B&B [GF,NS,GO] 105 W Morris Rd **360/678-0939, 866/440-1555** *restored 1908 farmhouse on 10 acres, lesbian-owned*

Edmonds

CRUISY AREAS

Edmonds City Park [AYOR] by ferry dock

Everett

INFO LINES & SERVICES

AA Gay/ Lesbian 2624 Rockefeller **425/252-2525** *7pm Sun*

NIGHTCLUBS

Twisted [MW,D,F,K,WC] 1212 California St (enter in the alley) **425/438-4111** *4:30-2am, from 6pm Sat, till midnight Sun*

Men's Services

▶ **Megaphone 425/322-2200** *Meet and Chat Live with HOT local men. FREE to listen & respond to ads. Video and text chat at GayMates.com. Use FREE code 4889.*

Erotica

Airport Video 11732 Airport Rd (1 block W of Hwy 99, at 128th St) **425/290-7555** *24hrs*

Cruisy Areas

Forest Park [AYOR] off 41st St

Glacier

Accommodations

Mt Baker B&B & Cabins [GS,NS] 9434 Cornell Creek Rd **360/599-2299** *modern chalet, full brkfst, hot tub*

Issaquah

Cruisy Areas

Sammamish State Park [AYOR] I-90 & SR 900

Kennewick

Cruisy Areas

Columbia Park [AYOR] *days only, cops & bashers after dark*

Kent

Bars

Swank [MW,D] 24437 Russell Rd **253/854-2110** *3pm-2am, from noon wknds, patio*

Vibe [MW,D,K] 226 1st Ave S (btwn Titus & Gowe) **253/852-0815** *noon-2am, till midnight Sun-Mon*

Men's Services

▶ **Megaphone 253/234-0700** *Meet and Chat Live with HOT local men. FREE to listen & respond to ads. Video and text chat at GayMates.com. Use FREE code 4889.*

Erotica

The Voyeur 604 Central Ave S **253/850-8428** *videos, toys, clothing*

La Conner

Accommodations

The Wild Iris [GF,NS,WC,GO] 121 Maple Ave **360/466-1400, 800/477-1400**

Long Beach Peninsula

Accommodations

Anthony's Home Court [GS,NS,WI,GO] 1310 Pacific Hwy N, Long Beach **360/642-2802, 888/787-2754** *cabins & RV hookups*

The Historic Sou'wester Lodge, Cabins & RV Park [GF,NS] Beach Access Rd (38th Pl), Seaview **360/642-2542** *inexpensive suites, cabins w/ kitchens & vintage trailers*

Senator TC Bloomer's Mansion [GF,GO] 1004 41st Pl (at Oceanfront), Seaview **360/642-8598, 800/747-2096** *rental home*

Lynnwood

Retail Shops

Colorbomb Tattoo 15315 Hwy 99, #7 (at 153rd) **425/742-8467**

Mt Vernon

Restaurants

Deli Next Door [WC] 202 S 1st St (at Memorial Hwy) **360/336-3886** *8am-9pm, 9pm-8pm Sun*

Cruisy Areas

Lions Park [AYOR] Freeway Dr (along the river)

Oak Harbor

Cruisy Areas

Joseph Whidbey Park [AYOR] Swantown & Crosby

Olympia

Info Lines & Services

Free at Last AA 11th & Washington #106 (at United Church) **360/352-7344** *call for info*

Gay Men's Social Network **360/923-1267** *events, newsletter*

Accommodations

Swantown Inn B&B [GF,NS,WI] 1431 11th Ave SE (at Central St) **360/753-9123, 877/753-9123**

Bars

Hannah's [GS,NH,F] 123 5th Ave W (at Columbia) **360/357-9890** *11am-2am, till midnight Sun-Mon*

Nightclubs

Jakes on 4th [MW,D,K] 311 E 4th **360/956-3247** *4pm-2am*

Cafes

Darby's Cafe [GS,GO] 211 SE 5th Ave (at Washington) **360/357-6229** *7am-2pm, 8am-2pm wknds, clsd Mon-Tue*

Restaurants

Saigon Rendez-Vous 117 5th Ave SW (btwn Columbia & Capitol Wy) **360/352-1989** *Vietnamese, plenty veggie*

Urban Onion [WC] 116 Legion Wy SE (at Capitol) **360/943-9242** *7am-9pm, till 10pm Fri, 8am-10pm Sat, till 9pm Sun, plenty veggie*

Retail Shops

Dumpster Values 302 4th (at Franklin) **360/705-3772** *10am-8pm, noon-6pm Sun, clothing, zines, records, toys*

Erotica

Desire Video 3200 Pacific Ave SE (off I-5, at exit 107) **360/352-0820** *24hrs, videos, toys, 100-channel video arcade, extensive LGBT section*

Cruisy Areas

Capitol Lake Marathon Park *take 5th Ave E to the parkway, follow signs to park*

Pasco

Nightclubs

Out & About Restaurant & Lounge [MW,D,F,K,C,DS,WC] 327 W Lewis **509/543-3796, 877/388-3796** *6pm-2am, clsd Mon, all ages Fri*

Port Townsend

Accommodations

The James House [GF,NS,WI] 1238 Washington St **800/385-1238, 360/385-1238** *Victorian B&B, full brkfst, gardens*

Ravenscroft Inn [GF,NS] 533 Quincy St (at Clay St) **360/385-2784, 800/782-2691** *seaport inn w/ views of Puget Sound, gourmet brkfst, hot tub*

Quinault

Accommodations

Lake Quinault Lodge [GF] South Shore Rd (off US 101) **360/288-2900, 800/562-6672**

Redmond

Cruisy Areas

Marymoor Park [AYOR] *days (cops evenings)*

San Juan Islands

Accommodations

Inn on Orcas Island [GF,NS,GO] **360/376-5227, 888/886-1661** *waterfront, full brkfst*

Lopez Farm Cottages & Tent Camping [GS,NS] 555 Fisherman Bay Rd, Lopez Island **360/468-3555, 800/440-3556** *hot tub, also camping*

Spring Bay Inn on Orcas Island [GS,NS,WI] Orcas Island **360/376-5531** *full brkfst, hot tub, kayak tour included in price*

Entertainment & Recreation

Western Prince Whale & Wildlife Tours 2 Spring St (at Front), Friday Harbor **360/378-5315, 800/757-6722** *whale-watching & wildlife tours April-Oct*

Seattle

Info Lines & Services

Capitol Hill Alano 1900 E Madison St **206/860-9560 (club), 206/587-2838 (AA#)** *12-step meetings daily*

Seattle LGBT Community Center [WC] 1122 E Pike St (btwn 11th & 12th Aves) **206/323-5428** *10am-9pm, 11am-8pm Sun*

Accommodations

11th Avenue Inn [GF,NS,WI] 121 11th Ave E **206/720-7161, 800/720-7161** *full brkfst*

The Ace Hotel [GS,NS,WI,GO] 2423 1st Ave (at Wall St) **206/448-4721** *modern & stylish, some shared baths*

Alexis Hotel [GF,WI,WC] 1007 1st Ave (at Madison) **206/624-4844, 800/426-7033** *luxury hotel w/ Aveda spa*

Arctic Club Hotel [GF,F,WI] 700 Third Ave (at Cherry) **206/340-0340, 800/600-7775**

Artist's Studio Loft B&B [GF,NS] 16529 91st Ave SW, Vashon Island **206/463-2583** *on 5 acres, garden, hot tub*

Bacon Mansion [GS,NS,WI,WC] 959 Broadway E (at E Prospect) **206/329-1864, 800/240-1864** *Edwardian-style Tudor*

Barclay Court East [GS,NS,GO] 1206 E Barclay Ct **206/329-3914** *2 studios, private sunken garden patio*

Bed & Breakfast on Broadway [GF,NS,WI] 722 Broadway Ave E (at Aloha) **206/329-8933**

Chambered Nautilus B&B Inn [GF,NS] 5005 22nd Ave NE (at N 50th St) **206/522-2536, 800/545-8459** *full brkfst, sundecks*

Gaslight Inn [★GS,SW,NS,GO] 1727 15th Ave (at E Howell St) **206/325-3654** *B&B in Arts & Crafts home*

Grand Hyatt Seattle [GF,WI,WC] 721 Pine St **206/774-1234** *views of Puget Sound, Lake Union & the Olympic & Cascade Mtns*

Hill House B&B [GF,NS] 1113 E John St (at 12th Ave) **206/323-4455, 866/417-4455** *full brkfst*

Hotel 1000 [GF,WI] 1000 First Ave **206/957-1000**

Hotel Monaco [GF,WI,WC] 1101 4th Ave (at Spring St) **206/621-1770, 800/945-2240** *gym, also Sazerac Cajun restaurant*

Hotel Vintage Park [GS,WI,WC] 1100 5th Ave (at Spring) **206/624-8000, 800/853-3914** *ultraluxe sleep in Seattle*

Inn at Queen Anne [GS] 505 1st Ave N (at Republican) **206/282-7357, 800/952-5043** *kitchenettes*

Pioneer Square Hotel [GF,NS,WI,WC] 77 Yesler Wy (btwn 1st Ave & Alaskan Wy) **206/340-1234, 800/800-5514**

W Seattle [GF,WI,WC] 1112 Fourth Ave **206/264-6000, 877/WHOTELS (reservations only)** *also restaurant*

Warwick Seattle Hotel [GS,SW,WC] 401 Lenora St (at 4th) **206/443-4300**

Wild Lily Cabins B&B [★GS,SW,NS,GO] 25 miles W of Steven's Pass, Index **360/793-2103** *cabins on Skykomish River, 1 hour from Seattle, cedar sauna*

Bars

The Baltic Room [GS,E] 1207 Pine St (at Melrose) **206/625-4444** *9pm-2am, clsd Wed & Sun*

Beacon Pub [GS,NH,K] 3057 Beacon Ave S **206/726-0238** *2pm-2am, from noon wknds*

The Bottleneck Lounge [GS,GO] 2328 Madison St **206/323-1098** *4pm-midnight, till 2am Th-Sat*

Cafe Metropolitain [GS] 1701 E Olive Way **206/324-0771**

The Can Can [GS,F,C] 94 Pike St (in the Pike Place Market) **206/652-0832** *4:30pm-2am*

Canterbury Ale and Eats [GF,NH] 534 15th Ave E **206/322-3130** *11am-2am*

CC Attle's [★M,NH,F,V,WC] 1501 E Madison (at 15th Ave) **206/323-4017** *noon-2am, patio, also Veranda Room & Men's Room*

Cha Cha Lounge & Bimbo's Cantina [GF,NH,GO] 1013 E Pike St **260/322-0703** *5pm-2am*

Changes [M,NH,F,K,V,WC] 2103 N 45th St (at Meridian) **206/545-8363** *noon-2am*

Chapel [GS,D,F] 1600 Melrose Ave (at E Pine) **206/447-4180** *5pm-1am, till 2am Fri-Sat, upscale*

The Crescent Lounge [GS,NH,K,WC] 1413 E Olive Wy (at Bellevue) **206/720-8188** *noon-2am, karaoke nightly*

▶ **The Cuff** [★M,D,CW,B,WC] 1533 13th Ave (at Pine) **206/323-1525** *2pm-2am, after-hours wknds, T-dance Sun, levi crowd, patio*

Double Header [GS,NH] 407 2nd Ave S Extension (at Washington) **206/464-9918** *10am-11pm, till 1am Fri-Sat*

Elite Tavern [MW,NH] 1520 E Olive Way (at Denny Way) **206/860-0999** *noon-2am*

Hula Hula [GF,K] 106 1st Ave N (at Denny) **206/284-5003** *4pm-close, tiki bar*

Madison Pub [★M,NH,F,WI,WC] 1315 E Madison St (at 13th) **206/325-6537** *noon-2am*

Martin's Off Madison [M,NH,F,P,WC] 1413 14th Ave (at Madison) **206/325-7000** *11am-2am, from 9am wknds*

Poco Wine Room [GS,F] 1408 E Pine St (at 14th Ave) **206/322-9463** *5pm-close*

R Place [M,NH,D,F,K,S,V,WI] 619 E Pine St (at Boylston) **206/322-8828** *4pm-2am, from 2pm wknds*

Rendezvous [GF,C,E] 2322 2nd Ave (at Battery) **206/441-5823** *4pm-2am, live shows, also restaurant*

The Seattle Eagle [M,L,WC] 314 E Pike St (at Bellevue) **206/621-7591** *2pm-2am, patio, rock 'n' roll, theme nights*

Sonya's Bar & Grill [M,NH,F] 1919 1st Ave (btwn Virginia & Stewart) **206/441-7996** *1:30pm-2am*

Temple Billiards [GF,F] 126 S Jackson **206/682-3242** *11am-2am, from 3pm wknds*

Nightclubs

Club Heaven [GS,D,F,$] 172 S Washington St (at 2nd) **206/622-1863** *6pm-2am, call for events*

Contour [GF,D,F,E] 807 1st Ave (at Columbia) **206/447-7704** *11:30am-2am, till 4:30am Th, till 6am Fri, 2pm-6am Sat, till 2am Sun, 3pm-2am Mon, fire performances*

Dimitriou's Jazz Alley [GF,F,E,NS,$] 2033 6th Ave (at Lenora) **206/441-9729** *call for events & reservations*

Neighbours Dance Club [★MW,D,YC,WC] 1509 Broadway (at Pike & Pine) **206/324-5358** *9pm-2am, till 3am Th, till 4am Fri-Sat, 2 flrs, also [18+] room Th-Sat*

Purr [M,F,K] 1518 11th Ave (at Pike St) **206/325-3112** *3pm-2am, till midnight Sun, cocktail lounge, Mexican-inspired food*

Re-bar [★GS,D,E,C] 1114 Howell (at Boren Ave) **206/233-9873** *10pm-2am, clsd Mon, DJ Wed-Sun*

Showbox [GF,E,$] 1426 1st Ave (at Pike) **206/628-3151** *live music venue, no cover charge in Green Room*

Cafes

The Allegro [WI] 4214 University Wy NE (at NE 42nd St) **206/633-3030** *7am-10:30pm, from 8am Sun*

Animals [WI] 550 12th Ave **206/726-9600** *6:30am-5pm, 8:30am-3pm Sat, clsd Sun*

Cafe Besalu 5909 24th Ave NW **206/789-1463** *7am-3pm, clsd Mon-Tue, great pastries*

Fuel Coffee [WI] 610 19th Ave E **206/329-4700** *6am-9pm, pastries*

Insomniax Coffee & Juice [WI] 102 15th Ave E **206/322-6477** *7am-5pm, clsd wknds*

Kaladi Brothers Coffee 511 E Pike St (at Summit) **206/388-1700** *6am-9pm, from 8am wknds*

Louisa's 2379 Eastlake Ave E **206/325-0081** *7am-7pm, 8am-2pm Sun*

Restaurants

Al Boccalino 1 Yesler Wy (at Alaskan) **206/622-7688** *lunch Tue-Fri, dinner nightly, classy southern Italian*

Bamboo Garden 364 Roy St (at Mercer St) **206/282-6616** *11am-10pm, Chinese vegetarian & kosher*

The Broadway Grill [★] 314 Broadway E (at E Harrison) **206/328-7000** *11am-11pm, from 8am wknds, full bar*

Cafe Flora [BW,NS,WC] 2901 E Madison St **206/325-9100** *lunch, dinner, wknd brunch*

Cafe Septieme [★MW] 214 Broadway Ave E (at Thomas & John) **206/860-8858** *9am-11pm, till midnight Fri-Sat, also bar*

Campagne [R] 86 Pine St (at 1st) **206/728-2800** *dinner only, clsd Mon, French, also full bar; also Cafe Campagne, 206/728-2233*

Capitol Club [E] 414 E Pine St **206/325-2149** *tapas menu*

Dahlia Lounge 2001 4th Ave (at Virginia) **206/682-4142** *lunch Mon-Fri, dinner nightly, wknd brunch, full bar*

Dick's Drive In 115 Broadway E (at Denny) **206/302-1300** *10:30am-2am, excellent fries & shakes*

Flying Fish 2234 1st Ave (at Bell) **206/728-8595** *5pm-midnight, bar till 2am*

Fresh Bistro 4725 42nd Ave SW (btwn Alaska St & Edmunds) **206/935-3733** *11am-11pm, till midnight Fri-Sat*

Glo's [★] 1621 E Olive Wy (at Summit Ave E) **206/324-2577** *7am-3pm, till 4pm wknds, brkfst only*

Julia's [E] 300 Broadway E (at Thomas) **206/860-1818** *8am-11pm, till midnight Fri-Sat, full bar, [DS] Sat*

Kabul 2301 N 45th St **206/545-9000** *5pm-9:30pm, till 10pm Fri-Sat, Afghan, some veggie*

Mae's Phinney Ridge Cafe [★WC] 6412 Phinney Ridge N (at 65th) **206/782-1222** *8am-2pm, till 3pm wknds, brkfst menu*

Mama's Mexican Kitchen 2234 2nd Ave (in Belltown) **206/728-6262** *lunch & dinner, cheap & funky*

Paseo 4225 Fremont Ave N (at N 43rd St) **206/545-7440** *11:30am-9pm, clsd Sun-Mon, Cuban*

Queen City Grill [★WC] 2201 1st Ave (at Blanchard) **206/443-0975** *dinner only, fresh seafood, full bar*

Rosebud Restaurant & Bar [NS] 719 E Pike St (at Harvard Ave) **206/323-6636** *dinner nightly, wknd brunch*

Snappy Dragon 8917 Roosevelt Wy NE **206/528-5575** *11am-9:30pm, 4pm-9pm Sun, Chinese, plenty veggie*

Sunlight Cafe [BW,WC] 6403 Roosevelt Wy NE (at 64th) **206/522-9060** *8am-9pm, vegetarian*

Szmania's 3321 W McGraw St (in Magnolia Bluff) **206/284-7305** *lunch Tue-Fri, dinner nightly, clsd Mon, full bar*

Teapot Vegetarian House 345 15th Ave E **206/325-1010** *11am-10pm, vegan*

Thaiger Room 4228 University Wy NE **206/632-9299** *11am-10pm, from noon wknds, Thai*

Tidbit Bistro 2359 10th Ave E (at E Miller) **206/323-0840** *dinner nightly, tapas, full bar, patio*

Wild Ginger Asian Restaurant & Triple Bar [★] 1401 3rd Ave (at Union) **206/623-4450** *lunch Mon-Sat, dinner nightly, bar till 1am*

Wild Mountain 1408 NW 85th St **206/297-9453** *8:30am-9:30pm, clsd Tue*

Entertainment & Recreation

Alki Beach Park 1702 Alki Ave SW, West Seattle *popular on warm days*

Century Ballroom [MW,D,F] 915 E Pine, 2nd flr **206/324-7263** *Outdancing 9:45pm 3rd & 4th Fri, lessons at 9:15pm, also restaurant*

Garage [★F,21+] 1130 Broadway **206/322-2296** *3pm-2am, way-cool pool hall, full bar, also bowling alley*

Gay Bingo 860 Terry Ave N (at S Lake Union Naval Reserve Bldg) **206/323-0069, 206/328-8979** *2nd Sat only, Jan-June*

Harvard Exit 807 E Roy St (at Harvard) **206/781-5755** *rep film theater*

Northwest Lesbian & Gay History Museum Project 206/903-9517 *exhibits & publication*

The Paramount Theatre [E] 911 Pine St **206/467-5510** *historic Beaux Arts-style theater, tours 10am 1st Sat*

Richard Hugo House [C,WC] 1634 11th Ave **206/322-7030** *noon-6pm, till 5pm Sat, clsd Sun; Zine Archive & Publishing Project; open later for events; also cafe*

Seattle Men's Chorus 206/323-0750 *world's largest & most successful gay men's chorus*

Tacky Tourist Clubs *fabulous social events*

The Vera Project [GF] corner of Warren Ave N & Republican St (in Seattle Center) **206/956-8372** *all-ages music arts center*

Bookstores

Bailey/ Coy Books [WC] 414 Broadway Ave E (at Harrison) **206/323-8842** *10am-10pm, till 6pm Sun*

Edge of the Circle 701 E Pike (at Boylston) **206/726-1999** *noon-9pm, alternative spirituality store*

Elliott Bay Book Company 101 S Main St **206/624-6600, 800/962-5311** *9:30am-10pm, 11am-7pm Sun, in historic Globe building, also cafe*

Fremont Place Book Company 621 N 35th (at Fremont Ave N) **206/547-5970** *10am-8pm, noon-6pm Sun*

Left Bank Books 92 Pike St (at 1st Ave) **206/622-0195** *10am-7pm, 11am-6pm Sun, worker-owned collective, LGBT section*

Twice Sold Tales 1833 Harvard Ave (at Broadway E) **206/324-2421** *10am-8pm, till 10pm Fri-Sat*

Retail Shops

Archie McPhee 1300 N 45th St (at Stone Way) **206/297-0240** *10am-7pm, till 6pm Sun, weird & wonderful toys & trinkets*

Broadway Market [★] 401 Broadway E (at Harrison & Republican) *mall full of funky, hip stores*

Lifelong Thrift Store 1017 E Union St **206/328-8979** *all proceeds to AIDS organization*

Metropolis 7220 Greenwood Ave N (at 73rd) **206/782-7002** *10am-7pm, till 6pm Sat, noon-5pm Sun, cards & gifts*

Publications

'Mo Seattle 410 Broadway Ave E **206/235-3320** *monthly LGBT mag*

SGN (Seattle Gay News) 206/324-4297 *weekly LGBT newspaper*

The Stranger 206/323-7101 *queer-positive alternative weekly*

Men's Clubs

Basic Plumbing [PC] 1505 10th Ave (btwn Pike & Pine) **206/323-2799** *24hrs; HIV testing Tue & Th*

Club Z [PC] 1117 Pike St (at Boren) **206/622-9958** *24hrs daily, discounts for out-of-towners*

Steamworks [★WI,PC] 1520 Summit Ave (btwn Pike & Pike Mailing) **206/388-4818** *24hrs*

Men's Services

► **Megaphone 206/877-0877** *Meet and Chat Live with HOT local men. FREE to listen & respond to ads. Video and text chat at GayMates.com. Use FREE code 4889.*

Erotica

Castle Superstore 206 Broadway Ave E **206/204-0126**

The Crypt Off Broadway 1516 11th Ave (at E Pine) **206/325-3882**

Deja Vu Adult Superstore 1510 1st Ave (at Pike) **206/624-1784** *24hrs*

Fantasy Unlimited 2027 Westlake Ave (at 7th) **206/682-0167** *24hrs*

Hollywood Erotic Boutique 12706 Lake City Wy NE **206/363-0056** *24hrs, theater, toys, lingerie*

Taboo Video 1012 1st Ave **206/622-7399** *24hrs*

Cruisy Areas

Arboretum [AYOR] *days*

Green Lake Park [AYOR] 5500 blk of W Green Lake Wy (btwn putting course & aqua theater) *evenings*

Spokane

Info Lines & Services

AA Gay/ Lesbian 301 S Freya (at Bethany Presbyterian Church) **509/624-1442** *7pm Wed*

Inland NW LGBT Center 508 W 2nd Ave **509/489-1914** *support groups, events, also art gallery*

Accommodations

Montvale Hotel [GF,TG,F,NS,WI,GO] 1005 W First Ave (at Monroe) **509/747-1919, 866/668-8253** *luxury, boutique hotel*

Nightclubs

Dempsey's Brass Rail [★MW,D,F,S,WC] 909 W 1st St (btwn Lincoln & Monroe) **509/747-5362** *3pm-2am, till 4am Fri-Sat, DJ Th-Sat, also restaurant*

Restaurants

Mizuna 214 N Howard **509/747-2004** *lunch Mon-Fri, dinner Mon-Sat, full bar*

Bookstores

Auntie's Bookstore & Cafe [WC] 402 W Main St (at Washington) **509/838-0206** *9am-9pm, 11am-6pm Sun*

Men's Services

▶ **Megaphone 509/777-2100** *Meet and Chat Live with HOT local men. FREE to listen & respond to ads. Video and text chat at GayMates.com. Use FREE code 4889.*

Erotica

Hollywood Erotic Boutique 9611 E Sprague Ave **509/928-9499** *24hrs*

Suquamish

Info Lines & Services

Kitsap Lesbian/ Gay AA 18732 Division Ave NE (at Congregational Church of Christ) **360/475-0775** *7:30pm Sun*

Tacoma

Info Lines & Services

AA Gay/ Lesbian 759 S 45th (at New Heart MCC) **253/474-8897** *7:30pm Fri*

Rainbow Center 741 St Helens Ave **253/383-2318** *10am-3pm Mon-Fri, community center, call for meetings & events*

Accommodations

Chinaberry Hill—An 1889 Grand Victorian Inn [GF,NS,WI] 302 Tacoma Ave N **253/272-1282** *full brkfst, jacuzzis, bay views, fireplaces, romantic*

Hotel Murano [GF,WC] 1320 Broadway Plaza (at S 15th) **253/572-3200, 888/862-3255** *restaurants & bars*

Bars

Airport Bar & Grill [MW,NH] 5406 S Tacoma Wy (at 54th) **253/475-9730** *2pm-2am*

Nightclubs

▶ **Club Silverstone** [MW,NH,D,F,K] 739 1/2 St Helens Ave (at 9th) **253/404-0273** *11am-2am*

Cafes

Shakabrah Java Cafe [E,WC] 2618 6th Ave **253/572-2787** *7am-10pm, till midnight Fri-Sat, 8am-4pm Sun*

Men's Services

▶ **Megaphone 253/882-0882** *Meet and Chat Live with HOT local men. FREE to listen & respond to ads. Video and text chat at GayMates.com. Use FREE code 4889.*

Erotica

Castle Superstore 6015 Tacoma Mall Blvd **253/471-0391**

Cruisy Areas

Wright Park [AYOR] 6th & G Sts

Vancouver

see also Portland, Oregon

Bars

Northbank [MW,D,F,K,C,DS,NS,WC] 106 W 6th St (at Main) **360/695-3862** *2pm-2am*

Men's Services

▶ **Megaphone 360/433-6100** *Meet and Chat Live with HOT local men. FREE to listen & respond to ads. Video and text chat at GayMates.com. Use FREE code 4889.*

Walla Walla

Accommodations

The Boyer House [GS,SW,NS,GO] 741 Boyer Ave **509/200-9931** *full brkfst*

Cruisy Areas

Fort Walla Walla Park [AYOR]

Pioneer Park [AYOR]

Wenatchee

Cafes

The Cellar Cafe [BW,GO] 249 N Mission St (at 5th) **509/662-1722** *9am-5pm, 10am-4pm Sat, clsd Sun, patio*

Cruisy Areas

River Walk [AYOR] at 19th St

Whidbey Island

Accommodations

Whidwood Inn [GS,NS,GO] **360/679-7472** *near historic Coupeville, hot tub*

Winthrop

Accommodations

Chewuch Inn [GF,NS,WI,WC] 223 White Ave **509/996-3107, 800/747-3107** *E of N Cascades Mtns*

Yakima

Erotica

Yakima Magazine Center 18 S 1st St **509/248-8598**

West Virginia

Statewide

Publications

Graffiti 304/485-1891 *alternative entertainment guide*

Beaver

Erotica

Airport Video 1194 Airport Rd (off I-64 at exit 125, 10 miles E of Beckley) **304/250-0263** *10am-2am*

Beckley

Erotica

Blue Moon Video 3427 Robert C Byrd Dr (at New River Dr) **304/255-1200**

Eccles Video 3517 Harper Rd, Harper **304/250-0068** *noon-10pm, clsd Sun, arcade*

Berkeley Springs

Accommodations

The Lodge [M,NS,WC,GO] **304/258-9454** *in Sleepy Creek Mtns, shared bath, also bar*

Erotica

Action Books & Video [AYOR] US 522 (7 miles S of town) **304/258-2529** *24hrs, arcade*

Bluefield

Cruisy Areas

East River Mountain Overlook [AYOR] off Rte 460 (take lane nearest mtn & turn off, go all the way up mtn)

Charleston

Accommodations

Long Fork Campgrounds [MW,SW,N,WI,GO] 114 Long Fork Camp Rd (at Charleston Rd), Walton **304/577-9347** *40 minutes from Charleston*

Nightclubs

Broadway [M,D,DS] 210 Leon Sullivan Wy (at Lee) **304/343-2162** *4pm-3am, from 1pm Sat-Mon*

Entertainment & Recreation

Living AIDS Memorial Garden corner of Washington St E (at Sidney Ave) **304/346-0246**

Bookstores

Taylor Books 226 Capitol St **304/342-1461** *7:30am-8pm, till 10pm Fri, 9am-10pm Sat, till 5pm Sun, independent, also cafe, art gallery & boutique*

Men's Services

▶ **Megaphone 888/634-2628** *Meet and Chat Live with HOT local men. Call for your local number or visit us online at GayMates.com. Use FREE code 4889.*

Erotica

Bookmart Video 4100 Maccorkle Ave SE (at 41st St SE) **304/925-9000**

Crazy Mitch's Adult Books 6721 Maccorkle Ave, St Albans **304/768-0947** *24hrs*

Cruisy Areas

Coonskin Park [AYOR] Greenbriar St (take Greenbriar St exit from I-77 heading from Beckley)

Daniel Boone Park [AYOR] Kanawha Blvd (just N of Capitol) *evenings*

Clarksburg

Erotica

Adult News 835 Philippi Pike (1/8 mile from Rte 58) **304/622-7909** *24hrs*

Fairmont

Cruisy Areas

Morris Park [AYOR] Pleasant Valley Rd

Follansbee

Bars

Wild Coyote Saloon [MW,D,DS] 869 Main St **304 /527-7191** *6pm-close*

Ghent

Erotica

▶ **The Lion's Den Adult Superstore** 302 Odd Rd (exit 28 off I-77) **304/787-3333**

Harpers Ferry

Accommodations

Laurel Lodge [GF,NS,WI,GO] 844 Ridge St **304/535-2886** *rustic stone bungalow overlooking scenic Potomac River gorge, full brkfst*

Huntington

Accommodations

Pullman Plaza Hotel [GF,SW,NS,WI,WC] 1001 3rd Ave (at 10th St) **304/525-1001, 866/613-3611** *downtown, full brkfst*

Bars

Jackhammer [M,NH,D,B,L,MR,K,S,WC,GO] 2127 Manchester Ave (at 22nd St & 3rd Ave) **304/781-2520** *5pm-3am, clsd Sun*

Polo Club [M,D,B,DS,PC,WC] 1037 7th Ave (at 11th St) **304/522-3146** *5pm-2am, from 2pm wknds*

The Stonewall [★MW,D,K,DS,18+,WC,GO] 820 7th Ave (enter in alley) **304/523-2242** *8pm-3am, clsd Mon*

Restaurants

Sharkey's 410 10th St **304/523-3200** *4pm-2:30am, clsd Sun, full bar*

Cruisy Areas

Rotary Park [AYOR] near 8th Ave & 29th St (off Rte 60 E, take 29th St exit)

Lewisburg

Accommodations

Lee Street Inn B&B [GF,WI,GO] 200 N Lee St **304/647-5599, 888/228-7000** *grand 1876 house, jacuzzi, garden*

Cruisy Areas

Tuckwiller Park [AYOR] off Rte 60 (from I-64 take exit 161 & head E for 1 mile)

Logan

Cruisy Areas

Chief Logan State Park

Lost River

Accommodations

Guest House at Lost River [MW,F,SW,NS,WI,GO] 288 Settlers Valley Wy (at Mill Gap Rd) **304/897-5707** *full brkfst, hot tub, restaurant & bar*

Restaurants

Lost River Grill & Motel [WI] St Rd 259 **304/897-6482** *11:45am-9pm, 8am-10pm Sat, till 9pm Sun, 4pm-9pm Mon, full bar, also motel & cabins*

Martinsburg

Erotica

Variety Books & Video 255 N Queen St (at Race) **304/263-4334** *24hrs*

Cruisy Areas

I-81 Rest Area 1/2 mile past exit 20 (in closed weigh station) *evenings*

Milton

Erotica

▶ **The Lion's Den Adult Superstore** 325 Summers Addition (exit 28, off I-64) **304/743-0190** *24hrs*

Mineral Wells

Erotica

▶ **The Lion's Den Adult Superstore** State Rte 14 & I-77 (exit 170, off I-77) **304/489-9690** *24hrs*

Morgantown

Info Lines & Services

BiGLTM (Bisexual, Gay, Lesbian, Transgendered Mountaineers) **304/293-8200** *counseling, referrals & social group*

Nightclubs

Vice Versa [MW,D,K,DS,S,PC,18+,WC] 335 High St (enter rear) **304/292-2010** *8pm-3am Th-Sun*

Weezie's Pub & Club [MW,D,E] 3438 University Ave **304/292-3939** *8pm-close, clsd Sun*

Erotica

Adult Toy Boxxx Hartman Run Rd **304/296-3428** *clsd Sun, bookstore w/ arcade*

Cruisy Areas

Cooper's Rock State Park [AYOR] 10 miles E of town (off I-68, take Cooper's State Park exit) *parking lot & woods*

Marilla Park [AYOR] E Brockway Ave (btwn Morgantown & Sabraton) *midday & evenings*

Parkersburg

Nightclubs

Woodstarr [MW,D,K,DS] 322 5th St **304/422-3711** *clsd Sun-Tue*

Erotica

Bookmark Video & Books 2602 Ohio Ave **304/485-2263** *bookstore w/ arcade*

Pioneer Adult Books & Videos 6603 Emerson Ave **304/428-8604**

Cruisy Areas

Corning Boat Ramp [AYOR] Staunton Ave (off I-77)

Pliny

Erotica

Route 35 Adult Video & Books 1651 US Rte 35 N (near Buffalo) **304/937-4900** *24hrs*

Proctor

Accommodations

Roseland Guest House & Campground [MO,F,SW,N,NS,GO] **304/455-3838** *222 secluded acres w/ campsites, theme wknds, hot tub*

Shepherdstown

Accommodations

Thomas Shepherd Inn [GF,NS,WI] 300 W German St (at Duke St) **304/876-3715, 888/889-8952** *B&B, full brkfst*

Bookstores

On the Wings of Dreams 139 W German St **304/876-0244** *11am-6pm, metaphysical*

Sissonville

Restaurants

Topspot Country Cookin' 7139 Sissonville Rd **304/984-2816** *7am-8pm, till 7pm Sun, clsd Mon*

Summerville

Erotica

Fantasy Video 102 Lake Rd (off Rte 19), Mt Nebo **304/872-9030**

Upper Tract

Accommodations

Wildernest Inn [GF,NS] **304/257-9076, 888/621-2948** *April-Dec, full brkfst*

Wheeling

Erotica

Fritz the Cat Coventry Rd (at I-70), Dallas Pike **304/547-0250**

Market St News 1437 Market St (at 14th St) **304/232-2414** *24hrs, till midnight Sun-Mon*

Wisconsin

Algoma

Retail Shops

The Flying Pig [GF,GO] N6975 Hwy 42 (at Tenth) **920/487-9902** *9am-6pm (May-Oct) clsd Tue-Th (Nov-April), art gallery & coffee bar*

Appleton

Bars

Rascals Bar & Grill [MW,F] 702 E Wisconsin Ave (at Lawe) **920/954-9262** *5pm-2am, from noon Sun, fish-fry Fri, patio*

Ravens [M,D,K,DS] 215 E College Ave **920/364-9559** *8pm-2am, clsd Sun-Mon*

Cafes

Harmony Cafe [GS,E,YC] 233 E College Ave **920/734-2233** *7am-9pm, 9am-9pm Sat, clsd Sun, also educational & support groups*

Men's Services

► **Megaphone 920/243-0043** *Meet and Chat Live with HOT local men. FREE to listen & respond to ads. Video and text chat at GayMates.com. Use FREE code 4889.*

Erotica

Eldorado's 2545 S Memorial Dr (at Hwys 47 & 441) **920/830-0042**

Cruisy Areas

Lutz Park [AYOR]

Ashland

Cruisy Areas

Prentice Park [AYOR]

Baileys Harbor

Accommodations

Blacksmith Inn on the Shore [GF,NS,WI,WC] 8152 Hwy 57 **920/839-9222, 800/769-8619**

Beloit

Bars

Club Impulse [MW,D] 132 W Grand Ave **608/361-0000** *4pm-2am, till 2:30am Fri-Sat, from 7pm Sat, from 3pm Sun*

Eagle River

Accommodations

The Edgewater Inn & Cottages [GS,NS,WI] 5054 St Hwy 70 W **715/479-4011, 888/334-3987** *also waterfront cottages*

Eau Claire

Info Lines & Services

LGBT Community Center of the Chippewa Valley 510 S Farwell St **715/552-5428** *drop-in 7pm-10pm Fri, call for other hours, library & variety of events*

Accommodations

Fireside Lake Lodge [GF,WI,GO] W 12745 Fireside Lake Rd, New Auburn **715/868-1172**

Nightclubs

Scooters [MW,D,K,DS,WC] 411 Galloway (at Farwell) **715/835-9959** *3pm-2am*

Erotica

Adult Video Unlimited 1518 Bellinger St **715/834-3393**

Green Bay

Info Lines & Services

Gay AA 920/469-9999 *call for times & locations*

Bars

Home Base [GF,K] 301 S Broadway **920/455-1005** *2pm-close, from 5pm Mon*

Napalese Lounge [M,NH,F,DS,WC] 1351 Cedar St **920/432-9646** *11am-close, DJ Fri-Sat*

Sass [MW,D,K] 840 S Broadway **920/437-7277** *6pm-2am Tue, Fri & Sat*

Nightclubs

The Shelter [MW,D,CW,B,L,TG,F,K,DS,V,GO] 730 N Quincy St (at 54302) **920/432-2662** *4pm-2am, theme nights*

Cafes

Harmony Cafe [E] 1660 W Mason St **920/569-1593** *7am-9pm, 10am-6pm Sun, also educational & support groups*

Publications

Quest 920/655-0611, 800/578-3785 *news & arts reviews for WI's LGBT community*

Men's Services

▶ **Megaphone 920/227-0077** *Meet and Chat Live with HOT local men. FREE to listen & respond to ads. Video and text chat at GayMates.com. Use FREE code 4889.*

Erotica

▶ **Lion's Den Adult Superstore** 836 S Broadway (at 5th) **920/433-9640**

Hayward

Accommodations

The Lake House [MW,SW,NS,WI,WC,GO] 5793 Division, Stone Lake **715/865-6803** *full brkfst, lesbian-owned*

Hurley

Accommodations

Anton-Walsh House [GF] 202 Copper St (at US Hwy 51) **715/561-2065** *historic B&B, full brkfst*

Whitecap Mountains Ski Resort & Skye Golf [GF,SW,WI,WC] County Hwy E (at Hwy 77), Montréal **715/561-2227, 800/933-7669** *golf & ski resort, full brkfst, kids/ pets ok*

Kenosha

see also Racine

Bars

Club Icon [MW,D,K] 6305 120th Ave (on E frontage road of 94) **262/857-3240** *7pm-2am,from 3pm Sun, clsd Mon*

La Crosse

Accommodations

Rainbow Ridge Farms B&B [GF,NS] N 5732 Hauser Rd (at County S), Onalaska **608/783-8181, 888/347-2594**

Trillium B&B [GF,NS] **608/625-4492** *2 cottages, full brkfst, 35 miles from La Crosse*

Bars

Chances Are [MW,NH] 417 Jay St (at 4th) **608/782-5105** *3pm-close, from noon wknds*

My Place [MW,NH,GO] 3201 South Ave (at East Ave) **608/788-9073** *3pm-close, from noon wknds*

Players [★MW,D,MR,TG,WC,GO] 214 Main St (at 3rd) **608/784-2353** *5pm-2am, from 3pm Fri-Sun, till 2:30am Fri-Sat*

Erotica

Pleasures [GS] 405 S 3rd **608/784-6350**

Cruisy Areas

Pettibone Park [AYOR] on the Mississippi River (off of North Beach, across from the Holiday Inn) *days only*

Lake Geneva

Accommodations

Eleven Gables Inn on the Lake [GF,NS,WI,WC] 493 Wrigley Dr **262/248-8393** *lakeside inn, full brkfst wknds*

Madison

Info Lines & Services

LesBiGay Campus Center 800 Langdon, 2nd flr Memorial Union, UW **608/265-3344** *drop-in 9am-5pm, till 2:30pm Fri, clsd wknds*

OutReach, Inc 600 Williamson St #P-1 **608/255-8582** *9am-9pm, noon-3pm Sat, clsd Sun*

Accommodations

Hawks Nest Log Home Rentals [MW,NS,GO] 2459 Fairview (at Door Creek Rd), Stoughton **608/445-7468** *log homes on Lake Kegonsa, lesbian-owned*

Bars

Club 5 [★MW,D,K,DS,V] 5 Applegate Ct (btwn Fish Hatchery Rd & W Beltline Hwy) **608/277-9700, 877/648-9700** *4pm-2am, dance club, also Barracks leather bar & Planet Q video bar, [18+] Tue*

Green Bush [GF,F] 914 Regent St (at Park) **608/257-2874** *4pm-midnight, clsd Sun, also restaurant*

OUT Restaurant and Nightclub [MW,D,DS,E,WC] 1262 John Q Hammons Dr **608/203-8338** *11am-9pm, later Th-Sat, clsd Sun*

Shamrock [★MW,F] 117 W Main St (at Fairchild) **608/255-5029** *11am-close, brunch wknds*

Woof's [MW,NH,D] 114 King St **608/204-6222**

Nightclubs

Cardinal [GF,D] 418 E Wilson St (at S Franklin) **608/251-0080** *8pm-2am, clsd Mon, more gay 2nd Tue & early Fri, call for events*

IQ/ IndieQueer [MW,D] *weekly & monthly queer parties in Madison, check local listings for dates & info*

Cafes

Java Cat [F,WI] 3918 Monona Dr (at Cottage Grove Rd) **608/223-5553**

Restaurants

Fromagination 12 S Carroll (on Capital Sq) **608/255-2430** *9:30am-6pm, 8am-4:30pm Sat, clsd Sun, cheese shop, sandwiches*

La Hacienda [★] 515 S Park St **608/255-8227** *9am-3am, Mexican, popular & cruisy post-Club 5 spot*

Monty's Blue Plate Diner [BW,WC] 2089 Atwood Ave (at Winnebago) **608/244-8505** *7am-9pm*

Retail Shops

Look At That [GO] 917 Williamson St **608/663-2453** *11am-7pm, till 8pm Fri-Sat, clsd Sun-Mon, biker leather, clothing & accessories, toys, lesbian-owned*

Publications

Our Lives *LGBT publication*

Men's Services

Erotica

Red Letter News 2528 E Washington (btwn North & Milwaukee) **608/241-9958** *24hrs*

Cruisy Areas

Burrows Park [AYOR]

Olin Park [AYOR] W shore of Lake Monona (parking lot near Sheraton) *afternoons*

Manitowoc

Bars

RiverBank Lounge [GF,D,GO] 902 Jay St (at 9th St) **920/482-0032** *4pm-midnight Fri & 7pm-1am Sat*

Mazomanie

Cruisy Areas

Mazo Nude Beach [AYOR] Madison *30 miles NW on Hwy 4, then 14 miles N to Laws Dr, turn left & go 1/2 mile to gravel rd*

Milwaukee

Info Lines & Services

AA Galano Club 315 W Court #201 (in LGBT Community Center) **414/276-6936** *call 6:30pm-9pm for meeting schedule*

Gay People's Union Hotline **414/645-0585**

Milwaukee LGBT Community Center 315 W Court St #101 (btwn W Cherry & Galena) **414/271-2656** *10am-10pm, from 6pm Sat, clsd Sun*

Accommodations

Acanthus Inn B&B [GF,NS] 3009 W Highland Blvd **414/342-9788, 800/361-3698** *in 1897 mansion, some shared baths*

The Brumder Mansion [GF,NS,WI] 3046 W Wisconsin Ave **414/342-9767, 866/793-3676** *B&B, fireplaces, some whirlpools, 3 dogs on premises*

Comfort Inn & Suites [GF,WI,WC] 916 E State St (at Marshall) **414/276-8800, 800/328-7275** *also restaurant*

The Milwaukee Hilton [GF,F,SW] 509 W Wisconsin Ave (at 5th St) **414/271-7250, 800/445-8667** *also indoor waterpark*

Bars

Art Bar [GS,E,GO] 722 E Burleigh St (at Fratney) **414/372-7880** *4pm-1am, till 2:30am Fri-Sat, boys' night Th, also gallery*

Ballgame [M,NH] 196 S 2nd St (at Pittsburgh) **414/273-7474** *2pm-2am, from 11am wknds*

Boom/ The Room [MW,NH,F,V] 625 S 2nd (at W Bruce) **414/277-5040** *5pm-2am, from 11am Sun, patio, also martini bar*

Boot Camp Saloon [M,NH,L] 209 E National Ave (at Barclay) **414/643-6900** *3pm-2am, from 9pm Sat*

City Lights Chill & Grill [MW,NH,F] 111 W Howard Ave **414/481-1441** *4pm-2am*

Fluid [M,NH] 819 S 2nd St (at W National) **414/643-5843** *5pm-close, from 2pm wknds*

Harbor Room [M,L] 117 E Greenfield Ave **414/672-7988** *6am-2am, till 2:30am Fri-Sat*

Kruz [M,L] 354 E National Ave (at S Water St) **414/272-5789** *3pm-close, patio, cruisy*

M's [MW,TG,E] 1101 S 2nd St (at W Washington St) **414/383-8900** *4pm-close, from 3pm wknds*

The Nomad [GF,E] 1401 E Brady St (at Warren) **414/224-8111** *2pm-close, from noon wknds, soccer pub*

Redroom Cocktail Lounge [GF,D,WC] 1875 N Humboldt (at Kane) **414/224-7666** *5pm-close, from 8pm wknds, also coffee bar, patio*

Taylor's [GS,NH,WC,GO] 795 N Jefferson St (at Wells) **414/271-2855** *4pm-close, from 5pm wknds, patio*

This Is It [★M,OC] 418 E Wells St (at Jefferson) **414/278-9192** *3pm-2am, till 2:30am Fri-Sat*

Triangle Bar [M,NH,WC] 135 E National Ave (at Barclay) **414/383-9412** *noon-close, from 6am wknds*

Two [GS] 718 E Burleigh St (at Fratney) **414/372-7880** *romantic hideaway*

Woody's [M,NH] 1579 S 2nd St (at Lapham St) **414/672-0806** *4pm-close, from 2pm wknds, sports bar*

Nightclubs

Babylon Thursdays [M,D] 722 N Milwaukee St (at Three nightclub) **414/225-0003** *9pm Th only*

Club Anything [GS,D,A,E] 807 S 5th St (at National) **414/383-5680** *9pm-close, from 7pm wknds, gothic/ industrial*

Jack [GS,D] 200 E Washington **414/389-3596**

La Cage [★M,D,S,V,YC,WC] 801 S 2nd St (at National) **414/383-8330** *10pm-close Wed-Sat, also martini bar 6pm-close nightly*

Mad Planet [GF,D,A,E] 533 E Center St **414/263-4555** *retro dance Fri, live rock venue*

MONA'S [MW,F,GO] 1407 S 1st St (at Greenfield) **414/643-0377** *4pm-close, from 6pm Sat-Mon, also restaurant*

Purr [MW,D,DS,MR] 3945 N 35th (at Capitol Dr) **414/442-7007** *8pm-close*

Wherehouse [MW,D] 818 S Water St **414/383-7593** *gay Fri only, check web for theme nights*

Cafes

Alterra Coffee Roasters 2211 N Prospect Ave (at North) **414/273-3753** *6:30am-10pm, till 11pm Fri, 7am-11pm Sat, 7am-10pm Sun*

Bella Caffe 189 N Milwaukee St **414/273-5620** *6:30am-9pm, till 11pm Fri-Sat, 8am-6pm Sun*

Fuel Cafe 818 E Center St **414/374-3835** *7am-10pm, till 11pm Fri-Sat, infamous for their strong coffee*

Restaurants

Beans & Barley 1901 E North Ave (at Oakland Ave) **414/278-7878** *8am-9pm, vegetarian cafe & deli*

Cafe Vecchio Mondo 1137 N Old World 3rd St (at Juneau) **414/273-5700** *dinner, Sun brunch, full bar*

Coquette Cafe 316 N Milwaukee St (btwn Buffalo & St Paul) **414/291-2655** *11am-10pm, till 11pm Fri, 5pm-11pm Sat, clsd Sun, bistro fare*

Harvey's [E] 1340 W Towne Sq Rd, Mequon **262/241-9589** *dinner nightly, cont'l*

The Knick [★WC] 1030 E Juneau Ave (at Waverly) **414/272-0011** *11am-midnight, from 9am wknds, full bar*

La Perla 734 S 5th St (at National) **414/645-9888** *11am-10pm, till 11:30pm Fri-Sat, Mexican, also bar*

Lulu [E] 2261 & 2265 S Howell Ave **414/294-5858** *11am-10pm, also bar till late, live music wknds*

Meritage 5921 W Vilet St **414/479-0620** *5pm-10pm, till 11pm Fri-Sat, clsd Sun-Mon, American*

Range Line Inn [R] 2635 W Mequon Rd, Mequon **262/242-0530** *4:30pm-9:30pm, till 10:30pm Fri-Sat, clsd Sun-Mon, American*

Sanford Restaurant 1547 N Jackson St **414/276-9608** *dinner only, clsd Sun, Milwaukee fine dining Euro-style*

Entertainment & Recreation

Boerner Botanical Gardens 9400 Boerner Dr (in Whitnall Park), Hales Corners **414/525-5650** *8am-dusk, 40-acre garden & arboretum, garden clsd in winter*

Hotcakes Gallery 3379 N Pierce St **414/961-7714** *noon-5pm Fri-Sat only*

Milwaukee Gay Arts Center 703 S 2nd St **414/383-3727** *performance, classes & more*

Mitchell Park Domes 524 S Layton Blvd (27th St, at Pierce) **414/649-9800** *9am-5pm, botanical gardens*

Rosebud Cinema & Drafthouse 6823 W North Ave, Wauwatosa **414/607-9446** *mainstream & art house films, food served, full bar*

Bookstores

OutWords Books, Gifts & Coffee [WC] 2710 N Murray Ave (at Park) **414/963-9089** *11am-7pm, till 9pm Th-Sat, noon-6pm Sun, LGBT, pride items*

Peoples' Books 2122 E Locust St (at Maryland) **414/962-0575** *noon-6pm, clsd Sun*

Woodland Pattern 720 E Locust St **414/263-5001** *11am-8pm, noon-5pm wknds, clsd Mon*

Retail Shops

Adambomb Gallerie 2028 N Martin Luther King Dr **414/276-2662** *11am-8pm, from noon Sun, clsd Mon, tattoo studio*

Miss Groove 1225 E Brady St (btwn Arlington & Franklin) **414/298-9185** *11am-7pm, 10am-6pm Sat, noon-5pm Sun, accessories & apparel*

Yellow Jacket 1237 E Brady (at North Ave) **414/372-4744** *noon-7pm, till 5pm Sun, vintage clothes*

Publications

Quest 920/655-0611, 800/578-3785 *news & arts reviews for WI's LGBT community*

Men's Clubs

Midtowne Spa—Milwaukee [PC,WC] 315 S Water **414/278-8989** *24hrs, sauna, whirlpool*

Men's Services

▶ **Megaphone 414/342-2222** *Meet and Chat Live with HOT local men. FREE to listen & respond to ads. Video and text chat at GayMates.com. Use FREE code 4889.*

Erotica

Booked Solid 7035 Greenfield Ave (at 70th), West Allis **414/774-7210**

Cruisy Areas

Juneau Park [AYOR] *beware after 10pm*

Oshkosh

Bars

Christopher Allan's Club 1226 [M,DS,GO] 1226 Oshkosh Ave (at Sawyer) **920/651-1226** *8pm-close Wed-Sat*

Erotica

Crave [18+] 1911 S Washburn St **920/235-2012**

▶ **The Lion's Den Adult Superstore** 1650 Plainview Dr (at Hwys 41 & 26) **920/235-9040** *24hrs*

Pure Pleasure 1212 Oshkosh Ave (off Hwy 21) **920/235-9727**

Racine

Nightclubs

JoDee's International [MW,D,E,K,DS,S] 2139 Racine St/ S Hwy 32 (at 22nd) **262/634-9804** *7pm-close, park in rear*

Rhinelander

Accommodations

Musky Bay Resort [GF,NS,GO] 3724 N Limberlost Rd (at County Hwy C) **262/554-6763, 866/855-9971** *3 cabins on the Moens Chain of Lakes, lesbian-owned*

Woodwind Health Spa & Resort [GS,SW,NS,WC,GO] 3033 Woodwind Wy (at S River Rd & Hwy 8) **715/362-8902** *retreat & spa, full gourmet brkfst, lesbian-owned*

Sheboygan

Bars

The Blue Lite [MW,NH,D] 1029 N 8th St (off Rte 143) **920/457-1636** *7pm-close, from 3pm Sun*

Stevens Point

Bars

Club Night Out [M,NH,D] 2533 County Rd M (4 miles W of town) **715/342-5830** *8pm-close, clsd Mon-Tue*

Erotica

Eldorado's 3219 Church St (at Business 51 S) **715/343-9877**

Sturgeon Bay

Accommodations

The Chadwick Inn [GF,NS,GO] 25 N 8th Ave **920/743-2771** *1890 Queen Anne, lesbian-owned*

The Chanticleer Guest House [★GS,SW,NS,WC,GO] 4072 Cherry Rd **920/746-0334, 866/682-0384** *hot tub, on 70 acres*

Superior

Bars

The Flame [MW,D,E,K] 1612 Tower Ave **715/395-0101**

JT's Bar & Grill [★MW,NH,D,F,K,DS,S,WC] 1506 N 3rd St (at Blatnik Bridge) **715/394-2580** *11am-2am, from 1pm Sat-Sun, patio*

The Main Club [★M,D,CW,L,E,WI,WC] 1217 Tower Ave (at 12th) **715/392-1756** *3pm-2am*

Wausau

Nightclubs

Oz [M,D,K,DS,V] 320 Washington **715/842-3225** *7pm-close*

Wisconsin Dells

Bars

Captain Dix [MW,K] 4124 River Rd (at Rainbow Valley Resort) **608/253-1818, 866/553-1818** *4pm-close, from 11am wknds, from 6pm Mon-Tue, theme nights*

Wyoming

Alpine

Accommodations

The Nordic Inn/ Brenthoven's Restaurant [GF] 1 Colonial Ln (1 mile E of junction Hwys 89 & 26) **307/654-7556** *inn & cottages, also 4-star restaurant, open June-Oct*

Casper

Erotica

Emporium Video Exchange 1210 East F St **307/265-9726**

Cruisy Areas

Morad Park [AYOR] Cy Ave (at Wyoming Blvd)

Cheyenne

see also Fort Collins, Colorado

Info Lines & Services

Wyoming Equality/ United Gays & Lesbians of Wyoming 307/778-7645 *10am-2pm Mon-Fri, info, referrals & newsletter, social activities*

Bars

Choice City Shots [MW,NH,D,K,S,WC,GO] 124 LaPorte Ave (at College), Fort Collins, CO **970/221-4333** *5pm-midnight, till 2am wknds, DJ Fri-Sat, men's night Tue*

Erotica

Cupid's Adult Books 511 W 17th St **307/635-3837** *arcade*

Cruisy Areas

I-25 Rest Area Southbound [AYOR] traveling S from Cheyenne, take exit 7 (turn right at McDonald's) *parking lot & woods, late nights*

Lions Park [AYOR] near skating pond

Etna

Retail Shops

Blue Fox Studio & Gallery 107452 N US Hwy 89 **307/883-3310** *open 7 days, hours vary, pottery, jewelry & mask studio, local travel info*

Evanston

Erotica

Romantix Adult Superstore 1939 Harrison Dr **307/789-0800** *6am-2am*

Gillette

Cruisy Areas

Camplex Park [AYOR] Garner Lake Rd (off I-90, Garner Lake Rd exit, go S 1 mile) *parking lot & woods*

Jackson

Accommodations

Spring Creek Ranch [★GF,F,SW,WC] 1800 Spirit Dance Rd **307/733-8833, 800/443-6139** *nonsmoking rooms available, also condos & mtn homes*

Lander

Cruisy Areas

City Park 3rd St (at City Park Ave)

Laramie

Info Lines & Services

Rainbow Resource Center [WC] Knight Hall, Rm 112, 1000 E University Ave (at University of Wyoming) **307/766-3478** *8am-5pm, clsd wknds, safe & supportive place for LGBT & questioning individuals & allies, open to community members*

Accommodations

Cowgirl Horse Hotel [W] 32 Black Elk Trail **307/745-8794 or 399-2502** *specializing in women travelers & their horses, men welcome*

Bookstores

The Second Story 105 Ivinson Ave **307/745-4423** *10am-6pm, clsd Sun, independent*

Cruisy Areas

I-80 Rest Area [AYOR] Happy Jack Rd (13 miles E, take Happy Jack Rd exit off I-80) *afternoons, late evenings*

Riverton

Restaurants

Country Cove [WC] 301 E Main (at First) **307/856-9813** *7am-3pm, till noon Sat, clsd Sun*

Rock Springs

Erotica

Exit 107 Video 1554 9th St (off I-80, exit 107) **307/362-0700** *arcade*

Sheridan

Cruisy Areas

Sheridan Information Center [AYOR] take 5th Ave exit off I-90 *parking lot & woods*

Thermopolis

Bookstores

Storyteller 528 Broadway **307/864-3272** *8am-5pm*

International Section

Canada

ALBERTA

Banff

see also Lake Louise

ACCOMMODATIONS

Fairmont Banff Springs [GF] 405 Spray Ave **403/762-2211** *in Canadian Rockies, also Willow Stream Spa*

Simpson's Num-Ti-Jah Lodge [GF] **403/522-2167** *overlooks Bow Lake & Canadian Rockies, 40km N of Lake Louise*

Spruce Grove Inn [GF,SW,NS,WC] 545 Banff Ave **403/762-3301, 800/879-1991**

Calgary

INFO LINES & SERVICES

Calgary Outlink: Centre for Gender & Sexual Diversity #4, 1230-A 17th Ave SW **403/234-8973, 877/688-4765 (24hr crisis & support line)** *11am-5pm Mon & Wed, 1pm-7pm Tue & Th, by appt Fri, clsd wknds, many groups*

Front Runners AA 1227 Kensington Close NW (at Hillhurst United Church) **403/777-1212** *8:30pm Tue, Th & Sat*

Inside Out #4, 1230-A 17th Ave SW **403/234-8973** *7pm Mon, support group for LGBTQ ages 15-25*

ACCOMMODATIONS

11th Street Lodging [GS,R,NS,GO] **403/209-1800** *"no shoe" policy inside*

Calgary Westways Guest House [GS,NS,WI,GO] 216 25th Ave SW **403/229-1758, 866/846-7038** *full brkfst, hot tub*

Executive Royal Inn North Calgary [GF] 2828 23rd St NE **403/291-2003, 888/388-3932** *restaurant, fitness center, close to City Centre*

The Westin Calgary [GF,SW,NS,WC] 320 4th Ave SW **403/266-1611** *downtown 4-diamond hotel, also restaurant*

BARS

The Back Lot [M,WC] 209 10th Ave SW (at 1st St SW) **403/265-5211** *2pm-2am, martini lounge, patio*

Calgary Eagle [M,B,L,F,OC,GO] 424-A 8th Ave SE **403/263-5847** *5pm-midnight, till 2am Fri-Sat, clsd Mon-Tue, dress code Fri-Sat from 10pm, dark night Fri, cruisy*

Ming [GF] 520 17th Ave SW **403/229-1986** *4pm-2am, martini lounge*

Money Pennies [MW,NH,F,K,WC] 1742 10th Ave SW (near 14th St) **403/263-7411** *4pm-11pm Tue-Th, 11am-2am wknds, clsd Mon, rooftop patio*

Texas Lounge [MO] 308 17th Ave SW (enter rear) **403/229-0911** *11am-2am*

NIGHTCLUBS

The Twisted Element [M,D,K,DS,S,WI] 1006 11th Ave SW **403/802-0230** *9pm-close, clsd Mon, 2 levels*

The Warehouse [GF,D,E,YC,PC] 731 10th Ave SW (alley entrance) **403/264-0535** *9pm-8am Fri-Sat only*

CAFES

Cafe Beano [WC] 1613 9th St SW (at 17th Ave) **403/229-1232** *6am-midnight, from 7am wknds*

RESTAURANTS

Halo 13226 Macleod Trail SE **403/271-4111** *lunch & dinner, steak, seafood & wine bar*

Melrose Cafe & Bar 730 17th Ave SW (at 7th St) **403/228-3566** *11am-2am, from 10am wknds, full bar till 2am, patio*

Thai Sa-On 351 10th Ave SW (at 4th) **403/264-3526** *lunch & dinner, clsd Sun, Thai*

Wicked Wedge Pizza 618 17th Ave SW (at 6th St) **403/228-1024** *11am-close, noon-10pm Sun*

ENTERTAINMENT & RECREATION

Calgary Men's Chorus PO Box 23217, Connaught RPO T2S 3B1

Bookstores

Daily Globe News Shop 1004 17th Ave SW (at 10th St) **403/244-2060** *9am-10pm, periodicals*

Self Connection Books 4004 19th St NW **403/284-1486, 866/735-3457** *10am-6pm, till 8pm Th, till 5pm Sat, clsd Sun; also 10816 Macleod Trail SE, 403/225-8887*

Retail Shops

Priape 1322 17th Ave SW (enter on 16th) **403/215-1800, 800/461-6969 #25** *noon-9pm, till 6pm Sun, clubwear, leather, books, toys & more*

Publications

Gay Calgary & Edmonton Magazine 888/543-6960 *monthly LGBT publication*

Men's Clubs

Goliath's Saunatel [F,PC,AYOR] 308 17th Ave SW (enter rear) **403/229-0911** *24hrs, cocktails*

Cruisy Areas

North Glenmore Park [AYOR] S end of Crowchild *down the ravine*

Edmonton

Info Lines & Services

AA Gay/ Lesbian 11355 Jasper Ave (at church) **780/424-5900** *7:30pm Mon; also 8pm Fri at 10804 119th St*

Pride Centre of Edmonton 9540 - 111 Ave **780/488-3234** *10am-10pm Tue-Fri, 2pm-6pm Sat, clsd Sun-Mon, youth group 7pm Sat*

Accommodations

Labyrinth Lake Lodge [GS,NS] **780/878-3301** *lodge on private lake, hot tubs, home of the Buck Naked Boys Club of Edmonton one wknd/ month*

McCracken Country Inn & Tea House [GF] 146 Brookhart St, Hinton **780/865-5662, 888/865-5662**

Northern Lights B&B [MW,SW,NS,GO] **780/483-1572** *full brkfst*

Bars

Boots [MW,D,E,DS,PC] 10242 106th St **780/423-5014** *4pm-close*

Woody's Pub & Cafe [MW,NH,F,K] 11723 A Jasper (above Buddy's) **780/488-6557** *3pm-midnight, till 3am wknds*

Nightclubs

Buddy's Nite Club [MW,D,DS] 11725-B Jasper **780/488-6636** *9pm-3am, from 8pm Fri*

Play [MW,D] 10220 103rd St (at 102nd Ave NW) **780/497-7529** *open Th-Sun, theme nights*

Restaurants

Cafe de Ville [NS,R] 10137 124th St (side entrance) **780/488-9188** *11:30am-10pm, till midnight Fri-Sat, 9:30am-2:30pm & 5pm-10pm Sun*

Garage Burger Bar & Grill 10242 106th St (at 103rd Ave) **780/423-5014** *11am-8pm*

Entertainment & Recreation

Edmonton Vocal Minority 780/479-2038 *LGBT chorus*

Gaywire CJSR FM 88.5 **780/492-2577** *6pm-7pm Th, LGBT radio*

Bookstores

Audrey's Books [WC] 10702 Jasper Ave (at 107th St) **780/423-3487** *9am-9pm, 9:30am-5:30pm Sat, noon-5pm Sun, large LGBT section*

Greenwood's Bookshoppe 7925 104th St (at 80th) **780/439-2005, 800/661-2078** *9am-9pm, 9:30am-5:30pm Sat, noon-5pm Sun*

Retail Shops

Divine Decadence 10441 82nd Ave (at 105th) **780/439-2977** *hip fashions, accessories*

Publications

Gay Calgary & Edmonton Magazine Calgary **888/543-6960** *monthly LGBT publication*

Men's Clubs

Down Under Bathhouse [MO] 12224 Jasper Ave **780/482-7960** *24hrs*

Steamers [MO] 9668 Jasper Ave (at 97th St) **780/422-2581** *24hrs*

Steamworks 11745 Jasper Ave (at 118th St) **780/451-5554** *24hrs*

Lake Louise

see also Banff

Accommodations

Lake Louise Inn [GF,SW] 210 Village Dr **403/522-3791, 800/661-9237** *mtn resort near Pipestone River*

Lethbridge

Info Lines & Services

GALA/LA (Gay/ Lesbian Alliance of Lethbridge & Area) 403/308-2893 *call for events*

Provincewide

Publications

Perceptions 306/244-1930 *covers the Canadian prairies*

Westrose

Accommodations

Pine Trails Getaway [MW] RR1 **780/586-0002**

British Columbia

Birken

Accommodations

Birken Lakeside Resort [GF,SW,GO] 9179 Portage Rd **604/452-3255** *cabins & campsites, hot tub, lesbian-owned*

Chilliwack

Restaurants

Bravo Restaurant & Lounge [WC,GO] 46224 Yale Rd (at Nowell St) **604/792-7721** *5pm-close, clsd Sun-Mon, Pacific NW food, martinis*

Gulf Islands

Info Lines & Services

Gays & Lesbians of Salt Spring Island (GLOSSI) PO Box 644, Salt Spring Island V8K 2W2 **250/537-7773**

Accommodations

Anne's Oceanfront Hideaway B&B [GF,NS,WI,WC] 168 Simson Rd, Salt Spring Island **250/537-0851, 888/474-2663** *full brkfst, hot tub*

Bellhouse Inn [GS,NS] 29 Farmhouse Rd, Galiano Island **250/539-5667, 800/970-7464** *historic waterfront inn, full brkfst*

Birdsong B&B [GS] 153 Rourke Rd, Salt Spring Island **250/537-4608** *ocean & harbor views*

Blue Ewe Cottage in the Woods [MW,NS,GO] 1207 Beddis Rd, Salt Spring Island **250/537-5827** *hot tub*

Fulford Dunderry Guest House [GF,NS,WI,GO] 2900 Fulford-Ganges Rd, Salt Spring Island **250/653-4860**

Hummingbird Lodge B&B [GF] 1597 Starbuck Ln (at Whalebone Dr), Gabriola **250/247-9300, 877/551-9383**

Island Farmhouse B&B [GS,NS,GO] 185 Horel Rd W, Salt Spring Island **250/653-9898, 877/537-5912** *kids/ pets ok, lesbian-owned*

Salt Spring Inn & Restaurant [GF] 132 Lower Ganges Rd (at Hereford Ave), Salt Spring Island **250/537-9339, 877/537-9339**

Kamloops

Accommodations

Mystic Mountain Acres B&B [GF] 1030 Bo Hill Pl, Blue River **250/674-2700**

Watauga Village B&B [GF] 734 Clearwater Village Rd, Blue River **250/674-0085** *cabins w/ kitchenettes*

Cruisy Areas

Mission Flats Beach [AYOR] off Mission Flats Rd (15 miles W of town) *popular nude beach*

Mission

Erotica

XXXtreme Adult 115-B 32423 Lougheed Hwy **604/814-0488**

Nanaimo

Cruisy Areas

Bowen Park [AYOR]

Okanagan Lake

includes Kaleden, Kelowna, Oliver, Penticton & Vernon

Accommodations

Eagles Nest B&B [M,NS,WI,GO] 15620 Commonage Rd (at Carrs Landing Rd), Kelowna **250/766-9350, 866/766-9350** *full brkfst, hot tub, overlooking Lake Okanagan*

Cafes

Bean Scene [WC] 274 Bernard Ave, Kelowna **250/763-1814** *7am-10pm, till 11pm Fri-Sat*

Restaurants

Greek House 3159 Woodsdale Rd, Kelowna **250/766-0090** *4pm-9pm, cont'l*

Okanagan Valley

Info Lines & Services

Okanagan Rainbow Coalition 1476 Water St, Kelowna **250/860-8555, 866/844-3444** *24-hr recorded info, support groups, social events & dances*

Port Alberni

Cruisy Areas

Harbor Quay Promenade [AYOR]

Powell River

Accommodations

Beacon B&B & Spa [GF,NS,WC] 3750 Marine Ave **604/485-5563, 877/485-5563** *full brkfst, hot tub*

Wilde Road Farm & Guesthouse [GS] 7420 Wilde Rd **604/483-4923** *farm-house & cabin, full brkfst*

Prince George

Info Lines & Services

GALA North 250/614-1661 *24-hr recorded info, call for drop-in hours & location*

Erotica

XXXtreme Adult 1412 Patricia Blvd **250/614-1411**

Qualicum Beach

Accommodations

Bahari Oceanside Inn [GF,NS,WI] 5101 Island Hwy W **877/752-9278** *full brkfst, hot tub, apt rental*

Richmond

Cruisy Areas

Richmond Nature Park [AYOR]

Surrey

Cruisy Areas

Green Timbers Park [AYOR] 144th St & 100th Ave

Tofino

Accommodations

Beachwood [GF,GO] 1368 Chesterman Beach Rd **250/725-4250** *private apt, steps to the beach*

BriMar B&B [GS] 1375 Thornberg Crescent **250/725-3410, 800/714-9373** *on the beach, full brkfst*

Eagle Nook Wilderness Resort & Spa [GF] Barkley Sound **800/760-2777** *private log cabins, gourmet meals, "all the comforts of a four-star resort"*

Restaurants

Blue Heron [WC] 634 Campbell St **250/725-4266** *5am-10pm, full bar*

Vancouver

Info Lines & Services

AA Gay/ Lesbian 604/434-3933

The Greater Vancouver Pride Line 604/684-6869, 800/566-1170 *7pm-10pm, info & support*

Vancouver Gay/ Lesbian Centre 1170 Bute St (btwn Davie & Pendrell Sts) **604/684-5307, 800/566-1170** *also Out on the Shelves LGBT lending library*

Accommodations

A Place at Penny's [GF,NS,WC] 810 Commercial Dr (at Venables) **604/254-2229**

Aberdeen Mansion [GF] 1110 Victoria Dr **604/254-2229** *B&B in 1905 Heritage House*

Arbutus Guest House [GF,GO] 1904 Arbutus St (at W Third Ave) **604/325-3013**

Barclay House B&B [GS,NS,GO] 1351 Barclay St (at Jervis) **604/605-1351, 800/971-1351** *restored Victorian, full brkfst*

The Buchan Hotel [GF,NS] 1906 Haro St (btwn Denman & Gilford) **604/685-5354, 800/668-6654** *built in 1926*

Columbia Cottage B&B [GF,NS] 205 W 14th Ave (at Manitoba) **604/874-7787** *1920s Tudor, full brkfst*

Comfort Inn Downtown [GS,F] 654 Nelson St (at Granville St) **604/605-4333, 888/605-5333** *boutique-style hotel, also Doolin's Irish Pub & Restaurant*

Granville B&B [GF] 5050 Granville St **604/307-2300, 866/739-9002** *Tudor Revival*

Hostelling International–Vancouver Central [GF,WI,WC] 1025 Granville St **604/685-5335, 888/203-8333** *hostel right on Granville St, kids ok, bar on-site*

Hostelling International–Vancouver Downtown [GS,WI,WC] 1114 Burnaby St **604/684-4565, 888/203-4302** *hostel located in West End, kids ok, travel agent in lobby*

The Langtry [GS,NS,GO] 968 Nicola St **604/687-7892, 800/699-7892** *B&B apts in West End, full brkfst*

The Listel Hotel [GS,F,SW,NS,WI] 1300 Robson Street (at Jervis) **604/684-8461, 800/663-5491** *boutique hotel, gym*

The Manor Guest House [GF,NS,WI] 345 W 13th Ave (at Cambie) **604/876-8494** *full brkfst, also apt available*

Moda Hotel [GS] 900 Seymour St (at Smithe) **604/683-4251, 877/683-5522** *also 3 bars [M,S]*

Mountain B&B [GF,NS,WI] 258 E Balmoral Rd (at Lonsdale) **604/987-2725** *full brkfst*

Nelson House B&B [MW,WI,GO] 977 Broughton St (btwn Nelson & Barclay) **604/684-9793, 866/684-9793** *Edwardian mansion, full brkfst*

"O Canada" House B&B [GS,WI,GO] 1114 Barclay St (at Thurlow) **604/688-0555, 877/688-1114** *restored Victorian, full brkfst*

Opus Hotel [GF,WC] 322 Davie St (Yaletown) **604/642-6787, 866/642-6787** *hip luxury boutique hotel, also bar & Elixer French brasserie*

Plaza 500 Hotel [GF,WI] 500 W 12th Ave (at Cambie St) **604/873-1811, 800/473-1811** *full brkfst, gym*

River Run Cottages [GF,WC] 4551 River Rd W, Ladner **604/946-7778** *on the Fraser River, full brkfst*

Rosedale on Robson [GF,SW,WI] 838 Hamilton St (at Robson) **604/689-8033, 800/661-8870** *all-suite w/ kitchenette*

Sandman Suites on Davie [GS,SW,NS,WC] 1160 Davie St (at Thurlow St) **604/681-7263, 800/726-3626** *West End suites*

Treehouse B&B [GF] 2490 W 49th Ave (btwn Larch & Balsam) **604/266-2962, 877/266-2960** *full brkfst, jacuzzi*

The West End Guest House [GS,NS,GO] 1362 Haro St (at Broughton) **604/681-2889, 888/546-3327** *full brkfst*

Bars

1181 [M] 1181 Davie St **604/687-3991** *4pm-close, upscale cocktail lounge*

The Fountainhead Pub [MW,NH,TG] 1025 Davie St **604/687-2222** *11am-midnight, till 2am Fri-Sat, wknd brunch, patio*

Gerard Lounge [GF,F] 845 Burrard St (in Sutton Place Hotel) **604/682-5511** *11:30am-1am, 4:30pm-midnight Sun, great martinis*

Lotus Lounge/ Honey [GS,D,E,F] 455 Abbott St (at Pender, in The Lotus Hotel) **604/685-7777 (hotel #)**

The Oasis [GS,NH,F,E,P] 1240 Thurlow (at Davie) **604/685-1724** *5pm-close Th-Sun, martini bar, tapas*

The PumpJack Pub [M,NH,L,WC] 1167 Davie St (off Bute) **604/685-3417** *1pm-1am, till 2am Fri-Sat*

Nightclubs

816 Granville/ The World [M,D] 816 Granville *midnight-6am Fri-Sun*

Celebrities [M,D] 1022 Davie St (at Burrard St) **604/681-6180** *theme nights*

Club 23 West [GS,D] 23 W Cordova (at Carrall) **604/662-3277** *10pm-4am Fri-Sat, call for events*

Numbers [★M,D,K,V] 1042 Davie (btwn Thurlow & Burrard) **604/685-4077** *9pm-2am, till 4am Fri-Sat, 8pm-2am Sun, cruisy*

The Odyssey [★M,D,DS,S,YC] **604/689-5256** *9pm-2am, till 3am Fri-Sat, patio, theme nights*

Pulse [M,D] 1138 Davie St **604/669-2013** *9pm-3am Wed-Sun*

Shine [GF,D] 364 Water St **604/408-4321**

Cafes

Coffee A Go-Go [F,WI] 829 Davie St **604/687-2909** *7am-9pm, 9am-6pm wknds*

Coming Home [GO] 753 6th St (at 8th Ave), New Westminster **604/288-9850** *10am-8pm, till 5pm Sun & Tue, clsd Mon*

Delaney's 1105 Denman St **604/662-3344** *6am-11pm, from 6:30am wknds, coffee shop*

Melriches Coffeehouse 1244 Davie St **604/689-5282** *6am-11pm, from 7am wknds*

Sweet Revenge [GO] 4160 Main St (at 26th) **604/879-7933** *7pm-midnight, till 1am Fri-Sat, patisserie*

Turk's Coffee Exchange [MW] 1276 Commercial Dr **604/255-5805** *6:30am-11pm*

Restaurants

Accents Restaurant [GO] 1967 W Broadway (at Arbutus) **604/734-6660** *lunch Tue-Fri, dinner Tue-Sun, clsd Mon, European/ int'l fine dining*

Bin 941 [★] 941 Davie St **604/683-1246** *5pm-2am, till midnight Sun, tiny tapas parlor; also 1521 W Broadway, 604/734-9421*

Brioche 401 W Cordova (at Homer, in Gastown) **604/682-4037** *7am-7pm, 9am-6pm wknds, Italian restaurant & bakery*

Cafe Deux Soleils [MW,E] 2096 Commercial Dr **604/254-1195** *8am-midnight, till 5pm Sun, vegetarian*

Cafe Luxy [E,WC] 1235 Davie St (btwn Bute & Jervis) **604/669-5899** *11am-10:30pm, wknd brunch 9am-3pm, full bar*

Cascade Room 2616 Main St (at 10th) **604/709-8650** *4pm-midnight, from noon wknds*

Cincin 1154 Robson St (off Bute) **604/688-7338** *dinner nightly, Italian/ Mediterranean, full bar*

Delilah's [WC] 1789 Comox St (at Denman) **604/687-3424** *5:30pm-11pm, prix-fixe menu, full bar, extensive martini menu*

The Dish [GO] 1068 Davie St **604/689-0208** *7am-10pm, 9am-9pm Sun, veggie fast food*

Elbow Room Cafe 560 Davie St (at Seymour) **604/685-3628** *8am-4pm, till 5pm wknds, great brkfst*

Foundation Lounge 2301 Main St **604/708-0881** *noon-1am, till 2am wknds, vegetarian*

Gastropod 1938 W 4th Ave **604/730-5579** *5:30pm-10:30pm, modern European*

Glowbal Grill & Satay Bar 1079 Mainland St (Yaletown) **604/602-0835** *also check out Afterglow next door, nightly 6pm-late*

Hamburger Mary's 1202 Davie St (at Bute) **604/687-1293** *8am-3am, till 4am Fri-Sat, till 2am Sun, full bar*

Havana [★] 1212 Commercial Dr **604/253-9119** *11am-11pm, from 10am wknds, Cuban fusion, full bar, patio, also gallery & theater*

India Gate 616 Robson St (at Granville) **604/684-4617** *lunch Mon-Sat, dinner nightly*

Jupiter Cafe [E] 1216 Bute St (at Davie St) **604/609-6665** *6pm-1am*

Lickerish 903 Davie St (at Hornby) **604/696-0725** *5:30pm-midnight, till 1am Th-Sun, cocktail lounge*

Lift Bar & Grill 333 Menchions Mews **604/689-5438** *11:30am-midnight, patio*

Lolita's 1326 Davie St (at Jervis) **604/696-9996** *4:30pm till late, wknd brunch, innovative Mexican, worth the wait*

Martini's Whole Wheat Pizza 151 W Broadway (btwn Cambie & Main) **604/873-0021** *11am-2am, from 2pm Sat, till 1am Sun, great pizza & full bar*

Naam [E,WC] 2724 W 4th St (at MacDonald) **604/738-7151** *24hrs, vegetarian*

Score 1262 Davie St (at Jervis St) **604/632-1646** *10am-late*

Tanpopo Sushi 1122 Denman (at Pendrell) **604/681-7777** *lunch & dinner, excellent, affordable sushi*

Zin Restaurant & Lounge 1277 Robson St (at Jervis St, in Pacific Palisades Hotel) **604/408-1700** *7am-midnight*

Entertainment & Recreation

Capilano Suspension Bridge 3735 Capilano Rd, N Vancouver **604/985-7474**

Cruisey T [MW,D,F,E,$] leaves from N foot of Denman St (at Harbor Cruises) **604/551-2628** *Sun (seasonal), 4-hour party cruise around Vancouver Harbour*

Queer FM CITR 101.9 FM **604/822-1242** *6pm-8pm Sun, political & social issues in queer community*

Rockwood Adventures 839 W 1st St #C, North Vancouver **604/741-0802, 888/236-6606** *rain forest walks & city tours for all levels w/ free hotel pickup*

Sunset Beach Beach Ave, right in the West End (near Burrard St Bridge) *home of Vancouver AIDS memorial*

Vancouver Men's Chorus 1270 Chestnut St **604/669-7464**

Vancouver Nature Adventures [$] 1251 Cardero St #2005 **604/684-4922, 800/528-3531** *orca-watching safari, guided kayaking day trip & beach BBQ, no experience required, free hotel pickup*

Bookstores

Little Sister's [★WC] 1238 Davie St (btwn Bute & Jervis) **604/669-1753, 800/567-1662 (in Canada only)** *10am-11pm, LGBT*

People's Co-op Bookstore 1391 Commercial Dr (btwn Kitchener & Charles) **604/253-6442, 888/511-5556** *LGBT section*

Spartacus Books 684 E Hastings **604/688-6138** *10am-8:30pm, 11am-7pm Sat, noon-7pm Sun, LGBT section*

Retail Shops

Cupcakes 1116 Denman St (at Pendrell) **604/974-1300** *10am-9pm, till 10pm Fri-Sat; also at 2887 W Broadway*

Liquid Amber Tattoo 1252 Burrard St #100 (at Burnaby) **604/738-3667**

Mintage 1714 Commercial Dr **604/871-0022** *vintage & future fashions*

Next Body Piercing 1068 Granville St (at Nelson) **604/684-6398** *noon-6pm, 11am-7pm Fri-Sat, also tattooing*

Priape 1148 Davie St (btwn Bute & Thurlow) **604/630-2330** *clubwear, leather, books, toys & more*

State of Mind 1100 Davie St (at Thurlow) **604/682-7116** *10am-6pm, designer queer clothes*

TopDrawers [WC] 1030 Denman St #115 **604/684-4861** *10am-7pm, till 9pm Th-Sat, men's clothing & underwear*

Publications

Xtra! West 604/684-9696 *LGBT newspaper*

Gyms & Health Clubs

Fitness World [GF] 1214 Howe St (at Davie) **604/681-3232** *day passes*

Spartacus Athletic Club 1522 Commercial Dr **604/254-6267**

Men's Clubs

Fahrenheit 212° [PC] 1048 Davie St (at Burrard) **604/689-9719** *24hrs; also 430 Columbia St, 604/540-2117*

M2M [L,PC] 1210 Granville, downstairs (S of Davie) **604/684-6011** *24hrs*

Steamworks 123 W Pender St **604/974-0602** *24hrs*

Erotica

Love's Touch 1069 Davie St **604/681-7024**

Source Video 2838 E Hastings St **604/251-9191** *24hrs*

Tom's Video 2887 Granview Hwy (at Renfew) **604/433-1722** *24hrs*

Womyn's Ware [GO] 896 Commercial Dr (at Venables) **604/254-2543, 888/WYM-WARE (orders only)** *11am-6pm, till 7pm Th-Fri, till 5:30pm Sun, toys for men too*

Cruisy Areas

Central Park [AYOR] S side of the Boundary & Kingsway intersection *on the Vancouver/ Burnaby border*

Stanley Park [AYOR] Lee's Trail

Wreck Beach [AYOR] below UBC

Victoria

Accommodations

Ambrosia Historic B&B [GS,NS] 522 Quadra (at Humboldt) **250/380-7705, 877/262-7672** *5-star B&B 3 blocks from Victoria's inner harbor, full brkfst, jacuzzi*

The Fairmont Empress [GF,SW,NS,WC] 721 Government St **250/384-8111, 800/257-7544** *Victoria landmark, famous afternoon tea*

Hostelling International–Victoria [GF,WI,WC] 516 Yates St **250/385-4511, 888/883-0099** *hostel located in West End, kids ok, travel agent in lobby*

Howard Johnson Hotel & Suites Victoria [GF,SW,WC] 4670 Elk Lake Dr **250/704-4656, 866/300-4656** *hot tub, restaurant & lounge*

Ifanwen B&B [MW,GO] 44 Simcoe St **250/384-3717** *full brkfst, gardens*

Oak Bay Guest House [GF,NS] 1052 Newport Ave **250/598-3812, 800/575-3812** *1912 Tudor-style house, full brkfst, near beaches*

Prior House [GF,NS] 620 St Charles (at Rockland Ave) **250/592-8847, 877/924-3300**

Ryan's B&B at Albion Manor [GS,NS,WI,WC,GO] 224 Superior St **250/389-0012, 877/389-0012** *full brkfst, jacuzzi*

Sandman Hotel Victoria [GF,SW] 1852 Douglas St **250/388-0788, 888/388-0787**

Bars

Paparazzi [MW,D,K,DS,V,WC] 642 Johnson St (enter on Broad St) **250/388-0505** *3pm-2am, from 1pm wknds*

Nightclubs

Hush [GS,D] 1325 Government St (in basement) **250/385-0566** *9pm-2am, clsd Sun-Tue, more gay wknds*

Restaurants

Green Cuisine 560 Johnson St #5 (in Market Square) **250/385-1809** *10am-8pm, vegan, also juice bar, bakery*

Rosie's Diner [WC,GO] 253 Cook St **250/384-6090** *8am-9pm, '50s & '60s music & videos*

Santiago's Cafe [GO] 660 Oswego St **250/388-7376** *11am-9pm, tapas bar, patio*

Entertainment & Recreation

Butchart Gardens 800 Benvenuto Ave, Brentwood Bay **250/652-5256, 866/652-4422**

Bookstores

Bolen Books 1644 Hillside Ave #111 (in shopping center) **250/595-4232** *8:30am-10pm, LGBT section*

Retail Shops

Oceanside Gifts [WC] 812 Wharf St, Ste 102 (across from Empress Hotel on the lower causeway) **250/380-1777** *10am-10pm, gifts from across Canada*

Men's Clubs

Steamworks [MO,V] 582 Johnson St (at Gov't St, look for red alley) **250/383-6623**

Erotica

Kiss & Tell 531 Herald St **250/380-6995**

Cruisy Areas

Albert Head Beach [AYOR] Colwood

Beacon Hill Park [AYOR] Dallas Rd, near totem pole

Island View Beach [AYOR] Saanichton

Saxe Point Park [AYOR] take Esquimalt Rd to Fraser St, Esquimalt

Thetis Lake Park [AYOR] Highland Rd exit, toward Duncan (off Hwy 1) *look for parked cars & pathway to "Blowjob Hill"*

Whistler

Accommodations

Alpine Vacation Accommodation [GF,NS] **604/938-0707, 888/938-0707** *ski-in/ ski-out luxury townhouses*

Best Western Listel Whistler Hotel [GF,SW,WC] 4121 Village Green (at Whistler Way) **604/932-1133, 800/663-5472** *hotel w/ pool, sauna & outdoor hot tub*

Fairmont Chateau Whistler [GF,SW,NS,WC] 4599 Chateau Blvd **604/938-8000, 800/257-7544** *ski-in/ ski-out hotel & spa*

Four Seasons Resort Whistler [GF,SW,NS,WC] 4591 Blackcomb Wy **604/935-3400, 800/268-6282** *luxury resort & spa*

Hostelling International—Whistler [GF,NS,WI] 5678 Alta Lake Rd **604/932-5492**

Westin Whistler [GF,SW,NS,WI,WC] 4090 Whistler Wy **604/905-5000** *full-service resort hotel, full bar & restaurant*

Restaurants

Araxi 4222 Village Square **604/932-4540** *lunch & dinner, local ingredients, also seafood bar & lounge*

The Bearfoot Bistro [R] 4121 Village Green **604/932-3433** *6pm-midnight, excellent wine cellar*

Boston Pizza 2011 Innsbruck Dr **604/932-7070** *11am-11pm, till midnight wknds, full bar*

La Rua 4557 Blackcomb Blvd **604/932-5011** *6pm-close, clsd Tue, Italian/ cont'l*

Monks Grill 4555 Blackcomb Wy **604/932-9677** *11:30am-10pm, grill menu, full bar*

Quattro 4319 Main St **604/905-4844** *dinner nightly, Italian*

Sachi Sushi 106-4359 Main St **604/935-5649** *lunch & dinner*

Southside Diner 2102 Lake Placid Rd (off Hwy 99) **604/966-0668** *7am-midnight, hosts monthly Gay Social*

Trattoria di Umberto [R] 4417 Sundial Crescent **604/932-5858** *lunch & dinner*

Entertainment & Recreation

ZipTrek EcoTours PO Box 734 V0N 1B0 **604/935-0001, 866/935-0001** *ziplines crisscross the Fitzsimmons Creek btwn Whistler & Blackcomb*

Erotica

The Love Nest #102-4338 Main St **604/932-6906**

Cruisy Areas

Lost Lake *from the parking lot, walk 1 km counter-clockwise around the lake to Dick Dock*

White Rock

Cruisy Areas

Marine Dr/ White Rock Beach [AYOR] walk E toward Crescent Beach

Manitoba

Provincewide

Publications

Perceptions 306/244-1930 *covers the Canadian prairies*

Winnipeg

Info Lines & Services

Rainbow Resource Centre 170 Scott St (at Wardlaw) **204/474-0212, 204/284-5208** *1pm-4:30pm Wed-Fri, 7:30pm-10pm Mon-Fri, clsd wknds, also info line, many social/ support groups*

Bars

Club 200 [MW,K,DS,S,WC] 190 Garry St (at St Mary Ave) **204/943-6045** *4pm-2am, 6pm-midnight Sun*

Nightclubs

The Estate [GF,D,K] 441 Main St **204/956-5544, /943-2623** *9pm-2am Fri, 9pm-4am Sat, multi-level, theme nights*

Gio's Club & Bar [MW,D,E,DS,PC] 155 Smith St (at York St) **204/786-1236** *4pm-11pm, till 2am Wed-Sat, till midnight Sun, screened patio*

Restaurants

Buccacino's Cucina Italiana [E] 155 Osborne St **204/452-8251** *11am-11pm, till 1am Fri, till midnight Sat, 10am-10:30pm Sun, full bar, patio*

Pizza Place 2140 McPhillips **204/940-6720** *3pm-10pm, till midnight Fri-Sat*

Right There! 472 Stradbrook Ave (at Osborne) **204/775-5353** *noon-11pm, from 1pm wknds, till 10pm Sun, from 4pm Mon-Tue, Korean*

Step'N Out [WC] 157 Provencher Blvd **204/956-7837** *lunch Mon-Fri, dinner Mon-Sat, clsd Sun*

Entertainment & Recreation

Queer in Your Ear CKUW 95.9 FM **204/786-9782** *9pm Mon*

Bookstores

McNally Robinson [WC] 1120 Grant Ave #4000 (in the mall) **204/475-0483, 800/561-1833** *9am-10pm, till 11pm Fri-Sat, noon-6pm Sun*

Publications

Outwords 204/942-4599 *LGBT newspaper*

Men's Clubs

Adonis Spa [MO] 1060 Main St (at Burrows) **204/589-6133** *24hrs*

Aquarius Baths 457 Notre Dame Ave **204/947-1763** *men only Mon, Wed & Fri, other times co-ed*

Erotica

Discreet Boutique 340 Donald (at Ellice) **204/947-1307, 800/247-0454** *also Discreet Video next door*

Dominion News 262 Portage Ave (btwn Garry & Smith) **204/942-6563** *8am-9pm, from 9am Sat, noon-6pm Sun*

Love Nest 172 St Anne's Rd **204/254-0422** *also 1341 Main St, 204/589-4141; also Portage & Westwood, 204/837-6475*

Cruisy Areas

Assiniboine Ave [AYOR] parking lot (btwn Main & Smith Sts) *nights by car*

Assiniboine Park [AYOR] parking lot of central picnic area (1/4 km W of pavilion) *weekday afternoons*

Bonnycastle Park [AYOR]

Osborne St Village [AYOR]

NEW BRUNSWICK

Fredericton

ACCOMMODATIONS

River's Edge Campground [MW,SW,WI,GO] 19 Cottage Ln, Durham Bridge **506/458-1049, 800/370-1644**

NIGHTCLUBS

boom! [MW,D] 474 Queen St **506/463-2666** *8pm-2am, 4pm-7pm Sun, clsd Mon-Wed*

RESTAURANTS

Molly's Cafe 554 Queen St **506/457-9305** *9:30am-11pm, noon-close Fri-Sun, full bar, garden patio, some veggie*

EROTICA

X-Citement 558 Queen St **506/458-2048** *videos, magazines, adult novelties*

CRUISY AREAS

The Green [AYOR]

Lower Sackville

EROTICA

X-Citement 295 Sackville Dr **902/864-4159** *videos, magazines, adult novelties*

Moncton

ACCOMMODATIONS

Auberge Au Bois Dormant Inn [GF,NS,WI,GO] 67 rue John (at Birch) **506/855-6767, 866/855-6767** *affordable luxury inn, full brkfst*

NIGHTCLUBS

Triangles [MW,NH,D,K] 234 St George St (at Archibald) **506/857-8779** *8pm-2am*

RESTAURANTS

Calactus Cafe 125 Church (at St George) **506/388-4833** *11am-10pm, vegetarian*

EROTICA

X-Citement 651 Mountain Rd **506/388-2226** *videos, magazines, adult novelties*

CRUISY AREAS

The Block [AYOR] Main St (btwn Highland & Fleet Sts)

Champlaine Place [AYOR]

Petit-Rocher

NIGHTCLUBS

Club GNG [MW,D,19+] 702 rue Principle, Bloc C **506/783-3277** *10pm-2am Sat, call for info*

St Andrews

ACCOMMODATIONS

Fairmont Algonquin [GF,SW] 184 Adolphus St **506/529-8823, 800/441-1414**

St John

ACCOMMODATIONS

Mahogany Manor [GS,NS,WC,GO] 220 Germain St **506/636-8000, 800/796-7755** *full brkfst*

BARS

A Khord [GF,D,WI] 30 Water St **506/657-8474** *7pm-2am, clsd Sun-Mon, bar, cafe & gallery*

NIGHTCLUBS

Element [MW,D] 112 Prince William St **506/693-4671** *10pm-2am Th-Sat, 2pm-8pm Sun*

Happinez Wine Bar [GF] 42 Princess St **506/634-7340** *4pm-midnight, till 2am Fri-Sat*

RESTAURANTS

Opera Bistro 60 Prince William St **506/642-2822** *lunch & dinner*

CRUISY AREAS

Rockwood Park [AYOR] at beach & on trails

NEWFOUNDLAND

Dildo

ACCOMMODATIONS

Inn by the Bay [GF,NS,WI] 78-80 Front St **709/582-3170, 888/339-7829** *B&B inn, full brkfst*

L'Anse aux Meadows

RESTAURANTS

The Norseman Harbour Front **709/623-2018, 877/623-2018** *9am-10pm seasonally*

St George's

ACCOMMODATIONS

The Palace Inn [GF] 2 School Rd (at Main St) **709/647-1377, 877/999-1377**

St John's

ACCOMMODATIONS

Abba Inn B&B [GS,NS] 36 Queen's Rd (at Prescott St) **709/754-0058, 800/563-3959** *full brkfst, fireplaces*

Banberry House [GS,NS] 116 Military Rd (at Rawlins Cross) **709/579-8006, 877/579-8226** *full brkfst*

Bluestone Inn [GF,NS,GO] 34 Queen's Rd (at Water St) **709/754-7544, 877/754-9876** *also studio apts*

Gower House B&B [GS,NS] 180 Gower St (at Prescott St) **709/754-0058, 800/563-3959** *in downtown, full brkfst, some shared baths*

NaGeira House [GF,NS] 7 Musgrave St (at Water St), Carbonear **709/596-1888, 800/600-7757** *B&B, full brkfst, jacuzzi*

NIGHTCLUBS

Zone 216 [MW,D] 216 Water St **709/754-2492** *9pm-close Fri-Sat*

RESTAURANTS

Oliver's 160 Water St **709/754-6444** *11am-10pm, till 11pm Fri, 10am-11pm Sat*

Zapatas [E] 10 Bates Hill (off Queens Rd) **709/576-6399** *lunch & dinner, full bar*

NOVA SCOTIA

Annapolis Royal

ACCOMMODATIONS

Bailey House B&B [GF,WI] 150 St George St (at Drury Ln) **902/532-1285, 877/532-1285**

King George Inn [MW,NS] **902/532-5286, 888/799-5464** *seasonal, full brkfst*

Baddeck

ACCOMMODATIONS

The Dunlop Inn [GF,NS,WI] **902/295-1100, 888/263-9840** *waterfront B&B inn*

Chester

ACCOMMODATIONS

The Mecklenburgh Inn [GF,WI] 78 Queen St **902/275-4638** *century-old inn constructed by shipwrights, full brkfst, cat on premises*

ENTERTAINMENT & RECREATION

The Chester Playhouse 22 Pleasant St **902/275-3933, 800/363-7529** *eclectic programming March-Dec*

Digby

ACCOMMODATIONS

Harbourview Inn [GF,SW,NS,WI,WC,GO] 25 Harbourview Rd (at Hwy 1), Smith's Cove **902/245-5686, 877/449-0705** *century-old country inn*

Seawinds Motel [GF,NS,GO] 90 Montague Row **902/245-2573, 877/245-2570** *views of Annapolis Basin & Digby Harbour*

Thistle Down Country Inn [GF,NS,GO] 98 Montague Row (at Warwick) **902/245-4490, 800/565-8081** *full brkfst*

Guysborough

ACCOMMODATIONS

Barrens at Bay Coastal Cottages [GS,NS,WC,GO] 6870 Hwy 16 (at Halfway Cove) **902/358-2157** *jacuzzi*

DesBarres Manor Inn [GF,NS,WI] 90 Church St **902/533-2099**

Halifax

Accommodations

Forevergreen House B&B [GF,NS] 5560 Hwy 1, St Croix **902/792-1692** *Victorian farmhouse, full brkfst, women-owned*

Fresh Start B&B [GF,NS] 2720 Gottingen St (at Black) **902/453-6616, 888/453-6616** *Victorian mansion, women-owned*

Bars

Menz Bar & Parts Dept [M,NH,F,K] 2182 Gottingen St, Level 2 **902/446-6969** *3pm-2am*

Reflections Cabaret [MW,D,E,C,DS,WC] 5184 Sackville St (at Barrington) **902/422-2957, 877/422-2957** *10pm-4am, clsd Tue-Wed*

Cafes

Coburg Coffee House 6085 Coburg Rd **902/429-2326** *7am-9pm*

The Daily Grind 5686 Spring Garden Rd (near South Park) **902/429-6397** *7am-9pm, till 10pm Th-Sat, 8am-6pm Sun, also newsstand*

The Second Cup 5425 Spring Garden Rd **902/429-0883** *7am-11pm, till midnight Th-Sat, internet access*

Uncommon Grounds [GF,WI] 1030 S Park St **902/404-3124** *7am-10pm*

Restaurants

Chives Canadian Bistro 1537 Barrington St **902/420-9626** *5pm-9:30pm*

Heartwood 6250 Quinpool Rd **902/425-2808** *11am-8pm, clsd Sun, vegetarian*

Jane's on the Common 2394 Robie St **902/431-5683** *lunch Tue-Sat, dinner nightly, Sun brunch, clsd Mon*

Satisfaction Feast 3559 Robie (N of Lady Hammond Rd) **902/422-3540** *10am-9pm, vegetarian, patio*

Trinity Restaurant [WC] 1333 S Park (near Spring Garden Rd) **902/423-8428** *11am-9pm, full bar*

Entertainment & Recreation

The Khyber 1588 Barrington St **902/422-9668** *noon-5pm, clsd Sun-Mon, visual & performing arts center*

Bookstores

Atlantic News 5560 Morris St (at Queen) **902/429-5468** *8am-10pm, from 9am Sun, periodicals*

Smithbooks 5201 Duke St (in Scotia Square) **902/423-6438** *9:30pm-6pm, till 8pm Th-Fri, clsd Sun*

Trident Booksellers & Cafe [WI] 1256 Hollis St (at Morris St) **902/423-7100** *8am-5:30pm, 8:30am-5pm Sat, 11am-5pm Sun, used, popular cafe*

Publications

Wayves PO Box 34090 Scotia Square B3J 3S1 **902/889-2229** *monthly magazine "for the rainbow community of Atlantic Canada"*

Men's Clubs

SeaDog's Sauna & Spa [MO,V,18+,PC,GO] 2199 Gottingen St (at Cunard St) **902/444-3647, 888/837-1388** *24hrs wknds, steam, darkroom, internet access*

Erotica

Night Magic Fashions 5268 Sackville St **902/420-9309** *clsd Sun, lingerie, toys, videos*

X-Citement 6260 Quinpool Rd **902/492-0026** *videos, magazines, adult novelties*

Cruisy Areas

Citadel Hill [AYOR] *evenings*

Crystal Crescent Beach [N,AYOR] 45 minutes from Halifax *for nude beach, head S from parking lot; 20-minute walk*

Kemptville

Accommodations

Trout Point Lodge [GF,WC,GO] 189 Trout Point Rd (off East Branch Rd & Hwy 203) **902/761-2142, 902/761-2142**

Lunenburg

Accommodations

1880 Kaulbach House Historic Inn [GF,NS,WI,GO] 75 Pelham St **902/634-8818, 800/568-8818** *full brkfst*

Atlantic Sojourn B&B [GF,WI] 56 Victoria Rd **902/634-3151, 800/550-4824** *teddy bear museum in lower level, also beautiful garden w/ fish pond*

North Sydney

Accommodations

Chambers Guest House [GS] 64 King St **902/794-7301, 866/496-9453**

Scotsburn

Accommodations

The Mermaid and the Cow [MW,SW,GO] West Branch **902/351-2714** *cabin & campsites*

Windsor

Bookstores

Readers' Haven 40 Water St **902/798-0133** *9am-5pm, till 3pm Sat, clsd Sun*

Wolfville

Restaurants

Tempest 117 Front St **902/542-0588, 866/542-0588** *lunch wknds, dinner nightly, clsd Mon, world cuisine*

Yarmouth

Accommodations

MacKinnon-Cann Historic Inn [GF,NS,WC,GO] 27 Willow St (at Collins St) **902/742-9900, 866/698-3142**

Murray Manor B&B [GF] 225 Main St (at Forest St) **902/742-9625, 877/742-9629**

Ontario

Provincewide

Publications

fab 416/925-5221 *Ontario's gay scene magazine*

Belleville

Cruisy Areas

Zwick's Park [AYOR]

Brighton

Accommodations

Apple Manor [GF,NS] 96 Main St, Box 11 **613/475-0351** *150-year-old Victorian, full brkfst, shared baths*

Burken Cottage [GF,NS,WI,GO] 14257 County Rd # 2 **613/475-5267**

Bookstores

Lighthouse Books 65 Main St **613/475-1269** *9:30am-5:30pm, clsd Sun-Mon*

Brockville

Accommodations

The Calico Cat B&B [GF,NS] 193 Brockmere Cliff (at Hwy 401) **613/342-0363** *located in the beautiful 1000 Islands*

Cambridge

Erotica

Stag Shop 561 Hespeler Rd **519/624-9492**

Cobourg

Accommodations

Victoria View B&B Retreat [GS,GO] 198 Bagot St (at Albert) **905/377-0620** *1874 heritage home, "an elegant & peaceful retreat destination"*

Elora

Accommodations

Log Cabin Heaven [GS,SW,NS] 7384 Middlebrook Rd (at Wellington Rd) **519/846-9439** *spa amenities*

Gananoque

Accommodations

Boathouse Country Inn & Heritage Boat Tours [GS,NS,WC] 17-19 Front St, 1000 Islands, Rockport **613/659-2348, 800/584-2592** *full brkfst, also tavern*

Trinity House Inn [GF,NS,GO] 90 Stone St S, 1000 Islands **613/382-8383, 800/265-4871** *historic country inn & sailing charters*

Grand Valley

Accommodations

Rainbow Ridge Resort [MW,F,SW,GO] Country Rd 109 (at Hwy 25 S) **519/928-3262** *trailers & tents, located on 72 acres on Grand River, restaurant, dance hall, day visitors welcome, seasonal*

Guelph

Info Lines & Services

Out Line 519/836-4550 *volunteer hours vary*

Bookstores

Bookshelf Cafe 41 Quebec St **519/821-3311** *9am-9pm, cinema, also restaurant & bar*

Hamilton

Accommodations

Cedars Campground [MW,D,SW] 1039 5th Concession W Rd, Millgrove **905/659-3655, 905/659-7342** *private campground, also bar, restaurant wknds*

Bars

The Embassy Club [MW,D,TG,K,DS,V] 54 King St E (at Houston) **905/522-1100** *noon-3am, nightclub from 8pm wknds*

The Werx [MW,NH,D,K,GO] 121 Hughson St N (at Canon) **905/972-9379, 866/796-0701** *11am-3am, pub, dance bar & dungeon [MO,B,L]*

Men's Clubs

Central Spa [GO] 401 Main W **905/523-7636** *24hrs Th-Sat*

Karel's Steambaths 12 Holton Ave N (at King St) **905/549-9666**

Erotica

Show World XXX Theater [AYOR] King St (at John St)

Stag Shop 58 Centennial Pkwy N **905/573-4242** *also 980 Upper James St, 905/385-3300*

Cruisy Areas

Jackson St [AYOR] from Catherine to City Hall

Kingston

Cruisy Areas

Little Cataraqui Conservation Area [AYOR] King St W

MacDonald Park [AYOR]

Kitchener

Nightclubs

Club Renaissance [MW,D,F,DS] 24 Charles St W **519/570-2406, 877/635-2352** *9pm-3am, clsd Sun-Tue, also billiards lounge*

Erotica

Stag Shop 10 Manitou Dr **519/895-1228** *also 30 King St E, 519/593-2303*

London

Bars

Buck Wild Bar [MW,D,DS,K,GO] 722 York St (at Central Spa) **519/438-2625** *8pm-close Th-Sat*

The Junction [MO,F,WC] 722 York St (in Central Spa) **519/438-2625** *patio*

Restaurants

Blackfriars Cafe [★] 46 Blackfriars (2 blocks S of Oxford) **519/667-4930** *lunch & dinner, Sun brunch, full bar*

Veranda [GO] 546 Dundas St (at William St) **519/434-6790** *dinner nightly, clsd Sun-Mon*

Men's Clubs

Central Spa [F] 722 York St (at rear, Complex 722) **519/438-2625** *24hrs, also bar w/ light meals*

Erotica

Adult Superstore 389 Lyle St (at Dundas) **519/672-4252**

Stag Shop 1548 Dundas St E **519/453-7676** *also 371 Wellington Rd S, 519/668-3334*

Maynooth

Accommodations

Wildewood Guesthouse [MW,NS,WC,GO] **613/338-3134** *brkfst & dinner included, hot tub*

Mississauga

Erotica

Lovecraft 2200 Dundas St E (W of Hwy 427) **905/276-5772** *toys, lingerie, videos*

Stag Shop 6020 Hurontario Rd **905/501-9855**

Morrisburg

Accommodations

The Village Antiques & Tea Room B&B [GF,F,NS,GO] 4326 County Rd 31, Williamsburg **613/535-2463, 877/264-3281** *full brkfst, dining room w/ excellent wine list, also antique shop & tea room*

Niagara Falls

see also Niagara Falls & Buffalo, New York, USA

Accommodations

Absolute Elegance B&B [GS,NS,GO] 6023 Culp St (at River Rd) **905/353-8522, 877/353-8522** *restored Victorian near Niagara Falls, full brkfst*

Amelia's [GS,SW,GO] 15526 Niagara River Pkwy, Niagara-on-the-Lake **905/468-5550** *full brkfst*

Angels Hideaway [GS,NS] 4360 Simcoe St (at River Rd) **905/354-1119** *B&B, full brkfst, jacuzzi*

Bampfield Hall B&B [GS,NS,WI,GO] 4761 Zimmerman Ave **905/353-8522, 877/353-8522** *historic Gothic home near Niagara Falls, full brkfst, jacuzzi*

Britaly B&B [GF,GO] 57 The Promenade (at Charlotte & John), Niagara-on-the-Lake **905/468-8778** *B&B, full brkfst*

Fairbanks House/ Ellis House [GS,NS,GO] 4965 River Rd **905/371-3716, 866/246-6616** *1877 restored Victorian, full brkfst*

Gretna Green B&B [GS,NS] 5077 River Rd **905/357-2081, 888/504-3565** *full brkfst*

Niagara Inn B&B [GF,NS,WI,GO] 4300 Simcoe St (at River Rd) **905/353-8522, 877/353-8522** *restored Victorian near Niagara Falls, full brkfst*

Oasis Niagara Guesthouse [M,NS,GO] 4266 Elgin St (at River Rd) **905/353-0223** *close to falls*

Peer Haven Guest House [M,NS,WI,GO] 5618 Peer St (btwn Main & Ferry) **905/371-2372**

Sheraton Fallsview Hotel & Conference Centre [GF,SW,WC] 6755 Fallsview Blvd (at Stanley) **905/374-1077, 800/267-8439** *300 yds from Niagara Falls, full brkfst, kids/ pets ok*

Stone Boutique Suites [GF,NS] 5225 River Rd (at Otter St) **905/357-4366** *2 self-contained cottage suites, 10 minutes to falls*

Cruisy Areas

Clifton Hill [AYOR]

Oshawa

Nightclubs

Club 717 [MW,D,DS] 717 Wilson Rd S #7 **905/434-4297** *9pm-midnight, till 2am Fri-Sat, clsd Mon-Wed*

Erotica

Forbidden Pleasures 1268 Simcoe St N **905/728-0834**

Ottawa

see also Hull, Province of Québec

Info Lines & Services

237-XTRA 613/237-9872 *touch-tone LGBT info*

Pink Triangle Services 251 Bank St #301 **613/563-4818** *many groups & services, library, call for times*

Accommodations

Ambiance B&B [GS,NS,WI,GO] 330 Nepean St **613/563-0421, 888/366-8772** *some shared baths, lesbian-owned*

Fairmont Château Laurier [GF,NS,WC] 1 Rideau St **613/241-1414, 800/441-1414** *in heart of Ottawa; landmark hotel w/ magnificent limestone edifice, turrets & masonry reminiscent of a French château*

Home Sweetland Home B&B [GS,NS,WI,GO] 62 Sweetland Ave (at Laurier Ave) **613/234-1871** *full brkfst*

Inn on Somerset [GS,NS] 282 Somerset St W (at Elgin) **613/236-9309, 800/658-3564** *3-story Victorian, full brkfst, some shared baths*

Rideau Inn [GS,NS,GO] 177 Frank St **613/688-2753, 877/580-5015** *Victorian town house, some shared baths*

Bars

Centretown Pub [MW,D,V] 340 Somerset St W (at Bank) **613/594-0233** *2pm-3am; also Cell Block [L] & Silhouette Lounge [P] wknds*

Collection/ Bar 56 [GS] 56 Byward Market **613/562-1120** *popular martini lounge*

The Edge [M,D,DS,YC] 212 Sparks (at Bank)

The Lookout [MW,F,WC,GO] 41 York, 2nd flr (in Byward Market) **613/789-1624** *noon-2am, men's night Th*

Swizzles [MW,D,K,DS] 246 Queen St **613/232-4200** *11am-2am*

Nightclubs

Mercury Lounge [GS,D] 56 Byward Market Sq (side door upstairs) **613/789-5324** *8pm-3am, clsd Sun-Tue, poplular Wed Hump night party*

Zaphod Beeblebrox [GS,NH,D,S] 27 York **613/562-1010** *4pm-2am, live music*

Cafes

Bridgehead Coffee [GO] 366 Bank St (at Gilmour) **613/569-5600** *7am-9pm*

Restaurants

Ahora Mexican Cuisine [GO] 307 Dalhousie St (below Sweet Art) **613/562-2081**

The Buzz 374 Bank St **613/565-9595** *dinner nightly, Sun brunch, also bar*

Elgin Street Freehouse 296 Elgin St **613/233-5525** *lunch Wed-Fri, dinner nightly, full bar, patio*

Kinki [E] 41 York St **613/789-7559** *lunch & dinner, Asian fusion, full bar, DJ*

Savana Cafe 431 Gilmour St (at Bank) **613/233-9159** *lunch wkdays, dinner nightly, Caribbean, popular patio in summer*

Shanghai Restaurant [K] 651 Somerset St W (at Bronson Ave) **613/233-4001** *lunch Tue-Fri, dinner nightly, clsd Mon, also bar, DJ*

Bookstores

After Stonewall 370 Bank St (near Gilmour) **613/567-2221** *10am-6pm, till 5pm wknds, LGBT*

Mags & Fags 254 Elgin St (btwn Somerset & Cooper) **613/233-9651** *gay magazines*

Octopus Books 116 3rd Ave (at Bank) **613/233-2589** *noon-5pm, clsd Sun-Mon*

Retail Shops

Wilde's [WC] 367 Bank St (at Gilmour) **613/234-5512** *11am-9pm, noon-6pm Sun, pride items*

Publications

Capital Xtra! 613/237-7133 *LGBT newspaper*

To Be Publications 613/236-8888 *LGBT magazine covering Ottawa & Montreal*

Men's Clubs

Club Ottawa Health Club [★PC] 1069 Wellington St **613/722-8978**

Steamworks 487 Lewis (at Bank St) **613/230-8431** *24hrs*

Sex Clubs

Breathless [GS] 318 Lisgar St (at Bank St, above Venus Envy) *sexual community center for alternative lifestyles*

Erotica

One in Ten [V] 216 Bank St (at Nepean) **613/563-0110** *noon-11pm, 1pm-8pm wknds, XXX video cinema, videos, toys*

Wicked Wanda's 382 Bank St **613/820-6032**

Cruisy Areas

Elgin St [AYOR]

Remic Rapids Lookout [AYOR] *parking spot along Ottawa river*

Perth

Accommodations

Perth Manor Boutique Hotel [GS,NS,WI,GO] 23 Drummond St W (at D'Arcy & Boulton) **613/264-0050** *boutique hotel, English gardens*

Peterborough

Accommodations

Riverside B&B [GF,NS,WI] 510 Monaghan Rd **705/742-3999, 866/295-4660** *private 2-bdrm suite on river, kitchen, private deck*

Erotica

Forbidden Pleasures 91 George St N #4 **705/742-3800**

Picton

Accommodations

Henderson House B&B [GS,SW,NS,GO] 116 Main St (at Hwy 33), Consecon **613/394-5093** *full brkfst, along Consecon River, lesbian-owned*

Plantation House B&B [GS,NS,WI,GO] 33 E Mary St **613/471-1116** *full brkfst*

Puslinch

Accommodations

Cedarbrook Farm B&B [GS,NS,GO] 812 8th Conc Rd W, RR 3 **905/659-1566** *full brkfst, lesbian-owned*

Scarborough

Erotica

Stag Shop 7 Progress Ave **416/412-1826**

St Catharines

Bars

The New Vouz [MW,NH,GO] 151 Queenston St **905/684-0451** *8pm-2am, clsd Sun-Mon*

Erotica

Stag Shop 387 Ontario St **905/687-3310**

Stratford

Accommodations

A Hundred Church Street [GS,NS,WI,GO] 100 Church St **519/272-8845** *full brkfst, hot tub*

Rundles-Morris House [MW,GO] 7-9 Cobourg St **519/271-6442**

Restaurants

Down the Street [★] 30 Ontario St **519/273-5886** *11am-midnight, clsd Mon, bar till 2am, int'l*

Rundles [BYOB,GO,WC] 9 Cobourg St **519/271-6442** *dinner Tue-Sun, lunch wknds*

Cruisy Areas

Shakespeare Memorial Gardens [AYOR]

Sudbury

Accommodations

Rainbow Guest House [MO,GO] 43 Lorne St **705/688-0561** *some shared baths*

Nightclubs

Zig's [MW,NH,D,B,L,TG,K,DS] 54 Elgin St (at Elm St) **705/673-3873** *8pm-close, clsd Mon-Tue*

Thunder Bay

Erotica

Rainbow DVD & Video 264 Bay St (at Court St) **807/345-6272** *11am-10pm, noon-6pm Sun, some books*

Toronto

Info Lines & Services

519 Church St Community Centre [WC] 519 Church St (on Cawthra Park) **416/392-6874** *9am-10pm, till 5pm wknds, LGBT info center, cafe open 10am-3pm Mon-Fri*

925-XTRA 416/925-9872 *touch-tone LGBT visitors info*

AA Gay/ Lesbian 416/487-5591

Canadian Lesbian/ Gay Archives 34 Isabella **416/777-2755** *7:30pm-10pm Tue-Th & by appt*

Accommodations

213 Carlton Street—Toronto Townhouse [GS,NS,WI,GO] **416/323-8898, 877/500-0466** *upscale town house, full brkfst, some shared baths*

312 Seaton [GS,NS,GO] 312 Seaton **416/968-0775, 866/968-0775** *B&B, also rental apt, dog on premises*

Banting House Inn [MW,NS,WI,GO] 73 Homewood Ave (at Wellesley) **416/924-1458, 800/823-8856** *restored Edwardian home, private entrances*

The Bearfoot Inn [MO,B,N,WI] 30-A Dundonald St **416/922-1658, 888/871-2327**

Bent Inn [M,L,WI,GO] 107 Gloucester St **416/925-4499** *B&B w/ well-equipped cellar dungeon*

Bonnevue Manor B&B [GS,NS,WI] 33 Beaty Ave (at Queen St & Roncesvalles) **416/536-1455** *B&B, full brkfst*

Cawthra Square Bed & Breakfast Inns [MW,NS,GO] **416/966-3074, 800/259-5474** *multiple Heritage homes, some shared baths, meeting rooms, spa*

Drake Hotel [GF,NS] 1150 Queen St W **416/531-5042, 866/372-5386** *boutique hotel*

Dundonald House [M,NS,WI,GO] 35 Dundonald St (at Church) **416/961-9888, 800/260-7227** *full brkfst, hot tub, sauna, gym, shared baths*

The Gladstone Hotel [GS,NS] 1214 Queen St W **416/531-4635** *artistic, also Melody bar*

The Grange Hotel [GF] 165 Grange Ave (at Queen) **416/603-7700, 888/232-0002** *kitchenettes*

Hazelton Hotel [GF,NS] 118 Yorkville Ave **416/963-6300, 866/473-6301** *luxury property*

Hotel Victoria [GF,WC] 56 Yonge St **416/363-1666, 800/363-8228**

House on McGill [GS,NS,GO] 110 McGill St (at Church & Carlton) **416/351-1503, 877/580-5015** *Victorian town house, shared baths, garden w/ deck, cat on premises*

Pimblett's Rest B&B [GS,NS,GO] 242 Gerrard St E **416/929-9525, 416/921-6896** *Victorian, full brkfst, hot tub, theme rooms*

Toronto Downtown Bed & Breakfast® [GS,NS,GO] 57 Chicora Ave **416/921-3533, 877/950-6200** *luxurious, full brkfst*

Two Aberdeen B&B [MW,NS] 2 Aberdeen Ave **416/944-1426** *Victorian in historic Cabbagetown, full brkfst*

Victoria's Mansion Guest House [GF,NS,WI] 68 Gloucester St **416/921-4625** *converted mansion*

Bars

Andy Poolhall [GS] 489 College St (at Markham) **416/923-5300** *6pm-2am, from 7pm Tue-Fri, clsd Sun, Pop Art pool hall*

Baby Huey [GS] 70 Ossington **416/992-5462** *7pm-2am*

Beaver Cafe [MW,D,F,GO] 1192 Queen St W **416/537-2768** *10am-2am, patio*

The Black Eagle [M,B,L,F] 457 Church St (btwn Maitland & Alexander) **416/413-1219** *2pm-2am, 3 bars, theme nights, heated rooftop patio*

The Cameron House [GS,E] 408 Queen St **416/703-0811** *4pm-close, also theater*

The Cellblock/ Yard [M,D,DS] 72 Carlton St (behind Zipperz) **416/921-0066** *noon-2am, from 9pm Sun, clsd Mon-Tue*

The Churchmouse & Firkin [MW,NH] 475 Church St (at Maitland) **416/927-1735** *11am-2am, English pub, leather brunch 3rd Sun*

Dakota Tavern [GF,CW,F] 249 Ossington Ave (at Dundas) **416/850-4579** *live country music, bluegrass brunch Sun*

George's Play [M,DS,K] 504 Church St (at Alexander) **416/963-8251** *11am-2am, bingo daily, theme nights, Latin wknds*

Gladaman's Den [M,NH,K,C,E] 502-A Yonge St (at Alexander) **416/961-5808** *11am-2am, theme nights*

The Hair of the Dog [GS,NH,F] 425 Church St (at Wood) **416/964-2708** *10am-2am, pub & restaurant, patio*

The House on Parliament Pub [GS,NH,F] 456 Parliament St **416/925-4074** *11:30am-2am, patio*

LeVack Block [GS,D,F] 88 Ossington St **416/916-0571** *5pm-close, from 11am wknds*

Lo'la [M,D] 7 Maitland (at Yonge) **416/920-0946** *5pm-2am, clsd Sun-Tue, martini lounge*

Melody Bar [GS,E,K] 1214 Queen St W (at Gladstone Hotel) **416/531-4635**

O'Grady's [GS] 518 Church St (at Maitland) **416/323-2822** *11am-2am, till 3am Fri-Sat, from 9am wknds, casual dining, huge patio, also lounge upstairs, [B] Fri*

Pegasus on Church [MW,NH] 489-B Church St (at Wellesley, upstairs) **416/927-8832** *11am-2am*

The Raq [GS,D] 739 Queen St W, 2nd flr **416/504-9120** *4pm-2am, 5pm-1am Mon-Wed, upscale pool hall*

Remington's Men of Steel [MO,S,WC,GO] 379 Yonge St (at Gerrard) **416/977-2160** *5pm-2am, strip bar*

Slack's Restaurant & Bar [★W,NH,D,F,V] 562 Church St (at Wellesley) **416/928-2151** *5pm-2am, clsd Mon, also restaurant, upscale pub fare, brunch wknds, comedy Th*

Smiling Buddha [GS,F,K,C,YC] 961 College St **416/516-2531** *4pm-2am*

Sneaky Dee's [GF,F] 431 College St (at Bathurst) **416/603-3090** *live bands, kitchen open late, Mexican*

Statlers [M,E,P,OC] 487 Church St (at Maitland) **416/962-1209** *4pm-2am*

Voglie [MW,D,F] 582 Church St **416/929-9108** *5pm-close, clsd Sun-Mon, martini bar, also restaurant, patio*

Woody's/ Sailor [★M,NH,E,DS,V,18+,WC] 465-467 Church (at Maitland) **416/972-0887** *1pm-2am, theme nights, cruisy*

Zipperz [M,P] 72 Carlton St (at Church) **416/921-0066** *noon-2am, patio*

NIGHTCLUBS

The Annex Wreck Room [GS,D,A,E] 794 Bathurst St **416/536-0346** *10pm-close Fri-Sat only, alternative music venue*

AsianXpress (AX) [M,D,MR-A] **416/410-5126** *quarterly, call for more info*

The Barn [M,D] 418 Church St (at Carlton) **416/593-9696** *theme nights*

Big Primpin' [MW,D] 1279 Queen St W (at Wrongbar) *10pm 1st Fri, monthly hip-hop, dancehall, R&B club, check local listings*

The Boat [GS,D] 158 Augusta **416/593-9218** *9pm-2am, pirate theme*

Circa [GS,D] 126 John St (at King St W) **416/979-0044**

The Comfort Zone [GS,D] 480 Spadina Ave (N of College) **416/763-9139** *after-hours wknds only*

El Convento Rico [★GS,D,MR-L,TG,DS] 750 College St (at Crawford) **416/588-7800** *9pm-4am, 7pm-3am Sun, clsd Mon-Th, [DS] Fri-Sat*

Fly Nightclub [★M,D,$] 8 Gloucester St (2 streets N of Yonge & Wellesley) **416/410-5426, 416/925-6222** *open Fri-Sat only, circuit crowd (you may recognize this club as Babylon from the 1st season of Queer As Folk!)*

Goodhandy's [M,TG,S] 120 Church St, 2nd flr (at Richmond) **416/760-6556, 416/760-6514** *9pm-close, clsd Sun-Tue, [M] Wed, trans-themed club, theme nights*

Lee's Palace/ Dance Cave [GS,D,E] 529 Bloor St **416/532-1598** *live bands, dance club upstairs*

The Mod Club [GS,D] 722 College (at Crawford) **416/588-7625** *9pm Sat, Mod-themed club*

Pink Mafia *alternative queer & straight events in hip locations, check www.pinkmafia.ca*

Straight [MW,D] 553 Church St **416/926-2501** *sophisticated lounge & danceclub*

Wrongbar [GS,D] 1279 Queen St W *Big Primpin 1st Fri, check listing for other queer events*

CAFES

Alternative Grounds 333 Roncesvalles Ave **416/534-5543** *7am-7pm, till 8pm Fri-Sat, from 8am wknds*

Cafe Diplomatico [★] 594 College (at Clinton, in Little Italy) **416/534-4637** *8am-3am, patio*

Croissant Tree 625 Church St **416/925-8379** *7am-7pm*

JetFuel 519 Parliament St **416/968-9863** *7am-8pm*

Timothy's [★MW] 500 Church St (at Alexander) **416/925-8550** *7am-midnight, till 3:30am wknds*

RESTAURANTS

Allen's Restaurant [E] 143 Danforth Ave (at Broadview) **416/463-3086** *lunch & dinner, great scotch selection, patio*

Big Mammas Boy 554 Parliament St **416/927-1593, 416/927-7777** *4:30pm-1am, 11am-midnight Sun, pizza*

Bistro 422 422 College St **416/963-9416** *4pm-2am, full bar*

Byzantium [M,GO] 499 Church St (S of Wellesley) **416/922-3859** *5:30pm-11pm, Sun brunch 11am-3pm, chic, cont'l/ global, also martini bar till 2am, patio*

Cafe 668 885 Dundas St W **416/703-0668** *lunch & dinner, vegetarian*

Commensal 655 Bay St (enter on Elm St) **416/596-9364** *brkfst, lunch & dinner, vegetarian*

Easy Restaurant 1645 Queen St W **416/537-4893** *9am-5pm*

Fire on the East Side 6 Gloucester St (at Yonge) **416/960-3473** *noon-1am, 10am-midnight wknds, clsd Mon, Southern comfort food, patio*

Flo's Diner [GO] 70 Yorkville Ave (near Bay St) **416/961-4333** *7:30am-10pm, till 9pm Mon, from 8:30am Sat, 9am-9pm Sun*

Fresh 147 Spadina (at Queen St W) **416/599-4442** *lunch & dinner, vegetarian, patio; also at 894 Queen St W, 416/ 913-2720*

Fressen 478 Queen St W (at Denison) **416/504-5127** *dinner nightly, wknd brunch, upscale vegan*

Fuzion 580 Church St **416/944-9888** *4pm-2am, also martini bar*

Get Real Cafe 135 Ossington Ave **416/532-4564** *11am-7pm, 10am-4pm wknds, clsd Mon, vegan/ vegetarian*

Golden Thai 105 Church St (at Richmond) **416/868-6668** *11:30am-9pm, from 5pm wknds*

Il Fornello 1560 Yonge St (1 block N of St Clair) **416/920-7347** *lunch Mon-Fri, dinner nightly, Sun brunch, Italian, plenty veggie; also 214 King W (at Simcoe), 416/977-2855 & 576 Danforth Ave (at Carlaw), 416/466-2931*

Jamie Kennedy Wine Bar 9 Church St **416/362-1957** *11:30am-11pm, tapas-style dishes*

Joy Bistro [NS] 884 Queen St E **416/465-8855** *11am-10pm, from 8am wknds, patio; also Over Joy lounge upstairs 6pm-2am Th-Sat*

Kalendar 546 College St **416/923-4138** *11am-midnight, till 1am Th, till 2am Fri-Sat, wknd brunch from 10:30am, eclectic, patio*

La Hacienda 640 Queen St W (near Bathurst) **416/703-3377** *noon-11pm, from 11am wknds, Mexican*

Mitzi's Cafe [★GO] 100 Sorauren Ave (at Pearson) **416/532-2570** *7am-4pm, popular wknd brunch*

Mitzi's Sister [★E,GO] 1554 Queen St W **416/532-2570** *4pm-2am, popular wknd brunch from 10am, upscale pub eats, full bar*

OddFellows 936 Queen St W **416/534-5244** *6pm-10pm, brunch wknds, bar till 2am Fri-Sat*

River 413 Roncesvalles Ave **416/535-3422** *lunch Th-Fri, dinner Tue-Sat, wknd brunch, also lounge Tue-Sun, upscale, supports homeless & at-risk youth*

Saving Grace 907 Dundas St W (at Bellwoods) **416/703-7368** *brkfst & lunch*

Splendido [WC] 88 Harbord St (at Spadina) **416/929-7788** *5pm-10pm, great decor & gnocchi, full bar*

The Superior Restaurant [WC] 253 Yonge St (across from Eaton Centre) **416/214-0416** *11:30am-11pm, till 9pm Mon, clsd Sun, oysters, full bar*

Supermarket 268 Augusta Ave (at College) **416/840-0501** *lunch & dinner, Thai, also bar w/ DJs*

Urban Herbivore 64 Oxford St (at Augusta) **416/927-1231** *9am-7pm, vegetarian*

Veda 506 Church St (at Maitland) **416/961-9797** *noon-9pm, Indian, plenty veggie/vegan*

The Village Rainbow 477 Church St (at Maitland) **416/961-0616** *8am-midnight, till 1am Th-Sat, 8am-1am Sun, full bar, big patio*

Xyclo Lounge 459 Church St **416/923-2695** *Vietnamese, also bar, DJs*

Zelda's [★MW,DS] 542 Church St **416/922-2526** *11am-11:30pm, till 12:30am Fri-Sat, 10am-10:30pm Sun, full bar, patio*

Entertainment & Recreation

AIDS Memorial in Cawthra Park

The Bata Shoe Museum 327 Bloor St W **416/979-7799** *10,000 shoes from over 4,500 years—including the platforms of Elton John & the pumps of Marilyn Monroe*

Buddies in Bad Times Theatre 12 Alexander St (at Yonge) **416/975-8555** *LGBT theater; also Tallulah's cabaret Fri-Sat [D]*

Hanlan's Pt Beach Toronto Islands *nude beach 10 minutes from downtown*

Bookstores

Glad Day Bookshop [★] 598-A Yonge St (at Wellesley) **416/961-4161, 877/783-3725** *10am-6:30pm, till 9pm Th-Fri, noon-7pm Sat, noon-6pm Sun, LGBT*

This Ain't The Rosedale Library [★] 86 Nassau **416/929-9912** *11am-10pm, till 11pm Fri-Sat, 1pm-9pm Sun, LGBT*

Retail Shops

Out on the Street 551 Church St **416/967-2759, 800/263-5747** *10am-8pm, till 9pm Th-Fri, 11am-6pm Sun, LGBT accessories*

Passage Tattoo 473 Church St, 2nd flr **416/929-7330** *noon-7pm, clsd Sun-Mon*

Take a Walk on the Wild Side [TG] 161 Gerrard St E (at Jarvis) **416/921-6112, 800/260-0102** *"hotel, boutique & club for crossdressers, transvestites, transexuals & other persons of gender"*

Publications

The Pink Pages 416/926-9588 *annual LGBT directory*

Xtra! 416/925-6665 *LGBT newspaper*

Men's Clubs

Cellar 78 Wellesley St E (at Church) **416/975-1799** *24hrs, no sign, enter through black door*

Central Spa 1610 Dundas St W **416/588-6191** *11am-midnight, till 3am Fri-Sat*

Club Toronto Baths & Health Club [SW,PC] 231 Mutual St (at Carlton) **416/977-4629** *24hrs, gym equipment*

Spa Excess [★] 105 Carlton St **416/260-2363, 877/867-3301** *24hrs*

St Marc Spa [★WC] 543 Yonge St, 4th flr (at Wellesley) **416/927-0210** *24hrs*

Steamworks [★WI] 540 Church (level 2) **416/925-1571** *24hrs*

EROTICA

Come As You Are 701 Queen St W (at Bathurst) **416/504-7934** *co-op-owned sex store*

Lovecraft 27 Yorkville Ave (btwn Bay & Yonge) **416/923-7331** *toys, lingerie, videos, books*

North Bound Leather [WC] 586 Yonge (W of Wellesley St) **416/972-1037** *toys & clothing*

Priape [★] 501 Church St **416/586-9914, 800/461-6969** *club-wear, leather, books, toys & more*

Seduction 577 Yonge St **416/966-6969**

Stag Shop 239 Yonge St **416/368-3507** *also 449 Church St, 416/323-0772*

CRUISY AREAS

Balfour Park [AYOR]

Cawthra Park [AYOR] Church St *summer sunbathing*

Hanlan's Pt Beach [AYOR] Toronto Islands *summers*

High Park [AYOR]

Yonge Street Walkway [AYOR]

Turkey Point

ACCOMMODATIONS

The Point Tent & Trailer Resort [M,L,SW,N,GO] 918 Charlotteville Rd #2, RR 1, Vittoria **519/426-7275** *on 50 acres*

Waterford

ACCOMMODATIONS

Cockshutt House B&B [MO,SW,WI,GO] 2140 Cockshutt Rd (at RR 1) **519/410-4339**

Waterloo

RESTAURANTS

Ethel's Lounge 114 King St N (at Spring) **519/725-2361** *11:30am-2am, full bar, patio*

EROTICA

Stag Shop 7 King St N **519/886-4500**

Windsor

see also Detroit, Michigan

ACCOMMODATIONS

University Place Accommodations [GS,NS,WI,WC] 3140 Peter St (btwn Sandwich & Mill) **519/254-1112, 866/618-1112**

Windsor Inn on the River [GF,NS] 3857 Riverside Dr E (at George Ave) **519/945-2110, 866/635-0055** *full brkfst*

BARS

Club 783 [MW,NH,K] 783 Wyandotte St E **519/973-4916** *5pm-2am*

The Honest Lawyer [GF,F] 300 Ouellete Ave **519/977-0599** *11am-2am, from 4pm Sun*

Phog [GF,F,E] 157 University Ave W (at Church St) **519/253-1605** *art & events*

Vermouth [GF] 333 Ouellette **519/977-6102** *4pm-2am, from 6pm Sat, clsd Sun, popular martini lounge*

NIGHTCLUBS

The Loop [GF,D,A,E,YC] 156 Chatham St W (at Ferry St) **519/256-9844** *9pm-2am, theme nights*

Rise [MW,NH,D] 800 Wellington **519/258-7473** *9:30pm-2:30am Fri-Sat only*

CAFES

The Coffee Exchange [WI] 266 Ouellette **519/971-7424** *7am-11pm, 8am midnight wknds*

MEN'S CLUBS

Vesuvio Steam Bath [PC] 563 Brant St **519/977-8578** *24hrs*

Erotica

Stag Shop 2950 Dougall Ave **519/967-8798**

Cruisy Areas

Jackson Park [AYOR] area at Ouelette Overpass

River Front Park [AYOR] at foot of Ouelette St *evenings*

Woodstock

Accommodations

Nunn's Hollow Guest Suites [GS,GO] 21 Delatre St (Dundas St) **519/539-9780** *full brkfst, jacuzzi, also self-catering apt*

Prince Edward Island

Albany

Accommodations

Evening Primrose [GF,NS,WI,GO] 114 Lord's Pond Rd **902/437-3134** *40 minutes from Charlottetown, B&B & cottage, full brkfst, seasonal, lesbian-owned*

Brackley Beach

Restaurants

The Dunes RR #9 **902/672-2586** *11:30am-10pm, also gallery & art studio*

Charlottetown

Info Lines & Services

Abegweit Rainbow Collective 144 Prince St (in AIDS PEI bldg) **902/894-5776, 877/380-5776** *24-hr info line, drop-in hrs 6:30pm-7:30pm Mon, monthly dances & other social activities*

Accommodations

Blooming Breezes Executive Cottage [GS,GO] 108 Lowe Ln, Blooming Point **902/626-4475** *cottage, close to beach*

Charlottetown Hotel [GF,SW,WI] 75 Kent St (at Pownall) **902/894-7371, 800/565-7633** *sauna, hot tub, also restaurant & lounge (clsd Sun)*

Delta Prince Edward [GF,SW] 18 Queen St **902/566-2222, 888/890-3222** *in heart of Olde Charlottetown, also restaurant*

Dunescape Cottages [GF,NS] 629 Queen St C1A 9C8 **902/368-3603, 800/719-3603** *waterfront properties near golf*

The Great George [GF,NS,WC,GO] 58 Great George **902/892-0606, 800/361-1118**

Rainbow Lodge [MW,NS,GO] **902/651-2202, 800/268-7005** *full brkfst, 15 minutes outside of town*

Shipwright Inn Heritage B&B [GF,NS,WI] 51 Fitzroy St **902/368-1905, 888/306-9966** *award-winning inn, central location, full brkfst*

Bars

Baba's Lounge [GF,F,E] 81 University Ave **902/892-7377** *noon-2am, 5pm-midnight Sun, live bands; also Cedars Canadian/ Lebanese restaurant*

Restaurants

Off Broadway Restaurant 125 Sydney St (at Queen St) **902/566-4620** *11am-10pm, till 11pm Fri-Sat; also 42nd Street Lounge*

Entertainment & Recreation

Blooming Point Blooming Point *nude beach*

Bookstores

Book Mark 172 Queen St (in mall) **902/566-4888** *9am-8pm, till 9pm Th-Fri, till 5:30pm Sat, noon-5pm Sun*

Erotica

Afternoon Delight 22 Exhibition Dr **902/892-3469, 877/424-5469** *woman-owned/ run*

Hunter River

Accommodations

Baywatch [GS,GO] 6921 Rustico Rd RR2 (at Camp Rd) **902/963-2206** *private oceanfront rental*

Souris

ACCOMMODATIONS

Johnson Shore Inn [GS,WC,GO] RR #3 Rte16 **902/687-1340, 877/510-9669** *full brkfst, ocean views, lesbian-owned*

York

ACCOMMODATIONS

Little York B&B [GF,WI,GO] 775 Rte 25 **902/569-0271, 800/953-6755** *1840 B&B, near beaches & Confederation trail, full brkfst, cats on premises*

Stanhope Beach Resort [GF,SW,WI,GO] 3445 Bayshore Rd **902/672-2701, 866/672-2701** *ocean views, golf, tennis*

PROVINCE OF QUÉBEC

Bromont

ACCOMMODATIONS

Auberge-Spa Le Madrigal [GF,NS] 46 boul Bromont **450/534-3588, 877/534-3588** *variety of spa treatments available, full brkfst*

Drummondville

ACCOMMODATIONS

Motel Alouette [GS,GO] 1975 boul Mercure **819/478-4166, 866/478-4166**

Havre-Aubert

CAFES

Cafe de la Grave [GF] 969 ch de la Grave **418/937-5765** *9am-3pm, from 10am Sun, local LGBT hang-out*

Hull

see also Ottawa, Ontario

RESTAURANTS

Le Twist 88 Montcalm St, Gatineau **819/777-8886** *opens 11am daily, full bar*

CRUISY AREAS

Meech Lake Beach [AYOR]

Îles de la Madeleine

ACCOMMODATIONS

La Butte Ronde [GF] 70 chemin des Buttes, Havre-aux-Maisons **418/969-2047, 866/969-2047** *converted country school, near beach*

Joliette

ACCOMMODATIONS

L' Oasis des Pins [MW,SW] 381 boul Brassard, St-Paul-de-Joliette **450/754-3819** *camping May-Sept, restaurant open year-round*

La Malbaie

ACCOMMODATIONS

Auberge au Petit Berger [GF,SW] 20 rue Desbiens **800/314-4428** *tennis court, near casino*

Laurentides (Laurentian Mtns)

ACCOMMODATIONS

Auberge de la Gare [MW,SW] 1694 chemin Pierre-Peladeau, Ste-Adèle **450/228-3140, 888/825-4273 (in Québec only)** *B&B, superb ancestral home, near slopes*

Havre du Parc Auberge [GS,F,GO] 2788 Rte 125 N, St-Donat **819/424-7686** *quiet lakeside inn for nature lovers, full brkfst*

Le Septentrion B&B [MW,SW,NS,WI,GO] 901 chemin St-Adolphe, Morin-Heights/ St-Sauveur **450/226-2665, 866/355-2665** *Victorian, full brkfst, sauna*

Le Bic

Accommodations

Auberge du Mange Grenouille [GF,NS] 148 rue Ste-Cecile **418/736-5656** *May-Oct only, also restaurant*

Gîte de la Baie Hâtée [GF] 2271 Rte 132 E **418/736-5668** *circa 1820 home decorated w/ antiques, shared baths*

Les Eboulements

Restaurants

Les Saveurs Oubliées [BYOB,R] 350 rang St-Godefroy (route 362) **418/635-9888** *dinner, specializes in lamb*

Magdalen Islands

Accommodations

Les Réfugiés [GF,NS,GO] L'Etang du Nord **418/986-4192** *B&B, full brkfst*

Magog

see also Sherbrooke

Accommodations

À Tout Venant [GF,WI] 624 rue Bellevue **819/868-0419, 888/611-5577** *massage, full brkfst, on cycling path "La Route Verte," near beach & skiing*

Au Gîte du Cerf Argenté [GS,NS,GO] 2984 chemin Georgeville Rd (off Hwy 10) **819/847-4264** *B&B in century-old farmhouse*

Auberge aux Deux Pères [GF,SW] 680 chemin des Pères **819/769-3115, 514/616-3114** *near golf, biking & other outdoor activities*

La Maison Ô Quatre Pattes [GF,NS] 30 chemin Gendron **819/847-4195** *very pet-friendly, shared baths*

Montréal

Note: M°=Metro station

Info Lines & Services

AA Gay/ Lesbian 514/376-9230 *call for meeting times & locations (in French or English)*

Gay/ Lesbian Community Centre of Montréal 2075 rue Plessis, local 110 (at Ontario) **514/528-8424** *10am-noon & 1pm-5pm, clsd wknds, library*

Gay Line/ Gai Ecoute 514/866-0103 (English), 888/505-1010 (in Canada only) *7pm-11pm*

The Village Tourism Information Center/ Gay Chamber of Commerce 240 St-Jacques #302 **514/522-1885, 888/595-8110** *10am-6pm, clsd wknds*

Accommodations

Le 3 Mai [M,WI,GO] 1607 rue Montcalm (at Maisonneuve) **514/524-8789** *located in heart of Gay Village*

Abri du Voyageur Hotel [GF] 9 rue Ste-Catherine Ouest **514/849-2922, 866/302-2922** *charming, good-value hotel in downtown Montréal, 15-minute walk to the Village*

Absolument Montréal B&B [GS,NS,WI,GO] 1790 Amherst (at Maisonneuve) **514/223-0017, 866/360-1351** *full brkfst, hot tub*

Accommodations International B&B [MO,WI,GO] 2002 Champlain #1 (at Ontario, above Citibar) **514/596-2317, 888/334-0348** *outside terrace*

Alcazar B&B [M,NS,GO] 1589 Alexandre de Sève (at Maisonneuve) **514/223-2622, 866/589-8964** *in heart of gay Village*

Alexandre Logan [GF] 1631 rue Alexandre de Sève **514/598-0555, 866/895-0555**

Alexandrie-Montréal [GF,NS,WI,GO] 1750 Amherst (at Robin) **514/525-9420** *rooms & apts in the Village*

Angelica Blue B&B [GS,NS,WI] 1213 Ste-Elisabeth (at Ste-Catherine) **514/844-5048, 800/878-5048** *theme rooms, full brkfst, some shared baths*

Auberge Belles Vues B&B [GF] 1407 rue Pânet #2 **514/521-9998** *in the Gay Village*

Auberge de la Fontaine [GS,WI,WC] 1301 rue Rachel Est (at Chambord) **514/597-0166, 800/597-0597**

Auberge La Raveaudiere B&B [GS,GO] 11 Hatley Center, North Hatley **819/842-2554, 866/272-2554** *19th-c country inn, full brkfst, 1.5 hours from Montréal, mtn views*

Auberge le Pomerol [GF,NS,WI] 819 boul de Maisonneuve E **514/526-5511, 800/361-6896** *many rooms w/ whirlpools*

Aubergell B&B [MO,F,NS,WI,GO] 1641 Amherst (at de Maisonneuve) **514/597-0878, 514/525-7744** *also full bar, rooftop terrace*

Aux Studios Montcalm—Guesthouse [M,GO] 1303 Montcalm St (at Ste-Catherine St) **514/815-6195**

B&B L'escogriffe [MO,WI,GO] 1264 rue Wolfe (at rue Ste-Catherine E) **514/523-4800, 877/523-6105**

B&B Le Cartier [GS,NS,WI,GO] 1219 rue Cartier (at Ste-Catherine Est) **514/917-1829, 877/524-0495** *newly renovated 100-year-old stone house in Gay Village*

B&B Le Terra Nostra [GF,NS,WI] 277 Beatty (at Lasalle) **514/762-1223, 866/550-5235** *full brkfst*

BBV (B&B du Village) [M] 1279 rue Montcalm (at Ste-Catherine) **514/522-4771, 888/228-8455** *jacuzzi*

Big Boys Guesthouse [MO,WI,GO] 1478 de Maisonneuve Est (at Alexandre de Sève) **514/525-4222, 866/889-2697**

Le Bliss [GS,NS,GO] 1282 rue Pânet (at Ste-Catherine) **514/277-0170** *rental apt, short- or long-term stays*

Les Bons Matins Au Village [MW,NS,WI] 1805 Ontario East **514/931-9167, 800/588-5280** *B&B*

Brigadoon B&B [GF,NS] 29 Main Rd, Hudson **450/458-0233** *nestled on the "Lake of Two Mtns," 1 hour from Montréal*

Le Chasseur B&B [GS,GO] 1567 rue St-André (at Maisonneuve) **514/521-2238, 800/451-2238** *Victorian row house, summer terrace*

Chateau Cherrier [MW,NS,GO] 550 rue Cherrier (at St-Hubert) **514/844-0055, 800/816-0055** *seasonal, full brkfst*

Chez Roger Bontemps [GS] 1441 rue Wolfe (at Ste-Catherine) **514/598-9587, 888/634-9090** *B&B & furnished apts*

La Claire Fontaine [GF] 1652 rue la Fontaine **514/528-9862** *B&B in quiet neighborhood*

▶ **La Conciergerie Guest House** [★M,N,NS,WI,GO] 1019 rue St-Hubert (at Viger) **514/289-9297** *hot tub, gym & sundeck*

Delta Montréal [GF,SW,WC] 475 Ave President Kennedy (at City Councilor) **514/286-1986, 877/286-1986** *hot tub, restaurant, bar, garden terrace*

Four Points by Sheraton [GF,WI,WC] 475 Sherbrooke St W **514/842-3961** *complimentary pool & fitness center across the street, also restaurant, bar & cafe*

Gingerbread House B&B [MW,NS,WI,GO] 1628 St-Christophe (at Maisonneuve) **514/597-2804** *full brkfst, shared bath*

Hotel Bourbon [★M] 1574 rue Ste-Catherine Est (at Champlain) **514/523-4679, 800/268-4679** *also Bar Cajun, Le Tube & La Track disco*

Hôtel Dorion [GS] 1477 rue Dorion **514/523-2427, 877/523-5908** *in the Gay Village*

Hotel du Fort [GS,WC] 1390 rue du Fort (at Ste-Catherine) **514/938-8333, 800/565-6333**

Hotel Dynastie [GS,NS,GO] 1723 St-Hubert **514/529-5210, 877/529-5210**

Hôtel Gouverneur Montréal Place Dupuis [GF,SW] 1415 rue St-Hubert **888/910-1111**

Hotel La Tour Centre Ville [GF,SW] 400 René-Lévèsque Ouest (at Bleurry) **514/866-8861, 800/361-2790** *all units w/ kitchenettes*

Hotel le St-André [GS,WI] 1285 rue St-André (at Ste-Catherine) **514/849-7070, 800/265-7071** *B&B inn, on edge of Gay Village*

Hotel Lord Berri [GF,WC] 1199 rue Berri (at Ste-Catherine) **514/845-9236, 888/363-0363** *nonsmoking rooms available, also Italian resto-bar*

Hotel Manoir des Alpes [GF] 1245 rue St-André (at Ste-Catherine) **514/845-9803, 800/465-2929**

Hotel XIXe Siècle [GF,WI] 262 rue St-Jacques **514/985-0019, 877/553-0019** *large, modern rooms*

Le Houseboy B&B [MO,NS,WI,GO] 1281 rue Beaudry (at Ste-Catherine Est) **514/525-1459, 866/525-1459** *full brkfst, shared baths, jacuzzi*

Immeuble Avenue Lacombe [GF] 3536 av Lacombe **514/738-5787 (fax only)** *furnished apts*

Jade Blue B&B [GS,NS,WI] 1225 de Bullion **514/878-9843, 800/878-5048** *theme rooms, full brkfst*

Loews Hotel Vogue [GF,WC] 1425 rue de la Montagne (near Ste-Catherine) **514/285-5555, 800/465-6654** *full-service 5-star hotel*

La Loggia Art & Breakfast [GS,NS,WI,GO] 1637 rue Amherst (at Maisonneuve) **514/524-2493, 866/527-7975** *in Gay Village, sundeck, no unregistered guests*

Montréal Boutique Suite Guesthouse [MW,NS,WI,GO] 1269 rue de Champlain (at Ste-Catherine) **514/521-9436, 514/521-3523**

Nuzone B&B [M,N,WI,GO] 1729 rue St-Hubert **514/524-5292** *in Victorian house, full brkfst*

Ruta Bagage [GS] 1345 rue Ste-Rose (at Panêt) **514/598-1586** *Victorian B&B, full brkfst, shared baths*

Sir Montcalm [M,NS,WI,GO] 1455 Montcalm (at Ste Catherine St) **514/522-7747** *B&B*

Le St-Christophe [MO,N,NS,GO] 1597 rue St-Christophe (at Maisonneuve) **514/527-7836, 888/521-7836** *full brkfst, hot tub, sundeck*

St-Lawrence Apartments [GS,WI] 65 René-Lévèsque Est (at St-Laurent) **514/961-1577** *fully furnished apts, near Gay Village*

Turquoise B&B [M,GO] 1576 rue Alexandre de Sève (at Maisonneuve) **514/523-9943, 877/707-1576** *Victorian B&B, shared baths*

W Montréal [GF,WI,WC] 901 Square Victoria **514/395-3100, 877/WHOTELS (reservations only)** *also spa, restaurant & 3 bars*

BARS

L' Adonis [MO,S] 1680 rue Ste-Catherine Est (at Papineau) **514/521-1355** *3pm-3am, from 6pm Mon-Wed*

Bar Rocky [M,V,OC] 1673 rue Ste-Catherine Est (at Papineau) **514/521-7865** *8am-3am, [E] wknds*

Black Eagle Bar (Aigle Noir) [M,L,PC] 1315 Ste-Catherine Est (at Visitation) **514/529-0040** *8am-3am, theme nights*

Cabaret Mado [★MW,D,K,C,DS,WC] 1115 rue Ste-Catherine Est (at Amherst, below Le Campus) **514/525-7566** *11am-3am, theme nights, owned by the fabulous Mado!*

Le Campus [M,S] 1111 rue Ste-Catherine Est, 2nd flr (at Amherst) **514/526-3616** *3pm-3am, from 1pm wknds, nude dancers, ladies night Sun*

Citibar [GS,NH] 1603 Ontario Est (at Champlain) **514/525-4251** *11am-3am*

Club Bolo [MW,D,CW,$] 2093 rue de la Visitacion (at Association Sportive) **514/849-4777** *10pm-2am Fri, events Sat, T-dance from 4pm-9pm Sun, also lessons*

Club Date [MW,NH,K,P,S] 1218 rue Ste-Catherine Est (at Beaudry) **514/521-1242** *8am-3am*

Cocktail [MW,NH] 1669 Ste-Catherine Est **514/597-0814** *8am-3am*

Le Drugstore [★MW,F] 1366 rue Ste-Catherine Est (at Panêt) **514/524-1960** *10am-3am, 8 bars on 3 flrs*

Foufounes Electriques [GF,D,E] 87 Ste-Catherine Est (at St-Laurent) **514/844-5539** *4pm-3am, patio*

Fun Spot [MW,NH,D,TG,K,DS] 1151 rue Ontario Est (at Wolfe) **514/522-0416** *11am-3am, poker machines*

Le Gotha [M,NH,E] 1641 Amherst (at Maisonneuve) **514/526-1270** *4pm-3am*

Le Mystique [MW,NH] 1424 rue Stanley (at Maisonneuve) **514/844-5711** *4pm-3am, English underground pub*

Normandie [MW,NH,V] 1295 Amherst (at Ste-Catherine) **514/522-2766** *10am-3am, terrace, one of Montréal's oldest taverns, popular happy hour*

La Relaxe [M,NH] 1309 rue Ste-Catherine Est, 2nd flr **514/523-0578** *noon-3am, open to the street—as the name implies, a good place to relax & people-watch*

St-Sulpice [GS] 1680 rue St-Denis (at Ontario) **514/844-9458** *11am-3am, till midnight Sun, 3 flrs, large terrace*

Stock Bar [MO,S] 1171 Ste-Catherine **514/842-1336** *shows start at 8pm nightly, nude dancers*

Le Stud [MO,D,B,L] 1812 rue Ste-Catherine Est (at Papineau) **514/598-8243** *10am-3am*

Taboo [MO,S] 1950 boul de Maisonneuve Est (at Dorion) **514/597-0010** *7pm-3am, nude dancers*

Woof [M,B,L] 1661 rue Ste-Catherine Est (at Champlain) **514/523-1481** *8am-3am*

NIGHTCLUBS

Beat Me Up [GS,D] 3699 St-Lauernt (at Ave des Pins, at Club Saphir) **514/284-5093** *Th only, popular electronica dance party*

Circus After Hours [GS,D] 915 rue Ste-Catherine Est **514/844-0188** *2am-10am Th-Sat only*

Cirque du Boudoir [GS,D,E] **514/789-9068** *opulent quarterly theme parties*

Club Parking [★M,D,L,YC] 1296 rue Amherst **514/282-1199** *10am-3am, clsd Tue-Wed, 2 flrs, [MO] Fri-Sat*

Club Tools [★M,D] 1592 Ste-Catherine Est **514/523-4679 (hotel)** *9pm-close Fri-Sun only, '70s, '80s & '90s club disco, 3 flrs w/ large back patio, sex club*

Complexe Sky [★MW,D,A,L,F,C,DS,S] 1474 rue Ste-Catherine Est (Alexandre de séve) **514/529-6969, 514/529-8989** *11am-3am, 3 levels, cabaret & dance club Fri-Sat, T-dance Sun*

Faggity Ass Fridays [MW,D,E] 5656 Ave du Parc (at The Playhouse) *10pm Fri, benefits Head & Hands sex ed organization*

Red Lite (After Hours) [★GF,D,$] 1755 rue de Lierre, Laval **450/967-3057** *Fri-Sun only, after-hours club*

Stéréo [★GS,$] 858 rue Ste-Catherine Est **514/286-0325** *after-hours Fri-Sun only*

Unity [★MW,D,S,YC] 1171 rue Ste-Catherine Est (at Montcalm) **514/523-2777** *9pm-close, clsd Sun-Tue, 4 flrs & great rooftoop terrace*

CAFES

Cafe Titanic [★WI] 445 St-Pierre (in Old Montréal) **514/849-0894** *7am-4:30pm, clsd wknds, salads & soups*

Kilo 6744 rue Hutchison **514/270-3024, 877/270-3024** *9am-5pm, clsd wknds, cakes, coffee & light meals*

The Second Cup [NS,WI] 1351 rue Ste-Catherine Est **514/598-7727** *24hrs, très gay coffee shop*

RESTAURANTS

L' Anecdote [MW] 801 rue Rachel Est (at St-Hubert) **514/526-7967** *7:30am-10pm, burgers*

Après le Jour [MW,BYOB,WC] 901 rue Rachel Est (at St-Andre) **514/527-4141** *5pm-9pm, till 9:30pm wknds, Italian/ French, seafood*

Bato Thai [★MW,BW] 1310 rue Ste-Catherine Est **514/524-6705** *lunch weekdays & dinner nightly*

Beauty's [★] 93 Mont-Royal Ouest **514/849-8883** *7am-4pm, till 5pm wknds, diner/ Jewish deli, worth the wait*

La Binerie 367 Mt-Royal **514/285-9078** *brkfst, lunch & dinner, Québecois*

Le Cagibi 5490 boul St-Laurent **514/509-1199** *9am-1am, from 10:30am wknds, 6pm-midnight Mon, vegetarian, live music & events*

Chu Chai [★] 4088 rue St-Denis (at Rachel) **514/843-4194** *lunch & dinner, vegetarian Thai, full bar*

Cluny Art Bar 257 rue Prince (at rue William) **514/866-1213** *8am-5pm Mon-Fri, Mediterranean*

La Colombe [BYOB] 554 Duluth Est **514/849-8844** *5:30pm-midnight, clsd Sun-Mon, French*

Commensal [BW,WC] 1720 rue St-Denis (at Ontario) **514/845-2627** *11am-10:30pm, till 11pm Fri-Sat, vegetarian*

Ella Grill [GO] 1237 Amherst **514/523-5553** *upscale Mediterranean*

L' Exception 1200 rue St-Hubert (at Réné-Lévèsque) **514/282-1282** *11am-11pm, clsd wknds, burgers & sandwiches, plenty veggie, terrace*

L' Express [★R,WC] 3927 rue St-Denis (at Duluth) **514/845-5333** *8am-2am, from 10am Sat, 10am-1am Sun, French bistro & bar, great pâté*

Fantasie [GO] 1355 rue Ste-Catherine Est **514/523-3466** *lunch & dinner, sushi*

La Strega [WC] 1477 rue Ste-Catherine Est **514/523-6000** *10am-midnight, from 4:30pm wknds, inexpensive Italian, some veggie*

La Paryse [MW,GO] 302 rue Ontario Est (near Sanguinet) **514/842-2040** *lunch & dinner, clsd Mon, '50s-style diner*

Piccolo Diavolo [★WC] 1336 rue Ste-Catherine Est (at Panêt) **514/526-1336** *dinner nightly, Italian, charming waiters*

Le Planète [YC,BW] 1451 rue Ste-Catherine Est (at Plessis) **514/528-6953** *lunch weekdays & dinner nightly, brunch only Sun, global cuisine*

Resto du Village 1310 rue Wolfe **514/524-5404** *24hrs, "cuisine canadienne"*

Saloon Cafe [★] 1333 rue Ste-Catherine Est (at Panêt) **514/522-1333** *dinner nightly, lunch wknds only, int'l cuisine, big dishes & even bigger drinks*

Santropol 3900 St-Urbain (at Duluth) **514/842-3110** *11:30am-10pm, unique sandwiches*

Schwartz's Deli 1895 boul St-Laurent **514/842-4813** *8am-12:30am, till 1:30am Fri, till 2:30am Sat*

Thai Grill 5101 boul St-Laurent (at Laurier) **514/270-5566** *lunch Mon-Fri, dinner nightly, one of Montréal's best Thai eateries*

Entertainment & Recreation

Ça Roule 27 rue de la Commune Est **514/866-0633, 877/866-0633** *join the beautiful people skating up & down Ste-Catherine*

Cinéma du Parc 3575 Parc (btwn Milton & Prince Arthur) **514/281-1900** *repertory film theater*

Prince Arthur Est at boul St-Laurent, not far from Sherbrooke Métro station *closed-off street w/ tons of outdoor restaurants & cafés—it's touristy but oh-so-European*

Retail Shops

Cuir Mont-Royal 826-A Mont Royal Est (at St-Hubert) **514/527-0238, 888/338-8283** *leather, fetish*

Priape [★] 1311 Ste-Catherine Est (at Visitation) **514 /521-8451, 800/461-6969** *clubwear, leather, books, toys & more*

Screaming Eagle 1424 boul St-Laurent **514/849-2843** *leather shop*

Publications

Fugues 514/848-1854, 888/848-1854 *glossy LGBT bar/ entertainment guide*

The Mirror 514/393-1010 *free queer-positive weekly, reviews, event listings & more in English*

RG 514/523-9463 *monthly newsmagazine*

La Voix 514/522-8204, 888/244-5429 *monthly magazine for men*

Men's Clubs

5018 Sauna [M] 5018 boul St-Laurent (at St-Joseph) **514/277-3555** *24hrs, hot tub*

Colonial Bath 3963 av Colonial (at Napoléon) **514/285-0132** *noon-midnight, till 2am Fri-Sat, from 7am Sun*

GI Joe [★L,E,V,PC] 1166 Ste-Catherine Est **514/528-3326** *24hrs, hot tub, specials for leather crowd*

L' Oasis [★V,PC] 1390 Ste-Catherine Est **514/521-0785** *24hrs, hot tub*

Sauna 1286 [M] 1286 chemin Chambly (at Breggs), Longueuil **450/677-1286** *24hrs, 3 flrs, hot tub*

Sauna 456 [★SW,PC] 456 rue de la Gauchetière Ouest (at Metro Square) **514/871-8341** *24hrs, 3 flrs, hot tub, also gym*

Sauna Centre-Ville 1465 rue Ste-Catherine Est (at Plessis) **514/524-3486** *24hrs*

Sauna du Plateau 961 rue Rachel Est (at Boyer) **514/528-1679** *24hrs*

Sauna Pont-Viau [M] 1-A rue de Nevers, Laval **450/663-3386** *24hrs*

Sauna St-Hubert [M] 6527 rue St-Hubert (at Beaubien) **514/277-0176** *24hrs Th-Sun*

Sauna Ste-Catherine 1836 rue Ste-Catherine Est **514/523-5355** *24hrs*

Erotica

La Capoterie 2061 St-Denis **514/845-0027** *adult novelties, condoms*

Il Bolero 6842-46 St-Hubert (btwn St-Zotique & Bélanger) **514/270-6065** *fetish & clubwear emporium, ask about monthly fetish party*

Cruisy Areas

Angrignon Park [AYOR]

De Maisonneuve Park [AYOR]

Parc Mont-Royal [AYOR] Park Ave *summer nights*

North Hatley

see Sherbrooke

Orford

Accommodations

Au Chant du Coq [GF] 2387 Chemin du Parc **819/843-2247** *near cycling, hiking, skiing & other outdoor activities*

Provincewide

Info Lines & Services

Gay Line/ Gai Ecoute [TG] **888/505-1010, 514/866-5090** *7pm-11pm*

Québec City

Accommodations

Le 727 Guest House (Chambres et Pension) [M,GO] 727 rue d'Aiguillon (btwn St-Augustin & Côte Ste-Geneviève) **418/523-7705, 866/523-7705** *B&B in private home, full brkfst, terrace*

ALT Hotel Québec [GF,WC] 1200 av Germain des Prés (at Laurier Blvd), Sainte-Foy **418/658-1224, 800/463-5253** *modern & elegant hotel, restaurant*

L' Auberge du Quartier [GS,NS] 170 Grande Allée Ouest (at av Cartier) **418/525-9726, 800/782-9441** *cont'l brkfst*

Auberge Place D'Armes [GF,NS,WI] 24 rue Ste-Anne **418/694-9485, 866/333-9485**

Le Château du Faubourg [GF,NS,GO] 429 rue St-Jean **418/524-2902** *B&B in château w/ 2nd French Empire Napoleon III architecture, also beauty salon, also rental cottage 50 minutes from the city*

Le Coureur des Bois Guest House [MW,NS,GO] 15 rue Ste-Ursule (at St-Jean, in Old Québec) **418/692-1117, 800/269-6414** *also apts, shared baths*

Dans les Bras de Morphée [GF,SW] 225 chemin Royal, St-Jean-De-L'Ile d'Orléans **418/829-3792, 866/220-4061** *full brkfst, near beach, shared baths, lesbian-owned*

Domaine Vagabond [MO,SW,18+] 1878 rang 5 Ouest (exit 266, off Rte 20), Joly **418/728-5522** *camping, full brkfst, also bar & restaurant*

Gîte aux Deux Lions [GF,WI] 25 boul René-Lévesque Est **418/780-8100, 877/777-9444** *cozy B&B in refined 1909 home*

Hôtel Dominion 1912 [GF,WI,WC] 126 rue St-Pierre **418/692-2224, 888/833-5253** *boutique hotel in city's 1st skyscraper*

Hotel Le Clos Saint-Louis [GS,NS,WI] 69 St-Louis (at St-Ursule) **418/694-1311, 800/461-1311** *small Victorian-style boutique hotel*

Hôtel-Motel Le Voyageur [GS,SW] 2250 boul Ste-Anne (at Estimauville) **418/661-7701, 800/463-5568** *restaurant, 2 bars*

Loews Le Concorde [GF,SW,WC] 1225 cours du Général De Montcalm **418/647-2222, 800/463-5256** *4-stars, located on Grand Allée, w/ revolving restaurant*

Maison du Cocher [GF,WI] 31 rue Dauphine **418/261-6610, 888/694-1388**

Le Moulin de St-Laurent Chalets [GS,SW,NS] 754 chemin Royal, St Laurent, Ile d' Orleans **418/829-3888, 888/629-3888** *cottages, also restaurant*

Bars

Bar 321 [M,NH,TG,S] 321 de la Couronne (at La Salle) **418/525-5107** *11am-3am*

Bar 889 [MW,NH] 889 côte Ste-Geneviève **418/524-5000** *11am-3am, patio*

Bar de la Couronne [★M,S] 310 rue de la Couronne (btwn rues de la Reine & de la Salle) **418/525-6593** *9pm-3am, nude dancers, [MO] Th-Sat*

Bar Le Drague [★M,NH,D,F,K,C,DS,WC] 815 rue St-Augustin (at St-Joachim) **418/649-7212** *10am-3am, 3 bars, DJ Fri-Sun, terrace*

ForHom [MO,OC,PC] 221 rue St-Jean (entrance at 225) **418/523-4918** *5pm-1am, till 3am Fri-Sat, good place for quiet conversation*

Nightclubs

Le Gai Serpentin [M,S] 101 boul du Pont (on Hwy 132), St-Nicolas **418/831-4055** *7pm-3am Th-Sat*

Restaurants

Le Commensal 860 rue St-Jean **418/647-3733** *11am-9pm, till 10pm Th-Sat, vegetarian/ vegan*

Le Hobbit 700 rue St-Jean (at Ste-Geneviève) **418/647-2677** *9am-10pm*

Le Moulin de St-Laurent Restaurant 754 chemin Royal, St Laurent, Ile d' Orleans **418/829-3888** *lunch & dinner, May-Oct only, live music Sun*

La Piazzetta 707 rue St-Jean **418/521-4393** *11am-11pm, till midnight Fri-Sat*

Le Poisson d'Avril 115 quai St-André (at St-Thomas) **418/692-1010, 877/692-1010** *5pm-close, name is French for "April Fools"*

Entertainment & Recreation

Fairmont Le Château Frontenac [GF,SW] 1 rue des Carrières **418/692-3861, 866/540-4460** *this hotel disguised as a castle remains the symbol of Québec—even if you can't afford the princess' ransom to stay the night, come & enjoy the view from outside*

Ice Hotel [GF] Sainte-Catherine-de-la-Jacques-Cartier **418/875-4522, 877/505-0423** *sometimes getting put on ice isn't a bad thing—check it out before it melts away, 9 km E of Québec City in Montmorency Falls Park (Jan-March only)*

Men's Clubs

Bloc 225 [PC] 225 St-Jean (at Turnbull) **418/523-2562, 877/523-2562** *24hrs, also Capital Gym*

Sauna Backboys [V] 264 rue de la Couronne (at Prince Edward) **418/521-6686, 877/523-6686** *24hrs*

Sauna/ Hotel Hippocampe [★V] 31 rue McMahon **418/692-1521, 888/388-1521** *24hrs, bar, also small hotel (www.hotelhippocampe.com)*

Erotica

Empire Lyon 225A rue St-Jean (at Turnbull) **418/648-2301** *DVDs, toys, lubes, magazines, underwear & more*

Importation André Dubois [TG,WC] 46 côte de la Montagne (at Frontenac Castle) **418/692-0264**

Cruisy Areas

Rue St-Denis [AYOR]

Rouyn-Noranda

Bars

Station D [MW,D,K,DS] 63 Perreault Ouest **819/797-8696** *2pm-close, clsd Mon, terrace*

Sherbrooke

Bars

L' Otre Zone [MW,D,F] 252 rue Dufferin **819/565-5333** *4pm-3am, from 8pm Sat, till midnight Tue-Wed, clsd Mon, more men Sat*

Nightclubs

Complex 13-17 [MW,D,S] 13-15-17 Bowen Sud (at rue King) **819/569-5580 (sauna), 819/562-2628 (club)** *11am-3am, pub & dance club, [S] Fri-Sun, also sauna*

St-Alphonse-de-Granby

Accommodations

Bain de Nature [MO,SW,N,GO] 127 rue Lussier **450/375-4765** *B&B & free-form camping, beautiful small lake, all meals included, hot tub, day visitors welcome*

St-Ferréol-les-Neiges

Entertainment & Recreation

Les Sept Chutes 4520 Ave Royale **877/725-8837, 418/826-3139** *historical village w/ hiking trails*

St-François-du-Lac

Accommodations

Domaine Gay Luron [MO,F,SW,N,GO] **450/568-3634** *seasonal, cabins, camping, RV spots & rental condos, also restaurant & bar*

St-Georges-de-Beauce

Bars

Bar L'Envol [MW,D,DS] 11270 1ère Ave, 5th flr, St-Georges **418/227-5550** *4pm-3am Th-Sat only*

St-Hubert

Men's Clubs

3481 Sauna [MO] 3481 Montee St-Hubert **450/462-3481** *24hrs*

St-Hyacinthe

Bars

Bar L'Illusion [GF,D] 460 ave Mondor **450/252-4011** *4pm-3am Wed-Sun, patio (summer)*

St-Joachim

Entertainment & Recreation

Cap Tourmente 570 chemin du Cap-Tourmente **418/827-4591** *nat'l wildlife area*

Ste-Anne-de-la-Pérade

Accommodations

Auberge à l'Arrêt du Temps [GS,NS,GO] 965 boul de Lanaudière **418/325-3590, 877/325-3590** *also restaurant*

Ste-Julienne

Accommodations

Camping de la Fierté [MO,SW,N,18+] 2905 Montée Hamilton **450/834-2888** *theme wknds summers, tent & RV spots, cabin, also bar/ restaurant/ rec hall*

Ste-Marthe

Accommodations

Camping Plein Bois [MO,D,SW,N,GO] 550 chemin St-Henri **450/459-4646, 888/459-4646** *seasonal, DJ Fri-Sat, also restaurant & bar, volleyball, 350 campsites & 200 trailer sites*

Trois Rivières

Accommodations

Le Gîte du Huard [GF] 42 rue St-Louis **819/375-8771** *B&B*

SASKATCHEWAN

Provincewide

Publications

Perceptions 306/244-1930 *covers the Canadian prairies*

Ravenscrag

Accommodations

Spring Valley Guest Ranch [★GS,F,NS,GO] **306/295-4124** *1913 character home, also cabin, full brkfst*

Regina

Info Lines & Services

The Gay & Lesbian Community of Regina 2070 Broad St (at Victoria) **306/569-1995, 306/522-7343** *4pm-2am*

Nightclubs

The OUTside [MW,D] 2070 Broad St (at Victoria, at Gay Center) **306/569-1995** *5pm-3am, from 8pm Sun-Wed*

Restaurants

Abstractions Cafe 2161 Rose St **306/352-5374** *9am-6pm, from 11am Sat, clsd Sun, some veggie*

The Creek in Cathedral Bistro 3414 13th Ave **306/352-4448** *lunch & dinner, clsd Sun, contemporary*

Pacific Fresh Fish 3005 13th Ave (at Robinson) **306/525-9147**

Cruisy Areas

Douglas Park [AYOR]

Wascana Park [AYOR] at College Dr & Lorne St

Saskatoon

Info Lines & Services

Avenue Community Centre 201-320 21st St W **306/665-1224, 800/358-1833** *10am-5pm, till 9pm Wed-Fri, clsd wknds, library, many social/ support groups, queer gift store*

Circle of Choice Gay/ Lesbian AA 505 10th St E (at Grace Westminster United Church) **306/665-5626** *8pm Wed*

Nightclubs

Diva's [MW,D,DS,PC] 220 3rd Ave S #110 (alley entrance) **306/665-0100** *8pm-2am, till 3am wknds, clsd Mon-Tue*

Restaurants

2nd Ave Grill 10-123 2nd Ave **306/244-9899** *11am-11pm, 5pm-9pm Sun*

The Berry Barn 830 Valley Rd **306/978-9797** *open daily, seasonal, home-style eatery w/ views of river*

The Ivy Dining & Lounge 24th St E & Ontario St **306/384-4444** *lunch & dinner Mon-Fri, dinner only Sat-Sun*

Prairie Ink 3130 8th St E **306/955-3579** *9am-10pm, till 11pm Fri-Sat, 10am-9pm Sun, also bookstore & cafe*

Seasons Cafe & Eatery 102 Cardinal Crescent (at Heritage Inn) **306/665-8121** *6:30am-10pm, 6am-11pm Fri-Sat, 7am-9pm Sun, fresh soups & salad bar*

Entertainment & Recreation

AKA Gallery 424 20th St W **306/652-0044** *noon-6pm, clsd Sun-Mon, contemporary art & performance*

Bridge City Chorus *LGBT chorus*

Rainbow Radio 306/664-6678 *9:30pm Sun*

Bookstores

Turning the Tide 525 11th St E **306/955-3070** *noon-8pm, till 10pm Th-Sat, till 5pm Sun, Saskatoon's alternative bookstore*

Retail Shops

The Trading Post 226 2nd Ave S **306/653-1769** *10am-5:30pm, clsd Sun, clothing*

Cruisy Areas

Lakewood Park [AYOR] *nights*

YUKON

Whitehorse

Info Lines & Services

Gay/ Lesbian Alliance of the Yukon Territory PO Box 31678, Y1A 6L3 **867/333-5800** *events, newsletter, check web for current event listings: www.gaycanada.com/galayukon*

Accommodations

Inn on the Lake [GF,NS,WI] **867/660-5253** *luxury lakefront log inn*

Caribbean

Bahamas

Nassau

Nightclubs

Club Waterloo [GF,D,F,E,SW] E Bay St (1/2 mile E of Paradise Island Bridge) **242/393-7324** *4pm-close, indoor/ outdoor complex w/ 5 bars, 2 dance flrs, live music & restaurant*

Barbados

Bridgetown

Restaurants

The Waterfront Cafe [E] The Careenage **246/427-0093** *10am-midnight, clsd Sun, trendy, also bar, live music, outdoor seating (not surprisingly, on the waterfront)*

British Virgin Islands

see also US Virgin Islands

Leverick Bay

Accommodations

Coconut Grove Villa [GF,SW,WI,WC] 36 Oleander Dr **284/495-7313** *hillside rental villa, great views, gourmet kitchen*

Tortola

Accommodations

Fort Recovery Villa Beach Resort [GF,SW,WC] Road Town, Tortola **284/495-4467, 800/367-8455 (wait for ring)** *grand home on beach & private beachfront villas*

Entertainment & Recreation

Yacht Ferdinand [GF] **284/499-1420**

Dominican Republic

Boca Chica

Accommodations

Costalunga [GF] 3 Av del Sur **809/523-6883** *closest beach to Santo Domingo*

Puerto Plata

Accommodations

Casa de la Luna [GS] La Catalina Cabrera (at Calle 5) **518/274-9463** *villa rental close to La Playa Grande Beach*

Tropix Hotel [GF,SW,GO] **809/571-2291** *garden setting near center of town & beach, full brkfst*

Santo Domingo

Accommodations

Camilo House Apartments Calle Padre Billini 455, Zona Colonial (btwn Palo Hincado & Pina) **809/221-1842, 809/768-5461** *apts w/in walking distance of historical architecture, gay nightlife, restaurants & the seaside boulevard*

Caribe Colonial Hotel [GF] Isabel Catolica 159 **809/688-7799** *boutique hotel*

Foreigners Club Hotel [MW,NS,WI,WC,GO] 102 Calle Canela (at Estrelleta) **809/689-3017**

Hotel Aida [GF] Calle El Conde 464 **809/685-7692** *near gay bars*

Hotel Venezia [GF] Av Independencia 45 (Gazcue) **809/682-5108**

Residencial El Candil [GS,SW,GO] Calle Juanico Garcia 2 (at 20 de Deciembre), Boca Chica **809/523-4252, 809/523-4253** *apts, 5 minutes from beach*

Bars

Esedeku [MW,F] 341 Mercedes (at Santome) **809/869-6322** *8pm-close, from 5pm Sun, clsd Mon*

Jay Dee's [M,NH,S,V] Jose Reyes 10, Zona Colonial **809/335-5905**

NIGHTCLUBS

Cha [M,D,DS,E] Av George Washington 165 (btwn Lincoln & Maximo Gomez) *Fri-Sun only, opened by local gay celbrity Chachita Rubio*

Eukliptus [M,D,S] Mercedes (at Espaillat)

Gazela Club [M,D,S] Av Bolivar 72 (at Dr Delgado)

RESTAURANTS

El Conuco 152 Casimiro de Moya (behind Jaragua Hotel) **809/686-0129** *touristy local landmark*

CRUISY AREAS

Avenida el Conde *pedestrian mall*

DUTCH & FRENCH W INDIES

Aruba

ACCOMMODATIONS

Little David Guest House [M,SW,N,GO] Seroe Blanco 56L, Oranjestad **297/583-8288** *private guesthouse w/ tropical garden, full brkfst*

BARS

Jimmy's Place [★MW,NH,D,F] Kruisweg 15 (at Digicel), Oranjestad **297/582-2550** *5pm-2am, till 4am Fri-Sat, from 8pm Sun, clsd Mon*

The Paddock [GS,NH,F] LG Smith Blvd #13, Oranjestad **297/583-2334, 297/583-2606** *10am-2am*

RESTAURANTS

Cafe the Plaza Seaport Marketplace, Oranjestad **297/583-8826** *10am-2am, lunch & dinner specials*

CRUISY AREAS

Eagle Beach [AYOR] btwn La Quinta Resort & Dutch Village Hotel, Oranjestad *afternoons*

Barbados

ACCOMMODATIONS

Inchcape Seaside Villas [GF,WI] Silver Sands **246/428-7006**

Bonaire

ACCOMMODATIONS

Coco Palm Garden/ Casa Oleander [GS,SW,WC] Kaya Statius van Eps 9 **599/717-2108** *studios, apts & houses*

Ocean View Villas [GS,R,WI,GO] Kaya Statius van Eps 6 **599/717-6105** *luxury apts w/ secluded patios & outdoor showers*

Curaçao

ACCOMMODATIONS

The Avila Beach Hotel [GF] 130 Penstraat, Willemstad **800/747-8162 (from US & Canada), 5999/461-4377**

Floris Suite Hotel [GF] Piscadera Bay **800/781-1011 (in US & Canada), 5999/462-6111**

Kura Hulanda [GF] Langestraat 8, Willemstad **888/264-3106 (from US & Canada), 5999/434-7700** *also Jacob's Bar*

Papagayo Beach Resort [GF] Willemstad **800/652-2962 (from US), 5999/747-4333**

BARS

Lyric's Cafe [MW,D] Punda (Waterford Arches), Willemstad *10pm-4am Th-Sat*

NIGHTCLUBS

Wet & Wild Beach Club [GF] Seaquarium Beach & Marina, Willemstad **5999/561-2477, 5999/562-0400** *9am-6pm, till 2am Fri & Sun, till 4am Sat, more gay wknds*

RESTAURANTS

Mambo Beach Bapor Kibra, Seaquarium Beach **5999/461-8999** *full bar, more gay Sat*

ENTERTAINMENT & RECREATION

Dolphin Academy at Curaçao Aquarium, Bapor Kibra z/n (east of Willemstad, at Sea Aquarium Park) **5999/465-8900, 5999/465-8300** *swim w/ dolphins!*

Museum Kura Hulanda Klipstraat 9, Willemstad **5999/434-7765** *African history & culture, Antillean art*

Saba

Restaurants

Eden Restaurant The Road, Windwardside **599/416-2539** *11am-8:30pm, clsd Sun, some veggie, patio*

Rainforest Restaurant Windwardside **599/416-3888, 599/416-5507** *brkfst, lunch & dinner, fresh, homemade food, seafood, some veggie, full bar*

St Barthélémy

Accommodations

Hotel le Village St-Jean [GF,SW] St-Jean Hill **590-590/27-61-39, 800/651-8366** *hotel & cottages*

Hotel Normandie [GF] Quartier Lorient **590-590/27-61-66**

Hotel St-Barth Isle De France [GF,F] Plage des Flamands **508/528-7727, 800/421-3396** *ultraluxe hotel*

Nightclubs

Le Sélect [GF] Gustavia **590-590/27-86-87** *more gay after 11pm*

Entertainment & Recreation

Anse Gouverneur St-Jean Beach [N]

Anse Grande Saline Beach [N] *gay section on the right side of Saline*

Orient Beach *gay beach*

St Maarten

See also St Martin

Accommodations

Blue Ocean Villas [GF] **352/505-2805** *private villa rentals*

Holland House [GF] 43 Front St, Philipsburg **599/542-2572** *on the beach, restaurant, bar*

Restaurants

Cheri's Cafe [★D,E,WC] Rhine Rd #45 (Maho Reef) **599/54-53-361** *11am-1:30am, clsd Tue, full bar, live music, touristy*

St Martin

see also St Maarten

Accommodations

Orient Bay Hotel & Jardins de Chevrise [GF,SW] Mont Vernon 1 **59-0590/87-31-10** *1- & 2-bdrm villas*

Villa Rainbow [MO,SW,NS,WI,GO] Pic Paradis **590/690-766-235** *stone villa w/ view of Caribbean*

Bars

Tantra [MW] Rhine Road, Maho Bay, Marigot (at the Marina Royale) **599/545-2861** *6pm-close*

Restaurants

L' Escapade [R] 94 Blvd de Grand Case **590-590/87-75-04** *French*

Le Pressoir 30 Blvd de Grand Case **590-590/87-76-62** *dinner nightly, clsd Sun, French*

Cruisy Areas

Cupecoy Beach [AYOR] park at established lot w/ blue & white "Cupecoy Beach" sign (near French border) *gay beach, take a friend & avoid if beach is empty*

Jamaica

Montego Bay

Accommodations

Half Moon Golf, Tennis & Beach Club [GF,SW] **876/953-2211, 866/648-6951** *upscale resort*

Negril

Accommodations

Seagrape Villas [GS] The Cliffs, West End Rd **831/625-1255 (US#)** *3 seafront villas*

Ocho Rios

Accommodations

Golden Clouds Villa [GF,SW,WC,GO] North Coast Rd, Oracabessa **941/922-9191, 888/625-6007** *private estate, full brkfst, fully staffed, jacuzzi, kids ok*

Port Antonio

ACCOMMODATIONS

Hotel Mocking Bird Hill [GF,F,SW,WC,GO] **876/993-7267, 876/993-7134** *eco-friendly inn, lesbian-owned*

Westmoreland

ACCOMMODATIONS

Moun Tambrin Retreat [GS,F,SW,NS] set in the mtns 28 miles from Montego Bay **876/437-4353, 876/357-6363**

PUERTO RICO

Please Note: For those with rusty or no Spanish, "carretera" means "highway" and "calle" means "street."

Aguada

BARS

Franky's Bar [MW,D,DS] Carr 115 en el Bo Asomante

Aguadilla

EROTICA

Condom World 18065 Punto Oro, Ste 205 **787/819-1418** *condoms, toys, videos & more—18 locations in Puerto Rico*

CRUISY AREAS

Las Ruinas [AYOR]

Bayamon

BARS

Start Night [MW,DS] 31 Ongay St (behind Clendo lab) **787/536-3579** *open Th-Sat*

Boqueron

BARS

El Schamar Bar [M,DS,GO] at corner of Muñoz Rivera & Jose de Diego **787/851-0542** *also hotel*

Sunset Sunrise [GS] Cabo Rojo **787/255-1478** *10am-close*

Cabo Rojo

ACCOMMODATIONS

Condominium Vistamar on the Beach [GS,SW,NS,GO] 403 Vistamar Condominium Combate (at Carretera 3301, km 2.7) **386/937-0735** *penthouse SW of Puerto Rico in quiet area, sleeps 10*

NIGHTCLUBS

Crash Boat Club [M,D,DS,S] Carr 100 Km 8 (at Hotel Highway Inn) **787/358-0123** *Sat-Sun only*

Camuy

BARS

Distortion [MW,D,SW] Carr 119 Norte, KM 7.6 (Barrio Membrio) **787/614-3404** *10pm Sat only*

Guaynabo

NIGHTCLUBS

Pride Night at Club Eggo [GS] Carazo 53 **787/708-4982** *gay night Wed only*

Isabela

NIGHTCLUBS

Acquamares [M,D,DS,E] Carretera 459 (near Carretera 466, by Brendy's Pizza) *open from 9pm*

Luquillo

ACCOMMODATIONS

Coqui Villa [GS,SW,NS] **787/889-2098** *treehouse villa, private veranda*

RESTAURANTS

Ely's Place Kiosk 10, at the beach **787/889-1761** *beach bar & restaurant*

CRUISY AREAS

Luquillo Beach [AYOR] from the beach, walk toward town

Manati

CRUISY AREAS

Playa de los Tubos [AYOR]

Mayaguez

Bars

Cafe Nova Ley [GS,D,DS,E,K] Calle Munoz Rivera 15 *also art gallery*

Patillas

Accommodations

Caribe Playa Beach Resort [GF,SW,NS,WC] Road #3, Km 112.1 Guardarraya **787/839-6339** *hotel, full brkfst, jacuzzi*

Ponce

Nightclubs

Backstage [M,D,DS,S] Ave Ponce de Leon, Las Delicias **787/259-5739** *Th-Sun*

Rincon

Accommodations

Bunger's Bon-Accord [GS,SW,WC] Barrio Buntas Carr 413, km 3.3 Int, Sector Sandy Beach **787/823-2525, 866/461-8936** *jacuzzi, also restaurant, near beach*

Horned Dorset Primavera Hotel [GS,SW] Apartado 1132 **800/633-1857**

Lemontree Oceanfront Cottages [GS,NS,WI,WC] Carr 429, km 4.1 (at Carr 115) **787/823-6452, 888/418-8733**

Villa Orleans Beachfront Vacation Home [GF,NS,WI] **787/433-6013** *vacation home on secluded beach*

San Juan

Info Lines & Services

Tanama [TG] **787/274-8445**

Accommodations

Acacia Seaside Inn [GF,SW,WI] 8 Taft St (at McLeary) **787/727-0626, 800/946-3244**

Andalucia Guesthouse & Vacation Rentals [M,WI,GO] 2011 McLeary St (at San Miguel St, Ocean Park) **787/309-3373** *guesthouse*

At Wind Chimes Inn [GF,SW,NS,WI,WC] 1750 McLeary Ave, Condado **787/727-4153, 800/946-3244** *restored Spanish villa, 1 block from Condado beach*

Caribe Mountain Villas [GF,SW,GO] Carr 857, km 6.0, Carolina **787/769-0860** *resort in Carolina rain forest (25 miles from San Juan)*

Casa del Caribe Guest House [GF,NS,WI] Calle Caribe 57, Condado **787/722-7139, 877/722-7139** *B&B in Condado*

Condado Inn [MW,GO] Av Condado 6 (at Av Ashford) **787/724-7145** *also bar*

Coqui del Mar [GF,GO] 2218 Calle General del Valle (at General Patton, Ocean Park) **727/459-4663** *apt rental*

Hotel El Convento [★GF,SW] Calle Cristo 100, Old San Juan (btwn Caleta de las Monjas & Calle Sol) **787/723-9020, 800/468-2779** *17th-c former Carmelite convent, gym*

Miramar Hotel [GF,WI] 606 Ponce de Leon Ave **787/977-1000, 877/647-2627** *also restaurant & bar*

Normandie Hotel [GF,WI] 199 W Muñoz Rivera Ave **787/729-2929** *art deco hotel, also restaurant & lounge*

Numero Uno on the Beach [GS,SW,WC] Calle Santa Ana 1, Ocean Park (near Calle Italia) **787/726-5010, 866/726-5010** *also Pamela's restaurant & bar*

The San Juan Water & Beach Club Hotel [GF,SW,NS,WI,WC] 2 Tartak St (Isla Verde), Carolina **787/728-3666, 888/265-6699** *boutique hotel on beach, restaurant & lounge*

Studio by the Sea [GS,WI,GO] 1123 Calle Seaview 2B (at Ashford) **787/525-9398** *free parking, laundry*

Bars

Angelu's Cafe [GS] Calle Eleanor Roosevelt 239, Hato Rey **787/294-2169**

Cafe Bohemio [GF,E] Calle Cristo 100, Old San Juan (in Gran Hotel El Convento) **787/723-9200, 787/723-9202** *11am-2am, clsd Wed, more gay Tue, also restaurant, food till 11pm, professional crowd, live music Th-Sat*

Downstairs Cafe [M] Av Condado 6 (at Condado Inn) **787/724-7145** *1pm-close, near beach, hustlers*

La Esquina del Cojo [GF,NH] 12 de Octobre (at Eleanor Roosevelt), Hato Rey **787/594-0074** *5pm-5am, clsd Sun-Mon*

El Paraiso [M,NH] 402 Calle 12 de Octubre (at Eleanor Roosevelt), Hato Rey *clsd Sun-Mon*

El Quenepo [M] Calle de Parque 411, Parada 23, Santurce **787/721-7420** *5pm-close, popular happy hour*

Rabanal Petit Club [M,NH] 1700 Ave Ponce de Leon (at Hotel San Jorge), Santurce **787/390-0336** *6pm-close Wed-Sun*

Sahara Bar [MW] 2440 Loiza St, Isla Verde (upstairs from Restaurante Tierra Santa), Isla Verde **787/661-9010, 787/425-7110**

Starz [MW,D,TG,DS,S] 365 de Diego Ave (at Ponce de Leon), Santurce **787/721-8645**

Tia Maria's [★MW,NH] Av Jose de Diego, Stop 22 (at Ponce de León), Santurce **787/724-4011** *noon-2am, professional crowd, also liquor shop*

VIP Bar [★M,NH,MR-L,TG,E,DS,S,YC] Calle Condado 613 (btwn Calle del Carmen & Av Ponce de León), Santurce **787/722-5509** *9pm-5am, leather & bear crowd Th, drag & bingo Sun*

NIGHTCLUBS

Circo Bar [M,D,K,DS] 650 Calle Condado, Santurce **787/725-9676** *9pm-5am, theme nights*

Club Babylon [MO,D,DS,S] Marginal San Agustin, 65 de Infanteria, Rio Piedras **787/765-7704** *10pm-close Th-Sun, theme nights*

Club Lazer [GF,D] Calle Cruz 251, Old San Juan **787/725-7581, 787/721-4479** *8pm-close, popular w/ gay cruises*

Junior's [★MW,NH,DS,S] Calle Condado (btwn Calle del Carmen & Av Ponce de León), Santurce **787/723-9477** *8pm-close, local crowd, 2 doors down from VIPs*

Krash Klub [★MW,D,DS,S,V,GO] Av Ponce de León 1257 (btwn Calles Villamil & Labra), Santurce **787/722-1131** *10pm-4am, clsd Mon & Tue, theme nights*

S Lounge [MW,D,DS] 1109 Roosevelt **787/783-8332**

CAFES

Cafe Berlin [★] Calle San Francisco 407, Plaza Colón, Old San Juan (btwn Calles Norzagary & O'Donnel) **787/722-5205** *9am-11pm, espresso bar*

Kasalta Bakery 1966 McLeary Ave **787/727-7340** *6am-10pm, bakery & deli*

RESTAURANTS

Aguaviva 364 Calle La Fortaleza, Old San Juan **787/722-0665** *dinner nightly, fresh seafood & ceviche*

Al Dente 309 Calle Recinto S, Old San Juan **787/723-7303** *lunch & dinner, clsd Sun, Italian, also wine bar*

La Bombonera [★] Calle San Francisco 259, Old San Juan **787/722-0658** *7:30am-8pm, come for the strong coffee & pastries, since 1903!*

La Casita Blanca 351 Calle Tapia (off Ave Eduardo Conde, near Laguna Los Corozas) **787/726-5501** *amazing local cuisine, best reached by car, no English spoken, beware of neighborhood*

Colombo [WI] 1024 Ashford Ave (at Aguadilla St) **787/725-1212** *8am-1am, till 3am wknds, American, also bar*

Dragonfly 364 S Fortaleza St, Old San Juan (across from Parrot Club) **787/977-3886** *6pm-11pm, till midnight Th-Sat, full bar, Latin/Asian fusion*

Fleria 1754 Calle Loiza, Santurce **787/268-0010** *lunch & dinner, clsd Sun-Mon, Greek, some veggie*

El Jibarito Calle Sol 280 **787/725-8375** *Puerto Rican/ criolla, also bar*

The Parrot Club [E] Calle Fortaleza 363, Old San Juan (btwn Plaza Colón & Callejón de la Capilla) **787/725-7370** *lunch & dinner, chic Nuevo Latino bistro & bar, live music*

Pinky's [★] La Placita, Santurce **787/289-8080** *sandwiches, smoothies & more, plenty veggie*

Vidy's Cafe Ave Universidad 104 (Rio Piedras) **787/767-3062** *10:30am-2am, plenty veggie*

Entertainment & Recreation

Nuyorican Cafe San Francisco 312 (enter on Capilla St) **787/977-1276, 787/366-5074** *live music & arts venue*

Saliendo del Closet WIAC 740AM **787/607-3939** *7:30pm-9pm Th*

Retail Shops

The Rainbow Shop Av Ponce de León 1418 #202 (upstairs), Santurce **787/645-1859**

Publications

Conexion G 787/607-3939 *LGBT paper, in Spanish*

Gyms & Health Clubs

International Fitness [GS] Av Ashford 1131, Condado (btwn Avs Cervantes & Caribe) **787/721-0717** *5am-10pm, till 9pm Fri, call for wknd hours*

Men's Clubs

Male Depot [MO,PC,S,V,GO] 1527 Ponce de Leon, Local 101 (at Ana G Mendez) **787/767-4118** *from 10pm Th-Sun*

Erotica

Pleasure Paradise Av Roosevelt 1367 (in Plazoleta Julio Garriga), Hato Rey **787/706-0855**

Cruisy Areas

La Playita [AYOR] in front of capitol bldg in Old San Juan

Scenic Overlook [AYOR] off Muñoz Rivera Dr *observation parking area near capitol bldg*

Vieques Island

Accommodations

Bravo! [GS,SW,GO] North Shore Rd (at Lighthouse) **787/741-1128** *Vieques' "first true beachside designer hotel" w/ beautiful ocean views*

Casa de Amistad [GS,SW,WI,GO] 27 Benitez Castano **787/741-3758** *guesthouse in heart of Isabel Segunda*

Crow's Nest Inn [GF,SW,NS] **787/741-0033, 877/276-9763** *restaurant*

Inn on the Blue Horizon [GF,SW,F,NS,WI] **787/741-3318**

Rainbow Realty [GS,GO] **787/741-4312** *20 fully equipped properties available, most w/ views, some on the water*

Vieques Realtor [GS] **787/741-0023, 787/741-0366**

St Vincent & the Grenadines

Bequia

Accommodations

Bequia Beachfront Villas [GF,SW,WC] La Pompe, Friendship Bay Beach, **284/495-4467, 800/367-8455 (wait for ring)** *1-4-bdrm villas on Friendship Bay Beach*

Trinidad & Tobago

Tobago

Accommodations

Grafton Beach Resort [GF,F,SW] **868/639-0191, 888/790-5264**

Kariwak Village Hotel & Holistic Haven [GF,F,SW,WI,WC] Store Bay Local Rd, Crown Point **868/639-8442, 868/639-8545** *1-room cabañas, outdoor jacuzzi w/ waterfall*

US Virgin Islands

see also British Virgin Islands

St Croix

Accommodations

King Christian Hotel [GF,F,SW] 59 Kings Wharf, Christiansted **340/773-6330, 800/524-2012** *also restaurant*

The Palms at Pelican Cove [MW,F,SW,GO] 4126 La Grande Princesse **340/778-8920, 888/790-5264** *beachfront resort*

Pink Fancy Hotel [GF,SW] 27 Prince St, Christiansted **340/773-8460, 800/524-2045**

Sand Castle on the Beach [★MW,SW,WI,GO] 127 Smithfield, Frederiksted **340/772-1205, 800/524-2018** *gay resort (from rooms to beachfront villas), also restaurant & bar*

Sugar Mill Villa [GS,SW,WI,WC] 301 Lorraine Ln, Christiansted **340/778-5466, 714/335-0484**

St John

Accommodations

Estate Concordia Preserve [GF,SW,WC] 20-27 Estate Concordia (at Rte 107) **800/392-9004** *upscale eco-lodge, month-long volunteer program available*

Gallows Point Suite Resort [GF,F,SW,WC] Cruz Bay **340/776-6434, 800/323-7229** *beachfront resort*

Island's End [GS,SW,NS,GO] Hanson Bay **800/341-2532, 734/274-0015** *vacation villa w/ panoramic views, lesbian-owned*

Maho Bay Camps & Harmony Studios [GF] VI National Park **340/715-0501, 800/392-9004** *environmentally aware resort*

St John Inn [GF,SW,NS,WI] **800/666-7688, 340/693-8688**

Restaurants

Asolare Rte 20, Cruz Bay **340/779-4747** *5:30pm-9:30pm, Asian/ French fusion, hip & elegant*

Entertainment & Recreation

Salomon Bay *20-minute hike on Salomon Beach Trail*

St Thomas

Accommodations

Hotel 1829 [GF,F,SW] Government Hill **340/776-1829, 800/524-2002**

Pavilions & Pools Hotel [GF,SW] 6400 Estate Smith Bay **340/775-6110, 800/524-2001** *1-bdrm villas each w/ own private swimming pool*

Restaurants

Oceana Restaurant & Wine Bar Historic Pointe at Villa Olga **340/774-4262** *on the water's edge, owned by renowned chef Patricia LaCorte*

Entertainment & Recreation

Beach at Emerald Beach Resort up hill (near airport runway) *walking distance from cruise ship dock*

Little Magens Beach *gay nude beach, near main beach at Magens Bay*

Morning Star Beach *popular gay beach*

Mexico

MEXICO

Please Note: Mexican cities are often divided into districts or "Colonias," which we abbreviate as "Col." Please use these when giving addresses for directions.

Acapulco

ACCOMMODATIONS

Acapulco Las Palmas Resort Hotel [MO,F,SW,N,GO] Av Las Conchas 155, Fracto Farallon (next to Restaurant El Chivo) **52-744/487-0843** *private villas, near gay beach, also bar*

Acapulco-Villa Roqueta [M,GO] **305/677-3525 (US#), 52-744/483-8503** *former estate of disco queen Gloria Gaynor, jacuzzi*

Casa Condesa [M,SW] Bella Vista 125 **52-744/484-1616, 800/816-4817 (US & Canada)** *full brkfst*

Fiesta Americana Condesa [★GF,F,SW] Av Costera Miguel Alemán 97 **52-744/489-2828, 800/343-7821** *deluxe hotel above the gay beach, 4-star dining, no guests allowed in room*

Las Brisas [GF,SW,WC] Carretera Escenica 5255 **52-744/469-6900, 888/559-4329 (US#)** *luxury resort, private pools*

Quinta Encanto [GF,SW,GO] Privada Roca Sola 108, Col. Club Deportivo (off Costera Blvd) **310/276-0752, 52-744/460-1112** *rental villa (sleeps 6), full staff, 1 1/2 blks to Condessa (gay) Beach & bars*

Sunscape Acapulco [GF,F,SW] Calle Caracol 70 (Fracc. Amiento Farallón) **52-744/484-3707, 866/496-3478**

Villa Estrella [GF,SW,GO] 169 Anahuac **775/445-6243** *6-bdrm villa (rent 4 rms or whole), 180° view of bay, fully staffed*

BARS

El Bar [MO,F,SW,N,GO] Av Las Conchas 155 (at Las Palmas Hotel) **52-744/487-0843** *noon-midnight*

Parranderías [MW,D,S] Av Cuauhtémoc (Col. Progresso, around corner from Hotel Palacio) *11pm-close*

Picante [★GS,D,S,AYOR,$] Privada Piedra Picuda 16 (behind Demas) **52-744/484-2209** *9pm-5am, popular male dancers, hustlers*

Plaza del Mariachi [GF,TG,DS,S,AYOR] Legazpi y Diego Hurtado de Mendoza (on the beach) *10pm-4am, more gay after midnight, popular w/ locals, patio*

NIGHTCLUBS

Baby 'O [GS,D] Costera Miguel Alemán 22 **52-744/484-7474** *10:30pm-5am, till midnight Sun*

Cabaré-Tito Beach [MW,D] Privada de Piedra Picuda 17 PA (nr Torres Gemelas) **52-744/484-7146** *9pm-close, clsd Sun-Tue*

Demas [★MO,D,S,$] Privada Piedra Picuda #17 (behind Carlos & Charlie's) **52-744/484-1370** *10:30pm-3am*

Prince [★M,D] Calle Juan de la Cosa 12 (across from Hotel Continental) **52-744/484-7601** *after-hours*

Relax [★MW,D,DS,S,V,YC] Calle Lomas de Mar 4 (Zona Dorada) *10pm-late, clsd Mon-Wed, [DS,S] wknds*

RESTAURANTS

100% Natural Av Costera Miguel Alemán 200 (near Acapulco Plaza) **52-744/485-3982** *24hrs, fast (healthy) food, plenty veggie*

Becco al Mare Carretera Escénica 14 **52-744/446-7402** *lunch & dinner, Italian, nice views*

Beto's Beach Restaurant [MW] Av Costera Miguel Alemán 99 (at Condesa Beach) **52-744/484-0473** *11am-midnight, full bar, seafood, palapas*

El Cabrito Av Costera Miguel Alemán 1480 (near Convention Center) **52-744/484-7711** *2pm-midnight, till 11pm Sun*

Carlos & Charlie's [E] Blvd de las Naciones #1813 (in La Isla Shopping Village) **52-744/462-2104** *lunch & dinner, int'l*

Coyuca 22 Av Coyuca 22 **52-744/483-5030** *open Nov-April, dress code, great views*

Le Jardin des Artistes [R] Vincente Yanez Pinzón 11 (in front of Hotel Continental Plaza) **52-74/84-8344, 52-74/84-3422** *7pm-close, French*

Kookaburra [★] Carretera Escénica (at Marina Las Brisas) **52-744/84-4418** *lunch & dinner, int'l, expensive*

La Cabaña de Caleta Playa Caleta Lado Oriente s/n (Fracc. las Playas) **52-744/469-8553, 52-744/469-7919** *9am-9pm, seafood, right on Playa Caleta, great magaritas*

La Tortuga [GO] Calle Lomas del Mar 5 **52-744/484-6985** *noon-midnight, clsd Mon, full bar, patio*

Le Bistroquet [MW,GO] Calle Andrea Doria 5 (Fracc. Costa Azul) **52-744/484-6860** *6pm-11pm, French, reservations recommended*

Madeiras Carretera Escénica 33-B (past La Vista shopping center) **52-744/446-5636** *7pm-11pm, 4-course prix fixe, Latin-Asian, reservations recommended, incredible view*

Su Casa/ La Margarita Av Anahuac 110 **52-744/484-1261, 52-744/484-4350** *seafood, great views*

Suntory de Acapulco Costera Miguel Alemán 36 **52-744/484-8088** *2pm-midnight, Japanese, gardens*

Zorrito's Av Costera Miguel Alemán (at Anton de Alaminos) **52-744/485-3735** *traditional Mexican, several locations along Costera, some all night*

Cruisy Areas

Playa Condesa & Beto's Beach near Hotel Fiesta Americana *cruisy by the rocks, at sundown*

Plaza Alvarez/ Zócalo [AYOR] *hustlers (chichifos)*

San Diego Fort [AYOR] along the Costera

Aguascalientes

Nightclubs

Mandiles [MW,D] Av Lopez Mateos 730 W (btwn Agucate & Chabacano) **52-449/153-281** *10pm-3am Fri-Sat only*

Cruisy Areas

Plaza Principal [AYOR]

Cabo San Lucas

Accommodations

Cabo Villas Resort [GF,SW] Callejon del Pescador s/n (Col. El Medano) **52-624/143-9199** *resort on Medano Beach w/ 2 restaurants*

Posada Chabela [GS,SW] Calle Tropico y Arcoiris, San Jose del Cabo **310/492-5629** *private hideaway*

Solmar Suites [GF,SW] Av Solmar 1 **800/344-3349, 310/459-9861 (US#)** *oceanfront suites at southern-most tip, 2 pools, hot tub*

The Todos Santos Inn [GS,SW,NS,GO] Calle Legaspi #33 (Topete), Todos Santos **52-612/145-0040** *colonial inn w/ bar*

Bars

The Rainbow Bar [★MW,D] Blvd de la Marina #39-E (Marina Cabo Plaza) **52-624/143-1455** *4pm-3am, patio*

Restaurants

Mi Casa [R] Av Cabo San Lucas (at Lazarus Cardenas) **52-624/143-1933** *clsd Sun, lunch & dinner, great chicken molé*

Cancún

see also Cozumel & Playa del Carmen

Accommodations

Casa de los Amigos [GS,WI,GO] Isla Mujeres **52-998/877-1169** *quiet cottage on Mexican Caribbean*

Dreams Cancun Resort & Spa [GF,SW] Paseo Kukulcán **52-998/848-7000, 866/237-3267** *2 beaches, several bars & restaurants including famous María Bonita*

Rancho Sak Ol [GF] Puerto Morelos **52-998/871-0181** *beachfront palapa-style B&B, 30 minutes from Cancún*

Zona Hotelera (The Hotel Zone) Blvd Kukulcán *Cancún's answer to the Las Vegas Strip: resorts ranging from the Sheraton Cancún's Mayan pyramids to small boutique hotels*

Bars

Cappucino Cafe Calle Magaritas (at Calle Azecenas) *early evening gay hangout*

Picante Bar [★M,D,DS,S,YC] Av Tulúm 20, Centro (E of Av Uxmal, next to Plaza Galerías) *9pm-5am, hustlers, [DS,S] Wed-Sat*

Risky Times [GS,AYOR] Av Tulúm (at Av Coba) **52-998/884-7503** *24hrs, rowdy after-hours, best after 4am*

Nightclubs

Glow [★MW,D,DS,S] 30 Avenida Tulum (Tulipanes, around the corner from Karamba) **52-998/898-4552** *11pm-6:30am, clsd Sun-Mon, huge dance flr & rooftop terrace lounge*

Karamba [★MW,D,K,DS,S] Av Tulúm 11 (Azucenas 2nd flr, SM 22) **52-998/884-0032** *10:30pm-close, clsd Mon, go-go boys Fri*

Restaurants

100% Natural Sunyaxchen 62 **52-998/884-3617** *healthy fast food: sandwiches, salads & shakes; plenty veggie*

Cafe D'Pa [★GO] Ave Alcatraces (at corner of Las Palapas Park) **52-998/884-7615** *opens afternoons, streetfront French restaurant, popular crêpes, also bar*

Casa Angelus Av Sayil 10 (Smza 4 Lote 72 y 73 Mza 12) **52-998/887-9444** *upscale int'l, full bar*

Modern Art Cafe Kukulcán Blvd, km 12.5 (at La Isla Shopping Center) **52-998/883-4511** *5pm-3am, full bar, gallery*

Perico's Av Yaxhilan 61 **52-998/884-3152** *noon-1am, traditional Mexican served up w/ huge theatrical flare—run, don't walk if you love your waiters dressed as Mexican revolutionaries, want a sombrero put on your head when you enter, like to dance in conga lines & drink strong margaritas*

Entertainment & Recreation

Chichén Itza *the must-see Mayan ruin 125 miles from Cancún*

Playa Delfines in the Hotel Zone (next to Hilton's beach) *gay beach*

Erotica

Cine Perlitas [AYOR] Calle 10 (near Plaza Cancún 2000) *porn theater, opens after 5:30pm*

Cruisy Areas

Avenida Tulúm [AYOR] Centro *take a stroll & take your pick, late*

El Mirador (Ruinas del Rei) [AYOR] next to Hilton Hotel (near the lighthouse)

Parque de las Palapas [AYOR] opposite Cinema Blanquita *near the Cine Blanquita*

Playa Delfines [AYOR] at S end of hotel zone *afternoons, beware cops (!) back in the bushes*

Ciudad Juárez

see also El Paso, Texas, USA

Bars

Bananas [S,AYOR] Ramon Corona & Ignacio Pena **52-656/222-5557** *till 2am, nude dancers, beware hustlers outside*

Club La Escondida [GS,NH] Calle Ignacio de la Peña 366 W

Club Olímpico [★M,NH,P] Av Lerdo 210 S (city center) **52-656/612-5742** *noon-2am*

Nightclubs

G&G Disco [★M,D,S,V,$] Av Lincoln 1252, Córdoba-Américas *9pm-3am, strippers wknds*

Men's Clubs

Baños Roma Calle Ignacio Mejía 881 E (at Calle Constitución) **52-656/612-7732** *9am-9pm*

Cruisy Areas

Plaza de la Constitución [AYOR] Plaza Hidalgo

Cordoba

Bars

Salon Bar El Metro [MW,D] Av 7 no. 117-C (btwn Calles 1 & 3)

Cruisy Areas

Mercado Juárez [AYOR] btwn Calles 7 & 9

Sidewalk Cafes [AYOR] El Portal Zevallos

Costa Alegre

Accommodations

El Tamarindo Beach & Golf Resort [GS,SW] Km 7.5 Carretara Barra de Navidad, Cihuatlan **52-315/351-5031, 866/717-4316**

Cozumel

see also Cancún & Playa del Carmen

Accommodations

Villa Las Anclas [GF,WI,GO] S 5th Ave #325 (btwn 3rd & 5th Sts) **52-987/872-5476, 52-987/872-6103** *suites-hotel, 1 block from main plaza*

Cuernavaca

Accommodations

Casa del Angel [GS,NS,GO] Calle Clavel 18, Col. Satelite (at Begonia) **52-777/512-6775** *contemporary guesthouse on hill overlooking 16th-c city of Cuernavaca, hot tub, full brkfst*

Las Mañanitas [GF,SW] Ricardo Linares 107 **52-777/312-8982 & 314-1466, 888/413-9199 (US only)** *gardens, restaurant, peacocks!*

La Nuestra [GS,SW,NS,WI,GO] Calle Mesalina 18 (at Calle Neptuno) **52-777/315-2272, 404/806-9694** *B&B, full brkfst*

Quinta Las Flores [GF,SW] Tlaquepaque 1 (Col. Las Palmas) **52-777/314-1244, 52-777/312-5769** *small hotel, gardens, near downtown*

Bars

Barecito [MW,F,GO] Comonfort 17 (at Morrow) **52-777/314-1425**

La Casa del Dictador [M,D] Jacarandas 4 (at Av Emiliano Zapata) **52-777/317-3186, 52-777/317-2377** *wknds only, garden*

Nightclubs

Cabaré-Tito Oxygen [MW,D,18+] Av Vicente Guerrero 1303 **52-777/317-2714** *from 9pm Th-Sat*

Club RA [MW] Ave Francisco Madero 503 (at Col. Miraval) **52-777/310-0504**

Oxygen Dance Hall & Lounge [M,D,F,E,DS,S,V,18+,YC] Av Vincente Guerrero 1303 (near Sam's Club) **52-777/317-2714 &** *10pm-close, Fri-Sat only*

Restaurants

La India Bonita Morrow 15 (btwn Morelos & Matamoros) **52-777/312-5021** *9am-9pm, till 5pm Sun-Mon, Mexican, in historic home of former US ambassador & father-in-law of Charles Lindbergh*

La Maga [E] Morrow, Altos 9 **52-777/310-0432** *clsd Sun, popular lunch buffet, plenty veggie*

Marco Polo Calle Hidalgo 30, Altos 9 (in front of cathedral, 2nd flr) **52-777/312-3484, 52-777/318-4032** *1pm-close, Italian (pasta & pizza), overlooking cathedral*

Entertainment & Recreation

CETLALIC (Centro Tlahuica de Lenguas e Intercambio Cultural) Fl Madero 721 (Col. Miraval) **52-777/313-2637, 52-77/317-0850 & 313-5450** *offers intensive Spanish language & culture classes, including ones just for LGBTs w/ gay-friendly Mexican homestays; check out www.cetlalic.org.mx*

Diego Rivera Murals Plaza de Museo (in Cuauhnáhuac Regional Museum)

Men's Clubs

Banos San Carlos Amado Nervo 111 (Col. Carolina) **52-777/317-2796**

Tepoz Spa [MO,18+,SW] Carretera San Andres de la Cal #69 (at Col Carolina), Tepoztlan, Morelos **739/395-8457** *open noon Fri-noon Mon*

Cruisy Areas

Mercado [AYOR] *Sun*

Plaza Morelos [AYOR]

Zócalo [AYOR] *also adjacent bar, Fri-Sat only*

Durango

Cruisy Areas

Cathedral Park [AYOR] Avenida 20 de Noviembre (across from cathedral)

Ensenada

Nightclubs

Scandalosas [MW,D,DS,S] Blvd Costero Plaza Marina **52-646/113-5769** *Fri & Sat only*

Sublime [M,D] Primera & Alvarado **52-646/128-8798** *9pm-close*

Restaurants

Casamar [★] Blvd Lázaro Cárdenas 987, Centro (at Blvd Costero) **52-646/174-0417** *8am-10:30pm, seafood, also bar, Ensenada landmark for 30 years*

Guadalajara

Accommodations

Casa de las Flores B&B [GF,WI] Santos Degollado 175, Tlaquepaque **52-33/3659-3186** *B&B 15 minutes from Guadalajara, great brkfsts & margaritas*

Casa Rayon [GS,WI,GO] Calle Rayon 179 (at Lopez Cotilla) **415/692-0126**

Casa Venezuela [GS,NS,WI,GO] 459 Venezuela (at Col. Americana) **52-33/3826-6590** *B&B in 100-year-old colonial house, full brkfst*

Casita GDL [M,NS,GO] Calle 68 A #312 SL (btwn Frc. de Aiza & Josefa Ortiz) **310/518-3445 (US #), 33/364-5622**

Escape B&B [MO,WI] Enrique Gonzalez Martinez 446 **52-33/3613-4140**

Hotel Calinda Roma [GF,SW] Av Juárez 170 (Sector Juárez) **52-33/3614-8650** *also rooftop restaurant*

Hotel Casa Campos B&B [GF,WI] Francisco de Miranda 30-A (Col. Centro), Tlaquepaque **52-33/3838-5296, 52-33/3838-5297** *hotel 15 minutes SE of Guadalajara, also bar & restaurant*

Hotel Puerta del Sol [GF,SW] Av López Mateos Sur 4205 (Col. Loma Bonita), Zapopan **52-33/3133-0808, 52-33/3133-0852 & 0862** *also bar & restaurant*

Hotel San Francisco [GF,F] Degollado 267 **52-33/3613-8954, 52-33/3613-8971**

Old Guadalajara B&B [GS,NS,GO] Belén 236 (Centro Histórico) **52-33/3613-9958** *elegant private 16th-c home in downtown historic district*

La Perla B&B [GS,NS,WI,GO] Prado 128, Col. Americana (Vallarta y Lopez Cotilla) **52-33/3330-2798** *full brkfst*

La Villa del Ensueño [GS,NS] Florida St 305, Tlaquepaque **52-33/3635-8792, 800/777-8792**

Bars

Arizona's Bar Saloon [M,B,DS,S] Av La Paz 1985 (at Av Chapultepec, Zona Rosa) **52-33/3826-3743** *11pm-3am, clsd Mon*

Bar Sótano [M] Galeana 159 (Centro) **52-33/3613-3436** *1pm-1am*

El Botanero [M,D,F,K,DS,YC,$] Calle Javier Mina 1348 (at Calle 54, Sector Libertad) **52-33/3643-0545** *6pm-3am, till 1am Sun, open Wed, Fri, Sat & Sun, drag shows, T-dance Sun*

Cactus Beer Bar [GS,NH,F] Galeana 279 (btwn Priscilliano Sanchez & Miguel Blanco) *5pm-1am, wide selection of int'l beers, western theme*

California's [M] Pedro Moreno 652 (at 8 de Julio, Col. Centro) **52-33/3614-3221** *6pm-3am, 5pm-5am Sat, Mexican cantina bar*

Cantina Ti@s [MW] Degollado 138 (Zona Centro, across from Hotel Universo) **52-33/3614-8326** *8am-1am*

Castro Street [MW,F] Av Vallarta 1840 *also cafe/ restaurant*

Caudillos Bar [★M,D,F,YC] Calle Prisciliano Sánchez 305, Centro (at Ocampo) **52-33/3613-5445** *5pm-3am, dancing from 9pm, friendly bar, also restaurant*

Chueca [M] López Cotilla 1988 (Zona Centro Magno) **52-33/3615-5940** *from 6pm, clsd Sun, lounge, tapas menu, Singles Night Th*

El Ciervo [M,D] 20 de Noviembre 797 (at Los Angeles, Sector Reforma) **52-33/3619-6765** *cruisy*

Club YeYe [MW,V,F] Prisciliano Sánchez 395 (Zona Centro) **52-33/1337-5253** *5pm-3am, chic video lounge*

Codice [M,D,F,DS] Enrique Gonzalez Martinez # 216 (Centro Historico) **52-33/3658-5760** *6pm-3am, clsd Mon, special events*

Condado [MO,CW] Colon 434 (btwn Leandro Valle & Nueva Galicia) *6pm-3am Wed-Sun*

Link Bar [M,D] Ave La Paz 2199 (at Simon Bolivar, Zona Rosa) **52-331/3331-3840** *4 bars, garden, special events*

Los Panchos Jr [M,D,F,S] Calle Galeana 180-A, 2nd flr (Zona Centro) **52-33/3613-5325** *9pm-2am, hustlers*

Luminare [MW] Hospital 882 (btwn Puebla & Federalismo) **52-33/3825-2085** *6:30pm-12:30am, clsd Sun, lounge, terrace, also cafe & gallery*

Maskaras [MW,NH,F,E] Calle Maestranza 238 (at Prisciliano Sánchez) **52-33/3614-8103** *9pm-3am, colorful atmosphere, live music*

Mundo Cool [MW,K] Prisciliano Sánchez 410 (Zona Centro) **52-33/3614-7481** *6pm-3am Wed-Sun*

Pink [MW,D,DS] Pavo 114 (btwn Lopez Cotilla & Juarez Ave)

Placeres [M] Calle 66 #30 (at Gigantes) **52-33/3655-9549**

La Prisciliana [GF,YC] Prisciliano Sánchez 395 (Zona Centro) **52-33/3562-0725** *5pm-3am, mellow vibe*

Rendibu Bar & Deli [M,F,V] 8 de Julio #5 (at Morelos, Zona Centro) **52-333/613-1521** *5:30pm-2am, clsd Sun-Mon, movie night Wed, art & culture*

Sexy Bar [MW,D,DS] Degollado 273 (Zona Centro) **52-33/3658-2838** *6pm-3am*

Sunrise [M] López Cotilla 497 (at Donata Guerra) *6pm-3am, clsd Mon, laid back lounge*

Nightclubs

7 Sins [M,D] Pedro Moreno 532 (at Donato Guerra, Zona Centro)

Angels [★M,D,F,DS,V,$] López Cotilla 1495-B, Col. Americana (btwn Av Chapultepec & Marsella, Zona Rosa) **52-33/3615-2525 & 3630-5478** *10pm-4am Fri-Sat, till 3am Wed, after-party Sun 6am-10am, performance wknds, restaurant*

Azul Disco [MW,D,K] Ocampo 270 (Centro Historico) *8pm-4am, clsd Mon-Tue*

Babylon Disco Bar [MW,DS,S] Morelos #84 (Plaza Tapatia) **52-33/1287-9628** *women's night Wed*

Black Cherry [M,D] Popocatepetl 40 (at Adolfo Lopez Mateos Sur) *10pm-5am Sat only*

Caudillo Platino [MW,D,TG,DS,S] Av Hidalgo 838 (Zona Centro) **52-33/3563-4332** *8pm-4am, clsd Mon*

Circus [★MW,D,E,DS] Galeana 277 (at Prisciliano Sánchez, Centro Histórico) **52-33/3613-0299** *9pm-5am*

Enigma [GF,D,C,DS,V,18+,YC,GO] Galeana 378 (at 9 Las Esquinas) *9pm-5am*

Mónica's [★M,D,DS,S,YC,$] Av Álvaro Obregón 1713 (btwn Calles 68 & 70, Sector Libertad; no sign, look for canopy under a big palm tree) **52-33/3643-9544** *9pm-5am, clsd Mon-Tue, packed after midnight, [DS,S] wknds, take a taxi to & from*

Romanos [M,D,S] Calle 68 (btwn Esteban Allatore & Federacion) **52-33/3808-4792** *10pm-5am Fri-Sat*

SOS Club [★MW,D,DS,S,$] Av La Paz 1413 (Sector Hidalgo, Zona Centro) **52-33/1201-0892** *9pm-3am, till 5am wknds, clsd Mon, [S] Fri-Sat, patio*

Tribu Bar [M,D,V,18+,GO,WC] Calle Mexicaltzingo 1521 (at enrique Diaz de Leon) *9pm-4am*

Cafes

Efebo Av Chapultepec 29-2 (btwn Pedro Moreno & Morelos) **52-33/3827-5133, 52-33/1380-9236** *cybercafe*

Restaurants

Mondo Caffe [GS,MR,BW,WI] Av Chapultepec 48 (at Pedro Moreno) **52-33/3630-2232** *8am-11pm, brkfst, lunch & dinner, coffee, smoothies, free internet access*

Sanborns Av 16 de Septiembre 127 **52-33/3613-6264** *int'l, many locations*

Sanborns Cafe Vallarta Av Vallarta 2037 **52-33/3615-7236** *int'l*

Retail Shops

Queer Nation López Cotilla 611 *5pm-midnight, clsd Sun, souvenirs, also cafe*

Publications

GAYGDL *online magazine at www.gaygdl.com, includes guide to gay Guadalajara*

Revista Estilo Libre **52-33/1410-3806** *LGBT lifestyle magazine*

Urbana Revista *gay lifestyle magazine w/ bars & clubs for Guadalajara & Puerto Vallarta*

Gyms & Health Clubs

Renacer Day Spa [★MO] Amado Nervo 106 (Col. Ladrón de Guevara) **52-33/3616-4441 or 4442** *noon-9pm, European-style day spa, sauna, steam room, jacuzzis, solarium*

Men's Clubs

La Academia [★PC] Prisciliano Sánchez 484 (btwn Donato Guerra & Enrique González Martínez) **52-33/3124-1154** *gym, steam, massage, darkroom, private rooms*

Baños La Fuente Calle Manuel Acuña #1107 (btwn Nicolas Romero & Gregoria Davila) **52-33/3826-3618** *clsd Sun*

Riilax [MO] Venustiano Carranza 313 (at Angulo) **52-33/3331-1062**

Erotica

Mundo Cool Ocampo 245 (at Prisciliano Sánchez) **52-33/3614-7481** *10:30am-9pm*

Cruisy Areas

Parque Revolución [AYOR] Av Juárez at Av Federalismo

Plaza Tapatía [AYOR] near Degollado Theater *days*

Isla Mujeres

Accommodations

Casa de los Amigos [GS,WI,GO] Col. La Gloria **52-998/877-1169**

Casa Sirena on Isla Mujeres [GF,GO] **52-998/161-2424**

Jalapa

NIGHTCLUBS

La Mansión [MW,D,DS,S,$] take a cab toward Banderillas (20 minutes NW of town, turn right at sign for El Paraíso Campestre & go past RR tracks) *9pm-4am Fri-Sat only*

CRUISY AREAS

Parque Juárez/ Zócalo [AYOR] at Enriquez & Zaragoza

La Paz

ACCOMMODATIONS

La Casa Mexicana Inn [GS,NS,WI,WC] Calle Nicolas Bravo 106 (btwn Madero & Mutualismo) **52-612/125-2748** *open Nov-June, 1 blk from La Paz Bay*

Hotel La Casa Jalisco [GS,SW,WI] 480 Jalisco (at Ignacio Ramierez) **52-612/128-4311**

Hotel Mediterrane [GS,F,NS,WI,GO] Allende 36 (at Malecón) **52-612/125-1195** *sundeck, also bar & restaurant*

BARS

Cafe La Pazta [GS,NH,YC,GO] Allende 36 (at Hotel Mediterrane) **52-612/125-1195** *7am-11pm*

NIGHTCLUBS

Las Varitas [GF,D,E] Calle Independencia 111 (at Malecón) **52-612/123-1590** *9pm-3am, clsd Mon, rock 'n' roll bar*

CRUISY AREAS

Malecón (Seawall) [AYOR] *afternoon & early evening*

León

BARS

G*bar [M,YC] Madero 226 (at Gante, Centro Histórico) **52-477/716-3695** *6pm-2am, café-bar w/ terrace*

NIGHTCLUBS

Bagoas [M,D,PC,$] Mar Báltico 1332, Col. Rinconada del Sur (at Alfredo Valadez) **52-477/771-0236** *Fri-Sat only*

Biza Club [★M,D,S] 20 de Enero 204, Centro (off Calle Pedro Moreno) **52-477/217-8083 & 8084** *11am-3am, clsd Sun, go-go boys Sat*

Bule Club [M,D] Mar Báltico 125 (at Alfredo Valadez) **52-477/761-9228**

La Madame [M,D,DS] Blvd A López Mateos 1709 Oriente (in front of Torre Banamex) **52-477/763-3086** *10pm-3am, clsd Mon-Wed, go-go boys*

Malinalco

ACCOMMODATIONS

Casa Mora B&B Malinalco [GF,SW,WI] Calle de la Cruz 18 (Barrio de Santa Maria) **52-714/147-0572** *full brkfst*

Manzanillo

ACCOMMODATIONS

Las Hadas [GF,SW] Av Vista Hermosa s/n (Fracc. Península de Santiago) **52-314/331-0101, 888/559-4329** *great resort & location*

Mexico's Villa Montaña Adventure Outpost [GF,NS,WC] 46 Los Angeles Locos, La Manzanilla **206/937-3882** *2-bdrm hilltop villa, ocean views, 1/2 hour N of Manzanillo*

Red Tree Melaque Inn [GF,SW,NS,WI,GO] Primaveras (30 miles N of Manzanillo), Melaque-Villa Obregon **52-315/355-8917** *bungalows, near ocean*

BARS

OK [M,D,DS,$] Independencia 42 (Centro) *Th-Sun only, drag shows*

CRUISY AREAS

Santiago Beach [AYOR]

Mazatlán

ACCOMMODATIONS

El Cid Resort [GF,SW] **866/306-6113, 52-669/913-3333** *4-hotel complex on 720 acres*

Hotel Los Sábalos [★GF,SW] Av Playa Gaviotas 100 (Zona Dorada) **52-669/983-5333, 800/528-8760 (US#)** *upscale resort w/ 2 pools, beach, health club, also popular Joe's Oyster Bar*

The Pueblo Bonito Emerald Bay [GF,SW] Ernesto Coppel Compaña **52-669/989-0525, 800/990-8250** *resort on 20 acres, jacuzzi, gym, also piano bar*

Bars

La Alemana [GS] Calle Zaragoza 16 (at Benito Juarez & Serdan) *sports bar*

Pepe Toro [★M,D,DS,S] Av de las Garzas 18 (1 block W of Av Camarón Sábalo, Zona Dorada) **52-669/914-4176** *9:30pm-4am, clsd Mon-Th*

Vitrolas Bar [MW,F,K,DS,S] Heribertos Frías 1608 (in El Centro) **52-669/985-2221** *6pm-2am, clsd Mon, lunch menu, [DS,S] Sun*

Restaurants

Panamá Restaurant Pastelería [GS] at Avs de las Garzas & Camarón Sábalo (Zona Dorada) **52-669/913-6977** *regional & int'l*

Roca Mar [★] Av del Mar (at Calle Isla de Lobos, Zona Costera) **52-669/981-6008** *till 2am, seafood, full bar*

Señor Frogs [D] Av del Mar s/n, Zona Costera (Col. Palo Prietov) **52-669/985-1110** *10am-1am, expensive menu, seafood, full bar*

Men's Clubs

Baños Juan Carlos [AYOR] Calle Genaro Estrada 712 (btwn Benito Juarez & Arquiles Serdan) **52-669/981-7205** *sleazy, busy after 5pm, closes early*

Mérida

Accommodations

Angeles de Mérida [GF,SW,NS] Calle 74-A, #495-A x 57 y 59-A (at Calle 57 & Calle 59) **52-999/923-8163** *restored 18th-c home, full brkfst, spa services available*

Los Arcos B&B [GF,SW,GO] Calle 66 **52-999/928-0214**

Casa Ana B&B [GF,SW,NS] Calle 52 #469 (btwn 51 & 53) **52-999/924-0005** *B&B in colonial home*

Casa San Juan B&B [GS,NS,WC,GO] 545-A Calle 62 (btwn Calle 69 & Calle 71) **52-999/986-2937, 305/394-9551 (US #)**

Casa Santiago B&B [GS,SW,NS,WI,WC,GO] Calle 63 #562 (btwn Calles 70 & 72) **52-999/928-9375** *colonial restored house*

Gran Hotel [GF,F] Calle 60 #496 (nr Parque Cepeda Peraza) **52-999/924-7730 & 923-6963** *historic turn-of-the-century hotel, courtyard w/ balconies, also restaurant*

Las Arecas Guesthouse [GF,GO] Calle 59 #541 (btwn Calle 66 & Calle 68) **52-999/928-3626** *guesthouse, full brkfst*

Posada Santiago Guesthouse [GS,SW,NS,WI,WC,GO] Calle 57 No 552 (between Calle 66 & 68, Centro Historico) **52-999/928-4258**

Villa Azul Rental and Restaurant [GS,SW,NS,W,IGO] Calle 74A # 496 (btwn 59A & 57) **713/208-2482**

Bars

El Establo [★GF,D,F] Calle 60 #482-A (btwn Calle 56 & 58) **52-999/924-2289** *popular w/ tourists & locals*

Nightclubs

Angeluz [M,D] Highways 180 & 261 (btwn Ctra Libramiento and Itzincab Palomeque) *all taxi drivers know where it is located, near Pride Disco*

Kabuki's Jacinto Canek 381

Pancho's Bar Avenida Juarez 33

Pride Disco [M,D,S] **52-999/946-4401** *south of town, all taxi drivers know where it is located*

Scalibur [M,D,S] Calle 4-B X 39-A No. 308 (Cól San Camilo II) **52-999/108-2046** *from 11pm, also wknd T-dance from 2pm, difficult to find but worth the ride*

Restaurants

Cafe La Habana Calle 59 #511-A (at Calle 62) **52-999/928-6502** *24hrs, also bar & café*

Cafe Pop [BW] Calle 57 (btwn Calle 60 & 62) **52-999/928-6163** *cafeteria w/ brkfst, lunch & "light dinner"*

La Bella Época Calle 60 #447 (upstairs in the Hotel del Parque) **52-99/928-1928** *4pm-1am, Yucatécan, try for a balcony table, some veggie*

Villa Maria Hotel & Restaurant Calle 59 No. 553 x 68 **52-999/923-3357**

Men's Clubs

La Banana Azul 514 Calle 70 (btwn 65 & 67, 3 blocks from Parque Santiago) **52-999/923-3957** *steam room, massage, gym*

Hotel Colón Calle 62 #483 (btwn 57 & 59 Centro) **52-999/923-4355, 52-999/923-4508** *upscale steam baths, 3pm-9pm, also hotel*

Cruisy Areas

Calle 60 [AYOR] btw the Zocalo and Santa Lucia park

Santa Lucia Park [AYOR] *late afternoons & evenings*

Zócalo [AYOR] near corner of Calle 60 & 61

Mexicali

Bars

La Linterna [M,NH,OC,AYOR] Blvd Juárez (btwn Calles Azueta & Altamirano) *1pm-1am, hustlers*

El Rey de Copas [MW,NH] Av Baja California (at Av Tuxtla Gutierrez, Pueblo Nuevo) *open till 3am*

El Taurino [★MW,D] Av Juan de Zuazua 480 (near Morelos) *1pm-2am, clsd Mon, cruisy*

Nightclubs

Mirage Disco [★D] Av Lerdo #430 (Zona Centro) *6pm-2am Wed-Sun*

Men's Clubs

Baños San Jose [GS] Av Juan de Zuazua 475 (enter rear) *7am-8pm*

Cruisy Areas

Chapultepec Park [AYOR] *afternoons*

Mexico City

Note: M°=Metro station

Note: Mexico City is divided into "Zonas" (ie, Zona Rosa) & "Colonias" (abbreviated here as "Col."). Remember to use these when giving addresses to taxi drivers.

Info Lines & Services

Cálamo (LGBT AA) Av de Chapultepec 465, desd 202 (Col. Juárez) *8pm Mon-Fri, 7pm Sat, 6pm Sun, LGBT AA group*

Centro Cultural de la Diversidad Sexual Colima 267 (Col. Roma) **52-55/5514-2565, 52-55/1450-9511** *Mexico City's LGBT center, also cafe*

Jovenes La Villa Calle 521 #248 (nr Ave 510) **52-55/2603-7696**

Accommodations

6M9 Guesthouse [MO,SW,WI,GO] Marsella 69 (at Havre) **52-55/5208-8347** *in gay area; jacuzzi, steam room, gym, complimentary brkfst & drinks; "an oasis in Mexico City"*

Best Western Majestic Hotel [GF,WC] Madero 73, Col. Centro **52-55/5521-8600, 800/528-1234** *4-star hotel on the Zócalo Plaza, rooftop restaurant*

Calinda Geneve [GF,SW] Calle Londres 130 (Col. Juárez, Zona Rosa) **52-55/5080-0800, 800/714-6549 (in Mexico)** *3-story colonial-style hotel, Sanborns restaurant, also bar*

Condesa Haus [GF,WI,GO] Cuernavaca 142 (at Campeche) **52-55/5256-2494**

Hostal San Sebastian [GF,GO] Havre 41 (at Av Insurgentes, in Zona Rosa) **52-55/5208-6528**

Hotel Casa Blanca [GF,F,SW] Lafragua 7 (Col. Tabacalera) **52-55/5096-4500, 800/905-2905 (US & Canada #)** *5-star hotel, also restaurant & bar*

Hotel Gillow [GF,F,WI] Isabel la Católica 17 (Col. Centro) **52-55/5518-1440, 52-55/5510-2636**

Hotel Polanco [GF] Edgar Allan Poe 8 (Col. Polanco) **52-55/5280-8082, 800/221-9044**

Marco Polo [GF] Amberes 27, Col. Juárez (Zona Rosa) **52-55/5080-0063, 800/448-8355 (US#)** *small boutique hotel*

NH Mexico City [GF,F,SW] Liverpool 155 (Col. Juárez, Zona Rosa) **52-55/5228-9928** *upscale, 2 restaurants*

W Mexico City [★GF,WI] Campos Eliseos 252 **52-55/9138-1800** *in trendy Polanco, 2 restaurants & bar*

Bars

El Almacen/ El Taller [MO,D,B,L,S,V] Av Florencia 37-A, Zona Rosa (basement, no sign so look for big nuts & bolts above door) **52-55/5207-0727** *5pm-3am, clsd Mon, cruisy leather/ levi crowd, also sex shop, theme parties*

Amsterdam 219 [GS] Amesterdam 219 (in Condesa) **52-55/5564-3034**

Black Out [GS] Amberes 11 (Zona Rosa) *upscale lounge, also restaurant*

Boy Bar [M] Amberes 14 (Zona Rosa) **52-55/5511-3915, 52-55/5207-5591** *10pm-close Th-Sat, fetish party for "hot, hard boys," w/ dance flr, lounge & "hot room"*

Cafeína [GF,D] Nuevo Leon 73 (in Condesa) **52-55/5212-0090** *7pm-4am, 6pm-10pm Sun, co-owned by Diego Luna of Y Tu Mama También fame*

La Cantina del Vaquero [★MO,L,S,V] Calle Algeciras 26, Col. Insurgentes Mixcoac (in Centro Armand) **52-55/5598-2195** *5pm-close, strict leather/ levi dress code (cowboy heaven)*

El Celo [★M,NH,D,F,S,$] Calle Londres 104 (Zona Rosa) **52-55/5514-4766** *5pm-close, clsd Mon*

Enigma [MW,D,S,$] Calle Morelia 111, Col. Roma (4 blocks from M° Niños Héroes, Zona Rosa) **52-55/5207-7367** *9pm-3:30am, 6pm-2am Sun, clsd Mon, go-go boys*

Gayta Freezing Bar [MW,NH,YC] Amberes 18 (Zona Rosa) **52-551/055-5873**

Lipstick [GS,DS,V] Amberes 1 (at Paseo de la Reforma, Zona Rosa) **52-55/5514-4920** *clsd Sun, lounge, more gay Fri-Sat*

New Cine Club [M,D] Colón 1 (Centro) **52-55/2243-1258** *nightly*

Tom's Leather Bar [M,L,S,V,$] Av Insurgentes 357 (Col. Condesa) **55-84/5564-0728** *9pm-4am, clsd Mon*

La Victoria [M,D,E] Coahuila 92 (at Calle Tonalá, Col. Roma) **52-55/5574-1762** *Wed & Sun*

Viena Bar [★M] República de Cuba 3 (Centro Historico) **52-55/5512-0929** *11am-11pm, clsd Mon-Tue, beer bar, packed nightly*

Nightclubs

Anyway/ Exacto/ The Doors [★MW,D,F,DS,S,$] Calle Monterrey 47, Col. Roma (Zona Rosa) **52-55/5533-1691** *9pm-4am, 3 flrs: The Doors, 1st flr, is a mixed restaurant/ bar; Exacto, 2nd flr, is for women; Anyway, 3rd flr, is men's bar w/ drag & strip shows*

Butterflies/ Buttergold [★MW,D,DS,S,$] Calle Izazaga 9 (at Av Lazaro Cárdenas S, Centro Historico) **52-55/5761-1351 & 1861** *9pm-3am, till 4:30am Fri-Sat, clsd Mon, 2 flrs, lavish drag shows Fri-Sat*

Cabaré-Tito Fusion [MW,18+] Londres 77 (Zona Rosa) **52-55/5511-1613** *open 4pm, clsd Mon-Tue, drag shows Th*

Cabaré-Tito Neón [MW,D,DS,S] Calle Londres 161, Local 20-A, Plaza del Angel (Zona Rosa) **52-55/5514-9455** *6pm-close*

Cabaré-Tito VIP [MW,D,DS,S] Calle Londres 104 (Zona Rosa) **52-55/5208-2305** *6pm-close, strippers, women's night Th, [DS] Sun-Mon*

Hibrido [MW,D] Calle Londres 16, Plaza del Angel, 2nd flr (Zona Rosa) **52-55/5511-1197** *Th-Sun*

Liverpool 100 [M,D] Liverpool 100 (Col. Juarez) **52-55/5208-4507** *9pm-close Wed, Fri & Sat only*

Living [★M,D,DS,S] Paseo de la Reforma 483 (Col. Cuauhtemoc) **55-55/5286-0069** *10pm-close Fri-Sat only, theme nights*

Nicho [MO,B] Calle Londres 179 *8pm-3am Th-Sat, 6pm-1am Sun*

Cafes

Coffee Station Londres 167-A (Zona Rosa), Mexico **52-55/5525-2705** *clsd Mon-Tue*

Restaurants

La Antigua Cortesana Chiapas 173-A (Col. Roma) **52-55/5584-4678** *1pm-11pm, till midnight Fri-Sat, till 7pm Sun, popular Mexican cuisine, also bar*

El Cardenal Calle de Palma 23 **52-55/5521-8815** *incredible pastries*

Casa Merlos Victoriano Zepeda 80 (at Obsevatoria) **52-55/5277-4360** *traditional poblano food, definitely try the molé*

Fonda San Ángel Plaza San Jacinto 3, Col. San Angel (across from Bazar San Angel) **52-55/5550-1641 & 1942** *popular after 7pm Fri-Sat, classic Mexican dishes*

Ligaya Nuevo Leon 68 (in Condesa) **52-55/5286-6268** *nouvelle Mexican, dinner nightly, outdoor seating*

La Nueva Opera [P] Calle Cinco de Mayo 10 (Centro Historico) **52-55/5512-8959** *1pm-midnight, clsd Sun, legendary cantina since Pancho Villa fired a bullet into the ceiling*

Open Cafe Florencia 35 (Zona Rosa) **52-55/5525-3298, 52-55/5525-3299**

Punto y Aparte [GS] Amberes 62 (btwn Calles Londres & Liverpool, Zona Rosa) **52-55/5533-5442** *int'l menu*

El Takón Liverpool 164 (at Florencia, Zona Rosa) **52-55/5511-2384** *24hrs, also bar [M,DS,S,V]*

Xel-Ha Parral 78 Bis (in Col. Condesa) **52-55/5553-5968** *traditional cuisine of the Yucatan*

Entertainment & Recreation

Centro Cultural Contempo Calle Londres 161, Local 20-A, Plaza del Angel (Zona Rosa) **52-55/5208-4044, 52-55/5208-4488** *LGBT cultural center, films, entertainment, also cafe*

El Hábito [S] Madrid 13 (Coyocán District) **52-55/5659-1139, 52-55/5554-6414** *avant-garde theater & bar*

Museo de Arte Carrillo Gil Av Revolución 1608 (San Angel) **52-55/5550-6260, 52-55/5550-3983** *10am-6pm, clsd Mon, contemporary art*

Museo de Frida Kahlo Calle Londres 247 (Coyoacán) **52-55/5617-4310** *10am-5:45pm, clsd Mon, original paintings, furniture, letters & Frida's dresses, also garden & café*

Museo Templo Mayor Calle Seminario 8 (at República de Guatemala, enter on plaza, near Cathedral) **52-55/5542-0256** *9am-5pm, clsd Mon, artifacts from the central Aztec temple at Tenochtitlán*

National Museum of Anthropology Paseo de la Reforma (at Calle Gandhi) **52-55/5553-6266** *9am-7pm, clsd Mon*

Bookstores

El Armario Abierto Agustín Melgar 25 (Col. Condesa) **52-55/5286-0895** *Mexico's only bookstore specializing in sexuality, some LGBT titles*

Retail Shops

Roshell [DS,TG] Lorenzo Boturini 440 **52-55/5768-1317** *drag emporium, hair styling, also monthly shows & events*

Publications

Homópolis 52-55/2616-0456, 52-55/2616-0457 *twice-weekly LGBT magazine & guide*

Rola Gay *national monthly LGBT newspaper, see: www.rolaclub.org.mx*

Ser Gay 52-55/1450-9511 *quarterly magazine, covers all Mexico nightlife, limited resources*

Gyms & Health Clubs

Club San Francisco [M] Calle Rio Pánuco 207 (Col. Cuauhtémoc) **52-55/5525-0936**

QI Amsterdam 317 (in Condesa) **52-55/5574-5095** *super-modern, 4-story gym w/ spa*

Men's Clubs

Baños Finisterre [AYOR] Calle A Contreras 11, Col. San Rafael (4 blocks W of M° San Cosme) **52-55/5555-3543** *traditional bathhouse where men go, hang out & get a massage; not "anything goes" like in US or Europe*

Baños San Juan [F,AYOR] Calle López 120 (N of M° Salto de Agua, in Centro Historico) **52-55/5521-3376** *also salon*

Baños Señorial [AYOR] Calle Isabel la Católica 92 (Centro Historico) **52-55/5709-0732, 52-55/5709-3120** *erotic massages available*

La Casita I [V,YC,PC,AYOR] Viaducto Miguel Alemán 72, Col. Algarín (near Bolivar—no sign/ number on door) **52-55/5519-8842** *24hrs, gym equipment, porn shop, ages 18-35 only*

La Casita II [V,YC,PC,AYOR] Insurgentes S 228 (Col. Roma) **52-55/5514-4639, 52-55/5514-4591** *24hrs, gym equipment, bar, porn shop, ages 18-35 only*

Fuck [S,$] Paseo de la Reforma 169 (Col. Cuauhtémoc) **52-55/5566-7342, 52-55/5559-7718** *24hrs, name says it all*

So Do Me Mariano Escobedo 716 (Col Anzures) **52-55/5250-6653**

Cruisy Areas

Alameda Central [AYOR] W side of park (Centro Historico) *afternoons & early evenings, dangerous later*

Bosque de Chapultepec [AYOR] either side of gate to monument (Zona Rosa) *afternoons*

Zona Rosa [AYOR] *nights, anywhere & everywhere, but especially Calle Florencia btwn Reforma & Liverpool, also Calles Génova, Hamburgo & Londres*

Monterrey

Accommodations

Holiday Inn Monterrey Centro [GF,SW] Av Padre Mier 194 N (at Garibaldi, Centro) **52-81/8228-6000** *also restaurant, near Zona Rosa*

Bars

Akbal [M,V] Abasolo 870B, 2nd Flr, Casa del Maíz **52-81/1257-2986** *9pm-2am, clsd Mon, trendy lounge*

Casa de Lola [M,D,K] Padre Mier 867 (btwn Porfirio Diaz & Vallarta) **52-81/8343-6210** *Th-Sat only*

Nightclubs

Parking [M,D] Allende 120 Ote (btwn Juarez & Guerrero) **52-81/8343-2624** *10pm-close Wed-Sat*

Taboo [MW,D,S,V] Ocampo 433 Puente (btwn Rayon & Aldama Centro) **52-81/8040-9458** *9pm-close, clsd Mon-Tue*

Venneno Club [MW,D,DS,S] Av de los Héroes 47 (at Av Francisco I Madero) *9pm-close, clsd Mon-Tue*

Men's Clubs

Baños Oasis [V] Democracia 413 (btwn Calle Jiménez & Calle Alfonso Reyes, Col. Sarabia) **52-81/8374-7645** *8am-10pm, steam baths, hustlers*

Baños Orientales Calle Hidalgo 310 Oriente, Guadalupe **52-81/8367-2843** *8am-10pm, till 3pm Sun, sauna, steam bath, hustlers, in SE Monterrey*

Cruisy Areas

Avenida Juárez [AYOR] btwn Calle Matamoros & Calle Padre Mier (Centro) *part of "El Circuito," hustlers*

Plaza Hidalgo [AYOR] Zona Rosa *late afternoons & early evenings*

Morelia

Bars

Amnesia Happy Bar [MW,NH] Gertrudis Bocanegra 905 (at Lázaro Cárdenas) **52-443/312-1578** *5pm-2am, clsd Sun, lounge w/ DJ*

NIGHTCLUBS

Con la Rojas [M,D,$] Aldama 343 (Centro) **52-443/312-1578** *9pm-3am,*

RESTAURANTS

La Capilla Ignacio Zaragoza 90 (at Posada de la Soledad Hotel) **52-443/312-1888, 800/716-0189** *in charming old hotel in converted convent*

Fonda Las Mercedes [★] Calle Leon Guzmán 47 **52-443/312-6113 & 313-3222** *inside beautiful colonial home*

Sanborns Campestre 376 **52-443/315-8306** *popular w/ gay men evenings*

MEN'S CLUBS

Baños Mintzicuri Calle Vasco de Quiroga 227 (enter through the Hotel Mintzicuri) **52-443/312-0664** *gay area through door marked "Ruso General"*

Oaxaca

ACCOMMODATIONS

El Camino Real Oaxaca [★GF,F,SW] Calle 5 de Mayo 300 **52-951/501-6100, 800/722-6466 (US reservations)** *5-star hotel in restored 16th-c convent, frescoes & courtyards abound*

Casa Adobe B&B [GS,WI,GO] Independencia 11, Tlalixtac de Cabrera **52-951/517-7268** *full brkfst, 15 minutes from center of Oaxaca*

La Casa de Don Pablo Hostel [GS,NS] Melchor Ocampo 412, Centro (at Rayon St) **52-951/516-8384** *hot tub, full brkfst*

La Casa de Mis Recuerdos [GF,NS] Pino Suárez 508 **52-951/515-5645** *full brkfst*

Casa Machaya B&B [GF] Sierra Nevada 164, Col. Loma Linda **52/951-1328203** *private level w/ patio & valley views*

Casa Sagrada [GS,NS,WC] Teotitlan del Valle **310/455-6085** *30 minutes from Oaxaca, full brkfst*

Hotel Villa Belmar [GF] Calle del Morro Sn, Puerto Escondido **52/954-5820244, 866/751-1440**

Mision de los Angeles Hotel [GF,F,SW] Calzada Porfirio Díaz 102 **52-951/515-1500 or 515-1000, 800/221-6509 (US#) or 800/446-2922** *resort w/ bungalows, restaurant & dance club, tennis courts*

BARS

La Chinampa [GS,NH] Bustamente 605 *11am-1am, friendly dive*

NIGHTCLUBS

Club Privado 502 (aka El Número) [GS,D,K,PC,$] Calle Porfirio Díaz 502 (Centro, ring to enter) *10pm-close, clsd Sun-Tue, tourists welcome w/ proper ID*

La Costa [M,D,S] Av 16 de Septiembre #517 (Col. Cinco Señores) **52-951/511-2908** *wknds only 9pm-close*

Gavana Dance Club [GS] Calzada Porfirio Diaz #216 (Col. Reforma) *9pm-close Th-Sat*

RESTAURANTS

El Asador Vasco [★] Portal de Flores 10-A (Centro) **52-951/514-4755** *great views & authentic Oaxacan cuisine (can you say ¡molé!)*

CRUISY AREAS

Parque Alemeda & Zócalo [AYOR] *early evenings*

Pátzcuaro

RESTAURANTS

Cha Cha Cha [GO] Buenavista 7 (at Jardines de la Basilica) **434/342-1627** *8:30am-9:30pm, clsd Wed*

Playa del Carmen

see also Cancún & Cozumel

ACCOMMODATIONS

Acanto Hotel & Suites [GF,SW,NS,WI] 16th St (btwn 5th Ave & the beach) **631/882-1986**

Aventura Mexicana Resort [GF,SW,N] Av 10 (at Calle 22) **52-984/873-1876** *jacuzzi, 15 minutes to gay nude beach, also restaurant & bar*

Pension San Juan [GF,NS] Sta Av 165 (btwn Calles 6 & 8 Norte) **52-984/873-0647**

Nightclubs

Playa 69 [M,D,GO] Av 5-A (btwn Calle 4 & Calle 6, ground flr) *wknds 9pm-4am, cruisy, int'l crowd*

Restaurants

100% Natural Av 5 (btwn 10th & 12th) **52-984/73-2242** *vegetarian*

Retail Shops

Jocks in Playa Avenida 15, enter Calle 2 & 4 (near 5th Ave) **984/140-6201** *mention Damron & receive 10% off your total purchases*

Puebla

Bars

La Cigarra [★M,S,V] Ave 5 Poniente 538 (at Calle 7, Centro) *6pm-3am, beer bar*

Franco's Bule Bar [E,DS,S] 5 Oriente 402 (Los Sapos) **52-222/232-3409** *11am-close, also cafe*

Nightclubs

Garotos [GF,D,$] 22 Orient E 602 (close to Blvd 5 de Mayo, Xenenetla) **52-222/242-4232** *9pm-3am Fri-Sat only*

Men's Clubs

Baños Las Termas [MO,V,PC] Av 5 de Mayo 2810, Centro **52-222/232-9562** *clsd Mon, 3 flrs, gym, sauna, "100% gay"*

Cruisy Areas

Zócalo/ Main Park [AYOR] at cathedral *late evenings*

Puerto Vallarta

Info Lines & Services

Discovery Vallarta **52-322/222-6918** *gay accommodations reservation service*

Accommodations

Abbey Hotel [MO,SW] Pulpito 138 (at Olas Altas) **52-322/222-4488** *full brkfst, also restaurant & lounge*

Apartmentos Esperanza [GS,WI,NS,GO] **206/632-2183** *furnished apt*

Arco Iris [M,SW,NS,WI,GO] 120 Paseo de los Delfines (at Conchas Chinas) **310/943-6366 (US#), 52-322/221-5527** *full brkfst*

Blue Seas [MW,SW] Malecon 1 Esq Abedul Col Emiliano Zapata **877/583-2583 (from US & Canada), 52-322/226-8152 (in Mexico)** *all suites*

Brisas de Mita [M,SW,NS,WI,GO] **52-329/298-4114** *all-inclusive oceanfront villa-style boutique hotel on beach, 45 minutes N of Puerto Vallarta, restaurant*

Bugambilia Blanca Condos [GS,GO] Carretera Barra de Navidad 602, Col. Emiliano Zapata (Off Hwy 200) **52-322/222-1152** *4 levels, suites, 2- & 3-bdrm apts, full brkfst, 6-minute walk to gay beach*

Casa Boana Torre Malibu [★GS,F,SW] Calle Amapas 325 **52-322/222-0999, 52-322/222-6695** *condo-hotel w/ bay views, poolside bar, near gay beach*

Casa Cúpula [★MW,SW,NS,WI,WC,GO] Callejon de la Igualdad 129, Col. Amapas **52-322/223-2484, 866/352-2511**

Casa de los Arcos [GS,SW] **52-322/222-5990, 212/561-5795 (US#)** *3-suite private villa, sleeps 8, terrace w/ amazing view of Bandera Bay*

Casa dos Comales [GF,SW,GO] Calle Aldama 274 **52-322/223-2042, 888/881-1822 (US#)** *guesthouse & apts, near Old Town*

Casa Fantasía [GS,SW,NS,WC,GO] Pino Suarez 203, Col. Emiliano Zapata (near the Rio Cuale) **52-322/223-2444** *B&B made up of 3 haciendas, terrace*

Casa Tranquila [GS,WI,GO] Morelos #7-A, Bucerias, Nayarit **52-329/298-1767** *apts w/ kitchens, near beach, massage, lesbian-owned*

Casa Tres Vidas [GS,SW] **888/640-8100 (US#), 801/263-9500** *3 luxury beachfront villas, hot tub*

Los Cuatro Vientos [GF,SW,WI] Matamoros 520 **52-322/222-0161** *hotel that's home to popular El Nido rooftop bar & Chez Elena restaurant*

▶ **Hotel Mercurio** [★MW,SW,WI,GO] **52-322/222-4793, 866/388-2689 (from US only)** *gay/ lesbian hotel in Vallarta's Gayborhood, 1 1/2 blocks from beach*

Hotelito Desconocido [GS,SW] Playon de Mismaloya, La Cruz de Loreto, Tomatlán **52-322/281-4010, 800/851-1143** *eco-resort on the beach, 60 miles S of Puerto Vallarta, sauna*

Mar Sereno [GF] Carretera a Barra de Navidad Km 15 **52-322/228-0879, 52-322/228-0285**

Quinta Maria Cortez [GS,SW] Calle Sagitario 132, Playa Conchas Chinas **888/640-8100 (US#)** *"Mexaterranian Villa" w/ sunny terraces & spectacular ocean views*

The San Franciscan Resort & Gym [GS,SW,WI] Calle Pilitas #213 (at Playa Los Muertos) **52-322/222-6473 x0**

Vallarta Cora [MO,SW,N,GO] Calle Pilitas 174, Col. Emiliano Zapata **52-322/223-2815 or 222-6234** *basic apts, often sexually charged atmosphere*

Vallarta Escapes [GS] Carratera a Barra Navidad 479 (at Col Alta Vista) **52-322/223-2745** *rents some of the finest properties in the Puerto Vallarta area*

Villa Amapas [M,GO] **52-322/205-3907** *luxury beachfront villa w/ heated pool & outdoor bar*

Villa del Cielo [GS,SW,GO] Paseo de los Delfines 121 (at Residencial Conchas Chinas) **206/285-3503 (US#)** *private villa on Conchas Chinas hillside, maid & houseman*

Villa Safari Condo [GS,SW,NS,GO] Francisca Rodriguez 203 **269/469-0468 (US #)** *hillside 2-bdrm condo, 2 blocks from Los Muertos Beach*

Villa Viva Vallarta [M,SW] Villas Altas Garza Blanca #210 Km 7, Carr. a Barra de Navidad (Zona Hotelera) **702/474-0963, 702/474-0264** *jacuzzi, near beach*

Villas David B&B [MO,SW,NS,WI,GO] Calle Galeana 348 (at Calle Miramar) **877/832-3315 (US#), 52-322/223-0315** *rooftop jacuzzi & pool, nude sunbathing & swimming*

Yelapa Casa/ Casa Perico [GS,GO] 51 El Camino Huachanango, Yelapa **888/213-7733** *full brkfst*

Bars

Los Amigos Bar [MW,NH] Calle Venustiano Carranza 237 (upstairs, next to Paco's Ranch) **52-322/222-7802** *6pm-4am, Mexican cantina, patio*

Apaches [GS,F,GO] Olas Altas 439 (at Rodriguez) **52-322/222-4004** *5pm-2am, till 1am Sun-Mon, classy cocktail bar, martinis & margaritas, tapas*

Blue Sunset Rooftop Bar [M,F,K,DS] Los Muertos Beach (at Blue Chairs Resort) *10am-midnight*

El Corralon [★M,F] Calle Pilitas 174 (at Vallarta Cora hotel) **52-322/222-6234** *3pm-11pm, pool-side bar, rumored to get quite wild*

Divas [MW,NH] 388 Francisco Madero (at South Side) **52-322/222-7774** *2pm-2am*

Encuentros [MW,F] Lazaro Cardenas 312 **52-322/222-0643** *6pm-2am, great pizza*

Frida [GS,F,GO] 301-A Insurgentes **52-322/222-3668** *1pm-2am, from 7pm Mon-Tue, Mexican cantina, more gay later in evening*

Garbo [★M,E,P,GO,18+] Pulpito 142 (at Olas Altas) **52-322/223-5753** *6pm-2am, upscale martini lounge, live jazz Fri-Sat*

Kit Kat Bar [★MW,F,DS,GO] Pulpito 120 (next door to Chiles restaurant) **52-322/223-0093** *5pm-1:30am, swanky New York-style cocktail lounge, drag shows some nights, also restaurant, pricey but fun*

La Noche [MW] Lázaro Cárdenas 257 (Zona Romantica) **52-322/222-3364** *7pm-2am, cocktail lounge*

Sama [MW,NH,18+] Olas Altas 510 (at Rodolfo Gomez) **52-322/306-1058** *5pm-2am, small martini bar w/ sidewalk seating*

Vanilla & Kinky [GS] 200 Basilio Badillo, upstairs **52-322/223-1797** *5pm-2am*

Nightclubs

Antropology [M,DS,S,YC,$] Calle Morelos 101, Plaza Río (at Rodriguez) **52-322/222-6392** *9pm-4am*

Los Balcones [★M,D,S,$] Calle Juárez 182, 2nd flr (at Calle Libertad) **52-322/222-0261** *10pm-4am, T-dance 6pm-11pm Sun, popular strippers late night*

Cheeky Monkey [GF] Dia Ordaz 556 (at Corona) **52-322/222-9040** *noon-2am*

Club Manana [★MW,D,DS,S,SW] Venustiano Carranza #290 (at Col Emiliano Zapata) **52-322/222-7779, 323/230-9876 (US)** *10pm-6am, till 8am Fri-Sun, clsd Mon*

Paco's Ranch [★M,D,P,GO,$] Calle Ignacio Vallarta 278 (at Carranza) **52-322/222-7667** *1pm-6am, cantina on 2nd flr, disco downstairs from 10pm, also rooftop terrace w/ live piano*

Ranch [★M,D,S,V,GO,$] Calle Venustiana Carranza 239 (walk thru Club Paco Paco to back of dance flr) **52-322/223-0537** *10pm-6am, clsd Mon-Tue, packed for nightly strip shows, also upstairs bar*

Stereo [MW,D] Lazaro Cardenas 267 (Emiliano Zapata Centro) **52-322/1114-243, 52-322/1238-030** *9pm-4am, small hip dance bar*

Cafes

A Page in the Sun [★] Olas Altas 299 **52-322/222-3608** *8am-11pm, coffee shop & English bookstore*

Cafe San Angel Olas Altas 449 **52-322/223-1273** *7am-1am, sidewalk café, also crêpes, smoothies, salads & sandwiches*

Choco Banana Calle Amapas 147 (at Calle Pulpito) **52-322/222-2114** *8am-10pm, clsd Sun, coffee, smoothies, shakes—& chocolate-covered bananas!*

The Coffee Cup [GO] Rodolfo Gómez 146-A (at Olas Altas) **52-322/222-8584** *7am-10pm, clsd Sun in summer*

CyberSmoothie [★] Rodolfo Gómez 111 **52-322/223-4784** *9am-9:30pm, internet cafe w/ smoothies, coffee, salads & sandwiches; owner is also certified massage therapist*

Dee's Coffee Company [WIFI] Rodolfo Gomez 120 (in Zona Romantica) **52-322/222-1197** *7am-10pm, homemade pastries*

Este Cafe [★GO] Libertad 336, Centro (around corner from flea market) **52-322/222-4261** *8am-10pm, clsd Sun, espresso & juice bar, desserts, ice cream*

Uncommon Grounds Buddha Lounge [F] Lazaro Cardenas 625 **52-322/223-3834** *5pm-close, clsd Mon-Tue, also aromatherapy & gifts*

Restaurants

El Arrayan [GO] Allende #344 (at El Centro) **52-322/222-7195** *6pm-11pm, clsd Tue*

Banana Cantina Calle Amapas 147 (at Calle Pulpito) **52-322/222-2114** *4pm-11pm, clsd Mon, Mexican*

Bianco [★E] Insurgentes 109 (Col. Emiliano Zapata) **52-322/222-2177** *6pm-11pm, bar till 2am, clsd Mon, chic restaurant & lounge, live jazz certain nights*

Blue Shrimp Morelos #779 (Col. Centro) **52-322/222-2280, 52-322/222-4246** *11am-midnight, seafood*

El Brujo [★] Venustiano Carranza 510 (at Naranjo) *1pm-9:30pm, clsd Mon, Mexican/ seafood, expect a wait*

Cafe Bohemio [★MW,GO] Rodolfo Gómez 127 (at Olas Altas) **52-322/134-2436** *5pm-2am, clsd Sun, open-air café, grilled food, late-evening happy hour*

Cafe de Olla [★] Calle Basilio Badillo 168 **52-322/223-1626** *10am-11pm, clsd Tue, Mexican, wait list an hour*

Cafe des Artistes [★R] Calle Guadalupe Sánchez 740 (at Leona Vicario) **52-322/222-3228** *6pm-11:30pm, upscale French w/ a Mexican twist*

Chez Elena [GO] Matamoros 520, Centro (at Los Quatros Vientos) **52-322/222-0161** *6pm-11pm, seasonal, garden restaurant, Mexican/ int'l, also rooftop bar*

Cilantros Abasolo 169 (at Morelos) **52-322/222-7147** *5:30pm-1am, clsd Sun, Mexican/fusion, rooftop deck, also bar*

Daiquiri Dick's [★] Olas Altas 314 (on Playa Los Muertos) **52-322/222-0566** *8:30am-1:30pm & 5:30pm-11pm, closed Tue & clsd Sept, Cal-Mex*

De Santos [D] 771 Morelos **52-322/223-3052** *5pm-4am, chic Mediterranean, also dance club*

Le Bistro Jazz Cafe [★GO] Isla Rio Cuale 16-A (on the island, at the East Bridge) **52-322/222-0283** *9am-midnight, clsd Sun, PV's classiest*

Mama Dolores Diner Olas Altas 534-B (Col. Emiliano Zapata) **52-322/223-5897** *4pm-11pm, clsd Mon, homestyle American & Mexican, daily happy hour*

Memo's Casa de los Hotcakes [★] Calle Basilio Badillo 289 **52-322/222-6272** *8am-2pm, long lines for cheap & good brkfst, indoor patio, cooking classes*

Mesa 61 Ignacio L Vallarta 264 **52-322/223-2175** *brkfst served, popular lounge upstairs*

Mezzogiorno Ristorante Italiano Avenida del Pacifico 33, North Beach Bucerias, Puerto Vallarta **52-329/298-0350** *6pm-11pm (clsd Mon off season)*

La Palapa Pulpito 103, Col Emiliano Zapata **52-322/222-5225** *brkfst, lunch & dinner, beachside dining*

La Piazzetta Rodolfo Gomez #143 (at Olas Atlas, Romantic Zone) **52-322/222-0650** *4pm-11pm*

Planeta Vegetariano Iturbide 270 (Centro) **52-322/222-3073** *8am-10pm, clsd Sun, buffet-style*

Red Cabbage [GO] Calle Rivera del Rio 204-A (at Basilio Badillo)
52-322/223-0411 *5pm-11pm, clsd Sun (Apr-Oct), Mexican, on Rio Cuale w/ great kitschy decor*

Trio [★] Guerrero 264
52-322/222-2196 *6pm-midnight, clsd Sun, Mediterranean/ Mexican, patio, live music*

Entertainment & Recreation

Boana Tours Calle Amapas 325 (at Casa Boana Torre Malibu)
52-322/222-0999, 52-322/222-6695 *horseback tours daily*

Diana's Cruise the Bay Tour [MW,F] meet at Los Muertos pier
52-322/222-1510 *9:30am-5pm Th, cruise on 33-ft trimaran, limited to 20 people, food served, open bar*

Ocean Friendly [GF] Paseo del Marlin 510-103, Col. Aralias
52-322/225-3774, 044-322/294-0385 (cell) *whale watching tours, Dec 15-March 31*

Playa Los Muertos/ Playa del Sol [★] S of Rio Cuale *the gay beach, now spans "Blue Chairs" & "Green Chairs"*

Rainbow Dancer [M,F,GO] Francia #487
52-322/299-0936 *gay yacht trips on Banderas Bay*

Retail Shops

Best Rodolfo Gómez 111 (at Hotel San Marino) **52-322/222-5128** *10am-8pm, men's beachwear & underwear*

Liquid Men [GO] Ignacio Vallarta 245
52-322/223-3165 *10am-10pm, men's clothes & accessories, also tickets to gay events like Latin Fever*

Publications

Revista Estilo Libre
52-33/1410-3806 *LGBT lifestyle magazine*

Urbana Revista 52-333/844-6471 *gay lifestyle magazine w/ bars & clubs for Guadalajara & Puerto Vallarta*

Gyms & Health Clubs

Acqua Day Spa & Gym Calle Constitución 450 **52-322/223-5270** *7am-9pm, till 5pm Sat, clsd Sun, spa w/ massage, pedicures & manicures, steam room & sauna, also small gym*

Gold's Gym Calle Pablo Picasso s/n (Zona Hotelera Las Glorias)
52-322/225-6671 *6am-10pm, 7am-7pm Sat, 9am-3pm Sun, full gym w/ classes, sauna, jacuzzi*

Men's Clubs

Plasma Labyrinth [MO] Pino Suárez 235 (Zona Romantica)
52-322/134-5415 *7pm-2am, dance club/ sex club*

Erotica

Condom House Lazaro Cardenas 239
52-322/126-7722 *noon-9pm, clsd Sun*

Cruisy Areas

Malecón (Seawall) [AYOR] facing Calle Morelos (esp near benches across from Presidencia Municipal at Iturbide) *evenings*

Playa Los Muertos [AYOR] near green chairs at The Beach Café & further S by the rocks *afternoons*

Plaza Caracol Mall [AYOR]

Querétaro

Cruisy Areas

Alameda Parque [AYOR]

El Jardín Guerrero [AYOR] 3 blks from Centro Historico

Plaza de Armas [AYOR]

Zócalo/ Obregón Plaza [AYOR]

Rosarito Beach

Accommodations

Rosarito Beach Hotel [GF,SW] Blvd Benito Juárez 31 **52-661/612-0144 or 1111, 866/ROSARITO (reservations)** *restaurant & full-service spa*

RosaritoRental.com [GF,SW,WI,GO] La Paloma Beach & Tennis Club
760/318-9672 (US#) *condo rentals, private beach*

San Jose del Cabo

ACCOMMODATIONS

El Encanto Inn [GF] 133 Calle Morelos **210/858-6649, 52-614/142-0388**

RESTAURANTS

Voila Bistro & Catering [★] Plaza Paulina (Calle Comonfort & Morelos) **52-624/130-7569** *noon-10pm, from 4pm Sun, Mexican w/ French twist, full bar, patio*

San Miguel de Allende

ACCOMMODATIONS

Casa de Sierra Nevada [GF,SW] Calle Hospicio 42 (Centro) **52-415/152-7040** *suites w/ fireplaces, horseback riding, also spa*

Casa Schuck Boutique B&B [GF,SW] Garita 3, Centro **52-415/152-0657, 937/684-4092 (US#)** *boutique hotel, private gardens & rooftop deck*

Dos Casas [GF] Calle Quebrada 101 (Guanajuato) **52-415/154-4073** *full brkfst*

Las Terrazas San Miguel [GS,NS,WI,GO] Santo Domingo 3 **52-415/152-5028, 707/534-1833 (US#)** *4 rental homes*

Santiago de Querétaro

ACCOMMODATIONS

Casa Santiago Queretaro [GF,NS,WI,GO] 20 de Noviembre #22 (Centro Historico) **52-442/212-6352** *renovated house in historic center of colonial city, rms available for holiday rental by week or month*

Sayulita

ACCOMMODATIONS

Casa Brava Sayulita [GS,SW,WI,GO] Calle del Cielo **530/432-2211, 415/692-0075** *2-bdrm/ 2-bath house*

Tijuana

BARS

DF [M,NH,OC] Plaza Santa Cecilia 1910 (near Calle 3) *open late*

Noa Noa [★MW,D,DS,YC] Av D 150/ Miguel F Martínez (at Calle 1) *5pm-3am, till 4am Fri, till 5am Sat, drag shows*

El Ranchero Bar [★M,NH,D,F,AYOR] Plaza Santa Cecilia 769 (btwn Calles 1, 2, Revolución & Constitución) *1pm-late, cruisy cantina, hustlers, use caution in bathrooms*

El Taurino Bar [M,NH,S] Av Niños Héroes 189 (at Calles 1 & Constitución) **52-664/685-2478** *3pm-2am, till 5am Fri-Sat, cruisy, hustlers, locals*

Villa Garcia [M,D] Plaza Santa Cecilia 751 (next to El Ranchero) *10am-late, small dance flr, cruisy*

NIGHTCLUBS

Los Equipales [★MW,D,DS,YC] Calle 7/ Galeana #8236 (at Av Revolución, opposite Jai Alai Palace) **52-664/688-3006** *9pm-3am, clsd Mon-Tue*

Extasis [★M,D,S,$] Larroque 213 (in Plaza Viva Tijuana, next to the border) **52-664/682-8339** *8pm-late, clsd Mon-Wed, go-go boys, more women Th*

Mike's Disco [★MW,D,DS,V,18+] Av Revolución 1220 (at Calle 6A) **52-664/685-3534** *8pm-5am, till 3am Th, clsd Wed*

Planet G [MW,V] Av Revolución 13238 (btwn 9 & 10 Sts) *video bar & art gallery*

Terraza [MW,D,DS,S,$] Calle 6/ Flores Magón #8150 (at Av Revolución) **52-664/685-3534** *5pm-2am, till 5am Fri-Sat, clsd Mon*

MEN'S CLUBS

Baños Enva Av Primero (nr Av Revolucion) *7am-9pm, mostly straight, covert*

Tulúm

Accommodations

Posada Luna del Sur [GF] Calle Luna Sur 5 **52-984/871-2984**

Veracruz

Accommodations

Casa de la Luz Tropical Guest House [GF] Tlacotalpan **52-288/884-2331** *charming studio apt,*

Hotel Villa del Mar [GF,SW] Blvd Miguel Ávila Camacho 2707, Col. Zaragoza (across street from Playa del Mar beach) **52-229/989-6500 & 6501, 800/322-1212** *hotel w/ separate motel & bungalows, near aquarium, moderate price*

Entertainment & Recreation

San Juan de Ulua Fortress *9am-4:30pm, clsd Mon, impressive early colonial-era floating fortress*

Veracruz Aquarium Blvd Avila (at Xicolencat) **52-229/932-7984** *10am-7pm, one of the largest & best in the world; don't miss it!*

Men's Clubs

Baños El Edén [AYOR] Av Hidalgo 1113, Centro (btwn Calles Juan Soto & Hernán Cortés) **52-229/932-4400** *buy tickets at rear counter of music store*

Cruisy Areas

Plaza de Armas/ Zócalo [AYOR]

Waterfront & Av República [AYOR]

Villahermosa

Accommodations

Hyatt Regency Villahermosa [GF] Av Juarez 106, Col. Lindavista (across from Tomas Garrido Park) **52-993/310-1234, 800/233-1234 (US#)**

Zacatecas

Accommodations

Quinta Real Zacatecas [GF] Av Ignacio Rayón 434 (Col. Centro) **52-492/922-9104 to 07, 866/621-9288 (US#)** *full-service, 5-star hotel built into grandstand of bull-fighting ring*

Cafes

Café Nevería Acrópolis Av Hidalgo (near cathedral) *Greek/ Mexican, even ice cream (!)*

Cruisy Areas

Av Juárez [AYOR] E from Av Hidalgo for 2 blks

Zihuatanejo

Accommodations

Casa Bulmaro [GS,WI,WC,GO] Calle Adelita **52-755/112-1295**

Hotel Las Palmas [GF,SW] Calle de Aeropuerto (at lot 5) **52-755/557-0634 (cell)** *full brkfst*

Nightclubs

Tequila Town [★GF,K,V] Cuauhtehoc 3 (off Malecon) **52-755/553-8587** *8pm-4am, more gay after 11pm*

Wilde's [MW,D,DS,S] Calle La Laja s/n (Col. Vicente Guerrero) **52-755/557-1042** *8pm-4am, [DS,S] Fri-Sun*

Central America

COSTA RICA

Alajuela

see San José

Arenal

ENTERTAINMENT & RECREATION

The Arenal Volcano *hourly eruptions*

Cocles

ACCOMMODATIONS

Casa Colibri [GF,GO] **207/725-4389** *rental house*

Casa Mariposa [GF,GO] **207/725-4389** *rental house*

Escaleras

ACCOMMODATIONS

Paradise Costa Rica [GS,SW,NS,GO] **800/708-4552** *vacation villas*

Guanacaste

ACCOMMODATIONS

Villa Decary [GF,GO] Nuevo Arenal, 5717 Tilaran **506-2/383-3012, 506-2/694-4330** *former coffee farm on 7 acres overlooking Lake Arenal*

Manuel Antonio, Quepos

ACCOMMODATIONS

Amigo Tico [GS,SW] **506-2/777-2812** *2- & 3-bdrm villas in jungle setting*

Casa Antonio [MW,GO] Enter at Arboleda Hotel **506-2/777-5174**

Casa Bumerango [GS,WC,GO] **213/330-0231**

Casa de Frutas [GS,GO] **506-2/825-3257 (cell), 800/936-9622** *luxury villa in Tulemar Gardens*

Casa Mono Congo [GS,SW,NS,WI,WC,GO] Manuel Antonio Nat'l Park Rd **773/472-7127** *vacation home, w/ excellent ocean view & monkey visits*

Casa Romano [GS,SW,WI,WC,GO] **404/290-6919** *near gay beach*

Casitas Eclipse [GS] KM 5 Manuel Antonio Rd **506-2/777-0408** *detached casitas*

Costa Verde [GS,SW,GO] **506-2/777-0584, 866/854-7958 (from US & Canada)**

Gaia Hotel & Reserve [GF,SW,WI,GO] km 2.7 Carretera Quepos a Manuel Antonio **506-2/777-9797, 800/226-2515** *boutique hotel, surrounded by wildlife refuge, full brkfst*

Géminis del Pacifico [GF,SW,NS,WI,GO] in the hills **506-2/777-5029** *luxurious vacation home, near beaches & bars*

Hotel Casa Blanca [MW,SW,WC,GO] **506-2/777-0253, 506-2/777-1790** *short hike to gay beach*

Hotel Del Mar [GS,WC,GO] 200 meters antes Playa Espadilla, apdo 6350-31 **506-2/777-0543** *near beach & Manuel Antonio Nat'l Park*

Hotel Parador [GF,SW,WI] **506-2/777-1414, 877/506-1414** *large luxury resort w/ mini golf course, health club, private helicopter pad (!), also gourmet restaurant*

Hotel Vela Bar [GF,F] 1st Beach (at Vela Bar Hotel) **506-2/777-0413** *apts surrounded by tropical garden, also bar & restaurant*

Hotel Villa Roca [M,SW,NS,WC,GO] **506-2/777-1349** *great ocean views*

Las Aguas Resort [M,SW,WI,GO] **813/784-7930 (US#), 305/760-4615** *mtn-resort in Costa Rican jungle, full brkfst, hot tub*

Makanda by the Sea [GF,SW] **506-2/777-0442, 888/625-2632** *private oasis, also restaurant*

La Mansion Inn [GS,F,SW,GO] **506-2/777-3489, 800/360-2071** *hot tub, ocean views, bar*

El Parque [GF,F,SW] **506-2/777-0096** *hillside condos w/ ocean views, waterfall pool, restaurant, spa*

La Posada [GF,SW,GO] **506-2/777-1446** *near beach*

Si Como No [★GF,SW,WC] **506-2/777-0777, 800/282-0488 x300** *30-acre wildlife refuge w/ butterfly garden across from hotel, also spa*

Villas Nicolas [GF,WC] **506-2/777-0481** *oceanview suites*

Bars

Tutu/ Gato Negro [★GS] KM 5 Manuel Antonio Rd (at Casitas Eclipse) **506-2/777-0408**

Restaurants

El Barba Roja [★] Carretera al Parque Nacional **506-2/777-0331** *7am-10pm, from 4pm Mon, American, great sunset location*

El Gran Escape & Fish Head Bar Quepos Centro **506-2/777-0395** *brkfst, lunch, dinner, clsd Tue, seafood, full bar*

La Hacienda Restaurante [E] Plaza Yara **506-2/777-3473** *5pm-11pm, clsd Sun*

The Plinio at the Hotel Plinio **506-2/777-0055** *int'l, full bar, Asian*

Rico Tico [★E] paved road to national park (in Hotel Si Como No) *lunch & dinner, Tex/ Mex, includes use of pool bar*

Entertainment & Recreation

La Playita N end of Playa Espadilla (w/ a steep hike over rocks) *the gay beach (impassable 2 hours before & after high tide)*

Osa Peninsula

Accommodations

Tierra De La Paz [MW,SW,NS,GO] Puerto Jimenez **212/981-9393** *yoga spa like retreat*

Playa Jaco

Accommodations

Hotel Poseidon [GF,SW,WI] Calle del Bohio (30 meters W of Jaco Centro) **506-2/643-1642, 888/643-1242** *also bar & restaurant, 50 meters to beach*

Playa Sámara

Accommodations

Casitas LazDívaz [GF,WI,WC,GO] 300 meters W of matapalo tree, entrance to beach, Playa Sámara, Guanacaste **506/2656-0295** *B&B, full brkfst, lesbian-owned*

Puerto Viejo de Limon

Accommodations

Banana Azul [M,WI,GO] 200 meters N of Perla Negra Hotel **506-2/750-2035, 506-2/351-4582 (cell)** *full brkfst*

Puntarenas

Cruisy Areas

Beach [AYOR]

Calle el Paseo de los Turistas [AYOR]

San José

Accommodations

Bohemian Paradise Hotel [M,GO] Calle 3 (btwn Avs 4 & 6, 125 meters S of the Teatro Nat'l) **506-2/258-9683** *hot tub, close to gay clubs*

Colours Oasis Resort [M,F,E,SW,GO] El Triangulo Noroeste, Blvd Rohrmoser (200 meters before end of blvd) **506-2/296-1880, 866/517-4390** *full brkfst*

Hotel Amon Plaza [GF,F,WI] Av 11 & Calle 3 bis **506-2/523-4600** *modern hotel, quiet location, also casino*

Hotel Don Carlos [★GF,WI] **506-2/221-6707, 866/675-9259**

Hotel Kekoldi [GS,WI,GO] Av 9 (btwn Calles 5 & 7, Barrio Amón) **506-2/248-0804, 786/221-9011 (from US)**

Melia Cariari [GF,SW] Autopista Grl Canas, Cruce San Antonio **506-2/239-0022, 888/956-3542** *luxury resort, great golfing*

Secret Garden B&B [GS,WI,GO] **506-2/224-1837** *in historic Rohrmoser district, private courtyard*

TV Hotel Costa Rica [GS,TG,NS,GO] **506-2/377-2503** *B&B for transgendered & admirers; t-girls, t-guys, cross-dressers & drag queens/ kings welcome*

Bars

Bar Al Despiste [GS,K] in front of Mudanzas Mundiales (W of Universal Zapote) **506-2/234-5956** *6pm-2am, 5pm-10pm Sun, clsd Mon*

Buenas Vibraciones [MW] Paseo de los Estudiantes **506-2/223-4573**

CeroEsTres Bar [MW,NH] nr the Int'l Airport in Alajuela (from the Fiesta Casino continue the old road into town) *traditional local bar*

Marguiss [GS,NH] in the suburbs of Alajuela *traditional local bar*

La Metro [MW,V] Calle 19 (btwn Ave 2 & Ave 4) **506-2/222-7167** *4pm-1am Tue, 8pm-4am Fri-Sat, 5pm-1am Sun, clsd Mon & Wed, darkroom*

WERD Bar & Lounge [GF,NH,F,E, 18+,WC,GO] 100 Metres Oeste de la Musmanni, Santa Ana **506-2/203-3624** *5pm-2:30am*

Nightclubs

La Avispa [MW,D] 834 Calle 1 (pink house btwn Avs 8 & 10) **506-2/223-5343** *8pm-2am, popular T-dance from 5pm Sun, clsd Mon-Wed*

El Bochinche [MW,D,V] Calle 11 (btwn Avs 10 & 12, Paseo de los Etudiantes), San Pedro **506-2/221-0500** *7pm-2am, till 5pm Fri-Sat, clsd Sun-Tue, also full restaurant, Mexican, dancing/DJ after 10pm*

Club Oh! [★GS,D] Calle 2 (btwn Avs 14 & 16) **506-2/248-1500, 506-2/810-1746** *9pm-close Wed, Fri-Sat, more gay wknds, 2 dance floors, take taxi to avoid bad area*

Puchos [M,F,DS,S] Calle 11 & Av 8 (knock to enter) **506-2/256-1147, 506-2/222-7967** *8pm-2:30am, from 4pm Sun, also restaurant*

Restaurants

Ankara San José de la Montaña (Heredia, San Antonio de Belén, S of church) **506-2/266-0303, 506-2/293-0089**

El Bochinche [MW,D,E,V] Calle 11 (btwn Avs 10 & 12, Paseo de los Etudiantes), San Pedro **506-2/221-0500** *8pm-4am, clsd Sun-Tue, [D] after 10pm, 3 bars, also restaurant*

Cafe Mundo [GO] Av 9 & Calle 15 (200 meters E of parking lot for INS, Barrio Amón) **506-2/222-6190** *11am-11pm, 5pm-midnight Sat, clsd Sun, garden seating, bar*

La Cocina de Leña [★R] in El Pueblo complex **506-2/255-1360, 506-2/256-5353** *11am-11pm, 5 minutes from downtown, Costa Rican*

Machu Piccu [★] Calle 32 (btwn Aves 1 & 3) **506-2/222-7384** *Peruvian*

Olio [★] Escalante, Bario California (N of Baselman's, San Pedro/ Los Yoses) **506-2/281-0541** *lunch & dinner, clsd Sun, Spanish, also full bar*

Ram Luna Aserri **506-2/230-3060** *dinner nightly, lunch & dinner wknds, clsd Mon, hillside restaurant w/ amazing views of San Jose & valley*

Vishnu Vegetarian Restaurant [★] Av 1 (btwn Calles 3 & 1) **506-2/256-6063** *8am-9:30pm*

Entertainment & Recreation

Gay Tours Costa Rica **506-2/305-8044** *daily events & excursions, Nov-April*

Mercado Central/ Central Market Central Avenida (btwn Calles 6 & 8) *bustling market selling food, clothing, souvenirs & more*

Publications

Gente 10 Apdo Postal 1910-2100, Sector Guadalupe **506-2/280-8886** *bi-monthly LGBT magazine, also map w/ listings*

Men's Clubs

Paris Sauna corner of Calle 7 & Av 7 (1 block from Morazan Park) **506-2/258-7254** *noon-2am, till 4am Fri-Sat*

Sauna Hispalis [★V] Av 2 #1762 (E of the Plaza de la Democracia, btwn Calles 17 & 19) **506-2/256-9540** *noon-1am, [N] Wed*

Cruisy Areas

Parque La Sabana [AYOR] next to Municipal Stadium (btwn airport & San José) *evenings & wknds*

Parque Nacional [AYOR] N of Av 1 (btwn Calles 15 & 19)

Plaza de la Cultura [★AYOR] in front of the Nat'l Theater (btwn Calles 3 & 5) *late afternoons & early evenings*

San Ramon

Accommodations

Angel Valley Farm B&B [GS,NS,WI,WC] 200m N & 300m E of Iglesia de Los Angeles (at Autopista to Arenal Volcano) **506-2/456-4084, 506-2/350-7647 (cell)** *full brkfst*

Inn at Coyote Mountain [GS,GO] Calle San Francisco 3 **506-2/383-0544, 902/482-8360** *full brkfst*

Santa Clara

Accommodations

Tree Houses Hotel Costa Rica [GS,NS,GO] **506-2/475-6507** *private treehouses in canopy of trees on wildlife refuge*

Tamarindo

Accommodations

Cala Luna Hotel & Villas [GF,SW] Playa Langosta (at Playa Tamarindo) **506-2/653-0214, 800/503-5202**

Hotel Sueño del Mar [GF,SW,NS,WI] Playa Langosta **506-2/653-0284** *private hacienda on the beach, full brkfst*

Uvita

Accommodations

Tucan Hotel [GF,WI,WC] Frente Ebais De Uvita (across from health clinic) **506-2/743-8140**

South America

Argentina

Buenos Aires

Info Lines & Services

Comunidad Homosexual Argentina Tomas Liberti 1080 **54-11/4361-6382**

Grupo Nexo [MW] Av Callao 339, 5th flr **54-11/4374-4484**

Accommodations

1555 Malabia House [GF,WI] Malabia 1555, Palermo Viejo (at Honduras) **54-11/4832-3345**

Bayres B&B [M,GO] Av Córdoba 5842 (in Palermo) **54-11/4772-3877**

The Cocker [GF,WI,GO] Av Juan de Garay 458 (at Defensa) **54-1/1436-28451**

Don Sancho Youth Hostel [GS,WI] Constitucion 4062 (at Boedo) **54-11/4923-1422** *full brkfst, some shared baths, hot tub*

Faena Hotel & Universe [GS,WI] 445 Martha Salotti St **54-11/4010-9000**

Hotel Axel [MW,F,WI] Venezuela 649 **54-11/4136-9393** *luxury gay hotel, pool parties*

Hotel Intercontinental Buenos Aires [GF] Moreno 809 **888/424-6835 (US#), 54-11/4340-7100**

Lugar Gay B&B [M,GO] Defensa 1120 **54-11/4300-4747**

Palermo Viejo B&B [GS,NS,WI,GO] Niceto Vega 4629 (at Av Scalabrini Ortiz) **54-11/4773-6092** *close to shopping & gay nightlife*

Solar Soler B&B [GF,NS] Soler 5676 (at Bonpland) **54-11/4776-3065**

Telmho Hotel Boutique [GF,WI] 1086 Defensa St (at Humberto Primo) **54-11/4116-5467**

Bars

Bach Bar [MW,E,K,V] Antonio Cabrera 4390 **54-11/5184-0137**

Bulnes Class [MW,D] Bulnes 1250 (Palermo) **54-11/4861-7492** *from 7pm Th & 11pm Fri-Sat*

Cero Consecuencia [MW] Cabrera 3769

Flux Bar [MW,D] Marcelo T de Alvear 980 (at 9 de Julio) **54-11/5252-0258** *7pm-close, from 8pm wknds, clsd Sun*

Goddess/ Secret [M,D] Av Córdoba 4185 (in Palermo) **54-11/4861-2961**

Inside [M,F,E,S,OC] Bartolomé Mitre 1571 **54-11/4372-5439** *[S] wknds*

Kim Y Novak [MW,NH,TG,A] Guemes 4900 **54-11/4773-7521** *kitschy cocktail lounge*

KM Zero [MW,D,DS,S,V] Av Santa Fe 2516 **54-11/4822-7530**

Men to Men [M,D,S,V] Anchorena 1347 (btwn Sante Fe & Pueyrredón) **54-11/5483-8840** *10pm-close, clsd Wed*

Parada Obligada [M] Charcas 4338 *10pm-close Fri-Sat only, darkroom*

Search Bar [M,D,DS,S] 1007 Azcuenaga (at Charcas) **54-11/4824-0932**

Sitges [★MW] Córdoba 4119 **54-11/4861-3763** *10:30pm-4am, till 6am Fri-Sat, clsd Mon-Tue*

Zoom [M,L,B$] Uriburu 1018 **54-11/4827-4828** *noon-3am, maze, lounge, cruisy*

NIGHTCLUBS

Alsina [MW,D] Alsina 940 (near Plaza de Mayo) **54-11/4334-0097, 54-11/4334-0098** *2am Fri & 10pm Sun only, darkroom Fri, T-dance Sun*

Amerik [M,D] Gascón 1040 (at Cordoba) **54-11/4865-4416** *darkroom*

Angel's Viamonte 2168 *midnight-7am Th-Sat*

Bahrein [GS,D,F] Lavalle 345 *6pm-7am Wed & Fri, from 10pm Sat, from midnight Tue*

Club 69 [GS,D,DS] Niceto Vega 5510 (btwn Humboldt & Fitzroy, Palermo) **54-1/4779-9396** *11:30pm Th only, over-the-top theme parties*

Cocoliche [GS,D] Rivadavia 878

Contramano [MO,D,B] Rodriguez Peña 1082 (at Av Santa Fe) *midnight-close, from 7pm Sun, clsd Mon-Tue, hustlers*

Fiesta Eyeliner [MW,D,A,DS] Campichuelo 472 *monthly queer/ alternative dance party, check web for dates*

Glam [★M,D] Cabrera 3046 **54-11/4963-2521** *midnight-close wknds, darkroom, patio*

Juana [MW,D] 775 Av 44 **54-1/557-6807** *from 11:30pm Fri-Sat only*

Pacha [GF,D] Av Costanera y Pampa **54-11/4788-4280**

CAFES

Gout Cafe [GO] Juncal 2124 **54-11/4825-8330** *sandwiches, pastries*

Pride Cafe [E] Balcarce 869 (in San Telmo) **54-11/4300-6435** *10am-10pm, live show Th night*

RESTAURANTS

Bio Humbolt 2199 (Palermo Viejo) **54-11/4774-3880** *lunch & dinner, vegetarian, organic market*

La Cabana [★] Rodriguez Peña 1967 (at Posadas) **54-11/4814-0001** *brkfst, lunch & dinner, upscale 2-flr steak house*

Casa Cruz 1658 Uriarte **54-11/4833-1112** *8:30pm-3am, later Fri-Sat, upscale, trendy restaurant, also bar*

Las Cholas Arce 306 **54-11/4899-0094**

Chueca [MW] Honduras 5255 (in Palermo) **54-11/4834-6373** *9pm-close, clsd Sun-Tue, popular gay restaurant, also bar*

Cumana [★] Rodriguez Pena 1149 (at Arenales) **54-11/4813-9207** *regional cuisine*

El Palacio de la Papa Frita [★] Lavalle 735 (at Maipu) **54-11/4393-5849** *also Av Corrientes 1612, 11/4374-8063*

Empire [★GO] Tres Sargentos 427 **54-11/4312-5706** *noon-midnight, 7pm-1am Sat, Thai food/ American bar*

La Farmacia Bolivar 898 (in San Telmo) **54-11/4300-6151** *brkfst, lunch, dinner, clsd Mon*

Filo San Martin 975 **54-11/4311-0312, 54-11/4311-1871** *8pm-close*

Mark's Deli & Coffeehouse [★] El Salvador 4107 (in Palermo) **54-11/4832-6244**

Milion [★] Parana 1048 **54-11/4815-9925** *swank lounge/ restaurant spread over 3-flr mansion, garden*

Pizza Que Charcas 4037 **54-11/4833-3165**

Rave [★] Gorriti 5092 **54-11/4833-7832**

Sucre Sucre 676 **54-11/4782-9082** *upscale contemporary*

Entertainment & Recreation

Casa Brandon [F] Luis Maria Drago 236 (at Lavalleja) **54-11/4858-0610** *events, dance parties, poetry readings, art & more*

Espanol al Sur [GF,GO] Pichincha 1031 #2 (at Carlos Calvo) **54-11/4942-9582, 54-11/6449-5447** *Spanish language & tango classes*

La Marshall Maipu 444 **54-11/4912-9043** *8:30pm Wed, exclusively gay tango lessons*

Museo Evita Peron Lafinur 2988 (in Palermo) **54-11/4807-9433** *2pm-7:30pm, clsd Mon*

Retail Shops

Gay Wine Store [MW] 995 Maipu **54-11/4313-2909, 54-11/4313-2896**

Publications

AG Magazine 54-11/4304-6357

G-Maps Buenos Aires Franklin 1463, Florida Oeste **54-11/4730-0729** *free pocket-size gay map of Buenos Aires*

La Otra Guía Apartado 78 (Suc Olivos) *free gay monthly guide*

The Ronda *gay pocket guide w/ local listings (www.theronda.com.ar)*

Gyms & Health Clubs

American Hot Gym Ayacucho 449 (M° Callao, Line B) **54-11/4951-7679** *clsd Sun*

Men's Clubs

A Full Spa [MO,V,GO] Viamonte 1770 (at Av Callao) **54-11/4371-7263** *noon-3am, 24hrs wknds*

Energy Spa [MO] Bravard 1105 (at Av Angel Gallardo, Villa Crespo) **54-1/4854-5625**

Homo Sapiens [MO] Gascon 956 **54-11/4862-6519**

Nagasaki [MO] Aguero 427 **54-1/4866-6335**

Sauna Unikus Av Pueyrredón 1180 (near Calle Mansilla) **54-11/4961-7792**

Tom's [V] Viamonte 638, in basement **54-11/4322-4404** *bar, [L] 2nd & 4th Fri*

Erotica

American Top Video Av Cabildo 2230 (Galeria Las Vegas) **54-11/4781-5343** *clsd Sun*

Box Laprida 1423 (at Santa Fe) *2pm-6am*

Cine ABC Esmeralda 506 (at the Microcentro)

City Libertad 429

Eden Av Santa Fe 1833 (gal Bozzini, B Norte)

Emporium [M] Cerrito 842 (btwn Marcelo T Alvear & Santa Fe) *sex store, also darkroom, cruisy*

Ideal Suipacha 378

Multicine Lavalle 750

Cruisy Areas

Avenida Santa Fe [AYOR] btwn Callao & Coronel Diaz

Bosques de Palermo [AYOR] Figueroa Alcorta & Dorrego St

Plaza Las Heras [AYOR] Coronel Dias & Av Las Heras

Brazil

Rio de Janeiro

Note: M°=Metro station

Info Lines & Services

Grupo Arco-Iris Rio de Janeiro Rua Monte Alegre 167, Santa Teresa **55-21/2215-0844** *1pm-7pm, till 11pm Sat, clsd Sun, LGBT community center*

Rainbow Kiosk [★MW,DS] Atlantic Av (in front of Copacabana Palace Hotel) **55-21/2275-1641**

Accommodations

Ananab Guesthouse Rio [GS,SW,WI,GO] Rua Alice (Laranjeiras) **55-21/2557-6789** *shared baths in guesthouse, also apt rental, full brkfst*

Casa Dois Gatos [M,SW,WI,GO] Rua Rosalina Terra 6, Cabo Frio **561/282-0023, 55-22/2645-5806** *free transportation from Rio airport*

Copacabana Panorama [M,GO] 3806 Av Atlantica (at Souza Lima) **617/803-9164** *oceanfront condo w/ gorgeous view of Copacabana Beach, short walk to gay night life*

Ipanema Plaza [GS,SW] Rua Farme Amoedo (at Rua Prudente de Morais) **55-21/3687-2000** *near gay beach, rooftop pool, also restaurant*

MyRioCondo.com [GS,WI,GO] 3150 Avenida Atlantica, Apt 901 (Copacabana) **808/536-4263 (HI #), 888/236-0799**

Nice Condos in Rio [M,SW,WC,GO] Rua Barata Ribeiro 669/ 604 **55-21/2227-5658, 55-21/9416-2665** *condos, near Copacabana & Ipanema beaches*

Bars

Blue Angel [MW,D,F,E,V] Rua Julio de Castilhos 15-B **55-21/2513-2501** *6pm-close*

Casa da Lua [W,NH,F,E] Rua Barao da Torre 240 **55-21/3813-3972** *11am-2am, clsd Mon*

Melt [GF] Rua Rita Ludolf 47 **55-21/2249-9309** *lounge, also restaurant*

Star's Club (Buraco da Lacraia) [★GS,D,DS,TG] Rua André Cavalcante 58 (Centro) **55-21/2242-0446, 55-21/2224-8880**

Nightclubs

Le Boy [★MW,D,S,YC] Rua Raul Pompeia 102 (Copacabana) **55-21/2513-4993** *11pm-close, clsd Mon*

Cabaré Casanova [M,D,E,DS,AYOR] Av Mém de Sa 25 (Centro) **55-21/2221-6555** *11pm-close*

La Cueva [M,D,B,L] Rua Miguel Lemos 51 (Copacabana) **55-21/2267-1364**

Dama de Ferro [MW,D] Rua Vinicius de Moraes 288 (Ipanema) **55-21/2247-2330**

Fosfobox [GS,D] Rua Siqueira Campos 143 **55-21/2548-7498** *open Th-Sun, underground techno*

Galeria Cafe [GS,D] Rua Teixeira de Mello 31 (Ipanema) **55-21/2523-8250** *10:30pm-close, clsd Sun-Tue, also gallery*

Ideal Party [GS,D] Rua da Carioca 64 **55-21/2252-3460** *huge club w/ visting big-name DJs*

Cafes

Copa Cafe Av Atlantica 3056 **55-21/2235-2947**

Expresso Carioca Rua Farme de Amoedo 76 **55-21/2267-8604**

Restaurants

Bar d'Hotel Av Delfim Moreira 696 (2nd Flr, inside Marina Hotel, Leblon) **55-21/2540-4990** *Mediterranean, food served all day, bar till late, see & be seen*

Bofetada [★] Rua Farme de Amoedo 87 (Ipanema) **55-21/2227-1675** *6pm-close, post-beach meeting place, also bar*

Sorelle Margherita Rua Farme de Amoedo 57 **55-21/2513-3775** *popular pizza place after the beach*

Tamino Rua Arnaldo Quintela 26 **55-21/2295-1849** *7pm-4am, clsd Mon-Wed*

Via Sete Rua Garcia D'Avila 125 (in Ipanema) **55-21/2512-8100** *noon-midnight, plenty veggie*

Zero Zero [★GS,D,F] Av Padre Leonel Franca 240 (inside planetarium) **55-21/2540-8041** *gay night Sun, upscale restaurant & nightclub*

Entertainment & Recreation

Copacabana Beach at Rua Rodolfo Dantas *gay across from Copacabana Palace Hotel*

Ipanema Beach *E of Rua Farme Amoedo*

Publications

Rio For Partiers 55-21/2523-9857 *great guide book*

Men's Clubs

Bonsucesso Sauna Rua Bonsucesso 252 **55-21/2260-9385** *1pm-10pm*

Club 117 Rua Cándido Mendes 117 (Gloria) **55-21/2252-0160** *clsd Mon, large sauna, steam, escorts*

Club 29 Rua Professor Alfredo Gomes 29 **55-21/2286-6380** *1pm-4am, bathhouse, cybercafe*

Copacabana Sauna [B] Rua Dias da Rocha 83 **55-21/2235-5563** *popular w/ bears*

Estação Rua Tonelero 217 (Copacabana) **55-21/2547-9953** *3pm-close*

Gaylígola [M,V] Rua Ubaldino do Amaral 50 (downtown) **55-21/9259-5625, 55-21/2224-6144**

Projeto SB Rua 19 de Fevereiro 162 (M° Botafogo) **55-21/2244-4263, 55-21/2541-8698** *also internet cafe*

Sauna Flamengo [OC] Rua Correia Dutra 68-A **55-21/2285-0197**

Spazio 18 [MO,DS,18+] Rua Santo Amaro 18 (near M° Gloria) **55-21/2224-3213** *also bar, theme nights*

Studio 64 [MO] Rua Redentor 64 **55-21/2523-5670, 55-21/2513-4229**

Termas Catete [MO,V] Rua Correia Dutra 34 **55-21/2265-5478** *dark-rooms, cabins*

Termas Kabalk [MO,V] Rua Santa Luiza 459 (near Varnhagem Square) **55-21/2572-6210** *3pm-11pm, bar, darkroom, very clean*

Termas Leblon [MO] Rua Barao da Torre 522 (at Rua Garcia d'Avila, Ipanema) **55-21/2247-9169, 55-21/2287-3762** *sauna, mature crowd*

Erotica

Iris Theater Rua Caroica 49 **55-21/262-1729**

Orly Theater Rua Alcindo Guanabara 17 **55-21/2533-3110**

Cruisy Areas

Avenida Copacabana & Av Atlantica

Barra Beach *across street from beach; look for flags & go past building into woods*

Chile

Santiago

Note: M°=Metro station

Info Lines & Services

Acciongay - Corporacion Chilena de Prevencion del SIDA Toesca 2311 **56-32/755-834, 56-32/755-285** *10am-10pm Mon-Fri, AIDS info, testing & workshops*

Accommodations

B&B Santiago [MW,GO] Corte Suprema 177 (Departamento B) **56-2/696-9499** *full brkfst*

Hotel Castillo [MW] Pio Nono 420 (Bellavista) **56-2/735-0243** *includes brkfst*

Bars

Bar 105 Bombero Nuñez 105 *9pm-late Th-Sat*

Bar de Willy [MW,E,S] Av 11 de Septiembre 2214 (Común Providencia) **56-2/381-1806** *10pm-4am, till 5am wknds, strippers on 1st flr*

El Closet [MW,K] Santa Filomena 138 (at Bombero Nuñez)

Farinelli [F,E,DS,S] Bombero Nuñez 68 (Recoleta) **56-2/732-8966** *5pm-2am, internet*

Pub Friend's [MW,E,DS] Bombero Nuñez 365 (at Dominica, barrio Bellavista) **56-2/777-3979** *9:30pm-4am, till 5am Fri-Sat*

Recoleta Bar de Vinos [GF] Loreto 75 *10am-2am, wine bar*

Vox Populi [M,F] Ernesto Pinto Lagarrigue 364 (Bellavista) **56-2/671-1267** *9:30pm-3am, clsd Sun-Mon, also restaurant, garden patio*

Nightclubs

Blondie [GS,D,A] Alameda 2879, loc 104 **56-2/681-7793** *theme nights*

Bokhara Discoteque [★M,D,F,DS,S] Pio Nono 430 (at Constitución, barrio Bellavista) **56-2/732-1050, 56-2/735-1271** *10pm-6am, till 7am wknds, darkroom*

Bunker [MW,D,F,E] Bombero Nuñez 159 (Bellavista) **56-2/738-2301, 56-2/738-2314** *11pm-close Fri-Sat*

Club Principe [M,D] Pio Nono 398 **56-2/777-6381**

Naxos [M,D,DS,S] Alameda 776 Subterraneo *theme nights*

Nueva Cero [M,D] Euclides 1204 par 2 Gran Avenida

Cafes

Mitos Diagonal Paraguay 477 (at Alameda) **56-2/632-7163** *10am-3am, 11am-5am Fri-Sat, 2pm-1am Sun, internet cafe*

Open Mind [WI] Von Schroeders 27 (Viña del Mar) **56-2/268-8663** *noon-1:30am, from 5pm Sun*

Tavelli [★] Andrés de Fuenzalida 34 (Providencia) **56-2/231-9862** *8:30am-10pm, from 9:30am Sat*

Restaurants

Ali Baba 102 Santa Filomena (Barrio Bellavista, Recoleta) **56-2/732-7036** *Middle Eastern*

Capricho Español Purisima 65 (barrio Bellavista) **56-2/777-7674** *dinner only, Spanish, full bar*

Holandesa [★M] Av Santa Rosa 31 *late-night hangout*

La Pizza Nostra Av Providencia 1975 & Pedro de Valdivia **56-2/231-8941** *Italian*

Santo Remedio [D] 152 Roman Diaz, Providencia **56-2/235-0984** *global cuisine, full bar*

El Toro Loreto 33 **56-2/737-5937** *noon-midnight*

Retail Shops

Dimension House Montijas 294 **56-2/683-7718**

Men's Clubs

Baños 282 Bellavista 282 **56-2/777-1709**

Banos Metro [MO,V] Almirante Montt 471 **56-2/633-1321** *1pm-midnight, also cafe, darkroom*

Mixhouse Loreto 260 *9pm-2am Wed-Th, 11pm-5am Fri-Sat, darkroom*

Sauna Mi Tiempo [V] Bombero Nuñez 230 **56-2/735-3949** *2pm-midnight, 24hrs wknds, cafe, darkroom*

Erotica

Sex Shop Amsterdam Nueva de Lyon 030

Sex Shop Multivariedades Paseo Las Palmas 2225, Local 111

Cruisy Areas

Paseo Las Palmas [AYOR] in Providencia neighborhood

Plaza de Armas [AYOR]

Europe

AUSTRIA

Vienna

INFO LINES & SERVICES

Gay & Lesbian AA 43-1/799-5599, 43-665/490-5603 (English)

Hosi Zentrum Novarragasse 40 **43-1/216-6604** *many groups & events, also publishes quarterly news magazine*

Rosa-Lila-Villa Linke Wienzeile 102 (near Hofmühlgasse, U4-Pilgramgasse) **43-1/586-8150 (women), 43-1/585-4343 (men)** *LGBT center, staffed 5pm-8pm Mon, Wed, Fri, info, gay city maps, also meeting place for various groups, also cafe-bar*

ACCOMMODATIONS

Arcotel Wimberger [GF] Neubaugürtel 34-36 (at Goldschlagstr) **43-1/521-650** *4-star hotel, restaurant & bar on premises*

Designapartment Vienna [GF,WI,GO] Glockengasse 25/ 9 **43-699/149-4140**

Golden Tulip Art Hotel Vienna [GF] Brandmayergasse 7-9 **43-1/5445-108** *stylish hotel, central location*

Hotel Urania [GF,F,WC,GO] Obere Weißgerberstr 7 (U-Schwedenplatz) **43-1/713-1711** *centrally located & inexpensive art hotel*

Le Méridien Wien [GF,SW] Opernring 13-15 **43-1/588-900, 800/543-4300** *sauna, hot tub, also restaurant & bar*

Pension Wild [M,F,GO] Lange Gasse 10 (off Lerchenfelder Str) **43-1/406-5174**

Das Tyrol [GF] Mariahilfer Str 15 **43-1/587-5415** *small luxury hotel*

BARS

Alte Lampe [★M,P,OC] Heumühlgasse 13 (at Rechte Weinzeile, U4-Kettenbrückengasse) **43-1/587-3454** *8pm-1am, clsd Mon-Tue, piano bar wknds, Vienna's oldest gay bar*

Arte Lampe [M] Heumühlgasse 13 **43-1/587-3454**

Bar Knast [M,L] Theobaldgasse 8 *10pm-4am, till 6am wknds, cruise bar*

Cafe Arte Bar [MW,E,C] Margaretenstr 34 *6pm-2am, clsd Sun-Mon*

Cafe Savoy [★MW,F] Linke Wienzeile 36 (at Köstlergasse) **43-1/586-7348** *5pm-2am, from 9am Sat, clsd Sun, upscale cafe-bar*

Cafe X Bar [M] Mariahilfer Str 45 (enter on Stiegengasse, U3-Neubaugasse) **43-1/585-2437** *4pm-2am, 6pm-midnight Sun, American bar*

Eagle Bar [★M,L,V] Blümelgasse 1 (at Gumpendorfer Str, U3-Neubaugasse) **43-1/587-2661** *9pm-4am, darkroom, also sex shop*

Felixx [MW,F,WI] Gumpendorferstr 5 **43-1/920-4714** *7pm-3am, from 10am Sat, 7pm-1am Sun*

Goldener Spiegel [★M,F,YC] Linke Wienzeile 46 (enter on Stiegengasse, U4-Kettenbrückengasse) **43-1/586-6608** *7pm-2am, hustlers*

Lo:sch [MO,L] Fünfhuasgasse 1 (at Sechshauserstr) **43-1/895-9979** *from 10pm Fri-Sat, also Sun in winter, call for events, leather/ uniform/ fetish club, strict dress code, 3 flrs*

Mango Bar [★M,YC,GO] Laimgrubengasse 3 (U4-Kettenbrückengasse) **43-1/920-4714** *9pm-4am*

Nightshift [★MO,L,V] Corneliusgasse 8 (at Kopernikusgasse, look for unmarked black door at bottom of stairs) **43-1/586-2337** *10pm-6am, clsd Sun, darkroom*

Peter's Operncafé Hartauer [GS,F] Riemergasse 9 (at Singer) **43-1/512-8981** *6pm-2am, clsd Sun-Mon, terrace*

Sling [M,L] Kettenbrückengasse 4 (at Grüngasse, U4-Kettenbrückengasse) **43-1/586-2362** *3pm-4am, darkroom, private rooms, sling, erotic shop, "piss cinema"*

Stiefelknecht [MO,L,V] Wimmergasse 20 (enter on Stolberggasse) **43-1/545-2301** *10pm-2am, till 4am Fri-Sat, darkroom, sling*

Studio 67 [GS,D] Gumpendorferstr 67 **43-1/966-7178** *6pm-2am, till 4am Fri-Sat*

Le Swing [M,TG,V,$] Hannovergasse 5 (at Wallensteinstr) **43-1/332-1670** *gay Tue only 9pm-2am, Transnight, sauna*

Das Versteck [GS,YC] Nikolaigasse 1 (at Grünangergasse, U1-Stephansplatz) **43-1/513-4053** *6pm-midnight, from 7pm Sat, clsd Sun*

Village Bar [★M,YC] Stiegengasse 8 (near Naschmarkt) *8pm-3am*

Wiener Freiheit [MW,D,TG,F,V] Schönbrunner Str 25 (U4-Kettenbrückengasse) **43-1/931-9111** *8pm-midnight, clsd Sun-Mon, 3 flrs, disco 10pm-4am Fri-Sat*

NIGHTCLUBS

Club Date/ Boys & Girls Club [M,D,V] Schikanedergasse 12 **43-1/581-2184** *9pm-4am, darkroom*

Heaven Gay Night [★M,D,TG,S,YC] **43-1/523-3063** *10pm-6am Sat*

Why Not? [M,D,S,V] Tiefer Graben 22 (at Wipplinger, U-Schottentor) **43-1/925-3024** *10pm-close Fri-Sat & before public holidays, darkroom*

CAFES

Bakul Margaretenstr 58 *10am-2am*

Cafe Berg [★MW,F,YC] Berggasse 8 (at Wasagasse, U2-Schottentor) **43-1/319-5720** *10am-1am, cafe-bar, T-dance 2nd & 4th Sun*

Cafe Central Herrengasse 14 (at Strauchgasse) **43-1/533-3763** *7:30am-10pm, from 10am Sun & public holidays, "world's most famous coffee-house"*

Cafe Raimann [M] Schönbrunner Straße 285 **43-1/813-5767** *8am-2am, till midnight Sat, clsd Sun*

Cafe Rifugio [M] Schönbrunner Str 10 **43-699/1138-0250** *10am-10pm*

Cafe Standard Margaretenstr 63 **43-1/581-0586** *8am-midnight, from 11am wknds*

Cafe Stein [GF,F] Währinger Str 6-8 (near U-Schottentor) **43-1/319-7241** *7am-1am, from 9am Sun, internet access, terrace*

Das Möbel Burggasse 10 (Spittelberg) **43-1/524-9497** *10am-1am, trendy, internet, also art gallery*

Point of Sale [WI] Schleifmuhlgasse 12 **43-1/941-6397** *8am-2am, cafe & deli, also vegan items, also bar*

Schik [MW,WI] Schikanedergasse 5 *5pm-2am, till 4am Fri-Sat, clsd Sun, also bar*

Smart Cafe [GS,F] Kostlergasse 9 **43-1/585-7165** *6pm-2am, Fri-Sat till 4am, clsd Sun-Mon, S/M & fetish cafe*

RESTAURANTS

Andino [GS,E] Münzwardeingasse 2 (U4-Pilgramgasse) **43-1/587-6125** *11am-2am, from 10am Sat, 11am-midnight Sun, Latin American, also full bar*

Aux Gazelles Rahlgasse 5 **43-1/585-6645** *French/ Moroccan restaurant 6pm-midnight; Arabian-style lounge, cafe & deli 11am-2am; also Turkish steam baths noon-10pm*

Bin Im Leo [BW] Servitengasse 14 **43-1/391-7763** *4pm-midnight, from noon wknds, plenty veggie*

Cafe-Restaurant Willendorf [MW] Linke Wienzeile 102 (near Hofmuhlgasse, U4-Pilgramgasse) **43-1/587-1789** *6pm-2am, food served till midnight, plenty veggie, full bar, terrace*

Halle Museumsquartier 1 **43-1/523-7001** *10am-2am, modern bistro, artsy crowd*

Kantine Porzellangasse 19 **43-1/319-5918** *6pm-2am, Thai*

Motto [★GS,R] Schönbrunner Str 30 (enter on Rüdigergasse) **43-1/587-0672** *6pm-2am, till 4am Fri-Sat, trendy, also bar, patio*

Santo Spirito [E] Kumpfgasse 7 **43-1/512-9998** *6pm-11pm, bar till 2am, classical music*

Schon Schön Lindengasse 53 (Ecke Andreagasse) *lunch & dinner, fashion-able restaurant, also bar; also clothing & hair salon*

Stöger Ramperstorffergasse 63 **43-1/544-7596** *11am-midnight, clsd Sun, Viennese*

Zum Roten Elefanten Gumpendorferstrasse 3 **43-1/966-8008** *lunch & dinner, open late Fri-Sat, clsd Sun*

Entertainment & Recreation

House of Music Seilerstätte 30 **43-1/516-4810** *10am-10pm, interactive museum*

Kunsthistorisches Museum Maria Theresien-Platz (enter Heldenplatz) **43-1/525-240** *10am-6pm, till 9pm Th, clsd Mon, not to be missed*

Bookstores

American Discount Rechte Wienzeile 5 (at Paniglgasse) **43-1/587-5772** *9:30am-6:30pm, till 5pm Sat, clsd Sun, int'l magazines & books; also Neubaugasse 39, 43-1/523-37-07*

Löwenherz Berggasse 8 (next to Cafe Berg, enter on Wasagasse, U2-Schottentor) **43-1/317-2982** *10am-7pm, till 8pm Fri, till 6pm Sat, clsd Sun, LGBT, large selection of English titles*

Publications

Coxx **43-1/595-3777-15** *Vienna gay news*

Vienna Gay Guide **43-1/789-1000** *city map & guide*

Men's Clubs

Apollo City Sauna [SW,V] Wimbergergasse 34 **43-699/811-65200** *bar, darkroom, gym equipment*

Kaiserbründl [F,V,SW] Weihburggasse 18-20 (at Grünangergasse, U1-Stephansplatz) **43-1/513-3293** *2pm-midnight, till 2am Fri-Sat, 3 flrs, 2 bars, darkroom maze, gym equipment*

Sauna Frisco [F,V] Schönbrunner Str 28 **43-1/920-2488** *3pm-midnight, 24hrs wknds, private rooms, full bar*

Erotica

Art-X Percostr 3 **43-1/02622-895550, 43-2622/89-555** *erotic supermarket, clsd Sun*

Man for Man [V] Hamburgerstr 8 (at Rechte Wienzeile, U-Kettenbrückengasse) **43-1/585-2064** *books, toys, videos, DVDs, private rooms*

Sexworld XXL Store [GS,V] Mariahilfer Str 49 **43-1/587-6656** *clsd Sun, cabins, darkroom, cruisy, special gay section*

Spartacus XXL Store Mariahilfer Str 49 (enter through Sexworld) **43-1/587-6656** *clsd Sun, toys, leather, books, videos, DVDs*

Tiberius [WC] Lindengasse 2 (at Stiftgasse, U3-Neubaugasse) **43-1/522-0474** *clsd Sun, leather, rubber, toys*

Wiscot Center Lerchenfelder Gürtel 45 **43-1/402-7822**

Cruisy Areas

Rathauspark [AYOR] *evenings only*

Schweizer Garten [AYOR] next to Südbahnhof

CZECH REPUBLIC

Prague (Praha)

Note: M°=Metro station

Prague is divided into 10 city districts: Praha–1, Praha–2, etc.

Prague (Praha)—Overview

Info Lines & Services

GayGuide.net Prague **36-309/323-334** *4pm-8pm, gay tourist info*

Accommodations

Apartments in Prague [GF,WI,WC] **420/251-512-502, 303/800-0858** *apt rental service*

Prague (Praha)—1

Accommodations

The Castle Steps [GF,WI] Nerudova 7 (at Malostranske Namesti) **420/257-216-337, 800/860-0571**

Hotel Metropol [GS] Narodni 33 **420/246-022-100** *design hotel, all-glass facade*

Old Town Apartments [M,GO] **36/309-323-334** *apts*

Prague Center Guest Residence [MW,GO] Stepanska Street (at Zitna) **36-309/323-334**

Vodickova Apartments [GF,WI,WC] Dusni 1 **420/222-242-431** *fully equipped flats w/ kitchen*

Bars

Friends Bar [★M,NH,D,V] Bartolomejská 11 **420/226-211-920** *6pm-4am, DJ Wed-Sat, internet access*

K.U. Bar [GS] Rytirská 13 (at Perlová, near Oldtown Square) **420/221-181-081** *7pm-4am, upscale & trendy*

Tingl Tangl [MW,D,F,C,DS] Karolíny Svetlé 12 **420/224-238-278** *11am-10pm, [C] 9pm-5am Wed & Fri-Sat, full restaurant*

U Rudolfa [M,BW,OC] Mezibranská 3 **420/605-872-492** *2pm-2am, from 4pm wknds*

Nightclubs

Celnice Club [GS,D] Celnici 4 **420/224-212-240**

Escape Club [MO,D,F,S,$] V Jame 8 (off Wenceslas Square) **420/602-403-744, 420/606-111-177** *9pm-4am, disco from 10pm, go-go boys, also restaurant, hustlers*

Roxy [GS,D,V,YC] Dlouhá 33 (M° Námestí Republiky) **420/224-826-296** *9pm-6am, cool events*

Cafes

Cafe Cafe Rytirská 10 (at Perlová, near Oldtown Square) **420/224-210-597** *10am-11pm*

Cafe Érra [GS,F] Konviktská 11 **420/222-220-568** *10am-midnight, salads, sandwiches & entrées*

Cafe Louvre [GS,F,NS] Národni 22 (M° Narodni Trida) **420/224-930-949** *8am-11:30pm, from 9am wknds, billiard tables*

Kafirna U Ceského Pána [★M] Kozí 13, Stare Mesto **420/222-328-283** *noon-11pm, from 3pm wknds, small bar popular w/ locals*

Noi [GO] Ujezd 19 **420/257-311-411** *11am-1am*

Restaurants

Casa Andina Dusni 15 **420/224-815-996** *lunch & dinner, Peruvian/ Latin American*

Petrinské Terasy [GO] Seminarská Zahrada 13, Petrin **420/257-320-688, 420/602-224-096** *noon-11pm, in a former monastery, great view*

La Provence [GO] Stupartska 9 (near Old Town Square) **420/296-826-155** *11am-1am, French*

Staromestska Restaurace Staromestske namesti 19 **420/224-213-015** *11am-midnight, local Czech specialties*

Entertainment & Recreation

Sex Machines Museum Melantrichova 18 **420/ 227-186-260** *10am-11pm*

Bookstores

Globe [E,F] Patrossova 6 **420/224-934-203** *English-language bookstore, also cafe*

Men's Clubs

Sauna Babylonia [★V] Martinská 6 **420/224-232-304** *popular w/ tourists, gym equipment, bar*

Erotica

Pink Shop U Pujcovna 6 **420/222-233-250** *clsd Sun-Mon, videos, DVDs, magazines*

Cruisy Areas

Hlavni Nadrazi [AYOR] Main Railway Station *gallery above ticket counters*

Prague (Praha)—2

Accommodations

Balbin Penzion [GF,WI] Balbinova 26 (near Wenceslas Square) **420/222-250-660** *located in city center, full brkfst*

Prague Saints [MW,GO] Polska 32 (office location) (at Trebizkeho, at Saints Bar) **420/775-152-041, 420/775-152-042** *apts in gay Vinohrady district*

Richard and Jirka [★] Gorazdova 11 **420/602-455-127** *also bar/ cafe, erotica store*

Bars

Club Ho Ho Ho [M,NH,TG,K] Luzická 26

Fan Fan Club [M,K] Dittrichova 5 **420/776-360-698** *5pm-2am*

Klub 21 [MW,F,YC] Rimska 21 **420/603-539-475** *6pm-close, clsd Sun, cellar bar/ gallery, mostly Czechs*

Klub Strelec [GF,BW] Zitna 51 **420/224-941-446** *5pm-2am, till midnight Sun*

Paprsek [M,WI] Vinohradska 34/ 30 **420/223-003-255** *11am-10pm, from 3pm Sun, bar/ cafe*

Saints [MW] Polska 32 (at Trebizkeho) **420/222-250-326** *7pm-4am*

Street Cafe [GS,D,F] Blanická 28 **420/222-013-116**

Nightclubs

Termix [★MW,D] Trebizkeho 4 **420/222-710-462** *8pm-5am, clsd Mon-Tue*

Valentino [MW,D,V] Vinohradska 40 **420/222-513-491, 420/776-360-698 (cell)** *2pm-5am, 3 levels, darkroom*

Restaurants

Bejkarna [WI] Slezka 19 **420/222-524-663** *11am-midnight, till 1am Fri-Sat*

Celebrity Cafe [GS] Vinohradska 40 (in Vinohrady) **420/222-511-343** *8am-2am, noon-3am Sat, noon-midnight Sun, also bar*

Radost FX [GS] Belehradska 120, Vinohrady **420/224-254-776, 420/603-193-711** *fabulous wknd brunch, vegetarian cafe, also nightclub [GF] w/ popular monthly gay party*

Sahara Cafe Namesti Miru 6 **420/222-514-987** *lunch & dinner; salad, pasta & meat*

Men's Clubs

Marco [★V] Lublanská 1916/17, Vinohrady **420/224-262-833** *2pm-3am, also bar, booths, small but popular*

Erotica

Heaven [★] Gorazdova 11 **420/224-912-282** *cinema, toys, books, videos, many US titles, darkroom*

Prague (Praha)—3

Accommodations

Studio Henri [M,GO] Jeseniova 52/1196 **420/271-773-837, 420/271-773-847** *apt, great view of Old Town Prague*

Bars

Club Temple [★M,D,DS,S,V,AYOR] Seifertova 3 **420/222-710-773** *7pm-4am, hustlers, also sex shop, rent boys*

Gulliver [MW,GO] Milicova 6 **420/721-031-965** *noon-10pm, from 5pm Sat, clsd Sun, wine bar*

Latimerie Club Cafe [MW] Slezska 74 **420/224-252-049** *4pm-close*

Piano Bar [★MW,F] Milesovská 10 **420/22-969-888, 420/775-727-796 (cell)** *7pm-close, mostly Czech*

Entertainment & Recreation

TV Tower Mahlerovy sady 1 **420/242-418-778, 420/242-418-766** *get a bird's-eye view of the city from the top of this tower, also restaurant 10am-11pm*

Gyms & Health Clubs

Bravo Fitness [MW,GO] Srobarova 9, Zizkov (at Pisecká) **420/271-731-412** *9am-10pm, 2pm-9pm wknds*

Men's Clubs

Alcatraz [MO,L,V,S] Borivojova 58 (off Seifertova, in Zizhkov) **420/222-711-458** *10pm-5am, S/M club, theme nights*

Real Club 2 [MO,18+] Ondrickova 15 **420/773-695-122** *cruisy, darkroom, also bar, theme nights*

Erotica

City Fox Pribenicka 12, Zizkov **420/222-540-358** *clsd Sun-Mon, small video store, Czech & US titles, cabins*

Prague (Praha)—5

Accommodations

Andel's Hotel [GF] Stroupeznickeho 21 **420/296-889-688**

Men's Clubs

Drake's [MO,F,S,V,$] Zborovska 50 (at Petrinska) **420/257-326-828** *24hrs, darkroom, maze, sex shop, free Sun buffet from 8pm*

Prague (Praha)—6

Cruisy Areas

Sarka Lake [AYOR] by metro to Dejvicka & tram 26 to end station *nude bathing, summers*

Prague (Praha)—7

Cafes

Duhova Cajovna [MW,F] Milada Horáková 73 (at Ovenecka) **420/775-269-699** *3pm-midnight, "Rainbow Tearoom"*

Cruisy Areas

Park Letna [AYOR] Park Letna *near Metronom & next to Belvedere Palace, April-Oct*

Prague (Praha)—8

Accommodations

Hotel Villa Mansland Prague [M,SW,GO] Stepnicná 9, Liben **420/286-884-405, 420/777-839-733** *wellness center including sauna, also restaurant*

Men's Clubs

Sauna David [M] Sokolovská 44, Karlin **420/222-317-869** *9am-11pm, from 11am wknds, oldest sauna in Prague, gym*

Sauna Labyrint [MO] Pernerova 4 *2pm-7am, sauna, steam room, dark room, also bar*

Prague (Praha)—10

Men's Clubs

Sauna Bonbon [MO] Cernomorska 6 **420/777-146-068** *1pm-1am, till 2am Fri-Sat, clsd Sun*

Accommodations

Arco Guest House [M,GO] Voronézská 24 (in Vinohrady) **36-309/323-334 (English & German)** *internet access*

Ron's Rainbow Guest House [GS,GO] Bulharska 4 (at Finská) **420/271-725-664, 420/731-165-022 (cell)** *jacuzzi*

Prague (Praha)—11

Accommodations

The ICON Boutique Hotel [GF,WI,WC] V Jame 6 (at Vodickova) **420/221-634-100** *full brkfst*

Cruisy Areas

Seberak Lake [AYOR] *from end station in Seberak, go to opposite side of lake to nude beach, summers*

Denmark

Copenhagen

Info Lines & Services

Wonderful Copenhagen Convention & Visitors Bureau Gammel Kongevej 1 **45/7022-2442 (tourist info)**

Accommodations

Amagerhus B&B [MW,WI,GO] Skovmarken 4A, Kastrup **45/3246-1920, 45/2339-1220 (cell)**

Carstens Guesthouse [MW,WI,GO] Christians Brygge 28, 5th flr **45/3314-9107, 45/4050-9107 (cell)** *B&B, hostel & apts, 5 minutes from gay area*

Copenhagen Rainbow Guest House B&B [MO,NS,WI,WC,GO] "Stroeget" Frederiksberggade 25 C, 1459 K **45/3314-1020** *centrally located, full brkfst*

First Hotel Skt. Petri [GF,F,WI,WC] Krystalgade 22 **45/3345-9100**

Hotel Fox [GS,NS] Jarmers Plads 3 **45/3395-7755, 45/3313-3000** *artistic rooms, central location, roof terrace; also lounge & restaurant*

Hotel Windsor [M,GO] Frederiksborggade 30, 1360 **45/3311-0830** *near gay scene, shared baths*

Bars

Cafe Intime [GF,P] Allegade 25, Frederiksberg **45/3834-1958** *6pm-2am, cafe-bar*

Can-Can [M,NH] Mikkel Bryggers Gade 11 **45/3311-5010** *2pm-2am, till 5am Fri-Sat*

Centralhjørnet [M] Kattesundet 18 **45/3311-8549** *noon-2am*

Chaca [W] Studiestraede 39 **45/3167-4655**

Code [MW,D,F,DS,MR,TG,E] Rådhusstraede 1 **45/3326-3626** *4pm-midnight, till 5am Fri-Sat, cafe/ bar*

Dunkel Bar [GS,D] Vester Voldgade 10 *6pm-5am, clsd Sun-Mon*

Masken [★MW,F] Studiestræde 33 **45/3391-0937** *2pm-3am, till 5am Fri-Sat*

Men's Bar [M,L] Teglgårdsstræde 3 **45/3312-7303** *3pm-2am, popular brunch 1st Sun*

Never Mind [GS] Nørre Voldgade 2 **45/3311-8886** *10pm-6am*

Oscar Bar Cafe [★M,F] Radhuspladsen 77 **45/3312-0999** *noon-2am, great happy hour*

Nightclubs

Dunst [★GS,D] *party-/event-planner in Copenhagen, check website for details at www.dunst.dk*

Rocco Party [M,D] Axeltorv 12 (Zum Biergarten, walk into garden thru gate)

SLM (Scandinavian Leather Men) [M,L,PC] 17-C Lavendelstraede (in back building) **45/3332-0601** *10pm-close Fri-Sat, theme nights Sat, strict dress-code*

Restaurants

Jailhouse Restaurant & Bar [★F] Studiestraede 12 **45/3315-2255** *3pm-2am, till 5am Fri-Sat*

Entertainment & Recreation

Amager Strandpark *beach 5 km from city center*

Bellevue Beach *mostly gay beach, left end is nude*

BLUS (Bøsse/ Lesbiske Studerende) [MW] Købmagergade 52 (at Studenterhuset) *7pm-midnight Tue, student-run GayDay cafe*

Tisvildeleje Beach N of the city (take S-train to Hillerød, then local train to beach) *gay beach*

Men's Clubs

Amigo Sauna [★V] Studiestræde 31 **45/3315-2028** *sauna, steam, tanning, cabins, mazes*

Body Bio [V] Kingosgade 7 *cabins, sauna, cruisy*

Copenhagen Gay Center [V] Istedgade 34-36 (behind erotica shop) **45/3322-2300** *2-flr sauna, tanning*

Erotica

EP-video Kattesundet 10 **45/3311-6406**

Men's Shop Viktoriagade 24 **45/3325-4475** *magazines, books, toys, leather/ rubber gear, videos & video cabin*

Cruisy Areas

Ørstedsparken [AYOR] btwn Nørre voldgade & Nørre farimagsgade *mainly at night*

Utterslev Mose [AYOR] off hwy toward Farum

Zigøjnerpladsen (Gypsy Square) [AYOR] near Arillerivej & Lossepladsvej

England

London

London is divided into 6 regions:
London—Overview
London—Central
London—West
London—North
London—East
London—South

London—Overview

Info Lines & Services

London Lesbian/ Gay Switchboard **44-(0)20/7837-7324** *10am-11pm*

Accommodations

London First Choice Apartments [GF] **44-(0)20/8990-9033** *short-term apt rentals, also hotel reservations*

Entertainment & Recreation

London Gay Symphony Orchestra **44-(0)79/6385-3099**

Publications

Boyz **44-(0)20/7025-6100** *fab gay boy newspaper w/ extensive club & event listings*

Gay Times 44-(0)20/7424-7400 *glorious gay glossy*

The Pink Paper 44-(0)20/7424-7414 *free LGBT newspaper*

QX International 44-(0)20/7379-7887

Time Out 44-(0)20/7813-3000 *weekly city scene guide w/ gay section*

London—Central

London—Central includes Soho, Covent Garden, Bloomsbury, Mayfair, Westminster, Pimlico & Belgravia

ACCOMMODATIONS

Checkin Accommodation London [GS,NS,WI,GO] 20 Trentishoe Mansions, 90 Charing Cross Rd (at Cambridge Circus) **44-(0)79/0983-6487** *3-bdrm flat in the heart of London's West End, rent a room or the whole apt*

Dover Hotel [GF,WI] 42/44 Belgrave Rd **44-(0)20/7821-9085**

Fitz B&B [MW,NS,WI,GO] Colville Place (btwn Charlotte St & Whitfield St) **44-(0)78/3437-2866**

George Hotel [GF] 58-60 Cartwright Gardens (N of Russell Square) **44-(0)20/7387-8777**

Hazlitt's [GF,WI] 6 Frith St (Soho Sq) **44-(0)20/7434-1771**

Holiday Rentals [MW,NS,GO] **44-(0)20/8846-3444** *also apt*

Lincoln House [★GS,WI,WC] 33 Gloucester Pl, Marble Arch (at Baker St) **44-20/7486-7630** *B&B, full brkfst*

London Gay Accommodation [MW,NS,GO] **44-(0)20/7486-0855** *room in private apt, shared bath, hot tub*

Manors & Co [GF,WC] 1 Baker St **44-(0)20/430-2006, 800/454-4385** *luxury apts*

Soho B&B [GF,NS,GO] Old Compton St (at Charing Cross Rd) **44-(0)78/3437-2866** *rent room or whole apt*

Waverley House Hotel [GF,F,WI] 130-134 Southampton Row (Bloomsbury) **44-(0)20/7833-3691, 44-(0)20/7833-2579**

BARS

Note: "Pub hours" usually means 11am-11pm Mon-Sat and noon-3pm & 7pm-10:30pm Sun

79 CXR [★M,D,WC] 79 Charing Cross Rd (Soho) **44-(0)20/7734-0769** *1pm-3am, till 10:30pm Sun, 2 flrs, cruisy*

The Admiral Duncan [★MW,NH,TG] 54 Old Compton St (Soho) **44-(0)20/7437-5300** *pub hours*

Bar Code [MW,D,E,YC] 3-4 Archer St (btwn Windmill & Rupert, off Shaftesbury, Soho) **44-(0)20/7734-3342** *4pm-1am, till 11pm Sun, Comedy Camp Tue*

Bar Soho [GS] 23-25 Old Compton St (at Frith St) **44-(0)20/7439-0439** *noon-1am, till 3am Fri-Sat, from 4pm Sun*

The Box [★M,D,F,V,WC] 32-34 Monmouth St (near Shaftesbury Ave, Covent Garden) **44-(0)20/7240-5828** *11am-11pm, noon-10:30pm Sun, cafe-bar*

Compton's of Soho [★M,L,F,WC] 51-53 Old Compton St **44-(0)20/7479-7961** *noon-11pm, till 10:30pm Sun, cruisy*

Duke of Wellington [MW,F] 77 Wardour (Soho) **44-(0)20/7439-1274** *pub hours*

The Edge [★MW,D,F,WC] 11 Soho Square **44-(0)20/7439-1313** *noon-1am, till 10:30pm Sun, 4 flrs, cafe-bar, live music, outdoor seating*

The Escape [★M,D,V] 10-A Brewer St (near Regent St) **44-(0)20/7734-2626** *5pm-3am, clsd Sun-Mon*

Freedom Bar [MW,D,F,YC] 66 Wardour St (off Old Compton St) **44-(0)20/7437-3490** *5pm-3am, from 2pm Fri-Sat, 2pm-11:30pm Sun*

Friendly Society [MW,YC] 79 Wardour St (the basement at Old Compton, enter Tisbury Ct) **44-(0)20/7434-3805** *4pm-11pm, ill 10:30pm Sun*

The G.A.Y Bar [MW,F,V] 30 Old Compton St **44-(0)20/7494-2756** *noon-midnight*

Geisha [MW] 75 Charing Cross Rd **44-(0)20/7734-6887**

Green Carnation [★MW,D,F] 4-5 Greek St (Soho) **44-(0)20/7434-3323** *4pm-2am, inspired by the life & times of Oscar Wilde*

Halfway to Heaven [★M,NH,K,C,OC,GO] 7 Duncannon St (at Charing Cross, West End) **44-(0)20/7930-8312, 44-(0)70/9042-1969** *noon-11pm, till 10:30pm Sun*

King's Arms [M,NH,B,F,K,V] 23 Poland St (Soho) **44-(0)20/7734-5907** *noon-11pm, till 1am Fri-Sat, 1pm-midnight Sun, popular bear hangout, 2 flrs*

Ku Bar/ Ku Klub [MW,K,YC,WI] 30 Lisle St (Leicester Sq) **44-(0)20/7437-4303** *12:30-2am, also Soho bar at 25 Frith St*

Kudos [MW,MR,F,V,WC,GO] 10 Adelaide St (off the Strand) **44-(0)20/7379-4573** *noon-midnight, till 11pm Sun, trendy cafe-bar, basement video bar open from 4pm*

Madam JoJo's [M,E,C] 8-10 Brewer St (near Regent St) *Tranny Shack Wed*

Profile [MW,D] 56 Frith St **44-(0)20/7734-8300** *4pm-close, from noon wknds, late night parties Fri-Sat, Sun T-dance*

The Quebec [M,NH,OC] 12 Old Quebec St (at Marble Arch) **44-(0)20/7629-6159** *pub hours, live DJs Fri-Sat, [C] Sun*

The Retro Bar [MW,NH,D,A,K] 2 George Ct **44-(0)20/7321-2811** *pub hours*

Rupert Street [★MW,F,WC] 50 Rupert St (off Brewer) **44-(0)20/7292-7141** *pub hours, upscale "fashiony-types"*

The Stag [M,F,C] 15 Bressenden Pl (near Victoria Stn) **44-(0)20/7828-7287** *noon-midnight, till 2am Fri, from 5pm Sat, till 10pm Sun, terrace*

Vault 139 [M] 139 Whitefield St (Warren St) **44-020/7388-5500** *4pm-1am, from 1pm Sun, theme nights/dress codes*

The Village Soho [★M,F,V,YC] 81 Wardour St (at Old Compton) **44-(0)20/7434-2124** *3pm-1am, till 11:30pm Sun, 3 flrs*

The Yard [★MW,F,E,YC,WC] 57 Rupert St (off Brewer) **44-(0)20/7437-2652, 871/426-2243** *pub hours, 2 levels*

Nightclubs

Discotec [M,D,$] 18 W Central St (at The End) **44-(0)20/7419-9199** *10pm-4am Th only, 2 rooms*

Electrogogo [GS,E] 184 High St (at Electric Ballroom, in Camden) **44-(0)20/07963-145138** *8pm-3am 1st Th, live music*

The Enclave [M,D,F] 25-27 Brewer St (Soho) **44-(0)20/7434-2911** *theme nights*

Exilio [MW,D,MR-L] Houghton St (at London School of Economics Underground) **44-(0)79/3137-4391** *10pm-3am Fri*

G.A.Y. [★M,D,E,YC,$] 157 Charing Cross Rd (at Oxford St, in London Astoria theatre complex) **44-(0)20/7734-6963** *11pm-3am*

Ghetto [MW,D,A] 58 Old Ct **44-(0)20/7287-3726** *10:30pm-3am, till 5am Fri-Sat, theme nights*

Heaven [★M,D] The Arches (off Villiers St) **44-(0)20/7930-2020** *the mother of all London gay clubs, call for hours/ events*

Lo Profile [M,D] 84-86 Wardour St **44-(0)20/7734-1053** *hip basement location*

Salvation [GS,$] Bloomsbury Ballrooms (Victoria House, Bloomsbury Sq) **44-(0)20/7287-3834 (venue), 44-(0)87/1474-6002 (tickets)**

The Shadow Lounge [MW,D] 5 Brewer St (Soho) **44-(0)20/7287-7988** *10pm-3am, from 9pm Th-Sat, clsd Sun*

T Tease [MW,TG] 93 Dean St (at the Black Gardenia) *Fri only*

Wish [MW,D] 60-62 Commercial St (at Gramaphone) *9pm-4am 1st Sat only, fashion fashion fashion!*

Cafes

Balans Cafe [★MW] 34 Old Compton St **44-(0)20/7439-3309** *8am-5am, till 2am Sun, terrace*

Caffe Nero 43 Frith St *cruisy cafe*

First Out [★MW,F] 52 St Giles High St (btwn Charing Cross & Shaftesbury) **44-(0)20/7240-8042** *10am-11pm, full bar*

Flat White 17 Berwick St **44-(0)20/7734-0370** *8am-7pm, 9am-6pm wknds, Australian-style cafe*

Restaurants

Asia de Cuba [R] 45 St Martin's Ln (near Leicester Square) **44-(0)20/7300-5588** *7am-midnight*

Bar Bruno 101 Wardour St **44-(0)20/7734-3750** *Italian cafe, hearty dishes*

Cha Cha Moon 15-21 Ganton St **44-(0)20/7297-9800** *noon-11pm, till 10pm Sun, inexpensive Chinese*

Eat & Two Veg 50 Marylebone High St (near Paddington St, Westminster) **44-(0)20/7258-8595** *brkfst, lunch & dinner, vegetarian American-style diner*

Food for Thought [BYOB] 31 Neal St, downstairs (Covent Garden) **44-0871/332-8808** *9:30am-8:30pm, noon-5pm Sun, vegetarian*

The Gay Hussar [WC] 2 Greek St (on Soho Square) **44-(0)20/7437-0973** *lunch & dinner, clsd Sun, Hungarian*

Just Falafs 155 Wardour St **44-(0)20/7734-1914** *9am-10pm, till 11pm Sat, clsd Sun, organic falafel*

Mildred's [★] 45 Lexington **44-(0)20/7494-1634** *noon-11pm, clsd Sun*

Nusa Dua 11-12 Dean St (Oxford Circus) **44-(0)20/7437-3559, 44-(0)87/1332-7468** *Indonesian*

Randall & Aubin 16 Brewer St (at Walkers Court) **44-(0)20/7287-4447** *noon-11pm, casual French, good people-watching*

Satsuma 56 Wardour St **44-(0)20/7437-8338** *Japanese*

Wagamama Noodle Bar [NS] 10-A Lexington St **44-(0)20/7292-0990** *noon-11pm, Japanese; many locations throughout city*

Entertainment & Recreation

Comedy Camp [★GS,$] 3-4 Archer St (at Barcode, btwn Windmill & Rupert, off Shaftesbury, Soho) **44-(0)20/7483-2960, 08-700/600-100 (TicketWeb)** *8:30pm Tue, amateur & established comedy acts*

Prince Charles Cinema [GF] 7 Leicester Pl (off Leicester Square) **44-020/7222-1234** *sing-alongs, often show LGBT & alternative films*

Bookstores

Gay's the Word 66 Marchmont St (near Russell Square) **44-(0)20/7278-7654** *10am-6:30pm, 2pm-6pm Sun, LGBT*

Retail Shops

Prowler Soho [★] 5-7 Brewer St (behind Village Soho bar) **44-(0)20/7734-4031** *11am-10pm, noon-8pm Sun, large gay dept store*

Gyms & Health Clubs

Soho Athletic Club [★M] 12 Macklin St (at Drury Ln, Covent Garden) **44-(0)20/7242-1290**

Sweatbox [GO] 1-2 Ramilies St, Soho

Men's Clubs

Chariots Waterloo 101 Lower Marsh **44-(0)20/7401-8484** *24hrs*

Pleasuredrome [F,V,NS] Arch 124, Alaska St (at Alaska St, Waterloo) **44-(0)20/7633-9194** *24hrs*

The Sauna Bar [F] 29 Endell St **44-(0)20/7836-2236** *also bar*

Erotica

RoB London [WC] 24 Wells St (near Berwick St) **44-(0)20/7735-7893** *leather/ fetish shop*

Soho Cinemas [V] 7-12 Walkers Court (off Brewer St, Soho) **44-020/7439-0835**

London—West

London—West includes Earl's Court, Kensington, Chelsea & Bayswater

Accommodations

Cardiff Hotel [GF,WI] 5, 7, 9 Norfolk Sq (Hyde Park) **44-(0)20/7723-3513, 44-(0)20/7723-9068** *B&B hotel in 3 Victorian townhouses, some share baths*

Millennium Bailey's Hotel [GF] 140 Gloucester Rd (at Old Brompton Rd, Kensington) **44-(0)20/7373-6000, 44-(0)20/7331-6331** *also restaurant & bar*

Parkwood Hotel [GF,NS] 4 Stanhope Pl (Marble Arch) **44-(0)20/7402-2241** *full brkfst*

Bars

The Culvert [M,NH,F,C,DS] 54 Cowley Mill Rd (Uxbridge) **44-(0)70/9042-1416** *4pm-close*

Infinity [M,D] 294 Old Brompton Rd (at Warwick Rd) **44-(0)20/7370-3494** *1pm-2am, noon-midnight Sun*

Queen's Head [M,NH,F,OC] 27 Tryon St (btwn King's Rd & Sloane Ave, Chelsea) **44-(0)20/7589-0262** *pub hours, professional crowd*

Richmond Arms [MW,D,K,C,DS] 20 The Square (at Princes, Richmond) **44-(0)20/8940-2118** *pub hours, professional crowd*

Ted's Place [M,D,TG,K,DS,V,PC] 305-A North End Rd (at Lillie Rd, Earl's Ct) **44-(0)20/7385-9359** *7pm-midnight, men-only Mon-Wed & Fri, TV/TG from 8pm Th & 6pm Sun, darkroom, cruisy*

West Five (W5) [MW,C,P] 5 Popes Ln (South Ealing) **44-(0)20/0871-971-4569** *6pm-midnight, open later Th-Sat*

Restaurants

The Churchill Arms 119 Kensington Church St **44-(0)20/7727-4242** *inexpensive, fantastic Thai, also pub*

The Gate 51 Queen Caroline St, Hammersmith *lunch & dinner, clsd Sun, vegetarian*

Star of India 154 Old Brompton Rd **44-(0)20/737-2901** *lunch & dinner, upscale*

Thai Princess [MW,TG,WC] 30-31 Philbeach Gardens **44-(0)20/7373-1244** *6pm-11:30pm*

Entertainment & Recreation

Walking Tour of Gay SOHO 56 Old Compton St (at Admiral Duncan Pub) **44-(0)20/7437-6063** *2pm Sun*

Retail Shops

Adonis Art Gallery 1b Coleherne Rd **44-(0)20/7460 3888** *gay art*

Clone Zone [GO] 266 Old Brompton Rd (Earl's Court) **44-(0)20/7373-0598** *10am-8pm, noon-6pm Sun; also Soho location, 64 Old Compton St*

London—North

London—North includes Paddington, Regents Park, Camden, St Pancras & Islington

Accommodations

Ambassadors Bloomsbury [GF,WI,WC] 12 Upper Woburn Pl (at Bloomsbury) **44-0207/693-5400**

Ossian Guesthouse [GF] 20 Ossian Rd **44-(0)20/8340-4331**

Bars

The Black Cap [★MW,D,TG,F,K,C] 171 Camden High St (Camden Town) **44-(0)20/7428-2721** *noon-2am, till-3am Fri-Sat, London's leading cabaret*

Catch 22 [MW,NH,K] 1a Wellington Ter, 679 Green Lanes (at Falkland Rd, Harringay) **44-(0)20/8881-1900** *4pm-12:30am, till 1am Th, till 3am Fri-Sat*

The George Music Bar [M,TG,C,GO] 114 Twickenham Rd (Isleworth) **44-(0)20/8560-1456** *5pm-close, from noon wknds, George Cabaret every Fri-Sat & every other Sun*

The Green [MW,F] 74 Upper St (Angel tube) **44-(0)871/971-4097** *4pm-midnight, till 1am Th, noon-2am Fri, 11am-2am Sat, 11am-midnight Sun, full menu*

King Edward VI/ Sunroom Cafe [★M,NH,F,WC] 25 Bromfield St (at Parkfield St, Islington) **44-(0)20/7704-0745** *noon-midnight, cafe-bar, beer garden*

King William IV [★MW,F] 77 Hampstead High St **44-(0)20/7435-5747** *pub hours, beer garden*

Klub Fukk [MW,D,TG] 37 Wharfdale Rd (at Central Station, King's Cross) **44-(0)20/7278-3294** *7pm-midnight 2nd Sat only, queer sex play space*

Nightclubs

Central Station [★MW,D,TG,F,C,DS,S,V,WI] 37 Wharfdale Rd (King's Cross) **44-(0)20/7278-3294** *complex includes theme nights and B&B, terrace*

Club Kali [★MW,D,MR-A,TG,E,$] 1 Dartmouth Park Hill (at The Dome) **44-(0)20/7272-8153 (Dome #)** *10pm-3am 3rd Fri, South Asian music*

Club Motherfu*ker [MW,D,E] 38-44 Stoke Newington Rd (at Bardens Boudoir) **44-(0)20/7249-9557** *8pm-2am 2nd Sat*

Egg [GS,D] 200 York Way (Kings Cross) **44-(0)20/7609-8364** *10pm Fri-10am Sat, 10pm Sat until late afternoon Sun, 3 flrs, theme nights*

Popstarz [★MW,D,$] 18 W Central St (at New Oxford St) **44-(0)20/7240-1900** *10pm-4am Fri, 4 rooms*

Restaurants

Manna [R] 4 Erskine Rd (at Ainger Rd, Camden) **44-(0)20/7722-8028** *lunch Tue-Sun, dinner nightly, vegetarian*

Providores/ Tapa Room 109 Marylebone High St (at New Cavendish St) **44-(0)20/7935-6175** *lunch & dinner, Asian fusion*

Entertainment & Recreation

Rosemary Branch Theatre [GS,F] 2 Shepperton Rd **44-020/7704-2730 (bar), 44-020/7704-6665 (theatre)** *also restaurant & bar, many gay-themed plays*

Retail Shops

Fettered Pleasures 90 Holloway Rd **44-(0)20/7619-9333** *11pm-7pm, clsd Sun*

Men's Clubs

Chariots Farringdon [F,V] 57 Cowcross St (across from Farringdon tube) **44-(0)20/7251-5553**

Play Pit [BYOB] 76 Caledonian Rd (at Kings Cross Cruising Club) **44-(0)77/7063-1385** *9pm-2am Th, till 3am Fri-Sat, 3pm-1am Sun*

Erotica

Regulation 17a St Albans Pl (Islington Green) **44-(0)20/7226-0665** *fetish gear & toys "made to measure"*

Cruisy Areas

Clapham Common [AYOR] *west side of the common near to the south circular road in the wooded area*

Earls Court Graveyard *summers*

Hampstead Heath [★AYOR]

Highgate Hill take Archway Tube *male sun bathing area at the Highgate Ponds*

London—East

London—East includes City, Tower, Clerkenwell & Shoreditch

Accommodations

The Hoxton [GF,NS,WI] 81 Great Eastern St **44-020/7550-1000**

Bars

Bar Music Hall [GF,D,E,F] 134 Curtain Rd (Shoreditch) **44-(0)20/7613-5951, 44-(0)20/7729-7216** *11am-midnight, till 2am Fri-Sat*

BJ's White Swan [M,D,TG,F,WC] 556 Commercial Rd (near Bromley St) **44-(0)20/7780-9870** *9pm-close, from 6pm Sun, clsd Mon*

Charlie's Bar [MW,NH] 124 Globe Rd (Stepney) **44-(0)20/7790-1007** *pub hours*

The George & Dragon [GF,NH] 151 Cleveland St **44-(0)20/7387-1492** *pub hours*

Joiners Arms [M] 116 Hackney Rd **44-(0)20/7739-9854** *cruisy & sleazy*

Lounge Lover [R,WC] 1 Whitby St (Old Street) **44-020/7012-1234** *fancy Japanese cuisine in a posh lounge*

The Macbeth [M,E,WI] 70 Hoxton St **44-020/ 7749-0600** *9pm-2am*

The Old Ship [MW,NH,C,WC] 17 Barnes St (Stepney) **44-(0)20/7790-4082** *4pm-11pm, from 7pm Tue-Th & Sat, from 5:30pm Sun*

Royal Oak [M,F] 73 Columbia Rd (Old St) **44-020/7729-2220** *6pm-11pm, from noon Sat-Sun*

Nightclubs

Backstreet [MO,L,PC] Wentworth Mews, Burdett Rd (at Mile End Rd, Bow) **44-(0)20/8980-8557, 44-(0)20/8980-7880** *10pm-2am, till 3am Fri-Sat, 11pm-1am Sun, clsd Mon-Wed, strict leather/ rubber dress code*

Dream Bags Jaquar Shoes [MW,D] 34-36 Kingsland Rd **44-020/7729-4192** *5pm-1am, jam packed club in a former shoe shop*

Images [M,D,TG,S,YC] 483 Hackney Rd **44-(0)20/7739-5213** *11pm-5am 1st & 3rd Sat*

Trailer Trash [★MW,D] 25 Kingsland Rd (at On the Rocks) *steamy Fri night party*

Unskinny Bop [MW,D,E] 359 Bethnal Green Rd (btwn Cambridge Heath Rd & Squirries St, at The Star) **44-(0)77/1466-0977** *9pm 3rd Sat only*

Way Out Club [MW,D,TG,S,PC,$] 9 Crosswall (at Charlie's) **44-(0)77/7815-7290** *9pm-4am Sat only, TV/TS & their friends*

Restaurants

Bistrotheque 23-27 Waderson St **44-(0)20/8983-7300** *expensive & glamorous, also cabaret shows after dinner*

Bonds Restaurant & Bar 5 Threadneedle St **44-(0)20/7657-8088** *hours vary*

Cafe Spice Namaste 16 Prescott St **44-(0)20/7488-9242** *lunch Mon-Fri, dinner nightly, clsd Sun, Indian*

Cantaloupe [★] 35-42 Charlotte Rd (Shoreditch) **44-(0)20/7729-5566** *11am-midnight*

Canteen [★] 2 Crispin Pl (Spitalfield) **44-(0)84/5686-1122** *place to be for brkfst*

Hoxton Square Bar & Kitchen [★] 2 Hoxton Square **44-(0)87/1971-3196** *great dark spot for brkfst, also popular gay scene Sun night*

Les Trois Garçons [R] 1 Club Row (at Bethnal, Shoreditch) **44-(0)20/7613-1924** *7pm-midnight, clsd Sun*

Rootmaster Old Truman Brewery, in Elys Yard, off Brick Ln (Algate East tube) **44-(0)79/1238-9314** *vegetarian restaurant in refurbished double-decker bus*

Saf 152-154 Curtain Rd, Shoreditch **44-(0)20/7613-0007** *lunch & dinner, also bar till midnight, upscale vegan/ raw food*

SoSho [★] 2 Tabernacle St **44-(0)20/7920-0701** *lounge and bar hours*

Men's Clubs

Chariots Limehouse [F,V] 574 Commercial Rd (near Limehouse tube) **44-(0)20/7791-2808** *24hrs*

Chariots Shoreditch [★SW,F,V] 1 Fairchild St (Shoreditch) **44-(0)20/7247-5333**

E15 Club 6 Leytonstone Rd **44-(0)20/8555-5455** *11am-11pm*

Erotica

Expectations 75 Great Eastern St (Shoreditch) **44-(0)20/7424-7493** *rubber store*

London—South

London—South includes Southwark, Lambeth, Kennington, Vauxhall, Battersea, Lewisham & Greenwich

Accommodations

Griffin House [MW,WI,GO] 22 Stockwell Green **44-(0)20/7096-3332** *2 rental apts near Vauxhall Gay Village & West End, kitchens*

Bars

Battersea Barge [GF,F,E,C,GO] Riverside Walk Nine Elms Ln (Vauxhall) **44-(0)20/7498-0004** *11:30am-late, clsd Mon, cabaret, comedy on the Thames River!*

The Chocolate Lounge [MW,D,F,E] 146-148 Newington Butts (Kennington) **44-(0)87/1971-4761**

The Eagle London [M,L] 349 Kennington Ln (Vauxhall) **44-(0)20/7793-0903** *9pm-close, from 8pm Sun*

Escape Bar & Art [GF,D] 214-216 Railton Rd (Herne Hill) **44-(0)20/7737-0333** *10am-midnight*

The Fort [M,L] 131 Grange Rd (off Tower Bridge Rd, Bermondsey) **44-(0)20/7237-7742, 44-(0)70/9042-1746** *pub hours, darkroom, theme nights, cruisy*

George & Dragon [MW,C] 2 Blackheath Hill (Greenwich) **44-(0)20/8691-3764** *6pm-2am, till 4am Fri-Sat, [K] Th*

Kazbar [MW,TG,V] 50 Clapham High St (Clapham) **44-(0)20/7622-0070** *4pm-midnight, till 1am Fri-Sat, from 1pm Sun, cafe-bar*

The Little Apple [MW,D,TG,F,WC] 98 Kennington Ln **44-(0)20/7582-7911** *noon-midnight, till 3am Sat, terrace*

The Two Brewers [MW,D,K,C,V] 114 Clapham High St (Clapham) **44-(0)20/7498-4971** *5pm-2am, till 3am Fri-Sat, 2pm-12:30am Sun*

Two8Six [MW,D,C,PC] 286 Lewisham High St **44-020/8690-5758** *11am-late, 7pm-1am Sun*

NIGHTCLUBS

Area/Embankment Bar [M,D] 67-68 Albert Embankment (Vauxhall) **44-020/7091-0173** *Th-Sat night,*

Black Sheep Bar [GS,D,A] 68 High St (Croydon) **44-(0)20/8680-2233**

Bootylicious [MW,MR] 1 Nine Elms (at Club Colosseum) *11pm 4th Sat, popular black gay club*

Ego [M,D,K] 82 Norwood High St **44-(0)28/971-4567** *from 8pm doors close at 11pm, ring bell for assistance*

Escape [M,D] 184 London Rd (Kingston) **44-(0)20/8549-9911** *7pm-midnight, till 3am Fri-Sat, clsd Mon-Tue*

Fire [MW,D,$] 47B S Lambeth Rd (Vauxhall) **44-(0)79/0503-5682** *Th-Mon nights & Sun afternoons*

The Fridge [★GS,D] 1 Town Hall Parade (Brixton Hill) **44-(0)20/7326-5100**

The Hoist [M,L] Railway Arch 47b&c, S Lambeth Rd (Vauxhall) **44-(0)20/7735-9972** *from 8:30pm, clsd Mon-Wed, S/M club w/ strict dress code*

Juicy [M,D] 47B S Lambeth Rd (at Fire, Vauxhall) **44-(0)79/0503-5682** *11pm-close Sat only*

Royal Vauxhall Tavern [M,NH,D,TG,F,WC] 372 Kennington Ln (Vauxhall) **44-(0)20/7820-1222** *8pm-late, 9pm-3am Fri-Sat, 2pm-midnight Sun*

Starkers [GS,D,N] 65 Goding St (at The Factory) **44-(0)77/3903-6056** *10pm-close 3rd Fri, naked club, not sex club, footwear required*

Union [M,D] 66 Albert Embankment (Vauxhall) **44-(0)20/7278-3294** *cruise mazes, dark corners, popular Fri*

Urban Desi [MW,D,MR-A] 61 Turnmill St (at Anexo Club) Farmington) **44-(0)79/5568-3144, 44-(0)79/5568-3134** *11pm-5am 2nd Sat, South Asian*

XXL [MO,D,B] 51-53 Southwark St (at London Bridge Arches) **44-(0)78/1204-8574** *10pm-6am Sat, till 3am Wed, "one club fits all"*

CAFES

Glow Lounge [F] 6 Cavendish Parade (Clapham Common S Side) **44-(0)77/3179-9530** *cafe by day, mellow club by night*

RESTAURANTS

Hidden at Hard On [MO,D,PC] 100 Tinworth St (at Hidden, in Vauxhall) **44-020/7820-1702 (Hidden)** *monthly parties, playroom*

ENTERTAINMENT & RECREATION

Oval Theatre Cafe Bar [F] 52-54 Kennington Oval **44-(0)20/7582-0080** *6pm-11pm Tue-Sat (cafe), inquire about current theatre & art*

RETAIL SHOPS

The Host 44a Parry St **44-(0)20/7793-1551** *rubber & fetish gear, by appt only*

GYMS & HEALTH CLUBS

Paris Gymnasium [MO] 73 Goding St (behind Vauxhall Tavern, Vauxhall) **44-(0)20/7735-8989** *£10 day pass*

Men's Clubs

Chariots Streatham 292 Streatham High Rd (at Babington Rd, enter rear) **44-(0)20/8696-0929** *24hrs wknds*

Chariots Vauxhall [F,V] Rail Arches 63-64 (Albert Embankment) **44-(0)20/7735-6709**

The Locker Room [V] 8 Cleaver St (Kennington) **44-(0)20/7582-6288** *24hrs wknds*

Star Steam [V] 38 Lavender Hill (Battersea) **44-(0)20/7924-2269** *noon-8pm*

Steamworks [V] 309 New Cross Rd **44-(0)20/8694- 0606** *24hrs wknds*

Cruisy Areas

Hyde Park [AYOR] *Southeast cornor of Hyde Park in the Rose Garden*

France

Paris

Note: M°=Métro station

Paris is divided by arrondissements (city districts); 01=1st arrondissement, 02=2nd arrondissement, etc

Paris—Overview

Note: When phoning Paris from the US, dial the country code + the city code + the local phone number

Info Lines & Services

Centre Gai et Lesbien 63 rue Beaubourg **33-1/4357-2147** *drop-in evenings, many groups/ events*

Gay AA 7 rue August Vacquerie (at St George's Anglican) **33-1/4634-5965** *7:30pm Tue*

Accommodations

Gay Accommodation Paris [GO] 271, rue du Faubourg Saint Antoine **33-1/4348-1382** *studios for rent in central Paris*

Marais Flats/ Studios [GO] 20 rue Pierre Lescot **33-6/3256-5727 (European daytime only)**

RentParis.com LLC [GS,NS,GO] **33-6/6703-5471** *fully furnished studios & apts*

Publications

PREF Mag 33-1/4087-1070 *bi-monthly magazine*

Têtu 33-1/5680-2080 *stylish & intelligent LGBT monthly (en français)*

Paris—01

Accommodations

Hotel Louvre Richelieu [GS,NS] 51 rue de Richelieu (M° Palais-Royal) **33-1/4297-4620**

Hotel Louvre Saint-Honoré [GS,WI,WC] 141 rue Saint-Honoré (at rue du Louvre) **33-1/4296-2323** *3-star*

Bars

Le Banana Cafe [★MW,D,E,P,S,YC,WC] 13-15 rue de la Ferronnerie (near rue St-Denis, M° Châtelet) **33-1/4233-3531** *6pm-dawn, go-go boys Th-Sat, theme nights, terrace*

Le Tropic Cafe [MW,D,TG,F,YC,WC] 66 rue des Lombards (M° Châtelet) **33-1/4013-9262** *4pm-5am, tapas, terrace*

Le Vagabond [M,F,OC] 14 rue Thérèse (at av de l'Opera, M° Pyramides) **33-1/4296-2723** *6pm-close, clsd Mon, oldest gay bar & restaurant in Paris*

Wolf [M,B] 37 rue des Lombards (M° Châtelet) **33-1/4028-0252** *5pm-2am, bear bar*

Nightclubs

Afrodisiack/ Lick'n Licious [W,D,MR,$] 14 rue St-Denis (at rue des Lombards, at Le Club, M° Châtelet) **33-1/4508-9625** *Sat only*

Le Club [MW,D,MR,YC,PC,$] 14 rue St-Denis (at rue des Lombards, M° Châtelet) **33-1/4508-9625** *midnight-close Fri-Sat only, theme nights*

Le Club 18 [★M,D,YC,PC,$] 18 rue du Beaujolais (at rue Vivienne, M° Palais-Royal) **33-1/4297-5213** *Wed, Fri-Sat only*

The Eagle [MO,D] 33 bis rue des Lombards, in basement (at boul de Sebastopol) **33-1/4233-4145** *6pm-dawn, clsd Mon, theme nights, darkroom*

Gay Tea Dance [M,D] 2 Place du Palais Royal **33-1/5862-5625** *8pm Sun only*

Gay Tea Dance [M,D] 2 place du Palais Royal (at Cab) *8pm Sun*

L' Insolite [★M,D,$] 33 rue des Petits-Champs (at rue Chabanais, enter through back courtyard, M° Pyramides) **33-1/4020-9859** *11pm-5am, till 6am Fri-Sat*

Rexy Club [GF,D] 9 rue de la Grande Truanderie (M° Etienne Marcel) **33-1/4026-5105**

Restaurants

L' Amazonial [MW,C,DS,WC] 3 rue Ste-Opportune (at rue Ferronnerie, M° Châtelet) **33-1/4233-5313** *lunch & dinner, brunch wknds, Brazilian/ int'l, heated terrace*

Au Diable des Lombards 64 rue des Lombards (at rue St-Denis, M° Châtelet) **33-1/4233-8184** *8am-1am, American, brunch till 6pm daily, full bar, terrace*

Au Rendez-Vous des Camionneurs [M] 72 quai des Orfèvres (M° Pont Neuf) **33-1/4354-8874** *lunch & dinner, traditional bistro*

Chez Max 47 rue Saint Honoré (M° Louvre) **33-1/4508-8013** *lunch & dinner, traditional French*

Jet Lag 4 rue Montmartre (M° Etienne Marcel) **33-1/4488-2230** *9am-2am, 2 patios*

Marc Mitonne [E,C] 60 rue de l'Arabe-Sec (M° Les Halles) **33-1/4261-5316** *6pm-2am, clsd Sun-Mon, theme nights*

La Poule au Pot 9 rue Vauvilliers (M° Les Halles) **33-1/4236-3296** *7pm-5am, clsd Mon & Aug, bistro, French*

Entertainment & Recreation

Forum des Halles 101 Porte Berger (M° Châtelet-Les Halles) **33-1/4476-9656** *underground sports/ entertainment complex w/ museums, theater, shops, clubs, cafes & more*

Gyms & Health Clubs

Club Med Gym [GS] 147 rue St-Honoré (M° Louvre) **33-1/4020-0303** *day passes available, many locations throughout city*

Men's Clubs

The Hole Next [MO] 87 rue St Honoré (at rue du Roule, M° Chatelet-Les Halles)

Til't [M] 41 rue Ste-Anne (near av de l'Opera, M° Pyramides) **33-1/4296-0743** *noon-7am, bar*

Le Transfert [MO] 3 rue de la Sourdiere (M° Tuileries) *midnight-7am, till 8am wknds, also open 4pm-10pm some wknds*

Erotica

Boxxman 2 rue de la Cossonnerie (M° Châtelet) **33-1/4221-4702** *videos, toys & fetish gear, also sex club, internet access*

Cruisy Areas

Quai des Tuileries [AYOR] on bank of The Seine (M° Louvre) *aka Tata Beach*

Paris—02

Bars

DMX [MW] 7 rue Chabanais (M° Pyramides) **33-1/4296-3917** *8pm-6am, cruise bar, theme nights*

L' Impact [MO,N,V] 18 rue Grenéta (M° Châtelet) **33-1/4221-9424** *8pm-3am, 10pm-6am Fri-Sat, from 3pm Sun, cruise bar, 100% naked, backroom, theme nights, free brkfst wknds*

Nightclubs

Rex Club [GF,D,$] 5 blvd Poissonière (M° Bonne Nouvelle) **33-1/4236-1096** *call for events, clsd August*

Cafes

Stuart Friendly [F] 16 rue Marie Stuart *noon-11pm, till midnight Fri-Sat, till 5:30pm Sun, "straight-friendly" cafe*

Restaurants

Aux Trois Petits Cochons [★MW,R,GO] 31 rue Tiquetonne (at rue St-Denis, M° Etienne-Marcel) **33-1/4233-3969** *8pm-1am, gourmet French*

Le César [MW] 4 rue Chabanais (M° Pyramides) **33-1/4296-8113** *6:30pm-5am, also bar*

Le Dénicheur 4 rue Tiquetonne (M° Etienne-Marcel) **33-1/4221-3101**

Le Loup Blanc [★MW] 42 rue Tiquetonne (M° Etienne-Marcel) **33-1/4013-0835** *7:30pm-midnight, till 1am Sat, also brunch 11am-4:30pm Sun, French/ int'l*

Pig'z [M] 5 rue Marie-Stuart (M° Etienne Marcel) **33-1/4233-0589** *8pm-midnight, clsd Sun-Mon*

Retail Shops

Galerie au Bonheur du Jour 11 rue Chabanais **33-1/4296-5864** *2:30pm-7:30pm, clsd Sun-Mon, gay art*

Men's Clubs

Euro Men's Club [V,SW,OC] 8-10 rue St-Marc (M° Bourse) **33-1/4233-9263** *run-down*

Paris—03

Accommodations

► **Absolu Living** [MW,GO] 236 rue St Martin **33-1/4454-9700** *fully furnished apts in central Paris, short & long-term stays*

Adorable Apartment in Paris [★GF,NS,GO] (M° Rambuteau) **415/397-6454 (US#)** *2-bdrm flat in heart of Marais*

Hôtel du Vieux Saule [GF] 6 rue de Picardie **33-1/4272-0114**

Republique Paris [M, GO] place de la République **33-6/6453-6450**

Bars

Le CUD Club [M,D,B] 12 rue des Haudriettes **33-1/4277-4412** *11pm-6am, till 7am wknds*

Le Dépôt [MO,D,S,YC,$] 10 rue aux Ours (btwn bd de Sébastopol & rue St-Martin, M° Rambuteau) **33-1/4454-9696** *2pm-8am, huge cruise bar on 3 flrs, backroom, T-dance 5pm Sun, go-go boys*

Le Duplex [MW,NH,S] 25 rue Michel-le-Comte (at rue Beaubourg, M° Rambuteau) **33-1/4272-8086** *8pm-2am, till 4am Fri-Sat, friendly, cruisy, internet access*

One Way [M,NH,B,L,F,V,OC] 28 rue Charlot (at rue des 4 Fils, M° République) **33-1/4887-4610** *5pm-2am, cruisy, darkroom, tapas*

Snax Kfé [M,F] 182 rue Saint Martin (M° Rambuteau) **33-1/4027-8933** *10am-2am, from 3:30pm Sat, clsd Sun*

Sun City [MO] 62 Blvd de Sébastopol (M° Rambuteau) **33-1/4274-3141** *noon-6am, sauna, swimming, gym, private cabins*

Le Tango/ La Boite à Frissons [★MW,F] 11 rue au Marie (M° Arts-et-Métiers) **33-1/4272-1778** *10:30pm-5am, clsd Mon, T-dance Sun*

Nightclubs

Les Bains Douches [★GF,D,F,$] 7 rue du Bourg-l'Abbé (at bd de Sébastopol, M° Etienne-Marcel) **33-1/4887-0180** *11pm-close, gay Sun-Mon*

Le Blue Square [DS] 8 rue Brantôme (at rue Rambuteau) **33-1/4029-0889** *drag T-dance 6pm Sun only*

Restaurants

La Fontaine Gourmande 11 rue Charlot **33-1/4278-7240** *lunch Tue-Fri & dinner Tue-Sun, French*

Entertainment & Recreation

Musée Picasso [WC] 5 rue de Thorigny (in the Hôtel Salé, M° St-Paul) **33-1/4271-2521** *clsd Tue*

Men's Clubs

The Glove [L] 34 rue Charlot (M° St-Sebastien-Froissard) **33-1/4887-3136** *10:30pm-close, 4:30pm-9pm Sun, clsd Mon-Wed, leather/ rubber/ uniform, theme nights, also bar, brkfst wknds*

Erotica

Rex 42 rue de Poitou (at rue Charlot, M° St-Sébastien-Froissard) **33-1/4277-5857** *clsd Sun, new, custom & secondhand leather & S/M accessories*

Paris—04

Accommodations

Chambres D'Hôte Rivoli [MW,WI,GO] **33-06/1991-5828** *B&B*

Hôtel Beaubourg [GS,WI] 11 rue Simon le Franc (btwn rue Beaubourg & rue du Temple, M° Hôtel-de-Ville) **33-1/4274-3424** *next to Centre Pompidou*

Hôtel Central Marais [M,WI,GO] 2 rue Ste-Croix-de-la-Bretonnerie **33-1/4887-5608** *central location, some shared baths, also gay bar*

Hôtel de la Bretonnerie [GF] 22 rue Ste-Croix-de-la-Bretonnerie (M° Hôtel-de-Ville) **33-1/4887-7763** *17th-c hotel w/ Louis XIII decor*

Hôtel du Vieux Marais [GF] 8 rue du Plâtre (M° Hôtel-de-Ville) **33-1/4278-4722** *centrally located*

Paris-Apart [GS,NS,GO] 14 rue François Miron *loft in old Le Marais*

Bars

Akhenaton Cafe [MW,NH] 12 rue de Plâtre (btwn rue du Temple & rue des Archives, M° Hôtel-de-Ville) **33-1/488-70-259** *5pm-2am, from 6pm Sun, cafe-bar*

L' Amnésia Café [★MW,D,F] 42 rue Vieille du Temple (at rue des Blancs-Manteaux, M° Hôtel-de-Ville) **33-1/4272-1694** *11am-close*

Au Mange Disque [M] 15 rue de la Reynie (at Boule de Sebastopol) **33-1/4804-7817** *6pm-2am, clsd Sun, theme nights, colorful modern decor*

Le Bar du Palmier [MW,F] 16 rue des Lombards (at bd de Sébastopol, M° Châtelet) **33-1/4278-5353** *2pm-6am*

Bears' Den [MO,D,B,V] 6 rue des Lombards (at rue St-Martin, M° Hôtel-de-Ville) **33-1/4271-0820** *4pm-2am, till 4am Fri-Sat, theme nights, T-dance Sun, darkroom, terrace*

Le Carré [MW,F] 18 rue du Temple (M° Hôtel-de-Ville) **33-1/4459-3857** *10am-4am, Sun brunch, lounge & restaurant, terrace*

Le Carrefour [M,NH] 8 rue des Archives (at rue de la Verrerie) **33-1/4029-9005**

Le Central [★M] 33 rue Vieille du Temple (below Hôtel Central Marais) **33-1/4887-5608** *4pm-2am, from 2pm Fri-Sun, int'l crowd, a Marais landmark*

Cox [★M] 15 rue des Archives (at rue Ste-Croix-de-la-Bretonnerie, M° Hôtel-de-Ville) **33-1/4272-0800** *noon-2am, cruisy, terrace*

L' Enchanteur [MW,P] 15 rue Michel Lecomte (M° Rambuteau) **33-1/4804-0238** *11am-2am*

Le Feeling [MW,NH,YC] 43 rue Ste-Croix-de-la-Bretonnerie (M° Hôtel-de-Ville) **33-1/4804-7003** *3pm-2am*

Free DJ [MW] 35 rue Ste-Croix-de-la-Bretonnerie (at rue du Temple, M° Hôtel-de-Ville) **33-1/4029-4440** *5pm-2am, till 4am Th-Sat*

Full Metal [M,L] 40 rue des Blancs-Manteaux (M° Rambuteau) **33-1/4272-3005** *5pm-4am, till 6am Fri-Sat, from 3pm Sun, well-stocked "hard backroom bar," theme parties, dress code*

L' Imprevu Cafe [M,NH,F] 9 rue Quincampoix **33-1/4278-2350** *noon-2am, from 1pm Sun, low-key cafe/ bar*

Les Jacasses [W] 5 rue des Ecouffes (M° St Paul) **33-1/4271-7551** *5pm-2am*

Le Mic-Man [M,NH,V] 24 rue Geoffroy-l'Angevin (at rue Beaubourg, M° Rambuteau) **33-1/4274-3980** *noon-2am, open later wknds, friendly bar w/ cruisy cave downstairs*

Le Mixer Bar [★MW,D,YC] 23 rue Ste-Croix-de-la-Bretonnerie (at rue des Archives, M° Hôtel-de-Ville) **33-1/4887-5544** *4pm-2am, 3-flr techno/ house bar, theme nights*

L' Oiseau Bariolé [MW] 16 rue Saint-Croix-de-la-Bretonnerie (M° Hotel de Ville) **33-1/4272-3712, 33-1/4272-3712** *5pm-close, quiet*

Okawa [★GS,F,C,P,YC] 40 rue Vieille du Temple (at rue Ste-Croix-de-la-Bretonnerie, M° Hôtel-de-Ville) **33-1/4804-3069** *9am-2am, trendy cafe-bar in 12th- & 13th-c caves, theme nights, [P] Tue-Wed, also restaurant*

L' Open Cafe [★MW,F] 17 rue des Archives (at rue Ste-Croix-de-la-Bretonnerie, M° Hôtel-de-Ville) **33-1/4887-8025** *11am-2am, till 4am Fri-Sat, sidewalk cafe-bar; also L'Open Coffee Shop, 23 rue du Temple (33-1/4887-8025), salads & sandwiches*

Le QG [MO,L,V] 12 rue Simon Lefranc (at rue du Renard, M° Rambuteau) **33-1/4887-7418** *4pm-8am, theme parties Fri, dress code, sex bar*

Quetzal [★M,NH,S] 10 rue de la Verrerie (at rue des Archives, M° Hôtel-de-Ville) **33-1/4887-9907** *5pm-5am, cruise bar, internet access, Latino night Mon, go-go boys/ shows Tue & Th, darkroom, terrace*

Le Raidd [M,D,S] 23 rue du Temple (M° Hotel de ville) *5pm-5am*

Secteur X [MO] 49 rue des Blancs-Manteaux (at rue du Temple, M° Rambuteau) **33-1/4027-9742** *5pm-2am, cruisy, backroom*

Les Souffleurs [MW,D,YC] 7 rue de la Verrerie (M° Hôtel-de-Ville) **33-1/4478-0491**

Yono [M,D,E,F] 37 rue Vieille du Temple *6pm-2am Tue-Sun, cozy basement bar*

Ze Baar [M,NH,F] 41 rue des Blancs Manteaux (at rue du Temple) **33-1/4271-7508** *5pm-2am, also restaurant*

Nightclubs

Le Scarron [MW] 3 rue Geoffroy l'Angevin **33-1/4277-4405** *clsd Sun-Mon, cozy dance club & piano bar*

Restaurants

Auberge de la Reine Blanche 30 rue St Louis en l'Ile **33-1/4633-0787** *romantic bistro*

Le Chant des Voyelles 3 rue des Lombards (M° Châtelet) **33-1/4277-7707** *lunch & dinner, traditional French, terrace*

Curieux Spaghetti Bar 14 rue Saint Merri (M° Rambuteau) **33-1/4272-7597** *noon-2am, till 4am Th-Sat, brunch wknds, home of scented vodka "Chup" shots*

Equinox [DS,P] 33 rue des Rosiers (M° St-Paul) **33-1/4271-9241** *7pm-midnight, Québecois/ French, full bar*

Etamine Cafe 13 rue des Ecouffes (at rue des Rosiers, M° Hotel de Ville) **33-1/4478-0962** *11am-midnight, also bar*

Le Gai Moulin [MW] 10 rue St-Merri (at rue du Temple, M° Hôtel-de-Ville) **33-1/4887-0600** *dinner, French/ int'l*

Le Kofi du Marais [MW] 54 rue Ste-Croix-de-la-Bretonnerie (M° Hôtel de Ville) **33-1/4887-4871** *coffee & light meals*

Le Petit Picard [MW] 42 rue Ste-Croix-de-la-Bretonnerie (M° Hôtel-de-Ville) **33-1/4278-5403** *lunch & dinner, clsd Mon*

Les Piétons [GS] 8 rue des Lombards (M° Châtelet) **33-1/4887-8287** *noon-4am, Spanish/ tapas, also bar, [D] Wed*

La Victoire Supreme du Coeur 27-31 rue du Bourg-Tibourg (M° Hôtel-de-Ville) **33-1/4041-9503** *lunch & dinner, vegetarian*

Entertainment & Recreation

Gay Beach E end of Ile St-Louis *sunbathing*

Bookstores

Les Mots à la Bouche 6 rue Ste-Croix-de-la-Bretonnerie (near rue du Vieille du Temple, M° Hôtel-de-Ville) **33-1/4278-8830** *11am-11pm, 1pm-9pm Sun, LGBT, English titles*

Retail Shops

Boy'z Bazaar Collections 5 rue Ste-Croix-de-la-Bretonnerie (at rue Vieille du Temple, M° Hôtel-de-Ville) **33-1/4271-3400** *noon-8:30pm, till 10pm Fri-Sat, clubwear to drag to leather*

Sweetman 17 blvd de Raspail **33-8/9270-5550** *10:30am-7pm, clsd Sun, men's underwear & more*

Erotica

BMC Store 21 rue des Lombards **33-1/4027-9809** *videos, DVDs, toys*

IEM Marais 16 rue Ste-Croix-de-la-Bretonnerie (M° Hôtel-de-Ville) **33-1/4274-0161** *leather, latex, uniforms & fetish gear*

Menstore 8 Square Ste-Croix de la Bretonnerie **33-1/4454-5115**

RoB Paris 6 Square Ste-Croix de la Bretonnerie **33-1/4454-5115** *leather/ fetish*

Cruisy Areas

Square du Pont de Sully [AYOR] at the end of Ile St-Louis (M° Sully-Morland) *along the side paths at night*

Paris—05

Restaurants

Le Petit Prince [★] 12 rue de Lanneau (M° Maubert-Mutualité) **33-1/4354-7726** *2:30pm-midnight, French*

Entertainment & Recreation

Open-Air Sculpture Museum Quai Saint-Bernard *along the Seine btwn the Jardin des Plantes & the Institut du Monde Arabe*

Gyms & Health Clubs

Hammam de la Mosque de Paris [GS] 39 rue Geoffroy St-Hilaire **33-1/4331-3820** *traditional Turkish baths; women welcome Mon & Wed-Sat; men welcome Tue & Sun*

Paris—06

Accommodations

Friendlyfrenchy's Gay B&B [M,WI] 104 rue d'assas (rue Michelet) **33-1/4354-3764**

Bookstores

The Village Voice 6 rue Princesse (M° Mabillon) **33-1/4633-3647** *10am-7:30pm, from 2pm Mon, noon-6pm Sun, English-language bookshop*

Paris—07

Cruisy Areas

Champs de Mars [AYOR] (M° Pont-de-l'Alma)

Paris—08

Accommodations

François 1er [GF,WI] 7 rue Magellan **33-1/4723-4404** *boutique hotel near les Champs-Elysées, also bar*

Bars

Le Day Off [MW,NH,F] 10 rue de l'Isly (M° Gare-St-Lazare) **33-1/4522-8790**

Nightclubs

Le Queen [★M,D,TG,DS,YC,$] 102 av des Champs-Élysées (btwn rue Washington & rue de Berri, M° Georges-V) **33-8/9270-7330** *midnight-dawn, very trendy, selective door, theme nights, drag shows, go-go boys*

Under [M,D] 22 rue Quentin Bauchart (at ave des Champs-Elysées, at Club 79) **33-1/4723-6917** *6am-noon 2nd Sun only*

Men's Clubs

Banque Club [S,V] 23 rue de Penthièvre (off Champs d'Élysées, M° Miromesnil) **33-1/4256-4926** *3pm-dawn, 3 levels, maze, theme nights, also bar*

Erotica

French Art [V] 64 rue de Rome (M° Europe) **33-1/4522-5735** *clsd Sun*

Vidéovision 62 rue de Rome (M° Europe) **33-1/4293-6604** *clsd Sun*

Paris—09

Accommodations

The Grand [GF] 2 rue Scribe **33-1/4006-0117, 800/327-0200 (US#)** *ultraluxe art deco hotel*

Bars

Mec Zone [M,L,V] 27 rue Turgot (M° Anvers) **33-1/4082-9418** *9pm-5am, 2pm-6pm wknds, cruisy, theme nights, darkroom*

Nightclubs

Folies Pigalle [GS,D,MR,$] 11 place Pigalle (M° Pigalle) **33-1/4878-5525, 33-1/4280-1203 (BBB info line)** *midnight-dawn Tue-Sat, theme nights*

Men's Clubs

IDM [★V] 4 rue du Faubourg-Montmartre (at bd St-Martin, M° Grand-Blvds) **33-1/4523-1003** *full gym, jacuzzi, bar*

Erotica

Yanko [AYOR] 10 place de Clichy (M° place de Clichy) **33-1/4526-7119** *videos & cinema*

Paris—10

Bars

Baxo [GS] 21 rue Juliette Dodu (M° Colonel Fabien) **33-1/4202-9971** *9am-2am, from noon Sun, trendy bar/restaurant, also brunch Sun, patio*

Cafe Moustache [M,NH,B,V] 138 rue du Faubourg St-Martin (at bd de Magenta, M° Gare-de-l'Est) **33-1/4607-7270** *4pm-2am, darkroom, patio*

Men's Clubs

Key West Sauna [★V,SW] 141 rue Lafayette (M° Gare-du-Nord) **33-1/4526-3174** *gym equipment, jacuzzi, 3 levels*

Erotica

Concorde 27 Blvd de Magenta **33-1/4249-1172** *also at 6 rue du Dahomey*

Cruisy Areas

Canal St-Martin Jean-Jaurès [AYOR] (M° Jaurès) *on the quais btwn the Jean-Jaurès & Louis-Blanc bridges*

Paris—11

Accommodations

Hôtel Beaumarchais [GS] 3 rue Oberkampf (btwn bd Beaumarchais & bd Voltaire, M° Filles-du-Calvaire) **33-1/5336-8686**

Bars

Le Bataclan [GF,E] 50 blvd Voltaire (at Bataclan club, M° Saint Ambroise) **33-1/4314-0030** *live music venue, more gay for the Follivores & Crazyvores, call for events*

L' Escalme [M,NH,F] 140 Blvd Richard Lenoir **33-1/4805-2955** *9am-2am, also restaurant*

Follivores/ Crazyvores [MW,D] 50 blvd Voltaire (M° Saint Ambroise) **33-1/4314-0030** *monthly sing-along dance parties; Follivores is 1960s-1990s French pop, Crazyvores is English-speaking; kitsch factor very high!*

Interface [M] 34 rue Keller (rue de La Roquette) **33-1/4700-6715** *3pm-2am, till 4am wknds, art exhibitions*

Keller's [MO,L,$] 14 rue Keller (M° Bastille) **33-1/4700-0539** *10:30pm-2am, till 4am Th-Sat, raunchy cruise bar, theme parties, strict dress code, darkroom*

Nightclubs

Beardrop [M,D,B] 2 bis rue des Taillandiers (M° Bastille, at La Scene) **33-1/4806-5070 (club)** *midnight-6am 3rd Sat only*

Les Disquaires [GS,D,E] 6 rue des Taillandiers (M° Bastille) *dance bar, live bands*

La Scène Bastille [GF,F,E] 2 bis rue des Taillandiers (M° Bastille) **33-1/4806-5070 (club), 33-1/4806-1213 (restaurant)** *also restaurant, live music, events*

Restaurants

Bistrot Guillaume 5 rue Guillaume Bertrand **33-1/4700-4350**

Sans Gêne 122 rue Oberkampf *5pm-2am, Sun brunch, also bar*

Le Sofa 21 rue St-Sabin (M° Bastille) **33-1/4314-0746** *6pm-midnight, till 2am Th-Sat, clsd Sun, also bar*

Le Tabarin [MW,P] 3 rue du Pasteur-Wagner (M° Bastille) **33-1/4807-1522** *lunch Sun-Fri, dinner Sun-Sat, full bar*

Entertainment & Recreation

L' ArtiShow [C] 3 cite Souzy **33-1/4348-5604** *cabaret, also lunch & dinner served*

O Chateau, Wine Tasting in Paris [GF,TG] 100 rue de la Folie Mericourt **33-1/4473-9780**

Bookstores

Violette & Co [GO] 102 rue de Charonne (at boulevard Voltaire) **33-1/4372-1607** *11am-8pm, 2pm-7pm Sun, clsd Mon, lesbian-owned*

Men's Clubs

Boys Video Club 8 rue de Nice (M° Charonne) *11am-2am, gloryholes, video rooms, cabins*

Bunker [V] 150 rue St-Maur (M° Goncourt) **33-1/4357-3382** *4pm-2am, till 3:30am Fri, till 4:30am Sat, till 1am Sun, backroom, theme nights*

Entre Deux Eaux [MO] 45 rue de la Folie Mericourt (at rue Oberkampf) **33-1/4357-7646** *naked sex club for men, theme nights*

Paris—12

Gyms & Health Clubs

Atlantide [GS,TG,V] 13 rue Parrot (M° Gare de Lyon) **33-1/4342-2243** *women & transgender welcome, cabins, tanning, also bar*

Cruisy Areas

Bois de Vincennes [AYOR]

Paris—13

Cruisy Areas

Quai d'Austerlitz [AYOR]

Les Sablières [AYOR] *along the quai d'Austerlitz, from library to blvds Perijheriques, at night only*

Paris—14

Entertainment & Recreation

Catacombes 1 rue du Colonel Henri Rol-Tanguy (M° Denfert-Rochereau) **33-1/4322-4763** *a ghoulish yet intriguing tourist destination, these burial tunnels were the headquarters of the Résistance during World War II*

Gyms & Health Clubs

Amphibi [GS,TG] 73 rue Hallé (at rue Bézout, M° Alesia) **33-1/4047-5090** *sauna where everyone is welcome: gay, straight, male, female, bisexual, transgendered*

Men's Clubs

Bains d' Odessa [MO, WI] 5 rue d'Odessa **33-1/4047-8343** *noon-10pm, sauna, swimming, massage, darkroom*

Les Bains d'Odessa [M,WI] 5 rue d'Odessa (at rue du Départ, M° Montparnasse) **33-1/4047-8343**

Paris—15

Bars

Mix [GS,D] 24 rue de l'Arrivée **33-1/5680-3737**

Entertainment & Recreation

Friday Night Fever [GS] Plaza Dautry (near Montparnasse Rail Station) *10pm-1am Fri (weather permitting), meet 9:30pm, rollerblading*

Paris—16

Accommodations

Keppler [GF,WI] 10 rue Keppler **33-1/4720-6505** *near major tourist stops, also bar*

Cruisy Areas

Bois de Boulogne [AYOR] (M° Porte Dauphine)

Paris—17

Men's Clubs

King Sauna [V] 21 rue Bridaine (near place de Clichy, M° Rome) **33-1/4294-1910** *1pm-7am, bar*

Paris—18

Bars

Karambole Cafe [GS,F] 10 rue Hegesippe (M° Place de Clichy or La Fourche) **33-1/4293-3068** *11:30am-2am, from 6pm Sat, artsy cafe by day, DJs by night*

Le Tagada Bar [M,F] 40 rue Trois-Frères (M° Abesses) **33-1/4255-9556** *6:30pm-2am, clsd Sun, upscale food*

Nightclubs

Blacks Blancs Beurs/ KELMA T-Dance [M,D,MR] 90 Blvd de Clichy (at rue Blanche, at Loco) **33-1/4205-7300 (infoline)+** *7pm-midnight Sun only, R&B & Arabic dance music*

Escualita [M,D,TG] 90 Blvd de Clichy (at rue Blanche, at Loco) *midnight Sun only, fabulous tranny dance party, all are welcome*

Entertainment & Recreation

Madame Arthur [F] 75 bis rue des Martyrs **33-1/4254-1592** *drag diva, dinner show*

Michou [F] 80 rue des Martyrs (at Blvd de Clichy, M° Pigalle) **33-1/4606-1604** *infamous drag cabaret, dinner show*

Men's Clubs

Sauna Mykonos [M] 71 rue des Martyrs **33-1/4252-1546** *noon-11:30pm*

Paris—19

Cafes

Cafe Cherie [GS,E] 44 Blvd de la Villette (M° Belleville) **33-1/4202-0205** *8am-2am, live music & DJs starting at 10pm*

Paris—20

Accommodations

Mama Shelter [GS,WI] 109 rue de Bagnolet **33-1/ 4348-4848**

Entertainment & Recreation

Père Lachaise Cemetery bd de Ménilmontant (M° Père-Lachaise) *perhaps the world's most famous resting place, where lie such notables as Chopin, Oscar Wilde, Sarah Bernhardt, Isadora Duncan, Gertrude Stein & Jim Morrison*

Men's Clubs

Le Riad [SW,V] 184 rue des Pyrénnées (M° Gambetta) **33-1/4797-2552**

GERMANY

Berlin

Berlin is divided into 5 regions:
Berlin—Overview
Berlin—Kreuzberg
Berlin—Prenzlauer Berg-Mitte
Berlin—Schöneberg-Tiergarten
Berlin—Outer

Berlin—Overview

INFO LINES & SERVICES

Gay AA for English Speakers at M-O-M **49-30/787-5188** *5pm Tue, also Gay AA 8pm Th*

Mann-O-Meter Bülowstr 106 (at Nollendorfplatz) **49-30/216-8008** *5pm-10pm, from 4pm wknds, gay switchboard & center, also cafe, also B&B referral service*

Sonntags Club Greifenhagener Str 28 (S/U-Schönhauser Allee) **49-30/449-7590, 49-30/442-3702 (transgender line)** *info line 10am-6pm daily, LGBT info & counseling, meetings, also cafe-bar [MW,TG,S,V] open 5pm-midnight Mon-Sun, regular parties*

ACCOMMODATIONS

Enjoy B&B [MW] Bülowstr 106 (at M-O-M, gay center) **49-30/2362-3610** *accommodations referral service, "on-the-cheap"*

CAFES

Sonntags Club Greifenhagener Str 28 (S/U-Schönhauser Allee) **49-30/449-7590, 49-30/442-3702 (transgender line)** *info line 10am-6pm daily, LGBT info & counseling, meetings, also cafe-bar [MW,TG,S,V] open 5pm-midnight Mon-Sun, regular parties*

RESTAURANTS

Paris Bar Kantstrasse152 **49-30/313-8052** *bistro, also bar*

ENTERTAINMENT & RECREATION

Fritz Music Tour 49-30/3087-5633 *visit the haunts of David Bowie, Nina Hagen, Iggy Pop & Rammstein, among other popular musical acts*

The Jewish Museum Berlin Lindenstr 9-14 **49-30/2599-3300** *10am-8pm, till 10pm Mon*

Schwules (Gay) Museum U6/U7 Mehringdamm 61 **49-30/6959-9050** *2pm-6pm, till 7pm Sat, clsd Tue, guided tours 5pm Sat (in German)*

PUBLICATIONS

Blu 49-30/443-1980 *free monthly gay magazine*

DU & ICH 49-30/235-5390 *bi-monthly nat'l gay magazine (in German)*

Siegessäule 49-30/235-5390, 49-30/2355-3932 *free monthly LGBT city magazine (in German), awesome maps*

Berlin—Kreuzberg

BARS

Barbie Bar [MW] Mehringdamm 77 **49-30/6956-8610** *4pm-close, lounge, terrace*

Barbie Deinhoffs [★MW,D,C] Schlesische Str 16 **49-173/434-6363** *6pm-2am*

Bierhimmel [GS,YC] Oranienstr 183 (U-Kottbusser Tor) **49-30/615-3122** *1pm-3am*

Club Trommel [M,D,TG] Thomasstr 53 **49-30/686-7345** *7pm-close, clsd Tue*

Ficken 3000 [M,D,L,V,YC] Urbanstr 70 (at Hermannplatz) **49-30/6950-7335** *10pm-close, cruisy, large darkroom*

Mobel Olfe [★MW] Reichenbergerstrasse 177 **49-30/2327-4690** *6pm-close Tue-Sun*

Rauschgold [MW] Mehringdamm 62 (U-Mehringdamm) **49-30/7889-9299** *8pm-close*

Roses [★MW,TG,YC] Oranienstr 187 (at Kottbusser Tor) **49-30/615-6570** *10pm-close*

NIGHTCLUBS

SchwuZ (SchwulenZentrum) [★M,D,S,YC,$] Mehringdamm 61 (enter through Café Sundstroem) **49-30/629-0880** *from 11pm Fri-Sat, 2 dance flrs, cocktail lounge, theme nights*

Serene Bar [MW,D] Schwiebusser Str 2 **49-30/6904-1580**

SO 36 [★GS,D,TG,S,V,YC,WC] Oranienstr 190 (at Kottbusser Tor) **49-30/6140-13067, 49-30/6140-1307** *theme nights, also live music venue*

Cafes

Drama Mehringdamm 63 **49-30/6746-9562** *also bar*

Melitta Sundström [MW,WC] Mehringdamm 61 (at Gneisenaustr, U-Mehringdamm) **49-30/692-4414** *10am-8pm, till 4pm Sat, clsd Sun, terrace, also gay bookstore*

Muvuca Gneisenaustr 2a (at Mehringdamm) **49-30/6165-6310** *4pm-close, radical/ political int'l cafe, Portuguese food*

Restaurants

Amrit Oranienstr 200 **49-30/612-5550** *noon-1am, Indian*

Kaiserstein Mehringdamm 80 **49-30/7889-5887** *9am-1am, int'l*

Locus [★MW] Marheinekeplatz 4 **49-30/691-5637** *10am-1:30am, Mexican, full bar*

Schwester Z Bergmannstr 3 **49-30/692-2716** *5pm-1am, Greek/ Mediterranean*

SUMO Bergmanstr 89 **49-30/6900-4963** *trendy Japanese*

Men's Clubs

Böse Buben [MO] Lichtenrader Str 32 (at Kienitzer Str) **49-30/6270-5610** *darkroom*

Triebwerk [M,L,V,WC] Urbanstr 64 (at Leinestr, U-Hermannplatz) **49-30/6950-5203** *10pm-close, cruise bar w/ darkroom*

Sex Clubs

Club Culture Houze [GS] Görlitzer Str 71 (off Skalitzer Str) **49-30/6170-9669** *gay theme nights 4 nights a week, open to all 3 nights a week*

Berlin—Prenzlauer Berg-Mitte

Accommodations

Hotel Transit Loft [GF] Greifswalder Str 219 (enter at Immanuelkirchstrasse 14) **49-30/4849-3773** *hotel in restored 19th-c factory, brkfst*

Kunstlerheim Luise [GF] Luisenstr 19 (Mitte) **49-30/284-480** *former palace w/ rooms re-imagined by local artists, near River Spree*

Le Moustache [M] Gartenstr 4 (at Rosenthaler Platz, U-Oranienburger Tor) **49-30/281-7277** *also Moustache Bar [M,L,F], open 8pm-close, clsd Mon-Tue*

Schall & Rauch Pension [MW] Gleimstr 23 (at Schönhauser Allee) **49-30/443-3970, 49-30/448-0770** *also bar & restaurant*

Bars

Bärenhöhle [M,B,BW] Schönhauser Allee 90 **49-30/4473-6553** *4pm-6am, beer bar*

Besenkammer Bar [MW] Rathausstr 1 (at Alexanderplatz, under the S-Bahn bridge) **49-30/242-4083** *24hrs, tiny "beer bar"*

Betty F*** [MW,NH] Mulackstrasse 13 (at Gormannstrasse)

Cafe Amsterdam [GS,TG,F,YC,WC] Gleimstr 24 (at Schönhauser Allee) **49-30/448-0792, 49-30/231-6796** *9am-3am, till 5am Fri-Sat, cafe-bar, terrace, also pension*

DarkRoom [MO,L] Rodenbergstr 23 (at Schönhauser Allee) **49-30/444-9321** *10pm-6am, uniform bar, darkroom, theme parties wknds*

Flax [M,F] Chodowieckistr 41 (off Greifswalder Str) **49-30/4404-6988, 49-30/441-9856** *5pm-3am, 3pm-5am Sat, brunch from 10am Sun*

Freizeitheim [MW] Schönhauser Allee 57 **49-30/17440-26444**

Greifbar [MO,L,V] Wichertstr 10 (at Greifenhagener Str, S/U-Schönhauser Allee) **49-30/444-0828** *10pm-6am, darkroom*

Grosse Freiheit 114 [MO] Boxhagener Str 114 (in Friedrichshain) *darkroom, cruisy*

Marietta [MW] Stargarder Str 13 **49-30/4372-0646** *popular gay night Wed*

Perle [MW] Sredzkistrasse 64 *8pm-close, innovative lighting & electronica*

Reingold [GS,GO] Novalisstr 11 (U-Oranienburger Str) **49-30/2838-7676** *lesbian-owned cocktail lounge, more gay Th*

Schoppenstube [M,D] Schönhauser Allee 44 (at Eberswalder Str) **49-30/442-8204** *8pm-close, from 10pm Fri-Sun, theme nights, terrace, cruisy*

Sharon Stonewall [MW] Kleinen Präsidentenstr 3 (at Hackeschen Market) **49-30/2408-5502**

Stahlrohr [MO] Greifenhagener Str 54 (off Wicherts Str, U-Schonhauser Allee) **49-30/4473-2747** *10pm-close, sex parties*

Stiller Don [★M,NH,L,F] Erich-Weinert-Str 67 (at Schönhauser Allee) **49-17/2182-0168** *8pm-close, terrace*

Zum Schmutzigen Hobby/ Nina's Bar [MW,D,DS,TG] Rykestrasse 45 *6pm-close*

NIGHTCLUBS

Berghain [MW,D] Am Wrietzener Bahnhof (off Strasse der Pariser Kommune, near Ostbahnhof station)

GMF [M,D] Alexanderstrasse 7 (at Week End, U-Alexanderplatz) **49-30/2809-5396** *Sun T-dance*

Irrenhouse [MW,D,DS,TG] Am Friedrichshain 33 (at Geburtstagsklub) *3rd Sat, Nina Queer's monthly drag party*

KitKat Club [GS,D,C] Kopenickerstrasse 76 (enter on Bruckenstrasse) **49-30/2173-6841** *8pm-close Th, 11pm-6am Fri-Sat, also S/M club*

Klub International [M,D,$] Karl-Marx-Allee 33 (at Kino International, U-Schillingstr) **49-30/2475-6011** *11pm-close 1st Sat, largest gay club in Berlin*

Sage Club [GS,D,TG] Köpenicker Str 76 (at Brückenstr) **49-30/278-9830** *11pm-7am Th-Sun, live music venue, more gay wknds*

Spy Club [MW,D] Friedrichstr/ Unter den Linden (at Cookies) **49-30/2809-5396** *2nd Sat only*

CAFES

Ackerkeller [D] Bergstrasse 68 *non-profit LGBT club and cafe from 6pm Sun, 8pn Tue & Fri*

November [MW] Husemannstr 15 (at Sredzkistr) **49-30/442-8425** *9am-2am, cafe-bar, terrace, brkfst buffet wknds*

RESTAURANTS

Drei Lychener Str 30 (U-Eberswalder Str) **49-30/4473-8471** *tapas bar*

Rice Queen Danziger Str 13 (U-Eberswalder Str) **49-30/4404-5800** *Asian*

Schall & Rauch Wirtshaus [MW,BW] Gleimstr 23 (at Schönhauser Allee) **49-30/443-3970, 49-30/448-0770** *10am-close*

Thüringer Stuben Stargarder Str 28 (at Dunckerstr, S/U-Schönhauser Allee) **49-30/4463-3391** *4pm-1am, from noon wknds, full bar*

MEN'S CLUBS

Gate Sauna [F,V,WI] Hannah Arendtstrsse 6 (U-Mohrenstr) **49-30/229-9430** *24hrs wknds, also bar*

Treibhaus Sauna [F,V,YC] Schönhauser Allee 132 (U-Eberswalder Str) **49-30/448-4503** *24hrs wknds, also bar*

EROTICA

Bad Boy'z [V] Schliemannstr 38 (U-Eberswalder Str) **49-30/440-8165** *sex parties*

Blackstyle Seelower Str 5 (S/U-Schönhauser Allee) **49-30/4468-8595** *clsd Sun, latex & rubber wear*

Duplexx Schönhauser Allee 131 (U-Eberswalder Str) **49-30/4849-4200** *videos, cruisy*

XXL Schönhauser Alle 98 **49-30/3289-8222** *large cruising cinema*

CRUISY AREAS

Volkspark Friedrichshain [AYOR] (at Märchenbrunnen, in Friedrichshain)

Berlin—Schöneberg-Tiergarten

Accommodations

Arco Hotel [GS,WC,GO] Geisbergstr 30 (at Ansbacherstr, U-Wittenbergplatz) **49-30/235-1480** *centrally located*

Art-Hotel Connection [MO,L,WI,WC,GO] Fuggerstr 33 (corner Welser Str, near U-Wittenbergplatz) **49-30/2102-18800** *also special "fantasy" apt for kink & S/M types, some shared baths*

Berlin B&B [MW,WI,GO] **49-30/2648-4756** *full brkfst*

Gaybed.de [GS,GO] Perleberger Str (at Stephan Str) **49-30/8185-1988** *B&B, hot tub, shared bath*

Hotel California [GF] Kurfürstendamm 35 (at Knesebeckstr, U-Uhlandstr) **49-30/880-120** *full brkfst, nonsmoking flr*

Hotel Hansablick [GF] Flotowstr 6 (at Bachstr, off Str des 17 Juni) **49-30/390-4800** *full brkfst*

Kinky Tulip [MO,L,N,GO] Welserstrasse 24 **49-30/2196-4240** *exclusively for leather/ fetish community*

The Mövenpick Hotel [GF] Schöneberger Strasse 3 **49-30/230-060**

RoB Play 'n Stay Leather Apartments [MO,GO] Fuggerstr 19 (behind RoB Berlin shop) **49-30/2196-7400** *in the heart of Berlin's gay scene, playroom*

Tom's Hotel [M] Motzstr 19 (at Eisenacherstr, U-Nollendorfplatz) **49-30/2196-6604**

Bars

Ajpnia eV [MO] Eisenacher Str 23 (U-Eisenacher Str) **49-30/2191-8881** *sex parties*

Blue Boy Bar [M,V] Eisenacher Str 3a (at Fuggerstr, U-Nollendorfplatz) **49-30/218-7498** *24hrs, ring bell, hustlers; also Fugger-Eck [GS,NH], 1pm-6am, clsd Sun, terrace*

Eldorado [M,F,E] Motzstr 20 (U-Nollendorfplatz) **49-30/213-2518** *24hrs, terrace*

Hafen [★M,TG,S,YC] Motzstr 19 (at Eisenacher Str, U-Nollendorfplatz) **49-30/211-4118** *8pm-close*

Harlekin [M,NH,F] Schaperstr 12-13 (at Lietzenburger Str, U9-Spichernstr, in Wilmersdorf) **49-30/218-2579** *4pm-close, from 2pm Sun, terrace*

Heile Welt [MW,F] Motzstr 5 **49-30/2191-7507** *6pm-close*

Kumpelnest 3000 [GF,D,TG,YC] Lützowstr 23 (at Potsdamer Str, U-Kurfürstenstr) **49-30/261-6918** *5pm-5am, till 8am Fri-Sat, cocktail bar*

Mario's Kneipe [MO,B] Fuggerstr 34 (at Welserstr, U-Wittenbergplatz) *4pm-5am, from 2pm Sun*

Mutschmann's [MO,L] Martin-Luther-Str 19 (at Motzstr, U-Nollendorfplatz) **49-30/2191-9640** *10pm-close, from 11pm Fri-Sat, clsd Sun-Mon, also bar, darkroom*

Neues Ufer [MW,OC] Haupstrasse 157 (U-Bahn Kleistpark) **49-30/784-1578** *9am-2am, clsd wknds, city's oldest gay bar*

New Action [★MO,L,V] Kleiststr 35 (at Eisenacherstr, U-Nollendorfplatz) **49-30/211-8256** *8pm-close, from 1pm Sun, uniform bar, darkroom, very cruisy*

Pinocchio Musikcafe [M] Fuggerstr 3 (at Schönhauser Allee, U-Nollendorfplatz) **49-30/2362-0333** *2pm-2am, till 4am wknds*

Prinz Knecht [★M] Fuggerstr 33 (U-Nollendorfplatz) **49-30/236-27444** *6pm-close, theme nights*

Scheune [★MO,L,V] Motzstr 25 (at Nollendorfplatz) **49-30/213-8580** *9pm-7am, till 9am Fri-Sat, uniform bar, darkroom, Naked Sex Party from 5:30pm Sun, rubber party last Fri*

Spot [M,NH,F] Eisenacher Str 2 (at Nollendorfplatz) **49-30/213-2267** *4pm-4am, open later wknds, from 6pm in winter, terrace*

Tabasco [M,F,AYOR] Fuggerstr 3 (at Schönhauser Allee, U-Nollendorfplatz) **49-30/214-2636** *6pm-6am, 24hrs wknds, hustlers*

Tom's Bar [★MO,L,V] Motzstr 19 (at Eisenacherstr, U-Nollendorfplatz) **49-30/213-4570** *10pm-6am, open later Fri-Sat, very cruisy, downstairs maze*

Tramps [M,NH,B,L] Eisenacher Str 6 *24hrs*

Woof [M,B] Fuggerstr 37 **49-30/2360-7870**

Nightclubs

Bangaluu [GS] Invalidstrasse 30 **49-30/969-3077** *Th-Sun, more gay Sun, glitzy supperclub w/ white beds*

Connection [★MO,D,L,V,$] Fuggerstr 33 (at Art-Hotel Connection) **49-30/218-1432** *11pm-close Fri-Sat only, cruisy, darkroom; also sex shop & cinema*

Propaganda [M,D,DS] Nollendorfplatz 5 (at Goya Theater) *2nd Sat only*

Cafes

Cafe Berio [★WC] Maaßenstr 7 (at Winterfeldtstr, U-Nollendorfplatz) **49-30/216-1946** *8am-1am, from noon wknds, int'l, brkfst all day, seasonal terrace, also bar*

Cafe Savigny Grolmanstr 53-54 (at Savignyplatz) **49-30/3151-9612** *9am-1am, full bar, terrace*

Inside Out [MW] Nollendorfstr 31-32 (at Maabenstr) **49-30/2128-0958** *2pm-9pm, noon-11pm Fri-Sat, also LGBT souvenirs & tourist info*

Men & Media [MW] Nollendorfstr 23 **49-30/2191-7524** *noon-midnight, gay cybercafe*

Windows [MW] Martin-Luther-Str 22 (at Motzstr, U-Wittenbergplatz) **49-30/214-2384** *2pm-2am, full bar, terrace*

Restaurants

Diodata Goltzstrasse 51 **49-30/2191-7884** *5pm-midnight, from 1pm wknds, Viennese*

Gnadenbrot Martin-Luther-Str 20a **49-30/2196-1786** *noon-1am, cheap & good*

Ma Vie Motzstrasse 28 **49-30/2363-1200** *8am-close, French bistro*

More [★] Motzstrasse 28 (at Martin-Lutherstrasse) **49-30/2363-5702** *9am-midnight*

Shima Schwabischestrasse 5 (at Barbarossastrasse) *6:30pm-close, California/ Asian*

Entertainment & Recreation

Xenon Kino Kolonmenstr 5-6 **49-30/7800-1530** *gay & lesbian cinema*

Bookstores

Bruno's [GO] Zeushofstrasse 1 (U-Nollendorfplatz) **49-30/6150-0381**

Prinz Eisenherz Buchladen [WC] Lietzenburger Str 9 A (in Schoeneberg) **49-30/313-9936** *10am-8pm, clsd Sun, LGBT books, magazines, DVDs "in all languages"*

Men's Clubs

Apollo Sauna [F,V] Kurfürstenstr 101 (in Charlottenburg, U-Wittenbergplatz) **49-30/213-2424**

Steam Sauna Club [L,F,V] Kurfürstenstr 113 (U-Wittenbergplatz) **49-30/218-4060** *24hrs wknds*

Erotica

Beate Uhse International Joachimstaler Str 4 (at Kantstr, at Erotic Museum)

The Jaxx Club [V] Motzstr 19 (U-Nollendorfplatz) **49-30/213-8103**

Mazeworld Kurfürstenstr 79 (at Keithstr) **49-30/2300-3251**

Pool Berlin [V] Schaperstr 11 (at Joachimsthaler Str, in Wilmersdorf, U-Kurfürstendamm) **49-30/214-1989** *clsd Sun, gay emporium*

RoB Berlin Fuggerstr 19 **49-30/2196-7400** *clsd Sun, leather/ fetish shop*

Cruisy Areas

Tiergarten [AYOR] along Str de 17 Juni (near the Siegessäule monument)

Berlin—Outer

Accommodations

Charlottenburger Hof [GF,F] Stuttgarter Platz 14 (at Wilmersdorfer Str) **49-30/329-070** *also bar*

Hotel Kronprinz Berlin [GF,WC] Kronprinzendamm 1 (at Kurfürstendamm, in Halensee) **49-30/896-030**

Bars

Himmelreich [MW] Simon Dach Str 36 (off Warschauer Str, in Friedrichshain, U-Frankfurter Tor) **49-30/2936-9292** *from 6pm Mon-Fri, 2pm-close wknds*

Nightclubs

Haus B [★MW,D,S,$] Warschauer Platz 18 **49-30/296-0800** *9:30pm-5am Wed & Sun, 10pm-6am Fri-Sat, terrace*

Cafes

Schrader's [GO] Malplaquetstr 16b (at Utrechter Str, Wedding) **49-30/4508-2663** *also bar*

Restaurants

Cafe Rix Karl-Marx-Str 141 (in Neükolln) **49-30/686-9020** *10am-5pm, also bar, open till 1am*

Kurhaus Korsakow Grunbergerstrasse 81 (in Friedrichshain) *6pm-close, from 9am wknds*

Cruisy Areas

Volkspark Wilmersdorf [AYOR]

Ireland

Dublin

Info Lines & Services

AA 105 Capel St (at Outhouse) **353-1/873-4932** *call for meeting times*

Gay Switchboard Dublin **353-1/872-1055** *7:30pm-9:30pm Mon-Th*

Outhouse 105 Capel St **353-1/873-4932** *LGBT community center, cafe, library, meetings*

Accommodations

The Clarence [GF,WI,WC] 6-8 Wellington Quay **353-1/407-0800** *owned by Bono & The Edge of U2*

The Dylan [GS] Eastmoreland Place **353-1/660-3000**

Hotel Capri [GF] 58-59 Middle Abbey St **353-1/872-0361**

The Merchant House [M,WI] 8 Eustace St (Temple Bar Area) **353-1/633-4400** *free access to Basic Instincts Cruise Zone*

Nua Haven Gay Guesthouse [MW,NS,WI] 41 Priory Rd **353-87/686-7062**

Waterloo House [GS,F] 8-10 Waterloo Rd **353-1/660-1888** *5-star hotel, resraurant & bar*

Bars

Centre Stage Cafe [M,F,C] 6 Parliament St **353-1/670-3390** *8pm-2am Th-Sat, also café 8am-3pm Mon-Fri*

The Dragon [MW,D] 64-45 S Great Georges St **353-1/478-1590** *5pm-11:30pm, till 2:30am Th-Sat, till 11pm Sun*

Front Lounge [★MW,D,TG,K] 33 Parliament St **353-1/670-4112** *noon-11:30pm, till 2am Fri-Sat, till 1am Sun*

The George [★MW,D,DS,E] 87 S Great George St **353-1/478-2983** *12:30pm-3am, till 1am Sun, Sun bingo*

Panti Bar [MW,D,F,DS,WC] 7-8 Capel St **353-1/874-0710** *5pm-close, theme nights*

Nightclubs

Furry Glen [M,D,B] 7-8 Capel St (at Panti Bar) **353-1/878-1032** *3rd Sat*

Glitz [MW,D] 2 Johnstons Place, Lr Stephens St (downstairs at Break for the Border) **353-1/478-0300 (Break for the Border), 353-85/727-3874** *11pm-2:30am Tue only*

Nimhneach [GS] 39-40 Arran Quay (at Voodoo Lounge) **353-1/873-6013** *fetish & BDSM party, strict dress code, call or see www.nimhneach.ie for dates*

PoD [★GS,D] Harcourt St (at Hatch St, at the Old Railway Station) **353-1/476-3374**

Q & A [MW,D,A,$] **353-1/670-9202 (Temple Bar Music Centre)** *"queer & alternative" dance party, check local listings for dates & location*

Spirit [GF,D,$] 57 Middle Abbey St **353-1/877-9999** *live music venue & dance club*

V.I.Q. [MW,D] Sycamore St (off Dame St, at Sin) *11pm-3:30am Mon only*

Cafes

Irish Film Institute Bar & Restaurant 6 Eustace St (in Temple Bar) **353-1/679-5744** *lunch & dinner, next to independent cinema, light meals, plenty veggie*

Lovinspoon Cafe 13 N Frederick St **353-1/804-7604** *7am-6pm, clsd Sun (except summers)*

Restaurants

Brasserie Sixty6 [WI] 66 S Great Georges St **353-1/400-5878** *brkfst, lunch, dinner, wknd brunch, meat & seafood*

La Cave 28 S Anne St **353-1/679-4409** *12:30pm-close, from 6pm Sun, French*

The Chameleon 1 Lower Fownes St **353-1/671-0362** *5pm-11pm, from 4pm Sun, clsd Mon, Indonesian*

Cornucopia [GS] 19 Wicklow **353-1/677-7583** *8:30am-8pm, till 9pm Th, noon-7pm Sun, affordable vegetarian*

L' Ecrivain [P,R] 109A Lower Baggot St **353-1/661-1919** *lunch Mon-Fri, dinner Mon-Sat, clsd Sun*

Eden Meeting House Square (entrance on Sycamore) **353-1/670-5372** *lunch & dinner, wknd brunch, patio dining*

Fire Restaurant Mansion House, Dawson St **353-1/676-7200** *5:30pm-close, noon-3pm jazz lunch Sat, clsd Sun*

FXB Crow St **353-1/671-1248** *5:30pm-close, clsd Mon, steak & seafood*

Gruel 68A Dame St **353-1/670-7119** *lunch & dinner*

Halo [R] Ormond Quay (in the Morrison Hotel) **353-1/878-2400** *dinner, creative fusion food, upscale, vegetarian dishes*

Juice [★] S Great Georges St (across from the Globe) **353-1/475-7856** *lunch & dinner, wknd brunch, vegetarian*

Mermaid Cafe [★GS] 69-70 Dame St **353-1/670-8236** *lunch & dinner, Sun brunch*

Odessa [★GS] 14 Dame Court **353-1/670-7634**

Shack 24 E Essex St **353-1/679-0043** *lunch & dinner*

Town Bar & Grill 21 Kildare St **353-1/662-4724** *lunch & dinner, Sun brunch, Italian*

Trocadero 4 Saint Andrew St **353-1/677-5545** *5pm-midnight, clsd Sun*

The Winding Stair Restaurant [YC] 40 Lower Ormond Quay **353-1/872-7320** *lunch & dinner, Irish*

Entertainment & Recreation

Dublin Devils Football Club Phoenix Park **353-86/805-9443** *gay men's soccer team, see www.dublindevilsfc.com for schedule*

Gloria 353-87/750-0062 (Deborah) *lesbian & gay choir*

Irish Queer Archive 35A Patrick St, Dun Laoghaire **353-87/953-1779** *reading room & reference library, call for hours*

Bookstores

Books Upstairs 36 College Green **353-1/679-6807** *10am-7pm, till 6pm Sat, 2pm-6pm Sun (summers only)*

Chapters Bookstore Ivy House, Parnell St **353-1/872-3297**

The Winding Stair Bookshop [YC] 40 Lower Ormond Quay **353-1/872-6576** *noon-5pm, clsd Mon, also restaurant*

Publications

GCN (Gay Community News) Unit 2 Scarlet Row, Essex St W, Temple Bar, 8 **353-1/671-0939, 353-1/671-9076** *monthly LGBT newspaper, many resources*

Men's Clubs

The Boilerhouse [★F,V] 12 Crane Ln **353-1/677-9578, 353-1/679-5128** *1pm-5am, till 6am Th, 24hrs wknds, sauna, steam, gym equipment, bar, dark-room*

The Dock [WI] 21 Upper Ormond Quay (at the Inn On the Liffey) **353-1/872-4172** *24hrs wknds*

Erotica

Basic Instincts 8 Eustace St (Temple Bar Area) **353-1/633-4400** *10am - 9pm, fetish supplies*

Condom Power 57 Dame St **353-1/677-8963, 353-1/671-0379**

Italy

Rome

Note: M°=Metro station

Info Lines & Services

Circolo di Cultura Omosessual Mario Mieli Via Efeso 2a (M° San Paolo) **39-06/541-3985 (help line)** *4pm-7pm Mon-Fri, switchboard, meetings & discussion groups*

Gay Help Line 800/713-713 *4pm-8pm, clsd Sun*

Accommodations

58 Le Real de Luxe [GS,NS,WI,WC] Via Cavour 58, 4th flr (near Colosseum) **39-06/482-3566, 39-399/805-2485 (cell)** *B&B inn a few steps from Colosseum*

Albergo Del Sole al Pantheon [GF] Piazza della Rotonda 63 **39-06/678-0441**

Ares Rooms [GF] Via Domenichino 7 **39-06/474-4525, 39-340/278-1248 (cell)** *some shared baths*

B&B Inandout Rome [GS,NS,WI,WC,GO] Via Arco del Monte (at Viale Trastevere) **39-339/784-0653**

Best Place [MW,R] Via Turati 13 **39-329/213-2320**

Bologna B&B [GF] 6 Piazza Bologna (at Via Sambucuccio D'Alando) **39-06/4424-0244, 39/34781-04781 (cell)**

Daphne Veneto [GF,NS] Via di San Basilio 55 **39-06/4782-3529, 39-06/8745-0086** *cozy inn in heart of historical Rome; also Daphne Trevi at via Degli Avignonesi 20*

Discover Roma [MW] Via Castelfidardo 50 **39-06/4938-2080**

Domus International [GS] **39-06/6889-2918** *short-term apt rentals in the heart of Rome*

Franklin [GF] Via Rodi 29 **39-06/3903-0165** *music-themed hotel w/ CD library*

Gaspare B&B [MW,WI] Via Balilla 16 **39-06/328-833-3486**

Gayopen B&B [GS,GO] Via dello Statuto 44, Apt 18 (at Via Merulana, Piazza Vittorio) **39-06/482-0013** *full brkfst*

Hotel Altavilla [GF] Via Principe Amedeo 9 **39-06/474-1186**

Hotel Claridge [GF] Via Liegi 62 **39-06/845-441** *near Borghese park, gym w/ sauna & Turkish bath*

Hotel Derby [GF,WC] Via Vigna Pozzi 7 (Largo delle Sette Chiese) **39-06/513-4955, 39-06/513-6978** *small hotel in heart of Rome*

Hotel Edera [GF] Via A Poliziano 75 **39-06/7045-3888**

Hotel Labelle [MW] Via Cavour 310 **39-06/679-4750** *near the Roman Forum*

Hotel Scott House [GF] Via Gioberti 30 **39-06/446-5379**

Italy-Accom [WI,WC,GO] Via Dei Greci 26 (at Spanish Steps) **39-06/3600-1394** *reservation service for Venice, Rome, Florence, Positano, Sicily, Calabria, & Tuscany, also tours, see www.italy-accom.com for more info*

Nicolas Inn [GF,NS,WI] Via Cavour 295 (at Via dei Serpenti) **39-06/9761-8483, 39-338/937-8387** *elegant rooms located near the Colosseum & Roman Forum*

Pensione Ottaviano [GF] Via Ottaviano 6 **39-06/3973-8138** *in quiet area near St Peter's Square, hostel*

The Rainbow B&B [MW,WI] Viale Giulio Cesare 151 **39-347/507-0344 (cell)**

Relais le Clarisse [GS,NS,WI,GO] Via Cardinale Merry del Val 20 (at Viale Trastevere) **39-06/5833-4437** *jacuzzis, Mediterranean garden, on historic site in central Rome, lesbian-owned*

Rentflatsinitaly.com [GF] Via Principe Umberto (at Piazza Vittorio Emanuelle) **39-069/784-3916**

Roman Reference [GF] Via dei Capocci 94 **39-06/4890-3612** *apts*

Rome Rental Apartments [GF] **33-338/389-4799**

Sandy Hostel [GF] Via Cavour 136 **39-06/4884-4585** *great location near Colosseum, Roman Forum & Spanish Steps*

Scalinata di Spagna [GS,NS,WI] Piazza Trinità dei Monti 17 (M° Piazza di Spagna) **39-06/6994-0896, 39-06/679-3006 (booking #)** *roof garden*

Welcome Residences [MW] Via Amendola 7 **39-06/4890-1248** *hot tubs*

www.romecityapartments.com [GF,NS] Via Quintino Sella 23 (at Via Boncompagni) **39-06/4201-6891**

BARS

Bear Butch [MO,B] Via Enea 34 (at Frequency Club) **39-06/785-1504, 39-340/693-9719** *2nd Fri only, bear cruising*

Coming Out [★MW,TG,F,E,K,V,GO] Via San Giovanni in Laterano 8 (near Colosseum) **39-06/700-9871** *5pm-2am*

Frequency [MO,S,V] Via Enea 34 **39-06/785-1504, 39-340/693-9719** *10pm-3am, till 4am Fri-Sat, darkrooms, cabins, sling*

Garbo [MW,F,GO] Vicolo di Santa Margherita 1a (in Trastevere, Tram 8) **39-06/5832-0782, 39-06/581-6700** *10pm-3am, clsd Mon, cocktail bar*

Il Giardino dei Ciliegi [MW] Via dei Fienaroli 4 **39-06/580-3423** *5pm-2am, from 1pm Sun, tea salon*

Hangar [★M,D,L,S,V,YC] Via In Selci 69 (M° Cavour) **39-06/488-1397** *10:30pm-2am, clsd Tue, int'l crowd, cruisy, live DJs, dark room*

Skyline [M,L,F,S,V,PC] Via Pontremoli 36 **39-06/700-9431** *10:30pm-3am, till 4am Fri-Sat, clsd Mon, 2-flr American bar, backroom, darkroom, monthly sex parties*

Sphinx [MO,L,V] Piazza Manfredo Fanti 40 **39-06/444-1312, 39-328/373-5887** *11pm-4am, clsd Mon, fetish, darkroom*

NIGHTCLUBS

L' Alibi [★MW,D,S,YC] Via di Monte Testaccio 40-44 (M° Piramide) **39-06/574-3448** *11pm-4am, clsd Mon-Tue, rooftop garden in summer, hosts Gloss & Tommy*

Il Diavolo Dentro [M,L,N] Largo Itri 23-24 **39-339/841-9298 (cell)** *11pm-5am Fri-Sat, 6pm-3am Sun (from 10pm winter), clsd Mon-Th & month of August*

Frutta e Verdura [MW,D] Via Placido Zurla 68-70 (in Casilina) **39-347/244-7621 (English), 39-348/879-7063 (Italian)** *4:30am-10am Sat-Sun & public holiday evenings, darkroom*

Gorgeous [M,D] Via del Commercio 36 (at Alpheus) **39-06/574-7826** *10pm-4am Sat*

Max's Bar [MO,D,L,V,$] Via Achille Grandi 7a (near Porta Maggiore, below Center Hotel 3, M° Manzoni) **39-06/7030-1599** *10:30pm-close, clsd Tue-Wed*

Muccassassina [★MW,D,K,S,YC,$] Via di Portonaccio 212 **39-06/541-3985** *10:30pm-5am Fri only (Sept-June), location changes so call ahead, darkroom*

Omogenic [MW,F] Via Casilina Vecchia 42 (at Circolo degli Artisti) **39-348/771-7725, 39-348/770-8420** *11pm-4am Fri only*

CAFES

Oppio Caffè [★MW,F,E] Via delle Terme di Titi 72 **39-06/474-5262, 39-347/510-8594 (cell)** *brkfst, lunch & dinner, open 24hrs in Aug, full bar, terrace w/ great view*

Restaurants

Asino Cotto Ristorante [R,GO] Via dei Vascellari 38 (in Travestere, Tram 8) **39-06/589-8985** *lunch & dinner, clsd Mon, creative gourmet Mediterranean*

La Carbonara Via Panisperna 214 **39-06/482-5176** *lunch & dinner, clsd Sun, classic Roman cuisine since 1906*

Città in Fiore [MW] Via Cavour 269 **39-06/482-4874** *lunch Th-Mon, dinner nightly, Chinese*

Ditirambo Piazza della Cancelleria 74-75 (near Campo dei Fiori) **39-06/687-1626**

La Focaccia Via della Pace 11 **39-06/6880-3312** *12:30pm-12:30am, pizza*

Gelateria San Crispino Via Panetteria 42 (near Trevi Fountain) **39-06/679-3924** *noon-12:30am, till 1:30am Fri-Sat, clsd Tue, gelato!*

Mater Matuta Via Milano 47 (basement) **39-06/4782-5746** *lunch Mon-Fri, dinner nightly, also wine bar*

Osteria del Pegno [WC] Vicolo Montevecchio 8 (Plaza Navona) **39-06/6880-7025** *lunch & dinner, clsd Wed winter, Italian, large pizza selection*

Ristorante da Dino Via dei Mille 10 (at Piazza Indipendenza) **39-06/491-425** *clsd Wed*

La Taverna di Edoardo II [MW,WC] Vicolo Margana 14 **39-06/6994-2419** *7:30pm-midnight, clsd Tue, full bar*

Entertainment & Recreation

Gay Village *gay summer festival*

Roma with Pride [MW] **39-349/372-0376** *guided walking tours*

Through Eternity [GO] Via Astura 2/B **39-06/700-9336** *walking tours of Rome*

Bookstores

La Libreria Babele Via dei Banchi Vecchi 116 **39-06/687-6628** *11am-7pm, clsd Sun, LGBT, some English titles*

Retail Shops

Hydra II [L] Via Urbana 139 **39-06/489-7773** *leather, vinyl, clubwear, western, vintage & more*

Gyms & Health Clubs

Roman Sport Center [GS] Via del Galoppatoio 33 **39-06/320-1667**

Men's Clubs

Apollion Sauna [V] Via Mecenate 59a (at Via Carlo Botta, M° Piazza Vittorio) **39-06/482-5389** *gym equipment, bar*

EMC-Europa Multiclub [V,YC,SW,PC] Via Aureliana 40 (M° Repubblica) **39-06/482-3650** *1pm-midnight, 24hrs wknds, 3 flrs, fountain whirlpool, gym, bar, massage, solarium, private rooms*

K Sex Club [L,V,PC] Via Amato Amati 6-8 (at Via Dulceri), Casilina **39-06/2170-1268, 39-349/587-6731** *10pm-4am, S/M club & bar, maze, darkroom*

Mediterraneo Sauna [F,V,PC] Via Pasquale Villari 3 (btwn Via Merulana & Via Labicana, M° Manzoni) **39-06/7720-5934** *3 flrs, full bar, jacuzzi, maze*

Rio's Sauna Club Via dei Colli Albani 10 **39-06/7814-7828**

Terme di Roma Internazionale [V] Persio 4 (M° Arco di Travertino) **39-06/718-4378** *jacuzzi, gym equipment, bar, labyrinth, popular Sun*

Erotica

Alcova Piazza Sforza Cesarini 27 (at Corso Vittorio Emanuele II) **39-06/686-4118** *fetish shop*

Cruisy Areas

Colosseo Quadrato [AYOR] (near Palazzo della Civiltà del Lavoro park)

Monte Caprino Park [AYOR] Capidoglio Hill

Villa Borghese [AYOR] (in front of the Architecture Academy)

NETHERLANDS

Amsterdam

Amsterdam is divided into 5 regions:
Amsterdam—Overview
Amsterdam—Centrum
Amsterdam—Jordaan
Amsterdam—Rembrandtplein
Amsterdam—Outer

Amsterdam — Overview

INFO LINES & SERVICES

COC Amsterdam Rozenstraat 14 (in the Jordaan) **31-20/626-3087** *info line 10am-5pm, also cafe 8pm-11:30pm Wed-Fri*

Gay/ Lesbian Switchboard 31-20/623-6565 *noon-10pm, 4pm-8pm wknds, English spoken*

Pink Point Westermarkt (Raadhuisstraat & Keizersgracht, in the Jordaan by Homomonument) **31-20/428-1070** *10am-6pm; info on Homomonument & general LGBT info; friendly volunteers; queer souvenirs & gifts*

SAD-Schorerstichting Sarphatistraat 35 **31-20/573-9444** *resource center for queer health & well-being*

ACCOMMODATIONS

Country & Lake [GS,NS,WI] IJsselmeerdijk 26, Warder **31-299/372-190** *3 beautiful apts in countryside 15 miles outside Amsterdam*

Flatmates Amsterdam [★MW,SW,NS,WI,WC,GO] **31-20/620-1545** *apts, studios, house boats & B&Bs*

Simply Amsterdam Apartments [GF,GO] **31-20/620-6608** *apts, studios, canal houses & houseboat*

NIGHTCLUBS

Club Stereo [GS,D] Jonge Roelensteeg 4 **31-20/770-4037** *7pm-close Wed-Sat*

ENTERTAINMENT & RECREATION

The Anne Frank House Prinsengracht 267 (in the Jordaan) **31-20/556-7100, 31-20/556-7105 (info tape)** *the final hiding place of Amsterdam's most famous resident*

Boom Chicago Leidseplein 12 (Leidseplein Theater) **31-20/423-0101 (tickets)** *English-language improv comedy; also dinner & drinks; distributes free Boom! magazine; € 18-20 (not including food/ drink)*

Homomonument Westermarkt (in the Jordaan) *moving sculptural tribute to lesbians & gays killed by Nazis*

MacBike Stationsplein 12 (next to Centraal Station) **31-20/620-0985** *rental bikes & map for self-guided tour of Amsterdam's gay points of interest*

De Pijp near Albert Cuypmarkt *gay-friendly neighborhood teeming w/ lots of interesting shops & restaurants*

The van Gogh Museum [WC] Paulus Potterstr 7 (on the Museumplein) **31-20/570-5200** *10am-6pm, till 10pm Fri, a must-see museum dedicated to this Dutch master painter*

PUBLICATIONS

COC Update 31-20/623-4596 *news & events calendar for COC*

Expreszo 31-20/359-0713 *for LGBT youth (in Dutch)*

Gay News Amsterdam 31-20/679-1556 *bilingual paper, extensive listings*

Gay & Night 31-20/788-1360 *free monthly bilingual entertainment paper w/ club listings*

GK Magazine 31-499/39-10-00 *nat'l LGBT newspaper in Dutch w/ English summaries*

Squeeze 31-09/684-1234 *glossy for boys, in Dutch*

Amsterdam — Centrum

ACCOMMODATIONS

Aloft Canal Apartments [GF,WI,GO] Singel 235 (at Paleisstraat) **31-62/445-7593**

Amsterdam B&B Barangay [★GS,NS,WI,GO] **31-6/2504-5432** *1777 town house near tourist attractions*

Amsterdam Canal Apartments [M,WI,GO] Kloveniersburgwal 55 **31-20/471-0272, 31-6/4748-4046 (cell)** *close to museums & nightlife*

Amsterdam Central B&B [MW,WI,GO] Oudebrugsteeg 6-II (Warmoesstraat) **31-62/445-7593** *near main gay area (Warmoestraat) & train station, in 16th-c guesthouse, also apartments, full brkfst*

Amsterdam Escape [GS] Geldersekade 106 (at Centrum) **800/216-7295 (reservations), 31-20/320-6402** *luxury apts & canal houses*

Anco Hotel-Bar [MO,L,N,NS,WI,GO] OZ Voorburgwal 55 (across from the Oude Kerk) **31-20/624-1126** *1640 canal house, some shared baths, also bar*

Avenue Hotel [GF,WI] NZ Voorburgwal 33 **31-20/530-9530**

The Black Tulip Hotel [★MO,L,R,WI,GO] Geldersekade 16 **31-20/427-0933** *luxury leather & S/M hotel*

Bob's Youth Hostel [GF,YC] Nieuwezijds Voorburgwal 92 **31-20/623-0063** *women's, men's & mixed dorms, brkfst included, 3am curfew*

Bulldog [GF,18+] Oudezijds Voorburgwal 220 **31-20/620-3822** *hostel in Red Light District, dorms & private rooms, brkfst included, coffeeshop & lounge/bar, no lockout or curfew*

Centre Apartments Amsterdam [GS,GO] Heintje Hoeksteeg 27 **31-20/627-2503, 31-65/371-3452 (cell)**

Club NL [GS,D] Nieuwezijds Voorburgwal 169 **31-20/622-7510** *10pm-3am, till 4am Fri-Sat, lounge w/ DJs*

Cosmos Hostel [GF,NS] Nieuwe nieuwstraat 17-1 **31-20/625-2438** *hostel in 17th-c hotel, dorms, no curfew, ages 18-35 only*

Crowne Plaza Amsterdam City Centre [GF,SW,WC] NZ Voorburgwal 5 **31-20/620-0500, 877/227-6963 (US#)**

Friendzz [MW,GO] Oudezijds Achterburgwal 34 **31-6/4140-4820**

NH Grand Hotel Krasnapolsky [GF,WI,WC] Dam 9 **31-20/554-9111**

Old Harbour Apartments [GS,NS,GO] Prins Hendrikkade 125-1 **31-20/428-5758** *private entrances & patio*

Palace B&B [GS,NS,WI,GO] Spuistraat 224 **31-6/4260-8847** *1794 bldg w/ indoor garden*

Stayokay Amsterdam Stadsdoelen [GF] Kloveniersburgwal 97 **31-20/624-6832**

Victoria Hotel Amsterdam [GF,SW,WC] Damrak 1-5 (opposite Centraal Station) **31-20/623-4255, 800/814-70000** *4-star hotel, gym, restaurants, bar*

Winston Hotel [GF,A] Warmoesstraat 129 **31-20/623-1380** *hipster hotel w/ alt-rock bar & decor, some shared baths*

Bars

Argos [★MO,L] Warmoesstraat 95 **31-20/622-6595** *10pm-3am, till 4am Fri-Sat, the oldest leather bar in Europe, popular darkroom, strict dress code, very popular SOS (Sex on Sunday) last of month (dress code: nude)*

De Barderij [M,NH,OC] Zeedijk 14 **31-20/420-5132** *noon-1am, till 3am Fri-Sat, large brown café*

Boys Club 21 [MO,S] Spuistraat 21 **31-20/622-8828** *noon-2am, boys' house (escorts) w/ full bar & live strip shows*

Cafe Mandje [GS] Zeedijk 63 **31-20/622-5375** *originally opened in 1927 as Amsterdam's first gay bar by dyke-on-bike Bet van Beeren*

The Cuckoo's Nest [MO,L,V,18+] NZ Kolk 6 **31-20/627-1752** *1pm-1am, till 2am Fri-Sat, cruisy, large play cellar*

Dirty Dick's (The Sleaze Pit) [MO,L] Warmoesstraat 86 **31-20/627-8634** *10am-4am Fri-Sat, till 3am Sun, very cruisy, darkroom*

The Eagle Amsterdam [MO,L] Warmoesstraat 90 **31-20/627-8634** *10pm-4am, till 5am Fri-Sat, darkroom, FF Party 1st Sun 3pm-9pm*

De Engel van Amsterdam [M] Zeedijk 21 **31-20/427-6381** *1pm-1am, till 2am Fri-Sat, patio*

Getto [★MW,F,K] Warmoesstraat 51 **31-20/421-5151** *4pm-1am, from 7pm Tue, 1pm-midnight Sun, clsd Mon, also restaurant, Sun brunch, live DJs*

Prik [MW,F] Spuistraat 109 **31-20/320-0002** *4pm-1am, till 3am Fri-Sat, clsd Mon, patio*

Queen's Head [M,DS,S] Zeedijk 20 (off Nieuwmarkt) **31-20/420-2475** *4pm-1am, till 3am Fri-Sat, bingo Tue*

The Web [★MO,B,L,V] St Jacobsstraat 6 (btwn Nieuwendijk & NZ Voorburgwal) **31-20/623-6758** *noon-1am, till 2am Fri-Sat, darkroom, rooftop patio, [B] Sat*

Nightclubs

Cockring [★MO,D,S,V] Warmoesstraat 96 **31-20/623-9604** *11pm-4am, till 5am Fri-Sat, cruisy darkroom, strippers/ sex shows Th, wknds*

Rapido/ Fresh/ Reflexx [M,D] *popular monthly dance parties, check clubrapido.com for dates & locations*

Cafes

Dampkring Handboogstr 29 (at Heiligeweg) **31-20/638-0705** *smoking coffeeshop*

Dolores Nieuwezijds Voorburgwal 289 **31-20/626-5649** *noon-6pm, till 9pm Th, healthy snacks*

Gary's Late Night [★] Witbolstraat 13 **31-20/637-3643** *noon-3am, till 4am Fri-Sat, fresh muffins & bagels*

Puccini Bomboni [★] Staalstraat 17 **31-(0)20/626-5474** *If you love chocolate, do we have a cafe for you!*

Restaurants

Cafe de Jaren [GS,YC] Nieuwe Doelenstraat 20-22 **31-20/625-5771** *10am-1am, till 2am Fri-Sat, int'l, full bar, terrace, cash only*

Cafe de Schutter Voetboogstraat 13-15 (upstairs) **31-20/622-4608** *noon-1am, till 3am Fri-Sat, popular local hangout, plenty veggie, full bar, terrace*

Cafe Latei [WI] Zeedijk 143 (in Red Light District) **31-20/625-7485** *8am-5pm, from 9am Sat, from 11am Sun, brkfst & lunch, great coffee hangout, everything you see you can buy, too*

Greenwoods Singel 103 (near Dam Square) **31-20/623-7071** *English-style brkfst & tea snacks*

Hemelse Modder [★WC,GO] Oude Waal 11 **31-20/624-3203** *6pm-10pm, clsd Mon, French/ int'l, popular w/ lesbians & gay men, full bar*

Kitsch [MW] Utrechtsestraat 42 *6pm-close, clsd Sun, kitsch & disco*

Krua Thai [WC] Staalstraat 22 **31-20/622-9533** *4pm-9pm, clsd Sun-Mon, Thai, terrace; also at Spuistraat 90a, 620-0623, full bar*

La Strada [★] NZ Voorburgwal 93-95 **31-20/625-0276** *4pm-1am, till 3am wknds, Mediterranean, full bar, terrace*

Het Land van Walem [WC,GO] Keizersgracht 449 **31-20/625-3544** *lunch & dinner, int'l, local crowd, canal-side terrace*

Maoz Muntplein 1 **31-20/420-7435** *11am-1am, till 3am wknds, vegetarian/ falafel*

Old Highlander Sint Jacobsstraat 8 **31-20/420-8321** *noon-1am, till 2am wknds, Scottish food, brkfst all day*

Pygma-lion [R,NS,GO] Nieuwe Spiegelstraat 5a (in Spiegelhof Arcade) **31-20/420-7022** *5:30pm-11pm, clsd Mon, South African cuisine, exotic meats & several veggie dishes*

't Sluisje [★MW,TG,DS] Torensteeg 1 **31-20/624-0813** *6pm-close, clsd Mon-Wed, steak house, full bar, drag shows nightly, cash only*

Song Kwae Kloveniersburgwal 14 (near Nieuwmarkt & Chinatown) **31-20/624-2568** *1pm-10:30pm, Thai, full bar, terrace*

Bookstores

The American Book Center [WC] Spul 12 **31-20/625-5537** *10am-8pm, till 9pm Th, 11am-6:30pm Sun, books & magazines in English imported from US & UK, large LGBT section*

Boekhandel Vrolijk Gay & Lesbian Bookshop [★] Paleisstraat 135 (near Dam Square) **31-20/623-5142** *10am-6pm, 11am-6pm Mon, 10am-5pm Sat, from 1pm Sun, LGBT books, videos & gadgets, also mail order*

Intermale Gay Bookstore Spuistraat 251 **31-20/625-0009** *11am-6pm Mon, from 10am Tue-Sat, till 9pm Th, noon-5pm Sun, wide selection of gay men's titles in English & Dutch*

Retail Shops

Conscious Dreams Kokopelli [★] Warmoesstr 12 **31-20/421-7000** *11am-10pm, "smart-warehouse," internet*

Gays & Gadgets Spuistraat 44 **31-20/330-1461** *cards, gifts & art gallery*

Magic Mushroom Spuistraat 249 **31-20/427-5765** *11am-7pm, till 8pm Fri-Sat, "smartshop": magic mushrooms & more; also Singel 524, 31-20/422-7845*

Sissy Boy Kalverstraat 199 **31-20/638-9305** *French & Dutch designers duke it out on the racks here*

Gyms & Health Clubs

Splash Looiersgracht 26-30 **31-20/624-8404** *gym & wellness center*

Erotica

4men Spuistraat 21 **31-20/625-8797** *cinema, darkroom, all-day ticket, private cabin, large sexshop*

Adonis [M] Warmoesstraat 92 **31-20/627-2959** *10am-1am, till 3am wknds, cinema, darkroom, large sexshop*

Alfa Blue Nieuwendijk 26 **31-20/627-1664** *porn store & video theater*

Christine Le Duc Spui 6 **31-20/624-8265** *video shop w/ private cabins*

Condomerie Het Gulden Vlies Warmoesstraat 141 **31-20/627-4174** *11am-6pm, clsd Sun, condoms in every size or color or configuration & the lube to go w/ them*

DeMask Zeedijk 64 **31-20/423-3090** *11am-7pm, clsd Sun, rubber & leather clothing*

Drake's of LA [★] Damrak 61 **31-20/627-9544** *videos & magazines, video cabins, cinema upstairs*

Mr B [WC] Warmoesstraat 89 **31-20/422-0003** *leather & rubber, also tattoo & piercing*

RoB Accessories Warmoesstraat 71 **31-20/428-3000** *leather, rubber, toys*

Robin & Rik Runstraat 30 (at Prinsengracht) **31-20/627-8924** *by appointment only, custom leatherwear*

Le Salon Nieuwendijk 20-22 (near the Spui) **31-20/622-6565** *sex supermarket, cinema*

Amsterdam—Jordaan

Accommodations

Budget Hotel Clemens Amsterdam [GF] Raadhuisstraat 39 (at Herengracht) **31-20/624-6089** *small hotel in Amsterdam's center, some shared baths*

Canal Apartments [GF] **31-20/626-4532, 877/283-7540 (US#)** *studio, 1-bdrm & 2-bdrm apts*

Chic and Basic Amsterdam [GF,NS,WI] Herengracht 13-19 **31-20/522-2345** *"the quiet hotel," full brkfst*

The Dylan [GF] Keizersgracht 384 **31-20/530-2010** *also restaurant*

En Suite Apartment [GF] Keizersgracht 320 **31-20/421-1887, 31-6/5234-3256 (cell)** *apt in historic 1675 canal house*

Hotel Acacia [GF] Lindengracht 251 **31-20/622-1460** *"homey hotel in heart of Jordaan"; also self-catering studios & houseboat*

Hotel Brian [GF] Singel 69 **31-20/624-4661** *cheap, no frills, but friendly, shared baths, no curfew*

Hotel Pulitzer [GF] Prinsengracht 315-331 **31-20/523-5235** *occupies 24 17th-c bldgs facing the Prinsengracht & Keizersgracht—2 of Amsterdam's most picturesque canals*

Hotel Rembrandt Centrum [GS] Herengracht 255 **31-20/622-1727, 31-20/623-6638** *canalside hotel near Dam Square*

Maes B&B [★GS,NS,WI,GO] Herenstraat 26 **31-20/427-5165** *renovated 18th-c home btwn 2 canals*

Marnixkade Canalview Apartments [★MW,NS,WI,GO] **31-6/1012-1296** *fully furnished apts in 19th-c canal house on a quiet canal in heart of Jordaan*

Sunhead of 1617 [★GS,NS,WI,GO] Herengracht 152 (at Leliegracht & Raadshuisstraat) **31-20/626-1809** *B&B, full brkfst*

Bars

Cafe de Gijs [GF,TG] Lindengracht 249 **31-20/638-0740, 31-6/2537-3674** *4pm-1am, 1st Wed of month hosts T&T, social gathering for transvestites & transsexuals, from 10pm (trans-friendly rest of the time, too)*

Nightclubs

de Trut [★MW,D,A,YC] Bilderdijkstraat 165 **31-20/612-3524** *11pm-4am Sun only, hip underground party in legalized squat, doors close when it's full (btwn 11:30pm-midnight) so come early*

Cafes

Cafe 't Smalle Egelantiersgracht 12 **31-20/623-9617** *10am-1am, till 2am wknds, brown cafe, full bar, outdoor seating*

Rokerij Singel 8 **31-20/422-6643** *smoking coffeeshop, 3 other locations*

Restaurants

Bojo [★] Lange Leidsedwarsstraat 49-51 (near Leidseplein) **31-20/622-7434** *11am-9pm, from 4:30pm wknds, Indonesian*

De Bolhoed Prinsengracht 60 (at Tuinstr) **31-20/626-1803** *vegetarian/vegan*

Burger's Patio 2e Tuindwarsstr 12 **31-20/623-6854** *6pm-1am, Italian, plenty veggie*

Foodism Oude Leliestraat 8 **31-20/427-5103** *11:30am-10pm, till 6pm wknds, great soups & sandwiches, funky & fun*

Granada [E] Leidsekruisstraat 13 **31-20/625-1073** *5pm-close, clsd Tue, Spanish, tapas, also bar*

De Vliegende Schotel Nieuwe Leliestraat 162 **31-20/625-2041** *4pm-11:30pm, kitchen till 10:45pm, vegetarian & fish, some vegan*

Entertainment & Recreation

De Looier Art & Antiques Market Elandsgracht 109 **31-20/624-9038, 31-20/427-4990** *11am-5pm, clsd Fri*

Retail Shops

Dare to Wear Buiten Oranjestraat 15 **31-20/686-8679** *noon-7pm, 1pm-6pm Sun, 1pm-7pm Mon, piercing, jewelry & accessories*

House of Tattoos Haarlemmerdijk 130c **31-20/330-9046** *11am-6pm, from 1pm Sun, great tattoos, great people*

Lust for Leather Lindengracht 220 **31-6/5573-4047** *2pm-6pm 1st Sat or by appointment, hip showroom, day & fetish wear*

Men's Clubs

Thermos Day [★SW,F] Raamstraat 33 **31-20/623-9158** *noon-8am, cruisy sauna on 5 flrs, also bar & cafe*

Sex Clubs

Sameplace [GS,TG,D] Nassaukade 120 **31-20/475-1981** *[MO] Mon, theme nights, darkroom*

Erotica

Black Body [WC] Lijnbaansgracht 292 (across from Rijksmuseum) **31-20/626-2553** *clsd Sun, rubber clothing specialists, also leather, toys, DVDs & more*

Amsterdam—Rembrandtplein

Accommodations

Amsterdam House [GF] 's Gravelandseveer 7 **31-20/626-2577 & 624-6607 (hotel), 800/618-1008 (US#)** *hotel, apts & houseboats*

Dikker & Thijs Fenice Hotel [GF] Prinsengracht 444 (at Leidsestraat) **31-20/620-1212** *4-star hotel overlooking canal, restaurant & bar*

Downtown Guesthouse [M,GO] Sint Jorisstraat 12 (at Reguliersdwarsstraat) **31-6/5087-2220 (cell)** *shared baths*

Eden Hotel [GF,WI,WC] Amstel 144 **31-20/530-7878** *3-star hotel overlooking Amstel River, brasserie*

Hotel Amistad & Apts [★M,NS,WI,WC,GO] Kerkstraat 42 (at Leidsestraat) **31-20/624-8074** *friendly staff, some shared baths, internet lounge*

Hotel de l'Europe [GF,SW] Nieuwe Doelenstraat 2-8 **31-20/531-1777** *grand hotel on the River Amstel*

Hotel Monopole [GF] Amstel 60 **31-20/624-6271** *also Cafe Rouge*

Hotel Orlando [GF,GO] Prinsengracht 1099 (at Amstel River) **31-20/638-6915**

Hotel The Golden Bear [★MW,B,OC,WI,GO] Kerkstraat 37 (at Leidsestraat) **31-20/624-4785**

ITC Hotel [★MW,GO] Prinsengracht 1051 (at Utrechtsestraat) **31-20/623-0230, 31-20/623-1711** *18th-c canal house, great location, also bar & lounge*

The Orfeo Hotel [M] Leidsekruisstraat 14 (at Prinsengracht) **31-20/623-1347** *exclusively gay (since 1969!), some shared baths, also bar & restaurant*

Seven Bridges [★GF] Reguliersgracht 31 **31-20/623-1329** *small & so elegant, canalside, view of 7 bridges (surprise!), brkfst brought to you*

Bars

Amstel Fifty Four [M,NH] Amstel 54 (at Rembrandtplein) **31-20/623-4254** *5pm-1am, till 3am Fri-Sat, classic brown café gone gay*

April [★M,V] Reguliersdwarsstraat 37 (at Rembrandtplein) **31-20/625-9572** *4pm-1am, till 3am Fri-Sat, 3 bars, 1 revolving*

ARC [★GS,D,F,YC] Reguliersdwarsstraat 44 **31-20/689-7070** *4pm-1am, till 3am Fri-Sat, hip 20-something crowd, also restaurant*

Cafe Mon Ami [M,NH,OC] Amstelstraat 34 **31-20/626-2243** *7pm-1am, till 3am Fri-Sat*

Cafe Rouge [M,NH] Amstel 60 **31-20/420-9881** *4pm-1am, till 3am wknds*

Entre Nous [MW,NH] Halvemaansteeg 14 (at Rembrandtplein) **31-20/623-1700** *8pm-3am, till 4am Fri-Sat*

Exit Cafe [M] Reguliersdwarsstraat 42 **31-20/638-5700** *1pm-4am, till 5am Fri-Sat, upscale, part of 4-bar Exit complex*

Habibi Ana [MW,MR,E] Lange Leidsedwarsstraat 93 **31-06/2192-1686** *7pm-1am, till 3am Fri-Sat, clsd Mon-Tue, Arabian clientele, Arabian & int'l music, bellydancing shows wknds*

Hot Spot Cafe [M,NH] Amstel 102 **31-20/622-8335** *4pm-3am, 8pm-4am Sat*

Het Leeuwtje Cafe [M,NH] Reguliersdwarsstraat 105 **31-20/622-2577** *3pm-1am, till 3am Fri-Sat*

Lellebel [★M,NH,TG,F,K,DS] Utrechtsestraat 4 **31-20/427-5139** *8pm-3am, till 4am Fri-Sat, from 3pm Sun, drag bar, very trans-friendly*

Mankind [M,F,WI] Weteringstraat 60 **31-20/638-4755** *noon-11pm, clsd Sun, cafe-bar, canalside terrace*

Mix Cafe [★MW,GO] Amstel 50 **31-20/420-3388** *8pm-3am, till 4am Fri-Sat*

Le Montmartre [★M,NH,YC] Halvemaansteeg 17 **31-20/625-5565** *5pm-1am, till 4am Fri-Sat, very Dutch*

Music Box [M,AYOR] Paardenstraat 9 (near Rembrandtplein) **31-20/620-4110** *8pm-2am, till 3am Fri-Sat, hustlers*

Reality [M,NH,MR-L] Reguliersdwarsstraat 129 **31-20/639-3012** *8pm-3am, till 4am Fri-Sat, Surinamese*

Soho [★MW,D,YC] Reguliersdwarsstraat 36 **31-20/638-5700** *6pm-1am, till 4am Fri-Sat, British pub 1st flr, lounge upstairs, happy hour 10pm-11pm*

Spijker [★MO,NH,L,V] Kerkstraat 4 **31-20/620-5919** *3pm-1am, till 3am Fri-Sat, darkroom, TVs showing hardcore porn & cartoons*

Het Wapen van Londen [★M,YC] Amstel 14 **31-6/1539-5317** *4pm-1am, till 2am Fri-Sat, clsd Mon, cafe-bar, terrace*

NIGHTCLUBS

Church [MO,D] Kerkstraat 52 *open Wed-Sat, theme nights w/ dress code*

Club Roque [MW,D] Amstel 178 (at Wagenstraat) **31-20/421-0900** *11pm-5am Fri-Sat, 6pm-midnight Sun, clsd Mon-Tue*

Exit [★MO,D,$] Reguliersdwarsstraat 42 **31-20/625-8788** *midnight-4am, till 5am Fri-Sat, clsd Mon-Wed, 4 bars, 4 kinds of music, darkroom*

Studio 80 [GS,D] Rembrandtplein 17 **31-20/521-8333** *9pm-5am Th-Sat*

CAFES

Downtown Coffeeshop [★M,GO] Reguliersdwarsstr 31 (at Koningsplein) **31-20/622-9958** *10am-8pm, till 10pm Fri-Sat, terrace open in summer*

Happy Feelings Kerkstr 51 **31-20/639-1154** *smoking coffeeshop*

The Other Side [M,GO] Reguliersdwarsstr 6 (at Koningsplein) **31-72/589-8498** *11am-1am, gay smoking coffeeshop*

RESTAURANTS

Garlic Queen [R] Reguliersdwarsstr 27 **31-20/422-6426** *6pm-close, clsd Mon-Tue, even the desserts are made w/ garlic!*

Golden Temple [NS] Utrechtsestr 126 **31-20/626-8560** *brkfst, lunch & dinner, mix of Indian, Mexican & Mediterranean, vegetarian & vegan*

De Huyschkaemer Utrechtsestraat 137 **31-20/627-0575** *noon-1am, till 3am wknds*

Le Monde [MW,GO] Rembrandtplein 6 **31-20/626-9922** *8am-11pm, brkfst till 4pm, terrace dining*

Rose's Cantina [★] Reguliersdwarsstr 38-40 (near Rembrandtplein) **31-20/625-9797** *5pm-11pm, Tex-Mex, full bar*

Saturnino [MW] Reguliersdwarsstr 5 **31-20/639-0102** *noon-midnight, Italian, full bar*

RETAIL SHOPS

Conscious Dreams Dreamlounge Kerkstr 113 **31-20/626-6907** *11am-9pm, noon-6pm Sun-Mon, "psychedeli-catessen," internet access*

MEN'S CLUBS

Thermos Night Kerkstraat 58-60 (near Leidseplein) **31-20/623-4936** *11pm-8am, till 10am Sun, sauna on 3 flrs, also bar*

EROTICA

B1 Cinema Reguliersbreestraat 4 **31-20/623-9546** *9am-midnight, from noon Sun*

The Bronx Kerkstraat 53-55 (near Leidseplein) **31-20/623-1548** *huge gay shop for sex supplies, videos, magazines & toys, also cinema*

De Stringslip Reguliersdwarsstr 59 **31-20/638-1143** *underwear, clothing, leather, rubber, accessories*

Amsterdam—Outer

ACCOMMODATIONS

Abba Budget Hotel [GF] Overtoom 122 (1st Constantyn Huygenstraat) **31-20/618-3058** *"smoker"-friendly*

Amsterdam B&B [GF,NS,WI,GO] Roeterstraat 18 **31-20/624-0174** *powered by green energy*

Amsterdam Room Service [GS,GO] 2e van der Helststraat 26 III **31-20/679-4941** *apt & B&B rooms in Amsterdam, cash only*

Between Art & Kitsch [GF,WI] Ruysdaelkade 75-2 **31-20/679-0485, 31-6/4744-2072 (cell)** *near museums*

Blue Moon B&B [GS,WI,GO] Weteringschans 123A **31-20/428-8800**

Chico's Guesthouse [GF] Sint Willibrordusstraat 77 (at Van Woustraat & Ceintuurbaan, near Sarphatipark) **31-20/675-4241** *in De Pijp*

The Collector B&B [GF,GO] De Lairessestr 46 hs (in museum area) **31-6/1101-0105 (cell), 31-20/673-6779** *full brkfst*

The Flying Pig [GF] Vossiusstraat 46-47 (at Leidseplein) **31-20/400-4187** *hostel, dorms, no curfew, kitchen facilities, also Centrum location*

Flynt B&B Amsterdam [MW,WI,GO] Eerste Helmerssraat 34 **31-20/618-4614, 31-(0)6/5260-1160 (cell)** *250 meters from Vondelpark*

Freeland Hotel [GF,WI,GO] Marnixstraat 386 **31-20/622-7511** *2-star hotel, full brkfst*

The Friendship B&B [GS,GO] Achtergracht 17G **31-20/620-9103** *houseboat sleeps up to 4*

Hemp Hotel Frederiksplein 15 **31-20/625-4425** *only in Amsterdam: sleep on a hemp mattress, eat a hemp roll (THC-free) for brkfst or drink hemp beer in the downstairs Hemp Temple bar*

Hotel Aadam Wilhelmina [GF] Koninginneweg 169 **31-20/662-5467** *charming, full brkfst buffet, some shared baths*

Hotel Arena [★GF,WI] Gravesandestraat 51 **31-20/850-2400** *hotel in former orphanage, popular nightclub in restored chapel*

Hotel Fita [NS] Jan Luykenstraat 37 **31-20/679-0976** *small family-owned hotel*

Hotel Kap [GS,GO] Den Texstraat 5 **31-20/624-5908** *bikes available to rent, also self-catering apt*

Hotel Rembrandt [GF,NS] Plantage Middenlaan 17 **31-20/627-2714** *beautiful brkfst rm w/ 17th-c art, near Rembrandtplein*

Hotel Sander [GF] Jacob Obrechtstraat 69 **31-20/662-7574** *also 24hr bar & coffee lounge*

InterContinental Amstel Amsterdam [WI] Professor Tulpplein 1 **31-20/622-6060** *5 stars (ultraluxe since it opened in 1867); for the queen (the royal kind) w/ money to burn: €500+*

International Budget Hostel [GF] Leidsegracht 76 (at Leidseplein) **31-20/624-2784** *in 17th-c warehouse on canal, lounge w/ internet, clean 4-person dorms*

Kerstin's B&B [GF,NS] Kwakerstraat 2h **31-20/612-6969** *B&B & self-catering apt overlooking new canal, kids ok*

Lloyd Hotel [★GF,F,WI] Oostelijke Handelskade 34 **31-20/561-3636, 31-20/561-3604** *hip hotel for all budgets in cool Eastern Harbor area*

NL Hotel [GS,WI,GO] Nassaukade 368 (at Leidseplein) **31-20/689-0030**

Prinsen Hotel [GF] Vondelstraat 36-38 (near Leidseplein) **31-20/616-2323**

Stayokay Amsterdam Vondelpark [GF,WI,WC] Zandpad 5 **31-20/589-8996** *dorms & rms, inside Vondelpark, also bar & restaurant*

NIGHTCLUBS

Melkweg [GS,E] Lijnbaansgracht 234 (at Leidseplein) **31-20/531-8181** *popular live-music venue, also restaurant/ cafe, cinema, theater*

ToNight @ Arena [★GF,D] Gravesandestraat 51 (at Hotel Arena) **31-20/850-2400** *theme nights; come to see the club itself—a restored chapel from an orphanage*

RESTAURANTS

An Weteringschans 76 (in Museum Quarter) **31-20/624-4672** *dinner only, clsd Sun-Mon, Japanese, full bar, patio, cash only*

Boom Chicago Leidseplein 12 (Leidseplein Theater) **31-20/423-0101** *lunch & dinner, patio, comedy/improv show at 8:30pm (tickets not included in price)*

De Peper Overtoom 301 **31-20/412-2954** *7pm-close Sun, Tue & Fri, sliding scale, volunteer-run vegan cafe, also monthly queer parties*

De Waaghals Frans Halsstraat 29 **31-20/679-9609** *5pm-9:30pm, clsd Mon, vegetarian*

CRUISY AREAS

Oosterpark [AYOR] at Linnaeusstr (behind the Tropenmuseum)

Sarphatipark [AYOR] *near baseball field*

Vondelpark [AYOR] at Vondelstr *in the rose garden*

Westerpark [AYOR] *at night, N of lake*

SCOTLAND

Edinburgh

ACCOMMODATIONS

94DR [GS,WI,GO] 94 Dalkeith Rd **44-131/662-9286** *guesthouse central location*

Alva House [M,NS,GO] 45 Alva Pl **44-0845/257-1475** *near gay bars & nightlife*

Ardmor House [★MW,NS,WC,GO] 74 Pilrig St (at Leith Walk) **44-(0)131/554-4944** *Victorian in city center near gay life*

Averon Guest House [GF,NS] 44 Gilmore Pl **44-0131/229-9932** *comfortable guesthouse in city center*

Ayden Guest House [GS,NS,WI,GO] 70 Pilrig St **44-0131/554-2187** *in-house chef cooks fabulous brkfst*

Garlands [GS,NS,WI,GO] 48 Pilrig St (off Leith Walk) **44-(0)131/554-4205** *Georgian town house, full brkfst*

Six Mary's Place Guest House [GF,NS] Raeburn Pl (Stockbridge) **44-(0)131/332-8965** *vegetarian brkfst*

Village Apartments [MO,GO] 5 Broughton Market **44-0131/556-5094**

The Witchery by the Castle [GF] Castlehill (The Royal Mile) **44-(0)131/225-5613** *theatrical suites at the gates of Edinburgh castle*

BARS

The Auld Hoose [GS,NH,F] 23-25 St Leonards St *11:30am-1am, from 12:30pm Sun*

Cafe Habana [MW,WI] 22 Greenside Pl **44-0131/558-1270** *noon-3am, from 12:30pm Sun*

Cafe Nom de Plume [F] 60 Broughton St (at Edinburgh Lesbian, Gay & Bisexual Centre) **44-0131/478-1372** *11am-11pm, till 1am Fri-Sat*

CC Bloom's [M,S,D,GO] 23 Greenside Pl (at Leith Walk) **44-0131/556-9331** *6pm-3am, from 7pm Sun*

Deep Blue [★MW,F,GO] 1 Barony St (below Blue Moon) **44-0131/556-2788** *4pm-1am*

Frenchies Bar [MW,NH] 89 Rose Street Ln N **44-0131/225-7651** *2pm-1am*

Newtown Bar [MW,D,F,WI] 26-B Dublin St **44-0131/538-7775** *noon-1am, till 2am Fri-Sat*

Planet [★MW,F] 6 Baxter's Pl (at Leith Walk) **44-0131/556-5551** *1pm-1am*

Priscilla's [M,K,C,DS] 17 Albert Pl (Leith Walk) **44-0798/659-1695** *noon-1am, from 5pm Sat*

The Regent [M,F,WI] 2 Montrose Terrace **44-0131/661-8198** *11am-1am, from 12:30pm Sun*

The Street [GS,D,F] 2 Picardy Pl **44-0131/556-4272** *4pm-1am, from noon wknds, patio*

Theatre Royal Bar [GF] 25-27 Greenside Pl **44-0131/557-2142** *noon-midnight, clsd Sun*

Nightclubs

DV8 Fetish Club [GS,PC] 258 Morrison St (in Spiders Web basement) **44-0131/228-1949**

Fever [MW,D] 207 Cowgate (at Faith Nightclub) **44-0131/225-9764, 44-0131/557-4656** *11pm-3am 3rd Sat*

GHQ [M,D] 4 Picardy Pl **44-0131/550-1780** *9pm-3am, fashionable gay crowd, theme nights*

Luvely [GS,D] Faith Nighclub, 207 Cowgate **44-(0)131/557-4656** *10:30pm-5am 1st Sat only*

Taste [GS,D] 37 Guthrie St (at GRV) **44-0131/220-2987** *11pm-3am 1st Sun*

Cafes

Blue Moon [★MW,F,GO] 1 Barony St **44-0131/556-2788** *11am-midnight, from 10am wknds*

Cafe Lucia 13-29 Nicolson St (next to Edinburgh Festival Theatre) **44-0131/662-1112** *10am-10pm*

Filmhouse Cafe [BW] 88 Lothian Rd **44-0131/229-5932, 44-0131/228-2688 (cinema)** *10am-11:30pm, till 12:30am Fri-Sat, also cinema*

Restaurants

Black Bo's Vegetarian Restaurant 57/61 Blackfriars St **44-(0)131/557-6136** *lunch & dinner, full bar*

Henderson's [BW] 94 Hanover St **44-0131/225-2131** *organic vegetarian, also deli & cafe*

Tower Restaurant & Terrace [WC] National Museum of Scotland, Chambers St (at George IV Brigde) **44-(0)131/225-3003** *lunch & dinner, panoramic views of Edinburgh's castle & historic skyline*

Valvona & Crolla [★] 19 Elm Row **44-(0)131/556-6066** *clsd Sun, oldest Italian deli in Scotland*

Entertainment & Recreation

The Luvvies 44-(0)131/ 6973-84513 *LGBT community theatre company*

Bookstores

Bobbie's Bookshop 220 Morrison St **44-(0)131/538-7069** *10am-5pm, clsd Sun*

Word Power 43-45 W Nicolson St **44-0131/662-9112** *10am-6pm, noon-5pm Sun, independent*

Retail Shops

Q-Store 5 Barony St **44-(0)131/477-4756**

Men's Clubs

No 18 18 Albert Pl **44-0131/553-3222** *noon-10pm, till 11pm Fri-Sun, sauna club*

Steamworks [SW] 5 Broughton Market (btwn Barony & Dublin) **44-0131/477-3567** *11am-11pm, steamroom, sauna, labyrinth, massage, cafe lounge, internet*

Erotica

Leather & Lace 8b Drummond St **44-0131/557-9413** *10am-9pm, from noon Sun, toys, clothing & videos*

Spain

Barcelona

Note: M°=Metro station

Info Lines & Services

Casal Lambda Verdaguer y Callís 10 (M° Drassanes) **34/93-319-5550** *5pm-9pm, community center & cafe, archives & library, also publish magazine*

Col-Lectiu Gai de Barcelona (CGB) **34/609-922-789** *staffed 7pm-9pm Mon-Sat, also publishess Info Gai*

Coordinadora Gai Lesbiana Vicant d'Hongria 156, E-08014 **34/900-601-601** *7pm-9pm Mon-Fri, 6pm-8pm Sat*

Accommodations

Agua Alegre [M] c/ Roger de Lluria 47 (M° Catalunya) **34/93-487-8032**

Barcelona City Centre [M,WI,GO] **34/653-900-039** *in Eixample District*

▶ **Beauty & the Beach B&B** [M,R,SW,N,NS,WI,WC,GO] **34/93-266-0562** *full brkfst, right across from gay nude beach*

California Hotel [GS] Rauric 14 (at Ferran, M° Liceu) **34/93-317-7766** *includes brkfst*

Casa de Billy Barcelona [GS,NS,WI,GO] Rambla Catalunya 85, Piso 5, Puerta 1 (at Mallorca) **34/69-326-6665** *shared baths, full brkfst*

Catalonia Albéniz [GF,F,WC] Aragó 591-593 **34/93-265-2626** *quaint, 3-star hotel, near the city center*

Catalonia Duques de Bergara [GF,WI] Bergara 11 **34/93-301-5151** *4-star hotel in the heart of old Barcelona*

Central Town Rooms & Apartments [M,WC,GO] Ronda San Pau 51 **34/93-442-7057, 24/687-911-460** *guesthouse*

Éos [MW,GO] Gran Via de los Corts Catalanes 575 (M° Universitat) **34/93-451-8772, 34/617-931-439** *B&B in gay district*

Fashion House [MW] Bruc 13 Principal **34/63-790-4044** *shared baths*

Friends Barcelona [M] Urgell 165 **34/652-32-1663**

HCC St Moritz [GF,WI,WC] Diputació 264 **34/93-412-1500, 34/93-412-1236**

Hostal Absolut Centro [M,GO] Casanova 72 (at Balmes) **34/649-550-238** *hostel, some shared baths*

Hostal Que Tal [M] Mallorca 290 (at Bruch) **34/93-459-2366**

Hotel Axel [MW,SW,WI,WC] Aribau 33 (at Consell de Cent) **34/93-323-9393** *full brkfst, rooftop bar*

Hotel Colon [GF] Avenida Catedral 7 **34/93-301-1404**

Hotel Majestic Barcelona [GF,SW,WC] Paseo de Gracia 68 (in city center) **34/93-487-3939** *5-star hotel, rooftop pool*

Bars

Aire/ Sala Diana [W,D,F,S,YC] Valencia 236 (btwn Enriq. Granados & c/ Balmes) **34/93-451-8462**

Am Bar [MW,NH] Casanova 71 (at Consejo de Ciento) *8pm-close*

Átame [M,E,V] Consell de Cent 257 (at M° Universidad) **34/93-454-9273** *6:30pm-2:30am, till 3am wknds*

Bacon Bear Bar [M,B] Casanova 64 (M° Urgell) *6pm-3am, theme nights*

Bar Lola [MW,F] Bruc 121 *open all day, also cafe*

Bar Platz [M] Consejo de Ciento 233 (at Urgell) *5pm-2am*

La Base [M,L,N] Carme 27 **34/933--017-396** *10pm-3am, till 5am Fri-Sat, leather & fetish, naked party Wed & Sat*

Berlin Dark [M,L] Pasage Prunera 18 (at de la Font Honrada) *10pm-3am Tue-Sun*

Burdel [M,DS] Carme 74 (at Joaquin Costa)

El Cangrejo [★MW,D] Villarroel 86 *10:30pm-3am Th-Sat*

La Chapelle [M] Muntaner 65 *small inexpensive bar*

El Chapulín [MW,F] Muntaner 92 (at Valencia) **34/93-452-5593** *1pm-late, clsd Sun*

La Concha del Barrio Chino [MW,D,TG] Guardia 14 (M° Liceu) **34/93-302-4118** *4pm-3am*

Dacksy [MW] Consell de Cent 247 *5pm-3am, trendy cocktail lounge*

El Dulce Deseo de Lorenzo [M] Playa de la Mar Bella *summer beach bar*

G Cafe [MW] Muntaner 24 (M° Universitat) **34/93-451-6536** *6pm-2am, till 3am wknds, funky decor*

Machín [MW,D,F] Casanova 48 **34/93-530-4656** *6pm-3am, clsd Mon, many events, internet*

Mandarina [MW,F] Diputació 157 (M° Urgell) **34/93-323-3393** *6pm-3am, terrace*

Milk House [D] Nou de la Rambla 24 (Raval) *cafe-bar*

Museum Cafe & Club [M] Sepulveda 178 (at Urgell) *6:30pm-3am*

New Chaps [M,L,S,V] Av Diagonal 365 (M° Diagonal) **34/93-215-5365** *9pm-3am, till 3:30am Fri-Sat, from 7pm Sun, darkroom*

Oui Cafe [★M,F] Consell de Cent 247 **34/93-451-4570** *6pm-2am, till 3am Fri-Sat, terrace*

Padam Padam [MW] Rauric 9 **34/93-302-5062** *7pm-3am, clsd Sun, also cafe, classical music*

People Lounge [M,OC] Villaroel 71 (at Diputacion) *8pm-3am*

Punto BCN [★M,WC] Muntaner 63-65 (enter on Consejo de Ciento Yragón, M° Universitat) **34/93-453-6123** *6pm-2:30am, till 3am wknds, upscale cafe-bar*

SM55 [M,L,V] Riera Sant Miguel 55 (M° Diagonal) **34/93-218-2471** *10pm-2:30pm, till 3pm wknds, clsd Wed*

Sweet Cafe [M,D,WC,GO] Casanova 75 (at Consell de Cent) *8pm-2:30am, till 3am Fri-Sat, clsd Sun-Mon*

Topxi [M,DS,V] València 358 **34/93-207-0120** *10pm-5am, dance bar, drag shows nightly,back room*

Z:eltas [M,D,E,V] Casanova 75 (M° Gran Vía/ Urgell) **34/93-454-1902** *10:30pm-3am, [DS] Th*

Zelig [GS,D,F] Carme 116 (M° San Antonio) **34/93-441-5622** *7pm-2am, till 3am wknds, clsd Mon*

NIGHTCLUBS

Arena Classic [★M,D,S,V,YC,$] Diputació 233 (at Balmes, M° Universitat) **34/93-487-8342** *12:30am-5am Fri-Sat only, theme nights, Spanish music*

Arena Dandy/ VIP [M,D,S,V,YC,$] Gran Via 593 (at Balmes, M° Universitat) **34/93-487-8342** *1am-6am Fri-Sat*

Arena Sala Madre [★M,D,F,S,V,YC,$] Balmes 32 (at Diputació, M° Universitat) **34/93-487-8342** *12:30am-5am, clsd Mon (except in Aug), darkroom*

Kiut [MW,D] Consell de Cent 280 (M° Universitat) *midnight-5:30am, clsd Mon-Wed*

Martin's [MO,D,L,S,V] Passeig de Gràcia 130, lower level (M° Diagonal) **34/93-218-7167** *midnight-5am, Sat only*

Metro [★M,D,L,DS,V,YC,$] Sepúlveda 185 (M° Universitat) **34/93-323-5227** *midnight-5am, from 1am Mon*

Tatu [★M,D,TG,DS,V,$] Cayo Celio 7 (M° Plaza d'Espanya) **34/93-425-3350** *10pm-4:30am, from 7pm Sun, patio, drag shows, darkroom*

CAFES

Camper Food Ball Carrer d'Elisabets 9 (M° Catalunya) **34/93-270-1363** *portable organic food & snacks*

Quizás [MW,F] Diputación 161 (M° Urgell) **34/93-451-5258** *9am-2:30am, also bar*

RESTAURANTS

7 Portes Passeig d'Isabel II, 14 **34/93-319-3033, 34/93-319-2950** *1pm-1am, Catalan*

El Bierzo a Tope Diputació 159 **34/93-453-7045** *specialize in lamb meat*

Botafumeiro [R] El Gran de Gràcia 81 **34/93-218-4230, 34/93-217-9642** *1pm-1am, Galician seafood specialities, full bar*

Castro [M,L,S] Casanova 85 (M° Urgell) **34/93-323-6784** *1pm-4pm & 9pm-midnight, clsd Sun, Catalan, full bar*

dDivine [MW,DS,R] Balmes 24 (M° Universitat) **34/93-317-2248** *9:30pm-1am, clsd Sun-Tue, dinner show hosted by "Divine"*

Eterna [MW,DS] Consell de Cent 127-129 (at Villarroel) **34/93-424-2526** *1pm-4pm Mon-Fri, 9:30pm-midnight Th-Sat, clsd Sun*

La Flauta Magica [WC] c/ de Banys Vells 18 (M° Jaume I) **34/93-268-4694** *dinner nightly, vegetarian/ organic*

Iurantia [R] Casanova 42 (M° Urgell) **34/93-454-7887** *lunch Mon-Fri, dinner Mon-Sat, clsd Sun, pizzeria*

Little Italy [E] c/ del Rec 30 (near Passeig del Born) **34/93-319-7973** *1pm-4pm & 9pm-midnight, live jazz*

Madrid-Barcelona [★] Carrer d'Arago 282 (M° Passeig de Gracia) **34/93-215-7027** *lunch & dinner, clsd Sun*

Marquette [★MW,TG,C,DS,R] Diputació 172 (M° Universitat) **34/93-454-6398** *1pm-4pm & 9:30pm-midnight, dinner only Sat-Sun*

Sazzerak Consejo de Ciento 211 **34/93-451-1138** *full bar*

Tafino Consejo de Ciento 193 *1pm-4pm Mon-Fri, 8:30pm-midnight Tue-Sat*

La Veronica Rambla de Raval 2-4 **34/93-329-3303** *1pm-1am, clsd Mon, popular pizzeria*

ENTERTAINMENT & RECREATION

Museu Picasso Montcada 15-23 **34/93-256-3000** *early Picasso works*

Parc Guell Mount Tibidado *mosiacs & sculpture by Gaudí*

BOOKSTORES

Antinous [WC] Josep Anselm Clavé 6 (btwn Las Ramblas & Ample, M° Drassanes) **34/93-301-9070** *LGBT, books & gifts, also cafe*

Cómplices Cervantes 2 (at Avinyó, M° Liceu) **34/93-412-7283** *10:30am-8:30pm, from noon Sat, clsd Sun, LGBT, Spanish & English titles*

Nosotr@s Casanova 56 (M° Urgell) **34/93-451-5134** *LGBT books, magazines, gifts, videos, DVDs*

RETAIL SHOPS

Ovlas [★] Layetana 33 **34/93-268-7691** *clothing, also cafe, Italian (DJ & shows Sat); also at Puertaferrisa 22 [93/301-4183]*

PUBLICATIONS

Gay Barcelona Av Roma 152 **34/93-454-9100** *monthly gay magazine*

Info Gai 34/93-453-4125 *free bi-monthly newspaper in Catalan*

Nois 34/93-454-3805 *free gay monthly*

Men's Clubs

Bruch Bruch 65 (Mº Passeig de Gracia) **34/93-487-4814** *11am-10pm*

Buenos Aires Urgell 114 (at Consell de Cent) **34/93-323-8199** *24hrs wknds*

Casanova [★F,V] Casanova 57 (at Diputació, M° Universitat) **34/93-323-7860, 34/65-016-5078** *24hrs, gym equipment, also bar*

Condal [F,V,SW] Espolsasacs 1 (at Carrer Condal, M° Catalunya) **34/93-317-6817** *24hrs,*

Corinto [★F,V] Pelayo 62 (at Rambla, M° Catalunya) **34/93-318-6422** *24hrs wknds*

Galilea Sauna [F,V,WI] Calabria 59 (M° Rocafort) **34/93-426-7905** *24hrs wknds*

Lesseps [V,SW] Mauricio Serrahima 9 (M° Lesseps) **34/93-218-0592** *also bar*

Sauna Barcelona [V,SW,WI] Tuset 1 (at Av Diagonal) **34/93-200-7716** *24hrs wknds*

Thermas [F,V,SW] Diputación 46 (at Entenza, M° Rocafort) **34/93-325-9346** *24hrs*

Erotica

Blue Star [GS] Av Roma 153 (Edificio Torre Catalunya) **34/93-452-5890**

Boyberry Calàbria 96 (Mº Rocafort) **34/93-426-2312**

Erotic Museum of Barcelona Ramblas 96 **34/93-318-9865**

Harmony Love Gran Via 562 **34/93-405-3300**

Kitsch Muntaner 17-19 (at Gran Vía) **34/93-453-2052**

Nostromo Diputació 208 (downstairs, M° Universitat) **34/93-451-3323** *video cabins, darkroom*

Sestienda Rauric 11 (at Farran, M° Liceu) **34/93-318-8676** *clsd Sun*

Skorpius [GS] Gran Vía 384-390 **34/93-423-4040**

Zeus Gay Shop Riera Alta 20 (M° Sant Antoni) **34/93-442-9795** *clsd Sun, ask for MENsual gay map, also info center*

Cruisy Areas

Parc de Montjuïc [AYOR] btwn Avs del Estadio & Rius y Taulet *behind the archaeology museum, by the cascade*

Parc Sagrada Familia [AYOR]

Playa de la Mar Bella [AYOR] *on the beach and in the park*

Las Ramblas [AYOR]

Madrid

Note: M°=Metro station

Info Lines & Services

COGAM (Colectivo de Lesbianas, Gays, Transexuales, y Bisexuales de Madrid) Infantas 40 (M° Tribunal) **34/91-522-4517** *LGBT center, groups, library, also cafe-bar*

Gai Inform 34/91-523-0070 *5pm-9pm Mon-Fri, helpline*

Accommodations

Chueca Pension [MW,WI] Gravina 4, 2nd flr (at Calle Hortaleza) **34/91-523-1473** *hostel, free internet access*

Hostal CasaChueca [MW,GO] San Bartolomé 4, 2nd flr **34/91-523-8127, 34/63-589-2805**

Hostal Hispano [GF] Hortaleza 38, 2nd flr (at Perez Galdos, M° Chueca) **34/91-531-4871, 34/91-531-2898**

Hostal La Fontana [MW] Valverde 6, 1° (M° Gran Vía) **34/91-521-8449, 34/91-523-1561**

Hostal la Zona [M,GO] Calle Valverde 7, 1 & 2 (at Gran Vía) **34/91-521-9904** *full brkfst, private balconies*

Hostal Odesa [★M,WI] Hortaleza 38, 3rd flr (at Perez Galdos) **34/91-521-0338, 34/91-521-5901**

Hostal Oporto [GF] Calle Zorilla 9, 1st flr (M° Sol) **34/91-429-7856** *10-minute walk to gay scene*

Hostal Puerta del Sol [M,WC,GO] Plaza Puerta del Sol 14, 4° (at Calle de Alcalá, M° Sol) **34/91-522-5126** *centrally located*

Hostal Sonsoles [M] Fuencarral 18, 2nd flr (M° Chueca) **34/91-532-7523**

Hotel A Gaudí Gran Vía 7-9 (at Alcalá) **34/91-531-2222** *4-star hotel in the heart of the city*

Hotel Suecia [GF] Marqués de Casa Riera 4 (M° Banco de España) **34/91-531-6900, 800/448-8355** *jacuzzis*

Hotel Urban Madrid [GF,SW] Carrera de San Jerónimo 34 **34/91-787-7770** *upscale hotel w/ 3 restaurants & rooftop pool*

Hotel Villa Real [GS,WI] Plaza de Las Cortes, 10 **34/91-420-3767** *located in the cultural, political & financial center of Madrid, full brkfst*

BARS

A Noite [M,D,DS,S,V] Hortaleza 43 (M° Chueca) **34/91-531-0715** *9pm-6am, darkroom, hustlers*

The Angel [M,D] Campoamor 11 **34/68-779-1452** *noon-5:30am, till 6am Fri-Sat, clsd Mon-Tue*

Bajo Cuerda [★M,NH,S,V,OC] Benito Pérez Galdós 8 (M° Chueca) *9pm-close, darkroom*

Bear's Bar [★MO,B,L,V] Pelayo 4 (M° Chueca, ring to enter) **34/91-521-7358** *6pm-2:30am, till 3:30am wknds, clsd Mon, 3 bars, darkroom, cruisy*

Black & White (Blanco y Negro) [★M,D,S] Libertad 34 (at Gravina, M° Chueca) **34/91-531-1141** *8pm-5am, till 6am Fri-Sat, disco downstairs*

Copper [MO,D,L,N] San Vincente Ferrer 34 (M° Tribunal) *2pm-3am, till 3:30am Fri-Sat, theme nights, dress code, sling, darkroom*

Cruising [★M,D,L,V,YC] c/ Benito Pérez Galdós 5 (M° Chueca) **34/91-521-5143** *8pm-close, till 3:30am Fri-Sat, cruise bar, darkroom*

Dumbarton [M,NH,OC] Zorrilla 7 (behind Congress bldg, M° Sevilla, ring to enter) **34/91-429-8191** *7pm-2am*

Eagle Madrid [M,L,F,V,N,PC] Pelayo 30 (M° Chueca) **34/91-524-1627** *2pm-close, from 5pm wknds, theme nights, darkroom*

Enfrente [M,B,L] Infantas 12 (M° Gran Vía) **34/68-779-1462** *8pm-3am, DJs Th & Sun*

Fu3l [M,B] San Marcos 11

Fulanita de Tal [W] Calle del Conde de Xiquena 2

Hot Bar [M,B,L,V] Infantas 9 (M° Chueca, ring to enter) *6pm-close, cruise bar, darkroom, [B] 1st Sat*

Leather [MO,D,L,S,V,OC] Pelayo 42 (at Gravina, M° Chueca) **34/91-308-1462** *7pm-3pm, from 8pm Sat, till 3:30am Fri-Sat, [S] Th-Sat, darkroom*

Liquid [M,D,V] Barquillo 8 (M° Banco) **34/91-532-7428** *9pm-close, trendy bar*

LL [★M,D,S,DS,V] Pelayo 11 (M° Chueca) **34/91-523-3121** *6pm-close, darkroom, cruisy*

La Lupe de Lavapies [MW,C] Torrecilla del Leal 12 (M° Antón Martín) **34/91-527-5019** *5pm-2:30am, flea market Sun*

El Mojito [MW,NH] Olmo 6 (M° Antón Martin) **34/91-531-1141** *10pm-3am, till 3:30am Fri-Sat, cocktail bar, great music*

Museo Chicote [GS] Gran Via 12 **34/915-326-737** *'50s style lounge*

O'Clock [M,B] Calle de San Marcos (M° Chueca) *5:30pm-close, cruisy*

The Paso [M,V] Costanilla de Capuchinos 1 (M° Gran Via) **34/91-522-0888** *6pm-close, darkroom*

Picardias [★M,NH,DS] Pérez Galdós 8 (M° Chueca) *7pm-3am*

Querelle [M,V] Lavapiés 12 (M° Tirso de Molina) **34/91-528-3860** *10pm-2am, 11pm-close Fri-Sat, sex club, darkroom*

Refugio [★M,D] Doctor Cortezo 1 (M° Tribunal) **34/91-369-4038, 34/91-523-4689** *midnight-6am, clsd Sun, hottest on Fri night*

Rick's [★M,D,YC] Clavel 8 (at Infantas, M° Gran Vía, ring to enter) **34/91-531-9186** *11pm-6am, open later Fri-Sat, 9pm-2am Sun, "see-and-be-scene"*

Rimmel [M,NH,V,YC] Luis de Góngora 2 (M° Chueca) *7pm-3am, darkroom, hustlers*

El Rincón Guay [MW] Embajadores 62 **34/914-683-769**

Soho [MW] Plaza de Chueca 6 *patio*

Sunrise [MW,D,S] Barbieri 7 (btwn San Marcos & Infantas, M° Chueca) **34/91-523-2808, 34/91-522-4317** *midnight-close, clsd Mon-Tue*

Truco [★W,D] Gravina 10 (at Plaza de Chueca) **34/91-532-8921** *8pm-close, clsd Mon-Tue, dance bar, seasonal terrace*

Why Not? [★GF,$] San Bartolomé 6 (M° Gran Vía) **34/91-523-0581, 34/91-521-8034** *10pm-close, fun dance bar*

Nightclubs

Bangalá [M,MR,V,YC,N] Escuadra 1 (M° Antón Martin/Lavapiés) *9pm-2:30am, till 3am Fri-Sat, darkroom*

Boite [GS,D] Calle Tetuan 27 (Plaza del Carmen) *check listings for gay club nights*

Delirio [M,D,S] Libertad 28 **34/91-531-1870** *11pm-5:30am, go-go boys Wed*

Griffin's [M,D,DS,E] Marqués de Valdeiglesias 6 (M° Banco de España) **34/91-522-2079** *midnight-5am, till 6am Fri-Sat, theme nights*

Heaven @ Sala But [★GF] Barceló 11 (M° Tribunal) *12:30am-6am only, mixed metrosexual party*

Joy Eslava [★GS,D,DS,S] arenal 11 (M° Sol) **34/91-366-3733** *11:30pm-6pm, fabulous crowd*

Long Play [MW,D] Plaza de Vázquez Mella 2 *midnight-6am wknds only*

Mito [MW,NH,D,DS] Augusto Figueroa 3 (M° Chueca) **34/65-793-9124** *11pm-6:30pm*

The Moon [GF,D] Aduana 21 *after-hours club*

Ohm [★M,D,S] Plaza de Callao 4 (at Sala Bash, M° Callao) **34/91-531-0132** *midnight-close Fri-Sat*

Pasapoga [M,D] Gran Via 37 *10pm Wed*

The Paw [M,N] Calatrava 29 (M° La Latina) **34/91-366-6093** *9pm-5am, 11pm-close Wed-Sat, 5pm-close Sun, sex club, darkroom, slings*

Polana [MW,D,C] Barbieri 10 (M° Chueca) **34/91-532-3305** *10pm-5am, trendy*

Royal Dance Coolture (Cool) [GS,D] Isabel la Católica 6 (M° Santo Domingo) **34/91-542-3439** *sleek 2-flr ballroom, more gay Sat for "Bunker Bears Club"*

Sachas [MW,D,DS] Plaza de Chueca 1 (M° Chueca) *8pm-5am Th-Sun, bar open 8pm-3am nightly, terrace*

Space of Sound [MW,D] Sala Macumba (at Estación de Chamartin) **34/90-249-9994** *10pm-close Sun only*

Strong Center [M,D,L,S,V,$] Trujillos 7 (M° Santo Domingo) **34/91-541-5415** *midnight-close, the main attraction is its enormous darkroom*

Tábata [MW,D,YC,$] Vergara 12 (next to Teatro Real, M° Opera) **34/91-547-9735** *11:30pm-late Wed-Sat*

Trip Family [M,D] *gay theme dance parties, check web for events & details*

Week-end [★MW,D,A,$] Plaza de Callao 4 (at Sala Bash, M° Callao) **34/91-541-3500** *midnight-6am Sun*

Cafes

BAires Cafe [MW] Gravina 4 (M° Chueca) **34/91-532-9879** *4pm-2am, also bar, hip crowd*

Cafe Acuarela [MW] Gravina 10 (M° Chueca) **34/91-522-2143, 34/91-570-6907** *3pm-3am, from 11am Sat-Sun, bohemian cafe-bar*

Cafe Figueroa [★MW] Augusto Figueroa 17 (at Hortaleza, M° Chueca) **34/91-521-1673** *also bar*

Cafe la Troje [★MW] Pelayo 26 (at Figueroa, M° Chueca) **34/91-531-0535** *2pm-2am, till 2:30am wknds, full bar*

D'Mystic [★GS,F] Gravina 5 (M° Chueca) **34/91-308-2460** *9:30am-close, hip cafe-bar in Chueca area*

El Jardin [MW] Infantas 9 (M° Gran Via) **34/91-521-9045, 34/91-523-1218** *10am-2am, till 3am wknds*

Mama Inés [★GS] Hortaleza 22 (M° Chueca) **34/91-523-2333** *10am-2am, sandwiches, pies*

La Sastrería [★MW] Hortaleza 74 (at Gravina, M° Chueca) **34/91-532-0771** *10am-2am, till 3am Fri-Sat, from 11am wknds, trendy, internet access*

Star's [MW,D] Marqués de Valdeiglesias 5 (at Infantas, M° Banco) **34/91-522-2712** *9am-6pm & 11pm-close, clsd Sun, cafe-bar, DJ Th-Sat*

XXX Cafe [M,F,C] Clavel 2 (M° Gran Vía) **34/91-532-8415** *10am-close, [C] wknds*

Restaurants

A Brasileira Pelayo 49 (M° Chueca) **34/91-308-3625** *lunch & dinner, Brazilian*

Al Natural Zorrilla 11 (M° Sevilla) **34/91-369-4709** *lunch & dinner, vegetarian*

El Armario [MW,S] San Bartolomé 7 (btwn Figueroa & San Marcos, M° Chueca) **34/91-532-8377**

Artemisa [MW] Ventura de la Vega 4 (at Zorrilla) **34/91-429-5092** *vegetarian*

Botin Cuchilleros 17 **34/91-366-4217** *one of the oldest restaurants in the world*

Chez Pomme Pelayo 4 (M° Chueca) **34/91-532-1646** *lunch & dinner, clsd Sun, int'l/ vegetarian*

Colby Fuencarral 52 (M° Chueca) **34/91-521-2554** *9:30am-close, from 11:30am Sun*

La Coqueta [MW] Libertad 3 **34/91-523-0647** *clsd Sun, lunch & dinner, Mediterranean*

Divina La Cocina [MW] Colmenares 13 (at San Marcos, M° Chueca) **34/91-531-3765** *lunch & dinner, elegant & trendy*

Ecocentro Esquilache 2, 4, y 6 (at Pablo Iglesias, M° Rios Rosas) **34/91-553-5502** *open till midnight, vegetarian, natural foods, also shop, herbalist school*

Gula Gula [★MW,E,DS,R] Gran Via 1 (M° Gran Via) **34/91-522-8764** *lunch & dinner, buffet/ salad bar, full bar*

Lombok Augusto Figueroa 32 (M° Chueca) **34/91-531-3566** *lunch & dinner, clsd Sun, int'l*

Momo [NS,GO] Augusto Figueroa 41 (M° Chueca) **34/91-532-7162** *lunch & dinner, charming staff*

Moskada Francisco Silvela 71 (at General Oraa) **34/91-563-0630** *lunch Mon-Fri, dinner Mon-Sat, clsd Sun*

Nina Manuel Malasana 10 (M° Bilbao) **34/91-591-0046** *contemporary Spanish food, open every day*

Pink Pollo Infantas 18 (near Plaza Vazquez de Mella) **34/91-523-7628** *12:30pm-12:30am, till 2:30am Fri-Sat, open daily for light meals/ snacks*

Restaurante Miau Plaza Santa Ana 6 **34/91-429-2272** *Madrileño cuisine & tapas*

El Rincón de Pelayo [★MW] Pelayo 19 (M° Chueca) **34/91-521-8407** *lunch & dinner*

Sama-Sama San Bartolomé 23 (M° Chueca) **34/91-521-5547** *lunch & dinner, clsd Sun, Balinese decor*

Vegaviana Pelayo 35 **34/913-080-381** *lunch & dinner, clsd Sun-Mon, vegetarian*

Bookstores

A Different Life Pelayo 30 (M° Chueca) **34/91-532-9652** *11am-10pm, LGBT, books, magazines, music, videos, sex shop downstairs*

Berkana Bookstore [WC] Hortaleza 64 **34/91-522-5599** *10:30am-9pm, from 11:30am Sat, from noon Sun, LGBT, Spanish & English titles, ask for free gay map of Madrid*

Retail Shops

AKM Pelayo 14 (M° Chueca) **34/91-531-1388** *clsd Sun, military-style fashion & fetish store*

Ovlas Augusto Figueroa 1 (M° Chueca) **34/92-522-7327** *10:30am-9:30pm, men's clothing, clubwear*

Publications

Odisea Espiritu Santo 33 **34/91-523-2154** *free monthly magazine (en español)*

Shangay Express 34/91-445-1741 *free bi-weekly gay paper, also publishes Shanguide*

Zero 34/91-701-0089 *stylish & intelligent LGBT monthly (en español)*

Gyms & Health Clubs

Energy Gym [★GF] Hortaleza 19 (M° Gran Via, Chueca) **34/91-531-1029, 34/91-522-3073**

Gimnasio V35 [M] Valverde 35 (M° Gran Via) **34/91-523-9352**

Holiday Gym [GF] Serrano Jover 3 (M° Argüelles) **34/91-547-4033** *central location*

Men's Clubs

Adán [V,SW] San Bernardo 38 (M° Noviciado) **34/91-532-9138** *24hrs wknds, 3 flrs, darkroom, also bar, hustlers*

Alameda [SW] Alameda 20 (M° Atocha) **34/91-429-8745** *1pm-11pm, darkroom, also bar, no steam room*

Caldea's [YC,V] Valverde 32 (at Gran Vía, M° Chueca) **34/91-522-9956** *24hrs, gym equipment, bar*

Comendadoras [★OC,V] Plaza Comendadoras 9 (M° Noviciado) **34/91-532-8892** *24hrs, also bar*

Cristal [V,SW] Augusto Figueroa 17 (M° Tribunal y Gran Via) **34/91-531-4489** *3pm-3am, also bar*

Hell [MO,L] Buenavista 14 (M° Antón Martín) *10:30pm-3am, 11:30am-3:30am Fri-Sat, clsd Mon, rubber/ leather/ uniforms welcome, selective entry policy*

Men [V] Pelayo 25 (M° Chueca) **34/91-531-2583** *3pm-8am, 24hrs wknds, bar*

Octopus [M,V,SW] Churruca 10 (M° Tribunal/ Chueca) **34/91-183-2832** *3pm-midnight, darkroom, bar*

Odarko [MO] Loreto & Chicote 7 (M° Callao) **34/91-522-9251** *10pm-close, from 6pm Sun, "pervy & fetish sex club in Madrid"*

Paraíso [★V] Norte 15 (at San Vicente F, M° Noviciado) **34/91-522-4232, 34/91-531-9891** *2pm-midnight, 24hrs wknds, gym equipment, also bar, darkroom*

Sauna Center [M] Cuesta de Santo Domingo 1

Sauna Gran Via [M] Barco 6 **34/915-230-468**

Sauna Príncipe [F,V] Travesia de las Beatas 3 (M° Opera) **34/91-559-5353, 34/91-548-2218** *2pm-midnight, also bar, darkroom*

Sauna Puerta de Toledo Cuesta de las Descargas 6 (M° Puerta de Toledo) *2pm-11pm*

Erotica

Amantis Pelayo 46 **34/91-702-0510**

City Sex Store c/ Hortaleza, next to #18 (in Chueca) **34/91-181-2723** *open every day*

La Jugueteria Travesia de San Mateo 12 **34-91/308-7269**

Play Pelayo 29 (M° Chueca) **34/91-523-0841** *sex shop, open daily*

SR [GO] Pelayo 7 (M° Chueca) **34/91-523-1964** *clsd Sun, fetish, military, leather*

Cruisy Areas

Casa de Campo [AYOR] *at night on top of hill—travel along only road going up from lake*

El Corte Ingles [AYOR] Puerta del Sol *large department store, men's lounge on 3rd & 5th flrs*

Parque El Retiro [AYOR] (M° Atocha) *at night in garden around statue of fallen angel*

Plaza de Toros [AYOR] *car cruising at night*

Sitges

ACCOMMODATIONS

Antonio's Guesthouse [MW,WI,GO] Passeig Vilanova 58 **34/93-894-9207** *also apts*

El Baobab B&B [M,SW,GO] Calle Mercuri 25, Olivella **34/620-162-293** *5 miles from Sitges, full brkfst, lovely views*

Los Globos [MW,WI,WC,GO] Avda Ntra Sra de Montserrat 43 **34/93-894-9374** *also bar, terrace*

Go Gay Sitges [M] Balmes 28, 08007 Barcelona **34/93-513-5560** *rental apts*

Hotel Antemare [GF,SW] Verge de Montserrat 48-50 **34/93-894-7000** *1 block from beach, great service*

Hotel Liberty [★MW,NS,WI,WC,GO] Isla de Cuba 45 (at Artur Carbonell) **34/93-811-0872** *seasonal*

Hotel Renaixença [MW] Sant Isidre 33, 08070 **34/93-894-8375** *some shared baths, hotel bar*

Hotel Romàntic [★GS] Sant Isidre 33 **34/93-894-8375** *full brkfst, some shared baths, seasonal, also full bar*

Hotel Santa Maria Paseo de la Ribera 52 **34/93-894-0999** *clean & modest, great restaurant*

Masia Casanova [M,SW,N,WI,GO] Pasaje Casanova 8, Canyelles **34/93-818-8058** *guesthouse, 10 minutes from town, 3-night minimum stay, full brkfst, jacuzzi*

Parrot's Hotel [MW] Joan Tarrida 16 **34/93-894-1350**

Pensión Espalter [★GF] Espalter 11 **34/93-894-0300** *balconies, in city center*

Sitges Holiday Apartments [GF] Francisco Gum 25 **34/93-894-1333** *centrally located 1-brdm apts, near beach*

Sitges Royal Rooms [M,WI,GO] C/ Sant Bonaventura 14 bajos (at Sant Francesc **34/64-998 -1148**

El Unicornio [GS] Av Mas den Puig 51 **34/93-811-3407, 34/61-907-2075** *verandas*

El Xalet [GF,F] Isla de Cuba 21 **34/93-811-0872** *bkfst included*

BARS

Azul [★M,NH,V] Sant Bonaventura 10 **34/93-894-7634** *9pm-3am*

B-Side [★M,F,S,V] San Gaudencio 7 **34/61-799-0926** *10pm-3:30am, cafe-bar, darkroom*

Bar Amura [M] Sant Pere 3 *6:30pm-3am, also darkroom*

Bears' Bar [M,B,V] Bonaire 17 **34/93-894-6296** *10pm-3am (Fri-Sat only off-season), theme nights, 2 darkrooms*

Blondies [GS,F] Port Alegre 10 (at San Sebastian Beach) *5pm-3am, till 3:30am Fri-Sat, seasonal, terrace*

Bourbon's [★M,D,V,YC] Sant Bonaventura 13 **34/93-894-3347** *10:30pm-3:30am (Sat only off-season), darkroom*

El Candil [★M,D,V,YC] Carreta 9 **34/93-894-1632** *seasonal, 10pm-3am, till 3:30am Fri-Sat, darkroom*

Casablanca [M,NH,B,F] Pau Barrabeitg 5 **34/93-894-7082** *8pm-close (clsd Mon off-season), cafe-bar, darkroom*

Comodín [M,D,DS] Tacó 4 **34/93-894-1698** *10pm-3am, till 3:30am Fri-Sat (Fri-Sat only off-season), drag shows Sat, darkroom*

Dark/ DSB [M] Bonaire 14 *5pm-3am, sleek lounge*

El Horno [★M,B,L,F,V] Joan Tarrida Ferratges 6 **34/93-894-0909** *5:30pm-3am, underwear parties Tue, darkroom, darkroom*

La Locacola [M] Bonaire 35 *7pm-close*

Le Male à Bar [M,D,F,V] Centro Comercial Oasis 28 *after-hours bar, 11pm-late (only wknds in winter), underwear parties Mon & Wed, terrace, dancing till 10am, darkroom*

Man [M,L] Bonaventura 19 *10pm-3:30am, darkroom, theme nights, underwear parties Sun & Th summers*

Mediterraneo [★M,D,YC] Sant Bonaventura 6 **34/93-894-3347** *10pm-3:30am, patio*

Mojito & Co [M] Plaza Industrial 1 *breezy lounge w/ outdoor seating*

New Port [MW,D,DS,S,V] Taco 1-3 **34/93-452-0356**

Orek's [M,D,S,V] Bonaire 13 *10pm-3am (only Fri-Sat in winter), darkroom*

Parrot's Pub [★MW,L,S] Plaza Industria 2 (at Primero de Mayo) **34/93-894-7881** *5pm-close, seasonal, patio, also restaurant*

Perfil [M,NH,D,L,DS,V] Espalter 7 **34/656-376-791 (cell)** *10:30pm-3am, [DS] Fri, darkroom, small local bar*

El Piano [MW,C,P] Bonaventura 37 **34/93-814-6245** *10pm-3am*

Prinz [M,C,DS,S] Nou 4 **34/93-894-6736** *11pm-3:30am*

Privilege [M,D] Bonaire 24 *seasonal, 10:30pm-3:30am, darkroom, Dog Meat Disco 1st Sat*

Queenz [M,D,DS,C] Bonaire 17

Ricky's [GS] San Pau 25 *local bar, more gay Fri*

El Seven [M,D,S,V] Calle Nou 7 *10pm-3am (wknds only off-season), clsd Nov, terrace, darkroom*

XXL [★M,D,L,V] Joan Tarrida Ferratges 7 *11pm-3:30am (wknds only off-season), industrial-style bar, darkroom*

NIGHTCLUBS

L' Atlántida [M] at Playa Les Coves *gay beach party from midnight on Tue (summers)*

Organic [M,D,TG,S,$] Bonaire 15 **34/93-894-2230** *midnight-6am (wknds only off-season), singles party Th, darkroom*

Trailer [★M,D] Angel Vidal 36 *1am-6am, seasonal, foam parties in summer*

CAFES

Cafe Al Fresco Carrer Major 33 **34/93-811-3307** *9am-midnight*

Cafe Sitges [F] Sant Pau 32 *11am-3pm, also 6pm-late Wed-Sun, clsd Tue*

Cine Cafe [M,GO] Jesus 55 **34/662-560-050** *10am-midnight, Anglo-American, Hollywood kitsch*

Mont Roig Cafe [★WI] Marques de Montroig 11-13 **34/93-894-8439** *9am-3am, patio, also full bar*

RESTAURANTS

Air Bahia [★R] Paseo Maritim 2 **34/93-894-2445**

Alma [MW,F] Tacó 16 **34/93-894-6387** *8pm-close (clsd Tue-Wed off-season), French, terrace*

Beach House [GO] Sant Pau 34 **34/93-894-9029** *brkfst & dinner, full bar*

Can Pagès [MW] Sant Pere 24-26 **34/93-894-1195** *1pm-4pm & 8pm-midnight, clsd Mon, seafood & grilled meats*

El Celler Vell Bonaventura 21 **34/93-811-1961** *dinner nightly, lunch Fri-Sun, clsd Wed, traditional Catalan*

Doré Restaurant & Lounge Carrer Sant Pau 11 **34/93-894-6782** *from 7pm, also bar, gay theme dinners*

Flamboyant [M,WC] Pau Barrabeitg 16 **34/93-894-5811** *8pm-11pm, seasonal, int'l, full bar, terrace dining*

Kento Calle Bonaire 25 **34/938-948-011** *sushi*

Ma Maison [★MW] Bonaire 28 **34/93-894-6054** *lunch & dinner, French, full bar, terrace*

Mezzanine Espalter 8 **34/93-894-9940** *dinner only, French*

Monroes Sant Pau 36 **34/93-894-1612** *dinner nightly, clsd Tue, Drag Queen Bingo Fri (winter only)*

Nuestro Mini Himalaya [M] Jesús 57 **34/93-810-2643** *English brkfst, theme nights*

Pic Nic Paseo de la Ribera **34/93-811-0040** *in front of gay beach, also internet cafe*

So Ca/ Southern California Sant Gaudenci 9 **34/93-894-3046** *1pm-close, Southern CA cuisine, also bar*

Sucré-Salé [MW] Sant Pau 39 **34/93-894-2302** *lunch & dinner, clsd Tue off-season, crêpes, terrace*

El Trull [★MW] Mossèn Felix Clará 3 (off Major) **34/93-894-4705** *dinner only, clsd Wed, French/ int'l*

ENTERTAINMENT & RECREATION

Gay Beach (Platja de la Bassa Rodona) *in front of Calipolis Hotel & Picnic cafe*

RETAIL SHOPS

Boyzone Sant Bonaventura 18 **34/93-894-6466** *clubwear, swimwear*

Jazz Boutique Bonaire 20 **34/93-894-9963** *men's clothing*

Oscar Marqués de Montroig 2 (at Plaza Industria) **34/93-894-1976** *designer clothing for men & women*

Ovlas San Francisco 22 **34/93-894-1521** *original clothing & accessories*

GYMS & HEALTH CLUBS

Gym Squash Sitges Barrachina 10 **34/93-894-5005** *gym, also sauna & bar*

MEN'S CLUBS

Parrots Sauna [MO] Joan Tarrida 16 **34/93-894-1350**

Sauna Sitges [V] Espalter 11 **34/93-894-2863** *4pm-9am, bar, darkroom, theme parties, foam parties*

EROTICA

The Mask Bonaire 22 **34/93-811-2214** *24hr wknds*

CRUISY AREAS

Espigon Beach [AYOR] *beware of cops!*

L' Estanyol Beach [AYOR] *go right, past gay beach—beware of cops!*

Gay Beach [AYOR] *in front of Calipolis Hotel & Picnic cafe (beware of cops!)*

Playa del Muerto [AYOR] *in woods near Terramar Hotel, daytime (beware of cops!)*

Asia

JAPAN

Tokyo

INFO LINES & SERVICES

Akta Daini Nakae Bldg #301 (Shinjuku 2-15-13) **81-3/3226-8998** *4pm-10pm, community center & HIV/AIDS resource*

ACCOMMODATIONS

24 Kaikan [M,F,V] Shinjuku 2-13-1 **81-3/3354-2424** *hotel & sauna; also Asakusa 2-29-16 (81-3/5827-2424) & Kita-Ueno 1-8-7 (81-3/3847-2424)*

Capitol Tokyu [GF] 10-3 Nagata-cho 2-chome (Chiyoda-ku) **81-3/3581-4511** *near the Diet, renovated hotel coming 2010*

Four Seasons Hotel [GF,SW,WC] 10-8 Sekiguchi 2-chome (Bunkyo-ku) **81-3/3943-2222** *surrounded by historic Japanese garden*

Hotel Century Southern Tower [GF] 2-2-1 Yoyogi (Shibuya-ku) **81-3/5354-0111** *near gay district*

Keio Plaza Hotel [GF,SW] 2-2-1 Nishi Shinjuku **81-3/3344-0111** *several restaurants & bars*

Park Hyatt [GF,SW] 3-7-1-2 Nishi Shinjuku **81-3/5322-1234** *luxury hotel featured in Lost in Translation; also restaurants & lounge*

Shinjuku Prince Hotel [GF,WI] 30-1 Kabuki-cho 1-chome (Shinjuku-ku) **81-3/3205-1111, 800/542-8686 (US)**

Shinjuku Washington Hotel [GF] 3-2-9 Nishi-Shinjuku (Shinjuku-ku) **81-3/3343-3111**

Tokyo International Hostel [GF] 18F Central Plaza (1-1 Kagurakashi, Shinjuku-ku) **81-3/3235-1107** *11pm curfew*

BARS

Advocates [MW,YC] 1-F, Dai-7 Tenka Bldg (Shinjuku 2-18-1) **81-3/3358-3988** *6pm-4am, café-bar*

Advocates Cafe [GS] 1/F 7th Tenka Bld (2-18-1 Shinjuku Ni-Chome) **81-3/3358-3988** *6pm-4am, till 1am Sun, outdoor seating*

Alamas Cafe [MW] 1/F Garnet Bldg, Shinjuku 2-12-1 **81-3/3358-3988** *6pm-2am, till 5am Fri-Sat, 3pm-midnight Sun*

The Annex [M,F,OC] 1F, Futami Bldg (Shinjuku 2-14-11) **81-3/3356-5029** *3pm-5am*

Arty Farty [★M,F,YC] 2F, #33 Kyutei Bldg (Shinjuku 2-11-7), Shinjuku-ku **81-3/5362-9720** *6pm-5am, from 7pm Fri, from 5pm wknds, till 3am Sun, clsd Mon*

Bravo! [M] 2F Shinbashi 2-9-17 **81-3/3503-8805** *6pm-midnight, clsd Sun*

Fuji [M,K] St Four Bldg, B104 (Shinjuku 2-12-16), Shinjuku-ku **81-3/3354-2707** *8pm-3am, till 5am wknds*

GB [★M] B1, Shinjuku Plaza Bldg (Shinjuku 2-12-3), Shinjuku-ku **81-3/3352-8972** *8pm-2am, till 3am Wed*

Hatch 3/F Tozaki Bldg, 2-7-4 Dougen-zaka Shibuya

Janny's [M] 2F Dai 3 Tenka Bldg (Shinjuku 2-14-8) **81-3/3341-3333** *6pm-5am, hustlers*

Joker [TG] B1/F Nakae Bldg, 2-4-9 Shinjyuku-ku **81-3/3358-5562** *7pm-2am, till 4am wknds*

Keivi [M,NH] 4F Yoshino Bldg, 17-10 Sakuragaoka **81-3/3496-0006** *6pm-midnight*

Kinsmen [MW] 2F Shinjuku 2-12-16 (near Shinjuku Sanchome Station) **81-3/3354-4949** *7pm-1am, till 3am Fri-Sat, clsd Mon*

Kusuo [M] 3F Sunflower Bldg (Shinjuku 2-17-1) **81-3/3354-5050** *8pm-4am, till 5am wknds*

Lamppost [M,P] 201 Yamahara Heights (Shinjuku 2-12-15) **81-3/3354-0436** *7pm-3am*

Magnum [M,B] 3-11-12, B1 Nagatani Teikueito Bld, Shinjuku **81-3/3358-5245** *8pm-2am, till 4am Fri-Sat*

Papi Chulos [M] Shinjuku 2-12-15 8F (Shinjuku-ku) **81-3/3356-9833** *6pm-5am*

Pau Hana [M] 2-11-10 Shinjuku (Shinjuku-ku) **81-3/3226-6369** *Hawaiian theme*

Poplar [M,OC] B1 St Four Bldg (Shinjuku 2-12-16) **81-3/3350-6929** *6pm-2am, till 4am Sat*

Tac's Knot [MW] 2F, Rm 202 (Shinjuku 3-11-12) **81-3/3341-9404** *8pm-2am, also art exhibitions*

Tactics [M,B] 105, 2-7-3 Shinjuku 2-chome **81-70/5086-9048** *8pm-2am, till 4:30am Fri-Sat*

Wordup Bar [M,D] 2-10-7 2F TOM Bld Shinjuku **81-3/3353-2466**

Nightclubs

Arch [★MW,D,DS] B1F Hayakawa Bldg (Shinjuku 2-14-6) **81-3/3352-6297** *call for info on men-only & women-only nights*

Club Dragon [M,D,L,V] 1/F Stork Nagasaki, 2-11-4 Shinjuku **81-3/3341-0606** *6pm-3am, till 5am Fri-Sat*

Dragon Men [M,D] 1F Stork Nagasaki (2-11-4 Shinjuku Ni-Chome) **81-3/3341-0606** *6pm-3am, till 5am Fri-Sat, cruisy*

Hijoguchi [GF,D] 1F (Shinjuku 2-12-16) **81-3/3341-5445**

Shangri-La [M,D] Yume no Shima, Koto ward (at Ageha, Studio Coast)

Restaurants

Angkor Wat 1-38-13 Yoyogi (Shibuya-ku) **81-3/3370-3019** *lunch & dinner, Cambodian*

Ban Thai 1-23-14 Kabuki-cho, 3rd flr (Shinjuku) **81-3/3207-0068** *lunch & dinner*

Chin-ya 1-3-4 Asukusa **81-3/3841-0010** *lunch & dinner, serving shabu-shabu & sukiyaki since 1880*

Edogin [★] 4-5-1 Tsukiji (Chuo-ku) **81-3/3543-4401** *11am-9:30pm, clsd Sun, sushi*

Gonpachi 1-13-11 Nishi Azabu, 1F, 2F (Minato-ku) **81-3/5771-0170** *11:30am-5am, izakaya*

Kakiden 3-37-11 Shinjuku, 8th flr **81-3/3352-5121** *lunch & dinner, upscale Japanese*

Kitchen Five [★] 4-2-15 Nishi-Azabu (Minato-ku) **81-3/3409-8835** *6pm-9:45pm, Mediterranean*

Las Chicas Jingumae 5-47-6 (off Shibuya), Shibuya-ku **81-3/3407-6865** *11:30am-11pm, English spoken*

Maisen 4-8-5 Jingu-mae (Shibuya-ku) **81-3/3470-0071** *specializes in tonkatsu*

Moti 3F Roppongi Hama Bldg (6-2-35 Roppongi) **81-3/3479-1939** *noon-10pm, Indian*

New York Grill [R] 3-7-1-2 Nishi Shinjuku (at Park Hyatt Hotel, 52nd flr) **81-3/5323-3458** *lunch & dinner, American*

Sasa-no-yuki 2-15-10 Negishi (Taito-ku) **81-3/3873-1145** *11am-9pm, clsd Mon, serving homemade tofu for 300 years*

Tenmatsu 1-6-1 Dogen-zaka (Shibuya-ku) **81-3/3462-2815** *tempura*

Gyms & Health Clubs

Shinjuku Tipness Kaleido Bldg 5-7F (Nishi-Shinjuku 7-1), Shinjuku-ku **81-3/3368-3531** *many locations throughout city*

Men's Clubs

24 Kaikan [M,F,V] Shinjuku 2-13-1 **81-3/3354-2424** *24hrs, darkroom, sauna, restaurant, hotel; also Asakusa 2-29-16 (81-3/5827-2424) & Kita-Ueno 1-8-7 (81-3/3847-2424)*

Babylon Tokyo [MO] Sendagaya Bldg 3F-5F (Sendagaya 5-30-9, near Yoyogi Station), Yoyogi *3pm-1am, till 7am Fri-Sat, [N] Wed & Fri*

HX [MO,YC] 1F, UI Bldg (Shinjuku 5-9-6) **81-3/3226-4448** *3pm-10am, 24hrs wknds*

Treffpunkt [MO] 4F Fukutomi Bldg (Akasaka 2-13-4) **81-3/5563-0523** *wknds naked*

Cruisy Areas

Hibiya Park [AYOR] near Yurakucho Station

Shin Kiba Park [AYOR] near Shin Kiba Station

Ueno Park near Tokyo Metropolitan Festival Hall

Southeast Asia

Thailand

Bangkok

Accommodations

Aquarius Gentlemen's House [MO,F,GO,AYOR] 243 Soi Huthayana, Soi Suan Phlu, S Sathorn Rd **66-2/679-3180, 66-2/677-2174** *massage & more, food served 7am-9pm; also bar, roof garden*

Baan Saladaeng [GF,WI] 69/2 Soi Saladaeng 3, Saladaeng Rd (Silom, Bangrak) **66-2/2636-3038** *upscale, near gay scene*

Babylon B&B [MO,SW,WI,AYOR] 34 Soi Nandha, Sathon Soi 1, S Sathon Rd **66-2/679-7984** *also spa & saunas, foam party 1st Fri*

Bangkok Rama Place, City Resort & Hotel [GF,SW,WC,GO] 1546 Pattanakarn Rd (in Suan-Luang District) **66-2/722-6602-10** *full brkfst, also restaurant*

Chatra Court [M,SW,WI] 49 Soi Sukhumvit 19 (Wattana) **66-2/651-1310** *residential hotel in the heart of Bangkok*

D&D Inn [GF,SW] 68-70 Khaosan Rd (Phranakorn) **66-2/629-0525-8**

Elephantstay [GS,GO] Royal Elephant Kraal & Village (74/1 M3 Tumbol Suanpik), Phra Nakhon Si Ayutthaya **66-81/745-7064, 66-87/116-3307** *live w/, care for & learn about elephants; Thai-style bungalows; near Lopburi River; 1 hour to Bangkok; lesbian-owned*

Homduang Boutique Hotel Sathorn [GF,SW,NS] Chan Road Soi 2 (at Naratiwas), Sathorn **66-2/678-6487** *near gay areas of Patpong & Sukhumvit*

Hotel de Moc [GF,SW,WI,WC] 78 Prajatipatai Rd, Pra-Nakorn **66-2/282-2831-3, 66-2/629-2100-5**

Lub d [GF] 4 Decho Rd (Silom, Bangrak) **66-2/634-7999**

Luxx [GF,WI] 6/11 Decho Rd **66-2/635-8800** *style-conscious, minimalist design hotel, full brkfst*

Old Bangkok Inn [GF,NS] 607 Pra Sumen Rd (at Rajdamnern Ave, in Pra Nakhon) **66-2/629-1787** *environe-mentally-friendly hotel*

Omyim Lodge [GS,NS,WI,GO] 72-74 Naratiwat Rd Silom **66-2/635-0169** *also restaurant*

Pinnacle Hotel [GS] 17 Soi Ngam Duphli, Rama 4 Rd, Sathorn **66-2/287-0111** *sauna, fitness center, hot tub*

Plaza Hotel Bangkok [GF,SW] 178 Surawong Rd **66-2/677-6240** *extra "joiner" charge for guests*

Regency Park Hotel [GF,SW] 12/3 Sukhumvit 22, Soi Sainamthip **66-2/259-7420** *located in heart of Bangkok, full brkfst*

Sheraton Grande Sukhumvit [GF,SW,WI,WC] 250 Sukhumvit Rd **66-2/649-8888**

Tarntawan Place Hotel [MW,WI,WC] 119/ 5-10 Surawong Rd **66-2/238-2620** *centrally located, deluxe boutique hotel, modern ameni-ties, bar & lounge*

The Unico Grande Silom [GF,SW] 533 Silom Rd (Bang Rak) **66-2/237-8300, 66-2/635-0378** *also gym, sauna, restaurant & bar*

White Orchid [GF] 409 - 421, Yaowaraj Road **66-2/226-0026**

Bars

70's Bar [MW,D] 231/16 Sarasin (Chitlom) **66-2/253-4433** *retro lounge*

The Balcony Pub & Restaurant [★M,F,K] 86-88 Silom Soi 4 (off Silom Rd) **66-2/235-5891** *5:30pm-close, Bangkok Metro Magazine's "Best Gay Bar 2000," terrace*

Balls Sports Bar [M,F] Duangthawee Plaza, 894 Soi Pratoochai, Surawong Rd **66-2/637-0078** *5pm-1am, from 1pm wknds*

Bearbie Bar [M,B,K] 82 Silom Soi 4, 2nd flr **66-2/632-8446**

Bed Supperclub [GS,D] 26 Soi Sukhumvit 11, Sukhumvit Rd, Klongtoey-nua, Wattana **66-2/651-3537** *7:30pm-close, more gay Sun for Think Pink*

Big Bearz [M,B,K] 130/2 Silom Soi 6 **66-4/681-1655, 66-81/206-2480** *6pm-1am*

Blue Club [M,D] 3161 Ramkhamhaeng Rd (btwn Soi 81 & 83, 2nd floor, above Duan Chai) **66-2/732-2360** *mostly Thai*

Club Cafe [M] 8/5 Silom Soi 2 (Bang Rak) **66-86/978-5221** *3pm-3am*

Club Love Remix [GS,D,F] Ramkhamhaeng Soi 89/2 **66-2/378-4345, 66-1/987-4946** *also restaurant*

E-Male [M,C,DS] 62-64 Ramkhamhaeng, Soi 24 **66-2/319-6772**

Expresso [M] 8/10-11 Silom Rd, Soi 2 (Bang Rak) *relaxed café-bar*

Finallé [M,D,C] Ramkhamhaeng Soi 89/2 **66-1/503-5398** *8pm-2am*

Future Boys [★M,S] 894/ 4-6 Soi Pratoochai (Duangthawee Plaza) **66-2/637-0507** *7pm-2am*

G.O.D. [M,D] 60/18-21 Silom Soi 2/1 (at Soi Thaniya) *"guys on display," till 6am*

Golden Cock [M] 39/27 Soi Rajanakarindra 1, Surawong Rd (Bang Rak) **66-2/236-3859** *1pm-1am*

Golden Dome [MW,C] 252/5 Ratchadapisek Rd Soi 18 (Huay Kwang) **66-2/692-8202** *shows nightly at 5pm, 7pm & 9pm*

Hamilton's Hideaway [M,F,E,NS] Soi Silom 2/1 (Saladeang BTS Station, Silom) **66-866/143-644** *6pm-1am, live jazz*

Ichub [M,B,K] 297 Sarasin Rd, Lumpini **66-1/208-5069** *7pm-1am, "chubs & chasers"*

JJ Park [GS,F,E] 8/3 Silom Rd, Soi 2 (Bang Rak) **66-2/233-3247** *9pm-3am, live music*

Jupiter 2002 [M,S] 31/1-33 Surawong Rd, Thaniya Soi 2 **66-2/237-4050** *8pm-2am*

Maxi's Bar [M] 38/1-2 Duangthawee Plaza, Soi Pratoochai, Suriwong Rd **66-2/2266-4225** *10am-2am*

Mogue [M,D] 362 Kamphangphet Rd, Chatuchak **66-2/618-6681** *8pm-2am*

MTV Remix [GS,D] Ramkhamhaeng Soi 24 **66-2/319-8340**

@Richard's Pub & Restaurant [M,NH,F] 10/17 Silom Soi 2/1 **66-2/234-0459** *6pm-2am*

Solid [M] 39/2 Soi Anuman Ratchathon, Suriwong, Bangkok **66-2/2634-2664**

Tawan [★M,S] 2/2 Soi Thantawan, Silom Soi 6 (off Suriwong Rd) **66-2/234-5506** *8:30pm-2am, specializing in muscular go-go boys*

Telephone Pub & Restaurant [★MW,F] 114/ 11 Silom Rd, Soi 4 **66-2/234-3279** *6pm-1am, numbered telephones on all the tables*

Vega [MW,F,K,GO] Sukhumvit 39 **66-2/258-8273, /662-6471** *11am-2am, lesbian-owned*

NIGHTCLUBS

9 Nightclub [M,D,S,C,DS] 90-96 Silom Rd, Soi 4 **66-2/266-3682**

The Boys [★M,S] 38/3-6 Duangthawee Plaza (at 38 Surawong Rd, Bang Rak) **66-2/235-5715** *8pm-2am, go-go boys*

Disco Disco [M,D] 8/12-13 Silom Rd, Soi 2 (Bang Rak) **66-2/234-6151, 66-2/266-4029** *9pm-3am*

DJ Station [★MW,D] 8/6-8 Silom Rd, Soi 2 (Bang Rak) *11pm-2am*

Dream Boy [★M,S] 38/3-6 Duangthawee Plaza (at 38 Surawong Rd, Bang Rak) **66-2/233-2121** *8pm-2am, go-go boy shows nightly at 10:30pm & 12:30am, 2 stages*

Ick [M,D,E] Ramkhamhaeng Soi 89/2 **66-9/119-3635, 66-1/442-9472** *8pm-2am*

Pharaoh's Music Bar [GS,F,K] 104 Silom Soi 4 (above Sphinx) **66-2/234-7249** *7pm-2am*

Sa-Ke [M,D] Kok Wau Intersection (at Tanao Rd & Ratchadamnoen Rd) **66-9/748-0212** *10pm-2am*

TG Street [M,D] Kok Wau Intersection (at Tanao Rd & Ratchadamnoen Rd) **66-89/748-0212** *10pm-2am*

CAFES

Babylon Galleria Cafe [M] 34 Soi Nandha, S Sathorn Rd, Soi 1 (at Babylon B&B) **66-2/679-7984** *11:30am-midnight*

Bug & Bee 18 Silom Rd, Suriyawong (Bang Rak) **66-2/233-8118**

Coffee Society [F,WI] 12/3 Silom Rd (Suriyawong, Bang Rak) **66-2/235-9784** *24hrs, also art gallery*

Dick's Cafe Bangkok 894/7-8 Soi Pratoochai (Duangthawee Plaza, off Surawong Rd) **66-2/637-0078** *11am-1am, European-style cafe*

RESTAURANTS

Anna's Cafe [★] Diethelm Tower B (ground floor), Wireless Rd **66-2/252-0864** *10am-10pm, clsd Sun, Thai & European fusion, other locations also*

Cabbages & Condoms 6 Soi 12 Sukhumvit Rd **66-2/229-4611** *11am-10pm, Thai food w/ safe-sex education*

Coyote on Convent Sivadon Building, 1/2 Convent Rd, Silom Bangrak **66-2/631-2325** *Mexican*

Crêpes & Co 18/1 Sukhumvit Soi 12 (Klongtoey) **66-2/653-3990** *terrace, lounge, full bar*

Eat Me Soi Pipat 2 (off Soi Convent) **66-2/238-0931, 66-2/233-1767** *art restaurant*

Food Loft 1027 Ploenchit Rd, Lumpini, Pathumwan (Central Chisholm, 7th flr) **66-2/655-7777** *upscale int'l food*

Full Moon [GO] 144/2 Silom Soi 10 **66-2/634-0766** *Thai food*

Indigo [GS] 6 Convent Rd (off Silom Rd) **66-2/235-3268** *noon-1am, clsd Sun, patio, full bar, French*

Loy Nava Dinner Cruises [R] 37 Charoen Nakorn Rd, Klongsan **66-2/437-4932** *traditional Thai cuisine on rice barge on Chao Phraya River*

Mali 43 Sathorn Soi 1 **66-2/679-8693** *8am-11pm, Thai & int'l*

Mango Tree [★E, R] 37 Soi Tantawan (off Suriwong Rd) **66-2/236-2820** *traditional Thai food, live music nightly*

May Kaidee 11-1 Racha Damnuem Rd, Banglampoo **66-9/137-3173, 66-2/281-7137** *9am-11pm, innovative vegetarian restaurant; also 33 Samen Rd (Soi 1), also guesthouse & massage*

O...Ho... [GO] 2/8 Soi Sri Bumphen **66-2/286-5292** *9am-midnight, Thai & Western menu*

Omyim Restaurant [GO] 106 Soi Sribumpen Rama 4 Rd (Sathorn District) **66-8/1300-1778**

Once Upon a Time 32 Soi Petchaburi 17, Pratunam **66-2/252-8629** *11am-11pm, Thai*

Sphinx [★M,K] 100 Silom Soi 4 **66-2/234-7249** *6pm-1am, Thai & Western, full bar, terrace*

Sweet Basil [★] 1 Soi Sriwiang (off Silom Soi Pramuan) **66-2/234-1889, 66-2/238-3088** *Vietnamese food*

Thaipaz 69/5 Saladaeng Rd (Bang Rak) **66-2/636-3220** *4pm-midnight, int'l tapas*

Entertainment & Recreation

Calypso Cabaret [MW,C,DS] 296 Phaya Thai Rd, Pathumwan (at Asia Hotel) **66-2/261-6355** *shows nightly at 8:30pm & 10pm*

Mambo [MW,C] 496 Sukhumvit Soi 22 (at Washington Theatre) **66-2/259-5128** *shows nightly at 8:30pm & 10pm*

Publications

Spice 66-3/983-0256, 66-81/941-6769 *monthly gay magazine*

Gyms & Health Clubs

Hercules Health Club [M,F,K] 91/194 Siam Park City, Sukhapiban 2 Rd, Siam Park Ave (Bangkapi) **66-2/919-9609** *gym w/ sauna & steam room; also restaurant & bar*

Men's Clubs

Adonis Massage [★MO] 44/11 Convent Rd (Silom) **66-2/236-7789, 66-9/010-3399** *massage by men for men*

Albury Men's Club [MO] 71/1 Sukhumvit Soi 11 **66-2/255-8920, 66-2/255-4768** *restaurant, bar, gym & steam room*

Aqua Spa Club [F] 11/5 Soi Sathorn 9 **66-2/286-5233, 66-2/286-4535** *massage, tarot readings*

Arena [MO] 491/19-21 Silom Rd, Silom Plaza, 2nd flr **66-2/635-3645** *Thai massage*

Banana Club [MO,F] 41/9 Sukhumvit Soi 11 **66-2/651-0002** *3 flrs, massage, also restaurant*

Body Club [M] 4/24-25 Sukhumvit Soi 8 **66-89/171-9009, 66-81/613-6095** *massage for men by men*

Chakran [F,K,V,SW] 32 Soi Ari 4, Phaholyothin Soi 7, Phayathai **66-2/279-1359** *darkroom, gym, poolside bar*

GQ [MO] 253/4 Soi Suan Phlu 6 **66-2/677-5915, 66-2/679-4490** *massage for men*

Sauna Mania [M] 35/2 Soi Pipat 2 (off Soi Convent, Silom) **66-2/817-4073** *3pm-2am, enter on 2nd flr*

V Club [MO,F] 52/1 Soi Aree Phaholyothin 7 **66-2/279-3322, 66-2/271-2464**

Australia

New South Wales

Sydney

Info Lines & Services

The Gender Centre 61-2/9569-2366 *free services for transgender/ transsexual people & their partners/ friends/ families, also publishes magazine Polare*

Lesbian & Gay Counselling Service 61-2/8594-9596, 1-800/18-4527(outside Sydney) *5:30pm-10:30pm*

Accommodations

Apartment Hotel East Sydney [GS,NS] 150 Liverpool St, E Sydney (at Oxford St) **61/404-793-159** *2-bdrm apts, terrace*

Brickfield Hill B&B Inn [GS,WI,GO] 403 Riley Street (at Foveaux), Surry Hills **61-2/9211-4886** *in gay district, near beaches*

Chelsea Guest House [GS,NS,GO] 49 Womerah Ave (at Oswald Ln), Darlinghurst **61-2/9380-5994** *Victorian w/ courtyard*

Footprints Westend [GF,NS,WC] 412 Pitt St **61-2/9211-4588, 1800/013-186** *budget/ backpacker's accommodations*

Governors on Fitzroy B&B [M,GO] 64 Fitzroy St, Surry Hills **61-2/9331-4652** *Victorian B&B, 3 blocks from Oxford St, full brkfst, hot tub, shared baths, garden*

Hotel Stellar [MW,WI] 4 Wentworth Ave **61-2/9264-9754** *kitchenette in each room*

Kirketon Boutique Hotel [GF,WI] 229 Darlinghurst Rd **61-2/9332-2011, 800/332-920 (Australia only)** *also restaurant & bar*

Medusa [GF,WI] 267 Darlinghurst Rd, Darlinghurst **61-2/9331-1000** *modern boutique hotel*

Oasis on Flinders [MO,N,GO] 106 Flinders St, Darlinghurst **61-2/9331-8791** *gay naturist men B&B*

Park Lodge Hotel [MW,GO] 747 S Dowling St (near Cleveland St), Moore Park **61-2/9318-2393** *"Sydney's friendliest gay-owned & operated 3-star boutique hotel"*

Pensione Hotel [GF] 631-635 George St **61-2/9265-8888, 800/885-886** *also restaurant & bar*

Sydney Star Accommodation [GS] 273-275 Darlinghurst Rd (at Liverpool), Darlinghurst **61-2/9358-1445**

Victoria Court Hotel Sydney [GF] 122 Victoria St (at Orwell) **61-2/9357-3200, 1800/630-505 (in Australia)**

Bars

Bar Cleveland/ Hershey Bar [GS,F,A,YC] 443 Cleveland St (at Bourke), Surry Hills **61-2/9698-1908** *11am-4am, noon-midnight Sun, cocktail lounge, DJ*

The Beauchamp [★GS,NH,GO] 267 Oxford St, Darlinghurst **61-2/9331-2575** *noon-2am*

The Colombian [★MW,D] 117 Oxford St (at Crown St), Darlinghurst **61-2/9360-2151** *9am-6am*

Flinders [MW,D,F,S,YC] 63-65 Flinders St, Darlinghurst **61-2/9356-3622** *popular late*

Green Park Hotel [GS] 360 Victoria St (at Liverpool), Darlinghurst **61-2/9380-5311** *10am-2am, noon-midnight Sun, very gay Sun, stylish bar*

Manacle [M,B,L] 450 Parramatta Rd (at the Clarence Hotel), Petersham **61-2/9560-0400** *8pm-late, clsd Mon, big, cruisy butch bar, DJ*

Mars Lounge [GS,D,F] 16 Wentworth Ave **61-2/9267-6440** *5pm-midnight, till 3am Th-Fri, 7pm-3am Sat, 7pm-1am Sun, clsd Mon-Tue, more gay Sun for Flash*

Mr Mary's [MW,D] 106-110 George St (at Redfern St) **61-2/9690-0610**

The Oxford [★MW,B,L,TG,OC] 134 Oxford St (at Taylor Square), Darlinghurst **61-2/9331-3467** *24hrs, 3 bars*

The Palace Hotel [GS,D,YC] 122 Flinders St (at S Dowling St) **61-2/9361-3611** *4pm-1am*

The Palms On Oxford [DS,P] 124 Oxford St, Darlinghurst **61-2/9357-4166** *8pm-late, clsd Mon-Tue*

The Phoenix Bar at Exchange Hotel [MW,D,DS] 34 Oxford St, Darlinghurst **61-2/9331-2956** *10am-5am, till 7am Fri-Sun, clsd Mon-Tue, 3 bars*

The Stonewall [★M,D,K,DS,S] 175 Oxford St, Darlinghurst **61-2/9360-1963** *11am-6am, pub downstairs, cocktail lounge 2nd flr, dance club 3rd flr, karaoke Tue, male dancers, patio*

The Taxi Club [M,D,TG,F,K,DS,PC,$] 40-42 Flinders St (at Grosvenor Club), Darlinghurst **61-2/9331-4256** *24hrs, [K] Th, [DS] Sun*

Nightclubs

ARQ [★M,D,F,DS,$] 16 Flinders St (at Taylor Square), Darlinghurst **61-2/9380-8700** *9pm-late Th-Sun, clsd Mon-Wed, drag shows Th*

Diamonds & Pearls [MW,D,DS,$] Heathcote Rd (at Moorebank Sports Club), Hammondville **61-4/3323-2425 (cell), 61-2/9825-3300 (Moorebank Sports Club)** *8pm-2am, monthly dance party*

Golden Palace Hotel [GS,D,K,DS] 68 Dixon St, Haymarket **61-2/9281-0821** *24hrs, more gay Sun for Gaymarket*

Hellfire [GS,D,A,L,E,S,$] 16-18 Oxford Square (on corner of Riley, at Rogues), Darlinghurst **61-2/9380-9244** *9:30pm-late 3rd Fri, fetish party, live shows*

Home [★GF,D,$] Cockle Bay Wharf (Darling Harbour) **61-2/9266-0600** *open Fri-Sun, hosts Homesexual (www.homesexual.com.au)*

The Midnight Shift [★M,D,V] 85 Oxford St, Darlinghurst **61-2/9360-4319** *10pm-2am Fri-Sat*

Slide [MW,D,F,E,C] 41 Oxford St *6pm-3am, 5pm-4am Fri, 7pm-4am Sat-Sun, clsd Mon-Tue*

Cafes

Cafe Sopra [★] 7 Danks St **61-2/9699-3174** *10am-3pm, from 8am Sat, clsd Sun-Mon, Italian vegetarian*

Coffee, Tea or Me? 536 Crown St **61-2/9331-3452**

Numero Uno Coffee 63 Nickson St **61-2/8399-0111** *bean roaster*

Victoire 285 Darling St **61-2/9818-5529** *great bread*

Vinyl Lounge Cafe [MW,F] 17 Elizabeth Bay Rd, Elizabeth Bay **61-2/9326-9224** *7am-4pm, from 8am wknds, clsd Mon, light menu, plenty veggie, cash only*

Restaurants

Bentley Restaurant & Bar 320 Crown St **61-2/9332-2344** *noon-late, clsd Sun- Mon, tapas & small plates, excellent wine*

Bertoni Casalinga 281 Darling St **61-2/9818-5845** *6:30am-7:30pm, till 7pm Sat, 7:30am-6:30pm Sun, Italian*

Betty's Soup Kitchen [MW] 84 Oxford St, Darlinghurst **61-2/9360-9698** *noon-11pm, till midnight Fri-Sat, healthy homecooking, plenty veggie*

Bills Surry Hills 359 Crown St **61-2/9360-4762** *7am-10pm, great ricotta pancakes*

Billy Kwong [★R,WC] 3/355 Crown St **61-2/9332-3300** *Chinese*

Bird Cow Fish 500 Crown St **61-2/9380-4090** *8am-10pm, till 5pm Sun, bistro & espresso bar*

The Boathouse on Blackwattle Bay [R] End of Ferry Road (Glebe) **61-2/9518-9011** *lunch & dinner Tue-Sun, gourmet seafood, some veggie, great view*

Chu Bay 312a Bourke St, Darlinghurst **61-2/9331-3386** *5:30pm-11pm, Vietnamese, some veggie*

Danks Street Depot 2 Danks St **61-2/9698-2201** *great brkfst*

Fu Manchu [NS] 249 Victoria St, Darlinghurst **61-2/9360-9424** *lunch & dinner, chic noodle bar, cash only*

Iku Wholefood Kitchen [NS] 25a Glebe Point Rd, Glebe **61-2/9692-8720, 800/732-962** *lunch & dinner, creative vegan/ macrobiotic fare, outdoor seating*

Lo Studio 53-55 Brisbane St (upper ground flr) **61-2/9212-4118** *noon-3pm Mon-Fri & 6pm-11pm Mon-Sat, clsd Sun, Italian*

Pink Peppercorn [GO] 122 Oxford St (near Taylor Square, Darlinghurst) **61-2/9360-9922** *6pm-10:30pm, Laotian & Thai*

Sean's Panaroma 270 Campbell Parade, Bondi Beach **61-2/9365-4924** *lunch Sat-Sun, dinner Wed-Sat, clsd Mon-Tue*

Thai Kanteen [★GO] 541 Military Rd, Mosman **61-2/9960-3282** *lunch Th-Fri, dinner Tue-Sun, clsd Mon, modern Thai*

Thai Pothong 294 King St (Newtown) **61-2/9550-6277** *lunch Tue-Sun, dinner nightly*

Entertainment & Recreation

Sydney by Diva departs from Oxford Hotel (in Taylor Square, Darlinghurst) **61-2/8004-0789** *5pm-8pm Sun, tour Sydney w/ drag queen host*

Sydney Gay/ Lesbian Mardi Gras 297-299 Trafalgar St, Petersham 2049 **61-2/9568-8600** *the wildest party under the rainbow on this planet (see www.mardigras.org.au)*

Bookstores

The Bookshop Darlinghurst 207 Oxford St (near Darlinghurst Rd), Darlinghurst **61-2/9331-1103** *10am-10pm, Australia's oldest LGBT bookstore, staff happy to help w/ tourist info*

Gertrude & Alice 46 Hall St (Bondi Beach) **61-2/9130-5155** *second-hand books, also coffee shop*

Publications

DNA 61-2/9764-0200, 888/263-2624 (US #) *monthly gay men's magazine*

SX Weekly 61-2/9360-8934 *free gay/ lesbian weekly*

Sydney Star Observer 61-2/8263-0500 *weekly newspaper w/ club & event listings*

Gyms & Health Clubs

City Gym 107-113 Crown St **61-2/9360-6247** *day passes available*

Gold's Gym Sydney 58 Kippax St (level 1), Surry Hills **61-2/9211-2799** *5:30am-9pm , 8am-8pm Sat, till 6pm Sun*

Men's Clubs

Bodyline Spa & Sauna [★V] 10 Taylor St (off Flinders), Darlinghurst **61-2/9360-1006** *24hrs wknds*

Headquarters [V] 273 Crown St (near Oxford), Darlinghurst **61-2/9331-6217** *24hrs, theme rooms, theme nights*

Ken's at Kensington [SW,18+] 83 Anzac Parade, Kensington **61-2/9662-1359** *24hrs wknds*

Kingsteam 38-42 Oxford St (next to Exchange Hotel), Darlinghurst **61-2/9360-3431, 61-2/8250-1818 (info line)** *24hrs*

Signal [V] at Riley & Arnold Sts (upstairs), Darlinghurst **61-2/9331-8830**

Sydney City Steam [WI] 357 Sussex (Darling Harbour) **61-2/9267-6766** *24hrs wknds*

Sex Clubs

Aarows [MW,TG,18+] 17 Bridge St, Rydalmere **61-2/9638-0553, 61-2//1300-062-541** *24hrs*

Erotica

Pleasure Chest 161 Oxford St, Darlinghurst **61-2/9356-3640** *24hrs; also 56 Darlinghurst Rd, Kings Cross*

The Probe [S] 159 Oxford St, upstairs, Darlinghurst **61-2/9361-5924** *24hrs*

Sax Fetish [GO] 110a Oxford St (Taylor Square) **61-2/9331-6105**

Toolshed 81 Oxford St, Darlinghurst **61-2/9332-2792** *191 Oxford St, Taylor Sq*

Cruisy Areas

Beare Park [AYOR] Ithaca Rd

Bondi Beach Pavilion [AYOR] Bondi Beach

Gunnamatta Park [AYOR] Cronulla

Lady Bay Beach [AYOR] at N tip of South Head, Cronulla

Loftus Oval [AYOR] Princes Hwy (Loftus), Cronulla *park*

Marks Park [AYOR] S end of Bondi Beach, Cronulla *head toward the cliffs, evenings*

Rushcutters Bay Park [AYOR] New Beach Rd

Sydney Park [AYOR] King St & Mitchell Rd, Newtown *behind Old Brick Works*

2010 Tours & Tour Operators

2010 Calendar

CRUISES

Mostly Men

All-Gay Windjammer Barefoot Cruises 407 Lincoln Rd #6B, Miami Beach, FL 33139 ☎ **305/672-9779, 800/768-7238** www.SourceEvents.com • one gay cruise per year, call for exact dates

Atlantis Events 9200 Sunset Blvd, Ste 500, West Hollywood, CA 90069 ☎ **310/859-8800, 800/628-5268** www.atlantisevents.com • largest LGBT tour operator in the world • all-gay cruise, resort & tour vacations

Pied Piper Tours 330 W 42nd St, Ste 1804, New York, NY 10036 ☎ **212/239-2412, 800/874-7312** www.gaygroupcruises.com • gay group cruises

Gay/Lesbian

Aquafest 4801 Woodway #400-W, Houston, TX 77056 ☎ **800/592-9058** www.aquafestcruises.com • LGBT groups mingle w/ mixed clientele on major cruise lines

Gayribbean Cruises Dallas, TX ☎ **214/311-2264, 877/560-8318** www.gayribbean-cruises.com • gay & lesbian group cruise organizer • fabulous destinations • annual Halloween cruise from Galveston, TX

Ocean Voyager 4098 Judith Ave, Merritt Island, FL 32953 ☎ **321/454-2083, 800/321-8264** www.oceanvoyager.com • hosted gay groups on mainstream upscale cruise ships

Port Yacht Charters 9 Belleview Ave, Port Washington, NY 11050 ☎ **516/883-0998, 877/DO-A-BOAT** www.portyachtcharters.com • custom charters worldwide, specializing in the Caribbean • commitment ceremonies • gourmet cuisine

R Family 5 Washington Ave, Nyack, NY 10960 ☎ **866/732-6822** www.rfamilyvacations.com • family-friendly vacations designed especially for the LGBT community

Rainbow Charters 939 Kawaiki Pl, Honolulu, HI 96825 ☎ **808/347-0235** www.RainbowChartersHawaii.com • gay & lesbian weddings • custom sailing cruises • whale-watching • snorkeling • sunset cruises

RSVP Vacations ☎ **800/328-7787** www.rsvpvacations.com • gay & lesbian cruise vacations

Sailing Affairs 58 E 1st St #6-B, New York City, NY 10003 ☎ **917/453-6425** www.sailingaffairs.com • gay sailboat charters, day trips, sunset sails & sailing vacations on 47-foot Beneteau • East Coast, Caribbean, Europe & Mediterranean

Travelpride Gay Vacations 710 NE 26th St, Wilton Manors, FL 33305 ☎ **954/689-2558, 877/774-3342** www.travelpride.com • all-gay cruise charters on smaller luxury ships free of crowds

LUXURY TOURS

Men Only

Hanns Ebensten Travel, Inc 923 White St, Key West, FL 33040 ☎ **305/294-8174, 866/294-8174** www.hetravel.com • worldwide adventures for the uncommon traveler • Peru, India, Morocco, Southeast Asia, Greece, Italy, Egypt & more

Mostly Men

EuroPanache 410 Park Ave, 15th flr, New York City, NY 10022 ☎ **888/600-6777** www.europanache.com • unique, elite vacation experiences w/ an appealing mix of themes • offices in New York, Paris & Sydney

Gay/Lesbian

DavidTravel 310 Dahlia Pl, Ste A, Corona del Mar, CA 92625-2821 ☎ **949/723-0699** www.DavidTravel.com • full service travel agency & tour operator • small luxury group departures & customized travel for individuals & groups

Out Traveller 45 Amarja, Johannesburg, Gauteng 2188, South Africa ☎ **27-074/171-8924** www.out-traveller.com • guided safaris to South Africa & East Africa • also Thailand, Bali & New Zealand • destination weddings • lesbian-owned

Steele Luxury Travel New York City, NY 10011 ☎ **646/688-2274** www.steeletravel.com • unique travel experiences to exotic destinations worldwide

GREAT OUTDOORS ADVENTURES

Men Only

Adventure Bound Expeditions 711 Walnut St, Boulder, CO 80302 ☎ **303/449-0990, 877/440-0990** www.adventureboundmen.com • outdoor adventure worldwide • hiking, kayaking, safaris, wildlife viewing

Mostly Men

Scuba Scotty 1731 California St, Berkeley, CA 94703 ☎ **831/233-2880** www.scubascotty.com • scuba instruction • local & exotic destinations • gay-owned

Touring Cairns Kewarra Beach, Cairns, QLD, Australia ☎ **61-7/4055 6462** www.touringcairns.com.au • rain forest tours in the Cairns hinterland

Mostly Women

Rainbow Rafting 1602 W Hays St #306, Boise, ID 83702 ☎ **208/331-2358** www.rainbowrafting.com • luxury multi-day rafting adventures in Idaho

Gay/Lesbian

• **Alyson Adventures, Inc** 923 White St, Key West, FL 33040 ☎ **305/296-9935, 800/825-9766** www.AlysonAdventures.com • award-winning adventure travel & active vacations • hiking, biking & multi-sport activities

OutWest Global Adventures PO Box 2050, Red Lodge, MT 59068 ☎ **406/446-1533, 800/743-0458** www.outwestadventures.com • specializing in gay/ lesbian active & adventure travel • worldwide

Undersea Expeditions PO Box 9455, Pacific Beach, CA 92169 ☎ **858/270-2900, 800/669-0310** www.UnderseaX.com • gay & lesbian scuba adventures worldwide

Gay/Straight

Come 2 Africa 75 Impala St, Hazyview 1242, South Africa ☎ **27 13/737-7482, 27 72/394-7625** www.come2africa.com • custom tours, including Kruger Nat'l Park

GoNorth Alaska Adventure Travel Center 3500 Davis Rd, Fairbanks, AK 99709 ☎ **907/479-7272, 866/236-7272** www.gonorthalaska.com • guided tours throughout Alaska & the Arctic • air taxis & transportation • camper, canoe & bike rentals • hostel accommodations • RV & SUV rental

Himalayan High Treks 241 Dolores St, San Francisco, CA 94103 ☎ **415/551-1005, 800/455-8735** www.hightreks.com • experience indigenous Buddhist & Hindu cultures

Natural Habitat Adventures PO Box 3065, Boulder, CO 80307 ☎ **303/449-3711, 800/543-8917** www.nathab.com • up-close encounters w/ the world's most amazing wildlife in its natural habitat

Open Eye Tours PO Box 324, Makawao, HI 96768 ☎ **808/572-3483, 808/280-5299 (cell)** www.openeyetours.com • customized private land tours of Maui & other islands • visit popular spots or places seldom seen, walking or not • sharing Maui's best-kept secrets since 1983

Paddling South & Saddling South PO Box 827, Calistoga, CA 94515 ☎ **707/942-4550, 800/398-6200** www.tourbaja.com • horseback, mountain-biking & sea-kayak trips in Baja • call for complete calendar

Puffin Fishing Charters PO Box 606, Seward, AK 99664 ☎ **907/224-4653, 800/978-3346** www.puffincharters.com • guided charter fishing • almost 30 years of experience • halibut, salmon & rockfish on vessels custom-built for Alaskan waters

Voyageur North Outfitters 1829 E Sheridan, Ely, MN 55731 ☎ **218/365-3251, 800/848-5530** www.vnorth.com • canoe outfitting & trips

SPIRITUAL/HEALTH VACATIONS

Gay/Lesbian

Spirit Journeys 134 River Rd, New Milford, NJ 97646 ☎ **201/483-3111, 800/754-1875** www.spiritjouneys.com • spiritual retreats, workshops & adventure trips throughout the US & abroad

Thematic Tours

Men Only

Absolute Sultans Istiklal Caddesi Hidivyal Palas # 465 Kat 4, 34420 Beyoglu, Istanbul, Turkey ☎ **90-532/243-5296** www.absolutesultans.com • discover Turkey w/ luxury & style

Pete's Tours PO Box 14373, San Francisco, CA 94114 ☎ **415/621-2915** home.pacbell.net/psgreene/ • specializing in big fun adventures • family vacations • Windstar, Windjammer, gay & straight cruises

Toto Tours 1326 W Albion Ave #3W, Chicago, IL 60626 ☎ **773/274-8686, 800/565-1241** www.tototours.com • unique worldwide adventures for gay men

Travel Keys Tours PO Box 162266, Sacramento, CA 95816-2266 ☎ **916/452-5200** • tours of dungeons & castles in Europe • also antique tours (gay/straight)

Mostly Men

Coda International Tours, Inc 12794 Forest Hill Blvd #1A, West Palm Beach, FL 33414 ☎ **561/791-9890, 888/677-2632** www.coda-tours.com • culturally focused travel programs

Connections Tours & Hotels 14362 SW 96 Terrace #1, Miami, FL 33186 ☎ **305/385-384** www.connectionstours.com • wholesale bookings worldwide • best rates under the sun

Gay/Lesbian

Africa Outing 3 Alcyone Rd, Claremont, Capetown 7708, South Africa ☎ **27-21/671-4028** www.afouting.com • gay/lesbian safaris & more • tours customized to your needs

Brazil Fiesta Tours & Visa Service 268 Bush St #3531, San Francisco, CA 94104 ☎ **415/986-1134, 800/200-0582** www.brazilianvisas.com • tours to Brazil • Brazilian visa service

Carlos Melia New York City www.carlosmelia.com • gay travel agency for South America

Ecuador InSitu Roca E4-115 & amazonas Av, Quito, Pichincha, Ecuador ☎ **593-2/256-4703** www.ecuadorinsitu.com • exclusive LGBT tour operator in Ecuador & Galapagos Islands

Gay Bali Tours Griya Anyar 76A, Br. Kajeng-Suwung, 80361 Bali, Indonesia ☎ **62-361/722 483** www.bali-rainbows.com • professional tour operator for GLBT & their friends • travel to Bali & beyond

Go Pink China Beijing, China ☎ **86/1366-124-6689** www.gopinkchina.com • adding queer elements to city tours & national trips in China

Going Your Way Tours 123 Ledgewood Rd #509, Groton, CT 06340 ☎ **860/447-9180** www.goingyourwaytours.com • upscale customized group & individual itineraries worldwide

Kuyay Travel Puerto Rosales 46, 5550000 Puerto Varas, Los Lagos, Chile ☎ **56-65/438-990** www.gaypatagonia.com • gay-owned/run travel planner & tour host in Patagonia

Mantrav International 130 W 42nd St #401, New York City, NY 10036 ☎ **212/398-0999, 407/816-7084** www.mantrav.com • international tour operator • European White Parties

MexGay Vacations 333 S Grand Ave, Floor 25, Los Angeles, CA 90071 ☎ **213/383-9491, 866/639-4299** www.mexgay.com • specializing in gay travel to Mexico

National Gay Pilots Association PO Box 7271, Dallas, TX 75209 ☎ **214/336-0873** www.ngpa.org • several annual gatherings • call for more info

Pacific Ocean Holidays Honolulu, HI ☎ **808/545-5252, 800/735-6600** www.gayhawaiivacations.com • Hawaii vacation packages

Planetdwellers 1/33A Davies St, Surry Hills, NSW 2010, Australia ☎ **614-1/923-0670** www.planetdwellers.com.au • LGBT tours of Australia • come to OZ!

Venture Out 575 Pierce St #604, San Francisco, CA 94117 ☎ **415/626-5678, 888/431-6789** www.venture-out.com • high-end escorted tours to a variety of countries around the world

Winelovertours.com 123 Ledgewood Rd #509, Groton, CT 06340 ☎ **860/861-2301** www.winelovertours.com • upscale group tours & individual itineraries for foodies & winelovers

Gay/Straight

Alaska Railroad Anchorage, AK 99510-7500 ☎ **907/265-2494, 800/544-0552 (reservations)** www.alaskarailroad.com • rail & tour packages

Brazil Ecojourneys Estrada Rozalia Paulina Ferreira 1132, 88063-555 Armação, Florianopolis, SC, Brazil ☎ **55-48/3389-5619** www.brazilecojourneys.com • incoming tour operator • South Brazil specialists

Earth Walks PO Box 8534, Santa Fe, NM 87504 ☎ **505/988-4157** www.earthwalks.org • custom, guided journeys of American Southwest & Mexico • experience traditional, nature-based healing practices of indigenous cultures

Ecotour Expeditions, Inc PO Box 128, Jamestown, RI 02835 ☎ **401/423-3377, 800/688-1822** www.naturetours.com • small group boat tours of the Amazon & more • call for color catalog

Heritage Tours Private Travel 121 W 27th St #1201, New York, NY 10001 ☎ **212/206-8400, 800/378-4555** www.htprivatetravel.com • custom trips to Portugal, Turkey, Spain, Morocco & all of Southern Africa

Holbrook Travel 3540 NW 13th St, Gainesville, FL 32609 ☎ **352/377-7111, 800/451-7111** www.holbrooktravel.com • natural history tours in Central America, South America & Africa • small groups

Lebtour.com 00961 Beirut, Lebanon ☎ **961-3/004-572** www.lebtour.com • professional travel in Lebanon, Syria & Jordan • gay packages available

Lima Tours Belen 1040, Lima, Peru ☎ **51-1/619-6900** www.limatours.com.pe • customized, gay-friendly tours to Peru

New England Vacation Tours PO Box 560, West Dover, VT 05356 ☎ **802/464-2076, 800/742-7669** www.newenglandvacationtours.com • gay/ lesbian tours (including fall foliage) conducted by a mainstream tour operator

Pacha Tours 37 E 28th St #708, New York City, NY 10016 ☎ **800/722-4288** www.pachatours.com • trips to Turkey & Greece

VIP Tours of New York 205 W 57th St, New York, NY 10019 ☎ **212/247-0366, 800/300-6203** www.viptoursny.com • private, custom-designed tours of New York • specializing in theater, architecture, gay life & more • groups from one to 100+

Welcome Rajasthan Umaid Bhawan Bani Park, Jaipur, Rajasthan 30216, India ☎ **91-931/450-3423** www.welcomerajasthan.com • tours & car rentals for Rajasthan, India

Wild Rainbow African Safaris 308 Jones St, Ukiah, CA 95482 ☎ **707/467-9676** www.wildrainbowsafaris.com • unique excursions to Tanzania, South Africa, Zambia, Botswana & more

Custom Tours

Costa Rica Experts 3166 N Lincoln Ave #424, Chicago, IL 60657 ☎ **773/935-1009, 800/827-9046** www.costaricaexperts.com

Embassy Travel 927 N Kings Rd #310, West Hollywood, CA 90069 ☎ **323/656-0743** • personalized tours to southern Africa & other worldwide destinations

Travel & Culture 702 Panorama Center Office Plaza, 75530 Karachi, Pakistan ☎ **92-321/242-4778** www.travel-culture.com • tours, safaris & hotel reservations in Pakistan

Various Tours

Mostly Men

Source Events 700 NE 90th St #E, Miami, FL 33138 ☎ **305/672-9779, 888/768-7238** www.sourceevents.com • we create inspiring travel experiences & adventures around the globe for our gay community

Gay/Lesbian

Above & Beyond Tours 230 N Via Las Palmas, Palm Springs, CA 92262 ☎ **760/325-0702, 800/397-2681** www.abovebeyondtours.com • several annual departures to South Pacific, Latin America, South Africa & Europe • cruises • also independent vacations year-round

Distinctive Travel 6515 N 7th St, 85014 Phoenix ☎ **602/604-1995, 800/249-4932** www.azdistinctivetravel.com • full-service travel agency • airline tickets • cruises • pride events • union ceremonies

Footprints 19 Madison Ave #300, Toronto, ON M5R 2S2, Canada ☎ **416/962-8111, 888/962-6211** www.footprintstravel.com • custom-designed, private tours arranged to worldwide destinations

Friends of Dorothy Travel® 1177 California St #B, San Francisco, CA 94108 ☎ **415/864-1600, 800/640-4918** www.fodtravel.com • unique gay & lesbian adventures • individual & group arrangements

Out & About Travel 161 Federal St, Providence, RI 02903 ☎ **800/842-4753** www.gaytravelpros.com • full-service travel agency specializing in gay & lesbian tours, cruises, adventure travel, ski trips, honeymoons, customized packages & more • serving the GLBT community since 1999!

Postcard Destinations 188 Crystal St, Johnstown, PA 15906 ☎ **814/539-4999, 800/484-3250 x2621** www.postcarddestinations.com • purveyors of gay travel worldwide since 1985 • tours, cruises, groups, customized trips, air, hotel • Europe/ Croatia specialists • gay-owned

Zoom Vacations 2338 N Monticello Ave, Chicago, IL 60647 ☎ **773/772-9666, 866/966-6822** www.zoomvacations.com • takes gay group travel to the next level • experience the best of a destination w/ surprises, insider events & a sense of magic

EVENTS

January

ongoing throughout the year: Tranny Roadshow *TBA, USA*
on-going, touring, performance art extravaganza • check website for shows near you ☎ 207/**778-6274** ✉ 118 Sandy River Terr, Farmington, ME 04938
Email: trannyroadshow@yahoo.com **Web:** www.trannyroadshow.com

6-10: Utah Gay & Lesbian Ski Week *Park City, UT*
☎ 877/**429-6368**
Email: wehojohn@aol.com **Web:** www.gayskiing.org

9-16: Arosa Gay Ski Week *Arosa, Switzerland*
mostly men • 500 attendees ☎ 41-81/**378-7100** ✉ Hotel Eden, CH-7050 Arosa, Switzerland
Email: info@arosa-gayskiweek.com **Web:** www.arosa-gayskiweek.com

17-24: Aspen Gay Ski Week *Aspen, CO*
LGBT • 3000+ attendees ☎ 970/**948-7743** ✉ c/o *Roaring Fork Gay & Lesbian Community Fund*, PO Box 3143, Aspen, CO 81612
Email: info@gayskiweek.com **Web:** www.gayskiweek.com

17-Feb 7: Midsumma Festival *Melbourne, Australia*
arts, culture & community • LGBT ☎ 61-3/**9415-9819** ✉ Room C1.17 The Convent
1 St Heliers St, Abbotsford, VIC, Australia 3067
Email: admin@midsumma.org.au **Web:** www.midsumma.org.au

20-24: Winter Rendezvous *Stowe, VT*
annual week of gay skiing & winter sports ☎ 587/**445-7198** ✉ c/o *www.MJWAdventures.com*, 50 Victory Rd, Boston, MA 02122
Email: info@winterrendezvous.com **Web:** www.winterrendezvous.com

February

12-15: Winter Explosion *Hudson Valley, NY*
popular LGBT African-American winter event w/ skiing & lots of entertainment • LGBT ☎ 202/**489-1032**
Email: info@winterexplosion.com **Web:** www.winterexplosion.com

16: Mardi Gras *New Orleans, LA*
mixed gay/ straight ☎ 800/**672-6124** ✉ c/o *New Orleans Convention & Visitors Bureau*, 2020 St Charles, New Orleans, LA 70130 **Web:** www.neworleanscvb.com

20-27: Telluride Gay Ski Week *Telluride, CO*
Email: info@telluridegayskiweek.com **Web:** www.telluridegayskiweek.com

21-March 6: Sydney Gay Mardi Gras *Sydney, Australia*
extravagant season of festivities, arts & culture, culminating in the parade & world-famous Mardi Gras party ☎ 011-61-2/**9568-8600** ✉ 297-299 Trafalgar St, Petersham, NSW, Australia 2049 **Web:** www.mardigras.org.au

March

1-8: WinterPRIDE: Whistler Gay Ski Week *Whistler, BC, Canada*
annual gay/ lesbian ski week • parties for boys & girls! • top-notch DJs & venues • popular destination 75 miles N of Vancouver • LGBT • 3000+ attendees
☎ 604/**288-7218** ✉ c/o *GayWhistler*, 102-4369 Main St, Whistler, BC, Canada V0N 1B4
Email: dean@gaywhistler.com **Web:** www.gaywhistler.com

6: Chicago Takes Off *Chicago, IL*
burlesque show to fight HIV/AIDS in the Chicagoland area • LGBT • 1400 attendees
☎ 773/**989-9400** ✉ c/o *TPAN*, 5537 N Broadway, Chicago, IL 60640
Email: r.lindsay@tpan.com **Web:** www.chicagotakesoff.org

20-27: European Gay Ski Week *Tignes, France*
hit the slopes for Gay Ski Week • mostly men ☎ 44-020/**7183 0823**
Email: jonathon@europeangayskiweek.com **Web:** www.europeangayskiweek.com

TBA: OutBoard *Breckenridge, CO*
annual lesbian/ gay snowboarding festival • 300+ attendees ☎ 303/**885-9655** ✉ 3724 Walnut St, Denver, CO 80205
Email: ryan@outboard.org **Web:** www.outboard.org

April

17: Boybutante Ball *Athens, GA*
LGBT • 1000+ attendees ☎ 706/**227-3530** ✉ c/o *Boybutante AIDS Foundation, Inc*, PO Box 6013, Athens, GA 30604-6013
Email: missthing@boybutante.org **Web:** www.boybutante.org

26-May 2: Equality Forum *Philadelphia, PA*
largest nat'l & int'l LGBT civil rights forum w/ 60+ programs, parties & special events
☎ 215/**732-3378 x116** ✉ 1420 Locust St #300, Philadelphia, PA 19102
Email: info@equalityforum.com **Web:** www.equalityforum.com

30: Queensday *Amsterdam, Netherlands*
huge street festival to celebrate what was originally the birthday of the Queen Mother • LGBT **Web:** www.queensdayamsterdam.eu

TBA: Philadelphia Black Gay Pride *Philadelphia, PA*
a weekend of social & cultural activities • films, BBQ, spoken word, parties & more • LGBT ☎ 877/**497-7247** ✉ c/o *Philadelphia Black Pride, Inc*, PO Box 40926, Philadelphia, PA 19107
Email: phillyblackpride@gmail.com **Web:** www.phillyblackpride.org

May

3-16: Int'l Dublin Gay Theatre Festival *Dublin, Ireland*
☎ 353-87/**657-3732** ✉ 179 S Circular Rd, Dublin, Ireland 8
Email: info@gaytheatre.ie **Web:** www.gaytheatre.ie

7-10: Blatino Oasis *Palm Springs, CA*
pool parties, DJs & hot porn stars draw hot black & Latino men from across the country • men only ☎ 213/**785-7336**
Email: rimshot4you@yahoo.com **Web:** www.clubrimshot.com/Blatino_Oasis.html

16: **AIDS Walk New York** *New York City, NY*
AIDS benefit • mixed gay/ straight ☎ 212/**807-9255** ✉ c/o *Gay Men's Health Crisis*, PO Box 10, Old Chelsea Stn, New York, NY 10113-0010
Email: awnyinfo@aidswalk.net **Web:** www.aidswalk.net

16: **Minnesota AIDS Walk** *Minneapolis, MN*
enjoy a 10K walk from Minnehaha Park & raise money for MN AIDS Project • mixed gay/ straight • 10,000 attendees ☎ 612/**341-2060** ✉ c/o *Minnesota AIDS Project*, 1400 Park Ave S, Minneapolis, MN 55404
Email: info@mnaidsproject.org **Web:** www.mnaidsproject.org

26-31: **Annual Gay Bowling Tournament** *Columbus, OH*
check site for local tournaments throughout the year ☎ 302/**202-5146** ✉ c/o *IGBO*, 6490 W 5th Ave, Lakewood, CO 80226
Email: president@igbo.org **Web:** www.igbo.org

27-30: **Int'l Association of Country Western Dance Clubs Annual Convention** *Austin, TX*
also semi-annual conventions in March (Fort Lauderdale, FL) & October (San Francisco, CA) • LGBT • 400-600 attendees ☎ 757/**456-5615**, 416/**923-8247 (in Canada)** ✉ c/o *IAGLCWDC*, 5534 Edmondson Pike, PMB 107, Nashville, TN 37211
Email: information@iaglcwdc.org **Web:** www.outcountrydance.com

27-31: **Pensacola Memorial Day Weekend** *Pensacola, FL*
many parties on beaches & in bars • LGBT • 35,000+ attendees ☎ 850/**438-0333**

28: **Gay Day at Great America** *Santa Clara, CA*
join 10,000 men & women for an exclusive LGBT night at Great America • rides • live performances • dancing till 2am
Email: rsvp@freshsf.com **Web:** www.gaydaycga.com

28-31: **Mondo Homo Dirty South** *Atlanta, GA*
queer-centric festival featuring music, dance, crafts, performance & more ☎ 404/**243-3476** ✉ 251 Tye St SE, Atlanta, GA 30316
Email: homosouth@yahoo.com **Web:** www.mondohomo.com

28-31: **San Juan Brothas** *San Juan, PR*
festival for African American & Latino gay men & their friends • men only ☎ 404/**474-3841**
Email: info@sanjuanbrothas.com **Web:** www.sanjuanbrothas.com

28-June 13: **Spoleto Festival USA** *Charleston, SC*
one of the continent's premier avant-garde cultural arts festivals • 140+ performances of dance, theater & music from around the world • mixed gay/ straight ☎ 843/**579-3100** ✉ c/o *Spoleto Festival USA*, PO Box 157, Charleston, SC 29402-0157
Email: info@spoletousa.org **Web:** www.spoletousa.org

TBA: **Gay Night at Knott's Berry Farm** *Orange County, CA*
amusement park rides, dancing & gay comedy ☎ 661/**250-1827** ✉ c/o *Odyssey Adventures*, PO Box 2566, Santa Clarita, CA 91386
Email: odsyadv@pacbell.net **Web:** www.odysseyadventures.com

TBA: **Queer Up North** *Manchester, England*
queer culture & arts festival in Manchester, England ☎ 161/**234-2942** ✉ Greenfish Resource Centre
46-50 Oldham St, Manchester, England M4 1LE
Email: contact@queerupnorth.com **Web:** www.queerupnorth.com

TBA: Splash: Houston Black Gay Pride *Houston, TX*
LGBT ☎ 832/**443-1016** ✉ c/o *Houston Splash*, PO Box 667248, Houston, TX 77266 **Web:** www.houstonsplash.com

TBA: We're Funny That Way *Toronto, ON, Canada*
comedians from around the world perform at Canada's International Gay/Lesbian Comedy Festival • LGBT ☎ 416/**975-8555** ✉ c/o *WFTW Productions*, 2060 Queen St E #45, Toronto, ON, Canada M4E 1C9 **Web:** www.werefunnythatway.com

June

ongoing: LGBT Pride *Cross-country, USA*
celebrate yourself & attend one - or many - of the hundreds of Gay Pride parades & festivities happening in cities around the world
Email: info@interpride.org **Web:** www.interpride.org

ongoing: Music in the Mountains *Nevada City, CA*
summer music festival • mixed gay/ straight ☎ 530/**265-6173** ✉ c/o *Music in the Mountains*, 530 Searls Ave #B, Nevada City, CA 95959
Email: mim@musicinthemountains.org **Web:** www.musicinthemountains.org

ongoing: National Queer Arts Festival *San Francisco, CA*
performances & exhibitions in the San Francisco Bay Area highlighting artists from around the country • LGBT ☎ 415/**864-4124** ✉ c/o *Queer Cultural Center*, 934 Brannan St, San Francisco, CA 94103
Email: director@QueerCulturalCenter.org **Web:** www.QueerCulturalCenter.org

1-7: Gay Days Orlando *Orlando, FL*
including Gay Day at Disney • 7 days of parties & fun for boys & girls alike! • LGBT ☎ 407/**896-8431** ✉ c/o *GayDays, Inc*, 775 S Kirkman Rd #111, Orlando, FL 32811
Email: chris@gaydays.com **Web:** www.gaydays.com

6: AIDS Walk & 5K Run Boston *Boston, MA*
mixed gay/ straight • 12,000 attendees ☎ 617/**437-6200** ✉ c/o *AIDS Action Committee*, 294 Washington Street, 5th floor, Boston, MA 02108
Email: info@aac.org **Web:** www.aac.org

6-12: AIDS LifeCycle *San Francisco to Los Angeles, CA*
bike from San Francisco to Los Angeles to raise money for HIV/AIDS services ☎ 415/**581-7077** ✉ c/o *LA Gay/Lesbian Center & SF AIDS Foundation*, 995 Market St #200, San Francisco, CA 94103
Email: info@aidslifecycle.org **Web:** www.aidslifecycle.org

11-13: PrideFest *Milwaukee, WI*
celebrate LGBT pride at Henry W Maier Festival Park ☎ 414/**272-3378** ✉ c/o *PrideFest*, PO Box 511763, Milwaukee, WI 53203-0301
Email: info@pridefest.com **Web:** www.pridefest.com

20: Unofficial Gay Day at Cedar Point *Sandusky, OH*
wear red to show your support on the unofficial Gay Day at this popular amusement park • mixed gay/ straight

24-27: Black Pride *Columbia, SC*
☎ 803/**799-9190** ✉ c/o *Carolinas Black Pride Movement*, PO Box 8191, Columbia, NC 29202
Email: info@southcarolinablackpride.com **Web:** www.southcarolinablackpride.com

26-27: San Francisco LGBT Pride Parade/ Celebration *San Francisco, CA*
LGBT ☎ 415/**864-3733** ✉ c/o *SFLGBTPCC*, 1800 Market St PMB 5, San Francisco, CA 94102
Email: info@sfpride.org **Web:** www.sfpride.org

TBA: Black Gay Pride *Memphis, TN*
LGBT ☎ 901/**522-8459** **Web:** www.brothersunited.com

TBA: Black Gay Pride Boston *Boston, MA*
celebrate Black pride in Boston ☎ 508/**245-9700** **Web:** www.mac-boston.org

TBA: Idapalooza Fruit Jam *Dowelltown, TN*
queer music festival in backwoods TN • camping • vegetarian feasts
☎ 615/**597-4409** ✉ 904 Vickers Hollow Rd, Dowelltown, TN 37059
Email: idapalooza@gmail.com **Web:** www.planetida.com

TBA: In The Life: Portland Black Pride *Portland, OR*
films, workshops, parties & more • LGBT ☎ 503/**847-3039** ✉ c/o *Unity Project of Oregon*, PO Box 3182, Portland 97209
Email: info@unityprojectoregon.org **Web:** www.unityprojectoregon.org

TBA: Juneteenth Jamboree of New Plays *Louisville, KY*
annual theater festival • new works about the African American experience • many w/ gay themes • mixed gay/ straight ☎ 502/**636-4200** ✉ c/o *Juneteenth Legacy Theatre*, PO Box 3463, Louisville, KY 40201
Email: juneteenthlegacy@aol.com **Web:** www.juneteenthlegacytheatre.com

July

1-4: Int'l Gay Square Dance Clubs Convention *Chicago, IL*
☎ 303/**722-5276** ✉ c/o *IAGSDC*, PO BOX 9176, Denver, CO 80209
Email: information@iagsdc.org **Web:** www.iagsdc.org

2-5: At the Beach Weekend *Los Angeles, CA*
celebrate a weekend of Black gay pride in Malibu • LGBT ☎ 323/**571-1724** ✉ c/o *At The Beach Shorey, Inc*, 6005 Ladera Ave, Los Angeles, CA 90056
Email: atbla@aol.com **Web:** www.atbla.com

10-11: Ride for AIDS Chicago *Chicago, IL*
2-day bike ride to fight HIV/ AIDS in the Chicagoland area • LGBT • 200 attendees
☎ 773/**989-9400** ✉ c/o *TPAN*, 5537 N Broadway, Chicago, IL 60640
Email: r.lindsay@tpan.com **Web:** www.rideforaids.org

11-18: IMEN Gathering *near Baltimore, MD*
all-inclusive summer camp for gay men • party naked w/ 300 guys for an entire week • theme parties, pool parties & great food • airport transportation to/from BWI ☎ 603/**841-5636** ✉ PO Box 578, Rising Sun, MD 21911
Email: info@imeninc.org **Web:** www.imengonude.org

17: EuroPride 2010 *Warsaw, Poland*
parties, politics, performance & more • there is something for everyone at this massive celebration of gay pride ✉ c/o *European Pride Organisers Assoc*, Buelowstrasse 106, Berlin, Germany D-10783 **Web:** www.europride.info

17-25: Hotter Than July Weekend *Detroit, MI*
the Midwest's oldest black same-gender-loving pride celebration • LGBT
☎ 888/**755-9165** ✉ c/o *Black Pride Society*, PO Box 7378, Detroit, MI 48207
Email: info@hotterthanjuly.com **Web:** www.hotterthanjuly.com

18: AIDS Walk San Francisco *San Francisco, CA*
mixed gay/ straight • 27,000+ attendees ☎ 415/**392-9255** ✉ c/o *Miller Zeichik & Assoc*, PO Box 193920, San Francisco, CA 94119-3920
Email: sfinfo@aidswalk.net **Web:** www.aidswalk.net

26-31: Black & White Men Together Convention *Fort Lauderdale, FL*
mostly men • 100+ attendees ☎ 412/**421-1000** ✉ c/o *National Association of Black & White Men Together*, PO Box 81236, Pittsburgh, PA 15217
Email: nabwmt@nabwmt.org **Web:** www.nabwmt.org

31: Crape Myrtle Festival *Raleigh-Durham, Chapel Hill, NC*
weeklong festival to raise money for AIDS & LGBT concerns • gala Saturday • also supporting events throughout the year • mixed gay/ straight • 500+ attendees ☎ 919/**616-0615** ✉ c/o *Crape Myrtle Festival, Inc*, PO Box 12201, Raleigh, NC 27605
Email: info@crapemyrtlefest.org **Web:** www.crapemyrtlefest.org

31-Aug 7: IGLFA World Championship *Cologne, Germany*
Int'l Gay & Lesbian Football Association's annual soccer tournament
Email: info@iglfa.org **Web:** www.iglfa.org

TBA: Gay Games 2010 *Cologne, Germany*
8 days of sports, cultural events, arts & ceremonies • LGBT ☎ 773/**907-2006**
Email: info@gaygameschicago.org **Web:** www.gaygameschicago.org

TBA: Outburst UK Black Pride Festival *London, England*
☎ 0844/**357-8681** ✉ PO Box 65118, London, England SW16 9BS
Email: info@outburstfestival.org **Web:** www.outburstfestival.org

TBA: Tampa Black Pride *Tampa, FL*
celebrate African American gay pride in sunny Tampa • LGBT **Web:** www.tampablackpride.com

TBA: Windy City Black Pride *Chicago, IL*
a weekend of parties, seminars & more • LGBT ☎ 888/**922-7244** ✉ PO Box 803425, Chicago, IL 60680 **Web:** www.windycityblackpride.org

August

4-8: Rendezvous 2010 *Medicine Bow Nat'l Forest, WY*
5-day camping festival to celebrate LGBT pride • 400+ attendees
☎ 307/**778-7645** ✉ c/o *Wyoming Equality*, PO Box 2531, Cheyenne, WY 82003
Email: info@wyomingequality.org **Web:** www.wyomingequality.org

6-8: Black Pride NYC *New York City, NY*
multicultural LGBT festival w/ a wide array of entertainment, forums, workshops & events • LGBT **Web:** www.prideinthecity.com

12-15: Homo A Go Go *San Francisco, CA*
queer music, film, art, performance & activism festival • LGBT ☎ 415/**347-5802**
Email: info@homoagogo.com **Web:** www.homoagogo.com

13-15: Fire Island Black Out *Fire Island, NY*
premier 3-day beach event for the LGBT community of color & friends • all are invited to attend & enjoy • LGBT ☎ 215/**751-0808** ✉ c/o *FIBO*, 2201 Race St, 2nd flr, Philadelphia, PA 19103
Email: info@fireislandblackout.com **Web:** www.fireislandblackout.com

15-21: Provincetown Carnival *Provincetown, MA*
☎ 800/**637-8696**, 508/**487-2313** ✉ c/o *Provincetown Business Guild*, PO Box 421, Provincetown, MA 02657
Email: info@ptown.org **Web:** www.ptown.org

20-29: GNI (Gay Naturist Int'l) Gathering *Poconos, PA*
weeklong gathering of gay nudists • price includes food, beverages, lodging & entertainment • workshops • men only • 800 attendees ☎ 954/**567-2700** ✉ c/o *GNI*, 5175 W Ajo Hwy #A-14, Tucson, AZ 85735
Email: gni@gaynaturists.org **Web:** www.gaynaturists.org

22-29: "Camp" Camp *Porter, ME*
summer camp for LGBT adults • sports, pottery, theater, yoga & more • LGBT
☎ 888/**924-8380** ✉ c/o *Camp Camp*, 545 Prospect Pl #2J, Brooklyn, NY 11238
Email: info@campcamp.com **Web:** www.campcamp.com

TBA: Black Pride *Jacksonville, FL*
celebrate African American gay/ lesbian culture • 2nd wknd in August • LGBT
☎ 904/**858-3757** ✉ PO Box 18841, Jacksonville, FL 32229
Email: info@jaxxblackpride.org **Web:** www.jaxxblackpride.org

TBA: Gay Ski Week Queenstown *Queenstown, New Zealand*
Email: ski@gayskiweeknz.com **Web:** www.gayskiweeknz.com

TBA: Indiana Black Pride Festival *Indianapolis, IN*
LGBT ☎ 317/**592-9529** ✉ PO Box 11471, Indianapolis, IN 46201
Email: indianablackgaypride@yahoo.com **Web:** www.indianablackpride.com

TBA: National Gay Softball World Series *Milwaukee, WI*
LGBT ☎ 412/**362-1247** ✉ c/o *NAGAAA*, 1014 King Ave, Pittsburgh, PA 15206
Email: volunteer@nagaaafest.com **Web:** www.nagaaafest.com

TBA: Northalsted Market Days *Chicago, IL*
a good ol' summer block party on Main St of Boys' Town, USA • LGBT
☎ 773/**883-0500** ✉ 3656 N Halsted St, Chicago, IL 61613 **Web:** www.northalsted.com

TBA: St Louis Black Pride *St Louis, MO*
☎ 314/**531-2284** ✉ PO Box 4854, St Louis, MO 63108
Email: info@stlouisblackpride.org **Web:** www.stlouisblackpride.org

TBA: West Coast Gathering *Malibu, CA*
swimming, parties, workshops & more with fellow gay male naturists • men only • 400 attendees ☎ 877/**683-4781**
Email: info@cmen.info **Web:** www.cmen.info

September

1-6: Atlanta Black Pride Weekend *Atlanta, GA*
celebrate Black Pride over Labor Day weekend in Atlanta • LGBT ☎ 678/**799-8526** ✉ c/o *In The Life Atlanta*, 346 Auburn Ave NE, Atlanta, GA 30312
Email: info@inthelifeatl.com **Web:** www.inthelifeatl.com

1-6: Southern Decadence *New Orleans, LA*
mostly men ☎ 504/**522-8049** ✉ c/o *Official Southern Decadence*, 828-A Bourbon St, New Orleans, LA 70116
Email: info@southerndecadence.com **Web:** www.southerndecadence.com

2-6: Inferno Dominican Republic *Punta Cana, Dominican Republic*
the premier Labor Day pride celebration • deluxe, all-inclusive accommodations • LGBT ☎ 305/**891-7536** ✉ c/o *Worldwide Travel Partners*, 10800 Biscayne Blvd #201, Miami, FL 33161
Email: info@infernodr.com **Web:** www.infernodr.com

3-5: Howl Festival *New York City, NY*
a cabaret from the underworld • outdoor murals • hip hop howl • all in Tompkins Square Park • mixed gay/ straight ☎ 212/**243-3413** ✉ 335 E 10th St, New York City, NY 10011
Email: Clarity32@gmail.com **Web:** www.howlfestival.com

5: Splash Days *Austin, TX*
weekend of parties in clothing-optional Hippie Hollow, highlighted by the beer barge on Sunday
Email: info@splashdays.com **Web:** www.splashdays.com

19: Out in the Park *Springfield, MA*
unofficial gay day at Six Flags New England • wear red to show your support • LGBT • 1000+ attendees **Web:** www.outinthepark.com

23-26: Get Wet Weekend *Curaçao, Netherlands Antilles, Caribbean*
discover the Caribbean Dutch Paradise of Curaçao! • gay/ lesbian
Email: curacaogayplasa@hotmail.com **Web:** www.gaycuracao.com

TBA: AIDS Walk Colorado *Denver, CO*
☎ 303/**837-0166** ✉ c/o *Colorado AIDS Project*, PO Box 48120, Denver, CO 80204 **Web:** www.aidswalkcolorado.org

TBA: Black Gay Pride *Dallas, TX*
LGBT ☎ 214/**540-4494** ✉ 3100 Main St #208, Dallas, TX 75226 **Web:** www.dallasblackpride.com

TBA: IAGLBC Annual Bridge Tournament *Palm Springs, CA*
Int'l Association of Gay & Lesbian Bridge Clubs
Email: wehojohn@aol.com **Web:** www.GayBridge.org

TBA: Minnesota AIDS Trek *Twin Cities, MN*
annual 175-mile bike ride to fight AIDS • mixed gay/ straight ☎ 763/**522-8067** ✉ 3017 York Ave N, Robbinsdale, MN 55422
Email: info@aids-trek.org **Web:** www.aids-trek.org

October

1-3: Gay Days Anaheim *Anaheim, CA*
celebrate the unofficial gay days at Disneyland • wear red to show your support
Email: gaydaysinfo@gaydaysanaheim.com **Web:** www.GayDaysAnaheim.com

3: Castro Street Fair *San Francisco, CA*
arts & community groups street fair • co-founded by Harvey Milk ☎ 415/**841-1824**
Email: info@castrostreetfair.org **Web:** www.castrostreetfair.org

7-Nov 7: Glasgay! *Glasgow, Scotland*
UK's largest lesbian & gay multi-arts festival ☎ 44-141/**552-7575** ✉ c/o *Q Gallery & Studio*, 87-91 Saltmarket, Glasgow, Scotland G1 5LE
Email: info@glasgay.co.uk **Web:** www.glasgay.co.uk

11: National Coming Out Day *Cross-country, USA*
check local listings for events in your area or visit www.hrc.com/ncop
☎ 202/**628-4160**, 800/**777-4723** ✉ c/o *Human Rights Campaign*, 1640 Rhode Island Ave, Washington, DC 20036
Email: hrc@hrc.org **Web:** www.hrc.org/issues/coming_out.asp

14-17: Sundance Stompede *San Francisco, CA*
San Francisco's annual country/ western dance weekend • LGBT ☎ 415/**820-1403** ✉ c/o *Sundance Assoc*, 2261 Market St PMB 225, San Francisco, CA 94114
Email: info@stompede.com **Web:** www.stompede.com

17: AIDS Walk Atlanta *Atlanta, GA*
mixed gay/ straight • 10,000+ attendees ☎ 404/**876-9255** ✉ PO Box 78187, Atlanta, GA 30357
Email: info@aidswalkatlanta.com **Web:** walk.aidatlanta.org

17: AIDS Walk LA *Los Angeles, CA*
annual AIDS fundraiser in West Hollywood • mixed gay/ straight ☎ 213/**201-9255** ✉ c/o *MZA Events, Inc*, PO BOX 933005, Los Angeles, CA 90093
Email: awlainfo@aidswalk.net **Web:** www.aidswalk.net

21-24: International Gay Rodeo Finals *Laughlin, NV*
check w/ local chapters for events throughout the year in your area
☎ 303/**766-5630** ✉ c/o *International Gay Rodeo*, 20140 E Maplewood Ave, Centennial, CO 80016
Email: RodeoDirector@finalsrodeo.com **Web:** www.finalsrodeo.com

22-31: Fantasy Fest *Key West, FL*
10 days of parties, costume contests, street fairs, masquerade balls & parades • 70,000 attendees ☎ 305/**296-1817** ✉ c/o *Fantasy Fest*, PO Box 230, Key West, FL 33041
Email: kwfanfest@aol.com **Web:** www.fantasyfest.net

29-31: Black Pride *Nashville, TN*
gay/ lesbian ☎ 615/**974-2832**, 800/**845-4266x269** ✉ c/o *Brothers United*, PO Box 68335, Nashville, TN 37206
Email: nashblackpride@aol.com **Web:** www.brothersunited.com

TBA: Fantasia Fair *Provincetown, MA*
annual 7-day fair for trannies & those who love them • costume ball, workshops, talent show, wine-tasting • all genders welcome ✉ 522 Pine Dr, Pine Lake, GA 30072
Email: info@fantasiafair.org **Web:** www.fantasiafair.org

TBA: Gaylaxicon *TBA, USA*
LGBT science fiction, fantasy, horror & gaming convention
Email: info@gaylaxicon2010.org **Web:** www.gaylaxicon2010.org

TBA: Seattle AIDS Walk *Seattle, WA*
mixed gay/ straight • 4000+ attendees ☎ 206/**957-1648**, 206/**323-9255** ✉ c/o *Lifelong AIDS Alliance*, 1002 E Seneca, Seattle, WA 98122
Email: events@llaa.org **Web:** www.SeattleAIDSWalk.org

TBA: US & Int'l Mr Gay Competitions *TBA, USA*
✉ c/o *Noble Beast Foundation*, 2080 Vallejo St #2, San Francisco, CA 94123
Email: dspradlin@MrGayCompetition.com **Web:** www.MrGayCompetition.com

November

6-7: Greater Palm Springs Pride *Palm Springs, CA*
free entertainment, dance parties, lots of people & a parade on Sunday ☎ 760/**416-8711** ✉ 777 N Palm Canyon Dr #102, Palm Springs, CA 92262
Email: administration@PSPride.org **Web:** www.PSPride.org

TBA: Tranny Fest *San Francisco, CA*
transgender multi-arts festival ✉ 3128 16th St PMB 240, San Francisco, CA 94103
Email: info@trannyfest.com **Web:** www.trannyfest.com

December

31: Mummer's Strut *Philadelphia, PA*
big New Year's Eve party • followed by New Year's Day Parade • mixed gay/ straight • $40-50 ☎ 215/**336-3050** ✉ c/o *Mummers Museum*, 1100 S 2nd St, Philadelphia, PA 19147
Email: parade@mummers.com **Web:** www.mummers.com

TBA: Holly Folly *Provincetown, MA*
lesbian/ gay holiday celebration • fabulous parties • holiday concert • open houses
Web: www.ptown.org

TBA: Skin Two Rubber Ball *London, England*
pansexual fetish party drawing celebrities & guests from around the world • theme parties • retail fair & expo • mixed gay/ straight ☎ 44-020/**8878-2488** ✉ c/o *Skin Two Events*, BCM Box 2071, London, England WC1N 3XX **Web:** www.skintworubberball.com

FILM FESTIVALS

January

29-Feb 6: Zinegoak *Bilbao, Spain*
LGBT film festival ☎ 34-94/**415-6258** ✉ c/o *HEGOAK*, C/Dos de mayo 7, bajo, Bilbao, Spain 48003
Email: info@zinegoak.com **Web:** www.zinegoak.com

TBA: Pride Film Festival *Bloomington, IN*
weekend of films • dance party in Buskirk-Chumley Theater • LGBT ☎ 812/**323-3021** ✉ c/o *Buskirk-Chumley Theater*, 114 E Kirkwood Ave, Bloomington, IN 47404
Email: info@buskirkchumley.org **Web:** www.pridefilmfestival.org

TBA: Reel Out Queer Film & Video Festival *Kingston, ON, Canada*
celebrating the best of queer independent film & video ☎ 613/**549-7335** ✉ 336A Bader St, Kingston, ON, Canada K7K 3T1
Email: reelpublicity@yahoo.ca **Web:** www.reelout.com

February

16-21: CineKink NYC *New York City, NY*
film festival exploring a wide variety of sexualities through documentary, comedy, porn, drama & more • mixed gay/ straight ✉ 1092 St Georges Ave #190, New York City, NY
Email: info@cinekink.com **Web:** www.cinekink.com

TBA: Mardi Gras Film Festival *Sydney, Australia*
Sydney film festival corresponds with massive Mardi Gras event
☎ 61-2/**9332-4938** ✉ c/o *Queer Screen LTD*, PO Box 1081, Darlinghurst, NSW, Australia 1300
Web: www.queerscreen.com.au

TBA: Out at the Movies *Canton, NY*
LGBT film festival for Northern New York **Web:** www.outatthemovies.org

March

14-18: QFest *St Louis, MO*
☎ 314/**289-4152**
Email: chris@cinemastlouis.org **Web:** www.stlqfest.org

17-28: Melbourne Queer Film Festival *Melbourne, Australia*
☎ 613/**9662-4147** ✉ c/o *MQFF*, PO Box 21244
Little Lonsdale St, Victoria, Australia 8011
Email: info@mqff.com.au **Web:** www.mqff.com.au

17-31: London Lesbian & Gay Film Festival *London, England*
grab your tickets for the largest LGBT film fest in Europe ☎ 44 (0)20/**7928-3232**
Web: www.llgff.org.uk

TBA: Fusion *Los Angeles, CA*
Los Angeles' LGBT people of color film festival ☎ 213/**480-7088** ✉ c/o *Outfest*, 3470 Wilshire Blvd #1022, Los Angeles, CA 90010
Email: outfest@outfest.org **Web:** www.outfest.org/fusion.html

TBA: Verzaubert Int'l Queer Film Festival *Berlin, Germany*
screening in Berlin, Cologne, Frankfurt & Munich • LGBT ☎ 49-30/**861-4532** ✉ c/o *Rosebud Entertainment*, Oranienburger Str 39, Berlin, Germany D-10117
Email: fans@verzaubertfilmfest.de **Web:** www.verzaubertfilmfest.com

April

16-22: FilmOut San Diego *San Diego, CA*
LGBT film festival ✉ 1010 University Ave #1869, San Diego, CA 92103
Email: info@filmoutsandiego.com **Web:** www.filmoutsandiego.com

23-May 2: Miami Gay & Lesbian Film Festival *Miami, FL*
☎ 305/**534-9924** ✉ PO Box 530280, Miami Beach, FL 33153
Email: info@mglff.com **Web:** www.MGLFF.com

TBA: Birmingham Shout *Birmingham, AL*
LGBT film festival ☎ 205/**324-0888** ✉ c/o *Alabama Moving Images*, 2312 1st Ave N, Birmingham, AL 35203
Email: info@bhamshout.com **Web:** www.bhamshout.com

TBA: Brisbane Queer Film Festival *Brisbane, Australia*
Email: info@brisbanepowerhouse.org **Web:** www.bqff.com.au

May

5-15: Boston LGBT Film Festival *Boston, MA*
☎ 617/**233-1190** ✉ c/o *Museum of Fine Arts*, 465 Huntington Ave, Boston, MA 02115 **Email:** info@bostonlgbtfilmfest.org **Web:** www.bostonlgbtfilmfest.org

13-16: Translations: Transgender Film Festival *Seattle, WA*
☎ 206/**323-4274** ✉ c/o *Three Dollar Bill Cinema*, 1122 E Pike St #1313, Seattle, WA 98122
Email: info@threedollarbillcinema.org **Web:** www.threedollarbillcinema.org

20-30: Inside Out: Toronto LGBT Film Festival *Toronto, ON, Canada*
☎ 416/**977-6847** ✉ c/o *Inside Out*, 401 Richmond St W #219, Toronto, ON, Canada M5V 3A8
Email: inside@insideout.ca **Web:** www.insideout.ca

27-June 5: Out Film CT *Hartford, CT*
☎ 860/**586-1136** ✉ PO Box 231192, Hartford, CT 06123
Email: glff@yahoo.com **Web:** www.outfilmct.org

TBA: Fairytales Int'l LGBT Film Festival *Calgary, AB, Canada*
☎ 403/**244-1956** ✉ #4 1230A 17th Avenue SW, Calgary, AB, Canada T2T 0B8
Email: info@fairytalesfilmfest.com **Web:** www.fairytalesfilmfest.com

TBA: Honolulu Rainbow Film Festival *Honolulu, HI*
☎ 808/**381-1952** ✉ c/o *Honolulu Gay & Lesbian Cultural Foundation*, 758 Kapahulu Ave #168, Honolulu, HI 96816
Email: info@hglcf.org **Web:** www.hglcf.org

TBA: Out Takes LGBT Film Festival *Wellington, New Zealand*
festival also travels to Auckland & Christchurch, NZ ☎ 64-4/**972-6775** ✉ c/o *Reel Queer Inc*, PO Box 27070, Wellington, New Zealand 6141
Email: info@outtakes.org.nz **Web:** www.outtakes.org.nz

June

3-10: Diversa Int'l Gay Lesbian Trans Film Festival *Buenos Aires, Argentina*
LGBT films from Argentina & beyond • art • theater • debates
☎ 0054911/**4773-2156** ✉ c/o *PRISMA*, Lavalleja 1030 2° "D", Buenos Aires, Argentina 1414
Email: festival@diversa.com.ar **Web:** www.diversa.com.ar

3-6: Q Cinema *Fort Worth, TX*
annual celebration of LGBT-themed movies ☎ 817/**723-4358** ✉ c/o *Q Cinema Inc*, 9 Chase Ct, Fort Worth, TX 76110
Email: todd@qcinema.org **Web:** www.qcinema.org

16-20: Provincetown Int'l Film Festival *Provincetown, MA*
mixed gay/ straight ☎ 508/**487-3456** ✉ PO Box 605, Provincetown, MA 02657
Email: info@ptownfilmfest.org **Web:** www.ptownfilmfest.org

17-27: **Frameline: San Francisco Int'l LGBT Film Festival** *San Francisco, CA*
get your tickets early for a slew of films about us • LGBT • 65,000+ attendees
☎ 415/**703-8650** ✉ c/o *Frameline*, 145 9th St #300, San Francisco, CA 94103
Email: info@frameline.org **Web:** www.frameline.org

22-26: **TLVFest: Israel Int'l LGBT Film Festival** *Tel Aviv, Israel*
films will also show in Jerusalem & Haifa ✉ c/o *TLVFEST*, Yair Hochner
2 Sprinzak St, Tel Aviv, Israel 64738
Email: tlvfest@gmail.com **Web:** www.tlvfest.com

TBA: **Milano Int'l Lesbian & Gay Film Festival** *Milan, Italy*
Email: info@cinemagaylesbico.com **Web:** www.cinemagaylesbico.com

TBA: **NewFest: New York LGBT Film Festival** *New York City, NY*
☎ 718/**923-1950** ✉ c/o *The New Festival*, 68 Jay St #218, Brooklyn, NY 11201
Email: info@newfest.org **Web:** www.newfest.org

July

TBA: **Gaze: Dublin Int'l Lesbian & Gay Film Festival** *Dublin, Ireland*
✉ The Priory
John West St, Dublin, Ireland 8
Email: info@gaze.ie **Web:** www.gaze.ie

TBA: **Mostra Lambda Barcelona** *Barcelona, Spain*
LGBT film festival ✉ c/o *Casal Lambda*, Verdaguer i Callis 10, Barcelona, Spain 08003
Email: mostra@lambdaweb.org **Web:** www.cinemalambda.com

TBA: **Outfest** *Los Angeles, CA*
Los Angeles' lesbian/ gay film & video festival in mid-July ☎ 213/**480-7088** ✉ c/o *Outfest*, 3470 Wilshire Blvd #1022, Los Angeles, CA 90010
Email: outfest@outfest.org **Web:** www.outfest.org

TBA: **Philadelphia QFest** *Philadelphia, PA*
☎ 267/**765-9800** **Web:** www.phillycinema.org

TBA: **Tokyo Int'l Lesbian & Gay Film Festival** *Tokyo, Japan*
✉ 3-10-18-401, Takada, Toshima-ku, Tokyo, Japan 171-0033 **Web:** www.tokyo-lgff.org

August

10-15: **Rhode Island International Film Festival** *Providence, RI*
don't miss the Gay & Lesbian Film Fest • mixed gay/ straight ☎ 401/**861-4445** ✉ c/o *RIIFF*, PO Box 162 , Newport, RI 02840
Email: info@film-festival.org **Web:** www.film-festival.org

TBA: **North Carolina Gay & Lesbian Film Festival** *Durham, NC*
☎ 919/**560-3040** ✉ c/o *Carolina Theatre*, 309 W Morgan St, Durham, NC 27701
Web: festivals.carolinatheatre.org/ncglff

TBA: **Vancouver Queer Film & Video Festival** *Vancouver, BC, Canada*
LGBT ☎ 604/**844-1615** ✉ c/o *Out on Screen*, 405-207 West Hastings St, Vancouver, BC, Canada V6B 1H7 **Web:** www.outonscreen.com

September

7-12: Austin Gay & Lesbian International Film Festival *Austin, TX*
☎ 512/**302-9889** ✉ c/o *AGLIFF*, 1216 E 51st St, Austin, TX 78723
Email: info@agliff.org **Web:** www.agliff.org

15-19: Fresno Reel Pride *Fresno, CA*
annual lesbian & gay film festival in central California ☎ 559/**999-7971** ✉ PO Box 4647, Fresno, CA 93744
Email: info@reelpride.com **Web:** www.reelpride.com

17-27: Out in Africa *Cape Town, South Africa*
the only film festival of its kind on the African continent • also in Johannesburg Sept 10-12 ☎ 27 21/**461 40 27 63** ✉ PO Box 15707, 8000 Vlaeberg, South Africa
Email: info@oia.co.za **Web:** www.oia.co.za

TBA: Milwaukee LGBT Film/ Video Festival *Milwaukee, WI*
☎ 414/**229-4758** ✉ Film Dept/ UWM
Mitchell Hall B70, Milwaukee, WI 53211
Email: lgbtfilm@uwm.edu **Web:**
www4.uwm.edu/psoa/programs/film/lgbtfilm/index.html

TBA: Pikes Peak Lavender Film Festival *Colorado Springs, CO*
☎ 719/**386-6843** ✉ PO Box 1987, Colorado Springs, CO 80901
Email: info@pplff.org **Web:** www.pplff.org

TBA: Southwest Gay & Lesbian Film Festival *Albuquerque, NM*
also in Santa Fe, NM ☎ 505/**243-1870** ✉ c/o *Closet Cinema*, 1209 7th St NW #A, Albuquerque, NM 87102
Email: info@closetcinema.org **Web:** www.closetcinema.org

October

2-8 Out on Film *Atlanta, GA*
LGBT ☎ 678/**237-7206** **Email:** jim.farmer@outonfilm.com
Web: www.outonfilm.com

7-9: Sacramento Int'l Gay & Lesbian Film Festival *Sacramento, CA*
☎ 916/**689-3284** ✉ 1017 L St #379, Sacrmento, CA 95814
Email: general@siglff.org **Web:** www.siglff.org

14-23: Reel Affirmations:
The Nation's LGBT Film Festival *Washington, DC*
lesbian/ gay films ☎ 202/**986-1119** ✉ c/o *One In Ten*, PO Box 73587, Washington, DC 20056
Email: mmurray@oneinten.org **Web:** www.reelaffirmations.org

15-24: Seattle Lesbian & Gay Film Festival *Seattle, WA*
☎ 206/**323-4274** ✉ c/o *Three Dollar Bill Cinema*, 1122 E Pike St #1313, Seattle, WA 98122
Email: info@threedollarbillcinema.org **Web:** www.threedollarbillcinema.org

19-24: Hamburg Int'l Lesbian & Gay Film Festival *Hamburg, Germany*
☎ 49-40/**348-0670** ✉ c/o *Querbild e.V.*, Schanzenstr 45, Hamburg, Germany D-20357
Email: mail@lsf-hamburg.de **Web:** www.lsf-hamburg.de

28-Nov 7: Madrid LGBT Film Festival *Madrid, Spain*
☎ 34-91/**593-0540** ✉ c/o *Fundación Triángulo*, Meléndez Valdés, 52 1ro D, Madrid, Spain 28015
Email: info@lesgaicinemad.com **Web:** www.lesgaicinemad.com

TBA: Copenhagen Gay & Lesbian Film Festival *Copenhagen, Denmark*
☎ 45/**2843-4217** ✉ Oster Farimagsgade 16B, Copenhagen, Denmark DK-2100
Email: kontakt@cglff.dk **Web:** www.cglff.dk

TBA: image+nation: Montréal Int'l LGBT Film Festival *Montréal, QC, Canada*
LGBT ☎ 514/**285-4467** ✉ c/o *Image + Nation*, 4067 boul St Laurent #404, Montréal, QC H2W 1Y7
Email: info@image-nation.org **Web:** www.image-nation.org

TBA: Out OK *Tulsa, OK*
Oklahoma's int'l LGBT film festival ☎ 918/**682-4654 x3** ✉ PO Box 2757, Muskogee, OK 74402
Email: pau@out-ok.com **Web:** www.out-ok.com

TBA: Pittsburgh Int'l Lesbian & Gay Film Festival *Pittsburgh, PA*
☎ 412/**422-6776** ✉ c/o *PILGFF*, PO Box 81237, Pittsburgh, PA 15217
Email: info@plgfs.org **Web:** www.pilgff.org

TBA: Portland Lesbian & Gay Film Festival *Portland, OR*
✉ c/o *Film Action Oregon*, 4144 NE Sandy Blvd, Portland, OR 97212
Email: info@plgff.org **Web:** www.plgff.org

TBA: Q Film Festival *Long Beach, CA*
showcasing films of interest to the queer community ☎ 562/**434-4455** ✉ c/o *The Center Long Beach*, 2017 E 4th St, Long Beach, CA 90814
Email: info@centerlb.org **Web:** www.centerlb.org

TBA: Reel Pride *Winnipeg, MB, Canada*
LGBT film festival ☎ 204/**775-6457** ✉ c/o *Winnipeg G&L Film Society*, 393 Portage Ave #Y300, Winnipeg, MB, Canada R3B 3H6
Email: reelpride@hotmail.com **Web:** www.reelpride.org

TBA: Tampa Bay Int'l Gay & Lesbian Film Festival *Tampa Bay, FL*
☎ 813/**879-4220** ✉ c/o *Friends of the Festival*, PO Box 18445, Tampa, FL 33679
Web: www.tiglff.com

November

4-13: Reeling: Chicago Lesbian & Gay Int'l Film Fest *Chicago, IL*
☎ 773/**293-1447** ✉ c/o *Chicago Filmmakers*, 5243 N Clark St, 2nd flr, Chicago, IL 60640
Email: reeling@chicagofilmmakers.org **Web:** www.reelingfilmfestival.org

TBA: Florence Queer Festival *Florence, Italy*
LGBT film festival
Email: info@florencequeerfestival.it **Web:** www.florencequeerfestival.it

TBA: Long Island Gay & Lesbian Film Festival *Huntington, NY*
✉ PO Box 360, E Northport, NY 11731
Email: info@liglff.org **Web:** www.liglff.org

TBA: Mezipatra *Prague, Czech Republic*
Czech LGBT film festival ✉ c/o *STUD Brno*, Smejkalova 75, Brno, Czech Republic 61600 **Email:** info@mezipatra.cz **Web:** www.mezipatra.cz

TBA: Mix: New York Lesbian & Gay Experimental Film Fest *New York City, NY*
film, videos, installations & media performances • write for info ☎ 212/**742-8880** ✉ c/o *MIX NYC*, 79 Pine St PMB 132, New York, NY 10005
Email: info@mixnyc.org **Web:** www.mixnyc.org

TBA: OUT TAKES Dallas *Dallas, TX*
LGBT film festival ☎ 972/**988-6333** ✉ c/o *The OUT TAKES Foundation*, 3818 Cedar Springs #405, Dallas, TX 75219 **Web:** www.outtakesdallas.org

TBA: Paris Gay & Lesbian Film Festival *Paris, France*
✉ 8 rue du Repos, Paris, France 75020
Email: info@ffglp.net **Web:** www.ffglp.net

Leather, Fetish & Bears

January

1-6: Bears Empire *Rome, Italy*
decadent, int'l bear gathering in Rome, Italy ☎ 39-392/**795-9441**
Email: info@@goodbear.net **Web:** www.bearsempire.com

14-18: La Fiesta de Los Osos *Tucson, AZ*
a winter bear gathering in the warmth of the desert sun • men only ☎ 520/**829-0117** ✉ c/o *Bears of the Old Pueblo*, 3938 E Grant Rd #193, Tucson, AZ 85712
Email: bop@botop.com **Web:** www.botop.com

15-17: Mid-Atlantic Leather Weekend *Washington, DC*
LGBT ☎ 202/**388-1010** ✉ c/o *Centaur MC*, PO Box 77416, Washington, DC 20013
Email: registration@leatherweekend.com **Web:** www.leatherweekend.com

22-24: Southwest Leather Conference *Phoenix, AZ*
workshops, vendors & fetish ball • MASTER/slave, Bootblack & Daddy/boy contests • LGBT ✉ c/o *SWLC*, 4757 E Greenway Rd #107B PMB 225, Phoenix, AZ 85032 **Web:** www.southwestleather.org

24-31: Beef Dip: Int'l Leather & Bear Week *Puerto Vallarta, Mexico*
beach parties, BBQs & hot DJs • local tours • cruises • bring sunscreen! • men only ☎ 416/**922-1018** ✉ c/o *BeefDip.com*, 135 Isabella St, Toronto, ON, Canada M4Y 1P4 **Web:** www.beefdip.com

February

11-15: Int'l Bear Rendezvous 2010 *San Francisco, CA*
☎ 415/**541-5000** ✉ c/o *Bears of San Francisco*, 584 Castro St #266, San Francisco, CA 94114
Email: info@bosf.org **Web:** www.bosf.org

March

TBA: Sugarbear Weekend *Montréal, QC, Canada*
Quebecois bear party with lots of maple syrup • men only
Email: sugarbearweekend@hotmail.com **Web:** www.sugarbearweekend.com

TBA: Washington State Leather Pride Week *Seattle, WA*
Email: info@seattlemeninleather.org **Web:** www.seattlemeninleather.org

April

1-5: Easter 2010 Berlin *Berlin, Germany*
annual leather & fetish weekend • German Mr Leather contest ☎ 49 30/**215 0099** ✉ c/o *Berlin Leder und Fetisch*, Nollendorfstrasse 28, Berlin, Germany 10777 **Web:** www.blf.de

9-11: Leather Leadership Conference *Detroit, MI*
join us to develop & strengthen problem-solving & camaraderie in the leather community • LGBT ✉ c/o *LLC c/o Larry Manion*, PO Box 190482, St Louis, MO 63119
Email: info@leatherleadership.org **Web:** www.leatherleadership.org

9-11: Rubbout *Vancouver, BC, Canada*
don't miss this annual gay rubber weekend • men only ☎ 604/**683-8000** ✉ 901-1238 Seymour St, Vancouver, BC, Canada V6B 6J3
Email: mitchkenyon@shaw.ca **Web:** www.rubbout.com

29-May 3: Phurfest *Phoenix, AZ*
let the fur fly in Phoenix ☎ 602/**370-3260** ✉ c/o *Bears of the West*, PO Box 33215, Phoenix, AZ 85067
Email: phurfest@bearsofthewest.com **Web:** www.bearsofthewest.com

30-May 2: Northwest Leather Celebration *San Jose, CA*
also Master/slave contest • gay/ lesbian
Email: info@northwestleathercelebration.com **Web:** www.northwestleathercelebration.com

May

27-June 1: Bear Pride *Chicago, IL*
1000+ attendees ☎ 773/**509-5135** ✉ c/o *Great Lakes Bears*, PO Box 578840, Chicago, IL 60657
Email: bearpride09@bearpride.org **Web:** www.bearpride.org

28-31: International Mr Bootblack Contest *Chicago, IL*
contest takes place during International Mr Leather weekend ☎ 800/**545-6753** ✉ c/o *International Mr Leather*, 5015 N Clark St, Chicago, IL 60640
Email: info@imrl.com **Web:** www.imrl.com

28-31: International Mr Leather *Chicago, IL*
weekend of leather events, capped by contest Sunday, Black & Blue Ball on Monday ☎ 800/**545-6753** ✉ c/o *International Mr Leather*, 5015 N Clark St, Chicago, IL 60640
Email: info@imrl.com **Web:** www.imrl.com

June

10-13: Southeast Leatherfest *Atlanta, GA*
LGBT ✉ c/o *Southeast Leatherfest*, PO Box 487, Hiram, GA 30141 **Web:** www.seleatherfest.com

20: Folsom Street East *New York City, NY*
New York City's answer to the famous San Francisco fetish street fair • LGBT
☎ 212/**727-9878** ✉ c/o *GMSMA*, 332 Bleecker St #D-23, New York City, NY 10014
Email: info@folsomstreeteast.org **Web:** www.folsomstreeteast.org

TBA: International Deaf Leather *Las Vegas, NV*
weekend of events, including Mr & Ms Deaf Leather Contest ✉ c/o *Int'l Deaf Leather*, 1128 Carlton Ave, Stockton, CA 95203
Email: president@@internationaldeafleather.org **Web:** www.internationaldeafleather.org

TBA: Southern HiBearnation *Melbourne, Australia*
a week of furry fun down under, culminating in the Mr Australasia Bear Contest, bringing bears from Australia, New Zealand, Southeast Asia, the South Pacific & beyond • 500+ attendees ☎ 61-412/**278-858** ✉ c/o *VicBears*, PO Box 1408, Collingwood, VIC, Australia 3066
Email: secretary@vicbears.org.au **Web:** www.southernhibearnation.com

July

22-25: International LeatherSIR/ Leatherboy *San Francisco, CA*
also Int'l Community BootBlack • check website for regional contest info
☎ 214/**534-8989** ✉ c/o *Leather Heritage Productions, LLC*, 3817 N Drexel Blvd, Oklahoma City, OK 73112
Email: domlevileatherman@cox.net **Web:** www.leathersir.com

25: Up Your Alley Fair *San Francisco, CA*
local SM/ leather street fair held in Dore Alley, South-of-Market • thousands of local kinky men & women attend ☎ 415/**777-3247** ✉ c/o *Folsom Street Events*, 965 Mission St #200, San Francisco, CA 94103
Email: info@folsomstreetevents.org **Web:** www.folsomstreetevents.org

TBA: Lazy Bear Weekend *Russian River, CA*
no contests, no pageants, no frills–just fur! • FUNdraiser benefits AIDS charities in Northern California & beyond • check web for details • mostly men ✉ c/o *Castrobear Presents*, 584 Castro St PMB 374, San Francisco, CA 94114
Email: joinus@lazybearweekend.com **Web:** www.lazybearweekend.com

TBA: Bear Week Provincetown *Provincetown, MA*
come to Provincetown for a relaxing week of parties & events • men only ✉ c/o *Provincetown Bears*, PO Box 1724, Provincetown, MA 02657 **Web:** www.ptownbears.org

TBA: Thunder in the Mountains *Denver, CO*
weekend of pansexual leather events & seminars • kinky comedy revue • talent show • LGBT • 800+ attendees ☎ 303/**698-1207** ✉ c/o *Thunder in the Mountains, LLC*, 258 Acoma St, Denver 80223-1339
Email: MrLthrCO@aol.com **Web:** www.thunderinthemountains.com

August

12-15: Pantheon of Leather *Los Angeles, CA*
annual leather/ SM/ fetish community service awards • int'l Mr & Ms Olympus Leather• mixed gay/ straight ✉ 5306 Romaine, Hollywood, CA 90029
Email: tljandcuir@aol.com **Web:** www.theleatherjournal.com/pantheon

TBA: Mr SE Rubber *Atlanta, GA*
hot weekend dedicated to rubber • Mr SE Rubber contest ✉ PO Box 133046, Atlanta, GA 30333 **Web:** www.mserubber.com

September

3-5: West Coast Rubber Weekend *Palm Springs, CA*
hot weekend dedicated to rubber, spandex, dive gear, BDSM • also Winter Warm Up event in Feb • men only ☎ 760/**880-7470** ✉ c/o *L8X Guys*, 5160 Vineland Ave #107-149, N Hollywood, CA 91601
Email: info@westcoastrubber.com **Web:** www.westcoastrubber.com

4: Folsom Europe *Berlin, Germany*
✉ c/o *Folsom Europe e.v.*, Nollendorfplatz 8/9, 10777 Berlin, Germany
Email: info@folsomeurope.com **Web:** www.folsomeurope.com

26: Folsom Street Fair *San Francisco, CA*
huge SM/ leather street fair, topping a week of kinky events • LGBT • thousands of local & visiting kinky men & women attendees ☎ 415/**861-3247** ✉ c/o *Folsom Street Events*, 965 Mission St #200, San Francisco, CA 94114
Email: info@folsomstreetevents.org **Web:** www.folsomstreetevents.org

TBA: Hairrison Street Fair *San Francisco, CA*
San Francisco's bear street fair weekend ☎ 415/**255-8658** ✉ c/o *PrideWorks*, 584 Castro St #714, San Francisco, CA 94114
Email: info@hairrison.org **Web:** www.hairrison.org

TBA: Oktobearfest *Munich, Germany*
join the Munich bears ☎ 49-089/**7093-9152** ✉ c/o *Munichbears*, Postfach 140406, München, Germany 80454
Email: munichbears@munichbears.de **Web:** www.munichbears.de

October

1-3: Mates Leather Weekend *Provincetown, MA*
sexy leather, rubber & uniform theme parties all weekend, including the First Mate contest ☎ 800/**330-9413** ✉ PO Box 1845, Provincetown, MA 02657
Email: info@matesleatherweekend.com **Web:** www.matesleatherweekend.com

1-4: OctobearFest *Denver, CO*
men only ✉ c/o *Front Range Bears*, PO Box 300534, Denver, CO 80203
Email: info@octobearfest.org **Web:** www.octobearfest.org

TBA: Bear Bust *Orlando, FL*
men only ✉ c/o *Bears of Central Florida*, PO Box 647, Orlando, FL 32802
Email: info@bearbust.org **Web:** www.bearbust.org

TBA: Leather Pride Amsterdam *Amsterdam, Netherlands*
weekend of hot leather events • men only ✉ c/o *Leather Pride Nederland*, PO Box 2674, 1000 CR Amsterdam, Netherlands
Email: info@leatherpride.nl **Web:** www.amsterdamleatherpride.eu

November

5-7: Santa Clara County Leather Weekend *San Jose, CA*
3 days of leather celebration in the San Jose area • LGBT ✉ c/o *Santa Clara County Leather Assoc*, c/o Billy deFrank LGBT Ctr
938 The Alameda, San Jose, CA 95126
Email: info@sccleather.org **Web:** www.SCCLeather.org

TBA: Bear Pride Week *Cologne, Germany*
☎ 49-179/**65 20 399** **Web:** www.bearpride.de

TBA: Mr Int'l Rubber & Rubber Blowout *Chicago, IL*
largest rubber event in US • market, parties • men only ☎ 773/**665-8064** ✉ c/o *MIR Contest*, PO Box 13385, Chicago, IL 60613
Email: info@MIRubber.com **Web:** www.MIRubber.com

TBA: Mr Leatherman Toronto Competition *Toronto, ON, Canada*
hot parties all weekend, including the competition & Victory Ball on Saturday • mostly men ☎ 416/**471-0222** ✉ c/o *MLTC, Inc*, 552 Church St, Box 500-35, Toronto, ON, Canada M4Y 2C3
Email: president@mrlt.com **Web:** www.mrlt.com

CONFERENCES & RETREATS

March

3-7: Creating Change Conference *Dallas, TX*
for lesbians, gays, bisexuals, transgendered people & queers into social activism • 2500+ attendees ☎ 202/**393-5177** ✉ c/o *National Gay & Lesbian Task Force*, 1325 Mass Ave NW #600, Washington, DC 20005
Email: creatingchange@thetaskforce.org **Web:** www.creatingchange.org

TBA: Transgender Leadership Summit *TBA, USA*
join transgender activists to help create a unified voice to advance the movement for transgender equality • 200+ attendees ☎ 415/**865-0176** ✉ c/o *Transgender Law Center*, 870 Market St #823, San Francisco, CA 94102
Email: info@transgenderlawcenter.org **Web:** www.transgenderlawcenter.org

May

TBA: Lambda Literary Awards *West Hollywood, CA*
the Lammies are the Oscars of LGBT writing & publishing • LGBT ☎ 212/**239-6575** ✉ c/o *Lambda Literary Foundation*, PO Box 1957, New York, NY 10113
Email: asklambda@earthlink.com **Web:** www.lambdaliterary.org

TBA: Saints & Sinners *New Orleans, LA*
LGBT writers & readers from around the country gather for a hot weekend of readings, panels & performance • 300 attendees • $100 ☎ 504/**821-2601 x217** ✉ c/o *NO/AIDS Task Force*, 2601 Tulane Ave, Ste 500, New Orleans, LA 70119 **Web:** www.sasfest.com

September

2-5: Nat'l Lesbian & Gay Journalists Assoc Convention *San Francisco, CA*
workshops • keynote speakers • entertainment ☎ 202/**588-9888 x10** ✉ c/o *NLGJA*, 1420 K St NW #910, Washington, DC 20005
Email: info@nlgja.org **Web:** www.nlgja.org

TBA: Gender Odyssey *Seattle, WA*
3 days of panels, workshops & meetings • entertainment, art exhibit & vendors • focus on transmen, transwomen & other gender variant people • open to all ☎ 206/**306-8252** ✉ c/o *Gender Spectrum*, PMB 796, 1122 E Pike St, Seattle, WA 98122
Email: info@genderodyssey.org **Web:** www.genderodyssey.org

TBA: Southern Comfort Conference *Atlanta, GA*
entertainers & leaders from the entire spectrum of the transgender community offering 5 days of learning, networking & fun ☎ 702/**336-1202** ✉ 2107 N Decatur Rd #207, Decatur, GA 30033
Email: info@sccatl.org **Web:** www.sccatl.org

October

TBA: National LGBT MBA Conference *TBA, USA*
career fair & discussions of sexual orientation, gender & leadership in the workplace by MBA students & out Fortune 500 company leaders • LGBT • 800+ attendees
Email: info@reachingoutmba.org **Web:** www.reachingoutmba.org

Spiritual Gatherings

February

12-15: PantheaCon *San Jose, CA*
pagan convention • mixed gay/ straight ☎ 510/**653-3244** ✉ c/o *Ancient Ways*, 4075 Telegraph Ave, Oakland, CA 94609
Email: store@ancientways.com **Web:** www.ancientways.com

May

19-23: Ancient Ways Festival *Stone City Pagan Sanctuary, CA*
annual 4-day mixed gender/orientation spring festival • pan-pagan rituals, workshops & music w/ lesbian/gay campsite • mixed gay/ straight ☎ 510/**653-3244** ✉ c/o *Ancient Ways*, 4075 Telegraph Ave, Oakland, CA 94609
Email: store@ancientways.com **Web:** www.ancientways.com

June

20-27: Pagan Spirit Gathering *near Salem, MO*
summer solstice celebration in Ohio • primitive camping • workshops • rituals • advance registration required • mixed gay/ straight ☎ 608/**924-2216** ✉ c/o *Circle Sanctuary*, PO Box 9, Barneveld, WI 53507
Email: circle@circlesanctuary.org **Web:** www.circlesanctuary.org/psg

August

TBA: BC Witchcamp *near Vancouver, BC, Canada*
weeklong Wiccan intensive at Evans Lake • mixed gay/ straight ☎ 250/**598-9229** ✉ c/o *Wtich Camp of BC Society*, 1266 Gladstone Ave, Victoria, BC, Canada V8T 1G6
Email: witchcampbcinfo@gmail.com **Web:** www.bcwitchcamp.ca

The Circuit

February

11-18: Latin Fever Puerto Vallarta *Playa del Carmen, Mexico*
4 days of parties in Puerto Vallarta • mostly men ☎ 213/**407-0542** ✉ c/o *Will Gorges & Canboy Productions*, PO Box 5943, Beverly Hills, CA 90209
Email: wgorges@cox.net **Web:** www.willgorges.com

12-15: Red Party Weekend *Montréal, QC, Canada*
AIDS benefit dance • mostly men • 2500+ attendees • $50+ ☎ 514/**875-7026** ✉ c/o *Bad Boy Club Montreal*, 94 Ste-Catherine Est #5, Montreal, QC, Canada H2X 1K7
Email: information@bbcm.org **Web:** www.bbcm.org

March

1-8: WinterPRIDE: Whistler Gay Ski Week *Whistler, BC, Canada*
annual gay/lesbian ski week • top-notch DJs & venues • popular destination 75 miles N of Vancouver • LGBT • 3000+ attendees ☎ 604/**288-7218** ✉ c/o *GayWhistler*, 102-4368 Main St #1025, Whistler, BC, Canada V0N 1B4
Email: dean@gaywhistler.com **Web:** www.gaywhistler.com

3-8: Winter Party Festival *Miami Beach, FL*
celebration of dance & cultural events for the for the LGBT community • 10,000 attendees ☎ 305/**571-1924** ✉ c/o *National Gay & Lesbian Task Force*, 3510 Biscayne Blvd #202, Miami, FL 33137
Email: winterparty@thetaskforce.org **Web:** www.thetaskforce.org

TBA: Saint-at-Large Black Party *New York City, NY*
LGBT • $100 ☎ 212/**674-8541** ✉ c/o *Saint-at-Large*, 382 Lafayette St, 8th flr, New York, NY 10003
Email: thesaint@saintatlarge.com **Web:** www.saintatlarge.com

April

8-11: Cherry Weekend *Washington, DC*
gay/ lesbian ☎ 703/**389-1238** ✉ c/o *Cherry Fund*, PO Box 53169, Washington, DC 20009
Email: info@cherryfund.com **Web:** www.cherryweekend.org

30-May 2: Purple Party *Dallas, TX*
a weekend of dance parties & social events benefiting AIDS Services of Dallas ✉ c/o *Purple Foundation*, 4027 Bowser Ave, Dallas, TX 75219
Email: blake@dallaspurpleparty.org **Web:** www.dallaspurpleparty.com

May

13-17: Hot & Dry *Montréal, QC, Canada*
AIDS benefit dance • mostly men • 5000+ attendees • $50+ ☎ 514/**875-7026** ✉ c/o *Bad Boy Club Montreal*, 94 Ste-Catherine Est #5, Montreal, QC, Canada H2X 1K7
Email: information@bbcm.org **Web:** www.bbcm.org

27-June 1: Sizzle 2010 *Miami, FL*
Miami's original circuit party ☎ 954/**938-9612** ✉ 1001 N Federal Hwy #365, Hallandale Beach, FL 33009
Email: mail@sizzlemiami.com **Web:** www.sizzlemiami.com

July

3-5: Summer Camp *Provincetown, MA*
celebrate the week of the 4th w/ cute boys & big name DJs ☎ 888/**887-8696** ✉ c/o *David Flower Productions*, PO Box 1947, Provincetown, MA 02657
Email: davidflower@comcast.net **Web:** www.davidflower.com

August

TBA: Sundance *Russian River, CA*
hot fun in the sun! • weekend of parties in sunny Russian River resort town • mostly men ✉ c/o *Gus Presents*, 1459 18th St PMB#141, San Francisco, CA 94107
Email: gus@guspresents.com **Web:** www.guspresents.com

TBA: Twist Party Weekend *Montréal, QC, Canada*
celebrate gay pride in Montréal • several dance events, including Mega T-Dance Saturday afternoon • mostly men • $40+ ☎ 514/**875-7026** ✉ c/o *Bad Boy Club Montreal*, 94 Ste-Catherine Est #5, Montreal, QC, Canada H2X 1K7
Email: information@bbcm.org **Web:** www.bbcm.org

September

25: Magnitude *San Francisco, CA*
the official, hottest dance & play party of the Folsom Street Fair • mostly men ☎ 415/**777-3247** ✉ c/o *Folsom Street Events*, 965 Mission St #200, San Francisco, CA 94103
Email: info@folsomstreetevents.org **Web:** www.folsomstreetevents.org/magnitude

26: Real Bad *San Francisco, CA*
"Be Bad... Do Good" • annual fundraiser immediately following the Folsom Street Fair • proceeds go directly to beneficiaries • mostly men ✉ c/o *GRGR/WEST*, 584 Castro St #495, San Francisco, CA 94114
Email: info@realbad.org **Web:** www.realbad.org

October

6-12: Black & Blue Festival *Montréal, QC, Canada*
North America's biggest & most innovative dance event & cultural festival • mostly men • 25,000+ attendees • $60-100+ ☎ 514/**875-7026** ✉ c/o *Bad Boy Club Montreal*, 94 Ste-Catherine Est #5, Montreal, QC, Canada H2X 1K7
Email: information@bbcm.org **Web:** www.bbcm.org

28-31: Halloween in New Orleans *New Orleans, LA*
mostly men • 5000+ attendees ☎ 504/**945-5546** ✉ PO Box 52171, New Orleans, LA 70152-2171
Email: web@halloweenneworleans.com **Web:** www.halloweenneworleans.com

TBA: Blue Ball *Philadelphia, PA*
benefit wknd for the LGBT community highlighted by Saturday night dance at Nat'l Constitution Center • open to all lifestyles • mostly men ☎ 267/**514-2088** ✉ c/o *Sapphire Fund*, 1315 Spruce St, Philadelphia, PA 19107
Email: blueball@sapphirefund.org **Web:** www.blueballphilly.com

November

24-28: White Party Week *Miami Beach, FL*
6 days of festivities capped by the annual White Party at Vizcaya • benefitting Care Resource • LGBT ☎ 305/**576-1234** ✉ c/o *CARE Resource*, 3510 Biscayne Blvd #300, Miami, FL 33137 **Email:** info@whiteparty.org **Web:** www.whiteparty.net

December

31: Metropolis New Year's Eve 2011 *San Francisco, CA*
12-hour dance marathon • largest gay New Year's party in San Francisco • mostly men ✉ c/o *Gus Presents*, 1459 18th St PMB#141, San Francisco, CA 94107
Email: gus@guspresents.com **Web:** www.guspresents.com

RUSSIAN RIVER PARTY WEEKEND 2010

gus presents

SUNDANCE

Blue Angel vodka

Russian River Resort

GUSPRESENTS.COM

THE OFFICIAL DANCE EVENT OF FOLSOM STREET FAIR®
MAGNITUDE®
SATURDAY SEPTEMBER 25, 2010
SAN FRANCISCO
FOLSOM
FOLSOM STREET EVENTS
FOLSOMSTREETFAIR.ORG/MAGNITUDE

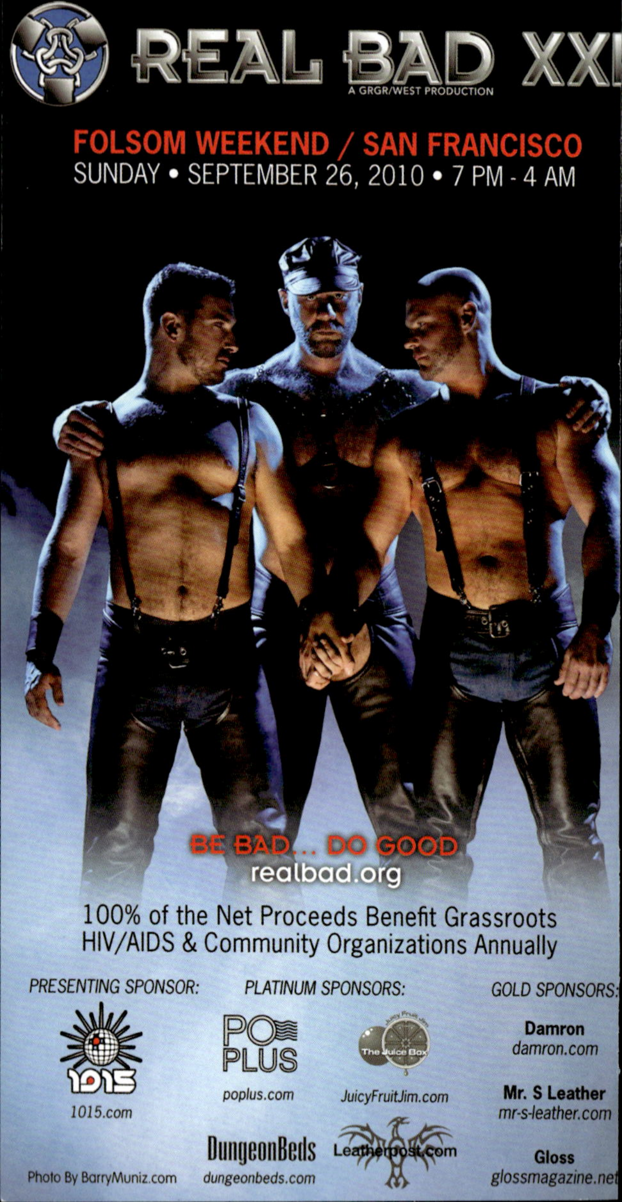

REAL BAD XX
A GRGR/WEST PRODUCTION
FOLSOM WEEKEND / SAN FRANCISCO
SUNDAY • SEPTEMBER 26, 2010 • 7 PM - 4 AM
BE BAD... DO GOOD
realbad.org
100% of the Net Proceeds Benefit Grassroots HIV/AIDS & Community Organizations Annually
PRESENTING SPONSOR:
1015
1015.com
PLATINUM SPONSORS:
PO PLUS
poplus.com
The Juice Box
JuicyFruitJim.com
DungeonBeds
dungeonbeds.com
Leatherpost.com
GOLD SPONSORS:
Damron
damron.com
Mr. S Leather
mr-s-leather.com
Gloss
glossmagazine.net
Photo By BarryMuniz.com

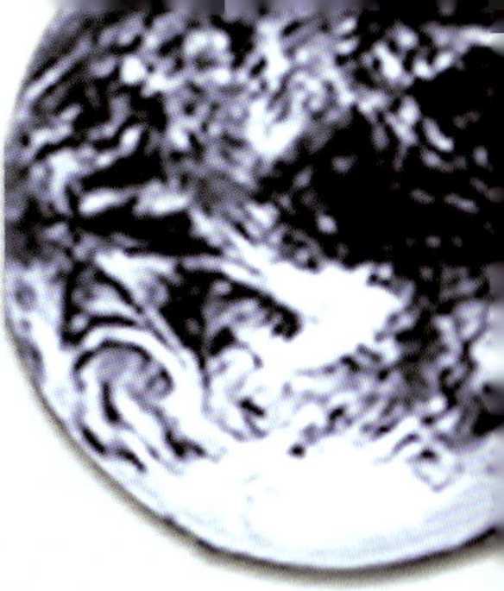

Male Order

FunMaps®
...finding art, culture, history, and adventure in the places you visit.
SAN FRANCISCO
SONOMA COUNTY/RUSSIAN RIVER
FunMaps
www.funmaps.com
NEW YORK CITY
FIRE ISLAND
FunMaps
www.funmaps.com
come OUT HERE
Onlyinsanfrancisco.com
Miami FunMap
FunMaps
www.funmaps.com